P9-CFE-442

DATE DUE

FOR REFERENCE

Do Not Take From This Room

Demco, Inc. 38-293

DISCARD

Nineteenth-Century
Literature Criticism

Guide to Gale Literary Criticism Series

For criticism on	Consult these Gale series
Authors now living or who died after December 31, 1959	*CONTEMPORARY LITERARY CRITICISM (CLC)*
Authors who died between 1900 and 1959	*TWENTIETH-CENTURY LITERARY CRITICISM (TCLC)*
Authors who died between 1800 and 1899	*NINETEENTH-CENTURY LITERATURE CRITICISM (NCLC)*
Authors who died between 1400 and 1799	*LITERATURE CRITICISM FROM 1400 TO 1800 (LC)* *SHAKESPEAREAN CRITICISM (SC)*
Authors who died before 1400	*CLASSICAL AND MEDIEVAL LITERATURE CRITICISM (CMLC)*
Authors of books for children and young adults	*CHILDREN'S LITERATURE REVIEW (CLR)*
Dramatists	*DRAMA CRITICISM (DC)*
Poets	*POETRY CRITICISM (PC)*
Short story writers	*SHORT STORY CRITICISM (SSC)*
Black writers of the past two hundred years	*BLACK LITERATURE CRITICISM (BLC)*
Hispanic writers of the late nineteenth and twentieth centuries	*HISPANIC LITERATURE CRITICISM (HLC)*
Native North American writers and orators of the eighteenth, nineteenth, and twentieth centuries	*NATIVE NORTH AMERICAN LITERATURE (NNAL)*
Major authors from the Renaissance to the present	*WORLD LITERATURE CRITICISM, 1500 TO THE PRESENT (WLC)*

ISSN 0732-1864

Volume 83

Nineteenth-Century Literature Criticism

Excerpts from Criticism of the
Works of Novelists, Poets, Playwrights,
Short Story Writers, Philosophers, and Other
Creative Writers Who Died between 1800
and 1899, from the First Published Critical
Appraisals to Current Evaluations

Suzanne Dewsbury
Editor

GALE GROUP

Detroit
New York
San Francisco
London
Boston
Woodbridge, CT

STAFF

Suzanne Dewsbury, *Editor*
Gianna Barberi, *Associate Editor*
Lynn Spampinato, *Managing Editor*

Maria L. Franklin, *Permissions Manager*
Kimberly F. Smilay, *Permissions Specialist*
Kelly A. Quin, *Permissions Associate*
Erin Bealmear, Sandra K. Gore, *Permissions Assistants*

Victoria B. Cariappa, *Research Manager*
Tracie A. Richardson, *Project Coordinator*
Tamara C. Nott, *Research Associate*
Timothy Lehnerer, Patricia Love, *Research Assistants*

Dorothy Maki, *Manufacturing Manager*
Stacy Melson, *Buyer*

Michael Logusz, *Graphic Artist*
Randy Bassett, *Image Database Supervisor*
Robert Duncan, *Imaging Specialist*
Pamela A. Reed, *Imaging Coordinator*

This book is printed on acid-free paper that meets the minimum requirements of American National Standard for Information Sciences—Permanence Paper for Printed Library Materials, ANSI Z39.48-1984.

Library of Congress Catalog Card Number 84-643008
ISBN 0-7876-3259-7
ISSN 0732-1864
Printed in the United States of America

10 9 8 7 6 5 4 3 2 1

Contents

Preface vii

Acknowledgments xi

Preface

Since its inception in 1981, *Nineteenth-Century Literature Criticism* has been a valuable resource for students and librarians seeking critical commentary on writers of this transitional period in world history. Designated an "Outstanding Reference Source" by the American Library Association with the publication of its first volume, *NCLC* has since been purchased by over 6,000 school, public, and university libraries. The series has covered more than 300 authors representing 29 nationalities and over 17,000 titles. No other reference source has surveyed the critical reaction to nineteenth-century authors and literature as thoroughly as *NCLC*.

Scope of the Series

NCLC is designed to introduce students and advanced readers to the authors of the nineteenth century, and to the most significant interpretations of these authors' works. The great poets, novelists, short story writers, playwrights, and philosophers of this period are frequently studied in high school and college literature courses. By organizing and reprinting commentary written on these authors, *NCLC* helps students develop valuable insight into literary history, promotes a better understanding of the texts, and sparks ideas for papers and assignments. Each entry in *NCLC* presents a comprehensive survey of an author's career or an individual work of literature and provides the user with a multiplicity of interpretations and assessments. Such variety allows students to pursue their own interests; furthermore, it fosters an awareness that literature is dynamic and responsive to many different opinions.

Every fourth volume of *NCLC* is devoted to literary topics that cannot be covered under the author approach used in the rest of the series. Such topics include literary movements, prominent themes in nineteenth-century literature, literary reaction to political and historical events, significant eras in literary history, prominent literary anniversaries, and the literatures of cultures that are often overlooked by English-speaking readers.

NCLC continues the survey of criticism of world literature begun by Gale's *Contemporary Literary Criticism (CLC)* and *Twentieth-Century Literary Criticism (TCLC)*, both of which excerpt and reprint commentary on authors of the twentieth century. For additional information about *TCLC, CLC,* and Gale's other criticism series, users should consult the Guide to Gale Literary Criticism Series preceding the title page in this volume.

Coverage

Each volume of *NCLC* is carefully compiled to present:

- criticism of authors, or literary topics, representing a variety of genres and nationalities
- both major and lesser-known writers and literary works of the period
- 4-8 authors or 4-6 topics per volume
- individual entries that survey critical response to an author's work or a topic in literary history, including early criticism to reflect initial reactions, later criticism to represent any rise or decline in reputation, and current retrospective analyses.

Organization

An author entry consists of the following elements: author heading, biographical and critical introduction, list of principal works, excerpts of criticism (each preceded by a bibliographic citation and an annotation), and a bibliography of further reading.

- The **Author Heading** consists of the name under which the author most commonly wrote, followed by birth and death dates. If an author wrote consistently under a pseudonym, the pseudonym will be listed in the author heading and the real name given in parentheses on the first line of the biographical and critical introduction. Also located at the beginning of the introduction to the author entry are any name variations under which an author wrote, including transliterated forms for an author whose language uses a nonroman alphabet.

- The **Biographical and Critical Introduction** outlines the author's life and career, as well as the critical issues surrounding his or her work. References are provided to past volumes of *NCLC* in which further information about the author may be found.

- Most *NCLC* entries include a **Portrait** of the author. Many entries also contain reproductions of materials pertinent to an author's career, including manuscript pages, title pages, dust jackets, letters, and drawings, as well as photographs of important people, places, and events in an author's life.

- The list of **Principal Works** is chronological by date of first publication and identifies the genre of each work. In the case of foreign authors with both foreign-language publications and English translations, the English-language version is given in brackets. Unless otherwise indicated, dramas are dated by first performance, not first publication.

- **Criticism** in each author entry is arranged chronologically to provide a perspective on changes in critical evaluation over the years. All titles of works by the author featured in the entry are printed in boldface type to enable the user to easily locate discussion of particular works. Also for purposes of easier identification, the critic's name and the publication date of the essay are given at the beginning of each piece of criticism. Unsigned criticism is preceded by the title of the journal in which it appeared. Publication information (such as publisher names and book prices) and some parenthetical numerical references (such as page and line references to specific editions of works) have been deleted at the editors' discretion to provide smoother reading of the text. Footnotes that appear with previously published pieces of criticism are reprinted at the end of each essay or excerpt. In the case of excerpted criticism, only those footnotes that pertain to the excerpted text are included.

- A complete **Bibliographic Citation** provides original publication information for each piece of criticism.

- Critical excerpts are prefaced by **Annotations** providing the reader with a summary of the critical intent of the piece. Also included, when appropriate, is information about the critic's reputation, individual approach to literary criticism, and particular expertise in an author's works, as well as information about the relative importance of the critical excerpt. In some cases, the annotations cross-reference excerpts by critics who discuss each other's commentary.

- An annotated list of **Further Reading** appearing at the end of each entry suggests secondary sources on the author. In some cases it includes essays for which the editors could not obtain reprint rights.

Cumulative Indexes

■ ' Each volume of *NCLC* contains a cumulative **Author Index** listing all authors who have appeared in Gale's Literary Criticism Series, along with cross-references to such biographical series as *Contemporary Authors* and *Dictionary of Literary Biography*. Useful for locating authors within the various series, this index is particularly valuable for those authors who are identified with a certain period but who, because of their death dates, are placed in another, or for those authors whose careers span two periods. For example, Fyodor Dostoevsky is found in *NCLC*, yet Leo Tolstoy, another major nineteenth-century Russian novelist, is found in *TCLC* because he died after 1899.

■ Each *NCLC* volume includes a cumulative **Nationality Index** which lists all authors who have appeared in *NCLC*, arranged alphabetically under their respective nationalities.

■ Each new volume in Gale's Literary Criticism Series includes a cumulative **Topic Index**, which lists all literary topics treated in *NCLC, TCLC, LC 1400-1800*, and the *CLC* Yearbook.

■ Each new volume of *NCLC*, with the exception of the Topics volumes, contains a **Title Index** listing the titles of all literary works discussed in the volume. In response to numerous suggestions from librarians, Gale has also produced a **Special Paperbound Edition** of the *NCLC* title index. This annual cumulation lists all titles discussed in the series since its inception. Additional copies of the index are available on request. Librarians and patrons have welcomed this separate index: it saves shelf space, is easy to use, and is recyclable upon receipt of the following year's cumulation. Titles discussed in the Topics volume entries are not included in the *NCLC* cumulative index.

Citing *Nineteenth-Century Literature Criticism*

When writing papers, students who quote directly from any volume in Gale's Literary Criticism Series may use the following general forms to footnote reprinted criticism. The first example pertains to material drawn from periodicals, the second to material reprinted from books:

[1]Kim McQuaid, "William Apes, Pequot: An Indian Reformer in the Jackson Era," *The New England Quarterly*, 50 (December 1977), 605-25; excerpted and reprinted in *Nineteenth-Century Literature Criticism*, Vol. 73, ed. Janet Witalec (Farmington Hills, Mich.: The Gale Group, 1999), pp. 3-4.

[2]Richard Harter Fogle, *The Imagery of Keats and Shelley: A Comparative Study* (Archon Books, 1949); excerpted and reprinted in *Nineteenth-Century Literary Criticism,* Vol. 73, ed. Janet Witalec (Farmington Hills, Mich.: The Gale Group, 1999), pp. 157-69.

Suggestions Are Welcome

In response to suggestions, several features have been added to *NCLC* since the series began, including annotations to excerpted criticism, a cumulative index to authors in all Gale literary criticism series, entries devoted to criticism on a single work by a major author, more illustrations, and a title index listing all literary works discussed in the series.

Readers who wish to suggest authors, single works, or topics to appear in future volumes, or who have other suggestions, are cordially invited to write: The Editors, *Nineteenth-Century Literature Criticism,* The Gale Group, 27500 Drake Rd., Farmington Hills, MI 48331-3535; call toll-free at 1-800-347-GALE.

Acknowledgments

The editors wish to thank the copyright holders of the excerpted criticism included in this volume and the permissions managers of many book and magazine publishing companies for assisting us in securing reproduction rights. We are also grateful to the staffs of the Detroit Public Library, the Library of Congress, the University of Detroit Mercy Library, Wayne State University Purdy/Kresge Library Complex, and the University of Michigan Libraries for making their resources available to us. Following is a list of the copyright holders who have granted us permission to reproduce material in this volume of *NCLC*. Every effort has been made to trace copyright, but if omissions have been made, please let us know.

COPYRIGHTED EXCERPTS IN *NCLC*, VOLUME 83, WERE REPRODUCED FROM THE FOLLOWING PERIODICALS:

American Studies, v. 17, June 20-July 11, 1976 for "Horatio Alger and American Modernism: The One-Dimensional Social Formula" by W. T. Lhamon, Jr. Copyright © Mid-American Studies Association, 1976. Reproduced by permission of the publisher and the author.—*Canadian Slavonic Papers: Revue Canadienne des Slavistes,* v. XXII, March, 1980. Copyright ©, *Canadian Slavonic Papers,* Canada, 1980. Reproduced by permission.—*Children's Literature,* v. 17, 1989. © 1989 by The Children's Literature Foundation, Inc. Reproduced by permission.—*College English,* v. 47, October, 1985 for "'The House-Band': The Education of Men in Little Women" by Anne Dalke. Copyright © 1985 by the National Council of Teachers of English. Reprinted by permission of the publisher and the Literary Estate of Stanley Cooperman.—*The Horn Book Magazine,* v. XLIV, October, 1968. Copyright, 1969, by The Horn Book, Inc., 11 Beacon St., Suite 1000, Boston, MA 02108. All rights reserved. Reproduced by permission.—*International Journal of Women's Studies,* v. 5, November-December, 1982 for "Alcott's Portraits of the Artist as Little Woman" by Elizabeth Lennox Keyser. Reproduced by permission of the author.—*Journal of Popular Culture,* v. X, 1976. Copyright © 1976 by Ray B. Browne. Reproduced by permission.—*The Lion and the Unicorn,* v. 18, 1994. © 1994 by The Johns Hopkins University Press. Reproduced by permission of The Johns Hopkins University Press.—*Neophilologus,* v. LXXXI, January, 1997. © 1997 Kluwer Academic Publishers. Reproduced by permission.—*PMLA,* v. 100, May, 1985. Copyright © 1985 by the Modern Language Association of America. Reproduced by permission of the Modern Language Association of America.—*Representations,* n. 19, Summer, 1987 for "'The Gentle Boy from the Dangerous Classes': Pederasty, Domesticity, and Capitalism in Horatio Alger" by Michael Moon. Copyright © 1987 The Regents of the University of California. Reproduced by permission of the publisher and the author.—*Russian Literary Triquarterly,* n. 3, 1972-73; v. 10, 1974. © 1972, 1974, by Ardis Publishers. All reproduced by permission.—*Slavic Review,* v. 28, September, 1969; v. 42, Summer, 1983. Copyright © 1969, 1983 by the American Association for the Advancement of Slavic Studies, Inc. All reproduced by permission.—*The Slavonic and East European Review,* v. 64, January, 1986. © University of London (School of Slavonic and East European Studies) 1986. All rights reserved. Reproduced by permission and the author.—*Soviet Literature,* n. 6 (315), 1974. Reproduced by permission of the Russian Authors' Society (RAO).

COPYRIGHTED EXCERPTS IN *NCLC*, VOLUME 83, WERE REPRODUCED FROM THE FOLLOWING BOOKS:

Auerbach, Nina. From an Afterword in *Little Women.* By Louisa May Alcott. Bantam Books, 1983. Afterword copyright © 1983 by Nina Auerbach. All rights reserved. Reproduced by permission of

Rupture: Narrative Desire and Duplicity in the Tales of Guy de Maupassant. The University of Michigan Press, 1994. Copyright © by the University of Michigan Press 1994. All rights reserved. Reproduced by permission of the author.—Vickery, Walter N. From *Alexander Pushkin.* Twayne Publishers, Inc., 1970. Copyright © 1970 by Twayne Publishers, Inc. All rights reserved.

PHOTOGRAPHS AND ILLUSTRATIONS APPEARING IN *NCLC,* VOLUME 83, WERE RECEIVED FROM THE FOLLOWING SOURCES:

Little Women

Louisa May Alcott

The following entry presents criticism on Alcott's novel *Little Women*. For a discussion of Alcott's complete career, see *NCLC*, Volumes 6 and 58.

INTRODUCTION

What is now known as *Little Women* includes both the original work by that title and its sequel, *Good Wives*. Written by Louisa May Alcott in 1868 and 1869 respectively, together these works have been long established as primary within the canon of juvenile literature and are considered by many to be the first children's books in America to break with the didactic tradition. Alcott introduced realism and entertainment to American children's literature, thereby achieving commercial success unknown to her moralizing contemporaries. *Little Women* is still read worldwide today.

Louisa May Alcott was born in Germantown, Pennsylvania in 1832, and raised in Concord, Massachusetts, and Boston. She was the second of four daughters of Abigail May Alcott and Amos Bronson Alcott, a Transcendentalist, educational reformer, and well-known writer. Louisa, though more commercially successful than her father, faced many obstacles to the literary career she envisioned for herself. As a woman writer, she was expected to write sentimental and moralizing tales, and in order to earn a living as a writer, she was expected to cater to the sensational cravings of her audience. Although she did both successfully until her death in 1888, many critics argue that with *Little Women,* Alcott countered sensationalism with realism and subverted the moralizing purpose she often appeared to embrace.

Plot and Major Characters

In Part I, while Mr. March is away as a volunteer chaplain in the Civil War, the March girls, Meg, Jo, Beth and Amy, embark on "pilgrimages" toward self-improvement, with the inspiration of John Bunyan's religious allegory, *The Pilgrim's Progress* (1678). Their journeys, though, are largely determined by their own consciences and will rather than by dogma. Meg learns to overcome her vanity, Jo to overcome excessiveness and temper, Amy, greed and selfishness. Beth is already saintly and seems not to need change, but ironically, it is an act of charity—a visit to a sick infant—which results in the scarlet fever that weakens her health and precipitates her death.

Welcomed into this haven are neighbors Theodore Laurence (Laurie) and his grandfather, who are far from stock patriarchal figures; they are, rather, admirers who crave and aspire to the domestic peace enjoyed by the Marches. Laurie and Jo develop a close friendship that intrigued Alcott's readers, but she avoided the conventional romantic plot by refusing to have them marry. Jo, an unconventional girl who thinks of herself as the "man of the house" while her father is away, is more interested in developing her art and financially supporting her family than marrying.

Part II of *Little Women,* originally published separately as *Good Wives,* focuses on the girls' transitions into adulthood. Meg marries John Brooke, Laurie's tutor—a financially difficult but happy match. Amy loses some of her passion for art and marries Laurie after he has been refused by Jo and has recovered from the blow. Beth dies before she can reach adulthood, but her loss inspires Jo to take up her domestic role. Jo eventually marries Professor Bhaer, a middle-aged academic with whom she shares philosophical interests. They open a boys' school, where she, no longer a tomboy, becomes a mother-figure for the students.

Major Themes

Alcott's earlier work, often published under the pseudonym A. M. Barnard, is generally characterized by sensational characters and plots, violence, melodrama, and romance—all consistent with the expectations of her readers. When asked to write a "girl's book," Alcott was yet again forced to write according to others' interests, but in this case she opted for more realism than sensationalism by choosing the only girlhood she knew for her subject—her own. Based on her life, and that of her sisters, Anna, Elizabeth, and May, *Little Women* follows the adolescence of the girls into adulthood, captures their private, domestic experience concretely, delineates their matriarchal haven of comfort and frugality, dramatizes their creative play, and explores their struggles to become artists, good sisters, and eventually happy wives. Although the culture of her time demanded that Alcott produce moralizing tales, she displayed a certain amount of resistance to that mandate in *Little Women*, preaching moderation rather than excessive religious molding. The girls are guided less by rigid moral strictures than by their strong sense of family, sometimes conveyed by words of wisdom from mother Marmee, but more often by a need to get along as a sisterly community. In part II this theme of sisterly love expands to include marriage and the formation of new families, with new roles for the three surviving sisters as good wives. Self-improvement, social responsibility, domestic cooperation, and matriarchal power, as well as the importance of play and artistic development, all serve as prominent themes in *Little Women*.

Critical Reception

The influence of *Little Women* has been vast, but historically limited to a female readership. Early critics received the novel with sentimental praise and an appreciation of Alcott's ability to meet the minds of her child readers, a view shared by Angela Brazil in her 1922 review. In the late nineteenth and early twentieth centuries, Alcott was appreciated, like many American women writers, as merely a local colorist with a talent for portraying the domestic sphere concretely. In academia, her novel was studied only by the scholars of children's literature until the 1960s and 1970s, when it came under closer scrutiny by feminist critics, some of whom were frustrated with its outdated sentimentality, others of whom dismissed it because it seems to uphold the traditional separation of men's and women's spheres (public vs. private). In the 1980s, the new emphasis on expanding the canon to include marginalized writers and works associated with popular culture brought more attention to *Little Women*. It has achieved importance within Women's Studies and the American literary canon in general for its detailed descriptions of nineteenth-century family life and of female struggles for social identity. As Carolyn Heilbrun suggests, *Little Women* has been particularly influential on female readers in the twentieth century who, craving models of female autonomy, found one, at least briefly, in Alcott's character Jo. Recent critics have continued in this positive vein, calling further attention to the subversive elements in *Little Women*, recasting Jo as an early feminist who, like her creator, made the most of the limited possibilities open to women in her time.

PRINCIPAL WORKS

Flower Fables (fairy tales) 1855
Hospital Sketches (letters and sketches) 1863
Moods (novel) 1864; revised edition, 1882
On Picket Duty, and Other Tales (short stories) 1864
The Rose Family. A Fairy Tale (fiction) 1864
Little Women; or Meg, Jo, Beth, and Amy 2 vols. (novel) 1868-69; also published as *Little Women and Good Wives,* 1871
An Old-fashioned Girl (novel) 1870
Little Men; Life at Plumfield with Jo's Boys (novel) 1871
Transcendental Wild Oats (memoir) 1872
Aunt Jo's Scrap Bag. 6 vols. (short stories) 1872-82
Work: A Story of Experience (novel) 1873
Eight Cousins; or, The Aunt-Hill (novel) 1875
Rose in Bloom. A Sequel to "Eight Cousins" (novel) 1876
A Modern Mephistopheles (novel) 1877
Under the Lilacs (novel) 1878
Diana and Persis (unfinished novel) 1879
Jack and Jill: A Village Story (novel) 1880
Proverb Stories (short stories) 1882
Jo's Boys and How They Turned Out (novel) 1886
A Whisperer in the Dark (novel) 1888
Louisa May Alcott: Her Life, Letters, and Journals (letters and journals) 1889
Comic Tragedies (drama) 1893
Behind a Mask: The Unknown Thrillers of Louisa May Alcott (short stories) 1975
Plots and Counterplots: More Unknown Thrillers of Louisa May Alcott (short stories) 1976
A Double Life: Newly Discovered Thrillers of Louisa May Alcott (short stories) 1986
The Selected Letters of Louisa May Alcott (letters) 1995
A Long Fatal Love Chase (novel) 1995

CRITICISM

Angela Brazil (review date 1922)

SOURCE: *"Little Women: An Appreciation," The Bookman,* Vol. LXIII, No. 375, December, 1922, pp. 139-40.

[*In the following review, Brazil praises Alcott's ability to write convincingly of childhood experiences as an adult.*]

To girls one of the most acceptable gift-books of the Christmas season will surely be this new and beautiful edition de luxe of **Little Women,** by Louisa M. Alcott.

In the days of my own youth I had revelled in the story, despite the bad print and lack of illustrations of a cheap edition, so I confess that when I saw it in this glorious new dress, with the lovely pictures giving such charming portraits of those dearest of old friends and playmates, Meg, Jo, Beth and Amy, I just sat down at once, and started to re-read it with all the rapture of my early teens. There are some girlhood tales which we skim through again, and wonder how our callow taste ever tolerated them, but to make re-acquaintance, after a gap of many years, with Miss Alcott's immortal masterpiece is to rejoice in it afresh, with the added appreciation of its true literary value.

What is the secret of the fascination of this story, which for more than fifty years has remained a prime favourite on both sides of the Atlantic? Why are the names of the members of the March family household words? Why are their little doings as familiar to most of us as the remembrance of the adventures of our own sisters and brothers? The answer to these questions lies, I think, in the fact that Louisa May Alcott had the genius to present to us, in her lovable heroines, four absolutely human girls exactly as she knew them in real life. She painted their pen-portraits with the faithfulness of a mistress of her craft, exaggerating neither virtues nor faults, and making us sympathise alike with their heroic little sacrifices or their many imperfections. In this style of writing she was a pioneer. Turn to most of the juvenile stories of fifty or sixty years ago, and you will find that the heroine was not so much a study of a real girl as a peg upon whom the authoress might hang her pet opinions, and into whose mouth were often put sentiments of so stilted a character that we can hardly imagine anybody young— outside a book—would ever express them, and certainly not in such flowery language.

How different are Meg, Jo, Beth and Amy! Their conversation is so natural that you can fancy you are sitting by their fireside and listening to them as they chat. How we love their grumbles and their little vanities, and are thrilled when Jo burns Meg's curls with the hot tongs, or when Amy goes to sleep with a clothes-pin on her nose, to try to uplift that offending feature in preparation for a party. We get to know them all so well, Meg with her girlish craving for the pretty things of life, brusque, hot-tempered, amusing Jo, gentle sweet-tempered Beth, and artistic, ambitious, little Amy, with her mispronounced long words, and her sense of sedate self-importance. Although they lived and worked during the time of the great American Civil War, they never seem out of date. Bob their hair, and dress them in knitted jumpers, and they would take their places as easily in 1923 as in 1861.

It is only an author who has the greatness and the simplicity to write of girls as she sees them, and not of girls as she thinks they ought to be, whose creations will thus outlast the march of the years.

One point worthy of special notice in the story of **Little Women** is Miss Alcott's skilful treatment of the struggles of a family of small means to make ends meet. There is never anything sordid in the descriptions, and the reader is carried away with enthusiasm for the little economies that go hand-in-hand with the charities, and sympathises heartily with the very natural longings expressed by the four heroines for the goods of this world. The humour of the book is delightful. Its racy language and joyousness of style carry us on from page to page with an interest that never flags from start to finish. We follow Meg through Vanity Fair, and Amy through the Valley of Humiliation, with equal enjoyment, and laugh over Jo's unsuccessful efforts at cookery, and at the effusions of the Pickwick Club.

There is nothing sentimental about **Little Women,** though of true sentiment we have tender touches. Can anything equal the pathos of the passage where Jo, mistaking sleep for death, believes that her favourite Beth has slipped over the divide?

> To her excited eyes a great change seemed to have taken place. The fever flush and the look of pain were gone, and the beloved little face looked so pale and peaceful in its utter repose, that Jo felt no desire to weep or to lament. Leaning low over this dearest of her sisters, she kissed the damp forehead with her heart on her lips, and softly whispered, Good-bye, my Beth; good-bye!

As if waked by the stir, Hannah started out of her sleep, hurried to the bed, looked at Beth, felt her hands, listened at her lips, and then, throwing her apron over her head, sat down to rock to and fro, exclaiming, under her breath, "The fever's turned; she's sleeping nat'ral, her skin's damp, and she breathes easy. Praise be given! Oh, my goodness me!"

Admirers of Miss Alcott's works have only one regret—that she did not live longer and write more. Personally I always wished she had given us a school story. My favourite chapter was the episode of the pickled limes at Mr. Davis's establishment, and while appreciating the spirit with which Amy bore her trying ordeal, snatched her things, and dramatically left the place "forever," I often regretted she had not patched up the quarrel, and gone back for further interesting scuffles with the irate master, or the sharp-tongued Jenny Snow, who made cutting remarks about "some persons whose noses were not too flat to smell other people's limes, and stuck up people who were not too proud to ask for them."

Oh, Amy March! How I lived with you in that supreme peep at your school days! Why did you let it all end so soon?

Louisa May Alcott must have been a very lovable personality, for it is an open secret that she put herself and her sisters into this most natural of stories, and that nearly all the experiences, grave or gay, pathetic or humorous, are bits from her early biography. She had the priceless gifts of laughter and of tears, and the talent which enabled her to express to other girls the charm and glamour of her own girlhood—no easy matter, for, by the time the necessary literary skill is obtained, the vision of youth is often lost to the writer, and only an elect soul can compass both.

I have heard of a boy who used to read the tales in a certain magazine until he came to the words "and now my dear young friends"—at which point he always flung the book violently away, knowing that he had skimmed the cream of the story and was getting to the more unpalatable portion which he wished to avoid. The "Sandford and Merton" type of composition was happily far away from Miss Alcott's ideals. She did not write "with a purpose," nor had her books any definite "mission." Yet her influence has been very great; she placed before growing girls a pure and high standard of conduct and aspiration, and showed the possibilities of heroism in "the daily round, the common task," though all in such a delightful, wholesomely human, and humorous fashion that nobody can accuse her heroines of priggishness or label them as "goody-goody." She wrote throughout for girls from a girl's point of view.

The illustrations by M. E. Gray for this beautiful edition of *Little Women* will meet with cordial appreciation; they are pictures in themselves, and give a most happy and realistic representation of how our friends, Meg, Jo, Beth and Amy, must have looked in the dear, old, brown house in America, which was their home. Beth with her dolls, Amy at Aunt March's, Meg as a fine lady, and Jo with her hair cut, are particularly attractive, also the frontispiece group of the sisters, and the sketch of the scene where they play *Pilgrim's Progress* in the fields. Is it too much to hope that we may have their further adventures in a companion volume, and that we can look forward, at another Christmas, to meeting "Little Women Wedded" in an equally delectable and delightfully illustrated edition de luxe?

Madeleine B. Stern (essay date 1943)

SOURCE: "The Witch's Cauldron to the Family Hearth: Louisa M. Alcott's Literary Development, 1848-1868," *More Books: The Bulletin of the Boston Public Library,* Vol. XVIII, No. 8, October, 1943, pp. 363-80.

[*In the following article, Stern provides the biographical and literary context behind Alcott's creation of* Little Women.]

When Louisa Alcott first began to write in the Hillside attic, she dipped her pen into the romantic, melodramatic ink that has ever been the property of sixteen-year-old authors. Wandering through a stormy world where noblemen unsheathed their daggers and stamped their boots, Louisa and her sister Anna produced a series of "lurid" plays aptly termed by the latter *Comic Tragedies.*[1]

"Norna; or, The Witch's Curse" and **"The Captive of Castile; or, The Moorish Maiden's Vow"** were produced in the barn with the aid of red curtains, ancient shawls, and faded brocades. The young actresses tossed roses from balconies, gathered herbs in dark forests, and boldly encountered those accommodating witches who brew magic potions in their cauldrons.[2] Nobles in green doublets were pursued by peasant girls disguised as pages. Suicide was a convenient panacea.[3] Strange grottos and death phials, forged letters and lovers' rings appeared at proper intervals for the delight of the Concord neighbors.

A Shakespearean twist was given to the plot now and then, when Rodolpho hired Hugo to murder Louis,[4] or when Ione was disguised as her own living statue.[5] Occasionally, the playwright took a suggestion from Milton, making Ion exclaim, "Thou mayst chain my limbs, thou canst *not* bind my freeborn soul!"[6] Even childhood fairy tales were grist for a mill that could grind out any number of counts and lords with appropriate destinies and costumes for each.

For the benefit of her neighbor, young Ellen Emerson, Louisa left the dark domain of melodrama to spin her *Flower Fables.*[7] In this sweeter, though no less marvelous fairyland, the only villains are droning bees; glow-worms and dew-elves ply a peaceful way; cakes of flower-dust with cream from the yellow milkweed provide a suitable diet for Concord fairies. Dr. Dewdrop, the Water Cure physician, ministers to the village elves.[8] The love of the tender Violet conquers the Frost King;[9] thorny Thistledown is redeemed;[10] Ripple, the Water-Spirit, restores the life of a child with flame from the Fire Spirits,[11] and, between the gray marbled covers of notebooks tied with pink ribbons, all is for the best in this best of all impossible worlds. Merely substituting Guido and Madeline for her flower heroes, Louisa Alcott continued in this fairytale vein, receiving five dollars from the Rev. Mr. Thomas F. Norris of the *Olive Branch* for her first published story, **"The Rival Painters. A Tale of Rome."**

All was for the best even when the author turned her attention to the more possible, though no less marvelous world that delighted Mr. W. W. Clapp, Jr., editor of the *Saturday Evening Gazette.* Though Louisa Alcott abandoned her fairies for human beings, she clung to the realm of cloying sweetness and cloudless light in order to increase her worldly stores by six or ten dollars. Having decided to make her fortune, "L. M. A." donned rose-colored glasses and followed the example of the Dickens of *Dombey and Son* and *The Old Curiosity Shop*[12] to see the benign influence that little children can exert upon an unyielding grandfather or upon an actress and her perfidious lover.[13] Alice's magic brings **"A New Year's Blessing"** into a cheerless home, and Little Genevieve, even in her death, ends a tearful, sentimental tale with the atonement of her erring parents. In a world where "white doves softly cooed" and "a cloudless morning sky arched overhead," Bertha[14] persisted in her loyalty to her music teacher until both character and author found virtue rewarded. Bertha herself won the love of Ernest Lennartson, and the author not only pocketed her ten dollars, but saw great yellow placards posted to announce the tale. In the course of the year 1856, while Louisa Alcott sewed cambric neckties and pillow-cases, she planned her stories and scribbled them down on Sundays, with the result that one tale after another covered the first page of the *Gazette.* **"Mabel's May Day"**[15] followed **"Bertha"** and again all was right with the world, for pride was conquered in the spirit of the wilful heroine. The year's output was concluded with the appearance of **"Ruth's Secret,"**[16] a tedious narrative in which an industrious young housekeeper takes care of her mother, "a poor lost creature," and for her virtues is blessed with the love of her employer's brother. Even the cloud of the "Magdalen" theme, later to reappear in **Work,** had a silver lining when the author was reaching a sentimental public that delighted in virtuous heroines who, after tearful trials, earned their well-merited rewards.

Thus far Louisa Alcott's literary effusions gave almost no hint of her future powers. Any talented youngster with an eye for the spotlights might have turned a barn into the haunt of villainous counts and witches; any imaginative girl might have given flowers a language or gazed through rose-colored glasses on a too cheer-

ful world. As one would expect from a youthful writer in the mid-century, it was, for the most part, the unreal, the magical, the supernatural that seized her attention. She wrote not of the real flowers that brightened the winding lanes along the Concord River, but of petals that harbored the folk of elfland; she saw no destinies at work among the neighboring farmers of the quiet village, but only such fates as lured to their doom the darkly unreal shadows of her dreams. If she viewed the world of reality at all, it was through a roseate haze that cloaked each story with a happy ending. To embellish the trappings of her imagination, she needed merely to draw down a copy of Mr. Emerson's Shakespeare or a volume of Dickens and borrow a touch here and there. This eclectic world of marvels has started many a writer along his path, and has brightened the lives of youthful dreamers who dropped their pens even before they dropped their dreams. Up to this point, then, Louisa Alcott differed not a whit from many another such dreamer. She might still have laid down her pen for a needle, if she wished, or locked up her scripts for a new broom.

Louisa Alcott, however, needed money, and she enjoyed the "lurid," melodramatic tales that had turned the Hillside barn into a haunt of witches. The penny dreadfuls would pay as much as two or three dollars a column for a sensation story to lift a reader from the humdrum world where the flow of gossip had ebbed. What was simpler, then, than to turn the dark-browed villains and the unloved wives to work and earn a carpet for the floor or a few new gowns to fit up the girls?

Little more than a year before Louisa was rewriting a fairy tale about the reformation of three little roses[17] for James Redpath, she was scribbling away at top speed on a "lurid" sensation story for *Frank Leslie's Illustrated Newspaper.* And this seems as good a place as any to interpose the thought that it is well nigh impossible to categorize and neatly label certain years of Louisa Alcott's—or indeed of any author's—life as the period in which certain works were exclusively produced. One phase leads gradually, almost imperceptibly, to another in every writer who is approaching maturity, and Louisa Alcott was no exception. There is no set date on which she stopped writing sentimental tales, for example, to start sensation stories at two dollars or so the column. Nor, indeed, is there any marked day on which one can record in red letters that now by the calendar Louisa Alcott stopped writing sensation stories and took up the more realistic domestic tales that were to make her fortune. These threads are all interwoven in more or less complex fashion in an author's life. With the pointer of analysis they may be marked out until the gradually changing warp and woof of the author's loom are lucidly traced.

An astute observer who had read Miss Alcott's first contribution to *The Atlantic Monthly* might have seen in **"Love and Self-Love"**[18] many of the elements that were to appear in later sensational stories. The relations between Little Effie and Basil Ventnor, the elderly gentleman who marries the child to provide her with a home, happen to be knit together with a respectable and happy ending, but the themes of incompatibility and attempted suicide were to appear subsequently in pseudonymous works that might bring perhaps better payment, but, if their authorship were recognized, a less savory reputation.

Miss Alcott was ever loath to append her signature to the stories that she wrote for Frank Leslie or James Elliott,[19] but there is little doubt that she enjoyed inventing strange names for her heroes, or providing them with a "savage element," or endowing her heroines with "indignant bosoms" and a spirit of revenge. Though her own critical instinct, never too well developed, rebelled against attaching her name to tales of murder and infidelity, she herself seems to have been fascinated by the details she wove into her sensational plots. Though the stories appeared before the public cloaked either in anonymity or pseudonymity, they did appear with striking regularity, for Miss Alcott enjoyed not merely the writing, but the fifty or one hundred dollar rewards that they brought.

It was, therefore, to a "lady of Massachusetts" that the first prize of one hundred dollars was awarded by Frank Leslie for **"Pauline's Passion and Punishment,"**[20] a story in which Pauline Valary's revenge for Gilbert Redmond's infidelity is interwoven, against a Cuban background, with details of forgery and brutality, capped with a fitting murder. The repartee of the protagonists consists of such remarks as, "Traitor! Shall I kill him?" to which the retort is, "There are fates more terrible than death." Even for Frank Leslie, however, the "moral tendency" must be considered, and so with the murder—"with that moment of impotent horror, remorse, and woe, Pauline's long punishment began,"—but the story itself ended.

James Elliott might not enrich his publications with such "appropriate illustrations" as characterized Frank Leslie's newspaper, but his prices were almost as high. For the firm of Elliott, Thomes, and Talbot, Miss Alcott, under the pseudonym of A. M. Barnard,[21] created her most incredible thriller. **"V. V.: or, Plots and Counterplots"**[22] is, as the title indicates, a long and involved story that boasts for its heroine Virginie Varens, a danseuse on whose white flesh "two dark letters"—V. V.—have been tattooed above a lover's knot. The yarn contains several disguises or impersonations, a mysterious iron ring, drugged coffee, and four violent deaths, one of which is perpetrated by a villain who falls upon his prey "with the bound of a wounded tiger." In a tale in which a viscount parades as a deaf and dumb Indian servant named Jitomar, in which poison vies with pistols or daggers for "the short road

to . . . revenge," and a murdered man has as his champion a cousin who looks like his twin, Miss Alcott reached the heights—or depths—to which a writer of sensational thrillers could possibly aspire. Suffice it to say she outdid even herself, and the stories that followed "V. V." must appear as anticlimaxes after this flight into the darkly impossible.

"A Marble Woman,"[23] **"Behind a Mask," "The Abbot's Ghost"** appeared with appropriate subtitles over the signature of the mysterious A. M. Barnard in *The Flag of Our Union,* but it was Louisa Alcott who collected the fifty or sixty-five dollars in payment for such effusions. The stories written for *The Flag* differ little in substance from **"Pauline's Passion"** except perhaps that they are more sensational. **"A Marble Woman"** has been modeled from the mold of **"Love and Self-Love,"** but to the basic theme of marital incompatibility has been added a dramatis personae including an ex-convict, a hero appropriately styled Bazil Yorke who moves in an aura of sorrow and mystery, and a benighted heroine who eats opium in her spare moments.

It is a credit to the ingenuity of Louisa Alcott that she could with impunity interpolate a sensational story into so respectable a narrative as **Work**.[24] Yet the chapter entitled "Companion" differs not at all from the tales that were flung across the pages of the penny dreadfuls. Insanity, suicide, and thwarted love provide the destinies that pursue such characters as "a mad Carrol" and a lad who frequents the "gambling tables and the hells where souls like his are lost." It is the companion herself, the sympathetic observer, who integrates the chapter with the rest of the book and contrives to make of it a fairly respectable interlude. Miss Alcott had not been long in discovering that the narrative powers she was gaining from scribbling her tales of horror could be combined with other themes and put to good use against other backgrounds.

The sensation stories carried by the penny dreadfuls, with their vitriolic burden of murder and vengeance, might be even more enticing to the public if they were timely. The Civil War was bearing in its wake the great tide of long-oppressed slaves, the flotsam and jetsam of a weakening South, humanity turned fugitive, "contraband." Here was a theme at hand, so malleable that it could be integrated with a sensation plot and a reader would scarcely know when he had escaped from the real world of the Rebellion to the nightmarish domain of melodrama. Even before the Civil War, the South could provide the mulatto, a type becoming more and more familiar to the North, as a character for a tale. The slave owners would brand his hand with mysterious initials that might lead to a weird and sinister plot. The technique of the sensation yarn would suggest a white woman to love the mulatto, and Louisa Alcott could despatch to a prospective publisher **"M. L.,"**[25] a story that was at once antislavery and melodramatic.

Even the ambitious *Atlantic* would not refuse a tale in which the tempestuous story of a stolen wife and a vengeful plan for murder was carefully worked round such characters as the contraband Bob and his white brother Ned, a wounded Reb. By placing the brothers in the same hospital room and introducing a nurse who could evoke from Bob the sad story of his past, Louisa Alcott created a plot with its roots in abolition and its branches in the realms of blood-and-thunder. Forgetting the latter, no doubt, and concentrating on the virtues of the former, Fields paid fifty dollars for **"My Contraband"**[26] and published it in November, 1863 for his Brahmin public.

The technique was simple, the rewards tempting. Louisa Alcott, recalling possibly the life of Fanny Kemble on her husband's plantation, wove another yarn about an island where the slaves plotted a sanguinary escape for liberty, and Gabriel, the righteous convictions of the North within him, freed them all, wrenched away "the rattle of fetters," baptized them with his own repentant tears. For **"An Hour,"**[27] compounded thus of the abolitionist doctrine and the stormy passions of a Dismal Swamp, Louisa Alcott reached the readers of *The Commonwealth* and received thirty-five dollars to pay the family debts.

Such stories could be manufactured easily once the pattern had been established. A little variety might be introduced by a slight change of character so that, for example, a Reb would lie next to a Northerner in a hospital ward. Poison could take the place of attempted strangulation. The result would be **"The Blue and the Gray"**[28] instead of **"My Contraband."** The elements of the story were violence, jealousy, and the will to murder—elements that Louisa Alcott had offered, and was still offering to the editors of the penny dreadfuls, but they were stirred now in a new crucible in which contrabands and mulattoes were heroes and abolition the loud, staunch war-cry. And so Louisa Alcott could serve the Union cause at the same time as she fulfilled her longings for the "lurid" and the sensational. The rewards of such patriotism were two-fold, for the author found she could reach a more respectable public and still place a fifty-dollar bill into the ever gaping family coffers.

The step from stories in which the Civil War theme was combined with a sensational plot to stories from which melodrama was eliminated and simple scenes of the Rebellion delineated in a straight and forthright manner, was one of the most significant in Louisa Alcott's career. She herself perhaps did not realize how important to her future was the laying aside of murder, poison, and jealousy for the depiction of **"A Hospital Christmas"**[29] in which a meagre dinner, the arrival of

a holiday box, the news of a child's birth, and the death (from natural causes) of a patient formed the sole elements of a simple, moving narrative. Surely the day on which Louisa Alcott turned thus to a realistic portrayal of an everyday war scene was as significant for her as the day, some four years later, when she sat down to write a girls' story for Thomas Niles. For, having once discarded the wild, tumultuous impossibilities that had peopled her imagination, she was left with little or no plot, and hence with the necessity of expanding her characters. This change from the alloy to the simple, from the "lurid" to the true, carrying with it an emphasis upon character instead of narrative, may—if one can mark any climacteric in a writer's life—be called the turning point of Louisa Alcott's career. She was developing now as the literary world was developing, from the strange to the natural, from the romantic to the realistic. She was paving the way for her future triumphs. She was beginning at last to write stories of a more lasting nature.

It would, no doubt, be convenient if Louisa Alcott had in every instance followed her sensational war stories with the more realistic variety. Dates, however, are not so important as themes. Even if the two types had appeared simultaneously, still the flow of truthful and simple war scenes from her pen would have marked her out for growth and indicated that she was approaching maturity. As it is, a few months did intervene between **"My Contraband"** and **"A Hospital Christmas,"** months during which Louisa Alcott had been able to pay for May's drawing lessons, had turned assiduously to her Dickens, and had realized, no doubt, that if the public could enjoy his more realistic characterizations it might also be ready for "straight" war stories without benefit of terror, mad passion, and strangulation.

The whining grumbler on the hospital cot, the kind attendant,[30] the mental courage of a wounded man awaiting death,[31] the heroism of two loyal brothers,[32] the embittered Massachusetts volunteer too early old[33]— these enlisted her attention now, and though **"A Hospital Christmas,"** for example, brought only eighteen dollars from *The Commonwealth* in contrast to the fifty dollars Louisa Alcott had received for "My Contraband," she gained more than she lost by this turn from the heavy-booted villains of old to the living men who moved about her. Now, if she wished, she could turn the key on her murderous counts and scarred mulattoes, and open the door through which a host of human beings, simple, kindly, and real, would walk as they did in life.

She herself had seen them—the willing nurse with her bandages and lint, her brown soap and sponge, the withered old Irishman on a cot, "overpowered by the honor of having a lady wash him," the tall New Hampshire man with his memories of his fallen mate, the doctor who regarded a dilapidated body as a damaged garment and set to work on it "with the enthusiasm of an accomplished surgical seamstress." At the Union Hotel Hospital in Georgetown, during six long weeks, Louisa Alcott had received enough impressions of human beings to carry her through a lifetime of story writing without the necessity of manufacturing such heroes as were never seen on land or sea. After she returned home, she brushed up her *Hospital Sketches,*[34] taking the details from the letters she had written to Concord, and laid the foundations of an art that would lead her to fame and fortune. Once again she washed feverish faces and smoothed tumbled beds, went the rounds with the doctors, observed the watchman's crooked legs and the tears of a twelve-year-old drummer boy, heard again the direful stories of Fredericksburg, and wrote what she had witnessed. No need now to invent a clash of arms between a darkrobed scoundrel and a noble lord. These men had met on the battlefield and had come to her for succor. War was as much a story of basins and lint, bandages and spoons, as of daggers and shields and gunpowder. All this she had experienced and put on paper. Romance was evicted and in its stead a crowd of living people thronged the page. Louisa Alcott had risen from her dreams and gazed on Truth, the never-failing source for story-tellers.

The source might have risen in a Georgetown hospital, but the author would not be long in discovering that there was a fountainhead of Truth bubbling freely in her home at Concord. Even before the Civil War she had begun to sip of it, evolving in Mark Field[35] a realistic character who finds himself after struggle and sacrifice and arrives at success through humanitarianism and humility. Closer home there had been the lives of four sisters compelled to earn their living in the ways best suited to their talents. Without romanticizing too much, Louisa Alcott had been able to sketch in **"The Sisters' Trial"**[36] one year in the careers of the actress Agnes, the writer Nora, the artist Amy, and the governess Ella. Four "little women" had found their way into print long before they had made the author's fortune. When Anna Alcott fell in love with John Pratt, her sister had once again found grist for her mill, seeing in their wholesome romance ample foundation for **"A Modern Cinderella."**[37] A pundit might very well declare that the early date of this significant story, 1860, sets askew any attempt to trace Louisa Alcott's penchant for domestic life as an outgrowth of her work on realistic war scenes. Here again, therefore, let it be stated that the seeds of a writer's interests may be early planted, but they germinate slowly. Needless to say, the bulk of the stories that eventually grew about the Alcott family hearth *followed* the author's sojourn in Georgetown and finally accorded to her a niche in literary history. The inference is that once the author discovered the saleability of truthful war scenes, she returned to Concord ready to find in the actual figures of her daily life characters for her stories. If realism

were an interesting and even profitable technique to apply to the soldiers of the Civil War, surely it could be extended to the Concord neighbors, to her sisters, to herself. Louisa Alcott was back where she had started—in the Hillside barn—but she had begun to search the minds of the youthful actors instead of the black-robed villains, to see in the easily gratified audience as wide a scope for stories as in the ghouls and spirits with which she had tried to enchant them.

In its way, **"A Modern Cinderella"** is as significant in Louisa Alcott's development as *Hospital Sketches,* for the story is, even more markedly than **"The Sisters' Trial,"** a skeleton of *Little Women.* She began, as she confessed, "with Nan for the heroine and John for the hero,"[38] but it was impossible to write a story about Anna's romance without introducing both her sister May and herself. The emphasis may be upon the simple, wholehearted love of Anna and her John, but realism demanded that the writer incorporate into the picture a sister who looked picturesque before her easel and another who could lose herself in the delights of *Wilhelm Meister* but hardly knew a needle from a crowbar. Laura is clearly a preliminary sketch of Amy; Nan needs only a touch here and there to emerge as the capable eldest sister, Meg; and Di, putting her mind through "a course of sprouts . . . from Sue to Swedenborg," corking her inkstand to plunge "at housework as if it were a five-barred gate," drowning "her idle fancies in her washtub," but determined one day to "make herself one great blot"[39] when the divine afflatus chose to descend upon her—surely Di is a Jo March in miniature. The course of Nan's love, despite the proverb, did run smooth, and Louisa Alcott was forced once again to resort to expanding her characters since her "plot" consisted of nothing more involved than a hardware clerk's wooing of her own sister.

In her own way, Louisa Alcott also traveled widely in Concord, finding in her neighbors and her family the groundwork for her tales. Gradually she began to inject into her simple stories of domestic life the humor that played about the corners of her mind. Her experience in acting in the "tavern" comedies[40] of the day was useful, teaching her to heighten an amusing situation or introduce a bit of homely and humorous dialogue.

As she had seen the wounded men of Georgetown, she had observed the tyro-gymnasts who made up "in starch and studs what they lost in color," the old ladies who "tossed beanbags till their caps were awry,"[41] the masquerades where little Bo-Peep was more interesting than the best-draped villain of the theatre, for her scarlet overdress concealed a being of flesh and blood. **"The King of Clubs,"** worked out of such details as these, has more than a passing interest, for just as Di is Jo March in outline, so August Bopp, the new leader of the class in gymnastics, may well have been an adumbration of Professor Bhaer. Like his successor, Mr. Bopp was a German who had come to America to earn a home for himself and his dependent. His "eminent nose" and blonde beard, his crop of "bonnie brown hair" were to appear later adorning the face of Professor Bhaer, and his gentle strength, his patient courage would shine once again reflected in the life of the better known professor of Plumfield.

The little white village of Concord harbored many such characters, gave material for many such tales. Simple, wholesome Debby, "the young crusader against established absurdities," lived not too far from the Lexington Road, and her affected Aunt Pen, who lost a set of teeth in the water, could not dwell much farther than Boston.[42] Surely Mrs. Podgers lived and moved and had her being in one of the neighboring farms; surely her teapot graced a tidy table of actuality, and the generosity of Mr. Jerusalem Turner was not untraceable.[43] Nelly's little hospital for the spiders and mice of the fields, modeled after that of the United States Sanitary Commission, might well have been planned by one of the Concord children.[44]

If the neighbors suggested so many lively character sketches, Louisa Alcott could find in her own life the material for a long and truthful story. Her travels both in America and Europe were already providing the source for many an amusing sketch.[45] Finally, in *Work,* on which she scribbled on and off for several years, she produced the sort of autobiographical novel with which most young authors today begin their careers. With her, however, it was not a beginning but an end, for after many forays into the dark forest of dreams the author had at last returned to that family hearth which was to brighten her days forever. Here she could sketch her own experiences in private theatricals, glorify somewhat her career in domestic service, enlarge upon her trials as a seamstress and a nurse, add to the humdrum lot of a girl who sought a living, a touch of romance, and unearth among the episodes of her life her own character, strong and unflinching before the world. The actual technique embarked upon in *Work* was to become a mannerism, a stereotype later on. Louisa Alcott would never forget that she had been apprenticed as a writer of short stories. Her full-length novels consist almost always of a series of episodes more or less related, a scrap-bag of stories tied together with the knot of character. From *Work* to *Little Women* the bridge is short. Louisa Alcott needed only to reduce the tragedies of mature life to the more sentimental tears of youth; her form of humor, inducing a chuckle at a homely phrase, would stand her in good stead when she wrote for children. If *Work* had centered upon her own trials and tribulations abroad in the world, she must simply return for a second look at her place in the family circle before taking up her pen to write the story for girls that was to establish her fame.

There is one exception always that proves the rule. Before she undertook *Little Women,* there was another novel in which Louisa Alcott took a fling at the world of dark, if not "lurid" passion. In the early edition of *Moods*[46] Sylvia discovers a solution to her romantic problems only in death, that ever convenient ending for melodramatic heroines who find themselves at odds with convention. Death, sleep-walking, shipwreck—the details of plot remind one of the violent deeds in *Comic Tragedies.* The author had matured, however, for she took space to interweave among the glaring threads of Sylvia's turbulent loves many a verbose remark on goodness and godliness, books and nature, dreams and visions, marriage and death. These deviations mark her growth. Passion and violence were not so all-sufficing that they could not be interrupted by a little essay on wisdom or a rambling account of intellectual love. *Moods,* meagre enough in worth, is yet better knit together than most of the episodic novels that were to follow. And within the account of stormy passion and death is imbedded a chapter that recalls the substance of **"A Modern Cinderella"** and points forward to *Little Women.* The golden wedding,[47] where Sylvia, Adam, and Geoffrey find themselves as uninvited guests, is an episode in which the melodramatic is forgotten and the simple delights of country songs and dances, hearty goodwill and honest generosity take the stage. And so the exception does actually prove the rule. The stormy Moods were to be exorcised and in their place would come the songs and dances of Concord, for Louisa Alcott was once again back at the family hearth from which no bearded villains or witches' wands would lure her away for long.

Though *Moods* sold rapidly at first, it would be but a short time before the author discovered that stories from her own roof-tree would sell far more rapidly. The fantastic would be buried; the realistic resurrected. Healthful romance would displace exotic passion, hygienic clothing would be recommended to the exclusion of flowing draperies and tightfitting boots, mischievous boys and grouchy aunts would take a stage deserted by Spanish nobles, and all such themes would be exalted on the altar of domesticity.[48] When Thomas Niles asked her for a girls' story,[49] Louisa Alcott would know to which girls she must turn for her characters, and would be ready to draw from the circle at home enough tales to satisfy her admirers. The fire in the family hearth was to send out a glow that would warm and comfort the author to the end of her days.

Notes

[1] *Comic Tragedies* Written by "Jo" and "Meg" and acted by the "Little Women." (Boston: Roberts, 1893). The plays were written and acted at Hillside principally in 1848.

[2] Louisa Alcott did not lose her interest in melodramatic plays. Years later, she dramatized her own story,

"The Rival Prima Donnas," issued under the pseudonym of Flora Fairfield in the *Saturday Evening Gazette* (November 11, 1854). The dramatized version, the MS of which is in Orchard House, was never produced.

[3] See "The Mysterious Page or Woman's Love," MS in Orchard House. The plot strongly resembles that of *Twelfth Night.*

[4] "Norna, or, the Witch's Curse," *Comic Tragedies,* p. 34 ff. Cf. *Macbeth.*

[5] "The Greek Slave," *Ibid.,* pp. 197 and 203 ff. Cf. *A Winter's Tale.*

[6] "Ion," *Ibid.,* p. 229.

[7] Louisa May Alcott, *Flower Fables* (Boston: George W. Briggs, 1855). It brought the author $32. Though the book was not published until 1855, it was written "for Ellen E. [merson] when I was sixteen." See Ednah D. Cheney, editor, *Louisa May Alcott Her Life, Letters, and Journals* (Boston: Roberts, 1889), p. 79.

[8] "The Fairie Dell," MS in Concord Public Library.

[9] "The Frost-King; or, The Power of Love," *Flower Fables.*

[10] "Lily-Bell and Thistledown," *Ibid.*

[11] "Ripple, the Water-Spirit," *Ibid.*

[12] For the more specific influence of *Dombey and Son* upon Louisa Alcott, see "Little Paul," *Saturday Evening Gazette* 16 (April 19, 1856), a poem patterned by Louisa upon the life of Paul Dombey. One of the author's favorite rôles in private theatricals was that of Mrs. Jarley, of *The Old Curiosity Shop.* In her childhood Louisa had organized "The Pickwick Club" with her sisters and produced "The Olive Leaf," scattered copies of which are extant.

[13] See "A New Year's Blessing," *Saturday Evening Gazette* 1 (January 5, 1856) and "Little Genevieve," *Ibid.* 13 (March 29, 1856).

[14] "Bertha," *Ibid.* 16 and 17 (April 19 and 26, 1856).

[15] "Mabel's May Day," *Ibid.* 21 (May 24, 1856).

[16] "Ruth's Secret," *Ibid.* 49 (December 6, 1856).

[17] *The Rose Family. A Fairy Tale.* (Boston: James Redpath, 1864). In a diary entry for December 1863, Louisa Alcott writes: "Rewrote the fairy tales, one of which was published; but . . . it was late for the holidays, . . . so the poor 'Rose Family' fared

badly." Cheney, p. 155. The story was reprinted in *Morning-Glories, and Other Stories.*

[18] "Love and Self-Love," *The Atlantic Monthly* V:XXIX (March, 1860). The story appeared anonymously, but is identified by a letter from A. B. Alcott to Sister Betsey, Concord, June 5, 1860, MS in *Family Letters* V, Concord Public Library. Reference to this letter is made through the courtesy of Mr. F. W. Pratt of Concord, Mass.

[19] There are some exceptions to this statement. "Enigmas" appeared under the signature of Miss L. M. Alcott in *Frank Leslie's Illustrated Newspaper* XVIII: 450 and 451 (May 14 and May 21, 1864). This story is a mildly exciting mystery about Italian refugees who are spied upon by a gentleman who finally falls in love with a woman disguised as a man. The element of mystery supersedes that of sensationalism here, and the absence of those incredible details that accompanied Miss Alcott's thrillers probably induced her to allow the story to appear under her own name.

"A Whisper in the Dark" was appended to a later edition of *A Modern Mephistopheles* (Boston: Roberts, 1889), but though Miss Alcott considered it "rather a lurid tale," (Cheney, p. 379) and though it does contain the theme of a marriage offer from an elderly man to a young girl, with a plot complicated by the clauses of a will, this story bears almost no comparison, in respect to shocking details, with the blood-and-thunder narratives issued anonymously or pseudonymously.

The same is true of "The Baron's Gloves," which Miss Alcott allowed to be reprinted in *Proverb Stories* (Boston: Roberts, 1882). The statement in the preface explains her point of view: "As many girls have asked to see what sort of tales Jo March wrote at the beginning of her career, I have added 'The Baron's Gloves,' as a sample of the romantic rubbish which paid so well once upon a time. If it shows them what *not* to write it will not have been rescued from oblivion in vain." It must be noted, however, that "The Baron's Gloves" centers about the romantic pursuit of a man with the initials S.P., and contains none of the horrifying themes in the tales that Miss Alcott declined to rescue "from oblivion." Incidentally, the background is that of a Europe that Louisa had come to know in her travels, rather than that of an exotic, untraveled Spain or Cuba. The story contains many actual details of Miss Alcott's life in Europe in 1865, even to the extent of the encounter with Ladislas Wisinewski—here appearing as Sidney Power, wounded in the Polish war, and afflicted with an interesting cough. Incredibly enough, the outlines of Amy's Laurie may be found in the hero of "The Baron's Gloves."

"The Skeleton in the Closet" (In Perley Parker, *The Foundling.* Boston: Elliott, Thomes and Talbot, [1867]) is another mildly exciting tale to which Louisa Alcott signed her name. Mme. Mathilde Arnheim, the heroine, has an idiot husband to whom the title refers, and to whom she is "bound by a tie which death alone can sever." Death finally does sever the tie and leaves the lady free, after one other trial by which the plot is complicated, to marry her beloved Gustave. Madame's steel bracelet, the symbol of her union with the imbecile, is removed, and in its place appears "a slender chain of gold." This not too shocking thriller is devoid of murder and brutality, the usual appendages of sensational stories.

The Mysterious Key, and What It Opened (Boston: Elliott, Thomes and Talbot, [1867]), published under the signature of L. M. Alcott, is a mystery of the type of "Enigmas" in which an Italianate boy spies on an English home, unlocks a casket with a silver key, and uncovers the secret of a hidden marriage. "Lurid" details have been laid aside for a stratagem which consists of nothing more exciting than a few false keys and feigned sleepwalking. The ending is anti-climactic, and the basis of the mystery sufficiently mild to allow Louisa Alcott to claim authorship. Here, too, the motif of the elderly gentleman married to a young wife reappears.

The conclusion does not seem unwarranted that Louisa Alcott did not allow the identity of the author of her most shocking thrillers to be known. All the stories whose authorship she claimed may be "romantic rubbish" indeed, but they appeared without benefit of the sensational details that accompanied her most daring flights for the penny dreadfuls. The latter, it must be repeated, remained either anonymous or pseudonymous.

20 "Pauline's Passion and Punishment," *Frank Leslic's Illustrated Newspaper* XV: 379 and 380 (January 3 and January 10, 1863). The story appeared anonymously, but is identified by a letter from the editor of Leslie's paper, E. G. Squier, to Miss Alcott, c. December 18, 1862, MS in the Orchard House.

21 For the discovery and identification of Louisa Alcott's pseudonymous works, see Leona Rostenberg, "Some Anonymous and Pseudonymous Thrillers of Louisa M. Alcott," *The Papers of the Bibliographical Society of America* 37:2 (June, 1943).

22 "V. V.: or, Plots and Counterplots" appeared originally in *The Flag of Our Union* XX: 5, 6, 7, 8 (February 4, 11, 18, 25, 1865), and was reprinted under the pseudonym of A. M. Barnard as a ten-cent novelette by Thomes and Talbot (Boston, [1865]).

23 "A Marble Woman: or, The Mysterious Model," *The Flag of Our Union* XX: 20, 21, 22, 23 (May 20, 27, June 3, 10, 1865). The other stories cannot be read now for, as Miss Rostenberg points out, the issues in

which they appeared have been stored away for the duration of the War by the Library of Congress.

24 *Work. A Story of Experience* (Boston: Roberts, 1873). The story was begun as "Success" in 1862. See Cheney, p. 129.

25 "M.L.," though written before February, 1860 (see Cheney, p. 120) was not published until 1863. It appeared originally in *The Commonwealth* I: 21, 22, 23, 24, 25 (January 24, 31, February 7, 14, 22, 1863). It was reprinted in *The Journal of Negro History* XIV: 4 (October, 1929).

26 "My Contraband; or, The Brothers," first appearing as "The Brothers" in *The Atlantic Monthly* XII:LXXIII (November, 1863) was written in August, 1863 and brought $50. It was reprinted in *Hospital Sketches and Camp and Fireside Stories* (Boston: Roberts, 1869).

27 "An Hour" was apparently rejected by *Our Young Folks* and sent in November, 1864 to *The Commonwealth,* where it was published, III: 13 and 14 (November 26 and December 3, 1864). Louisa received $35 for it. The story was reprinted in *Camp and Fireside Stories.*

28 "The Blue and the Gray, A Hospital Sketch," first appeared in *Putnam's Magazine* I: VI (June, 1868) and was reprinted in *Camp and Fireside Stories.*

29 "A Hospital Christmas" first appeared in *The Commonwealth* II: 19 and 20 (January 8 and 15, 1864). It brought $18, and was reprinted in *Camp and Fireside Stories.*

30 The characters appear in "A Hospital Christmas."

31 See "The Hospital Lamp," *The Daily Morning Drum-Beat* III and IV (February 24 and 25, 1864). The story reappears as an episode in "The Romance of a Summer Day."

32 See "Love and Loyalty," begun in April, 1864 and first published in *The United States Service Magazine* II: 1, 2, 3, 5, 6, (July, August, September, November, December, 1864). Charles B. Richardson promised $100 for the story. It was reprinted in *Camp and Fireside Stories.*

33 See "On Picket Duty," *On Picket Duty, and Other Tales* (Boston: James Redpath, 1864).

34 *Hospital Sketches* (Boston: James Redpath, 1863). The Sketches appeared originally in *The Commonwealth* I: 38, 39, 41, 43 (May 22, May 29, June 12, June 26, 1863). "Night Scene in a Hospital," taken from the Sketches, was published in *The Daily Morning Drum-Beat* Extra Number (March 11, 1864). Louisa Alcott's

interest in the soldiers was not confined to her attendance upon them in the hospital. See L.M.A., "Colored Soldiers' Letters," *The Commonwealth* II:44 (July 1, 1864).

[35] "Mark Field's Mistake" and its sequel, "Mark Field's Success," were published in the *Saturday Evening Gazette* XLV: 11 and 16 (March 12 and April 16, 1859).

[36] "The Sisters' Trial" appeared in the *Saturday Evening Gazette* 4 (January 26, 1856).

[37] "A Modern Cinderella: or, The Little Old Shoe" written in March, 1860, first appeared in *The Atlantic Monthly* VI:XXXVI (October, 1860), bringing $75. It was reprinted in *Camp and Fireside Stories.*

[38] Cheney, p. 120.

[39] The quotations are from "A Modern Cinderella," *Camp and Fireside Stories,* pp. 274, 286, 287, and 262 respectively.

[40] Many of the plays in which Louisa Alcott acted were set in taverns. "The Crooked Billet," a roadside inn, is the scene of *The Jacobite* by J. R. Planché, for example, in which Louisa Alcott played Widow Pottle in July, 1855, and on September 11, 1855.

[41] The quotations are from "The King of Clubs," *Camp and Fireside Stories,* pp. 99-100. "The King of Clubs and the Queen of Hearts" was written in April, 1862 and brought $30 when it was first published in *The Monitor* (Concord, Mass.) I:1, 2, 3, 4, 5, 6, 7 (April 19, April 26, May 3, May 10, May 17, May 24, and June 7, 1862). It was reprinted in *On Picket Duty.* It is interesting to note that the character of August Bopp was, in all probability, suggested by a Concord boy, Seymour Severance. See Louisa Alcott to Alfred Whitman, Concord, January 25, 1860, MS in Houghton Library.

[42] See "Debby's Début," *The Atlantic Monthly* XII:LXX (August, 1863). The story is reminiscent of "The Lady and the Woman," *Saturday Evening Gazette* 40 (October 4, 1856) in which strong-minded Kate Loring fights against fashionable absurdities and is rewarded with the love of Mr. Windsor.

[43] See "Mrs. Podgers' Teapot, A Christmas Story" written in November, 1864, first published in the *Saturday Evening Gazette* L:52 (December 24, 1864) and reprinted in *Camp and Fireside Stories.*

[44] See "Nelly's Hospital," *Our Young Folks* I:IV (April, 1865), reprinted in Washington by the United States Sanitary Commission, 1868.

[45] See "Letters from the Mountains," *The Commonwealth* I:47, 48, 49, 51 (July 24, July 31, August 7, August 21, 1863), "Up the Rhine," *The Independent* XIX:972 (July 18, 1867), and "Life in a Pension," *The Independent* XIX:988 (November 7, 1867).

[46] *Moods* was first published in Boston by Loring, 1865. The story was revised, with the ending changed, and published in Boston by Roberts in 1882. In the preface to the later edition the author comments on her changes resulting in "a wiser if less romantic fate" for the heroine than in the former edition.

[47] See also "A Golden Wedding: and What Came of It," *The Commonwealth* II:35 and 36 (April 29 and May 6, 1864).

[48] See *Kitty's Class Day.* (Boston: Loring, 1868); *Aunt Kipp* (Boston: Loring, 1868); and *Psyche's Art* (Boston: Loring, 1868).

[49] *Little Women* was not the first manuscript submitted in response to a request. Louisa Alcott had had experience in writing to order. See, for example, "Happy Women," *The New York Ledger* XXIV:7 (April 11, 1868). She had also had experience in writing for specific occasions. See, for example, the Christmas story, "What the Bells Saw and Said," *Saturday Evening Gazette* LIII: 51 (December 21, 1867), reprinted in *Proverb Stories.*

Lavinia Russ (review date 1968)

SOURCE: "Not to Be Read on Sunday," *The Horn Book*, Vol. XLIV, No. 5, October, 1968, pp. 521-26.

[*In the following essay, Russ examines the widespread appeal of* Little Women *one hundred years after its original publication.*]

Nineteen sixty-eight seems a strange time to talk about **Little Women,** and I seem a strange choice to do the talking. Of course there is an obvious reason for the date: October 3, 1968, will make it a neat one hundred years since **Little Women** was first published—published because an editor, Thomas Niles, nagged, in a Boston gentleman's kind of way, at Louisa M. Alcott to write the book. "I think, Miss Alcott," he told her, "you could write a book for girls. I should like to see you try it." He had to ask her twice. Her swift reaction the first time was that she knew nothing about girls, that she understood boys better. Circumstances—her family's—were on Mr. Niles's side when he asked her the second time. Her family, who always lived on the edge of economic disaster, was teetering perilously then, and she agreed to try. So Louisa M. Alcott, who before that had saved the family she loved by writing wild tales of blood and thunder, rescued them this time by writing about them—rescued them and created immortality for them. And for herself.

But 1968 seems a strange year to talk about the books she sent Mr. Niles at Roberts Brothers (*Little Women* was originally two books), strange to talk about these books in this year of violence that has already seen the most terrifying of all the faces of violence—assassination—not once, but two times. To think, let alone to write, about a book remembered as a story of a loving New England family in the nineteenth century seems about as timely as a history of antimacassars.

And I seem a strange choice to be writing about it. Though I write some reviews of children's books, I am no authority on children's literature, am not equipped by degrees to evaluate *Little Women* academically, nor by temperament—I loved it too much when I was young to evaluate it dispassionately, loved it so much when I was a girl that Jo was the second most important person in my life.

She must have been loved by other girls, millions of other girls, for Jo's book—and *Little Women is* Jo's book—has survived one hundred years. Survived! It has flourished like a New England oak! There are no exact figures available. Publishers did not keep sales figures back in the nineteenth century; and Little, Brown and Company did not take it over from Roberts Brothers until 1898. And nowadays with the countless editions of *Little Women* around, both in hardback and paperback, a search for the sales figures for one year would be a five-year project.

But Augusta Baker, Coordinator of Children's Services of the New York Public Library, who *is* an authority, told me that the two most circulated titles on the New York City Public Library's shelves are *The Diary of Anne Frank* and *Little Women.*

And Virginia Haviland, head of the Children's Book Section of the Library of Congress, who is *also* an authority, sent me a list of the countries, and in some instances the languages, in which *Little Women* has been published. Listen to their names. Together they form a musical wreath around the world—Argentina, Belgium (Flemish), Brazil, Czechoslovakia, Denmark, Egypt (Arabic), Eire, England, Finland, France, Germany, Greece, Hungary, Iceland, India (Urdu), Indonesia, Israel, Italy, Japan, Korea, Netherlands, Norway, Persia, Poland, Portugal, Russia, Spain, Sweden, Taiwan, and Turkey.

Not everybody loves *Little Women.* Brigid Brophy didn't love it—she took six full columns in the *New York Times Book Review* to say why, ending her blast against sentimentality by calling it "a masterpiece, and dreadful," a blast which shot her readers straight to their bookshelves to reread their copies of *Little Women.*

Ernest Hemingway did not love the idea of it—in Paris, when he and this century were young, Hadley and he once asked me up to their flat. When I walked in with a copy of Ibsen's plays under my arm, Ernest put me down with "You're so full of young sweetness and light you ought to be carrying *Little Women.*" (He had never read it.)

The unknown critic who wrote one of its first reviews didn't dislike *Little Women,* but did not announce the birth of a masterpiece with any ruffle of drums. "Louisa Alcott is a very spritely and fascinating writer, and her sister, May Alcott, always makes beautiful pictures to illustrate the books. Their books and stories are always interesting and instructive about everyday life. They are not religious books, should not be read on Sunday, and are not appropriate for the Sunday School. This is the character of the book before us. It is lively, entertaining, and not harmful."

Why did *I* love it? Why did all the millions of girls who have read it in the last hundred years love it? Why do all the girls who are reading it all around the world today love it? To find out, I reached for my copy of *Little Women* with its title page "Little Women or Meg, Jo, Beth and Amy, by Louisa M. Alcott, with illustrations in color by Jessie Willcox Smith, Boston, Little Brown and Company, 1915," with its inscription on the fly leaf from the most important person in my life—"Lavinia Faxon—To a Little Woman—Father." And for the first time in fifty years, I read it straight through, from the very beginning—"'Christmas won't be Christmas without any presents,' grumbled Jo, lying on the rug"—to the very end, to the sunny afternoon at Plumfield, where all the Marches had gathered to celebrate Marmee's sixtieth birthday with presents and songs—"Touched to the heart, Mrs. March could only stretch out her arms as if to gather children and grandchildren to herself, and say, with face and voice full of motherly love, gratitude, and humility, 'Oh my girls, however long you may live, I never can wish you a greater happiness than this!'"

I read it all, and I found out, I found out why I loved it. I had a strong hunch I had found out why when I read earlier Cornelia Meigs's splendid biography of Miss Alcott, *Invincible Louisa,* and when I read *Louisa M. Alcott: Her Life, Letters and Journals,* edited by Ednah D. Cheney. I found out for sure when I reread *Little Women.* I loved it because Louisa M. Alcott was a rebel, with rebels for parents. I found out why other girls loved it—because Jo was a rebel, with rebels for parents. Not the rebels of destruction—they never threw a brick—but rebels who looked at the world as it was, saw the poverty, the inequality, the ignorance, the fear, and said, "It isn't good enough" and went to work to change it.

They did not attack poverty by buying a ticket to a charity ball at the Waldorf. Poverty was their neighbor, often their star boarder. Charity was no Lady Bountiful; charity was another name for compassion.

Mrs. Alcott ran an informal employment service, "a shelter," Louisa Alcott describes in her journal, "for lost girls, abused wives, friendless children, and weak or wicked men." In her journal Louisa tells how "One snowy Saturday night, when our wood was very low, a poor child came to beg a little, as the baby was sick and the father on a spree with all his wages. My mother hesitated at first, as we also had a baby. Very cold weather was upon us, and a Sunday to be got through before more wood could be had. My father said, 'Give half our stock, and trust in Providence; the weather will moderate, or wood will come.' Mother laughed, and answered in her cheery way, 'Well, their need is greater than ours, and if our half gives out we can go to bed and tell stories.'"

The Alcotts attacked inequality by working for Abolition. Louisa, who had a memory, so far back in her childhood that she couldn't remember where or when, of finding a slave hidden in the vast oven of one of the houses they lived in, wrote of a meeting to protest the return of a runaway slave, which she went to when she was nineteen—"I should be horribly ashamed of my country if this slave is taken back."

Louisa M. Alcott was among the first to work for suffrage for women. In an 1881 letter to Mr. Niles—"I can remember when Antislavery was in just the same state that Suffrage is now, and take more pride in the very small help we Alcotts could give than in all the books I ever wrote or ever shall write." Then in characteristic salty fashion she adds, "I, for one, don't want to be ranked among idiots, felons, and minors any longer, for I am none of the three, but very gratefully yours, L. M. A."

The Alcotts attacked ignorance with truth—truth they looked for constantly and found in the inward life, not in the established manners and mores of their time. Always with Ralph Waldo Emerson nearby to offer advice, encouragement, and practical help, they sought for truth. Louisa's father, Bronson Alcott, taught truth as he found it. He was one of the first teachers to respect his pupils and to trust their instincts as he respected and trusted the instincts of his own children. He found such joy in learning that to teach was a joyful experience, and he taught children that to learn was a joyful experience.

They attacked fear with faith. And laughter. When poverty threatened to change from a familiar who was a constant annoyance to have around, to an enemy who could destroy them, they routed him with faith. When Bronson Alcott came back from what we would now call a lecture tour, Louisa recorded in her journal, "In February Father came home. Paid his way but no more.

A dramatic scene when he arrived in the night. We were waked by hearing the bell. Mother flew down crying 'My husband.' We rushed after her, and five white figures embraced the half frozen wanderer, who came in hungry, tired, cold and disappointed, but smiling bravely and as serene as ever. We fed and warmed and brooded over him, longing to ask if he had made any money, but no one did till little May said after he told all the pleasant things, 'Well, did people pay you?' Then with a queer look he opened his pocketbook and showed one dollar, saying with a smile that made our eyes fill, 'Only that. My overcoat was stolen and I had to buy a shawl. Many promises were not kept, and traveling is costly. But I've opened the way and in another year shall do better.' I shall never forget how beautifully Mother answered him, though the dear hopeful soul had built much on his success. With a beaming face she kissed him, saying, 'I'd call that doing *very well.* Since you are safely home, dear, we don't ask anything more.' Anna and I choked down our tears and took a little lesson in real love which we never forgot. Nor the look that the tired man and the tender woman gave one another. It was half tragic and half comic, for Father was very dirty and sleepy, and Mother in a big nightcap and funny old jacket."

And when death knocked uninvited at their door, they welcomed him, serene in their faith that death was not an enemy, but the darker brother of life.

Brigid Brophy was wrong about *Little Women.* A girl in Russia cries over Beth's death, not because it is sentimental, but because it is brave. And a girl in India cries when Jo refuses Laurie, because she realizes suddenly that life is not going to hold a neat, happy ending for her.

Ernest Hemingway was wrong about *Little Women.* If he had read *Little Women,* he would have realized that it is not "sweetness and light," it is stalwart proof of his definition of courage: grace under pressure.

Its early reviewer was wrong about *Little Women,* because if religion is living Faith, Hope and Charity every minute of your life, the Alcott-Marches were a truly religious family.

Above all, girls are right to love *Little Women,* every word of it, because it is a story about *good* people. And if there is one generality that is true (and it is the only generality I will ever make about them), it is that young people love goodness. And if there is one hope for us in 1968, the only one, it is that the young recognize the power of goodness, and the responsibility that goodness demands of men and women of good will—the responsibility to their brothers, the responsibility to look at the world as it is—at the poverty, the inequality, the ignorance, the fear—and to say "It isn't good enough" and go to work to change it.

Kate Ellis (essay date 1977)

SOURCE: "Life with Marmee: Three Versions," in *The Classic American Novel and the Movies,* edited by Gerald Peary and Roger Shatzkin, Frederick Ungar Publishing, 1977, pp. 62-72.

[*In the following essay, Ellis claims that unlike the film adaptations of* Little Women, *which stereotype girls, Alcott's book represents them as serious and capable people.*]

In times of economic and social upheaval, the sphere of home and mother is always there to fall back on. This at least is what popular literature and the media would have us believe. Yet war and economic depression often necessitate changes in the family that bring reality into conflict with the ideal of a single male breadwinner and his flock of happy dependents. Men in wartime leave home to fight, while female members of the household are drawn into the labor force—paid and unpaid—in support of the war effort. And when employment is scarce, women's menial jobs do not disappear as quickly as men's work. It is therefore not surprising that, in the aftermaths of wars or depressions, books and films idealizing the domestic sphere should find an especially receptive market. It is in this light that I would like to look at Louisa May Alcott's novel *Little Women* and its two film versions, appearing in 1868, 1933, and 1949 respectively.

The novel *Little Women* opens in the middle of the Civil War. Father is away, and does not appear until the middle of the book, after which his presence is confined mainly to his study—"offstage," so to speak. His ineptitude as a breadwinner is mentioned in the opening chapter, though none of the daughters makes an issue of it the way the spoiled, selfish Amy (played by Elizabeth Taylor) does in the 1949 film version. Fiscal authority in the March family lies mainly with the women throughout the novel, and Meg and Jo are proud to contribute to the family income, though neither particularly likes her work—as governess and paid companion respectively.

This deviation from the ideal is rectified by the pre-eminence of Father as the source of moral authority, a role that he can play from a distance since Marmee is the agent through whom his wisdom is transmitted to his four "little women." We can see this downward flow of authority in the scene where Marmee reads Father's Christmas letter to his daughters and wife, written from the front and quoted in full, incidentally, in both film versions.

> Give them all my dear love and a kiss. Tell them I think of them by day, pray for them by night, and find my best comfort in their affection at all times.

A year seems a very long time to wait before I see them, but remind them that while we wait we may all work, so that these hard days will not be wasted. I know that they will be loving children to you, will do their duty faithfully, fight their bosom enemies bravely, and conquer themselves so beautifully, that when I come back to them I may be fonder and prouder than ever of my little women.

This letter, replete with Biblical echoes ("a cloud by day and a pillar of fire by night"), suggests a modern Christ urging his faithful disciples to love one another, to carry out his work in his absence, and to await with patience and hope his return ushering in the millenium.

Father does communicate directly with his family after he returns, but Alcott reproduces almost nothing of these conversations. Those she does show us are between Marmee and her girls, where father is a supreme but absent God who teaches gently and by example. We see this in a conversation between Jo and Marmee about anger, the "bosom enemy" that Jo must conquer if she is to be a source of pride to her father. "You think your temper is the worst in the world," says Marmee to her daughter, "but mine used to be just like it." Jo is astounded, since she has never seen her mother show anger, but Marmee insists that she feels anger every day of her life, and felt it particularly strongly when Father lost his money and she had four small children to deal with, economically and emotionally. "Poor mother!" Jo exclaims. "What helped you then?" to which Marmee replies:

> Your father, Jo. He never loses patience—never doubts or complains—but always hopes and works, and waits so cheerfully that one is ashamed to do otherwise before him. He helped and comforted me, and showed me that I must try to practice all the virtues I would have my little girls possess, for I was their example.

Marmee exemplifies a warmth and openness with her daughter that is a departure from the Puritan model of child-rearing, where the emphasis was on "breaking the will" of the naturally willful, intractable, sinful child. Observers from Europe coming to America after the Civil War noted the precociousness of American children, to whom their parents were companions rather than distant authorities. The frequency with which American mothers and children were thrown on their own resources while the males of the community were engaged in "civilizing" a new land undoubtedly laid the groundwork for this development even before the Civil War took men from their homes in a systematic way. But it was in the 1860s that the new freedom began to attract comments, most of them unfavorable. One American observer in 1863 warned his fellow citizens of "an irreverent, unruly spirit [that] has come to be prevalent, an outrageous evil among the young people of our land."[1] The demise of family discipline, in other words, was lamented in the same language that we hear used today.

What Alcott did in her novels about children was to show how this method of teaching by example rather than by severity could be made the basis of a new family ideal: a modified "little commonwealth" that might reflect the democratic spirit stirring in the larger society, and which might at the same time preserve the moral preeminence of Father even in his physical absence. Previous children's literature had presented life as a grim *Pilgrim's Progress*, as the title of one frequently reprinted work, first published in 1700, suggests:

> A Token for Children; Being an Exact Account of the Conversion, Holy and Exemplary Lives and Joyous Deaths of several young children. To Which is added A Token for the Children of New England of Some Examples of Children in whom the Fear of God was remarkably budding before they died in several parts of New England, Preserved and Published for the Encouragement of Piety in Other Children.

The spirit behind this document was softened slightly over the next century and a half, but religious tracts conveying essentially this message remained the principal reading material for children up to the time that Alcott began writing.

In *Little Women* we see her making conscious use of this exemplary tradition of her predecessors. The Christmas letter, the references to John Bunyan's *Pilgrim's Progress* in the early chapters, and the use of his characters and place names for chapter headings ("Playing Pilgrims," "Burdens," "Beth Finds the Palace Beautiful," "Amy's Valley of Humiliation," "Jo Meets Appolyon," "Meg Goes to Vanity Fair") all suggest a spiritual progress that ends, for three out of the four girls, in the presence of a husband who takes Father's place as their moral authority. It is significant, I think, that Jo's Professor Bhaer, the most overtly paternal of the three husbands, is first shown romping spontaneously with children. He thus has character traits that make him eligible to head the kind of modified patriarchal family that Alcott accommodates to her other vision of economically capable, self-sufficient women.

Writing at a time when the Civil War had not only loosened the bonds of parental authority but given impetus to the movement for women's rights, Alcott endowed the March women not only with an appreciation of female earning power but with the high spirits that tend to accompany such competence in the world. All the girls dream of fame and wealth, building "castles in the air," and Jo and Amy do more than dream: they work hard at their writing and painting. Moreover, the negative side of these high spirits is neither whitewashed nor turned into trivial bickering, as it is in both film versions. Rather, it is expressed in real temptations that are portrayed vividly before they are overcome. For instance, Amy burns a notebook in which Jo has been writing her stories, and Jo in retaliation allows Amy to skate where the ice is thin, with the result that she falls into the freezing river and risks drowning. Amy's anger has been set off by the discovery that her older sisters have excluded her from an expedition they were planning. The painful lesson she is resisting, and which Jo resists right up to her meeting with Professor Bhaer, is that exclusion is part of growing up, that the four sisters cannot do everything together as they did as children. Yet her feelings, as Alcott portrays them, are simultaneously childish and serious, and set off a chain of increasingly severe retaliation that ends only when Jo turns to Marmee for help and they have the talk about anger mentioned above. In presenting family harmony as a product of struggle against strong negative emotions that would have condemned children in earlier literature to the fires of everlasting damnation, Alcott made a real contribution to the representation of children in fiction.

What makes *Little Women* more than an innovative book for children is Alcott's portrait of Jo as an economic force in her family's household and later behind her husband and his school. Before Jo leaves for New York she has won a hundred dollars in a short story contest, published a novel that receives mixed reviews, and tasted the joys of self-sufficiency. Her father's advice, which he probably follows himself, is to "aim at the highest, and never mind the money," but Jo's head is not so far in the clouds. Alcott comments:

> Wealth is certainly a most desirable thing, but poverty has its sunny side, and one of the sweet uses of adversity is the genuine satisfaction that comes from hearty work of head or hand; . . . Jo enjoyed a taste of this satisfaction, and ceased to envy richer girls, taking great comfort in the knowledge that she could supply her own wants, and need ask no one for a penny.

Later in New York, "her emaciated purse grew stout," and fed her dream of "filling home with comforts." These comforts may be seen as luxuries and thus not a threat to Father's position as prime breadwinner, but a trip to the seaside for her mother and dying sister, Beth, is hardly a "frill." Jo's role in the economy of her household is one of the contradictions of the March ménage, as it was of the Alcott home.

At the end of *Little Women* Jo apparently gives up her writing and thus her access to money of her own. Yet it is her inheritance of Aunt March's house that provides the building for her husband's school for boys. She may become "Mother Bhaer" to the pupils he teaches, but she does not become his economic dependent. Much later, in *Jo's Boys* (1886), the school runs into financial hard times and she takes up her pen to earn money. After having lost her girlish dream of success and fame, she becomes a celebrated American author, a New England tourist attraction, in fact. She is thus always, either potentially or actually, the economic moving force behind whatever household she is in.

Alcott is able to get away with this partly because Bhaer, like Father whom he replaces, is so clearly the moral authority in Jo's life, particularly when it comes to ending her career as a writer of sensational stories. But also Alcott was writing at a time when the feminist movement, though small, was strong and growing. In the 1930s, when the first film version of the novel came out, feminism was perceived to have run its course and died. By 1949 there was strong backlash against the idea of women working outside the home at all. Moreover, the portrayal of working women by Hollywood has always been somewhat ambiguous. The thirties produced the most serious and extensive treatment of the subject, but the focus of many thirties films on stage careers is not accidental: actresses and chorus girls were not taking jobs from men. Katharine Hepburn could therefore rise to stardom in *Stage Door* (1937) without upsetting the all too visible apple cart, while *Gold Diggers of '33*, though it focuses on the plight of unemployed chorus girls, ends with a moving plea by Joan Blondell for full male employment.

It is not surprising, then, that Hollywood had difficulty both with the unfeminine exuberance of young Jo and with her later earning power as a writer. The problem with both of these attributes is that our culture views them as masculine qualities, and did so particularly in the periods of difficult social adjustment when the two films appeared. This was also true in Alcott's day, though the fact that the economy was still for the most part rural gave a scope for female competence that waned after World War I with the advent of home appliances and processed foods, and had all but disappeared in the suburban home of the late forties. This development affects not only women but also children who, having no useful economic function in relation to their families the way children in a rural economy do, are reduced to paradigms of cuteness. The media contributed to this new image of the cute child and the child-centered family, giving us the "Our Gang" series in the twenties, Shirley Temple in the thirties, followed by Mickey Rooney, Margaret O'Brien, Roddy McDowell, and a host of other child stars. The problem with Jo March is that she is not merely cute,

yet Hollywood found it difficult to deal with any other qualities in children. This impoverishment of the media notion of family life is particularly visible in the later version of the book, which is simply a showcase for stars as stars: Janet Leigh, June Allyson, Elizabeth Taylor, and Margaret O'Brien, with Peter Lawford adding a heavy dose of precocious virility.

Unlike media adolescents in the twentieth century, Alcott's Jo is both a serious person and a tomboy. She is also quite maternal, and the first time she visits the orphaned Laurie she gives the gloomy living room of the Laurence mansion the benefit of a woman's touch. When he tells her his mother died, and turns away "to hide a little twitching of the lips that he could not control," Alcott comments:

> The solitary, hungry look in his eyes went straight to Jo's warm heart. She had been so simply taught that there was no nonsense in her head, and at fifteen she was innocent and frank as any child. Laurie was sick and lonely; and, feeling how rich she was in home love and happiness, she gladly tried to share it with him. Her face was very friendly and her sharp voice unusually gentle. . . .

The George Cukor version of 1933 has some of this innocence in it; but the Mervyn Le Roy remake (1949) with June Allyson and Peter Lawford is a stereotyped boy-meets-girl encounter, and at no point during the youth of Jo are the sharp voices of either actress who played the role "unusually gentle." Apparently a tomboy cannot walk or talk normally, let alone gently. She must be constantly swaggering, stomping, thrusting out her chin and exclaiming, "Christopher Columbus!" Then to offset Jo's masculinity and give us a hint of things to come, both directors give us a touch of comic eroticism. Hepburn and Douglass Montgomery fence in the style of Hamlet until Hepburn falls and the audience, along with Laurie, get a brief view up her skirt until her gallant partner helps her up. June Allyson, a little more restrained, burns her skirt, falls to the ground face down, and lets Peter Lawford beat the back of her skirt with a broom.

For Hepburn this boyish image changes dramatically and without explanation in the last third of the film, as the heroine who has sold her hair to help finance Marmee's trip to Father's sickbed in Washington, and who climbs out of windows and talks out of the side of her mouth, suddenly becomes (such is the transforming power of the right man) the subject of dreamy, soft-focus close-ups. She positions herself next to the piano while Professor Bhaer is singing "None But the Lonely Heart" (a scene not in the novel) and leans back in a way that allows his head to be outlined against her breast and torso. Later, when they return from the opera, she who vowed to wear her hair in

Scene from the 1949 film Little Women *starring June Allyson and Peter Lawford.*

pigtails till she was twenty is wearing a low-cut dress and leans back seductively against the bannister while she responds to the professor's broken English. From being Hepburn the tomboy she suddenly becomes, under Cukor's loving direction, Hepburn the star, as Alcott's image of the true-woman-as-mother gives way to the glamorous image of escapist thirties films: top hats and evening dresses.

June Allyson's portrait of adolescence is more consistent, but reflects the increasingly stereotyped view of adolescence. Despite the period costumes, she is a suburban teen-ager on her way to the altar. This effect is created partly by Allyson's acting style: she is one of those wholesome actresses, perpetually virginal and smiling, who gave to the forties and fifties films in which they starred their peculiar brand of premarital unreality. It is also created by the sets, which were not researched as Cukor's were, and have the low-ceilinged coziness of suburban colonial living. Further, even the few references to the world beyond the home that appear in the novel and the Cukor film are cut out of this one. The Cukor film begins, for instance, with

soldiers marching through town and Marmee at the commissary giving a coat to an old man who has lost four sons. In 1949 studios were discreet about invoking the war dead on screen.

One other unmentionable in both 1933 and 1949 was the pride of a woman at the sight of her "emaciated purse" growing stout. In the earlier film, the first money Jo receives for a story is not a hundred dollars but a dollar fifty. In 1949 the value of that first check has dropped to a dollar! When Professor Bhaer confronts Jo with his opinion of her stories (something that does not happen in the novel: he only suspects, and, like an understanding father, forgives a poor girl her desire to make money), Katharine Hepburn mentions briefly and apologetically the things she has been buying for her family. June Allyson does not mention her purchases, but simply resolves to Rossano Brazzi (one could not have a real German in this romantic role in 1949) never to err again. In the novel, the "simple stories" that Jo writes after she returns home from New York are sent by her own hand to a publisher, and win her some real success that she can acknowledge to her family. In the films, she sends everything she writes to Bhaer, and he takes care of her career, bringing her finally a copy of the novel for which his friend has "great hopes," but which do not translate, as far as we can see, into cash for his author.

One final eradication that is performed in the 1949 version, but not in the earlier one, is the passage of time itself. In the Cukor film, Spring Byington is a not very intelligent looking middle-aged Marmee who wears her gray hair in the style we find in photographs of nineteenth-century matrons in their fifties. A nineteenth-century woman whose oldest daughter was fifteen would probably be in her late thirties but no attempt is made by Cukor to make Marmee look youthful. The same is true for Father, who comes home from the war emaciated and white-haired. It seems that such an image of a returning soldier was not acceptable to those in charge of casting the later film. In this version Leon Ames as Father looks only a few years older than Peter Lawford, his daughter's admirer, while Mary Astor's Marmee has exquisite red hair with not a streak of gray to be seen.

This attempted annihilation of the generation gap is in part a by-product of the fact that all members of the younger generation except Beth are played by adult actors trying to look ten years younger than they are. But I suspect that a large part of the message of this film to its postwar audiences was that home was a place where men could return to wives who had not aged, and where wives could greet men whose experiences overseas could be wiped out and forgotten. Home, then, was a place where both parties could begin again as if time had stood still for five years, and where Father's preeminence was not only economic and moral. It was physical as well, which meant that he wanted his "little women" to have become in his absence not so much virtuous as attractive. It was in the early fifties that Ivory Soap ran a series of ads which pictured a mother and a daughter and asked if you could tell the difference. If you look at Jo and Marmee in this film it is, in fact, hard to tell which one is more successful in canceling out the effects of time.

Notes

1 Quoted in John Demos and Virginia Demos, "Adolescence in Historical Perspective," in *The American Family in Social-Historical Perspective,* edited by Michael Gordon (New York: St. Martin's Press, 1973), pp. 211-12.

Elizabeth Lennox Keyser (essay date 1982)

SOURCE: "Alcott's Portraits of the Artist as Little Woman," *International Journal of Women's Studies,* Vol. 5, No. 5, November-December, 1982, pp. 445-59.

[*In the following essay, Keyser discusses the functions of stories and play in* Little Women—*as escape, as training, and as allegory for the novel as a whole.*]

I

Recently an Indian friend of mine told how, as a girl growing up in Kerala, she had won a contest for a speech in English and, as a prize, received a copy of Louisa May Alcott's *Little Women.* She especially remembered the words of the man who presented it to her: "Read this, and be a great woman!" Initially I was struck by the irony of this injunction, for, according to my own and other feminist readings of the novel, to become a little woman is to relinquish one's dream of becoming a great one.[1] But there is a sense in which *Little Women,* if read aright, can help us avoid the stumbling blocks of self-denial which, no less than those of self, obstruct a woman's path to creativity.

The book opens as the four March sisters receive a letter from their absent father, a Union Army chaplain, exhorting them to "fight their bosom enemies bravely and conquer themselves so beautifully that when I come back to them I may be fonder and prouder than ever of my little women."[2] The girls' mother, Marmee, aids them further by suggesting that they play in earnest their childhood game of Pilgrim's Progress. Marmee's doctrine that life is a spiritual journey seems trite but unexceptional until one reflects on the way Pilgrim's Progress is played in the March household. Marmee reminds the girls of how they used to "travel through the house from the cellar, which was the City of Destruction, up, up, to the housetop, where you had all the lovely things you could collect to make a Celestial City." When twelve-year-old Amy claims to be too old for such games Marmee reproves her: "We never are too old for this, my dear, because it is a game we are playing all the time in one way or another. . . . see how far on you can get before Father comes home." Thus, the doctrine implies first that women's pilgrimage is merely a game, an imitation of men's, and second that it takes place within the confines of the home for the purpose of winning male approval. To reinforce the constricted nature of women's sphere, Alcott has the girls divide the sheets they are sewing into continents "and in that way [they] got on capitally, especially when they talked about the different countries as they stitched their way through them."

Part I of *Little Women* is filled with accounts of the girls' games, amusements, and entertainments, most of which have a symbolic function. The amateur theatricals in Chapter 2, which are juxtaposed with the playing of Pilgrim's Progress in Chapter 1, are as significant as the theatricals in *Mansfield Park* or the charades in *Jane Eyre.* In "The Witch's Curse," written by Jo, there are eight parts, thus requiring that each of the four girls play two of them. Jo plays both the hero and the villain, which suggests not only her longing for male freedom and her major role in the larger drama of *Little Women* but, more importantly, the way she is divided against herself. Meg, the most conventional of the girls and the quickest to reprove Jo, plays both the witch, whose curse destroys the villain, and Don Pedro, "the cruel sire" whose patriarchal authority would thwart the hero. Amy is cast as both the airy sprite and Zara, the heroine, but her hopeless stiffness in the latter role and the way she brings the romantic-looking tower tumbling down suggest that she, no less than Jo, is too solid and substantial to permit herself to be etherealized. Finally, Beth plays a rosy retainer, the role she habitually plays in the March household, but before that she plays an ugly black imp, which implies a darker side to her nature.

Playing, pretending, acting—these activities loom large in the lives of the March girls and would seem to offer compensation for and temporary liberation from poverty, irksome tasks and, above all, the constricting roles of little women. Jo in Chapter 1 complains that "I can't get over my disappointment in not being a boy" and consoles herself with playing "the man of the family now Papa is away." Her dramas allow her to play "male parts to her heart's content" and the girls' Pickwick Club, which publishes its own newspaper, also enables her to simulate the masculine world from which she is excluded. But the futility of their efforts to escape their destined roles becomes clear at the one meeting we witness of the Pickwick Club. When Jo recommends admitting Laurie, the boy next door, Meg and Amy object: "We don't wish any boys, they only joke and bounce about. This is a ladies club, and we wish to be private and proper." In fact, by learning to make-believe and play various parts, the girls are rehearsing for the games and roles they will, as Marmee says, be playing all their lives. Significantly, Meg, not swashbuckling Jo or stiff Amy, is described as the most accomplished actress. Although she professes to be too grown up to continue acting in Jo's productions, she is simply ready to play the part in life assigned her, a part for which, more than the other girls, she has a talent.

The Gardiners' party in Chapter 3 points up both the opposition between Meg and Jo, suggested by their roles in "The Witch's Curse," and the nature of the part that Meg is anxious to play. Meg is concerned that Jo's party dress is torn and burned in back because of Jo's habit of standing too close to the fire. Thus she warns Jo to "sit still all you can and keep your back out of sight; the front is all right." Because, according to Meg, "a real lady is always known by neat boots, gloves, and handkerchief," Jo must wear one of Meg's clean gloves, even though her hand is larger and will stretch it, and carry a strained one crumpled in her other hand. As they enter the party Meg admonishes Jo not to shake hands if introduced to anyone because "it is not the thing." At first Jo is miserable, standing

against the wall to conceal the back of her dress, but she is hardly more so than Meg whose "tight slippers tripped about so briskly that none would have guessed the pain their wearer suffered smilingly" and who pays for her dubious pleasure with a sprained ankle. The simple details of this chapter skillfully suggest that girls like Jo, who burn their frocks and soil their gloves, who, in other words, are too full of passion and life or who lack the refinement of a "true lady," must acquire the art of concealment and that even girls like Meg, to whom the art comes almost naturally, must hide their pain and suffer injury in consequence. Before Meg's accident, however, Jo meets Laurie, forgets her dress, and dances a spirited polka with him in the freedom and privacy of a long hall. Thus, Alcott would seem to suggest that there are a few, like Laurie, to whom a woman may freely show both sides of her nature, even if one side is slightly soiled or singed. But Jo's few relaxed moments simply sharpen the images of pain, concealment and constriction. Jo's comment on the evening, "I don't believe fine young ladies enjoy themselves a bit more than we do," can thus be read ironically. The irony, if anything, is reinforced by the narrator's ambiguous comment, "And I think Jo was quite right."

Such ambiguity is typical of the narrator even when she seems to be affirming the life of selfless service and patient, silent suffering. To Beth, the sister who comes closest to embodying the ideals of little womanhood, such service is second nature. Just as she was the rosy retainer in Jo's play, so Beth, "a housewifely little creature," ministers to the wants of her mother and sisters. Not content with that, she amuses herself by setting up a hospital for infirm dolls. Later, she insists on visiting a family with typhoid while Jo is too engrossed in her writing to do so, and as a result she nearly dies of the disease. Even after she recovers at least enough to resume her household chores, Beth is unable to conceive of a future beyond the confines of her parents' home, and with the approach of adulthood she wanes and finally dies. In one of the many passages which cloy if not read ironically, Alcott, doubtless for the sake of her Victorian audience, has the narrator glorify Beth's passive, retainer role: "There are many Beths in the world, shy and quiet, sitting in corners till needed, and living for others so cheerfully that no one sees the sacrifices till the little cricket on the hearth stops chirping, and the sweet, sunshiny presence vanishes, leaving silence and shadow behind." The modern reader, however, is struck by the vision of thankless martyrdom and the connection between self-sacrifice and death.[3]

Marmee, as well as the narrator, seems to express the author's doctrine of compensation for self-discipline and self-denial. But even when Marmee's moralistic judgments seem unequivocal, the incidents that prompt them admit of more than one interpretation. For example, in Chapter 4 ("Burdens") what at first reading appears to be a sermon on the need for cheerful resignation becomes, on a closer reading, a protest against women's ignorance, passivity, vulnerability and dependence. In this chapter each girl gives an account of her day after which Marmee extracts a single moral from them all: "When you feel discontented, think over your blessings and be grateful." Jo, who resents her dependent position as paid companion to crotchety Aunt March, discovers she is lucky because, unlike her aunt, she can appreciate the magnificent library "left to dust and spiders" since her uncle's death. Jo does not speculate as to why the old woman is so severely limited, why the library her husband prized is no resource to her. But *we* wonder, especially later when we see the good use to which Mr. Laurence, as old and lonely as Aunt March, puts *his* library. Meg, like Jo, resents her dependent position, but she concludes she is luckier than the wealthy family she serves as governess because she hasn't "any wild brothers to do wicked things and disgrace the family." Meg does not reflect, as we do, that at least boys *can* be wild and wicked while their sisters remain passively at home to be disgraced by them. Amy stops envying a friend when that friend is punished in a most humiliating way for having made a caricature of the schoolmaster; what *we* see, however, is the danger of ridiculing the male power structure. Finally, Beth tells how, in the fish market, Mr. Laurence presented a big fish to a poor woman who had nothing with which to feed her family. Although Beth's point is the goodness of Mr. Laurence and her own comparative good fortune, what *we* see is the working class woman's dependence on the patriarchal establishment. Alcott, by having Meg laughingly accuse Marmee of turning their stories against them in order to extract a moral, indicates her recognition that each story, far from pointing up the girls' good fortune, exposes something about the unfortunate condition of women, a condition in which they all share.

II

As Jo was both hero and villain of her own play, so she is the complex character of the novel, the one who undergoes inner conflict. The nature of that conflict is defined by her relationships with her sisters, her mother and her friend Laurie. That the other girls represent alternate possibilites for Jo is, in fact, suggested by Laurie's role. He is, as has been pointed out, a suitor for each girl in turn:[4] he is regarded in the "Vanity Fair" chapter and later by Jo as a potential suitor for Meg, is an actual, if unsuccessful, suitor for Jo, is regarded by Jo as a suitor for Beth, and is finally a successful suitor for Amy. But Laurie not only points up how Meg, Beth and Amy all represent aspects of Jo; he too represents an important aspect. As mentioned earlier, he is the one with whom Jo can be completely natural. Confined, almost imprisoned in the big house next door, he is freed by Jo in a reversal of

the Sleeping Beauty tale. In boldly entering the house which she regards as "a kind of enchanted palace, full of splendors and delights," and by confronting gruff old Mr. Laurence, Jo seems to be appropriating male power and freeing part of her own nature. In fact, the shabby old brown house containing the five women, and the stately but lifeless stone mansion which contains Laurie, his grandfather and the tutor, John Brooke, could represent the feminine and masculine spheres. Jo and Laurie, whose friendship brings the spheres into contact and thus enlarges both of them, seem together to make up a whole, androgynous person; Jo's nickname suggests her longing for masculine freedom and independence whereas Laurie's nickname, "Dora," and even "Laurie" itself suggest the feminine in his nature, the kinship with his artist mother. Although Jo draws him into the March girls' charmed feminine circle, she seems to bring out the manliness in "Teddy," as she alone calls him. With Laurie, "her boy," Jo is able to enjoy the male camaraderie for which she has always longed.

Although each offers and accepts so much from the other, a barrier, represented by Jo's horsehair pillow, remains between them. When Laurie threatens to run away to Washington and take Jo with him, "Jo looked as if she would agree, for wild as the plan was, it just suited her. She was tired of care and confinement, longed for change." But then she puts the temptation from her. "If I was a boy, we'd run away together and have a capital time; but as I'm a miserable girl, I must be proper and stop at home." Later, when Jo, for reasons she finds difficult to explain, rejects Laurie's much more serious offer of marriage, she feels "as if she had stabbed her dearest friend, and when he left her without a look behind him, she knew the boy Laurie would never come again." Alcott's description of this parting makes it clear that Jo has not only betrayed a friend but a crucial part of herself which she cannot hope to recover.

The boy in Jo, as represented by Laurie, is successfully opposed by Meg, Beth and Marmee. Meg and Jo, as the two oldest sisters, have a special relationship rather like that of Jane and Elizabeth Bennet. Jo writes her mother that Meg "gets prettier every day, and I'm in love with her sometimes." Whereas Elizabeth encouraged Jane's romantic interest in Bingley, Jo is frightened and angry when John Brooke seems to be courting Meg: "I just wish I could marry Meg myself, and keep her safe in the family." The threat to Meg seems a threat to Jo herself, and in her desire to protect her sister, she exposes her fear and suspicion of masculine domination. In Jo's play, we remember, Meg had been the witch and Don Pedro, the symbol of patriarchal authority. In her unquestioning acceptance of that authority, and in her affinity for the traditional female role, she does, much as Jo loves her, represent a threat and a curse. Despite their closeness, she and Jo are always at odds. Jo's "good strong words that mean something" are "dreadful expressions" to Meg. Jo enters the "enchanted palace" for the first time partly because she loves "scandalizing Meg by her queer performances." Like the benign witch in the play, Meg opposes what to her seems villainous or shocking in Jo, but, like Don Pedro, she also opposes what is heroic or creative. She does not realize that to subdue the one is to stifle the other. As the model lady, wife and finally, mother, Meg represents the patriarchal pattern imposed on women that Jo would escape. This explains Jo's outrage when, breaking in on the proposal scene, she finds "the strong-minded sister enthroned upon [John Brooke's] knee and wearing an expression of the most abject submission."

Although Amy is stronger-minded and less sweet-tempered than Meg, they are both outwardly feminine and concerned with appearance and propriety. Thus they, too, have a special bond, leaving Jo to form one with her younger sister Beth. In one of the many significant juxtapositions in **Little Women,** Alcott, as though to point up the striking contrast between Jo and Beth, has Beth enter the "Palace Beautiful" shortly after Jo's first visit to the "enchanted palace." But whereas Jo enters boldly, without a formal invitation, Beth creeps in only after being assured that she will see no one. She is as drawn to the grand piano as is Jo to the library, but Mr. Laurence, recognizing that her timidity almost cancels out her pleasure, provides her with a "cabinet piano" so that she can remain at home. Yet, despite her meekness, "over her big, harum-scarum sister Beth unconsciously exercised more influence than anyone in the family." Jo refers to Beth as her conscience, and when she looks at Beth's hood "the submissive spirit of its gentle owner seemed to enter into Jo." As Jo's conscience, Beth, as in the play, is both Jo's retainer and her black imp. Her influence is more subtle and insidious than Meg's because Jo is not conscious of a need to struggle against it.

Marmee, who like Jo possesses a quick temper, teaches the self-repression which Beth alone has completely achieved, as well as the feminine and domestic virtues so readily acquired by Meg. Although Marmee admits to Jo that she is still "angry nearly every day of my life," she has "learned not to show it" and hopes "to learn not to feel it." When Jo asks her how she has learned to "keep still," Marmee explains that Jo's father made "it easy to be good." But the lesson is not so much that men make it easy to be "still" and "good"; rather, they demand it, and women, being economically dependent, learn to comply.[5] Although Marmee gives Meg tips for dealing with her husband's temper as though it were Meg's duty to govern both his and her own, she still insists that "To be loved and chosen by a good man is the best and sweetest thing which can happen to a woman." But to so insist is not, as has been argued, to allow "her girls a great freedom . . .

the freedom to remain children and, for a woman, the more precious freedom *not* to fall in love."[6] Although Marmee does not make worldly matches for her girls as she is accused of doing in a conversation Meg overhears, she makes it clear that marriage is the desired event for which to wait, if not to strive. There is, then, a sense in which Mrs. March *does* allow the girls to remain children: by denying them other options and by repressing the parts of themselves that would make other options available, she keeps them dependent, undeveloped, diminutive—like Beth, who literally fails to attain adulthood.

In another sense, though, Marmee is for denying the pleasure-loving child, and the consequences of such denial are implied when Jo endangers Amy's life. Just as Jo is closest to Beth, the sister she least resembles, so she resents Amy, the sister whose self-assertiveness mirrors her own.[7] In Chapter 8, Amy wheedles Meg and Jo to let her accompany them to the theatre with Laurie. Meg is willing but Jo refuses, calling her a little girl and a baby. Amy warns Jo she will be sorry, and retaliates by destroying Jo's "loving work of several years." Jo is unable to forgive her, and later, when Amy tags after her and Laurie, Jo spitefully neglects to warn her of some thin ice. The resulting accident points up the consequences not only of strong emotion but of trying to repress it. In punishing and nearly killing Amy, Jo is trying to punish and exorcise the needy, greedy, demanding and childish part of herself that Amy represents, but Amy's near-tragedy suggests the futility and danger of attempting to do so.[8] Further, Amy's destruction of Jo's book after having been spurned by Jo implies that such repression interferes with creativity. As has been argued, Jo is in a double-bind: "as a girl, [she is] constantly being told that she is not supposed to express what's in her—yet her vocation is to be a writer."[9] Just as Amy was the heroine in Jo's play, the issue at stake between the hero and the villain, so she seems to represent something crucial in Jo's nature, something towards which Jo is deeply ambivalent. Unfortunately, Jo and Marmee see this episode as calling for more repression and self-control rather than for a recognition of the feelings that prompted it.

After Laurie is rejected by Jo, he marries Amy who, like him, seeks happiness and self-fulfillment, and who is not afraid to assert herself, take risks and appear foolish or selfish. Jo, too, desires self-fulfillment, what she calls independence, but she has so internalized her mother's values that she cannot seek it without guilt. Jo views the publication of her first story as the first step in realizing "the dearest wishes of her heart"—"to be independent and earn the praise of those she loved." But the two wishes are incompatible: to achieve independence she will have to assert herself in such a way as to incur blame; and to win the praise of those she loves best, she will have to curtail her striving for independence.[10] When Meg is staying with the worldly

Moffats, she slips Marmee's note "into her pocket as a sort of talisman against envy, vanity, and false pride." Similarly, Jo pins Marmee's note inside her frock "as a shield and reminder, lest she be taken unaware." Jo must guard against her emotions at all times; otherwise she will disappoint her mother and, through her, her father. When, upon his return, Mr. March praises Jo, causing her to blush with pleasure, it is for having become a "young lady who pins her collar straight, laces her boots neatly, and neither whistles, talks slang, nor lies on the rug as she used to do"—in short, a lady as defined earlier by Meg.

Part I ends with Laurie wishing he could look three years ahead into their futures. But Jo, significantly, does not wish to, "for I might see something sad, and everyone looks so happy now, I don't believe they could be much improved." Comparing the end of Part I with the end of Part II, we can appreciate Jo's wisdom. Each part ends with a family tableau: in Part I Mr. and Mrs. March sit together, the engaged couple, Meg and John, sit together, and Laurie leans on the back of Jo's chair so that the two are reflected in a long glass; in Part II, John and Laurie play cricket with the boys, Mr. March strolls deep in conversation with Professor Bhaer, Jo's husband, and Jo sits with her mother and the two surviving sisters. Masculine and feminine spheres, momentarily united by the friendship of Jo and Laurie, are once again separate.

III

Meg's marriage, with which Part II begins, is an extreme but not unusual case of separate spheres. Meg is described as "growing womanly in character, wise in housewifely arts." What strikes the reader, though, is the constriction—physical, mental and emotional—to which Meg must adapt. The lawn of Meg's home, which she refers to as "my baby home," is "about as big as a pocket handkerchief" and her dining room is described as a "tight fit." Just as Meg at the Gardiners' party had to smile although her slippers pinched her feet, so now she must gracefully, even gratefully, accept her cramped and narrow lot in life. While John takes "the cares of the head of a family on his shoulders," Meg's greatest challenge is the making of currant jelly. Her failure touches off the one quarrel we witness between Meg and John, during which Meg declares "I'm sick, dead—anything." Rash as these words are, the imagery surrounding Meg's marriage does indeed suggest a living death.[11] After the birth of her twins, Daisy and Demi, Meg complains to Marmee that she is "on the shelf." Marmee, to do her justice, exhorts Meg not to "shut yourself up in a bandbox because you are a woman, but understand what is going on and educate yourself to take your part in the world's work." In other words, Marmee urges Meg to enter, at least through reading and conversation, her husband's sphere and, by teaching him how to help in the nurs-

ery, to draw John into hers. Although John succeeds in teaching *her* how to cope with their son, Demi,[12] years of little womanhood have ill-prepared Meg to enter John's world of ideas. Having asked John to read her something about the election, Meg soon "decided that politics were as bad as mathematics" and regarded her bonnet "with the genuine interest his harangue had failed to waken."

After a few such domestic experiments, Meg learns "that a woman's happiest kingdom is home" and achieves "the sort of shelf on which young wives and mothers may consent to be laid, safe from the restless fret and fever of the world, finding loyal lovers in the little sons and daughters who cling to them."[13] These loyal lovers, Meg's Daisy and Demi, perpetuate the sexual stereotypes Jo tries in vain to escape.[14] At three, Daisy begins to sew "and managed a microscopic cooking stove with a skill that brought tears of pride to Hannah's [the March's servant's] eyes, while Demi learned his letters with grandfather" and "developed a mechanical genius which delighted his father." Whereas Daisy demands a "needler," Demi actually tries to construct a sewing machine. Furthermore, in their relationship to each other they also reflect age-old stereotypes: "Demi tyrannized over Daisy, and gallantly defended her from every other aggressor, while Daisy made a galley slave of herself and adored her brother as the one perfect being in the world." Daisy is so angelic, such a perfect little woman, that she reminds her family of Beth. "Her grandfather often called her 'Beth,' and her grandmother watched over her with untiring devotion, as if trying to atone for some past mistake, which no eye but her own could see." But it is unlikely that even her keen eye detects what the reader's can: that in rewarding Beth, and now Daisy, for angelic or slavish, self-abnegating behavior they fail to prepare them for full participation in the adult world.

Ironically, it is Jo, not Daisy, who, as we shall see, eventually succeeds Beth as "angel in the house." At the beginning of Part II, however, Jo is still defiant of sex role stereotypes and determined to expand her sphere. When Laurie returns from college, Jo can hardly refrain from "imitating the gentlemanly attitudes, phrases, and feats, which seemed more natural to her than the decorums prescribed for young ladies." In an attempt to reconcile the selfless homebody role with masculine assertiveness, Jo boasts that "if anything is amiss at home, I'm your man." Recognizing marriage as a threat to her independence, Jo prefers "imaginary heroes to real ones, because when tired of them, the former could be shut up in the tin kitchen [where she keeps her manuscripts] till called for, and the latter were less manageable."[15] She uses her pillow, "hard, round, covered with prickly horsehair," as a "weapon of defense, a barricade," against Laurie, who she senses is becoming romantic about her. But in evading Laurie, Jo walks into the very domestic trap she has sought to avoid. Encouraged by Marmee, who believes Jo and Laurie "are too much alike and too fond of freedom," Jo goes to New York where, just as she is getting a taste of independence, she finds in Professor Bhaer the "something sweeter" than freedom that Marmee had wished for her.

Whereas Laurie had always encouraged Jo's writing without attempting to direct it, Jo's parents and later, Professor Bhaer, are as ruthless as her opportunistic publishers. While still at home, Jo had tried seriously to write and described her fits of inspiration as falling into a "vortex." After earning several checks for her stories, "she began to feel herself a power in the house." But although she enjoys both the process and the proceeds of her writing, it does not, as she had hoped, bring her the praise of those she loves. The process disturbs Marmee, who always "looked a little anxious when 'genius took to burning'" and when her sensation story wins a prize, her father says "You can do better than this, Jo. Aim at the highest, and never mind the money." Unlike her father, however, she cannot ignore the money her fiction earns, for "she saw that money conferred power." But she does try to reconcile her desire for power with her duty, as a woman, to be self-less: "Money and power, therefore, she resolved to have, not to be used for herself alone, but for those she loved more than self." When, after attempting a serious novel, her family offers suggestions for improvement, "the young authoress laid her firstborn on the table, and chopped it up as ruthlessly as any ogre." Later, the newspaper to which she takes her sensation stories asks her to edit out all moral reflections, and she feels "as a tender parent might on being asked to cut off her baby's legs in order that it might fit into a new cradle." Jo's work, no less than Meg's life, must accommodate itself to a "tight fit," and the strikingly similar passages equate her parents' moral with her publishers' amoral influence.

Professor Bhaer, who saves Jo from "the frothy sea of sensational literature," is, like John Brooke, a tutor, and his romance with Jo, like John's with Meg, begins in German lessons. For Christmas, Bhaer gives Jo what he calls a "library" between two "lids," an edition of Shakespeare, which he takes from its "place of honor with his German Bible, Plato, Homer, and Milton"— patriarchal works and authors all. Bhaer, in giving her Shakespeare, hopes "the study of character in this book will help you read it in the world and paint it with your pen." However, as Virginia Woolf points out in *A Room of One's Own,* women cannot write like Shakespeare until, freed from the fetish of chastity, they are allowed to experience life as Shakespeare and other male authors have done.[16] Jo, under the stimulus of her sensation writing, has begun to free herself and to experience life, at least vicariously: "as thrills could not be produced except by harrowing up the souls of the read-

ers, history and romance, land and sea, science and art, police records and lunatic asylums, had to be ransacked for the purpose." As a result, Jo begins to catch "glimpses of the tragic world which underlies society," but the narrator, like Professor Bhaer, reproves her for "beginning to desecrate some of the womanliest attributes of a woman's character," and as Woolf continues, "Chastity . . . has so wrapped itself round with nerves and instinct that to cut it free and bring it to the light of day demands courage of the rarest."[17] Sadly, Jo, for all her spirit, lacks this courage.

Professor Bhaer is described as "a genial fire"; "people seemed to gather about him as naturally as about a warm hearth." But in a sense, Bhaer's fire is less than genial in that it throws a damper on Jo's creative powers. After Bhaer, in disgust, burns a sheet of the despised *Weekly Volcano* for which Jo writes, she rereads her work, feeling as though she is wearing the Professor's glasses (significantly, he is short-sighted). Jo "had tried them once, smiling to see how they magnified the fine print of her book; now she seemed to have got on the Professor's mental or moral spectacles also, for the faults of these poor stories glared at her dreadully and filled her with dismay." She ends by stuffing the whole bundle into her stove and, after a few vain attempts to write didactic fiction, corking up her inkstand. Professor Bhaer is satisfied to see she has "stood the test" and "given up writing." Having sacrificed the *Weekly Volcano* and the vortex of creativity to Bhaer's "genial fire," Jo goes on to sacrifice "my boy," as she calls Laurie, to "my Professor." Ironically, in rejecting Laurie, Jo tells him, to his indignation and disbelief, "You'd hate my scribbling, and I couldn't live without it." This seems disingenuous as Laurie, unlike Professor Bhaer, has always championed her writing; when Jo first went to sell a story to a newspaper, Laurie waited outside the office with a "Hurrah for Miss March, the celebrated authoress!" Alcott further associates Laurie with Jo's writing by having her feel, after she has rejected him, as though she "had murdered some innocent young thing and buried it under the leaves," a feeling, we recall, which Jo had when editing her work against her better judgment.

IV

With the departure of Laurie from Jo's life, the dying Beth gains ascendancy. Jo takes Beth to the shore where "they were all in all to each other." When they return home, Jo devotes herself "body and soul to Beth," whose room becomes a shrine, "a little chapel, where a paternal priest taught his flock the hard lesson all must learn." For Jo, "My Beth" replaces "my boy," and in a poem Jo asks Beth to "Give me that unselfish nature." Gradually, Jo begins to feel "that I won't lose you, that you'll be more to me than ever, and death can't part us." Beth promises "I shall be your Beth, still" and urges Jo to take her place, assuring her, "you'll be happier in doing that than writing splendid books or seeing the world." "And then and there Jo renounced her old ambition, pledged herself to a new and better one." After Beth's death, Jo assumes her role: she takes shelter in her mother's arms, sits in Beth's little chair close beside her father, and assumes Beth's house-keeping duties with Beth's implements. Although it has been argued that Beth "dies so that the others can marry,"[18] her death seems to perpetuate childish dependency. Specifically, in Jo's case, her death signifies the internalization of the values that Beth represents, the values of little womanhood. In turning from Laurie as she earlier turned from Amy, and in turning towards Beth and Professor Bhaer, Jo relinquishes her dreams of success and independence in order to secure the approval of those she loves. In exacting such a sacrifice, Beth is not only Jo's conscience or retainer; she is also the "black imp" of "The Witch's Curse."[19]

At this time Jo also turns to Meg and begins to contemplate the advantages of marriage and domesticity. Meg recommends them as a means of bringing out "the tender womanly half of your nature." Marmee, realizing it is safe now to do so, encourages Jo to write "something for us, and never mind the rest of the world." After she has done so, her father mails the piece to a popular magazine where it is accepted and much acclaimed. Jo wonders, "What *can* there be in a simple little story like that to make people praise it so?" Her father tells her, "you have found your style at last"; but Jo demurs: "If there *is* anything good or true in what I write, it isn't mine; I owe it all to you and mother and Beth." Jo's works are described now as "little stories," "humble wanderers," received by a "charitable world" and sending back "comfortable tokens to their mother, like dutiful children." The image of the female artist as mother, her works as dutiful children, suggests how Jo has withdrawn into the feminine sphere from which she had sought to escape. Even the word "charitable" reminds us of women's economic dependence and implies Jo's acceptance of it. The tension between Jo's desire for success and her desire for love has dissolved at last, and she cares more for being loved and approved than for anything else in the world.[20]

Jo, then, for all her engaging qualities, cannot provide us with a model of the female artist. Amy, on the other hand, appears to reconcile her love of art with her desire for love, perhaps because, unlike Jo, she never attempts to appropriate the male role. Significantly, she plays the heroine in Jo's play, whereas Jo attempts to play both hero and villain. Always ladylike, Amy shrewdly defines Jo's version of independence as a desire to "go though the world with your elbows out and your nose in the air." Jo's unconventionality, while genuine, is, as Amy implies, a matter of appearance and manners; she is only independent of those for whom she cares nothing. Amy, on the other hand, moderates her behaviour so as to please those who can help her, but she is truly independent of those upon whom it is most tempting to rely. In the chapter "Artistic Attempts," Amy, despite the derision of Jo, who accuses her of truckling to people, plans a luncheon party for the wealthy girls in her drawing class, and she retains her composure when, as Jo predicted, only one of them shows up. In the chapter "Calls," Amy's decorous and graceful behavior contrasts with Jo's too stiff or too relaxed style. As Amy says, "Women should learn to be agreeable, particularly poor ones, for they have no other way of repaying the kindnesses they receive." While Jo would flaunt her unconventionality, Amy would conceal hers in order to preserve and foster her genuine independence and what would appear to be the rudiments of a feminist consciousness. During their last call, on Aunt March and Aunt Carrol, Jo asserts "I don't like favors, they oppress and make me feel like a slave. I'd rather do everything myself, and be perfectly independent." But Amy's willingness to accept patronage "when it is well meant" earns her the coveted trip to Europe and the chance to develop her art abroad.

In the chapter describing Amy's luncheon party, the narrator pokes fun at her "artistic attempts," and Alcott, by juxtaposing them with her social ambitions, seems to imply that both are equally vain.[21] Yet in one of these attempts, Amy casts her own foot and has to have it dug out of the plaster by Jo, who "was so overcome with laughter while she excavated that her knife went too far" and "cut the poor foot." The image would suggest that Amy, perhaps more than Jo, puts herself into her work, and that Jo, in an attempt to extricate life from art, does injury to both. Further, at the end of the long passage which seems to disparage Amy's art, the narrator adds that Amy "persevered in spite of all obstacles, failures, and discouragements, firmly believing that in time she should do something worthy to be called 'high art'." As some have pointed out, Amy is not only socially but also artistically more ambitious than Jo; Jo wants to be successful and to make money, whereas Amy wants to achieve greatness.[22] Nor does Amy give up her art for a man as Jo does. By the time she meets Laurie in Europe she has already discovered that "talent isn't genius." As she tells Laurie, "Rome took all the vanity out of me." While Jo subjects her work to Professor Bhaer's "moral spectacles," Amy submits hers to a far sterner test—comparison with the greatest masterpieces. Even when her work fails that test, she continues drawing, which suggests that she values the process itself.

In Europe, Amy begins to take Jo's place with Laurie just as she becomes the more self-directed artist. During their courtship she is assertive: when driving with Laurie it is she who holds the reins, and, unlike the other girls, who marry their tutors, she plays Mentor to

Laurie's Telemachus. While Laurie is still languishing for Jo, looking like "the effigy of a young knight asleep on his tomb," Amy wakes him up as he had thought only Jo could do. As Laurie later tells Jo, Amy's lecture was "a deal worse than any of your scoldings." It is Amy, then, who makes a man of Laurie, whereas Jo would keep him "her boy." As Amy says, "I know you'll wake up and be a man in spite of that hardhearted girl." Laurie, in turn, encourages Amy with her art after her sketch of him excites his admiration. Having had artistic aspirations himself, and having suffered the pain of having them discouraged, he is sympathetic and nonjudgmental. As a consequence, her letters to Laurie are filled with "captivating sketches." After Amy has finally taught Laurie to forget Jo, he gathered up "all Jo's letters, smoothed, folded, and put them neatly into a small drawer of the desk," laid Jo's ring with the letters, and locked the drawer, "feeling as if there had been a funeral." The funeral marks not only the death of his old relationship with Jo but the death of her imagination and striving for independence. Amy and Laurie, significantly far removed from the dying Beth, have the only joyous union in the book. The European chapters close with the image of them rowing side by side, and the letter they send home is described as a "duet."

Amy, then, by combining an appropriate and satisfying relationship with artistic integrity and self-direction, seems to succeed where Jo fails. Why, if this is true, does she remain, like Jo, instructive more as a negative than as a positive example? For one thing, although she says she has learned the difference between talent and greatness, we never see her in the process of making that agonizing discovery. Nor do we see her, as we see Jo, acquiring "glimpses of the tragic world which underlies society." Most important, however, Amy triumphs not because she has questioned the values of little womanhood and consciously rejected them, but because she has never felt them to be incompatible with her artistic goals. For example, during Beth's first illness, Amy is sent to stay with Aunt March (significantly, Amy, unlike the other girls, is always removed from scenes of pain and suffering). Here Amy, with the help of a Catholic maid, fits up a closet as a little shrine in which she thinks "good thoughts" and prays for Beth's recovery. This little womanly activity, however, is also an aesthetic one. Amy takes great pleasure and a pardonable pride in the careful disposition of her few treasures, and her "beauty-loving eyes were never tired of looking up at the sweet face of the divine mother." Similarly, after Beth dies, Amy's gentle melancholy seems graceful, almost aesthetic compared to Jo's raw grief and subsequent despair. When Laurie finds Amy grieving in the chateau garden, "everything about her suggested love and sorrow—the blotted letters in her lap, the black ribbon that tied up her hair, the womanly pain and patience in her face; even the little ebony cross at her throat seemed pathetic to Laurie,

for he had given it to her, and she wore it as her only ornament." Amy's greatest art, we begin to suspect, is not her painting or her sculpture but rather the graceful way in which she exploits her little womanhood to further her own interests. Whereas Jo finally refuses to be drawn into the vortex of creativity, Amy, just as she once tried to cast her own foot, appears to give herself unreservedly to her art. But the incident of the foot is instructive: Amy gives herself to art by becoming an art object. As object she preserves, in her studied gracefulness, something not unlike the stiffness that prevented her from being a convincing heroine in Jo's play. So, too, in the novel Amy is no real heroine and offers no real solution to the problem of woman as artist, for, unlike Jo, she evades rather than confronts the problem, and in so doing perpetuates the myth of woman as artifact rather than artificer.

In the last analysis, as throughout, out deepest sympathies lie with the real heroine, Jo, for although she lacks Amy's self-assertiveness and single-mindedness, she is right in her recognition of the need for sacrifice and self-denial. She is simply wrong about what to sacrifice and what to deny herself. After learning of Amy's happiness with Laurie, Jo's craving for affection is intensified to the point where it triumphs finally over her drive to create.[23] Although she had promised to take Beth's place with her parents and with old Mr. Laurence, that place is compatible with her place at the side of Professor Bhaer. Further, on inheriting Plumfield from Aunt March, Jo decides to open a school for boys and become a retainer on a large scale. "Fritz [Bhaer] can train and teach in his own way, and Father will help him. I can feed and nurse and pet and scold them, and Mother will be my stand-by." We are told that "Jo made queer mistakes; but the wise Professor steered her safely into calmer waters" just as he had earlier rescued her from "the frothy sea of sensation fiction." But Jo now finds "the applause of the boys more satisfying than any praise of the world, for now she told no stories except to her flock of enthusiastic believers and admirers." While Jo wistfully expresses the hope that "I may write a good book yet," Amy in the final scene is sketching still and has just modelled a figure much praised by her husband. Yet Amy is not entirely happy, for the child whose figure she has successfully modelled is dying, a further sign that Amy's graceful blend of art and domesticity is too easy and thus doomed to failure.[24] For Amy to become a true artist, she must both give up something and do so consciously and painfully. The sickly child, significantly named Beth, thus represents the need for women to relinquish, however tenderly and regretfully, those self-denying values which Beth, or little womanhood, has come to mean in the course of the novel. In other words, to break the pattern of self-denial we must deny ourselves its comforting familiarity. *Little Women* ends with Marmee stretching out her arms as though to embrace the final sex-divided tableau at Plumfield: "Oh, my girls, however long you may live, I never can wish you a greater happiness than this." But although Marmee has the last words, we are prepared by the time we read them to detect their devastating irony. Although the mother can wish nothing better for her "girls," the artist who conceived *Little Women* has wished something better for us.

Notes

[1] For a persuasive feminist reading of the novel which in many ways anticipates my own, see Judith Fetterly's "*Little Women:* Alcott's Civil War," *Feminist Studies,* 5 (1979), 369-83. Martha Saxton, in *Louisa May: A Modern Biography of Louisa May Alcott* (1977; New York: Avon Books, 1978), sees the process of becoming "little women" as the process of "achieving complete diminution" (p. 41).

[2] *Little Women* (1868 and 1869; New York: Collier Books, 1962), p. 19. All further references will be to this edition.

[3] Patricia Meyer Spacks, in *The Female Imagination* (1972; New York: Avon Books, 1976), has also equated Beth's pure selflessness with death (p. 125).

[4] See Nina Auerbach's *Communities of Women* (Cambridge: Harvard Univ. Press, 1978), p. 61.

[5] As Fetterly points out, female anger in the novel produces, or threatens to produce dire consequences whereas male anger is permissible.

[6] Auerbach, p. 62.

[7] Anne Hollander, in "Reflections on *Little Women,*" *Children's Literature 9* (New Haven: Yale Univ. Press, 1981), views the younger Amy as unlike the other March girls in that she is unpleasant, selfish, and genuinely bad (p. 32).

[8] According to Fetterly, Amy's accident is part of a "pattern of maximum possible consequences for a minimal degree of self-absorption and selfishness" (381). In other words, a woman's anger is criminal, tantamount to murder.

[9] Spacks, p. 125.

[10] In *Diana and Persis,* a manuscript novella recently edited by Sarah Elbert (New York: Arno Press, 1978), Alcott explores the possibility that such wishes are compatible. Both of her heroines strive for "success and happiness; but with Diana success came first, with Percy [Persis] happiness; both being conscious at times of that secret warfare of thwarted instincts and imperious ambitions, the demands of temperament as well as talent" (p. 65).

When Percy becomes a wife and mother, her husband insists that she will "be the greater artist for being a happy woman" (p. 128), but Diana, the character more closely resembling Alcott herself, remains skeptical.

[11] Auerbach also argues that in Part II of *Little Women,* Alcott connects "the departures of marriage and death" (p. 63).

[12] Fetterly, 376.

[13] Jane Van Buren, in "Louisa May Alcott: A Study in Persona and Idealization," *Psychohistory Review,* 9 (1981), sees Alcott as recommending "an idealized version" of marriage in this passage (297-298). However, an initiated reader can detect the author's irony beneath what Van Buren calls the narrator's "suffusion of florid prose."

[14] As Carolyn Heilbrun as written in *Reinventing Womanhood* (New York: Norton, 1979), "Perhaps only in America, with its worship of 'manliness,' could boy-girl twins, elsewhere universally a literary phenomenon characterized by their resemblance to one another, be so sharply defined and differentiated by sex roles" (p. 191).

[15] This passage explains Jo's contribution to the game of rigamarole played at Camp Laurence in Part I. John Brooke begins a story of a knight and captive princess— a thin disguise for himself and Meg; Jo reduces the romantic tale to absurdity by beheading the knight and packing him in a tin box with eleven other headless knights (p. 148).

[16] (1929; New York: Harcourt, 1957), pp. 48-52.

[17] Woolf, p. 51.

[18] Auerbach, p. 62.

[19] Sarah Elbert Diamant, in her 1974 Cornell University dissertation, *Louisa May Alcott and the Woman Problem,* finds it significant that "Jo is the least conventional of the March girls but is also the one to whom sisterhood means the most" (p. 167). Thus she suggests that Alcott, through Jo, equates unconventionality, freedom from oppressive sex role stereotypes, with the strength to be found in sisterhood - sisterhood, that is, in our modern sense of solidarity among women. Jo's sisterhood, however, the expression of which is her attachment to Beth, means loyalty to the patriarchal family, and far from strengthening her in her unconventionality, it compels her to conform. The fact that Jo turns Plumfield into a school for boys and thus surrounds herself with males confirms that, far from valuing sisterhood in our modern sense, Jo accepts the concept of male superiority.

[20] As Fetterly comments, "Good writing for women is not the product of ambition or even enthusiasm, nor does it seek worldly recognition. Rather it is the product of a mind seeking solace for private pain, that scarcely knows what it is doing and that seeks only to please others and, more specifically, those few others who constitute the immediate family. Jo has gone from burning genius to a state where what she writes isn't even hers" (374).

[21] Critics too have disparaged Amy's art. Spacks contends that Jo "is interested in the occupation itself, unlike Amy, for example, whose narcissistic desire to paint disappears promptly when she is married" (p. 126). Some have speculated that Alcott sympathizes with Jo, who resembles herself, and withholds sympathy from Amy, who, like Alcott's sister May, goes after what she wants and always seems to get it. (See, for example, Saxton, Ch. 1.) In *Diana and Persis,* Percy, the May-Amy figure, is portrayed more sympathetically. In this story it is Percy who cares for happiness or love at least as much as she cares for art, and it is Diana, the Louisa-Jo figure, who is willing to live without love in order to achieve artistic greatness. The sisterhood that Elbert and Auerbach find in *Little Women* is a much stronger theme in this later work.

[22] Hollander, p. 33.

[23] Obviously I disagree with John Seelye who believes that "in marrying a much older man, while refusing the beautiful Childe Byron, Laurie, Jo most certainly continues her subversive operation." See "Notes on the Waist-High Culture," *Children's Literature 9,* p. 180.

[24] Fetterly interprets Amy's sickly child as another indication that art, for most women, "is the product of a mind seeking solace for private pain" (374).

Carolyn G. Heilbrun (essay date 1982)

SOURCE: "Louisa May Alcott: The Influence of *Little Women,*" in *Women, the Arts, and the 1920s in Paris and New York,* edited by Kenneth W. Wheeler and Virginia Lee Lussier, Transaction Books, 1982, pp. 20-26.

[*In the following essay, Heilbrun argues that* Little Women's *Jo has been a model of female autonomy for twentieth-century women artists.*]

The influence of *Little Women* upon women artists in Paris between the wars is a matter of faith. As the Bible tells us, faith is the evidence of things not seen. If only Gertrude Stein had written of Jo March, or at least stopped into Sylvia Beach's bookshop and requested *Little Women.* What she requested, I am con-

strained by truth to report, is *The Trail of the Lonesome Pine* and *A Girl of the Limberlost.*[1] There is a reference to Alcott in Stein's writing, but not to *Little Women.* It is to *Rose in Bloom,* and Stein is reminded of it by the New Englanders' fear of drinking: "I always remembered it in *Rose in Bloom* and how they worried about offering any one a drink and even about communion wine, any one in that way might suddenly find they had a taste for wine."[2]

Sylvia Beach mentions *Little Women* only as the source of a joke on Frank Harris who, rushing to make a train, was in search of something "exciting" to read. Beach asked him if he had read *Little Women* which, rendered into French as *Petites femmes,* connoted something exciting to a man of Harris' tastes. He was resentful of being locked in a train for hours with such an appalling lack of eroticism.[3] Thornton Wilder, who knew Stein and many of the others, evokes *Little Women* in *The Eighth Day,* supposedly not for the first time. But is any of this evidence?

Yet I do not admit that my faith in *Little Women* as an influence consists solely of the substance of things hoped for. Everyone read *Little Women*—there is evidence enough for that; certainly every prepubescent female absorbed that book with the air she breathed. My own children—just to show you the extent and persistence of the influence—went to school with four sisters named Meg, Jo, Amy, and Beth. Unfortunately, no one could notice that Jo differed perceptibly from the others. But in the book itself, Jo differed more than perceptibly: Jo was a miracle. She may have been the single female model continuously available after 1868 to girls dreaming beyond the confines of a constricted family destiny to the possibility of autonomy and experience initiated by one's self.

We literary critics welcome complexities which challenge our carefully honed talents and enable us to unravel novels whose profundities can be suspected of escaping the untrained reader. Complex novels and poems are meat and drink to critics, but children are more in the position of the puzzled ice cream manufacturer who asked Wallace Stevens if in "The Emperor of Ice Cream" he was for ice cream or against it. We forget sometimes, though Frank Kermode has reminded us, that "fictions are for finding things out."[4] One of the things they are for finding out is the process of growing from a girl into a woman. Men may ask pretty girls: "Are there any more at home like you?" Most girls may, in the past, have considered that a pretty question. But girls who were going to grow up and go to Paris were more likely to have exclaimed with Jo: "I hate affected, niminy-piminy chits. I hate to think I've got to grow up, and be Miss March, and wear long gowns and look as prim as a China-aster. . . . I can't get over my disappointment in not being a boy." Beth soothes Jo by assuring her she can be a brother to them all, and Jo, to be sure, in her father's absence, recognizes herself as "the man of the family."

Jo's is an identification only possible in those innocent days when one could say what one felt without being accused of nameless, or worse, named Freudian perversions. Jo recognized (along with her readers) that girls such as she, few enough in number, *were* ideally the fathers of their families because there was no other model. Such girls might want to care for their mothers; they certainly did not wish to imitate them. Who in her right mind (which few girls were in those dark days) would want to imitate such a creature? Marmee's vision of a woman's role in marriage is enough to turn the stomach, and the exceptional young reader could declare with Jo: "I wasn't meant for a life like this."

Great books are so identified because they turn out, a century or so later, to have been amazingly prescient. Today, armed with the data and insights of all those social sciences focusing their attention upon achieving women, we recognize that Alcott provided for Jo those conditions likeliest to produce this interesting creature. While Alcott depended upon the facts of her own life, she nonetheless transmuted them into a pattern of female selfhood. Reviewers might attribute the success of **Little Women** to the threefold accomplishment of preserving the family as the foundation of the republic, making female adolescence into a life stage, and picturing loving self-sacrifice according to female dreams[5]—but beyond all this is Alcott's recognition of the opportunity her all-girl family had provided for her own development.

Bronson Alcott, at the birth of his fourth female child, noted that her birth manifested God's will that the Alcotts be content to "rear women for the future world."[6] Whatever God's will, if any, in the matter, girls without brothers are far likelier to end up as true women of the future world, questioning the conventional female destiny. Achieving women are statistically likely to be from all-girl families. Margaret Hennig, for example, examining top-range women managers in business firms, of whom there were not many, discovered that all the women in her sample were only children or from all-girl families—an extraordinary statistical finding. These girls were brotherless and therefore qualified as "sons." Louisa and her older sister were objects of educational experiments by their father: he had no sons on whom to apply them. Not uncommonly, if the unconventional woman is not the only or oldest child, she will be the one among a father's daughters selected by him as his "son." Writer Dorothy Richardson, for example, was "odd girl out" for her father: third among his four daughters, the child with whom he formed a union against a household of "women."[7] Louisa, we know, was Bronson Alcott's "son."[8]

While the tomboy character has long been a staple of life and fiction, most tomboys exist in relation to boys; certainly those of fiction do so, emulating and envying their brothers. These tomboys may be teased as hoydens, but they are not recognized as sons, as the independent ones among weaker women. Maggie Tulliver, for example, in George Eliot's *The Mill on the Floss,* creates herself in emulation and adoration of her brother Tom. Their father may mourn that it is the wench who is the smart one, but it is Tom who will get the education. For Jo, male destiny may be envied, but not in the person of a brother. Similarly, in an all-girl school girls may win the attention of teachers and aspire to positions not automatically considered the property of males: there are no males. Laurie in this eccentric book is made to look with envy on the happy female world.

A word of caution is necessary regarding girls chosen by their fathers as "sons." He does not think of her nor does the girl think of herself as a boy. Penis envy, despite Freud's strictures rigidified with the eager help of his female followers, is not the issue. These young women never doubt their core gender identity. They inhabit female bodies gladly, and dream, not of male anatomy, but of male autonomy. Here Alcott was again both naive and, in the wonderful freedom of that naiveté, prescient. She knew that for women who considered Marmee's destiny, or Meg's, impossible for themselves, the only model was a male model—she adopted it.

Women have been trapped here. The world, wishing to keep them in their place, where the world found it very convenient for them to be, warned them that if they did not accept the female role they would lose their femininity and become, moreover, monsters: imitation men. It followed that in imitating men they were also robbing them of their masculinity. This has to be the most extraordinary double bind in history. Jo could be so clear about her choice between male and female destinies, at least for half the book, because no one had arrived to tell her that she was courting some hideous Freudian disaster. The chosen "son" within the all-girl family, Jo was free to follow the male model, the only acceptable one around.

Jo plays the male parts in plays, wears a "gentlemanly" collar and has a gentlemanly manner, thinks of herself as a businessman and cherishes a pet rat. (The pet rat is male and has a son, "proud of his whiskers," who accompanies him along the rafters.) Jo finds it easier to risk her life for a person than to be pleasant when she does not want to, and she admires the "manly" way of shaking hands. The point is clear: men's manners speak of freedom, openness, comradery, physical abandon, the chance to escape passivity. Who would not prefer such a destiny, except those taught to be afraid?

Strictures against women imitating the male model are universal. Even today if one recommends the male model for women (shorn of its machismo and denigration of women), one is likely to startle everyone. But Jo knew that there was no other, and that to search for female models makes good history but poor consolation. Jo knew that in a conventional family pattern, where the mother could recommend only her own confinement, there was no other model than the father. Some women indeed provided another model. Where did they discover it? Partly, in a young fictional creature who, as Natalie Barney was to say of Gertrude Stein, "had such faith in herself as passeth understanding."[9]

In the end, Alcott betrayed Jo. Women have great difficulty imagining autonomous females (even if they have managed to become one) and sustaining the imaginative creation once they have achieved it. Jo had to be more or less conventionally "disposed of."[10] Those who hold to the romantic view of tomboys resent the fact that Jo had to marry a German twice her age. Alcott could not, apparently, prevent Jo's marrying, but she could and did prevent her marrying Laurie, despite the demands of her publisher and public. When Jo's father returns from the war to this female world, he "compliments" Jo by saying that he does not see the "son, Jo" whom he left a year hence. "I see a young lady who . . ." and there follows an account of a young lady's attributes. We feel sold. Alcott will tell us at the end of **Little Women** that spinsters "have missed the sweetest part of life" (how persistently women buy that line!) despite the fact that she signed her letters from Europe in the months following the success of **Little Women** "spinsterhood forever," and when asked for advice to give girls, told them of "the sweet independence of the spinster's life."[11] Alcott was confused in her fictional, if not in her usual mind, but her biographers muddle the two. The latest, Martha Saxton, writes as though not finding a man to marry were a failure explicable only by psychological wounds.

Of course, Jo starts a school for boys. Who would want to mess around with silly girls? If you cannot change the destiny of girls, you can at least take on the education of the sex with some chance of freedom and accomplishment outside of domesticity. The feeling is most commonly reflected in the woman's wish for male children, as Adrienne Rich tells us: "When I first became pregnant I set my heart on a son. (In our childish, acting-out games I had always preferred the masculine roles and persuaded or forced my younger sister to act the feminine ones.) I still identified more with men than with women; the men I knew seemed less held back by self-doubt and ambivalence, more choices seemed open to them. I wanted to give birth, at twenty-five, to my unborn self—someone independent, actively willing, original."[12]

Once one has opted to support the male system and put one's ambitions, as Jo does, into the raising of boys, one writes of Meg's twins as though stereotyped destinies for the sexes were among the eternal verities. There may be something more sickening than little Daisy, but where to find it outside the precepts of the Total Woman movement, I do not know. It has been argued, most persuasively by Nina Auerbach in her excellent study of female communities, that in the end Jo becomes "a cosmic mother," the greatest power available in that domestic world.[13] Jo was the girl who embodied the impossible girlhood dreams, and not the young female who became—heaven forbid—a mother.

Jo's readers probably overlooked the conventional ending. Jo wanted to end up, when she knew she could not become free as a man, as a "literary spinster," an apt way to describe the women in Paris between the wars. Jo's youthful experiences may have provided a model for sisterhood, as Nina Auerbach so well demonstrates. The all-girl family in Austen's *Pride and Prejudice,* Auerbach points out, lives in an empty world, awaiting rescue by men.[14] The March world is complete in itself; there women suffice to each other for happiness, and "permanent sisterhood is a felt dream rather than a concrete possibility."[15] Auerbach further suggests that in giving the family the name of a month, Alcott took her mother, whose maiden name was May, as the true progenitor of the family, the source of energy and possibility. To me Alcott's portrayal of sisterhood is too sentimental, too doomed by marital conventions both as to its present and future; yet it is, for all that, a memorable dream of sisterhood, perhaps the one fictional world where young women, complete unto themselves, are watched with envy by a lonely boy.

Alcott's other literary works, with Jo or without her, are certainly of interest, especially **Work,** yet they appeal perhaps more to the feminist historian and critic than to the girl reader. We recognize with pleasure that in **An Old Fashioned Girl** there is a community of women artists, and that in an unpublished fragment of an adult novel Alcott, most enticingly, has a woman say: "Do not look for meaning in marriage, that is too costly an experiment for us. Flee from temptation and do not dream of spoiling your life by any commonplace romance."[16] But these fragments, these interpretations, are what the critics find. For youngsters, reading in search of legends they need not even consciously acknowledge or remember, it is Jo who is immortal.

What must be emphasized is her uniqueness. She is a myth, alone and unchallenged—peerless. For she has the whole business absolutely straight as a child, an adolescent. Maybe Alcott did not know what to do with her when she grew up, but Barney, Stein, and Flanner knew what to do with themselves when they grew up, and I am inclined to give Jo part of the credit. Perhaps remembered only dimly, children's literature, safe as homes, she nonetheless expressed, as few had, what it felt like to be a girl who was not going to grow up conventionally female and knew it when she was very young. Because there was no fantasy in Jo's end, her beginnings were believable. Romance promised a prince. *Little Women* promised whatever you could make of your life; anyway, not the boy next door. What Stein, Barney, Toklas, and Beach made of their lives, we know or will learn here. I want to suggest Jo as the daimon, the unique girl who dared to speak as they felt. Alcott, who created her, was not the mother of us all, but Jo was, and not because she became a cosmic mother in fiction. In fiction her children were boys. In life, her true children were girls who grew up and went to Paris and did wonderful things.

Notes

1 Sylvia Beach, *Shakespeare and Company* (New York: Harcourt, Brace, 1959). p. 28.

2 Gertrude Stein, *Everybody's Autobiography* (New York: Random House, 1937), p. 237.

3 Beach, *Shakespeare,* p. 92.

4 Frank Kermode, *The Sense of an Ending* (New York: Oxford University Press, 1967), p. 39.

5 Sarah Elbert, Introduction to *Work* by Louisa May Alcott (New York: Schocken Books, 1977), p. xviii.

6 Ibid., p. xi.

7 Horace Gregory, *Dorothy Richardson: An Adventure in Discovery* (New York: Holt, Rinehart, & Winston, 1967), p. 19.

8 Martha Saxton, *Louisa May Alcott* (Boston: Houghton Mifflin, 1977), p. 256.

9 Linda Simon (ed.), *Gertrude Stein: A Composite Portrait* (New York: Discus Books, 1974), p. 44.

10 Patricia Spacks, *The Female Imagination* (New York: Knopf, 1975), p. 100.

11 Mary Jane Moffat and Charlotte Painter (eds.), *Revelations: Diaries of Women* (New York: Random House, 1974), p. 29.

12 Adrienne Rich, *Of Women Born* (New York: Norton, 1976), p. 193.

13 Nina Auerbach, "Austen and Alcott on Matriarchy," Radcliffe Institute Reprint, p. 24. See Nina Auerbach, *Communities of Women: An Idea in Fiction* (Cambridge, Mass.: Harvard University Press, 1978).

14 Idem, "Austen and Alcott," p. 17.

15 Ibid., p. 24.

16 Quoted in ibid., p. 23.

Nina Auerbach (essay date 1983)

SOURCE: Afterword, *Little Women* by Louisa May Alcott, Bantam, 1983, pp. 461-70.

[Auerbach's look at Alcott's life and work suggests that although Meg, Jo, and Amy had to accept marriage as their fates, Alcott actually idealized feminist utopias that excluded marriage and men.]

For those of us who entered the March household as children, its power is unabated. Adult women remember life with Meg, Jo, Beth, and Amy when their own childhoods have grown dim. For better or worse, the March family has passed into American folk mythology. Though Alcott had hoped only for transient commercial appeal, by 1890 Ednah Cheyney, her first biographer, could claim: "Already twenty-one years have passed, and another generation has come up since she published [*Little Women*], yet it still commands a steady sale; and the mothers who read it in their childhood renew their enjoyment as they watch the faces of the little girls brighten with smiles over the theatricals in the barn, or moisten with tears at the death of the beloved sister." More than a century has passed without breaking this chain of generations. Women's situation has changed rapidly over the decades, but Marmee's is one family we all have lived in.

Little Women begins with an invocation from Bunyan's *Pilgrim's Progress,* a work that inspires the sisters on their separate pilgrimages toward self-conquest and self-perfection. Apart, the sisters must undergo strenuous journeys to equip them for adulthood but together they have reached perfection from the first page. "'We've got father and mother and each other,' [says] Beth contentedly, from her corner," hushing the grumbling of her more aspiring sisters. Accordingly, the first half of *Little Women* celebrates the abundance of this impoverished household. Its inner treasure is as precious as it is precarious, because their noble father has left for the Civil War as a chaplain, and exists only through intermittent lofty letters to the circle of women. He may die, or he may return. Either way, the girls are living an interim life.

The struggles, games, letters, rituals, jokes, the abundance within poverty, entice the reader, of whatever age, to enter the charmed circle as a fifth sister. For though *Little Women* is famous as a children's classic, actual children do not toddle into the saga until the arch whimsy of *Little Men.* Alcott places her girls at an intermediate stage of life in which they are endowed with adult consciousness, but have not yet moved into restricted wifely roles. Once married, Meg will be "on the shelf," living a new life of submission and seclusion. Their childhood home provides the March girls with a sanctuary for energy and assertion, not with a protected children's world: the girls understand poverty, war, and envy as well as their mother, Marmee, does. Home under Marmee's guidance cherishes this adult understanding while sheltering the girls from the pressure to sell themselves in a "good" match: "better be happy old maids than unhappy wives, or unmaidenly girls, running about to find husbands." With these words, Mrs. March bestows upon her girls a rare dowry in any century, the freedom to remain in a sanctuary that nourishes self-possession in the face of the compromising demands of official adulthood.

This underlying faith in the spiritual self-sufficiency of women may explain why the March family has been cherished for decades by women readers. The essential liberty of Marmee's reign is a greater treasure than her sometimes sententious moralizing against vanity, ambition, and anger (those concomitants of a healthy ego) might suggest. Jo and Beth understand the value of her dispensation, an awareness that explains the otherwise strange alliance between the hoyden sister and the frail one. The intense affinity between Jo and Beth throws Meg and Amy together as the most conventionally feminine of the sisters; both are eager to grow into the stylized rituals of "ladies." But Beth knows that "father and mother and each other" produce an almost magical harmony in a threatening world. Jo, too, clings to home as the essence of freedom, raging when Meg's marriage breaks the circle: "I just wish I could marry Meg myself, and keep her safe in the family."

The family is "safe" because it is uncompromised, not because it is free from rage and violence. Marmee sadly understands that these are essential components of female existence. A strangely homicidal love exists between Jo and Amy. Jo nearly kills Amy three times in the course of their young lives; Amy kills Jo's best hopes by stealing both the trip to Europe and her dashing, understanding comrade, Laurie. Relations among the sisters are fractious but never dishonest. Their household is a model of integrity rather than sentiment. Their harmony is worked for, not inherent. Under the guise of a childhood haven, family union is a dynamic test for the complications of the adult self. The March girls' boisterous plays, their songs, Jo's vertex when she writes, Beth's rapture at the piano, Amy's sometimes violent absorption in her art, combine to give the cottage the atmosphere of a modern-day artist's colony, where creative energy is sheltered from the falsifying demands of daily life. At its best, the March family itself is a mobile, dynamic work of art, achieving a difficult harmony that survives only when the family is together. In the classic film version of

Little Women, Katharine Hepburn flounces about while her faceless sisters strike picturesque attitudes, but in Alcott's novel, the sisters take mutual life from each other; not even Jo is a star. Marmee is the god of this intense little world, half-magical in her wisdom and the spell of her presence, while the loyal servant, Hannah, is its obligatory chorus, providing awed commentary on the family doings.

The richness of the March household—its plenitude reproaches the scantness of the world outside—has to do with the absence from it of controlling men. When Mr. March does return, the ghostly invalid is scarcely more present than he was in Washington: his philosophic mind is immune from the book's energy, its crises, its human life, which are the property of the women alone. Charming Laurie and his wealthy grandfather are equally peripheral. A more conventional novel would cast them as romantic rescuers, but here, wealthy men are wistful mendicants, forever soliciting access to the charmed circle. After a series of cavalier rejections, of which Jo's is the most dramatic, Beth's death makes a place for Laurie at last. Amy is heartsick and vulnerable, and so he manages to win the one sister who is "left for him"; so immune is the March family from the world's lure that an eligible suitor can enter it only by default. In this American classic, so dutiful on the surface, only women can build Utopias. For Louisa May Alcott, better worlds are the creation, not of high-minded men, but of practical women who understand the art of work and so transform their home into a self-sustaining work of art.

Little Women derives much of its power from Louisa's secret battle against her adored father, whom Emerson called New England's "most refined and advanced soul," but whose unworldly spirituality was a torment to the women who depended on him. One wonders about Louisa's mixed feelings when Bronson Alcott, Concord sage, revered educator, and Transcendentalist Philosopher, was transformed in the public eye from "the American Plato" to "the father of *Little Women*." Bound as she was to Bronson in life, Louisa virtually excluded him from her passionate vision of the family his eccentricities created and dominated. *Little Women* begins with a spiritual triumph whose victory is hunger: at Marmee's instigation, the girls give their Christmas breakfast to a pauper family, thus translating themselves into "funny angels in hoods and mittens" who have elected themselves to grace. That night, their neighbor Mr. Laurence rewards their renunciation with a Christmas feast, the first link between the two families. In the novel, hunger is a chosen and instantly rewarded discipline.

For the Alcott sisters, hunger was a perpetual fact, and no benevolent gentleman canonized it with pink-and-white ice cream. Bronson's vegetarianism, his elevated ideals of spiritual development and purification, and his inability to earn a living, determined what they ate. The girls endured a virtual prisoners' diet of apples, unleavened bread, cold water, and enforced cheerfulness at meals. On one occasion when Abba, Marmee's original, rebelled and sent Bronson out for meat for the children, he bought the wrong piece and purified himself by writing in his diary: "What have I to do with butchers? . . . Death yawns at me as I walk up and down in this abode of skulls." In real life the father made this florid gesture of denial on the mother and sisters' behalf. In *Little Women,* the father's absence places moral choice in the hands of the women, raising their hunger from mysterious punishment to voluntary self-glorification.

Bronson Alcott's educational experiments were notorious throughout Boston and Concord; thus, his shaping power gave their family life a public dimension. The March girls live in virtuous obscurity among their richer neighbors; their private struggles, their occasional bursts of glory, are known only to each other and their small approving audience. The Alcott girls were the public property of Concord: they were Bronson's dearest experiments, his "model children." Thoreau, Margaret Fuller, and other Transcendental luminaries came to study their development. Eccentric as he was, Bronson's controversial reputation bestowed immediate public significance on his daughters, while most Victorian families were protectively shrouded from outside scrutiny. Louisa's early awareness of the import of her family tribulations fuels the Utopianism of *Little Women,* where the family is not merely a refuge for intimacy, but a model society in itself. Moreover, her public role as model child fed her guilty lust for the stage, which she neither indulged not outgrew. In *Little Women,* and throughout Alcott's works, play and performance are woman's dangerous compensations for self-denial. The power of acting contains all the potential aggression that a grown-up little woman must renounce.

Like the March girls, the four Alcott sisters put on plays in the barn. As an adult, Louisa continued to perform in amateur productions and in charity performances, but she never acted professionally, though one of her plays was produced in Boston. Before her success as a writer, she had been a nurse, seamstress, domestic servant, teacher, and governess, but acting, which she loved, was a tabooed profession. At midcentury the stage could offer more money and personal power than any other occupation open to women. Perhaps because of that very fact, it was considered a disreputable life for a lady, no matter how gifted or impoverished she may have been. Louisa both gravitated toward and shunned a public assertion of identity that broke through women's sanctioned domestic sphere. Though Bronson called his writing daughter "an arsenal of powers," an acting daughter was at the center of her most explosive dreams. For many of her domestic heroines, acting

is the forbidden fruit; the darker heroines of her sensation fiction are born actresses, onstage and off, releasing through the medium of performance what one of them calls the "power in a woman's wit and will."

After the March girls have renounced their Christmas breakfast, they turn their turbulence outward and put on a play. Rife with villainy, demonism, and violence—some of which is impromptu, for a massive set falls on demure Amy, the ingenue—the play embodies the dynamic potential of their communal art. In the somber second half of the novel, there are no more private theatricals, but play is not forgotten. We learn in *Jo's Boys* that even placid Meg once pined to be an actress; in this final novel, the theater stands for the faded dreams of the now matronly sisters. Only there do we meet an actual diva, Miss Cameron, who is both beautiful and good. Since "this great and happy woman who could thrill thousands by her art and win friends by her virtue, benevolence, and beauty" is working in some vague manner for "the purification of the stage," Meg's daughter Josie, the most vibrant of the sisters' children, is permitted to act: the next generation lives in a wider world than their mothers did. The March trilogy begins with a play; once it produces an actress, it can let "the curtain fall forever on the March family." In the story itself, acting becomes a symbol of the public power the little women must renounce. Its forbidden allure is intensified in two of Alcott's adult works.

Work: A Story of Experience (1873) stars Christie Devon, stalwart orphan. Christie's pilgrimage carries her, not through domestic life, but through the available women's professions. In the course of her hard life she assumes the women's roles of servant, actress, governess, companion, seamstress, near-suicide, wife, nurse, mother, and public speaker for women's rights. Only as an actress is personal triumph possible: her other choices involve various sorts of self-renouncing service. But Christie sternly forbids herself the stage, feeling contaminated by power and ambition: "better *be* a woman than *act* a queen." With similar sternness, Alcott changed the title of Christie's story from *Success* to *Work.* Artistically as well as physically, her good women are forced to thrive on hunger.

Alcott's best bad woman, Jean Muir, is also her best actress. **"Behind A Mask, or A Woman's Power"** (1866) is the story of her triumph and a brilliant example of the sensation fiction Alcott published pseudonymously throughout her career. Jo March obediently burned her sensation stories when Professor Bhaer rumbled about their danger to children, but Louisa May Alcott's have been recovered for us in Madeleine Stern's two recent collections, *Behind a Mask* (1975) and *Plots and Counterplots* (1976). Jean Muir, diabolical and witty manipulator, abandons Jo March's humility, retaining her initials and her performing verve. Like Christie Devon, Jean Muir is an actress turned governess for a proud, patriarchal family. She acts her servitude with such flexible brilliance that she seduces father and sons, humbling their pride and solidifying her power before she is unmasked. For this heroine, acting does not enliven the family but destroys it. In story after story Alcott's womanly heroines renounce this power, for they understand its potential destruction as well as Jean Muir does. In the book for which Alcott is best known and loved, recurrent renunciations, great and small, are the little women's only sanctioned display of corporate strength.

We first meet the family in its glory, but the second half of the novel, originally published separately as *Good Wives,* is a mournful counterpoint to this early buoyancy. Home changes and everyone must leave. Father returns, Meg marries, Beth dies, Amy marries; finally, even Jo succumbs in a downpour to portly Professor Bhaer, a destiny that has depressed readers from Alcott's day to our own. But the family, not Jo, is the heroine, and the sadness of its ending is corporate. Beth's lingering death symbolizes the marriages of the remaining sisters, for with her dies the spirit of the all-sufficing home. When we mourn for Beth, we mourn for all the girls as they bravely give up their "castles in the air" for worthy but subduing marriages. As Mother Bhaer, Jo presides over a more institutionalized Utopia than Marmee's, which she could not have done as "lady" to the more dashing Laurie's "lord": her idyllic Plumfield, the setting of *Little Men* and *Jo's Boys,* is not merely school, but farm, great family, just society, and small world. At the end of *Little Women,* though, we remember Amy weeping furtively over her sickly little daughter. Marmee's is a castened "harvesttime," with none of the vital promise of the play with which we began, but this elegiac conclusion was the only one Alcott could forsee for the March girls.

For *Little Women* was a book she never wanted to write: her publisher pressured her to capitalize on the new market for girls' books. The success of the first half depressed her: the woman who "never liked girls, or knew many, except my sisters" had become the reluctant patron saint of proper female development. Her own life defied the pattern to which her little women submit. She was presumed to dote on children, but she did not, celebrating her single life with gusto: the refrain of *Shawl Straps*—her little-known account of three American women traveling through Europe—is the ringing "Spinsterhood forever!" She resented the commercial pressures that forced her to conclude *Good Wives* with suitable marriages: "Publishers are very perverse & wont let authors have their way so my little women must grow up & be married off in a very stupid style." She consoled herself by writing at the same time a defiant counterpoint, **"Happy Women,"** in which

a community of spinsters flourishes as physician, author, artist, philanthropist, actress, and lawyer. This alternative ending, in which energy, ambition, and community are not renounced was dearest to the author's heart, but sentimental love stories were dearer to her audience, and she complied. Her reward was fame for turning out what she wearily called "moral pap for the young." The anger and defiance behind the mask of nursery angel left her innocent readers untouched.

Her own life was full of a drama and division, masked by the apparent normalcy of *Little Women.* As Bronson's hungry and hard-worked child, her legacy was a sense of grand and inescapable sins. At the age of ten, she wrote in the journal she was encouraged to keep for purposes of soul-searching: "I was cross today, and I cried when I went to bed. I made good resolutions and felt better in my heart. If I only *kept* all I make, I should be the best girl in the world. But I don't, and so am very bad." Forty years later, she added: "Poor little sinner, She says the same at fifty!" The wickedness she felt lurked in her nature brought both torment and self-importance to this little woman who never evolved into a good wife. Nathaniel Hawthorne, her family's friend and neighbor, made art out of the gnawing sins he scrutinized in his soul. Louisa May Alcott tried to conquer sin in her girls' books, while in her anonymous sensation fiction she reveled in it. This doubleness in her writing pervaded the decisions of her life.

In *Little Women* Jo dutifully stays home while Mr. March faces the danger of Civil War. In life the roles were reversed: Louisa bravely enlisted as an army nurse, celebrating herself in ringing soldierly language as the son of the house. As Ednah Cheyney slyly puts it: "Mr. March did not go to the war, but Jo did." This impulse to better her father and find a heroic life beyond the family cost her dearly: she was soon sent home with typhoid fever. Her adventure made her a writer, inspiring *Hospital Sketches,* her first successful book, but lost her her heroism and her hair, which, like Jo, she saw as her strength as well as her "one beauty." Like Beth, she was never well after her first illness, transformed at the age of thirty from hoyden to semiinvalid. Jo March sells her hair and keeps her vitality; the vocation of invalidism is Beth's. Home from the war with thinning hair, Louisa sold stories, but she was shorn of the strength for physical adventure.

Thus, from the beginning, her career as a writer descended on her almost as a punishment. She wrote one of America's enduring books, but she would not have done so with a stronger body and in a better world. For from the beginning, Louisa May Alcott longed less for art, success, or fame than for escape from the dependence and confinement of being what Jo calls "a miserable girl." She aimed to become the son of the household, to support herself and the family, to earn the money that eluded Bronson. Vigorously and with some scorn, she declared her creed: her life proved that "though an *Alcott* I *can* support myself. I like the independent feeling; and though not an easy life, it is a free one, and I enjoy it. I can't do much with my hands; so I will make a battering-ram of my head and make a way through this rough-and-tumble world." The violent assault of this first declaration is not apparent in the sequestered life of the children's writer Louisa later became, but the fervor of its resolve was the guiding emotion of her divided life.

She was eleven when she vowed to become self-supporting and to support the family. The Alcotts were suffering one of their many inflictions of homelessness. Bronson's Masonic Temple School had collapsed; with the help of William Lane, an English philosopher, the family moved to Harvard, Massachusetts, to found a holy community. Their Fruitlands was one of the many valiant efforts by Victorian Americans to found a "New Eden" within the larger Eden of their burgeoning new country. For these visionary nonfarmers, it bred misery. Hunger, hard labor, division, and betrayal invaded this Utopia as they had invaded all of Bronson's purest dreams. Louisa's counter-dream of moneymaking was born from the deprivations of Fruitlands. Her private Utopia was to be solid, ample, vehemently competitive in a "rough-and-tumble world," rooted in the captalist system, and inspired by the ideal family values Fruitlands destroyed. For William Lane blamed the colony's failure on the Alcott women, claiming that families corrupted the purer bonds of the new Eden. When he defected to the celibate Shakers, Bronson's dream colony disbanded, leaving Abba to nurse her broken husband back to life and hope.

"Transcendental Wild Oats," Louisa's essay about life at Fruitlands, characteristically subdues its agony in favor of fun and jolly misadventures. Characteristically, too, her March girls are led on no strenuous experiments, for their new Eden is their home, though Jo's Plumfield in *Little Men,* where some mild farming goes on, may be a more orderly and woman-centered corrective of Bronson's failed experiment. But if Fruitlands failed both as farm and holy community, it did produce the Louisa May Alcott we know. Fearing and delighting in her own energy, passionately committed to keeping the family together through her moneymaking power, full of Utopian hopes for American institutions, Alcott discovered herself at Fruitlands; while repudiating its conditions, she cherished its spirit. For though in conventional terms Bronson was a disaster as a father, his determined unworldliness allowed his daughter space in which to be vehement. Bronson's financial ineptitude generated Louisa's strenuous commitment to moneymaking and independence, a more substantial legacy than most nineteenth-century fathers granted their daughters.

For Louisa, its toll on her art was her greatest loss. She deplored writing for the market, enforcing nursery pieties she did not believe in, relinquishing her adult ambitions and instead becoming "the children's friend." Her anonymous novel, **A Modern Mephistopheles,** may be inspired by her own sense that, like Faust, she has sold her soul, though in her case the buyer was virtue rather than vice. But for all its compromises, *Little Women* is a deathless book, one that contains its author's best self. Its hopes and defeats are those of all women.

Whatever one might say about the later children's books, *Little Women* is not "moral pap for the young." Its energy, sadness, and anger, its sense of joyous potential, are too real for that. Its reluctant author resisted her material, calling her first account of life among the Alcotts *The Pathetic Family.* Her publisher thought it would have only modest life as a girls' book; yet its tribute to the vivid lives of girls raises it above the category of children's literature, aligning it with the great themes of nineteenth-century America.

The crowded, spiritually energized life of the March cottage—like that of Melville's *Pequod* in *Moby-Dick* or of Huck Finn's raft—embodies the vigorous energy of a human community in a torn and empty world. Like its literature, nineteenth-century America dreamed of holy communities, of transfigured little Americas within America: Bronson Alcott's Fruitlands joined Brook Farm, the Oneida Community, the Shakers, Thoreau's Walden (a sanctified community of one), the small, visionary world of Transcendentalist Concord itself, as attempts to enthrone a new Eden within the larger and less controllable new world. In life as in literature, this holy nation within a nation must invariably be renounced for struggles with the fallen world outside; so must the wholeness of the March cottage.

Louisa May Alcott is part of this visionary tradition of American letters. Her family of women takes its energy and its poignancy from the knowledge that Father must return and the community must be left. But the ideal of the March household translates an important dream of our heritage into female terms. It does so with all the energy of rebellion, but unlike *Huckleberry Finn,* Alcott's book need never strike out beyond civilization. The glowing sanity of an independent female family allows revolt at the same time that it cherishes home. Its amplitude is Louisa May Alcott's happiest compromise.

Anne Dalke (essay date 1985)

SOURCE: "'The House-Band': The Education of Men in *Little Women*," *College English,* Vol. 47, No. 6, October, 1985, pp. 571-78.

[In the following essay, Dalke argues that Little Women, *particularly the second part, redefines family according to matriarchal values.]*

Seven years ago, Nina Auerbach elevated *Little Women* from children's classic to a place on the college syllabus. She did so by re-visioning the book, by instructing us, as we in turn gleefully instructed our students, in the "plenitude" and "primacy" of the sisterhood set forth in the novel's first half. The "world of the March girls," Auerbach told us, is "rich enough to complete itself" (*Communities* 58, 61, 55).

In Auerbach's vision of the fiction, the happy marriages at the end of *Little Women* are irrelevant. Auerbach not only exalted the novel's first half at the expense of the second, but offered an alternative ending. She described Alcott's article on **"Happy Women,"** published in *The New York Ledger* at the time she was writing the book, as offering "the idyll lying behind Marmee's new wives' training school: a community of new women, whose sisterhood is not an apprenticeship making them worthy of appropriation by father-husbands, but a bond whose value is itself" (64).

Auerbach's reading of *Little Women* excited me when it first appeared, and continues to do so today. But I have come increasingly to feel that it is false to Alcott's intention and achievement. To re-write the novel into a forum for the autonomous development of women is, I think, to do violence to Alcott's fiction. To embrace only half the book, and to dismiss the rest as compromised, is to misread the whole. Like *Pilgrim's Progress,* on which she drew so heavily, Alcott's novel offers a "stereoscopic" view of two journeys: the first individual and the second communal (cf. Frye 97). The second journey is the appropriate culmination of the first. Auerbach observes that the "March girls had to relinquish the art they all aspired toward" (66); Judith Fetterley has charted in some detail the subjugation of the artistic ambitions of both Jo and Amy into family service. But at the same time that Alcott creates, in the novel's second half, a balance for the female ambitions expressed and sought after in the first, she gives the males in the family the opportunity to participate in a new, expanded family life.

The strength of the novel lies in the combination of its parts. In the first section, Alcott acknowledges "the opportunity her all-girl family had provided for her own development" (Heilbrun, "Influence" 22). In the novel's second half, she envisions the entire March family, most insistently including the men who are incorporated into it, in a non-patriarchal arrangement.

The fascination *Little Women* holds for me now lies less in Jo's ease in adopting males manners and behavior (cf. Heilbrun, "Influence" 23), than in the facility with which her whole family restructures itself on a female pattern. Auerbach argues that the sisterhood of the March girls is "dissolved by marriage" (68). But the book does not fall apart when Meg, Jo, Beth and Amy leave the family. It reaches a climax when Father, John, Friedrich and Laurie join their ranks. Ultimately, the novel celebrates less Jo's reinvention of girlhood (Heilbrun, *Reinventing* 212) than the opportunities provided by the strength and stability of the March matriarchy for reinventing manhood. The sons, husbands, and fathers of Alcott's fiction are reeducated by the women they love. They slowly discover new ways of being men: affectionate, expressive and nurturing (cf. Rich 209-211). With the help of their female associates, they rework masculinity on a female model. Love becomes, by the novel's end, not the power play described by Fetterley, but rather an act of service performed mutually by both sexes.

In her selective adaptation of a preface from John Bunyan, Alcott makes it very clear that her primary focus is on the pilgrimage to be undertaken by the "young damsels" in her story. The "tripping maids" are aided in their stumbling progress by a number of older, seemingly wiser, males (Fetterley 381-382; Spacks 95-101). Certainly the March girls' initial resolve to play Pilgrim's Progress in earnest is prompted by a desire to please their absent parent with their improvement, or, as Marmee says, to "see how far you can get before Father comes home" (*Little Women* 11).

The girls are assisted in that attempt by a male closer to their own age, whom they acknowledge as "a remarkable boy" (278), and whom they use as a standard to measure both other young men and their own behavior. Vain Meg first realizes the extent of her misconduct when she meets Laurie's disapproval in "Vanity Fair" (87); angry Jo's ill temper is certified when "even good-natured Laurie had a quarrel with her" (104); shy Beth is offered Laurie as a model of accomplishment without conceit (67); and selfish Amy is saved from thin ice by his self-possession, from dull Aunt March by his powers of entertainment, and from an inappropriate marriage by his reproof (74, 180, 397).

Laurie offers the girls reward as well as censure. His home becomes the "Palace Beautiful" for them all: it allows Meg the pleasures of a garden, Jo a library, Beth a piano, and Amy art. If his house is a metaphoric heavenly retreat, Laurie himself fulfills the role of substitute deity. Jo, for example, finds him a great comfort when "'God seems so far away I can't find Him'" (173).

Laurie satisfies more mundane needs as well. His sociability saves a dismal dinner party, and his appetite a poorly attended one. He is bodyguard to the girls in their mother's absence; his initiative brings her back. He names Meg's son, and even after he leaves for college, provides, with his "weekly visit . . . an important event in their quiet lives" (229).

Auerbach and Carolyn Heilbrun have both made much of Laurie's initial, wistful solicitation of entrance into the happy community of women next door (*Communities* 57-58; "Influence" 22). But both critics dismiss Laurie, along with all the other men in the novel, as essentially "peripheral" to the rich March household (Auerbach, Afterword 463). Neither acknowledges that self-fulfillment, in Alcott's world, is discovered in relations with others, and that Laurie's eventual admission into the closed circle of women is testimony both to their achievement and to his own.

The relationship between Laurie and the March girls is very much a reciprocal one. He helps them in their journey toward self-improvement, but needs and receives instruction himself in return. Anne Hollander is right to identify Laurie "as a student of the March way of life" (34). Indeed, a major subplot to the story of the four pilgrims' progresses is the *bildungsroman* of their "fifth sister" (Hoyt; cf. Auerbach, *Communities* 60), a young man who goes on a journey much longer and harder than the ones they must undertake, a journey which is incomplete even when the young women exult, at Harvest Time, over their own accomplishments.

Laurie's pilgrimage differs from that of his neighbors, and is correspondingly longer, both because he is wealthy and because he is male. Jo worries about the temptations and amusements usually associated with affluence: billiards, gambling, and drink (140). But Laurie's worst failing is passivity. Poverty provides for the Marches an impetus to occupation; for Laurie, prosperity has the opposite effect.

Like each of his neighbors, Laurie has a central fault. Although his solitary state is soon remedied by his inclusion in the activities of the March family, it requires the length of the novel for him to conquer his indolence. The juxtaposition of the single male against the group of women is succeeded by the juxtaposition of his laziness with their vigor, and that juxtaposition lasts.

On his first encounter with the Marches, Laurie finds that "their busy, lively ways made him ashamed of the indolent life he led" (55). Ashamed, perhaps, but not shamed into action. Months after he has made friends with the girls, he lounges "luxuriously swinging to and fro in his hammock . . . wondering what his neighbors were about, but too lazy to go and find out" (130). When he does pursue them on an expedition, he is admitted to their group only on the condition that he "'do something; it's against the rules to be idle'" (131). Although full of "gratitude for the favor of admission into the 'Busy Bee Society'" (132), Laurie's employment there, as subsequently in college, is only intermittent; he does not learn to emulate the directed energy of the sisters. His visit to Amy, five years later in Nice, is chronicled in a chapter entitled "Lazy Laurence," in which he lives up to his name: "Laurie made no effort of any kind, but just let himself drift along as comfortably as possible" (374).

Not until Amy reproves him directly, and harshly, for his "dreadful . . . indolence" (376) does Laurie consider reform. It takes Amy's denunciation to provoke him to activity: "'you are faulty . . . and miserable. . . . you have grown abominably lazy. . . . and waste time. . . . you can do nothing but dawdle'" (380-381). When Laurie departs to prove Amy wrong, he addresses her as his "dear Mentor," and signs himself off as "Telemachus" (385). The appellations he chooses are fitting. Amy's role is not unlike that of Athena, who in *The Odyssey* assumes the disguise of Mentor and encourages Telemachus to action. The journey of the nineteenth-century Telemachus leads him not in search of a father figure, however, but back to the instructor who with her scolding has proved herself an appropriate match for the erring boy.

Laurie has been posited as a potential suitor for each of the March sisters in turn, and till now found wanting in each case (Auerbach, *Communities* 61). His final mating with Amy is apt because they can learn the most from each other. Fetterley describes the marriages in the novel as "excessively hierarchical" (381-382), but the term is inappropriate as a description of Laurie and Amy's match. She is his best educator, as he is hers. Their bethrothal takes place as they are rowing together, and they pledge in their marriage to always "pull in the same boat" (428).

Amy claims that Laurie "made a princess of me, as the king does the beggarmaid" (429), but his transformation by marriage is even greater than hers. Like Jo, he finds that his heart "was asleep til the fairy prince came through the wood, and waked it up" (445). It is Amy who exhorts Laurie to "wake up and be a man" (384), and he himself speaks with a great deal of decision and energy about his intentions to act on his newly acquired "manly" virtues (395): "'I'm going into business with a devotion . . . and prove . . . that I'm not spoiled. I need something of the sort to keep me steady. I'm tired of dawdling, and mean to work like a man'" (426).

But we never see a demonstration of such work. For marriage to Amy liberates Laurie into another form of activity entirely, not working like a man, but loving like a woman. He does not appear at the office, for example, but instead is deeply involved in family matters: "Laurie devoted himself to the little ones, rode his small daughter in a bushel basket, took Daisy up among the birds' nests, and kept adventurous Rob from breaking his neck" (455).

Laurie is too vigorously engaged in such romps to take part in the final summing up of the novel, in which his wife and her sisters compare their earlier "castles in the air" with their present lives. But Amy reports that she has "'Laurie to take more than half of every burden. . . . He . . . is so sweet and patient with me, so devoted to Beth, and such a stay and comfort to me always that I can't love him enough'" (458). The comparison with Laurie's early hopes to "'just enjoy myself and live for what I like'" (134) is here implicit.

Laurie had been right to predict that his arrival, in the married life that constitutes the this-worldly paradise of the novel's conclusion, would be delayed: "'I shall have to do a good deal of traveling, before I come in sight of your celestial city'" (133). But he eventually earns his place in the March family, a place denied him at first because of his wealth, his indolence, and his sex. With Amy's help, he learns to put the first to good use, to overcome the second, and to subjugate the customary prerogatives of the third to those of the female.

Ironically, his masculinity first attracted Jo to Laurie. She gave him a nickname more masculine than the one he gave himself, and solicited his entrance into the "P.C." (a "ladies' club" in which the March girls assumed male personae), because he would restrain their sentimentality (99). But the primary lesson that his neighbors have to teach Laurie is the same one which Jo learns: the value of female occupation, the worth not only to others, but to the self, of the traditional female virtue of "taking care."

Laurie is taught by the March girls how to respond to women, children, and to other men. Fetterley emphasizes Alcott's portrayal of "the love that exists between women" (379); such love also serves as a model for male relationships. The interaction of Laurie and his grandfather, for example, is carefully coached by Jo. She suggests a course of apology and reconciliation when the two strongwilled men quarrel (*Little Women* 198-203). When she herself refuses Laurie's offer of marriage, she prepares Mr. Laurence to be kind to his grandson. Her preparation enables the older man to handle the situation in a motherly mode: "'I can't stand this,' muttered the old gentleman. Up he got, groped his way to the piano, laid a kind hand on either of the broad shoulders, and said, as gently as a woman, 'I know, my boy, I know'" (344).

As the result of such instruction, Laurie acknowledges that he owes Jo "for a part of my education" (429). But his finishing comes from Amy. The structure of the final quarter of the novel, in which chapters alternate between Jo's experience at home and Laurie's abroad, suggests that the two erstwhile companions are simultaneously undergoing similar learning experiences, for which they will receive similar rewards. Jo discovers in Beth's example the "solace of a belief in . . . love," and acknowledges finally the concomitant "poverty of

other desires" (391). With less pathos, Laurie learns the same lessons from Amy. She teaches him the emptiness of ambition; he comes to accept not the limitations of the conventional act of nurturing, but rather the limits of male autonomy and striving.

Laurie is not the only man in the novel to move past the egocentric self to an appreciation of, and involvement in, the family. All of the men in the novel long for home, all of them solicit access to the circle formed by the March women. Compelled to express such desires, each of them thinks himself "unmanly" for doing so. Laurie is visibly emotional in his plea for admission to the March family circle: his voice "*would* get choky now and then in spite of manful efforts to keep it steady," while his lashes were "still wet with the bitter drop or two her hardness of heart had wrung from them" (339-341). Professor Bhaer's tears come when Jo gives him a different answer, but that experience of happiness is preceded by one of solitary gloom: "he sat long before his fire, with the tired look on his face and . . . homesickness lying heavy at his heart. . . . He did his best and did it manfully, but . . . [didn't find] a pair of rampant boys, a pipe, or even the divine Plato . . . a satisfactory substitute for wife and child and home" (337).

Admission to the family group comes easier to John Brooke than to Laurie or the Professor, but even John shows himself a "domestic man" (363) at a time when the March girls are dreaming dreams which are explicitly not home-bound. When Meg teases him, "Poor Mr. Brooke looked as if his lovely castle in the air was tumbling about his ears" (214).

The girls' father, like their prospective husbands, is distinguished less for activity in the outside world than for his role within the family. Father spends his service in Washington longing to return home. Once arrived, he resumes the function of "household conscience, anchor and comforter . . . in the truest sense of those sacred words, husband and father" (223). His position in the family, like the "unmanful" roles assumed by his sons-in-law, is emphatically female: "Like bees swarming after their queen, mother and daughters hovered about Mr. March" (211).

The men in Alcott's novel participate little more than the women in the world outside of the family. All significant activity is located in the home. Auerbach is mistaken in her conclusion that the March girls are unable to accomplish "the final amalgamation of their matriarchate with the history it tries to subdue. . . . history remains where we found it at the beginning of *Little Women*: 'far away, where the fighting was'" (*Communities* 73). Rather history has been refocused, by Alcott, on the family. Like the homes described by Jane Tompkins in her discussion of *Uncle Tom's Cabin*, the household in *Little Women* is "the center of all meaningful activity . . . physical and spiritual, economic and moral, whose influence spreads out in ever-widening circles." The family offers a blueprint for revising the world, for reforming the human race (95-98). Alcott offers the March home as an alternative to the fashionable and pugnacious activity conducted outside its boundaries.

Men are not incidental to this endeavor (cf. Tompkins 98 and Marsella 9, 130). Both they and the women spend the novel learning to understand the central role of the male in this new scheme. Boys are "almost unknown creatures" to the March girls at the novel's beginning (28), and the young women are perfectly satisfied not to include men in their group. Meg reports, in fact, that she is "'rather glad I hadn't any wild brothers to do wicked things and disgrace the family'" (40). But just as Laurie must learn not to be wild and wicked, his neighbors must learn that men have the capacity for fulfilling other functions. The March family is slowly educated on the necessity of including men in their circle, slowly taught that marriage will not, as Jo claims, "make a hole in the family" (191), but rather fill in the gaps which already exist. Meg is only the first to discover the "treasuries of . . . mutual helpfulness. . . . walking side by side, through fair and stormy weather, with a faithful friend, who is, in the true sense of the good old Saxon word, the 'house band'" (373).

The stewards who join the group bring with them wisdom and wealth, but most emphatically a refusal to abide by the traditional separation between love and work. There is no "Two-Person Career," no "Dual-Career Family" in *Little Women* (cf. Heilbrun, *Reinventing* 193). The novel offers instead a family unit in which husband and wife share the economic and, more significantly, the emotional responsibilities of group existence. John, Friedrich and Laurie all learn to participate in the pattern established by Father March. As Marmee tells Meg,

> "don't shut [your husband] out of the nursery, but teach him how to help in it. His place is there as well as yours, and the children need him; let him feel that he has his part to do . . . and it will be better for you all. . . . That is the secret of our home happiness: [Father] does not let business wean him from the little cares and duties that affect us all. . . . Each do our part alone in many things, but at home we work together, always." (366)

Marmee's plea for the equal involvement of both partners in the demands of family life is put into increasingly successful practice by each of her sons-in-law in turn. Meg is house-bound while John goes out to work. Laurie and Amy have a more equitable arrangement: both stay at home. But it is Jo's marriage which is most explicitly made over on the matriarchal pattern. She chooses the life work for herself and her partner,

and provides the setting for their new school. She and her professor enlarge the family beyond the ties of blood, putting women's traditional strengths to work in an arena wider than that of the immediate household. As Jo says, "'no one can say I'm out of my sphere now, for women's special mission is supposed to be drying tears and bearing burdens. I'm to carry my share, Friedrich, and help to earn the home'" (449). He learns to carry his share as well, in making that home.

As the male characters enter the family, they are successively remodeled on the female mode. The family which incorporates them is not dead (cf. Auerbach, Afterword 466-467), but thriving, growing, and ever more influential. The "wholehearted antagonism to traditional family life" that so many feminist critics have observed in *Little Women* (Auerbach, "Feminist Criticism" 267) thus finds its locus in the role men are taught to play in the novel.

Little Women is the first book in a trilogy. The next two novels both focus clearly on the education of men. What is subplot in *Little Women* becomes main plot in *Little Men* and *Jo's Boys:* the need to reeducate young men for a new world, one that demands their active participation in those activities conventionally reserved for women. Heilbrun suggests that Jo takes in motherless boys because she has no interest in insignificant girls (*Reinventing* 190). I would suggest instead that she does so as a vehement assertion of Alcott's belief in the salvation available to males through the power of motherly love. Jo does not need to make fighting and business accessible to women. Her real work involves remaking men on a female pattern, by granting them admission to female activities, and by teaching them the values of nurturance.

Works Cited

Alcott, Louisa May. *Little Women*. 1868-69. New York: Bantam, 1983.

Auerbach, Nina. Afterword. *Little Women*. By Louisa May Alcott. New York: Bantam, 1983. 461-470.

———. *Communities of Women: An Idea in Fiction*. Cambridge: Harvard UP, 1978.

———. "Feminist Criticism Reviewed." *Gender and Literary Voice: Women and Literature* 1 n.s. (1980): 258-268.

Fetterley, Judith. "*Little Women:* Alcott's Civil War." *Feminist Studies* 5 (1979): 369-383.

Frye, Roland Mushat. *God, Man and Satan: Patterns of Christian Thought and Life in* Paradise Lost, Pilgrim's Progress *and the Great Theologians*. Princeton: Princeton UP, 1960.

Heilbrun, Carolyn. "The Influence of *Little Women*." *Women, the Arts, and the 1920s in Paris and New York*. Ed. Kenneth W. Wheeler and Virginia Lee Lussier. New Brunswick, NJ: Transaction Books, 1982. 20-26.

———. *Reinventing Womanhood.* New York: Norton, 1979.

Hollander, Anne. "Reflections on *Little Women*." *Children's Literature* 9 (1981): 28-39.

Hoyt, Sarita. "The Fifth Sister." Unpublished essay, English 015.01, Bryn Mawr College, Fall 1983.

Marsella, Joy. *The Promise of Destiny: Children and Women in the Short Stories of Louisa May Alcott*. Westport, CT: Greenwood, 1983.

Rich, Adrienne. *Of Woman Born: Motherhood as Experience and Institution*. New York: Bantam, 1976.

Spacks, Patricia Meyer. *The Female Imagination*. New York: Knopf, 1975.

Tompkins, Jane P. "Sentimental Power: *Uncle Tom's Cabin* and the Politics of Literary History." *Glyph* 8 (1981): 79-102.

Ruth K. MacDonald (essay date 1985)

SOURCE: "Louisa May Alcott's *Little Women*: Who is Still Reading Miss Alcott and Why," in *Touchstones: Reflections on the Best in Children's Literature,* Children's Literature Association, 1985, pp. 13-20.

[*MacDonald contrasts recent responses to* Little Women *with those of child readers in Alcott's time, suggesting that although modern critics often consider the book sentimental and romantic, when compared to other works of the time, it is radical and realistic.*]

Louisa May Alcott's books continue to occupy space on library shelves, and some of her novels can still be found in bookstores. At least part of the reason that children, especially girls, continue to read Alcott is that her books are highly recommended by adults who read them when they were children, and who find re-reading them similar to visiting an old friend. For children today, however, the experience of Alcott cannot be so comfortable; her books are certainly not as exhilarating as much of the modern fiction available for children, and Alcott's style, with its frequent copious descriptions and occasional authorial intrusions, is somewhat archaic, perhaps even obsolete, quite different from the simplified vocabularies and syntax of many

modern novels. Certainly the multi-cultural, quickly paced urban lives that many American children lead today would not predispose them to the leisurely, sentimental journey that Alcott offers. Yet that journey still has much to offer them.

There is another large group of readers who keeps Alcott's reputation alive. One need only note the many titles of critical and biographical works on Alcott in the past decade to realize that academic women find Alcott fascinating. Perhaps this interest exists because, as Janice Alberghene has pointed out, Alcott deals with many of the issues that modern women still face: how to combine marriage and a career, how to be a professional in a world which may judge women's efforts to be inferior, how to assert one's principles and rights without so offending the powers that be that the granting of those rights is jeopardized. In short, Alcott is a feminist, who struggles to combine both womanly duties and manly pursuits; the tension that results from this struggle keeps academic readers interested, and they in turn help to keep Alcott's reputation alive.

Little Women, Alcott's first and best novel for children, continues to receive the most attention. Once a reader is hooked on Jo March's conflict between societal expectations about "little women" and her own aspirations to be somebody, to do something worthy of praise, he (or more likely she, as I will call the reader from now on) is likely to continue through the whole Alcott canon. The other books are less satisfactory, but good enough so that the reader keeps on reading. If she is lucky, she will discover Alcott's gothic short stories, and perhaps even her adult novels, though modern editions of these works are few, and unlikely to be found anywhere but in college libraries. If she does find these adult works, the vivid contrast between Miss Alcott, "the children's friend," and the sometimes anonymous or pseudonymous voice of the adult works, may force her to pause and reevaluate those works otherwise uncritically perceived as perfectly charming and appropriate for children.

Of course, Alcott's children's books seem to be quite safe to recommend, especially from the point of view of the modern censor; unlike a good deal of modern "problem literature" or "new realism" for children, Alcott no longer shocks the reader with her subject matter. There are no promiscuous, drug-dealing anorexics here, and ever since "Christopher Columbus," Jo March's favorite expletive, ceased to offend even the most delicate sensibility, no one has seen fit to criticize the language. Alcott and her family were all believers in and pursuers of social reform throughout their lives, but there is nothing in *Little Women* that reveals that authorial predisposition, and even in Alcott's time, most readers found little to take exception to. Even those readers, past or present, who know

Frontispiece for the first volume of Little Women.

that the South won the War Between the States, find this Civil War novel set in New England worthy of their total approbation.

From the point of view of the child reader, furthermore, there is much real appeal in the warmth of the family relations. Marmee is hardly ever really angry; certainly she never raises her voice at her daughters, and she is always willing to explain why she says what she says and does what she does. She is never peremptory, never harried, and only occasionally does the reader see a crack in her maternal veneer. The sisters may have on-going squabbles, but even these, for the most part, seem under control. The girls are basically good and easy to sympathize with. And like good girls in fairy tales, they get the traditional reward at the end: parental approval for their hard work and achievements, and loving husbands and children. Though the sisters never get to be princesses, their husbands are attractive and attentive, and their lack of wealth is not so troubling, since there always seems to be enough to keep the families happy, without spoiling them on the one hand and depriving them on the other.

Americans have always celebrated the golden isolation of the home from the turbulence of the outside world. From Puritan times, colonists saw the family as the model upon which the commonwealth was based and believed in the sanctity of the family unit. Americans are inventors of the idea of home as more than just a dwelling, of the terms "hometown" and "homesick." So as a group, we like and enthusiastically recommend portrayals of such happy homes, in the faith that such portrayals can perpetuate a sense of the value of home in our young.

Little Women seems to offer that sort of portrayal and to be a safe, unthreatening book. But Alcott deserves the benefit of the doubt about her conventionality. We need to suspend our modern standards of judgment, and try to see the work through the eyes of Alcott's contemporaries.

In its own time, *Little Women* was unique in its restrained impulse to preach. By modern standards, Alcott intrudes herself into the novel entirely too often to be acceptable; but by the standards of her time she stood on her soapbox hardly at all. She did not preach to children about right behavior, but rather let characters and readers work out their own conclusions through the situations and actions in the novel. Marmee may be full of good advice, but she does not offer it unless asked, and only in amounts appropriate to the situation.

To the reader used to dealing with juvenile delinquents in realistic fiction, the girls may seem nearly perfect already; but before Alcott, no one else had even tried to create faulty characters worthy of improvement. Good characters were models; bad characters incorrigible and

exemplars of the negative results of their actions. Alcott's abilities in fully-rounded characterization alone earn this novel a place in the canon.

Modern readers have lost their taste for the sentimental novel and may find Alcott somewhat treacly and lacrimose; but here too Alcott shows her restraint. By the standards of her time she was not manipulating the reader to tears to the extent that other sentimental writers did, and though she does have one deathbed scene, it is short by comparison to those of her contemporaries, and certainly short of melodramatic excess. She did not introduce the death simply to indulge the readers' demands for bathetic release, but because her readers had demanded a continuation of her original March family story. The original story was based on her own family; and since her own sister had died, she felt justified in presenting her death as part of the autobiographical reality of the narrative.

It is clear, then, that the March family story is not a simple sentimental formula without any dramatic tension or interest. And while children are hardly literature's best or most articulate critics, I think that at some level even they realize that Alcott has more on her mind and in her writing than just her loving, charming, fictional family happily living together in genteel poverty. For the young reader old enough to read and remember carefully, there will be a clear message about the value of being comfortable in clothing rather than being stylish, about the intrigue of a personality that is not restrained in saying what it wants and in laughing out loud, however boisterously, at jokes. As modern as parents are now be trying to be in raising their daughters, there are still a number of rules about being a "lady" which every little girl at some time comes to resent. Jo March articulates clearly her resentment at the restraints that the "little woman" role imposed upon her. She may be admonished by her sisters and mother for her frankness in responding, but she articulates for the reader socialized enough to know that one does not always say what one thinks that such strictures are unfair and uncomfortable. Jo receives little rebuke; the reader receives none. So there is vicarious criticism of the prevailing social order on behalf of the reader, and yet she need not worry about the consequences.

For Alcott, the only way to do manly things in a man's world while still being a woman was to be competent at the housewifely arts, such as cooking, cleaning, and sewing, while at the same time pursuing other interests outside the home. The compromise she posits here is a workable answer to the modern girl's and woman's dilemma about combining male and female. In fact, it is one which will probably guarantee success in both sexes' domains. In her last book, *Jo's Boys,* Alcott complained more stridently about the burdens which such a dual role places on a woman, and encouraged the co-eds at Laurence College to consider spinster-hood and career as an acceptable alternative to combining marriage and family; but she did not dare to take such an outspoken stand earlier in her career. And even in *Jo's Boys,* homemaking is still a worthy choice of career for a woman to dedicate her life to. At the same time, Alcott did not discourage women from pursuing careers outside the home. And she suggests quite clearly that work is ennobling and rewarding; having one's own money, however small the sum, gives one status in the world and a feeling, if not the actual achievement, of independence and autonomy. Work is also a healthy solution to depression about the unfairness of life, and to the langor of inactivity. Though her solution may have encouraged several generations of readers to try it for themselves—after all, if Marmee and Jo March could do it, why shouldn't they?—it has also led contemporary women to question the stress that such a burden places on such "Super Women." But for many readers, Alcott solves a problem to which there seemed to be no solution.

Even though the surface of the novel suggests that everything is placid and graceful in the relations of the family members, the careful reader realizes that there is a great deal of sibling rivalry going on in *Little Women.* The tension, subtly presented so that Alcott's less perceptive readers could not object to the novel's surface, does much to enhance the novel's appeal. When Amy burns Jo's notebook, Jo's anger surfaces, and the reader feels that Jo would be more than justified in killing Amy. After all, Amy's provocation is simply childish pique; Jo will not let her come along to a theater outing with Laurie and herself, certainly not a substantial enough provocation to justify Amy's heinous destruction of Jo's hard and irrecoverable work. When Jo goes skating with Laurie later in the same chapter, Amy once again traipses after them, invading their comaraderie the same way she wanted to in the first place. Once again, Amy provokes, and Marmee, as idealized as she is, does not intrude to prevent Amy from being a brat. When Amy nearly drowns by falling through the ice, Jo feels remorse, and all is forgiven between the sisters—but not for long. Throughout the novel, Jo and Amy continue to irritate each other. Amy criticizes Jo's mannish manners; Jo criticizes Amy's social pretensions. Though the rivalry is never again as clearly demonstrated as in this chapter, it is always present as a continuous source of interest and realism.

Marmee's status as the ideal American mother was not nearly as clear in Alcott's original version of the novel. For example, when Marmee first enters the door in chapter one, in the version that most girls read today, a revision that Alcott substituted after the first two editions, Alcott describes her as "a tall, motherly lady, with a 'can-I-help-you' look about her which was truly delightful. She was not elegantly dressed, but a noble-looking woman . . ." (Orchard House Edition 8). The

first edition gives a much more revealing description, one perhaps much closer to Alcott's estimation of her own mother: "a stout, motherly lady, with a 'can-I-help-you' look about her which was truly delightful. She wasn't a particularly handsome person, but mothers are always lovely to their children . . ." (Modern Library Edition 14). Alcott edited out her frankness about her mother's physical appearance here and elsewhere, and eliminated many of the mother's quick retorts and willingness to comment on others' faults; yet the traits still persist, revealed primarily in Marmee's pursed lips, which Marmee tells Jo and the reader is her way of containing her temper. When irascible Aunt March ungraciously consents to lend Marmee the money she needs to rush to the side of her stricken husband, Marmee reads the letter containing Aunt March's reply with the telltale configuration of lips.

When Marmee lets the girls follow their own self-indulgent inclinations to do no work for the summer in order to pursue idleness, she again reveals her humanity as she forces the experiment to a disastrous ending. During the first week of the experiment, she and the household servant try to fill in the gaps that the girls' idleness have left in the household labor force; but by the end of the week she gives the servant a day off to rest and deliberately absents herself, so that the girls will have to shift for themselves, and will appreciate more sincerely the efforts made on their behalf during the earlier part of the week. Marmee does not really allow events to follow their own course to calamity; she forces the issue, giving play to her own anger about having been unacknowledged and unappreciated in the early part of the week. As sister Meg reports,

> Mother isn't sick, only very tired, and she says she is going to stay quietly in her room all day, and let us do the best we can. It's a very queer thing for her to do, she don't act a bit like herself; but she says it *has* been a hard week for her, so we mustn't grumble, but take care of ourselves. (Modern Library Edition 139)

As the reader soons finds, there is much more anger beneath Marmee's surface than implied by the charming, loving, maternal bosom presented to the world.

As Nina Auerbach has pointed out, there is a lot to be said for the seductive power of that maternal bosom. As much as Marmee's maternal instincts are otherwise innocuous, her love is so all-accepting and her desire to be a mother to all comers so all-consuming, that she manages to convince her daughters, and even the boy next door, that life as her child is a permanent status. Auerbach notes that although the novel purports to be about growing up, its equally salient message is that, in the fictional world of this novel, one need never grow up. One can remain Marmee's chosen and cherished darling forever if one so desires. The sisters seldom chafe at the maternal apron strings. Even when they marry, they barely move away from home, being able to stand a separation of only a few houses down the street. This offer of eternal childhood explains much of the book's charm. Not only is Marmee the perfect mother, she is also eternally available, both to the reader in the stasis in which she exists in the book, and to her daughters. As Marmee herself says when a troubled Jo comes to her for advice about Meg's impending marriage, "It is natural and right you should all go to homes of your own, in time; but I do want to keep my girls as long as I can" (Modern Library Edition 251).

The book also continues to be read, I think, because of its appeal to the pleasures of consumerism—an apparent contradiction to the spiritual values it proclaims. John Bunyan's spiritual guide *The Pilgrim's Progress* is a specifically posited model for the March sisters to follow, for as early as chapter one they all decide to shoulder their burdens and go forward in their earthly progresses to their eventual heavenly perfection. But as spiritual and high-minded as the sisters are supposed to be, the reader tends to agree with Jo March's famous opening line in the novel, "Christmas won't be Christmas without any presents" (Modern Library Edition 7). Though the line shows Jo and her sisters to be utterly misguided spiritually, it also shows them thoroughly and sympathetically possessed by the pleasures of consumption inevitably associated with the Yuletide season. Though the girls complain of their poverty, they do not seem so poor to the modern reader, who has lost the conception of genteel poverty as socially embarrassing. And for all their protestations about their material sacrifices since the family's financial reverses, they don't miss out on much: they still go to the fancy balls and have special dress-up clothes and hair styles to match. They may not have fancy foods, but certainly there is always enough at the table, and their simple gustatory pleasures are so convincingly described that it hardly seems as though they are missing anything. Even something as simple as a cup of coffee, a rare treat for the sisters, is offered to them in the novel at a time when both they and the readers particularly appreciate its aroma, flavor, and caffeine-derived stimulation. Just after their mother rushes off to be with their stricken father at his Civil War post, the household servant and long-time friend realizes that the sisters need something both to distract them from the parental absences and to lift their spirits. The coffee, not only because it is a rarity but also because it is a physical stimulus at a point in the book where spiritual and emotional descriptions have predominated, cheers both fictional character and reader. As important as prayer and self-examination are supposed to be in the novel, sometimes nothing works as well as a new dress or a snack.

Though *Little Women* is not the educational novel that *Little Men* or *Eight Cousins* is, still Alcott's concern for educational reform according to the precepts of her father's rather unconventional ideas does much to attract the modern young reader. Bronson Alcott did not believe in corporal punishment, but rather, in correction by moral suasion and learning from the consequences of one's actions. He did not believe in rote memorization, but rather in learning from experience. Most of all, he did not believe that most education went on in the classroom. His educational ideas were rooted in his conception of the child as innately good, someone who was willing to learn and to be good if only learning and goodness were put in his way. These ideas do not seem so radical now, but in his daughter's time, they were nearly scandalous—especially when one considers that they were combined with his ideas about co-education of the sexes and racially integrated classrooms. Perhaps the attraction for the modern young reader is that these educational ideas are centered on what children are and not on what they are supposed to be; and as theoretical and irrelevant as Bronson's ideas might seem to today's reader, she will no doubt find appealing the fact that none of his characters ever seem to spend much time in a dreary classroom.

Little Women established for Louisa May Alcott a popular and critical success, which her writing for adults had failed to do for her. Perhaps because *Little Women* was so lucrative, and because her family had long been destitute, she continued to use some of the formulae from *Little Women* in her later novels. The reader who continues on through the Alcott canon finds much that is familiar, if not as vigorous as in the original presentation. There are more comments about women's rights and about education; there are more good characters who appear in the novels in order to be made better. There is even a recreation of Jo March, in a niece of Jo's, also named Josie, who appears in *Jo's Boys*. There are other dying children, other girls trying to find careers for themselves and proper mates. Alcott did not tamper with a good thing once she found it, but repeated it as long as her public would continue to buy and read. But she never achieved again what she had in *Little Women,* and it is on this one book that her reputation continues to be based.

Works Cited

Alcott, Louisa May. *Little Women: or Meg, Jo, Beth, and Amy.* Orchard House Edition. Boston and Toronto: Little, Brown, 1915.

———. *Little Women.* Boston: Roberts Brothers, 1869. Reprint with introduction by Madelon Bedell. New York: Modern Library, 1983.

Auerbach, Nina. "Austen and Alcott on Matriarchy: New Women or New Wives?" *Novel* 10 (Fall 1976): 6-26.

Sarah Elbert (essay date 1987)

SOURCE: "Reading *Little Women*," in *A Hunger for Home: Louisa May Alcott's Place in American Culture*, Rutgers University Press, 1987, pp. 195-218.

[*In the following chapter, Elbert identifies major themes in Alcott's work as exemplified in* Little Women, *tying them all to an ideal of "domestic democracy."*]

> I may be strong-minded, but no one can say I'm out of my sphere now, for woman's special mission is supposed to be drying tears and bearing burdens. I'm to carry my share, Friedrich, and help to earn the home. Make up your mind to that, or I'll never go.

Jo March in Little Women, chapter 46

The title of Louisa May Alcott's most famous book is a common-place nineteenth-century expression. In the opening chapter, Marmee reads a Christmas letter from her absent husband to his daughters, which tenderly admonishes them to "conquer themselves so beautifully that when I come back to them I may be fonder and prouder than ever of my little women."[1] This sentimental diminutive is puzzling in an author who was concerned with enlarging, rather than diminishing, woman's status. Such belittlement was part of the woman problem, as Alcott knew. This title appears even more puzzling when we consider that *Little Women* deals with the problems common to girls growing into womanhood.

Alcott had no intention of depreciating the struggles of young women, so we must look elsewhere for explanations of the title. We find one in the works of Charles Dickens, which Alcott read and took with her to the Union Hotel during the Civil War. For several decades Dickens had moved English and American readers to tears with his tender depictions, imitated but never equaled, of childhood woe. Dickens cared most deeply for the misery of exploited children—abused strangers in a venal adult world, but often remarkably capable of fending for themselves. Dickensian girls are particularly self-reliant, able to care for their siblings by the time they are "over thirteen, sir," as the girl "Charlie" says to Mr. Jarndyce in *Bleak House*. In this novel the term "little women" makes a prominent appearance when Esther, ward of the generous, sweet-hearted Mr. Jarndyce, is told by her guardian, "You have wrought changes in me, little woman," indicating that she has widened and deepened his sensibilities and hence his philanthropy.[2]

Esther saves many people during the course of the novel, including the girl Charlie whom she takes in and nurses through a bout of smallpox. Charlie herself had contracted the disease from Jo, another pathetic Dickensian orphan. Inevitably, Esther comes down with smallpox, which leaves her face scarred and sets her musing about the meaning of "little woman."

Although only twenty-one, Esther has been close to death and realizes now how short time is for "little women." No longer a child, yet not an adult, she finds life fleeting and precious. Dreadfully confused, she talks about the stages of her life, feeling herself at once "a child, an elder girl, and the little woman I had been so happy as." The problem, she thinks, is that the stages are not so distinct as she had once innocently supposed. Rather, they seem joined together and weighted down by similar "cares and difficulties," which are hard to reconcile or understand.[3]

When Louisa May Alcott employed the term "little women," she infused it with this Dickensian meaning. *Little Women* portrays just such a complex overlapping of stages from childhood to elder child, little woman to young woman, that appears in *Bleak House*. Like Esther, each of Alcott's heroines has a scarring experience that jars her into painful awareness of vanished childhood innocence and the inescapable woman problem.

Esther's role as part-time narrator in *Bleak House* is given to Jo in *Little Women*, but the resemblance between the two characters ends there. Jo comes close to bounding off the pages of her book; an American heroine, she has fits of exuberance alternating with moments of half-chastened humility. Unlike Esther, and very much like her creator, Jo writes a story that succeeds miraculously even though she "never knew how it happened." "Something," Jo declares, "got into that story that went straight to the hearts of those who read it." She put "humor and pathos into it," says saintly Mr. March, sure that his daughter had "no thought of fame or money in writing" her story.[4]

Louisa May Alcott of course, unlike Jo, produced the story of *Little Women* in record time for money. As she reviewed the first page proofs, she found that "it reads better than I expected; we really lived most of it and if it succeeds that will be the reason of it."[5] Five succeeding generations have laughed and cried over *Little Women*. Each generation may well have its own favorite incidents and lessons. And every generation's readers indisputably love Jo, who is never an orphan though she often feels like one in moving from girlhood to womanhood.

Alcott's acknowledged mentors in the writing of *Little Women* also include Susan B. Warner and Charlotte M. Yonge. Contemporary readers could not miss the significance of Jo sitting in the family's apple tree, crying over *The Wide Wide World*.[6] The March sisters, in fact, name their apple tree "Ellen-tree" after Ellen Montgomery, the orphaned heroine of that story. Amy and Jo put a saddle on a "nice, low branch," and use the tree as a hobby horse, not being fortunate enough to get a real pony as Ellen does in Warner's novel. Jo is also discovered eating apples and crying over *The Heir of Redclyffe* in the privacy of a garret inhabited only by her pet rat, Scrabble, who probably also witnessed Jo's reading of another Yonge novel, *The Daisy Chain.*[7] Yonge's heroine in the latter novel, like Ellen Montgomery in *The Wide Wide World,* is by nature a rebellious, moody girl. Ethel May is a "thin, lank, angular, sallow girl, just fifteen, trembling from head to foot with restrained eagerness as she tried to curb her tone into the requisite civility."[8]

Women's fiction in the nineteenth century has been characterized as following a formula in which the heroine, often orphaned, progresses through a series of lonely ordeals that prove her inherent worth and her ability to survive independently. She finds help along the way, usually in the form of an expanding female network. A heroine's ordeals prompt her perceptual transformation or change of heart; she grows considerably during the process.[9] In Alcott's time, *The Wide Wide World* was the most popular rendition of this women's fiction formula. Juvenile literature, in this categorization, merely simplifies women's fiction; young heroes and heroines grow up because circumstances force them out into a cruel and heartless world where they see the light and become the best they can be, converting others in the process.

Because it is juvenile literature, *Little Women* seems to some critics to represent a decline in the radical power of women's fiction.[10] The novel may also be considered a diminishment of women's capacity for independence precisely because Alcott's heroines are not orphans or widows but members of a particularly embracing family. And, since the Victorian middle-class family leaves women's work famously unpaid and undervalued, it hardly seems an environment conducive to empowering little women. Just as American heroines are portrayed provoking Civil War and ending slavery, they are seemingly remanded to a private sphere in *Little Women.* Historians of juvenile fiction consequently join with many historians of women's literature in placing *Little Women* at the top of a downward spiral.[11]

Domestic Realism

Romanticism provided two powerful impulses to the development of juvenile literature. Shaping our modern view of "human nature," the Romantic perspective insists that children are born as pure, unique wellsprings of creativity. Building upon this belief, children's vision of the world seems particularly honest and sincere. Placing children at the center of the action, Romantic juvenile fiction also encourages them to reveal adult hypocrisy. Sometimes, childhood ends with the pragmatic necessity of growing up to join the hypo-

crites. In sentimental novels, however, a pure child's ability to convert adults conversely restores grownups to the lost world of children's innocence.[12]

The golden age of children's literature in England produced a remarkable glow emanating from fairy rings and fictional children who stubbornly refused to grow up; as runaways, they poked sharply at both the bourgeois family and the deadening blights of industrial capitalism. Historians of childhood and juvenile literature understandably revel in analyses of *The Water Babies, Alice in Wonderland, Peter Rabbit, Peter Pan,* and *The Wind in the Willows;* all these works, like the women's fiction categorized by Nina Baym, provide significant social commentary and criticism. America, with the same Romantic heritage to inspire its juvenile genre, produced the *Little Women* series, followed by a host of imitators from *Rebecca of Sunny-brook Farm* to the Pollyanna books and the Bobbsey Twins series.

Little Women does not betray the author's Romantic birthright, nor does it belittle women's fiction. Louisa May Alcott combines many conventions of the sentimental novel with crucial ingredients of Romantic children's fiction, creating a new form of which *Little Women* is a unique model. In it Alcott created the American Girl reflecting her myriad facets in the diverse personalities of Meg, Jo, Beth and Amy March. Alcott's work indisputably enlarges the myth of American womanhood by insisting that the home and the women's sphere cherish individuality and thus produce young adults who can make their way in the world while preserving a critical distance from its social arrangements. All the March sisters are engaged in a search for their adult selves and all—Jo most painfully and powerfully—fear that their unique human potential will be lost or destroyed in the process of growing up. Balancing their fears with castles in the air, the sisters also hope that their individuality will somehow be recognized and specially rewarded in the adult world.

Jo writes the first part of *Little Women* in the second half of the novel. As a story based on her own childhood, her narration signals a successfully completed adolescence. She has preserved the unique child within herself, disciplining her talent to create a work of art which is also a recipe for achieving an adult self. The trial or ordeals as well as the perception of a change of heart necessary to a heroine's progress in adult women's fiction are also present in *Little Women.* Alcott's added ingredient is the social arrangements defining the March family. A loving female creation, the March cottage is a nest from which the sisters fly out, testing themselves in the larger world. Marmee counsels and rules, but also lets her daughters go, one by one. *Little Women* significantly reassures young readers, who are generally younger than Amy March in the first part, that they will remain truly themselves in growing up. The March girls, after all, are easily recognizable in the persons of the March women. Readers need only the bit of "gossip" provided by the author to fill in what has transpired between the end of childhood and the beginning of young womanhood.

Adult women still reread **Little Women,** traveling backward to recover toys in the attic, precious objects that have been mislaid or put away over the years. The gap between an authentic self and a modern identification with functional social roles grows wider with each decade. As it widens adult readers return longingly to **Little Women** where the source of fragile individuality rests, Alcott argues, in the memories of those who knew us in childhood—in our families. The March sisters share the same parents and the same stable childhood environment yet each little woman has a unique self; the recognition of their differences and their bond is an important aspect in **Little Women's** domestic realism. Jo, the self-proclaimed historian of the family, has custody of objects and memories connecting past to present in March history. And the family history reassures readers that each of them has a human value beyond the marketplace.

Themes in Little Women: *Domesticity*

The novel develops three major themes: domesticity, work, and true love. All of them are interdependent and each is necessary to the achievement of a heroine's individual identity. The same motifs appear in **Little Men, Jo's Boys, Eight Cousins, Rose in Bloom,** and **An Old-Fashioned Girl.** None of these novels has been out of print since first published. Together they comprise a fictional record of liberal woman's rights ideology, process, and programs from 1867 through 1886 in America.

From the outset Alcott established the centrality of household democracy, underscoring the importance of "natural" cooperation and mutual self-sacrifice within family life. The March cottage shelters the sisters and their parents, all of whom love and depend upon one another. Even the family poverty, so reminiscent of Alcott's own, serves to reinforce democratic practice in the family. With the help of Hannah, who worked as a maid for Mrs. March in better days and now considers herself a member of the family, all the women work together to accomplish household chores, making the most of meager means by sharing everything.

The virtues of mutual self-sacrifice and domestic cooperation, however, must be proven to the March girls before they can recognize the importance of such virtues to their self-realization. Independent-minded and childishly selfish, the girls must learn how to shape their individualities in harmony with the interests of the family. In an important episode Alcott describes the tactics used by Mrs. March to win her daughters to a higher social standard, which is in a sense to "conquer themselves."

After listening to Jo, Meg, Beth, and Amy pine for the "vacations" enjoyed by wealthier friends, Marmee agrees to release them from domestic duties for one week. She allows them to structure their time in any way they please. On the first morning, the neat inviting cottage is suddenly a different place, and after a day of small troubles, the girls are grumpy and ill-tempered. The experiment, however, is not over. Excessive attention to self-pleasure produces a scarcity of necessities, including food. Emulating the little red hen, Mrs. March decides that those who do not work shall not eat. She gives Hannah a holiday, and the maid leaves with these parting words: "Housekeeping ain't no joke." Unable to rely on the experience and counsel of Hannah and their mother, the girls produce a breakfast featuring boiled tea, very bitter, scorched omelette, and biscuits speckled with saleratus. Jo caters a luncheon for friends, forgetting that she can't make anything "fit to eat" except "gingerbread and molasses candy." So she sails off to purchase "a very young lobster, some very old asparagus, and two boxes of acid strawberries." She boils the asparagus for an hour until the heads are "cooked off" and the stalks "harder than ever." She undercooks the lobster and the potatoes, and sprinkles salt instead of sugar on the strawberries.

In the midst of this culinary chaos, Beth discovers that her canary, Pip, is dead from lack of water and food. Her sisters and the assembled guests, including Laurie, try to help, but to no avail. Amy proposes that they warm the bird in an oven to revive him. "Overcome with emotion and lobster," sickened by the death of her bird, Beth rebels. "He's been starved," she says of her bird, "and he shan't be baked, now he's dead . . . and I'll never have another bird . . . for I am too bad to own one."

Returning home to find her daughters miserable over their failures as homekeepers, Mrs. March easily persuades them to admit that "it is better to have a few duties, and live for others." This experiment, she says, was designed to show "what happens when everyone thinks only for herself. Now you know that in order to make a home comfortable and happy," everyone in it must contribute to the family welfare. Marmee has also proven to the girls that domestic work is real work, giving women a "sense of power and independence better than money or fashion." She has shown them that home life becomes a "beautiful success" only if work alternates with leisure, independence with cooperation and mutual concern.[13]

Although this episode deals almost exclusively with girls, Alcott integrated men into her vision of co-operative family life. Men too should benefit from and participate in this family experience, but only on the grounds that they respect the independence and equal authority of women within the home.

Accepting, even glorifying the importance of women's domestic work, Alcott emphasizes that men are homeless without women. Since the ability to create a home and sustain a family supercedes fame and money as evidence of success and civilization, it follows that women have already proved themselves in the world; thus their ability to extend their sphere is unquestioned in *Little Women.* Homeless men, despite wealth, wages, and worldly experience, are motherless children. Meg's suitor, John Brooke, is attracted to the March cottage in large part because he is a lonely young man who has recently lost his mother. Laurie is motherless, which excuses most of his faults, and Mr. Laurence, his grandfather, has no wife, daughter, or granddaughter. Mr. March alone has a proper home and knows his place in it, returning from the war to enlarge, but not supercede, Marmee's authority. He wholly accepts the female abundance around him, tending the flock of his tiny parish and leaving domestic arrangements to his womenfolk.

The question of whether men can be integrated into domestic life on democratic terms first appears in the relationship between young Laurie and the March sisters. Laurie starts out right. The offer of food is an excellent way to gain acceptance into an alien tribe. Meg, Jo, Beth, and Amy, having given up their Christmas breakfast for a starving German immigrant family, are happily surprised by a compensatory feast sent over by the Laurences. Mrs. March has encouraged her daughters to pack up their hot muffins, buckwheat cakes, bread, and cream early Christmas morning and deliver the meal to the hungry Hummels. After a full day spent giving gifts to Marmee and then performing a homemade opera for their friends, a fashionable supper of "ice cream—actually two dishes of it, pink and white—cake and fruit and distracting French bon-bons" is exactly what the unfashionable March girls crave. Three huge bouquets of hothouse flowers complete the Laurence boy's offerings. With the proper motive of rewarding their self-sacrifice, he is also courting them.[14]

Laurie and Jo reverse the gift giving and also their sexual personas when Jo visits her new friend on his home ground, the mansion next door.[15] She suggests a visit from girls, because her sex ordinarily is "quiet and likes to play nurse." Jo arrives and unpacks a maternal abundance of gifts, including her own womanly touch; she brushes the hearth, straightens books and bottles, and plumps Laurie's pillows. It is this shy confession that he has been watching them together, coupled with the "hungry, solitary look in his eyes," that turns Jo from boy to little woman to foster mother in a twinkling. Juvenile readers are warned away from any other interpretation of the unchaperoned visit by Alcott's firm assertion that Jo "had been so simply taught that there was no nonsense in her head, and at fifteen, she was as innocent and frank as any child."[16]

A boy's acceptance of motherly abundance encourages an innocent young girl to treat him as her sister or alternatively to make him, as Jo says, her "boy" or foster son. An adult romance emerging out of this familiar relationship is fraught with incestuous complications. The worst one, from Jo's viewpoint, is that such frozen domestic roles preclude female independence within marital union; democratic households cannot be incestuous.

Alcott advances ideas about the place of men in the family which emerged out of her domestic experiences with her parents, despite her belief in universal laws of progress and democracy. On the whole, she does not paint a compelling picture of marital equality in *Little Women.* Instead she presents the possibility of educating a new generation of little men and little women. In the second part of *Little Women* Alcott describes the married life of John and Meg Brooke. Theirs is not a modern egalitarian marriage. The single wage earner for his family, John provides a domestic servant but does not share domestic chores himself, except for disciplining his son in the evening. Meg is totally dependent upon his income for both household and personal expenses.

In a chapter called "On the Shelf," Meg's docility appears as her greatest virtue and her most serious domestic flaw. Docility is a fine quality in a daughter, even a sister, Alcott admits, but dangerous in a wife. Meg becomes dowdy and dependent, isolated in her little cottage with two small children.[17] Mrs. March shares her domestic secret with her daughter: a good marriage is based on mutuality of interests and responsibilities: "We each do our part alone in many things, but at home we work together, always."[18]

According to Alcott, the reform of domestic life required restoration of a mutuality that had vanished with the separation of home and work. Yet of all the domestic advice presented in *Little Women,* this lesson carries the least conviction. As we shall see, Alcott can offer model domesticity only in utopian settings where cooperative communities reappear in sexually democratic forms.

Flying up: Little Women Grow up to be Themselves

When Alcott finished writing part two of *Little Women,* she suggested "Wedding Marches" as a possible title. She changed it, however, to "Birds Leaving the Nest," or "Little Women Grow Up," because she did not wish to suggest that marriage should be the focal event for growing girls. Instead she argues that girls who take trial flights from secure homes will find their own paths to domestic happiness. They might choose an independent single life or some form of marital bonds that range from partial to complete "household democracy." For Alcott, sisterhood and marriage, though often contradictory, are equally valuable possibilities for women. Fully realized sisterhood becomes a model for marriage, not simply an alternative to it. Together, marriage and sisterhood guarantee that individual identity and domesticity will be harmonious.

Meg, the eldest and most docile daughter, does not attain Alcott's ideal womanhood. Democratic domesticity requires maturity, strength, and above all a secure identity that Meg lacks. Her identity consists of being Marmee's daughter and then John's wife. When Meg leaves home to work as a governess she accepts a three-year engagement period, dreaming that she will have much to learn while she waits. But John says, "You have only to wait; I am to do the work." Alcott accepts the limitations of temperament and circumstance in Meg, as she does in all her characters. In *Little Men,* however, Meg's widowhood grants her the circumstances to develop a stronger side of her character.

Fashion provides a counterpoint to woman's rights in *Little Women.* Jo's strong sense of self is established in part by her rejection of fashion, which she perceives as a sign of dependency and sexual stereotyping. Amy, on the other hand, struggles against her burden of vanity, which has its positive side in her "nice manners and refined way of speaking." Amy must learn that appearances can be deceiving, whereas Jo must learn that appearances do count in the larger world.

Jo's lack of vanity about clothes at first conceals her pride both in her writing talent and in her exclusive relationship to Laurie. Laurie enjoys Jo's vivid imagination; it gives color and vivacity to his own lonely childhood. Keeping Amy out of pleasurable excursions with Laurie is one of Jo's main "faults." Left at home once too often, Amy burns a collection of Jo's painstakingly written fairy tales as revenge. Furious, Jo leaves her behind again when she and Laurie go skating. Amy follows behind and is almost killed by falling through the thin ice. Penitent, Jo vows to curb her temper and cherish Amy. Jo realizes that she is not the only independent and talented member of the family; accepting that fact is part of her growing up.[19]

Her notion that she is "the man of the family" is a more serious problem in the story. In a strange way this too plays itself out around fashion. Jo has her first serious encounter with Laurie at a neighborhood dance, where she is uncomfortably dressed up. She finds her sartorial model in the opposite sex and decides she can grow up to be a splendid woman with neatly laced boots and clean linen. She does not want Laurie as a sweetheart; she wants to adopt both him and his air of freedom and elegant comfort.[20]

Amy's trials are rewarded when Aunt Carrol, hearing of her niece's delicate manners, talented fancy work, and Christian forbearance at the charity fair, rewards her with a trip to Europe as her companion. Poor Jo is left behind, too unfashionable and forthright to be patronized. On one occasion Jo tells Amy, "It's easier for me to risk my life for a person than to be pleasant to him when I don't feel like it." Amy replies that "women should learn to be agreeable, particularly poor ones; for they have no other way of repaying kindnesses they receive. If you'd remember that, and practice it, you'd be better liked than I am because there is more of you." It is precisely because Jo is indeed more substantial that the author grants Amy a free holiday in Europe and eventually a wealthy indulgent husband.[21]

Amy and Laurie grow up together in Europe. Both are fashionable, inclined to coquetry. Both have talent, Amy for painting and Laurie for music, but only enough to please friends in polite salons. Neither is put to the test of earning a living. Both are also inclined toward "illusion" in dressing themselves and appreciating each other's refined taste. Their growing up, however, does require a degree of honesty: they admit that "talent isn't genius and you can't make it so."

Despite the sniping and competition for parental love, social approval, and material rewards, Amy and Jo share one great loss that matures them both. The central tragedy of *Little Women* is Beth's death in the final part of the book.[22] Loving home the best, gentle Beth never wants to leave it; perhaps she would never have done so. She grows more fragile each year, and in her last months confides to Jo the feeling that she was never intended to live long. Her short speech is also her longest in the novel:

> "I'm not like the rest of you; I never made plans about what I'd do when I grew up; I never thought of being married, as you all did. I couldn't seem to imagine myself anything but stupid little Beth, trotting about at home, of no use anywhere but there. I never wanted to go away and the hard part now is the leaving you all. I'm not afraid, but it seems as if I should be homesick for you even in heaven."[23]

Jo's maturation is sealed by her grief over Beth's decline. The chapter entitled "Valley of the Shadow" sketches a household that revolves around Beth's room for one year. Everyone, including Beth, knows she is dying. Jo writes a long poem to her sister in which she acknowledges that true sisterhood is born in shared domestic experiences, and that such loving ties cannot be severed:

> Henceforth, safe across the river,
> I shall see forevermore
> A beloved, household spirit
> Waiting for me on the shore.
> Hope and faith, born of my sorrow,
> Guardian angels shall become,
> And the sister gone before me
> By their hands shall lead me home.[24]

Wasted away, suffering with "pathetic patience," Beth's death releases her parents and sisters to "thank God that Beth was well at last." Beth's self-sacrifice is ultimately the greatest in the novel. She gives up her life knowing that it has had only private, domestic meaning. Only the March family knows and loves her sweet "household spirit."

Nobody mourns Beth more than Jo, her opposite temperament as well as her partner in the bonds of sisterhood. Their commonality lies in the simple fact that both of them value their sororal relationship above any other unions.

When Meg becomes engaged and Jo feels she is about to lose her "best friend," Laurie declares that he will stand by Jo forever. But Laurie turns out to be a boy, not Jo's sister after all. Jo rejects Laurie's suit, which is her first grown-up act, and her trip to New York to become a writer is her first flight into the world. Beth's death, through which she escapes the awful problem of growing up, triggers Jo's maturation. Jo's journey is the only fully complete one in *Little Women* and it involves her learning to tell true love from romantic fancy. She must do so in order to reproduce her lost sisterhood in a new, democratic domestic union.[25]

True Love Found

The ability to distinguish true love from romantic fancy is one of the prerequisites for a woman's growing up in *Little Women.* True love involves mutual self-sacrifice and self-control and requires the kind of man who can make the household the center of his life and work. Romance, on the other hand, is inherently selfish, passionate, and unequal.

Ultimately the surviving heroines are paired off in true love. Jo, however, proves closest to Alcott's ideal because she rejects Laurie Laurence. At one point she tells him that they are unsuited to one another because both have strong wills and quick tempers. Unpersuaded and unreasonable, the spoiled young man presses his suit, forcing her to tell him a harder truth: she does not love him as a woman loves a man, and never did, but feels simply motherly toward him.

Jo does not want to be an adoring adornment to a fashionable man's home. Nor will she give up her writing to satisfy Laurie, and his proposal reveals just how much "scribbling" really means to her. If merely saving her "pathetic family" from poverty were her only motivation, she might marry Laurie and enrich them all. She might even produce leisured, graceful literature under his patronage. But she won't be patronized and she won't concede. "I don't believe I shall ever marry," she declares. "I am happy as I am, and love my liberty too well to be in any hurry to give it up for any mortal man."[26] Possibly, Jo also recognizes passions in herself, how-

ever hard she struggles to keep them under control. She certainly experiences more than "moods"; she has genuine emotional depth and active fantasies, which she usually transforms into tragicomic family operas or melodramatic stories just as Alcott did.

In the nineteenth-century world of *Little Women,* there are only two alternatives following the relative sexual equality of childhood: romantic love or rational affection. With considerable regret Jo chooses the latter, because she must forgo forever the equality she once knew with Laurie, her exuberant companion in childhood. Jo's decision, as Alcott knew, presents the reader with a bitter pill, for nearly everyone wants Laurie to win Jo. Yet the author has her heroine firmly reject any "silliness" from the start. She enjoys being Laurie's chum, plays at being his mother, but is never tempted to be his domestic companion; once wed they will cease to be equals.

It is precisely because Alcott makes Laurie such an irresistible boy-man that the reader must take Jo's refusal seriously. The youthful sweet surrogate sister develops into a handsome, passionate suitor. Moreover, Jo is physically attracted to Laurie, and she frequently observes his handsome face, curly hair, and fine eyes. The reader as well as Jo feels the power of Laurie's sexuality and the power he tries to exert over her. Yet if he calls her "my girl," meaning his sweetheart, she calls him "my boy," meaning her son.

Jo's refusal is not prompted by love for a rival suitor. In New York she works as a governess to children in her boardinghouse and writes for the penny-dreadful newspapers. She soon encounters Friedrich Bhaer helping a serving maid. Bhaer's life, unlike Laurie's, is not the stuff of romance. Forty years old, "learned and good," he is domestic by nature and darns his own socks. He loves flowers and children and reads good literature. Moreover, he insists that Jo give up writing blood-and-thunder tales and learn to write good fiction. He gives her his own copy of Shakespeare as a Christmas present. "A regular German," Jo says,

> rather stout with brown hair tumbled all over his head, a bushy beard, good nose, the kindest eyes I ever saw, and a splendid big voice that does one's ears good, after our sharp, or slipshod American gabble. His clothes were rusty, his hands were large, and he hadn't a really handsome feature in his face, except his beautiful teeth; yet I liked him, for he had a fine head, his linen was very nice, and he looked like a gentleman, though two buttons were off his coat, and there was a patch on one shoe.[27]

Bhaer is a man Jo can love and marry without fear of inequality.

A mature adult capable of raising his two orphaned nephews, he does not need Jo to mother him, although she is drawn to do so. Bhaer is more attracted to her youth and independent spirit. Nevertheless, he bestows his affection upon her by appreciating both her Old World "gemutlichkeit" and her American self-reliance. In a way he is Santa Claus, giving gifts despite his poverty to friends and servants alike. In one scene Bhaer buys oranges and figs for small children while holding a dilapidated blue umbrella aloft for Jo in the rain. Unlike Father March, who is a fragile invalid, Father Bhaer is a strapping, generous man.

There is no end to his domesticity or his capacity for cooperative self-sacrifice. Matching his paternal benevolence to Jo's maternal abundance, Bhaer does the shopping for both himself and Jo. As Alcott describes him, he "finished the marketing by buying several pounds of grapes, a pot of rosy daisies, and a pretty jar of honey, to be regarded in the light of a demijohn. Then, distorting his pockets with the knobby bundles, and giving her the flowers to hold, he put up the old umbrella and they travelled on again."[28] Contrast this fulgent account of a man who understands the "household spirit" with Laurie, who cannot even direct the maids to plump his pillows properly, or with John Brooke, who magisterially sends the meat and vegetables home to Meg (no knobby bundles in his pockets!).

Meanwhile, Laurie has returned from Europe with Amy, and they tell the story of their Swiss romance. Laurie has found a perfect mate in Amy, who will be very good at giving orders to their servants, having practiced in her imagination for years. Theirs will also be an equal marital partnership, though somewhat different from that of Jo and Fritz, and very different from the frugal conventions of Meg and John.

Jo, the last sister to leave home, might never have accepted Professor Bhaer's proposal were it not for Beth's death. Fritz has found a poem of Jo's expressing the deep love and devotion she feels for Meg, Amy, and Beth. We are "parted only for an hour, none lost," she writes, "one only gone before." Tenderly Bhaer declares: "I read that, and I think to myself, she has a sorrow, she is lonely, she would find comfort in true love. I haf a heart full for her."

Bhaer has all the qualities Bronson Alcott lacked: warmth, intimacy, and a tender capacity for expressing his affection—the feminine attributes Alcott admired and hoped men could acquire in a rational, feminist world. As Marmee says, he is "a dear man." He touches everyone, hugs and carries children about on his back. Bronson, despite all his genuine idealism and devotion to humanity, was emotionally reserved and distant. Fritz Bhaer loves material reality, is eminently approachable, and values all the things that Bronson Alcott rejects, such as good food, warm rooms, and appealing domestic disorder.

They decide to share life's burdens just as they shared the load of bundles on their shopping expedition. Jo hopes to fulfill "woman's special mission," which is "drying tears and bearing burdens," so that nobody will ever again call her unwomanly. She resolutely adds the feminist postscript: "I'm to carry my share, Friedrich, and help to earn the home. Make up your mind to that, or I'll never go."[29] The marriage contract they arrange is very different from that of Meg and John at the end of the first part of *Little Women*.

Love and Work

Having grown up with a working mother, each surviving March sister tailors her marital arrangements with work appropriate to her talent and temperament. At the opening of *Little Women* Marmee's arrival is anticipated in a manner generally reserved for welcoming working men: "The clock struck six; and, having swept up the hearth, Beth put a pair of slippers down to warm. . . . Meg stopped lecturing, and lit the lamp, Amy got out of the easy-chair without being asked, and Jo forgot how tired she was as she sat up to hold the slippers nearer to the blaze."[30]

Arriving home after a day of Civil War relief work, Mrs. March does not repair to the kitchen; instead her daughters fly round and serve tea, sharing the day's news, and generally demonstrating that a fully employed female household is commonplace, at least in the middle of a war.

Vanity, envy, selfishness, and pride are conquered by work in *Little Women*. Unlike the shallow, gossiping ladies of fashion in the novel, Marmee March is a true woman largely because she is a working woman; her employment is an extension of her motherly duties, the entire world is therefore her sphere. Marmee's management abilities and her self-discipline are examples to her daughters. She knows how to delegate work and does so from her entrance in the first scene to her last crisis management when Mr. March and Beth are ill.

Meg's marketable talents are those most commonly associated with a modern American wife. She is very pretty, with good taste and acting ability, and she develops her mother's managerial sense. Marriage to John provides Meg with a full-time job once she has children. Alcott does take marriage-as-work seriously, and Meg's growing household staff reflects myriad chores: child raising, domestic planning, nursing, shopping, accounting, and entertaining preclude any other career.

Impatient Jo has a harder time reconciling domestic duties, talent, and work. Starting off as a paid companion to her wealthy aunt, she gains access to a good library but cannot sharpen her literary skills in the scant "leisure" time gleaned from earning her bread and helping to bake it. She begins her writing career as an unpaid contributor to a cheap newspaper just as Alcott did. When the family can finally spare her domestic services, Jo goes off to New York and works full time as a governess, writing sensational stories at night. She has already noted that what the public considers a "first-rate story" is really the "usual labyrinth of love, mystery, and murder," in which "the passions have a holiday, and when the author's invention fails, a grand catastrophe clears the stage of one-half the dramatis personae, leaving the other half to exult over their downfall."[31] A good living is to be had writing such stories, and "Mrs. S.L.A.N.G. Northbury" is Alcott's version of E.D.E.N. Southworth, ebullient author of *The Hidden Hand, The Curse of Clifton, Ishmael,* and *Self-Raised.* Southworth wrote for *The New York Ledger* and also completed fifty novels.[32] As Northbury Jo imitates Southworth and wins a prize for what we know was "Pauline's Passion and Punishment." Scarcely bothering to hide behind her pseudonym, Alcott then credits Jo with writing "The Duke's Daughter," "A Phantom Hand," and "Curse of the Coventrys" *(Behind a Mask).* Work, while remunerative, is not yet a fulfillment of Jo's vocation. The sensation stories give Jo satisfaction because with the money she earns "she could supply her own wants, and need ask no one for a penny."

Having entered the market as a paid writer, Jo then rewrites her novel for a fourth time and submits it to three publishers. Finally she gets it accepted on condition that she cut it, and omit all the parts she particularly admired. In a family council, much like the one Alcott herself convened to discuss *Moods,* Jo's father advises her to maintain artistic integrity and wait for recognition. Mrs. March has faith in publishers and in critics' taste; she counsels following their advice. Jo admits that she really cannot judge the quality of her own work. Meg likes the novel as it is; Amy says to make "a good, popular book, and get as much money as you can." Achieving success, she says, an author can then afford such luxuries as "philosophical and metaphysical" characters.[33]

Jo's first novel suffers the same fate as Alcott's *Moods.* And, like Alcott, Jo also keeps on trying because the second part of *Little Women* makes clear that writing is her true vocation. Jo wants to do "something splendid," and after Beth's death. Alcott lifts her heroine up once more from the Slough of Despond; Jo takes up writing again "as a comfort." And, ignoring both market and immortality, she writes the "simple little story" that is *Little Women.*[34] It is this departure from the actual truth of writing *Little Women* which troubles modern feminist scholars. In reality, we know that *Little Women* was suggested by Alcott's publisher Thomas Niles and was written posthaste as a juvenile story for money. Alcott does not disguise the truth in her journals.[35]

One explanation for the discrepancy between the real writing of the novel and the fictional rendition is that

Alcott's life is telescoped in *Little Women.* Louisa was thirty-five years old when she wrote the novel and Jo is ten years younger. Elizabeth Alcott had been dead for ten years before Louisa began *Little Women;* in the novel Beth's death occurs the same year that Jo takes up writing as a comfort. The difference between real and fictional time surely does not explain the difference between writing a solicited juvenile story and writing as comfort. Also Louisa May Alcott's journals show that she had no idea of the power in her *Little Women* serial as she wrote the first part. She was the hard-working editor of *Merry's Museum,* and she labored overtime as a writer of children's fairy tales and sensation thrillers for adults.[36]

Louisa Alcott was often the worst judge of her own writing. But there is more to her bewilderment over *Little Women*'s reception. The novel *is* "something splendid" and Alcott searches, in the second part of the story, for the key to its success. She has Jo's father acknowledge it, "There's truth in it, Jo—that's the secret, humor and pathos make it alive, and you have found your style at last."[37] The real question is what prevented Alcott from developing *Little Women*'s successors with the power and skill she demonstrated in the first history of the March family? Louisa May Alcott was a conscious student of good literature as well as a professional writer. Her ideal of a splendid work included *The Scarlet Letter, Faust, Jane Eyre,* the essays and poetry of Emerson and Whittier, and the works of Charles Dickens. She loved *Uncle Tom's Cabin* and frequently quoted from it: Stowe was, moreover, a commercial success and Alcott aspired to the same reward.

Louisa May Alcott found it almost impossible to include *Little Women* in the canon of good literature as she knew it. Contemptuous of an audience that loved "Mrs. S.L.A.N.G. Northbury," perfectly cognizant of the commercial basis for the growing genre of juvenile fiction, and brought up on Concord's canon of "splendid" works, it is no wonder that *Little Women*'s author was skeptical of her own achievement.

Professor Bhaer respects Jo's dedication to writing; his literary tastes accord with her own. Her real passion was expressed in writing, and marriage to impoverished, scholarly Bhaer makes Jo's writing career not only possible but necessary. Jo's castle in the air, the one she builds while still a little woman, consists of writing books, and "getting rich and famous." It is only at the end of *Little Women* that Jo, while on a sort of "maternity leave," admits to hoping that she may "write a *good* book yet."[38]

Unquestionably Alcott intends Jo to go on writing and to make good writing more important than being "rich and famous."[39] Jo's partner in this harvest time is Amy, her temperamental opposite but a kindred spirit in attempting serious work. Jo and Amy both wanted to be artists but Amy is more certain of her talents, as was May Alcott. Her "modest desire," as Alcott wrote of Amy, was to be the "best artist in the whole world." She works hard to this end but Louisa May Alcott does not yet know how to predict the outcome of her sister's aspirations. In Europe with "lazy Laurence," Amy says that "Rome took all the vanity out of me." She insists that talent isn't genius and she wants "to be great or nothing." Not wishing to be a "common-place dauber," she intends to polish up her other talents and "be an ornament to society, if I get the chance." Amy, bluntly, during one stage of growing up, intends to marry for a living if she can't be a great artist. Alcott cannot abandon her beloved sister and rival to such a fate however and Amy has a change of heart. She falls in love with Laurie and seems to be making matrimony her career, in an upper-class version of Meg and John's union.

Amy ultimately proves to be a complex heroine, who changes her perspective on life and work several times. Having married and borne a baby, she again revises her work plan:

> "like Jo, I don't relinquish all my artistic hopes, or confine myself to helping others fulfill their dreams of beauty. I've begun to model a figure of baby, and Laurie says it is the best thing I've ever done. I think so myself, and mean to do it in marble, so that, whatever happens, I may at least keep the image of my little angel."[40]

The marble image of Amy's fragile daughter, named after Beth, has an ambiguous meaning. It appears to make Amy's work merely a memorial keepsake. Amy's explicit alliance with Jo and her words about her work are clear indications that Alcott validates her own as well as her sister May's determined vocation. Neither of them will be confined simply to domestic self-sacrifice or ornamental status.

The Model Society: A Harvest of Rationalism

Jo March and Friedrich Bhaer embark on more than a model marriage in the second part of *Little Women.* Together they set out to construct a model society which institutionalizes many of Jo's (and Louisa Alcott's) feminist ideals. Both Jo and Professor Bhaer are keenly interested in new ideas and reforms. In New York City, during Jo's trial flight away from home and from Laurie's unwelcome attentions, the new friends attend a symposium together where they participate in a wide-ranging discussion in which the "world was being picked to pieces and put together on new and according to the talkers, on infinitely better principles than before."

At first disturbed by the flirtations and by the disillusioning talk around her, Jo soon becomes enthralled by the debate. Speculative philosophy fascinates her, "though Kant and Hegel were unknown gods, the subjective and objective unintelligible terms." Less delighted by the discussion, Bhaer defends older beliefs, standing "his colors like a man." Not the intellectual equal of the philosophers in the room, he nevertheless insists upon speaking up because "his conscience would not let him be silent." It is that conscience that Jo so admires. "Character," she believes, "is a better possession than money, rank, intellect, or beauty and to feel that if greatness is what a wise man has defined it to be, 'truth, reverence, and good will,' then her friend Friedrich Bhaer was not only good but great."[41]

If Bronson moves through the second part of *Little Women* idealized as Mr. Bhaer, he takes on a more "muffled" guise as Mr. March. Madeleine Stern observes that Bronson "would be atypical in a book on the American home . . . with his vegetarianism, his fads, and his reforms."[42] Hence Louisa divides him into two characters. The older Bronson surely resembles Mr. March, and in Friedrich we see the man he might have been with the aid of a rational, feminist reform movement. Bhaer's devotion to humanity—embodied in his acceptance of a "merry little quadroon" at Plumfield and also by his brave speech at the symposium—are direct homages to Bronson.

Alcott's modified view of her father paralleled the emergence of her conception of a model society. At the end of *Little Women,* she remakes her father's experiment at Fruitlands into her own fictional experiment at Plumfield. A fortunate inheritance from Jo's former employer, Aunt March, enables her to turn the suburban estate of Plumfield into a "good happy, homelike school" with herself as headmistress and Friedrich Bhaer as headmaster. Laurie and Amy provide scholarships and Meg sends her son and daughter as model pupils, which ensures that the school will be coeducational from the start. Mr. and Mrs. March beam like benevolent household gods at the assembled, extended family as the book closes on Mrs. March's sixtieth birthday celebration.

As Jo watches John and Laurie playing cricket with the boys at Plumfield, she speaks to Amy in a "maternal way of all mankind." Jo, the tomboy, has attained the final stage of true womanhood; she has accepted maternal responsibility for the whole world. The conflict between feminist selfhood and domestic self-sacrifice has been resolved by expanding the home to include the world, making everyone equally responsible for human nurturance. If woman's rights are enlarged with her responsibilities, men's rights are also granted to them—but "nothing more," as Elizabeth Cady Stanton demanded in *The Revolution.*

Sororal bonds, Alcott argues, are forged between equals. A female family, therefore, is naturally democratic;

while accepting conflict, like "birds in a nest," sisters must share household tasks, pool their incomes, and lend one another their personal treasures. The Marchs' household democracy is perfectly represented by Hannah's daily provision of hot turnovers, which warm Jo and Meg's hands on the way to work. Meg and Jo, even while they labor outside the home, have no special exemption from domestic chores in *Little Women*.[43]

Alcott made little attempt to conceal the parallels between her life and her fiction. The family name of March is a simple substitute for May. Unlike Fruitlands, however, with its disappointing poverty, Plumfield is a feminist utopia that promises an abundance of puddings, free fields to roam in, and festivals in apple-picking season. Having admitted the "female element" to full equality with the male, Plumfield's harvest will have "more wheat and fewer tares every year." Commemorating the the bittersweet fall of Fruitlands, Alcott tucks in a reference to Mr. March strolling about with Mr. Laurence enjoying "the gentle apple's winey juice." Since Alcott admitted that Mr. Laurence was modeled on Grandfather May, we can assume that the Mays would smile approvingly on Plumfield. And unlike Sam May, who withdrew family money from Fruitlands, the Laurence family provides scholarships to Plumfield. True love is not denied at the end of *Little Women;* it is linked, as Fritz Bhaer put it, "to the wish to share and enlarge that so happy home."[44]

Unquestionably *Little Women's* message was powerfully transmitted not only to Alcott's readers but to her best imitators. Within three years of *Little Women's* publication as a book, stories for young readers were advertised in *Our Young Folks* as "likely to find popularity in the large circles that read Miss Alcott's books." And, *The Boston Traveller* noted that *Little Women* "is a book that parents will be glad to have their sons and daughters read, but so interesting that they will be apt to insist on reading it through for themselves first." Elizabeth Stuart Phelps, Harriet Beecher Stowe, and Louisa May Alcott were advertised in the same pages of juvenile magazines. Their names lent prestige to the notices of *Oliver Optic, Farming for Boys,* and *History of My Pets.*[45]

Phelps's serialized story, "Our Little Women," exemplifies one version of Alcott's new form.[46] A prosperous widow and her two daughters, Hannah and Mary Alice, are tried and almost found wanting by the visit of their half-cousins. The relations are another widow and her daughter, Margaret and Lois McQuentin. Mrs. McQuentin is a paid housekeeper who comes to Boston seeking surgery for an incurable tumor. Her daughter arrives from her work in a Lynn shoe shop to nurse her mother. Hannah, the narrator, and Mary Alice are deeply embarrassed by their poor relations. Although Lois does not wear a "red feather and a purple veil" as

expected, her gruff manner and her callused hands offend the genteel sisters. Their change of heart is occasioned by Mrs. McQuentin's pitiful suffering but also by Lois's gentle courage and innate sensitivity. She has, as her mother says, never had "a chance." Hannah takes a long time trying to understand the meaning of this remark. In fact the dying widow scarcely says anything else besides muttering, "little woman, little woman," as she strokes "Lois's short, thin hair."[47]

Lois goes back to working in the shoe shop after her mother's death; she must support herself and she is seeking some solace in hard work. Mary Alice gets engaged and Hannah is left particularly lonely and depressed, being in love with her sister's fiancé. Lois McQuentin then comes back to visit announcing that earning her own living is a necessity but she has sought and found a deeper meaning in work. Lois has lost her earlier incentive; both she and her mother were working and saving for a home of their own. Having "always had something to earn *for*," Lois plans to earn her way through school and become a doctor. Confronted with the years of required education, her lack of means, and the prejudices against women physicians, Lois coolly replies that she will live on "shoes" while studying. She·is accustomed to hard work and will go into the shop on vacations and Saturdays too.[48]

Hannah remarks that Mrs. McQuentin used to call her daughter "little woman," and being a doctor seems so "strong minded, and that." Lois replies very much in the manner of Jo March:

> And don't suppose that I know, and my mother knows, and you ought to know, that if it means *anything* to be a 'little woman',—I don't care whose,—it means to be the most, and the best, and the noblest, and the most needed thing that you can get or make the chance to be.[49]

Notes

[1] Louisa May Alcott, *Little Women* (Boston, 1868, 1869), chap. 1, "Playing Pilgrims." References to *Little Women* are cited by chapter numbers and titles which remain consistent in all editions.

[2] Charles Dickens, *Bleak House,* 2 vols. (London, 1854). The first reference is in chapter 8. Mr. Jarndyce tried out several versions of "good little woman."

[3] Esther's relationship to Charlie, whom she nurses through smallpox, is crucial to understanding Alcott's version of domestic democracy. Charlie is a servant and Esther is a lady; nevertheless, housekeeping duties and mutual nurturance unite them. Esther, "attached to life again" after her near-fatal illness, for she too got smallpox, recalls "the pleasant afternoon when I was

raised in bed with pillows for the first time, to enjoy teadrinking with Charlie!" Charlie has taken over Esther's housewifely tasks (2:15). The same relationship occurs between Phoebe and Rose in *Eight Cousins* and *Rose in Bloom*.

4 Louisa May Alcott, *Little Women,* chap. 42, "All Alone."

5 Ednah Cheney, ed., *Louisa May Alcott: Life, Letters and Journals* (Boston, 1928), p. 164.

6 Susan B. Warner [Elizabeth Wetherell], *The Wide, Wide World* (New York, 1852).

7 Charlotte M. Yonge, *The Heir of Redclyffe* (New York and London, 1853); *The Daisy Chain* (New York and London, 1856).

8 Humphrey Carpenter notes the resemblance between Ethel May and Jo March in his witty study, *Secret Gardens: A Study of the Golden Age of Children's Literature* (New York, 1985), pp. 86-102.

9 Nina Baym identifies this "overplot" of nineteenth-century women's fiction in *Women's Fiction: A Guide to Novels by and about Women in America, 1820-1870* (Ithaca, N.Y., 1978). She names several other characteristics of the typical woman's novel: a heroine and a villainess are paired; the heroine's childhood is miserable and only her mother's memory comforts her; heroines often acquire surrogate families; husbands are not as important to heroines as fathers, guardians, and brothers; women's faith is removed from a patriarchal setting. *The Wide, Wide World* does not conform to all of Baym's characteristics, but it is generally representative of her model.

10 See Baym, *Women's Fiction,* pp.' 296-299. Judith Fetterley in "*Little Women:* Alcott's Civil War," *Feminist Studies* 5, no. 2 (Summer 1979):369-393, argues for an "over reading" and a "subliminal" reading of Alcott's work, claiming that the rage expressed in *Behind a Mask* is repressed but still evident in *Little Women.* For a representative selection of *Little Women* analyses see Madeleine B. Stern, ed., *Critical Essays on Louisa May Alcott* (Boston, 1984).

11 See Carpenter, *Secret Gardens,* pp. 86-102, and the following other historians and writers who recognize *Little Women* as a positive contribution to juvenile literature: Joy A. Marsella, *The Promise of Destiny: Children and Women in the Short Stories of Louisa May Alcott* (Westport, Conn., 1983); Anne Scott MacLeod, *A Moral Tale: Children's Fiction and American Culture, 1820-1860* (Hamden, Conn., 1975); R. Gordon Kelley, *Mother Was a Lady: Self and Society in Selected American Children's Periodicals, 1865-1890* (Westport, Conn., 1974).

12 See Carpenter, *Secret Gardens;* Martin Green, "The Charm of Peter Pan," in *Children's Literature* 9 (New Haven and London, 1981): 19-27; Elizabeth Cripps, "Alice and the Reviewers," *Children's Literature* 11 (New Haven and London, 1983): 32-48.

13 Louisa May Alcott, *Little Women,* chap. 11. "Experiments." Nina Auerbach understands the "primacy of the female family" in the novel "both as moral-emotional magnet and as work of art"; see *Communities of Women* (Cambridge, Mass., 1978), pp. 56, 73. She argues, however, that Alcott's female family is a closed circle. Domestic democracy, I think, provides a launching pad for the "little" women's flight into the larger world.

14 Louisa May Alcott, *Little Women,* chap. 20, "Confidential."

15 Ibid., chap. 5, "Being Neighborly." Auerbach (in *Communities of Women*) writes with sensitivity about the role of Laurie in *Little Women.* Laurie needs the March family's harmony, but in order to gain entrance to the feminist household he must acquire some feminist virtues. A balanced domesticity, Alcott maintains, also depends upon the girls' acquisition of "masculine" courage, independence, and comfortable elegance. Elizabeth Lennox Keyser brilliantly observes that Jo's rescue of Laurie from the "enchanted palace" is a "reversal of the Sleeping Beauty tale; see "Alcott's Portraits of the Artist as Little Woman," *International Journal of Women's Studies* 5, no. 5 (1978): 445-459.

16 Louisa May Alcott, *Little Women,* chap. 5, "Being Neighborly." Anne Hollander notes that "fellowship, insisted on by Jo, appears here as an American ideal for governing the conduct between sexes"; see her "Reflections on *Little Women,*" in *Children's Literature* 9:28-39.

17 Louisa May Alcott, *Little Women,* chap. 38, "On the Shelf." Meg has already made the case for true love, telling rich Aunt March, "I shall marry whom I please, and you can leave your money to anyone you like."

18 Ibid. See Patricia Spacks in *The Female Imagination* (New York, 1972), pp. 125-28. She argues that there is "no doubt about which sex really does things" in *Little Women.* According to Spacks, it is men who do things in the novel; hence female readers "yearned somehow to be boy and girl simultaneously" (p. 120). For a view closer to my own see Carolyn Heilbrun, *Reinventing Womanhood* (New York, 1979), p. 191.

19 Louisa May Alcott, *Little Women,* chap. 8, "Jo Meets Apollyon." Elizabeth Keyser views this incident quite differently, arguing that Amy is Jo's repressed greedy, childish self ("Alcott's Portraits," p. 450).

[20] Louisa May Alcott, *Little Women,* chap. 3, "The Laurence Boy."

[21] Ibid., chap. 29, "Calls."

[22] Beth's death is not the sentimental artifact so brilliantly discussed by Ann Douglas in "The Meaning of Little Eva"; see *The Feminization of American Culture* (New York, 1972), chap. 1, Elizabeth Keyser argues that Beth's death relegates Jo to her younger sister's role of childish dependency ("Alcott's Portraits," p. 454).

[23] Louisa May Alcott, *Little Women,* chap. 36, "Beth's Secret."

[24] Ibid., chap. 42, "All Alone."

[25] Ibid., chap. 24, "Gossip." Douglas *(The Feminization of American Culture)* finds Little Eva's death merely decorative in *Uncle Tom's Cabin.* Jane Tompkins argues for a different reading of this death in *Sensational Designs: The Cultural Work of American Fiction, 1790-1860* (New York, 1985), chap. 6. Beth March's death is closer, I think, to Tompkins's method of analysis. Jo is deeply affected and she is "all alone" as Alcott notes, a situation that occasions her change of heart and her reevaluation of Professor Bhaer's meaning in her life.

[26] Louisa May Alcott, *Little Women,* chap. 35, "Heartache." Fetterley ("*Little Women:* Alcott's Civil War") sees Jo March's refusal as part of her internal battle between passivity and sexual rage.

[27] Louisa May Alcott, *Little Women,* chap. 33, "Jo's Journal." Professor Bhaer has a younger, handsomer fictional counterpart in August Bopp, a twenty-three-year-old German immigrant gym teacher in Alcott's "King of Clubs and the Queen of Hearts," *Camp and Fireside Stories* (1869), pp. 99-142. His heavy German accent and his sincere romanticism appeal to Dolly, an all-American girl in his gym class. He is working to bring his little niece to America and he calls Dolly his "heart's dearest" or "mein liebchen."

[28] Louisa May Alcott, *Little Women,* chap. 46, "Under the Umbrella."

[29] Ibid.

[30] Ibid., chap. 1, "Playing Pilgrims."

[31] Ibid., chap. 27, "Literary Lessons."

[32] See Baym, *Women's Fiction,* pp. 110-139.

[33] Louisa May Alcott, *Little Women,* chap. 27, "Literary Lessons."

[34] Ibid., chap. 42, "All Alone."

[35] Cheney, ed., *Alcott,* p. 199 (June, July, August, 1868). In 1876 she appended, "Too much work for one young woman. No wonder she broke down."

[36] Ibid. Having sent off 402 pages of *Little Women,* Alcott wrote, "Hope it will go, for I shall probably get nothing for *Morning Glories.* Very tired, head full of pain from overwork, and heart heavy about Marmee, who is growing feeble."

[37] Louisa May Alcott, *Little Women,* chap. 42, "All Alone."

[38] Ibid., chap. 47, "Harvest Time."

[39] See Fetterley, "*Little Women:* Alcott's Civil War"; Keyser, "Alcott's Portraits"; Eugenia Kaledin, "Louisa May Alcott: Success and the Sorrow of Self-Denial," *Women's Studies* 5 (1978): 251-263.

[40] Louisa May Alcott, *Little Women,* chap. 47, "Harvest Time." Anne Hollander's provocative reading of *Little Women* points to the complex character of Amy March and its development. See "Reflections on *Little Women*" in *Children's Literature* 9:28-39.

[41] Louisa May Alcott, *Little Women,* chap. 34, "A Friend."

[42] Stern, *Louisa May Alcott,* p. 176.

[43] Louisa May Alcott, *Little Women,* chap. 1, "Playing Pilgrims."

[44] Ibid., chap. 47, "Harvest Time."

[45] "Our Young Folks Advertizer," in *Our Young Folks,* no. 95 (Nov. 1872).

[46] Elizabeth Stuart Phelps, "Our Little Woman," serialized in *Our Young Folks,* pts. 1, 2, no. 95 (Nov. 1872): 654-662; pts. 3, 4, no. 96 (Dec. 1872): 727-737.

[47] Ibid., pt. 2, pp. 728, 729.

[48] Ibid., pt. 4, p. 734.

[49] Ibid., pt. 4, p. 736.

Beverly Lyon Clark (essay date 1989)

SOURCE: "A Portrait of the Artist as a Little Woman," *Children's Literature.* Vol. 17, 1989, pp. 81-97.

[*In the following essay, Clark discusses Alcott's ambivalence toward the role of writing, particularly as self-expression, in* Little Women.]

Alcott as submissive, Alcott as subversive, Alcott as ambivalent—these are dominant themes in recent reflections on Louisa May Alcott.[1] The same themes appear in Alcott's own writing about writing, when she writes about Jo March. Though Alcott gives some play to subversive ideas of self-expression, her overt message is that girls should subordinate themselves and their language to others. A little woman should channel her creativity into shaping the domestic space or shaping her soul. She can enact *Pilgrim's Progress* and learn to live as a Christian—to live by God's Word, or by John Bunyan's word, not by her own.[2]

Nineteenth-century male authors send a very different message to their readers. Jan B. Gordon notes that in works as diverse as the Alice books, Mill's *Autobiography,* and *David Copperfield,* the child "must reverse or otherwise overturn a prescriptive text that had kept him in a figurative prison" (179). The opposite is true for the girls in **Little Women.** Laurie may complain that "a fellow can't live on books" (62), rebelling against prescribed texts as other males do, but Jo must learn to stifle her rebelliousness and to forgive Amy for burning the only manuscript of her book, Jo's attempt to find her own voice.

In her other works Alcott shows a similar reluctance to rebel. Her adult novel **Work** may in effect rebel against its predecessor *Jane Eyre,* but only in the service of a higher submission. The heroine, Christie, objects to Charlotte Brontë's portrayal of Rochester: "I like Jane, but never can forgive her marrying that man, as I haven't much faith in the saints such sinners make" (80). Then Christie enacts her objection to *Jane Eyre* by marrying not the Rochesterlike Mr. Fletcher but David Sterling, a type of St. John Rivers, with whom she undertakes missionary work at home; and a symbolic bedroom fire is caused not by the madwoman in the attic but by Christie's dangerous penchant for books. Alcott rebels against the romance of *Jane Eyre* not so much to find her own voice as to submit herself to the divine and masculine allegory of *Pilgrim's Progress.* Christie's very name recalls those of Christian and Christiana, and in her progress through temptations she eventually achieves a state of grace, with the help of a character compared to Mr. Greatheart. Thus Alcott's rebellion against a predecessor text is not so rebellious after all: it is a reworking of the secular *Jane Eyre* in order to submit to the higher truths of *Pilgrim's Progress,* a reworking that underscores the searing dangers of books to women. She rebels not to find her own voice but to modulate it in the heavenly chorus.[3]

In **Work** Alcott stifles her predilection for the lurid and sensational, much as she has suppressed her blood-and-thunder tales (first by publishing them anonymously or under a pseudonym and then by turning instead to juveniles). In a telling entry in her diary, at age eigh-teen, she notes, "Reading Miss Bremer and Hawthorne. The 'Scarlet Letter' is my favorite. Mother likes Miss B. better, as more wholesome. I fancy 'lurid' things, if true and strong also" (Cheney 63). Eighteen years later, in her own writing, Alcott has submitted to the preferences of her mother, the arch-representative of the family, giving up the gothic for domestic realism, banishing the "skeleton in the closet." Or hiding "behind a mask," as so many of Alcott's strong gothic heroines do, concealing her passions and longings behind the passionless and virtuous facade of her "marble women."[4] Alcott's reworking of *Jane Eyre* (one of fifteen items in an 1852 list of books she liked) is more a self-chastisement for her sneaking fondness for things gothic, more an act of penitent submission to Christian godliness than a rebellion against a predecessor text.[5]

In **Little Women,** too, Alcott stifles the sensational—or at least hides it. In the first volume it still lurks just below the surface. Thomas H. Pauly points to the contrast between the romantic literature that the girls read and their plain lives, a contrast that signals both Alcott's innovation, the way she calls "attention to the drama and impact that could attend the commonplace," and also the "notable deficiencies that Alcott perceived in the very environment she strove to recommend" (123). Or perhaps in **Little Women** the two tendencies are in creative tension, the sensational not yet as fully repressed as it will later be: Ann Douglas suggests that "Alcott hoped to let sensational and domestic fiction educate each other" (238).

Still, the surface message in **Little Women** is that the March sisters should aspire to domesticity and moral goodness. **Little Women** may not enforce submissiveness as much as some of Alcott's other books for girls do—Jo is remarkably rebellious for a nineteenth-century girl. And some of her eventual taming may result from Alcott's sense that fiction for girls ought to teach feminine virtues—Alcott may simply have been acceding to the constraints of the form. Yet she chooses to submit to these constraints (and also to the constraint of writing popular books that will earn money for her family). Jo, too, eventually submits to the constraints of what her culture considered seemly feminine behavior.[6]

According to this cultural definition of the feminine, art and fiction are suspect, self-control preferable to self-expression. Such self-control requires control of language; and, significantly, the two girls with artistic aspirations, Amy and Jo, are also the two who need to learn greater control of their language. Janice Marie Alberghene has suggested that each tries "to forge a personal style," Amy having too great a weakness for the ornamental, Jo for the sensational (21). Certainly Jo is fond of slang and strong language, of saying "pegging away" for "studying," and of using phrases like "desperate wretches," making Meg chide her for using such "dreadful expressions." Later, in volume two, Jo is largely cured of her weakness, perhaps in part because she has acted out its extreme manifestation by becoming Mrs. Malaprop at a masquerade party (much as she seems to be cured of writing partly from having sampled the extremes of thrillers and virtual sermons).

Amy, too, is guilty of excess in both art and language in volume one but overcomes both excesses by the end of volume two. Early on, she tries to use impressive words but commits malapropisms, using "label" for "libel," "samphire" for "vampire," "fastidious" for "fascinating." Likewise, she is fond of drawing ludicrous caricatures, which "came fluttering out of all her books at unlucky moments" (49). By the end of the first volume, though, she has learned to control her language and to channel her creativity into religion, to model her life after *Pilgrim's Progress,* to meditate in front of a picture of the Madonna instead of drawing one herself. What creativity she does allow herself is a tribute to domestic bliss: she sketches the engaged Meg and Mr. Brooke. By the end of the second volume she recognizes her own lack of genius and happily submerges personal in domestic achievement, tastefully arranging curtains rather than an artist's draperies. She may be allowed the indulgence of molding a model of her baby, but only in case this second Beth dies, "so that, whatever happens, I may at least keep the image of my little angel" (531).[7]

Much as art should not be Amy's supreme goal, writing should not be Jo's. Jo should outgrow it, like her strong language and her tomboy exuberance.[8] Alcott undermines the value of writing, yet she cannot dismiss it altogether, for she herself is Jo, she herself is writing. Initially, Alcott endorses writing; especially in the first volume, fiction allows Jo to enact her masculine fantasies of power. She can assume male roles in the plays that she writes and in meetings of the Pickwick Club, where, as Augustus Snodgrass, she gives her word as a gentleman. Writing fiction gives her an arena where she can express herself, express her anger, instead of just tightening her lips to suppress it as her mother teaches her.

The other girls, too, though less strikingly, find in the stories they invent an outlet for self-expression—and also self-revelation—before they submerge themselves in domesticity. For *The Pickwick Portfolio,* the family newspaper, Meg writes a romantic story of the Lady Viola's wedding to an apparently impoverished suitor, unconsciously anticipating her own marriage to John Brooke. Housewifely Beth writes a homely tale of the life of a squash, grown by a farmer, baked by a little girl, and eaten by the Marches. Irresponsible Amy writes a note of apology for not writing anything.

Stories similarly allow self-expression and self-revelation when a group of young people plays Rigmarole, a game in which players take turns telling a story, one picking up the thread where another leaves off. Although the game affords Alcott a chance to display stylistic virtuosity—the segments are variously romantic, gothic, adventurous, humorous, or Polonius-like combinations thereof—it also sheds light on the characters. It reveals the tellers' literary tastes and hints at matters important to them. Mr. Brooke, for instance, tells of a poor knight who tames a colt and longs for a captive princess, much as he has been taming Laurie and longing for Meg. Shy Beth characteristically prefers not to participate—as if she knows the dangers of fiction and chooses not to indulge.[9]

The game also celebrates creativity and self-expression, as becomes clearer if we compare it to a similar game in Charlotte Yonge's popular family story, *The Daisy Chain* (1856). Quite possibly Alcott wrote her episode in response to the British one, for Alcott's game is introduced by a British visitor, and the whole chapter plays Britain against America: the American friends, as if inspired by "the spirit of '76," defeat the British family at croquet, even though one of the British boys has cheated; nor is the British young lady's tendency to condescend to young women who earn money, as Meg does, endorsed. On some level, it seems, Alcott wants to show how the American family story can outdo the British, and how accepting money for one's writing (instead of channeling it to religious and other charitable causes, as Yonge did) is worthy. In any case, while all the players of Alcott's Rigmarole have been influenced by their favorite reading, the segment told by the boy who cheated at croquet is even more derivative, jumbling together phrases and facts from a single book—from *The Sea-Lion,* as Laurie recognizes. And it's clear that such plagiarism is not praiseworthy. In *The Daisy Chain,* however, a kind of plagiarism is endorsed. The story game is, to begin with, rather different: various people tell someone stories incorporating an agreed-upon word until the person can guess what the word is. The story segments are related semantically rather than syntactically, metaphorically rather than metonymically. The game thus invites allegorical stories, focused on the key word, rather than the wide-ranging inventiveness fostered by Rigmarole. The young girl Flora tells of a girl who becomes the first woman to achieve the glory of ascending Mont Blanc; the story is a thinly veiled allegory of Flora's own ambitions, particularly her later political ambitions for her dullard husband. Her father tells of a hummingbird who considers itself "vain and profitless" but whose master tells it that by valuing its own bliss and praising its master it "conduces to no vain-glory of thine own, in beauty, or in graceful flight, but . . . art a creature serving as best thou canst to his glory" (287, 288). As for the heroine, Ethel, an engaging and lively girl like Jo, she too tells a story distinguishing between worldly and heavenly glory, about princes competing to serve the ladies Vana Gloria and Gloria: the one prince, trying to conquer worlds, finally discovers Vana Gloria to be vain and ugly; the other, staying at home and being good to his subjects, finds his Gloria, still lovely, as he dies. Here is an allegory particularly apt for Ethel, who learns to seek her glory—to glory in her duties—close to home.

Significantly, Ethel does not invent her story; she has modified a tale from an old French book. Yet such plagiarism does not call forth censure here, implicit or otherwise, as it does in *Little Women.* Far from it. Ethel has enacted what the story preaches—by not seeking earthly glory through her own originality but, in a devout and womanly fashion, assimilating the moral in another's work.

As for the secret word in Yonge's story game, it is, of course, glory. And much as we have learned its true meaning in these transparent allegories, so do we learn it in the book as a whole. The young people are not to pine after earthly glory, we are later told, but to discover that "charity is the true glory" and that letting God's will be done can release an exulting "cry of Glory" (600, 641).

Thus is the reader invited to read *The Daisy Chain,* more chained by religious allegory than *Little Women,* just as its language game is more constrained. For, compared to Ethel, Jo is granted considerable freedom; Ethel is more willing than Jo to accept her constraints, more willing to give up her writing. The differing imports of their nicknames are emblematic. Josephine lays claim to male prerogatives when she becomes Jo. Ethel, on the other hand, is short for Etheldred. As a younger child she had been nicknamed King Etheldred the Unready—King for short—the overt significance being her childhood tendency to be a little slapdash with household duties. Yet the nickname is also male, appropriate for someone who chafes more than her sisters do against traditional expectations for women. She finally settles, however, for the feminine Ethel, thus reversing Jo's progress, outgrowing the male and becoming female. Or rather, Jo's progress is a little more complex, for when in later volumes Jo becomes Aunt Jo or Mrs. Jo, both gender oxymorons, she highlights the tensions between the two tendencies toward domestic and literary creativity that she continues to embody.

Not all the stories in *Little Women* are as self-expressive as the Rigmarole ones are; some are constrained by allegorical shaping. In the chapter called "Burdens" each girl tells a story, or rather a vignette, of her experiences that day. These stories are not so much outlets for self-expression as reflections on each pilgrim's progress. The girls are morally shaping their lives, allegorizing them, rather than creatively expressing their

feelings. Jo tells of interesting Aunt March in *The Vicar of Wakefield* in lieu of Belsham's Essays; Meg tells of a disgrace in the society family where she works as a governess; Amy tells of the embarrassing punishment meted out to a fellow pupil; Beth tells of seeing Mr. Laurence's act of kindness to a poor woman. True, the stories are expressive insofar as the girls reveal aspects of themselves. It is fitting that Jo tell a story about the attractions of fiction, that Meg tell a story about the attractions of society, that Beth tell a story of selfless generosity, that Amy tell a story of the horrors of embarrassment (anticipating her own experience later at school). Yet the girls are learning, in their monitory stories, to channel their feelings in socially acceptable ways: they are learning both how to behave (like Mr. Laurence, not like the fellow pupil) and how to channel storytelling.

The culmination they should aim for is the selflessness of Marmee—a selflessness and devotion she then enacts by glossing their stories. For Marmee tells a transparent allegory about four girls who learn to become happy by counting their blessings:

> "One discovered that money couldn't keep shame and sorrow out of rich people's houses; another that, though she was poor, she was a great deal happier, with her youth, health, and good spirits, than a certain fretful, feeble old lady, who couldn't enjoy her comforts; a third that, disagreeable as it was to help get dinner, it was harder still to have to go begging for it; and the fourth, that even carnelian rings were not so valuable as good behavior. (54).

Just as the girls tell stories here to shape their lives more than to express their feelings, Marmee provides a final shaping, one that unifies the stories, much as she unifies the family. Furthermore, she subtly revises the moral of Jo's potentially subversive story— from the pleasures of fictional escape to the advantages of Jo's own lot—much as she subtly revises, redirects, Jo herself.[10]

Writing is thus double-edged, enabling expression or repression, or both. Some of Jo's other fictions likewise aim not so much at self-expression as at accommodation: they allow her, as she grows older, to come to terms with domesticity. She works through her adjustment to domesticity, in part, by writing of it in "A Song from the Suds." The poem joins the virtues of domesticity and moral goodness. She can physically "wash and rinse and wring" and wants further to "wash from our hearts and souls / The stains of the week away" (190). Her writing here has been tamed to laud domestic and moral virtues—as has Alcott's own in *Little Women.* And again Jo follows a male model, Bunyan, for she creates an allegory out of the ordinary. Yet for all its surface compliance the poem is subtly subversive. There's humor in the mere idea of "A Song from the Suds" as moral literature. And instead of simply living *Pilgrim's Progress,* as Marmee has enjoined, Jo is rewriting it, much as Alcott herself has done.

Thus Alcott remains ambivalent—about writing, about self-expression, and about gender roles. A key emblem of her ambivalence is Jo's cutting of her hair, ambiguously masculine and feminine. The daring action itself may be "masculine," as may the shorn hair, but the sacrifice of a prized possession for the benefit of others—so that Marmee can travel to her ailing husband—is "feminine." Further complicating the gender valence is the echo of Samson and Delilah. For Delilah was active, not passive, and Samson's shorn hair became a sign of masculine weakness. The traditional gender boundaries were blurred, decisive action associated with the female, long hair associated with physical strength. Moreover, Jo plays Delilah to her own Samson—she is ambiguously, perhaps ambivalently, both artist and art object, both Samson and Delilah.[11]

By the end of the first volume, though, Jo becomes more object than artist, more conforming, less wildly imaginative: her father is proud of her for becoming "a young lady who pins her collar straight, laces her boots neatly, and neither whistles, talks slang, nor lies on the rug as she used to" (294). Jo learns to restrain her exuberance, in both writing and action, and to submit to her proper role—and to God: to submit both to the Word and to the words of Bunyan's text. She must learn to curb her "abominable tongue"; she must channel her creativity into living, "replac[ing] her pen with a broom" (137); she must forgive Amy for burning a precious manuscript. Thus Jo's writing recedes into the background, eventually stopping. At the end of the first volume she is presumably still writing, but we see less of it and its fruits. It could be that she no longer needs to act out her melodramas and instead channels her earlier public exuberance into writing done behind the scenes. More likely, though, Alcott simply had to submerge this self-expressive writing since, according to the ethic she wanted to espouse, submerging the self and caring for others are more suitable to a little woman than self-dramatization and self-expression.

Jo's submersion in domesticity can be gauged, in part, by the submersion of her fictions, including her dramatic fictions. On the first Christmas the melodramatic adventures of Don Roderigo and Zara are so compelling that both stage scenery and "dress circle" collapse. Even here, though, Alcott feels the need to justify staging Jo's play: "It was excellent drill for their memories, a harmless amusement, and employed many hours which otherwise would have been idle, lonely, or spent in less profitable society" (24). She is not altogether comfortable about giving free reign to creativity. Certainly such exuberant self-expression is not appropriate for the grown women the little women

want to become. As Karen Halttunen suggests, the play "permits Jo's theatrical violation of true womanhood only within a larger ritual of family harmony," enabling Jo to act out "the moral struggle raging within her" and thereby "to control the destructive potential of her inner demon" (244, 245). The following year the drama is muted and more fully absorbed into the life of the family—the girls seem to follow Marmee's early advice and recognize that *Pilgrim's Progress* "is a play we are playing all the time in one way or another . . . not in play, but in earnest" (17). The melodramatic romance of Don Roderigo and Zara has become the more prosaic one of John Brooke and Meg. The play is absorbed not only into the plot but also into metaphor: the volume has become "the first act of the domestic drama called 'LITTLE WOMEN'" (258). Much as Jo learns to suppress anger, all the girls—and the narrator—learn to suppress melodramatic fictions.

And much as drama gives way to drama metaphor, fiction gives way to fiction metaphor: the stories of the Pickwick Club and the game of Rigmarole dwindle, by the end of the first volume, to story metaphors. Meg no longer needs romantic fictions because she lives her own novel: she "felt like the girls in books"; John might act "like the rejected lovers in books"; he then "looked decidedly more like the novel heroes whom [Meg] admired" (229, 249, 251). As the narrator tells us, "Now and then, in this work-a-day world, things do happen in the delightful story-book fashion" (241). The volume concludes when "Father and Mother sat together, quietly re-living the first chapter of the romance which for them began some twenty years ago" (258).

This taming of exuberance, this attempt to control it through metaphor, reverses the movement of the contemporary *Alice's Adventures in Wonderland* (1865). Lewis Carroll did not attempt to justify his excursion into fiction by making it moral. He simply sought to entertain Alice Liddell and to find a means of self-expression. Thus the book literalizes metaphor: "mad as a hatter" engenders a Mad Hatter; "mock turtle soup," a Mock Turtle. The book is profoundly liberating, granting the imagination creative freedom—even if Carroll does try to recant at the end, making the adventure just a dream. *Little Women,* on the other hand, metaphorizes the literal. It grounds Jo's early imaginative flights, and it similarly grounds the dangerously fictive, constraining it in metaphor. Like the budding poet in Alcott's "Mountain Laurel and Maidenhair," Jo "put her poetry into her life, and made of it 'a grand sweet song' in which beauty and duty rhymed so well that the . . . girl became a more useful, beloved, and honored woman than if she had tried to sing for fame which never satisfies" (158-59). Still, the mere existence of the fiction metaphors may remind us of the earlier fictional flights, of the potential for imaginative, not just imaginary, freedom.

The effects of this shift in *Little Women,* this absorption of fictions into the plot, are several. One is to show the domestication and maturing of the little women: they have outgrown their childish reliance on stories and now live them, as they try to live *Pilgrim's Progress.* Another is to lift the book itself into the never-never land of story: the book loses some of its reality, becoming more of a romance, receding from our everyday world in part because of its saccharine sweetness but also because of its metamorphosis into the fiction it has previously enclosed. The fiction metaphors may remind us that we are, after all, reading a fiction—and thereby give us enough distance to call the pronouncements it seems to endorse into question. In any case, because of the shift from fiction making to living, Jo is no longer primary author and mover; she can no longer direct Meg in a play or in life. And her loss of authority may account for some of her indignation that Meg wants to marry and leave her sisters.

The devaluation of writing continues in the second volume. For here writing is a means, not an end. It is, first of all, a means of earning money, to send Beth and Marmee to the seashore. Writing is more womanly if its goal is self-sacrifice and kidness to others, if self-expression is subordinate to self-abnegation. Alcott's ambivalence is nowhere so clear as in the kind of writing that she allows herself and Jo to pursue—"popular" writing to earn money for others, not "serious" writing for the selfish purposes of art.

Elsewhere in the second volume writing is similarly a means, though not always unambiguously so. When Jo is feeling despondent, Marmee urges her to write to make herself happy—a therapy that largely works. Some degree of self-expression is permissible, it seems, as medicine, though the line dividing therapy and creativity is not entirely clear. But the two samples of Jo's writing that we see in the second volume, both poems, are less ambiguous: both achieve crucial nonartistic ends, their artistry subordinated to utility. Compared to the lively pieces in the first volume, these two are plodding and pedestrian. The first, Jo's poem about Beth's dying, allows Jo to express some of her grief and to tell Beth that she has not lived in vain, that others have benefited by her example. The second, a meditation on four trunks in the garret, revealing some of Jo's loneliness and longing for love, appears in a publication that Professor Bhaer reads—and it brings him courting. Jo acknowledges that it is "very bad poetry," but the Professor points out that "it has done its duty" (519), beauty once again subordinated to—made to rhyme with—duty.

Even more striking is how dangerous art has become. At first, in volume two, the effects are relatively benign. Jo's overdeveloped imagination leads her to believe Beth in love with Laurie, "and common sense,

being rather weakened by a long course of romance writing, did not come to the rescue" (354). The consequences here are trifling. Later, as Jo is lured to write thrillers for the sake of money, a worse danger looms:

> "She thought she was prospering finely; but, unconsciously, she was beginning to desecrate some of the womanliest attributes of a woman's character. She was living in bad society; and, imaginary though it was, its influence affected her, for she was feeding heart and fancy on dangerous and unsubstantial food, and was fast brushing the innocent bloom from her nature by a premature acquaintance with the darker side of life, which comes soon enough to all of us. (381).

Beyond such possible excesses, though, writing is simply not what a little woman should aim for. Jo's beloved Beth urges her to follow the claims of love and duty: "you'll be happier in doing that than writing splendid books or seeing all the world; for love is the only thing that we can carry with us when we go, and it makes the end so easy" (455).[12]

Jo essentially does stop writing when she marries, and she channels her creativity into telling stories to her household of boys and composing a song for a festive occasion. True, bookishness has brought Jo and her Professor together: they read Hans Christian Andersen; he gives her a volume of Shakespeare; they attend a literary dinner. Yet the Andersen is simply sugarcoating for Jo's German lessons, the dinner a disappointment. Books are insufficient in themselves, but they may serve a useful end. And that end is marriage and domesticity. Early on, Jo is bookish, with a metaphoric family: her stories are "dutiful children whom good fortune overtakes"; she herself, a "literary spinster, with a pen for a spouse, a family of stories for children" (474, 478). She ends, though, with a true family, and bookishness is metaphoric; when the Professor becomes intimate with Jo he will read "all the brown book in which she keeps her little secrets" (519). The metaphoric family becomes actual, the actual bookishness metaphoric. At the end of volume two as at the end of volume one, fiction is channeled into metaphor. Jo does state, "I haven't given up the hope that I may write a good book yet, but I can wait, and I'm sure it will be all the better for such experiences and illustrations as these" (530). Such a teasing reminder of Jo's earlier bookishness may subvert some of Alcott's surface message—and may also remind us that we are reading a book, only a book, and can thus question its pronouncements. But the surface message remains clear: as long as she is happy and busy and dutiful—as a proper woman, a wife and mother—Jo should feel no great call to write.

In the first continuation of *Little Women,* in fact, she feels none. The only writing she does in *Little Men* is in her Conscience Book, where each week she records the virtues and follies of the boys at Plumfield. Again, the writing is instrumental, here (as in Alcott's own works) an instrument of moral growth. Not until *Jo's Boys,* published nearly twenty years after *Little Women,* does Alcott allow Jo the writing she allowed herself. And then it is only because Jo has been fretting for something to do while sick, has hoped to lighten her family's financial burdens, and has wanted to buy Marmee some peace and comfort at the end of a hard life. Furthermore, it's not dangerous gothic tales that Jo indulges in but domestic realism. Still, Alcott calls this return to writing "Jo's last scrape"—and not just because Jo's popularity makes her the prey of autograph hounds. Despite all the rationalizations, writing remains morally dubious. Later, Jo and Laurie collaborate on a Christmas production, one far different from the melodrama of Don Roderigo and Zara in *Little Women.* For this one is a tribute to motherhood: "I'm tired of love-sick girls and runaway wives. We'll prove that there's romance in old women also" (243). The play thus provides closure to the family saga that began with a Christmas play so long ago. But the tenor of the final play exalts the everyday rather than the exotic, the dutiful rather than the beautiful, echoing the shift in Alcott's own writing from the gothic to the domestic.[13]

Fortunately, even if she was dubious about its justification, Alcott herself continued to write. She could justify her writing by doing it out of a sense of duty: she earned money to feed her family, and her fiction was an instrument of good, teaching girls how to become proper women. Alcott may have espoused women's rights, including suffrage, but in her books as in her life the greatest good was not individual rights and self-fulfillment but loyalty and service to the family; she was a "domestic feminist," seeing the family as the key to reforming society (see, for example, Strickland 145). Though she sometimes needed to escape her family in order to write and rented a room in Boston, the family almost always took precedence over her liberal causes, over herself, over her writing.

Alcott couldn't write just for the sake of writing, for the joy of creating. She may have continued beyond the point of financial necessity partly because she liked indulging in writing, but her avowed goal was always security for the family. Perhaps the only way she could permit herself to write was to pretend, even after her family was secure, that she was writing only for the sake of the family (see Strickland 56, Elbert 132). Or, to put it another way, the act of writing itself may have been liberating, but Alcott paid for such self-indulgence by making the writing instrumental, by sacrificing herself and her writing to duty. The liberating pen was also its homonym: confinement could give birth to creativity but could also abort it.

Notes

Even though my title echoes one of Elizabeth Keyser's, "Alcott's Portraits of the Artist as a Little Woman," I came up with it independently and can't resist the temptation to use it. Perhaps my slight swerve from her wording can be taken as a sign of my swerve from her reading. I read Alcott as less intentionally subversive; Keyser concludes "Portraits" by suggesting that although Marmee can hope for nothing better than marriage for her daughters, "the artist who conceived *Little Women* has wished something better for us" (457). Perhaps, too, the similarity of my title to Keyser's can be taken as a sign of my indebtedness to her, both to her published work—her bracing reminders that "instead of offering facile or partial solutions to social problems, [Alcott] exposed their complexity and the imperfect nature of all solutions, not excluding her own" ("Domesticity" 174)—and to her careful and generous reading of this essay.

[1] See, for instance, Habegger and Kaledin, who stress submissiveness, the former suggesting that Alcott's fantasies are politically regressive; Janeway and Keyser, who emphasize subversion, the latter with more sophisticated, potentially deconstructive readings; and such proponents of ambivalence as, in their varying ways, Fetterley, Halttunen, Langland, and O'Brien.

[2] Even a male character may say, in Alcott's story "Psyche's Art," that "Moulding character is the highest sort of sculpture, and all of us should learn that art before we touch clay or marble" (65). With respect to the March sisters' game of imitating the *Pilgrim's Progress,* Keyser notes "that the women's pilgrimage is merely a game, an imitation of men's" ("Portraits" 446). For a more general examination of domesticity and Christian redemption in sentimental fiction, demonstrating the convergence of the two by means of typology, see Tompkins.

[3] Or (in contrast with Gilbert and Gubar's notion of women seeking rather than rebelling against female predecessors out of an "anxiety of authorship") Alcott is not so much seeking a predecessor in Brontë as disavowing her, rejecting her in the name of God.

For further discussion of *Work,* one that assesses its radical aims and its failure to convey moral development convincingly, see Yellin.

[4] In her Introduction to *Plots and Counterplots,* Madeleine Stern discusses the theme of the marble woman, which appears in such Alcott thrillers as "Behind a Mask" and "A Marble Woman."

Only once after publishing *Little Women* did Alcott indulge in the gothic—to write and publish the anonymous *Modern Mephistopheles* in her publisher's No

Name Series. The novel also gives curious expression to some of Alcott's ambivalence about authorship. Not only did she publish it anonymously, but the plot hinges on the Mephistophelian Jasper Helwyze's power over the young Felix Canaris: the former allows the latter to publish Helwyze's work as his own and to bask in the ensuing fame and success, which the young man is reluctant to give up. Alcott seems to be expressing some of her ambivalence about fame, about owning one's own work, about the satanic power an author can have. For further discussion of Alcott's exploration of such issues, see Cowan xi-xii.

[5] A similar message, though it stresses domestic virtues more than religious ones, appears in Alcott's *Rose in Bloom.* A woman like Phebe may sing in public for a while, to prove her self-restraint and worthiness of Archie, but a woman should not write. When Rose bemoans her lack of talent for poetry or singing or painting, her uncle assures her that she has "one of the best and noblest gifts a woman can possess"—"the art of living for others so patiently and sweetly that we enjoy it as we do the sunshine, and are not half grateful enough for the great blessing." He adds that "the memory of a real helper is kept green long after poetry is forgotten and music silent" (322-23). Likewise, in "Mountain Laurel and Maidenhair," a young girl is encouraged to "Write your little verses, my dear, when the spirit moves—it is a harmless pleasure, a real comfort, and a good lesson for you; but do not neglect higher duties or deceive yourself with false hopes and vain dreams" (150). It's true that *An Old-Fashioned Girl* contains women characters—minor characters—who are allowed some measure of success as artists. But the writer looks sick and overworked. And the sculptor's statue of the coming woman includes not only a symbolic ballot box, pen, and palette, but also a needle and a broom. It's likewise true that the fragmentary *Diana and Persis,* which Alcott never published, holds out some hope for women artists, while exploring the possibilities for uniting art and domesticity. Will Percy be able to pursue her art after becoming a mother? Will Diana's art be enriched by a budding relationship with a fellow sculptor and his son? Alcott's inability to finish the novel suggests her inability to resolve such questions—much as the death of her sister May, the model for Percy, soon after the birth of her child curtailed any resolution in her own family. And perhaps the differences among critics about the sequencing of chapters, with significant implications for the resolution of the story (see Showalter xxxviii, xli), hints that such perplexity continues to resonate.

[6] Nina Auerbach explores the subversive qualities of *Little Women*—how it subverts cultural prescriptions by validating the March family's community of women. True, the book is subversive in this respect. But belonging to a community of women is not necessarily liberating for an artist: the family's communal values may allow a little woman to deviate somewhat from the values of the larger community, but they do not foster individual self-expression. As Keyser suggests, "Jo's sisterhood . . . means loyalty to the patriarchal family, and far from strengthening her in her unconventionality, it compels her to conform" ("Portraits" 458). Or as Halttunen suggests, "Through the character of Jo March, Alcott performed literary penance for her greatest sins against the cult of domesticity: her flight to Washington, her Gothic period, her consuming literary ambition, and her refusal to marry" (243).

[7] It's true that Laurie, a male, submerges his own yearning for musical achievement, but we've never sensed that he is as accomplished as Amy. His dabbling at a requiem and an opera seems more an attempt to overcome Jo's rejection than a whole-hearted commitment to music. In other novels Alcott allows men to be artists—in *Jack and Jill,* for instance, Ralph receives no censure for becoming a sculptor, and Mac of *Rose in Bloom* becomes a successful poet. Even in the fragment *Diana and Persis* we may see Diana as a talented sculptor, yet in her budding relationship with the well-known sculptor Stafford it is clear who is metaphorically the master and who the pupil, whose genius is established and whose is not, at least not yet. Although it could be that Alcott wants to distinguish between talented dabbling and professional genius—those who are merely talented dabblers should subordinate their talents to serving others—there does seem to be a gender bias. For further discussion of the ambiguities of Amy's artistry, see Keyser, "Portraits" 455-56.

[8] Sharon O'Brien provides an illuminating discussion of the contradictions inherent in the nineteenth-century encouragement of tomboyism.

[9] In her other works as well Alcott hints at the dangers of fiction. The one story that Rose of *Eight Cousins* tries to tell has disastrous consequences. She tells a pointed story of a little girl who takes a rolled bandage from a basket, without asking permission—thus making guilty little Pokey, who has behaved like the girl in the story, overwhelmingly remorseful and confused. It's bad enough that Dr. Alec then chides Rose for publicly embarrassing Pokey, but Pokey's champion Jamie also tells Rose's secret—that she has had the vanity to pierce her ears. The moral is not just that Rose should beware of embarrassing others, but that she shouldn't tell stories. She may marry a poet, not become one.

[10] Yet Marmee can't erase the traces of the original stories, traces that are potentially subversive: Keyser suggests that "Alcott, by having Meg laughingly accuse Marmee of turning their stories against them in order to extract a moral, indicates her recognition that each story, far from pointing up the girls' good fortune, exposes

something about the unfortunate condition of women, a condition in which they all share" ("Portraits" 448).

[11] See Madelon Bedell: "In this modern female version, the legend of Sampson and Deliah is . . . turned upside down. To shear a woman's hair is to give her power" (xxi). Elizabeth Langland suggests that the episode "equates Jo's cutting her hair with a masculine assertion of responsibility. Jo not only acts like the man of the family in this episode, but she now looks 'boyish.' Yet, she cries for the loss of her beauty, and this detail endears her to us as a woman" (122).

[12] I agree with Anne Hollander that Alcott "demonstrates that to achieve a good character the practice of patience, kindness, discretion, and forbearance among one's fellows must totally absorb one's creative zeal. Such zeal may not be expended on the committed practice of any art, or any intellectual pursuit which might make the kind of demand that would promote the unseemly selfishness of the creative life" (38). But I disagree with her argument that, for Alcott, the driving force of creativity is sexuality, and that Jo cannot become a true artist until she accepts her sexuality. Hollander claims, for instance, that "Jo can write as a true artist only later, when she finally comes to terms with her own sexual self and thus rather belatedly grows up. . . . " (34). But when Jo marries she stops writing.

In any case, the praise of duty reverberates throughout Alcott's fiction. In *Jack and Jill* a mother knows "that it was better for her romantic daughter to be learning all the housewifery lessons she could teach her, than to be reading novels, writing verses, or philandering about with her head full of girlish fancies, quite innocent in themselves, but not the stuff to live on" (201-02). In *Eight Cousins* Dr. Alec tells Rose that housekeeping "is one of the most beautiful as well as useful of all the arts a woman can learn. Not so romantic, perhaps, as singing, painting, writing, or teaching, even; but one that makes many happy and comfortable, and home the sweetest place in the world" (185). In *Under the Lilacs* a young girl follows the advice of a young woman and loses an archery contest to a boy, sacrificing her own achievement for that of another: "Losing a prize sometimes makes one happier than gaining it" (247). Even in "Psyche's Art," in which a woman's art is not stifled but enriched by attending to home duties, and in which Alcott allows the possibility that the heroine may not marry the hero, the hero wins "fame and fortune" as an artist while the heroine grows "beautiful with the beauty of a serene and sunny nature, happy in duties which became pleasures, rich in the art which made life lovely to herself and others, and brought rewards in time" (83)—not happy and rich in the art of sculpture.

[13] Although most of the young women in the novel end up marrying, Alcott does allow one to become a doctor and to remain a spinster. For a discussion of Jo's ambivalence about her own achievements and those of the next generation of women, see Keyser, "Women and Girls."

Works Cited

Alberghene, Janice Marie. "From Alcott to *Abel's Island:* The Image of the Artist in American Children's Literature." Ph.D. diss., Brown University, 1980.

Alcott, Louisa May. *Eight Cousins; or the Aunt-Hill.* 1875. Illus. Ruth Ives. Garden City, N.Y.: Doubleday, 1958.

———. *Jack and Jill: A Village Story.* 1880. Boston: Little, Brown, 1910.

———. *Jo's Boys, and How They Turned Out: A Sequel to "Little Men."* 1886. Boston: Roberts, 1890.

———. *Little Women: or Meg, Jo, Beth and Amy.* 2 vols. 1868-69. Boston: Roberts, 1893.

———. "Mountain Laurel and Maidenhair." *A Garland for Girls.* 1886. Rpt. in *Glimpses of Louisa: A Centennial Sampling of the Best Short Stories by Louisa May Alcott.* Ed. Cornelia Meigs. Boston: Little, Brown, 1968.

———. "Psyche's Art." *Proverb Stories.* 1882. Boston: Roberts, 1896. 55-83.

———. *Rose in Bloom.* 1876. Illus. Hattie Longstreet Price. Boston: Little, Brown, 1927.

———. *Under the Lilacs.* 1877. New York: Grosset and Dunlap, 1919.

———. *Work: A Story of Experience.* 1873. Introd. Sarah Elbert. New York: Schocken, 1977.

Auerbach, Nina. *Communities of Women: An Idea in Fiction.* Cambridge: Harvard Univ. Press, 1978.

Bedell, Madelon. Introduction. *Little Women.* By Louisa M. Alcott. New York: Modern Library, 1983. ix-xlix.

Cheney, Ednah D., ed. *Louisa May Alcott: Her Life, Letters, and Journals.* Boston: Roberts, 1891.

Cowan, Octavia. Introduction to *A Modern Mephistopheles,* by Louisa May Alcott. Toronto: Bantam, 1987. v-xiii.

Douglas, Ann. "Mysteries of Louisa May Alcott." *New York Review of Books* 28 Sept. 1978. Rpt. in Stern, *Essays.* 231-40.

Elbert, Sarah. *A Hunger for Home: Louisa May Alcott and* Little Women. Philadelphia: Temple Univ. Press, 1984.

Fetterley, Judith. "*Little Women:* Alcott's Civil War." *Feminist Studies* 5 (1979): 369-83.

Gilbert, Sandra M., and Susan Gubar. *The Madwoman in the Attic: The Woman Writer and the Nineteenth-Century Literary Imagination.* 1979. New Haven: Yale Univ. Press, 1980.

Gordon, Jan B. "Lewis Carroll, the *Sylvie and Bruno* Books, and the Nineties: The Tyranny of Textuality." In *Lewis Carroll: A Celebration,* ed. Edward Guiliano. New York: Potter, 1982. 176-94.

Habegger, Alfred. "Precocious Incest: First Novels by Louisa May Alcott and Henry James." *Massachusetts Review* 26 (1985): 233-62.

Halttunen, Karen. "The Domestic Drama of Louisa May Alcott." *Feminist Studies* 10 (1984): 233-54.

Hollander, Anne. "Reflections on *Little Women.*" *Children's Literature* 9 (1981): 28-39.

Janeway, Elizabeth. "Meg, Jo, Beth, Amy, and Louisa." *New York Times Book Review* 29 Sept. 1968. Rpt. in *Only Connect: Readings on Children's Literature,* ed. Sheila Egoff, G. T. Stubbs, and L. F. Ashley. 2d ed. Toronto: Oxford Univ. Press, 1980. 253-57.

Kaledin, Eugenia. "Louisa May Alcott: Success and the Sorrow of Self-Denial." *Women's Studies* 5 (1978): 251-63.

Keyser, Elizabeth. "Women and Girls in Louisa May Alcott's *Jo's Boys.*" *International Journal of Women's Studies* 5 (1983): 457-71.

Keyser, Elizabeth Lennox. "Alcott's Portraits of the Artist as Little Woman." *International Journal of Women's Studies* 5 (1982): 445-59.

———. "Domesticity versus Identity: A Review of Alcott Research." *Children's Literature in Education* 16 (1985): 165-75.

Langland, Elizabeth. "Female Stories of Experience: Alcott's *Little Women* in Light of *Work.*" In *The Voyage In: Fictions of Female Development,* ed. Elizabeth Abel, Marianne Hirsch, and Elizabeth Langland. Hanover, N.H.: Univ. Press of New England, 1983. 112-27.

O'Brien, Sharon. "Tomboyism and Adolescent Conflict: Three Nineteenth-Century Case Studies." In *Woman's Being, Woman's Place: Female Identity and Vocation in American History,* ed. Mary Kelley. Boston: Hall, 1979. 351-72.

Pauly, Thomas H. "*Ragged Dick* and *Little Women:* Idealized Homes and Unwanted Marriages." *Journal of Popular Culture* 9 (Winter 1975). Rpt. in Stern, *Essays.* 120-25.

Showalter, Elaine. Introduction to *Alternative Alcott,* by Louisa May Alcott. Ed. Elaine Showalter. New Brunswick: Rutgers Univ. Press, 1988. ix-xliii.

Stern, Madeleine B., ed. *Critical Essays on Louisa May Alcott.* Boston: Hall, 1984.

———, ed. *Plots and Counterplots: More Unknown Thrillers of Louisa May Alcott.* New York: Morrow, 1976.

Strickland, Charles. *Victorian Domesticity: Families in the Life and Art of Louisa May Alcott.* University, Ala.: Univ. of Alabama Press, 1985.

Tompkins, Jane P. "Sentimental Power: *Uncle Tom's Cabin* and the Politics of Literary History." *Glyph* 8 (1981): 79-102.

Yellin, Jean Fagan. "From *Success* to *Experience:* Louisa May Alcott's *Work.*" *Massachusetts Review* 21 (1980): 527-39.

Yonge, Charlotte M. *The Daisy Chain; or, Aspirations, a Family Chronicle].* 1856. Preface Susan M. Kenney. New York: Garland, 1977.

Ellen Butler Donovan (essay date 1994)

SOURCE: "Reading for Profit *and* Pleasure: *Little Women* and *The Story of a Bad Boy,* "The Lion and the Unicorn, Vol. 18, No. 2, 1994, pp. 143-53.

[*In the following excerpt, Donovan places* Little Women *in the context of the development of children's literature. Though Alcott incorporated lessons for self-improvement in her work, she opposed didacticism.*]

Fiction written in the United States specifically for children changed fundamentally in 1868 and 1869 with the publication of Louisa May Alcott's **Little Women,** part I, and Thomas Bailey Aldrich's *The Story of a Bad Boy.* In these two novels, we see the development of a new narrative strategy that mirrors a new awareness or understanding of children's experience and a trust in the child reader's abilities to interpret and judge.

Alcott's **Little Women** and Aldrich's *The Story of a Bad Boy* were written in opposition to the didacticism of contemporary children's literature. In both novels, we see a greater degree of realism in the characters. The children behave in childlike (and frequently childish) ways. Unlike most of the children in the juvenile fiction of the decade, the characters in these novels are not examples of ideal or wrong behavior. Moreover, the characters are not overshadowed by adults who constantly guide them into proper behavior. Most significantly, the authors of these novels consistently attempt to prevent an adult judgment of the childlike behavior by shifting the narrative point of view from omniscient adult narrators to the children's consciousness.

The innovations in the narrative perspective in the novels may not be readily apparent because Alcott's and Aldrich's novels are didactic and sentimental compared to children's literature of the late twentieth century. However, a brief discussion of the literature available to children in the 1860s will provide the yardstick by which we can measure the changes the novels initiate.

It is commonplace now to assert that, in the antebellum period, fiction for children was only countenanced if it was read in moderation and if it had a clear didactic message. Fiction, because it is not true, was suspect unless used for a higher cause, such as teaching moral and religious lessons. MacLeod emphasizes the didactic nature of children's fiction written between 1820 and 1860:

> Tender minds were given . . . innumerable small tales of temptation resisted, anger restrained, disobedience punished, and forbearance learned. Countless desirable traits of character were developed and strengthened, and undesirable ones "rooted out" in the pages of fictional books for children. (*Children's Literature* 42-43)

Kelly points out that, after the Civil War, constraints loosened somewhat and children were allowed to read for pleasure. The gentry "resolutely turned their faces away from what they now were pleased to recognize as the cheerless didacticism and the overt religiosity of their predecessors" (92). However, moralistic stories still dominated the pages of children's literature. *Our Young Folks,* the magazine in which Aldrich's novel was serialized, represents the literature available to this audience. In addition to Aldrich's novel, in the 1869 volume of *Our Young Folks,* children read eight stories with clearly stated moral or ethical lessons, seven sentimental stories with clearly implied ethical or moral lessons, six quasi-fictional stories that use adult characters to impart factual information about a variety of subjects, and six installments of "The William Henry Letters," and only one adventure story.[1]

The sentimental and moralistic stories from *Our Young Folks* are barely tolerable today. For example, in "The Beautiful Gate," a little slave boy made lame by his short-tempered master warns the Union Army of an impending Confederate attack and then dies and thereby enters the "beautiful gate" of the title. In "The Spray Sprite," a little girl who likes to play at the shore discovers that work is the best blessing God gave the world. Reading *Our Young Folks* reveals that, at the close of the decade, children's fiction was still predominantly didactic and sentimental.

Both Alcott and Aldrich recognized the need for novels that repudiated the sentiment and moralistic lessons found in children's literature. Using the third-person pronoun to refer to himself, Aldrich remarks in the preface (1894) to *The Story of a Bad Boy* that he "wished simply to draw a line at the start between his hero—a natural, actual boy—and that unwholesome and altogether improbable little prig which had hitherto been held up as an example to the young" (vi). Alcott recorded in her diary, "lively, simple books are very much needed for girls, and perhaps I can supply the need" (Myerson 166). Later, when she was reviewing the proofs of the novel, her judgment is firmer: "It reads better than I expected. Not a bit sensational, but simple and true, for we really lived most of it; and if it succeeds that will be the reason of it" (Myerson 166).

A fundamental way for both authors to repudiate the didactic was to make the characters of the novels more complex. In other words, the children are not simply examples of good or bad behavior but are children who are both good and bad. Typically, children's fiction of the period limited the child's role to illustrate the moral of the story; however, Alcott's March children and Aldrich's Tom Bailey are both good and bad. From the very beginning of the novel, Alcott contrasts the March children with the ideal her readers might expect: in the first chapter of the book the girls complain that their work is distasteful and trying. They all long to have the money to do the things they desire: Meg wants to be fashionable, Jo wants to write, Amy wants to draw, and Beth wants to play piano. Instead of thankfully accepting the position in society that has been ordained for them (as good girls should), the girls chafe at their station in life.

Alcott gives each of the girls her own individual faults and, in doing so, suggests the faults that characterize American girlhood and reflect child development. Meg longs to be fashionable and to make a good impression on the class in society to which she aspires. Jo is short-tempered and boyish.[2] Amy is vain and conceited. Beth is bashful.

In Aldrich's *Story of a Bad Boy,* this strategy is taken even further. Tom Bailey, the bad boy of the title, manages to involve himself in all sorts of scrapes. He fights the school bully and wins. He burns up Ezra Wingate's coach, finds himself in jail because of it, and escapes from jail. He, along with his friends, cheats the storekeeper out of twelve sixpenny ice creams. He participates in a snowball fight that is so dangerous that the constables are called upon to stop it. He is the mastermind of the plan to shoot off an abandoned cannon in the middle of the night and send the town into confusion.

Given the general immaturity or lack of moral fortitude of the characters of these novels, a nineteenth-century reader might expect that the adults of the novels would provide firm guidance in correcting the faults of the children. However, *Little Women* and *The Story of a Bad Boy* can both be distinguished from contemporary children's fiction by the minimal roles adults play in the novels. Much has been made of the absent Mr. March and the centrality of Marmee in *Little Women*.[3] This centrality is not surprising because, in the mid-nineteenth century, the mother in particular was considered the moral center of the child's life. More important for the purposes of this argument, in children's literature of the period, moral and parental authority is an inherent attribute of adult characters. The ideal parent, particularly but not exclusively the mother, is all wise, all knowing, and all good (MacLeod, *A Moral Tale* 51). Good children respected, obeyed, even anticipated their parents' commands.

Compared to this literature, however, Marmee's role is limited. She is not all powerful. For example, when Amy burns Jo's book and Jo loses her temper, the narrator remarks:

> No one spoke of the great trouble—not even Mrs. March—for all had learned by experience that when Jo was in that mood words were wasted, and the wisest course was to wait till some little accident, or her own generous nature, softened Jo's resentment and healed the breach. (96-97)

Moreover, Alcott takes pains to show that the moral authority that Marmee does possess is the result of a process that identifies her with each of the girls. When Marmee explains to Jo that she too once had a bad temper and she learned to control it, the image of inherent power associated with the adult is somewhat dispelled: Marmee is just an older, more experienced version of the girls.

Another way in which Alcott limits Marmee's moral authority is by allowing the girls to recognize their own faults and confess them without reprimand or prompting on Marmee's part. Kelly has pointed out that self-regulation and self-control were important virtues to writers of children's popular fiction (76).[4] Frequently, as in Jacob Abbott's Rollo stories, that self-examination was prompted by the adult characters of the story; however, in *Little Women,* all self-examination and confessions are initiated by the girls. For example, when Meg returns from the Moffats, she

confesses to having been "powdered, and squeezed and frizzled," that she "drank champagne and romped and tried to flirt and was altogether abominable" (121). Even more surprising is Marmee's response—she does not condemn her daughter's behavior. The narrator remarks, "Mrs. March looked silently at the downcast face of her pretty daughter, and could not find it in her heart to blame her little follies" (121). When Meg tells Marmee that she overheard gossip that Mrs. March is trying to arrange a match between Meg and Laurie, Marmee blames herself for the predicament in which Meg found herself: "I was very unwise to let you go among people of whom I know so little. . . . I am more sorry than I can express for the mischief this visit may have done you, Meg" (122). Again, Alcott limits Marmee's authority by including her apology to Meg and Meg's acceptance of the apology. In doing so, Alcott inverts the conventional pattern of behavior in children's literature. . . .

By minimizing the adult roles in their narratives, Alcott and Aldrich focus the reader's attention on the child and the child's experience rather than on the teaching or guiding relationship between the parent and the child. Also, because the child's experience is not frequently judged by the parent, the reader can see that experience in accordance with the child's values rather than the parent's.

Both authors further minimize an adult interpretation of the child's experience by limiting the adult narrator's interpretive role. Though both novels are, for the most part, narrated from an adult perspective, the narrative perspective is very sympathetic to the child's experience and frequently refrains from adult judgment upon the child's experience.

Alcott avoids the necessity of emphasizing the adult narrator's judgment by shifting the narrative perspective to the character central to the event taking place. Most often, Jo's perspective is used because she is the most dominant of the March sisters. Her freedom and tomboyishness allow her to act and initiate more adventures than the other girls. Alcott's narrative innovation lies in her choice of Jo's perspective rather than Beth's perspective. By choosing Jo rather than Beth for the narrative perspective, Alcott is validating Jo's character type over Beth's.[5]

Alcott uses the other girls' perspectives when she narrates their experiences. For example, when Meg is visiting her friend, the narrative provides her thoughts and judgments about the events she sees:

> When the evening for the "small party" came, she found that the poplin wouldn't do at all, for the other girls were putting on thin dresses and making themselves very fine indeed; so out came the tarlatan, looking older, limper, and shabbier than ever beside

Sallie's crisp new one. Meg saw the girls glance at it and then at one another, and her cheeks began to burn, for with all her gentleness she was very proud. No one said a word about it, but Sallie offered to dress her hair, and Annie to tie her sash, and Belle, the engaged sister, praised her white arms; but in their kindness Meg saw only pity for her poverty, and her heart felt very heavy as she stood by herself, while the others laughed, chattered, and flew about like gauzy butterflies. (108-109)

The narrator has already briefly informed readers that Meg's host family is "kindly" but "frivolous," that "they were not particularly cultivated or intelligent people, and that all their gilding could not quite conceal the ordinary material of which they were made" (109). However, Meg's perceptions and experience dominate the account; we experience her feelings even while we know that her judgment about her relative merit is misguided.

As in Meg's case, so too are the readers presented the experiences of Amy and Beth from their perspectives. When Amy is disgraced by corporal punishment at school and when Beth overcomes her shyness in order to play the piano in the Lawrence house, their experiences are presented with immediacy and sympathy. Cornelia Meigs, in her biography of Louisa May Alcott for younger readers, explains the success of the novel using this criterion:

> Part of the magic of Louisa's charm for young people surely lies in the fact that she sees things through their eyes, that she depicts the ups and downs of the early adventures of life, all from the young point of view. The youthful readers all feel, entirely, that Louisa is *on their side.* (227)

By using Jo's narrative perspective consistently and by shifting the narrative perspective from character to character as the plot demands, Alcott limits the interpretive authority of the adult narrative perspective. This narrative strategy provides a more immediate and intimate experience of the children's lives. . . .

Alcott and Aldrich may have discovered the usefulness of shifting the narrative perspective to the child because they were using material from their own childhoods. Identification with the child's perceptions would be relatively easy because those perceptions were part of the authors' experiences.

Moreover, the autobiographical element that is emphasized in *The Story of a Bad Boy* and was assumed in *Little Women*[6] diminished the force of the cultural constraint against fiction for children: the work was "true" and thus did not need an adult narrator to interpret events and teach lessons. Publication records of the novels suggest that this new emphasis on the

child's experience was acceptable to the book-buying public. The novels were immediately popular. Both publishers found the demand great enough to merit reprinting the novels almost yearly: Fields, Osgood, and Company reprinted *Story of a Bad Boy* eight times between 1870 and 1880, and Roberts Brothers reprinted *Little Women* nine times between 1868 and 1878. Both books were considered immensely successful.[7]

Other cultural values or ideas also probably contributed to the success of these two novels and their emphasis on the child's experience. In her study of British Victorian children's literature, Gillian Avery argues that fiction written for Victorian middle- or upper-class children frequently portrayed the characters as essentially good-hearted but embroiled "in pickles" as a result of foolish choices or misbehavior. However, literature intended for cottage children continued to be overtly didactic. Avery concludes that British writers assumed that cottage children had not internalized middle-class ethical standards and so could not be trusted to interpret naughty characters properly. Though clearly written within the American literary tradition, *Little Women* and *The Story of a Bad Boy* follow Avery's pattern. Both novels portrayed gentry families (though unusual ones) and gentry values.

Moreover, studies of the American family note the increasing recognition of adolescence as a stage between childhood and adulthood at about this same period. John Demos notes that "by 1850 shrewd observers detected new patterns of behavior, and 'special problems,' among some of the nation's youth" (442). Joseph Kett mentions that most educators and parents saw a transition in child behavior around the age of twelve or thirteen and that, while the adolescent was not considered an adult, the formative years in which the child's behavior could be shaped were ended (112). In *Jack and Jill,* Alcott suggests that such a development was familiar to her. She remarks that characters "stepped out of childhood into youth" (Kelly 155). The greater trust in the ability and judgment of child readers required by the narrative perspectives illustrates this new stage of childhood that was emerging in the mid-century.

A consequence of this new stage of development is the liberation of the child's reading pleasure and interpretative role. No longer was reading merely an opportunity for a moral lesson. Alcott and Aldrich offered to child readers the opportunity to experience another child's reality, to see the world or events from a child's point of view. The narrative strategies used by the authors also provided the readers an opportunity to think and judge independently. No adult narrator or character metaphorically leans over the readers' shoulders to explain the lesson of the tale. If there is a lesson in these novels, readers have to discover it on their own. Both Louisa May Alcott and Thomas Bailey Aldrich provided children the chance to read for pleasure as well as profit.

In this essay, I want to view *Little Women* against the other literature available to children in order to show how the novel was groundbreaking and not how it supported or illustrated the cultural values that we now find so troubling. For example, feminist interpretations see Jo's repression of her temper or her control of her tomboyishness as a coercion or denial of her personality. However, Alcott's plot suggests that Jo is not fully grown until she accepts the fact that she is female and accepts the ways in which the society governs her behavior because of her gender. More important for my purposes is the fact that Jo, the central character of the story, is a tomboy and is portrayed with such sympathy that being a tomboy, at least in the early years of adolescence, is represented as acceptable behavior.

Notes

[1] "The William Henry Letters" by Mrs. A. M. Diaz are most like the novels under discussion in their emphasis on the boy's experience and the use of his perspective by means of the epistolary form.

[2] Feminist scholars have focused much attention on *Little Women* because of its continuing popularity among girls and because it so clearly reveals both Alcott's and her culture's assumptions about what growing up as a girl involves and what demands are placed on a woman in American society. The need for those interpretations is especially evident to me, for, when I teach *Little Women,* the female students who read the book as girls invariably remark about how much they loved it and are not at all troubled by the process of denial and restraint that the March girls must experience.

[3] See the articles by Kornfield and Jackson, Fetterly, and Auerbach.

[4] See also MacLeod, "For the Good of the Country," 44; and MacLeod, *Moral Tale,* 73-82.

[5] O'Brien points out that those who encouraged tomboy childhoods for girls in post-Civil War advice manuals were "seeking to preserve rather than to challenge woman's essential role as wife and mother" (354). O'Brien also notes that this advice created a difficult adolescent transition for young women (355). However Alcott's desire that Jo remain unconventional—she refuses to marry Jo to Laurie and resists marrying Jo to anyone at all (see Myerson, *Journals,* 167; and Myerson, *Letters,* 120, 121-22, 124-25)—distinguishes Alcott from the authors of advice manuals.

[6] An anonymous reviewer for *Harper's New Monthly Magazine* (August 1869) commented: "Autobiographies, if genuine, are generally interesting, and it is shrewdly suspected that Joe's [*sic*] experience as an author photographs some of Miss Alcott's own literary mistakes and misadventures" (qtd. in Stern 83). Zehr also discusses that readers' and reviewers' assumptions that Jo and Alcott were one and the same (324). The accuracy of that assumption is not of importance here.

[7] *Little Women* made enough money for Alcott that she achieved financial security for the rest of her life.

Works Cited

Alcott, Louisa May. *Jack and Jill.* Boston: Little, 1880.

———*Little Women.* New York: Modern Library, 1983.

Aldrich, Thomas Bailey. *The Story of a Bad Boy.* Rpt. Hanover, NH: UP of New England with Strawbery Banke Museum, 1990.

Auerbach, Nina. *Communities of Women: An Idea of Fiction.* Cambridge: Harvard UP, 1978.

Avery, Gillian. *Childhood's Pattern: A Study of the Heroes and Heroines of Children's Fiction 1770-1950.* London: Hodder, 1975.

Demos, John. 'The American Family in Past Time." *The American Scholar* 43.3 (1974): 422-46.

Fetterly, Judith. "*Little Women:* Alcott's Civil War." *Feminist Studies* 5.2 (1979): 369-83.

Kelly, R. Gordon. *Mother Was a Lady: Self and Society in Selected American Children's Periodicals, 1865-1890.* Westport: Greenwood, 1974.

Kett, Joseph. *Rites of Passage: Adolescence in America, 1790 to the Present.* New York: Basic, 1977.

Kornfield, Eve and Susan Jackson. 'The Female *Bildungsroman* in Nineteenth-Century America: Parameters of a Vision." *Journal of American Culture* 10.4 (1987): 69-75.

MacLeod, Anne Scott. *A Moral Tale: Children's Fiction and American Culture 1820-1860.* Hamden: Archon, 1975.

———. "For the Good of the Country: Cultural Values in American Juvenile Fiction, 1825-60." *Children's Literature* 5 (1976): 40-51.

Meigs, Cornelia. *Invincible Louisa.* Boston: Little, 1951.

Myerson, Joel and Daniel Shealy, eds., with Madeleine B. Stern, assoc. ed. *The Journals of Louisa May Alcott.* Boston: Little, 1989.

Myerson, Joel and Daniel Shealy, eds. *The Selected Letters of Louisa May Alcott.* Boston: Little, 1987.

O'Brien, Sharon. "Tomboyism and Adolescent Conflict: Three Nineteenth Century Case Studies." *Woman's Being, Woman's Place: Female Identity and Vocation in American History.* Ed. Mary Kelley. Boston: Hall, 1979. 351-72.

Stern, Madeleine B., ed. *Critical Essays on Louisa May Alcott.* Boston: Hall, 1984.

Zehr, Janet S. "The Response of Nineteenth-Century Audiences to Louisa May Alcott's Fiction." *American Transcendental Quarterly* 1.4 (1987): 323-42.

Christy Rishoi Minadeo (essay date 1994)

SOURCE: "*Little Women* in the Twenty-First Century," in *Images of the Child,* edited by Harry Eiss, Bowling Green University Press, 1994, pp. 199-214.

[*In this essay, Minadeo considers the relevance of* Little Women *to today's readers for whom gender roles are less limiting than in Alcott's time.*]

Reading *Little Women* used to be easy. Before feminism changed the way American girls looked at the future, Louisa May Alcott's book was simply a manual showing girls how to be ideal women. From Alcott's book girls learned to serve others and forget themselves, to put ambition aside for marriage and family, and to hide their negative feelings. Reading *Little Women* these days is much more confusing because feminism has helped girls understand the future isn't limited by gender—that biology is *not* destiny. It is difficult to read *Little Women* anymore without resisting its overt messages about the nature of femininity. The March sisters' journey to little womanhood seems to involve a degree of self-renunciation that is no longer realistic, emotionally healthy, or even fashionable. Contemporary readers feel let down by Jo March's eventual capitulation to marriage and motherhood after her long-standing insistence on "paddling her own canoe." Yet if we remember the novel is a product of its time and place, post-Civil War New England, and that the outcomes of the plot are dependent on those factors, we're left with a novel of female development that reflects not only the cultural norms of its time, but also specifically female conflicts that are not significantly reduced despite the passage of more than 100 years. Even so, *Little Women* has a strong undercurrent of resistance to cultural restrictions placed on girls; the

March girls' gentle rebellion against the cultural imperative that makes domestic work their domain suggests the possibility that there are (or should be) choices.

Still, modern girls are no more exempt from expectations they be agreeable, nurturing, and giving than the March sisters were. If they are to achieve success in school and in the workplace, girls are expected to do so without unseemly displays of ambition, aggression, or competitiveness. In the end, as Marmee March tells her daughters, many modern females are still taught that "to be loved and chosen by a good man is the best and sweetest thing which can happen to a woman" (118). As regressive as Marmee's philosophy sounds, an updated version would likely sound like a description for Superwoman (modern women *should* have successful careers, happy marriages, well-behaved children, home-cooked meals, and spotless homes), a role as restrictive in its way as that of "little woman." *Little Women* does depict limited roles for women, and the plot of the novel does serve to rein in the one character who doesn't fit the mold, but modern expectations differ only in specifics—girls must now be high achievers in academics, athletics, and the arts as well as cultivate many old-fashioned girlish virtues, such as selflessness, docility, and patience. The trajectory of girls' lives remains carefully defined, and that is why *Little Women* remains relevant to contemporary readers.

That modern readers still identify with Jo, the rebellious March sister, suggests they too feel at odds with social and cultural expectations. The central problem for Jo in becoming a woman is deciding how she will reconcile her unwomanly ambitions and tendencies with the immutable fact of her gender. What does it mean to be a woman? What can a woman have in life and still be acceptable to society? What must she give up? This is the basis for Jo's conflict; her resolution of these questions and the reconciliation of seemingly irreconcilable desires is at the core of *Little Women.* It is this theme that elevates what many have seen as a sentimental girls' book into an important work in the American canon. The struggle to find a definition of womanhood one can live with is a critical, perhaps universal rite of passage for girls.

And yet there's much in *Little Women* to make any self-respecting feminist cringe. The entire novel seems bent on maintaining the health of the patriarchy by stamping out any tendencies toward feminine self-reliance and self-esteem. The March sisters learn to renounce themselves and serve others, to repress anger and other negative feelings, but most of all that nothing is more important than to be "loved and chosen by a good man."

Marmee March is the model of little womanhood for her girls. Never angry, always ready to serve others,

and in possession of a good (though thoroughly useless) husband,[1] Marmee guides her girls toward fulfillment of their destinies. Expressing her dreams and
hopes for her girls, she says:

> I want my girls to be beautiful, accomplished, and
> good; to be admired, loved and respected; to have
> a happy youth, to be well and wisely married, and
> to lead useful, pleasant lives with as little care and
> sorrow to try them as God sees fit to send. (118)

The only challenges and ambitions Marmee foresees
for her daughters are domestic; there seems to be no
room for worldly success and achievement. The March
sisters must suppress any ambitions beyond the domestic sphere; that they are successful in doing so is perhaps the most difficult plot outcome for modern readers to accept. Yet this discomfort is useful to girls
reading *Little Women* today, allowing them an intimate view of how girls' lives used to be, and enabling
them to favorably contrast their own options with those
of the March sisters.

In contrast to Marmee's hopes for her girls are their
own dreams for the future; each girl reveals her fond-
est hopes in a chapter titled "Castles in the Air." Their
innocent wishes contrast in varying degrees with the
path their mother envisions for them; the extent to which
each girl's dream reflects the ideal of little womanhood reveals just how difficult each one's fulfillment
of it will be.

Beth's "castle in the air" is to "stay at home safe with
Father and Mother and help take care of the family"
(173). She is "perfectly satisfied" with that and her
piano. A perfect specimen of little woman, Beth has
successfully collapsed almost all interest in self into a
desire to serve others. She is associated with domestic
accoutrements—"a little mop" and an "old brush," and
is so diligent in serving others without thought of her
own safety that she contracts scarlet fever. There are
no struggles for Beth in becoming a little woman,
because wherever there might be a conflict, she gives
in. Tired from her domestic labors, Beth forces herself
to visit the destitute (and ailing) Hummel family their
mother has adopted. Not able to give in to her own
selfish desire to skip the visit, Beth dutifully carries a
basket of food to the Hummels, and returns with the
scarlet fever that causes her death.

According to feminist scholar Judith Fetterley, the implication is that "to be a little woman is to be dead"
(380). The character and history of Beth March do not
provide a good rebuttal to Fetterley's view. Beth is
saintly, and although readers often weep at her death,
they do not usually identify with her. Beth's selflessness is so extreme it leeches the life out of her as
effectively as the scarlet fever does. Despite her apparent perfection in meeting the ideals of little woman-

hood, Beth has a terrible self-image; everyone loves
her, but she thinks of herself as "stupid little Beth."
She even provides justification for her own death, telling Jo that she is "of no use anywhere but [at home]"
(452). There is no need to indoctrinate Beth into the
role of little woman; she has embraced the definition
wholeheartedly, obliterating herself literally and symbolically in the process.

Meg, the eldest sister, is also destined to fulfill the
ideal with a minimum of difficulty, but her outcome is
much less extreme than Beth's. Meg's "castle in the
air" is a nearly perfect reflection of her mother's hopes
for her:

> I should like a lovely house, full of all sorts of
> luxurious things—nice food, pretty clothes, handsome
> furniture, pleasant people, and heaps of money. I am
> to be mistress of it, and manage it as I like, with
> plenty of servants, so I should never need to work a
> bit. . . . I wouldn't be idle, but do good, and make
> everyone love me dearly. (172)

The deviations from the ideal are relatively minor, and
are disposed of in due course. Meg struggles
with a longing for luxury from the beginning, but
when she vacations with wealthy friends she gives
in to pressure to dress in the latest fashions and
preen before stylish lads. But having been raised
well, she is ashamed of her foolish vanity when she
finds herself face to face with Laurie, the boy next
door, who clearly prefers the unaffected Meg. When
Meg returns home after her visit, she confesses her
foolishness to Marmee, who is well pleased that the
lesson was not lost on Meg. While Marmee wishes
good and wise marriages for her girls, she tells Meg
and Jo that it is "better [to] be happy old maids than
unhappy wives or unmaidenly girls running about to
find husbands" (119). It is obviously not acceptable
for a little woman to choose and pursue a good
husband; she must be chosen and pursued by *him*.

Humility is not taught in one simple lesson, however,
and Meg must fall a few more notable times before she
finally accepts her place. Falling in love with John
Brooke, while sweet for Meg, poses a bit of a conflict
for her. He is not wealthy, and will probably never be
able to build her the castle in the air she dreamt of.
Still, she accepts this, because she has internalized her
mother's teaching about wise marriages, and because
she loves John. After her marriage, when Meg rebels
against the limitations of his modest income, the consequences for her are understated but pointedly clear.
Meg gives in to the urge to buy a $50 silk dress in
order to keep up with a wealthy friend. John is kind
and understanding, but he cancels his own order for an
overcoat, telling Meg it is too expensive. Consumed
with guilt, Meg prevails upon her wealthy friend to
buy the dress so John can have his coat. The selfish

desire to satisfy herself falls out in two ways for Meg: first, she realizes that John earns money for his work, so he is entitled to whatever he wants to get: he has earned it. On the other hand, Meg's work carries no economic value so she feels she isn't entitled to buy things for herself. Second, Meg learns that domestic harmony is ensured only when she puts herself and her needs after her husband and his needs.

In Marmee, Meg finds the role model for the kind of wife she was raised to be: always sweet, happy, and smiling, with dinner ready at the end of the day. Meg desires to be a good wife, and so tells John that he should feel free to bring home dinner guests any time he pleases; he needn't so much as warn her, because she will always be prepared to welcome guests with open arms. Predictably, John takes her at her word, but chooses a day when Meg has tried all day (without success) to make currant jelly. The house is closed up, uninviting, no dinner is ready, and Meg is hot and tired; most unforgivably, she is angry with John for not warning her he was bringing a guest. John quietly but effectively punishes her by going away with his friend. When he returns, she is still angry, but while they peck at each other, Meg recalls her mother's advice:

> Be careful, very careful, not to wake John's anger against yourself, for peace and happiness depend on keeping his respect. Watch yourself, be the first to ask pardon if you both err. . . . (338)

A husband's anger and lack of respect are to be feared and avoided at all costs. A wife must repress her perhaps justifiable anger, because domestic peace rests on her willingness to ensure it by avoiding the expression of negative feelings. So Meg internalizes the suggestion that the whole problem is hers, the necessary repairs to the relationship her responsibility alone. She apologizes, and bliss is thus restored. Meg successfully submerges herself in John's superiority.

Later when Meg is frazzled with caring for newborn twins, she neglects her appearance, her housework, and her husband. Once again John's reaction and her mother's advice serve to remind Meg of the consequences of not placing John first. He is driven to look for companionship elsewhere, which he finds in the parlor of another young couple whose wife is not worn down by the demanding chores of young motherhood. Marmee does not hesitate long in letting Meg know she is to blame for John's desire to avoid home.

> You have only made the mistake that most young wives make—forgotten your duty to your husband in your love for your children. . . . Make it so pleasant he won't want to go away. (472)

The sermon is not wasted on Meg, who desires to be a good little woman, and who runs herself ragged to

give the appearance that the management of house and children doesn't impede her ability and desire to please her husband. Meg must bear the responsibility for keeping the marriage happy, and if her husband doesn't want to be at home, she must be at fault. There's no mandate for the husband to participate in needed changes; it's the wife's duty to be forever pleasant, attractive, and available to her husband.

The major differences between Meg's girlish "castle in the air" and her married reality is that she is *not* to manage her home as she likes, but rather how her husband prefers it. And she learns the necessity of work, because without some work to do, she is left to feel useless, as if she doesn't deserve anything of value if she doesn't create some work by which to earn her keep. With husband and mother guiding her to the correct path, Meg is finally indoctrinated into the ways of little womanhood, with hardly a whimper of protest. Her reward is, by the time she has finally reached little womanhood, everyone loves her as dearly as she had wished in her girlhood fantasy. Clearly, to be loved and chosen by a good man is indeed the sweetest thing that could happen to Meg, and she recognizes the necessity of keeping herself in his good graces.

The kind of oppression Meg endures in her marriage is not extinct today, a fact not likely to be lost on modern adult readers, but perhaps not fully understood by the book's usual audience of 10-13-year-olds. Still, a modern girl will be certainly be dismayed by Meg's subservience, thus increasing the value of *Little Women* to postfeminist generations. Rather than being an exemplary model of young womanhood, Meg's gradual capitulation to the restrictions imposed on her can help emphasize the degree to which things have changed for the better. Young women of the postfeminist generation often claim they're not feminists, but faced with a portrait of prefeminist attitudes about women, they find they are more feminist than they thought.

Meg's inability to buy a dress for herself because she believes she doesn't do anything to earn it is echoed in the modern need women have to delineate the value (both economic and cultural) of traditional women's work: housework, child-rearing, and family management. Though attitudes have changed a good deal since *Little Women* was written, housewives still aren't valued much. Meg's story serves as an excellent cautionary tale. As a result, many girls will respond to Meg's subservience with repugnance, rather than admiration, and may even feel renewed dedication to achieving equality for women.

The youngest March daughter, Amy, is perhaps the most unsympathetic character in the novel, but she is also useful in shaping the images of themselves that contemporary readers hold. Being of an artistic bent, Amy's "castle in the air" involves going to Rome, painting fine pictures and becoming "the best artist in the whole world" (172). Notably absent from Amy's castle is any mention of traditional womanly fulfillment, but even so, it is not too difficult to tame her aspirations. Amy, like Meg, delights in the finer things in life, and because she possesses a disposition that pleases, she gains opportunities her less socially adept sisters miss. In spite of her pronounced vanity, Amy works hard at her art, and is often depicted working on her projects with single-minded zeal. But faced with the genius of Michelangelo on her European tour, she gives up on her art, realizing that talent isn't genius. Claiming "I want to be great or nothing" (489), Amy opts for nothingness, which opens her up to the new possibility of fulfillment through marriage to Laurie. Through him she becomes a patron of the arts, thus fulfilling the womanly dictum that she serve others, not herself.

Amy does not even require a motherly sermon to accept the tenets of little womanhood. The model of genius Amy finds in Michelangelo is enough to suggest to her that she cannot be a great artist and be a woman. As a woman, Amy can never be more than a dabbler, if she is also to fulfill her womanly roles. It does not occur to her to create a new, uniquely female model of artistic achievement; she gracefully capitulates to socially acceptable pursuits, like philanthropy, which always appealed to her anyway. Again, the pattern is reinforced; in the world of *Little Women,* the only acceptable pursuits are in service to others and fulfillment lies in being loved and chosen by a good man.

Like Amy, Jo's ambitions have nothing to do with fulfillment in the domestic sphere. Meg characterizes Jo's "castle in the air" as full of "nothing but horses, inkstands, and novels"; Jo wants to do "something heroic or wonderful that won't be forgotten after I'm dead. I don't know what, but I'm on the watch for it and mean to astonish you all someday" (172). Jo's conflicts are the most difficult because of all the girls, she is the farthest from the ideal. Her journey to little womanhood is fraught with disappointments, bitter lessons and bewilderment, leaving Jo and her readers with the unmistakable impression that becoming a woman is a series of compromises of one's individuality. The novel resolves neatly because even ornery Jo finally accepts the role society defines for her by the end, although she does put her own imprint on it.

Jo refers to herself as "the man of the house" while her father serves in the Civil War, introduces herself to Laurie as a "businessman—girl, I mean," and generally bemoans the great injustice in her fate of being born female. She seems to suffer from rather serious gender confusion, enjoying playing all the swashbuckling, romantic male roles in the sisters' homemade melodramas, and fancying the role of breadwinner for her genteel (but poor) family. The action of the novel serves to help Jo discover and relish her place among women. In a society with distinctly drawn roles for men and women, it is critical for Jo to recognize and accept her womanly attributes.

The first and most difficult fault Jo is asked to overcome is her wild temper. Alcott writes that "[P]oor Jo tried desperately to be good, but her bosom enemy was always ready to flare up and defeat her, and it took years of patient effort to subdue it" (90). Jo's lessons in repressing her anger come, as many do, at her mother's knee. Having been angry for days at Amy for burning a treasured manuscript, Jo fails to warn Amy about thin ice when they are skating. Amy falls through and nearly drowns, but is rescued in time by Laurie. Jo is tearfully repentant for not forgiving Amy sooner, thus connecting her anger to guilt for Amy's accident. She calls her temper "savage," and fears she will do great harm with it someday. Jo is astonished to learn that Marmee used to have an even worse temper than Jo.

> I've been trying to cure it for forty years and have only succeeded in controlling it. I am angry nearly every day of my life, but I have learned not to show it, and I still hope to learn not to feel it. . . . I've learned to check the hasty words that rise to my lips, and when I feel that they mean to break out against my will, I just go away a minute and give myself a little shake for being so weak and wicked. (97)

The consequences for Jo "having her feelings" is that her sister nearly dies. As Judith Fetterley points out, "in the world of "little women,' female anger is so unacceptable that there are no degrees to it;" all anger has terrible consequences. Marmee reinforces this view by her firm repression of all angry feelings. This is a turning point for Jo; she is deeply penitent, and vows to repress her anger in the same purportedly admirable way her mother has demonstrated (Fetterley 380).

The reasons for Marmee's anger are never articulated; indeed it seems possible she has repressed her feelings so well that she might be unable to articulate them herself. But the overt message of this episode teaches that women should *not* be angry, regardless of whether there might be just cause for it. The barely disguised message is that a woman is "weak and wicked" if she gives vent to her anger. Still, the idea of anyone trying so sincerely to eliminate all hints of anger, even to herself, is so preposterous it seems reasonable to wonder if Alcott wasn't perhaps being ironic. It does seem like an absurd notion to contemporary readers: encouraged everywhere to express our feelings, good or bad, Marmee ends up looking like the hopelessly repressed Victorian she was. By presenting an extreme characterization, Alcott imbedded a message of protest in her homily. Jo is never completely successful in repressing her feelings (and readers applaud because her individuality is her most appealing characteristic), but with the simple passage of time and the indoctrination she receives, she finds more acceptable outlets for her sometimes unmanageable feelings. While Jo is still somewhat "wild" at novel's end, the fact that girls sometimes feel disappointed by the path she chooses points to one of Alcott's most important covert messages. There is value in this disappointment readers feel as it helps girls see that they needn't give up whole parts of themselves to fit a mold. It was a cultural and social necessity for Jo, but needn't be for her readers.

Jo and Amy have ambitious dreams in common, but unlike Amy, Jo has a true vocation for writing; Jo doesn't much care if her work fits standard notions of what literature is. She simply *must* write. The action of the plot, then, pushes Jo to place her writing in its proper place—in a secondary position at best. The desire to be a genius doesn't drive Jo so much as her enjoyment of the power she has in earning a living for herself and her family. Skilled at writing "sensation fiction," Jo makes good money selling her stories. She is, however, ashamed of her subject matter, publishing her work without attribution while hoping her family will not recognize her style. Jo

> thought she was prospering finely, but unconsciously she was beginning to desecrate some of the womanliest attributes of a woman's character. Wrongdoing always brings its own punishment, and when Jo most needed hers, she got it. (*Little Women* 422-23)

Jo's real crime was not writing lurid fiction, but rather in straying from the confines of subject matter deemed appropriate for women. Appropriately enough, it is a man, in the form of her future husband, who chastens her. Discreetly, Professor Bhaer tells Jo that sensation stories are "bad trash" and making a living from selling them is dishonest—like putting "poison in a sugar plum" and letting others eat it.

Thoroughly ashamed, Jo burns all her manuscripts and resolves to hold herself to higher standards in her future writings. Her next tale is moral and didactic, but no one will buy it. The public, it seems, wants only their women to be morally correct, not their fiction. Soon after this episode, Jo returns to her family home to take up the more acceptable vocation of caring for her dying sister, putting aside her writing for the time being.

Jo doesn't takes her writing seriously, calling it "scribbling," but when she writes, it consumes her. After a period of intense writing, Jo returns to the real world, cross and hungry. Her art is not romanticized; it is literary "labors," and eventually Jo feels it is not enough to sustain her. With Meg happily tucked in her nest,

and Amy crooning blissfully with Laurie, Jo is finally bothered by her solitude. "An old maid, that's what I'm to be. A literary spinster with a pen for a spouse, a family of stories for children, and twenty years hence a morsel of fame, perhaps" (530). This is clearly an unhappy vision, for despite Marmee's sermon to the contrary, it is apparently not all right to be an old maid under any circumstances. Jo's discomfort at the prospect of old-maidhood reinforces the notion that a little woman is happily and wisely married. It isn't possible to be an old maid and a little woman; old maids do not meet the criteria.

After Beth's death, Jo plunges into a deep depression. With Beth's shining example no longer before her, Jo finds it difficult to keep her promise of self-abnegation. She despairs at the thought of spending the rest of her days tied to her parents' house, endless duty, and few pleasures. She is guided out of her grief by her parents, who try to teach her to "accept life without despondency or distrust, and to use its beautiful opportunities with gratitude and power" (522). But she is also converted to domesticity at this stage; she begins to see the beauty in "brooms and dishcloths [that] could never be as distasteful as they had once been" because they were Beth's magic implements (522). And, as if sprinkled with fairy dust, Jo begins to take pride in making home cozy and clean. She notices and appreciates Meg's domestic wizardry for the first time, noting "Marriage is an excellent thing after all. I wonder if I should blossom out half as well as you have if I tried it" (523). Jo has nearly made it. Now she is ready to be accept Professor Bhaer's courtship with gratitude and pleasure, but not necessarily because he's perfect for her. Looking about her, seeing everyone neatly paired off, and wondering what morsels will be left for her, Jo essentially jumps at her last chance to become a little woman.

And here the notion of a woman being "little" must be discussed. Jo cannot marry Laurie when he proposes, because not only are they too much alike, they're also too equal in age, intellect, and personality. Laurie is more properly married to Amy who is immature enough and young enough to be his clear inferior—not unlike a parent/child relationship (Fetterley 381). Meg, as we have seen, has also learned her place as the lesser half of her marriage to John. These two couples, interestingly, do interact on a fairly equal level until they marry, when their roles revert to socially acceptable form. Professor Bhaer is significantly older than Jo, but more important, his educational and moral superiority to Jo are immediately evident. Temperamentally, intellectually, morally, and chronologically, Bhaer is depicted as superior to Jo, making him the ideal mate for her to play little woman to. The end of *Little Women* shows Jo and the professor happily ensconced at Plumfield, a home and school for orphan boys (she always did feel more akin to boys) where Professor Bhaer does all the teaching and Jo presides over the meals, contenting herself with mothering her own two boys and all the other needy lads. She doesn't seem to be writing at all (she will, however, return to her vocation in the sequels), although she claims that marriage and motherhood will make her a better writer. A radical thought for its time, and while it sounds like rationalization, there is no hint of irony in Jo's philosophy. Alcott validates female life experiences by having Jo believe they will enrich her art. But for all Jo's spunkiness and creativity, she ends up taking the only socially acceptable path in life available to her.

Having enumerated the ways in which the ideology of *Little Women* is antifeminist, it seems reasonable to wonder if the novel has any value today, and if it might not actually give future feminists some very regressive ideas. Feminists are no more monolithic than any other group, so their responses to the novel do vary. Judith Fetterley writes that it is difficult to see Jo's capitulation to the doctrines of little womanhood with "unqualified rejoicing" (382), and indeed, many readers seem disappointed with Jo's marriage, or at least by her rejection of Laurie. She has married a man who is a father figure and mentor, rather than the soul mate she might have had in Laurie. Her marriage to an authority figure serves to dampen her considerable vitality—symbolized by her renunciation of writing—and to severely curtail her image of herself as a person of value. During the first months of their friendship, Jo darns Professor Bhaer's socks in return for German lessons, clearly signaling that the only thing of value she has to barter with is her domestic skills. In marrying Bhaer, Fetterley asserts, Jo's rebellion is neutralized and she proves once and for all that she is a good little woman who wishes for nothing more than the chance to realize herself in the service of some superior male (382). It is difficult to argue against this vision; Jo is indeed tamed, and brought into her proper sphere. By the end of the novel, Mr. and Mrs. March are pleased with the fruit borne by their teaching, and note that all their "little women" have realized their parents' brightest hopes for them. It is the reader who cannot forget that Jo's own dreams have been severely restricted as she internalized the cultural norm of self-abnegation in women.

Yet Elaine Showalter sees in *Little Women* "Alcott's belief that the fullest art came from women who had fulfilled both their sexual and intellectual needs, and her effort to imagine such a fulfillment for Jo" (61). Seen in this light, Jo's story is one of discovery of her whole self, not simply buying into the acceptable role for women, or completely rejecting it in favor of an alternative lifestyle either. Jo's marriage to Bhaer can then be seen as a positive step for her, given Jo's unconventional style, for Bhaer is no conventional man. Nurturing, loving and expressive, Bhaer does eventually give Jo a room of her own to pursue her vocation as a writer, which does not diminish after her marriage. This marriage provides Jo with the framework that eventually allows her to see her writing for the gift it is, rather than denigrating it as merely "scribbling." Showalter points out that although modern readers might wish Jo had gone off and lived independently, such a wish is really not true to Jo's time, place, or personality. Jo is rather a foremother to those women who came after her, who had fewer limitations than Jo had to contend with (64).

Women readers of many generations have identified with Jo, in spite of her limited options. My octogenarian aunt read *Little Women* as a young girl, admiring Jo for being the "doer." Though she wouldn't describe herself as a feminist, this aunt supported herself and her family, put herself through college and graduate school, and married late by choice. My mother, growing up in the conformist early 1950s, thought Jo a "brick." A college sophomore likes Jo because she was the "hard worker who intended to do something outside the house." Apparently girls still feel that they are housebound, and admire Jo because she didn't want to be burdened with domestic duties either. Few girls can truly put themselves in Beth's saintly shoes, for how many girls are as good at erasing themselves as Beth was? Amy also fails as a role model, primarily because, through Jo's eyes, we see her as selfish and vain. Meg may be admired by a scattered few readers, but she fails to sustain interest because she is brought into line with such ease.

If my attempt to find out what young girls think of *Little Women* is any indication, this book is not much in fashion any more.[2] It is easy to see why—at nearly 600 pages, it takes fairly sustained concentration to complete, something that may be difficult for a generation weaned on Sesame Street, the Berenstein Bears, and MTV. Unlike those contemporary shapers of adolescent self-image, the messages in the novel are subtle and require active intellectual engagement. *Little Women* asks its readers to compare themselves to each of the characters to find where they stand. Among women who have read *Little Women,* it is a time-honored tradition to compare which March sister was the favorite. And the answer to that question always seemed to reveal a great deal about the character of the reader. The differences in the characters seem to invite self-examination, asking each girl, who are you most like? Are you vain like Amy? Or sweet and loving like Beth? Or spunky like Jo? Is that what you want to be like? The act of sizing herself up helps the young reader define herself, perhaps for the first time, even if it is by negative comparison (I know I'm not like *that!*). Yet those I found who had read it share with previous generations of readers an appreciation of Jo's strength and empathy with her struggles to fit in. They seem to understand that, for her time, Jo did what was right for her.

And while the plot of *Little Women* inarguably reinforces androcentric stereotypes of womanhood, it also makes some covert suggestions that run contrary to those stereotypes. For all its reinforcement of the superiority of men, or "the lords or creation," the world of the novel is that of self-reliant, self-sustaining women. Father March is physically absent in the first half of the book, tucked away in his study for most of the second half, and while he is the nominal head of the household, it is his wife and daughters who hold it together, physically, financially, and emotionally. But it is through Jo that Alcott makes her veiled suggestions resisting social norms for women. Jo steadfastly clings to a platonic relationship with Laurie despite social pressure to view male/female relationships as possible only within marriage. While readers are invariably disappointed that Jo rejects Laurie's proposal of marriage, they still admire her for going her own way.

Jo is also the only member of her family, including her father, who is able to earn a living, and although she later puts it aside, this fact serves to emphasize her strength and self-reliance, attributes she never entirely puts aside. Although Jo does put aside her writing to take care of domestic duties, her mother recognizes its importance to Jo's sense of self, and suggests that Jo write to work through her grief over Beth's death. Writing is then seen as an acceptable outlet through which Jo can express her feelings. The result of this therapeutic writing is that she finds, as her father proudly notes, her "true style." It is clear that through her life experiences, *as a woman,* Jo has finally come into her own as an artist, creating her best work thus far. In making an unconventional marriage, Jo completes her own unique definition of womanhood, blending her own needs with the expectations of society, and thus creating a new female model of artistic and marital success.

I suggest readers tend to identify with Jo because so many girls have experienced Jo's conflicts. The desire for independence, rebellion against the drudgery of domestic burdens, and straining against the limits placed on girls' horizons are far more universal in women's literature and lives than often recognized. Reading *Little Women* at age ten, Simone de Beauvoir focused on the choices Jo made, identifying with Jo and learning that

> marriage was not necessary for me. . . . I saw that all the March girls hated housework because it kept them from what really interested them, the writing and drawing and music and so on. And I think somehow, even when very young, I must have perceived that Jo was always making choices and sometimes they were neither well reasoned nor good. The idea of choice must have frightened me a little, but it was exhilarating as well. (qtd. in Showalter 64)

Little Women is, as many others have asserted, *the* American female myth, having profoundly influenced generations of women, and not simply to be good little wives and mothers who never lose their tempers. In 1989, there were only three women govemors in America; two of them named *Little Women* as their favorite childhood book (Showalter 42). While the novel explicitly extols the place of women in the home, implicitly it suggests the availability of options. With each succeeding generation of readers interpreting the message through the lens of their times, *Little Women* continues to be a vital role model of the passage from girlhood to womanhood.

Notes

[1] Although a warm and loving man, Mr. March contributes little to the financial and emotional health of his family. Having lost the modest family fortune, Mr. March is away serving with the Union forces for the first half of the novel. Although he comes home for the second half, he is mostly in his study, above and beyond the machinery of daily living. Incapable of managing day-to-day affairs, or even earning a living, Mr. March leaves it all in the capable hands of his wife and daughters.

[2] I handed out over 100 reader surveys to female middle-schoolers in Ann Arbor, Michigan, seeking answers to the following questions:

> 1. How old were you when you first read *Little Women?*
>
> 2. Which of the four sisters did you identify with most closely? Why?
>
> 3. Did you identify with the March sisters' struggle to become "little women"? Why or why not?
>
> 4. Do you feel pressured by your family, teachers, or friends to behave a certain way because you're female? What is it like? How do you feel about that pressure?

Having no means by which to require the return of my surveys, I received a disappointing five completed surveys. While I have no way of knowing, I do suspect the wording of the questions encouraged girls who had not read the book to simply toss out the questionnaire.

I also asked another dozen women, ranging in age from 20-82, what their memories were of reading *Little Women*. Without exception, these women felt that reading *Little Women* was a special and important part of their growing up years. Each found something to admire in at least one of the March sisters (usually Jo) and each recognized the specifically female growing pains experienced by their fictional counterparts.

Works Cited

Alcott, Louisa May. *Little Women*. 1869. New York: Dell-Yearling, 1869. . . .

Baym, Nina. *Woman's Fiction*. Ithaca, NY: Cornell UP, 1979. . . .

Fetterley, Judith. "*Little Women*: Alcott's Civil War." *Feminist Studies* 5.2 (1979): 369-83. . . .

Showalter, Elaine. *Sister's Choice: Tradition and Change in American Women's Writing*. Oxford: Clarendon, 1991. . . .

Shirley Foster and Judy Simons (essay date 1995)

SOURCE: "Louisa May Alcott: *Little Women*," in *What Katy Read: Feminist Re-readings of 'Classic' Stories for Girls,* University of Iowa Press, 1995, pp. 85-106.

[*In the following chapter, Foster and Simons explain that critics tend to be emotionally engaged with* Little Women *because its subject, female development, is universally mythic, and its realism keeps it timeless.*]

Louisa May Alcott's *Little Women* (1868) is probably the most famous of all the works discussed in this study, and of the nineteenth-century texts certainly the most enduring in popularity. Although it is over a hundred and twenty years since its first appearance, it remains a best-seller in both the United States and in Britain. The original novel is available in both hardcover and paperback editions on the permanent classics list of mainstream publishing houses, selling alongside abridged, adulterated and cartoon versions of the adventures, and even the further adventures, of Meg, Jo, Beth and Amy. The book has been dramatized for stage and screen, and television and radio adaptations continue to be broadcast for audiences who, habituated to a cultural diet of comic strips and soap operas, can have at best only a limited understanding of mid-nineteenth-century New England life. Elaine Showalter, in an essay on the phenomenon of *Little Women,* has noted how a number of twentieth-century women, as diverse in their origins and achievements as Gertrude Stein, Simone de Beauvoir and Adrienne Rich have all been prepared to admit to the impact of the novel as a formative influence on their lives.[1]

A text with such an established and central position in the female reading experience carries its own particular problems. Indeed one of the difficulties encountered by recent critics of *Little Women* has been the perceived disparity between emotional engagement with the text and evaluative criteria. As Lavinia Russ ob-served, it is difficult to view any text objectively when it has been deeply embedded in early imaginative experience and the empathy with characters and episodes has blurred the boundaries between fiction and fact.[2] Going further, Catherine Stimpson suggests that the problematics of reading *Little Women* highlight an important area of concern for feminist criticism, a concern which, in the remit of this study, has particular bearing on the reception of children's literature. As a child, Stimpson memorized and could quote whole chapters of *Little Women,* a text she locates as central in the 'paracanon', that alternative but complementary literary hierarchy, composed of works whose 'worth exists in [their] capacity to inspire love', whether or not they are judged by the critical establishment to have literary value.[3] As Stimpson argues, *Little Women,* like *Huckleberry Finn* or *Tom Sawyer* (the male equivalents with which it is often compared), is indubitably a work that makes an indefinable but fundamental appeal to a collective readerly imagination. In the years since its original publication it has acquired mythic status, occupying a special place in American culture as '*the* American female myth, its subject the primordial one of the passage from childhood, from girl to woman.'[4]

British audiences are not immune from responding to this story of female progression: in the first survey of the most borrowed 'classic' authors in British libraries, undertaken by the Public Lending Rights Office in 1993, Alcott was placed twentieth, just below Shakespeare and above Conrad and the Brontës.[5] Certainly *Little Women* is the childhood text most frequently analysed by feminist critics for its reflection and exploration of female culture and for the complicated narrative tensions it reveals. The story of the four March sisters and their mother, Marmee, during a year when their father is away at the American Civil War, provides a paradigm of female struggle whose literary influence can be seen in texts as dissimilar as Susan Coolidge's *What Katy Did* and E. Nesbit's *The Railway Children,* works which also explore the processes of growing up in fictional frameworks that reinforce the problematic nature of specifically female adolescence. Stories for children frequently stress their protagonists' ability to survive in a world without adults. When such a narrative also focuses on girls who are removed from obvious patriarchal influence, the emphasis on possibilities of female autonomy becomes intensified. Yet *Little Women* is by no means a simple text to interpret in the revised feminist critical framework of the enterprise undertaken in this study. In addition to the issues of critical evaluation referred to above, it raises questions about ideologies of the feminine, their impact on women's roles in both domestic and professional spheres, and literary reception. Close analysis of the text elicits unresolved tensions in the depictions of girlhood and the narratives available to women, whether realized or projected, and in turn

this poses intriguing lines of enquiry about the requirements for women authors to produce work in prescribed
genres and with strictly controlled subject matter.

Little Women is one of the first fictional texts for
children to convey the difficulties and the anxieties
of girlhood, and which suggests that becoming a 'little
woman' is a learned and often fraught process, not an
instinctual or natural condition of female development.
In its ability to promote a double set of value systems,
the book maintains a precarious balancing act, simultaneously providing for its readers a positive image of
the values of home and female domesticity *and* arguing for the importance of creative independence for
women. Indeed it is the very coexistence of these apparently conflicting elements that has contributed to
the novel's continued appeal, and that more recently
has exposed it to the rigorous critical scrutiny of feminist literary scholars, who find in the text evidence of
teasing contradictions about female authorship and
consequent ambivalent messages as to its conformist
or subversive intent. The use of Jo March as a projection of her creator's aspirations further serves to emphasize the frustrations that women's imaginative creativity encounters. Jo is perhaps the first of the heroines in this study who act out their own psychic fragmentation through adopting the role of author, and who
figure prominently in fiction for girls, and whose uncertainties provide scope for readers' empathetic response. As Stimpson has observed:

> Possibly . . . both female and male readers love
> any text that gives an experience of division and
> self-division. . . . the female reader's love of *Little
> Women* becomes a synechdoche for both a female
> and a male love of a textual escape from any
> psychological and ethical coherence that seems as
> pre-formed as a slab of concrete.[6]

In its portrayal of adolescence as a transitional period
from girlhood to womanhood, the novel registers a crucial point of tension in many women's lives. The March
girls are encouraged to develop their distinctive talents
as separate individuals, and readers are invited to engage imaginatively with the challenge that Jo offers to
certain traditional modes of female behaviour. Her longing for action and her careless disregard for passive
and decorative femininity is visualized as both desirable and natural, and adolescence is perceived as the
period of opportunity for self-expression and acceptable rebellion. At the same time, however, the women's
world which Marmee and her four daughters inhabit is
offered as a positive model of the civilizing and the
necessary, a feminizing and thus taming influence on
the harsh rationalism of the coexistent but non-intrusive
all male Laurence household. In addition, the little
women's struggle to please, to conform simultaneously
to several incompatible demands, reflects the pressures
placed on women in a society that made personal inde-

pendence into a political manifesto, while clearly
establishing a demarcation of gender roles that excluded women from decision-making processes. In a
review of recent Alcott scholarship, Ann B. Murphy
has usefully summarized the possible polarized critical positions: 'Is *Little Women* adolescent, sentimental, and repressive, an instrument for teaching girls
how to become "little", domesticated and silent?' Alternatively, is it 'implicitly revolutionary, fostering
discontent with the very model of female domesticity
which it purports to admire?'[7] It is the refusal of the
book ultimately to resolve the intractable questions it
raises that creates it anew as a dynamic text for modern
readers, who recognize in Jo March's confusion about
her gendered identity and the pull between the demands of family and those of individualism a withdrawal from the overarching sentimental structure that
apparently controls the novel's narrative direction.

Little Women was a book written to commission by an
author who was intensely professional in her attitude
to what she saw only as an uncomfortable and difficult
task. 'I don't enjoy this sort of thing', Alcott confessed
to her diary, in the process of struggling with the story
for girls she had been asked to produce so as to fill
what her publisher saw as a profitable gap in the market. 'Never liked girls', she admitted revealingly, 'or
knew many, except my sisters; but our queer plays and
experiences may prove interesting, though I doubt it.'[8]
Filled with misgivings, she plodded on with the work,
her distaste for the enterprise undoubtedly a major con-
tributory factor in its ultimate success. For it is important to recognise the innovatory calibre of *Little Women*
as a 'girls' story'. Although produced specifically for
a female juvenile audience, it is a text that deliberately
avoids many conventional features of contemporary
American children's fiction by substituting comic incident for sentimental pathos, and by rejecting the paradigms of female fictional propriety (such as were found
in Susan Warner's Ellen Montgomery) for the vital,
androgynous Jo March and the talented if overexuber-
ant Amy. Despite the clear moral directive of *Little
Women,* Alcott refused, as Ruth K. MacDonald has
noted, to follow the conventional format of didactic
literature for children. Neither did she use the novel to
advance political and ethical causes, such as the temperance movement, abolition of slavery or progressive
education, all issues taken up in the reformist tendency
that characterized much children's writing of the period.[9] Recoiling from the fashionably sentimental structures of juvenile narrative, Alcott relied instead on the
genre of domestic realism which she had exploited so
successfully in her earlier *Hospital Sketches* (1865), a
work firmly rooted in her personal grim experience of
nursing at a field hospital in Georgetown during the
Civil War. Despite her initial reluctance for the task,
her decision to base the work for girls on her own
family was to be a major turning-point, not just in her
own career, but in the history of children's literature,

and when in August 1868 Alcott read the proofs of *Little Women,* she was surprised by the power of its immediacy: 'Not a bit sensational, but simple and true, for we really lived most of it; and if it succeeds that will be the reason of it.'[10]

Alcott's open acknowledgement of her own departure from the sentiment and the didacticism of contemporary fictional practice is present throughout *Little Women,* where she makes explicit comparative reference to the difference between her heroines and their literary counterparts. 'If she had been the heroine of a moral storybook', the narrator observes about Jo, bereft of companionship after Beth's death in the second section of the novel,

> she ought at this period of her life to have become quite saintly, renounced the world, and gone about doing good in a mortified bonnet, with tracts in her pocket. But, you see, Jo wasn't a heroine; she was only a struggling human girl, like hundreds of others.[11]

Alcott's quasi-satirical treatment of religious sentimentality and moral sententiousness effectively promotes her own stance as realist. In contrast to the idealized portraits of heroines in conventional novels, Meg, Jo, Beth and Amy are no paragons of perfection, but adolescent girls sensitive to their own personality deficiencies and for whom social gaucherie and the lack of new clothes are very genuine concerns. The intertextual dimension of *Little Women* indicates its degree of literary sophistication in its response to wellestablished genres: the evangelical, sentimental and heroic narratives that were characteristic of popular literature. References to other fictions in the novel include, among others, Bunyan's *The Pilgrim's Progress,* Scott's *Ivanhoe,* Goldsmith's *The Vicar of Wakefield* and, significantly, Warner's *The Wide, Wide World,* classic examples of respectively, a moral allegory, a historical romance, a sentimental comedy and what had already become a highly influential story of female self-development. These are the literary models which both serve as inspiration for Alcott's heroines and expose their realist foundation.

For, as Jo points out, the economic materialities that determine the March family's existence are far removed from the fantastic scenarios of popular romantic fictions, where

> "some rich relative [would] leave you a fortune unexpectedly; then you'd dash out as an heiress, scorn everyone who has slighted you, go abroad and come home my Lady Something, in a blaze of splendour and elegance." (213)

The inclusion in the novel of parodies of clichéd scenes from contemporary children's literature also enhances the distinction between *Little Women* and its predecessors. During the account of Beth's first, almost fatal, attack of scarlet fever for instance, as the illness approaches its crisis Alcott shifts the focus of attention from the sickroom to Aunt March's house. Here Amy has prepared her childish and misspelled Last Will and Testament, a comic foil which undermines the potentially sentimental excesses of the stock deathbed tableau. And when Beth's death does occur, in the second volume of *Little Women,* later to be retitled *Good Wives,* the authorial voice draws attention to the dying girl's refusal to fade away according to type, for:

> Seldom, except in books, do the dying utter memorable words, see visions, or depart with beautified countenances.[12]

Similarly the March sisters' deviation from standard conduct book behaviour is a pronounced feature of episodes which could have been used as exemplary. At the smart New Year's Eve party at the Gardiners' house, Meg sprains her ankle dancing in high heeled shoes that are too tight, and Jo spills coffee on a dress that she has already ruined with a scorch mark. The incidents offer a striking contrast to Ellen Montgomery's Christmas visit to Ventnor in *The Wide, Wide World,* where the heroine functions as an exemplar of decorum and moral superiority.

It is, however, *The Pilgim's Progress* which provides the most explicit model for the narrative and the spiritual schema of the novel. Receiving the book as a gift from their mother on Christmas morning, the girls are encouraged to see themselves as unworthy pilgrims on the symbolic journey towards self-improvement, and the naming of episodes in *Little Women* after Bunyan's own chapter headings reinforces the analogy at every stage of the story. Yet the male text offers no easy solutions for female adaptation, as Marmee, herself a victim of patriarchal control, is prepared to admit. As a literary construct *The Pilgrim's Progress* presents a behavioural ideal which in the literal absence of the father takes on the power of the Logos, the all-powerful word which carries the authority to determine female conduct and which negates female identity. Struggling to obey the dicta of this fictional text, the sisters succeed only partially in conforming to its template of spiritual perfection, and the existence of alternative literary identities within *Little Women* indicates the inadequacy of Bunyan's powerfully simple ideal in resolving the contemporary problems which the girls encounter.

This is conveyed most tellingly through the conceptualization of Jo March as author, a role which embodies Alcott's ambitions and forms an eloquent comment on women's position in the literary market place. Like Alcott, Jo's first literary inclination is towards the Gothic, the sensational genre that liberates her fantasies of violence, aggression and cross-dressing. The sexually transgressive implications of their context and the latent subversion they encode are, however, not allowed to flourish in the world that is dominated by a patriarchy which represses the unacceptable female text. Her encounters with publishers and later with Professor Bhaer force Jo to confront the tension between commercial practice and conventional family values, and she ultimately tones down her exotic taste for thrillers to the more domestic, acceptable mode of moral fables for children. Jo's hopes for her future echo those of her creator. ' "I want to do something splendid before I go into my castle" ', she declares, ' "something heroic or wonderful, that won't be forgotten after I'm dead. I shall write books, and get rich and famous". ' (196). The remark makes explicit the connection between personal ambition, literary practice and the parameters of achievement for women. Although for both Alcott and her heroine the dream was to materialize, it was in a dimension which Alcott certainly saw as compromising her early idealism.

As discussed in the introductory chapter, children's writing in the nineteenth as in the twentieth century lacked literary prestige, and writing for girls in particular, largely the province of women, ranked even lower in status than other forms of children's literature. In part this has been used as evidence of the campaign to trivialize women's literary achievement, what one feminist critic has called a general 'belittling . . . of women and women's culture.'[13] In this context it is highly significant that Jo's ultimate professional destination is as an author of books for boys, not for girls, a sphere where she can continue to allow her boisterous imagination to have free rein, and where her subjects will not be tied to domestic or matrimonial affairs. Alcott's personal resistance to stereotyped categorization as female novelist continued well after she had recognized the need to satisfy market forces. Working on the sequel to the first section of *Little Women,* she was infuriated by the public demands for the expected romantic conclusion to the narrative. 'Girls write to ask who the little women marry, as if that was the only end and aim of a woman's life. I *won't* marry Jo to Laurie to please anyone,'[14] she declared passionately, almost wilfully providing her dynamic heroine with a deliberately anti-romantic lover, twice her age. Alcott's disaffection from the literary niche in which she found herself was profound, and despite the financial triumph of *Little Women,* she could not rekindle the sense of exhilaration she had experienced after her first appearances in print. *Little Women* ensured the family's economic security but it consigned Alcott to a career path which fractured her sense of artistic integrity as she became bitterly aware of the treadmill to which she had committed herself. In April 1869, just after the publication of *Little Women,* she confessed to her journal, 'Feel quite used up but the family seem so panic-stricken and helpless when I break down, that I try to keep the mill going.'[15] The frustration and self-division which Alcott personally experienced and which is a running theme throughout her personal writings,

her journal and her letters, surfaces most provocatively in her most famous work. As noted earlier, it is this refusal to be easily codified or to be reduced to any single or simple interpretation that forms a significant factor in understanding why *Little Women* has acquired its 'classic' status.

Alcott's four heroines, and in particular her self-portrait, Jo, the unruly second daughter of the March family, embody the anxieties of female adolescence and social insecurity at a time when such problems went formally unacknowledged. The March sisters span the ages from twelve to sixteen, the period of female puberty, each sister a discrete component in the exploration of the processes of women's acculturation. Amy, the youngest and the nearest to childhood, has apparently the simplest lessons to learn, those closest to the conventional moral tutelage of the time: the need to subdue vanity, to work in harmony with others and to control selfish impulses. The educational precepts that are exemplified through her story recur in more developed form with Meg, the daughter at the other end of the age spectrum, and the one who at the conclusion of *Little Women* has to embark on her own domestic career, the goal that implicitly she and the others are working towards in their preparation for adulthood. Although Marmee tells her two eldest daughters that it is better to ' "be happy old maids than unhappy wives, or unmaidenly girls, running about to find husbands"' (141), she also makes it plain that spinsterhood comes a poor second to the main purpose of a woman's life. '"To be loved and chosen by a good man is the best and sweetest thing which can happen to a woman" ' (40), she advises Meg and Jo in direct opposition to the author's privately declared opinions. It is this definitive statement of Marmee's which signposts most strikingly the critical contradictions of the text, for her injunction seems to undermine the novel's sympathetic identification with the issue of female independence and the importance of the creative life for women.

Despite Marmee's insistence on the passive roles that women must adopt as they wait for 'a good man', the March household, as it functions in the first significant section of *Little Women,* is presented as a self-contained and self-supporting female unit and all four daughters must address the need to earn their own living. Creativity, whether perceived as a conventionally feminine or as a transgressive act, is a central ingredient in the text's conceptualization of female autonomy. Each sister realizes her individuality through artistic self-expression: Meg's embroidery, Jo's writing, Beth's music and Amy's drawing and sculpture are not merely leisure pursuits for bourgeois young women who wish to occupy their time, but serious activities which double in providing vital imaginative sustenance and, in Meg's and Jo's case, a practical source of income. Marmee, as the focus and the guiding spirit of this all-female household, thus paradoxically encodes both the traditional values of domesticity *and* the more progressive move towards female self-sufficiency and individual fulfilment.

The contradictions are made more forcibly apparent with the portrayals of Beth and Jo, who are paired as twinned but antithetical extremes of the growth to womanhood. Beth, the third sister, although at one level seemingly a stereotype of female virtue, is also used by Alcott to address the complex issue of compatibility between image and reality. Conforming to the traditional iconography of the 'angel in the house', delicate, frequently compared to a rose, with large, soft eyes, self-effacing and tranquil, Beth must learn to overcome her natural timidity in order to achieve full social integration. Her blushing shyness and feminine modesty operate as both positive and negative attributes, for, while her fragility and gentleness encourage masculine protection (she is the automatic recipient of largesse from the Laurence menage), her failure to cope with external community structures results ultimately in her death. The spiritual perfection that she embodies, whilst offering an inspirational source of guidance to her sisters, is doomed in a world which demands that women must ultimately function outside the family which has nurtured them.

Beth's reluctance to integrate is complemented by Jo's boisterousness and sociability, qualities which she must learn to curb or at least channel into appropriate outlets. Jo's energy must be subdued because, as the book demonstrates, it can lead to moral unruliness: her inability to control her temper for instance results in an accident where Amy nearly drowns skating on thin ice. And her longings to chat with boys and men as equals carry dangerous overtones of sexual freedom: at the Gardiners' party, Meg has to restrain her sister from joining a group of 'half a dozen jovial lads [who] were talking about skates' (50), because of the impropriety involved.

At fifteen, Jo is the sister who most powerfully projects the physiological and psychological disturbances of adolescence, and for virtually all readers she is the character in whom the emotional substance of the novel is invested. Yet, as Anne Scott MacLeod has argued, Jo as a fictional creation merely extends the reality of the experience that many American girls encountered in their journey from girlhood to womanhood, when the childhood licence they had enjoyed was brought to an abrupt end by the realization that the time had come to embark on adulthood.[16] As noted in the introduction, the nineteenth-century American experience of growing up for girls was significantly different from the Victorian insistence on silence and inactivity that English middle-class children were expected to submit to, and this difference becomes apparent in the alternative scenarios that American and British authors contrive for their heroines. Even Ethel May in Yonge's

The Daisy Chain is allowed only a brief, temporary excursion into tomboyhood. The point is reinforced emphatically in *Little Women* in the scene when the free and easy demeanour of the March sisters is contrasted with the formality of Laurie's English visitors, whose reliance on rigid class division is seen as 'starched-up' and inhibiting. The inhibitions are not merely manifestations of outward codes of dress and behaviour but relate crucially to a revised ideology of girlhood that problematizes conventional notions of the feminine. "'Young ladies in America love independence as much as their ancestors did'" (193), says John Brooke in defence of Meg, with a consciousness of the separate origins of the two cultures that is implicit throughout the novel. It is this very sense of liberation, the 'psychic as well as physical freedom' as MacLeod notes,[17] that Jo March is so reluctant to relinquish as she moves inexorably towards the position of maturity that society demands of her.

In a cultural climate where, as Warner's *The Wide, Wide World* demonstrates, fictional literature for girls most frequently emphasized the growth of a perfectible moral sensibility and seemed to provide role models of femininity that could go unchallenged, Alcott broke with the prescriptive barriers of her age in order to articulate her own uncertainties about gender relations and the latent power structures of family life. As critics have pointed out,[18] such uncertainties were to a certain extent a reflection of the current debate about women's nature as well as symptomatic of nineteenth-century American economic concerns about the sexual division of labour. *Little Women* contributes in part to this debate by dramatizing the difficulties of establishing clear gendered identities in the pre-adult stage of development. Alcott's own upbringing had been highly unconventional, and *Little Women* as an autobiographical, if somewhat sanitised, text is based upon its author's own childhood experience of repression and a consciousness of difference in a family that was ostensibly progressive in its social and educational practice. As the second in a family of four girls, Louisa May Alcott was continually reprimanded by her father for her failure to live up to his ideal of the pattern of feminine behaviour, and in particular to be like her sisters, especially her older sister, Anna, who was mildmannered, docile and naturally home-loving. 'I don't care much for girls' things', she wrote pathetically in her diary in March 1846, at the age of thirteen, as she imagined her mind to be 'a room in confusion, and I was to put it in order',[19] a task at which she failed miserably.

Like her creator, Jo's inability to keep tidy exhibits itself most noticeably in her excess of physical energy, her body refusing to behave decorously, 'her long limbs . . . very much in her way' and 'a fly-away look to her clothes' (23). References to Jo's appearance characterize her resistance to conventional femininity, and the opening pages of *Little Women* portray her as a classic study in physical awkwardness, a 'colt', 'uncomfortable' with 'large hands and feet'. Jo is a character who is unwilling to acknowledge the changes that are taking place in her own body and who is reluctant to leave behind the androgynous world of childhood, where boys' games and wild energetic play are permissible pursuits for New England pre-adolescent girls. She is torn between the attractions of the female role, as represented by Marmee, and evident in her own spontaneous mothering of the sick Laurie (whose disorderly room she is able to transform with a few quick feminine touches) and her distaste for adult sexuality to which her adolescent awakenings uncomfortably alert her. She is shocked by the fact of Meg's romance with John Brooke and the physical intimacy she witnesses between them provokes in her a reaction of disgust. Similarly, despite the obvious mutual attraction between them, Jo is appalled by the suggestion that she and Laurie might become lovers.

This confusion about her own gendered identity is further illustrated in the hair-cutting episode, when she sells her long chestnut locks to a wig-maker as her contribution to the family finances. Proud of her independence and defiant about the social solecism she has committed by displaying herself with cropped hair, Jo is nonetheless deeply disturbed at the sacrifice of 'my one beauty', the symbol of her femininity. The incident is recounted in images of violence and mutilation. '"Didn't you feel dreadful when the first cut came?"' asks Meg, 'with a shiver', and Jo, despite her pose of indifference, is forced to confess that, '"It almost seemed as if I'd an arm or a leg off"' (223). Weeping in bed at night for the loss of her hair, she cannot understand the reason for her tears. The episode can be read in Freudian terms as a re-enactment of the experience of female castration. Jo's recognition of lack is commensurate with her loss of innocence and exposes her fear of initiation into adult sexuality, a fear that continues to be manifest throughout both *Little Women* and its sequel, *Good Wives*. There are also interesting autobiographical correspondences between the character's and the author's condition of deprivation. In 1862 when she was nursing at the military hospital in Georgetown, Alcott's own hair was shorn during her attack of typhoid. The projection of the experience in such graphic detail onto her fictional persona hints at the psychological damage inflicted by such an act and the anxieties that underlie the bravado which characterizes the tomboy awkwardness of both Jo and her creator. The scene suggests too the polarization within the text between a desire for independence and a need to express femininity, an opposition that Jo negotiates with only partial success.

A reading of the diary, which Alcott was encouraged to keep by her parents as a necessary adjunct to self-scrutiny and improvement, provides some insight into the context of Jo March's creation. Early entries in the diary suggest how the difficulties Alcott confronted as a child were internalized to produce a fraught individual whose only way of coming to terms with her own psychic tensions was to redraw their boundaries through artistic means. According to Bronson Alcott's interpretation of Puritan doctrine, with which his daughter was instilled, the rigid demarcation of gender characteristics made it impossible for her desire for action to be contained within the remit of condonable female behaviour. Her wish for masculinity became an imaginative and expressive retreat and her diary, reticent in style, indicates the close correlation between psychological and linguistic control. 'I long to be a man', wrote Alcott at the outbreak of the Civil War, while in 1865 she confessed dispiritedly that, 'I was born with a boy's spirit under my bib and tucker.'[20] Both statements are private but desperate testimonies to her discomfort with the straitjacket of adult female propriety, a dictate which was at odds with the passionate energies which she could only interpret as freakish and incompatible with womanhood.

It is a masculine discourse to which Alcott reverts in order to articulate Jo March's rejection of the feminine. From the opening chapter of the book, where she vigorously asserts that '"I like boys' games and work and manners! I can't get over my disappointment in not being a boy"' (22) and claims the right to be '"the man of the family now papa is away"' (24), Jo echoes Alcott's own strategies of evasion in her refusal to be formed into the mould of adulthood prepared for her. Whistling, sprawling, untidy, and full of ambitions that transcend her domestic destiny, Jo March reflects the self-assertion and the self-doubt that characterize adolescence in its search for an individual identity. Without clear examples of strong, independent women to follow, Jo, like her creator, is forced back on male role models for inspiration. As Elaine Showalter has observed, as girls, 'both Jo and Amy measure themselves continually against the most towering and unapproachable models of male genius: Shakespeare for Jo, Michelangelo for Amy.'[21] Lacking any comparable female sources of inspiration outside the home (Aunt March provides only a negative image of singleness, as a woman who has repressed her capacity for love), they turn to the male fields of action and achievement for stimulus, and in measuring themselves against inappropriate standards of excellence, become conscious only of their own inadequacy. Personal and artistic creativity in *Little Women* is thus without any appropriate female yardstick and the debate about woman's nature which Jo enacts is extended through the discussion of her artistic practice which forms a complement to her self.

The division that manifests itself in *Little Women* and in the Gothic tales of power, revenge and dark desire that Alcott wrote effortlessly for contemporary magazines is indicative of her personal experience of re-

pression, an experience that speaks tellingly to her female audience. Both Jo's literary productions, and the
roles she creates for herself in the family's amateur theatricals, suggest subversive tendencies and the need to
enact fantasies of power. In the plays the children perform and in male disguise, Jo can release the aggressive
impulses that would otherwise be unacceptable. In a
perfect illustration of the personality split she embodies,
she can cast herself as both hero and villain simultaneously, taking on adventurous and romantic parts in
her home-made dramas, while her alternative persona
engages in deeds of murder and violence.

The same fantasies of the forbidden are projected in
her commercial literary life, where, like her progenitor, Jo writes sensational thrillers of madness, eroticism, death and despair, subjects of which she is taught
to be ashamed, her very knowledge of them reprehen-
sible because it encourages her to 'desecrate some of
the womanliest attributes of a woman's character'.
'"They are trash, and will soon be worse than trash if
I go on; for each is more sensational than the last"', Jo
is forced to acknowledge, looking at her stories in a
bitter moment of self-assessment, when Professor Bhaer
has shown her the error of her ways with his 'mental
or moral spectacles'. '"I can't read this stuff in sober
earnest without being horribly ashamed of it; and what
should I do if they were seen at home?"'[22] In *Little
Women,* the tension between masculine precepts of
morality that determine behavioural codes, and female
imaginative energy and expressive resources creates a
problem for the woman artist that can only be resolved
through compromise. Literary creation is Jo's only outlet for the passionate and rebellious elements in her
nature, and while the writing of thrillers is seen as
acceptable as a stage in adolescent development, or a
genre that is appropriate for men rather than women,
once Jo approaches adulthood she must cast aside such
delinquent tendencies. As Marmee makes abundantly
clear, the subversive impulses that Jo satisfies through
her writing are incompatible with the contemporary
versions of selfhood for women, where anger must be
kept hidden and a silent conformism cultivated.

For, as Mrs March admits, the image of unruffled saint-
liness that she presents to the world is an illusion, and
one acquired with the help of her husband's insistence
on female self-control:

> "I am angry nearly every day of my life, Jo; but I
> have learned not to show it; and I still hope to learn
> not to feel it, though it may take me another forty
> years to do so." (118)

The model that Jo March yearns to emulate is thus
closer to her own nature than she at first realizes, and
as a source of inspiration consequently more powerful.
In Jo's ultimate union with Professor Bhaer she, like
her mother, exchanges her father's moral instruction

for that of her husband, unable to function independently in a patriarchal world without the guidance of a
male authority figure.

Little Women then maintains an uneasy equilibrium
between the fantasies of rebellion it dramatizes and
the moral message it claims to promote. Whilst on
the one hand it endorses Jo March's defiance of the
womanly, and invites support for a reinterpretation
of women's roles generally, it also reinscribes the
traditional myths of femininity in its valuation of the
ideals erected by the patriarchal order: motherhood,
marriage and the values of home. The uneasiness
which exists between Alcott's own deeply felt feminism and the conventional models of family which
the text promotes thus reflects the contemporary political and cultural debates of midcentury American
society. The progressive theories about women's nature and the move towards political emancipation
contend with economic requirements which rely on
the maintenance of a strict sexual division of labour,
the production of children and the consequent centrality of the domestic role for women.

In the March household which acts as the magnetic
power centre of *Little Women* the concept of woman-
liness is explored in ways which only serve to perpetuate the ambivalence that marks the novel as a whole.
The home, with Marmee as its symbolic centre, functions as a matriarchy within the overriding patriarchal
system. As such it facilitates an examination of female
strength and the mutual support network that women
are seen to construct but without finally allowing that
strength any political influence. During the first part of
the narrative Mr March is conveniently absent from
home, his shadowy but prevailing presence making its
impact through the medium of his letters and through
the moral legacy he has left behind which continues to
direct the women's behaviour. Even after his return, he
remains a vague figure, officiating at Meg's wedding
and providing fatherly advice when necessary, but
barely registering as a character on the reader's sensibilities.

By removing Mr. March as a major focus of interest from
Little Women, the novel limits the possibilities of marital
discord and parental tyranny in its analysis of the power
structures of family life. Any acknowledgement of the
existence of potential tensions between husband and wife
is reserved for the depiction of Meg's marriage to John
Brooke where it can be presented as suitably educative.
As well as underplaying family difficulties that its author
found particularly painful to confront, the novel develops
a strategy which left Alcott free to focus her domestic
history on mother/daughter relationships and on the
interactions of sisters, relationships which had more
positive significance for her than the failures in marital
harmony to which she had personally been witness. As
Nina Auerbach has argued,[23] Mr. March's removal from

the main action of *Little Women* results in a celebration of the primacy of the female family and in turn this foregrounds the special qualities of womanhood which male outsiders, such as Laurie and Professor Bhaer covet. The women's close knit and self-sufficient society is presented as culturally and psychologically necessary both for the girls whose identity it shapes and for the men for whom it provides the elements that are missing in their otherwise sterile lives. Laurie, the isolated boy next door, gazing wistfully through the window at the illuminated tableau of women, in what Auerbach has pointed to as a reverse of the fictive norm, can only long for entry into the privileged feminine world, with its symbolic referents of flowers, light and fire, the magic circle of women representing the family support network which he has been denied. Similarly Jo, despite her impulses towards independent action and the freedom of masculine role-play, finds solace and sustenance through her identification with Marmee as mother figure, the prime source of nurturing and psychological protection.

To some extent the debate about female values which *Little Women* enacts reiterates the Victorian intellectual dilemma of 'the woman question', the quandary as to whether women were capable of functioning independently, equal to and competing with men, or whether their strengths were something other, a natural complement to masculine qualities. In *Little Women,* Jo and Marmee posit two extremes of the ideological spectrum, through Jo's self-assertiveness and her transgression of gender boundaries, and through Marmee's undeviating adherence to the iconization of womanhood. Ultimately, because Jo is in a transitional stage of development and irresistibly bound by the psychological ties of family (and because Alcott was sensitive to the responsibilities of her position as children's author and driven by the need to find success in the market place), she does conform to Marmee's strictures, but not before her challenge to that behavioural model has been made the imaginative heart of the novel. At the same time, the identification between mother and daughter is emphasized so as to highlight the inner conflicts surrounding female development in a society which harboured profound contradictions in its teachings. Marmee's confession to Jo of her own feelings of rage and her efforts at self-control bring the two women together, and Jo's aspirations for self-assertion are tempered by her wish to emulate the role model her mother provides her with. Jo's confusion has its source in this psychic split between 'masculine' and 'feminine' norms, a split that her mother too has experienced in a revealing insight into generational patterning. The two warring impulses, between the aggressive independent self and the mothering instinct, are perceived as irreconcilable in the contemporary culture that Alcott depicts. Marmee's role and Jo's eventual decision to adopt a version of it is, however, at one level fully satisfying, for it allows Jo to remain

in the childish state she does not want to relinquish, finding approval by being seen to adhere to her parents' criteria.

As in a number of more conventional texts of the period, motherhood remains a sanctified institution in *Little Women,* and the values of family that Alcott presents as irresistible ultimately reinforce the return to the conservative model as propounded by Bronson Alcott and which in its denial of women's individuality informed his daughter's upbringing. Recent feminist psychoanalytic theory, in its deconstruction of Freudian models of infant development, has emphasized the centrality of the mother both in psychological and in cultural terms. As Ann B. Murphy has argued, the mother is seen:

> not as scapegoat or saviour, but as the primary, if inadvertent, enforcer of patriarchal values as well as their victim, and thus as fulcrum of the private and public. . . . The institution of motherhood in a patriarchal culture achieves not only the reproduction of mothering but the perpetuation of patriarchy.[24]

Aware of the importance of women's work within the home and the essential psychological framework that the family creates, Alcott's investigation of female identity formation and family structures in *Little Women* can find no practical solution to Jo's problem in the prevailing ideological and literary climate.

In its concentration on women's culture and its values, *Little Women* stresses the significance of sisterhood and female bonding in a male world that is cold, commercially oriented and ignorant of female value systems. An example of an unmediated patriarchy is to be found in the Laurence household with its luxurious environment and its prioritization of individual achievement, a household which is inhabited by men who are unable to communicate their deepest feelings to one another. Old Mr. Laurence, after the death of his daughter, retreats into himself and becomes a crabby, quicktempered old man, while his grandson, Laurie is, at the beginning of *Little Women,* an emotionally repressed adolescent, hungry for tenderness and expressions of love. In contrast, the relationships between the sisters, although not without occasional disagreements and jealousies, are intimate and mutually supportive. Through Marmee's inspirational presence, the March women are seen to have a transforming effect on the lifeless palace of the Laurences, constructing a sleeping beauty myth in reverse as they reinvigorate the dormant male emotional territory.

In contrast to the isolated male establishment next door, the female community, materially poor but spiritually wealthy, is grounded on principles of sharing, mutual support, self-sacrifice and generosity. The first actions in which the little women engage are those of self-denial and communal charity, banishing thoughts of personal Christmas presents, preparing the parlour to welcome Marmee home from work, and, on Christmas morning, giving up their breakfast to help a poor family in need. The sisters' interdependence is constantly emphasized, and the dangers of uncaring individualism are made apparent in the episode where the girls are too absorbed in their own activities to notice Beth's plea for help in visiting the suffering Hummel family. Their indifference results in Beth's attack of scarlet fever, which is caught from the Hummels, and which proves almost fatal (an incident which also suggests Alcott's acquiescence in contemporary literary forces and their moral lessons). From Laurie's perspective, the March sisters continually form a composite, symbolic portrait of womanhood, a work of art in which each girl takes her place in the collective illustration of femininity: whether they be gathered around the parlour fire, or setting out on a picnic, each girl has her allocated task. The sisters' individual identities are thus succoured by the communal experience, which they carry with them to the male world of rationalism and paternal authority, a world which, apart from Beth, they must learn to negotiate to their advantage.

In what could be interpreted as a return to a dangerously essentialist view of gender, *Little Women* ascribes domestic skills to women only: even Jo can exercise a positive feminizing influence on Laurie, and, later, on Professor Bhaer, tidying Laurie's sickroom and helping Professor Bhaer sew on buttons and darn socks, tasks at which he proves to be incompetent. Despite the fantasies of independence that the novel licenses, self-assertion ultimately cannot prosper. The disasters of Jo's dinner party where the oven won't light, the bread burns and she serves strawberries with salt instead of sugar form a salutary lesson on the organizational and cooperative skills necessary for a smooth domestic life. The promise of an autonomous childhood world which *Little Women* offers its readers is an illusion which fails to materialize in the practical domestic environment in which girls are inevitably positioned. Marmee in *Little Women* consequently becomes a model of practical as well as symbolic maternity, capable in the domestic sphere, charitable in her deeds outside the home, the repository of wisdom and tact. In the examination of the development of female identity which the novel conducts, Marmee is invested with the primary twin functions of psychological prop and cultural role model for her daughters. Perfect because she has contained and controlled her impulse for autonomous life, she is thus created as the emblematic centre of the multi-dimensional metaphor of home.

In contrast to this dramatization of female strength, Alcott's men form a revealing, if separate, study in gender relations. Neither in *Little Women* nor in her other domestic fictions does Alcott portray men as virile or exhibiting traditional attributes of masculinity. Their power is either economic, as in the character of Mr Laurence, or moral, as in the conception of Mr March and Professor Bhaer. Even Laurie, the most dynamic male figure in *Little Women* and the potential romantic lead, is described from Jo's perspective as atypically masculine. Indeed he is compared with Jo herself, an indeterminately gendered figure:

> 'curly hair; brown skin; big, black eyes; handsome nose, fine teeth, small hands and feet; taller than I am, very polite for a boy.' (54)

His features effectively combine the exotic and the delicate. As Madeleine Stern has pointed out, this description itself is a modification of the original version of the manuscript where Laurie is not 'taller than' but the same height as Jo and suggestions of his effeminacy are more pronounced.[25] And although, as a boy, Laurie can get into scrapes and display a natural physical athleticism, this is always tempered by a sensitivity and a yearning to be loved as he seeks the girls' company. In what most readers find a disappointingly inadequate alternative to Laurie's vitality and charm, Professor Bhaer, Jo's ultimate lover and husband, lacks any suggestion of sexual dynamism. A deliberately anti-heroic character, he is introduced through a series of negative characteristics, being 'neither rich nor great, young nor handsome, in no way what is called fascinating, imposing or brilliant.'[26] His redeeming personality traits are benevolence, wisdom and an unerring moral sensibility, all qualities which Jo can respect intellectually, but, more significantly, which can provide her with a moral touchstone in her own dealings. Her difficulties in coming to terms with her sexual identity are resolved in fictional terms as Professor Bhaer becomes a fathersubstitute for a woman whose reluctance to mature can it seems only be satisfied through alliance with a paternal surrogate.

Little Women forms a fascinating study of gender politics in a society which established strict guidelines for women's roles in the domestic sphere. Although the novel formally accedes to these conventional guidelines, for reasons that are complex both professionally and personally on Alcott's part, it also projects a profound mistrust of the principles and practices that confined women to roles of wives and mothers and that led to the apotheosis of femininity as a cultural icon. Through the story of Jo March and her fraught adolescence, Alcott suggests the complexities that underlie essentialist concepts of definitive gendered identity, and the consequent difficulties which girls experienced in their attempt to conform to clear-cut behavioural models. In addition, the admitted autobiographical correspondences between Jo and Alcott reflect the discordance of the woman artist with her society and the pressures on her to conform to public requirements in her choice of genre and subject matter. Jo's move from sensational to realistic fiction does not merely replicate Alcott's own career change. It also has important implications for thinking about **Little Women** as a response to the demands from a male publisher for books for girls which perpetuate the prevailing ideology that would continue to dictate their artistic and behavioural limits.

Notes

[1] Elaine Showalter, *Sister's Choice: Tradition and Change in American Women's Writing,* (Oxford: Clarendon Press, 1989), p. 42.

[2] Quoted in Ann B. Murphy, 'The Borders of Ethical, Erotic and Artistic Possibilities in *Little Women',* *Signs: Journal of Women in Culture and Society,* vol. 14 (3), Spring 1990, p. 564.

[3] Catherine R. Stimpson, 'Reading for Love: Canons, Paracanons and Whistling Jo March', *New Literary History,* 21, 1990, p. 958.

[4] Stimpson, p. 967.

[5] Reported in *The Guardian,* 7 January 1993.

[6] Stimpson, p. 970.

[7] Murphy, p. 564.

[8] Louisa May Alcott, *Life, Letters and Journals,* ed. Ednah D. Cheyney (London: Sampson, Low, Marston; Searle & Rivington, 1889).

[9] Ruth K. MacDonald, *Louisa May Alcott* (Boston: Twayne, 1983), p.15.

[10] Cheyney, p.199.

[11] Louisa May Alcott, *Little Women* (London: Puffin Books, 1953), p.231. All subsequent references are to this edition and will be included in the text.

[12] Louisa May Alcott, *Good Wives,* (London and Glasgow: Blackie, n.d.), p.136.

[13] Stimpson, p.967.

[14] *Life, Letters and Journals,* p.201.

[15] Ibid., p.202.

[16] Anne Scott McLeod, 'The Caddie Woodlawn Syndrome: American Girlhood in the Nineteenth Century', *A Century of Childhood 1820-1920,* ed. Mary Lynn Steven Heininger, (Rochester, NY: Margaret Woodbury Strong Museum, 1984), pp.98-119.

[17] McLeod, p.104.

[18] See particularly Sarah Elbert, *A Hunger for Home: Louisa May Alcott's Place in American Culture* (New York: Rutgers University Press, 1987) for a full discussion of this issue.

[19] *Life, Letters and Journals,* p.48.

[20] Ibid., p.127.

[21] Showalter, op.cit., p.58.

[22] *Good Wives,* p.136.

[23] Nina Auerbach, *Communities of Women: An Idea in Fiction* (Cambridge, Mass: Harvard University Press, 1978).

[24] Murphy, p.574.

[25] Madeleine B. Stern, *Louisa May Alcott* (University of Oklahoma Press, 1971), quoted in Showalter, p.56.

[26] *Good Wives,* p.137.

FURTHER READING

Delamar, Gloria T. *Louisa May Alcott and "Little Women": Biography, Critique, Publications, Poems, Songs and Contemporary Relevance.* London: McFarland and Co., 1990, 350 p.

> As its title suggests, this source is more than biographical. Delamar creatively draws from diverse evidence to illuminate Alcott's life and influence.

Fetterley, Judith. "*Little Women:* Alcott's Civil War." *Feminist Studies* 5.2 (1979): 369-83.

> Fetterley argues that Alcott's novel has tiered messages: one, which reflects the views of male-dominated culture, encouraging women to marry, work domestically, and not complain; the other, a subversive undermining of such views.

Grasso, Linda. "Louisa May Alcott's 'Magic Inkstand': Little Women, Feminism, and the Myth of Regeneration." *Frontiers: A Journal of Women's Studies* 19.1 (1998): 177-92.

> Contrasts Gillian Armstrong's 1995 film adaptation of *Little Women* with Alcott's novel, arguing that Hollywood romanticizes the past in order to mask the harsh reality of women's experience in the nineteenth century.

Kerber, Linda K. "Can a Woman Be an Individual? The Limits of Puritan Tradition in the Early Republic" *Texas Studies in Literature and Languages* 25.1 (1983): 165-78.

> Kerber explores the possibility that Alcott and her characters struggle not only with the social limitations

of femaleness, but from the legacy of guilt and repression inherent in the Puritan tradition.

Keyser, Elizabeth Lennox. *Whispers in the Dark: The Fiction of Louisa May Alcott.* Knoxville: University of Tennessee Press, 1993, 228 p.

Keyser suggests that Alcott's work is not radically subversive, but it "enables a critique of the exemplars" of repressive womanhood.

Meigs, Cornelia. *Invincible Louisa.* Boston: Little, Brown, and Co., 1933, 260 p.

As an early biography of Alcott, this source provides an example of early literary study, which, as many critics have pointed out, has been somewhat sentimental in Alcott's case.

Pauly, Thomas H. "*Ragged Dick* and *Little Women:* Idealized Homes and Unwanted Marriages." *Journal of Popular Culture* 9 (1975): 583-92.

Pauly places *Little Women* in the context of early children's literature, which was meant to morally instruct and socially mold young people, but he argues that Alcott tended to subvert these purposes.

Shealy, Daniel. "'Families Are the Most Beautiful Things': The Myths and Facts of Louisa Alcott's March Family in *Little Women.*" *The Child and the Family: Selected Papers from the 1988 International Conference of the Children's Literature Association, 19-22 May, 1988,* 86 p.

Shealy provides background information for Alcott's creation of *Little Women,* focusing on the influence of earlier works and identifying real persons said to inspire Alcott's characters.

Showalter, Elaine. "*Little Women:* the American Female Myth." *Sister's Choice: Tradition and Change in American Women's Writing.* Oxford: Clarendon Press, 1991. 42-64.

Showalter provides an overview of critical responses to *Little Women,* casting the novel as central to feminist myth in America and abroad.

Stern, Madeleine B., ed. *Critical Essays on Louisa May Alcott.* Boston: G. K. Hall and Co., 1984, 295 p.

Stern has compiled a comprehensive collection of reviews on Alcott's larger works from the time of their publication to the 1980s. Useful for reception studies and historical contextualization.

Additional coverage of Alcott's life and works can be found in the following sources published by the Gale Group: *Children's Literature Review,* **Vols. 1 and 38;** *Dictionary of Literary Biography,* **Vols. 1, 42, and 79;** *Short Story Criticism,* **Vol. 27;** *Something about the Author,* **Vol. 100; and** *World Literature Criticism, 1500 to the Present.*

Horatio Alger, Jr.

1832-1899

(Also wrote under the pseudonyms of Arthur Lee Putnam, Arthur Hamilton, and Julian Starr). American novelist, biographer, short story writer, poet, and essayist.

For additional information on the life and career of Alger, see *NCLC,* Volume 8.

INTRODUCTION

Alger was one of the most widely-read authors of juvenile fiction in the United States during the late nineteenth and early twentieth centuries. He wrote more than a hundred books, all based on the principle that honesty, perseverance, and industry are certain to be rewarded. Almost invariably, his novels described a virtuous boy's rise from poverty to prosperity. In an era of rapid industrial growth when many Americans were accumulating vast personal fortunes, Alger captured the imaginations of millions of young readers and underscored the ideals and aspirations of a changing American society. Alger's works lost their relevance and popularity during the twentieth century, but they have been regarded by historians and popular culturalists since the 1970s as definitive American mythology. Alger did not invent the "rags-to-riches" formula for fiction, but he is often credited with popularizing it. Although Alger's stories are generally considered devoid of literary merit, he is of historical interest to the student of American culture since, as the critic Rychard Fink expressed it: "It is dangerous to ignore a man whose ideas hang on so stubbornly."

Biographical Information

Born in Revere, Massachusetts, Alger was the oldest child of a Unitarian preacher and his wife. When he was twelve, the family moved to Marlborough, Massachusetts, where he attended Gates Academy in preparation for admission to Harvard College. In 1853, after his graduation from Harvard, Alger entered Cambridge Divinity School but withdrew shortly afterwards in order to become an assistant editor for the *Boston Daily Advertiser.* He held this post until the spring of 1854, when he was hired to teach at a boarding school in East Greenwich, Rhode Island. After briefly serving as the principal of a boys' academy in Deerfield, Massachusetts, Alger reentered Cambridge Divinity School and was ordained a minister in 1861.

Little is known of Alger's personal life. Prior to 1961, his only biographer was Herbert R. Mayes, who issued *Alger: A Biography without a Hero* in 1928. A fictitious account of Alger's life based on a diary and letters that never existed, Mayes's biography was accepted as authoritative by the majority of Alger's critics for nearly forty years and is quoted as a reliable source in most reference texts. Almost all of the criticism of Alger's works written since 1928 relies to some degree on this fabrication, which was made partly plausible by a thread of biographical fact and a detailed listing of Alger's works, some of which Mayes invented. Mayes portrayed Alger as the repressed child of a stern Unitarian preacher who insisted on training his son for the ministry almost from birth. After graduating from divinity school, Mayes wrote, Alger rebelled against his father by fleeing to Paris, where he engaged in a series of ill-fated romances. According to Mayes, Alger returned to the United States to write a "great novel" for an adult audience but succeeded only in producing an endless stream of stories for juveniles. The irony of Alger's life, Mayes concluded, was that the creator of the "rags-to-riches" myth died a frustrated and impoverished man. The first major attempt to discredit Mayes's biography, Frank Gruber's *Horatio Alger, Jr.: A Biography and Bibliography,* was published in 1961. In 1964, Ralph D. Gardner published his *Horatio Alger, or the American Hero Era,* another study devoted to dispelling the misconceptions about Alger's life generated by Mayes. Yet it was not until 1972 that Mayes first admitted that his biography "literally swarms . . . with countless absurdities." Since Mayes's admission, several critics, most notably Jack Bales and Gary Scharnhorst, have documented the hoax.

Major Works

During several years of irregular employment, Alger contributed essays, poems, and short stories to a variety of magazines and newspapers. His earliest literary efforts were directed toward adults; it was not until 1864 that he published his first novel for juveniles, *Frank's Campaign; or, What Boys Can Do on the Farm for the Camp.* In 1866, encouraged by the favorable reception of *Frank's Campaign* and its sequel, *Paul Prescott's Charge,* Alger resigned from his ministerial position at the Unitarian Church in Brewster, Massachusetts, and moved to New York City, where he devoted himself to writing. The following year, his most successful novel, *Ragged Dick; or, Street Life in New York with the Boot-Blacks,* was serialized in the children's magazine *Student and Schoolmate.* The hero of the story, Dick Hunter, is a New York City bootblack who, by a combination of luck, pluck, hard work, thrift, and piety, gains the opportunity to become a respected and influential member of society. Alger followed the pattern set in *Ragged Dick* with little variation in a steady succession of enormously popular novels, including the *Tattered Tom* and *Luck and Pluck* series, sales of which almost equaled those of the *Ragged Dick* books. In addition, Alger composed several biographies of self-made statesmen, among them *From Canal Boy to President; or, The Boyhood and Manhood of James A. Garfield,* and *Abraham Lincoln, the Backwoods Boy; or, How a Young Rail-Splitter Became President.* Most of his novels are set in New York City during the latter half of the nineteenth century, and critics praise his accurate descriptions of the city's streets, boarding houses, hotels, and restaurants. Alger gathered much of the information for his stories from conversations with young boys who lived in the Newsboys' Lodging House, a philanthropic institution in New York City with which he was closely connected until his death.

Critical Reception

Alger's novels reached the height of their popularity during the decade following his death. As economic opportunities in American cities narrowed during the 1920s and 1930s, the books began to lose their credibility and appeal. There was little scholarly interest in Alger's works until the publication in 1945 of *Struggling Upward, and Other Works,* a reprinting of *Ragged Dick,* and *Struggling Upward.* Most commentators share Richard Wright's opinion that Alger "was, is and will forever be the most terribly bad of writers," and his stories are consistently denounced for their stock characterization, repetitive plots, and stilted dialogue. Alger's historical and cultural significance is still debated. In the 1940s and 1950s, he was generally viewed as an apologist for business success, a man who applied the Protestant ethic to the urban world of the Gilded Age. Van Wyck Brooks faulted him for vulgarizing Ralph Waldo Emerson's doctrine of self-reliance by writing about boys whose motive was self-advancement instead of self-improvement. Russel Crouse, Kenneth S. Lynn, and Wright emphasized the monetary value which Alger placed on the virtues of hard work, thrift, and obedience and interpreted his heroes as would-be captains of industry who exploit every opportunity to succeed financially. Since the 1960s, Alger's role as a propagandist of capitalism has been repeatedly challenged and it is frequently argued that his stories do not sustain the "rags-to-riches" myth with which his name has become synonymous. John G. Cawelti, Michael Zuckerman, and Frank Shuffleton maintain that Alger was not an exponent of entrepreneurial individualism, because his typical hero's success is largely due to a chance encounter with a benevolent patron. They also point out that Alger's heroes aspire to middle-class respectability rather than wealth. Scharnhorst contends that Alger was primarily a moralist who hoped to imitate on a juvenile level the novels of Charles Dickens, which helped to expose social injustices in England. Critics often note, however, that *Phil, the Fiddler,* which called attention to the *padrone* system, by which young street musicians were brought to New York from Italy and kept as virtual slaves, was the only Alger novel that contributed to social reform.

Speculation often centers on Alger's move from the ministry in Brewster to writing in New York, which Mayes explained as Alger's rebellion against his father and the church. Scharnhorst, Alan Trachtenberg, and Michael Moon have suggested that, in fact, the move was prompted by a scandal in which Alger was accused of making "unnatural" advances towards boys in his congregation. This evidence has brought a new twist to Alger criticism in the 1980s and 1990s, which sometimes focuses on the homoeroticism of his works. At the same time, scholars like Carol Nackenoff draw attention away from exploring Alger's personal motives by encouraging a more historical understanding of the social contexts he represented.

Critics have offered varying explanations for Alger's apparent transformation in the middle of the twentieth century from a minor writer of popular children's stories into a prophet of business enterprise. Some commentators argue that after the Depression, Alger made a convenient scapegoat for the evils of unrestrained capitalism. Others contend that Mayes, who stated in his biography of Alger that all his heroes "started poor and ended up well-to-do," was instrumental in creating the Alger legend. While today it is generally agreed that the fictional hero created by Horatio Alger does not embody the myth that has been ascribed to him, Alger remains significant as a cultural and historical phenomenon.

---

*PRINCIPAL WORKS

Bertha's Christmas Vision (short stories and poetry) 1856

Frank's Campaign; or, What Boys Can Do on the Farm for the Camp (novel) 1864

Paul Prescott's Charge (novel) 1865

Fame and Fortune; or, The Progress of Richard Hunter (novel) 1868

Ragged Dick; or, Street Life in New York with the Boot-Blacks (novel) 1868

Luck and Pluck; or, John Oakley's Inheritance (novel) 1869

Mark, the Match Boy; or, Richard Hunter's Ward (novel) 1869

Rough and Ready; or, Life among the New York Newsboys (novel) 1869

Ben, the Luggage Boy; or, Among the Wharves (novel) 1870

Rufus and Rose; or, The Fortunes of Rough and Ready (novel) 1870

Sink or Swim; or, Harry Raymond's Resolve (novel) 1870

Paul the Peddler; or, The Adventures of a Young Street Merchant (novel) 1871

Strong and Steady; or, Paddle Your Own Canoe (novel) 1871

Tattered Tom; or, The Story of a Street Arab (novel) 1871

Phil, the Fiddler; or, The Story of a Young Street Musician (novel) 1872

Slow and Sure; or, From the Street to the Shop (novel) 1872

Strive and Succeed; or, The Progress of Walter Conrad (novel) 1872

Bound to Rise; or, Harry Walton's Motto (novel) 1873

Try and Trust; or, The Story of a Bound Boy (novel) 1873

Brave and Bold; or, The Fortunes of a Factory Boy (novel) 1874

Julius; or, The Street Boy Out West (novel) 1874

Risen from the Ranks; or, Harry Walton's Success (novel) 1874

Grand'ther Baldwin's Thanksgiving, with Other Ballads and Poems (ballads and poetry) 1875

Herbert Carter's Legacy; or, The Inventor's Son (novel) 1875

Sam's Chance; and How He Improved It (novel) 1876

Shifting for Himself; or, Gilbert Greyson's Fortunes (novel) 1876

The Western Boy; or, The Road to Success (novel) 1878; also published as *Tom, the Bootblack; or, The Road to Success*, 1880

The Young Adventurer; or, Tom's Trip across the Plains (novel) 1878

From Canal Boy to President; or, The Boyhood and Manhood of James A. Garfield (biography) 1881

Abraham Lincoln, the Backwoods Boy; or How a Young Rail-Splitter Became President (biography) 1883; also published as *The Backwoods Boy; or, The Boyhood and Manhood of Abraham Lincoln*, 1883

Do and Dare; or, A Brave Boy's Fight for Fortune (novel) 1884

Hector's Inheritance; or, The Boys of Smith Institute (novel) 1885

Bob Burton; or, The Young Ranchman of the Missouri (novel) 1888

The Erie Train Boy (novel) 1890

Five Hundred Dollars' or, Jacob Marlowe's Secret (novel) 1890; also published as *The Five Hundred Dollar Check*, 1891

Struggling Upward; or, Luke Larkin's Luck (novel) 1890

Facing the World; or, The Haps and Mishaps of Harry Vane (novel) 1893

In a New World; or Among the Gold-Fields of Australia (novel) 1893

Victor Vane, the Young Secretary (novel) 1894

The Young Salesman (novel) 1896

Frank and Fearless; or, The Fortunes of Jasper Kent (novel) 1897

Walter Sherwood's Probation (novel) 1897

The Young Bank Messenger (novel) 1898; also published as *A Cousin's Conspiracy*, date unknown

Jed, the Poorhouse Boy (novel) 1899

Adrift in New York; or Tom and Florence Braving the World (novel) 1904

Struggling Upward, and Other Works (novels) 1945

Alger Street: The Poetry of Horatio Alger, Jr. (poetry) 1964

*Many of Alger's works were originally published in periodicals.

CRITICISM

Bruce E. Coad (essay date 1972)

SOURCE: "The Alger Hero," in *Heroes of Popular Culture*, edited by Ray B. Browne, Marshall Fishwick, and Michael T. Marsden, Bowling Green University Press, 1972, pp. 42-51.

[*In the following essay, Coad argues that though Horatio Alger's work has been relatively neglected by scholars, Alger's ideals are still reflected in America's materialistic culture.*]

Hidden on one of the inside pages of a recent edition of *The New York Times* was a small article announcing the recipients of the Annual Horatio Alger Awards, an event that has been going on for some years now.[1] Certainly few people would dispute that the day has passed when simple country boys can become sole owners of large enterprises merely by climbing through the ranks from errand-boy to president. And contemporary sociologists, supported by much impressive statistical data, have been quick to point out that the majority of successful businessmen do not, and never did, struggle to the top solely by way of their own "pluck" and industry. Yet, even though it is no longer front-page news, a remnant of that era when the Carnegies, Rockefellers, and Vanderbilts were held up as national heroes who pulled themselves up by their bootstraps continued to cling to its place in the minds of many Americans.

The fact is that social engineering has largely replaced pioneering and profiteering as fertile ground for prospective national heroes—the Kennedys, Dr. King, and Malcolm X being examples that most easily come to mind; nonetheless, when the media refer to a "typical Alger hero," one can still consistently anticipate a formula-like report on the uniquely American phenomenon of successful businessmen whose careers, as the Horatio Alger Awards Committee puts it, "typify the results of individual initiative, hard work, honesty, and adherence to the traditional ideals, . . . who by their own efforts had pulled themselves up by their bootstraps in the American tradition."[2] Whether or not today's reader finds any degree of reality in such accounts, or whether he even has seen an Alger book, the rags-to-riches formula has clearly taken on mythic proportions in the past decades and has made "Alger hero" an American cliche.

With rare exceptions though, twentieth century literary critics have not considered Alger's fiction important enough to demand their serious attention. They not only have overlooked the possibility that he may be the most widely read author in American literature,[3] but with the exception of several recent studies largely concerned with disputing the accuracy of the three or four Alger biographies,[4] critics have singularly ignored the real message that Alger indefatigably portrayed for his young readers. Doubtless, Alger must be called extraliterary and "popular"—always for most "respectable" critics a pejorative term. Nor is it possible to argue that he is not a very minor influence in American literature; however, he still appears to hold a durable, if unexamined, position as a major influence in American folk ideals, thus suggesting that perhaps some critics and historians have unwisely neglected the substance of his fiction.

Despite this dearth of "respectable" scholarly interest, the Alger hero is decidedly still with us, if a bit tarnished and misunderstood. One has only to recall, for instance, the recent national interest in Texas billionaire, H. Ross Perot (would that the "H" have stood for "Horatio!"). Mr. Perot, who started seven years ago to develop a computer software company on an initial investment of $1000, has emerged today as one of the world's wealthiest men.[5] Curiously though, the national attention given to this latest "contemporary Luke Larkin" cannot in fact be attributed to his financial accomplishments, incredible as they might seem. Rather, in much of the newspaper and broadcast journalism that has discussed Mr. Perot's sudden-found prominence there was a consistent emphasis on his humanitarian exploits, e.g., his attempts to deliver mail and supplies to American prisoners in North Vietnam or his financial grants to experimental schools in Dallas, Texas.[6] Further, this same emphasis on the heroic nature in social responsibility was clearly apparent when in 1970 Mayor Carl Stokes of Cleveland, Senator Hiram Fong of Hawaii, and former governor Luther Hodges of North Carolina were selected to join such earlier recipients of the Horatio Alger Awards as Dwight D. Eisenhower, Ralph Bunche, Herbert Hoover, and Bob Hope.[7] It is implicit, then, that what is expected of the contemporary "typical Alger hero" is something more than a talent for piling up huge sums of money. He must reveal a new role: an acceptance of public responsibility far beyond making a profit. In the past one gained the status of "Alger hero" by working hard and maximizing profits. Now he cannot gain such a distinction without becoming deeply involved in furthering the aspirations of his fellow Americans.

Lest the confusion about the Luke Larkins and Herbert Carters be further compounded (indeed, more than a few of my students thought "Horatio Alger" was the name given to the young hero in the stories), it seems necessary to reassess (not debunk) the motives of those original characters, who in the process of becoming the most articulated element in the larger American dream of success, have lost a certain amount of their authenticity and are today being exalted for deeds they rarely performed.

A close reading of virtually any Alger novel would substantiate the claim that the humanitarian interests so prominent, for example, in Mr. Perot's activities were simply nonexistent in the original Alger version. On the contrary, in such novels as *Grit, The Young Boatman, Chester Rand;* or *A New Path to*

Fortune, Try and Trust, and others, Alger reflects an almost obsessive predilection for money-making. And even though this observation has been made many times before, what seems to have been forgotten is that seldom does "our young hero" attempt to remedy social problems or improve the quality of life for anyone but himself (admittedly, these young men eventually manage to assume the overdue payments on their widowed mothers' mortgages). Consequently, after re-reading the novels, one might conclude that it is more accurate to label the Alger hero a "hustler" (an enterprising person determined to succeed in business at any cost) rather than a humanitarian—as the Alger hero is seemingly defined today.

There is little question that success in the Alger novel is virtually always measured in material assets and liabilities. Moses Rischin, writing in *The American Gospel of Success,* puts it this way: Alger's economic ethic "followed logically from the Puritan ethic which instructed men to lay up wealth for the greater glory of God."[8] Of course, if one recalls the complementary side of the dual calling—what John Cotton named a "deadnesse to the world,"[9] Alger's novels become revealing examples of the tendency to make original seventeenth century religious doctrine into a secular expression. Consequently, when H. L. Mencken argues that in original Puritan creed there was no distinction between religious and economic interests, and that "later, Piety degenerated into hypocrisy and people seized this as the original,"[10] he is also making a perceptive assessment of what goes on in an Alger novel.

Not only is money in the forefront of almost every story—how much the hero earned on his first job, how much he spent on food and rent, and how much of a fortune he indubitably gained (to the penny), but the equation of the pursuit of happiness with the pursuit of money is made explicit again and again. Simply noting the titles of several novels may begin to suggest their content:

> *Five Hundred Dollars*
> *Herbert Carter's Legacy; or, The Inventor's Son*
> *Luck and Pluck; or, John Oakley's Inheritance*
> *Striving for Fortune; or, Walter Griffith's Trials and Successes*
> *Timothy Crump's Ward; or, The New Year's Loan and What Came of It*
> *The Tin Box; or, Finding a Fortune*
> *Tom Turner's Legacy; or, The Story of How He Secured It*
> *Room at the Top; or, How to Reach Success, Happiness, Fame, and Fortune*

The overriding single subject of these and numerous other examples is money, and the things that go with money: power, respectability, and position. In a typical moral argument that could be dropped into almost any of these stories, Alger would say that playing pool leads to drinking, which leads to idleness, which leads to stealing, which sometimes leads to jail, but more often to poverty—poverty being the ultimate punishment for Alger's villains and the hell of his own brand of theology. It is not peculiar, for example, that in *The Tin Box* the only punishment that young Philip Ross incurs for stealing twenty dollars is the loss of his financially profitable position. Thus, while Alger's heaven may be little more than making a great deal of money, likewise everything and/or everyone in this world has a cash value, e.g., a boy who earns ten dollars a week is likely to consider himself twice as deserving as a boy who earns only five. Of course, it would be unfair to claim that Alger's heroes were without some ethical principles. But it nonetheless would also seem difficult for any perceptive reader today to imagine Herbert Carter or Bob Burton or any of the others as likely volunteers for service in organizations like VISTA or the Peace Corps. They simply did not have the time for such non-profit organizations.

Probably the most extreme example of Alger's obsession with the dollar is *Herbert Carter's Legacy.*[11] The story opens with a detailed description of young Herbert's "one source of income" and it sets the pattern throughout the novel. Alger's young man was employed to deliver letters and papers to families living some distance from the village post office (oddly, no young hero ever seemed to have time to "play" with the other boys, unless of course it was to compete for a prize—usually a Waterbury pocketwatch). As the reader might expect, Alger is careful to report any cash earnings to the exact penny:

> For this service he received a regular tariff of two cents for each letter, and one cent for each paper. He was not likely to grow rich on this income, but he felt that, though small, it was welcome. (p. 13)

Later, in a letter delivered to his own cottage, Herbert learns that his Uncle Herbert has died. The news excites considerable interest in our young hero:

> "Uncle Herbert was rich, wasn't he, mother?"
>
> "Yes, he must have left nearly a hundred thousand dollars."
>
> "What a pile of money!" said Herbert. "I wonder how it feels when a man is so rich. He ought to be happy." (p. 13)

That night Herbert fell asleep with thoughts of the inheritance well in mind:

> He dreamed that his uncle left him a lump of gold so big and heavy that he could not lift it. He was

considering how in the world he was going to get it home, when all at once he awoke. (p. 18)

When Herbert actually attends the reading of his uncle's will, he soon learns that he is only one of many impatient relatives with hopes of changing their financial situations. This is how one of them described his intentions:

"Well, I'm a second or third cousin. I don't know which. Never saw him to my knowledge. In fact, I wouldn't have come, on to the funeral, if I hadn't heard that he was rich." (p. 31)

What young reader, selecting this novel from the Sunday-school library, would guess that Alger is *not* here preparing the ground for some larger attack on the callous greed of these people? And although Alger's fiction rarely displays any degree of subtlety, would not this be the precise time for "our young hero" suddenly to come to his senses and denounce this bizarre event? But curiously, the direction of the novel does not change. To be sure, Herbert is saddened that his legacy turns out to be nothing more than a trunk of old clothes and a "paltry one hundred dollars," but Alger makes it clear that neither Herbert nor the young reader should be disappointed:

"I would rather make a fortune for myself than inherit one from another," said Herbert.

"I respect your independence, my boy," said the lawyer, who felt favorably disposed toward our hero. "Still, a legacy is not to be despised." (p. 42)

If Alger's heroes seem obsessed with money-making, what might one expect from the villains? Interestingly enough, Alger carefully notes that, although both hero and villain are intent on financial success, it is "industriousness" that motivates the hero, while "greed" is what makes the villain run. Whether or not the perceptive reader can accept this thesis, the author makes it explicit that Herbert seeks his fortune with pluck and luck; Squire Leech seeks his fortune with covetousness:

Squire Leech was a covetous man. He had a passion for making money, and he availed himself of all the opportunity which the country afforded, and until this moment he had fancied himself successful. But Temple's talk about the large amounts to be made in the city influenced his imagination. Why might not he, too, rise to a half a million in five years? (p. 201)

As happens midway through almost every Alger story, Herbert decides to follow the well-worn path of other heroes and villains and heads for the city in search of his fortune and/or happiness. Before he departs he asks, "Is it easy to make money in the city?" "Yes, if a man is sharp and has some money to start with," answered the lawyer (p. 185).

Consequently, when Herbert finally arrives in the city, he is confident that "poor boys don't always stay poor" (p. 192), and he begins selling newspapers. Once again Alger takes pains to calculate the exact profits:

The first day was not successful, chiefly because of his inexperience. He was "stuck" on nearly half of his papers, and the profits were less than nothing. But Herbert was quick to learn. The second day he cleared twenty cents. The third day he netted seventy-five. He felt now that he had passed the period of experiment, and that he would be able to pay his board. (p. 269)

Although there was probably little doubt in the young reader's mind that Alger would soon allow Herbert to find success, e.g., a financially profitable position in business, the remainder of the story is devoted to fleshing out the rags-to-riches formula. Alger makes it clear that his hero has "arrived" when Herbert returns to the village in time to rescue his widowed mother from Squire Leech who wishes to swindle her and gain the little cottage. Herbert displays his sudden adeptness in financial matters by shrewdly making this offer to the Squire:

"If you choose to pay six hundred and fifty, we will sell. If you don't want to buy, we will make another offer. We will rent the house for ninety dollars a year. That is the interest on fifteen hundred dollars at six per cent." (p. 323)

Whether one likes it or not, then, *Herbert Carter's Legacy* does not appear to be part of what has been called "Alger's wonderful world of virtue rewarded."[12] Rather, in this novel and numerous others, the Alger hero is part of a society that has largely forgotten everything but money, making it the measure and source of all other value.

One may also argue that Alger is neither clear nor consistent about the ultimate significance of wealth. To be sure, at the outset of most of the novels Alger pays lip-service to the Puritan economic ethic: success comes to the thrifty, industrious young man because of his thrift and industry. And yet, despite this seemingly rigid formula of cause and effect, a close reading of the novels reveals that, in the end, the young hero routinely gains success because of an accident—saving a rich man's child from drowning, finding and returning a wallet to a wealthy businessman, or, as in *Grit, The Young Boatman,* finding a rich merchant's lost son.

Nor is there any convincing evidence that Alger holds providence responsible for such activities. Over and above the direct causal relation of virtue and prosperity, the Puritan tradition claimed the advantage of having God on its side. But conspicuously absent in most Alger novels is any indication that God might be even partially responsible for financial success. Instead, Alger asserted that "by pluck and luck" any young man could conquer poverty. One might look, for example, at the noticeably secular conclusion to *Struggling Upward:*

> So closes this eventful passage in the life of Luke Larkin. He has struggled upward from a boyhood of privation and self-denial into a youth and manhood of prosperity and honor. There has been some luck about it, I admit, but after all he is indebted for most of his good fortune to his own good qualities.[13]

The point is that Alger vacillates between his orthodox Puritan background and the reality of the social mores of the late nineteenth century. While he extolls work as virtuous in itself and the means to financial success, and accordingly, happiness, nonetheless the wealthy characters in the novels are more than often portrayed as avaricious or inhumane. Alger intrudes into *Herbert Carter's Legacy* to remind the reader,

> How a rich man like Squire Leech can deliberately plot to defraud a poor woman of a portion of her small income, you and I, my young reader, find it hard to understand. Unfortunately, there are too many cases in real life where just such things happen, so that there is really a good deal of truth to the old adage that prosperity hardens the heart. (p. 38)

But unlike Dickens in, for example, *Our Mutual Friend,* Alger was never quite convincing when he set out to attack society's lust for money. Indeed, he seemed obsessed with formulating a blueprint for financial success, and only infrequently did he allude to the humanitarian responsibilities (the "right" use of wealth) that traditionally went along with attaining success. Money spreads out to define the lives of virtually all the characters in his novels, heroes and villains alike. And even though in some instances Alger takes pains to introduce a "benefactor"—usually a successful businessman interested in giving aid to the struggling young men — character invariably is part of a contrived ending or unbelievable circumstance that has little effect on the true shape of the book. Furthermore, no matter how often Alger reminds the reader that "prosperity hardens the heart," one cannot ignore the hollowness of such epitaphs when he recalls that in the last chapter of *Herbert Carter's Legacy,* and humerous others, Alger admits his hero into this supposedly sterile and "hardening" world as though he were opening the gates of paradise.[14]

In sum, the general line of my thesis is simple enough: money, and little else, is what makes the Alger hero run. A close reading of the novels provides virtually no evidence to support the claim that public service was ever an integral part in Alger's original formula for success. My contention, in this paper, is that critics who dwell, for example, on the "intense idealism of his parables, the selflessness of his heroes, and the kindly benevolence of their patrons"[15] have overlooked the larger and more prevalent thrusts of an Alger novel.

Further, by identifying today's "typical Alger hero" largely on the basis of his humanitarian activities, while glossing over the original heroes' singular talents for simply making money, scholars and journalists are adding confusion to an already dimly perceived piece of popular American literature. Perhaps this latest distortion of the Alger myth in part reflects the efforts of a society that is straining to create traditional heroes in a time when few are to be found.

Notes

[1] *The New York Times,* May 7, 1970, p. 4.

[2] From "Opportunity Still Knocks," the publication distributed at the 24th Annual Horatio Alger Awards held May 6, 1970, at the Waldorf Astoria in New York City. Officially called The Horatio Alger Awards Committee of the American Schools and Colleges Association, this non-profit organization publicizes its concern about "the trend among young people towards the mind-poisoning belief that equal opportunity was a thing of the past," and takes at its central purpose the need to provide tangible evidence that "the American way of achieving success still offers equal opportunity to all." After surveying campus leaders at some 500 colleges and universities for nominations, the Alger Committee, not surprisingly with Norman Vincent Peale presiding, selects approximately ten "successful" business and professional leaders to serve as examples that "the American Way is the highest type of human relationship conceived by the mind of man."

[3] Ralph D. Gardner, *Horatio Alger; or, The American Hero Era* (Mendota, Illinois, 1964), p. 346. Several other commentators have speculated on Alger's sales. F. L. Mott in *Golden Multitudes* (New York, 1947) conservatively sets the figure at sixteen or seventeen million. But Frank Gruber in *Horation Alger, Jr.: A Bibliography and Biography of the Best-Selling Author of All Time* (Los Angeles, 1961) argues that "estimates of their sales range from one hundred to three hundred million copies," and adds, "I am inclined to favor the latter figure" (p. 41). Certainly sales figures alone are not the whole story, since for each copy sold there were probably several readers, and frequently copies were passed on to succeeding generations.

4 See, for instance, John Seelye, "Who Was Horatio? The Alger Myth and American Scholarship," *American Quarterly*, XVII (Winter, 1965), 749-756.

5 For more complete accounts of Perot's financial prowess, see Arthur M. Louis, "The Fastest Richest Texan Ever," *Fortune*, LXXVII (November, 1968), 168-170, 228, 231; "Texas Breeds New Billionaire," (anon.) *Business Week* (August 30, 1969), 73-74; and Jon Nordhiemer, "Texan Fights Social Ills," *The New York Times*, November 28, 1969, p. 41.

6 The opening remarks by Bill Lawrence on ABC's news interview program, "Issues and Answers," Sunday, January 11, 1970.

7 See "Opportunity Still Knocks."

8 Moses Rischin, *The American Gospel of Success* (Chicago, 1965), p. 21. See also Robert Falk, "Notes on the Higher Criticism of Horatio Alger," *Arizona Quarterly*, XIX (Summer, 1963), 151-167.

9 Quoted by Perry Miller in *The New England Mind* (New York, 1939), p. 42.

10 H. L. Mencken, "Puritanism as a Literary Force," *A Book of Prefaces* (New York, 1917), p. 235.

11 Horatio Alger, Jr., *Herbert Carter's Legacy; or, The Inventor's Son* (New York, John C. Winston Company, no date available).

12 Seelye, "Who Was Horatio?" p. 756.

13 Horatio Alger, Jr., *Struggling Upward; or, Luke Larkin's Luck* (Akron, Ohio, Superior Printing Company, no date available), p. 280.

14 See William Coyle's introduction to the Odyssey Press reprint of Alger's *Adrift in New York* (New York, 1966). The same conclusion has been voiced by Robert Falk, "Notes on the Higher Criticism."

15 Seelye, p. 755.

Gary F. Scharnhorst (essay date 1976)

SOURCE: "The Boudoir Tales of Horatio Alger, Jr.," in *Journal of Popular Culture*, Vol. X, No. 1, 1976, pp. 215-26.

[In the following essay, Scharnhorst looks at the humanitarian moralism of Alger's adult fiction.]

Horatio Alger, Jr., whose fame rests upon his prodigious output of over a hundred juvenile novels written between 1864 and his death in 1899, also had a career as a writer of adult fiction, although it is generally ignored. Alger published a total of eleven adult novelle between 1857 and 1869, by which time the demand for his juvenile work had substantially increased following the publication in 1867 of his first best seller for boys, ***Ragged Dick, or Street Life in New York.*** In addition, during his career Alger published nearly two hundred different short tales in such family and women's magazines as *Home Circle, Yankee Blade,* and *Gleason's Literary Companion.* Most of these were also originally written prior to his success in the juvenile genre, however, and later reprinted in various publications.[1] Finally, late in life, after his reputation as a juvenile fictionist was secure, Alger wrote three more adult novels, one of which remains unpublished and in manuscript. This complete body of work, particularly the short apprenticeship pieces, still await a more thorough anlysis than is possible here; however, a few representative adult works, by providing a context apart from the juvenile fiction for examining Alger's thought, amply reveal that important themes in the juveniles have usually been missed because of the emphasis on the success motif.

The standard interpretation of the Alger Myth holds that Our Hero rose, if not from rags to riches, to at least a comfortable middle-class standard of living by exploiting every available opportunity to succeed financially. For example, Bruce E. Coad asserts that, in his novels, "Alger reflects an almost obsessive predilection for money-making."[2] According to the usual interpretation, Alger explicitly equated the pursuit of happiness with the pursuit of wealth. In short, Our Hero is usually viewed as a fortune-hunter, his creator as a success ideologue, and the novels as mere capitalistic tracts.

A dissenting interpretation of the Alger Myth, however, holds that Our Hero was a humanitarian rather than a ruthless exploiter, and that he was rewarded in the denouement of each initiation novel for his acts of charity.[3] This interpretation, which suggests that the author was more concerned with morality and the moral uses of money than with money itself, is supported by a reading of Alger's adult fiction. To be sure, in the juveniles Alger did describe the increase of Our Hero's bank account or detail the steps taken in the acquisition of his birthright, but this money-making was symbolic of Our Hero's initiation into adulthood and was a badge of his innate moral goodness, conferred by a Benevolent Patron who, like God, recognized his worth and rewarded him. Because most of the virtuous characters in Alger's adult fiction already have been initiated, the importance of money to them is drastically reduced. Because Alger in his adult fiction labored under no requirement to elevate his characters' stations as a sign of their election, as was required in the juveniles, the wage-earning and wealth of the juvenile hero is replaced in the adult fiction by courtship and marriage among the mature characters. This correspondence between money and marriage in turn suggests that Alger conceived of personal happiness as the ultimate reward of moral people. In other words, Alger's adult fiction, which develops certain themes of the juvenile fiction, informs the myth he created by correcting the usual impression that the author praised wealth-gathering alone or considered it a sufficient end unto itself.

Alger's first eleven adult novelle, written during a period of as many years, tended to be weaker in plot and characterization than his earliest juvenile fiction. Between 1857 and 1860, while a student at Harvard Divinity School, Alger published a total of eight novelle in *The New York Sun* newspaper, entitled as follows: **"Hugo, the Deformed," "Madeline, the Temptress," "The Secret Drawer, or the Story of a Missing Will," "The Cooper's Ward, or the Waif of the New Year," "Herbert Selden, the Poor Lawyer's Son," "Manson the Miser, or Life and Its Vicissitudes," "The Gipsy Nurse, or Marked for Life,"** and **"The Discarded Son."**[4] Each of these works exhibited the trappings of popular sentimental romance, although by all indications they atracted slight popular attention. For example, the hunchbacked villain of **"Hugo, the Deformed"** commits suicide rather than suffer apprehension by the police, while the romantic hero and his betrothed at length attain "that peaceful and tranquil happiness which mutual love can alone bestow."[5] This was hardly an auspicious beginning for the man whom Kenneth S. Lynn has hailed as "one of the great mythmakers of the modern world."[6] After printing this series of eight novelle cut from the same sentimental fabric, the *Sun* editors rejected further offerings for adult consumption from Alger's pen. *Marie Bertrand,* his ninth adult novel, set in Paris and at least partially autobiographical, was finally serialized in *The New York Weekly* in 1864.[7] Alger's tenth adult novel appeared in 1866 and was a lengthly revision of **"The Cooper's Ward,"** and was retitled *Timothy Crump's Ward.*[8] Alger's eleventh attempt to write a substantial adult work, *Ralph Raymond's Heir,* was serialized in *Gleason's Literary Companion* in 1869 and later issued in bookform.[9]

On the basis of these eleven early works, it would seem that Alger was not overburdened with wealth-obsessions. Sentimental and melodramatic, they describe a world in which the consequences of good and evil have been inexorably predetermined. The heroic characters strive not for fortune but for marital bliss. The ideal of Marriage, as in all of Alger's adult fiction, operates as a correlate of happiness, the highest human good in the fictional world. With no young heroes in transit struggling upward, the virtuous characters harbor few thoughts of money. Indeed, only

the evil characters in them dream of filthy lucre and its perverse sexual correlate, seduction. In the tradition of melodrama, these works employ as a recurrent plot device the abduction of the chaste by the vile.[10] Also as in conventional melodrama, in them the virtuous inevitably are rewarded (by marriage, not necessarily by wealth) and the evil inevitably punished. In *Ralph Raymond's Heir,* for example, the two criminals who temporarily deprive an heir of his modest birthright and hope to appropriate it for themselves die in a grisly murder-suicide similar to the violent end of Hugo. The sordid quest for personal profit is righteously condemned by Alger in every instance. Characters who are guilty of avarice are without exception portrayed as miserable. For example, Peter Manson dies at the end of **"Manson the Miser"** with "a few gold pieces firmly clutched in his grasp. He had received a sudden summons" while engaged Scrooge-like in counting his fortune.[11] Justice is meted out in this fictional world not on a sliding scale of monetary gain or loss; rather, goodness is rewarded with happiness and evil is punished with spiritual and/or legal conviction or death. These works, in short, belie the interpretation of Algerism as unbridled capitalism, and suggest that Unitarian minister Alger believed moral behavior to be its own reward.

Also during these early years of his writing career, Alger frequently published short fiction for adults which contained quaint moral lessons. A volume of short tales, entitled *Bertha's Christmas Vision: An Autumn Sheaf,* appeared in 1856, and was in fact Alger's first published book.[12] Most of his short pieces, however, appeared in magazines. Of Alger's nearly two hundred adult stories, perhaps the best three appeared in two major magazines—*Graham's* and *Harper's*—and merit individual attention. Alger's story **"Five Hundred Dollars"** appeared in an 1858 issue of *Graham's,* then edited by Charles Godfrey Leland.[13] This tale essentially rebuts the allegation that the climate of Alger's world was always favorable to fortune-hunting, for in it the author acknowledged the moral snare always implicit in the urge to become rich. Gregory Flint, the narrator of the retrospective tale, explains to the reader that a few years earlier his late aunt had bequeathed to him five hundred dollars, and that immediately thereafter he had begun to search for an appropriate investment for his legacy. "There was something exhilarating in the idea of being a capitalist—with money to invest," he recalls. One morning Flint had met "a sleek personage, of very plausible address" whose name was Lynx. This mysterious stranger told Our Gullible Hero about an investment that he had recommended to a friend. With an investment of only two hundred dollars, he explained, his friend had realized a fortune of twenty thousand dollars after only two years. Flint immediately had calculated that "at that rate my five hundred dollars would have become fifty thousand." The mode of investment, Lynx explained, was quite simple: "'I purchased for him a quarter section in a rising town in Minnesota,'" Supposedly, the purchased land had been required for building lots, so its value soared. Lynx also had assured Our Hero that such an opportunity was not unique, and that his advice would insure success. Flint remembers that "my imagination set fire at once. No more chance of my letting out my aunt's legacy at a paltry six per cent., when such golden harvests were to be had for the gathering." As a result, Flint had purchased within the hour one hundred and sixty acres in Constantinople, Minnesota. The cost of the land, plus the commission that Flint paid the stranger, exhausted the five hundred dollar bequest. Flint had walked home "with the broad consciousness that I was a landed proprietor, and on the high road to fortune." Here, perhaps, the later Alger juvenile would end, for the "Benevolent Patron" who had "placed more than one young man with small means on the road to fortune" seemingly again had accomplished his self-appointed task. In two or three years, Flint had anticipated, he would be able to offer a comfortable living to his intended wife, the lovely Julia Mackintosh.

Flint's vain aspirations are, of course, built on sand, for the mysterious stranger had deceived him. Two years later he had traveled to Minnesota to visit his claim, spending his nights in rude log huts, until finally arriving at his village destination—"three miserable log-houses, in front of one of which a pig was rooting very composedly." Half of his quarter section, he then learned, was swampland and the other half uncleared forest. In short, like many investors during the Florida land scandals of the 1920's he had lost his money. Flint returned from this journey "with all my daydreams effectually dispelled. I am quite as far from marrying Julia Mackintosh as ever. The revenues of my Western property will scarcely justify me in assuming so expensive a responsibility."

Although this apprenticeship piece introduces dramatic contrivances Alger would subsequently employ in his juvenile novels, the plot itself is an inversion of the success stories. On the one hand, there appear such devices as the confidence man who robs of bilks Our Hero, the pilgrimage to the West (a device used by Alger especially after his own first journey to California in 1877), and the hero's investment in land at the direction of a patron.[14] No less than in his later juvenile fiction, Alger instructs his readers in a moral lesson—a modern, secular equivalent of the Biblical parable of the Lost Son. On the other hand, the protagonist of this story is victimized by his desire to gain fortune and, unlike the heroes of the juveniles, sinks to destitution instead of rising to respectability. In this way, Alger expressly cautioned against money-mongering. The worldly invitation to rise to a higher economic station could be revoked, Alger averred, for the pristine innocence of people had been corrupted by the Original Sin of avarice.

Alger's second major story for adults, entitled **"Job Warner's Christmas,"**[15] was obviously inspired by, and nearly plagarized from, Dickens' *A Christmas Carol*. It describes the pathetic situation of an assistant bookkeeper in the counting room of Bentley and Co. and his family as they prepare to celebrate the holiday on his modest salary. Although the Warners are poor, the authorial voice explains, "there [are] few happier or more thankful hearts than those of the shabby book-keeper and his good wife." Still, economic hardship in the Warner house has been increased by the Civil War-induced inflation. Necessities have become expensive and "made a rigid economy needful. Months ago the family had given up sugar, and butter was only used on Sunday." Rather than asking for a holiday from work as Bob Cratchit, Job asks his employer for a small raise to partially compensate for his lost purchasing power. However, a penny-wise Mr. Bentley agrees only to consider the matter. Job's wish to buy a few gifts for his family on this Christmas Eve seems doomed to frustration. Nevertheless, Job offers to aid a street urchin who appeals to him for help as he walks home. He exclaims, "I am poor, my child, but not so poor as you, thank God! I had intended to buy some little presents for my children, but they will be better pleased if I spend the money in making you comfortable." Employer Bentley overhears Job's offer, and he in turn resolves to become more charitable. He is, after all, "not naturally a selfish man, only inconsiderate. Now that his benevolent impulses were excited he would not rest till they were embodied in action." The upshot of this resolution is that Bentley swears off frugality. He increases Job's salary from seven hundred to a thousand dollars per year, and he grants Job and his wife an additional two hundred dollar annual allowance to care for the orphan found begging on the street. He accounts for his new beneficience by explaining to them that "prosperity had begun to harden my heart. At any rate it had made me thoughtless of the multitudes who are struggling with ills which my wealth could alleviate." The earlier, unredeemed Bentley is the prototype of the callous capitalist who stalks Alger's juvenile world; the stock character's conversion in this tale, however, attests to Alger's abiding faith in the efficacy of good works and selflessness in a world sullied by war and privation. Predictably, Warner spends part of his new-won fortune on gifts. With no Tiny Tim to squeak the final words, the story closes instead with a text from the gospel of Luke, read aloud by Warner to his family: "Glory to God in the highest, and on earth peace, good-will to men!" Without question, Alger's ministerial training shaped the moral caliber of his tales.

The third adult story which Alger published in a major periodical, **"Ralph Farnham's Romance,"**[16] concerned with the hero's struggle to become a renown author rather than a rich man. Ralph journeys to the small town where the tale is set in order to write a romance. He hopes, as he writes to his sister, to earn enough by his pen to "provide a home for you, however, humble, so that we might be again united." If only that would happen, he "should feel happy." Significantly, his pursuits are literary, not mercantile; indeed, he comes to the village after rejecting an offer of a clerking position in the city, although he begins to second-guess his decision. "Though it would bind me to a life I detest, it would have given me a secure income, while now I may only experience mortifying failure . . . *I must succeed!*"

Ralph, who boards near the mansion of Judge Henderson, one day saves the life of the Judge's daughter Ellen. As a reward for his rescue of the distressed heroine, he becomes a frequent guest in the Judge's home. Through the intervention of the grateful Ellen, Ralph also becomes a weekly columnist for the local newspaper, which enables him to stave off starvation while he completes his romance. At length, they are betrothed, and their wedding date is set to coincide with the date that Ralph's manuscript is to be published. Ellen's father pronounces the benediction upon the happy couple—with whom Ralph's sister will come to live—when he tells Ralph, "You have talent, and Ellen has money . . . It is a fair exchange." In other words, success in the story's terms is not identical with prosperity, but with the happiness assured by artistic achievement, marriage, and economic security.

Although these adult stories each speak to the question of what money means in the Alger canon, the author developed in them common themes that clarify his appraisal of fortune hunting. For example, all of them promote the Biblical virtues of economy and charity, not entrepreneurship. Gregory Flint assumes the role of the man who squandered his legacy in foolish living, in contrast to the wise economy of Ralph Farnham and Job Warner. Economy is practiced by these characters not to raise investment capital, but to satisfy the Biblical injunction that each person be a faithful steward of God's bounty. Moreover, because the Warners are willing to share their livelihood, meager as it may be, with the orphan, they become the exemplars of this faith that converts thrifty Bentley into a fount of generosity. In this world, contagious charity is practiced in order to reduce the suffering of the less fortunate, to act upon Christ's command to "do unto others as you would have them do unto you." Although it is not the Social Darwinists' world of cutthroat competition, neither is it always a bright, innocent world. On its fringes appear "street Arabs," orphaned and hungry children in the supposed land of milk and honey. Finally, the two

stories in which the hero plans to marry reveal Alger's conscious irony. The protagonist who seeks artistic success is rewarded with it, a bride, and financial security; however, the one who seeks crass wealth and a bride receives neither. The difference between them is that Ralph Farnham's ambition is honorable and his reward acquired in part through his own industry, whereas in contrast Gregory Flint is motivated by greed and exerts no effort of his own by investing his inheritance in distant land on a sham-promise of wealth. Each of them merits his fate.

Between his initial success with *Ragged Dick* and his death, Alger wrote juvenile novels almost exclusively—often as many as four or five in a single year. However, he upon three occasions returned to writing for an adult audience, and these later works command particular attention for they silhouette Alger's mind long after the exigencies of his literary apprenticeship. The first of these three novels in the style of the newer genteel sentimentalism, entitled *Mabel Parker: or The Hidden Treasure. A Tale of the Frontier Settlements,* was never published and a manuscript copy of it has only recently come to light.[17] Transcribed in a copyist's hand with corrections by Alger himself, the manuscript was submitted to the publishing firm of Smith and Smith, judging from internal evidence, in the early 1880's.[18] Its rejections by their editors may be explained by Alger's earlier unpopularity among adults—Street and Smith were publishers of the *Sun,* and it would have been familiar with the situation—or by their fear that if successful Alger would abandon the more lucrative juvenile market. These occasional forays into adult fiction, in short, were not to be encouraged by his publishers.

The plot of *Mabel Parker* is hardly distinguishable from that of other melodramatic romances of the period; its most salient feature is a thinly-disguised similarity to Fenimore Cooper's *The Pioneers,* which might have been another reason that Street and Smith declined to issue it.[19] Set in the lake region of central New York state around 1820, the story is basically another variation on the seduction theme then popular.[20] The central conflict involves the attempt by the villainous Dick Clarke to extort from the widowed Squire Parker permission to wed his beautiful daughter Mabel, who loves the honorable Henry Davenport. "A selfish as well as a proud man,"[21] Parker is tempted to accede to the perverse Clarke's demand when he is promised the recovery of his lost inheritance, some fifty thousand dollars in gold. Eventually, however, the rightful heir recovers his fortune without Clarke's help, and Mabel and Davenport are wed with the Squire's blessing.

Explicit in this novel is the admission that money is neither a necessary no[r] sufficient condition for human well-being. The quest for fortune alone, the author observed in this novel, is irrelevant to the larger questions of human happiness. Just as the only self-made men in the juveniles are villains, so too does Mabel's undeserving father, who resembles a snob from one of the boy-books grown to adulthood, receive his inheritance and live a life of unmerited leisure. With neither guile nor rapacity, Mabel also becomes rich, deservedly so according to the determinism which steadfastly governs the lives of the virtuous in Alger's world, but she would willingly have spurned material wealth to insure spiritual happiness, and indeed distinguishes between the two states. As she tells her father, "I care not for money. To me it is of no value compared with the happiness which I shall enjoy as Henry's wife"(93). Even the villain Clarke has "the good taste to value youth and beauty above the mere dross of gold"(61); otherwise, he would have kept the missing treasure for himself.

Like the other stock characters in Alger's adult fiction, those in this drama cherish not wealth, but home and family. This novel is unique, moreover, for it reveals Alger's increasingly complex economic vision in the 1880's. Goodness and evil had become less distinct moral categories to him, and Clarke and Squire Parker inhabit that widening gray zone between virtue and depravity. The incongruity of Parker's undeserved wealth indicates, as Alger would explicitly admit years later in a juvenile, that "the evil are sometimes prospered" in this world.[22] In short, Alger was not an unequivocal proponent of business success. He found it necessary to qualify his earlier, reductive determinism that equated goodness with success in order to account for the success of the vile. Rebate scandals, investigations of trusts and monopolies, and exposes of child labor convinced him by the final decade of his life that "'business is business'" is a phrase "used to excuse all manner of vile acts."[23] Morality, not money, was his chief concern.

In *A Fancy of Hers* (1892), the first new adult work by Alger to appear in decades, the author praised the life of self-sacrifice, of giving rather than receiving.[24] The heroine, wealthy debutante Mabel Frost Fairfax, who scorns her class privilege in genteel New York society, assumes the name Mabel Frost and comes with the airy grace of the *ingenue* to the village of Granville, New Hampshire to accept a teaching position in the middle school there. Alger explains her motives by insisting that sheer wealth is a curse, her bugbear:

> She had all the advantages of wealth. She had youth, beauty, and refinement. She had the entree to the magic inner circle of metropolitan society. And yet there was in her an ever present sense of something lacking. She had grown weary of the slavery of fashion. Young as she was, she had begun to know its hollowness, its utter insufficiency as the object of existence. She sought some truer interest in life.

She had failed to secure happiness, she reasoned, because thus far she had lived only for herself (701).

Mabel performs her pedagogical tasks well and succeeds "in inspiring an interest in study such as had not been known before. She offered to teach a class in French and one in Latin, though it entailed extra labor"(712). Alger's choice of a teaching career for Mabel evinces his belief that a classical or humanistic education, "the birthright of every citizen"(707), would aid in the amelioration of social problems and was a prerequisite of personal advancement.[25]

Mabel eventually is amply repaid for her kindness, although not in dollars. She meets the mature version of Our Hero, artist Allan Thorpe, who recognizes her from a reception he attended in New York several seasons earlier. Thorpe writes to a friend (for Alger often employed even in his juveniles the epistolary technique for entering the mind of a character) that

> between the struggling artist and the wealthy heiress there was a distance too great to be spanned even by love, but now that her estate is on a level with my own I need not hesitate. The same spirit that has enabled her to meet and conquer adversity will sustain her in the self denial and self sacrifice to which she may be called as the wife of a poor man. I have resolved to put my fortune to the test (734).

Social status is an artificial barrier among people, Alger infers, for the success of Thorpes suit is not dependent upon Mabel's social position. Thorpe proposes marriage to the princess-in-disguise just before she reveals to him that they will not need to grovel for their livelihood. When Thorpe asks why, if still rich, she had become a schoolmarm, she replies, "Because I wished to be of some service to my kind; because I was tired of the hollow frivolity of the fashionable world. I don't regret my experiment. I never expected to be so richly rewarded"(744). A happy marriage is again the reward of the virtuous.

Moreover, an unhappy union is the deserved punishment of two other characters in a subplot which ratifies Mabel's decision to flee the superficialities of fashionable society. After his own condescending proposal to the "poor" Mabel is rebuffed, Randolph Chester, who is the middle-aged version of Alger's juvenile snob, marries a girl whom he ironically believes to be very rich, but who is "in truth, considerably straitened"(728). Marriage again is the vessel dispensing justice, for by their irrevocable unhappiness together Randolph and his wife are penalized for their snobbery and aristocratic pretensions.

Alger's final adult work, *The Disagreeable Woman: A Social Mystery,* was published in 1895 under the pseudonym Julian Starr, which may in part account for the dearth of attention it attracted. Only one known copy survives, and it is in the Library of Congress.[26] The story is narrated from the point of view of a young physician, Dr. Fenwick, who has recently moved to New York from a small village in order to partake of the "wider opportunity" available to him in the city, and it involves a menage of characters at his boarding house. The novel thematically explores the sinister city and the irony of its purported opportunity, especially during the economic depression that followed the Panic of '93.[27] One resident of the house, a young clerk at Macy's, for example, finally returns to her "country home and is now the wife of her rustic admirer." According to the narrator, whose insight anticipates that of Dreiser in *Sister Carrie,* she has chosen wisely, for "life in the great stores is a species of slavery, and she could save nothing from her slavery."[26] The doctor also ponders his own commitment to the city, as he recalls that "in the country village, where I knew everybody, I always looked forward to [Sunday] as the pleasantest day of the week. Here is the crowded city, I felt isolated from human sympathy."[17] The doctor often complains in the course of his narration about his failure to become financially independent in the city, and he particularly resents the selfish upper class. "Rich men with large incomes keep [doctors] out of their pay for a long time."[15] However, when one resident criticizes the doctor for wasting his time with charity cases, arguing that he "will never get rich in that way," Fenwick responds that "I do not expect to. I shall be satisfied if I can make a living."[20] Forever charitable, the doctor ministers to a distressed family whose poverty is enforced by the low wages offered by city employers. The doctor prescribes rest and wholesome food, but is unable to give them any money, so on their account he appeals to another boarder, the Disagreeable Woman. Although she is considered by the other characters to be a callous, indifferent woman, the doctor realizes that she merely scorns their frivolities. At heart, indeed, she is a charitable, cultured woman whose past remains a mystery to them all. "Under a brusque exterior she certainly possesses a kind heart, and consideration for others," the doctor writes of her. "Upon everything in the shape of humbug or pretension she is severe, but she can appreciate worth and true nobility. In more than one instance I have applied to her in behalf of a poor patient, and never in vain"[26].[28] Because she privately volunteers money for the doctor's needy patients, she too is eventually rewarded for her charity. In the novel's final chapter, she learns from Fenwick of the illness of her long-lost fiance, and Evangeline-like she attends his sickbed. When she learns that the patient will live, "a look of grateful joy lighted up the face of the Disagreeable Woman"[28]. The final Alger adult novel ends, like most of its predecessors, with a long-deferred marriage on the verge of consummation.

This novel, like the other adult works, supports the view that in Alger's world happiness is earned by charity and other forms of moral behavior, and that money is at best an accessory guage of success. Moreover, the city is not portrayed in this work as an Elysian Field of unlimited opportunity, but as a fester of social depravity. The same sense of the city often is conveyed in Alger's juvenile novels. For example, *Julius, or The Street Boy Out West*(1874) was inspired by Charles Loring Brace's pioneering document of urban reform, *The Dangerous Classes of Society,* which described the program at the Children's Aid Society of New York through which orphans in the city were adopted by families in the West. In *Julius,* Our Hero must be transplanted from the city into the frontier before he can prosper.[29] In *Joe's Luck,* similarly, Alger admitted that "a boy needs to be strong and self-reliant and willing to work if he comes [to the city] to compete for the prizes of life."[30] As in *Julius,* the hero of this novel abandons the brick and mortar mountains of the city for wider opportunities in the West.

This reading of Alger's adult fiction challenges the standard view of the world Alger created and the type of quest he described. The adult tales reveal by inference that Alger wrote essentially American morality fables, not business tracts or indiscreet celebrations of the American entrepreneur. The virtuous Alger protagonist invariably receives Good Fortune, but not necessarily wealth.[31] In the Alger canon, money may be a means to attain success, but it alone never constitutes success. Rather, the hero earns success and happiness by his virtue, especially by his charity, never by business acumen. A character who covets wealth or his neighbor's wife-to-be usually receives his just reward: however, Alger's later novels presuppose a world of more complex economic transactions in which the underserving occasionally frustrate the Fates and gain wealth. Still, as the wise guardian of one Alger boy-hero observes, "This world is not all."[32] Nearing the end of his life, seasoned by his knowledge that unethical business practices in a dark real-world could profit the culprit, Alger could only hope for an eschatological vindication of the moral principles that animate his fictional world, instead of a temporal one.

Notes

[1] The most complete bibliography of Alger's short works has been printed in the *Newsboy,* the newsletter of the Horatio Alger Society, 13 (December 1974), pp. 6-11.

[2] Bruce E. Coad, "The Alger Hero," in *Heroes of Popular Culture,* ed. Ray B. Browne et al. (Bowling Green, Ohio: Bowling Green U. Popular Press, 1972), p. 44. See also Moses Rischin, *The American Gospel*

of Success (Chicago: Quadrangle, 1965), p. 21; Kenneth S Lynn, *The Dream of Success: A Study of the Modern American Imagination* (Boston: Little, Brown, 1955), p. 7.

[3] See especially John Cawelti, *Apostles of the Self-Made Man: Changing Concepts of Success in America* (Chicago: U. of Chicago Press, 1965), pp. 108-120; Rychard Fink "Horatio Alger as a Social Philosopher," intro. to *Ragged Dick and Mark the Match Boy,* by Horatio Alger (New York: Collier, 1962), pp. 27-30.

[4] The respective dates of publication of these serials in the *Sun* are as follows: Jan. 27 to Feb. 7, 1857; Aug. 7 to Sept. 4, 1857; June 14 to July 5, 1859; Dec. 8, 1858 to Jan. 10, 1859. Mar. 5 to Apr. 12, 1859; May 18 to June 21, 1959; Aug. 15 to Sept. 14, 1859; Feb. 3 to Mar. 2, 1860. "The Discarded Son" was published in book form in 1866 under the title *Helen Ford,* and still later (1885) printed in *Golden Argosy* under the title "A Child of Fortune." For a plot summary, see John Tebbel, *From Rags to Riches* (New York: Macmillan, 1963), pp. 168-184. "Manson the Miser" was slightly rewritten for a juvenile audience and published in 1866 under the title *Charlie Codman's Cruise* (Newsboy, 12 (August 1973), pp. 8-9; letter from Gilbert K. Westgard II of Des Plaines, Ill., to Scharnhorst, July 12, 1974; Ralph D. Gardner, *Horatio Alger, or The American Hero Era* (Mendota, Ill.: Wayside Press, 1964), pp. 394-486).

[5] *New York Sun,* Feb. 7, 1857; rpt. in *Newsboy,* 12 (December 1973), p. 20.

[6] Lynn, p. 6.

[7] For a brief plot summary, see Gardner, pp. 437-438. *Marie Bertrand* is a precursor of Alger's urban novels which employ a guidebook description of the city, in this case to Paris rather than to New York or Chicago.

[8] For a plot summary, see Tabbel, pp. 184-193. This adult novel was also rewritten for a juvenile audience and published, in 1875, under the title *Jack's Ward.*

[9] Slightly rewritten, this story appeared as a juvenile in 1892 under the same title.

[10] This device is employed in "Hugo," "The Cooper's Ward," "The Secret Drawer," *Timothy Crump's Ward, Marie Bertrand,* and *Ralph Raymond's Heir.*

[11] *New York Sun,* June 21, 1859.

[12] For a plot summary of three of the stories, see Tebbel, pp. 145-152.

[13] Horatio Alger, "Five Hundred Dollars," *Graham's Illustrated Magazine,* 52 (January 1858), pp. 30-32.

[14] For an example of the latter, see Alger's *Digging for Gold: A Story of California,* rpt. with an introduction by John Seelye (New York: Collier, 1968). Our Hero gains his fortune in this juvenile novel when his patron on his behalf purchases with his meager fortune in gold a tract of land around which, the reader learns, the city of San Francisco will mushroom.

[15] Horatio Alger, Jr., "Job Warner's Christmas," *Harper's New Monthly Magazine,* 28 (December 1863), pp. 119-124.

[16] Horatio Alger, Jr., "Ralph Farnham's Romance," *Harper's New Monthly Magazine,* 28 (March 1864), pp. 500-507.

[17] The only previous mention in print of this manuscript appeared in the bibliography section of Gardner, p. 436. Gardner merely reported its existence, however, since he did not read the manuscript. The ms. was apparently used by Edward Stratemeyer, the creator of the Rover Boys series, to "complete" a novel, entitled *Jerry the Backwoods Boy,* which he published in 1904 under Alger's name. However, the unrevised ms. is the only authentic *adult* version of this novel.

[18] The time setting, since Mabel's grandfather had been contemporaneous with the American Revolution, seems to be around 1820. Alger mentions that the events occurred sixty years before he wrote.

At 203 pages, divided into 21 chapters intended for publication in seven installments, it is the longest adult novel Alger wrote. Because the few corrections in Alger's hand seem to be mainly of copying errors, the manuscript evidently is a revision of a prior draft. Whether Alger was always so careful is not certain. This is the only extant book-length manuscript of his work, unfortunately, so its condition cannot be compared with others.

[19] Similarities between the works, in addition to setting, include an archery match reminiscent of Leatherstocking's turkey-shoot, the simultaneous shooting of a deer by two characters and their ensuing argument, and parallel characterizations, notably Mabel with Elizabeth Temple and Henry with Edward Effingham.

[20] See Leslie A. Fiedler, *Love and Death in the American Novel,* 2nd ed. (New York: Dell, 1966), pp. 209-287.

[21] Horatio Alger, Jr., "Mabel Parker; or, The Hidden Treasure. A Tale of the Frontier Settlements," unpublished novel, c. 1882, p. 57, From the Street and Smith

Collection, George Arents Research Library for Special Collections at Syracuse University. Quoted by permission of the Conde Nast Publications Inc. Subsequent references in the text to the manuscript are indicated parenthetically.

[22] Horatio Alger, *A Cousin's Conspiracy* (New York: New York Book Co., 1909), p. 12.

[23] Horatio Alger, *Andy Grant's Pluck* (Chicago: M. A. Donahue, n.d.), p. 241.

[24] Horatio Alger, Jr., "A Fancy of Hers," *Munsey's Magazine,* 6 (March 1892), pp. 697-744; rpt. in *Newsboy,* 13 (March-April 1975), pp. 7-31. Subsequent references in the text to this work, indicated parenthetically, are to the original printing.

[25] Among the books in which the juvenile hero studies a classic language while on the way to success are *Try and Trust, Andy Grant's Pluck,* and *The Young Salesman.* Ragged Dick even studies French and world geography at night while earning his living by blacking boots during the day.

[26] Julian Starr (Horatio Alger), *The Disagreeable Woman: A Social Mystery* (New York: G. W. Dillingham, 1895); rpt. in *Newsboy,* 13 (October-November 1974), pp. 1, 8-28. subsequent references in the text to this work, indicated parenthetically, are to the latter printing.

[27] Alger himself lost an editorial position with *True Flag* magazine as a result of the business slump of 1857 (Gardner, p. 125). That event would be recreated later in several juveniles, among them *Rupert's Ambition* and *The Young Salesman,* that were written soon after the Panic of '93.

[28] Like her, Alger's juvenile heroes invariably are charitable, often "loaning" money to the less fortunate. For only two examples of this, see *Ragged Dick,* p. 193, and *Digging for Gold,* p. 196.

[29] *Strive and Succeed: Two Novels by Horatio Alger,* intro. S. N. Behrman (New York: Holt, Rinehart and Winston, 1967), pp. 1-146.

[30] Horatio Alger, *Joe's Luck* (Akron, Ohio: The Superior Printing Co., n.d.), p. 37.

[31] Cawelti (p. 109) notes that it has been estimated that the average Alger hero ended with only about $10,000. It would seem that on those infrequent occasions that Alger hoisted his young hero to the top of the economic ladder, he did so only to accommodate the stranger-than-fiction success mythology of men such as Carnegie and Rockefeller.

[32] Alger, *A Cousin's Conspiracy,* p. 12.

W. T. Lhamon, Jr. (essay date 1976)

SOURCE: "Horatio Alger and American Modernism: The One-Dimensional Social Formula," in *American Studies,* Vol. 17, No. 2, June 20-July 11, 1976, pp. 11-27.

[*In the following essay, Lhamon places Alger as a central influence in defining American mores and developmental ideals, especially in regard to the relationship of the individual to society.*]

Imamu Amiri Baraka's story, "The Death of Horatio Alger," is an important overlooked benchmark in the history of American literature because it so consciously marks the end of America's one-dimensional culture.[1] Baraka says even "Poets climb, briefly, off their motorcycles, to find out who owns their words. We are named by all the things we will never understand [and] all the pimps of reason who've ever conquered us." He speaks of the white, majority culture as a "complete and conscious phenomenon." And when Horatio Alger died for him, Baraka experienced his "first leap over the barrier." That is, he began to be free when he saw that serious literature was part of the complete and conscious phenomenon that owned his earlier words. By holding him in Horatio Alger's sort of life, literature, too, pimped his reason. It, too, conquered him. Serious literature was the cultural arm of social oppression. It was war carried on by other means.

I

And there is a measure of truth in that claim, because Alger's influence outlived his 107 novels and even the 118 published in his name. Among the "highbrow" authors who kept Alger alive were Dreiser and Fitzgerald—in *An American Tragedy* and *The Great Gatsby,* both published in 1925. Also Faulkner's *Snopes* trilogy breathed life into the Alger pattern from 1925 until 1959. But what sort of life? Alger died, in fact, in 1899. Between that year and the 1960s his formula may be said to have had a transcendent afterlife in the books of American modernism which made lasting fictions structured on Alger's paradigm. His afterlife terminated in the 1960s with the publication of such works as Baraka's story. Alger's prime bequest to American fiction was the complacent plot of the outsider breaking into society's structure, and its sustaining premise was that the only valuable life was within society. And so even such an expatriate as Hemingway finally falls within Alger's values when Jake and Brett follow the policeman's baton on the last page of *The Sun Also Rises.* It would be merely "pretty" to think they might build an alternative together. In saying that, Hemingway unconsciously illustrates William Burroughs' comment that "A *functioning* police state needs no police," for living outside society "does not occur to anyone as conceivable behavior." And yet alternative existences had been conceivable before Alger—in Twain, for instance—and they are conceivable again today in the works of post-modernism. Which is to say that the limits of modernism are now available to us as they have never been before, largely because the era is now sandwiched between times of contrast.

Preceding Alger was a period of tremendous ambivalence and consequent rich complexity in American literature. His slightly older contemporaries included Sinclair, Norris, Howells, Twain, Wharton and James. That is, the wide thematic diversity in the nineteenth century included illiterate boys on rivers, educated American girls in Europe. Lithuanian immigrants in Chicago, wheat growers in California and gentility in New York drawing-rooms. The literature reflected the society's genuine pluralism. Alger's novels, however, came at the time when that pluralism began to decline toward the seeming one-dimensionality of modern society and modern literature. After him and after the First World War, by all accounts, American society had gone a long way toward the centralizing bureaucratization of late urban life. These social forms moved increasingly to shunt aside the complex, often confused, but still rich stimuli of nineteenth-century American experience. Alger's novels helped perform the same function in American literature. And they helped provide the comforting mood of mind that would allow Americans to become accommodated to one-dimensionality.

Part of my title comes from Herbert Marcuse's famous book, *One-Dimensional Man* (1964), but I use the phrase carefully. Marcuse's thesis is desperate. He suggests that there is no chance anymore in highly integrated—one-dimensional—modern societies for an alternative vision even to be *felt,* much less realized. But his book had the misfortune to appear in 1964—the very year of Mississippi Freedom Summer. SDS, SNCC, SCLC, CORE, RYM, RYM II, PLP and ERA—that whole inscrutable thicket of capital letters—were either on the scene that year, or shortly would be. So Marcuse's theory is not so truthful as it is important. It is important because in extreme form it expressed, or nearly did, the social despair of the modern intellectual. Yet in Marcuse's own year a burgeoning reform movement belied him. So that was Paradox One about Marcuse's book and the idea of one-dimensionality. Paradox Two is that for all his book's dire fears, Marcuse did not go far enough at least in one respect: whereas he thought drastic unification was a new phenomenon, America, in fact, had had a one-dimensional *culture* for at least a century.

Henry James may not have been the first to notice the philistine limits to American culture, but in 1879 he noticed them most negatively: "no personal loyalty, no aristocracy, no church, no clergy, . . . no literature, no novels, no museums, no pictures." And so on. James left the country. Not much after James wrote that, Huck Finn, seemingly a very different sort of person, left the country too. But they both left for the same fundamental reason: so fully had the middle taken over, so fully was the bourgeois figure the one figure America was beginning to support, that no inroads could be made from the top or bottom.

So forceful was the Alger formula in the culture that it excised alternative patterns preceding—and emerging during—his time. Twain's influence, for instance, was relegated to filling in niches in the Alger pattern. That is, modern characters after Alger and Twain have talked in Twainian dialect, but the dialect most often merely expresses Algeresque platitudes. The formula was the same no matter who was pronouncing it and no matter the attitude toward it. If American modernists disliked or hated the formula, they still felt constrained to follow it in order to talk about their country and culture. The Alger formula took occupation in the land. We recognize that occupation only retrospectively because our heroes and our few heroines have been to the reading public just as the psychotic is to the neurotic: the same as everyone else, only a little more so, and a little before us. But what were the laws of that occupation?

There have been three central creeds to the literature America inherited from the industrial age and from Alger. The first was: Join America or Leave Her—as Christopher Newman and Huck Finn found out (in James's *The American,* 1877, and Twain's *Adventures of Huckleberry Finn,* 1884). A little later came the second creed: Join America or Die—as Edna Pontellier and Quentin Compson discovered (in Chopin's *The Awakening,* 1899, and Faulkner's *The Sound and The Fury,* 1929). This second creed developed as it seemed there was no escaping the totality of America, and as it seemed there was no territory to light out to. Then came a third creed: Join America and Die Anyway—as happened to characters as different as Jay Gatsby, Lemuel Pitkin and the eventual Flem Snopes (in Fitzgerald's *The Great Gatsby,* 1925; West's *A Cool Million,* 1934; and Faulkner's *The Mansion,* 1959). And that was the beginning of the end for one-dimensional literature. Because all the options within society were played out, the pendulum swung away. Postmodernism began in the late fifties when Burroughs went into withdrawal and Ginsberg howled; and it continued in the sixties when Yossarian "took off" for Sweden, Brautigan went trout fishing in his mind, Rojack went to Guatemala and Yucatán, Rabbit ran, Pynchon began digging under the rose and Baraka ended his *Tales* with a story about a revolution in progress.[2]

This contemporary literature demonstrates the inevitability of cultural pluralism. There are times when an economy and its culture can tighten like a noose, more and more narrowly defining the ways to be in the world. But there comes another time when everyone climbs down off the motored cycles of culture, as Baraka argues, to see who owns the words, who has been "pimping" reason. As "The Death of Horatio Alger" suggests, the perception that somebody else has been possessing one's language is a finding of some surprise. By the discovery of loss there is also the plausible repossession of one's words. And the perception also advises that escape is less spatial than cultural. One escapes not to a Woolfian "room of one's own," but rather to a dialect of one's own.

Every cultural period says both yes and no to its social and economic structure. Sometimes, as with American modernism, the period says No! in thunder, but in the end sighs, yes. The next generation—post-modernism, in this case—has arisen out of that capitulation. For we have not yet had a one-dimensional society, no matter how truly one-dimensional the literature and larger culture have become. Always there has been the profound drama of what America has done to her disinherited and what they have done for themselves. And what is true for the literally disinherited is also true for everyone else. In letting literature give us words which, in time, ossify into shibboleths, we all let literature possess us. One of the highest missions of culture, therefore, is paradoxically to allow people their own words, thus to possess themselves, thus to create their own sub-cultures—which will need to be negated in turn, again and again. For that to happen, however, there must be an understanding of how peoples are culturally disinherited, of how they have been possessed. This paper is a study of the roots of one of the ways literature contributed to that processed, one-dimensional, culture.

II

Alger did not determine the largely one-dimensional topic of subsequent modern American fiction, but he prompted and anticipated it. He gave youths agreeable images of what they could expect in life. In over a hundred novels, he defined the sense of what was plausible in America. And though those definitions were bogus in their simplicity, they nevertheless stuck. He recorded the shift in late nineteenth-century American culture from pluralism to monism—from many heroes and heroines, for instance, to a repeated bourgeois hero. Because his novels were so widely read and because the need was presumably so great for authors to address that theme, Alger established the topic. His lifetime was so happily congruent with the mushrooming national communications and transportation systems that his fiction was able to supplant regional folktales. Thus he represents the beginning of the pop industry as opposed to organic folk sources. In fact, Alger began the urban, national "poptale." It

is no accident that Edward Stratemeyer—the later author of all the Tom Swift, Rover Boys, Nancy Drew and Hardy Boys novels (among many other series)—began by pirating Alger's formula and imprimatur. There is a significant line connecting Alger, Stratemeyer and the children's industry today, a pop industry which fixes certain images early so that serious adult literature will have to deal with them later. This is one of the reasons contemporary ambitious fiction now draws so heavily on pop culture. For these historical reasons, then, it is important to pay attention to Alger's legacy. Whether one considers his formula a great sourcepool or a great cesspool of modern American fiction, Alger has been very important.

The American dream was a lode by the time Alger mined it. That perhaps as many as four hundred million copies of his books have been sold is testament both to the reality and fragility of the dream: clearly readers liked what Alger told. Clear, too, is that they needed to be reminded over and over again, as if the clarity he provided did not last long and soon left them confused again in a world resistant to his formula. That he probably wrote 107 novels along the lines of *Ragged Dick, Risen from the Ranks and Hobart the Hired Boy,* often in periods as short as from two weeks to a month, signifies that Alger worked from a substantial vein, but that it was deliquescent, constantly in need of being rediscovered.[3]

The social dilemma of a highly mobile society existed before Alger published his first novel, *Frank's Campaign* (1864). Moreover, the convention of self-help literature was as old as America and just as noble since it was well under way with Jefferson and Franklin.[4] Alger's important function, therefore, was to catch the social stimuli at their great point of change as America became urban, industrial, and nationally conscious. Equally important, he almost monopolized the literary projection of those elements. While sharing substantially in the stream of the Adamic myth, he fixed a new sluice lending the flow its own distinctive features. The literature of the present century has had to account for them willy-nilly.

Alger's novels had three common plots: country boy goes to city and thus from rags to riches (*Ragged Dick*); city boy goes West and from poverty to respectability, so he can return to the city (*Joe's Luck*); wealthy city boy loses his luxury and then must provide for himself on the streets before regaining his just deserts (*Strong and Steady*). But in each case the dominant elements are the same. In the city novels, some people (usually, lesser people) go west; in the novels of the West, the heroes are urban and return to the city. The city is the starting and ending point for most of the novels; the focus is there. If only for this reason, the country-boy-in-the-city is the most important version of the Alger formula and would deserve primary attention. But it is also this version which has stuck in the popular consciousness of Alger, the version most thoroughly passed on into the twentieth century.

Like all fiction, Alger's is a departure from reality. If one definition of Romance, as Henry James said, is an authorial world cut loose from actuality like a balloon with severed string floating away from the ground, then Alger's "novels" are Romances. But directly proportionate to his severance from the common ground is his insistence that his novels are guidebooks constituting urban realism. This silent contradiction in his work goes far to account for the success Alger enjoyed in his own time. It is also the fundamental reason Alger is useful to read a century later as we try to understand the problems of the present.

Perhaps the best place to demonstrate his departure from the world then and now is in the populace of Alger's fiction. Always there is a hero with an Anglo-Saxon name, quick wit and appealing features: "attractive," "frank, straight-forward," "a share of pride, and a bold, self-reliant nature"; "if he had been clean and well-dressed he would have been decidedly good-looking." The villain of the story is equally recognizable: "slender and dark," with "a soft voice and rather effeminate ways"; he "never played baseball," was "sprucely dressed," and had "hands encased in kid gloves." The villain is never a poor boy, finally, but always represents scheming effeteness and luxury. When poor boys at first appear evil, as Micky Maguire does in *Ragged Dick,* they eventually knuckle under to the authoritarian system, often as valets to the hero.

This knuckling under and attendant obsequiousness occur, for instance, in *Joe's Luck,* an Alger novel of some importance because Nathanael West transcribed whole sections of it into his *A Cool Million.* Especially revealing are those passages in *A Cool Million* having to do with the "rip-tail roarer from Pike County" who terrorizes West's Lemuel Pitkin, rapes Pitkin's girl and is last seen carrying her off to Mexico on his horse.[5] Alger's significantly tamer version had had the Pike County man end as janitor and chief bottlewasher in a restaurant owned by the hero. He had became "a reformed roarer . . . remarkably industrious." Likewise, in *Ragged Dick,* Micky Maguire is the poor boy who seems at first villainous. But Dick bests him at every point, verbally and physically. In the sequel, *Mark, the Match Boy,* it turns out that, "by his magnanimity, [Dick] had finally wholly overcome the antipathy of his former foe. . . . Micky had become an enthusiastic admirer of Richard." Micky's villainous threat is tamed, as was the rip-tail roarer's.

Untamed villains are scourged. These true villains, once discovered and shamed from the city, typically move "to Chicago, and perhaps further West." Having failed to dupe New Yorkers, they can always try again in the Midwest, moving successively to older frontiers, where it is easier to make one's way. Thus New York is a trial by fire and the rest of the continent, increasingly as the distance from the City is greater, becomes a fool's green pastures. Alger thus reversed expectations from earlier nineteenth-century popular literature by changing the locus of man-testing hardships from the mountain passes and river valleys to the alleys and concrete canyons. The change is an important indication of the new dispensation Alger was formed by, as well as forming. It is also a fascinating example of how a culture moves into a new period by inappropriately reapplying past values to new stimuli.

Perhaps because he admired Henry James, Alger included in many of his novels a ficelle, who is normally younger, weaker, "less confident, and not so well fitted as [the hero] to contend with the difficulties of life, and fight his way upward." The ficelle allows authorial comment on the perils of smoking, drinking, and bad company. More significantly, however, he is another of the means Alger uses to place the hero in a setting of the golden mean—this time between the pole of slothful wealth (against which the ficelle counsels) and that of timid ineffectuality (which the ficelle embodies).

The hero normally has paternal problems.[6] His real father is thwarted, lost or dead. If the father is thwarted, the hero reinstates him; if he's lost, the hero finds him; if he's dead, the hero erects a surrogate. Between the real and substitute fathers, however, there is often a wicked father who takes shape as one of the challenges the hero must overcome to prove himself. And the hero always does overcome these ultimately ineffectual adults. Mothers also appear in this self-reliant world. Whether they are real mothers (and thus good) or false mothers (and thus wicked), our hero finds ways either to protect them or to expose them. Thus Alger manipulates the plot so that society is finally reaffirmed. Heroes spend all their time rejecting parents but not parental values and structure, which they always embrace at the end. The enduring mythic dimension of this resolution is best stated by Ellison's Invisible Man, in his Epilogue: "we were to affirm the principle on which the country was built, and not the men, or at least not the men who did the violence." All of this is to say that evil in Alger's fiction, and in its heirs, is pervasive but personal: aberrant, not systemic, not structural.

The chief personae in Alger's novels are interesting in themselves. But against the panoply of the minor characters Alger's vision relaxed the largest social tensions, for his resolutions of social conflicts provided for readers a very comforting way of shaping the world. Indeed, there is a formula of enduring dimensions lying in his dramatized social interactions. Ragged Dick is fourteen, admittedly an awkward age. Were he to grow much older he would be an adult—an adult shining shoes. The message of the story is that Dick is an exceptional youth; through luck and pluck, grit and wit, health not stealth, Ragged Dick becomes Richard Hunter, Esq. But whatever happened to the other urchins—the ones who hadn't the stuff of greatness?

In the early chapters of *Ragged Dick* they are everywhere on the streets and sleeping in doorways. Yet by book's end and Richard's ascent the streets are purified. In life as we know it, just as boys will be boys, they will also be men. In life as Alger formulized it, boys will be boys; some boys will be men; but no boys will be visibly poor men. When poor men do appear, it is as thieves or confidencemen, whom the hero always catches and ships to Blackwell's Island, or the Tombs, or sends scurrying westward. When, toward the end of a novel, occasional representatives of the honest poor remain, Alger heroes always lend them a helping hand. Good Samaritanism, therefore, takes care of anything left over from the scourges. Poor men who fail to succeed in the system disappear and rich men who wallow in their luxury are shipped to Chicago. As symbolic action, this rise of one man with concomitant social cleansing action is serious. An ultimate world without threatening villains, without evil adults, without poor people, without problems: this is how the literary contribution to the one-dimensional society is made.

The hero enters manhood by affirming shopkeeper values. The novel documents to the nickel the money he saves, the cost of his room, the value of his accoutrements and furniture. He aims to inhabit an Astor hotel suite, because in this pattern adulthood is marked by respectability and its furnishings. Unless one has these—otherwise symbolized by a gold pocket watch, a desirable fiancée, and a ticket (to New York City from the West, or up in a business firm)—one is not a man either in the sense of adulthood, or of simple effectuality. It may therefore be that the term "boy" is not entirely a racial slur, but is also class-related, for at least in Alger's fictive world all men worthy of the name are middle-class.

Alger lived in a time when it was still possible to have a distinct middle-class consciousness. No Alger hero ever aspires to or achieves the upper class, for the upper class is divorced from "fighting upward." Living in lassitude is perhaps the lowest form of life; it certainly is reserved for the sallowest villains. The Old Bowery is a bad place; poor boys squander pennies there to relieve their sordid street lives. But Alger's final scorn falls on the likes of the boys at the fancy Madison Club where, for instance, Roswell

Crawford deals down cards and drinks up dollars. Part of Alger's hate for grand wealth results from his Calvinstic doctrine of sin; part certainly stems from the demands of his conscious realism (one can't credibly rise *too* far from rags and bootblack); part is due to a simplistic rendering of finance ("there came a great catastrophe, and I found my brilliant speculations were but bubbles").

Still, the chief part of his hostility toward wealth is doubtlessly rooted in an unconscious sense that the real danger to an aspiring middle class was the concentration of wealth and power in the hands of an upper class. He had to dramatize such a class as ineffective and had to dismiss its constituents if his formula was to work, if Ragged Dicks were to make it. The novels too repeatedly display the author's animosity toward the very wealthy and too often show the poor boy vanquishing them for any reader to doubt either that Alger had a great anger toward an over-monied class or that he saw them as invincible. In our history, Horatio Alger, Jr. is the first popular partisan of what we now call a managerial class.

The Alger legacy designates the way one makes a heap of money through a clean life and diligent work: from rags to riches through luck and pluck. Such is the shape of the Algeresque experience. But in so pronouncing the phrase we trip past luck, the most submerged but most important part of the cliché. The Alger hero typically shines shoes and sells matches for 153 pages, and then inherits $50,000. Or he saves a rich man's son from drowning, and is adopted by the newly-found benefactor, who sends him to college. Or he drifts through New York until finally discovered by his father, a rich man the hero thought was long dead. Alger's heroes, although seeming to fight upward, must actually mark time passively until the critical juncture in their lives. Even when he attains success, the hero further hides his luck by maintaining a humble facade for a proper initiative period so that social change, while actually portrayed as fortuitous and saltatory, seems to be oiled and gradual.

Alger carefully suppresses luck's significance because if its importance were apparent, the formula would lose its credibility. But the obvious fact in each novel is that good fortune falls on the hero while mischance rains on villains. Therefore, in direct proportion to the number of incredibly lucky accidents in the novels, Alger obfuscates their necessity by repeatedly and rhetorically underscoring the overwhelming reliability of manly pluck, grit and prudential virtue. In short, Alger was skirting a central problem in his formula. It is luck that makes the man, but not obviously, because the formula and authorial rhetoric hide the luck. Nor is the luck simple—because really random chance would offer opportunity at least as often to pauper and crook as to hero and ficelle. Nevertheless, in Alger's formula, it is always the boy with manly pride who discovers the long-lost father, chances across a wealthy child drowning in the river or discovers that his paupered mother's farm is oil-rich. Unmanly types chance across wallets in other people's pockets; and when they try to capitalize on their discoveries, they are caught and sent to the Tombs. Therefore, although luck is finally necessary to success, only the plucky are lucky. Horatio Alger and his middle class are happy to spread around beneficences—but only to latent versions of themselves.

From the character of the relationships that casually occur—it's nothing for two boys to meet one afternoon and be bed partners that night—to the nature of the social ascent, Alger assiduously presents this society as open. But to consider this openness in a closer look and a comparison is to see something else in these novels. The movement in an Alger novel seems to resemble most closely the mode of the Bildungsroman—with one critical difference. Central to the Bildungsroman is the notion that a man's important period of development takes place in his youth, at roughly the age of Alger's heroes when they walk the streets. In the Bildungsroman, characters struggle with values in their youth and establish a lasting adult relationship to their society. Essentially, the Bildungsroman is a celebration of Pauline values in their struggle with Corinthian ways; and the struggle is every bit as serious as in the biblical model. Young rogues learn in the Bildungsroman to put away childish things, but only slowly and reluctantly, because the childish things are initially attractive. The point of the form is that the rogue tries to remain Corinthian (or childish) as long as possible. The adult society of Pauline respectability must prove its superiority to the skeptical, self-pleased, and Corinthian hero. It does; and he puts away his childish things. In the formula of the Alger novel, however, there is no struggle with values, nor is there an important period of development. Boys struggle with material hardships, then are rewarded by a nice, middle class that was waiting only to see if the boys had gumption. Youths undergo economic transformations, but never develop new values. Boys on the street always knew they wanted to wear starched collars and eat petits fours; boys in the townhouses were glad they had advantages and were respectable, even if it was boring. In fact, only those boys with pluck—native capitalistic competitiveness—are allowed to transform their lives. A struggle with values is out of the question. Everyone who will endure in this Algeresque world is Pauline from the beginning. None of them actually liked his childish irresponsibility; each of them was always plucky.

Indeed, there is an important punning sense to the way Alger's heroes rise on pluck. They have assiduous pluck, yes, but more important is the way the good merchants "pluck" the hero out from a mob of street boys. This last understanding of action in the novels at least accounts accurately for the locus of responsibility and power in Alger's world. Except insofar as he was genetically endowed with gumption, the boy has had little to do with anything in his career. Alger has stood the Bildungsroman on its head and written a new genre instead—the Sky Hook Romance. But he has concealed the Sky Hook in the realistic machinations of his mode. Thus his audience grew up indoctrinated with luck but not knowing it, just as they believed they were reading about a struggle with values when they were actually reading about how a society scourges alien values.

Never do the police, the visible arm of the government, fail to aid the hero and his friends; authority is only appropriately heavy-handed, always friendly, always understanding of the distinction between honest hero and stealthy villain. Consonance exists between the authority of the social elements represented in the story and the authority of the narrative plot. All elements—of the formula and of the social form—dovetail agreeingly: policeman and author agree about who is bad and who is good. For Alger, there is but one possible rapprochement with the flux of society. Despite the narrator's speeches in every novel to the effect that boys make their own way, the obvious plot formulations show that society promotes certain boys. That is, despite the promise of great openness in the content and narrative rhetoric of the novels, the shape of each plot is tightly closed.

Fully continuous with this is the way the names in Alger novels telegraph the outcome before the events even begin to unfold. The characters' names do not individualize them, but class them; the names are as formulaic as the plots. There are contemptuously fancy names for upperclass characters (Roswell Crawford, Randolph Briggs, Philemon Carter); sturdy, monosyllabic names for the boys who will succeed (Dick Hunter, Ben Barclay, Frank Courtney, Joe Mason); and finally the ethnic and/or deprecatory names for "street arabs" whose fate it will be to disappear (Micky Maguire). When there is any confusion of heroes' names with those of villains, Alger calls the "street arabs" only by the surname, i.e., "Travis" and "Hawley." Likewise, Alger is not subtle when he dislikes a business firm which is exploiting the public or treating its employees badly; thus he names a lottery "Grabb & Co." and a publishing firm "Pusher & Flint." In another novel, a carpenter is "Mr. Plank," a detective is "Mr. Lynx" (who "ferrets" out information), and one attractive girl is "Rose Gardiner."

The real social divisions will ultimately dominate despite their apparent shuffling at any random point. Walter Conrad, in *Strong and Steady,* may be thrown into poverty by the death of his father and attendant conspiracies, may have to struggle desperately to maintain himself in a hostile world, but his due will come. He will be restored to his right place above hoi polloi. The hortatory message is that there are no class divisions in this society that cannot be overcome. But the form suggests very differently that the class divisions are absolute and never to be overcome, always to be fulfilled.

Alger's impact is ominous: in the way he grants potency and even existence only to those fully in accord with bourgeois values, while scourging alternative modes of being; in the way he assures solid consensus by closing society, while righteously insisting it is open; and in the personal cost to the few who succeed (to which we shall return). Most ominous of all is that this pattern sold so many books, presumably because it satisfied such great needs, and thus, at least in part, indicated that the reading audience participated in Alger's anxieties. His heroes acted out the resolutions his audience wanted. They were like the boys who bought the books, only a little more so.

III

How did it happen that Alger's form, with all its imitators and detractors and believers, came so tenaciously to occupy the American mind? A partial explanation worth exploring here is that the dream, for Alger and his readers, was a necessary logomachy—prompted by their position, their guilt and their competition with a vital working-class subculture.

Alger's public was decidedly middle-class. The internal evidence indicates such an audience: the polite and formally written diction, excitement about schooling and the attention to details of clothing. And the external evidence also indicates a middle-class audience: Alger books were selling at the price of a dollar a copy at the turn of the century (A. L. Burt Company). Alger's books were not penny pamphlets, not were they distributed gratis by churches or other philanthropic organizations; try as he might, Alger was no Dickens. Tax-supported libraries were flourishing in American cities throughout the nineteenth century. Like the bookstore, theater, music hall and fine restaurant, however, libraries "could for the most part be enjoyed only by the few."[7] This question of middle-class readership is of some significance because Alger has often been seen as a man writing guidebooks for the poor on how to get rich. For example, one recent critic has said of Alger's intentions. "Youngsters surrounded by poverty and sickness needed something to sustain them in their early years. Deprived of virtually all material comforts, they must at least be given the hope of a better future."[8] Nevertheless, it was precisely because they were deprived of all material comforts—in addition to the fact that a great many of the poor did not even speak or read English—that "youngsters surrounded by poverty" did *not* read Alger. He wrote about the poor, and perhaps for them, but he was read by youngsters who resided in at least moderate comfort.

Equally insufficient to explain Alger's extraordinary popularity and his name's later crystallization into a household word denoting special success is the kind of blurb with which his publishers promoted him: "books that are good and wholesome, with enough 'ginger' in them to suit the tastes of the younger generation . . . healthy and elevating" (from the last page included in the Hurst & Co. reprints). However, James Otis, Edward Ellis and G. Harvey Ralphson ("The Great Nature Authority and Eminent Scout Master . . . of the Black Bear Patrol") also wrote healthy and elevating books with ginger in them. Yet there are no James Otis societies or Edward Ellis Awards presented annually, no G. Harvey Ralphson success stories headlined in the newspapers, although there still are Alger societies, awards and headlines. To explain the prominence Alger held in his day and his name's persistent appropriateness for a part of the American experience, it is important to review the needs of his audience.

The social facts of the years between 1865 and 1914 are familiar. It was the age when the city rose and the railroad too, when the West filled, when America developed a national to replace a regional consciousness, when centralization became possible in education and media and government. There was a tremendous rise in wealth; between the Civil War and 1890 the number of American millionaires grew from a handful to four thousand. In 1865, America was predominantly agrarian, but by 1914 only thirty percent of the population lived off the land. Between 1860 and 1910 the proportion of the population living in cities and towns increased from less than a quarter to almost half. Jay Martin reports that: "By 1890 a third of all Bostonians were of foreign birth. New York held as many Germans as Hamburg, twice as many Irish as Dublin, and two-and-a-half times as many Jews as Warsaw . . . four of every five residents [of New York City were] of foreign birth or parentage."[9] The thirty thousand miles of railroad track in 1860 had become one hundred ninety-three thousand miles just thirty years later in 1890—a growth of six hundred forty-three percent. Growth in industrial output was similar. Surely, these are figures of seeming growth and openness.

There was, however, another side to the coin of growth. In 1885 there were nearly a thousand foreign language newspapers in the United States, signifying, among other things, large pockets of as yet "unmelted" ethnic audiences—people who either resisted or were repelled by open assimilation. These were also the early days of labor organizing—with police, industrial and labor violence probably more widespread than it has been since. These were the years of the AFL, IWW, ILGWU, ARU, railroad and coal strikes, Haymarket Riots, Knights of Labor, Prohibition Party, Women's Christian Temperance Union, Greenback and Socialist-Labor and Socialist Parties, Mugwumps and Populists. In short, growth was making some people satisfied, angering others, but hardly providing consensus. Restlessness and discontent were growth's flipside. Indeed, even at this period of great productive leaps, there was a strong feeling that for many Americans opportunity was closed. This central paradox in American history is central also to the appeal Alger had, for he silently spoke to it.

From our perspective in the next century, these conflicting versions of what it meant to live between the Civil War and the First World War seem hopelessly irresolvable. Nor are historians, for the most part, much help. Liberal scholars like Eric Goldman and Richard Hofstadter have emphasized the period's opportunity, its "sheer vitality," "unbridled ambition and audacity."[10] Directly opposed to them, however, has been the solidly entrenched theory of historical sociologists (and sociological historians) which is argued by scholars like the Lynds and Lloyd Warner. They argue that industrialization rigidified class lines and implicitly, therefore, the whole notion of social mobility in America is a sham. Fortunately, there is a somewhat recent resolution in the iconoclastic historiography of Stephen Thernstrom.[11]

Thernstrom dismisses the dramatic rags-to-riches paradigm as "absurd" on two counts. First, it is "clear that growing up in rags is not in the least conducive to the attainment of later riches, and that it was no more so a century ago than it is today." Second, that a few people rose from poverty to grand wealth is no indication of an authentically open society, only that "organizers and manipulators" come from all its segments. Like Alger, Thernstrom is more interested in the moderate success pattern, in the man who rose from laborer to the middle levels of the class structure. Thernstrom's surprising findings are that there were three types of mobility—geographical, occupational and propertied—with a different dynamic for each.

There was extensive geographic mobility, but it did not mean vertical mobility, except for people who were already middle-class. At "the lower reaches of the social order, getting out of town did not ordinarily mean a step up the ladder somewhere else." This type of keeping on, but not moving up, was the dominant feature of life in the nineteenth-century American city for the very poor, who were "buffeted about from place to place, never quite able to sink roots." However, for those working-class people with property who were able to stay in one place—usually skilled laborers—there was "very impressive upward mobility, though not always of the kind we might expect." Here the claims become very complex: there are differences in success patterns between native-born and second-generation workers, for instance, and between WASP families and those of other ethnic origin. But Thernstrom suggests "the most common form of social advance for members of laboring families . . . was upward movement *within* the working class, mobility into the stratum between the lower middle class and the floating group of destitute unskilled families." Also, "the sons of exceptionally prosperous laborers did *not* enjoy generally superior career opportunities; the sacrifice of their education and the constriction of their occupational opportunities, in fact, was often a prime cause of the family's property mobility."[12] Which is to say, a Ragged Dick's new job hardly meant he could bequeath a nest egg, as a new job traditionally meant that a middle-class person could, Although there was enough mobility in Alger's day to suggest his faith in an open society was plausible, the mobility entailed very different possibilities for different groups. Today it may be true that "Once families escape from poverty, they do not fall back into it." And that "Middle-class children rarely end up poor," as Christopher Jencks claims.[13] But Thernstrom demonstrates that very often the opposite was true in the nineteenth century. In fact, the parents' rise frequently lowered the children's chances. There was a cost to moving up for working-class people. This point marks not so much where Alger contradicts the historical record as where he unconsciously most submits to it.

The symbolic expense of success in the Alger formula is parallel to the material expense described by Thernstrom. A fundamental attraction of every Alger hero is the way each behaves so colorfully, so self-reliantly, during his period on the streets. During his street days he is as witty as he will ever be. For instance, while he was on the street, one of his companions told Ragged Dick he had seen Dick "before"; Dick replied, turning around, "Oh, have you? Then p'r'aps you'd like to see me behind." If such is not the zenith of humor, it is still enough to make adolescents chuckle. Dick faced danger, and coped; he fought sin, and won; he faced poverty, and succeeded. In the success, however, he changed by definition.

To succeed is to become middle-class, and that necessitates effacing the features that made him interesting all along. To succeed means to change from Ragged Dick, boy of colorful diction, to Richard Hunter, Esq., man of correct rhetoric. Here is the key moment when a merchant offers Dick his first position in a mercantile establishment:

> "How would you like to enter my counting-room as clerk, Richard?" [the merchant] asked.
>
> Dick was about to say "Bully," when he recollected himself, and answered, "Very much."

When it had sunk in that he was really to be a clerk in a respectable establishment,

> Dick was so elated that he hardly restrained himself from some demonstration which would have astonished the merchant; but he exercised self-control, and only said, "I'll try to serve you so faithfully, sir, that you won't repent having taken me into your service."

It is no coincidence that the novel ends just two pages later. The reader's cathexis has been to Ragged Dick: that is, to a figure who is spontaneous, clever, textured, and empowered to elicit excitement precisely because he is working-class. When Dick becomes Richard, that interest stops; and so must the novel.

In literary terms the paradox is simply that the shopkeeping society that one is urged to join will not sustain emotional commitment. And the lumpen society one is urged to leave, while exciting millions of readers through several generations, is so self-embarrassed that it repeatedly represses itself. Each Alger novel defuses its own lively conflict: it arouses then souses itself.

That essential contradiction is why the historiographic controversy is significant to the literary issue. Even Thernstrom's sophisticated answers to the question of nineteenth-century social mobility thornily retain the ambiguity of the historical debate about an open society. And his answers suggest the suspense of living through that experience. Therefore, both current scholarship and the covert conflicts in nineteenth-century literature tell us that American social agreement was superficial during the nineteenth century and that the culture was embedded instead in profound conflict. Alger's fictions were one way that the middle class assured its youths that theirs was an open, fair world, in which all might make their way equally if they had proper pluck.

But then Alger's readers, his middle-class adolescent boys, must also have felt that tension. They must have sensed the difference between their world and the working-class world, between the couplings of middle-class material possibilities and emotional effacement, on the one hand, and working-class material privation and emotional vitality, on the other hand. Such are the clichés Alger unconsciously dealt in and to which his readers subconsciously assented. His audience must have sensed the excitement, too, in the promise that some working children, if diligent enough, would fall heir to luck. Surely Alger's young readers, free to visit libraries and given allowances by parents to buy books, realized the difference between their own condition and that of the working children they passed on the way to the library or the newsvendor's. Here were children dressed in poor clothes and talking "low," as Alger describes them, who offered to sell matches, newspapers, or shoeshines to well-dressed rich children talking Standard English. There must have been an anxious distance—even guilt and fear—between the "vagabone" and the "respectable" child. The Alger novel laid itself over that gap between the two. It posed as a bridge but was more a rampart.

Alger's novels participated in that underlying dream of a loving fraternity between boys and among races (Irish and "Arabs" representing people of color) brilliantly identified by Leslie A. Fiedler.[14] When Micky Maguire eventually becomes valet to Richard Hunter, or the Pike County Man washes dishes faithfully for Joe Mason, there is a manifest dream of racial understanding that is, in Fiedler's and Huck Finn's words, "too good to be true." It is, in other words, self-serving for the (white) middle class. But Alger's imprimatur was to make the dream not adolescently, innocently, beautiful (as in Cooper, Twain, Melville, Dana), but vicious. There is no period of equality between Richard and Micky as between Ishmael and Queequeg, no sense of Richard's learning from Micky as Leatherstocking learned from Chingachgook, no sharing of terms nor mingling of ethnic values. Richard and Joe conquer Micky and the Pike County Man. The Irish boy and the bluff barbarian meet the WASPs only on WASP terms. Their options are to knuckle under or be erased from existence in the Alger world.

Alger addressed the problem of a closed society by projecting a fictional world which he thought was open. At least in part, guilt prompted his novels. But he soothed guilty feelings in his middle-class readers by showing what he thought was a world in which all could rise equally. In fact, he even gave a kind of advantage to the street boys because he showed them going through the "school of hard knocks." He took the felt sense of distance and difference and defused it. We have seen how the actual contemporary predicament was chock full of profound disagreement. But Alger's process of defusion is rooted in the way conflicts *in his novels* is only superficial, and is, Alger claims, embedded in profound agreement.

That so many of America's best novelists—among them, James, Fitzgerald, Faulkner, Dreiser, West, Mailer, Ellison and Baraka—have written in Alger's vein shows that Alger suggested parameters which have held sway persuasively through the first half of the twentieth century. But, impenetrable as those parameters may have seemed, they and literary modernism in general are presently under attack—an attack that has begun to look like a real alternative. A good test of the novels now billing themselves as post-modern is this final question: Do they avoid the tracks Alger laid down?

Notes

[1] LeRoi Jones, "The Death of Horatio Alger," in *Tales* (1967; rpt. New York, 1968). LeRoi Jones has since changed his name to Imamu Amiri Baraka.

[2] The references in this sentence are respectively to: *Naked Lunch* (1959), *Howl and Other Poems* (1956), *Catch-22* (1961), *Trout Fishing in America* (1967), *An American Dream* (1964-65), *Rabbit Run* (1960), "Under the Rose" (*The Noble Savage,* No. 3 [1961], incorporated into *V.* [1963], chapter III), and *Tales* (see note 1). For a discussion of the social formula of post-modernism, see W. T. Lhamon, Jr., "Break and Enter to Breakaway: Scotching Modernism in the Social Novel of the American Sixties," *boundary* 2, 3 (1975), 289-306. The distinction between modern and contemporary literature is now widely assumed by literary critics ranging from Leslie Fiedler to Frank Kermode. Current disputes are over the terms of difference and elements of (dis)continuity between the periods. My assumption in this paper is that the root of the issue lies in the period preceding both-in the popular culture of the late nineteenth century.

[3] Both the number of copies sold, and the number of novels Alger wrote are variously estimated. The most careful bibliography is the revised one by Ralph D. Gardner, *Horatio Alger, or The American Hero Era* (Mendota, Ill.: The Wayside Press, 1971). My figures are from this edition. But for another account, see Frank Luther Mott, *Golden Multitudes* (New York, 1947), 153. Edward Stratemeyer added eleven more volumes to Alger's 107, making a total of 118 "Alger Novels." For information on Stratemeyer, see Gardner, 21-23, and Arthur Prager, *Rascals at Large, or, The Clue in the Old Nostalgia* (Garden City, N.Y., 1971), 101-02, and throughout; also see Russel Nye, *The Unembarrassed Muse: The Popular Arts in America* (New York, 1970), 76-87.

[4] For this early history, see John G. Cawelti, *Apostles of the Self-made Man* (Chicago, 1965).

[5] For a sense of how very much of *A Cool Million* West appropriated from Alger, see Douglas H. Shepard, "Nathanael West Rewrites Horatio Alger, Jr.," *Satire Newsletter,* 3, No. 1 (1965), 13-28.

[6] For an analysis of Alger's oedipal content, see Norman Holland, "Hobbling with Horatio; or the Uses of Literature," *Hudson Review,* 12 (1959), 549-57.

[7] Charles N. Glaab and A. Theodore Brown, *A History of Urban America* (New York, 1967), 101-02.

[8] Richard Weiss, *The American Myth of Success* (New York, 1969), 55.

[9] *Harvests of Change* (Englewood Cliffs, N.J., 1967), 55. My sources in these paragraphs are Martin, Glaab and Brown (cited above, footnote 5), and Ray Ginger, "Introduction," in *The Nationalizing of American Life, 1877-1900,* Ray Ginger, ed. (New York, 1965), 1-27.

[10] This is especially true of Goldman. The quoted phrases are from his *Rendezvous with Destiny* (1952; rpt. New York, 1956), 3.

[11] The most concise summary of his work is in "Urbanization, Migration, and Social Mobility in Late Nineteenth-Century America," in *Towards a New Past,* Barton J. Bernstein, ed. (1968; rpt. New York, 1969), 158-75. This article is the source for my account of his work in the following paragraphs, except where separately noted. Also see his full-length book, *Poverty and Progress* (1964; rpt. New York, 1969); and his paper, "Immigrants and WASPs: Ethnic Differences in Occupational Mobility in Boston, 1890-1940," in *Nineteenth-Century Cities,* Stephen Thernstrom and Richard Sennett, ed. (New Haven, 1969), 125-64.

[12] These last two quotations are from Thernstrom, *Poverty and Progress,* 160 and 155, respectively. The italics are his.

[13] "Inequality in Retrospect," *Harvard Educational Review,* 43, No. 1 (1973), 139.

[14] "Come Back to the Raft Ag'in, Huck Honey!" in *An End to Innocence* (Boston, 1955), 142-51.

Gary Scharnhorst and Jack Bales (essay date 1985)

SOURCE: "Cast Upon the Breakers (1887-1899)," in *The Lost Life of Horatio Alger, Jr.,* Indiana University Press, 1985, pp. 127-48.

[*In the following chapter, Scharnhorst and Bales provide biographical and historical information on the last decade of Alger's life, with special attention to his politics and economic ideology.*]

I

Rupert did not envy his father's old partner. "I would rather be poor and honest," he reflected, "than live in a fine house, surrounded by luxury, gained by grinding the faces of the poor."

—HORATIO ALGER, JR., *Rupert's Ambition*

Alger was a mugwump, a liberal Republican committed to principles of fair prices and decent wages, a critic of sharp business practices and cutthroat competition. He was neither an apologist for the wealthy class nor a stalking horse for industrial capitalism.

Rather, his appeal was fundamentally nostalgic. He often set his tales in idealized villages modeled upon preindustrial Marlborough. His heroes never worked in mechanized factories, and in his later stories they were more often sons of poor farmers than indigent street Arabs. Whereas Alger wrote his early juvenile fiction to publicize the work of the Children's Aid Society and kindred institutions, many of the stories he wrote in the 1880s and 1890s were thinly-disguised critiques of the corrupt captains of industry.

Alger was dismayed by the rebate scandal, for example. Soon after government investigators first revealed, in 1879, that railroads often granted special rate concessions or "midnight tariffs" to oil companies, especially the Standard, he joined his voice to the chorus protesting the practice. He later described it by analogy in his novel *Number 91* (1886): A corrupt housekeeper, like a robber baron, levies tribute from every merchant whom she patronizes "as a compensation for turning the trade in his direction." As a result, the consumer, "without being aware of it, paid a larger price than any one else for what articles she purchased, the storekeeper and others compensating themselves in this way for the percentage they had to pay the housekeeper."[1] A simple enough scheme, however unfair.

Alger also indicated in his stories the unscrupulous investors who profited by manipulating stock values to personal advantage. The most notorious case of market plunder also occurred in 1879, when Jay Gould, James R. Keene, and their confederates circulated exuberant reports of the profitability of the Union Pacific railroad and the dividends to be realized from prudent investment in Union Pacific stock. According to contemporary accounts, "widows and orphans and lady stockholders rushed to buy the stock," whereupon Gould quietly sold most of his shares on the bull market and reaped a windfall profit of about ten million dollars.[2] Later the artificially inflated stock crashed, of course, though Gould stoutly fended off charges of malfeasance by maintaining he still owned stock in the railroad and thus shared in the loss. He neglected to add that it was a paper loss only. In Alger's *The Store Boy* (1883), a character who has lost money speculating in the stocks complains that "Keene or Jay Gould or some of those fellows" had upset the market.[3] Alger alluded to the scheme again in *Luke Walton.* He transferred the scene to Chicago and substituted the "Excelsior Mine" for the Union Pacific railroad, but otherwise the story remained the same. A "mock philanthropist" named Thomas Browning explains how, like Gould, he profited by a stock swindle with a modest initial investment:

> "I hired an office, printed circulars, distributed glowing accounts of imaginary wealth, etc. It cost considerable for advertising, but I sold seventy thousand shares, and when I had gathered in the money I let the bottom fall out. There was a great fuss, of course, but I figured as the largest loser, being the owner of thirty thousand shares (for which I hadn't paid a cent), and so shared the sympathy extended to losers. It was a nice scheme, and after deducting all expenses, I made a clean seventy-five thousand dollars out of it."

A widow, the mother of two children who has lost all her money in this confidence game, comes to Browning to plead her case.

> "One of your circulars fell into my hands. The shares were two dollars each, and it was stated that they would probably yield fifty per cent. dividends. That would support me handsomely. . . . You endorsed all that the circular contained. You said that within a year you thought the shares would rise to at least ten dollars. So I invested all the money I had. You know what followed. In six months the shares went down to nothing, and I found myself penniless. . . . But you seem to be a rich man."[4]

Alger's opinion of the profiteer is obvious: "He has done more harm than he can ever repair."

His modern reputation as a capitalist ideologue notwithstanding, Alger was a doctrinaire advocate of neither wage- nor price-competition. As early as 1871, in *Paul the Peddler,* he explained to his young readers that when too many workers compete for jobs in the marketplace, the entire labor force suffers from depressed wages and economic hardship.[5] Later, the mother of Luke Walton, who works as a seamstress in a glutted market, estimates that she earns only about three cents an hour sewing shirts.[6] On the other hand, her newsboy son enjoys the "advantage of diminished competition" when two other newsies quit the business. Alger often invoked in his fiction the biblical injunction "the laborer is worthy of his hire," arguing that employers should pay a living wage, not the lowest wage the market would bear. He even advocated organization or unionization of the working class in such novels as *Ben the Luggage Boy* and *Slow and Sure.*

He also recognized the advantages of economic cooperation, at least on a modest scale, in fixing fair prices. Though he was no socialist, he was interested in cooperative experiments as early as 1877, when he visited the Zion Cooperative Store in Salt Lake City. In 1885, he sent Edwin Seligman, by then an economist investigating the merits of socialism, a circular about a cooperative store recently opened in Natick. In an accompanying letter, the supposed champion of free enterprise opined that the store

> has been a remarkable success, and paid extraordinary dividends. Yet I do not know that there has been

anything exceptionally favorable in the circumstances attending its formation and history. The secret of its success has been good management, and where coöperation fails, I suspect that failure is due to poor management.[7]

Alger sometimes went so far in his late fiction as to criticize the profit motive. In *Tom Tracy* (1886), he complained that some haberdashers aim "to get their clothing made for the lowest market prices, and to make the best possible bargain with the customers." In *Luke Walton,* he endorsed usury laws which would limit the interest charged on loans.[8]

Despite his mugwumpish inclinations, Alger carefully hewed the Republican party line on election days.[9] His correspondence reveals that he proudly voted for Rutherford Hayes in 1876, William Henry Harrison in 1888, and William McKinley in 1896. "With the election of McKinley," he accurately predicted in September 1896, two months before the vote, "an era of confidence and prosperity will be ushered in." He wrote the same friend in December, after the election, that "All eyes are now turned to Washington. I have great hopes of the success of the coming administration."[10] He supported anti-Tammany candidates in New York municipal elections and advocated civil service reforms. He believed that tariffs were necessary to protect the business interests of the nation, and he opposed the campaigns to inflate American currency with greenbacks and Free Silver.[11] To their everlasting credit, as he reported in his juvenile biographies, Garfield and Webster had battled for "sound" or "hard" money. On the other hand, as he observed in June 1896. "The Democrats seem to be all at sea with the silverites predominating."[12] At least the Gold Democrats had "nominated a good ticket," which was more than he could say of the populist supporters of William Jennings Bryan.[13]

He reserved his strongest endorsements for two politicians with whom he enjoyed some personal acquaintance. He was first attracted to Russell A. Alger by reports that the former governor of Michigan, a distant cousin, had generously contributed money to help a thousand poor boys in Detroit. General Alger was a candidate for the Republican nomination for President in 1888, and Horatio wrote to assure him that spring that he "should be glad of an opportunity to vote" for him and that he would "be glad to meet one who has made our family name so honorably conspicuous." A few weeks later, Horatio lurked in the lobby of the Fifth Avenue Hotel in New York and sent up his card to General Alger's room, though his kinsman was not receiving visitors. On June 30, after the Republican national convention, the defeated candidate wrote Horatio to ask his support of the party in the fall. Horrified by the prospect of Grover Cleveland's reelection, Horatio was amenable to the appeal. "I think you would have been a stronger candidate than Harrison," he replied on July 4. "However, the strongest feeling with me as with you is the hope that our party may win against an Administration which is unAmerican." A decade later, Secretary of War Russell Alger became the target of intense criticism when spoiled meats and other substandard supplies were shipped to American troops fighting the Spanish in Cuba. Horatio again wrote his cousin to express both his displeasure "at the senseless and unreasonable criticisms on your official course" and his confidence that "the public will do you justice in the end."[14] This prediction fell far short of the mark. On July 19, 1899, the day after Horatio died, Russell Alger resigned under fire from McKinley's cabinet.

Horatio was also favorably impressed by young Theodore Roosevelt, a patrician New Yorker and graduate of Harvard, whose father had helped Charles Loring Brace found the Children's Aid Society. Alger was acquainted with the foppish Roosevelt through the Harvard Club as early as 1881 and watched his star rise over the next eighteen years. Late in 1895, John Downie passed a civil service exam, one of Roosevelt's innovations while the New York City police commissioner, and became "one of Roosevelt's reform police," as the proud foster father bragged. A few weeks later, Alger went to Railroad Hall on Madison Avenue to hear Roosevelt speak, and, when the commissioner failed to appear, he was called to the podium as a stopgap. Late in 1896, Alger was disturbed to learn that Roosevelt was shopping "for a position in Washington" in the McKinley administration, for he "will be a loss to New York."[15] Roosevelt was subsequently appointed to the post of Assistant Secretary of the Navy and, less than two years later, elected governor of New York. Unfortunately, Alger did not live long enough to learn he would be elected Vice-President in 1900 and assume the presidency upon McKinley's assassination the next year.

II

I am content to share in the successes of my young friends, and feel satisfied with the little I have myself achieved. My work has been chiefly satisfactory because it has brought me so many friends whom I value.

-HORATIO ALGER, JR.,
7 October 1894

For a decade before he retired in 1896, Alger was so prolific that he had to invent a new pseudonym to prevent confusion. In all, he wrote thirty-nine serials during the decade, in large part because Frank Munsey, the entrepreneur who launched *Golden Argosy* on a string in 1882, had succeeded beyond all expectations. Munsey had built the circulation of the weekly simply by pricing it below the competition. Each issue cost but a nickel, an annual subscription but a dollar and a half. Alger contributed so much pulp fiction to it that in 1886, even as its circulation peaked at 115,000, his serials began to overlap. Some numbers contained both the closing chapters of one of his stories and the opening installment of another. Between the spring of 1886 and the summer of 1894, Alger published a total of thirty serials in the *Golden Argosy,* eleven of them under the penname "Arthur Lee Putnam." Meanwhile, circulation dipped to about nine thousand. The more Alger wrote for the magazine, the fewer copies it sold.[16]

The fault was not entirely Alger's, to be sure. Munsey increasingly aimed the paper at semi-literate adults rather than at juveniles, and he raised the subscription price about the time the national economy turned sour in 1893. But Alger was one more albatross around the masthead. As his career sputtered, he abandoned all pretense of writing stories in thematically-organized series. He wrote hurriedly, haphazardly, without pride, for the cash. Publicly, he continued to assert that "If a writer finds his own interest in the story he is writing failing, he may be sure that the same effect will be produced on the mind of the reader."[17] Privately, he wished he "could enjoy work as I used to" and allowed, for example, that he "did not care much" for his story *Adrift in the City.*[18] Most of the juveniles he wrote during these years, including most of the serials "Putnam" wrote for *Golden Argosy,* appeared in book format only after his death.

Partly to collect more material for stories in the style of the "Pacific series," partly to escape the harsh New York winter, Alger returned to the West Coast in the fall of 1890. He left New York, "stopped at Niagara Falls, but only for a few hours, and spent a day in Chicago," where he visited Jackson Park, soon to be the site of the Columbian Exhibition. He headed on to St. Paul and Minneapolis, where he boarded the cars of the Northern Pacific for the trip "over the broad plains of North Dakota and through the mountains of Montana." He reached Helena on Saturday, October 25, where he passed the weekend with Albert Seligman, another of Joseph's nephews, and his wife. He left Helena two days later and passed Arlee, Montana, on October 28, reached Portland a day or two later, and arrived in San Francisco on November 2.[19] A week later, the *Morning Call* reported in a feature article that Alger had "a host of warm personal friends" in the city whom he had come to visit.[20] He wintered in California and returned east the next spring. As late as June 1896 he considered another trip to California, one via the Canadian Pacific road.[21]

Unfortunately, the western stories Alger researched in 1890-91 were neither popular nor critically well received. His novel *Digging for Gold,* for example,

was panned in the *Dial:* Alger "attempts to mine the wealth that lies hidden in the early history of California, but he brings back little to enrich us." In fact, reviewers usually reviled Alger's late stories. The *Bookman* concluded that *Adrift in the City* evinced "mediocre ability," and the *Literary World* damned it with faint praise as "written in the most polished Oliver Optic style." Some reviewers reiterated the old charge of sensationalism. The *Literary World* in December 1893 asserted that Alger "might do something better than pour forth this unceasing stream of sensational, impossible literature." Other readers found fault with his weak characterizations: He "could not possibly be more puerile in the selection of characters or more clumsy in their delineation," the *Literary World* concluded. Still others lamented the predictability of his plots: The *Critic* complained in 1895 that Alger always finds an audience of boys

> no matter how bad his rhetoric, how unreal his situations, or how crude his workmanship. His latest book, "Victor Vane, the Young Secretary," tells, as usual, of the impossible virtues, triumphs and successes of a boy of seventeen, who becomes private secretary and confidential adviser and friend to a Western Congressman, and transacts a large amount of important business in the most experienced fashion. Such stories as this call for little comment.

Similarly, according to the *Dial,* in *The Young Salesman* Alger "tells how a poor young English orphan, landing in New York with a small sum of money, becomes, without apparent effort, an earl's friend, a merchant prince, and a general philanthropist to small boys." The *Critic* averred that "there is nothing new" about *The Five Hundred Dollar Check* "except the cover and the paper and possibly the pictures. . . . It is such an obvious, worn-out theme for a story that we wonder any author with the instinct of literary self-preservation should employ it." Still other reviewers chided Alger for his overreliance on coincidence as a plot contrivance: In *Rupert's Ambition,* according to the *Dial,* "everything happens at precisely the right moment, in precisely the manner in which everything fails to happen in real life."[22] Reviewers rarely rallied to Alger's defense. Yet some young readers thought well of these late, limp stories. To judge from his autobiographical novel *Look Homeward, Angel,* Thomas Wolfe read dozens of Alger's books, including *Jed the Poorhouse Boy* (1892). In 1890, two of Alger's stories were even translated into Russian and published in a juvenile magazine issued in St. Petersburg.[23]

Alger readily admitted whenever asked that he wrote his stories without outlining their plots in advance. Instead, he chose an opening incident and began to write without regard to subsequent chapters, with no preconceptions about pace or direction.[24] He built each novel at the rate of a chapter or so per day, usually writing only in the afternoons amid the noise and bustle of a group of boys in his room.[25] Quiet confused him, he said. His rationale for this strategy echoed, if on a lower frequency, Henry James's argument in "The Art of Fiction" that a story should grow organically from its original conception like a plant from a seed. "I never fully understand a character, to begin with," Alger explained, "but gradually become acquainted with it as I go on. The characters, once introduced, gradually develop and in turn shape the story."[26] As in the cases of Johnny Nolan and Micky Maguire, he tried to model characters upon real boys whom he met, whenever it was "possible for me to find a character" suited to his tale. "I have always made a close study of boys in order that my characters might seem to be drawn from life," he added.[27] "I have a natural liking for boys, which has made it easy for me to win their confidence and become intimately acquainted with them."[28] Once a week, usually on Friday evening, he invited boys to his room, where he sat at his writing desk and asked questions. As George Steele Seymour, a minor poet who as a boy once attended the circle, recalled years later, "I did not see him take any notes," but "it was understood that he was gathering material—that boys' personalities were somehow in process of filtering through to the printed page."[29] Alger identified some of these boys by name in the stories, such as Arthur Burks, John Schickling, Eugene Sweetland, and Tommy Keegan.[30]

Even in old age he centered his routine both in New York and in Natick around boys. "What gratifies me most," he wrote privately in 1897, "is that boys, though strangers, seem to regard me as a personal friend."[31] He went so far as to claim that in his experience boys were "natural" and girls "artificial."[32] James Montgomery Flagg, later a popular artist, as a boy in the 1890s often visited Alger, that "dear little pink old gentleman from Natick." In his autobiography, Flagg recalled attending "some of his parties for Ragged Dicks and other Alger characters. He fed them ice cream and told them stories and they loved him."[33] Like Flagg, Seymour later supplied one of the few eyewitness descriptions of Alger's appearance in his declining years. He was a "short, almost bald man wearing nose glasses, with a protruding lower lip and an upward tilt of the head." He thought there was "a New England air about Mr. Alger, and something birdlike too."[34] Arthur Burks's brother Ernest also remembered Alger fondly years later. "He was very stout and short," he recalled, with a fair complexion. He was "very near sighted" and "almost completely bald" but for a few tufts of white hair.[35]

Fortunately, a few letters Alger wrote to his young friends during these years have survived. Most are filled with banal amenities and gossip. In some of them, however, Alger told of his disappointment when one of his boys was arrested. His moral maxims were no fail-safe deterrent to crime. In 1892, Oren Trott, a boy he knew from his summer vacations at Peak's Island, Maine, near Portland, was persuaded by a young thief to fence a few watches. "The sum realized was only a dollar and a quarter, but the fact that Oren sold them makes him an accomplice in the eyes of the law," Alger explained to Ernest Burks.

> If Oren knew that the watches were stolen he was very weak and foolish to consent to sell them, and he realizes this now. I hope his previous good character will help him. . . . Of course I shall stand by him whatever happens. I always do stand by a friend in time of trouble.[36]

Similarly, Alger later wrote his friend Irving Blake that

> one of the boys who used to frequent my room— not to my satisfaction—is now at Sing Sing prison, confined for burglary. I exerted myself to obtain a mitigation of his sentence, and was very successful. . . . I don't think he realized what he was doing. I have sent him an autoharp to fill up his time as the prisoners are not now employed.[37]

Occasionally, Alger lost patience with boys who demanded his favors, and he changed apartments every three or four years to shake hangers-on. "I gave up my room on 34th St. because I had too many young callers who were unwelcome," he explained to Blake in March 1896. "For this reason please don't mention where I am."[38]

Over the years he increasingly indulged his taste for popular theater and classical music. In New York during the 1870s and 1880s, he frequented the Grand Opera House, Niblo's Theatre, and Lester Wallack's playhouse on the Great White Way, where he struck up friendships with members of the stock companies.[39] He praised in his books and letters such period actors as James Lewis, Sir Henry Irving, Edwin Booth in the role of Cardinal Richelieu, Richard Mansfield as Jekyll/Hyde, Joseph Jefferson as Rip Van Winkle and, of course, Edwin Forrest.[40] While in New England for Christmas in 1877, he commuted from Natick to Boston to attend "two or three amusements including 'Pippin,' the new American Opera bouffe."[41] He saw Mark Twain perform on stage on three occasions ("peculiar lectures, but interesting"),[42] and, in 1890, he befriended little Elsie Leslie, child star of "The Prince and the Pauper" stage adaptation.[43] During the winter of 1896-97, after his retirement to Natick, Alger regularly attended Boston theaters. "I go with young friends and consult their tastes as to the plays," he explained.[44] On December 3, 1896, for example, he saw Bret Harte's new play

Sue, with Annie Russell in the title role, at the Museum Theatre. He was not particularly impressed. "The plot is faulty," he remarked candidly to Irving Blake a few days later. Some of the minor characters are quite picturesque, especially those who take part in a lynching court scene. I don't think, however, the piece can on the whole be regarded as a success."[45] Alger was also fascinated by such musical prodigies of his day as the Brazilian violinist Maurice Dengremont, who toured the United States in 1881 at the age of fifteen ("I became acquainted with Degremont with whom I could converse a little in French").[46] On April 23, 1890, he attended the farewell concert at Steinway Hall in New York of the young German pianist Otto Hegner ("He has promised to write to me").[47] On December 11, 1896, he heard the thirteen-year-old Polish violinist Bronislaw Huberman play a classical program at the Music Hall in Boston ("He is not good looking but in his childish costume he produced a pleasing impression").[48]

In short, despite the fragility of his health, Alger remained reasonably active until he was long past sixty, he wrote four serials a year as late as 1895, though he had begun to exploit opportunities to escape his desk. He attended the forty-year reunion of his college class at Young's Hotel in Boston on July 21, 1892,[49] and, as Class Odist, he once more penned a lamentation on lost youth for the occasion:

> Grown older now, we will not mourn
>   Those exhalations of the dawn;
> The heroes that we hoped to be
>   Will never live in History.
> No knights or paladins are we,
>   Plain toilers only in the mart;
> Yet let us hope on Life's broad stage
> That we have played a worthy part.[50]

In the early 1890s, he began to spend more time each summer in Natick and at the coastal resorts of Maine and Massachusetts. He quit working for months at a time to relax in the sun. He had not written a word for publication in two months, he wrote Blake from Natick in August 1894, and he was about to leave to rusticate further at Old Orchard Beach and Martha's Vineyard.[51] He thought the sea breezes cleared his lungs and restored his strength, and he certainly ranked his health above the stories he might have wrung from a more active career.

He centered his life no less than his stories on boys during these years, but he still experimented with adult fiction. Frank Munsey had serialized *Helen Ford* in *Golden Argosy* in 1885-86 under the title "A Child of Fortune" and the old pseudonym "Arthur Hamilton." Early in 1889, Alger contributed a series of new adult short stories to the *Yankee Blade* which were subsequently syndicated in newspapers

throughout the country. Munsey reprinted a slightly revised version of *The New Schoolma'am* in *Munsey's Magazine* in March 1892 under the title "A Fancy of Hers."[52] In short, Alger found the urge to write for adults difficult to suppress, especially when he read popular fiction by writers, such as Beatrice Harraden and Florence Marryat, who were no more talented than he. In fact, the idea for a new adult novel, *The Disagreeable Woman,* occurred to him as he read Harraden's *Ships That Pass in the Night* in the spring of 1895. The more telling influences on this story, however, were Holmes's Breakfast Table books and Longfellow's "Evangeline." Narrated by a young physician who has lately moved to New York from the country, the plot involves a menage of characters at a boarding house who try to cope with the economic depression of the mid-1890s. One of them, whom the others call the Disagreeable Woman, seems callous and indifferent, though the doctor understands that she merely disdains frivolities. In the final chapter, he tells her the whereabouts of her long-lost fiance and she hurries to his sickbed. She nurses him back to health, and the story concludes, like most of Alger's adult romances, with a long-deferred marriage on the threshold of consummation.[53] Because Porter & Coates had exclusive rights to Alger's fiction, this novel, published in July 1895 by G. W. Dillingham of New York, appeared under the new pseudonym "Julian Starr."

Though it retailed for only seventy-five cents per copy, the novel was Alger's personal worst seller. Dillingham issued it in attractive hardcover, and even the author admitted he "hardly thought this story worth such a setting."[54] Henry B. Blackwell in the *Woman's Journal* commended the feminist overtones of the "bright, lively charming book," and Munsey loyally plugged it as "good, easy reading for a summer's day," but a reviewer for the *New York Times* intimated that the story was more disagreeable than the title-character.[55] By any measure the novel was a resounding flop. Only two copies of the original edition are known to exist, one of those deposited for copyright in the Library of Congress.

In June 1895, Alger declared a moratorium on work and left New York for New England "a little earlier than I intended. I find the rest and quiet very grateful."[56] He loafed around his sister's house in Natick for several weeks, gave his niece Annie away in marriage to the submaster of the Chapman School in East Boston on July 1, and left for Peak's Island on July 7.[57] "I have done no work since I've been away," and "I do not expect to do anything till fall," he wrote Blake from the Aldine Hotel, Old Orchard Beach, on July 11.[58] "Horatio Alger, Jr., is staying on the Maine coast during the summer, making his headquarters at Old Orchard and Peak's Island," the *Critic* reported later that month.[59] "The paragraph in the Critic may convey the misleading impression that I have given up work," Alger reassured a friend. "I do not propose to do this however, only to work less."[60] He returned to Natick via Manchester and Gloucester towards the end of the month, and left for two weeks in the Catskills on August 5 in company with his sixteen-year-old cousin, Frank Cushman, who also was descended "from Rev. Robert Cushman of Mayflower memory." They cruised down the Hudson to New York, where Alger took young Cushman to Central Park and the Statue of Liberty, before they returned to Natick on the 24th. Alger spent another week in Maine in early September and at last returned to New York and to work on October 9.[61]

The winter of 1895-96 would be his last season in the city. He was besieged by a nagging case of bronchitis, complicated by overwork, which lingered for weeks. In January, fearing an onslaught of fever, he hurried to Natick to be near his sister. "I considered myself in imminent danger of the *grip*," he wrote Blake on February 5. "I have staved it off, but still have a bad cold. . . . I may stay here some weeks."[62] Though nearly exhausted, Alger pushed his pen to finish **A Cousin's Conspiracy,** eventually serialized in the *New York Weekly* between April and August 1896. "I took special pains with it," he admitted later, because "I hope to leave a good impression on the readers, should that [story] be my last."[63] "I have been working very hard," Alger told a reporter in the lobby of the Adams House in Boston on April 9, "and it is a pleasure to be able to rest a little. I am staying out at Natick with relatives now. . . . I do not feel as energetic as I used to."[64] The reporter noted that Alger's closely cropped moustache was gray and his complexion "rather florid." Two weeks later, Alger wrote that his "general health is fair, but I find it difficult to rally from mental overwork."[65] For all practical purposes, he had retired, though not formally or voluntarily. He would never again work more than a day or two at a stretch. Eventually, he would realize that, at the age of sixty-four, he was past trying.

III

I wonder, Irving, how it would seem to be as young and full of life and enthusiasm as you are. I shouldn't dare to go back to 19 again, lest my share of success should prove to be less than it has been.

—HORATIO ALGER, JR.,
12 May 1897

At first, Alger treated his retirement as a period of recuperation. At the invitation of his sister Augusta, he recited a poem at a meeting of the Natick Woman's Suffrage League.[66] He still traveled occasionally—to New York in May 1896 on business; a day journey to Marblehead in late May with A. K. Loring, seventy

years old and in straitened circumstances; several days on the Maine coast in August and two weeks at Woodstock, Connecticut, in September.[67] "My summer travel is doing me good," he reported to Blake. "I feel brighter & better than I did."[68] But early in November he took another brief business trip to New York—it would be his last visit to the city—and he "contracted so severe a cold that I thought it the part of prudence" to return to Natick earlier than planned.[69]

Predictably, he had begun to worry about how he might live on a reduced income. Soon after he moved to Natick, he bemoaned the fact that "There are plenty of good writers for boys. If there were not I should occupy a larger field & have more abundant sales." Early in 1897 he expressed the vain hope that "my books have sold well."[70] He was expecting any day to receive a royalty check from Henry T. Coates & Co., successor to the firm of Porter & Coates. When it arrived, it was not as large as he would have liked, though he presently concluded that his income was "adequate" to meet his reduced expenses.[71] In each of the last four years of his life, he sold book rights to two of his old serials to Coates at the flat rate of five hundred dollars per serial— this in addition to his royalties on earlier books still in print.[72] He had also become a silent partner in a small business in Boston to supplement his income.[73] "I still find writing up hill work," he complained to Blake in February, "and if things go well I shall not write any this year." "On account of overwork," he explained a week later in reply to an inquiry from an editor, "I shall not *for some time* be able to undertake any new work."[74] Though his health improved slightly over the summer, especially while he was at Old Orchard Beach in August, he continued to fret about the future.[75] He had earned, by his own estimate, about $100,000 as a writer during his thirty years in New York, but he had earned little money since moving to Natick.[76] "My royalties this year have been less than usual," he diplomatically observed in a letter to Coates in September, "but I hope we shall do better in the coming year."[77]

Unfortunately, Alger's anxieties, both financial and physical, only grew worse over the next twelve months, aggravated by a sluggish economy and a palpitating heart. "I suppose Coates is to publish a book or two for me this fall but I don't think any have appeared," he carped to Blake in October 1897.[78] His sales were still slow, and Coates was unwilling to saturate the market with more than two new Algers a year. Meanwhile, his health continued to fail. He cancelled a business appointment in New York in December because he was "afraid of taking cold" on the trip.[79] His precautions merely postponed the inevitable. The winter in Massachusetts was unusually severe that year, and in early February 1898 he suffered another attack of bronchitis, a fulminating infection "which to one of my physique would probably have been fatal" had it settled in the lungs.[80] "My bronchitis still hangs on," he wrote Blake on March 21, "and probably will for a week or two yet. The worst feature of it is the difficulty of breathing."[81] His condition was complicated by atherosclerosis, hardening of the arteries around the heart, which caused severe anginal pain. In May he took to his bed and wrote letters in a crabbed scrawl. "My most serious trouble is a too rapid heart," he complained in early June. "I have always been short breathed."[82] He tried to recuperate that summer in Nantucket and Old Orchard Beach, but to no avail. In October his eyesight began to fail as the flow of blood to his head was occluded. "I am not at all well," he admitted to Blake on October 21. "I am quite lacking in strength."[83] He still maintained a lively correspondence—he wrote or dictated as many as thirty letters a week to Blake, John Trowbridge, Edward S. Ellis, Louise Chandler Moulton, and others.[84] He still tried to read the *Atlantic Monthly* and other magazines, but he was merely marking time.[85] Even his sister thought he had aged beyond his years.[86]

"It is more than two years since I broke down in New York from over-work and removed to Natick, Mass.," he wrote his cousin Russell Alger on November 10, 1898. "I have been able to do little since then, and it has been somewhat discouraging, particularly as it has cut down my income considerably."[87] Most disturbing to him was his inability to support his eighteen-year-old ward, Tommy Downie, who had gone to work for a magazine dealer in New York. Alger was determined to send him to the Brooklyn Business College, the same school his brother John had attended, so that he might enter a profession and earn a good living. "I may not be able to leave Tommy much," he grieved, "but I want to leave him a better education at any rate."[88] "With such means as I had I have been able to do a good deal of charitable work," he added in his letter to Secretary of War Alger, "but I doubt if I shall be able to [do] very much more."[89] He was not penniless—he owned a lot in North Chicago and had over a thousand dollars in the bank[90]— but on Tommy's account he needed extra cash. When he left New York in 1896, he had written over half of a juvenile novel entitled ***Out for Business***.[91] He had been unable to finish the story during his illnesses, however, so in the fall of 1898 he began to search for a ghostwriter who might complete it for him.

He settled on Edward Stratemeyer. Alger had corresponded with Stratemeyer, a sometime editor who had serialized his novel ***The Young Acrobat*** in the magazine *Bright Days* in 1896, for over two years. "He is an enterprising man and his stories are attractive and popular," Alger thought. "Under favorable circumstances I think he will win a book reputation."[92] In November 1896, during his last trip to New York,

he had called on Stratemeyer and found him both polite and personable.[93] When he decided to recruit a ghost to round out his manuscript, he thought first of Stratemeyer, who had completed William T. Adams's last manuscript a few years before. On October 26, 1898, Alger wrote to solicit the help of the younger writer. He was "in a state of nervous prostration," he began,

> and not only can't write, but can't invent the rest of the story for some time to come. I think of all the juvenile writers you can write most like me. Of course I want this help to be *sub rosa*. Can you take my story and finish it in my style? You will be left to your own discretion pretty much. By way of compensation, if satisfactory to you, you shall take the story & sell it to some periodical under *my name*. You will divide the proceeds *equally* with me but I shall retain the copyright and it will appear as my book. . . . Do you think you could easily find a market for a *new book of mine?* Of course we can't get a high price but whatever you can get that is reasonable will satisfy me. You can collect the money & pay me.

> If this proposal suits you I will send [the manuscript] out by express. I fancy it would be *easy* work for you as you have a fluent & facile style.[94]

Alger quickly concluded negotiations with Stratemeyer and, on November 21, mailed him two hundred manuscript pages.[95] The story *"is a good deal below my average,"* he confessed, "having been written when I was in a state of nervous depression" back in New York.[96] Barely three weeks later, Stratemeyer returned an outline of his projected final chapters. His suggestions pleased Alger, though he admitted he had "only taken a casual glance at the M.S. my eyes being a good deal affected by my illness." In a brief note on December 18, he promised to get back to Stratemeyer when he had a chance "to go through it" in greater detail. "Go ahead with any other work," he added. "Will communicate with you as soon as ready."

He did not write Stratemeyer again, despite the best of intentions. His health steadily deteriorated through the winter. In February 1899, perhaps the last time he touched pen to paper, he scribbled a request to Blake to send him an account of the latest Harvard Club dinner.[97] In April, he was permanently confined indoors. During his final illness he expressed a wish to his sister Augusta that as little publicity as possible attend his death—he did not even want his true age reported—and he acquiesced to her suggestion that his remains be cremated before burial.[98] He died in her home on Florence Street in Natick shortly after midnight on July 18. His physician listed heart disease as the cause of death.

The funeral on the 20th was a quiet, modest affair in keeping with Alger's wish.[99] In the morning his body lay in a plain coffin at Augusta's home, and, early in the afternoon, it was carried to the Eliot Church in South Natick, "one of those huge, shapeless, barn-like structures," as Harriet Beecher Stowe had described it, lit on the interior by "two staring rows of windows, which let in the glare of summer sun."[100] The Reverend George F. Pratt, the elder Horatio's successor in the pulpit, officiated at the service and delivered a brief eulogy. Both A. K. Loring and Henry Denny, the secretary of his college class, sat quietly in the pews. Four Natick boys, among them Arthur Burks and Eugene Sweetland, served as pallbearers. After cremation, his ashes were interred at Glenwood Cemetery, South Natick.

Alger's will contained no surprises.[101] Seventeen months before his death, he had decided to leave bequests of cash totaling $950 to young friends and family members, his calendar gold watch to a grandnephew in California, his lot in North Chicago to his niece Annie, his library to Annie's and Augusta's husbands. He willed his copyrights and future royalties to Annie, Augusta, and the Downie brothers, and he directed his sister, as executor of the will, to sell as part of the estate any manuscripts or serials not yet published as books. "All the rest and residue of my estate"—including his private papers—"I bequeath to my sister to be used at her discretion in the furtherance of my wishes, privately communicated to her," he concluded. The files were to be destroyed. The long-kept secret of Brewster was not even to be divulged posthumously.

Augusta did her part to protect her brother's legacy and reputation. On the day he died, she explained to a reporter from the *Boston Post* that, although "he enjoyed ladies' company very much," he had never married because he "apparently never found one whom he particularly fancied."[102] She sold the fragment of *Out for Business* outright to Stratemeyer for $150.[103] "By arrangement with a friend, the book is to be finished and published," she announced.[104] In fact, Stratemeyer would divide the two hundred pages of Alger's manuscript between *Out for Business* and a sequel largely of his own invention, *Falling in with Fortune*.[105] He would rewrite the unpublished **"Mabel Parker"** for juvenile readers and publish it under the title *Jerry the Backwoods Boy*.[106] Over the next decade, he would complete eight more novels published under Alger's name. These stories were genuine collaborations, based at least in part on Alger's notebooks and other material which Augusta sent him. With her help, Stratemeyer became Alger's official literary heir.

Outside the immediate circle of his friends and family, Alger's death was not much noticed. There were no public outpourings of grief, though his college roommate George Cary visited Augusta to extend condolences on behalf of the Class of '52.[107] "He was continually doing some kind act to assist the boys," Augusta observed. "I never walked down town with him but that some boy or other would have something to say to him."[108] The published tributes to his memory were gracious but few in number. In a brief obituary he prepared for the *New York Tribune,* Irving Blake described him as "a short, stout, bald-headed old gentleman with cordial manners and whimsical views,"[109] Stratemeyer wrote a memoir of Alger published in the October 1901 issue of *Golden Hours Junior,* a promotional supplement to *Golden Hours.* Though Augusta thought it "the most satisfactory article about him which has yet appeared," no known copy of it survives.[110] In 1907, eight years after Alger's death, Frank Munsey apotheosized his old friend and contributor in a privately-printed history of his publishing company. "He was one of the most human men I have ever known," Munsey declared, "a man with the simplicity of a child and the sweet, pure soul of God's best type of woman."[111] *De mortuis nil nisi bonum.* Alger was gone and, but for his books, mostly forgotten.

In addition to his books and the bequests in his will, Alger left another legacy of boys whose lives he had influenced as tutor, father, and friend. In most cases the boys did well by him. Joseph Dean became a banker in Palatka, Florida. Isaac Seligman succeeded his father and uncle as head of J. & W. Seligman Co. Edwin Seligman became, at the age of thirty, Professor of Political Economy at Columbia and spent a distinguished career in the study of public finance. In 1885, he helped organize the American Economic Association, and, in 1902, he was elected its president. Gilbert Hitchcock, to whom Alger dedicated a novel in 1878, subsequently succeeded his father in the Congress of the United States, served as wartime spokesman for the Wilson administration as chairman of the Senate Foreign Relations Committee, and was a dark-horse candidate for President in 1920. Alger's pupil Benjamin Cardozo became one of the outstanding jurists of his generation, and, in 1932, he was appointed by Herbert Hoover to the U.S. Supreme Court. Alger's pupil Lewis Einstein enjoyed an eminent career as an American diplomat in France, England, China, Turkey, and Czechoslovakia. Alger's ward John Downie served honorably on the New York Police Department for nearly forty years until his retirement in 1935. Alger's friend Irving Blake served as private secretary to Whitelaw Reid, editor of the *New York Tribune* and ambassador to the Court of St. James. Edward Stratemeyer went on to write the Tom Swift and Rover Boys books and hundreds of other juveniles.[112]

But the ledger was not filled entirely with credits to his memory. In 1871, Alger had dedicated a novel to Washington and Jefferson Seligman, nephews of Joseph, "in the hope that they may emulate the virtues of the distinguished men whose names they bear."[113] As an adult, Washington gambled heavily, concealed a mistress in his room, and subsisted mostly on whiskey, pieces of cracked ice he carried in a zinc-lined pocket, and chunks of charcoal which blackened his teeth. When he was broke he extorted money from his father, Jesse, by threatening to kill himself if refused. In 1903, he attempted suicide by slashing his wrists, and, in 1912, he succeeded with a gun. In 1886, Jefferson Seligman married for money, and, in 1915, he separated for love. He spent the rest of his life and most of his fortune giving fur coats to young women and advocating the kiss as social ritual. In 1889, Alfred Seligman, the youngest of Joseph's sons, married Florine Arnold, a young family friend to whom Alger had once dedicated a novel. Through the years they conducted a salon for Bohemian artists. Their marriage nearly ended in divorce in 1901 when Florine confessed to an affair. A. Florine ("Boisie") Henriques, the son of the vice-chairman of the New York Stock Exchange, to whom Alger dedicated a novel in 1873, became as an adult a notorious *bon vivant,* and, in 1892, he was arrested and jailed for passing a bad check. Lorin Bernheimer, another friend of the Seligmans to whom Alger dedicated a novel in 1879, suffered a nervous breakdown in 1906; began to claim he possessed incredible wealth; was declared mentally incompetent two years later; and was committed to a sanatorium, where he boasted continually of his fabulous, albeit nonexistent, fortune until his death in 1913.[114] It was an insidious delusion Alger would have understood and perhaps perversely appreciated.

Notes

I

Previous biographers sing one note in the same key: HA preached a gospel of wealth. Mayes claims (pp. 214-15) that the "most omnivorous readers of Horatio Alger were poor boys" or "boys who wanted to grow rich." He suggests that HA aimed his pitch at incipient robber barons. Like a catalyst in a chemical reaction, according to Mayes, HA's stories inspired entrepreneurs to join the scramble for wealth and prestige. Gruber chimes in (p. 11) that "Generations of successful men read Alger in their youth and many, many hundreds, thousands of them give Alger at least partial credit for their success," Gardner asserts (p. 346) that "Innumerable American leaders of today—and of recent memory—once read Alger and believed in him." The folklore of rags to riches, the celebration of free enterprise—HA's critics and his admirers alike agree to debate his merits in these terms. Unfortunately, his stories, especially those he wrote after 1880, harp on different themes—especially the rascality of the rich and the potential of money and power to corrupt.

[1] *Number 91* (New York, 1887), 181-82.

[2] Matthew Josephson, *The Robber Barons* (New York, 1934), 198.

[3] *The Store Boy,* pp. 279-80.

[4] *Luke Walton,* 115, 117.

[5] *Paul the Peddler,* 9-48.

[6] *Luke Walton,* 18, 35.

[7] HA to E. R. A. Seligman, 14 Nov 1885 (CU).

[8] *Tom Tracy* (New York, 1888), 42. Luke Walton, 246.

[9] HA to E. R. A. Seligman, 9 Nov. 1876 (CU); to R. Alger, 4 July 1888 (Mich); to Blake, 9 Sept. 1896 (Hunt).

[10] HA to Blake, 12 Dec. 1896 (Hunt).

[11] Anti-Tammany: HA to Blake, 7 Nov. 1897 (Hunt). Pro-civil service: *From Canal Boy to President,* 293, 300. Pro-tariff: *Abraham Lincoln, the Backwoods Boy,* 117. "Sound" money: *From Canal Boy to President,* 251-252; *From Farm Boy to Senator,* 175.

[12] HA to Blake, 26 June 1896 (Hunt).

[13] HA to Blake, 9 Sept. 1896 (Hunt).

[14] HA to R. Alger, 2 May 1888, 28 June 1888, (1 July?) 1888, 4 July 1888, 10 Nov. 1898 (Mich).

[15] *NYTi,* 22 Feb. 1881, 5:3; HA to Blake, 23 Dec. 1895, 5 Feb. and 3 Dec. 1896 (Hunt); HA to R. Alger, 10 Nov. 1898 (Mich).

II

[16] Mott, *A History of American Magazines 1885-1905,* 419.

[17] "WSfB."

[18] "Could enjoy": HA to Blake, 7 Sept. 1895, 3 Jan. 1896.

[19] Route west: *Chester Rand,* 335. Jackson Park: *Rupert's Ambition,* 260. Reached Helena: *Helena Herald,* 28 Oct. 1890, 5:2. Passed Arlee: Portland *Oregonian,* 30 Oct. 1890, 6:6. Reached San Francisco: *Alta California,* 3 Nov. 1890, 5:4.

[20] SF*MC,* 9 Nov. 1890, 12.

[21] HA to Blake, 2 June 1896 (Hunt).

[22] Reviews: S&B, 39-43; *Dial,* 16 Dec. 1896, 391-92; and 1 Dec. 1899, 434.

[23] SF*MC,* 9 Nov. 1890, 12.

[24] *Frank Leslie's Pleasant Hours,* NS 1 (March 1896), 354.

[25] *BDG,* evening ed., 18 July 1899, 10:6.

[26] HA to C. T. Scott, 25 March 1895 (LC).

[27] "AMBR."

[28] *Writer,* 6 (Jan. 1892), 16.

[29] *N,* 23 (Nov.-Dec. 1983), 10.

[30] *Chester Rand, 117; The Young Salesman* (Philadelphia, 1896), 15; *Rupert's Ambition, 285; Out for Business* (New York, 1900), 73-77.

[31] HA to Blake, 27 Feb. 1897 (Hunt).

[32] *BP,* 19 July 1899, 5:4.

[33] *Roses and Buckshot* (New York, 1946), 52.

[34] *N,* 23 (Nov.-Dec. 1983), 10.

[35] E. W. Burks to Frank Millner, 27 June [1939?] (LC).

[36] HA to Ernest Burks, 23 Nov. 1892 (Hunt). HA also mentioned young Trott by name in *Walter Sherwood's Probation,* 232-33.

[37] HA to Blake, 14 March 1898 (Hunt).

[38] HA to Blake, 17 March 1896 (Hunt).

[39] HA to E. R. A. Seligman, 1 July 1885 (CU).

[40] HA to Blake, 17 Sept. 1896 (Hunt); *Rupert's Ambition,* 206, 228; *A Boy's Fortune,* 69; *TF,* 1 May 1858, 2:5.

[41] HA to E. R. A. Seligman, 3 Jan, 1878 (CU).

[42] HA to Blake, 28 April 1896 (Hunt).

[43] HA to Elsie Leslie Lydes, 24 April 1890 (PML).

[44] HA to Blake, 28 April 1896 (Hunt).

[45] HA to Blake, 3 Dec. and 12 Dec. 1896 (Hunt).

[46] *NYTi,* 12 Jan. 1881, 4:7; HA to Blake, 12 Dec. 1896 (Hunt).

[47] HA to Elsie Leslie Lydes, 24 April 1890 (PML).

[48] HA to Blake, 12 Dec. 1896 (Hunt).

[49] *HGM,* 1 (Oct. 1892), 157.

[50] *AS,* 87-88.

[51] HA to Blake, 7 Aug. 1894 (Hunt).

[52] Munsey reprints: Bennett, 88, 130. Adult syndication: Bennett, 173-191; *N,* 22 (May-June 1983), 21-23.

[53] Synopsis: *The Disagreeable Woman* (New York, 1895), v and *passim.*

[54] HA to Blake, 4 April 1895 (Hunt).

[55] Reviews: S&B, 41-42; *Woman's Journal,* 3 Aug. 1895, 247.

[56] HA to Blake, 13 June 1895 (Hunt).

[57] HA to Blake, 7 July 1895 (Hunt).

[58] HA to Blake, 11 July 1895 (Hunt).

[59] *Critic,* 27 July 1895, 61.

[60] HA to Blake, 26 Aug. 1895 (Hunt).

[61] Returned to Natick: HA to Blake, 2 Aug. 1895 (Hunt). Visit to New York: HA to Blake, 26 Aug. 1895 (Hunt); *The Young Salesman,* 72. Maine and return: HA to Blake, 7 Sept. 1895 (Hunt).

[62] HA to Blake, 5 Feb. 1896 (Hunt).

[63] HA to Blake, 2 June 1896 (Hunt).

[64] *BA,* 10 April 1896, 9.

[65] HA to Blake, 28 April 1896 (Hunt).

III

Mayes and Gardner offer two contrasting views of HA in his sixties. According to Mayes (pp. 167-195)—and, of course, Tebbel as well (pp. 110-122)—HA had an affair with a middle-aged, married woman named Una Garth whom he pursued all the way to Paris. The waning of her affection caused him to return to New York sadder, wiser, and temporarily insane. His health broken, his ambition to write the Great American Novel turned to ashes, he died an invalid in his sister's home, destitute of money but rich in dreams. According to Gardner, on the other hand (pp. 289, 303), HA was infatuated late in life with the widowed mother of John and Tommy Down. Gardner explains in detail how HA, in the spring of 1891, bought a house in a quiet Brooklyn neighborhood, where he and the three Downs lived together in middle-class respectability. "Kate Down made for Horatio a snug home in Brooklyn," he writes, and as in most fairy tales they all lived happily ever after. Unfortunately, there is not a scrap of evidence to indicate that HA ever lived in Brooklyn or that "Kate Down" ever lived at all. Consider too the closing sentences of Gardner's biography:

Still holding the letter, appearing tiny and childlike on the large bed, he closed his eyes to slumber, nevermore to awaken. But on Horatio Alger's face was a relaxed expression of contentment, for he went to sleep knowing that when he joyously greeted his Kate, the first thing he would tell her was that he loved her.

Not only does Gardner invent the character of Kate Down, not only does he presume to read the mind of a man who would die in his sleep, he clearly suggests that HA had formed a heterosexual attachment, an unconscionable distortion of the Brewster records he claims to have examined.

Gruber, Gardner, and Hoyt are also misinformed about the so-called "Stratemeyer Algers." After HA's death, eleven novels were published under his name with the stipulation, at first explicit and later implied, that they had been completed by "Arthur M. Winfield," a pseudonym of Edward Stratemeyer. Gruber argues (p. 45) that all eleven "were actually written" by Stratemeyer. Gardner concurs (pp. 364-68; "Foreword" to *Cast Upon the Breakers,* p. 30): The novels "were actually written by Edward Stratemeyer." Hoyt echoes Gardner (p. 248): "They were books written by Edward Stratemeyer." Unfortunately, no earlier biographer checked with Stratemeyer's heirs. The MS of *Out for Business,* the first Stratemeyer completion, started in HA's hand and finished on Stratemeyer's typewriter, as well as HA's scrawled plea to finish the story for him, are still owned by the Stratemeyer Syndicate in Maplewood, New Jersey.

[66] HA to Blake, 26 Oct. 1896 (Hunt).

[67] To New York and Marblehead: HA to Blake, 2 June 1896 (Hunt). Maine coast: HA to Blake, 7 Aug. 1896 (Hunt). Woodstock: HA to Blake, 9 Sept. 1896 (Hunt).

[68] HA to Blake, 22 Aug. 1896 (Hunt).

[69] HA to Blake, 10 Nov. 1896 (Hunt).

[70] HA to Blake, 6 April 1896, 14 Jan. 1897 (Hunt).

[71] HA to Blake, 3 Feb. 1897 (Hunt).

[72] O. A. Cheney to Edward Stratemeyer, 2 Nov. 1899 (SS).

[73] HA to Blake, 16 Feb. 1897 (Hunt).

[74] HA to Edward Stratemeyer, 26 Feb. 1897 (SS).

[75] HA to Blake, 15 Aug. 1897 (Hunt).

[76] HA to Edward Stratemeyer, 18 Dec. 1898 (SS).

[77] HA to Henry T. Coates & Co., 24 Sept. 1897 (Bob Bennett).

[78] HA to Blake, 17 Oct. 1897 (Hunt).

[79] HA to Blake, 1 Jan. 1898 (Hunt).

[80] HA to Blake, 14 Feb. 1898 (Hunt).

[81] HA to Blake, 21 March 1898 (Hunt).

[82] HA to Blake, 2 June 1898 (Hunt).

[83] HA to Blake, 21 Oct. 1898 (Hunt).

[84] HA to Blake, 2 Feb. 1897 (Hunt).

[85] HA to Blake, 7 Nov. 1897 (Hunt). HA had been reading the excerpts of Mark Twain's *Following the Equator* published in *McClure's.*

[86] *BDG,* evening ed., 18 July 1899, 10:6.

[87] HA to R. Alger, 10 Nov. 1898 (Mich).

[88] HA to Blake, 1 Jan. 1898 (Hunt).

[89] HA to R. Alger, 10 Nov. 1898 (Mich).

[90] *N,* 18 (Jan.-Feb. 1980), 4.

[91] *BP,* 19 July 1899, 5:4.

[92] HA to Blake, 25 Sept. 1896 (Hunt).

[93] HA to Blake, 10 Nov. 1896 (Hunt).

[94] HA to Edward Stratemeyer, 26 Oct. 1898 (SS).

[95] HA to Edward Stratemeyer, 21 Nov. 1898 (SS).

[96] HA to Edward Stratemeyer, 18 Dec. 1898 (SS).

[97] HA to Blake, 24 Feb. 1899 (Hunt).

[98] *BP,* 19 July 1899, 5:3-4.

[99] Death and funeral: *BT,* 21 July 1899; *Natick Bulletin,* 21 July 1899, 1:4-6; S&B, 152-53.

[100] *Oldtown Folks* (Boston and New York, 1869), 2, 49-50.

[101] *N,* 18 (Jan.-Feb. 1980), 4-5.

[102] *BP,* 19 July 1899, 5:4.

[103] O. A. Cheney to Edward Stratemeyer, 2 Nov. 1899 (SS).

[104] *BP,* 19 July 1899, 5:4.

[105] *N,* 21 (May-June 1983), 5; 22 (July-Aug. 1983), 12.

[106] *Jerry the Backwoods Boy* (New York, 1904).

[107] *HGM,* 9 (Sept. 1900), 111.

[108] *BP,* 19 July 1899, 5:4.

[109] NY*Tr,* 19 July 1899, 7:3. Blake had prepared the copy 3 years before (HA to Blake, 16 July 1896 [Hunt]).

[110] *Golden Hours,* 28 Sept. 1901, 16:4; O. A. Cheney to Edward Stratemeyer, 11 Nov. 1901 (SS).

[111] *The Founding of the Munsey Publishing-House* (New York, 1907), 5-6.

[112] Joseph Dean: *Record of the Service of the Forty-Fourth Massachusetts Volunteer Militia,* 309. Isaac Seligman: *DAB* (New York, 1935), VIII, 570-71. E. R. A. Seligman: *Who Was Who in America* (Chicago, 1943), I, 1102-03. Gilbert Hitchcock: *NYTi,* 3 Feb. 1934, 13:1. Benjamin Cardozo: George Hellman, *Benjamin N. Cardozo: American Judge* (New York, 1940). Lewis Einstein: *Who Was Who in America* (Chicago, 1950), II, 171. John Downie: *NYTi,* 8 Dec. 1945, 17:2. Irving Blake: *NYTi,* 18 Nov. 1940, 19:4. Edward Stratemeyer: Russel Nye, *The Unembarrassed Muse* (New York, 1970), 76-84.

[113] *Strong and Steady* (Boston, 1871), v.

[114] Washington Seligman: *NYTi,* 13 Feb. 1912, 7:5; Peggy Guggenheim, *Confessions of an Art Addict* (New York, 1960), 19. Jefferson Seligman: *NYTi* 6 Aug. 1915, 18:5; Guggenheim, 19. Alfred Seligman and Florine Arnold: *The Telegraph Boy* (Boston, 1879), iii; Hellman, "The Story of the Seligmans," 296-301. A. F. Henriques: *Try and Trust,* iii; *NYTi,* 8 March 1892, 3:6; *GA,* 25 April 1885. Lorin Bernheimer: *The Telegraph Boy,* iii; *NYTi,* 30 Jan. 1913, 11:3.

Michael Moon (essay date 1987)

SOURCE: "'The Gentle Boy from the Dangerous Classes': Pederasty, Domesticity, and Capitalism in Horatio Alger," in *Representations.* No. 19, 1987, pp. 87-110.

[*In the following essay, Moon discusses Alger's blend of homoeroticism and capitalist nostalgia.*]

Throngs of Ragged Children bent on earning or cadging small sums of money filled the streets of mid-nineteenth-century New York, if we are to credit the testimony of a large number of chroniclers of city life of the period. These genteel observers—journalists, novelists, social reformers, early criminologists—professed to be alternately appalled and enchanted by the spectacle of street children noisily and energetically playing, begging, and hawking a multitude of services and goods—shoeshines, matches, newspapers, fruit. In considering the accounts of this scene made by those who first concerned themselves with it, one soon becomes aware that a significant number of writers respond to it with strong ambivalence. For many of them, there is an undeniable charm or beauty, strongly tinged with pathos, in the spectacle of the pauper children: the high style with which they collectively wage their struggle for subsistence exerts a powerful appeal. For some of the same observers, though, the charm of the street urchins is a siren song: beneath their affecting exteriors many of them are prematurely criminal, expert manipulators of the responses of naive and sentimental adults.

George Matsell, New York's first chief of police, initiated the vogue for writing "sketches" of the city's street children with his sensationalistic and strongly unfavorable report of 1849 on "the constantly increasing number of vagrants, idle and vicious children of both sexes, who infest our public thoroughfares."[1] The extensive testimony of minister and reformer Charles Loring Brace, who devoted a long career to "saving" street children, is more ambiguous, and consequently more representative of genteel response in general. While professing to detest the criminal tendencies that he believes street life encourages in poor children—indeed, the "philanthropic" plans for them that he and his colleagues in the Children's Aid Society (founded in 1853) framed and enacted involved systematically removing them from the city—Brace nevertheless often confesses to feeling a powerful attraction toward the children themselves, especially the boys. Brace seems to have possessed a remarkable capacity for "activat[ing] male sympathies," to borrow a phrase historian Christine Stansell has used to characterize his program: both the middle-class, reform-minded men who funded and worked in his programs and many of the ragged boys whom they housed, counseled, educated, and sent away to work seem to have found compelling the particular version of male community institutionalized in his charities.[2]

One often hears in the language Brace and his colleagues directed toward their boy charges the familiar intensities of evangelical piety, hortatory and emotionally charged. Unsurprisingly to readers familiar with the rhetoric of nineteenth-century American

Protestant revivalism. Brace's language frequently exhibits a markedly homoerotic character, as when in one of his *Sermons to News Boys* he appeals to his boy auditors' longings for an "older and wiser" male friend who would love and support them unreservedly:

> Though you are half men in some ways, you are mere children in others. You hunger as much as other children for affection, but you would never tell of it, and hardly understand it yourselves.

> You miss a friend; somebody to care for you. It is true you are becoming rapidly toughened to friendlessness; still you would be very, very glad, if you could have one true and warm friend.[3]

Although the "friendship" Brace is urging the street boys to accept here is ostensibly that of Christ, one can readily see how closely congruent a rhetoric of seduction could be with discourses of middle-class philanthropy like his, as when the adult male avows his willingness to recognize and respond (in various institutionally mediated ways) to adolescent male desires for dependency on an older, more powerful man for affection and support. The genteel gaze of Gilded Age New Yorkers seems always to descry disturbingly mixed qualities in pauper children, and the boundaries these imputed mixtures disturb are often ones of age and gender, as witness the ambiguous "half men" (adult males)/"mere children" (minors of indeterminate gender) to whom Brace addresses his exhortations.

Despite the pederastic overtones of some of their discourse, Brace and his fellow reformers seem to have been primarily interested in seducing poor children away from their underclass environments rather than actually engaging in sexual activity with them. However, at least one man who long associated himself with Brace's boy charities—Horatio Alger, Jr.—is known to have seduced boys sexually during at least one period of his career as well as to have actively participated in the reform movement to "seduce" New York street boys away from their milieu into an at least minimally genteel way of life. Alger has long been recognized as (in Hugh Kenner's phrase) "the laureate of the paradigms of ascent" in early corporate capitalist America; since 1971, his expulsion from the Unitarian ministry for pederasty in 1866 has been a matter of public record.[4]

In this essay I propose to explore how Alger's reformulation of domestic fiction as a particular brand of male homoerotic romance functions as a support for capitalism. Alger's writing provides a program cast in moralistic and didactic terms for maximizing a narrow but powerfully appealing range of specifically male pleasures: certain forms of social respectability and domesticity, the accumulation of modest wealth,

and the practice of a similarly modest philanthropy toward younger needy boys. As a number of critics have noted, Alger's tales generally prove on inspection to be quite different from what the "Alger myth"—"rags to riches" for industrious poor boys—has prepared readers to expect. Rather than promising riches to boy readers, they hold out merely the prospect of respectability; also, rather than presenting an example of "rugged" and competitive individualism, they show boys "rising" through a combination of genteel patronage and sheer luck. As Michael Zuckerman perceptively observed, "beneath [Alger's] paeans to manly vigor" one can discern "a lust for effeminate indulgence; beneath his celebrations of self-reliance, a craving to be taken care of and a yearning to surrender the terrible burden of independence." Alongside the apparent support of such capitalist ideals of the period as the self-made man and the cult of success, notions to which Alger's writing pays lip service but fails to narrativize or thematize effectively, another agenda inconspicuously plays itself out in tale after tale—one that would appear to be the antithesis of the idea commonly associated with Alger that any reasonably bright boy can rely on his own hard work and "pluck" to catapult him to a place near the top of the Gilded heap. Actually, Alger's tales hold out a considerably less grandiose prospect for boy readers; that any boy who is reasonably willing to please his potential employers can attain a life of modest comfort. Only a character as programmatically resistant to this prospect as Bartleby the Scrivener stands to lose out entirely in the new modest-demand, modest-reward ethos of the rapidly expanding corporate/clerical workplace. A characteristic authorial aside in Alger's 1873 **Bound to Rise; or, Up the Ladder** makes apparent in unmistakable terms the large part patient passivity, rather than competitive aggression, plays in the scheme of his stories:

> Waiting passively for something to turn up is bad policy and likely to lead to disappointment; but waiting actively, ready to seize any chance that may offer, is quite different. The world is full of chances, and from such chances so scized has been based many a prosperous career.[6]

"Rising" for Alger's heroes always remains a waiting game; within this pervasive passivity, there is an active and a passive position, but there is no way for a boy to take a more direct approach to the world of work and achievement in Alger's books.

How does one explain the gap that yawns between the reputation of Alger's books as heroic fables of ascents from the gutter to the pinnacle of power and wealth with their actual narrative contents: the achievement—with the benefit of considerable "luck" and patronage—of a mild form of white-collar respectability that releases the boy hero from the competitive struggle he has had to wage on the street? I propose that the answer lies not in some quirk in Alger's personality but in some basic contradictions in his culture that the tales engage. Alger's books can be read—and were by generations of young readers, albeit probably largely unwittingly—as primers in some of the prevailing modes of relationship between males in corporate/capitalist culture. I will argue further that the pederastic character of much of the "philanthropic" discourse about boys in this period is particularly marked in Alger's texts, and that what this sexual undercurrent reveals is not so much that the leading proponents of this discourse were motivated in large part by conscious or unconscious pederastic impulses—some, like Alger, no doubt were; perhaps others were not—but that there are determinate relations between social forms engendered by the emergent Gilded Age culture and some of the quasisexual ties and domestic arrangements between males that impel Alger's fiction.[7]

"Gentle-but-Dangerous" Horatio Alger

Alger arrived in New York City in 1866, eager to put his disgrace in Brewster, Massachusetts, behind him and to establish himself as a professional writer for boys (he had combined careers as a divinity student and fledgling juvenile author for a few years before his exposure). In one of the first pieces he published after moving to New York. Alger expresses the kind of fascination with the precocity of street boys familiar from other genteel writing:

> The boys looked bright and intelligent; their faces were marked by a certain sharpness produced by the circumstances of their condition. Thrown upon the world almost in infancy, compelled to depend upon their own energy for a living, there was about them an air of self-reliance and calculation which usually comes much later. But this advantage had been gained at the expense of exposure to temptations of various kinds.[8]

Struggling to establish himself as a popular writer in a competitive and demanding market, Alger may well have envied the ragged boys of Brace's Newsboys' Lodging House the "self-reliance" they had acquired not from reading Emerson (who is said to have once visited the home of Alger's parents) but from premature and extensive "exposure to temptations." The element of glamour he attributes to the street boy heroes of the books that followed ***Ragged Dick; or, Street Life in New York*** (1867) for a decade or so after is a quality that arises (as I shall try to show) from the way the figure embodies certain sexual and class tensions that were markedly present in the culture of Alger's period, tensions that had forcefully asserted themselves at critical points in his own life.

Unlike most of his genteel contemporaries, Alger shared with the street boys he began writing about in New York the experience of having been deemed outcast and "dangerous" to the community. That the boy ideal in his fiction should magically combine both "gentle" (genteel) and "dangerous" (underclass) qualities is the generative contradiction in Alger's work, but it bears closely on significant contradictions in his culture. Gentility and public disgrace, respectability and criminality were states that were not supposed to interact closely in mid-nineteenth-century America, but they did so with notable violence at several points for Alger, as when his Unitarian minister father, plagued with debt throughout the author's childhood, was forced to declare bankruptcy in 1844, or when Alger himself was ejected from the ministry for (in the words of the report of the church's committee of inquiry) "the abominable and revolting crime of unnatural familiarity with *boys.*"[9]

The Discourse of the "Dangerous Classes"

Alger's pederasty was an act that simultaneously transgressed a number of fundamental proscriptions in his culture: its object was male rather than female, and a child rather than an adult. Although apparently the boys with whom he was sexually involved during his days as a Unitarian minister were themselves middle class, Alger may have added a third form of transgression—sex across class lines—to his offenses against the dominant morality with some of the numerous underclass boys he fostered during his thirty years' residence in New York.[10]

Although there is no lack of documentary evidence to support the assertion that feelings of guilt and anxiety over real and imaginary wrongdoing were felt by many of Alger's middle-class contemporaries, a considerable amount of literary energy in America as well as in Europe in the two decades before he began producing his books was devoted to representing the actual states of being deemed outcast or criminal as conditions that properly happened only to the denizens of a segment of the urban world somehow fundamentally disjunct from the one middle-class readers inhabited—despite the physical proximity of the two worlds. Some of the most popular writting of the day served to provide these readers with a vicarious experience of the supposed color and romance of underclass life while reassuring them not only that the "honest" or "deserving" poor could readily transcend the worst effects of poverty but also that the squalor and violence of their lives could be readily contained—in slums, workhouses, charity wards, and prisons. Such experiences were likewise contained (and placed on exhibit, as it were) on the fictive level in such voluminous and widely read works as Eugène Sue's *Les Mystères de Paris* (1842), G. W. M. Reynolds's *Mysteries of London* (1845-18),

George Lippard's *The Quaker City* (1845), and Ned Buntline's *Mysteries and Miseries of New York* (1848). In the late 1850s, *Godey's Lady's Book* opined that the vogue for books like these, which depicted the lives of "rag-pickers, lamplighters, foundlings, beggars . . . murderers, etc.," was having what it saw as the undesirable effect of "widen[ing] the social breach between honest wealth and honest poverty."[11] In 1867 Alger would begin pursuing his own literary method of bringing the "gentle" and the "dangerous" back into touch with one another—by locating these supposedly mutually exclusive qualities in the person of the same boy character.

An abundance of stimulating scholarship published in recent years has established the interdependence of the discourse of "the dangerous classes" in mid- to late-nineteenth-century fiction with the forensic forms of the same discourse, in government reports, police dossiers, and sociological studies.[12] One of the most notable characteristics of this massive body of discourse is its frequent placement of the figure of the child in the foreground. From its inception, writing of all kinds about "the dangerous classes" took as its special concern the peril to the social order that the children of the urban poor allegedly posed.[13] Writing about the children of "the dangerous classes" frequently exceeded the ostensible purpose of alerting its readership to the minatory aspects of these "dangerous" children to celebrate their beauty or charm. This conflicting tendency reaches a culmination of sorts in the heroes of Alger's street-boy fictions, in which the child of "the dangerous classes" is presented as being an estimable and even desirable figure.

The Discourse of the "Gentle Boy"

The particular means by which the boy of the "dangerous classes" is idealized in Alger's texts involves his being conflated with another, older writerly construction, the "gentle boy." This figure was itself a hybrid, two of its principal antecedents being the exemplary "good little boy" (sometimes middle-class, sometimes not) of evangelical tract literature for children and (coming out of a quite different discursive formation) the boy version of the "natural aristocrat" central to Jeffersonian social mythology. This latter figure, the "natural little gentleman," the boy of lowly origins who manifests from early childhood the virtues and graces associated with "true gentility," was a staple of "democratic" writing for children. Alger's boy heroes are both a belated and an extreme version of him.[14]

One need not look far in the discourse of the "gentle boy" in nineteenth-century America to appreciate that the terms *gentle* and *gentleman* were extremely unstable markers of a broad spectrum of attributes ranging from purely moral qualities like chivalrousness and benevolence to purely economic ones like the source of one's income. Given the constantly shifting meaning that *gentleman* is given in the nineteenth century, one of the few generalizations about its usage it seems to me safe to hazard is that the term's exclusionary powers are usually more important than its inclusionary ones. That is, establishing who *is* a gentleman is usually secondary in importance to establishing who is *not;* a *gentleman* often is not so much a description of a type of person as an attempt to draw a line between two levels of social status. This yields widely various definitions of *gentle* and *gentleman,* such as (for example) the "high" or "aristocratic" sense of the term, "a man of 'good' family and independent financial means who does not engage in any occupation or profession for gain"—a sense of the term quite different from what one might call the "bourgeois" one, "a man who does not engage in a menial occupation or in manual labor to earn his living." By the first definition, to be a "true" gentleman one must be rich, leisured, and a member of an upper-class family; by the second, one need only not be a working man to qualify—that is, it excludes from its compass only lower-class men.[15]

Besides signifying rigid divisions and invidious distinctions between social classes, *gentle* and *gentleman* bore a number of other meanings. "Soft" definitions of *gentleman* were based not on the source of his income or on the lowest level of work that it was necessary for him to do, but on an unstable set of moral qualities that commonly included courtesy, chivalry, benevolence to "inferiors," and a lively sense of personal "honor." The range was even wider (and must have been even more confusing) for boys who aspired to be "gentlemen": to be considered "gentle," boys, besides possessing various combinations of the foregoing qualities, were also expected to be (in certain relations) tractable, docile, and mild—types of behavior neither required of nor even particularly admired in adult males. At the extreme of the "soft" end of the spectrum, we arrive at a stretch of potentially hazardous meanings for males living in a society in which gender roles were becoming ever more polarized, elaborated, and rigidly prescribed: "sweet," "delicate," "tender," "fond," "loving," "affectionate." Embodying such qualities, even when they were part of behaving in a "gentle" or "gentlemanly" manner, could be a treacherous business for nineteenth-century boys, especially if these qualities came into play not between the boy and an infant or female family member, where they might seem appropriate, but between one boy and another or between a boy and a man. At the "soft" end of the "gentle" spectrum, disgrace by (alleged) feminization threatened the unwary boy.[16] Social constructions of such matters as what success and security, manliness and "gentle" behavior are, as well as what is truly "dangerous" about the urban poor, are some of the basic elements of which Alger's tales are composed. His attempts to stabilize in didactic narratives the volatile field of meanings these terms represented in his culture remain instructive in ways he could not have anticipated.

Ragged Dick and Tattered Tom

Perhaps the master trope, insofar as there is one, for nineteenth-century attitudes toward the urban poor is the figure common to pictorial representations of the proletarian uprisings in Paris in 1830: that of the young or mature man, usually depicted half naked, who is possessed of a beautiful, muscular torso and a bestial face.[17] Middle-class facial beauty, lower-class muscle; middle-class mentality, lower-class bodiliness; middle-class refinement, lower-class brutality; lower-class vigor and middle-class malaise; an overbred middle class and an overbreeding lower class—these are some of the constants in the shifting spectrum of stereotypical paradigms of social class in which nineteenth-century sociologists, journalists, novelists, and illustrators traded. Ragged Dick, the prototypical Alger hero, is not composed of ugly face and muscular torso as a thoroughly "dangerous" youth in popular representation might be: other qualities are mixed in him. As the hero-to-be of Alger's particular brand of male homoerotic domestic romance, he conspicuously combines, to begin with, the qualities of appearing both dirty and handsome:[18]

> But in spite of his dirt and rags there was something about Dick that was attractive. It was easy to see if he had been clean and well dressed he would have been decidedly good looking. (*Ragged Dick*, 40)

Sexual attractiveness is the one characteristic Alger's heroes all have in common. "Luck" comes to them, and "pluck" they exhibit when it is required, but their really defining attribute is good looks. Statements like the following occur ritualistically on the opening pages of the books:

> Both [boys] had bright and attractive faces. . . . [Dick] had a fresh color which spoke of good health, and was well-formed and strong. (*Fame and Fortune*, 53)

> In spite of the dirt, his face was strikingly handsome. (*Phil the Fiddler*, 283)

> He was a strongly-made and well-knit boy of nearly sixteen, but he was poorly dressed. . . . Yet his face was attractive. (*Jed the Poorhouse Boy*, 401)

The narrators of Alger's tales are fierce discriminators of good looks in boys, which they suggest might

be obscured for other spectators by shabbiness and grime. The boy's initially mixed appearance, the good looks revealing themselves despite the physical evidence of poverty—dirt and rags—is the infallible sign that one of Alger's boy characters is likely to emerge from his outcast condition to become a "gentle/dangerous" boy.

Besides the handsome faces and comely bodies visible despite their shabby coverings, another strikingly homoerotic characteristic of Alger's writing is the element of seduction involved in the first steps of the ragged hero's conversion to respectability through his chance street encounters with genteel boys and men. Here the mixing is not figured on the hero's person (handsome/dirty) but on the social level: "dangerous" (street boy) and "gentle" (genteel boy or man) not only meet but make lasting impressions on one another. This impression making takes the form of a mutual seduction of sorts, as in the following representative episode from early on in **Ragged Dick**. When Dick puts himself forward for hire as a guide for a rich boy who is visiting the city, the boy's businessman uncle hesitates to entrust his nephew to him. After a moment's reflection the older man decides to take the risk: "He isn't exactly the sort of guide I would have picked out for you," the man says. "Still, he looks honest. He has an open face, and I think he can be depended upon" (55). The man's quick physiognomic assessment of Dick is amply borne out by the rest of the story: the ragged boy is not only honest, open, and dependable; his contact with Frank (the rich boy) is decisive in his transformation from "street pigeon" to young gentleman. It is Ragged Dick's looks that initially allay the older man's anxieties about him; on the rich boy's side, young Frank does some seducing of his own. Amidst the plethora of advice and encouragement Dick receives from Frank and his uncle in the course of the single day of their acquaintance, it is possible to overlook the significance that direct physical contact has in Frank's ability to convince Dick that he is capable of "rising." The first instance of this occurs when Dick lapses for a short time from his usual jocular tone to tell Frank about his occasional "blue spells" over the hard and lonely life he lives on the street. Frank replies. "'Don't say you have no one to care for you, Dick,' . . . lightly laying his hand on Dick's shoulder. 'I will care for you'" (99). There is another laying on of hands by Frank when the two boys part and Frank persuades Dick to give up his unthrifty (and, by Frank's lights, immoral) streetboy amusements: "'You won't gamble any more,—will you, Dick?' said Frank, laying his hand persuasively on his companion's shoulder" (110). "A feeling of loneliness" is said to overwhelm Dick after Frank leaves the city, as a result of the "strong attachment" he has rapidly formed for the rich boy, but this feeling

of loneliness soon gives way to Dick's overriding desire to be fully "gentle" (genteel). rather than merely Frank's "gentle" (sweet, fond, affectionate) ragamuffin.

A modest suit of new clothes is almost always the symbolic gift that enables the Alger hero to begin rising (Dick's is a "hand-me-down" from Frank), just as the gift of a pocket watch is often ritually made at a later point in his ascent. It is as a part of the ritual of donning his first suit that the matter of the boy's still mixed nature frequently arises for a second time: "He now looked quite handsome," the narrator says of Dick when he has put on Frank's gift, "and might readily have been taken for a young gentleman, except that his hands were red and grimy" (58). Alger's hero's face can simply be washed clean, and most of his body encased in suit and shoes, but his hands are the last part of his person to be divested of signs of hard toil and "dangerous" living.

A particularly interesting example of the mixed Alger hero is Tattered Tom, hero of a book of that title (1871) that inaugurated the Tattered Tom series, which soon followed the successful Ragged Dick series. The appropriately named Tom, a girl who has taken to living on the streets disguised as a boy, is the only "girl hero" in all of Alger's books for boys. She competes on an equal basis with other boys selling newspapers and carrying heavy luggage for nickels. Although the narrator makes passing gestures toward women's rights ("There seemed a popular sentiment in favor of employing boys, and Tom, like others of her sex, found herself shut out from an employment for which she considered herself fitted"; 71), the book, far from being a feminist fable, thoroughly endorses the privileging of the figure of the attractive boy that impels all of Alger's books. Of all of his heroes, only Tom does not "rise" as a consequence of her demonstrably enterprising and honest behavior; she is finally rescued from her plight on the street and restored to her mother, a rich Philadelphia lady from whom she had been abducted years earlier, whereupon she resumes her long-lost genteel, feminine identity as "Jane Lindsay."

Alongside this conventional story of a tomboy who attempts to live as a street boy but is rescued and reclaimed for genteel femininity it is possible to perceive a highly unconventional story of a partially feminized street boy who is drawn upward into genteel femininity by the irresistible magnetic force of Alger's model. This tale represents a twist on the standard one because its hero ends up becoming entirely feminine, instead of the mixed composite of putatively masculine and feminine qualities that Alger's heroes usually represent. *Tattered Tom* can be read not as a story of a literal sex change but of the "rise" from the street to the parlor usual in Alger

combined with an unusually complete reversal of gender roles from street boy to young lady.

While it might be difficult to support such a reading of *Tattered Tom* on the basis of that text alone, it is possible to do so by interpreting the tale in the context of the series it follows (the Ragged Dick series, and the first three volumes of the Luck and Pluck series) and the one it introduces and to which it gives its name. One of the characteristics of a proliferating multiple series like Alger's street-boy stories is that repetitions and variations in the writing from volume to volume can produce meanings that are not readily available to the reader of any single volume in the series. The unique degree to which *Tattered Tom* in its course completely refigures Alger's typical boy hero as a genteel young lady provides a good example of the way formulaic and apparently tautological and repetitious writing like that in Alger's serials can generate unexpected meanings. By inaugurating a major series of boys' books with the story of a "female street boy" and by frequently employing gender-related formulae from the other stories of the series with the gender-signifier reversed, *Tattered Tom* represents a point in Alger's writing where the dynamic interactions of the relative age, gender, and class positions of child and adult characters are revealed with particular clarity. When, for example, the narrator says that Tattered Tom's face is dirty but that if it were clean, "Tom would certainly have been considered pretty" (80), his use of the normative feminine-gender term *pretty* recalls at the same time that it momentarily reverses other descriptions of the boy heroes of the previous tales in the series who have been said to have dirty but *handsome* faces. Similarly, when the narrator says of the benevolent gentleman who takes an interest in Tattered Tom, "There was something in this strange creature—half boy in appearance—that excited his interest and curiosity" (42-43), the text exhibits with exceptional directness the primary role that ambiguities of age and gender play in the appeal of Alger's heroes (one thinks of Brace's "half men"/"mere children") to their genteel benefactors.

"The Fashionable Newsboy at Home": Alger's Reformulation of the Domestic Ideal

"The idea of a fashionable newsboy! It's ridiculous!"
—Alger, **Herbert Carter's Legacy** (1875)

Having attracted the attention and favor of a genteel man with his unmistakable good looks, and having in turn been "seduced" by the warm concern of a rich boy into embracing genteel aspirations, Alger's prototypical hero begins his transformation from "dangerous" child/vagrant into "gentle" youth. That Alger's books are not only homoerotic romances but also represent a genuine reformulation of popular domestic fiction is made evident by the regularity and narrative intensity with which the tales highlight the boy hero's moving from the street or from a transitional charity shelter into his own modest little home (usually a boardinghouse room).[19] That this transition is perhaps the most crucial in the boy's development is manifested in the elaborate care that Alger expends on discriminating the fine points of comparative domestic amenities at this point in his narratives. Once his boy hero reaches the point of setting up a little home of his own, Alger, otherwise often vague about "realistic" detail, shows himself to be as astute a recorder of the differences between the four or five lowest grades of boardinghouses as Balzac could have wished to be.

Having negotiated shifting one type of social construction of themselves ("dangerous") for another ("gentle"), Alger's heroes, in their culminating move into private lodgings, undertake the project of shifting another set of social constructions—those of gender identity and family role. As I have discussed above, gender confusion is thematized extensively in the street phases of Alger's tales only in the case of the female street boy, Tattered Tom. As long as he remains a poor boy on the streets, the Alger hero's behavior remains fairly conventionally gender bound. But once the "gentle boy" is removed from the street and street occupations and is placed in a private, at least minimally genteel domestic setting, he and his boy friends begin to differentiate themselves along (for boys of Alger's day, or of our own) highly unconventional gender-role lines. For example, as soon as fifteen-year-old (formerly Ragged) Dick can manage it, he moves his twelve-year-old friend Henry Fosdick (their very names suggesting they somehow belong together) into his lodgings with him. The two boys share a cult of domestic comfort and respectability that in many ways conforms to the standards of simplicity, cleanliness, and efficiency set in Alger's time by ideologues of "scientific" domesticity like Catharine Beecher.[20] As it is in her work, the Alger hero's first real home, like the poor but decent lodgings Dick and Fosdick take on Mott St., is a man's refuge from the demands of the marketplace and an appropriately ordered decor in which for him to pursue self-improvement.[21]

Dick and his friend and roommate Fosdick inaugurate the second major phase of their joint ascent by moving from their extremely modest digs in Mott St. to a more pleasant place uptown on Bleecker St. These are the opening lines of the sequel to *Ragged Dick:*

> "Well, Fosdick, this is a little better than our old room in Mott St.," said Richard Hunter, looking complacently about him.
>
> "You're right, Dick," said his friend. "This carpet's rather nicer than the ragged one Mrs. Mooney supplied us with. The beds are neat and comfortable, and I feel better satisfied, even if we do have to pay twice as much for it."

The room which yielded so much satisfaction to the two boys was on the fourth floor of a boarding-house in Bleecker St. No doubt many of my young readers, who are accustomed to elegant homes, would think it very plain; but neither Richard nor his friend had been used to anything as good. They had been thrown upon their own exertions at an early age, and [had] had a hard battle to fight with poverty and ignorance. Those of my readers who are familiar with Richard Hunter's experiences when he was "Ragged Dick" will easily understand what a great rise in the world it was for him to have a really respectable home. (*Fame and Fortune*, 9-10)

The Bleecker St. boardinghouse that is the boys' second home together is relatively luxurious; the narrator contrasts it with the minimal, unfastidious amenities that have been available to them back on Mott St.: "There once a fortnight was thought sufficient to change the sheets, while both boys were expected to use the same towel, and make that last a week" (52).

The practical, quotidian ideals of the domestic ideology in its "scientific" and privatizing aspect (a clean and comfortable home that serves as both a haven from the world and a suitable environment for continuous self-improvement) seem entirely congenial to Alger. Other aspects of the conventional domestic ideal that had come into being in the two or three decades preceding, such as its rigid polarization of gender roles, seem considerably less congenial to him. In order to consider how Alger represents these matters, one must attend not to those attitudes that Dick and Fosdick share, like their desire to live as "respectably" as they possibly can afford to, but those characteristics of either boy by means of which the text differentiates, and indeed to some degree dichotomizes (although not nearly as far as other domestic definers of gender roles would have done), their respective personalities.

Alger characterizes the younger boy, Fosdick, as a sweet, timid, quiet, and clever boy, obviously the stereotypically feminine version of the "gentle boy" type, in contrast with the stereotypically masculine Dick, who is thoroughly "gentle" in Alger's ambiguous sense (handsome, kind, nurturant, and, to all appearances, born with embryonic genteel values despite his actual origins in poverty) but is also self-confident, "handy," and generally competent in the realm of what Alger's culture defined as masculine affairs. The significant twist on the gender-role stereotypes in this representative tale of Alger's is that it is Dick, the "dominant" type of these two gentle boys, who plays the maternal role in Alger's version of domesticity and not, as one might expect, the "feminine" character Fosdick.

The relationship between the dominant boy in the maternal role and his partner (for example, Dick and Fosdick, respectively, in the first three volumes of the Ragged Dick series) is thoroughly familial; so much so, in fact, that Alger specifies (another significant example of his uncharacteristic precision about detail) that nine months after the two boys move in together ("at the end of nine months, therefore, or thirty-nine weeks"; chapter 20, "Nine Months Later," **Ragged Dick,** 166), Dick is said to bring forth a little bundle—a nest egg of $117 that has accumulated in his new savings account. But fascinating as the nursing of this nest egg is depicted as being for both boys, they eventually acquire a real human child: in the third volume of the series they adopt a small beggar boy to round out their family, and they make available to him in his turn the experiences—primarily domestic ones—that have aided their own earlier transformations from "dangerous but gentle" street boys to young gentlemen and members of an ideal, genteel, all-boy family.

This fantasmatic family serves as a lingering ideal in Alger's books, but, as he depicts it, it is a far from stable unit.[22] For example, Mark the Match Boy, the adopted "son" of Dick and Fosdick, is revealed at novel's end to be the missing and long-sought-for grandson of a rich merchant from Milwaukee. The old man rewards Dick and Fosdick handsomely for fostering the boy, who is then removed to Milwaukee to enjoy the life of the grandson of a rich gentleman. Dick and Fosdick revert to nursing a now considerably enlarged nest egg. Dick's intermittent maternity toward his "nest egg" and his temporary ward Mark, and the essential interchangeability of "baby" and capital in this scheme—the last in the series of transformations I have been describing—requires consideration in relation to one final aspect of domesticity in Alger, and that is the all-important habit of "saving." Good looks combined with other virtures—honesty, enterprise, male homosociability—are all qualifications for "good fortune" in the forms this takes in Alger. But once the hero begins to "rise" and achieves a modicum of domestic stability, the activity or habit that is represented as being indispensable to maintaining his personal ascendancy is that of "saving." It is by saving, i.e., thriftily and systematically accumulating bits of capital, that Dick produces his nest egg; it is by virtue of these habits that he shows himself to be a fit parent (mother) for Mark; and it is his "saving"—by rescuing from dead-end poverty—first Fosdick and then Mark that the cycle of ascent is renewed in the series. Just as Dick has been saved in order to learn to "save" himself, so will he save younger boys and provide them a model of "saving" both money and still more boys. This religion of accumulating (saving) both money and other boys is ubiquitous in Alger:

> The disposition to save is generally the first encouraging symptom in a street boy, and shows

that he has really a desire to rise above his circumstances, and gain a respectable position in the world. (**Mark the Match Boy,** 293)

> Of greater value than the [monetary] sum . . . was the habit of self-denial and saving which our hero had formed. (**Risen from the Ranks,** 141)

> Boys who have formed so good a habit of saving can be depended upon. (**Fame and Fortune,** 11)

> "All labor is respectable, my lad, and you have no cause to be ashamed of any honest business; yet when you can get something to do that promises better for your future prospects, I advise you to do so. Till then earn your living in the way you are accustomed to, avoid extravagance, and save up a little money if you can." (**Ragged Dick,** 109)

It is in the "saving" (i.e., salvific) habit of "saving" money and other boys that Alger's work represents its cycle of transformations—street boy into "gentle" boy, newly "gentle" boy into domestic partner and foster parent (mother), capital into baby and baby back into further capital—reaching a state of equilibrium: at the end of the narrative, there lies ahead for Alger's heroes a static future of endlessly pursuing the two "saving" projects (i.e., of money and other boys). I want now to consider the question of what is being "saved" in Alger's fantasmatic no-loss chain of transformations and exchanges, the process that begins at the lowest end of his society—at an isolated ragged boy—and extracts from this supposedly unpromising figure the particular combination of virtues and powers normally ascribed to his remote social superiors—gentility, domesticity, wealth, philanthropy.

"Taking an Interest": The Art of Saving Boys

As became apparent in the last section, the salvaging operation ongoing in Alger's writing is a complex one. In each book, a boy is "saved from ruin," from possibly becoming a criminal or a derelict, by being fostered as a candidate for recruitment into the petty bourgeoisie. Furthermore, an outmoded model of virtue (thrift, probity, self-restraint, ambition, hard work—"the Protestant work ethic") is reformulated to correspond more closely to the requirements of changed social and economic conditions: aspiring to and finally reaching the kind of low-level clerical position that brings "respectable" social status as well as access to a modest array of consumer "goodies" to its holder is presented as being a high moral achievement. What is ultimately being saved or recuperated in Alger's writing, though, is something more primal than the notion of the worldly efficacy of a certain combination of virtues: it is a belief that a kind of "magic" acts to secure his boy heroes in the corporate/capitalist network. As I have discussed earlier in this essay, critics of Alger have often decried the regularity with which an experience of sheer "luck" sets his boy heroes on their way, rather than some experience like a recognition of the workings in their world of some consistent notion of "character" or "self-making." It is crucial to notice in this regard that the ritualistic "lucky break" that initiates the boy's rising usually takes the form of his attracting the attention of a well-to-do male patron, usually through some spontaneous exhibition of his physical strength and daring. The "magic trick" that the Alger text ultimately performs is to recuperate the possibility of a man's taking an intense interest in an attractive boy without risking being vilified or persecuted for doing so—indeed, this "interest" is taken in a manner that is made thoroughly congruent with the social requirements of corporate capitalism on the sides of both parties: boy and potential employer alike "profit" from it.

Alger's 1876 *Sam's Chance; and How He Improved It,* in the second Tattered Tom series, provides a representative example of this in the interactions of fifteen-year-old Henry, a clerk in a shipping company, and his employer, James Hamilton. Although Henry is said not to be aware that Hamilton favors him or is even aware of his presence in the firm, the narrator relates that the older man has been "observing him [Henry] carefully, fully determined to serve him in the future if he should deserve it" (89). One day, after four years in the firm, Henry is called into Hamilton's office, where his employer interviews him about how he manages his life and his small income, and then, pleased with what he learns, invites the boy to make a substantial investment in a shipping venture the firm is about to undertake:

> Henry stared at his employer in surprise. How could he, a boy with thirty-five dollars capital, join in such an enterprise?
>
> "I don't see how I can," he replied. "I am afraid you take me for a capitalist."
>
> "So you are," said his employer, "Have you not money in the bank?"
>
> Henry smiled. (93)

Hamilton encourages Henry to participate in the venture, saying he will take the boy's savings bank book (with thirty-five dollars in the account) as security. "Thirty-five dollars will pay a year's interest on the five hundred dollars I lend you; so my interest is secure." Hamilton tells him. "I am willing to take the risk," the older man tells him (twice) to counter Henry's anxieties about becoming his "partner" (94-95). Henry finally happily agrees to the transaction and rises to leave Hamilton's office with the words, "Thank you, sir, I am very grateful to you for your kind interest in me."

With Hamilton's "interest" in Henry thus firmly secured, three months come and go, during which period nothing passes between man and boy except frequent "pleasant word[s] or smile[s]" (107). Henry is then called back into Hamilton's office, and then talk immediately turns to their mutual "interest": "I have just received a statement of [the outcome of the shipping venture]," Hamilton tells Henry, "and as you are interested, I have called you in to let you know how it has turned out." Henry is delighted to learn his investment has earned him a hundred dollars. The following conversation ensues:

> "I shall charge you interest on the five hundred dollars you borrowed of me, at the rate of seven per cent. You have had the use of the money for three months."
>
> "Then the interest will amount to eight dollars and three quarters," said Henry, promptly.
>
> "Quite right; you are very quick at reckoning," said Mr. Hamilton, looking pleased.
>
> "That is not a difficult sum," answered Henry, modestly.
>
> "I did not suppose you knew much about computing interest. You left school very young, did you not?"
>
> "At twelve, sir."
>
> "You had not studied interest then, had you?"
> "No, sir; I have studied it since."
>
> "At evening school?"
>
> "No, sir; I study by myself in the evening."
>
> "How long have you done that?"
>
> "For two years."
>
> "And you keep it up regularly?"
>
> "Yes, sir; occasionally I take an evening for myself, but I average five evenings a week at studying."
>
> "You are a remarkable boy," said the merchant, looking surprised.
>
> "If you flatter me, sir, I may grow self-conceited," said Henry, smiling. (108-9)

Once again, a mutually "profitable" encounter leaves Henry "smiling" and Hamilton looking "surprised" and "pleased," their "partnership" fulfilled. The boy has proven himself to be as quick and expert a computer of "interest" as his merchant employer; with a little further education in calculating "risk," one suspects, he will have little more to learn from Hamilton. (In their crucial first nine months together, Ragged Dick is said to learn everything from Fosdick that he has to teach, which includes reading, writing, and "arithmetic as far as Interest"; 167.)

The recognition and avowal of "interest"—one's own in other men and theirs in oneself—and the close study of calculation and risk in pursuing these "interests" are matters that have figured as highly problematic and emotionally charged concerns in male homosexual behavior in homophobic capitalist culture. As Michael Pollak has written of the institutions of the "sexual market" of the gay ghetto (bars, baths, cinemas, and so on), as these functioned between the time of the emergence of gay liberation in Western metropolises at the beginning of the 1970s and the decline of "casual sex" practices among many gay men in recent years in response to the AIDS epidemic: "Of all the different types of masculine sexual behavior, homosexuality is undoubtedly the one whose functioning is most strongly suggestive of a market, in which in the last analysis one orgasm is bartered for another."[23]

As is evident from passages like the dialogue from *Sam's Chance* quoted above, the network of calculation, risk, and interest that binds males together in Alger's work is a complex one; the economic working of the quasisexual marketplace of these "boys' books" leaves the crude barter system described by Pollak far behind. At a representative moment in an earlier entry in the Tattered Tom series. *Paul the Peddler,* distinctions between the boy hero or his body and corporate economic forms vanish; as Paul considers how to come up with thirty-five dollars to buy out another boy's necktie stand, the narrator observes:

> If Paul had been a railroad corporation, he might have issued first mortgage bonds at a high rate of interest, payable in gold, and negotiated them through some leading banker. But he was not much versed in financial schemes, and therefore was at a loss. (164)

Paul's being "at a loss" is a circumstance that "gets worse before it gets better"; his case provides a typical example of the way in which the networks of interest between males in Alger's fiction can be disrupted by the incursion of the feminine—a quality that is frequently represented in these stories as being equivalent to (in readily recognizable infantile-fantasy form) the quality of anality. Paul becomes involved in a series of misadventures when he attempts to sell a valuable "ring" his mother has found and given him to provide the capital for his "rise." A con man named

Montgomery who poses as "a jeweler from Syracuse" is said to overhear "with evident interest" a conversation between Paul and another boy about this ring. The man steps forward and avows his "interest in examining" and possibly buying Paul's ring; permitted to do so, he pronounces it "handsome" and valuable, and invites the boy to his hotel room to complete the transaction (199-200). Once at the hotel (called "Lovejoy's"), Montgomery grabs Paul and applies a sponge soaked in chloroform to his nose until the boy passes out. "Eyeing the insensible boy with satisfaction," he seizes the ring and flees (208-9).

Alger's fictions never allow such disruptions of the networks of male interest by the incursion of what it represents as the feminine/anal—a position of jeopardy into which every "gentle boy" can at least potentially be forced—to become more than temporary: Paul recovers his ring and completes his sale of it, then deposits most of the proceeds with his gentleman patron, who promises him "interest" on it (295). When the con man is sent off to Sing Sing after being convicted of assaulting and robbing Paul, according to the narrative, even the man's wife is said to be indifferent: "As the compact between her and her husband was one of interest rather than of affection, her grief at his confinement is not very deep" (304). Compacts of interest between man and wife, the narrative leads us to assume, are ignoble, but between man and boy "on the market," there is no comparably invidious distinction to be drawn between mutual "interest" and "affection": they come to the same thing, and both qualities are estimable.

Older men who might (but actually do not) stand in relation to Alger's boy heroes as fathers may "take an interest" in them that may eventuate (as we have seen) in actions as various as respectful advancement or rape, but none of these interactions with older men on the boys' part leaves any permanent trace in the lives of the boy characters except in the form of yet another accession of capital. Domestic arrangements are formed between boy and boy, but relations between man and boy remain casual, intermittent, and extradomestic: the "rise" of Alger's hero is fostered by "interested" older patrons, but (the informing, contradictory fantasy runs) the boy remains entirely self-fathering.

Alger's particular version of the "self-made man" takes the form of this "self-made" all-boy family that the boy protagonist generates with his money. This version of domesticity, as I have suggested above, derives from the infantilefantasy equivalence that the stories propose between femininity and anality. Drawing on the succinct psychoanalysis of the "magic-dirt" complex that Norman O. Brown makes in *Life Against Death,* I would argue that Alger's writing denies sexual difference—and privileges the figure of the formerly "dirty" boy-turned-gentle over figures of other age, gender, and class positions—"in the interest" of promoting this particular notion of self-making, of simultaneous self-mothering and self-fathering, that it takes over from capitalist culture:

> The infantile fantasy of becoming father of oneself first moves out to make magic use of objects instead of its own body when it gets attached to that object which both is and is not part of its own body, the feces. Money inherits the infantile magic of excrement and then is able to breed and have children: interest is an increment.[24]

Alger's all-boy families merely imitate the extraordinary propensities for self-reproduction, for apparently asexual breeding, that they are represented as discovering already ongoing in their first accumulations of capital. The chain of "magical" transformations I have charted in Alger's writing from ragged to gentle boy by way of a series of negotiations of capital into baby and then back into capital conforms entirely to Brown's Freudian reading of the fantasy of transformation of bodily excrement into capital increment by way of the metamorphosis of feces into baby and subsequently into "magical," self-engendering money.

Alger's tales sometimes manifest a modicum of self-awareness on the author's part with regard to his role of purveyor of a "magical thinking" that effectively links infantile fantasies of self-fathering with some of the fundamental formations of capitalist culture. In his recent study of forms of popular narrative in nineteenth-century America, Michael Denning has likened the function of Alger's street-boy heroes—"dangerous" figures drawn from contemporary popular, nongenteel fiction (story papers, dime novels) who enact what Denning (correctly) reads as unequivocally genteel moralistic fables—to the use of "a ventriloquist's dummy to recapture and reorganize working class culture."[25] I would supplement Denning's characterization of Alger as a ventriloquist across class lines (as well as, I would add, across lines of prohibited sexuality between man and boy) with a brief analysis of Alger's representation of himself in the figure of Professor Henderson, a magician/ventriloquist who figures as a patron/employer of the boy hero of *Bound to Rise*. Henderson first deceives the boy Harry Walton, who has come to work as his assistant, by throwing his voice into a trunk, from which emerges a child's voice pathetically pleading, "Oh, let me out! Don't keep me locked up in here!" Harry is said merely to "smile" when he realizes Henderson has tricked him with ventriloquism (102). Shortly thereafter, Henderson repeats the trick in the boy's presence, this time at the expense of an elderly woman character; Henderson and Harry have a good laugh at her chagrin. The trick is

more elaborate the second time: Henderson throws his voice into the boy's body and increases their mirth by making Harry seem to lie to the woman to the effect that the professor does indeed have someone locked away in the trunk; this time Henderson specifies (ventriloqually) that the child is female—in fact, his little daughter. The climax of the trick comes when the professor throws open the trunk and shows the woman that there is no one there (114-15).

The reader may share some of the woman character's discomfort over the "little girl in the trunk" trick that at a critical point in the episode turns into the "vanishing daughter" trick. Not much imagination is required to produce the biographical speculation that the little girl locked in the trunk, crying to be released, is a figure from Alger's psychological past who survived in encrypted and rejected form in his unconscious and whose ultimate fate was to be pressed into service as comic relief in texts like *Bound to Rise*. Even more thoroughly than the ambiguously feminine Tattered Tom, this fantasmatic "little girl" vanishes almost without a trace from the magical network of male interests through which she is passed in this text—leaving the reader to suspect, at this and other points in the Alger corpus, that the "dangerous" figures in his writing are not really at any point the ragged street boys whose labile qualities it celebrates but the little girls it almost totally excludes—along with the femininity they embody, a "threatening" quality insofar as it might permanently disrupt the smooth unfolding in the America of the time of the exclusively male homosocial institutions of corporate capitalism.

It was in the decade or so after Alger's death in 1899 that Lewis Hine began to produce his extraordinary photographs of the new, turn-of-the-century generation of urban street boys at their work of peddling, shining shoes, selling newspapers, and delivering parcels. What is striking about Hine's photographs is their self-conscious refusal to "gentle" their underclass subjects in the way that Alger and his philanthropist colleagues had done: Hine's boy subjects are not represented as picturesque ragamuffins or charming but dangerous "animals" or "savages," some of whom will inevitably make their way to affluence and respectability. Rather, his images of these boys reveal their sufferings as real, lasting deformations rather than as transient experiential way stations on the road to untroubled security and success: the child subjects of Hine's photographs characteristically look weary, depressed, and even bitter. In association with the Progressivist reform organization the National Child Labor Committee (NCLC), Hine wrote and lectured extensively on the need for legislation prohibiting the exploitation of poor children as laborers by either their parents or their employers: his photographs, he insisted, were his incontrovertible documentary evidence that children forced to support themselves by full-time employment at low-paying labor were generally destroyed physically and morally in the process. Hine supplemented his photographic record of street-boy life with his own antisentimental testimony about their plight: for example, a propos of his 1909 photograph of a Hartford, Connecticut, newsboy named Tony Casale, Hine records that the boy had recently shown his boss the marks on his arm where his father had bitten him "for not selling more papers"; Hine also mentions that the boy said he disliked being the object of verbal abuse from the drunken men with whom he constantly came in contact on the city streets.[26]

Hine and the NCLC encountered strong popular resistance to their movement; politicians and other members of their audiences vociferously denied that conditions for street-child laborers were as grim and brutalizing as Hine represented them as being. Hine's street boys, his opponents often argued, were Horatio Alger heroes, toiling their way up from paupery to comfortable, respectable lives.

It was during these years, between the turn of the century and the beginning of World War I, at the height of the Progressive Era, that Alger's books, republished in cheap reprints that suppressed substantial amounts of the books' didactic moralizing, sold in the millions of copies.[27] During his lifetime, Alger had had only one genuine bestseller, the early ***Ragged Dick;*** only posthumously did he achieve true mass popularity. It was also during the early years of the twentieth century that the term "a Horatio Alger story" became fixed in the language to mean a tale of a man's "rise" from boyhood poverty to a position of great wealth and power. The myth that Alger's are male-capitalist Cinderella tales has had an astonishing success of its own. How can one account for the ubiquity of this inaccurate characterization of the content of Alger's stories? With the benefit of hindsight, we can see that one thing that was being "saved" in Alger's writing was a notion of "virtuous poverty rewarded" that was already archaic when his first street-boy series appeared in the decade after the Civil War. The Alger mania of readers in the first fifteen years of this century might be said to have served as a reinoculation of American readers with the myth of "virtuous poverty rewarded," an article of faith that was being vociferously combatted from Progressivist, socialist, and organized-labor quarters during those years. I would attribute some of the popularity of Alger's stories with boy readers during and after his lifetime to their propensity for combining a not inaccurate representation of the conditions, requirements, and mild rewards to be expected on the extensive lower reaches of the corporate workplace with a version of boy life—idyllic, domestic, self-perpetuating, untroubled by direct intervention from parents or other adult figures of authority or by the "threat" (to male supremacy) of female enfranchisement—that may strike us as highly unrealistic at first glance but that is (again) a not inaccurate version of some of corporate culture's favorite modes of self-presentation (i.e., as fraternal, financially rewarding, benevolently hierarchical, open to individual talent or "merit").

I would attribute the extraordinary tenacity of the "rags-to-riches" misreading of Alger to corporate/capitalist culture's need for a serviceable mythology of "success" like Alger's—but one which entirely represses (as Alger's does not) the determinate relations perceptible in his stories between the achievement and maintenance of white-collar "lifestyles" and particular, exclusive modes of relationship between males. I first began to read Alger's writing out of an interest in thinking about ways in which his pederasty might have determined it, but I have come to think that the far more interesting way his work manifests male homosexuality is not as indirect autobiographical data for a single figure (i.e., Alger) but as an encapsulation of corporate/capitalist America's long-cherished myth, its male homoerotic foundations fiercely repressed, that the white males who control wealth and power have their eye out for that exceptional, "deserving," "attractive" underclass youth who defies his statistical fate to become (with the benefit of limited paternalistic "interest") yet another "gentle boy from the dangerous classes."

Notes

I wish to thank Jane Tompkins and Larzer Ziff for thoughtful readings of an earlier draft of this essay, and Jonathan Goldberg and Michael Warner for helpful advice on subsequent versions of it. I also wish to thank Michael Rogin for making valuable editorial suggestions.

[1] Quoted in Christine Stansell, *City of Women: Sex and Class in New York, 1789-1860* (New York, 1986), 194. I have depended on the chapter of Stansell's book in which this report is quoted ("The Use of the Streets," 193-216) for my brief opening account in this essay of genteel response to street children in New York City in the years just before Alger's arrival on the scene.

[2] Ibid., 212.

[3] Charles Loring Brace, *Short Sermons to News Boys* (1866), 140-41.

[4] Hugh Kenner's phrase occurs in his "The Promised Land," in *A Homemade World: The American Modernist Writers* (New York, 1975), 20. Richard Huber rediscovered the documentary material on Alger's

pederasty and discussed it in his book *The American Idea of Success* (New York, 1971).

[5] Michael Zuckerman, "The Nursery Tales of Horatio Alger," *American Quarterly* 24, no. 2 (May 1972): 209.

[6] Horatio Alger, Jr., *Bound to Rise; or, Up the Ladder* (New York, 1909), 101, in a chapter significantly entitled "The Coming of the Magician."

[7] My thinking about homoeroticism, homophobia, social class, and capitalism in this essay is indebted to Eve Kosofsky Sedgwick, *Between Men: English Literature and Male Homosocial Desire* (New York, 1985), especially her chapter "Homophobia, Misogyny, and Capital: The Example of *Our Mutual Friend*," 161-79. I am also indebted to Luce Irigaray, "Commodities Among Themselves," in *This Sex Which Is Not One,* trans, Catherine Porter with Carolyn Burke (Ithaca, N.Y., 1985), for her analysis of the determinate relation between homophobia and the foundations of patriarchal economics: "Why is masculine homosexuality considered exceptional, then, when in fact the economy as a whole is based upon it? Why are homosexuals ostracized, when society postulates homosexuality?" (192). In considering the profound effects of the requirements of the forms of corporate capitalism emergent in Alger's time on his culture, I have also profited from Alan Trachtenberg's treatment of this matter in *The Incorporation of America: Culture and Society in the Gilded Age* (New York, 1982).

[8] Alger's sketch of the boy residents of the Newsboys' Lodging House of the Children's Aid Society (Brace's organization) originally appeared in the pages of the *Liberal Christian.* It is reprinted in Gary Scharnhorst with Jack Bales, *The Lost Life of Horatio Alger, Jr.* (Bloomington, Ind., 1985), 79. The appearance at long last of a factually reliable biography of Alger like this one makes writing about his work substantially easier.

[9] I quote this formulation from Scharnhorst, ibid., 67.

[10] The boys involved were apparently all members of Alger's Unitarian congregation in the small Cape Cod community of Brewster. If Alger did cross class lines "for sex" in his later years in New York, where, according to Scharnhorst, he entertained hundreds of street-boy friends in his rooms (*Lost Life,* 77) and semi-officially adopted three of them (124-25), it was of course only the official version of the morality of his time and place that he was violating: the casual sexual exploitation of the poor by those economically and socially "better off" than they was of course a pervasive feature of nineteenth-century urban life. For the example of New York City in the decade before the Civil War, see Christine Stansell,

"Women on the Town: Sexual Exchange and Prostitution," in *City of Women,* 171-92.

[11] Quoted in Nina Baym, *Novels, Readers, and Reviewers: Responses to Fiction in Antebellum America* (Ithaca, N.Y., 1984), 210-11.

[12] Stansell gives a brief and useful history of the "sketch" of scenes, especially street scenes, of urban poverty in New York in the three decades before the Civil War in *City of Women,* 195-97, demonstrating as she does so how much what genteel observers of the time "saw" depended on expectations that writing about "the problem" had helped form. Stansell writes, "Although the *problems* of the streets—the fights, the crowds, the crime, the children—were nothing new, the 'problem' itself represented altered bourgeois perception and a broadened political initiative." She goes on to say, "Matsell's report and the writing Brace undertook in the 1850s distilled the particular way the genteel had designated themselves arbiters of the city's everyday life" (197). Louis Chevalier, *Laboring Classes and Dangerous Classes in Paris During the First Half of the Nineteenth Century,* trans. Frank Jellinek (New York, 1973), gives extensive documentation of the interdependence of the depictions of the urban poor to be found in Sue, Balzae, and Hugo with contemporary forensic writing. D.A. Miller has analyzed similar interdependences between contemporary "policing" techniques and the fiction of Wilkie Collins, Dickens, and Trollope in such articles as "From *Roman policier* to *Roman-police:* Wilkie Collins's *The Moon-stone,*" *Novel* 13 (Winter 1980): 153-70; "The Novel and the Police," *Glyph* 8 (1981): 121-47; "Discipline in Different Voices: Bureaucracy, Police, Family, and *Bleak House,*" *Representations* 1 (February 1983): 59-89; and "The Novel as Usual: Trollope's *Barchester Towers,*" in Ruth Bernard Yeazell, ed., *Sex, Politics, and Science in the Nineteenth-Century Novel,* Selected Papers from the English Institute, 1983-84 (Baltimore, 1986), 1-38. Mark Seltzer has explored the relation of the forensic discourse of surveillance to Henry James's writing in "*The Princess Casamassima:* Realism and the Fantasy of Surveillance," in Eric J. Sundquist, ed., *American Realism: New Essays* (Baltimore, 1982), 95-118.

[13] M.A. Fregier's influential 1840 study *Des Classes dangereuses de la population dans les grandes villes* has been called "a close study of the process by which the course of the lower-class child's life was shaped toward crime" by Louis Chevalier, *Laboring Classes,* 120.

[14] John G. Cawelti traces the lines of descent of this "democratic" boy hero in his chapter on Alger in *Apostles of the Self-Made Man: Changing Concepts of Success in America* (Chicago, 1965). See also in the same volume, "Natural Aristocracy and the New

Republic: The Idea of Mobility in the Thought of Franklin and Jefferson," 1-36.

[15] For comparative purposes, see the discussions of the shifting parameters of gentility in nineteenth-century England in the respective introductory chapters of the following two works: Robin Gilmour, *The Idea of the Gentleman in the English Novel* (London, 1981), 1-15; and Shirley Robin Letwin, *The Gentleman in Trollope: Individuality and Moral Conduct* (Cambridge, Mass., 1982), 3-21.

[16] All these senses of the term, and all these potential occasions of social unease ranging from simple embarrassment to disgrace and persecution, are alive in American Renaissance writing about the "gentle" and "gentlemen." The figure of the "gentle boy" reached an apogee of sorts in Hawthorne's 1832 tale of that name. A second key text for this figure as it appears in American Renaissance writing is Thoreau's poem, "Lately, alas, I knew a gentle boy . . . ," which he published in the "Wednesday" section of *A Week on the Concord and Merrimack Rivers* (1849).

[17] See Chevalier, *Laboring Classes,* 414.

[18] References to Alger's novels will be given by short titles in the text. The editions cited are: *Ragged Dick* (New York, 1962); *Fame and Fortune* (Boston, 1868); *Phil the Fiddler,* in *Struggling Upwards and Other Works* (New York, 1945); *Jed the Poorhouse Boy,* in *Struggling Upwards; Tattered Tom* (Boston, 1871); *Mark the Match Boy* (New York, 1962); *Risen from the Ranks* (Boston, 1874); *Sam's Chance, and How He Improved It* (Chicago, n.d.); *Paul the Peddler: The Fortunes of a Young Street Merchant* (New York, n.d.); *Bound to Rise; or, Up the Ladder* (New York, 1909).

[19] Nina Baym briefly but perspicaciously classifies Alger as a domestic writer in *Woman's Fiction: A Guide to Novels by and About Women in America, 1820-1870* (Ithaca, N.Y., 1978), 261.

[20] For an informative account of Beecher's theory of domesticity, see Kathryn Kish Sklar, *Catharine Beecher: A Study in American Domesticity* (New Haven, 1973), 158ff.

[21] See Mary Ryan, "Varieties of Social Retreat: Domesticity, Privacy, and the Self-Made Man," in *Cradle of the Middle Class: The Family in Oneida County, New York, 1790-1865* (Cambridge, 1981), 146-55, for Ryan's discussion of the compatibility and indeed the congruence of the cult of the "self-made man" with the cult of (feminine) domesticity.

[22] Fredric Jameson, *The Political Unconscious: Narrative as a Socially Symbolic Act* (Ithaca, N.Y., 1981),

employs the term *fantasm* to denote "the traces and symptoms of a fundamental family situation which is at one and the same time a fantasy master narrative" that "is an unstable and contradictory structure, whose persistent actantial functions and events . . . demand repetition, permutation, and the ceaseless generation of various structural 'resolutions'" (180). If, as Jameson suggests, a residue of fantasmatic thinking about "a fundamental family situation" is characteristic of all bourgeois narratives, then it becomes possible to perceive many more narratives as being fundamentally "domestic"—or antidomestic—in their emphases than most of us are probably used to doing.

[23] Michael Pollak, "Male Homosexuality; or, Happiness in the Ghetto," in Philippe Aries and André Béjin, eds., *Western Sexuality: Practice and Precept in Past and Present Times,* trans. Anthony Foster (Oxford, 1985), 44.

[24] Norman O. Brown, *Life Against Death: The Psychoanalytical Meaning of History* (Middletown, Conn., 1959), 279.

[25] Michael Denning, "Cheap Stories: Notes on Popular Fiction and Working-Class Culture in Nineteenth-Century America," *History Workshop* 22 (Autumn 1986): 6.

[26] Quoted in the catalog entry for Lewis Hine's photograph entitled *Bologna, Hartford, Connecticut, 1909,* in Julie R. Myers, et al., *Of Time and Place: American Figurative Art from the Corcoran Gallery* (Washington, D.C., 1981), 92.

[27] Scharnhorst, *Lost Life,* 149-56, provides an illuminating account of the "editorial reinvention" of Alger's work (often by silent abridgement) in the years after his death (149-56).

Carol Nackenoff (essay date 1994)

SOURCE: "Reading Alger: Searching for Alger's Audience in the Literary Marketplace," in *The Fictional Republic: Horatio Alger and American Political Discourse.* Oxford University Press, 1994, pp.181-203.

[*In the following chapter, Nackenoff identifies Alger's readership within the changing historical context of increased literacy and cheaper availability of books.*]

> Your kind and flattering letter reached me just as I was starting for the Geysers . . . It gives me great pleasure to find that I have friends and appreciative readers among the girls, as well as among the boys, and on the shores of the Pacific, as well as the Atlantic. I hope at an early date to write a story located in California, and I shall be glad if it proves acceptable to my friends here.
>
> Alger to Miss Harriet Jackson, March 3, 1877[1]

The marked surge in the production, dissemination, and reading of literature in the Gilded Age created new readers and new reading tastes. Rising literacy, increased leisure for some, a spreading national network of reading matter available for purchase and loan, and declining price of fiction helped make readers out of new classes. Especially after 1880, these factors worked in conjunction with growing family incomes to produce changes in reading propensities, buying habits, and tastes. Much of the reading was fiction.

But who read **Ragged Dick** or **Sam's Chance?** Discovering the real, potential, likely, and intended audience for Alger's fiction is no simple task. Popular fiction does not yield secrets easily, and "we know very little about the readers of the *New York World,* the *Ladies' Home Journal,* and **Ragged Dick.**"[2]

Whereas this book makes many text-based arguments, the object of Chapter 10 is to search for Alger's audience in the marketplace. One course is to follow the production, circulation, and exchange of the reading matter Alger generated. In doing so, Chapter 10 introduces the story papers, magazines, and the book trade through which Alger reached his public(s), along with the stores and libraries that carried his wares.

But the gap between macro- and microlevel data is large. Although we can paint a picture of who might have read Alger, following vehicles of communication to points of distribution cannot definitively identify the Alger reader. And current historians of the book and of other nineteenth century reading matter are highly skeptical of methods and inferences made about audiences in extant secondary sources.[3]

The best available evidence we can supply on who read Alger comes from a child's diary, fan mail, letters to magazine editors, and testimonials. Since the author directed that correspondence in his possession be destroyed upon his death, this important resource on reader response is lost. However, some recipients of Alger's letters treasured and preserved them. The data are supplemented by Alger's own reports about access and readership, and observations made of readers in the public library.

The individual-level data yields a marked class skew toward the middle-class reader. So, too, does clothbound novel pricing data. But there is reason to hold back from the conclusion that this is the best portrait of Alger's audience. Too often, scholars have forgotten that Alger tales appeared in forms other than clothbound novels.

In any investigation of how far Alger's works penetrated the working classes, there are many silences. Many readers left no testimonials, and the story papers through which many came to know Alger, were, like today's newspapers, discarded or recycled.

In only the rarest case can we *will* the reader to pick up the work and read. The sample is too small and not representative. The portrait of Alger's readers must, then, be further sketched by examining access to the different forms in which these stories found their way to their publics. This chapter draws upon a range of available tools and data to begin a sketch of this portrait. Much more detective work could productively be done.[4] However, this endeavor addresses a near void in our understanding and combats facile pronouncements about Alger's audience that are too often taken as fact.[5] Improving our portrait of the real or likely Alger reader by bringing disparate evidence together in the same place will help in the search to understand the locus of these texts in the space of political discourse.

READING ALGER: THE NORCROSS DIARY

Grenville Howland Norcross (1854-1937), the son of a former Boston mayor, was graduated from Harvard in 1875, acquired a Harvard law degree in 1879, and became a Boston lawyer. He was active in historical and literary organizations around Boston, including the American Antiquarian Society. As a boy, he attended dance school, took vacations with his family to the shore, visited grandmother in Jamaica Plain, studied Latin, and noted his reading habits in diaries.

While the Norcross diary affords evidence only of the reading habits of one middle-class Boston boy, it indicates that more and less reputable fiction are present in the diets of such young people in the early Gilded Age. The diet was a mix of history, fiction writers who would join the canon—Dickens, Swift, Cooper, Defoe; tales of Alger, Optic, Ellis, and Castlemon; dime novels and railroad literature. It also indicates that Alger became known without necessarily being purchased in book form.

In 1874, Alger supplied biographical data and a photo upon the request of George A. Bacon for use in a subsequent edition of the "Game of Authors."[6] The photo, one that Joseph H. Allen supplied gratis to *Student and Schoolmate* subscribers, appeared in the "'Moral and Religious' suit along with Henry Ward Beecher, Edward Everett Hale, and T.S. Arthur, author of the temperance tract *Ten Nights in a Barroom and What I Saw There.*"[7] One of Norcross's boyhood games was an earlier version of the Game of Authors. Other boys and girls of his class may have made Alger's acquaintance in this way a few years later.

Alger wrote the popular sentimental ballad **"John Maynard"** after he heard a speaker recount the tale of "a courageous if mythical sailor on a Lake Erie steamer who steers his burning ship and its passengers to shore and safety just before he is consumed by the flames." Alger went to the reading room of the local YMCA, found and read the story of Maynard, copied it, and then wrote the poem in a single sitting. His **"John Maynard, A Ballad of Lake Erie,"** was published in the *New York Ledger* in 1862, the *New York Sun* in 1866, and in *Student and Schoolmate* in January of 1868; for its publication in this last case, Alger received "the munificent sum of three dollars." It was anthologized, the author reported, at least a dozen times during his lifetime.[8] The poem became a popular declamation piece in the schools. One who declaimed it was Norcross. Young Norcross probably read it in *Student and Schoolmate,* for his diary of March 19, 1868 contains the entry: "Rehearsed 'John Maynard', which I am trying to speak." On Saturday, April 4, 1868, public day at school, the fourteen-year-old notes: "I spoke 'John Maynard, a ballad of Lake Erie.'"[9]

Had Norcross perused this same 1868 issue of *Student and Schoolmate* he would have found an installment of Alger's serial story, **Fame and Fortune,** a sequel to *Ragged Dick.* Indeed, picking up virtually any issue of *Student and Schoolmate* from 1867 through 1872 would have exposed Norcross or his acquaintances to Alger.[10] *Ragged Dick* had been serialized in this Optic magazine starting in January, 1867. Bound annual volumes of *Student and Schoolmate,* priced at $1.50 in 1865 and $2.00 toward the end of the decade, also contained the serialization of *Ragged Dick* and his companions.

However, the same spring that Norcross declaimed **"John Maynard,"** A. K. Loring issued an expanded version of *Ragged Dick* in book form. In addition to some stories, three novels bearing Alger's name were already published by Loring: **Frank's Campaign, Paul Prescott's Charge,** and **Helen Ford.**[11] An entry on Alger appeared in the new edition of Duyckinck's *Cyclopaedia of American Literature before* the appearance of **Helen Ford** or **Ragged Dick,** while *Student and Schoolmate* editor, Boston schoolteacher and principal William T. Adams, who was then "author of some twenty popular boys' books" under the pen name Oliver Optic, was omitted.[12]

In advertising the upcoming release of clothbound **Ragged Dick,** *Student and Schoolmate* readers were told "The story has been carefully re-written and enlarged by Mr. Alger, new and beautiful illustrations are in preparation . . . ." Readers of the earlier version were encouraged to become purchasers of the book:

> **RAGGED DICK,** or Street Life in New York. By Horatio Alger, Jr., is now before us, brought out in beautiful style by Loring, whose "Up Town

Bookstore" is so well known to Bostonians. The readers of the SCHOOLMATE looked with too much eagerness for the monthly chapters in our magazine, not to feel a desire to own a book of so much interest, in which *five* entirely new chapters appear . . . [13]

The announcement was in May, 1868; by August, the editors had to apologize for the delay in filling orders:

> The first edition was exhausted, and consequently a second edition must be issued at once. It is gratifying to perceive the great demand for this excellent book, and we shall now be able, from the new issue, to answer orders more promptly.[14]

During this rush on **Ragged Dick** and a few months after declaiming **"John Maynard,"** young Norcross began reading Alger novels. His first was one of the adult novels, published by Loring in 1866. His diary entry for Saturday, July 11, 1868 reads: "Took **'Helen Ford'** by H. Alger, Jr. from Burnham's Library and paid 10 cts. for 'Farming for boys.'" Burnham's, a private circulating library, surely operated much like Loring's own.

A. K. Loring's Select Library, begun in 1859, lent volumes for circulation at two cents per day apiece, and sold off surplus books no longer in circulation at cheap prices. Loring began publishing in 1863, and his first Alger novel appeared the following year. *Frank's Campaign,* set during the Civil War and appealing to young Northern boys to help the cause even in their local communities, combined the "action, emotional appeal, and moral lesson," that A. K. Loring made his publishing credo.[15] Loring published Alger titles until his firm collapsed in 1880.

On the 14th of July 1868, Norcross returned to Burnham's and took out **Ragged Dick.** The only indication of his reaction to Alger fiction was that he read a second volume. This was not unusual, because he rarely recorded his reaction to reading, except in a case where he noted that he did not enjoy something and did not intend to finish it; that month, he found "a great many lies in" Dickens's *American Notes* (July 7, 1868). These were among nine books the boy read in July, 1868 and among the eighty-eight books he read during the year.

For Christmas, 1868, Grenville Howland Norcross received from his father a subscription to one of Optic's magazines, *Our Boys and Girls.* Fiction was also arriving in the home by mail, facilitated by the postal rate structures. Other types of reading matter, such as dime novels, were also distributed by mail. This phenomenon did not escape the attention of the Comstock crusaders.

The postal system supplemented the book publisher's established distribution networks. Would-be readers with financial resources could have access to Alger's clothbound volumes so long as they could receive mail. Books included advertisements from the publisher, offering to send a volume or a series, such as the "Ragged Dick Series," "Tattered Tom Series," "Campaign Series," or "Pacific Series." Purchasers got a boxed set, with a specified number of volumes in cloth, sometimes "printed in colors," but no discount.

Readers of the monthly juvenile *Student and Schoolmate* were advised they could order copies of current and previous Alger volumes through that publication, sometimes at below retail: "**TATTERED TOM** will be mailed to any of our subscribers, *post-paid,* on receipt of $1.05, retail price being $1.25."[16] Book jobbers, clergymen, librarians, and anyone termed a "large buyer" could lay claim to some sort of publisher's discount and continue the process of book distribution.[17]

Young Norcross's family had, by the late 1860s, joined the class of fiction purchasers: Christmas, 1868 also brought the gift of an Oliver Optic novel from his aunt. Nonetheless, even this comfortably circumstanced boy appears to have owned few of the books he read. Not one individually owned clothbound volume of Alger fiction seems to have been in the Norcross home, yet his work crossed the threshhold in magazines and as lending library books. Public and private circulating libraries and borrowing from friends were prevalent means of acquiring juvenile fiction in his circles, so that a single book volume was likely to have multiple readers. The Norcross experience helps explain the fact that, while publishers generally reported no huge Alger sales, reviewers often noted that his stories were hits with the boys.

Many American families were not yet spending for fiction. During the era Alger wrote, "large portions of the public were using printed matter for the first time, magazines at the start and then an occasional bound volume."[18] The most likely books for a family to own at this time were religious books, an almanac, and perhaps a few practical works.[19] There was sustained interest in volumes that helped Americans in burgeoning communities and settlements plan a "design for living." Volumes of plans and designs for homes became popular in midcentury; books on accounting proliferated after 1870. Etiquette books and advice manuals remained strong sellers, with approximately the same number of distinct editions appearing in the thirty years preceding the war as were issued in the thirty years after 1861. The number of titles published in such genteel subjects as philosophy and poetry was in decline; so were drama, geography and travel.[20]

While the total number of book titles published remained roughly constant from 1869 to 1880, annual output practically doubled by 1890 and tripled by the turn of the century.[21] Some of the strongest selling works were works of fiction.

The publication of **Ragged Dick** assured Alger's status as a well-known author. Publishers of the era considered ten thousand copies to be about the smallest edition of a book that would make it a decided hit.[22] Gauged by volume of sales, **Ragged Dick** was apparently Alger's only "major" commercial success. One standard source, defining best sellers as only those volumes whose total sales approximated one percent of the population of the United States during the decade in which it was published, includes **Ragged Dick** for the 1860s; this achievement required sales of three hundred thousand copies. **Fame and Fortune** (1869), **Luck and Pluck** (1870), and **Tattered Tom** (1871) achieved runner-up status.[23]

By such a measure of popularity, a few of Alger's volumes placed him in the company of Charles Dickens, who made a second American tour in the year **Ragged Dick** appeared in serial form in *Student and Schoolmate* (1867), and English romance novelist Charles Reade. Alger was also in the company of female authors Harriet Beecher Stowe, Louisa May Alcott, Mary Mapes Dodge, and prolific sentimental novelist Mrs. E. D. E. N. Southworth, whose works were also widely purchased in the years immediately surrounding **Ragged Dick**.[24] Henry Ward Beecher's *Norwood* was one of the few comparably popular pieces of religious fiction. By 1870, Mark Twain and Bret Harte joined the list of best-selling authors.

But where publishers' records are absent, publication and sales estimates for any volume are necessarily poor. Alger himself made modest sales estimates. He once volunteered, of the six volume Ragged Dick series, that "the large sales, amounting to probably 150,000 volumes, show the public interest in the poor boys about whom the stories are written."[25] His obituary estimated total sales at 800,000 volumes. In 1910, when Alger sales were strong, *Publishers Weekly* reported that one bookseller estimated current sales of Alger books at a million a year, and dismissed such a claim as "probably very greatly exaggerated."[26]

Some members of the American public in the Gilded Age were initiated into book purchasing by "subscription."[27] A form of mass marketing that eliminated the retailer's profit, subscription publishing "reached the vast majority of the population that never entered a bookstore and perhaps did not live within geographical reach of one."[28] Audiences would not have acquired any Alger *fiction,* but if they looked carefully enough, they could have found Alger included in a subscription book on American authors.[29] They may well have made the acquaintance of various Alger publishers beginning around 1880, for quite a few of these generated a portion of their business through subscription volumes. Publishers' selection of authors, just as their selection of titles to go by subscription, underscored their attentiveness to mass audiences.[30]

Subscription books were designed as books of general interest. Drummers (salesmen) would canvas communities, distribute advertising fliers, and sell a volume house-to-house by showing sample covers and a few sample pages. Interested citizens would then "subscribe," entering their name and perhaps some payment in a ledger carried by the drummer.

Offerings included biographies and autobiographies of famous Americans (including P. T. Barnum), travel narratives (e.g., Livingstone's journals), religious works, temperance tracts by T.S. Arthur, and medical or other encyclopedias.[31] The subscription fare included success guides. In 1872, the salesman's prospectus (dummy) for Harriet Beecher Stowe's *The Lives and Deeds of our Self-Made Men* advertised that this volume, sold by subscription only, would contain over six hundred octavo pages and would be sold at $3.50 to $5.00, depending on style chosen. As an added inducement, subscribers were promised as a "Magnificent Premium, Free to All!" a beautiful engraving entitled "After the Nap," which would cost $1.00 if purchased separately.[32] William Makepeace Thayer's *Success and Its Achievers* first circulated as a subscription book in 1891. Alger was familiar with this version, which incorporated illustrations of famous statesmen, inventors, literary figures, and men of business.

Twain was the only fiction author who was a success in the subscription publishing business; during the 1870s, his bound volumes were sold by subscription only, through the American Publishing Company of Hartford. "'No book of literary quality was made to go by subscription except Mr. Clemens' books,'" William Dean Howells noted, "'and I think these went because the subscription public never knew what good literature they were.'"[33] Twain stood out in what has been called "a form of publishing only a step removed from the dime pamphlets and story weeklies."[34]

But the price of subscription volumes, was a major liability if the goal were to generate a mass literature. These volumes were considerably more expensive than other books. They were often elegantly produced and contained many illustrations, for "the subscription audience was fond of pictures and not discriminating in its appreciation of them."[35] The base price for Twain's *Sketches, New and Old* (1875) was $3.00; with gilt edges or a more elaborate half-turkey binding, the cost could rise to $4.50. Pinkerton's *Professional Thieves and the Detectives* (1881) sold for $2.75 in cloth, $3.25 in sheepskin.[36]

New clothbound novels published in 1876 that appeared on the *Publishers Weekly* list of popular titles ranged in price from $1.25 to $1.75. The trade publication's survey excluded elaborate bindings and special editions. These prices were comparable to the cost of acquiring books in the antebellum era.[37]

Most of Loring's Alger titles were offered at $1.25; an occasional volume during Alger's lifetime was priced at $1.50. While these prices were certainly moderate, Alger's clothbound books hardly represented an *inexpensive* price to many Americans in the 1860s and 1870s. The cost of such volumes probably placed purchase out of the reach of the families of tradesmen and skilled workers at least until 1880. The outlay easily represented a day's wages for a nonfarm earner.

A publisher's advertised book price did not mean very much, as the *Boston Globe* editorialized in 1876: "a book advertised for one dollar costs one dollar only to an inexperienced customer."[38] This following advertisement from The Troy *Times* (New York) sounds like it came from the now-defunct Crazy Eddie chain.

A CARD FROM THE BUTCHER

> In my advertisement in Saturday's Times I advised the people to go to the other booksellers and see the prices they charge, and then to come and see my prices; but to save them the trouble of doing so I have concluded to compare the prices of another bookseller with my own. The following quotations are taken from the advertisement of one of the leading bookselling firms in this city, and published in the Budget of last Sunday. They advertise "'Aunt Louisa's books,' reduced from $2.50 to $2"; my price has never been more than $1.50 . . ." 'Robinson Crusoe,' 'The Swiss Family Robinson,' and 'The Arabian Nights,' reduced from $1.50 to $1"; my price has always been 60 cents . . . These facts and figures will enable the people to judge where they can buy books cheapest. I never overcharge, therefore I never require to reduce my prices. I strike "rock bottom" every time.

THE BOOK BUTCHER, 281 River Street[39]

Publishers were outraged but apparently impotent.[40] For streetwise city folk, discounting could increase access to fiction and expand the class of book purchasers at the margins.

The $1.25 list price held until the turn of the century, while family incomes were rising. Porter and Coates of Philadelphia bought the stereotype plates and rights to Alger titles after Loring's bankruptcy and published forty-eight of Alger's novels, many of which were reprints of Loring titles.[41] But at the time of Alger's death, Porter and Coates dropped the price of these novels to twenty-five cents. Reincarnated as Henry T. Coates & Co, the firm also "permitted Hurst & Company, of New York, and Donohue & Henneberry, of Chicago, to do likewise. From this it was only a step to paper covers at a dime a throw . . ." Millions of boys would read Alger titles as dime novels during the next fifteen years.[42]

Prices and Audiences

> Went to Cohasset. Bought a book named "Munro's Ten cent novels no 18—'Wild Scout of the Mountains,'" to read in the cars."

Grenville Howland Norcross, July 27, 1864

If clothbound fiction remained too expensive for some would-be readers until late in the century, cheaper forms of fiction were available from mid-century. There were dime novels, railroad fiction, and story papers. There was considerable overlap. Authors and publishers in one of these genres were likely to be found involved in some of the others.[43] Alger did not publish dime novels, and Grenville Howland Norcross did not appear to read story papers, but one of Alger's key publishers was a major player in the production of both.

Ten-year-old Grenville Howland Norcross notes, on April 24, 1864, that he began "The Wrong Men," a "dime novel." He did not relish this book, but the boy appears to have devoured others. At least prior to the explosion of cheap fiction, some young genteel readers could read dime novels without hiding out behind the barn.

Norcross finished *Wild Scout of the Mountains,* the book he began for his July, 1864 train ride and probably purchased at the station or in the cars, four days later. The boy had validated Munro's and other publishers' belief that people would read railroad literature. Railroads carried passengers with leisure time, suggesting an immediate audience for fiction. Inexpensive reading matter designed specifically for train travel began to appear in the 1850s; the volumes were known as railroad novels.

Aaron K. Loring probably earned his designation as "a pioneer in cheap book publishing" for his early foray into paper covers. The term "cheap book," pervasive in the Gilded Age book trade, referred to books that, considering their character, were "conspicuously low in price in comparison with book prices in general."[44] In 1866, A. K. Loring published Alger's *Timothy Crump's Ward* anonymously in paper covers for

their Railway Companion Series.[45] Loring's anonymously published Alger adult novella, *The New Schoolma'am* was "of the paper-covered half-dollar variety" in 1877.[46]

After the demise of Loring's firm, the 1883 publication of *Tom, the Bootblack* by J. S. Ogilvie & Company (New York) may have marked the next earliest publication of Alger in paper covers. Although the railway audience seemed not overly fond of the series specifically designed for this purpose, Ogilvie, known as "the largest 'purveyor' of 'Railroad Literature' in the country" in the 1880s, made a large hit with *The People's Library.* Twelve paper-covered Alger titles appeared in this series, priced from ten to twenty cents per issue.[47] There were other such Alger publishers.

On the train, Norcross might have encountered the likes of Alger's young Paul Palmer, *Train Boy* (1883), who sells newspapers and other reading matter on the Chicago to Milwaukee line. His wares include *Harper's, Scribner's, Lippincott's,* and the *Atlantic Monthly;* he has "All the illustrated papers and magazines . . . [and has] besides some novels." On one better-than-average trip, Paul sold "three bound novels, which sale afforded him a handsome profit."[48] As he worked the aisles, he quite possibly sold Alger novels.

Among Paul Palmer's wares, newspapers, magazines, and story papers catered especially well to short-installment readers.[49] In the 1870s, large-circulation monthlies such as Paul sells on the railroad—specifically *Century, Harper's, Scribner's,* and *Atlantic*—showed a combined circulation (including overlap) of roughly 150,000, but the price of these magazines was still relatively dear; in Alger's *Train Boy, Harper's* costs thirty-five cents. But Paul also sells the illustrated papers. These were another matter.

In addition to *Ragged Dick,* two other mid-1860s Alger Loring novels had previous serial runs. The Alger pattern of publishing a serialized story prior to the issuance of a bound volume was not unusual. Newspaper and periodical previews of novel material were viewed as potential stimulators of interest in book sales. And, like the successful movie which is subsequently disseminated as a paperback, the timing could be reversed: Many cloth bound Alger novels were again serialized, or, toward the end of the century, reprinted in cheaper book form.[50] *Adventures of Huckleberry Finn* was serialized in a highly respectable publication and also circulated as a subscription novel.

But *Paul Prescott's Charge* and *Helen Ford* appeared in a rather different type of publication than *Student and Schoolmate.* The tales appeared anonymously in the story papers *New York Sun* and *New York Weekly Sun* in 1859 and 1860. These serial stories were among nine Alger published in the *New York Sun* between 1857 and 1860; eight of these ran in the *New York Weekly Sun* as well.[51] The *New York Sun* has been described as "a dreadful penny paper for the unwashed masses."[52] Poe wrote that the plan of this paper was to supply "the public with news of the day at so cheap a rate as to lie within the means of all."[53]

In January and February of 1864, the year of his first Loring novel, *Frank's Campaign*, Alger published his first serialized story for the firm of Street & Smith. The firm had been active and highly visible as publishers of dime novels and the story paper *New York Weekly* long before their foray into cheap book publishing in the late 1880s. The publishers had persuaded Alger to try his hand at a serial for their story paper, the *New York Weekly*.[54] Following **"Marie Bertrand, or the Felon's Daughter,"** seventeen more Alger stories were serialized therein. While the *New York Ledger* could claim the largest story paper circulation, the *New York Weekly* provided Alger a large potential audience.

Story papers, railroad fiction, and dime novels were joined by other kinds of inexpensive fiction by the time Norcross reached adulthood. At the commencement of the fourth quarter of the century, an observer could still claim that "the masses have not the means, if they had the inclination, to buy many papers and magazines"; this condition would soon change. For many publishers, magazine and book pricing became a key to new markets.

There was a tenfold increase in the number of copies of newspapers and magazines issued in 1890 compared with midcentury.[55] Advertising, publicity, and the availability of second-class postage rates played major roles in this phenomenon.[56] But while newspaper and magazine circulation skyrocketed, the combined circulation of *Century*, *Harper's*, *Scribner's* and *Atlantic* declined "in the face of competition from cheaper and less genteel magazines such as *Cosmopolitan*, *Collier's*, *McClure's*, and *Munsey's*."[57] Some publications dropped in price to ten and fifteen cents. Different kinds of publications were thriving.

Alger enjoyed a long association with Frank Munsey, a pioneer in cheap pricing of magazines, Munsey's *Golden Argosy*, begun in 1882, was priced at five cents an issue; the paper stock had more than a passing resemblance to newspaper. From early 1886 to mid-1894, Alger published thirty serials in Munsey's magazine under his own name and, when serials overlapped, under pen names. The circulation of the magazine peaked at 115,000 in 1886.[58]

When Street & Smith launched a new serial, *Good News*, on May 15, 1890, it was also priced for the masses at five cents an issue.[59] The lead-off story was by Oliver Optic; Alger's **"Only an Irish Boy"** also made its debut run.

Street & Smith "concentrated, perhaps more intensely and for a longer period of years than any other firm, in the marketing of ten-cent paperbacks and various cheap 'libraries' and popular fiction serials." Prior to entering this part of the business, they had apparently helped back the firm of J. S. Ogilvie. Advertising several series in 1890, Street & Smith claimed: "They are not cheap reprints, but are all written by popular American Authors . . . They are not sold in dry-goods stores, are returnable, and Newsdealers should be sure to have a complete stock."[60] The firm was one of the few survivors among the cheap publishers and piratical libraries after the International Copyright agreement of 1891.

Street & Smith issued almost all of Alger's *New York Weekly* serializations as novels; eighteen of Alger's stories were posthumously edited by Edward Stratemeyer for the firm.[61] This house published twenty-seven clothbound Algers, and well over one hundred appeared in five different paperback series after the author's death.[62] Their Medal Library, begun in 1898, sold books at ten cents in 1900; it was advertised as "a series of high-class books for boys and youth, written by the best authors."[63]

But before Street & Smith began to publish such books, Alger had already become a staple of the cheap book trade. "Of all the publishers of cheap books during the 1880's there were few to rival the cheapness of the F. M. Lupton publications," a firm responsible for one clothbound and eight paperbound Alger titles from the late 1880s until 1906. Some were priced at three cents per number, the size of a short "classic."[64] The imprint of the Mershon Company of Rahway, New Jersey appeared on thirty-five Alger reprints (often abridged) and graced many "cheap and nasty" volumes of fiction starting in the late 1880s. Mershon published a great deal of railroad fiction.[65] The United States Book Company issued Alger titles during its short existence, one in cloth and six in paper covers, and planned to issue others in their paperback Leather-Clad Tales of Adventure and Romance had bankruptcy not intervened.[66] G. W. Carleton, publisher of three Alger novels, was "particularly active in the low-price field."[67] Other cheap book publishers issuing Alger titles in cloth or paper included, but were not limited to, A. L. Burt, Hurst, John W. Lovell, Frank F. Lovell, W. L. Allison, DeWolfe-Fiske & Company, and M. A. Donohue and Company.[68] Toward the end of the century, cheap Alger publishing began to take place in new centers of the book trade outside the Northeast. Inexpensive copies of his work were also published in London.[69]

Although cheap reprints did not have an immediate impact on Alger's sagging popularity, there would be a posthumous payoff. Some of the greatest sales of Alger's works occurred in the first two decades of this century, and "more of his books were sold each year during the Progressive era than were sold in total during his life . . ."[70]

Pricing meant accessibility. But if the American public benefited from the low prices, they nonetheless generally received poorly made books that were often abridged and mutilated. Cheap reprints of Alger's works were no exception.

Working-Class Reading

Purchased reading matter in the latter half of the nineteenth century reached the American public through publishers and bookstores, drummers and train boys who peddled their printed wares. City sidewalk stands offered cheap fiction. Drug stores, stationery stores, and fancy goods stores served as retail outlets for the printed word, where books could be found alongside wallpaper and window curtains. And the railroad and postal system took books and magazines published in major northeastern publication centers to regions and communities in which they had not been available previously.[71] But how far did this proliferating and increasingly accessible fiction reach into the laboring classes?

Reviewing *Paul Prescott's Charge* in 1865, *The Nation* thought that "the tale is likely to prove a favorite in spite of occasional 'big words.'"[72] By the time Loring published *Frank's Campaign,* in 1864, the vast majority of the population was deemed literate, although the figure was lower in the South.[73] Reading English at an eighth-grade level was sufficient, except for some foreign phrases and a few large words, for the Alger novels.

This barrier excluded some of the street boys the author immortalized. There were other obstacles, especially for older readers. Until steel spectacles reached working-class audiences toward the end of the century, their prolonged reading, whether of fiction or of other printed matter, may have been unlikely.[74]

When neither of these problems presented itself, Loring and Porter & Coates clothbound Algers were beyond the *purchasing* power of urban newsboys and other young people struggling to earn a living. However, Alger advertised in *Fame and Fortune* that A. K. Loring was authorized "to send a gratuitous copy of the two volumes of the 'Ragged Dick Series' already issued, to any regularly organized Newsboys

Lodge within the United States."[75] Some copies of the novels in the "Ragged Dick Series" reached the newsboys' lodges, and some of these passed through many hands. *Student and Schoolmate* reports:

> The manager of the Newsboy's Home in St. Louis writes, "When on East last year, I got a copy of *Ragged Dick,* and the boys have enjoyed it so much, that it will not last much longer, and are continually asking for the second volume. You will oblige us very much by sending us a copy of both *Ragged Dick,* and *Fame and Fortune.*"[76]

Unless poor urban youth encountered these stories in newsboys' lodges, or unless they frequented libraries (and Alger gives us no example in which they do), they may never have seen Alger's fiction in clothbound novels. But they had access to Alger in the illustrated papers from the eve of the Civil War.

As Ben, the Luggage Boy, crossed the lower end of City Hall Park and walked up the Park Row side, "he saw a line of street merchants. Most conspicuous were the dealers in penny ballads, whose wares lined the railings, and were various enough to suit every taste."[77] Story papers appeared alongside other cheap printed matter on street corners of major cities. "Our story papers, damp from the press and printed very black, upholster all the news-stands," reports an 1879 observer.[78]

An Alger contemporary describes modes of dissemination of storypaper literature for the 1879 *Atlantic,* and also provides a valuable portrait of the audience. Entering a stationer's, where story papers are also found, this author describes the display:

> The story papers, the most conspicuous stock in trade, are laid out on the front counter, neatly overlapped, so as to show all the titles and frontispieces. Ten are already in, and more to come,—the Saturday Night, the Saturday Journal, the Ledger, the Weekly, the Family Story Paper, the Fireside Companion. Near them on the glass case, in formidable piles, are the "libraries." These are, omitting the prominent examples which do the same sort of service for standard works, pamphlets reprinting at a dime and a half dime the stories which have appeared as serials in the papers. There are papers which, finding this practice a diversion of interest, distinctly announce that their stories will not reappear, and that their fascinations can be enjoyed only at original sources.

Purchasers included a middle-aged woman carrying a basket with half a peck of potatoes; a shop-girl on her way home from work; "a servant from one of the good houses in the side streets"; but most of all come the boys—working boys, school boys, street boys.[79] As the information and story functions of newspapers diverged, the story paper came to be identified increasingly with a working-class readership.[80]

If the point of sale differed from the same story in hardback, there were other important differences. The format and surrounding material put the work in a context different from that of a novel sequestered between cloth or even paper covers. In the story paper, Alger, entertainer and moral crusader, narrated alongside sentimental tales and stories of the Molly Maguires, tramps, and highwaymen. Serial publication audiences got only a small piece of the story at a time, although this was not a new phenomenon: American audiences waited for the next installment of a current Dickens novel to arrive by boat and learned installment fiction reading of necessity.

The alternative to installment reading, demanding no delayed gratification, was the dime or half-dime novel. They were sold alongside the story paper. Alger works would have to vie with these novels for poor boys and working-class readers in the street battles and culture wars, and it was with these works that Alger stories were compared toward the end of the century.

Fiction consumption depended upon more than pricing, literacy, and availability. Reading and purchasing habits are factors in any tale of working-class reading. In a provocative study, David Nord probed the readership of popular fiction by sampling one hundred families in the cotton textile industry from the three chief cotton-milling regions in the United States, examining links between class, culture, and the disposition to read.[81] In doing so, he drew upon data on family spending for newspapers and books in family cost-of-living budgets developed by emerging bureaus of labor statistics.

Families in Nord's sample spent, on average, $4.23 per year for reading materials—about 2.4% of their discretionary expenditure and .75% of their total expenditures. New Englanders in the sample allotted more than 3% of their discretionary spending to reading materials; Southerners spend less than half of this.[82] Of the working-class families 77% reported at least some expenditure for newspapers and books. However, families in which children were engaged in the labor force were less likely to spend for reading matter than families whose children were not contributing to overall family income. Children in the factory made unlikely readers.

The most intriguing finding was that there appeared to be "a connection between reading and a feeling of arrival in a new culture, of involvement with the surrounding community—whether native or immigrant." Avid readers "seem to have been more at home with the institutions of the modern industrial community." Nord's workers who "had not yet acquired a permanent working-class culture"—who were new to the industrial system and who perhaps expected to return to the land—were "cultural transients" and were *not* spending money on reading materials.[83] Identifiable groups of "cultural sojourners," who participated more in traditional activities of family and clan (gemeinschaft) than in modern community activities (gesellschaft) were less likely to spend for reading matter.[84]

Among working-class families whose children were not employed, reading Alger (and any other fiction) might have been more likely the *greater* the sense of belongingness in the industrial community—quite the opposite from what some text-based projections claim.

Age and Gender

When popular fiction did arrive in the home, it is likely that various family members read it. It was not uncommon for adults to read juvenile fiction in this era, and when Alger sent copies of his works to adult correspondents, he surely hoped they would read them.[85] Although most frequently described as an author for boys, Alger aimed a small part of his fictional output at adult audiences, and he wrote several juvenile and adult novels with female heroines. Among these were ***Helen Ford, Tattered Tom, The Disagreeable Woman, Mabel Parker,*** and ***A Fancy of Hers.***

Oliver Optic's *Student and Schoolmate* advertised Alger's tales as having appeal across age and gender lines. ***Paul Prescott's Charge*** was described as "Another good book for the boys, and we presume that the girls will not object to reading it." The notice for ***Strong and Steady*** claimed: "It is not a book for boys—for from grandfather down to the wee ones all cry out for a chance to read **STRONG AND STEADY,** and all say' a splendid story.'"[86] The *Student and Schoolmate* statement was probably more wishful than factual, but was there any truth to the portrait? The observer of story paper purchasers revealed that the audience for this class of publication may have been mixed by age and gender, with boys overrepresented.

But what of the more expensive and respectable Alger vehicles? Fan mail and requests for autographs attest to Alger's popularity among young boys. There is at least some evidence that boys were not alone. Bookplates and inscriptions reveal that copies of Alger novels were given as gifts to girls as well; some were owned by Girl Scout leaders. Alger's letter to Miss Harriet Jackson, quoted at the outset of this chapter, reveals that his works were not only accessible in California, but they were being read by at least some young females.

BORROWING ALGER: LIBRARIES

> Though my sales of books have of course fallen off with the times, I am encouraged by my popularity at the libraries. In the Boston public library of over 250,000 vols. the sup'. reports that last year Optic and myself led all other authors in popularity, and father learned from the Harpers' Boston agent that on a recent Saturday there were *390* applications for my books 290 for Optic's who came next for that day. It is also very curious that the single book in that library wh. led all others in popularity last year according to the report was **"Timothy Crump's Ward"** wh. I published anonymously ten years since, and have never acknowledged. Loring always had a prejudice against it, and allowed it to pass out of print—though I had a considerably better opinion of it. I am very much surprised at its popularity at this late day.

> *Horatio Alger, Jr. to Edwin R. A. Seligman,*
> *August 6, 1877*[87]

National distribution publishers in the Gilded Age were located in New York, Boston, and Philadelphia, as were chief Alger publishers Loring, Porter & Coates, John C. Winston, and Street & Smith. While improved transportation and communication made possible "a far-flung net of travelling representatives and nationwide publicity campaigns," much of the West and the South remained outside main channels of literary distribution.[88] Nonetheless, Alger made his mark in some of these areas.

Fans and autograph-seekers wrote Alger from various points in the United States. A young male college boy in Georgia told Alger of the availability of his works in the library just around the time of McKinley's election.[89] In Portland, Oregon, during Alger's visit in 1877, henotes "I . . . find myself, rather to my surprise, well known here."[90]

On Alger's first trip to California in 1877, the author was pleased to note his novels in a public school library three thousand miles from the scene of action in **Ragged Dick.** Planning an upcoming visit to a San Francisco area public school, Alger wrote: "I hear the scholars are curious to see the historian of Ragged Dick, whose eventful story, with others of his kindred, is included in the Public School libraries."[91]

It was in no small measure due to the library that Alger was able to reach a book and magazine reading public that was so widely diversified by class and region. Alger proudly cited large Boston Public Library circulation figures for some of his works. His popularity was part of a boom in fiction circulation witnessed by the libraries. Until quite late in the century, Alger's works were widely available to young library patrons.

When Alger began to write, libraries came in many forms. The free reading room housed leading newspapers and magazines of the day.[92] Young Men's Christian Association libraries and libraries established by some manufacturers in working communities afforded additional access to somefiction.[93] There were subscription libraries and social libraries, supported by member contributions of perhaps five dollars per year; these last, generally known as mercantile libraries, were past their heyday by the fourth quarter of the century.[94] Noted an 1876 observer: "To many of these admission is by membership, fee, or introduction, but there are reasons for believing that in a few years public libraries, free to all, will be found in every city and hamlet in the land."[95]

Alger once bragged that "Hundreds of Sunday-school libraries bought them [his novels] . . . and they were read in every State and Territory in the Union."[96] According to one estimate, at least a third of the Alger volumes purchased "found their way into circulating libraries, particularly into Sunday school libraries."[97] Sunday School libraries appear especially important in providing rural youth with access to moralistic tales for youth.[98] Some turn of the century copies were gifts or awards to individuals from Baptist and Congregational Sunday Schools.

The Gilded Age was the era of great expansion for public libraries, a classification that included public school libraries, state libraries, college and university libraries, prison libraries, and theological seminary libraries. A large proportion of these libraries were nevertheless located in urban areas. Data on the distribution of public libraries in the United States circa 1875 are shown in the appendix to this chapter.

The U.S. Department of the Interior *Report on Public Libraries* (1876) included a revealing table entitled "Classified statistics of circulation of twenty-four public libraries in 1874-75." On average, 67.4% of all circulating works in this period were classed as "English prose, fiction, and juveniles"; the range was from 50% to 77.8% fiction. The averages reported by these libraries for some of the "better" classes of materials were 8.0% for history and biography, 6.7% for voyages and travels, 4.4% for science and art, 1.5% for religion and theology, and 1.1% for German and French literature.[99]

The pattern was mirrored at the Boston Public Library. A table of Boston Public Library (Lower Hall) reading for 1868-75 shows a range of 69 to 78.4% of circulating works in the category "prose fiction for adults and youths."[100] One librarian there opined that if novels, stories and jokes were excluded from the public library, this would, "in general, reduce the extent of its use to one-quarter of what it would otherwise be."[101]

The pattern persisted. In 1881, a librarian at Boston Public Library asserted that

> out of 14,950 books bought during the past five years for the Lower Hall,—the popular department of the Central Library,—10,417, or 70 per cent, were story-books, technically called "fiction" and "juveniles." This, however, by no means represents the whole amount purchased, since it includes only those stories published in book-form and not those printed in periodicals and magazines, of which great numbers are taken.[102]

These books were not collecting dust; in the same five year period, four-fifths of the material circulating from the Lower Hall and branches consisted of "juveniles" and "fiction," including in the category "the stories contained in the magazines and periodicals, and the very considerable number of novels not classified under 'fiction.'"[103]

Those concerned with patterns of library circulation did more than collect statistics: Librarians observed patrons, and provided some idea of who was thronging the halls of the public libraries to consume fiction. In 1876, one reported: "Most of those who read are young people who want entertainment and excitement, or tired people who want relaxation and amusement."[104] One crusader against most fiction circulating from the Boston Public Library thought that library use knew no class bounds: "Every boy and girl in Boston, over fourteen years of age, has free access to a collection of story-books amounting in the aggregate to 50,000 volumes; and a very large proportion make frequent use of the privilege."[105]

Noting the democratization of reading that accompanied universal education, this librarian-critic writes: "Never before have there been so many who, engaged in purely manual labor, turn almost instinctively for their recreation, at the end of the day, to a book or a paper." While this may be the case, he nonetheless observes that the chief part of the patrons "who throng the Lower Hall and Branches afternoon and evening" were not "poor persons, who must either have their reading free or go without it . . . but in fact they appear to be principally persons in apparently comfortable circumstances or the children of well-to-do parents."[106] If the laboring classes are beginning to make use of the library, they are doing so shoulder to shoulder with children of the elite, or of the middle classes, who appear to outnumber them as patrons.

TEXTS AND AUDIENCES: CLASS, CULTURE AND ALGER READING

Most text-based projections of Alger's audience claim that the predominant voice in Alger's tales spoke *most* coherently to and for an audience that had *not* been incorporated into the industrial life of the antebellum era. However, even the texts can reveal a more incendiary discourse, as we saw in Chapter 9. This chapter sought to be especially wary of "purely text-based projections of implied readers."[107]

Text-based projections about readership presume, in Stanley Fish's terminology, that there is *one* "text in this class." In the Alger case, it is readily apparent why there is not. Clothbound novels priced at $1.25, juvenile magazines, cheap magazines, Alger reprints, and story papers were not clearly the same texts.

Reading publics were becoming more segmented as they became class diversified. In developed markets of the Northeast, "the reading public became fragmented by sex, class, and religion in the face of the onslaught of new titles."[108] The expanding Gilded Age publishing industry began to target its audiences: "The varied components of the reading public began to be recognized and the mechanisms for the production and distribution of the staple commodity, fiction, were adjusted more precisely to the demands of the market."[109]

From the late 1850s, Alger had been able to sell story after story to the *New York Sun,* the *New York Weekly Sun,* the *New York Weekly,* the *Golden Argosy,* and other inexpensive publications. He was clearly successful enough that penny papers and cheap magazines continued to pay him for new and recycled stories. The mere appearance of an Alger story in a magazine or story paper does not tell us who read it. While pricing made it possible for a broader audience to read Alger, it could not compel their response. During the period Alger generated so many serials for Munsey, *Golden Argosy* circulation dropped to nine thousand.[110] Such evidence, accompanied by Alger's declining economic fortunes, has led one critic to conclude that, although Alger had the vehicles for reaching working-class audiences, his moralism fell upon deaf ears.[111]

This, too, is projection. Publishers made errors: Loring went bankrupt, and every indication was that he was overextended. Copyright books faced stiff competition from other and cheaper forms of fiction; living on copyright book royalties as well as one-time payments for stories, Alger was not likely to grow rich given the type of fiction and where and how it was produced.

We simply cannot know why the reader of these works did so, nor how actual Alger readers produced meaning. We can only speculate on how they "responded to" the author. The literary text is neither irreducibly given nor is it coercive or controlling of reading. Rather, reading is production. It is a process "governed by reading strategies and interpretive conventions that the reader has learned to apply as a member of a particular interpretive community."[12] Readers bring cultural codes to the task.

Reading matter is not always simply taken or left. If it *is* picked up, many things can occur, for "people do not injest mass culture whole but often make it into something they can use." Mass fiction readers were not "passive, purely receptive individuals who can only consume the meanings embodied within cultural texts, . . . powerless in the face of ideology."[113]

Grenville Howland Norcross's family did not object to Alger reading, and they did not appear unusual. But by the time F. Scott Fitzgerald read a cheap reprint of Alger's **Ralph Raymond's Heir** and Carl Sandburg read **Tom the Bootblack** (the reprint title of **The Western Boy**), Theodore Dreiser had to read **Brave and Bold** behind a barn. This way is precisely how some late Alger antiheroes would read dime novels and melodramas.[114]

Alger and Optic tales would only become "trash," or morally suspect, in broader circles beginning in the late 1870s. Many middle-class youth profess reading Alger tales in the late nineteenth and early twentieth centuries; some of them were engaged in clandestine or questionable activity. It is in the context of the rise of working-class reading and the booming dissemination of fiction of all sorts that the battle over fiction in the closing decades of the nineteenth century would take shape.

If purchasers of illustrated papers and cheap monthly magazines read his tales, then there is evidence of a wide class span for Alger's fiction. If one author reached both Grenville Howland Norcross's circles and working-class readers, he accomplished something that many moral reformers could not. To the extent Alger had the attention of the working-class story paper audience, one might at least *believe* that readers were united in the same universe of discourse.

With Gilded Age pleasures becoming increasingly class specific, if different classes read Alger stories through different vehicles, they were likely to be reading quite different stories. The same words could be transported to different worlds.

Notes

[1] Letter dated March 3, 1877 from the Grand Hotel, San Francisco; UVa.

[2] David Paul Nord, "Working-Class Readers: Family, Community, and Reading in Late Nineteenth-Century America," *Communication Research* 13 (April, 1986): 156-81.

[3] I am grateful to James Green, Library Company of Philadelphia, for pointing out some of the most egregious problems in this secondary literature. For an example of more current scholarship, see Michael Hackenberg, ed., *Getting the Books Out* (Washington: Center for the Book, Library of Congress, 1987).

[4] Extant publishers' magazine subscription and book order records; estate inventories and probate records, such as have been examined by Robert Darnton; library charging lists, checked against city directories were all left untouched.

[5] Scholars emphasizing Alger's cultural influence have tended to presume enormous circulation. Claims that Alger "is probably the most popular author America has ever had, and one of the most popular the world has ever known" are much overblown. For examples, see Scharnhorst, *Horatio Alger, Jr.*, 1980 and Chapter 1 above.

[6] Biographical sketch supplied by Alger and enclosed with letter to George A. Bacon, Esq., Jan. 26, 1874; UVa.

[7] Scharnhorst with Bales, *Lost Life*, pp. 90-91. This would be about 1869, possibly after Norcross's card game days.

[8] Scharnhorst with Bales, *Lost Life*, pp. 75-76. The inspirational lecture was by John B. Gough. Publication history from Benett, *Horatio Alger, Jr.*

[9] This and all subsequent references to Norcross are from the Grenville Howland Norcross Diaries, 1860-76. Unpublished manuscripts from the Children as Diarists collection, AAS.

[10] Optic's magazine ran *Ragged Dick* in 1867, *Fame and Fortune* in 1868, *Rough and Ready* in 1869, *Rufus and Rose* in 1870, *Paul the Peddler* in 1871, and *Slow and Sure* in 1872. The run for each story was January-December.

[11] He had also written *Nothing to Do* (anonymously), *Hugo, the Deformed,* and *Timothy Crump's Ward.*

[12] The quote is Alger. Letter to Duyckinck, 28 January 1866, from Brewster, Mass; NYPLd.

[13] "Tangled Threads," *Student and Schoolmate* 21 (March, 1868): 140; (May, 1868): 234.

[14] "Tangled Threads," *Student and Schoolmate* 22 (August, 1868): 376.

[15] Madeleine B. Stern in Stern, ed., *Publishers for Mass Entertainment in Nineteenth Century America* (Boston: G. K. Hall & Co., 1980), pp. 191, 193. Stern claims Loring published 36 Alger titles, and Bob Bennett, *Horatio Alger, Jr.,* pp. 148-49, finds 37.

[16] "At Our Desk," *Student and Schoolmate* 27 (June, 1871): 292. See also "Tangled Threads," in *Student and Schoolmate* 21 (May, 1868): 282. See below on discounting practice.

[17] John T. Winterich, *Three Lantern Slides* (Urbana, Il.: University of Illinois Press, 1949), p. 20. DeWolfe-Fiske and Company of Boston, publisher of Alger's biographies, also "sold new books to individuals and to libraries and acted as a wholesaler for small-town booksellers." Lehmann-Haupt et al., *The Book in America*, p. 243; p. 247 for a Chicago example. Bennett, *Horatio Alger, Jr.: A Comprehensive Bibliography*, p. 144.

[18] Lehmann-Haupt et al., *The Book in America*, p. 195.

[19] See Soltow and Stevens, *The Rise of Literacy and the Common School in the United States.*

[20] Lehmann-Haupt et al., *The Book in America*, pp. 197-99 and 321. They place the number of etiquette/advice manuals in each period at 170. There was also growing interest in volumes on fine arts late in the century, perhaps stimulated by the Philadelphia Exposition's exhibit of American painting.

[21] Lehmann-Haupt et al., *The Book in America*, p. 198.

[22] Ronald Zboray, "Antebellum Reading and the Ironies of Technological Innovation," *American Quarterly* 40 (March, 1988): 66.

[23] Frank Luther Mott, *Golden Multitudes, The Story of Best Sellers in the United States* (New York: Macmillan, 1947), pp. 158-59; 303; 307-13. By this definition, to be a best seller required a sale of 375,000 copies for 1870-79; 500,000 copies for 1880-89; and 625,000 copies for 1890-99. Runner-ups, pp. 315-22. With evidence that Alger's greatest volume of sales occurred in the two decades after his death, there were still no "bestsellers" in the lot according to Mott's data. Whereas Mott draws heavily on the fake Alger biography by Herbert Mayes, he does not use Mayes's grossly inflated estimates for publication figures.

[24] See Mott, *Golden Multitudes,* pp. 309-22.

[25] Alger, to Russell A. Alger, letter of May 2, 1888, UM. See also Scharnhorst and Bales, *Horatio Alger, Jr.: An Annotated Bibliography*, p. 17.

[26] Obituary, HUA. Mott, *Golden Multitudes,* pp. 158-59 quotes the 1910 figure, which he is inclined to accept as reasonable.

[27] The phenomenon of subscription bookselling probably peaked in the 1880s. Michael Hackenberg in Hackenberg, ed., *Getting the Books Out*, p. 45.

[28] Henry Nash Smith, *Democracy and the Novel*, p. 106.

[29] Alger noted his inclusion there in a January 28, 1898 letter to Blake; HL.

[30] C.N. Caspar, *Caspar's Directory of the American Book, News and Stationery Trade* (Milwaukee: Riverside Printing Company, 1889; copyright C. N. Caspar), listing approximately 450 subscription publishing houses, turns up five publishers of Alger's clothbound works; his paperback publishers were not included (pp. 1047-49). Among these, Hurst & Company of New York carried sixty-seven Alger titles. The Hurst firm, active in the 1870s and 1880s, leased their plates to the United States Book Company in 1890, and resumed publishing after that unique company failed shortly after (Raymond Howard Shove, *Cheap Book Production In The United States, 1870 To 1891*. Urbana, Il.: University of Illinois Library, 1937, pp. 70-71). See also Michael Hackenberg, "The Subscription Publishing Network in Nineteenth-Century America," in Hackenberg, ed., *Getting the Books Out*, p. 46. Alger's hard cover and paper cover publishers are listed in Bennett, *Horatio Alger, Jr.: A Comprehensive Bibliography*, pp. 139-71.

[31] Smith, *Democracy and the Novel*, p. 106; also collections of drummer's samples, AAS.

[32] Publishers' Broadsides/Prospectuses Collection, AAS. Stowe's *Lives and Deeds of our Self-Made Men* was published by Worthington, Dustin & Co., Hartford Conn. and Queen City Publishing Company, Cincinnati, and M.A. Parker & Co., Chicago, Il. in 1872.

[33] Howells (1893), quoted in Justin Kaplan, *Mr. Clemens and Mark Twain* (New York: Simon and Schuster, 1966), p. 62.

[34] Denning, *Mechanic Accents*, p. 208.

[35] Smith, *Democracy and the Novel*, p. 106.

[36] Publishers' Broadsides/Prospectuses collection; AAS. Salesman's dummy for *Mark Twain's Sketches, New and Old*. A sheet from N.D. Thompson & Co. of St. Louis and New York entitled "Confidential Terms to Agents for Professional Thieves and the Detectives by Allan Pinkerton" tells agents their profit for each $2.75 copy will be $1.10 and for each $3.25 leather copy, $1.30.

[37] On this occasion, *Publisher's Weekly* collected data on book pricing for popular titles. Titles were put on the list by ballot, presumably by those receiving the trade publication. The roster of pre-1876 popular titles showed several $2 titles and one or two at $2.50. Witnerich, *Three Lantern Slides*, pp. 14-15. On antebellum book pricing, Zboray, "Antebellum Reading," 74.

[38] Winterich, *Three Lantern Slides,* p. 15, quoting the *Boston Globe.*

[39] Winterich, *Three Lantern Slides,* pp. 17-18.

[40] *Publisher's Weekly* deplored underselling, but ran advertisements by book sellers advertising rock bottom prices. Winterich, *Three Lantern Slides,* p. 20.

[41] Anna Lou Ashby on Porter & Coates in Stern, ed., *Publishers for Mass Entertainment,* pp. 247-48. Many of these Alger titles appeared in 1882.

[42] The Alger plates would be passed along again; at the end of the century, the list was taken over by the rising house, John C. Winston and Company of Philadelphia, Chicago, and Toronto. It was classified as a subscription firm and carried fifty-nine Alger titles (Lehmann-Haupt et al., *The Book in America,* p. 232). The text quote is Mott, *Golden Multitudes,* p. 158. The price drop may well have reflected the fact that no royalties need be paid.

[43] The most prominent in the field was the Beadle dime and half-dime library.

[44] Shove, *Cheap Book Production In The United States,* p. 141; ix on the use of the term. Clothbound, paperbound, and books without a separate cover of any sort at all are included, although dime novels were generally not included in the designation.

[45] Bennett, *Horatio Alger, Jr.: A Comprehensive Bibliography,* p. 162.

[46] *The Nation,* October 6, 1877.

[47] According to the *American Bookseller* (1886) Ogilvie's output ranged "from works of worldwide reputation to stories that are never heard of in fashionable society." Quoted in Shove, *Cheap Book Production,* p. 95.

[48] Paul earns around eight dollars per week, though on lucky weeks, he earns as much as eleven—more than he could get in a store or office, we are told. Alger, *Train Boy* (Leyden, Mass.: Aeonian Press, Inc., 1975; originally copyrighted 1883 by Street & Smith), pp. 9, 12, 92.

[49] See Chapter 11, where this is also said of Alger novels.

[50] Lehmann-Haupt et al., *The Book in America,* p. 143.

[51] Bennett, *Horatio Alger, Jr.,* for serialization histories. *Frank's Campaign* was not serialized. Some stories were published anonymously or under pseudonyms. "Hugo, the Deformed," from 1857, was the one story not carried in the *New York Weekly Sun.*

[52] Scharnhorst with Bales, *Lost Life,* p. 39.

[53] Poe's 1846 article on Richard Adams Locke, quoted Terence Whalen, "Edgar Allan Poe and the Horrid Laws of Political Economy," *American Quarterly* 44 (September, 1992): 391.

[54] Quentin Reynolds, *The Fiction Factory* (New York: Random House, 1955; copyright Street & Smith Publications, Inc.), p. 37. "Marie Bertrand, or the Felon's Daughter" is one of the few Alger stories never to appear in book form. See Bennett, *Horatio Alger, Jr.* for the *New York Weekly* serial stories and subsequent publication histories.

[55] The number of copies in 1890 was about 4.5 billion. Nord, "Working-Class Readers," 161.

[56] Lehmann-Haupt et al., *The Book in America,* p. 154.

[57] Smith, *Democracy and the Novel,* pp. 104-5, citing Frank L. Mott's *History of American Magazines.*

[58] Scharnhorst with Bales, *Lost Life,* p. 132.

[59] Quentin Reynolds, *Fiction Factory,* p. 78.

[60] Quote is Shove, *Cheap Book Production,* p. 145; the citation is omitted but appears to be *Publisher's Weekly* (1890). Lehmann-Haupt et al., *The Book in America,* p. 237, relying upon Mott's *Golden Multitudes.* The Street & Smith inventory comes from Bob Bennett, *Horatio Alger, Jr.,* pp. 164-69.

[61] Quentin Reynolds, *Fiction Factory,* pp. 37, 83. Stratemeyer edited *Good News* for Street & Smith, which apparently occasioned the meeting with Alger around 1890 (Gardner, *Horatio Alger,* p. 283; pp. 364-65 on the unfinished works).

[62] The largest group of paperback titles—104—was issued largely between the end of 1915 and 1919, although several additional titles were added in the fall of 1926. Other paperback series were issued from 1900-1906, 1903-4, and 1906-11. Bennett, *Horatio Alger, Jr., passim.*

[63] Quentin Reynolds, *The Fiction Factory,* p. 79 on the origins of Medal Lobrary; *Publishers' Trade List Annual,* 1900. The Alger titles listed were *Erie Train Boy, From Farm Boy to Senator, Dean Dunham, Young Acrobat; Adventures of a New York Telegraph Boy* and *Tom Tracy* were attributed to Arthur Lee Putnam, one of Alger's pen names.

[64] Shove, *Cheap Book Production,* p. 142. The classification of publishers known mainly for cheap books is Shove's; the list of publishers derives from Shove and from Bennett's comprehensive bibliography in

Horatio Alger, Jr. The three titles were published from 1886 to 1900.

⁶⁵ Shove, *Cheap Book Production,* p. 143.

⁶⁶ Bennett, *Horatio Alger, Jr.,* pp. 156, 169-70; Gardner, *Horatio Alger,* p. 392.

⁶⁷ Lehmann-Haupt et al., *The Book in America,* p. 226; Bennett, *Horatio Alger, Jr.,* pp. 141, 144. Carleton's successor, George W. Dillingham, published one of Alger's adult novels.

⁶⁸ Stern, in *Publishers for Mass Entertainment.* See also Shove, *Cheap Book Production;* Bennett, *Horatio Alger, Jr.*

⁶⁹ Chicago was later joined by Cincinnati, Akron, Cleveland, and other cities in Alger reprint publishing. The Donnelly Lakeside Library, which began publishing in 1875, may have also been among the early contenders. Bob Bennett, *Horatio Alger, Jr.,* p. 163 and passim.

⁷⁰ Scharnhorst, *Horatio Alger, Jr.,* p. 141.

⁷¹ Lehmann-Haupt et al., *The Book in America,* pp. 242, 246.

⁷² Scharnhorst, *Horatio Alger, Jr.,* pp. 27-28, quoting *The Nation* for 14 December 1865, 757.

⁷³ See Soltow and Stevens, *The Rise of Literacy and the Common School in the United States,* Chapter 5, for a rich study of changes in illiteracy 1840-70.

⁷⁴ Zboray, "Antebellum Reading," 78.

⁷⁵ Preface to Alger, *Fame and Fortune* (Philadelphia: John C. Winston; copyright Horatio Alger, Jr., 1896), viii.

⁷⁶ "At Our Desk," *Student and Schoolmate* 24 (November, 1869): 530.

⁷⁷ Alger, *Ben, the Luggage Boy* (Philadelphia: Henry T. Coates; copyright A. K. Loring, 1870), p. 39.

⁷⁸ W. H. Bishop, "Story-Paper Literature," *Atlantic Monthly* 44 (September, 1879): 384.

⁷⁹ Bishop, "Story-Paper Literature," both quotes, 384.

⁸⁰ Michael Schudson, *Discovering the News* (New York: Basic Books, 1978). See also Denning, *Mechanic Accents,* Chapter 2. Story papers pure and simple were already in evidence by the 1840s.

⁸¹ Nord, "Working-Class Readers," 160. This appears to be the first use of such data to study reading behavior.

⁸² Nord, "Working-Class Readers," 162. This spending was greater than any other discretionary expenditures catalogued in the survey, and represents a figure comparable to 1929-68 data for media expenditures as a percentage of consumer spending. Regional differences (p. 164) are partly attributable to differentials in literacy between regions and the fact that Southerners were less well integrated into reading distribution networks; income differentials do not explain regional differences.

⁸³ Nord, "Working-Class Readers," 175, 177, 174 respectively for quotes.

⁸⁴ Nord, "Working-Class Readers," 178; 175-76. These groups were Southerners and French Canadians. Nord examined four categories of expenditures touching the life-style of the family in the community, treating expenditure for family amusements, church, and charity as traditional expenditures; insurance and organizational expenditure were treated as linked to formal, contractual community.

⁸⁵ On adult reading of juveniles, see Soltow and Stevens, *Rise of Literacy.*

⁸⁶ *Student and Schoolmate* 16 (October, 1865): 127. "At Our Desk," *Student and Schoolmate* 29 (January, 1872): 51.

⁸⁷ Written from South Natick, Mass.; letter in HL. Loring was apparently not happy with sales of *Timothy Crump's Ward,* which had been offered in both cloth and paper covers (Scharnhorst with Bales, *Lost Life,* p. 75).

⁸⁸ Lehmann-Haupt et al., *The Book in America,* p. 217 (quote); Charleston and Richmond, literary production and distribution centers in the prewar South, lost influence, and Cincinnati became the region's principal link to the book trade. See also Zboray, "Antebellum Reading," 79.

⁸⁹ Alger to Irving Blake, November 23, 1896; HL.

⁹⁰ Alger to Edwin R. A. Seligman, dated May 7 [1877]; CU.

⁹¹ Alger to Edwin R. A. Seligman, February 21, n.y. from Palace Hotel in San Francisco; CU.

⁹² William C. Todd, "Free Reading Rooms," *Public Libraries in the United States of America: Their History, Condition, and Management. Special Report.* Department of the Interior, Bureau of Education. (Washington, D.C.: Government Printing Office, 1876), pp. 460, 462.

⁹³ The Revere, Massachusetts Public Library, near the site of Alger's birthplace and housing a small Alger collection, is a Carnegie Library.

[94] U.S. Department of the Interior, Bureau of Education, *Public Libraries in the United States of America* (Washington, D.C.: Government Printing Office, 1876), p. 404 [henceforth, *Public Libraries*]. See Soltow and Stevens, *Rise of Literacy* for the member costs at social libraries.

[95] Todd, "Free Reading Rooms," p. 462 in *Public Libraries*.

[96] Alger quoted in Scharnhorst with Bales, *Lost Life*, p. 90, from *Golden Argosy* (October 17, 1885).

[97] Harvey, "Alger's New York," 3. His estimation of Alger's widespread popularity and sales antedates the Mayes hoax biography.

[98] Dee Garrison, "Cultural Custodians of the Gilded Age: The Public Librarian and Horatio Alger," *Journal of Library History* 6 (October, 1971): 325, footnote 18. Inscriptions and book plates of copies of Alger books provide evidence they were located here. Sunday Schools may possibly have given these books as gifts as they divested themselves.

[99] *Public Libraries*, p. 820. This table includes subscription as well as free libraries.

[100] The percentage rises then declines during this period, for which an account is given: "A comparison of this table with those showing the classifications of the reading at the branches indicates the beneficial effects of the notes in the Lower Hall Class-list for History, Biography, and Travel, which has reduced materially the percentage of fiction used, while it is maintaining its old predominance, and in some cases, increases in the branches." *Public Libraries*, p. 821.

[101] F. B. Perkins, of the Boston Public Library, in "How to Make Town Libraries Successful," p. 422 in *Public Libraries*.

[102] James Mascarene Hubbard, "Fiction and Public Libraries," *International Review* 10 (February, 1881): 170.

[103] Hubbard, "Fiction and Public Libraries," 170, again having recourse to the appendices to the annual reports of the Boston Public Library.

[104] Perkins, "How to Make Town Libraries Successful," *Public Libraries*, p. 420.

[105] Hubbard, "Fiction and Public Libraries," 171. His estimate includes those volumes lost or used up in service and is based on the 1880 report.

[106] Hubbard, "Fiction in Public Libraries," 168; 174-75.

[107] Davidson, "Towards a History of Books and Readers," 11.

[108] Zboray, "Antebellum Reading," 79.

[109] Smith, *Democracy and the Novel,* p. 104.

[110] Scharnhorst with Bales, *Lost Life,* p. 132.

[111] Denning, *Mechanic Accents,* pp. 203 and 235-36 (drawing on secondary sources) for a good, brief discussion of his reception over time by the "genteel culture" and by a mass audience.

[112] Radway, *Reading the Romance,* p. 11.

[113] Janice Radway, "Reading Is Not Eating: Mass-Produced Literature and the Theoretical, Methodological, and Political Consequences of a Metaphor," *Book Research Quarterly* (Fall, 1986): 7-29; second quote, Radway, *Reading the Romance,* p. 6

[114] Scharnhorst with Bales, *Lost Life,* pp. 94-95, 106; citing Sandberg's *Prairie-Town Boy* and the *Fitzgerald/ Hemingway Annual* (1978). Scharnhorst and Bales, *Horatio Alger, Jr.: An Annotated Bibliography,* p. 34.

FURTHER READING

Beauchamp, Gorman. "*Ragged Dick* and the Fate of Respectability." *Michigan Quarterly Review,* Vol. 31, No. 3 (Summer 1992): 324-45.

   In this discussion of *Ragged Dick,* Beauchamp argues that critics in the past overlooked the preeminent theme of respectability, an ideal he finds relatively scarce in contemporary American popular culture.

Hendler, Glenn. "Pandering in the Public Sphere: Masculinity and the Market in Horatio Alger." *American Quarterly,* Vol. 48, no. 3 (September 1996): 415-38.

   Hendler argues that Alger's novels were intended to indoctrinate boys in preparation for the male, financial, public sphere.

Nackenoff, Carol. "Of Factories and Failures: Exploring the Invisible Factory Gates of Horatio Alger, Jr." *Journal of Popular Culture,* Vol. 25, no. 4 (Spring 1992): 63-80.

   Nackenoff argues that Alger's moralism has been underestimated by past critics. She clarifies the urgency of his moral message by contextualizing his writings historically.

Pauly, Thomas H. "*Ragged Dick* and *Little Women*: Idealized Homes and Unwanted Marriages." *Journal of Popular Culture* 9 (1975): 583-92.

   Pauly places *Ragged Dick* in the context of early children's literature, which was meant to morally instruct and socially mold young people, but he argues that Alger tended to subvert these purposes.

Scharnhorst, Gary. *Journal of Popular Culture.* Vol. 15, No. 3 (Winter 1981): 175-82.

Scharnhorst explores Alger's literary influences, concluding that Alger's works are derivative but more diverse than generally considered.

Trachtenberg, Alan. Introduction to *Ragged Dick.* Signet, 1990.

Trachtenberg argues against the interpretation of Alger's novels as capitalist guide books, provides historical and biographical background, and concludes that Alger's ideals are pervasive because he wrote formulaically.

Additional coverage of Alger's life and career is contained in the following source published by the Gale Group: *Dictionary of Literary Biography*, **Vol. 42.**

(Henri René Albert) Guy de Maupassant

1850-1893

French short story writer, novelist, journalist, poet, dramatist, and travel writer.

For further information on Maupassant's complete career, see *NCLC*, Volume 1; for additional information on Maupassant's novel *Pierre and Jean*, see *NCLC*, Volume 42.

INTRODUCTION

Maupassant is generally considered to be one of the masters of the short story and a champion of the realist approach to writing (though he resisted any identification with literary movements). He also authored six novels, a volume of poetry, a number of plays, three travel journals, and several journalistic pieces. Short-story writing, however, was clearly his strength—he produced over three hundred short stories from 1880 to 1890, the decade during which he penned the majority of his other works as well. He would have preferred fame as a novelist and likely would have garnered more critical attention if he had published more novels; critics have tended to regard the short story as a "lesser" form of literature. As a result, at least in part, Maupassant, though widely recognized outside his native country, usually has not been numbered among the most acclaimed of France's nineteenth-century prose writers—Gustave Flaubert, Emile Zola, and Honoré de Balzac. Maupassant drew upon his own day-to-day life experiences as material for his works, focusing on the peasants native to his homeland, the service of government employees, the Franco-Prussian War of 1870, and his own private hallucinations and feelings of dread.

Biographical Information

Maupassant was born in Normandy, and both the setting and character of his childhood left a distinct impression on his life and work. His childhood home was a wealthy but unhappy one; his mother, though intelligent and educated, was prone to neuroses, and his father turned to other women for comfort. When Maupassant was twelve years old, his parents separated and he lived with his mother, seeing little of his father. The young Maupassant's cynicism regarding marriage seems to have stemmed from these early experiences and is evident in much of his work. His stories often center on the fate of a rejected woman and the children of an ill-fated liaison, exploring the problems of identity and the individual's place in a rigid social structure. In

1863 Maupassant's mother enrolled him in a Catholic boarding school, from which he was later expelled for the nature of the poetry he had written during what he called his "imprisonment." With the outbreak of the Franco-Prussian War in 1870, Maupassant left his law studies in Paris (which he had begun in 1869) to enlist in the army. His experiences during the war inform some of his finest short stories, expressing his disgust for the degradation and folly of war. After the war, he worked first in the Ministry of the Navy from 1872 to 1878, and then the Ministry of Public Education from 1878 to 1882. This experience provided the setting for many of his stories in which he depicted the hopeless, repetitious life of the civil servant. He regularly escaped the boredom of his work through encounters with women, often prostitutes. One of these encounters would prove fatal, as in 1877 he was diagnosed with syphilis, for which there was no known cure.

Maupassant devoted a great deal of time to writing during his tenure as a civil servant, writing plays, poetry, and narrative prose. Gustave Flaubert became his friend and mentor, helping him with his writing and introducing him to Flaubert's literary circles. After Flaubert's death, Maupassant became a regular contributor to *Le Gaulois,* a respected Paris newspaper, and eventually wrote for the periodicals *Gil Blas* and the *Figaro* as well, often using the pseudonyms Joseph Prunier, Guy de Valmont, and Maufrigneuse. After he left the ministry, his literary output increased dramatically, especially from 1883 to 1885, and he enjoyed much success. The syphilis he had contracted as a young man led to recurrent problems with his eyesight and eventually to a complete physical and emotional collapse. Struggling with bouts of a debilitating mental disorder, Maupassant attempted suicide in 1892 and was subsequently confined to a sanatorium in Passy until his death.

Textual History

Perhaps the greatest influence on Maupassant's life and career was Flaubert, a childhood friend of his mother, who personally asked Flaubert to take her son under his wing. In the company of Flaubert and his literary friends, which included Ivan Turgenev, Alphonse Daudet, and Emile Zola, Maupassant was truly at the center of European thought, and his work bears its legacy. His first published story, "Boule de suif" (1880) was part of a collaborative effort, *Les Soirées de Médan,* which includes the work of several young French Naturalists under the influence and direction of Zola. The work proved a minor success for the young Naturalists, but Maupassant's story was so clearly superior to those of his fellow contributors that it established him immediately as a strong young talent in short fiction. He subsequently broke with the Naturalist school, turning instead to the precepts of the Realist school. These principles, forged by Flaubert, called for a scrupulous concern with form and a dedication to precision of detail and exact description. Maupassant also shared with his mentor a severe pessimism toward life, as well as a disdain for bourgeois values. Indeed, his work met with problems of censorship as early as 1880, and his poem "Au bord de l'eau," whose subject matter was, according to a fellow poet, "a very banal copulation," shocked and offended bourgeois sensibilities. Maupassant's prolific literary output has often been remarked upon, but he constantly reshaped and reworked his material, repeating scenes, descriptions, and vignettes from his journal pieces in his stories and novels.

Critical Reception

Throughout Maupassant's lifetime and into the twentieth century, scholars and writers generally have been united in their favorable assessments of his work. Flaubert, Leo Tolstoy, and Anatole France all recognized his talent. Critics did, however, have concerns with some aspects of his work. Many early critics faulted his narration, which they found unaffected by emotion. In addition, they expressed ethical concerns with what appeared to be the erotic nature of his writing, and they disliked the way in which he presented human beings as being motivated by the basest instincts. Readers, however, have consistently found Maupassant's stories fascinating, and his works have been widely translated.

The novels Maupassant wrote are generally considered less consistently successful than his short stories, which in their diversity and quality mark him as one of the finest exponents of the genre. These stories are characterized by both the clarity of their prose and the objective irony of their presentation. To the realists' ideal of scrupulous diction Maupassant added an economy of language and created a narrative style outstanding in its austere power and simplicity. Many modern critics have found rich material for study in the women characters in his tales. Noting that fewer than sixty of Maupassant's stories have minor female characters or no female characters at all, critic Mary Donaldson-Evans (1986) concentrated on the connection between the role of women in the tales and the author's clear "contempt for the concept of God." Other critics have pointed out Maupassant's generally cynical view of women. Mary L. Poteau-Tralie (1995), for example, traced Maupassant's increasingly pessimistic portrayal of mothers, in particular; whereas his early tales contain a primarily idealistic vision of motherhood—referring to the role as "a unique and privileged position"—his later tales focus on horrific versions of motherhood, involving infanticide, sexual promiscuity, and madness. According to Poteau-Tralie, this increasingly negative characterization was directly related to Maupassant's deteriorating mental and physical health and his growing pessimistic view of the world in general. Studying the relationship between prostitutes and their primarily middle-class male clientele in Maupassant's tales, critic Charles J. Stivale (1994) argued that Maupassant subverted traditional social and gender hierarchies, as the women characters typically proved more powerful than the bond "between men."

Other twentieth-century critics have covered such subjects as the structure of Maupassant's stories and the erotic nature of Maupassant's tales. Angela S. Moger (1985), studying Maupassant's use of "framed" stories—a story within another story—contended that this embedded tale is actually the primary tale and maintained that Maupassant used this form to further influence the readers' response to the stories, equating the narrator of the embedded story with the external audience. Looking at the censorship issue relative to Maupassant's tales, P. W. M. Cogman (1997) pointed out that Maupassant's writings often mock those of his fellow writers who refused to refer to explicit matters—especially sexual ones. To create tension as well as amusement, Maupassant used both inhibited narrators who were hesitant to tell the tales, as well as narratees who expressed shock at the nature of the stories.

PRINCIPAL WORKS

(With Robert Pinchon) *A la feuille de rose: Maison turque* [*Turkish Brothel*] (drama) 1877

Histoire du vieux temps [*Story of the Old Days*] (drama) 1879

*"Boule de suif" (short story) published in *Les Soirées de Médan* 1880

Des vers (poetry) 1880

La Maison Tellier [*Madame Tellier's Establishment*] (short stories) 1881

Mademoiselle Fifi (short stories) 1882

Contes de la bécasse [*Stories of the Woodcock*] (short stories) 1883

Clair de lune [*Moonlight*] (short stories) 1883

Une Vie [*A Woman's Life*] (novel) 1883

Au soleil [*African Wanderings*] (travel essays) 1884

Miss Harriett (short stories) 1884

Les Soeurs Rondoli [*The Sisters Rondoli*] (short stories) 1884

Yvette (short stories) 1884

Bel-Ami (novel) 1885

Contes du jour et de la nuit [*Day and Night Stories*] (short stories) 1885

Contes et nouvelles (short stories and novellas) 1885

Monsieur Parent (short stories) 1885

La Petite Roque (short stories) 1886

Toine (short stories) 1886

Le Horla (short stories) 1887

Mont-Oriol (novel) 1887

Pierre et Jean [*Pierre and Jean: The Two Brothers*] (novel) 1888

Le Rosier de Mme Husson (short stories) 1888

Sur l'eau [*Afloat*] (travel sketches) 1888

Fort comme la mort [*Strong as Death*] (novel) 1889

La Main gauche [*The Left Hand*] (short stories) 1889

The Odd Number; Thirteen Tales (short stories) 1889

L'Inutile beauté (short stories) 1890

New Stories by Guy de Maupassant (short stories) 1890

Notre cœur [*The Human Heart*] (novel) 1890

La Vie errante [*In Vagabondia*] (travel sketches) 1890

Musotte (drama) 1891

La Paix du ménage [*Peace at Home—at Any Price*] (drama) 1891

La Maison Tellier (Madame Tellier's Girls) L'heritage (The Inheritance) Boule de suif (Butter-ball) (short stories) 1897

Le Père Milon [*Old Milon*] (short stories) 1899

Le Colporteur [*The Peddler*] (short stories) 1900

Les Dimanches d'un bourgeois de Paris (novel) 1901

The Life and Work of Henri Rene Guy de Maupassant,

Embracing Romance, Travel, Comedy, & Verse, for the First Time Complete in English (short stories, novels, plays, poetry, travel sketches) 1903

Yvette, and Other Stories (short stories) 1904

Oeuvres complètes de Guy de Maupassant. 29 vols. (short stories) 1907-10

Mademoiselle Fifi, and Twelve Other Stories (short stories) 1917

The Collected Novels and Stories of Guy de Maupassant (novels and short stories) 1922

Miss Harriett, and Other Stories (short stories) 1923

A la feuille de rose: Maison turque (novel) 1945

The Complete Short Stories of Guy de Maupassant (short stories) 1955

Romans (novels) 1959

Oeuvres complètes. 16 vols. (complete works) 1961-62

Oeuvres complètes. 17 vols. (complete works) 1969-71

Correspondance. 3 vols. (letters) 1973

Contes et nouvelles. 2 vols. (short stories) 1974-79

Chroniques. 3 vols. (short stories) 1980

Romans (novels) 1987

Lettres d'Afrique (letters) 1990

*Many of Maupassant's stories were published in periodicals before being collected in book form.

CRITICISM

Angela S. Moger (essay date 1985)

SOURCE: "Narrative Structure in Maupassant: Frames of Desire," in *PMLA,* Vol. 100, No. 3, May, 1985, pp. 315-27.

[*In the following essay, Moger discusses Maupassant's narrative technique of using "framed" stories, where the story within the story is actually the primary tale within the frame. To accomplish this effect, according to the critic, Maupassant used a secondary narrator—often a doctor-narrator—and allowed readers to be maneuvered into a reciprocal relationship with the story such that the tales are created as much by the reader as by the storyteller.*]

Here we might refer to G. K. Chesterton's remark that a landscape without a frame means almost nothing, but that it only requires the addition of some border (a frame, a window, an arch) to be perceived as a representation. In order to perceive the world of the work of art as a sign system, it is necessary to designate its borders: it is precisely these borders which create the representation. In many languages the meaning of the word "represent" is etymologically related to the meaning of the word "limit."

Boris Uspensky, *A Poetics of Composition*

A provocative constant of Maupassant's narrative technique is the rapid introduction, within a slender containing narrative, of a narrator persona responsible for presenting the drama at the heart of the story. The "primary," or initial, narrator exists only to introduce, on the first page of each story, this "authorial" figure and, on the last page, that teller's audience. This particular narrative structure, which prevails in so many of Maupassant's most arresting tales, invites scrutiny as a special version of the story within a story. It is unique since the "contained" story is clearly the main story and is not subordinate, other than syntactically, to the containing narrative, the frame. An examination of several such "framed" stories reveals the effects of this narrative procedure and allows us to speculate on the author's motives in relying so often on this device. Maupassant's invention of the narrator persona permits him, for example, to install a persona of his audience, a "listener" who is being told the internal narrator's story. The presence, in turn, of such a figure within the story enables him to influence our reading of his story—he can set things up in such a way that our reading must be a corrective of, or reaction to, the internal reader's response to what is told. It might be useful to consider two stories where the narrator persona is a physician. The frequent selection of a doctor as the agent of narration and, therefore, as the mediator between the two worlds, those told and those told about, seems to me revealing of Maupassant's general purposes and preoccupations.[1]

In **"La rempailleuse,"** a group of aristocrats is seated around the banquet table after dinner when the conversation turns to love, "l'éternelle discussion." The debate between the women and the men centers on whether "l'amour, l'amour vrai, le grand amour" can happen more than once for each mortal. The doctor in the party is approached as the authoritative mediator: "On prit pour arbitre le docteur . . . et on le pria de donner son avis. Justement il n'en avait pas" 'They chose the doctor as arbitrator and asked him to give his opinion. In point of fact, he had none.' He is without bias in the matter; he is the scientist, the impartial observer who believes that it all depends: "C'est une affaire de tempérament." But he offers to tell the story of a passion that lasted fifty-five years and ended only because of death. The women are delighted and eager until he says, with a smile (what kind of smile? indulgent? or mockingly ironic?), that the protagonists of his story are none other than the local pharmacist and the old woman who traveled the district for so many years, repairing cane chairs: "L'enthousiasme des femmes était tombé; et leur visage dégoûté disait: 'Pouah!' comme si l'amour n'eût dû frapper que des êtres fins et distingués, seuls dignes de l'intérêt des gens comme il faut" 'The enthusiasm of the women had subsided. The look of disgust on their faces said: "Pooh!" as if love could only strike those fine and distinguished beings worthy of the in-

terest of fashionable people' (650; translation mine). The implication that true love is an emotion experienced exclusively by the upper class is important to the rest of the story.

But the doctor goes on to tell the story he heard from the old peasant on her deathbed: she had loved the pharmacist, Choquet, since she had first seen him, had made him gifts of money throughout their childhood in order to be permitted to draw close to him and to embrace him occasionally (he willingly submitted to these caresses when the payment was large enough), and had continued to pass through his village whenever possible—even after they were both grown and Choquet no longer acknowledged her—just to catch a glimpse of him from afar. The doctor then recounts his subsequent meeting with Choquet, who is indignant to learn that such a creature harbored feeling for him. Had he known while she was alive, he assures the doctor, he would have had her arrested and put into prison. But when he learns of the legacy she has charged the doctor to deliver to him, he allows himself to be "violated" by her affection and, overcoming his scruples, fairly inhales the money. The doctor describes, finally, the details of Choquet's use of her money and her cart and concludes, "Voilà le seul amour profond que j'aie recontré, dans ma vie" 'There's the only deep love I have encountered in my life.' How does his audience react to this tale charged with misery and hypocrisy? These are the closing lines of the story: "Alors la marquise, qui avait des larmes dans les yeux, soupira, 'Décidément, il n'y a que les femmes pour savoir aimer!'" 'Then the marquise, with tears in her eyes, sighed, "It is certainly only women who know how to love" ' (655).

It is important to consider what would be the effect of the doctor's story without the *encadrement*. If Maupassant had simply begun, "There was once a *rempailleuse* . . . ," or even if he had had the story introduced directly by the doctor (who would then be the single narrator), "I attended a woman on her deathbed . . . ," where the story would end with Choquet's hypocrisy, the story would be touching but banal. Maupassant accomplishes several things by telling the story "once removed" in the person of this secondary narrator. Most important, he creates several levels of awareness. By installing listeners as characters, he can show that the story is understood in varying degrees. We realize, in spite of the marquise, that the thrust of the doctor's narrative is hardly that "only women . . . know how to love." A certain irony is implicit in the very architecture of the tale, for Maupassant's audience understands more than the doctor's audience does. We even begin to wonder if there is a game of mirrors going on when the doctor says at one point in his account: "Le lendemain je me rendis chez les Choquet. Ils achevaient de déjeuner, en face l'un de l'autre, gros et rouges, fleurant les produits pharmaceutiques, importants et satisfaits" 'The next day I went over to the Choquets. They were finishing lunch, sitting opposite each other, stout and red, smelling of their pharmaceutical products, important and satisfied' (654). Is an ironical mirror being held up to the group before him, who have also just finished dining and are surely feeling "importants et satisfaits"? Then, although these aristocrats may not have the shock of recognition, we are certainly invited to make the identification when the Choquets' snobbish reaction to the idea of a vagabond peasant's passion mirrors the initial reaction of the fine ladies as the doctor embarked on his tale. Furthermore, the inclusion at the end of the story of the vapid reaction of the marquise causes us to make a judgment about her, but such a judgment simultaneously implicates us. To form an opinion of how she "reads," the reader has to have formed an idea of the correct interpretation. A reader who entered and exited with the *rempailleuse* could remain rather passive to her troubles. But it is precisely because of the existence of the rhetorical audience that the reader becomes actively involved in the story. By placing an inadequate listener inside the story, Maupassant can smirk at the marquis and the guests, establishing a complicity between himself and the reader. But once there is complicity, there is participation, and the reader has been maneuvered into a reciprocal relationship with the story: he or she cannot be just a receiver. The marquise's reaction is so utterly inappropriate to the content of the story she has been told that the reader is compelled to an aggressive rejection of her interpretation; that is, the silly response of the marquise sets a dialectical process into motion since the reader's interpretation must act as a corrective of the earlier erroneous reading. In other words, the framing of the narrative goes beyond the creation of irony; it gives the author control over how the narrative is read. We are forced to do more than take the story in. The interference in our direct reception of it engages us in a much more active effort to grasp what we are being told. Because we have to assess the ways the internal reader has misread, we must read more meticulously and self-consciously than we ordinarily do. Since, moreover, we are aware that the listener figure is *our* persona, the syntax of the story obliges us to confront the relationships between storytellers and their audiences, between what is told and what is heard, and to realize that everything we have been doing—our smirk and our corrective reading—may, finally, "reflect" on us. Implicit in this narrative structure is the suggestion that we may be players in the game of mirrors and that we are in constant danger of reacting exactly as do the marquises and the Choquets of the world. The very name assigned to the pharmacist demonstrates that principle: while we immediately respond to the delicious irony in Maupassant's clearly deliberate invention of the name "Choquet" for one whose fundamental posture is to manifest superiority by being "(s)choqué," only gradually do we realize that

our own response to his response is to be similarly "shocked," betraying the same haughty indignation that "shocked" us in the pharmacist.[2] Thus, at the very moment we as readers are shaking our heads in amused superiority at the fools inside the tale, we recognize that this judgment has the potential for ricochet.[3] The presence of the reader's persona within the story (i.e., the framing of the story) permits the author, then, to dramatize the function of the addressee and the problems of transmitting any message or vision, given that considerable control of the narratee, to use Gerald Prince's term. . . .

But there are other effects and economies made possible by the framing of the narrative. Another story may illuminate even further the reasons for Maupassant's frequent reliance on this narrative form. **"En voyage,"** or, rather, the drama at its center recounted by the doctor, is extremely melodramatic and so charged with romantic clichés as to be a caricature. Because of the architecture of the whole, however, its credibility is not seriously questioned. Again it is fruitful to ask how we would judge the story of these two romantically stereotypical creatures—one a beautiful Russian noblewoman stricken with a mortal illness (respiratory, of course) and the other a dashing outlaw—if we were to come up on the story without the ingenious prologue and epilogue affixed to the love story by the doctor's "sponsor." To start with the obvious, the reader of the story of the Countess Marie Baranow and her mysterious admirer would find it quite improbable as it stands: they love each other from afar; she has extracted, in their only meeting, a promise that he will never attempt to speak to her again. That meeting takes place in her private compartment on a train bringing her from Russia to southern France.[4] The door of the compartment is suddenly flung open in the middle of the night, and the countess finds herself confronted by a young man in evening dress, bleeding profusely from a wound in the hand. He begs her to conceal him until they have crossed the border. "Je suis un homme perdu, un homme mort, si vous ne m'aidez à passer la frontière. . . . Si vous ne me secourez point, je suis perdu. Et cependant, Madame, je n'ai ni tué, ni volé, ni rien fait de contraire à l'honneur. Cela je vous le jure. Je ne puis vous en dire davantage" 'I am a lost man, a dead man, if you do not help me cross the border. . . . If you don't help me I am lost. And yet I have neither killed anyone, nor robbed, nor done anything contrary to honor. This I swear to you. I cannot tell you more' (639).

The countess does indeed help him cross the border, passing him off as her servant, and they part—never, indeed, to speak again. Over the next several years, she dies slowly; he stands under her window in the street, hoping to catch a glimpse of her, and follows her when she occasionally goes out. Finally, he takes to visiting the doctor to have news of her condition.

On the day she dies, the doctor grants him an audience with the corpse, whose hand he kisses violently before he disappears forever.

Who was this man? Why was he wounded and why was it a matter of life and death to get out of Russia? What was the state of Marie Baranow's marriage? Why did her husband send her away to die? What were her feelings for the singular man whom she liked to see beneath her window but whom she would not allow to speak to her in spite of their mutual desolation?[5] Without the formal cadre affixed to the story, which gives it at least the superficial appearance of fullness and completion, one would need more details and explanations to accept that things could have happened this way; and one would simply want more information about the principals. The author has been relieved of any obligation to develop character gradually and fully or to provide the detailed context of the lives of his protagonists. Because we meet the countess as a figure in another character's story, we accept the selection and compression of the portrait. We accept that the doctor's aim is to impart a certain story and not to describe in detail a certain woman. We would expect something different if our narrator had introduced her. The trompe l'oeil has worked, for in fact he has! By wielding his narrative device to alter our expectations, the author induces our credulity with regard to characterization, the passage of time, the outcome of events. We forget to be suspicious of the partial information or the caricatures because what we read is not the "main story"; it is only a sort of digression or intermission. It acts on us, nonetheless, with all the power of a main story.[6] There is a double standard here—the framed narrative has only limited accountability and the privilege of totally exploiting the resources of (unframed) narrative.

In point of fact, however, the paucity of information promotes an understanding that the dual level of narration is itself more central as a subject matter than the characters presumably under scrutiny. In the absence of any detailed explanation concerning them, our consciousness as readers shifts to the potential significance of having a character tell the story; indeed, this delegation of the telling to a secondary narrator may afford us a first insight into the real focus of the story. That is, we experience the refraction as gratuitous; we are vaguely aware that the narrator persona might more naturally have been the conventional invisible narrator, encountered only in his voice in the first line of the story. The awareness is distracting, and the distraction is then enhanced by the curious attitude of this arbitrary figure toward what he recounts.

At the end of **"En voyage,"** as at the conclusion of **"La rempailleuse,"** there is an equivocal comment on the whole by the internal narrator himself, followed again by a reaction from a female listener who is ex-

tremely moved. And there is the same short circuit in communication between the teller and the listener that obtained in the other story. The narrator persona, in contributing this story, has merely been observing the established theme set out in the beginning of the whole tale: passionate crimes and adventures befalling travelers in the course of their journeys. Thus the doctor observes only, "Voilà, certes, la plus singulière aventure de chemin de fer que je connaisse. Il faut dire aussi que les hommes sont des drôles de toqués" 'There you have, certainly, the strangest railroad adventure I know of. It must also be said that men are queer lunatics' (643). His detachment seems rather exaggerated, considering the tragic death and separation he has recounted. Is he teasing his listeners or is he genuinely unmoved by the situation he has described and presumably witnessed? Similarly, when the doctor-narrator in **"La rempailleuse"** says, "Voilà le seul amour profond que j'aie rencontré, dans ma vie," the reader is uncertain whether this is a sincere, carefully deliberated opinion or a bitterly ironic barb directed at all those around him who would think they alone had experienced "l'amour profond." As we have seen, the marquise ignores his comment and makes of the story what she chooses. Although it is less clear what the woman at the end of **"En voyage"** has concluded, the description of her reaction is similarly calculated to draw the reader into speculation and involvement: "Une femme murmura à mi-voix: 'Ces deux êtres-là ont été moins fous que vous ne croyez. . . . Ils étaient . . . ils étaient. . . . ' Mais elle ne pouvait plus parler, tant elle pleurait. Comme on changea de conversation pour la calmer, on ne sut pas ce qu'elle voulait dire" 'A woman murmured softly: "Those two people were less crazy than you think. . . . They were . . . they were. . . . " But she was crying so hard that she could no longer speak. As the subject was changed to calm her, no one ever knew what she meant' (643). By now the reader's attention has turned from the lovers and their plight to wondering what, indeed, "elle voulait dire" and what would have been the end of her sentence, had she voiced it.[7] More important, why is the story orchestrated so as to end with this ambiguity? Does the author just want to break the spell harshly, to bring us back to reality with a jolt, or does he want the reader to reflect, rather, on the relationship between the listener and the story? By leaving us to finish her sentence, he draws us into identifying with the listener. We cannot remain in the passive role of mere audience to his story—we are compelled to review the story in order to guess what she was on the verge of saying.[8] We do not know what the relation between the containing narrative and the one contained is supposed to be.

When, on rereading the story, we perceive that the structure of the relationship between the two lovers is analogous to the structure of the story, we begin to sense that the relationship between the two stories, not a specific aspect of plot, is meant to be the focus of our attention. A particular passage of **"En voyage"** is worth scrutinizing for its metaphoric value; the doctor is describing the distance that the two lovers reverently preserved:

> Alors, j'assistai à une chose surprenante et douloureuse, à l'amour muet de ces deux êtres qui ne se connaissaient point.

> Il l'aimait, lui, avec le dévouement d'une bête sauvée, reconnaissante et dévouée à la mort. Il venait chaque jour me dire: "Comment va-t-elle?" comprenant que je l'avais deviné. Et il pleurait affreusement quand il l'avait vue passer plus faible et plus pâle chaque jour.

> Elle me disait:

> "Je ne lui ai parlé qu'une fois à ce singulier homme, et il me semble que je le connais depuis vingt ans."

> Et quand ils se recontraient, elle lui rendait son salut avec un sourire grave et charmant. Je la sentais heureuse, elle si abandonnée et qui se savait perdue, je la sentais heureuse d'être aimée ainsi, avec ce respect et cette constance, avec cette poésie exagérée, avec ce dévouement prêt à tout. Et pourtant, fidèle à son obstination d'exaltée, elle refusait désespérément de le recevoir, de connaître son nom, de lui parler. Elle disait: "Non, non, cela me gâterait cette étrange amitié. Il faut que nous demeurions étrangers l'un à l'autre."

> Quant à lui, il était certes également une sorte de Don Quichotte, car il ne fit rien pour se rapprocher d'elle. Il voulair tenir jusqu'au bout l'absurde promesse de ne lui jamais parler qu'il avait faite dans le wagon.

Then I witnessed a sad and surprising thing, the mute love of these two beings who were not acquainted with each other.

He loved her with the devotion of a rescued animal, grateful and devoted to the death. He came every day to ask me, "How is she?" understanding that I had guessed his feelings. And he wept frightfully when he had seen her going by, weaker and paler every day.

She said to me:

"I have only spoken once to that singular man, and yet it seems as if I have known him for twenty years."

And when they met she returned his bow with a serious and charming smile. I felt that she was happy, that although she was given up and knew herself lost she was happy to be loved in this manner, with this respect and constancy, with this exaggerated poetry, with this devotion, ready for anything.

Nevertheless, faithful to her fanatical obstinacy, she absolutely refused to receive him, to learn his name, to speak to him. She said: "No, no, that would spoil this strange friendship for me. We must remain strangers to each other."

As for him, he was certainly a kind of Don Quixote too, for he did nothing to get closer to her. He wanted to keep to the end the absurd promise never to speak to her that he had made in the car. (642)

The particular aspects of the "love affair" that the doctor underlines in his summary of the relationship bear examination.

This love—as the doctor says in the first paragraph above—is "l'amour muet" between persons "qui ne se connaissaient point." They are separated as if by an invisible barrier, but they are also together. In the second and third paragraphs, each lover speaks of the other to the doctor, who plays the classic role of confidant in this drama. In the following paragraph the doctor assures his audience that the countess enjoyed being loved in this fashion, "avec cette poésie exagérée," and did not want any direct contact with the man who loved her so desperately: "'Non, non, cela me gâterait cette étrange amitié. Il faut que nous demeurions étrangers l'un à l'autre.'" "Gâter" and "il faut" amount to strong language; indeed, the expression of the thought is so emphatic that it arrests our attention on the principle being articulated. What is that principle? Distance—removal from the desired object—is proposed as a value. And the particular form of distance that is most important is silence. The countess is willing to look at her lover and even to smile at him in the street, but she will have nothing of him that words might convey. The text insists on this verbal distance from the outset. In the space of three pages there are so many explicit references to the absence of verbal communication between the lovers that the absence becomes a presence, an object of scrutiny to the readerly consciousness.[9] In their first meeting, we are not surprised, given the circumstances, that "Elle ne répondit rien" or that, a few sentences later, "Elle ne disait toujours rien" (639). Nor are we particularly distracted, on the same page, by the outlaw's returning her purse to her "sans ajouter un mot" 'without adding a word' (639) and by her remaining "immobile et muette" (640) in the face of apparent danger. But, something else begins to happen, although we may not perceive it consciously at that precise juncture; the silence begins to be loud when, on the next page, we find the somewhat redundant cluster of the following scene: "'Je ne mets qu'une condition à ce que je fais: c'est que vous ne me parlerez jamais, que vous ne me direz pas un mot, ni pour me remercier, ni pour quoi que ce soit.' 'L'inconnu s'inclina sans prononcer une parole'" "'I make only one condition to what I am doing: that is that you never speak to me, that you shall not say a word to me, either to thank me or for anything whatsoever." The stranger bowed without uttering a word' (640). A few sentences later, there is the (superfluous?) additional detail: "Pendant toute la nuit ils restèrent en tête-à-tête, muets tous deux" 'During the night they sat opposite each other, both mute' (641).

Part 2 of the story opens, moreover, with the sentence "Le docteur se tut une seconde, puis reprit" 'The doctor fell silent for a second, then began again' (641). Finally, when the countess confides to the doctor that this man whom she does not know follows her everywhere—"Je le rencontre chaque fois que je sors; il me regarde d'une étrange façon, mais il ne m'a jamais parlé" 'I meet him every time I go out. He looks at me in a strange way, but he has never spoken to me' (641)—the reader realizes what trouble she and the story have taken to make that statement possible. It has become clear that the absence of speech to which the countess refers is a positive value before the reader ever reaches Marie Baranow's ultimate revelation: "Non, non, cela me gâterait cette étrange amitié. Il faut que nous demeurions étrangers l'un à l'autre." The verbal removal preserves an apparently precious distance. The love duet has an intermediary, and we sense that this refraction somehow makes the duet more satisfying.

Should we regard this curious love affair as a kind of cryptogram, decipherable for an understanding of the story we are reading? **"En voyage"** presents the frame and the framed, a pair, joined together but also separated "as if by an invisible barrier." The two interact only because of a third party, the reader, who receives the statements of both and performs an interpretive act of combination, conferring meaningful integration on the disparate elements. Furthermore, the very gratuitousness of the structure of the story suggests that something important is invested in the distance created by the frame. What would be "spoiled" by direct contact with the main story? What is preserved by the story's inaccessibility?

Like **"La rempailleuse,"** **"En voyage"** contains another story, a self-sufficient unit that, in its proportions, dominates the story in which it has been inserted. Since the tale imparted by the doctor could easily be made complete in itself, why has the author not given it to us directly? Why is the reader forced to perceive it only at some distance, through the refractions of another tale? What has been accomplished by using the travelers-telling-each-other-stories topos to motivate the story of the countess and her admirer? Maupassant apparently saw some advantage in casting their situation as a tableau mounted in a frame and therefore not immediately available to the beholder. (For the purposes of my argument, I provisionally invoke the spatial model.)[10] Indeed the onlooker is conditioned to a particular interpretation by the angle of vision he or she is forced to adopt. The words of the countess come back: "cela me gâterait. . . . " She obviously wants this relationship to remain unrealized, to preserve the inaccessible, untouchable quality of the ideal. She wants none of the dynamism of process here—they are not going "to love"—she wants, instead, the stasis of the object: there is to be the substance, "their love," an entity, not an activity. Their love is essentially a story she tells: it seems to come into being as a result of the presence of the audience, the doctor. Where the Countess Baranow is concerned, the fixity inherent in definition as story not only gives permanency to their love: narrative removal permits the preservation of the ideal. In the story of their love, nothing has been metamorphosed into something (for nothing indeed has ever transpired between them after their first, brief meeting); the love is frozen at the moment of virtuality, which preserves it uncompromised and ensures its immortality. It seems that desire thrives on distance; the object of desire does not suffer the degradation provoked by familiarity, since its mundanity and its flaws are not perceptible from afar. Marie Baranow's love, then, is given permanency at the cost of dynamism; it is converted into a fictional object of art to ensure its duration and "integrity." To be constituted as story, however, it must have an addressee who, in receiving its details, confirms and perpetuates it as a love story. And this is the doctor. The way he characterizes the relationship between Marie Baranow and her admirer suggests the relationship's impulse to story status. When the doctor says things like "Je la sentais heureuse d'être aimée ainsi, . . . avec cette poésie exagérée" and "il était certes également une sorte de Don Quichotte," his self-consciously literary diction invites us to make an analogy between their love and our story. If it seems that the story of a love is more satisfying than the love itself, we can infer that the story of a particular story might have some advantages not enjoyed by the original, unframed narrative.

We cannot know much more of the story we are eager to possess than the young man can know of the woman whom he yearns to possess. As we have seen, there are many details missing—we would like to have had direct contact with the doctor instead of receiving his remarks through the narrator. But the story would seem less exciting, less irritating, and, therefore, less desirable if it were not mounted, like a jewel, in its setting. The *enchâssement* of the lovers' story has, perhaps, enhanced their sparkle for us, creating a kind of halo of otherworldliness about them, projecting them as platonized lovers, as archetypes, rather than as flesh-and-blood creatures with limitations. (We might have learned from interrogating the doctor that she coughed and spat constantly and that her lover had fled Russia in fear of a jealous husband's threats.)

We contemplate the story of the lovers from a point of removal that guarantees their perfection but, more important, allows blanks in their story, for (the reader's) pleasure proceeds from what is suppressed rather than from what is given.[11] Let us explore in what sense this is true. The frame story lends the symmetry and weight that, through a kind of trompe l'oeil, make the central story seem properly proportioned, formally complete. In fact, a story about Marie Baranow and the outlaw, told head-on (third-person narration), would demand greater detail and a more rounded treatment than we expect in a vignette of the sort tossed out by the doctor to his fellow travelers. But there is something quite provocative in the very partiality of their story; it is sustained at the delicious moment of incipience, when all pleasure lies ahead and much is yet to be known. There is intense excitement as a storyteller begins a tale, giving a few inviting details about whom and what will be described; and there is keen disappointment as we realize from the musical overvoice or from the paucity of pages beneath our thumbs that a compelling movie or novel is coming to a close. If we can know the whole story, eliminate all the mysteries present at the outset, we replace a presence with an absence; gratification of a desire, after all, cancels the desire. There is, finally, something more satisfying than satisfaction. Desire is made up of two conflicting impulses: the longing to overcome the distance between oneself and the object of desire, to "coincide," so to speak, with that object, and the impossibility of closing that gap if desire is to survive. In order to preserve her love the countess takes care to remain on its threshold. The story embedded in **"En voyage"** is in a similar state of virtuality—a condition, indeed, made possible by its being a story within a story. The presence of the frame legitimizes the internal narrative; it is that outer casing which makes the encased material appear to conform to the aesthetic and logical demands of the mechanism known as story. Thus the principal narrative can remain in the sketchy state that most stimulates a reader's fantasies, its desirability perpetuated by its inaccessibility. We have the illusion of possession without the deprivation engendered by possession. We enjoy simultaneous satisfaction of our desire for closure and for ever-renewed mystery.[12]

As we see in **"En voyage,"** a framed story can simulate a purposeful progression while actually remaining permanently in a provocative phase of anticipation and speculation. One wonders, indeed, if the unfinished sentence of the lady at the end of **"En voyage"** is to be read as an emblem of the principle incarnate in the story: the promise of something is more beautiful than the fulfillment, the suggestion more seductive than the definition. Her comment certainly draws us in all over again, sending us right back to dream anew over the story she has just heard.

In other words, the framed story can "have the cake and eat it"—and in more ways than one. For the frame both gives immediate structural support to the internal

narrative and allows the author preemptively to undercut that story. He not only gets to tell a rankly sentimental tale, he blocks our opportunity to find it so by making fun of it himself. In the frame his narrator figure deflates its pathos, and the listener figure is often mocked for having taken it seriously or misunderstood it. The author, then, can present these two mutually exclusive points of view because the reader is propelled into acting as mediator. Just as the countess, by using the doctor as intermediary, can have her love and yet not have to have it, the author can have it both ways because a link, a dialogue, is created between the members of this narrative pair by the reader, whose very act of reading holds the two together.

What has been said, however, would not account for one particular problem: the doctor-narrator is consistently undermined by the syntax of the narrative, if only by a few words of rejection (or simply by rejection of the narrator's own reaction to the story he tells, as in **"En voyage"**) or by misinterpretation of his story.[13] This recurrent pattern explicitly dramatizes the essential dilemma of the storyteller: he has no control over what is heard. Although he creates the message, he cannot control how it is read. The friction between the narrator and his audience establishes as a basic proposition that stories are not understood; they are transformed by their addressees, who respond to different texts from the ones that were dispatched. If Maupassant does indeed subscribe to this equivocal view of the efficacity of storytelling, a message his stories might work at transmitting, in their very articulation, is that stories do not signify of themselves and are "created" as much by their audience as by their originator.[14] But the reader senses more in this unwillingness to suppress the other point of view (whether "romantic" reading or simply uncomprehending rejection), this dramatization of the story's failure to transmit any message other than that failure. At the level of the text is the implicit suggestion that stories may not be understood, because someone will insist on approaching them from the standpoint of a truth-lie polarity when it is the fact of electing that polarity as an approach to fiction that is an issue under discussion. Thus, when the narratees in these stories evaluate what they have heard in terms of whether it corresponds to their experience—is it true or false of life?—the larger narrative problematizes that criterion. When the marquise finds that, ah yes, "only women . . . know how to love" and when the listener in **"En voyage"** assesses the reasonableness of the lovers' attitudes and ignores all other aspects of what she has been told (who is doing the telling? to what end? with what kind of connection to the "travel adventures" theme?), the text undermines the "content" their readings infer, shifting emphasis instead to the questioning of all such referentially oriented interpretations.[15] The compulsive cancellation of a story's intentions, in the reactions of its audience, may point to an underlying conviction that stories read as imitations of life are always lies, deserving of the rejection inherent in lack of comprehension. If, then, as we have said, the story is presented as a solid, circumscribed artifact surrounded by a frame, perhaps that frame is to be read as a parenthesis indicating that what is contained is unreal. Thus the frame would italicize the framed, implying that the story's mimetic status is a self-deception on the part of the reader, whose earnest attitude is implicitly derided. By the same token, then, the frame may be a means of discussing the limitations of stories—perhaps they are not meant to exalt any more than to reproduce reality—as much as the erroneous expectations of addressees. Consequently, the mechanization of life (analogous to the automatism of jokes), conveyed by the rhythm and caricaturing inherent in the framed structure, may exist as an equivocation concerning the true function of the enterprise rather than simply as the manifestation of a particular worldview.[16]

Furthermore, the professional identity of the narrator warrants consideration if we are to understand some other implications of these stories. Why does the author so frequently—in these and many other tales—assign the narrator role to a physician? It seems he does so not only because doctors are ubiquitous and powerful figures in the moments of highest drama in human life, becoming repositories of everyone's significant "stories," but also because their involvement differs from the involvement of others. They deal unemotionally with things that are greatly charged for the layperson. Maupassant creates a world devoid of governing principle; because he does not subscribe to any particular code, his logical choice of narrator is someone who accepts everything and does not make moral judgments (moral judgment is here replaced, in fact, by the doctor's apparent detachment). As a reporter of events, the physician can be assumed to have no moral or political or social bias and, moreover, as a scientist can be relied on for accuracy and careful observation. The doctor is called on as "arbitre" (to use Maupassant's own term) in matters hotly contested and is considered all-knowing about human events. Consequently, the deployment of the doctor-narrator enhances the credibility of the narrative and at least initially gains the confidence of the reader. If readers have begun to question the authority and reliability of writers of fiction, the refraction effected by the framing of the story permits the author to suggest to the mind's eye that the narrative is not the creation of a litterateur but the firsthand report of a scientist.

That is our initial experience of the doctor-narrator. But Maupassant has not really left matters there. We have a delayed reaction, as well, and find that the text propels us into a more problematic sense of the doctor. The fabled detachment appears to have further ramifications. At second glance, we appreciate that the choice of the physician as narrator permits Maupassant to

suggest not only "scientific" objectivity but also the price paid for that objectivity. The doctor's neutrality and prestige may induce our credulity on a certain level, but they do not prevent our being startled by that very detachment in his reactions and attitudes. Can we ultimately lend credence to the appraisal of someone so remote, so indifferent to chicanery and suffering?

In *Sur l'eau* Maupassant speaks of "cette seconde vue qui est en même temps la force et toute la misère des écrivains" 'that second sight which is at once the gift and the curse of writers' (*Œuvres* 80), describing the condition of the writer in the following terms:

> il vit condamné à être toujours, en toute occasion, . . . un reflet des autres, condamné à se regarder sentir, agir, penser, aimer, souffrir et à ne jamais souffrir, penser, aimer, sentir comme tout le monde, bonnement, franchement, simplement, sans s'analyser soi-même après chaque joie et chaque sanglot.

> he lives condemned to be always, on every occasion, . . . a reflection of others, condemned to watch himself feel, act, think, love, suffer and never to suffer, think, love, feel as everyone else does, plainly, frankly, simply, without analyzing himself after each joy and each sob. (82)

These remarks imply that only distance gives perspective and that vision is a kind of voyeurism indicative of estrangement from others and from the self. And when the author here suggests that if artists do indeed see well, it is because they do not live as others do, his comment provokes an analogy to the "unwholesome" condition of the physician as we encounter him in Maupassant's stories. That is, since the doctor, as dispenser of the narrative, is unquestionably a persona of the author and since his essence seems to be his cool removal from the passions he observes, it is interesting to reflect on his function in the light of Maupassant's description of the writer. Perhaps the doctor-narrator is itself a metaphor for nonintegration in the life process.[17]

The doctor, it seems, "knows," "understands" in just such measure as he has become separate, distant, alienated. Thus the recurring motif of the doctor as agent of narration operates on two levels simultaneously; it is both a trick played and the exposure of the trick, the calling of the question, through that author persona, of what fiction is and at what cost it is created. The doctor-narrator functions to make an equivocal statement about the story and the optic that produces it, and these matters finally displace, as the focus of the story, the little melodramas reported by the doctor.

Indeed, the tendency to frame stories betrays an awareness of a shift in what stories may validly take as their subject. That is, they must address the "predicament" of stories, a subject matter dramatized in the tension between teller and listener. The special structure of these narratives is emblematic of this new consciousness in the author. Putting himself at a distance from his own material (the narrator persona tells the story), raising questions about the function and meaning of that material (the theme of the story is the telling of a story—a story, moreover, that doesn't "work"), leaving those questions dangling (the reader is exposed to divergent points of view)—all these gestures indicate the neutralization of traditional content. The alienation implicit in the material is virtually organic. The French expression for a parenthetical unit that bisects a sentence, *une incision,* suggests, with its nuance of a threat to the organic integrity of the whole, the syntax particular to the framed tale. (Here is another reason for the choice of physician as narrator; the doctor is one who operates in the presence of pathology. Moreover, while an incision violates the body, it also ultimately restores it.) The narrative form, then, signifies the basic cleft in the artistic imagination whereby the author both performs the conventional telling and judges it, trying to reconcile conflicting impulses (through irony, if that is the only mode of reconciliation). It permits the author to express structurally the dilemma of the creative mind caught between the desire for the fully formed artifact, an entity that betokens certitude, and the awareness of the prevarication inherent in any such creation. Each story "means" to inquire into the way stories are made, "means" to confront the dubious relationship between certitude and wisdom.

The framing of a tale permits Maupassant to elucidate rhetorically the properties and potential effects of stories. At the same time, it affords the reader a dynamic function in the making of the story, a story kept interesting and vital because inaccessible to direct contact. But the framing device has further implications. In creating the reader who misreads in these stories, the narratee, Maupassant sets up a particularly disorienting paradox. Although the author himself shows that stories involve subterfuge, failed communication, and closure, he demonstrates those points by means of a frame that, revealing all this to the reader, simultaneously reopens the artificially closed narrative. A dynamism is thus reintroduced into the stasis that is a (contained) story. Therefore, in one sense the containing narrative cancels out the contained one, since this tendency to unravel what had been so neatly woven exposes the artifices and illusions that constitute a story for the teller and the listener. But it goes beyond disclosure.

This gesture of rhetorically uncovering the sleight of hand and the power dynamics intrinsic to stories creates the potential for the rectification of any such flaws. Given the importance, to the "successful" story, of blanks and unanswered questions, it should be clear that any dynamism in a given story results from an element of virtuality in the story's composition. At the same moment that Maupassant's frame points up (by implied contrast) the static reification of one contained narrative and supports the precarious but more vital partiality of another, it corrects both problems by compelling readers, almost in spite of themselves, to perform an integrative operation that releases meaning. The detraction implicit in the "undoing" performed by the frame automatically allows the frame to be read as a complement to the framed material instead of as a parenthesis or set of quotation marks stressing the unreality of the material set off. The frame and the framed can be integrated along a paradigmatic axis such that the dynamism results from the combinatory effort required of the reader and not from the mere "unsealing" of the tale by the frame of the stories we have considered. Thus meaning is not encoded into specific components of the story, awaiting discovery, but is created as a by-product of a process the reader undergoes in the very attempt to make sense of the seemingly arbitrary juxtaposition of frame and framed. Meaning is a do-it-yourself project that incidentally and paradoxically removes the story from any condition of stasis.[18]

We see, finally, that the cleft that the reader encounters in the syntax of the narratives—containing story and contained—and the compulsion to build in a dual perspective on the contained narrative—doctor and listener—may be the "reflection" of the conflict between the exigencies of truth and the exigencies of stories. That is, the creation may present itself as two unintegrated pieces because that form best expresses the conflicting desires we feel on writing and reading stories. Consequently, the self-analysis and dismemberment thematically and structurally manifest in these stories may constitute an awareness that the stories' only power lies in the preemptive assertion of impotence. The stories' exposition of their failure is, indeed, their success, given the author's ultimate preoccupations.

Maupassant's stories, in being framed, unravel themselves and, giving up their rights, sacrifice themselves to something that surpasses certitude and closure. The story is there but, mounted in the frame, raises questions about itself that carry it beyond mere answers to knowledge, if knowledge of ignorance.[19] A story that takes a frame can mythologize: it can use the failure it articulates to intimate things larger than life, greater than its own capacities. In removing to the plane of relation rather than of representation, in focusing on a dynamism that reflects on, and thereby transcends, mimesis, the framed narrative transmits a knowledge it does not master; it enacts the movement, not the fulfillment, of desire and hence affords us that fragile but lasting pleasure which is, perhaps, the essence of the literary.

Notes

[1] For a related analysis of a third framed story, "Une ruse," see my "That Obscure Object of Narrative." Quotations of Maupassant's stories in the present essay are from *Contes et nouvelles*.

[2] In an interesting discussion of another Maupassant story, Gerald Prince insists on the importance of nomination as a form of signification: "Mais l'économie nominative des textes littéraires est souvent, sinon toujours, un éminent directeur de lecture et, dans ce texte qui nous sollicite, la précision et l'insistance en sont telles que j'ai du mal à la croire fortuite" 'But the economy of naming is often, if not always, an eminent guide in reading; and, in the text that engages us here, the precision and the insistence of it are such that I have difficulty believing it accidental' ("Nom et destin" 268).

[3] There is, moreover, a complex snare implicit in our judgment: what is inappropriate about the reaction of the marquise is the narcissism of her concluding that the story shows the superiority of women. But when we make the decision that *she* is a misreader, we feel superior in the same way and thus repeat her narcissistic delusion.

[4] According to Jean Pierrot, there is a great deal of moving about in public conveyances throughout Maupassant's work, and these "displacements" are significant. One comment seems particularly pertinent to the story at hand:

> Mais surtout, le mouvement, le déplacement paraissent entretenir, dans cette oeuvre, des rapports particulièrement étroits avec la femme et avec la sexualité. Et d'abord parce que, sortant l'individu de son environnement habituel, ils offrent l'occasion par excellence de la rencontre amoureuse. On ne cesserait pas d'énumérer les textes de Maupassant dans lesquels une intrigue amoureuse se noue, ou s'esquisse, à la faveur d'un voyage ou d'un déplacement.

> But especially, moving about, traveling appear to be intimately related in this work to woman and sexuality. And first off because, removing the individual from his or her usual environment, they furnish the perfect opportunity for the amorous encounter. It would be difficult to enumerate all the texts of Maupassant in which an amorous intrigue is launched or developed by means of a trip or some other geographical displacement. (186)

[5] We are reminded of Tolstoy's assertion: "The thing that most tormented Maupassant, to which he returns many times, is the painful state of loneliness, spiritual loneliness, of man; of that bar which stands between man and his fellows; a bar which, as he says, is the more painfully felt, the nearer the bodily connection" (28).

[6] The framed story is then different from other story-within-a-story constructs (i.e., interpolated tales)—the very dimensions of the frame relative to the "framed" make clear that the latter is the principal story and the former a kind of commentary about the contained story's immediate and fundamental essence. Thus, Todorov comments: "L'importance de l'enchâssement se trouve indiquée par les dimensions des histoires enchâssées. Peut-on parler de digressions lorsque celles-ci sont plus longues que l'histoire dont elles s'écartent?" 'The importance of framing is indicated by the very dimensions of the stories bracketed in this manner. Can one call them digressions when they are longer than the story from which they digress?' (84).

[7] Maupassant's stories frequently end in this deflated manner; they simply stop instead of reaching a true climax. Chklovski's comment on this kind of narrative ending is provocative:

> Nous classerons à part les nouvelles à fin négative. Tout d'abord j'explique mon terme. Dans les mots "stola," "stolu," les sons "a," "u" sont des terminaisons, des désinences, la racine "stol" est le radical. Au nominatif singulier, nous trouvons le mot "stol" sans désinence, mais nous percevons cette absence de désinence en comparaison avec les autres formes fléchies, et elle est l'indice d'un cas. Nous pouvons l'appeler forme négative . . . désinence zéro. . . . Ces formes négatives sont assez fréquentes dans la nouvelle et surtout dans celle de Maupassant.

> We will put in a separate category stories with negative endings. First of all, I will explain my terminology. In the words *stola, stolu,* the sounds *a, u* are endings; the radical *stol* is the root. In the nominative singular, we find the word *stol* without an ending, but we note this absence of ending by comparison with the other inflected forms, and that absence itself indicates a particular case. We could call it the negative form, or the zero ending. . . . These negative forms occur quite frequently in the short story and especially in that of Maupassant. (177)

[8] Furthermore, this "lapse" in the text explicitly dramatizes the extent to which all readers "write" the story they read: "Le véritable auteur du récit n'est pas seulement celui qui le raconte, mais aussi, et parfois bien davantage, celui qui l'écoute" 'The real author of the tale is not only the one who tells it but also, and sometimes to an even greater extent, the one who listens to it' (Genette 267).

[9] I count nine such notations without including those that figure in the passage cited above ("l'amour muet," "elle refusait . . . de lui parler," "l'absurde promesse de ne lui jamais parler").

[10] In my extended study of framed narrative, I contend that the more deliberate our examination of the frame, the more absolute the disintegration of the spatial model. Just as the frame neutralizes an opposition between beginning and end, so also does it demonstrate the irrelevance of any distinction between inside and outside, focal object and surrounding margin. Since these particular stories are explicitly involved in a thematics of distance, however, I find the analogy useful and pertinent for this discussion, even if it does not account for Maupassant's ultimate effects.

[11] Wolfgang Iser is prominent among theorists who see structure as the element that controls interaction between reader and text. He has proposed that it is the abrupt juxtaposition of segments (the frame and the framed?) that engenders a "blank" in a text. Iser insists that these "blanks" provoke the readers' constitutive activity. The reader sets about filling in the blanks, and that activity, says Iser, brings about a referential field. Parts of Goffman's argument are also of interest on this subject.

[12] That is, the reader experiences a sense of closure without experiencing the letdown attendant to closure. Barbara Herrnstein Smith's discussion of a sonnet by Sidney elucidates the "duplicitous" potential of the framed work:

> In the last three lines, our attention is explicitly directed toward the very qualities of the process which would otherwise have made closure a problem: that is, its disorder and inconclusiveness. The problem has been solved, however, by the creation of two fairly distinct orders or levels of representation: first, the representation of interior speech, and second, framing it, the more traditional order of lyrical mimesis, the representation of direct non-literary speech. Most significant is the fact that, by making a rational and stable comment from "outside," the framing lines allow Astrophel's problems to retain the psychological realism of irresolution while leaving the reader with a sense of closure. (149-50)

[13] That is, the same story could be told—the disagreeing internal audience could even be present—without its being in this particular sequence. The return to the installed listener after the narrator persona's tale constitutes the *mise en question* of that story. If the "authorial" figure had the last word, his story would be read differently. It is, indeed, narrative syntax that suggests that the contained story is being discredited.

[14] The framing of the story would be not only a way out (the problem itself could be constituted as the "subject" of the story) but the only way of demonstrating that truth (the installed listener who "receives" something other than what was relayed by the teller). The failure to make connection is, in some sense, what the story is about.

[15] The story is "about" something different from what it might appear to be on the initial, constative level: says Greimas in his book on Maupassant, " . . . comment combler, plus précisément, le fossé entre ce que le texte paraît être dans son déroulement discursif et ce qu'il est du fait de son organisation sémiotique, à la fois narrative et sémantique. . . . Le paraître du discours renvoie, par mille allusions, à un *être* du texte sémiotique qui s'insinue comme son référent interne" 'More specifically, how shall we close the gap between what the text appears to be in its discursive unfolding and what it is from the point of view of its semiotic organization, both narrative and semantic. . . . The appearance of the text refers, through countless allusions, to a semiotic reality of the text that insinuates itself as the text's internal referent' (266-67). The distinction Greimas makes may be further illuminated by Crouzet's discussion of the rhetorical aspects of Maupassant's work:

> A coup sûr l'idée de "réalisme," plus que celle de sublime peut-être, est un déni rigoureux de toute rhétorique. . . . [L]a revendication de la "vérite," ou la perpétuelle tentative d'analogie de la littérature avec la science ou l'information, tend à substituer le constat à la construction, ou *la natura naturata* à *la natura naturans,* à opposer la passivité devant la chose à l'activité de l'esprit pour qui *la nature* ne peut être imitée qu'à condition d'être trouvée et inventée: tout ce qui est naturel n'est pas dans *la nature.* Ou bien, si l'on reprend une distinction de R. Barthes, l'on devra dire que le "discours réaliste" veut se placer tout entier du côté du "parce que," ou du mobile réel, et récuse le "pour que," ou l'exigence du discours lui-même, alors que toute écriture conserve cette duplicité, maintient ce tourniquet des deux instances, qui indissociables et inséparables ne pourraient rompre leur unité sans ruiner la rhétorique.

> The idea of "realism," more even than that of the sublime perhaps, definitely implies a rigorous denial of all rhetoric. . . . [T]he claim of "truth," or the constant attempt to draw an analogy between literature, on the one hand, and science or information, on the other, tends to substitute the content for the manner of presentation or *la natura naturata* for *la natura naturans,* tends to oppose passivity before the phenomenon to the activity of mind for which *nature* can be imitated only if it is discovered and invented: not everything that is natural is in *nature.* Or, if you will, if one were to adopt the distinction of Roland Barthes, one should say that the "discourse of realism" places itself entirely on the side of the "why," or the real intention, and impugns the "in order to," or the demands of discourse itself, whereas all writing preserves this duplicity, maintains a turnstile between these two indissociable and inseparable instances whose unity could not be disrupted without destroying rhetoric. (233)

[16] Thus, the choice of a narrative form that depicts persons devoid of will or interiority may be a way of

saying that a writer deforms and disfigures in order to accommodate the demands of his or her craft. The author's estimation of the enterprise and his or her worldview are, of course, related, as this critical lament makes quite evident:

> Maupassant's short story is the perfected expression of an age which has lost itself amid things. The story itself has the form of a thing. It is limited and confined like a thing. It has the self-containedness, the hardness and superficiality of a thing. Maupassant is the mightiest portrayer of his period. His stories exactly reflect the bourgeois materialistic epoch's conception of the universe and of man. The features that distinguish his short stories are the features of this particular state of civilization. Here the story's shortness discloses its meaning: it is the symptom of a world in a state of disintegration. Everything is a fragment, like the short story. There is no longer any great relating principle, there is no relation between the soul and the universe, between inner and outer, the surface and the depths, no relation between man and man. It is a world without love, a world without God, a world without meaning. Blind fate rules supreme; men are shackled, utterly helpless, to the iron law that dominates things.

(Spoerri 10)

What Spoerri misses, if I draw my conclusions from his tone, is that Maupassant's use of the frame indicates an awareness of much that Spoerri describes here.

[17] The nineteenth-century tale offers many examples of the voyeuristic physician, the outsider whose fate is to have his face pressed to the glass of others' lives rather than to participate in similar dramas himself. Two examples that come to mind are Balzac's "Etude de femme" and Barbey's "Le bonheur dans le crime." Both stories depict the parasitic affective life of the doctor.

[18] See Lubbock's remark on Maupassant's method:

> Maupassant's idea of a story . . . would suggest an object that you fashioned and abandoned to the reader, turning away and leaving him alone with it. . . . He relates his story as though he had caught it in the act and were mentioning the details as they passed. There seems to be no particular process at work in his mind, so little that the figure of Maupassant, the showman, is overlooked and forgotten as we follow the direction of his eyes. . . . but the effect is that he is not there at all, because he is doing nothing that ostensibly requires any judgment, nothing that reminds us of his presence. He is behind us, out of sight, out of mind; the story occupies us, the moving scene, and nothing else. (112-13)

Thus the narrative form obliges the reader to be "non plus un consommateur, mais un producteur du texte," to borrow Barthes's phrase (10).

[19] Stanley Fish describes the ending of a certain kind of poem (one that, indeed, has the same framed structure we encounter in "En voyage"), saying that what is devastating about such endings is that they "render superfluous the mode of discourse and knowing of which they themselves are examples" (158).

Works Cited

Barthes, Roland. *S/Z*. Paris: Seuil, 1970.

Chklovski, Victor. "La construction de la nouvelle et du roman." *Théorie de la littérature*. Ed. T. Todorov. Paris: Seuil, 1965. 170-96.

Crouzet, Michel. "Une rhétorique de Maupassant?" *Revue d'histoire littéraire de la France* 80 (1980): 233-61.

Fish, Stanley. *Self-Consuming Artifacts: The Experience of Seventeenth-Century Literature*. Berkeley: U of California P, 1972.

Genette, Gérard. *Figures III*. Paris: Seuil, 1972.

Goffman, Erving. *Frame Analysis: An Essay on the Organization of Experience*. Cambridge: Harvard UP, 1974.

Greimas, A. J. *Maupassant: La sémiotique du texte: Exercices pratiques*. Paris: Seuil, 1976.

Iser, Wolfgang. *The Implied Reader*. Baltimore: Johns Hopkins UP, 1974.

Lubbock, Percy. *The Craft of Fiction*. 1921. Rpt. New York: Scribner's, 1955.

Maupassant, Guy de. *Contes et nouvelles*. Ed. Albert-Marie Schmidt. Paris: Albin Michel, 1973.

———. *Œuvres complètes*. Paris: Louis Conard, 1947.

Moger, Angela S. "That Obscure Object of Narrative." *Yale French Studies* 63 (1982): 129-38.

Pierrot, Jean. "Espace et mouvement dans les récits de Maupassant." *Flaubert et Maupassant: Ecrivains normands*. Ed. Joseph-Marc Bailbé. Paris: PUF, 1981. 167-96.

Prince, Gerald. "Introduction à l'étude du narrataire." *Poétique* 14 (1973): 178-96.

———. "Nom et destin dans 'La parure.'" *French Review* 56 (1982): 267-71.

Smith, Barbara Herrnstein. *Poetic Closure: A Study of How Poems End*. Chicago: U of Chicago P, 1968.

Spoerri, Theophil. "Mérimée and the Short Story." *Yale French Studies* 2.2 (1949): 3-11.

Todorov, Tzvetan. *Poétique de la prose.* Paris: Seuil, 1971.

Tolstoy, Leo. *Guy de Maupassant.* Trans. U. Tcherkoff. 1898. London: Haskell, 1974.

Mary Donaldson-Evans (essay date 1986)

SOURCE: "Women and Religion," in *A Woman's Revenge: The Chronology of Dispossession in Maupassant's Fiction,* French Forum, Publishers, 1986, pp. 82-108.

[*In the following excerpt, Donaldson-Evans examines Maupassant's skepticism of traditional religion through his portrayal of various feminine types, including the pious woman; the woman who identifies herself with the Divinity; the woman as Virgin Mother; the sadistic woman incapable of love; and the cruel mother.*]

The disaffection for traditional religion that was prevalent at the end of the 19th century in France had many sources, literary, philosophical, scientific, historical. France's sobering defeat at the hands of the Prussians in the War of 1870 shattered French self-confidence; the horrors of the Commune even further shocked the nation and plunged her into an emotional depression from which she did not fully emerge until the end of the century. Marked by a resurgent interest in Romanticism's dark side,[1] the literature of this period reflects the pessimism of the day, a faithless pessimism that found the roots of its disbelief in the determinism of Darwin and Taine, the cynicism of Schopenhauer and the tradition of blasphemy going back to Sade.

A superficial reading of Maupassant's work suggests that he was in perfect step with the *fin-de-siècle* skepticism preached by his contemporaries. The profanatory spirit in which he makes use of religious themes and décors conforms precisely to what Jean Pierrot terms "le catholicisme esthétique" (*L'Imaginaire décadent,* 106) of the decade beginning in 1880, that is, the use by non-believing writers of religious subjects solely for artistic effect, for the *pittoresque.* And yet a closer analysis of Maupassant's treatment of religious themes reveals unsuspected complexities, as well as a contempt for the concept of God which cannot be traced uniquely to the "hors-texte" of his era, but which is closely bound to the role played by women in his fictional universe.

From the beginning Maupassant's women enjoy a privileged (one is tempted to say "sacred") relationship with the Divinity. With few exceptions (**"La Reine Hortense,"**[2] la comtesse de Brémontal

in **L'Angélus**), their faith knows no limits and their naturals expansiveness no greater outlet than that offered by religion. From this point of view prostitutes and nuns are indistinguishable; whether a woman gives herself to Christ or to men is of no importance, since it is generally the result of an accident of nature (in the case of the elder nun in **"Boule de suif,"** for example, a disfiguring smallpox is clearly responsible for the woman's "vocation"); whatever path she chooses to follow, a woman is guided by her emotions. It is this "éternelle tendresse" (I, 595) that l'abbé Marignan despises and fears in women and that seems to him to be an integral part of their emotional make-up. Even nuns are possessed of it:

> Il la sentait dans leurs regards plus mouillés de piété que les regards des moines, dans leurs extases où leur sexe se mêlait, dans leurs élans d'amour vers le Christ, qui l'indignaient parce que c'était de l'amour de femme, de l'amour charnel. . . . (**"Clair de lune,"** I, 595)

While it is obvious that Maupassant intended to ridicule his misogynistic priest, who, "port[ant] bien son nom de bataille" (I, 594), looked upon woman as the Enemy, a threat to his virtue, a blemish in God's otherwise flawless creation,[3] it is also true that the portrait of women as irrational creatures whose "âme aimante" governs all of their relationships, divine as well as human, is a cliché of the early work and is intimately connected with what is seen as woman's "piety." The legacy of Flaubert and the Goncourts is plain here, and, although Maupassant stops short of portraying woman's "weakness" for the trappings of religion as maliciously as had the latter in their *Madame Gervaisais* (1869), he is not above ridiculing what he sees as a feminine debility. The letter-writer of **"La Relique"** (1882), Henri Fontal, cutting through to the heart of women's "religious" sensibility, recognizes it as a purely emotional need, illogical, more akin to superstition than to faith. Having persuaded his fiancée Gilberte of the authenticity of a relic (which is in reality nothing but a piece of mutton bone) by telling her that he personally had stolen it from a *châsse* in the Cologne cathedral, he is amused by her reaction. Instead of expressing horror at the profanation that she believes he has committed, she falls into his arms, thrilled by his courage, even more thrilled to possess what she believes to be a bone chip from one of the 11,000 virgins, despite—perhaps even because of—the way in which it was acquired:

> J'avais commis, pour elle, un sacrilège. J'avais volé; j'avais violé une église, violé une châsse, violé et volé des reliques sacrées. Elle m'adorait pour cela; me trouvait tendre, parfait, divin. Telle est la femme. . . . (I, 592)

Fontal invites the reader to marvel at the contradictions in the feminine nature that are illustrated here. A "pious" young woman who condones—even rewards—sacrilege, Gilberte is typical of early heroines, passionately devout, yet flagrantly amoral.

This absence of scruples in even the most "religious" of Maupassant's heroines is everywhere apparent. Cogny has pointed out that, according to a common prejudice of the period, "un homme qui pratique est un sot, et une femme qui ne pratique pas une gourgandine" (*Maupassant,* 41). The corollary of this statement—the woman who does practice her religion is virtuous—does not apply to the world contained in Maupassant's fiction, where harlots are endowed with a religious fervor far exceeding that of most women, and for good reason. If the Goncourts had bequeathed to Maupassant the notion that religion satisfied a woman's sexual needs, or, put somewhat less crudely, that woman's sexuality and her religiosity had a common source ("La religion est une partie du sexe de la femme," they had proclaimed in an 1857 entry to their *Journal*),[4] Maupassant was quick to draw the obvious conclusion: the more "sexual" the woman, the greater her capacity for religious ecstasy. One has only to consider Boule de Suif, who derives immense satisfaction from prayer, or the prostitutes of **"La Maison Tellier,"** whose uncontrollable weeping during a First Communion service gains an entire congregation and causes the priest to assert with considerable emotion that a miracle has taken place in his church:

> Pendant que Jésus-Christ pénétrait pour la première fois dans le corps de ces petits, le Saint-Esprit, l'oiseau céleste, le souffle de Dieu, s'est abattu sur vous, s'est emparé de vous, vous a saisis, courbés comme des roseaux sous la brise. (I, 275)

It must have been with mirthful malice that Maupassant selected his priest's words, whose *double-entendre* brings to mind monstrous visions of Christ as rapist, the Holy Spirit as vulture and man not as *roseau pensant,* to use Pascal's image, but rather as a fragile reed battered by emotion in the "wind" of God's breath. The mockery that can be discerned at the lexical level is consistent with the symbolism of the narrative itself: the emotional frenzy into which the congregation has been thrown is not divinely, but humanly inspired, and the source of the inspiration is a prostitute whose reminiscences of childhood purity move her to tears. Inasmuch as their profession demands that they raise their customers to an orgasmic pitch of passion, in the communion scene the prostitutes have merely transferred from the physical to the emotional plane their role as *allumeuses,* and the renewed enthusiasm with which they undertake their normal duties later the same day appears not as alien, but as complementary to the contagious excitement they had felt in the church, *maison de Dieu* which is an obvious counterpart of the *maison de passe* in which the women work.[5] To the communion wine thus corresponds the champagne offered gratis

to all customers that evening. "Ça n'est pas tous les jours fête," explains the radiant madam in the story's closing line.

The *rapprochement* between church and brothel is in fact a leitmotif in Maupassant's work, **"La Maison Tellier"** being merely the first of several blasphemous identifications between the two. The following year (1882) saw the publication of **"Conflits pour rire"** in the *Gil Blas.* Here it is a priest who draws the analogy between church and bordello. Embarrassed by the rather explicit statue of Adam and Eve which adorns the portal of his country church and humiliated by the mocking laughter of passers-by, he reflects that in fact "son église portait au front un emblème de honte, comme un mauvais lieu" (I, 427). When dressing Adam fails as a permanent solution to the problem (for he is promptly undressed by one of the townspeople), the virginal young priest castrates him. The playful irreverence of this anecdote is but a thin disguise for the seriousness behind it: this country cleric is cut from the same cloth as the priest of **"Le Saut du berger"** (March 1882), whose frustrated sexuality led him from verbal to physical violence, from the cruel killing of a bitch that had just given birth to the murder of a couple discovered embracing in a shepherd's hut. According to Maupassant's clever formula, "une chose surtout le soulevait de colère et de dégoût: l'amour" (I, 378). Like Father Tolbiac of *Une Vie,* after whom he is modeled,[6] this obsessed clergyman is tormented by his celibacy. And just as l'abbé Tolbiac is linked by antithesis to the indulgent abbé Picot, Maupassant's apparent taste for binary oppositions led him to create, one week after the publication of **"Le Saut du berger,"** a curé for whom the dictum of chastity was certainly not to be taken seriously. Although the abbé Argence of **"Le Lit"** is present in the narrative only by implication, being the *destinataire* of several letters found sewn into the lining of a chasuble (thus playing the narratological role of *narrataire* insofar as the *récit enchâssé* is concerned),[7] the compromising nature of the letters leaves no doubts as to this priest's "virtue." The first three, which "fixaient simplement des rendez-vous" (I, 382), are not transcribed; the fourth, which is a meditation upon the subject of the bed (whence the title) by the priest's temporarily bed-ridden mistress, brings to mind once again the relationship between the sacred and the profane. Although the *maison de Dieu/maison de passe* metaphor does not reappear here, it is clear that for the writer of the letter the bed, "symbole de la vie" (I, 384) and locus of the three essential acts of human existence (*naissance, amour, mort*), is possessed of a religious transcendence. "*Tabernacle* de la vie" (I, 383) in which *one* life becomes *two,* the bed itself seems to come to life when it sets the scene of "le délirant *mystère* d'amour," an embrace "faisant de *deux* êtres *un seul*" and giving to each an ineffable joy "qui descend en eux comme un *feu dévorant et céleste.*" The

La Main Gauche

PAR

GUY DE MAUPASSANT

SEIZIÈME ÉDITION

PARIS

PAUL OLLENDORFF, ÉDITEUR

28 *bis*, RUE DE RICHELIEU, 28 *bis*

1889

proliferation of religious terms in the description of the bed and the acts that are accomplished upon it prepares us for the parodical distortion of one of Catholicism's most important dogmas: "Hors l'Eglise point de salut" becomes "Rien n'est excellent hors du lit" (I, 384). The narrative irony is strong here, and the perspicacious reader will note that the *épistolière,* for whom "le lit, c'est l'homme," treats Christ's divinity with unconscious malice when she links it to the absence of a bed at two of the three basic moments of human existence, birth and death: "Notre Seigneur Jésus, pour prouver qu'il n'avait rien d'humain, ne semble pas avoir jamais eu besoin d'un lit. Il est né sur la paille et mort sur la croix, laissant aux créatures comme nous leur couche de mollesse et de repos" (I, 384). The heretical theology of this statement, which ignores Christ's humanity, brings into sharp relief the subtly blasphemous nature of this "meditation" and the false piety of the "meditator." The allusion at the beginning of the story to a "marchande à la toilette" is thus given meaning by what ensues, for her dual role (according to Forestier, I, 1408, she serves both as saleswoman of used clothing, jewelry, fabrics, etc., and as *entremetteuse*) is reflected by that of the letter, which, ostensibly a reverent meditation, is in fact (like the three which preceded it) an invitation to an amorous encounter, its perlocutionary aspect being unequivocal: "Venez me voir demain à trois heures, peut-être serai-je mieux et vous le pourrai-je montrer."

The notion of commerce associated with prostitution provides an important foundation upon which the church/brothel metaphor is sometimes built. Just as *l'amour* is a prostitute's bread and butter, for Maupassant's priests *la mort* est un gagne-pain" (I, 446). The old peasant, Amable (**"Le Père Amable"**), is terrified of priests and never sets foot in church, which he regards as "une sorte d'immense maison de commerce dont les curés étaient les commis, commis sournois, rusés, dégourdis comme personne, qui faisaient les affaires du bon Dieu au détriment des campagnards" (II, 735). Amable's deprecatory view of priests and organized religion is typical of Maupassant's pre-1887 skeptics and free-thinkers, who for the most part regard clergy as money-grubbing hypocrites, "voleurs d'âmes . . . violeurs de consciences" (**"Le Marquis de Fumerol,"** II, 811). Only when their own material welfare is at stake do such heroes align themselves with the church and its traditions (**"Un Normand," "La Confession de Théodule Sabot"**).

Associated with many of Maupassant's heroines by their disgust of sexuality, early priests in particular are seen by the male protagonists as the enemy, the Other. Duroy's amusing comment in the Church of the Trinity to the priest who had just heard Virginie Walter's desperate confession and has thereby thwarted (temporarily at least) the young man's seduction strategy reflects this identification: "Si vous ne portiez point une jupe, vous, quelle paire de soufflets sur votre vilain museau!" ([**Bel-Ami (B-A)**], 411). Ironically, perhaps, the church becomes in Maupassant's work all things for all women. While the frigid ones can take the veil of religion ("elle . . . avait épousé Dieu, par dégoût des hommes," I, 445), the promiscuous ones can hide *behind* it, using as pretexts charitable activities in order to betray their husbands (**"La Confession," "La Chambre II"**); and the prostitutes can use religion as priests themselves do, soliciting customers in much the same way that the latter solicit converts, by appealing to their "spiritual" needs. Two stories, **"La Baronne"** (1887) and **"Les Tombales"** (1891), are exemplary in this respect.

In the first la baronne Samoris, a high society courtesan who attends Mass regularly and receives the sacraments "avec recueillement" (II, 909), goes to great lengths not to compromise herself for fear of jeopardizing her daughter's chances to marry well, but falls upon hard times. Unwilling to sell herself openly, she appeals to a close friend for a loan of 30,000 francs. The friend, an antique dealer and the story's principal narrator, decides instead to lend her an ivory statue of Christ dating from the 16th century, with the promise that he will give her address to appropriate clients who express an interest in seeing this precious *objet d'art.* Should she be successful in selling the Christ, 20,000 of the 50,000-franc selling price will be hers to keep. The antique dealer's ingenious idea does indeed save Madame Samoris from "degradation": after six months she is financially solvent enough to purchase the statue herself, upon condition that her friend will continue to send clients to her, "car il est encore à vendre . . . mon Christ" (II, 912). The desacralization—indeed, desecration—of a sacred icon could hardly be more obvious. This Christ, involuntary *proxénète* who, in an ironic reversal of the Biblical account of Mary Magdalene, makes it possible for this prostitute to continue the practice of her "profession," is on display in the chapel of Madame Samoris's daughter Isabelle: "C'était une sorte de boudoir pieux où brûlait une lampe d'argent devant le Christ . . . couché sur un lit de velours noir" (II, 911). To the sensuality of the setting corresponds the sybaritic comfort of the entire lodging, "une demeure confortable qui invitait à rester" (II, 912), where one detects the mingled fragrances of incense, flowers and perfume. The metaphoric identification between the carnal and the spiritual is nowhere more evident than in this story, bringing to mind once again the parallel established six years previously (in **"La Maison Tellier"**) between the house of ill repute and the house of God.

Liturgical ornaments, characterized by **"La Reine Hortense"** as "de la marchandise à pleureurs" (I, 802), can clearly be exploited in other ways as well. Given the depths of amorality and egotism to which

Maupassant's later heroines regularly sink, it is hardly unexpected to find in 1887 a woman violating the sanctity of a religious object.

In sum, however, Madame Samoris's profanation, dictated by need, is quite innocuous in itself, and Maupassant's treatment of the religious theme is patently derisive. The perverse exploitation of human emotion practiced by the charming prostitute of **"Les Tombales"** (1891), on the other hand, suggests a much darker view of the human female. Like clergymen who are envisioned by the dying Moiron as crows sent upon cadavers by a malicious God, the whore of this story is a friend of death, a "sépulcrale chasseresse" (II, 1245) who solicits in cemeteries rather than on sidewalks, gathering her customers from among the bereaved and the lonely. Her hypocrisy, her shameless exploitation of the grief of others, mirrors that of Maupassant's earlier priests and underscores her relationship with religion: for her, as for them, "la mort est un gagne-pain." From a relatively "innocent" complicity between women and priests in the early work (Jeanne consults l'abbé Picot about duping Julien into fathering another child in **Une Vie**) to the conscious use by the later heroines of religion's most persuasive schemes, from the redemptive heroine of **"Le Mariage du lieutenant Laré"** to the diabolical *femme fatale* of the later works, the growing depravity of Maupassant's heroine can also be measured by plotting on the chronological axis Maupassant's use of religious terminology in describing the male-female relationship. To do this, however, we must begin again at the beginning.

As with the aquatic imagery, one of the first things to strike the reader about the religious code in Maupassant's fiction is its versatility. Having briefly considered the role played by religion at the syntagmatic level of the plot, we now turn to religious metaphor to discover that it is brought into play primarily in portrayals of two sorts of love, filial and sexual. The false identification of the mother with the Virgin, with all that is holy and pure and irreproachable, finds its principal expression in **Une Vie, "La Veillée"** and **Pierre et Jean,** and offers an abundant source of such imagery. At her mother's wake Jeanne de Lamare has the consoling inspiration to read her mother's correspondence, "comme elle aurait fait d'un livre pieux" (**Vie,** 240). To do so would be to accomplish "un devoir délicat et sacré" (p. 240), and Jeanne begins to read the yellowing letters with filial tenderness and piety. Her horror upon discovering a packet of passionate love letters addressed to her mother by an old family friend is echoed six months later in **"La Veillée,"** which recounts the same anecdote with modifications dictated by the exigencies of a different genre, the short story.[8] Here it is a nun-daughter and a magistrate-son who read their mother's letters at her wake, an act the nun readily likens to "un chemin de la croix" (I, 447). As might be expected, their revulsion (unlike Jeanne's)

gives way to a judgmental pose: they close the curtain upon their mother's bed, condemning her to a symbolic isolation.

Equally judgmental is Pierre of **Pierre et Jean,** whose "amour religieux pour sa mère" (p. 84) is based upon the illusion of her inviolable purity. When the truth regarding her youthful transgressions dawns upon him, he tries at first to reject it, accusing his jealousy for giving rise to his suspicions, examining his psyche "comme les dévots leur conscience" (p. 84). His slow movement from doubt to certainty is punctuated by periods of remorse and self-flagellation in which he inculpates his own egotism, placing his mother once again upon the pedestal from which his doubts had pulled her. Such scenes are encoded in religious symbolism:

> Je suis fou, pensa-t-il, je soupçonne ma mère. Et un flot d'amour et d'attendrissement, de *repentir,* de *prière* et de désolation noya son cœur. . . . Oh! s'il avait pu la prendre en ses bras en ce moment, comme il l'eût embrassée, caressée, comme il se fût *agenouillé* pour *demander grâce!* (p. 104)

Increasingly moralistic as he becomes ever more certain of her perfidy, Pierre considers that it is he who has been betrayed, "volé dans son affection *sacrée,*" "trompé dans son *pieux* respect" (p. 131). His outrage at his mother's betrayal is spent when he shares his discovery with his brother; after this tirade he is still tormented by a sense of injustice, but he turns his harsh judgment upon himself. Feeling great remorse for having revealed the terrible secret, Pierre "se jugeait odieux, malpropre, méchant" (p. 219). Madame Roland's impenitence (she does not regret for a moment her long liaison with Maréchal) thus carries with it the sting of irony: it is she who has flown in the face of social norms through her illicit affair, yet it is Pierre who is exiled from "society"; it is she who has "sinned," yet it is her son Pierre who is made to feel guilty. One may of course protest, and with reason, that Pierre is condemned precisely because of his self-righteous condemnation of others; one may also consider that from a psychoanalytical perspective Pierre is indeed guilty, his overreaction suggesting an abnormal love for his mother. The fact still remains that **Pierre et Jean** "demythifies" maternity and abolishes the distance between *la mère* and *la femme* and between what Maupassant increasingly represents as their archetypes, the Virgin and the prostitute. The irreverent identification between the Virgin Mother and the fallen woman had, moreover, been explicit as early as 1882 in **"Un Normand"** and **"Nuit de Noël."**

Madame Roland's defensive stance (her deep sense of the propriety of her love affair with Maréchal) links her with many of Maupassant's heroines who readily transfer their religious sensibilities to the profane level of sexual love. Such heroines fall into two general categories: (1) those who indulge in a kind of "religious" eroticism, elevating their lovers to the status of the divine (such heroines are a phenomenon of the early work only) and (2) those to be found from beginning to end in Maupassant's literary production (but with important modifications) who confer divinity upon themselves, equating their lovers with worshippers. In the first group we find the archetypal bride evoked in **"Voyage de noce."** Engulfed by a feeling of immense tenderness during the magical days of her honeymoon, the newly married woman invests the man she has wed with divine attributes, placing all of her hopes in him: "Il est l'amour . . . il est l'espoir saisi; il est Celui à qui nous allons pouvoir nous dévouer, à qui nous nous sommes données; il est l'Ami, notre Maître, notre Seigneur, tout" (I, 510-11). In the case of the young bride the illusion does not last.

Unfaithful wives, on the other hand, bring to their extramarital affairs a religious fervor unequaled in its intensity, as **"Une Passion"** (1882) illustrates. When Madame Poinçot sacrifices her reputation and her previously unblemished virtue to a reluctant army officer with whom she falls deeply in love, it is in the spirit of a religious celebration, exalted, fanatical: she "avait tout jeté dans cette flamme de son cœur comme on jetait, pour un sacrifice, tous ses objets précieux en un bûcher" (I, 517). Her unrequited passion renders even more ridiculous her cult of her lover, Jean Renoldi ("Elle . . . s'abbattait à ses genoux pour le contempler longtemps dans une pose d'adoration," I, 517); for his part, Renoldi considers that this woman "[le] martyrise d'attentions, . . . [le] torture de prévenances, . . . [le] persécute de tendresses" (I, 517). It is Renoldi himself in fact who is the real sacrificial victim, his career ruined by this tenacious woman.

The same cannot be said for Duroy (1885), whose liaison with the formerly virtuous Madame Walter offers some thought-provoking refinements on the prototype. More resistant to the demands of her sexuality than Madame Poinçot had been, Madame Walter (whose first name, not coincidentally, is Virginie) still struggles in vain against the temptations of the flesh, even seeking support from a priest. Her deeply devout Catholicism established from the beginning, it comes as no surprise when this overly emotional, hypersensitive *adoratrice* prostrates herself before her lover as she once had before Christ. (One is reminded once again of the Goncourt influence.) Nor is it by accident that, in a scene no doubt owing much to *Madame Bovary,* Madame Walter arranges to meet Duroy in church. (Duroy cynically reflects that religion is an *en-tout-cas* for women "qui se fichent du bon Dieu comme d'une guigne, mais qui ne veulent pas qu'on en dise du mal et qui le prennent à l'occasion pour entremetteur," *B-A,* 398). Increasingly incapable of prayer, Madame Walter is assailed by worldly thoughts as she attempts to meditate: "Au lieu de l'apparition céleste attendue dans la détresse de son cœur, elle apercevait toujours la moustache frisée du jeune homme" (p. 405). Ironically, it is Madame Walter's Jewish husband who adds grist to the mill of his wife's obsessions when he purchases a painting of Christ walking on the water. The remarkable resemblance between the painted figure and Duroy results in the complete destruction of Madame Walter's delicate mental balance, and upon learning that her lover has abducted her daughter, she rushes to the greenhouse, where she throws herself before the painted Jesus, "balbutiant des mots d'amour, des invocations passionnées et désespérées" (p. 551), only to be greeted by the same dispassionate look which her exasperated lover had worn after he had tired of her:

> . . . ce n'était plus Dieu, c'était son amant qui la regardait. C'était ses yeux, son front, l'expression de son visage, son air froid et hautain!

> Elle balbutiait "Jésus!—Jésus!—Jésus!" Et le mot "Georges" lui venait aux lèvres. (p. 551)

Despite the clearly comic aspect of Madame Walter's confusion, the situation is not without pathos. The hallucinatory identification of one's lover with one's God that reaches its apex in *Bel-Ami* is founded upon the feeling of painful insecurity characterizing so many early heroines. Even Christiane Andermatt, whose growing independence is traced by the diachronic movement of the narrative in *Mont-Oriol,* adopts a posture of total submission and abdication of will when she first gives herself to Paul. To quiet her troubled conscience, she convinces herself that she is passionately in love with her lover and determines to give him her life and her happiness, "à lui sacrifier tout, selon la morale exaltée des cœurs vaincus mais scrupuleux qui se jugent purifiés par le dévouement et la sincérité" (pp. 165-66). Like Duroy, Paul Brétigny is deified by his mistress, and the tender words she utters to him the day following his amorous conquest ("Je vous appartiens corps et âme. Faites de moi désormais ce qu'il vous plaira," p. 169) appear as a parody of the Virgin Mary's response to the angelic salutation: "Be it unto me according to thy word." Brétigny's cruel betrayal of Christiane's love and her subsequent suffering strengthen her and lead her to draw a parallel between her situation and that of Christ. When her Jewish husband Andermatt comments that he would have liked to name what he naïvely assumes to be *their* infant daughter after her mother, Christiane replies: "Oh! cela promet trop de souffrances de porter le nom du Crucifié" (p. 415). Moreover, Brétigny's remorse, his humility and his anguish as he pays his respects to the new mother in the final pages of the novel are those of a repentant sinner in the presence of his God. He feels himself "enfoncé dans une de ces saletés morales qui tachent, jusqu'à la mort, la conscience d'un homme" (p. 423). As with the culinary metaphor which testified to Christiane's passage from a passive to an active role, the thematic and lexical use of the religious code records her development from "dévouée sublime" (the term is used to describe Clochette in a story of the same name) to a self-determining divinity. Where the role of women is concerned, **Mont-Oriol** must certainly be considered a pivotal work in Maupassant's fiction.

Whereas numerous early heroines engage unwittingly in idolatry, elevating their unworthy lovers to the ranks of the divine, the rare male protagonists of the pre-1885 works who exalt their mistresses (or would-be mistresses) are play-acting, their false humility being but one of several tactics in an artful seduction. Machiavellian to the quick, Duroy falls on his knees at Madame Walter's feet, gazes upon her "visage adoré" (p. 393), vows to respect her, promises his undying love for her, then takes her brutally, uses her to his own ends and casts her off with utter indifference when she begins to bore him. Duroy's insolence, his misogyny, his iconoclastic debasement of women mark him as an early hero who, his pride having been wounded by a woman (Madame Forestier), responds by building a wall of indifference around himself ("Toutes les femmes sont des filles. Il faut s'en donner et ne rien donner de soi," p. 358). This ruthless egotism would appear to render his likeness of Christ ludicrous; yet in the context of this novel it is not anomalous, for the Christ of Walter's painting is not a sympathetic figure, but a powerful one, not human, but superhuman. His disciples do not marvel at his feat; rather, they recoil in fear, "les figures . . . convulsées par la surprise" (p. 490). Christ's defiance of the laws of physical gravity as he walks upon the water, besides evoking Duroy's ability and willingness to trample upon women in his march to power, reflects the latter's contempt of social norms and prepares the reader for his final triumph, celebrated at the altar of the Madeleine: " . . . sur l'autel le sacrifice divin s'accomplissait; l'Homme-Dieu, à l'appel de son prêtre, descendait sur la terre pour consacrer le triomphe du baron Georges Du Roy" (p. 571). The bishop's farcical homily, addressed to Duroy, contains an implicit though unmistakable parallel: "Vous, Monsieur, que votre talent élève au-dessus des autres, vous qui écrivez, qui conseillez, qui dirigez le peuple, vous avez une belle mission à remplir, un bel exemple à donner" (p. 569). The irony, of course, is that Christ's mission led to the Crucifixion, whereas the only cross to be evoked in this novel is the crucifix that hangs on the wall of Georges's boyhood room. Duroy's is an infernal mission ("vous êtes l'être le plus vil que je connaisse," hisses Madame Walter, p. 568), and the priest's repetition of an adjective normally reserved for esthetic appreciation ("bel," "belle") suggests the true source of Duroy's success. Moreover, Walter's *Jésus marchant sur les flots* provides the central image. If, as Robert Artinian perceptively remarks ("Chacun son égout"),

the sewers of the first chapter clearly symbolize the sordid milieu in which Duroy will rise to glory, the aquatic imagery of the final chapter presents us with an ironic Christ standing above the sea of well-wishers who have come to acclaim him. A "*flot* de soleil" (p. 562) inundates the church through its immense entrance; the invited guests inside the church hear from without, "vague comme le bruit d'une *mer lointaine,* le grouillement du peuple amassé devant l'église" (p. 565); this sound is in turn dominated by the music of the powerful organ, "des clameurs prolongées, énormes, *enflées comme des vagues.*" And if, as he shakes hands and proffers banalities in the reception line, Duroy sees the crowd flow past him "comme un fleuve" (p. 572), his arrival at the threshold of the Madeleine reveals below him a dark sea of people, "une foule noire, bruissante, venue là pour lui, pour lui Georges Du Roy" (p. 573). This burlesque Christ, however, thinks only of himself, and in spite of his immense pride and his sense of superhuman power ("il lui sembla qu'il allait faire un bond du portique de la Madeleine au portique du Palais-Bourbon," p. 573), the only "miracle" performed by the all-too-human Duroy is the symbolic parting of the waters as he descends the steps of the church "entre deux haies de spectateurs" (p. 573).

The playful portrayal of an unscrupulous opportunist as a Christ-figure, although clearly ironic, is remarkably consistent with the early image of Christ in Maupassant's work, nearly always the symbol of victory, evoked with the tongue-in-cheek piety of a true skeptic. Aside from scattered allusions to the crucifix in descriptions of the décor in some stories (e.g., **"Tribunaux rustiques"**), the suffering Christ is not represented until 1886, when Christiane Andermatt compares her tribulations with His. There is, of course, some irony in this, for Christiane's equation fails to take into account the fact that Christ suffered for the sins of others, whereas she is expiating her own sin of infidelity. After 1886, however, and simultaneously with the growing anguish of Maupassant's male protagonists and their victimization by women, we find a far greater number of allusions to the suffering Christ, who is progressively transformed into a symbol for the martyrdom of the male.[9] Concurrently, woman becomes equated with God the Father, who, in keeping with Sadian philosophy, is viewed as a supreme sadist. Let us examine the steps in this transformation.

The notion of love as sacrifice, hardly consistent with the Decadent[10] view of love as mere submission to the instinct of self-preservation, is first elaborated in **"Amour"** (December 1886), where, as we have seen, the male teal's immolation is endowed with religious transcendence by the evocation of the cross. Two weeks after the appearance of this story, **"Clochette,"** another story of sacrificial love, was published. This time it is a young woman who risks her life and sacrifices her beauty for her suitor when she jumps from a second-story window in the school attic to avoid compromising him. Badly crippled by her fall, she never marries, and the cause of her disfiguring limp is revealed only after she dies many decades later. While she is never explicitly presented as a Christ-figure, the bewhiskered old maid is clearly regarded as a martyr who looks upon her misfortune as a well-deserved punishment for the transgression she was about to commit. As such, she is to be contrasted with Christiane, who was her literary contemporary (*Mont-Oriol* was published the same year). It was in 1886 as well that Christ's suffering was explicitly evoked and compared to that of another old woman, the "être innommable" of "Misère humaine," who, stooped with age and barely ambulatory, is observed shuffling painfully through crowded streets: "Et quelle route douloureuse! Quel chemin de la croix plus effroyable que celui du Christ!" (II, 752).

Male martyrs are ubiquitous as well, and the Romantic compassion for and interest in society's pariahs clearly survive in Maupassant's works. But the martyrdom of the lover is especially tragic and offers numerous insights into the mutations of the male-female relationship. One must wait until 1889 before the male-as-Christ motif is fully crystallized. We encounter the lover-martyr in **"Le Rendez-vous"** (February 23, 1889), although the symbolism is susceptible to a pluralistic reading because of the story's ironic mode. Here Madame Haggan, exasperated by the tedium of her weekly *rendez-vous d'amour,* "punishes" her lover by keeping him waiting. One day, just as she is about to take a carriage to his apartment, she encounters an attractive male friend, who easily persuades her to visit his "collections japonaises" (II, 1123). With thinly masked relief she dashes off a telegram to her lover, using illness as a pretext and asking him to come to dinner the following evening "pour que je me fasse pardonner" (II, 1124). The heroine looks upon herself as a martyr, upon her *rencontres amoureuses* as painful steps in her personal Calvary. She has long forgotten the ephemeral emotion that allowed her to abandon herself to her lover in the first place, but her memory of the countless meetings is vivid: "elle n'avait pas oublié . . . ce chapelet de rendez-vous, ce chemin de croix de l'amour, aux stations si fatigantes, si monotones, si pareilles . . ." (II, 1120). Her self-pity transforms her into a figure of ridicule, and her annoyance, which focuses upon the 120 dressings and undressings without a chambermaid, is frankly derisive. Clearly, the real victim here is not Madame Haggan (*à gants?*), but her lover, the vicomte de Martelet, whose name evokes first *martelé,* but also *martyr.* His constant disappointments, his tolerance, his forgiveness of his mistress's repeated cruelties, his unfailing love and above all his *patience* identify him with the sufferer, the *patient.* The religious metaphors must thus be understood in an ironic sense. Madame Haggan is *le bourreau,* the traitor, and it is

not mere coincidence that she bides her time in the park of Trinity Church while her lover anxiously awaits her.

Fort comme la mort, published the same year, presents similar ambiguities. Any de Guilleroy and her look-alike daughter Annette, heroines of Maupassant's penultimate novel, play an innocently diabolical role. Any has her own Calvary—aging—and she addresses an ardent prayer to "Celui qui avait aussi tant souffert" (p. 316), begging him to spare her the horror of a physical decline for at least a few more years. Although her anguish is very real, it is difficult not to see irony in this passage. After feverishly begging "le martyr divin" to preserve her beauty, she sits before her mirror carefully applying her man-made creams and powders "avec une tension de pensée aussi ardente que pour la prière" (p. 316). Furthermore, Maupassant had set the tone of her egotistical relationship with the Divinity in an earlier passage, asserting that when she doubted Olivier's constancy, she prayed for divine help, taking care not to reveal to God the shameful cause of her supplication, "traitant Dieu avec la même hypocrisie naïve qu'un mari" (p. 239). As was the case in **"Le Rendez-vous,"** it is not the heroine, but the hero who is to be identified with a tortured Christ, whence his name, Olivier, which evokes the olive grove of Christ's Passion. Any's acute jealousy of her daughter's fresh beauty leads her to the conviction that her lover is drawn to Annette not by paternal affection, but by passionate love. And while there is a grain of truth in this (Olivier is indeed troubled and confused by the emotions, long dormant, that this replica of a younger Any awakens in him), Any's accusation, together with her watchful, suspicious behavior, serves only to exacerbate the situation and cause Olivier untold mental anguish. Her egotism, her self-pity and her useless efforts to rival her daughter's youthful beauty show her relationship with the Divine in a properly ludicrous light (she calls upon God, "comme elle avait appelé un médecin, le matin même," p. 240) and make a mockery of her apparent concern for her lover's welfare.

"Le Champ d'Oliviers," which provides a much more dense treatment of the lover-as-Christ motif, was published almost exactly one year after **"Le Rendez-vous"** (February 19-23, 1890). The title itself evokes Christ's suffering, and the protagonist's name, l'abbé Vilbois, alludes quite obviously to the cross. Having met a pretty actress in his youth, the innocent Vilbois became violently enamored of this perverse young woman, who "sut le conquérir complètement, faire de lui un de ces délirants forcenés, un de ces déments en extase qu'un regard ou qu'une jupe de femme brûle sur le bûcher des Passions Mortelles" (II, 1182). The capitalization of the word *Passions* offers the reader a foreglimpse of Vilbois's eventual fate: he will indeed suffer at the hands of what he soon discovers to be his unfaithful mistress. Leaving her pregnant (she convinces him that the child she is carrying is not his), he joins the priesthood, offering to the church "une vie brisée qu'il avait failli lui donner vierge" (II, 1184). It is not until many years later that his past comes to haunt him in the form of his illegitimate son, a vulgar criminal sent by his mother on her deathbed. Anguished by the resemblance between himself and this sordid vagabond, the priest turns his eyes skyward and sees "tremblotant sur le ciel, le petit feuillage grisâtre de l'arbre sacré qui avait abrité sous son ombre frêle la plus grande douleur, la seule défaillance du Christ" (II, 1190). The symbolism is prophetic. Like Christ, the priest dies for the sins of others. That his death is a suicide could perhaps be seen as a not-so-subtle commentary on Christ's refusal to save Himself, and, given Maupassant's other playful distortions of Scripture (**"Le Père Judas," "Nos Anglais,"** etc.), a reading of this story as parody would certainly not be unwarranted. The fact remains, however, that from the perspective of the increasingly polarized male-female relationships, the priest's suffering at the hands of a woman typifies that of later heroes and cannot be discounted. Significantly, the cleric's coarse young son begins to resemble his *mother* as he boasts of past crimes:

> C'était à sa mère que l'enfant, à présent, ressemblait le plus, non par les traits du visage, mais par le regard captivant et faux et surtout par la séduction du sourire menteur qui semblait ouvrir la porte de la bouche à toutes les infamies du dedans. (II, 1196)

The resemblance has a metaphorical dimension: the young hoodlum is a messenger from his mother, who, having died three years previously, continues to torment her former lover from beyond the grave. Her sadistic cruelty has thus been immortalized.

If from very early in Maupassant's literary production his heroines have identified themselves with the Divinity, the identification is largely facilitated thanks to the precious "relics" provided by the lovers themselves in the form of love letters: "Ces petits papiers qui portent notre nom et nous caressent avec de douces choses, sont des reliques, et nous adorons les chapelles, nous autres, surtout les chapelles dont nous sommes les saintes" (II, 1030). The self-love of such heroines is innocent enough and does not necessarily exclude the capacity to love others. However, a progression through time reveals an increasing number of frigid heroines whose absolute egotism entails a growing inability to love others and hence a widening disjunction from the male. The continuing identification of such women with the Divine seems at first blush incompatible with their changing role. Quite the opposite is true, and an examination of the epithets attributed to God Himself from the early works to the last illustrates that the metamorphosis undergone by the fictional women is in fact closely paralleled by the striking changes wrought

in Maupassant's view of the Creator. As Author of the Universe, Maupassant's God had been associated with nature and biological reproduction—and hence with women—right from the beginning. However, whereas in the very early work He is merely accused of having been "trop . . . trop naturaliste" (**"Le Verrou,"** I, 491) in inventing the reproductive act, it is not long before the image of a deliberately malicious Divinity comes to the fore. In **"Les Caresses"** (August 14, 1883) a young woman, revolted by her suitor's demands, speculates that God, in whom she believes, was consciously malevolent when He fashioned the "sense" which in her eyes are "ignobles, sales, révoltants, brutaux . . . mêlés aux ordures du corps," a mockery of love, "la plus douce chose qui soit au monde" (I, 952). The lover, who responds with an impassioned plea for artificiality and excess, is a typical product of the Decadent sensibility, which, as we noted earlier, saw "refinements" on the *acte génésique* as a vehicle for outsmarting Nature.

In a somewhat different vein, the sadistic magistrate in **"Un Fou"** (1885) engages in an implicit rivalry with God by destroying His creatures. Yes, he reasons, killing must be "une volupté, la plus grande de toutes peut-être; car tuer n'est-il pas ce qui ressemble le plus à créer?" (II, 540). As representative of the Law, "Etat civil, glorieuse Divinité" (II, 543) who judges men and condemns the guilty to death, the venerable magistrate is an avatar of God right from the start. His hidden identity as pathological killer who derives intense excitement from his murders can thus be interpreted as the other side of the Divinity.

A year later the Divine Being comes under explicit attack when the madman of **"Un Cas de Divorce"** rails against the monotony of the created universe: "Comme tout est triste et laid, toujours pareil, toujours odieux. . . . Comme elle serait pauvre l'imagination de leur Dieu, si leur Dieu existait ou s'il n'avait pas créé d'autres choses, ailleurs" (II, 778). His cerebral lechery permitting him to escape from the *dégoût* of the human condition, the diarist-narrator no longer needs woman, whom he sees as an instrument of nature.

The diatribes against the Creator attain the status of "respectability" early in 1887 (**"Madame Hermet"**), when a doctor, recounting the tale of a female mental patient's obsession, reasons that it was her horror of aging that brought about her "crise," in which she abdicated maternal responsibility and refused to visit her dying son for fear of contracting the smallpox that was killing him. In the physician-narrator's view, God, "l'Inflexible Inconnu" (II, 878), is a sadistic "lender," lending youth in order to make old age more painful, lending beauty only to snatch it quickly back. The notion of a cruel God only sketched here is more completely fleshed out in **"Moiron"** (September 1887), but once again the distance established between narrator and reader by virtue of the former's insanity should not be overlooked. In a deathbed confession to the judge who spared his life many years previously, the schoolmaster Moiron avows that he had indeed poisoned several of his pupils in an attempt to get revenge upon God, who had allowed his three children to fall ill and die. This tragedy had enlightened Moiron as to the "true" nature of the Divine as spectator of a macabre comedy for which he is responsible:

> "Pourquoi avait-il tué mes enfants? J'ouvris les yeux, et je vis qu'il aime tuer. . . . Dieu, monsieur, est un massacreur. Il lui faut tous les jours des morts. Il en fait de toutes les façons pour mieux s'amuser. Il a inventé les maladies, les accidents . . . et puis, quand il s'ennuie, il a les épidémies, la peste, le choléra . . ." (II, 989)

Reminiscent of the Old Testament Moloch (the loathsome god to whom the Ammonites sacrificed their children), this diabolical Divinity (Moiron refers to him as a reptile) is in fact mirrored in Moiron himself. Indeed, the troubled schoolmaster admits to having engaged in a rivalry with the Divine: "j'en ai tué aussi, des enfants. Je lui a joué le tour. Ce n'est pas lui qui les a eus, ceux-là!" (II, 989). If the philosophical content of Moiron's invective is somewhat undermined by his naïve and perverse reaction to his own misfortune, the story nonetheless serves as a provocative introduction to the God-as-Sadist motif, which, after a three-year hiatus, finds eloquent expression in the mouths of two narrators somewhat more credible than Moiron, Roger de Salins of **"L'Inutile Beauté"** and Dr. Paturel of the unfinished novel, *Angélus.*

For Salins, God, "créateur économe" (II, 1216) who made each sense organ serve two purposes, was deliberately perverse in his creation of man's sexuality, entrusting the sacred mission of reproduction to organs that are "malpropres et souillés" (II, 1216). A cynic of the highest order, Salins's God tried to prevent man from idealizing his sexual encounter with woman. But man, undaunted, invented love. Echoing the sentiments of an earlier hero, Henri, the *épistolier* of **"Les Caresses"** (1883), Salins sings the praises of vice, asserting that refined debauchery is the best means of turning the tables on the Divinity. In Paul Brétigny's tradition, Salins looks upon procreation as bestial and the pregnant woman as ugly. God, an ignorant Creator, is pictured as a gigantic phallus: "Sais-tu comment je conçois Dieu . . . comme un monstrueux organe créateur inconnu de nous, qui sème par l'espace des milliards de mondes, ainsi qu'un poisson unique pondrait des Œufs dans la mèr" (II, 1217). The reduction of God to the bestial implicit in this (comic?) passage, the view of an androgynous Creator taking a peculiar, onanistic pleasure in solitary reproduction, appears to be a departure from the theme of a sadistic Deity. Here God is not held responsible for His creation: "stupidement

prolifique," He is ignorant of the consequences of His activities. Human intelligence is an accident of nature unforeseen by the Divinity, whose created universe, "cet inconfortable petit parc à bestioles, ce champ à salades, ce potager sylvestre" (II, 1218), is clearly not intended for Man, who has risen above the caveman status God intended. Although Salins makes no mention of the Bible, the reader familiar with the New Testament will not fail to draw a parallel between this passage and the Sermon on the Mount, in which man is told to forget his concerns for a terrestrial future:

> Behold the fowls of the air: for they sow not, neither do they reap, nor gather into barns; yet your heavenly Father feedeth them. Are ye not much better than they? . . . And why take ye thought for raiment? Consider the lilies of the field, how they grow; they toil not, neither do they spin. And yet I say unto you, that even Solomon in all his glory was not arrayed like one of these. (Matthew 6: 26, 28-29)

In Salins's view God provided for lesser creation only; man was obliged to work, to invent, to use his talent and ingenuity in order to make livable "ce sol de racines et de pierres" (II, 1219). It is thus man, not God, who is the true creator, who has idealized and poeticized the world, and Salins's panegyric on artifice has a distinctly Baudelairean ring to it. It is fitting that Salins's extemporization should take place within the confines of the Opera during an intermission of "Robert le diable." Salins, with an air of great theatricality, seems to be playing the devil's advocate and enjoying every moment of it. It is hardly coincidental, moreover, that his name is associated with sin through the story of Sodom and Gomorrha, in which Lot's wife was changed into a pillar of salt. Salins's friend Grandin, accustomed to "les surprises éclatantes de sa fantaisie" (II, 1218), is entertained by his ideas; and his somewhat amused condescension is amply justified by the parlor-talk style of Salins's remarks, full of flourishes, redundancies and contradictions (at one point Salins refers to biological reproduction as "cet abominable loi," II, 1216, at another as "la plus noble et la plus exaltante des fonctions humaines").

One is not surprised to learn that the entire scene, which forms Part III of **"L'Inutile Beauté,"** has often been regarded as a gratuitous digression, a major flaw in the story.[11] However, this judgment seems seriously out of step with Maupassant's own evaluation: "**L'Inutile Beauté** est la nouvelle la plus rare que j'aie jamais faite. Ce n'est qu'un symbole" (quoted by Forestier, II, 1709). Although Maupassant's remark may strike the reader as a trifle too self-indulgent, the judgment of the critics seems equally misguided, based upon only a superficial reading of the story. Viewed from the perspective of woman's role in the later work, Part III of this four-part story no longer seems merely a heavy-handed attempt at philosophical enrichment, but rather an integral part of the whole story. Salins, who begins and ends his diatribe with an allusion to the beauty of the countess de Mascaret, the story's heroine, expresses his anti-God, anti-Nature principles with a vocabulary very similar to hers. Grandin, on the other hand, is more fatalistic ("Que veux-tu? c'est la nature," p. 1216) and is to be identified rather with the comte de Mascaret, "un homme d'instinct, un homme d'autrefois" (p. 1221). Through her revenge upon her possessive husband (after bearing for him seven children in eleven years, she tells him that one of her children is not his, a lie that drives him from her bed for six years and causes him great mental anguish), the countess is identified as an enemy of Creation, she who had once been its victim. Now deliberately and obstinately non-productive, she is at the center of what Albert-marie Schmidt terms "une litanie de la femme stérile" (p. 70). Moreover, the sacrilege she commits when she perversely and consciously takes God as witness to her falsehood (in the church of St. Philippe du *Roule!*) is proof positive that the countess is a new breed in Maupassant's fiction. As such, she becomes the *porte-parole* of her sex, expressing with regard to the procreative role a disgust that had previously been the prerogative of the male: "Je suis, nous sommes des femmes du monde civilisé. . . . Nous ne sommes plus et nous refusons d'être de simples femelles qui repeuplent la terre" (II, 1223). Despite this attitude, her maternal sentiments are strong and durable; she is a rare creature who "réalise le phénomène de la famille dans le monde" (II, 1225). Indeed, Gabrielle de Mascaret, whose first name, not coincidentally, evokes the archangel Gabriel, divine messenger, is herself a phenomenon. Her loveliness is indestructible: time has not aged her (at 36, she appears 25). Her repeated pregnancies have not deformed her: she is described as "svelte" (II, 1205). Her emotional tribulations have not left their mark, and her "éclatante beauté" and ivory complexion give her "un air de statue" (II, 1215). It takes no great insight to realize that this heavenly creature whose tiara glistens in her dark hair, its diamonds "pareils à une voie lactée" (II, 1223), has replaced the King of Kings, rising to the realm of the Ideal just as surely as Salins's wisdom has dethroned the traditional God, equating Him with blind instinct. The celestial imagery (her gray eyes are "des ciels froids," her hair "cette nuit opaque," II, 1223) brings to mind Diana, the moon goddess, symbol of purity, a fitting emblem of the chaste mother represented by Gabrielle de Mascaret, untouchable, immortal *femme angélique.* Her husband's almost spiritual "conversion," his sudden recognition in his wife of a mystical being, the mysterious product of human desire, would have been quite impossible fifteen years earlier. One notes with some irony that Dr. Heraclius Gloss, who thought for a moment that he had found philosophical truth in a woman's beauty, was sorely mocked by his friend the rector: "Ce pauvre docteur! si la vérité lui apparaît

comme la femme aimée, il sera bien l'homme le plus trompé que la terre ait jamais porté" (I, 15). The count and countess de Mascaret, whose cosmic roles are implicit in their family name (meaning tidal wave), have indeed changed the face of Maupassant's fictional universe. Woman, free from phallocracy, rises to new heights of power in this story, and she does it without sacrificing either her femininity or her maternity. The final image with which the reader is left is that of a beautiful woman who, after having been victimized by her father (for he arranged her marriage) and her jealous husband, has thrown off the chains of her slavery, has become a self-determining being, an *inutile beauté* who refuses to remain an instrument of nature. An esthetic object (whence her likeness to a statue), she exists only to be admired, pure icon, cold, unfeeling. Mascaret himself, a revised and updated Pygmalion, no longer prays that life be breathed into the woman he loves. Truly representative of the spirit of the late 19th century, he accepts her as *objet d'art,* seeming to prefer, like Baudelaire, the Goncourts and his fictional elder Des Esseintes, "l'artifice de l'homme à la production du Créateur."[12]

This characteristic is to be found again, even more dominant, in the countess de Brémontal, the last of Maupassant's ideal women. Because *L'Angélus* (the novel of which she was to be the heroine) remained unfinished, it is quite impossible to draw any definitive conclusion relative to her role. What we know is this: she was to have been a "demi-fervente" ([*Œuvres posthurnes* (*OP II*)], 217) who, although not "ardemment croyante" (*OP II,* 215) and never dominated by religious laws and practices, was moved by "la si touchante légende chrétienne" (*OP II,* 217). Like the countess de Mascaret, she was unafraid of confrontation with those "higher authorities" who were in a position to brutalize her (in this case the Prussians); like her, she was extremely attractive; like her, she was a mother, and her all-engulfing maternal love left no room for the passions of the flesh. For her husband she felt only a fondness: "Germaine . . . l'aimait bien, sans grande passion, mais en compagne fidèle et dévouée, bien plus mère que femme . . ." (*OP II,* 217). Her quiet affection for her husband stands in sharp contrast to the intensity of her maternal passion, "cet amour qui est le seul indestructible, qui n'a point d'égal et de rival" (*OP II,* 201). Taking her small son into her arms one winter night, she kisses him on the top of his head, on his eyelids, on his mouth, trembling all the while "de cette joie délicieuse dont tressaillent les fibres des vraies mères" (*OP II,* 201). This countess does not become a symbol of human triumph over Divine will, as had the countess de Mascaret; however, she is hardly an "ordinary" woman, and the imagery indicates clearly that she is to be identified with the Virgin Mother, to whom she prays for a daughter. The child to whom she does give birth, a son, is crippled for life by damages incurred *in utero* when his mother was struck by the Prussian soldiers. Clearly a Christ-figure, born in a stable as church bells were pealing in the distance, the child is destined to suffer the pain of rejection, his infirmity rendering sexual normality impossible. Even his mother's love is insufficient to compensate for this sad fate: "partout, et toujours, il devait voir passer devant ses yeux, jusqu'au jour où il les fermait à la lumière, ce fantôme charmant dont il n'approcherait jamais, jamais . . . une jeune fille" (*OP II,* 235). This contemporization of Christ's Passion is indeed remarkable. Moreover, the remaining fragments of this unfinished work contain passages about both Christ and God the Father that suggest once again a profound sympathy for the Son of God and an ever-growing hatred of God Himself, sentiments that are echoed throughout the literature of the period (cf. Sagnes, pp. 423-74). Maupassant's personal tragedy—the absence of his father during his formative years and his feeling of disdain for this irresponsible womanizer—bears mentioning here as well. From the image of Father as phallus who has badly provided for His creatures and has condemned them to a destructive sexuality (*IB*) to this pathetic portrait of a child whose deformity can be attributed to the Absent Father, the work is obviously nourished as much by life as by literary tradition.

In *L'Angélus* it is a priest, l'abbé Marvaux, who reflects upon the role of Christ. As opposed to earlier representatives of the clergy, who are often portrayed as fanatical, Marvaux is clearly a credible, respectable character whose ideas are not to be dismissed lightly. He is cast in the same mold as Father Vilbois (**"Champ d'Oliviers"**): vigorous, courageous, intelligent, he took Holy Orders not as a virginal young lad, but as a man who had come to know life and who sought refuge from its sorrows. Decorated for heroism in one of Napoleon III's wars, he had married, then fathered a daughter. But the child had died, as had his wife, of typhoid fever. The reader is led to believe that it was this double tragedy that drove him into religious exile. Content to remain a country cleric, unwilling to compromise his integrity in order to rise in the hierarchy of the Church, he is known for "l'indépendance de son caractère, la hardiesse de sa parole" (*OP II,* 206). For him *God* is an empty word, incomprehensible to the mind of man, which can attain knowledge only through the senses. Christ, on the other hand, tangible and visible, is the true God. In response to the young Dr. Paturel's diatribe against a God who appears to condone suffering, the priest speculates that Christ, too, may have been deceived by God, as men are:

> Oui . . . le Christ doit être aussi une victime de Dieu. Il en a reçu une fausse mission, celle de nous illusionner par une nouvelle religion. Mais le divine Envoyé l'a accomplie si belle, cette mission, si magnifique, si dévouée, si douloureuse,

si inimaginablement grande et attendrissante, qu'il a pris pour nous la place de son Inspirateur. (*OP II,* 229-30)

The priest expresses his compassion for Christ's suffering and speaks movingly of Him as a personal God whom he loves "de tout mon cœur d'homme et de toute mon âme de prêtre" (*OP II,* 229). His insistence upon the crucified Christ, Christ as symbol of a suffering humanity, betrayed by an impersonal God, clearly owes something to the Jean-Paul tradition.[13] But it is also important in the context of Maupassant's work, for it is his last word on the subject. The priest is silenced by a sigh from the handicapped child at his side. It is the countess's second son, who has been moved to tears by the priest's words. The latter turns to the boy:

> Pauvre petit, toi aussi tu as reçu de l'impitoyable destinée un triste sort. Mais tu auras au moins, je crois, en compensation de toutes les joies physiques, les seules belles choses qui soient permises aux hommes, le rêve, l'intelligence et la pensée. (*OP II,* 230)

This *mise en valeur* of the joys of the mind to the detriment of sensual pleasures is consistent with the mounting wave of nausea with which sexual intercourse is regarded and an increasingly violent rebellion against the Creator who endowed His creatures with physical needs not for their pleasure, but for His own ends. In the last lines that he was to write before insanity struck, Maupassant again returned to Sade's philosophy of a cruel God, using another character, the young Dr. Paturel, to renew Moiron's fulminations against God, "destructeur infatigable" (*OP II,* 232). Sadistic spectator, God is "embusqué dans l'Espace" (*OP II,* 232), from where he gleefully satisfies his insatiable need for death and destruction. Only the animals, happily copulating with no sense of their mortality, are unaware of His ferocity. The passage ends with an unfinished sentence which alludes, like a haunting refrain, to the reproductive instinct that dictates the behavior of horses, goats, pigeons and nightingales.[14] The obsessive identification of sexuality as the instrument of divine malice thus persists to the very end.

How does the woman of the final works fit into the scheme of things? We have already seen that there is a distance established between heroes and heroines, an idealization of the woman who, having acceded to the sacred station of motherhood, becomes suddenly resentful of her biological destiny. Her refusal to serve out her sexual term has two results: on the one hand, it makes her inaccessible to the male, transferring her to the realm of the ideal (*IB*); on the other, it transforms her from a seductive mistress into a tender mother, that most beloved of all women

in Maupassant's fiction. Yet even in this most benevolent of roles she is as powerless to protect her
child from suffering as was the Mother of Christ.

The heroes, for their part, find little relief from their
pain, and the frequency with which we find allusion to
the Crucified Christ in the last works suggests that the
roles of hero-victim and suffering Christ were becoming increasingly assimilated. If André, the handicapped
child of *L'Angélus,* was martyred by his solitude and
his forced celibacy, his namesake André Mariolle of
Notre Cœur suffered a similar fate through an emotional (rather than a physical) handicap. So, too, did
Olivier Bertin of *Fort comme la mort.* In these cases,
as in many others, it is ultimately because of their
desperate need for women that the men of the later
works become sacrificial victims.

Conversely, the female of the final works who has
not been redeemed by motherhood is identified with
a sadistic divinity. Indifferent to sexual needs, she is
free to exploit her beauty for her own egotistical
purposes, and in so doing she robs the male of his
selfhood, victimizes him, crucifies him. Michèle de
Burne [*Notre Cœur* (*NC*)] provides a perfect example of this type of woman. Mariolle's love for her
is a perpetual martyrdom in which she takes a visible pleasure: "Elle l'avait cloué sur une croix; il y
saignait de tous ses membres, et elle le regardait
agoniser sans comprendre sa souffrance, contente
même d'avoir fait ça" (*NC,* 202). Mariolle, an unwilling Christ, is determined to wrench himself from
this cross, even if it means leaving upon it "des
morceaux de son corps, des lambeaux de sa chair et
tout son cœur déchiqueté" (*NC,* 202). Fragmented
and mutilated by this cruel mistress, Mariolle is the
archetypal victim of the last works, bearing the cross
of an unrequited love. Michèle de Burne, a frigid
mistress who is more drawn to women than to men,
is representative of a large group of later heroines in
whom sexual appetite is absent, who find pleasure
only in the company of members of their own sex.[15]
Despite her indifference to sexual love, however,
this society woman needs a man, needs his adoring
words, his presence, his loving looks, "comme une
idole, pour devenir vrai dieu, a besoin de prière et
de foi" (p. 167). By the same token, one worshipper
is hardly sufficient, and her divinity depends upon
her ability to attract many "believers" to her sanctuary: "Elle était bien cette sorte de déesse humaine,
délicate, dédaigneuse, exigeante et hautaine, que le
culte amoureux des mâles enorgueillit et divinise
comme un encens" (*NC,* 168). Mariolle is tormented
by Michèle's insatiable greed for male admirers, but
even more than this he is tortured by her inability to
love. A feminine Narcissus, she encloses herself daily
in a three-paneled mirror, surrounding herself with a
triple image of her own beauty. Childless, coquette,
an egotistical hunter for whom "love" is nothing more

than the sport of conquest, she pursues prospective
lovers "comme le chasseur poursuit le gibier, rien
que pour les voir tomber" (pp. 39-40). Like the God
of the last works, she is a spectator of the destruction
that she herself has wrought, and she gloats over each
new triumph: "Cela l'amusait tant de les sentir envahis
peu à peu, conquis, dominés par sa puissance invincible de femme, de devenir pour eux l'Unique, l'Idole
capricieuse et souveraine" (p. 39). As was the case
with the countess de Mascaret, Michèle de Burne had
suffered at the hands of her husband. Delivered from
her slavery by his sudden death, she seems determined to get revenge on all males. If her "fidèles," who
had slowly formed "une sorte de petite église . . . [dont]
elle . . . était la madone" (p. 12), were her victims, it
was precisely because of their devotion to her, a devotion which in its most extreme form kills artistic creativity. She scorns men who are unwilling to spend all their
energy upon winning her love (e.g., the sculptor Prédolé)
and demands total sacrifice, total submission of will.
Celebrated in Mariolle's love letters, she becomes the
unique object of his cult, an esthetic object replacing all
others, possessing him completely. Although somewhat
of a dilettante, Mariolle had achieved a measure of
recognition for his musical abilities and for a sculpture
entitled "Masseur tunisien" before meeting Madame
de Burne. Rather than help him to develop his talents,
Michèle de Burne had robbed him of what little inclination he had previously displayed toward the fine arts:
"Elle a tout remplacé pour moi, car je n'aspire plus à
rien, je n'ai plus besoin, envie ni souci de rien" (*NC,*
237). A jealous deity, Michèle de Burne tolerates no
departure from the "straight and narrow" path that
leads to her. Whereas Any and Annette and many
women before them (*Fort*) had inspired Bertin to
great artistic achievement and had in fact been the
source of his success as a portraitist, Michèle de
Burne is more demon than muse,[16] and the venom-
ous descriptions of *la mondaine* that spill from the
pen of the fictional novelist Gaston de Lamarthe are
offered to the world as a revenge against this cold
socialite and her ilk. In the badly smitten Mariolle
she inspires no more than florid love letters intended
for her eyes only; another hopelessly entangled admirer, the musician Massival, "avait subi cette espèce
d'arrêt qui semble frapper la plupart des artistes
contemporains comme une paralysie précoce" (*NC,*
19). Although it is true that the love-trap into which
Bertin falls eventually results in an artistic sterility,
such a fate is not *willed* by his mistress. With Michèle
de Burne, on the other hand, Maupassant has realized a new feminine type, the deliberately destructive, sadistic goddess who is associated not with the
procreative laws of a fertile universe, but with sterility, both biological and artistic. The resigned submission of her lover is that of a worshipper before
his god: "Il lui dit lentement, avec des mots presque
solennels, qu'il lui avait donné sa vie pour toujours,
afin qu'elle en fît ce qu'il lui plairait" (*NC,* 118).

Mariolle's idolatry—his solemn sacrifice of self to a woman—and the resultant disintegration of his personality point to the nefarious role played by the *femme du monde* in the later work. Although the religious terms used to describe the love relationship suggest the divinization of a profane love, the very fact that the affair is destructive and the mistress diabolical (she is explicitly likened to her friend, the baronne de Frémires, a young woman "inventée et créée par le diable lui-même pour la damnation des grands enfants à barbe," p. 132) hints at an evolution in Maupassant's heroine which parallels that of Maupassant's God.

The characterization of God as a force of evil that we find in the last few years of Maupassant's creative life is founded upon a pessimistic view of the world as inferno, "bagne pour les âmes tourmentées de savoir, et pour les corps en mauvaise santé" (***L'Angélus, OP II,*** 230). The image is apt: man is imprisoned in the world (just as, in a Manichean sense, the soul is imprisoned in the body), suffering both morally and physically and in so doing providing pleasure and entertainment for a sadistic Keeper. Whether transcoded in the hunting idiom or that of war, the theme of cruelty had been treated with an unrelieved pessimism from the earliest stories on. However, whereas in the pre-1889 work the tormentors are numerous and varied—ranging from the Prussian officer (**"Mademoiselle Fifi," "Deux Amis"**), the vengeful farm boy (**"Coco"**) and the vulgar pillagers (**"L'Ane"**) to the dignified judge (**"Un Fou"**), the newspaper columnist (***B-A***) and the doctor [***Pierre et Jean (P et J)***]—the writings of the last few years offer evidence of a convergence of all these various types into two quintessential sadists: God and Woman. Not surprisingly, when searching for metaphors to characterize their destructive powers, Maupassant digs into his storehouse of fictional sadists from which he draws such images as a God "embusqué dans l'espace" (***L'Angélus, OP II,*** 232) or a *femme-amazone:* "comme un pays dont on s'empare, elle accapara sa vie peu à peu par une succession de petits envahissements plus nombreux chaque jour" (***NC,*** 66). With Any de Guilleroy the domination had been represented as a solid chain ("elle en refaisait les anneaux à mesure qu'ils s'usaient," ***Fort,*** 61). In either case, what is important is the characteristic joy the women feel at the spectacle of their lovers' suffering. If Any is not fully aware of her true emotions (she is "engourdie dans un chagrin cruel de le voir souffrir, et ce chagrin était presque du bonheur," ***Fort,*** 40), Michèle de Burne is fully cognizant of the pain she is inflicting upon her lover, and she savors her victory "comme est heureux un épervier dont le vol s'abat sur une proie fascinée" (***NC,*** 290).

Instruments of man's damnation, such women bear no resemblance to the young woman of **"Le Mariage du lieutenant Lauré"** (1878) who delivers a troop of French soldiers from certain death. Moreover, the fact that the variants of this early story (**"Souvenir,"** 1882, and **"Les Idées du colonel,"** 1884) became progressively more satirical testifies to a breakdown in this optimistic image of the feminine role. I do not wish to suggest that *la femme inspiratrice* was a major theme in the early work or that all late heroines are *femmes fatales.* One must beware of oversimplification in the complex labyrinth of Maupassant's creative universe: the cruel women have antecedents going right back to 1880; similarly, one can find a current of angelism right through to the end. The paradox is only apparent: "angels"—when they are not represented as *la femme rêvée,* either imagined (**"A vendre," "Un Portrait"**) or met only fleetingly (**"La Mère Sauvage," "Rencontre"**), but never possessed—are for the most part those heroines who have been "purified" by maternity (and not infrequently by suffering as well) and who have shed their sexuality like a second skin.[17] They extend from Jeanne de Lamare through Christiane Andermatt to the countess de Brémontal—without forgetting that complex and problematical heroine, Gabrielle de Mascaret, who appears to bridge to gap between these Untouchable Madonnas and the Unfeeling Idols.

Of this latter group, a phenomenon of the later work only, Michèle de Burne is the archetype. Unnatural, ignorant of both sexual and maternal instincts, such a woman exists only to be admired; many are the men who are sacrificed upon the altar of her egotism. Satan incarnate, she coils around her victims, ensnaring them with the caress, "lien redoutable, le plus fort de tous, le seul dont on ne se délivre jamais quand il a bien enlacé et quand il serre jusqu'au sang la chair d'un homme" (***NC,*** 127-28). Yet, although her victims are absorbed, mutilated, in short, destroyed by her, she remains impassive, uninvolved, "incapable . . . d'amour" (***NC,*** 143-44).

As monstrous an aberration as she is, however, the society woman is not alone in Maupassant's gallery of satanic women. There is another group, alluded to earlier, which is equally well represented. This group consists of the cruel mothers, women who, unwilling to forgo personal aspirations for the good of their offspring, continue to seek the love and adulation of men. From the "innocent" perfidy of Madame Roland (***P et J***) and the compulsive behavior of Madame Hermet to the cold-blooded torture inflicted upon her unborn babies by "la mère aux monstres" (who is known in her village as "la diable"), mothers who violate the sanctity of the maternal bond are condemned as unnatural. Once again it is a *mondaine* who serves as supreme target for the author's wrath, who represents the truly satanic mother. The ignorant peasant woman of **"La Mère aux monstres,"** "demi-brute et demi-femme" (I, 843) who stumbled upon a sordid recipe for producing deformed children and who continues to do so at will for her own financial gain (she sells them to side-show promoters), is evil, to be sure; but it is precisely because she is so grotesque and animalistic that she does not represent the insidious threat of a real she-devil. The elegant *mondaine* described in the story's epilogue, on the other hand, slim, attractive, surrounded by admiring men, is equally contemptible and far more dangerous. Just a few yards away from where she is holding court on a popular beach, the narrator's eyes come to rest upon her children, deformed, crippled, "les résultats des tailles restées fines jusqu'au dernier jour" (I, 847). Vanity, both the root of all evil and the source of untold suffering [*Fort comme la mort* (*Fort*)], is the most characteristic vice insofar as Maupassant's *femmes fatales* are concerned.

Even if one excluded such "transitory" she-devils as the blacksmith's wife of **"Conte de Noël"** (who is devil-possessed) and La Rapet of **"Le Diable"** (who disguises herself as Satan), excluding also the innumerable heroines who exercise a "pouvoir fatal et souverain" (**"La Femme de Paul,"** I, 299) over the male through the seduction of their accursed flesh, it is clear that there is an ever-growing tendency to identify women as inherently evil, "ces êtres dangereux et perfides qui ont pour mission d'entraîner les hommes en des abîmes inconnus" (**"L'Inconnue,"** II, 447). Treated ironically in the early work (*Une Vie*, **"Clair de Iune,"** **"Une Surprise"**) as the warped idea of celibate priests, the notion of woman's infernal mission is no laughing matter after 1885. We have seen that, like madness and death, women are represented as parasitic creatures, feeding upon their unwilling host-victims in what now seems a cruel perversion of Holy Communion. The Sadian mockery of Christ as a "juif lépreux . . . né d'une catin et d'un soldat"[18] is conspicuously absent from Maupassant's vision;[19] and if, like Sade, he repeatedly vilified and derided the Creator, nowhere after 1885 does his satire seem to be directed against the Son of God. The fact that in his madness he was said to have claimed to be Christ[20] lends more weight to the hypothesis of a profound sympathy for the crucified Christ in the last works; and Cogny's statement regarding Maupassant's attitude vis-à-vis believers ("s'ils sont sincères, ce sont des sots et s'ils ne le sont pas, des canailles," *Maupassant*, 49) does not seem altogether justified in view of such late heroes as l'abbé Vilbois and l'abbé Marvaux (not to mention l'abbé Mauduit, the priest of **"Après,"** who is treated with sensitivity and compassion).[21]

If the suffering heroes of the final works are portrayed as modern Christs, if the callous, degrading heroines are Wickedness Incarnate, it seems only natural that the relationship between the two would be represented as a variation upon the struggle between Good and Evil or that the Feminine Power of Darkness should be identified with the infernal fires of her kingdom, Hades. . . .

Notes

[1] See [Mario Praz, *The Romantic Agony,* trans. Angus Davidson (London: Oxford Univ. Press, 1933)] for a faithful chronicle of the forms taken by this pathological interest.

[2] For a sensitive treatment of this story see E. D. Sullivan, *Maupassant: The Short Stories* (Great Neck, N.Y.: Barron's Educational Series, 1962), 23-25.

[3] His misinterpretation of Scripture is blatant: he sees in Christ's statement to his mother, made at the wedding feast of Cana—"Femme, qu'y a-t-il de commun entre vous et moi?" (John 2: 4)—evidence of God's dissatisfaction with this creature. Biblical commentaries, while conceding that Christ's remark represents a gentle rebuke, generally interpret it to mean that not even his mother should presume to control his course of action now that his ministry has started. See J. R. Dummelow, ed., *A Commentary on the Holy Bible* (London: Macmillan, 1952).

[4] Edmond and Jules de Goncourt, *Journal, mémoires de la vie littéraire, 1851-1896* (Paris: Fasquelle-Flammarion, 1956), I, 400.

[5] On the relationship between the two *maisons* see Michel Crouzet, "Une Rhétorique de Maupassant?" *Revue d'Histoire Littéraire de la France,* 80 (1980), 233-61.

[6] André Vial regards "Le Saut du berger" as "un tirage anticipé" of *Une Vie,* "conçu à des fins strictement alimentaires" (p. 487).

[7] The term *narrataire,* coined by Gerald Prince, "Introduction à l'étude du narrataire," *Poétique,* 14 (1973), 178-96, refers to the fictional receiver (explicit or implicit) of the narrative message.

[8] See [Louis Forestier, ed. *Contes et nouvelles,* by Guy de Maupassant, Bibliothèque de la Pléiade, 2 vols. (Paris: Gallimard, 1974-1979)] I, 1434, and Vial, 435-507.

[9] In Maupassant's peculiar Christology we find no mention of the Resurrection; and the emphasis, particularly in the later work, is clearly upon the Christ of Gethsemane. Such a restricted view distinguishes Maupassant from writers of the Romantic period, for whom, as Frank Paul Bowman reports in *Le Christ Romantique* (Geneva: Droz, 1973), Christ was often an image of revolutionary fervor, particularly in 1848. Some saw Woman as a Christ: "Tout comme la France, la femme a connu son Calvaire et va maintenant descendre de sa croix et ressusciter à la liberté" (Bowman, 106).

[10] I use this slippery term (in its generally accepted sense) as a convenience only and not without some

hesitation—cf. Robert L. Mitchell's caveats in "The Deliquescence of Decadence: Floupette's Eclectic Target," *Nineteenth-Century French Studies,* 9 (1981), 247-56.

[11] Cf. André Vial, 434: "Toute une partie, la troisième, n'est que dissertation abstraite: à ce morceau de bravoure, le prétexte de lieu et de temps confère une justification illusoire,—et une situation privilégiée, dans un enchâssement d'épisodes, un relief démesuré."

[12] Guy Sagnes, *L'Ennui dans la littérature française de Flaubert à Laforgue (1848-1884)* (Paris: Colin, 1969), 332. See also Villiers de I'Isle-Adam, *L'Eve future.*

[13] The German novelist Jean-Paul Richter was known in France largely through faulty and incomplete translations. A single part of his novel *Siebenkas,* "Le Discours du Christ mort," in which Christ proclaims the death of God, given undue prominence in France, served as inspiration (directly or indirectly) for two generations of French writers. In fact, as Claude Pichois amply demonstrates in his *L'Image de Jean-Paul Richter dans les lettres françaises* (Paris: Corti, 1963), the passage in question was most unrepresentative of Richter's thought.

[14] "Le cheval qui bondit au soleil dans une prairie, la chèvre qui grimpe sur les roches de son allure légère et souple, suivie du bouc qui la poursuit, les pigeons qui recoulent sur les toits, les colombes le bec dans le bec sous la verdure des arbres, pareils à des amants qui se disent leur tendresse, et le rossignol qui chante au clair de lune auprès de sa femelle qui couve ne savent pas l'éternel massacre de ce Dieu qui les a créés. Le mouton qui . . ." (op. 11 [*Œuvres posthumes*] 232).

[15] Also representative are the Baronne de Grangerie and the Marquise de Rennedon, heroines of "La Confidence" (August 1885), "Sauvée" (December 1885) and "Le Signe" (April 1886).

[16] My view is thus diametrically opposed to that of Chantal Jennings in "La Dualité de Maupassant: son attitude envers la femme," *Revue des Sciences Humaines,* 35 (1970), 565, who sees in Michèle de Burne "l'inspiratrice de l'artiste, une sorte de muse du poète."

[17] A detailed analysis of those stories in which *la femme rêvée* is evoked would surely prove revealing from a psychoanalytical viewpoint, for nearly all bear witness either on the surface level or symbolically to a preoccupation with maternity.

[18] D. A. F. Sade, *Justine ou les malheurs de la vertu,* in *Œuvres complètes,* II (Paris: Jean-Jacques Pauvert, 1955), 89.

[19] This is not to deny the existence in the early work of veiled allusions to the strange circumstances of Christ's birth (cf. "Nuit de Noël," which features a burlesque "Nativity").

[20] Lanoux (p. 405) reports that on January 14, 1893, Maupassant announced, "Dieu a proclamé du haut de la Tour Eiffel . . . que Monsieur de Maupassant est le fils de Dieu et de Jésus-Christ!" Some time later he offered the following variant, the Oedipal implications of which are plain: "Jésus-Christ a couché avec ma mère. Je suis le fils de Dieu."

[21] The work, although undated, is similar enough in perspective and subject to suggest that it was written near the end of the ten-year period that marked Maupassant's literary life. In this regard see Antonio Fratangelo, *Guy de Maupassant, scrittore moderno* (Florence: Olschki, 1976), 108. See also Forestier's remark (II, 1719) regarding the desacralization of the priest.

Select Bibliography

1. Maupassant's Works

Contes et nouvelles. Ed. Louis Forestier. Bibliothèque de la Pléiade. 2 vols. Paris: Gallimard, 1974-1979.

Œuvres complètes de Guy de Maupassant. 29 vols. Paris: Conard, 1907-1910.

2. Critical Works on Maupassant

. . . . .

Artinian, Robert. "Chacun son égout: A Metaphoric Structure in *Bel-Ami.*"

Nassau Review (Nassau, N.Y., Community College), 2 (1973), 15-20. . . .

Cogny, Pierre. *Maupassant, l'homme sans dieu.* Brussels: La Renaissance du Livre, 1968. . . .

Lanoux, Armand. *Maupassant le bel-ami.* Paris: Fayard, 1967. . . .

Pierrot, Jean. *L'Imaginaire décadent.* Paris: PUF, 1977. . . .

Vial, André. *Maupassant et l'art du roman.* Paris: Nizet, 1954. . . .

3. Other Works

. . . . .

Sagnes, Guy. *L'Ennui dans la littérature française de Flaubert à Laforgue (1848-1884).* Paris: Colin, 1969. . . .

Trevor A. Le V. Harris (essay date 1990)

SOURCE: "Maupassant's Journalism: The Conservative Anarchist," in *Maupassant in the Hall of Mirrors: Ironies of Repetition in the Work of Guy de Maupassant*, St. Martin's Press, 1990, pp. 25-36.

[*In the following essay, Harris focuses on Maupassant's journalistic writings, pointing out how understanding Maupassant's nostalgia for the past (including his elitism and nationalism) and his perceptions of scientific progress is essential in evaluating his narrative technique.*]

In **'Adieu mystères',** an article published in 1881, Maupassant argues that poetry draws its power from the unknown. Comparing the latter to 'une épaisse et redoutée forêt', Maupassant implores would-be poets to work quickly, since, 'Ô poètes, vous n'avez plus qu'un coin de forêt où nous conduire'.[1] This race against time is prompted by the advance of modern science, which drives the unknown before it. In an intriguing inversion of Herbert Spencer's famous image, Maupassant implies that human contact with the unknown is finite and that it decreases with the expansion of knowledge. It is clear that, for Maupassant, a watershed has been reached. He intimates that poets are hard-pressed to compete with men of science, whose thrilling discoveries and inventions reduce the artist's exploitation of the unknown to a rather feeble rivalry. Maupassant mocks and yet sympathises with poets, claiming that 'vos pauvres fantômes sont bien mesquins à côté d'une locomotive lancée' (i, 313-14).

Both Huysmans and Zola were later to dwell on the power and compelling beauty of the same machine, but Maupassant's own recourse to the train as icon proceeds less from any confident fascination than from an anxious recognition of the values the train appears to embody. Indeed, notwithstanding his condemnation of those 'qui ne sont pas de leur siècle', those whom he qualifies, in the opening lines of his article, as 'ces ankylosés, ces pétrifiés, ces empêcheurs de sonder les mystères du monde' (i, 311), the onward march of science arouses in him feelings of regret and loss for 'ce quelque chose de vague et de terrifiant' (i, 315) which shrouded the pre-positivistic age. Maupassant is quick to point out that measurements and laws which explain reality also divest it of a fundamentally important spiritual aspect, a tension which emerges fully in the following: 'malgré moi, malgré mon vouloir, et la joie de cette émancipation, tous ces voiles levés m'attristent. Il me semble qu'on a dépeuplé le monde. On a supprimé l'Invisible. Et tout me paraît muet, vide, abandonné!' (i, 314).

Maupassant's nostalgia, the way in which he emphasises the 'invincible besoin de rêve' (i, 313) as a general

human characteristic, might easily be taken as the expression of a somewhat banal truism, although its banality would have appeared less obvious to his contemporary reader than to a modern one. And yet, there is clearly a sense in which Maupassant is writing here within the context of what one might call the negative phase of positivism, a position of serious doubt with regard to the value of material progress. It is the manner in which his nostalgia is fleshed out, as well as its political corollary, elitism, which deserve more detailed consideration, and the aim of this chapter is to follow Maupassant's discussion of these and related themes through his *Chroniques* and to suggest how his journalistic writing necessarily informs and modifies one's view of his fictional works.

Maupassant's terminology throughout **'Adieu mystères'** offers a convenient point of departure in this respect, since the basic opposition he establishes between terms such as *mystères, croyances, légendes, fantômes, esprits, voiles, invisible,* on the one hand, and *lois, quantité, phases, figures, temps,* on the other, illustrates the polarisation of two notions, quality and quantity, which are explored in considerable detail in the *Chroniques.* The distinction between the intangible and the measurable, between vagueness and precision, embodies what Maupassant perceives as a struggle between two orders of knowledge, a struggle which the second, materialistic element of the opposition is in the process of winning. To put this another way, Maupassant sees the advance of science as the inexorable quantification of the qualitative. One example would be his description of electric lighting as 'l'antique foudre des dieux, la foudre de Jupiter et de Jéhova emprisonnée en des bouteilles!' It is this fencing in of the *insaisissable* which removes the intellectual pleasure and stimulus to be derived from speculation, the latter being replaced by calculation. As Maupassant puts it, 'les choses ne parlent plus, ne chantent plus, elles ont des lois! La source murmure simplement la quantité d'eau qu'elle débite!' (i, 314).

Maupassant's wistful musing on the dubious value of progress in the sciences, as expressed in **'Adieu mystères',** is symptomatic of a much broader preoccupation with the substitution of quantity for quality, a preoccupation which, not surprisingly, finds more elaborate expression in his thoughts on writing. Of his contemporaries only Flaubert excites his unqualified admiration.[2] Bourget, Goncourt and Zola are also singled out for favourable treatment.[3] Earlier figures, such as Balzac and Gautier, interest Maupassant too—the former, especially, being impressive by the sheer energy of his work.[4]

In general, however, Maupassant looks further back into the past for his articles of literary faith. He praises the 'grands maîtres sincères de l'Antiquité' (ii, 269), the most frequently mentioned among these being Aristophanes, Ovid and Virgil.[5] But, while his admiration for such giants as Boccaccio, Cervantes, Dante and Shakespeare is also clear, Maupassant's nostalgia for the greatness of the past almost invariably selects the eighteenth century as the period *par excellence* of sophistication. In the visual arts two names, Boucher and Watteau, recur frequently. In literature, Beaumarchais and Voltaire are mentioned whenever the eighteenth century is evoked.[6] On a more general, social level, Maupassant laments the passing of the 'charmants causeurs du siècle dernier' (i, 389) and the 'grâce poudrée de l'autre siècle' (ii, 82). In sum, the eighteenth century constituted the period 'qui est et qui restera le grand siècle de la France, le siècle de l'art par excellence, de la grâce et de la beauté' (ii, 185).

Again, a first reaction to this might be to see it as nothing more than a simple preference for the traditional, a not unusual admiration for the great figures of history: in short, a potentially banal conservatism. To be sure, on a superficial level it is all of these things. And yet, the implied absence of the truly artistic sensibility from late nineteenth-century society, and the nationalism lurking in the last quotation suggest a richer and more serious set of attitudes to be explored.

Indeed, the sterility of contemporary French intellectual life is the inevitable consequence, Maupassant argues, of a social order 'composé presque exclusivement de parvenus récents' (ii, 303). What motivates his resignation concerning scientific progress and his nostalgia for France's artistic heritage, is not merely an innocuous *passéisme,* but a profound anxiety fuelled by what he sees as the disappearance of the 'fines qualités' of the French nation, those traits of behaviour which formerly elevated the French above other nations. His yearning for 'le siècle de Watteau et de Boucher, le siècle de Voltaire, le siècle aussi de Diderot, le siècle de l'incroyance, de la galanterie et de l'amour, le siècle qui grise, même de loin, le siècle français' (i, 303) is prompted not so much by feelings of regret for the specific political order of the *Ancien Régime,* as by the individualism and flamboyance which were the hallmarks of the kind of society over which it held sway.

Throughout the ***Chroniques*** Maupassant returns, again and again, to the examination of these 'fines qualités': 'la politesse', 'la galanterie', and 'l'esprit', notably, are all discussed in detail. What emerges is a picture of a society steeped in mediocrity, condemned at every turn for its lack of sophistication, a society which has lost, in a word, its Frenchness. Manupassant unleashes a bitter cynicism against his compatriots, who seem to have become 'une race de goujats' and wonders at 'les causes secètes, les influences mystérieuses qui ont pu faire du peuple le plus courtois du monde un des plus grossiers qui soient aujourd'hui' (i, 289).

As a writer, Maupassant understandably dwells on linguistic issues, aiming to shore up what he sees as the inherent purity of the French language. In **'En lisant',** for example, published in 1882, he reviews a re-edition of *Themidore,* an eighteenth-century text, exclaiming 'voilà de bonne prose de notre vieux pays, de la prose bien transparente qu'on boit comme nos vins, qui scintille comme eux, et monte aux têtes, et rend joyeux' (ii, 11). Simplicity and playfulness: these are the natural qualities of the French language which, like French wine, seems to emanate from the very soil of France, as well as the history of the French people. Wit, especially, 'né sur le sol de France' (i, 242), and an essential characteristic of the French nation, is under threat from linguistic change and infiltration. As Maupassant puts it, 'l'esprit français semble malade' (ii, 300). The agile wit of former generations, characterised by subtlety and economy, is being overtaken by 'des sottises tellement lourdes qu'on en demeure confondu' (ii, 301). The superiority of the earlier form of wit was located in its lightness of touch and its 'ludic' qualities; in sarcasm, satire and irony. But Maupassant discerns only volume and clumsiness in contemporary attempts at witticism. Paradoxically, efforts to enrich the French language merely impoverish it.

In this linguistic context, Maupassant's disillusioned elitism and his nationalism converge to heap scorn on a work by a Swiss author: *La Ferme du Choquard,* by Victor Cherbuliez. The latter's 'français d'outre-monts', because of its close similarities to metropolitan French, embodies an especially insidious threat and is taken to task in the most strident terms for the 'invincible somnolence' it provokes, its 'pâleur' and its 'uniforme banalité' (ii, 197). But linguistic variation within France is also attacked, the authors of the 'Société des gens de lettres' being lambasted for their 'charabia négro-français' (iii, 66), and the marked regional accent of inhabitants of southern France for inducing in northerners the feeling of being 'des barbares étrangers à la patrie' (ii, 180). Maupassant's conclusion, in the face of such evidence, is that 'nous paraissons surtout être devenus beaucoup moins français' (iii, 35).

Given such attitudes, the diachronic enterprise of historical linguists attempting to analyse their way back through the Babel of late nineteenth-century language forms to the *Ursprache,* or proto-language, from which all others sprang would have been anathema to Maupassant. His own endeavour is to maintain the specificity of French at all costs.[7] Maupassant's own approach is achronic. Time, he seems to imply, cannot alter the fundamental nature of the French language, which bears the imprint of a set of French-language universals, outside history and embodying the very essence of the national character. It is as though, for Maupassant, the French language had sprung fully formed from the loins of France.[8]

In the context of *boulangisme* and the fanatical cries for revenge of Paul Déroulède and his 'Ligue des patriotes', Maupassant's linguistic and artistic nationalism is apt to appear understated. And yet, it is worth stressing its significance, because it clearly relates to such social and political issues, of great prominence during Maupassant's writing-career, issues from which his work is sometimes separated, perhaps because they are assumed to be irrelevant, to lie beyond his field of interest, even beyond his intellect.

That Maupassant was alive to the flavour of emerging debates on race and nationality seems a logical inference given his position and, indeed, might already be supposed from the preceding paragraphs. This becomes clearer, however, if one considers his assessment of Rabelais as someone who was 'Français dans les moelles', as someone who characterises 'notre race gaillarde, rieuse, amoureuse, en qui le sang et le propos sont vifs' (ii, 93). One can attempt to dismiss the terminology here as simple enthusiasm; there is something rather too insistent about the conflation of the national and the biological to be quite coincidental. This fact comes into focus more sharply still when Maupassant claims that 'la puissance absorbante de la race blanche devient irrésistible dans les climats qui lui conviennent' (iii, 148).[9] One is tempted to see in Maupassant's defence of the French language and culture the manifestation of a crude racism. His presentation of Walter in **Bel-Ami,** and Andermatt in **Mont-Oriol,** certainly appears to confirm the extent to which Maupassant was aware of, and perhaps a party to, an incipient anti-semitism, for example.

His use of the term *race,* however, is both extensive and unstable, being used to mean *social class, social group, type, sex* and even *clan.*[10] Moreover, it is unclear whether Maupassant had any precise knowledge of the ideas of such theorists as Broca and de Gobineau.[11] His repeated use of the term suggests, none the less, that contemporary discussions on the subject may well have influenced his own ideas. In the broader context of the development of theories of racial origins and superiorities, Maupassant's use of the term might be deemed amateurish, a pseudo-familiarity with current research in sociology and psychology. Within the context of his own nostalgia and nationalism, however, it is clear that he is attempting to underpin his elitist attitudes by appropriating and redefining *race.*

The core of his argument seems to be that, just as France was a great country in the past by virtue of the art and literature of a restricted number of brilliant artists, expressing the French genius for individualism primarily through the French language, so, at the end of the nineteenth century, the principal national characteristics and the greatness of French art are being diluted, not least through the linguistic channel, by a fundamentally different society and political system. What had once been the preserve of the few is now threatened by the advance of the many.

Indeed, the aristocratic and the artistic are synonymous for Maupassant. The artistic and the popular sensibilities are incompatible. When, for example, a proposal is put forward to extend military service for all Frenchmen to three years, Maupassant cannot contain his amazement: 'Trois ans de la vie d'un artiste, juste au moment où cet artiste se forme, où il va devenir *lui,* où il va s'affirmer, naître, mais cela vaut la vie entière de cent mille commerçants et de cent millions d'ouvriers!' (ii, 231).[12] The essentially qualitative difference between the artist and the masses excludes popular art, a contradiction in terms for Maupassant. In 'A propos de peuple', he underlines this when he writes, 'L'Art, quel qu'il soit, ne s'adresse qu'à l'aristocratie intellectuelle d'un pays. Je m'étonne qu'on puisse confondre' (ii, 274). Maupassant makes it clear that by 'intellectual aristocracy' he is referring not to any specific political group or class within society, but to 'la *partie vraiment intelligente d'une nation'* (ii, 274).

But Maupassant's anxiety in the face of the increasing importance of the masses in social terms and their resulting influence on the intellectual standards of the country renders direct political comment inevitable. His nostalgia for a political system which allowed individualistic talent to flourish inevitably entails a fundamental critique of the democratic principles of the Third Republic. Equality, for Maupassant, is a farcical notion, being defined as 'le mal dont nous mourrons' (ii, 233).

He frequently turns on the republican regime, denigrating it for its judicial system, its specious morality, or its attempts, ludicrous in his view, to encourage and protect artists, to collectivise that which is necessarily individualistic. He attacks France's democratically elected representatives, dismissing Gambetta as a 'charmeur de foules' (ii, 154) and tarring all the deputies of the National Assembly with the same brush, calling them 'les Dupont et les Durand qui nous gouvernent' (ii, 369). They are nothing more than 'pesants doctrinaires', whose principal distinguishing characteristic is their 'gravité pontifiante' (ii, 388). Following Tocqueville, Maupassant recognises the potential despotism of the majority. His own interest in the phenomenon, however, is driven by scepticism and fear.

A system based on the notion of number inevitably projects men from the masses forward into the arena of government, a fact which Maupassant sees as having incalculable consequences, given a social framework not yet in a position adequately to prepare those who may be required to assume responsibilities in government. The Chamber of Deputies is described as 'cette assemblée de provinciaux illettrés, élus et parvenus par l'aveugle volonté du nombre' (ii, 90) and Maupassant dismisses 'cette machine qu'on appelle le suffrage universel, inventée pour l'exaltation des médiocres, l'élimination des supérieurs et l'abaissement général' (ii, 370).

The consequences do not end at this point, since, erected as it is on the principle of number, France's republican government is drawn inexorably into committing that gravest of sins in Maupassant's eyes, the corruption of the French language. As a democratic institution, France's National Assembly, is, at least in part, accountable to its electors. It is to the masses of recently enfranchised Frenchmen that the Chamber necessarily directs much of its comment. The inevitable result of this is that speeches in the Assembly are 'rédigés en charabia' (i, 343). At the same time, in an effort to influence public opinion—'toujours aveugle' (ii, 252) in Maupassant's view—that other turbine of democracy, the press, is also tempted to reduce the intellectual demands it makes of its readers, with the result that 'les journaux, les trois quarts du temps, sont écrits en petit nègre, seule langue à la portée des foules' (i, 344).

There is a clear link here between Maupassant's denigration of contemporary writing and his criticism of the contemporary political scene. The implied foreignness of the language emanating from the Chamber of Deputies or the press matches the un-French babble he perceives in current abuse of the language in works of literature. Similarly, the false wit of the late nineteenth century, qualified as a 'robinet à banalités' (ii, 302), finds its political corollary in the sheer welter of words produced in the Assembly. The orators and demagogues of the Republic have been cut off from the great French tradition in which the political and the aesthetic appeal of the linguistic were closely interwoven. While the great orators of former times merited 'le surnom poétique de "Bouche-d' Or" ', for their latter-day counterparts 'si un surnom peut leur aller, c'est celui de "Bouche-d'Egout" ' (i, 291).

While Maupassant's treatment of this whole theme clearly reveals his affective involvement in political questions, the terms in which he presents his arguments effectively discount any direct or practical form of political action on his part. His elitist assessment of France under the Republic prevents him from participating, his anxious defence of individualism forcing a reticence in the face of a constant invitation to take up cudgels on behalf of a specific political ideology. Identification with any such cause, however closely related to his own position, would associate him with a group attitude and represent a dilution of precisely those values which he seeks to defend. In this sense his elitism contains an incipient right-wing anarchism.[13] He is unable to reconcile the idea of government of whatever political hue—legitimist, Orleanist, Bonapartist, republican—with the practical implications of the day-to-day implementation of policy.

Above all, Maupassant's critique of democracy is prompted by the feeling that the individual as a social entity is threatened with extinction. Within a republican system of government, under the terms of which 'le nombre imbécile seul est puissant' (i, 279), the downward trend of French artistic and cultural life affects even and especially those individuals who might flourish in other circumstances. Maupassant is prepared to admit that not all politicians are necessarily devoid of positive qualities. The difficulty, as he perceives it, is that they form only a small part of a vast structure which effectively neutralises their political impact. There may be exceptions, 'mais ils ne comptent pas, noyés dans la masse des représentants crottés du suffrage universel' (ii, 305). Just as vast numbers of cheap foreign ornaments swamp France, smothering the sophisticated French *bibelot,* so the Republic with its mass of electors drowns the few, the men who possess 'ce flair des races fines, manquant totalement à notre société utilitaire et lourdaude' (i, 106).[14]

It is the crowd which threatens to sweep away the France of old in a torrent of mediocrity, the crowd's incomprehension, its 'férocitiés inconscientes' (i, 179) and the 'tourbillon de sottises' (i, 218) it propagates. The crowd is 'crédule' (i, 260), possessed of a 'bêtise particulière' (i, 224), a 'bête à mille têtes' (i, 408), 'incapable de subtiles délicatesses' (ii, 120).

Maupassant's anxiety merely intensifies as he concentrates, drawn by a somewhat morbid fascination, on the psychology of the crowd and the conflict between the crowd and the individual. The crowd is a 'pâtée grouillante' (ii, 138), 'une épaisse bouillie humaine' (i, 375), into which the individual is absorbed. Anticipating theorists such as Gustave Le Bon and Gabriel Tarde, Maupassant perceives how the collectivity functions independently of the individuals which compose it. The collective body, he implies, is not simply the sum of its constituent elements, but something quite different. Turning again to France's legislative body by way of example, he claims that it shows how a structure operates to the detriment of all personal idiosyncrasies. It is the position which one occupies within the structure, the role one plays, rather than one's individual characteristics, which are most important. It is this which prompts Maupassant to suggest that a *député,* as an individual, is 'si facile à remplacer qu'on ne s'aperçoit pas du changement' (ii, 374). The legislative structure, despite periodic changes in its membership, continues to function according to a collective identity which ignores or subjugates the differences ordinarily pertaining between its individual members.

Maupassant is attracted by the subject to the extent that he devotes an entire article to the theme. In

'Les Foules', written in 1882, Maupassant opens with the following description of the crowd:

> Regardez ces têtes pressées, ce flot d'hommes, ce tas de vivants. N'y voyez-vous rien que des gens réunis? Oh! C'est autre chose, car il se produit là un phénomène singulier. Toutes ces personnes côte à côte, distinctes, différentes de corps, d'esprit, d'intelligence, de passions, d'éducation, de croyances, de préjugés, tout à coup, par le seul fait de leur réunion, forment un être spécial, doué d'une âme propre, d'une manière de penser nouvelle, commune, et qui ne semble nullement formée de la moyenne des opinions de tous. (ii, 15)

Maupassant's description underlines the difference between his own vision and that of others. As Susanna Barrows has shown, analysing the work of crowd psychologists and authors of the period, the vision of the crowd, in many cases, was shot through with metaphors which belied immense fears, 'fears deeply rooted in the social fabric of the time'. The crowds of many writers 'loomed as violent, bestial, insane, capricious beings whose comportment resembled that of the mentally ill'.[15]

It should be clear from the preceding paragraphs that Maupassant's view of the crowd does not perceive in it the bloodthirsty power and savagery which Susanna Barrows isolates in many accounts. Even the portrayal of the crowd in *Germinal,* for example, a near-contemporary of 'Les Foules' by an author often equated with Maupassant, seems alien to the perception of the crowd which the latter formulates. His own metaphors tend to emphasise the insidious at the expense of the gory. Panic and horror, to say nothing of sensationalist exploitation of a convenient image, give way to a description of the subtle ways in which the crowd operates at the physical and psychological levels. Its power is none the less unsettling and destructive for that, since the combination of individuals into a crowd 'fait que tous subitement, par suite d'une sorte de dégagement cérébral commun, pensent, sentent et jugent comme une seule personne, avec un seul esprit et une même manière de voir' (ii, 17).

The mysterious and spontaneous process engendered by the formation of a crowd both intrigues and unnerves Maupassant. Each member of a crowd, he seems to imply, sheds his usual personality and adopts another, a standardised psyche, a social self, which is reproduced as many times as there are people in the crowd. Those present, however intelligent, are incapable of preventing the transformation. On their return home, Maupassant surmises, they must ask themselves how they failed to resist such a change in their behaviour. The reason is simply that their individual will 's'etait noyée dans la volonté commune comme une goutte d'eau se mêle à un fleuve' (ii, 16).

There is a clear link here, in the recurrence of the metaphor of liquidity, between Maupassant's preoccupations in 'Les Foules' and his presentation of the crowd scenes in 'La Ficelle' and *Pierre et Jean.* Indeed, Maupassant's ideas on the social and political status of the individual in late nineteenth-century France must necessarily place consideration of his fictional writings in a new context, since one cannot fairly assume that his work as a journalist and *chroniqueur* was subject to some convenient, quite arbitrary separation from his work as a novelist and writer of short stories. Maupassant the journalist clearly had an extensive influence on Maupassant the writer of fiction, and it is the mistaken propensity to disregard the relationship between these two aspects of his work which has encouraged the misleading view of the author as an instinctive, unreflective producer of entertaining but only semi-serious fiction.

Among the important conclusions to emerge from a detailed consideration of the *Chroniques,* given the vast spread of subjects which Maupassant tackles there, is that it is very difficult to persist in seeing him as this gifted but intellectually limited craftsman of letters. Maupassant was in touch. Art, history, love, marriage, fashion, politics, religion: the list of themes running through his journalism could be extended almost indefinitely. Even more striking, as the preceding pages show, is the stability of tone in a body of material spanning a period of some fifteen years. Nostalgia and elitism are never out of view.

At the centre of the elitist consideration of contemporary French political life, of what he sees as the intellectual and artistic mediocrity which blights the country, is a profound anxiety about the function and status of the individual human being. It is not only that fewer great men seem to be coming forward, but also that even those intelligent individuals that do exist are reduced to insignificance by the standardising influence of the amorphous, anonymous mass around them. People, for Maupassant, especially men, are in danger of becoming reduced to a purely group function which robs them of their specificity, their personality. They are cast, as it were, in the same mould and therefore replaceable.

Notes

[1] Maupassant, *Chroniques,* ed. Hubert Juin, 3 vols (Paris: Union Générale d'Editions, 1980) i, 313. All quotations from Maupassant's journalism are from this edition. References are given in parentheses after quotations and consist of volume number, in Roman numerals (lowercase), followed by page number(s).

[2] See, for example, iii, 77-124.

[3] On Bourget, see ii, 393-8; on Goncourt, i, 175-80; on Zola, ii, 306-22.

⁴ On Balzac, see ii, 37 and 288; on Gautier, ii, 21 and 146.

⁵ See, for example, ii, 92, 281 or 329.

⁶ See i, 243, 291, 303, 353; and ii, 146, 167.

⁷ On the development of linguistic science in the late nineteenth century see, for example, Julia Kristeva, *Le langage, cet inconnu* (Paris: Seuil, 1981) pp. 190-214.

⁸ See, for example, 'Le Roman', where he writes, 'La langue française, d'ailleurs, est une eau pure que les écrivains maniérés n'ont jamais pu et ne pourront jamais troubler. Chaque siècle a jeté dans ce courant limpide, ses modes, ses archaïsmes prétentieux et ses préciosités, sans que rien surnage de ces tentatives inutiles, de ces efforts impuissants' (*R*, 714-15).

⁹ Elme Caro, in his *Le Pessimisme au XIXe siècle* (Paris: Hachette, 1878), uses the word in the same sense and emits a similar elitist view, insisting that physical suffering is most acute in 'les races les plus civilisées et, dans ces races, chez l'homme de génie' (p. 130).

¹⁰ See i, 106; i, 225; ii, 209; ii, 333; i, 70, respectively.

¹¹ Theodore Zeldin, in his *France 1848-1945,* 2 vols (Oxford: Clarendon Press, 1973 and 1977) II, 12, gives a brief account of the race theories having some currency at the time.

¹² Caro expresses a similar idea when he writes, 'je suppose que Newton, quand il trouva la formule exacte de l'attraction, condensa dans un seul moment plus de joie que tous les bourgeois de Londres réunis ne pouvaient en goûter durant une année entière dans leurs tavernes, devant leur pâté de venaison et leur pot d'ale' (*Le Pessimisme,* p. 134).

¹³ What Hubert Juin, in his preface to the *Chroniques,* has called 'un anarchisme de salon' (i, 7).

¹⁴ For Maupassant's thoughts on consumerism, which he sees as the inevitable social and commercial consequence of the political system, see i, 106-12, 'Chine et Japon'.

¹⁵ Susanna Barrows, *Distorting Mirrors: Visions of the Crowd in Late Nineteenth-Century France* (New Haven, Conn., and London: Yale University Press, 1981) p. 5.

Charles J. Stivale (essay date 1994)

SOURCE: "Figures of Male Repute," in *The Art of Rupture: Narrative Desire and Duplicity in the Tales of Guy de Maupassant,* University of Michigan Press, 1994, pp. 111-41.

[*In the following excerpt, Stivale examines Maupassant's portrayal of the struggle between prostitutes and their environment through their relationships with les hommes-filles (men-harlots). The critic does this in three ways: by analyzing Maupassant's depiction of registered prostitutes; by studying the interactions between filles (prostitutes) and hommes filles; and by considering how women are depicted as "other" (for example, the lesbian woman, the exotic woman, or the anonymous woman).*]

Maupassant's strategic maneuvers of narrative desire and duplicity situate the social type that he calls *l'homme-fille* as an ambiguous agent in various scenarios of the art of rupture. Writing in the *Gil Blas,* where he also published such *chroniques* as **"Politiciennes"** [**"Women politicians"**] and **"La Guerre,"** Maupassant seems implicitly to identify himself, through his narrator, with this group given that "the most irritating of the species is assuredly the Parisian and the *boulevardier*" ("L'Homme-fille," *CSS* 715; *CN* 1:757).¹ In this chapter, I wish to examine such scenarios within tales of the war-machine that functions to degrade women of the demimonde and *grand monde* while stressing the sexual difference among them and that simultaneously emphasizes the hypocrisy of their exploiters, diverse *mondains* and bourgeois who seek their company while rejecting them from society. Far from being "relatively banal" (Bernheimer 309), these tales depict incursions of the war-machine into the bourgeois activities that Maupassant presents as the "strange spectacle of a real harlot and an *homme-fille*" (*CSS* 715; *CN* 1:757)—the incessant combat between women and the *mondains* and bourgeois to whom I refer as figures of male repute. Furthermore, these tales are of particular interest in providing access to what Peter Brooks has identified (in Eugène Sue's fiction of prostitution) as "the modern narratable," "that eminently storied subworld, realm of power, magic, and danger" (*Reading* 162). It will therefore be useful to consider the manner in which these figures of male repute act as agents of a narrative as well as a discursive vengeance and are thus deployed as weapons of the war-machine, but also how they may become the unwitting victims of its shrewd manipulation by the dangerous objects of their pursuit.

One narrative trait of this strange spectacle is the prevalence of Maupassant's use of framed tales, embedded narration, usually to heighten the identification of the framed interlocutors with the narrator's own experiences and also, as we shall see, to limit significantly the possible meanings that the listener/reader might make of the framed tale.² Indeed, like many of his framed narrators, Maupassant seeks to appeal to as well as to draw in the Baudelairian "hypocrite reader" whose very nature, in fact, lends itself to his deceptive tactics. For, as the narrator of **"L'Homme-fille"** concludes: "Under the right circumstances, *l'homme-fille* will reveal weaknesses and commit infamies without even realizing it at all, since he obeys unquestioningly the oscillations of his ever susceptible mind" (*CSS* 715; *CN* 1:757), in other words, the ideal prey as well as weapon for the art of rupture.

Moreover, the attitude of constant, mutual struggle between *la fille* or *la femme du monde* and her environment in relationships with *l'homme-fille* suggests a critical approach other than simply examining "venal love" in Maupassant's writing through the different portraits of *filles*.[3] It is possible, then, to pursue the dual hermeneutic described in chapter 1 [of *The Art of Rupture*] by considering the diverse ways in which these portraits are determined through the depiction of the *hommes-filles* themselves in their responses to these women. As Maupassant insists in a number of *chroniques* and tales, whatever may be the innate limitations of woman, "created weak, changeable, capricious, easily influenced by nature itself," it is due to society's influence and to continued contact with men that woman is "raised to give pleasure" and is "instructed in this thought that love is her domain, faculty and sole joy in the world" (**"Le préjugé du déshonneur,"** *Chr* 1:232).

I propose, then, to examine various narrative and discursive developments of the "strange spectacle" of struggle that unfolds in these tales of prostitution: in section 1, I will study a textual counterpart to the ordeal of one *femme galante,* in **"Boule de suif,"** through the depiction of *filles soumises* (registered prostitutes) and their provincial bourgeois clientele, both under the protection of a wily madame at **"La Maison Tellier"** ("Madame Tellier's Establishment"). In section 2, I will explore the diverse relationships between *filles* and *hommes-filles,* examining in particular the discursive means by which the narrating *hommes-filles,* whether self-designating or duplicitous, situate their tales "between men."[4] This examination will prepare my consideration, in section 3, of the means by which this already inaccessible other is rendered even more alien as well as degraded through three narrative strategies of alterity, or *othering*. This perspective will allow us to see how Maupassant's representation of women as other is not limited to gender, but extends also to race, ethnic origin, and class distinctions. Throughout these three sections, I undertake a dual consideration, on one hand, of the relation of *l'homme-fille* to prostitutes, to women *du grand monde* (from the city) and *du petit* (from the country), and on the other hand, of *l'homme-fille* as counterpart to his interlocutor(s) and reader(s) alike. In turn, these considerations will prepare the study, in part 3, of Maupassant's narrative and discursive deployment of the art of rupture in terms of fidelity and conjugality, maternity and paternity, and through the hallucinatory register, of subjectivity and identity themselves.

1. La Maison That Is a Home

To situate the complex relations that reign within Madame Tellier's establishment as well as with the surrounding (and invading) community, let us consider the typology that we can derive from the elaboration of social regulation during the nineteenth century (cf. Corbin, *Women for Hire*). We may better understand these relations by contrasting them to the immediate tensions underlying Elisabeth Rousset's interactions in **"Boule de suif,"** in her status as a *femme galante* (translated as "coquette"), a kept woman freely sharing her "admirable qualities" (*CSS* 6) [qualités inappréciables (*CN* 1:91)]. As such, this unregistered prostitute is by definition *insoumise,* unsubmissive, to the official patriarchal scrutiny leveled at activities of all women.[5] It was her practice, therefore, to share her qualities outside the regulations of the moral order imposed by the bourgeois administration, increasingly obsessed in the late nineteenth century with the dangers of moral and physical "contagion" of unregistered prostitutes and *femmes galantes*. As Bernheimer notes in reviewing Parent-Duchâtelet's discourse of regulation (see 14-33), "through strategies of camouflage, role playing, and fictionalizing, the clothed body of the *insoumise* becomes a means to deceive the policing authority that attempts to translate it into knowledge" (27).[6]

In fact, in Maupassant's fiction, the focal point of activity of the *fille* with *l'homme-fille* rarely occurs within the confines of the regulated, registered *maisons de tolérance,* but rather "in contact with both the proletariat and with a 'slumming' potential in itself by way of erotic curiosity mediated by money" (Brooks, *Reading* 162). We have seen one such inhabitant, Rachel in **"Mademoiselle Fifi,"** who finally returns to "the establishment from which she came" (*CSS* 237) [le logis public (*CN* 1:397)], only to be rehabilitated through marriage, a miraculous feat given the prevailing sentiment regarding the immutably corrupt, and corrupting, nature of the prostitute. However, her unexpected elevation to the ranks of "Lady" is indeed consistent with the theme of the patriotic prostitute who serves as "guarantor of stability in morals and an obstacle to the increase in adultery and the development of erotic behavior in bourgeois women" (Corbin, *Women for Hire* 20).

In **"La Maison Tellier,"** the sole tale by Maupassant that focuses its primary attention on the brothel inhabitants and on their bourgeois clientele, the rupture between the characters is not explicitly internal, as in **"Boule de suif."**[7] Rather, the strategy consists of constructing the appearance of nearly blissful harmony while deploying the textual warmachine, in fact, against *l'homme-fille* through his relations with the *filles*. This strategy suggests a dual consideration of the tale: I will observe, on one hand, the function of the seemingly mystical transformation that the *filles* and the proprietress of the *maison,* Madame Tellier, undergo during their trip to attend a first communion in the latter's home village. On the other hand, I will scrutinize the role played by the bourgeois clientele in terms of the transformation of their relations with the occupants of the *maison.* By following the key moments of this transformation in the tale's three sections—the preparation for change implicitly announced with the *maison*'s unexpected closure on a Saturday night in rural Fécamp, the transformative trip on Saturday and Sunday, and the metamorphosis of activities in the re-opened *maison* on Sunday evening—I will study how Maupassant deploys the art of rupture as a weapon aimed at *filles* as well as at *hommes-filles.*

From the first sentence onward—"Men went there every evening about eleven o'clock, just as they went to the café" (*CSS* 43) [On allait là, chaque soir, vers onze heures, comme au café, simplement (*CN* 1: 256)]—,the tale suggests that its focus and frame consist precisely of the relationship of the *filles* to *hommes-filles,* of the *maison* to its clientele, between which occur the women's excursion and transformation. The nominative devices employed to designate the distinction of the proprietress are, first, the author initially placing her title, *Madame,* in italics and, second, the narrator noting emphatically that "Madame, who came of a respectable family of peasant proprietors in the department of the Eure, had taken up her profession, just as she would have become a milliner or dressmaker," for a simple reason:

> The prejudice against prostitution, which is so violent and deeply rooted in large towns, does not exist in the country places in Normandy. The peasant simply says: "It's a paying business," and sends his daughter to keep a harem of fast girls, just as he would send her to keep a girls' school. (*CSS* 43; *CN* 1:256)

That this observation is an extraordinary example of wish-fulfillment alerts us to the perspective of *l'homme-fille* preparing the tale's dénouement: whereas Madame Tellier's operation of the *maison* and management of the *filles* correspond to laudable business practices, this submission to bourgeois principles will nonetheless yield finally, during one golden evening at least, to the generative, seductive principle of the art of rupture. For not only does the reader observe the wise distribution of female resources in the *maison,* specifically, two *filles* (Louise, "nicknamed Cocote," and Flora, "called Balançoire [the swing] because she limped a little") for the commoners in the downstairs café, and three *filles* (Fernande, *la juive* Raphaële, and "a little roll of fat," Rosa la Rosse) (*CSS* 45; *CN* 1:258-59) for the bourgeois clients upstairs in the salon.[8] The reader also learns an important detail of the widow Tellier's character: that, besides exhibiting exemplary refinement, reserve, and maternal solicitude, "since Madame had

been a widow, all the frequenters of the establishment had wanted her, but people said that personally she was quite virtuous" (*CSS* 44) [absolument sage (*CN* 1:257)]. To her clients, her presence above the demands of her calling served the vital and shrewd marketing function of providing "a rest from the doubtful jokes of those stout individuals who every evening indulged in the commonplace amusement of drinking a glass of liquor in company with girls of easy virtue" (*CSS* 44; *CN* 1:258).[9]

Given that her *maison* had become for her bourgeois clientele "a resource" and that they "very rarely missed their daily meetings there" (*CSS* 45; *CN* 1:260), it is understandable that their finding the *maison* inexplicably closed one Saturday evening would throw the group into disarray. The depiction of their plight is quite instructive since Maupassant does not fail to attach each name to a civil status. Thus, M. Duvert ("the gunmaker"), M. Poulin ("timber merchant and former mayor"), M. Tournevau ("the fish curer"), M. Philippe ("the banker's son"), M. Pimpesse ("the collector"), M. Dupuis ("the insurance agent"), and M. Vasse ("the judge of the tribunal of commerce") all find the doors shut. M. Tournevau is especially "vexed" since "he, a married man and father of a family and closely watched, only went there on Saturdays—*securitatis causa,* as he said, alluding to a measure of sanitary policy which his friend Dr. Borde had advised him to observe. That was his regular evening, and now he would be deprived of it for the whole week" (*CSS* 46; *CN* 1:260). Joining four other regulars, the "sad promenaders" wander listlessly, M. Poulin ("timber merchant and former mayor") and M. Dupuis ("insurance agent") nearly coming to blows in their frustration, and a group of four eventually returns "instinctively" to the still "silent, impenetrable" *maison.* Much later, wandering alone, "exasperated at the police for thus allowing an establishment of such public utility, which they had under their control, to be thus closed," M. Tournevau discovers the notice that had been posted on a shutter all along, "Closed on account of first communion" (*CSS* 47; *CN* 1:262), a statement that "emphasizes the equation *maison-commercial establishment*" and partially clarifies the enigma of the *maison*'s closure that dominates the opening sequence (Dickson 45-46).

Madame Tellier's purpose for taking the five *filles* in her employ along to the country birthplace, in fact, follows sound business practice since the canny proprietress wants to avoid the consequences of difficulties that would inevitably arise in her absence: the "rivalries between the girls upstairs and those downstairs," the drunkenness of the footman, Frédéric, events that would upset the smooth functioning of her establishment. The majestic effect of these women on the quiet village—whether on a simple promenade that becomes "a procession" before the villagers (*CSS* 51; *CN* 1:268), on their way to the church as "Madame Tellier's regiment" (*CSS* 53; *CN* 1:271), or at the mass and communion ceremony in the tiny church—is indeed impressive, all the more so since their profession is unknown in this isolated rural community. But of greater importance for the implicit development of the narrative war-machine is the effect of this environment itself on these women that contributes to producing a profound metamorphosis. This process is initiated as much by the attitude of Madame's niece, "the well-behaved child, fully penetrated by piety, as if closed off through absolution" (*CN* 1:269) [l'enfant bien sage, toute pénétrée de piété, comme fermée par l'absolution (omitted from translation)], as by the "perfect repose of the sleeping village," causing the visitors to shiver, "not with cold, but with those little shivers of solitude which come over uneasy and troubled hearts" (*CSS* 51; *CN* 1:269). That night in the village is particularly difficult for one *fille,* Rosa the Jade (Rosa la Rosse), "unused to sleeping with her arms empty" (*CN* 1:269), until she goes to comfort Madame Tellier's sobbing and frightened niece, taking her back into her bed where Rosa "lavished exaggerated manifestations of tenderness on her and at last grew calmer herself and went to sleep. And till the morning the girl slept with her head on Rosa's naked bosom" (*CSS* 52) [Et jusqu'au jour la communiante reposa son front sur le sein nu de la prostituée (*CN* 1:270)].

This astonishing juxtaposition of the sacred and the profane and, following Michel Crouzet, the "permanent conflict between farce and its conjuration" (248), establish an implicit destabilization of bourgeois commonplace images, a fact not lost on the (anonymous) English translator who systematically distorts the original by rendering *communion* by *confirmation, communion recipient* by *confirmation candidate,* and extensively censoring the consecration scene that follows. During the mass, Rosa is again at the center, this time of the veritable outbreak of "contagious weeping." For having recalled her own first communion, her sobbing transmits throughout the church a "strange sympathy of poignant emotions" that affects everyone: "Men, women, old men and lads in new blouses were soon sobbing; something superhuman seemed to be hovering over their heads—a spirit, the powerful breath of an invisible and all-powerful being" (*CSS* 54; *CN* 1:274).[10] Receiving communion from the "old priest," the people "opened their mouths with spasms, nervous grimaces, eyes closed, faces pale" (*CN* 1:274; omitted from translation). Then,

> Suddenly a species of madness seemed to pervade the church, the noise of a crowd in a state of frenzy, a tempest of sobs and of stifled cries. It passed over the people like gusts of wind which bow the trees in a forest, and the priest remained standing, immobile, the host in his hand, paralyzed by emotion, saying: "It's God, it's God who is among us, who is manifesting his presence, who is descending as I speak to his kneeling congregation." And he stammered out incoherent prayers, those inarticulate prayers of the soul, in a furious burst toward heaven. (*CSS* 54; *CN* 1:274)[11]

His no doubt heartfelt final words are turned cruelly ironic from the perspective of the textual war-machine, for in seeking to calm the crowd, the priest bestows a special benediction on the visitors "whose presence among us, whose evident faith and ardent piety have set such a salutary example to all." "Without you," he continues, "this day would not, perhaps, have had this really divine character. It is sufficient at times that there should be one chosen to keep in the flock, to make the whole flock blessed" (*CSS* 54) [Il suffit parfois d'une seule brebis d'élite pour décider le Seigneur à descendre sur le troupeau (*CN* 1:274)]. Finally, "his voice failed him again from emotion, and he added, 'I wish for you divine grace. So be it'" [C'est la grâce que je vous souhaite. Ainsi soit-il (*CN* 1:275; omitted from translation)].[12]

The concluding scenes of this second section, as Dickson has remarked, alternate between "euphoric and dysphoric tonalities" (46), i.e., the spiritual elevation that returns to more sensual pursuits during the subsequent scenes of the village celebration, and especially of the attempts by Madame's brother, Rivet, to seduce Rosa. Following their departure and uneventful return to Fécamp, the impact of the women's "euphoric" experience is of considerable import to the clientele of the *maison* Tellier. For, with "the flock returned to the fold" at the start of the third section (*CSS* 57) [dans la bergerie le troupeau était revenu (*CN* 1:280)], the news spreads quickly throughout the town, and the customers swarm to the festive establishment, even M. Tournevau finding a ruse to absent himself from the imprisoning family gathering on this Sunday evening. The downstairs pair, Louisa and Flora, are already working hard with the sailors, drinking with one and all, thus earning more than ever "their nickname of the 'Two Pumps.'" Yet, they long to share the euphoric atmosphere upstairs that evening, running up to spend a few minutes "while their customers downstairs grew impatient, and then they returned regretfully to the café" (*CSS* 58; *CN* 1:282). Deprived of the transformative vigor still enjoyed by their colleagues, and two *filles* being hardly adequate for the work ahead, "for them, the night promised to be toilsome" (*CSS* 57) [la nuit pour elles s'annonçait laborieuse (*CN* 1:280)].

Upstairs, however, more delicate negotiations are in motion as M. Vasse, "the judge of the tribunal of commerce, Madame's usual platonic wooer, was talking to her in a corner in a low voice, and they were both smiling, as if they were about to come to an understanding" (*CSS* 57; *CN* 1:280). M. Poulin ("the former mayor") with Rosa; M. Pimpesse ("the tax collector") and the young M. Philippe ("the banker's son"), both with "la grande Fernande"; M. Dupuis ("the insurance agent") negotiating with Raphaéle who concludes their talk, "Yes, my dear, tonight I will. . . . Tonight, anything you want," and is then swept off her feet and out of the room by the determined M. Tournevau; Madame waltzing with M. Vasse, looking at him "with a captivated glance, with this gaze that answers 'yes,' a 'yes' that is more discreet and more delicious than any spoken word" (*CN* 1:281); the champagne that keeps flowing, ordered by the usually more economical men—all these events betoken excellent business, but not as usual. For it is not only the "demoiselles" that evening "who exhibit an inconceivable willingness" (*CN* 1:282); Madame also is involved in "long private talks in corners with M. Vasse, as if to settle the last details of something that had already been agreed upon" (*CSS* 58; *CN* 1:282). At the close of the evening, the men only had to pay the cost of the champagne, the details of which the narrator notes with peculiar insistence, "six francs a bottle instead of ten, which was the usual price" (*CSS* 58; *CN* 1:283).

However, as if to explain not only this truly inconceivable generosity, but also the general willingness that contributes to maintaining the euphoric atmosphere, Madame, "who was beaming, said to them: 'It's not every day that we have a holiday'" [Ça n'est pas tous les jours fête]. Yet, as has been amply noted (Crouzer 248-49; Dickson 49-50), this final statement contains not merely the focal ambiguity between the determining festive events, holy (first communion) and carnal (the homecoming). It also underscores the ambiguity of Madame's intentions: on one hand, she may provide a recapitulative "justification" of these activities, drawing into her radiant joy readers and customers alike. On the other hand, this justification may also serve as a prospective, business-like limitation to such generosity, to the *fête* that does and will not come everyday, when business as usual will certainly prevail. The latter reading is supported by the fact that, unlike the euphoric abandon of the women under her charge, Madame negotiates at length with M. Vasse before yielding anything from her precious "capital" amassed over the years—her reputation as being "absolument sage," not only virtuous, but wise. This reading situates the tale finally within the letter of the Law, albeit one that an empowered woman (relatively so, of course, within an oppressive patriarchal framework) chooses to exercise according to her principles of exchange and usage, but within an "establishment of public utility" (*CSS* 47; *CN* 1:262) that must respect its commercial function and thereby maintain the proper balance between conjugal and sensual pursuits.

The preceding analyses of **"Boule de suif'** and **"La Maison Tellier"** have shown two portrayals of pros-

titutes implicitly situated at opposite poles of the regulationist spectrum, the *filles soumises* in the hierarchized and well--established *maison de tolérance* of the widow Tellier, and the *femme galante,* therefore *insoumise,* represented by the independent Elisabeth Rousset. In each tale, the prostitute serves as the dual focal point for duplicitous narrative strategies: while the heterodiegetic narrators situate the *filles* so that they represent the least ridiculous and/or repellent subject-position, thus performing the subversive function (especially for nineteenth-century readers) of providing the *filles* as the most likely pole of attraction, the clients' social status is juxtaposed directly to their sensual pursuits so that their moral hypocrisy is all the more evident. However, just as Elisabeth Rousset, the model of a forthright, even principled patriot, is primarily represented in her professional role, symbolized by the nickname *Boule de suif,* she is first seduced, then abandoned by one (the Prussian) and all (the traveling companions) in an explicit manipulation of the art of rupture.

In contrast, while rupture is not at all evident in **"La Maison Tellier,"** it is the sincere religious fervor of Madame Tellier, the women under her care, and even the rural congregation that is, in fact, exploited for narrative ends. For the ultimate euphoric result of this experience is the effusive male enjoyment at the *maison* Tellier of an "inconceivable willingness, of the festive swoon by which every man's desire is satisfied, without a single chain attached. Furthermore, these representations (harlots as plump, religious, patriotic) not only rely on myths of the prostitute prevalent throughout the nineteenth century, but are "drawn up in virtually definitive form by Parent-Duchâtelet" (Corbin, *Women for Hire* 8). In each case, as well as generally in Maupassant's tales of prostitution, the *hommes-filles* necessarily render their counterparts other in order better to abandon them: *Boule de suif* is cast out of society, and the women of the *maison* Tellier succumb for a golden evening precisely to the sexual fantasies of *l'homme-fille,* after which he can retreat to the security of the conjugal surveillance. These overlapping analyses provide the necessary foundation for studying the depiction of *l'homme-fille* in relation to *filles* as well as the concomitant situation of the reader in relation to the diegetic and discursive strategies that animate Maupassant's art of rupture.

2. L'Homme-fille: "Sentiments like the Affections of Harlots"

Let us consider some additional details of the peculiar temperament of *l'homme-fille* and of the ongoing struggle that pits him in battle with *la vraie fille,* a struggle that Maupassant describes toward the end of the quasi-*conte* **"L'Homme-fille":**

For the relations of these *hommes-filles* are uncertain. Their temper is governed by fits and starts, their enthusiasms unexpected, their affection subject to sudden revulsions, their excitement is liable to eclipse. One day they love you, the next day they will hardly look at you, for they have, in fact, a harlot's nature, a harlot's charm, a harlot's temperament, and all their sentiments are like the affections of harlots. (*CSS* 715; *CN* 1:756)

Far from revealing the sympathy toward *filles* for which Maupassant has occasionally been noted (cf. Vial, *Faits* 240), these sentiments express a "reversal" that is hardly "chiasmic" (cf. Donaldson-Evans, "Doctoring" 357). That is, instead of degrading one type as the other is elevated (the case for the bourgeois vis-à-vis *Boule de suif*), here the temperament of one type is dragged down by the negative weight of the other's. After asserting that the *hommes-filles* "treat their friends as kept women treat their pet dogs" (*CSS* 715) [Ils traitent leurs amis comme les drôlesses leurs petits chiens (*CN* 1:756)], Maupassant's narrator paints a vivid portrait of the "strange spectacle" of the real harlot with *l'homme-fille*:

He beats her, she scratches him, they loathe each other, cannot bear the sight of each other, and yet cannot part, linked together by no one knows what mysterious bonds of the heart. . . . They cause each other to suffer atrociously without being able to separate. They cast invectives, reproaches and abominable accusations at each other from morning till night, and then, excessively excited and vibrating with rage and hatred, they fall into each other's arms and kiss each other madly, uniting their quivering mouths and harlots' souls. (*CSS* 715; *CN* 1:757)

Among the gripping examples of such combat that Maupassant provides in his fiction, it is in **"L'Épingle"** [The hat pin] (translated as "Doubtful Happiness"), that the ambivalence of such struggle is narratively portrayed most dramatically.[13] On one hand, the interlocutor of the first-person (homodiegetic), framing narrator thus describes his relationship with his mistress Jeanne de Limours: "For three years ours was a frightful but delicious existence. I was very near to killing her five or six times; she tried to jab out my eyes with the pin that you were just looking at." This relationship is only explicable for *l'homme-fille* within the ambivalent logic that we have located in the art of rupture:

How can I explain this passion? You could never comprehend it. There should be such a thing as a simple love, born of the dual transport of two hearts and two souls; but assuredly there is such a thing as an atrocious, cruelly torturous love, born of the invincible rapture of two beings totally unalike who detest while adoring each other. (*CSS* 617; *CN* 2:522)

On the other hand, having exiled himself abroad and there amassed a small fortune, the interlocutor responds to the question, "Will you try to see her again?" by indicating his plans for the final struggle, to return and keep this passion and himself alive, if only provisionally: "Surely! I have here now, in money and land, seven or eight hundred thousand francs. When the million is completed, I will sell everything and leave. I will have enough for a year with her, one solid year.— And then, adieu, my life will be finished" (*CSS* 618; *CN* 2:524).

We can consider more fully the role of *l'homme-fille* as he consorts with women on the end of the regulationist spectrum that corresponds to the activities of an Elisabeth Rousset, i.e., the numerous tales of *filles* who attempt to resist submission, *insoumises* as much to the patriarchal order of enforced surveillance as to the exploitive and often destructive art of rupture. However vague the designation of *fille insoumise* came to be during the nineteenth century (cf. Corbin, *Women for Hire* 128-32), Maupassant simplifies matters by portraying women belonging to three categories:

tales of *femmes galantes,* of which **"Boule de suif"** is one example (**"Yveline Samouris," "Yvette," "La Baronne,"** and **"Les Soeurs Rondoli"**);

tales of *filles de la rue* (streetwalkers) (**"L'Odyssée d'une fille," "Les Tombales," "Nuit de Noël,"** and **"L'Armoire"**); and

tales of *filles aux canotiers,* most likely female shop assistants (*demoiselles de magasin*) or dressmakers' assistants (explicitly the case in **"Ça Ira"**), who frequent the society of male canoeists on the Seine (**"Ça Ira," "Mouche,"** and, in terms of the tale's setting, **"La Femme de Paul"**).[14]

We may nuance this typology in light of the aforementioned narrative characteristic prevalent in nearly all of these tales, the device of embedding a tale within a narrative frame. In previously examining an example of this device in **"Les Idées du colonel,"** we saw the structure's duplicitous function in providing the author with even more control over the manner in which a tale is received. Angela Moger suggests that, on one hand, "the frame would italicize the framed, implying that the story's mimetic status is a self-deception on the part of the reader, whose earnest attitude is implicitly derided" (322). On the other hand, the assignment of the narrator's role to a physician, in the tales **"En voyage"** and **"La rempailleuse,"** Moger argues, "enhances the credibility of the narrative and at least initially gains the confidence of the reader," the narrative being posed not as "the creation of a litterateur but the first hand report of a scientist" (322). In **"Les Idées du colonel,"** and Forestier's objections notwithstanding (*CN* 2:1397), the idiosyncrasies of the colonel's remarks tend finally to reinforce his demonstration of the invigorating effects of *la femme* in ways that were perhaps impossible in the unframed predecessor, **"Le mariage du lieutenant Laré."**

But what are we to make of *l'homme-fille* as narrator, whose "temper is governed by fits and starts"? Following Chambers's remarks on the device of embedding, this type of narrator would seem the ideal practitioner of the textual art of rupture since the device would allow, on one hand, "for relatively intense interpretive involvement on the part of the reader." On the other hand, the device would limit "the reader's options in approaching the text," i.e., "opening up interpretive options while simultaneously programming them" (*Story* 35). At once volatile and constraining, *l'homme-fille* would, on both narrative and discursive levels, seemingly open up the polysemy of the tales recounted while seeking to determine their meaningfulness, directly among the interlocutors, indirectly for readers. Of the two tales in which the narrator remains ostensibly covert, **"La Femme de Paul"** and **"Yvette,"** the latter (which I will consider among tales of *femmes galantes*) is firmly anchored to embedding: it begins with a framing discussion between two *hommes-filles*/interlocutors, then proceeds to a longer, heterodiegetic narration of its earlier version (the framed tale, **"Yveline Samouris"**), with the maternal character appearing subsequently within yet another frame in **"La Baronne."** While **"La Femme de Paul"** appears exempt from the discursive manipulation imposed by narrational embedding, in section 3 we shall observe a different form of embedding that continually positions the reader discursively vis-à-vis the narrative agency, and thereby plays a crucial role in the deployment of the art of rupture.

Femmes galantes

Considering first the group of women whose professional stature makes them the colleagues closest to Elisabeth Rousset, the *femmes galantes*—and just as importantly, the men whose desire constitutes these women as such—we find in **"Les Soeurs Rondoli"** ["The Sisters Rondoli"] the depiction of what may be the beginnings of the career either of a *femme galante* (free agent) or *femme d'attente* (kept woman). Moreover, this presentation occurs explicitly from the perspective of *l'homme-fille*, Pierre Jouvenet, who frames his tale by explaining the "charming insights of the manners" of Italy that he received on his two unsuccessful attempts to "penetrate" the country beyond its borders (*CSS* 202; *CN* 2:133). The account of these evidently difficult circumstances, solicited obliquely by an undefined interlocutor, constitutes the material of his retrospective tale of seduction, abandonment, then the subsequent promise of renewed seductions.[15]

One fascinating aspect is how closely Jouvenet fits the type of *l'homme-fille*, his temperament governed by

the characteristic "fits and starts," "enthusiasms," and "revulsions" described in **"L'Homme-fille."** For example, Jouvenet's departure is forced on him by "the violent vigor of spring [that] infuses the fervor for love and adventure" (*CSS* 202) [la sève violente du printemps vous met au coeur des ardeurs de voyage et d'amour (*CN* 2:133)]. His obsessive character becomes evident concerning not only his own detailed collection of "little instruments of cleanliness" that he carries along on the trip, but especially the explicit details that he provides of Francesca's *lack* of cleanliness, for instance, her reluctance to use soap and her excessive use of perfumes and powders creating "such a violent odor that I was overcome with a migraine" (*CSS* 211; *CN* 2:149).[16] His inexplicably growing attraction to Francesca is based on "a secret bond, that mysterious bond of *animal love,* the secret attachment to a possession that does not satiate" (*CSS* 214; *CN* 2:153; my emphasis). The continued experience of fever and the memory of Francesca well after leaving her haunt Jouvenet "with strange persistency," torturing him "like a nightmare" (*CSS* 216-17; *CN* 2:157), forcing him to return to Genoa. The resolution of this dilemma is, of course, ideal for *l'homme-fille,* in that he has a continued intimacy with fresh and youthful females, similar enough to the original to evoke the same sensations in the same locale, but different enough to provide variety, all with the added attraction of maternal approval and no chains to bind.

However, what is perhaps less evident, yet is crucial for understanding the deployment of the war-machine by and against *l'homme-fille,* is the manner in which this tale of seduction, (dis)possession and renewal, rendered more spicy by Jouvenet's final reflections about Mme Rondoli's other daughters, obliquely presents the homosocial interactions of two *hommes-filles,* Jouvenet and Pavilly. For, Pierre Jouvenet initially has no intention of seducing the woman in their train compartment; it is Paul Pavilly who undertakes to impress her, as a man for whom "woman is everything, the world, life itself," all of whose acts and thoughts "have women for their motives" (*CSS* 203; *CN* 2:135), according to the framing narrator, Jouvenet. Once they discover that, speaking no French, she could not understand a single gallant word Pavilly has pronounced, Jouvenet must intervene as interpreter, a polyglot pimp of sorts, inviting her to share their food, and trying to discover her plans. When she finally volunteers to accompany them to their hotel in Genoa and chooses Pierre Jouvenet, not Pavilly, as her *patito* (the man who looks after a woman), Paul's enraged response is "All the better for you!'" (*CSS* 210) [Tant mieux pour toi (*CN* 2:146)].

The question that arises is who has Pavilly really lost through his linguistic impotence, the mysterious woman or the man who tempted him into the voyage in the first place with promises of charming Italian women and of Naples's refined society (*CSS* 204; *CN* 2:136)? I submit that it is truly more the latter than the former, since the tale of heterosexual intimacy is itself particularly uninteresting, rendered all the more so through Francesca's committed indifference repeatedly emphasized by "her perpetual 'Che mi fa?' or her no less perpetual 'mica'" (*CN* 2:154) [What's that to me? and Leave me alone (*CSS* 214)]. With Pavilly, however, we see a veritable lovers' struggle between men, Paul's "execrable temper," "rage and swearing" (*CSS* 211-15; *CN* 2:149-54) growing in direct proportion to the length of time he remains near the two, but strangely unable to travel or return to Paris alone, despite repeated threats to do so. Moreover, Paul evokes the bourgeois fear of contagion, prostitution's "terrible threat to the future of the race" (Corbin, *Women for Hire* 23), in order to separate the lovers:

> "You declare that she is not a tart! And you persuade yourself that you are not running any more risk than if you were to go and spend the night with a woman who had smallpox." He laughed with an unpleasant and angry laugh. I sat down, a prey to uneasiness. What was I to do, for he was right after all? A struggle began within me, between desire and fear. (*CSS* 212; *CN* 2:150)

But, desire wins out, a victory that Pierre exclaims to his friend: "You know the old saying: 'A victory without perils is a triumph without glory.'" Finally, given an opening by Francesca's absence one day, Paul counterattacks, insisting that the two men leave, and when she fails to return to the hotel that night, he presses his advantage with mockery. Claiming that a wait of twenty-four hours is enough for his "conscience to be quite clear" (*CSS* 216; *CN* 2:156), Pierre packs his belongings the next morning, and they return to Paris.

This homosocial bonding "between men" plays itself out time and again in Maupassant's tales of prostitution, and we can understand the framed *conte* as itself lending a formal basis to this implicit homosocial intimacy. For the act of orally re-presenting to one or several (male) interlocutor(s) the phases and circumstances of the heterosexual art of rupture is tantamount to reliving and relieving those "imperious needs," while whetting the appetite verbally for still more such carnal exchanges. Furthermore, the dual gesture of the art of rupture, of breaking with the grasping women, and yet having them all narratively again and again, enables *l'homme-fille* to render woman other and distant and still maintain that possession by sharing it/her with the same, that is, among *hommes-filles*.

Even a text that is not framed, such as **"Yvette,"** reveals textual similarities with the framed tale from which it is derived, **"Yveline Samouris,"** The opening section of each text, one with a framing device (**"Yveline"**), the other with an introductory exposi-

tion of two *hommes-filles*, Jean de Servigny and Léon Saval, conversing as they stroll along the boulevard, reveals the circumstances of the countess Samouris/ Obardi as courtesan and, more important, of her daughter Yveline/Yvette, "born an honest woman" (*CN* 1:684). However, as Servigny declares, Yvette "disturbs me, allures me, and makes me uneasy, at once attracts me and frightens me. . . . She provokes me and excites me like a harlot, and guards herself at the same time as if she were a virgin" (*CSS* 106-7; *CN* 2:238-39). In any case, he concludes, like a practical consumer, "If she has had lovers, I shall make one more. If she has not, I shall be the first to take my seat in the train" (*CSS* 107; *CN* 2:239).

In both tales, the girl is, in fact, naive and innocent, a virgin as well, but her discoveries of the mother's marginal status and, therefore, of her own circumscribed destiny (accurately defined by *l'homme-fille*, Servigny, in the initial, framing analysis of **"Yvette,"** [*CN* 2:239-40]), are the elements that lead to the culminating attempt at suicide. Whereas Yveline successfully takes the final step when her mother ignores her ultimatum to change their existence (*CN* 1:687), Yvette succeeds only in inducing a delightful chloroform high and in frightening the company assembled with her mother in a rented country retreat. However, according to the *hommes-filles*, these divergent outcomes result from differences in women's inherent constitutions, and even evaluation, within and by society. As Irigaray notes,

> Prostitution amounts to *usage that is exchanged*. Usage that is not merely potential: it has already been realized. The woman's body is valuable because it has already been used. In the extreme case, the more it has served, the more it is worth. Not because its natural assets have been put to use this way, but, on the contrary, because its nature has been "used up," and has become once again no more than a vehicle for relations among men. (*This Sex* 186)[17]

Since she was born an honest woman, Yveline seemingly has no choice *but* to die given her inevitable destiny of unacceptable *usage* (use as well as wear and tear), a death that leads the narrator to conclude, with convenient tardiness, "In truth, if I had known,—but one never knows,—I would have perhaps married that harlot" [cette fille-là (*CN* 1:687)].

Servigny, on the contrary, has no such illusions about Yvette: whether or not she is a virgin and whether or not he loves her, it is certain "that I shall never marry her" since, quite simply, by dint of her eventual *usage*, she is destined to be "a vehicle for relations among men" (Irigaray, *This Sex* 186). Servigny thus comments correctly, "she can't possibly marry ever. Who would marry the daughter of the Marquise Obardi, Octavie

Bardin? Clearly, no one, for any number of reasons" (*CSS* 107; *CN* 2:239). Yvette's drug-induced stupor and hallucinations function in exactly the same transformative manner as the divine ecstasy during the communion ceremony and the subsequent euphoria for Mme Tellier and her employees: Yvette's resistance to her fate and her will to die are swept aside in the euphoric reflections at the edge of death, strangely similar in their content as well as indirect form to Renardet's in **"La Petite Roque"**: "Why not live? Why should she not be loved? Why should she not live happily? Everything now seemed possible, easy, sure" (*CSS* 144; *CN* 2:300). It is Servigny who discovers her suicide note, "I die so that I may not be a kept woman. Yvette. Goodbye, Mother dear. Forgive me" (*CSS* 147; *CN* 2:305). As he kneels by her bedside, whispering, "Listen to me, mam'selle," she feels the happy, gentle "caressing breeze," no longer wishing to die, feeling instead "a strong, *imperious* desire to live, to be happy, no matter how, to be loved, yes, loved" (*CSS* 147; *CN* 2:306; my emphasis). So, Servigny's words of wisdom regarding existential and, here, sexual economy—"We must all accept our share of things, however sad" (*CSS* 148; *CN* 2:307)—fall on welcoming ears, and body, as "their lips met," and as she asks and promises softly, "You will love me very much, won't you?" [Vous m'aimerez bien, dites?], to which the only reply possible for the conquering *homme-fille* comes easily, "I adore you" (*CSS* 148) [Je vous adore (*CN* 2:308)].[18]

Filles de la rue

All the tales of the *filles de la rue* are embedded within narrative frames, and this device provides not only the possibility for homosocial bonding, more or less clearly defined depending on the tale's initiating frame, but also a means for the narrator to distance himself discursively from what is for him the uniformly disturbing, even distasteful experience with women from the lower end of the hierarchy of *filles*. As Dijkstra notes, "a confused mixture of sexual desire and guilt, a vague sense of class difference and exploitation, and a desire to hold onto privileges gained made the prostitute seem to these men, as the brothers Goncourt had remarked in their journal, the means whereby the proletariat revenged itself upon the rich" (358). In one such tale, **"L'Armoire"** ["Florentine"] the overt connivance between men is presented in the opening framing device: "We were talking about *filles,* after dinner, for what else is there to talk about among men?" (*CSS* 593; *CN* 2:401). However, at least this once, the man's disgust "in this public bed" (that he nonetheless entered readily) turns to pity, not so much from uncovering the lies in tales of her first lovers that the *fille* relates, as from finally discovering that the strange noise he has been hearing is her little boy, Florentine, hidden in a cupboard "at the head of our bed" (*CSS* 596; *CN* 2:406). The mother's angry, tearful explanation—"What can you expect? I do not earn enough to put the child in

school! I must take care of him somehow, and I cannot afford to rent another room"—and the "timid and pitiful" child's frightened weeping lead *l'homme-fille* to an uncharacteristic sympathy: "I, too, had a desire to weep. And I returned home to my own bed" (*CSS* 597; *CN* 2:407), a rupture that results, in fact, in minimal loss and no binding attachment.

In the other tales of *filles de la rue,* however, the narrator's impulse is implicitly to distance himself emotionally from the intrusive other. For example, the framing narrator in **"L'Odyssée d'une fille"** ["A Poor Girl"] responds to the story of a *fille*'s origins quite differently than the narrator of **"L'Armoire."** The path of prostitution that she describes, her betrayals by older bourgeois men, and the dangers she runs by dint of her unregistered status, all provoke in him "the sinister sensation of invincible fatality" and allow him "to comprehend fully how impossible an honest life is under some conditions" (*CSS* 695; *CN* 1:996). Yet, having identified himself as a married man, he insists then on a moral attitude of disgust as interlocutor of the *fille*. By thus distancing the framing narrator, Maupassant can safely depict the trajectory and perils of the *framed* narrator's (i.e., the *fille*'s) career, and can also unveil the hypocrisy of the upper bourgeois *hommes-filles* that renders inevitable the trusting girl's path to prostitution, notably the old, devout grain dealer, Lérable, and the old judge whose excesses result in his death and her imprisonment.

In another such tale, **"Nuit de Noël"** ["Christmas Eve"], the term *réveillon* (Christmas Eve supper) evokes for the framing narrator "the dirtiest trick in the world" [le plus sale tour du monde], a translation that includes an interesting pun on *trick,* since it is his taste for corpulent women that led him one Christmas Eve to invite back to his lodgings an appropriately proportioned *fille*. The "dirty trick" occurs after dinner with the delivery of a *petite fille,* a baby to which the *fille* gave birth in his bed. Despite his self-imposed obligation to support the child, the only real recourse for *l'homme-fille* is to the art of rupture: having lost weight quite understandably following the delivery, the *fille* "had grown as thin as a homeless cat, and I turned the skeleton out of doors" (*CSS* 835) [J'ai flanqué dehors cette carcasse (*CN* 1:699)]. Yet, she still continues to wait for him in the street, "enough to drive me mad. That is why I never keep Christmas Eve now."[19]

A third tale, **"Les Tombales"** ["Graveyard Sirens"], presents a *garçon* (bachelor) with the opportunity to relate to four other men (another bachelor and three married) *une aventure singulière* (a curious thing) that occurred as a result of an encounter in a cemetery: attracted by the tears of a weeping woman, supporting her as she fainted before the tomb of a navy captain killed in action, the narrator gradually found himself led to the woman's apartment, where she responded to his embrace, ambiguously crying, "Finish it, do finish it" (*CSS* 425) [Finissez . . . Finissez donc (*CN* 2:1243)]. He interprets this ambiguity to his sexual benefit, but after three weeks, he broke off the liaison since "man tires of everything, especially of women." A month later, however, he met her once again among the tombs at Montmartre, accompanied by an officer of the Legion of Honor. This encounter leads the narrator to wonder whether she was indeed "an inspired prostitute" who works the cemeteries "like the street," as a "graveyard siren" (*tombale*), or if it was her idea alone "to profit by the amorous regrets awakened in these awful places" (*CSS* 426; *CN* 2:1245). In each of these tales, then, the mixture of attraction to and repulsion by the *filles* reveals, on one hand, the implicit narrative investment of the *homme-fille* in the strategic alienation of the female other constitutive of the art of rupture, and on the other hand, by dint of the framing device, the evident connivance of *hommes-filles* and *garçons* established through the habitually shared pleasure, narrative and discursive, "among men" (*CSS* 593; *CN* 2:401).

Filles aux canotiers

It is clear from the third group of tales, those of the *filles aux canotiers,* that these women are treated the most fondly, perhaps due to Maupassant's own nostalgia for years spent on the river as an energetic and devoted canoeist (cf. Troyat 47-54). In one case, **"Ça Ira"** ["The Tobacco Shop"], the framing narrator explains how the proprietress of a rural *tabac,* into which he chanced to enter, had at one time been "a poor, thin girl who limped," employed for a Parisian *modiste* (dressmaker), and who became "a part of our band" of canoeists (*CSS* 691-92; *CN* 2:573-74). What makes this tale unusual is that rather than relate the story of her origins, the woman, nicknamed by the band *Ça Ira* (So-it-goes), tells the narrator "a thousand things of the secret life of a Parisian woman, . . . the whole story of the heart of a working girl, that sparrowhawk of the sidewalk who hunts through the streets" (*CSS* 692; *CN* 2:575). She reveals that she had distinguished between the *canotiers,* who she and her friends frequented "for pleasure" (*pour le plaisir*), and the men that they "hunted" in order to survive. Having employed an array of ruses concocted by her comrades *la belle* Irma and Louise, *Ça Ira* explains finally that her illegitimate son's father, previously a law student in Paris and eventually elected *député,* had arranged for her to occupy the functionary's position as tobacconist (a detail also recalling Maupassant's appointment through influence to a position in the naval ministry; cf. Troyat 37-45). The narrator's emphasis on the solemn moment of leave-taking as she introduces him to her son, Roger, "a future subprefect," is implicit recognition of the successful ascent of the woman in social rank, especially to a respectable position in which she

affirms, rather than threatens, the order of law and reason: "I saluted this functionary [the son] in a worthy manner and went back to my hotel, after having pressed with gravity the extended hand of *Ça Ira*" (*CSS* 695; *CN* 2:579).

In **"Mouche—Souvenir d'un canotier"** ["Mouche—A Boating Man's Reminiscence"], the frame is as slim as possible, as the tale begins, "He said to us: 'What queer things and queer women I have seen in those long-ago days when I used to go on the river'" (*CSS* 31) [Il nous dit: 'En ai-je vu, de drôles de choses et de drôles de filles aux jours passés où je canotais' (*CN* 2:1169)]. As Forestier notes, this tale is quite autobiographical, not merely evoking details from the 1873-79 period of Maupassant's canoeing life, but using the nicknames that his real comrades had adopted at that time (*CN* 2:1699-1700). As for the woman nicknamed *Mouche,* so called because she was "a little blister fly . . . strangely disturbing the whole crew of the *Feuille-à-l'envers*" (*CSS* 33; *CN* 2:1172), her adoption by and enjoyment with the crew results in a pregnancy which itself becomes a collective event for these *hommes-filles.* The group paternity, of which all, and no one in particular, are responsible, is cause for a second "adoption," when the miscarriage after an unfortunate boating accident is turned from tragedy into ironic comedy by *Mouche*'s total acceptance of and by the eager group. "Be comforted, little *Mouche,* be comforted," advises one canoeist, "we'll make you another one." The framed narrator and paternal candidate interprets her response in their favor: "The sense of humor that was bred in her bones woke suddenly, and, half convinced, half joking, still all tears and her heart contracted with pains, she asked, looking at us all: 'Promise?' And we all answered together: 'Promise'" (*CSS* 36-37; *CN* 2:1178). **"Mouche"** suggests quite clearly another facet of the art of rupture: how enjoyable it would be for group paternity to occur when, using the Maupassantian metaphor, the chains that might otherwise be attached individually can be shared "between men" and its consequences narratively aborted with little ado.

3. Narrative Strategies of "Othering"

Besides the different forms of tales as well as the repeated use of the narrative frame by which *l'homme-fille* can distance himself discursively and narratively from the women described, the war-machine is further deployed as means to render women into objects of masculine discourse through a number of textual strategies: the depiction of women as lesbians, that I will consider in the tale **"La Femme de Paul"**; the use of onomastic elements in different tales, especially related to the Semitic other; and the presentation of a specifically exotic object of desire, the Arabic *fille du sable* (harlot of the sand).

Lesbians

The first strategy concerns homosexuality, a subject about which Maupassant reveals himself to be distinctly uneasy. We have already seen the homosocial tension that emerges in certain tales like **"Les Soeurs Rondoli,"** of barely concealed desire between men, and in the discussion of Maupassant's liaison with Gisèle d'Estoc (chapter 2), I cited several examples of Maupassant's homoerotic fascination and anxiety. We should also recall that Maupassant incarnated the extension of this fascination in his role as the bisexual prostitute in *A la Feuille de Rose. Maison Turque.* The author's equivocal fascination brings us to the narrative depiction of lesbianism, the most dangerous form of love, not merely as perceived by the nineteenth-century regulationists (Corbin, *Women for Hire* 7-8, 124-26), but also in terms of the narrative consequences of this form of attachment. Indeed, the "lesbian scenario" was one aspect of a distinct narrative strain in nineteenth-century French literature, from the Romantic pornography of "Gamiani," attributed to Musset and well-known among Maupassant's contemporaries (36-57), to what Dijkstra calls "the turn of the [nineteenth to twentieth] century's emblem of [woman's] enmity toward man," her "desire to embrace her own reflection, her 'kiss in the glass'" (150; cf. 152-59).

In **"La Femme de Paul"** ["Paul's Mistress"], set in the context of joyful promiscuity of the canoeists, Maupassant depicts the fatal results not merely for a young woman, Madeleine, "corrupted" by other women renowned for their enjoyment of the pleasures of "Lesbos," but also for her companion, Paul Baron, a senator's son, floating on the wild side of the social *bas-fonds* (lower regions). Confronted by the presence on the river of lesbian canoeists, he shows himself to be unreasonably disturbed, "borne away by a male jealousy, by a profound, instinctive and ungovernable fury. He stammered, his lips quivering with indignation: 'It is shameful! They ought to be drowned like bitches, with a stone around their necks'" (*CSS* 1058; *CN* 1:297). Madeleine's angry response is significant: "And what has it to do with you? Aren't they free to do what they want, since they owe no one anything? Leave *us* alone with your manners and mind your own business" (*CSS* 1059; *CN* 1:297; my emphasis). The first person plural object of "fiche-*nous* la paix" could be interpreted simply as rejecting Paul's intrusive judgements on behalf of all women. However, given the events that follow, it is clear that Madeleine is at the very least susceptible to, if not having already participated in, lesbian activities.

Far from constituting the Baudelairian "innovation" of "the lesbian as heroine of modernity" (Walter Benjamin, qtd. in Buci-Glucksmann 85), the particular practice of dispossession of men by these distinct "others" is devastating for a budding *homme-fille* such as

Paul, particularly from the perspective of the art of rupture. For the tale's conclusion leaves no doubt: losing his mistress to an onomastic as well as sexual counterpart, "Mme Pauline," Paul is literally driven mad in his search for Madeleine along the Seine near Bougival. Like Renardet carried away by his visions, what Paul perceives as Madeleine's ecstatic, orgasmic shrieks leaves him "astounded and overwhelmed, as if he had discovered a mutilated corpse of one dear to him, a crime against nature, a monstrous, disgusting profanation" (*CSS* 1064; *CN* 1:306). That this description could apply to Renardet's crime as well is no mere coincidence; as we saw in **"La Petite Roque,"** and as is the case in **"La Femme de Paul,"** both men transgress the lines of Law and Reason imposed by bourgeois society and must therefore suffer the consequences. Paul's own desperate, "frightful cry: 'Madeleine!' . . . shot across the great silence of the sky, and sped over the horizon," announcing, as it were, the only recourse apparently left to an *homme-fille* driven so far from the safe confines of bourgeois regulations: "With a tremendous leap, with the bound of a wild animal, he jumped into the river" (*CSS* 1064; *CN* 1:306).

The focalization shifts finally to Paul's former companion, Madeleine, who intuitively understands the sound of his cry and rushes to the bank, only to find men dragging the hideously discolored corpse from the river. Already "green, with his mouth, his eyes, his nose, his clothes full of slime," the corpse seems in a state of decomposition not merely from drowning, but from the contaminating realization that had preceded and, in fact, caused his final act. Yet, rather than being horrified by the fatal event that she seemingly caused, Madeleine easily accepts not only Pauline's brutal insight, "It is not your fault, is it? It is impossible to prevent men from doing silly things," but also her comforting embrace and words of support, "Come, my dear . . . we will cure you," of her suffering, no doubt, but perhaps of her remaining attraction to heterosexual love as well. Madeleine's departure with "her head upon Pauline's shoulder, as though she had found refuge in a more intimate and more certain, a more familiar and more confident tenderness" (*CSS* 1065; *CN* 1:308), would offer, in another text and sociohistoric context, a rather beautiful vision of homosexual closure. Given the blatant exposition of cause and effect that precedes, however, the usurpation and deformation of the male practice of the art of rupture lays added emphasis on the profane impulses of "nurturance" displayed by a willful, dominant, yet ultimately doomed, feminine "other."

"La belle juive"

A second means by which women are distanced and rendered other in these tales is through the manipulation of key onomastic elements. As was common practice upon entering a *maison de tolérance,* a prostitute was given "a pseudonym, which she usually kept throughout her career, even when she moved to a different establishment" (Corbin, *Women for Hire* 77).[20] Onomastic elements in Maupassant's tales, as Forestier has noted (following commentary by Dr. Reuss in *La Prostitution, CN* 1:1416), correspond to the then current practice of nicknames (e.g., *Boule de suif;* in **"La Maison Tellier,"** *Rosa la Rosse, Louise Cocote,* and *Flora Balançoire; Mouche; Ça Ira;* and *Eve la Tomate* in **"Mademoiselle Fifi"**) and names ending in *a,* especially those borrowed from literature, theater, and *café-concerts* (e.g., *Pamela* and *Amanda,* in **"Mademoiselle Fifi"**).[21] However, we can specify three further ways in which the manipulation of onomastic elements determines women as objects and other. First, in all the tales in which *l'homme-fille* comes into contact with a *fille de la rue,* she remains anonymous, designated by the third person *elle,* or takes over the tale as *je* (as in **"L'Odyssée d'une fille"**) for scrutiny as an object/abject lesson in human misery. Even when nicknames are used, such as *Mouche* or *Ça Ira,* no christian name (except *Elisabeth Rousset* for *Boule de suif*) ever comes to replace them, or to personalize the women beyond the behavior that had earned them the particular appellation.

Second, besides several of the aforementioned nicknames that indicate physical characteristics, certain other names take on symbolic importance for *l'homme-fille:* appearing in **"La Maison Tellier"** and in **"Ça Ira,"** *Louise* is also the first name of *la petite Roque* and has a curious resonance in Maupassant's life, as the name of his aunt and of his first boat (*Louisette*). The use of *Madame* for the widow Tellier does not stand simply for her previously married status, but for her role as proprietress and desired woman somehow removed from directly carnal exchange. And *Madeleine,* in **"La Femme de Paul,"** clearly evokes the "fallen woman," here remaining unredeemed, even "condemned" to a life engulfed in a fatal "tenderness."[22]

A final means of manipulating onomastic elements occurs for the first time in **"La Maison Tellier"** with the use of the name *Raphaële* to designate the apparent exoticism provided in the establishment by "the indispensable role of the *belle juive* [beautiful Jewish woman]" (*CSS* 45; *CN* 1:259). Maupassant had previously adopted this name for his role in *A la Feuille de Rose. Maison Turque,* and while other women's names (for example, *Fatma* in *A la Feuille de Rose, Fernande* in **"La Maison Tellier,"** and the sisters *Rondoli, Francesca,* and *Carlotta*) also might be said to provide an exotic tonality, the recurring presence of the *belle juive* has particular value in Maupassant's tales. For, in each case, the woman's striking traits— Raphaële's "black hair, which was always covered with pomatum" (*CSS* 45; *CN* 1:259), and Rachel's features in **"Mademoiselle Fifi,"** "a very young, dark girl, with eyes as black as ink, a Jewess, whose snub

nose confirmed by exception the rule which allots hooked noses to all her race" (*CSS* 234; *CN* 1:392)—establish an exotically and ethnically distinct presence, seemingly an indispensable mainstay of the fully equipped *maison de tolérance.*[23]

This association of *fille* and *juive* in Maupassant's tales is hardly surprising since, as Buci-Glucksmann notes in her discussion of Otto Weininger's *Sex and Character,* the modern period reveals the confluence of the figures of "woman" and "Jew(ess)" as the time of "a non-subject possessed by his/her all-powerful sexuality, an 'a-moral' and 'anti-social' non-subject, prisoner of a libido of evil and 'ignorant of the State/Status'" (146). In fact, Buci-Glucksmann continues, "the parallelism between 'woman' and 'Jew,' the *simultaneous* rise of a philosophical anti-feminism stemming from Schopenhauer and a diversified anti-Semitism . . . is a veritable commonplace in the second half of the nineteenth century and the beginning of the twentieth" (149-50; see also Dijkstra 218-21). Indeed, the period of Maupassant's youth and particularly of his literary production (1860-91) saw, as well, the sharp rise of anti-Semitic sentiment in France (notably in Catholic, financial, and political milieus), the organization of the first explicitly anti-Semitic *ligues,* and the publication of influential anti-Semitic texts, e.g., by Gougenot des Mousseaux and the best-seller *La France juive* (1886) by Edouard Drumont.[24] Furthermore, Forestier suggests both cultural and personal connections for Maupassant's interest in Jews,[25] and Albert-Marie Schmidt goes further, pointing out that Maupassant's predilection for the "charm" of Jewish women was well known among his peers, for example, the Goncourt brothers.[26] Regarding the presence of Jews in Maupassant's work, Forestier concludes that by the mid-1880s, "Israelites begin to take hold of a large place in Maupassant's imagination: **Mont-Oriol** will soon confirm this" (*CN* 2:1511), referring to the character of the entrepreneur Andermatt in Maupassant's third novel (1887).[27]

It is Maupassant's use of this commonplace of the period that renders it so intriguing, notwithstanding Forestier's disclaimer of Maupassant's simple devotion to realism's "humble truth."[28] For example, the tale to which Forestier's commentary refers, **"Ça Ira,"** would seem to have little connection to Maupassant's growing "interest in Jews" except for a bizarre semantic slide that occurs concerning the eponymous nickname. Reflecting on his earlier life among the *canotiers,* the framing narrator notes:

> We baptized her "So-it-Goes" (*Ça Ira*), because she was always complaining of her destiny, of her misfortune and her sorrows. Each Sunday morning they would say to her: "Well, So-it-Goes, how goes it?" And she would always answer: "Not too well, but we must hope that it will go better someday." (*CSS* 691; *CN* 2:574)

Once this first, baptismal generation of *canotiers* moved on, however, "our successors, not knowing why we had christened her as we did, believed her to have an oriental woman's name and called her Zaïra." Continuing on to the next generations, "Zaïra had now become Zara, and later Zara was modified into Sarah. Then they thought she was an Israelite. The last ones, those with the monocles, called her simply 'the Jewess.' Then she simply disappeared" (*CSS* 692; *CN* 2:574). This onomastic displacement would seem to indicate, at the very least, that *hommes-filles* associated *la juive* quite easily, even expected to associate her, whether in a brothel or not, with the practice of "the trade which demands the most grace, tact, cleverness and beauty" (*CSS* 692; *CN* 2:574), not to mention exotic charm and mystery. These reflections of an *homme-fille*/narrator would stand as a mere curiosity if they did not take an even more sinister turn in another tale, **"L'Inconnue"** ("The Unknown"), written earlier the same year (1885) and appearing with **"Ça Ira"** in the same collection of tales, *Monsieur Parent* (December 1885). In fact, Schmidt refers to this tale as an example of Maupassant's "ambiguous feelings" toward Jewish women, a feeling "made of sadistic desire and sacred horror, that incites the outsider to slide into the beds of prophetesses and ghouls" (115). Such is the strange exotic force that *l'homme-fille* naturally attributes to *la juive* in this tale. Relating a (framed) anecdote "between men" of his fascination with and seduction of a *femme de la rue,* Roger des Annettes describes "a tall and rather sturdy young woman who made on me . . . an altogether amazing impression." According to des Annettes, she was dark-haired, hirsute even, with a slight mustache that set him "dreaming . . . dreaming . . . ," and had eyes "like ink stains on the gleaming white skin," eyes "through which one saw right into her, entered into her." Quite "naturally," then, des Annettes "imagined her to be a Jewess" (*CSS* 412; *CN* 2:443-44), a detail which seems to relate simply to the *homme-fille*'s need for exotic stimulation. However, at the end, as if to explain the obsession with this woman that has overwhelmed his every moment since meeting her, des Annettes slips into this final, delirious stream of consciousness: "Who is she? An Asiatic perhaps? Mostly likely an eastern Jewess. Yes, a Jewess. I am convinced she is a Jewess. But why? Yes, why indeed? I do not know!" (*CSS* 414-15; *CN* 2:447).[29] These ravings reflect the link between "threatening" women and "degenerate races" that the theories of Otto Weininger would systematize in *Sex and Character* at the turn of the century, views that "simply updated and made more fashionably diabolical what had already become a commonplace about the inherently dependent nature of woman" (Dijkstra 221).

La fille du sable

This fascination, even the imperious obsession with what is deemed to be the exotic, oriental object of

desire finds expression in the third strategy of "othering" in Maupassant's tales set in North Africa where he made three trips during the 1880s.[30] Even the titles of these tales of *la fille du sable,* **"Marroca"** (1882), **"Châli"** (1884), and especially **"Allouma"** (1889), suggest Maupassant's need to designate exoticism and alterity onomastically. However, this tendency is not isolated from the fiction and art of the author's period (cf. Said 166-97; Dijkstra 112-18), not even from "the whole history of European colonialism" (Behdad, "Eroticized" 122). Nor is this "orientalist desire" (cf. Behdad) exceptional in Maupassant's fiction, since one of Maupassant's earliest works, **A la Feuille de Rose. Maison Turque,** "illustrates how the harem conceit was used in pornography to signal a place where the phallus is fully mythified as a super-performative" (Apter, "Female Trouble" 210). And in the middle of his lengthy nautical reverie, *Sur l'eau,* Maupassant imagines the delight of living, like the protagonist of **"L'Épingle,"** far from society, "in one of these countries of the Orient," served by "handsome black slaves," and entertained by "five spouses from five parts of the world, who would bring me the savor of the blossoming feminine beauty of all races" (132-34).

Moreover, each of the aforementioned tales contains various thematic traits developed elsewhere: **"Marroca"** depicts, first, a woman caught unaware and framed within nature by the insistent male gaze while bathing, as in **"La Petite Roque."** Following this scene of the gaze is a distinct variation of marital relations in the form of Marroca's uniquely forceful mode of understanding "conjugal duties, love and hospitality" (*CSS* 582; *CN* 1:376) by implicitly threatening her husband with a hatchet in order to assert her right to keep a lover.[31] In **"Châli,"** the harem of pre-pubescent girls recalls not only **"La Petite Roque"** through Maupassant's continued interest, as Forestier points out, in "the delicate body of the child-woman" [le corps gracile de la fillette-femme (*CN* 2:1340)], but also **"Les Soeurs Rondoli,"** through the fantasy of a visiting male's temporary sensual attachment without obligation to the "naturally" solicitous female children. In **"Allouma,"** the Arab *fille* who herself dares to exercise the prerogative of the art of rupture is a direct descendent of the *Parisienne,* Jeanne de Limours from **"L'Épingle,"** especially in terms of the framed narrator's obsession with this woman, manifested in **"Allouma"** by his willingness to forgive everything for the sake of more pleasure since, as he pronounces finally, "where women are concerned, one must either forgive . . . or ignore" (*CSS* 1263; *CN* 2:1117).

What makes these tales important from the critical perspective that I have developed is the radical discourse by which the homodiegetic (and framed, in **"Châli"** and **"Allouma"**) narrators experience the eponymous women.[32] For the tales that the narrators relate "between men" situate the female objects of their gaze and desire as racially "other," specifically it terms of their animality. While the device certainly occurs elsewhere, e.g., *la Roque*'s "animal cry" emitted upon discovering her murdered daughter, the narrators all seem fixated upon these colonized women as belonging to a species distinctly different from humans. Not only does Marroca's body suggest "something of the animal," thus making her "a sort of inferior yet magnificent being" (*CSS* 579; *CN* 1:371), even her speech contains animal traits. Consider, for example, the manner in which she explains why she wants the narrator to sleep at her home in her husband's absence (omitted from translation): "When you are no longer here, I will think of it. And when I kiss my husband, it will seem to me to be you" [Quand tu ne seras plus là, j'y penserai. Et quand j'embrasserai mon mari, il me semblera que ce sera toi]. The narrator emphasizes the distinctive traits of her statements: "And the *rrrai* and the *rrra* took on in her voice the familiar rumblings of thunder" [Et les *rrrai* et le *rrra* prenaient en sa voix des grondements de tonnerres familiers (*CN* 1:372)]. In **"Châli,"** the "naturally" savage Indian prince, who is the traveler/narrator's host, offers the royal gift of a pre-pubescent harem, "the herd of children" (*CSS* 75; *CN* 2:88), "little human animals" (*CSS* 76; *CN* 2:89), "a pack of kittens" (*CSS* 76; *CN* 2:90). In contrast, the *fillette* chosen by the traveler "to become truly my woman" [ma femme pour de vrai] is consistently reified as "a little statue of ancient ivory" (*CN* 2:89; omitted from translation), with "her little sphinx's head" (*CSS* 76; *CN* 2:90), with the "hieratic pose of sacred statues" (*CSS* 76; *CN* 2:90). Yet, all of the activities of the narrator and the harem members are surrounded and observed by tamed apes of the prince's compound, providing a suggestive metonymic resonance to the visitor's reminiscences.

The conditions of sensual deprivation of the framed narrator in **"Allouma,"** Monsieur Auballe, "haunted by the lure of the female" (*CSS* 1252) [ce goût de la femme (*CN* 2:1100)], prepares his readiness to accept the Algerian "girl with the face of a statue" (*CSS* 1252) [fille au visage d'idole (*CN* 2:1101)] that his manservant introduces into the master's dwelling. His examination of her features includes such racist reflections as "she had an unusual face: with regular, refined features with a slightly animal expression, but mystical like that of a Buddha. Her thick lips . . . pointed to a slight mixture of Negro blood, although her hands and arms were *irreproachably* white" (*CSS* 1253; *CN* 2:1101; my emphasis). Later, the narrator expresses his general distaste for "the young women of this primitive continent. . . . They are too close to human animality, their hearts are too rudimentary, their feelings are too poorly refined to waken in our souls the sentimental exaltation that is the poetry of love" (*CSS* 1256; *CN* 2:1107). Still later, as Allouma sporadically disappears into her nomadic wanderings and

then returns to the narrator, he explains his love for her: despite his earlier desire to punish her disappearance "as I would have thrashed a disobedient dog," he admits, "I loved her, in fact, rather as one might love a very rare animal, a dog or a horse that one could not replace. She was a wonderful, a delightful animal, but no more, in the form of a woman." And he concludes, "I can hardly describe what a gulf separated our souls, although perhaps our hearts came into contact at times and responded to the touch. She was a pleasant object in my house and in my life, an extremely agreeable habit to which I had become attached and which appealed to the carnal man in me, the one with only physical senses" (*CSS* 1261; *CN* 2:1114-15).[33]

We must be suspicious, however, of these seemingly dispassionate descriptions, all the more so since they accompany abundant evidence of the effects of Allouma's alluring power. The narrator's reminiscence of their first encounter reveals not only the contradictions in his own responses, but also the obsessive force of her powers of attraction in terms of the imminent struggle by which *l'homme-fille* is always threatened:

> Her eyes, burning with the desire to bewitch, with that need of conquest that imparts a feline fascination to the immodest gaze of a woman, appealed to me, captivated me, robbed me of all power of resistance, and roused me to an impetuous passion. It was a short, silent and violent struggle carried on through the medium of the eyes alone, the eternal struggle between the primitive man and woman, in which man is always conquered. (*CSS* 1253; *CN* 2:1101-2)

This emphasis on the fundamental contradiction in the relations between *l'homme-fille* and the *vraie fille* points to an inner turmoil with which the framed narrator of **"Allouma"** simply cannot come to terms, the "left hand," says Didier Coste, that does not to speak "to the right."[34] When asked finally by the framing narrator if he would take her back, Monsieur Auballe's brief answer reveals these contradictory impulses: "The wicked girl!" [sale fille], says the conquering male, the man of Law and Reason. But then, "Yet I should be very glad all the same" (*CSS* 1263) [Cela me ferait plaisir tout de même (*CN* 2:1117)], responds the conquered male, caught in the grips of the war-machine against which *l'homme-fille* and all his strategic defenses cannot resist, except to "keep them all" in the contradictory, yet complementary, solution of the art of rupture.

While the contemporary resisting reader will no doubt see through the sexist and racist strategies that Maupassant deploys in these tales, the reader must still be attentive to the nuances created, and the narrative duplicity imposed, by the thematics of ethnic and racial "othering" and by the use of embedded narration that structures most of these tales on different narrative levels. From the perspective of recent analyses of "orientalism" (Said) and "orientalist desire" (Behdad), the art of rupture operates fully in these tales through the depiction of oriental sexuality that serves a simultaneous, dual function: to contain the effects of the threatening excess and danger posed by the seductive attraction to the oriental "other," yet also to offer "a simulacrum for the European domination and colonization of Asia and Africa, since [the fantasm of the harem] also embodied an oppressive power structure of the master-slave type" (Behdad, "Eroticized" 124). Indeed, the title of one of Maupassant's earliest creative efforts, the licentious *A la Feuille de Rose. Maison Turque,* includes at once a direct reference to the ultimate site of exotic "otherness," an "oriental" brothel, and an oblique homage paid to the final scene of Flaubert's *L'Éducation sentimentale,* i.e., the adventure at *la Turque*'s establishment presented retrospectively in the reminiscences of the aging Frédéric and Deslauriers, an event that represented "the very best" days of their youth (Flaubert 2:456-57).[35]

Moreover, the explicit circumstances of this play's mise-en-scène, Maupassant's and his young comrades' cross-dressing as prostitutes and engaging in their trade with successive customers, point to the more subtle narrative and discursive strategies that the author subsequently deploys. I refer to the formal basis that the framed tale lends to the implicit homosocial bonding "between men," as narrative and discursive processes through which the appetites of characters and narrators (and even duplicitous readers) are propelled verbally and carnally toward more such mutually stimulating intercourse. These strategies function, then, as effective tactics of engagement in the art of rupture, through the narrative repetition of "othering," yet exchanging tales among *hommes-filles.* Such exchange again raises questions about the implicit "hommo-sexuality" in Maupassant's works (to borrow a neologism from Irigaray). We have confronted this process not merely in tales of homosocial bonding, like **"Les Soeurs Rondoli,"** but especially in the foremost tale that exposes Maupassant's horror of, yet fascination with, the other and the same, in the lesbianism of **"La Femme de Paul."**[36] The homosocial/hommo-sexual specularity implied in these preceding tales of the socio-sexual war-machine provides, then, new grounds for rereading other networks of Maupassant's tales. . . .

Notes

[1] Two other "species" described in "L'Homme-fille," found at "our Chamber of Deputies" and newspapers, are the special targets of Maupassant's second novel, *Bel-Ami* (cf. Donaldson-Evans, "Harlot's Apprentice" 620-24).

[2] See Lehman (227-29), for a structuralist typology of narrative frames in Maupassant's tales.

[3] This has been the critical approach of choice; see Vial ("La Vénus vénale," *Faits* 231-41) as well as Alvado ("L'Amour vénal" 47-72), and Lecarme-Tarbone ("Enigme"). Edmond de Goncourt's expression, "les amours vénals," appears in the preface to *La fille Elisa* (qtd. Alvado 48).

[4] Chambers distinguishes "narratives that focus on their own status as narration," i.e., self-designating, often through narrational embedding, and "narratives that historically have tended to background their status as narrative act so as to focus attention on their content," i.e., duplicitous (*Story* 32-33). However, Chambers is careful to note that self-designating narratives, "although open as to their status as narrative, tend to be situationally duplicitous, their openness as narrative coinciding with seductive programs" (*Story* 217-18). In my own use of the term *duplicitous,* I identify this trait generally with the art of rupture so that all narrators are, in a broad sense, duplicitous.

[5] It is clear from the explanation of her reasons for leaving Rouen that *Boule de suif* did not share her "house full of provisions" with anyone, and certainly not with a Prussian (CSS 9; CN 1:96). As Corbin notes regarding *femmes galantes,* "All these women operated in isolation, at home, at whatever times suited them, whether they lived in an apartment, which was generally the case, or in a townhouse, as the wealthiest of them did. Their clientele was exclusively composed of rich men, foreign aristocrats, *grands bourgeois* of finance or industry, members of the Parisian *bonne bourgeoisie,* or rich provincials who specialized in immoral women on the decline. As good courtesans, the *femmes galantes* exercised choice and were able, therefore, to maintain the illusion with which they surrounded themselves" (*Women for Hire* 133).

[6] Corbin notes, "Threatened in its very health, the bourgeoisie was also threatened in its fortune. The *mangeardes* (women who 'eat up' men's money) . . . are now described as the terror of bourgeois mothers, who will look back fondly to the days when their sons were content to frequent the *maisons de tolérance.* The *femmes galantes* and all the unregistered prostitutes are partly responsible for the 'extraordinary mobility of money' which threatens the most apparently stable positions. . . . The *disorderliness* of vice, at once the cause and symbol of social disorder, was, by its essence, what haunted the regulationists most" (*Women for Hire* 24). Corbin cites Maxime Du Camp's "La prostitution" (in his 1872 *Paris, ses organes, ses fonctions et sa vie,* vol. 3, 116).

[7] Other tales employ the brothel as secondary narrative focus, e.g., "Les Vingt-cinq Francs de la supérieure"

["The Mother Superior's Twenty-five Francs"], and as a supportive function, e.g., as source of fortune, even of a curious respectability ("L'Ami Patience" ["A Way to Wealth"]), and of male potency ("Le Moyen de Roger" ["Roger's Method"]). While "Le Port" ["In Port"] is also set in a Marseille *maison* inhabited presumably by *filles soumises,* the focus of the tale leads to the discovery of incest between a brother, the sailor Celestin Duclos, and his sister, Françoise, who only recognize each other's identity after sexual relations. Another tale in which incest, between father and daughter, is discovered after the act, "L'Ermite" ["The Hermit"] presents another form of unregistered prostitution, the *femme de brasserie,* the barmaid who serves with no legal difficulties within an established workplace with a usually fixed clientele (Corbin, *Women for Hire* 168-71). Of course, Maupassant's very first production is set in a *maison,* the mise-en-scène of the licentious *A la Feuille de Rose. Maison Turque.*

[8] Referring to "La Maison Tellier" as an example of how the hierarchy within provincial *maisons de tolérance* is less subtle than in Paris, Corbin concludes, "This literary example, like the typology pertaining to the capital, is a good illustration of the influence of dominant modes of social life, since the bourgeois salon and the popular café were the models on which these establishments had been based" (*Women for Hire* 60).

[9] As Corbin emphasizes with specific reference to "La Maison Tellier," "The brothel became a place of escape, a place to get away from one's ordinary life, a place where one could make up for the austerity of life at home. There, new forms of sociability were developed between the petty-bourgeois men of the area and a society of women who, in a way, helped to refine their sensibility as well as their sensuality" (126-27). Maupassant fruitfully plays upon the word *maison* (house) in "Une soirée" ["The Noncommissioned Officer"]: a merchant having misunderstood the type of *maison* sought by a visiting quartermaster on leave, the latter faithfully follows the directions received and produces a marvelously embarrassing effect among the town's bourgeois elite.

[10] Donaldson-Evans also points out that "the *rapprochement* between church and brothel is in fact a leitmotif in Maupassant's work" (*A Woman's Revenge* 84-86), e.g., in "Conflits pour rire," "Le Saut du berger," and "Le Lit"; and in "Le Marquis de Fumerol," the eponymous character's death-bed caress, intended for one of two *filles* sitting at bedside, is interpreted by the receiver, his sister (and the framed narrator's mother), as a sign of religious conversion in extremis. See Jean Paris's exhaustive analysis of the generative disjunction of *bordelléglise* ("La Maison Tellier"), and MacNamara's study ("Feminity")

of "La Maison Tellier" as a locus of feminine enclosure. On space in Maupassant's novels, see Giacchetti (*Espaces*).

[11] In a blatant act of censorship, the translation at this point omits two full paragraphs that describe the distribution of holy communion to the children, clearly an essential moment in the tale, as well as the reference to the host held by the priest and his stammering statement. In the subsequent paragraphs, references to his distributing communion "in a state of overexcitement," his lengthy opening statement on feeling the presence of the Holy Ghost, and his brief closing blessing are also omitted (CSS 54-55; CN 1:274-75).

[12] "Conte de Noël" ["A Miracle"] provides a strange complement to the mystical effects of religious experience, since the Eucharist is employed as an instrument of exorcism; see Donaldson-Evans ("'Nuit de Noël'" 70-71).

[13] See also "Le Modèle" ["The Artist's Wife"] for the repercussions of a fatal passion between a susceptible male artist and a *demoiselle.* On the relationship between the painter and feminine sensibilities, see Bailbé.

[14] On the *contes de canotage,* see Delvaille. Although "Une Partie de campagne" ["A Country Excursion"] might be considered a tale of the *canotiers,* I will include it in chapter 6 among the tales of conjugal relations.

[15] Having successfully seduced the enigmatic, taciturn *Italienne,* Francesca Rondoli, whom he met while en route by train to visit the cities of Italy in 1874 with his companion, Paul Pavilly, Jouvenet remains in Genoa with Francesca, as well as with the reluctant Pavilly, for three weeks rather than continue the voyage. Succumbing eventually to Pavilly's incessant urgings, Jouvenet and he abruptly return to Paris, but the following year, traveling to Italy alone, Jouvenet attempts to locate Francesca at the address that she had given him, where he encounters her mother who welcomes him into her home. Explaining that Francesca is now happily situated with a painter in Paris, Signora Rondoli suggests that since he is alone in Genoa, Jouvenet accept the company of Carlotta, the eldest of three remaining daughters. Doing so, then leaving her behind after two weeks of (elided) enjoyment, Jouvenet recalls a final thought, "with a certain uneasiness, mingled with hope, that Mme Rondoli has two more daughters" (CSS 219; CN 2:161).

[16] See Corbin (*The Foul and the Fragrant*), on the "new calculus of olfactory pleasure" and the "perfumes of intimacy" in eighteenth- and nineteenth-century France (71-85 and 176-99, respectively).

[17] See also the reflections of Buci-Glucksmann, following Walter Benjamin, on the "political economy of the prostitute(d) body" (117-24).

[18] On "Yvette," see Danger ("La transgression" as well as, generally, *Pulsion et désir*) and Lecarme-Tabone ("La relation mère-fille"). In another tale of sexual economics recounted "between men," "La Baronne" ["Bric-à-Brac"], the framed narrator, the merchant Boisrené, describes his efforts on behalf of the Baroness Samoris, "a kept woman capable of making herself respected by her lovers more than if she did not sleep with them" (CSS 783; CN 2:909), to help her raise sufficient funds to maintain an economic level suitable for arranging an attractive marriage for her daughter. By himself furnishing her with a "Christ of the Renaissance" to sell at a profit on his behalf from her home, Boisrené unwittingly provides the Baroness with the proper tool to reimburse him and, more importantly, to attract wealthy suitors interested more in *usage,* i.e., of the *objet d'amour,* than in exchange, i.e., of the *objet d'art,* both of which, at the end of the tale, are "still for sale . . . my Christ . . ." (CSS 785; CN 2:912).

[19] For a study of the role of food in this tale, see Donaldson-Evans's comparison between "Nuit de Noël," published in the *Gil Blas* the day after Christmas 1882, and the more respectable "Conte de Noël," published the previous day in *Le Gaulois;* see also Donaldson-Evans (*A Woman's Revenge* 52-53).

[20] Corbin points out that just as "the most common baptismal names—Marie, Jeanne, Louise, Joséphine, Anne—do not appear on the list of pseudonyms," the most common pseudonyms—"Carmen, Mignon, Suzanne, Renée, Andrée, Marcelle, Simone, Olga, Violette, Vyette, Paulette—hardly appear at all on the list of given names" (*Women for Hire* 77). Furthermore, besides revealing the influence of literature and musical theater on determining the choice of pseudonyms, the purpose of names ending in -*ette,* 65 percent of the pseudonyms, "was probably to emphasize youth." Yet, "none of the pseudonyms has a specifically erotic character of its own, and none suggests sexual specialties or perversions" (*Women for Hire* 77). See also Valette's typology of proper names.

[21] Another perspective on onomastics in Maupassant's work is provided by Philippe Bonnefis ("Catoptrique du Nom").

[22] A complementary onomastic analysis would be necessary for another "Madeleine," Madeleine Forestier in *Bel-Ami,* so succinctly described in Maupassant's *chronique* "Politiciennes" [Women politicians] (Chr 1:316-20).

[23] While not explicitly identified as *juive,* the prostitute *insoumise* in *Bel-Ami,* Rachel, resembles her namesake: "She was a large brunette with skin whitened by make-up, with dark eyes, lengthened, emphasized by eyeliner, framed under enormous artificial eyelashes" (*Romans* 208).

[24] As Zeldin notes, "Anti-Semitism was an expression of the ignorance of the modern world that the [Catholic] church suffered from in the mid-nineteenth century rather than a close observation of [the Jewish community]. The anti-Semitic work that the aristocrat [H. R.] Gougenot des Mousseaux (commander of the Order of Pius IX) published in 1869 [*Le Juïf, le judaïsme et la judaïsation des peuples chrétiens*] was inspired by the belief that Jews were cabalistic worshipers of Satan" (2:1037). See Zeldin on anti-clericalism and anti-Semitism in the late nineteenth century (2:1036-39), Corbin on the place of Jewish prostitutes in the white slave trade (*Women for Hire* 275-98), Willa Silverman on anti-Semitism and occultism in fin de siècle France, and for a general reference and bibliography, see Berkovitz.

[25] Forestier comments: "*La Juive,* based on a libretto by Scribe, is an opera by Fromental Halévy, whose daughter, widow of Georges Bizet, remarried the lawyer Straus and maintained a literary salon attended by Maupassant which was the model for the salon of the duchess of Guermantes in Proust's work" (CN 2:1511).

[26] Schmidt qualifies as "false and cruel" a comment in the Goncourt memoirs, "Jewish society has been deadly for Maupassant and Bourget. It has turned these two intelligent beings into literary dandies, with all the pettiness of this race" (*Journal* 4:125 [22 July 1891], qtd. in Schmidt 115).

[27] See Forestier's commentary on the historicopolitical context of Maupassant's Jewish characters Walter (*Bel-Ami,* 1885) and Andermatt (*Romans* 1328-34; 1434-39). See also Hausmann who provides a thorough examination of the portrayal of Jews in nineteenth-century French literature.

[28] Forestier maintains that, "with Andermatt, the writer is not settling a score with the Jewish race, but is painting an actual figure of contemporary France. It is still 'the humble truth'" (*Romans* 1439). See an earlier example of Maupassant's depiction of Jews in his adaptation of the legend of the *Juif errant* (Wandering Jew), "Le Père Judas" ["Father Judas"] (*Le Gaulois,* 28 February 1883).

[29] On "L'Inconnue" see Christopher Lloyd's detailed analysis.

[30] From these trips resulted not only fiction, but *chroniques* and two books of essays, *Au Soleil* (1884) and *La Vie errante* (1890). See especially Maupassant's description of Algerian *filles* in "Prov-

ince d'Alger" in *Au Soleil* (54-91) and reminiscences of visits to brothels in Djelfa and Tunis in the 1889 *chronique* "Les Africaines" (Chr 3:367-77), partially reprinted in the chapter of *La Vie errante* entitled "Tunis" (159-68). On Maupassant's *chroniques,* see Chessex (18-22), Marsigli, and Delaisement (*Guy de Maupassant,* vol. 2, 41-45, including a selection of *chroniques coloniales* [211-23]; and "Les chroniques coloniales").

[31] As the "daughter of Spanish colonists" and wife of a French functionary in the Algerian town of Bougie, Marroca is not, strictly speaking, a *fille du sable,* but the circumstances in which the narrator finds her, as well as their subsequent relations, demonstrate abundantly her complete adaptation to the customs of native women, at least as related by *l'homme-fille.*

[32] The original versions of "Marroca" (entitled "Marauca") and "Châli," both published in the *Gil Blas,* contain significantly different frames and details from the versions adopted in volumes. The original of "Châli" is of particular interest since the framing narrator's depiction of the after-dinner discussion that precedes the tale, recounted by the old admiral de La Vallée, includes women interlocutors who debate with male counterparts diverse literary questions that treat *l'amour mondain* (CN 2:1340-42).

[33] This description of animality recalls another tale, "Boitelle," in which a "young *négresse*" is described, in the indirect mode, as "a little black animal" [un petit animal noir], and her marriage with the son Antoine Boitelle strikes his parents "as if he had proposed a union with the Devil" (CSS 1123) [comme s'il leur avait proposé une union avec le Diable (CN 2:1088-89)].

[34] Coste studies how "the primary structure of the interior separation of the subject" is figured in "Allouma" not only in topographical and cultural terms, but also in lexical, syntactic, and rhetorical traits. See also Donaldson-Evans's discussion of "Allouma" (*A Woman's Revenge* 115-19).

[35] Let us recall that Flaubert attended the second representation of this play and appreciated it greatly for its "freshness" (*Feuille de Rose* 23-30; Goncourt, *Journal* 2:1189).

[36] As Irigaray argues, "So there will be no female homosexuality, just a hommo-sexuality in which woman will be involved in the process of specularizing the phallus, begged to maintain the desire for the same that man has, and will ensure at the same time, elsewhere and in complementary and contradictory fashion, the perpetuation in the couple of the pole of 'matter'" (*Speculum* 103, 127).

Bibliography

[Selected] Works by Maupassant

Chroniques. Ed. Hubert Juin. 3 vols. Paris: U.G.E., 1980.

The Complete Short Stories of Guy de Maupassant. Garden City, NY: Hanover House, 1955.

Contes et nouvelles. Ed. Louis Forestier. 2 vols. Paris: Gallimard, 1974-79.

Selected Critical Works on Maupassant

. . . . .

Alvado, Hervé. *Maupassant ou l'amour réaliste.* Paris: La pensée universelle, 1980. . . .

Bailbé, Joseph-Marc. "Le peintre et la sensibilité féminine chez Maupassant." In Forestier, *Maupassant et l'écriture* 75-85. . . .

Bonnefis, Philippe. "La Catoptrique du Nom." In *La Chose Capitale.* Ed. Philippe Bonnefis and Alain Buisine. Lille: PU de Lille, 1981. 175-208. . . .

Chessex, Jacques. *Maupassant et les autres.* Paris: Éditions Ramsay, 1981. . . .

Coste, Didier. "Allouma, ou ce que la main gauche n'a pas dit à la main droite." *French Forum* 13.2 (1988): 229-42.

Crouzet, Michel. "Une rhétorique de Maupassant?" *Revue d'Histoire littéraire de la France* 80.2 (1986): 233-61. . . .

[Danger, Pierre.] *Pulsion et désir dans les romans et nouvelles de Guy de Maupassant.* Paris: Nizet, 1993.

———. "La transgression dans l'oeuvre de Maupassant." In Forestier *Maupassant et l'écriture* 151-59. . . .

[Delaisement, Gérard.] *Guy de Maupassant, le témoin, l'homme, le critique.* 2 vols. Orléans-Tours: CRDP de l'Académie de Tours, 1984. . . .

Delvaille, Bernard. "Bords de Seine." *Magazine littéraire* 310 (1993): 34-36. . . .

Dickson, Colin. "Théorie et pratique de la clôture: l'exemple de Maupassant dans 'La Maison Tellier'." *The French Review* 64.1 (1990): 42-53. . . .

[Donaldson-Evans, Mary.] "Doctoring History: Maupassant's 'Un Coup d'état'." *Nineteenth-Century French Studies* 16:3-4 (1988): 351-60. . . .

———. "The Harlot's Apprentice: Maupassant's *Bel-Ami.*" *The French Review* 60.5 (1987): 616-25. . . .

————. "'Nuit de Noël' and 'Conte de Noël': Ironic Diptych in Maupassant's Work." *The French Review* 54.1 (1980): 66-77.

————. *A Woman's Revenge: The Chronology of Dispossession in Maupassant's Fiction.* Lexington, KY: French Forum, 1986. . . .

[Forestier, Louis.] ed. *Maupassant et l'écriture.* Paris: Nathan, 1993. . . .

[Giacchetti, Claudine.] *Maupassant. Espaces du roman.* Geneva: Droz, 1993. . . .

Lecarme, Jacques, and Bruno Vercier, eds. *Maupassant: Miroir de la nouvelle.* Saint-Denis: PU de Vincennes, 1988.

Lecarme-Tabone, Éliane. "Enigme et prostitution." In Lecarme and Vercier 111-23.

————. "La relation mère-fille dans l'oeuvre de Maupassant." In Forestier, *Maupassant et l'écriture* 87-98. . . .

Lehman, Tuula. *Transitions savantes et dissimulées: Une étude structurelle des contes et nouvelles de Guy de Maupassant.* Helsinki: The Finnish Society of Sciences and Letters, 1990. . . .

Lloyd, Christopher. "Maupassant et la femme castratrice: lectures de 'L'Inconnue'." In Forestier, *Maupassant et l'écriture* 99-108.

MacNamara, Matthew. "Femininity and Enclosure in Maupassant's Nouvelles." In *L'Hénaurme Siècle. A Miscellany of Essays on Nineteenth-Century French Literature.* Ed. Will L. McLendon. Heidelberg: Carl Winter Universitätsverlag, 1984. 155-65. . . .

Marsigli, Marie-José Hoyet. "Paesaggio 'fantastique' e paesaggio 'féerique' nei 'Carnets de Voyage' di Guy de Maupassant." *Bérénice* 5.12 (1984): 153-70. . . .

Moger, Angela S. "Narrative Structure in Maupassant: Frames of Desire." *PMLA* 100.3 (1985): 315-27. . . .

Paris, Jean. "La Maison Tellier." In *Lisible/Visible: essai de critique générative.* Paris: Seghers/Laffont, 1978. 51-92. . . .

Schmidt, Albert-Marie. *Maupassant par lui-même.* Paris: Seuil, 1962. . . .

Troyat, Henri. *Maupassant.* Paris: Flammarion, 1989.

Valette, Bernard. "Le nom des personnages dans les contes de Maupassant." In Forestier, *Maupassant et l'écriture* 207-18. . . .

Vial, André. *Faits et significations.* Paris: Nizet, 1973. . . .

Other Critical and Literary Works

. . . .

Apter, Emily. "Female Trouble in the Colonial Harem." *differences* 4.1 (1992): 205-24. . . .

Behdad, Ali. "The Eroticized Orient: Images of the Harem in Montesquieu and his Precursors." *Stanford French Review* 13.2-3 (1989): 109-26. . . .

Berkovitz, Jay R. *The Shaping of Jewish Identity in Nineteenth-Century France.* Detroit: Wayne State UP, 1989.

Bernheimer, Charles. *Figures of Ill Repute: Representing Prostitution in Nineteenth-Century France.* Cambridge: Harvard UP, 1989. . . .

Buci-Glucksmann, Christine. *La raison baroque: De Baudelaire à Benjamin.* Paris: Galilée, 1984. . . .

[Chambers, Ross.] *Story and Situation: Narrative Seduction and the Power of Fiction.* Minneapolis: U of Minnesota P, 1984. . . .

Corbin, Alain. *The Foul and the Fragrant: Odor and the French Social Imagination.* Cambridge: Harvard UP, 1986. Trans. of *Le miasme et la jonquille.* Paris: Aubier-Montaigne, 1982.

————. *Women for Hire: Prostitution and Sexuality in France after 1850.* Trans. Alan Sheridan. Cambridge: Harvard UP, 1990. Trans. of *Filles de noce: Misère sexuelle et prostitution (19e et 20e siècles).* Paris: Aubier Montaigne, 1978. . . .

Dijkstra, Bram. *Idols of Perversity: Fantasies of Feminine Evil in Fin-de-siècle Culture.* New York and Oxford: Oxford UP, 1986. . . .

[Flaubert, Gustave.] *Oeuvres.* 2 vols. Paris: Gallimard, 1952. . . .

Hausmann, Frank-Rutger. "Juden and Judentum in der französischen Literatur des 19. Jahrhunderts." *Conditio Judaica: Judentum, Antisemitismus und deutschsprächige Literatur vom 18. Jahrhunderts bis zum Ersten Weltkrieg.* Ed. Hans Otto Horch and Horst Denkler. Vol. 2. Tübingen: Max Wiemeyer Verlag, 1989. 52-71. 2 vols. . . .

Irigaray, Luce. *Speculum of the Other Woman.* Trans. Gillian C. Gill. Ithaca: Cornell UP, 1985. Trans. of *Speculum de l'autre femme.* Paris: Minuit, 1974.

————. *This Sex Which Is Not One.* Trans. Catherine Porter. Ithaca: Cornell UP, 1985. Trans. of *Ce sexe qui n'en est pas un.* Paris: Minuit, 1977. . . .

Said, Edward W. *Orientalism.* New York: Random House, 1978. . . .

Silverman, Willa Z. "Anti-Semitism and Occultism in *fin-de-siècle* France: Three 'Initiates'." In *Modernity and Revolution in Late Nineteenth-Century France.* Ed. Barbara T. Cooper and Mary Donaldson-Evans. Newark: U of Delaware P, 1992. 155-63. . . .

[Zeldin, Theodore.] *Intellect, Taste and Anxiety.* Oxford: Clarendon P, 1977. Vol. 2. of *France, 1848-1945.* 1973-77. 4 vols.

Mary L. Poteau-Tralie (essay date 1995)

SOURCE: "Violating a Sacred Bond: Monstrous Mothers on Trial," in *Voices of Authority: Criminal Obsession in Guy de Maupassant's Short Works,* Peter Lang, 1995, pp. 45-87.

[*In the following excerpt, Poteau-Tralie traces the portrayal of the mother in Maupassant's works—focusing on the "good" mother, the criminal mother, the monstrous mother, and the "unnatural" mother—within the context of prevailing nineteenth-century thought; Maupassant's childhood; his thoughts on God, religion, and children; and his worldview.*]

2.1 Introduction

Maupassant paints a generally cynical picture of women in his fiction; however, one type of woman enjoys a unique and privileged position: the mother. There is a definite evolutionary process from the earliest short stories in which an idealization of the concept of motherhood is placed upon a pedestal, to the increasingly pessimistic portrayal of mothers which marks the final works. One could argue that Maupassant's relationship with his own mother, Laure Le Poittevin de Maupassant, caused him to dwell on the maternal figure and to find in her a constant source of inspiration. Maupassant's parents separated when he was quite young, leaving him only occasional contact with his father. His mother became the focal point of his life and the driving force behind his work. Much has been written regarding the extent of Laure's influence in Guy's life: some portray her as well-meaning in her excessive devotion to him and to his younger brother Hervé, while others simply see in her a domineering woman who hindered rather than helped her son.[1] One thing is certain: by far the greatest influence exerted by Guy's mother was in the cultivation of his writing talent. Thanks to a childhood friendship with Flaubert, Laure was able to persuade the master to take her son under his wing.

It would be difficult to understand how Maupassant's fictional mothers could be both saintly ("**Une Vendetta**") and monstrous ("**La Mère aux monstres**") without first examining the vision of motherhood and female nature in general which emerges in the short works. Maupassant portrays maternal feelings as natural, indeed instinctive, a parallel to his view that women operate by pure instinct, while the capacity for rational thought is seen as a strictly male domain. These are, of course, predominant notions of the time. New ideas regarding motherhood were proposed by writers in the eighteenth century, with Rousseau leading the debate. These notions profoundly influenced French society by the second half of the nineteenth century. Maupassant himself was a product of the new thinking in which the wet-nurse and practice of swaddling the child were now viewed as harmful, if not "unnatural." For example, his mother spoke proudly of the fact that she herself had nursed her son, and not the woman who claimed after Maupassant's death to have been his wet-nurse.[2]

So deeply ingrained had these ideas become, that those who did not conform to the new model for ideal motherhood were looked on as "guilty," because their behavior was now seen to go against a natural maternal instinct. Elisabeth Badinter documents the genesis in the nineteenth century of the notion of the guilty mother: "En ce sens, Rousseau a remporté un succès très important. La culpabilité a gagné le coeur des femmes."[3] Thus, Maupassant's ideas regarding motherhood could be viewed as simple reflections of the prevailing attitudes. However, the criminal context within which so many stories dealing with mothers are placed raises other questions regarding Maupassant's preoccupation with male-female relationships. One of the earliest stories which shows the instinctual nature of female behavior, to the exclusion of rational thought, is "**Histoire d'une fille de ferme**," published in 1881. A careful examination of this early story provides a fitting point of departure for a study of motherhood in Maupassant's work: many facets of the themes of motherhood and of female nature, which here appear in their simplest form, will be developed further or drastically modified in the writer's later works.

The story opens with Rose, a servant girl on a farm, watching the copulation of hens and roosters in an atmosphere of suffocating, dusty summer heat. The narrator highlights her absence of thought when he remarks, "La servante les regardait sans penser" (I, 226). This portrayal of purely animal instinct returns later, but is transposed into a scene involving the story's human protagonists. As the tale unfolds, Rose gives in to the advances of Jacques, the farm hand. When Jacques later finds out that she is pregnant, he leaves the farm. Rose gives birth secretly and hands the child over to others to raise. Her maternal instincts have been awakened, however, and her separation from the child renders her incomplete: "Mais alors, en son coeur si longtemps meurtri, se leva, comme une aurore un amour inconnu pour ce petit être chétif qu'elle avait laissé là-bas" (I, 231). Rose does visit the child occasionally, and her reunions with him become violently physical encounters in which the mother attempts to regain that which has been torn from her. The following description of one such visit, when the child is eight months old and no longer recognizes his mother, bears witness to the depth of Rose's maternal longings: "Elle se jeta dessus comme sur une proie, avec un emportement de bête, et elle l'embrassa si violemment qu'il se prit à hurler de peur" (I, 233). Once the child grows accustomed to her during this visit, the mutual physical bond is reestablished: "Elle prenait une joie infinie à le pétrir dans ses mains, à le laver, à l'habiller, et elle était même heureuse de nettoyer ses saletés d'enfant, comme si ces soins intimes eussent été une confirmation de sa maternité" (I, 233). Unfortunately, Rose's maternal love can never be completely satisfied, for these brief visits are inevitably followed by separation.

The sexual and maternal instincts which regulate the conduct of Maupassant's fictional women are manifested in Rose. Yet, Rose's maternal instincts outweigh her sexual ones, and when the farmer asks for her hand in marriage, Rose refuses, fearing an end to the secret visits to her son. One night, the farmer rapes her in her room. After initially attempting to fight him off, Rose finally gives in to her latent sexual desires, for as the narrator says: "Elle ne consentait pas, pour sûr, mais elle résistait *nonchalamment,* luttant elle-même contre l'instinct toujours plus puissant chez les natures simples, et mal protégées par la volonté indécise de ces races inertes et molles" (I, 239; emphasis mine). In this scene, the reader hears the echo of the opening scene of copulation between the rooster and the hens. Even the terms used to describe the two are identical: "La poule se levait *nonchalamment* et le recevait d'un air tranquille, pliant les pattes et le supportant sur ses ailes" (I, 226; emphasis mine). Only now does the reader fully realize the significance of the opening scene.[4] It is natural for Rose to give in "nonchalantly" to Jacques's sexual advances; she is seen as existing on the same level as the animals whose behavior is regulated by instinct, in the best of the Naturalist tradition.

What precisely is the effect of this link between the opening scene and the unfolding events in Rose's life? Although sympathetic to Rose's plight, the reader is left with a sense of fatalism, as if what happened to her had simply followed the natural course of events. At the conclusion of the tale, Rose is left with no choice but to marry the farmer who continues to take advantage of her. After many years of marriage, the couple remains childless, and the farmer further brutalizes Rose, both physically and verbally, as a result. In the following tirade, he tells Rose that a woman is worth-

less without a child, and once again the animal-human link is established: "Quand une vache n'a point de viaux, c'est qu'elle ne vaut rien. Quand une femme n'a point d'éfant, c'est aussi qu'elle ne vaut rien" (I, 241). Because the union has remained childless, the farmer beats Rose until, on the verge of death, she reveals that she is indeed a mother, and that her illegitimate son is now six years old. The farmer's violent temper is instantly transformed into joy, and he offers to adopt and raise the child as their own, creating a "happy" ending.

This early tale makes several assertions about motherhood which lie at the core of Maupassant's representations of women. First and foremost, a woman may find true happiness and worth only in her role as a mother. As noted, even though the reader might sympathize with Rose for her tremendous suffering, the narrator remains essentially detached, portraying life as it is. Hainsworth asserts that Maupassant's ability to transpose events—here, the copulation of farm animals and the details of a farm girl's life—is evidence of his technical sophistication: "In any event Maupassant's use of the symbolic or explicit detail, evoking a parallel and suggesting, pessimistically in most cases, behind what is particular what is general, must be taken as his most characteristic tendency."[5] In this case, the particular suggests that despite the cruelty to which she succumbs, Rose's life, indeed life in general, is simply following its predetermined course.

In this third-person account, the characters do not speak for themselves. One has the feeling that Rose is placed on the stage of life and is acted upon by others, without the ability to react in turn. The impotence and silence of mothers like Rose is a constant of what we might call "good mothers" in the short stories. Only the "good mother" remains silent and completely self-sacrificing, as evidenced in the various ways in which her voice in the narration is drowned out by other voices of authority. For example, even though the suffering mother is allowed to tell her sad tale to a stranger (the first-person narrator) in a story entitled **"Humble drame"** (1883), a reworking of **"Rencontre"** (1882), her words have no power to bring back the son she has lost.[6] She tells the stranger that her life had been spent trying to hold on to her son, who was constantly taken from her. Sent as a young boy to boarding school, at the time of the tale's unfolding he is married to a woman who refuses to allow the mother contact with him. The mother's parting words to the stranger reveal her pain: "Adieu, monsieur, ne restez pas près de moi, *ça me fait mal de vous avoir dit tout cela*" (I, 1020; emphasis mine). There is something heroic about the final image the narrator presents of the mother who suffers in silence, despite the brief and modest glimpse she has allowed us into her life:

> Et comme je redescendais la colline, m'étant retourné, j'aperçus la vieille femme debout sur

une muraille crevassée, regardant les monts, la longue vallée et le lac Chambon dans le lointain. Et le vent agitait comme un drapeau le bas de sa robe et le petit châle étrange qu'elle portait sur ses maigres épaules. (I, 1020)

Like Rose, she remains forever a victim of circumstances, and is meant to be admired for her silent suffering. Indeed, she wears her meager clothing which hides her figure as a "flag," a symbol of her motherhood.

Finally, although sexual drive is indeed strong in women, the maternal instinct should override this and any other instinct, including that of self-preservation, in order for a woman to fit into the "good mother" category. Transgression of this basic code leads to trial and judgment of the female characters throughout the short works, as will be seen by the varied complexities in narrative structure which serve to set up a voice of authority in leading the reader to a guilty verdict. The basic early portrait of a mother provided by Rose will serve as point of reference in our study of maternity.

2.2 Acquitting the Murderous Mother

As Maupassant continued to privilege the mother in his fiction, especially in the three years immediately following the publication of **"Histoire d'une fille de ferme,"** his views regarding motherhood crystallized to the point that any mother who deviated from the clearly established norm quickly became the focus of judgment in the stories. In the works dating from this period, the reader finds stories of good mothers who uphold the sanctity of motherhood juxtaposed with those of bad, indeed criminal, mothers. However, it is important to note that even if a mother commits a crime and is plainly guilty in legal terms, she is not necessarily judged "criminal" by the voice of authority in the tale. Two stories published a few months apart, **"Une Vendetta"** (1883) and **"La Mère sauvage"** (1884), suggest that even murder itself does not render a mother guilty, as long as her violent deed is in response to an affront against her maternity. These "innocent" mothers stand in striking contrast to those whom the narrator judges to be truly criminal in Maupassant's works.

Far from concealing or glossing over the fact that the mothers in **"Une Vendetta"** and **"La Mère sauvage"** commit murder, the narrators dwell at length on every detail surrounding the crime. Indeed, these stories are fascinating in their depiction of the anatomy of a crime. **"Une Vendetta,"** recounted by an omniscient third-person narrator, tells how an old widow suffers the loss of her only son, Antoine, who is stabbed to death in a dispute with Nicolas Ravolati, a Corsican bandit. The woman's maternal status is subtly underscored by the narrator who refers to her as "la mère Saverini"

and "la vieille mère." She speaks to her son's corpse in a lament reminiscent of a lullaby, promising:

> Va, va, tu seras vengé, mon petit, mon garçon, mon pauvre enfant. Dors, dors, tu seras vengé, entends-tu? C'est la mère qui le promet! Et elle tient toujours sa parole, la mère, tu le sais bien. (I, 1031).

Ironically, when la mère Saverini devises a plan of revenge, she goes to church to pray, not for forgiveness, but for the strength to carry out her plan. The narrator notes how the mother does not even question the gravity, in religious or legal terms, of the crime she is about to commit:

> . . . levée dès les approches du jour, elle se rendit à l'église. Elle pria, prosternée sur le pavé, abattue devant Dieu, le suppliant de l'aider, de la soutenir, de donner à son pauvre corps usé la force qu'il fallait pour venger le fils. (I, 1032)

In a sense, la mère Saverini is meant to be seen as the equivalent of the Virgin Mary who suffers as a result of the wrongful death of her son. Yet, her request for divine assistance in murderous revenge is clearly ironic.

Mary Donaldson-Evans writes: "A superficial reading of Maupassant's work suggests that he was in perfect step with the *fin-de-siècle* skepticism preached by his contemporaries," most notably, "the determinism of Darwin and Taine, the cynicism of Schopenhauer and the tradition of blasphemy going back to Sade."[7] Yet, as she rightfully argues,

> Maupassant's treatment of religious themes reveals unsuspected complexities, as well as a contempt for the concept of God which cannot be traced uniquely to the "hors-texte" of his era, but which is closely bound to the role played by women in his fictional universe.[8]

In addition to the ideas promoted by the religious skeptics of his time, Maupassant had a model for excessive female religiosity in one of the female creations of his mentor—Flaubert's Emma Bovary.[9] However, in the early **"Une Vendetta"** at least, Maupassant seems to suggest that there is indeed a certain complicity between God the Father and the mother who has been made to suffer as a result of the death of her offspring. In short, Maupassant does not regard La Mère Saverini's piety as entirely vain or senseless; rather, he leaves his reader with a sense of awe regarding the powerful bond between the suffering mother and God. La mère Saverini certainly stretches, to an almost blasphemous degree, the notion that the innocent may find comfort in God. Nonetheless, in this early work, Maupassant focuses exclusively on the maternal aspect of her womanhood, an aspect which he undeniably privileges at this point in his career.

The narrator makes no attempt to hide the details of la mère Saverini's complex plan for revenge. La mère Saverini carefully puts together a straw mannequin, attaching a strip of blood-sausage to its throat. For three months, she accustoms her dog to repeated fasts after which he is let loose to devour the sausage around the mannequin's neck. The narrator reveals that, "la mère Saverini alla se confesser et communia un dimanche matin avec une ferveur extatique," and, filled with confidence that God is on her side, seeks out her son's killer (I, 1033). When she arrives at Nicolas Ravolati's wood shop, she unleashes her starving dog which promptly goes for Nicolas' throat. The narrator ends the tale by stating quite simply: "La vieille, le soir, était rentrée chez elle. Elle dormit bien, cette nuit-là" (I, 1034). The reader is left shocked by the crime. The narrator highlights the mother's complete lack of remorse, although he does not explicitly condemn her. Maupassant has created a moral code which distinguishes mothers from others in society. For her part, the mother in the story never questioned her own innocence. Indeed, she would have found herself "guilty" only if she had failed to avenge her son's death.

As we have seen in the first chapter [of *Voices of Authority*], Maupassant is at his best when he weaves the plot around a much more complicated chain of witnessing which eventually includes the reader.[10] Just a few months after the publication of **"Une Vendetta,"** Maupassant published **"La Mère sauvage,"** a similar though more skillfully written tale of a mother's revenge. This story makes use of the technique of the narrative frame, thereby incorporating the reader into the narration process. The nameless first-person narratee begins the tale by telling of the pleasure he finds in returning fifteen years later to his favorite hunting spot in Virelogne with his friend, Serval. Nothing in the frame prepares the narratee, and in turn the reader who identifies with him, for the morbid tale of a mother's revenge which Serval will recount when the floor is handed over to him. In fact, the sensual impact of the atmosphere on the narratee leads the reader to think that perhaps the story will involve a beautiful young woman, and not an aging mother. The narratee, too, seems to be readying himself for such an encounter with a young woman in this lovely setting. In the following passage, woman and landscape are fused into one image, a frequent technique in the short stories:

> J'aimais ce pays infiniment. Il est des coins du monde délicieux qui ont pour les yeux un charme sensuel. . . . Quelquefois même la pensée retourne vers un coin de forêt, ou un bout de berge, ou un verger poudré de fleurs, aperçus une seule fois, par un jour gai, et restés en notre coeur comme ces images de femmes rencontrées dans la rue, un matin de printemps, avec une toilette claire et transparente, et qui nous laissent dans l'âme et dans la chair un désir inapaisé, inoubliable, la sensation du bonheur coudoyé. (I, 1217)

Once the reader has been won over, the narratee sees the burnt shell of an old farmhouse, and the mood changes dramatically.[11] He engages Serval as the narrator of the framed story by asking Serval to tell him what happened since his last visit to this house which was at that time owned by the Sauvage family. Serval tells him that during the Prussian invasion, la mère Sauvage (left widowed after the death of her husband at the hands of the gendarmes) was forced to take in four Prussian soldiers, her own son having been conscripted. She takes care of them, and over time, the soldiers appear "comme quatre bons fils autour de leur mère" (I, 1219). This surrogate mother never forgets her own son, however. In a long aside, Serval notes that this woman is first and foremost a mother for whom war and politics mean nothing next to the love she feels for her son. She is simply a victim of circumstances:

> Elle les aimait bien, d'ailleurs, ses quatre ennemis; car les paysans n'ont guère les haines patriotiques; cela n'appartient qu'aux classes supérieures. Les humbles, ceux qui paient le plus parce qu'ils sont pauvres et que toute charge nouvelle les accable, ceux qu'on tue par masses, qui forment la vraie chair à canon parce qu'ils sont le nombre, ceux qui souffrent enfin le plus cruellement des atroces misères de la guerre, parce qu'ils sont les plus faibles et les moins résistants, ne comprennent guère ces ardeurs belliqueuses, ce point d'honneur excitable et ces prétendues combinaisons politiques qui épuisent en six mois deux nations, la victorieuse comme la vaincue. (I, 1219-20)

La mère Sauvage's maternal instincts take over when she receives a letter informing her of her son's death, and like la mère Saverini in **"Une Vendetta,"** she devises an intricate plan for revenge. She has the soldiers write down their names and addresses on a piece of paper and sends them to bed in the attic which she has filled with fresh hay. La mère Sauvage sets fire to the house, and the soldiers perish while she stands impassively outside. In fact, her lack of remorse and the actual pride she takes in her "accomplishment" are highlighted when she openly admits her guilt to the Prussian soldiers who subsequently execute her against the wall. However, lest the reader be lulled into believing that this is simply a story of a mother's undying love for her son—a love so excessive that she will quite "innocently" commit murder—Maupassant has the narratee return at the end to offer his own commentary on the story he has just heard. Here, the outcome deviates dramatically from that of **"Une Vendetta,"** because the narratee ends the tale by declaring, "Moi, je pensais aux mères des quatre doux garçons brûlés là-dedans; et à l'héroïsme atroce de cette autre mère fusillée contre ce mur. Et je ramassai une pierre, encore noircie par le feu" (I, 1224). The reader cannot accept this act as entirely innocent, for if it were, the logical conclusion would be for the violence to continue through the four mothers who might now them-selves be justified in seeking revenge in such an "atro-ciously heroic" manner.

J. H. Matthews interprets this story as a comment on war:

> The effect provoked by this narrative tone is reinforced by the final image with which Maupassant leaves his readers: all that remains of so much suffering is a blackened pebble in the hand of a stranger, suggesting all the futility and sterility of war. So that it is only now that we fully understand the function of the frame within which Maupassant has placed his narrative.[12]

Given Maupassant's use of the Franco-Prussian war era as the setting for many of his stories, this assess-ment is correct. However, there is a second theme treated here directly related to the power of the ma-ternal instinct which one should not overlook, since Maupassant had similarly showcased a mother's re-venge only a few months earlier in **"Une Vendetta."** By taking his earlier story one step further, Maupassant appears to question the code of morality which had begun to emerge in **"Une Vendetta,"** whereby moth-ers seem to be exempt from moral guilt if acting in retaliation for the death of a child. The internal lis-tener, the narratee of the frame, guides our response to this violent act, and forces us to think of the pos-sible perpetuation of such violence if one accepts the mother's logic in committing the crime. He is left not only with the blackened stone, but with the disturbing thought of the four mothers left childless by la mère Sauvage, and indeed of all mothers so deprived by the tragedy of war. The two themes—war and the maternal instinct's savage hold on a woman—are intertwined. It is war which unleashes a potentially violent instinct in mothers, one which renders them capable of murder—this time a murder which is not treated so casually as in **"Une Vendetta."** We have in this story hints that Maupassant's view of mothers is no longer as rosy as it appeared in the early **"Histoire d'une fille de ferme."**

2.3 Maternal versus Sexual Instincts and the Crime of Infanticide

In the evolution of the short stories devoted to mater-nity, there is a definite shift in focus from the mother to the child. Indeed, the halo worn by Maupassant's early mothers fades in the many instances in which the sacred mother-child bond is violated by the mother. In these later stories, the nurturing function dictated by a woman's apparently overriding maternal instinct van-ishes. In its place is a conflict between the mother and her offspring: the child struggles for simple survival, while the mother denies her maternity in an effort to hold on to an identity which is closely linked to her sexuality. At the heart of the conflict is the inability of Maupassant's women to reconcile their sexual and

maternal roles. Either they become mothers who lose themselves in their children (tellingly, most of the "good" mothers are old and certainly physically un-appealing), or they remain childless and retain their attractiveness to men. This concept of the asexual mother has a rich literary tradition in the period, and Maupassant was certainly aware of its presence in Flaubert's work. In order for Emma Bovary to con-tinue her downward spiral with men, for example, her child Berthe had to be dropped from the plot or the story would have ended with her birth. The mother is by nature confined to the enclosed space of the ménage in which the public, sexual, aspect of her womanhood is concealed.

The theme of beauty, first in its inspiration found in the barren woman, and then in its transformation into art through the artist's imagination, is likewise appar-ent throughout Baudelaire's work. His is a "cult which glorifies beautiful sterility in the female," for "giving birth is to be the *intellectual* attribute of the poet, and his muse-mistress is not to be defiled by the all too *natural* horrors of child-bearing."[13] This notion is evident in Baudelaire's "Sed Non Satiata" which refers to the idealized woman, and her fetishized eyes as the locus: "Où tout n'est qu'or, acier, lumière et diamants, / Resplendit à jamais, comme un astre inutile, / La froide majesté de la femme stérile."[14] The artist could at least imagine a perfect beauty in beholding a woman, even if the illusion proved tran-sitory. The illusion could not be conjured up, let alone sustained, when the functional aspect of a woman's body was apparent through her maternity. In Baudelaire's poetry, one finds the "metamorpho-sis of the woman desired and dreamed about, through the cerebral alchemy with which moderns delight in complicating lust or sentiment."[15] As shown in chap-ter 1, the prostitute served the artist of the period well in this regard. Her appeal both in the social and literary history centered on her role as object of pure pleasure, distinct from the natural procreative role played by the wife and mother. Bernheimer summa-rizes Baudelaire's attraction/repulsion faced with the prostitute in the following: "When Baudelaire asks 'What is art?' and answers 'Prostitution,' it is to this kind of biologically sterile, but erotically stimulating, multiplication of the self that he is referring."[16]

Unlike other writers of the time, however, Maupassant does not abandon the child. Any attempt to fuse the maternal and the sexual in Maupassant's work requires that the child become the sacrificial victim of a now guilty mother. In addition, the potential for criminality on the mother's part is brought out in the actual and simulated courtroom settings of the stories. Ironically, while the mother attempts to gain some sort of control or power over her life or story by brushing the un-wanted child aside, it is the child who is given a voice in the narration, often becoming a witness to his or her own mother's guilt. Maupassant places great emphasis on the child who suffers when the mother abandons him for the sake of her sexuality.

Many of Maupassant's stories which employ the narrative frame rely on the voice of a doctor as narrator and expert witness. If the narratee in the frame is called upon at the end of the tale to comment upon the story just told by the doctor/narrator—that is, if the narratee in the frame does not simply function as one who merely serves to provide an introduction to the story—the layers of narration thus created isolate the subject of the tale from her (in this case) own story. When the story involves a mother's transgression, the child, too, often becomes a silent witness and judge of the mother. Such is the case in **"L'Enfant,"** published in *Gil Blas* in 1883. It is perhaps one of Maupassant's most graphic stories in its portrayal of a violent crime.

In the frame of **"L'Enfant,"** the anonymous third-person narrator observes, "On parlait, après le dîner, d'un avortement qui venait d'avoir lieu dans la commune" (I, 981). The setting takes on the aura of a courtroom as two of the speakers enter into a debate regarding the guilt or innocence of a woman accused of infanticide. The frame pits the baroness in the role of prosecutor against the doctor, who assumes the role of lawyer for the accused. Using the terminology of courtroom litigation, the doctor argues that society's creation of false honor and concern with moral "honnêteté" is "plus abominable que le crime." He seems to be arguing that society is at fault for making a crime of the free embrace of two beings. Thus, society's laws, which conflict with the laws of nature, or as he puts it, "la loi impérieuse de la vie," can only lead, "à l'assassinat, à l'infanticide de pauvres filles. . . . " (I, 980). Just as in **"Confessions d'une femme,"** the thrust of the argument for innocence rests on the fact that nature has provided these fallen women with a sexual appetite which can never be reconciled with man-made laws.[17]

The baroness's role as society's voice is established when she contrasts terms such as "le vice" and "la vertu," "la prostituée" and "l'honnête femme" (I, 981). However, she is only one presumably among several narratees—recall the opening: "*On* parlait après le dîner. . . . " (I, 981; my emphasis)—and her voice of authority is quickly eclipsed at the end of the frame by the doctor who responds to her charges. The anonymous third-person narrator intervenes, adding a detail concerning the doctor which further tips the scales in his favor as credible witness and one ultimately to be believed by the reader. He is not only a doctor, but also "un vieux homme qui avait touché à bien des plaies" (I, 982), implying wisdom gained through age and experience. Now having the third-person narrator's approval as authority, the doctor leaves the frame and becomes the first-person narrator of the new tale.

The doctor prefaces his story with general observations on human nature, with specific reference to that of women. Once again, nature's unyielding power over humans exculpates them. The doctor laments, "Malheur à ceux à qui la perfide nature a donné des sens inapaisables" (I, 982). In the following, the power of the senses and instincts are equated with forces in nature, much like the omnipotent forces which governed Rose's actions in **"Histoire d'une fille de ferme":**

> Pouvez-vous arrêter le vent, pouvez-vous arrêter la mer démontée? Pouvezvous entraver les forces de la nature? Non. Les sens aussi sont des forces de la nature, invincibles comme la mer et le vent. Ils soulèvent et entraînent l'homme et le jettent à la volupté sans qu'il puisse résister à la véhémence de son désir. (I, 982)

Through this equation, the baroness's authority as judge is further subverted, for if she condemns women who follow their natural instincts, it is only because she has been spared the high dose of sexual appetite granted to other women. In an off-handed affront to her femininity, the doctor suggests that the baroness is even perhaps one of those beings who is "désespérément jaloux des autres, sans le savoir" (I, 983). She is not given the chance to respond; instead, the doctor finally proceeds with the story of the events he witnessed.

The doctor gives the woman "on trial" before the baroness and the other narratees present at the dinner the name "Mme Hélène." We learn of her incredible sexual appetite, and of the fact that the doctor was consulted for his professional scientific opinion when the girl had reached puberty. His diagnosis at that time was that she was, at the age of twelve, biologically a woman already afflicted "par des désirs d'amour" (I, 983). This seemingly clinical diagnosis by an objective man of science contrasts sharply with his observations regarding her physical appearance. In fact, he seems to present us with a sort of male fantasy figure, which is clearly not objective at all:

> Elle avait des lèvres grasses, retournées, ouvertes comme des fleurs, un cou fort, une peau chaude, un nez large, un peu ouvert et palpitant, de grands yeux clairs dont le regard allumait les hommes. (I, 983)

The doctor seems to have fallen under her spell as other men had done. We are told that all three of her husbands died of exhaustion after spending only a short period of time with her. She is left with no honorable or legal way to relieve her nymphomania. Madame Hélène has accepted society's prejudices, and thus is unable to follow the doctor's suggestion that she take a lover. Instead, she becomes pregnant by her gardener, whom she pays for his services. Her behavior, then, is doubly shocking here: she goes beneath her social class to find a lover, and she *pays* him. This is typically male behavior, for she now becomes the female "client" of a working class male "prostitute." Already, she has overstepped the bounds of acceptable female behavior. At this point, the doctor recreates her private confession to him. He records her words as: "Oh! je me confesse à vous sans réserve et sans hésitations. J'ai essayé de me faire avorter" (I, 984). Once again, she does not take his advice to go away and give birth in secret.

It is interesting to note how the doctor in his role as first-person narrator, who presumably had limited vision on the events he witnessed, becomes omniscient in re-telling Hélène's story. He has access to and describes her private thoughts and her actions in her bedroom. Maupassant seems to have given this narrator a greater authority than one would expect from someone who could not possibly have been an eyewitness to all that is revealed here. For example, the doctor describes her emotions as she stands naked before her mirror gazing at her pregnant body. Indeed, he is almost a voyeur:

> Chaque soir elle se dévêtait devant son armoire à glace et regardait son flanc déformé; puis elle se jetait par terre, une serviette dans la bouche pour étouffer ses cris. Vingt fois par nuit elle se relevait, allumait sa bougie et retournait devant le large miroir qui lui renvoyait l'image bosselée de son corps nu. (I, 985)

The doctor was supposedly absent when the abortion was performed. Yet, he is able to describe in painstaking detail the crime and the psychological state of the woman as she commits it:

> Puis elle descendit, nu-pieds, à la cuisine, ouvrit l'armoire et prit le grand couteau qui sert à couper les viandes. Elle remonta, alluma quatre bougies et s'assit, sur une chaise d'osier tressé, devant sa glace. Alors, exaspérée de haine contre cet embryon inconnu et redoutable, le voulant arracher, et tuer enfin, le voulant tenir en ses mains, étrangler et jeter au loin, elle pressa la place où remuait cette larve et d'un seul coup de la lame aiguë, elle se fendit le ventre. (I, 985)

Surely, the doctor could have pieced together the clues left at the scene, but interwoven in his description of the crime are details regarding her thoughts and emotional state.

Up to this point, an interesting shift in focus has taken place, perhaps without the reader being at all aware of this manipulation. Details about the crime as well as the title Maupassant chose for the story change our perspective on what is really being judged here. The title is **"L'Enfant,"** and one cannot ignore the role given to the child in the final scene. It is noteworthy that the child assumes its own identity as it is clearly made to struggle repeatedly for survival: "C'était entre eux une lutte terrible. Mais il ne mourait pas: et, sans cesse, il s'agitait comme s'il se fût défendu" (I, 985). The child's role in the struggle must be kept in mind when we return to the frame at the end. The doctor asks his listener for a verdict: "Fut-elle bien coupable, madame?" (I, 986). The baroness offers no help in how we are to judge the tale, for she is silenced: "La baronne ne répondit pas" (I, 986). Her testimony as authority has already been dismissed, but her silence is now coupled with the revealing silence of the doctor himself who seems to pause, allowing the reader to enter into the chain of witnessing: "Le Médecin se tut et attendit" (I, 986).

It is certain that Madame Hélène is acquitted as far as her nymphomania is concerned. This innocence was established from the outset in the long description of nature's control of the senses, and is in keeping with the deterministic tendencies in Maupassant's work dating as far back as **"Histoire d'une fille de ferme."** Madame Hélène is not "guilty" for her sexuality, as the baroness, the official voice of society and society's law would have us believe. However, the issue of guilt and innocence is clouded in reference to the infanticide. The title makes the "child" the central issue. The child's uneven struggle with its mother is highlighted, and the final act seems to symbolize the "unnaturalness" of the woman's suppression of the maternal instinct. We are told that at the end, despite cutting the child physically from her own body, "il tenait par des liens qu'elle n'avait pu trancher" (I, 986). Literally, this "lien" is the umbilical cord, but symbolically, these ties refer to the unbreakable mother-child bond. Thus, although the doctor becomes the advocate for the woman in one sense, seeming to free her from guilt, he is really the advocate for the child against what is an unnatural act by a desperate mother. Maupassant gives the doctor/narrator within the framed tale tremendous freedom in his storytelling, even to the point of allowing him to become an eyewitness to what was apparently a private tragedy. The doctor's voice subverts the voice of the baroness and that of the original omniscient narrator in the frame who initially described the dinner conversation. Yet, in granting the doctor omnipotence as authority in matters of guilt and innocence, the reader's eventual judgment of the events is not to be left in doubt. Indeed, the distance between reader and author has been greatly reduced. This is coupled, of course, with Maupassant's revealing choice of a title, and his simulation of a courtroom atmosphere in the narration process.

The woman in **"L'Enfant"** is presented as having two irreconcilable roles. Either she is an overly sexual being and agent of death for the man—recall the way in which she killed off three husbands and even had power over the doctor—or she is the life-giving mother. Mme Hélène transgressed this code by attempting to fuse the two roles. Perhaps this is why she was unable to follow the doctor's advice that she take leave of society until her child could be born in secret. She could not bear to isolate herself and suppress the power she wielded through her sexuality, after pregnancy so transformed her once sensuous body.

Maupassant's focus on the child in **"L'Enfant"** as implicit judge of his mother bears witness, as we will see, to a novel child-centeredness in stories involving a mother's guilt. In addition, from an historic perspective, this particular story addressed a crime at the heart of legislative debates throughout the nineteenth century: infanticide. Louis Forestier notes that a *fait divers* involving a woman suspected of infanticide appeared in *Gil Blas* just two weeks before **"L'Enfant"** was published.[18] The very frequency of the crime in the period within which Maupassant wrote assured the author a large audience interested in this question. As Richard Lalou documents:

> Ainsi de 1856 à 1895, on compte en moyenne, tous les cinq ans, 4000 crimes contre l'enfant nouveau-né! Nous pouvons donc admettre que ce type de crime, loin d'être la persistance de pratiques moyenâgeuses, constitue bien un nouveau phénomène d'ordre social.[19]

Recent historiographers have questioned the relevance for the nineteenth century of Philippe Ariès's theories on the discovery of the child in light of the prevelance of the crime of infanticide in France just a century ago. Ariès traces the evolution of a new awareness of and concern for the child from the Middle Ages, when mortality alone made sentimentality toward the child difficult, to the nineteenth century when the nuclear family, with the child as its focal point, became the center of society.[20] Yet, reconciling this idea that the discovery of the child culminated in the nineteenth century with a crime against the child so prevalent that Maupassant clearly exploited it in his short stories is problematic, as Dominique Vallaud points out:

> Comment aborder alors, dans la mise en place de ce nouveau cadre, la pratique encore répandue de l'infanticide au XIXème siècle, et surtout, l'indulgence des Cours d'Assises à l'égard de crime, apparemment en contradiction avec ce nouveau statut donné à l'enfant dès sa naissance?[21]

Despite the frequency of infanticide, relatively few women brought to trial were ever actually found guilty.[22] Lalou estimates that, in the last half of the nineteenth century, seventy percent of those women brought to trial for infanticide were not found guilty by a jury. The indulgence of juries during such trials has several possible explanations,[23] but perhaps the most interesting in relation to **"L'Enfant"** pertains to the profile of the woman most often accused of infanticide. Typically, she is a "femme jeune, célibataire, illétrée et d'origine rurale."[24] Vallaud suggests that bourgeois society feared any child born outside the family structure: "Cette menace enfantine et juvénile dont serait responsable l'illégitimité contribue à éclairer l'absence de compassion du jury à l'égard de l'enfant d'une fille-mère."[25] She concludes, "l'horreur qu'inspire le crime, qui se mesure d'habitude aux souffrances de la victime, ne parait pas avoir été prise en compte."[26]

In writing **"L'Enfant,"** Maupassant chose not to portray the "typical" infanticidal mother, and to take into account the suffering of the crime's victim as well. Madame Hélène, widowed three times, was not the *fillemère* of most courtroom trials for infanticide, and she lived in a château complete with its own gardener. By creating such a criminal mother Maupassant was able to deflect the listener's pity away from the mother, who was often seen by actual juries as as much a victim of circumstances as the child, and toward the child himself.

The manipulation is quite subtle here, and the focus is indeed novel. But Maupassant showed that he was aware of and bowed to public sentiment in this regard when, in 1886, he published **"Rosalie Prudent,"** a story told entirely in the third person, and far inferior from a technical perspective to the earlier **"L'Enfant."** The young woman accused of infanticide in this actual courtroom drama fits the typical mold: she is an unmarried servant girl who gives birth in secret. When she reveals that she became pregnant by her employer's nephew, she elicits sympathy from the jury, and cries of indignation from the bourgeois couple for whom she worked. The only twist in an otherwise ordinary plot, which followed so many actual trials played out daily in the newspapers, was the addition of something of a surprise ending. Rosalie was seen preparing clothes carefully for her child before the birth, and thus the judge could not understand her murderous act. She tells the shocked jury that she gave birth not to one child, but to twins, and, in desperation at the overwhelming prospect of raising two children alone, killed them both. Rosalie tells the assembly where the second child is buried, and the narrator describes the scene as follows: "La moitié des jurés se mouchaient coup sur coup pour ne point pleurer. Des femmes sanglotaient dans l'assistance" (II, 702). In the end, "La fille Rosalie Prudent fut acquittée" (II, 702). **"Rosalie Prudent"** represents a small fray in a thread which otherwise runs unbroken through the whole of the short stories: mothers who refuse to relinquish their sexual role in favor of their maternal one are guilty of explicit (in the case of **"L'Enfant"**) and, as we shall see, implicit infanticide. And, more often than not, it is the child who is called upon to condemn the mother.

2.4 Indicting the Murderous Mother: The Child Witness

In **"L'Enfant,"** Maupassant takes the possible images conjured up of the horror of the crime committed against the child out of the shadows of the reader's imagination and places them onto the pages of a Naturalist text. Focusing on the child as victim is effective in convincing the reader of the guilt of the woman who refuses to give up the one thing that empowers her: her sexual attractiveness to men. Despite the fact that the plot of **"Rosalie Prudent"** is typical from a socio-historic point of view, **"L'Enfant"** is more "typical" of Maupassant's fiction wherein the child is called upon as a witness against his mother.

In **"L'Enfant,"** the child is a "silent" witness: his position in the struggle against his mother is made manifest through the intricate narrative structure. For Madame Hélène, the burden of guilt centers on her refusal to privilege her maternity over her sexuality. Every day she lingered in front of her mirror gazing in revulsion at "son flanc déformé" and "l'image bosselée de son corps nu" (I, 985). This is not the only time that Maupassant's characters look with such loathing on pregnancy and the pregnant body, which, as mentioned, is a constant in the literature of the period. One of the most fascinating treatments of the theme of a mother's guilt in refusing to accept her new status as a mother, beginning with the physical changes it brings, is found in a tale entitled **"Madame Hermet"** (1887) in which the child stands in judgment of the mother. Louis Forestier places this tale among those concerned with old age: "L'obsession dont souffre Mme Hermet est celle du vieillissement, que Maupassant lui-même éprouvait. . . . " (II, 1606). However, one must not overlook the fact that the link between her madness and her advancing age on one level is coupled with a link between her madness and her maternal status on another. The tale opens with an observation made by a first-person narrator identified only as "je," who will become the narratee in the framed tale:

> Les fous m'attirent. Ces gens-là vivent dans un pays mystérieux de songes bizarres, dans ce nuage impénétrable de la démence où tout ce qu'ils ont vu sur la terre, tout ce qu'ils ont aimé, tout ce qu'ils ont fait recommence pour eux dans une existence imaginée en dehors de toutes les lois qui gouvernent les choses et régissent la pensée humaine. . . . Eux seuls peuvent être heureux sur la terre, car, pour eux, la Réalité n'existe plus. (II, 874)

As the tale unfolds, it becomes evident that the optimistic portrayal of the insane in the introduction serves to mislead the reader.[27] The first-person narrator in the frame is so fascinated with the insane, that he visits an asylum where a doctor invites him to see "un cas intéressant" (II, 875). He opens the door upon a woman "âgée d'environ quarante ans, encore belle, assise dans un grand fauteuil, [qui] regardait avec obstination son visage dans une petite glace à main" (II, 875). At the sight of the visitors she runs and veils herself, lamenting to the doctor that she has discovered ten more pock marks on her face. He assures her that they are not there but she refuses to believe him. The doctor tells her that the visitor (i.e. the frame's narrator) is also a doctor and that she can take him into her confidence.

A careful reading both of Madame Hermet's words when she is given the brief opportunity to speak and of the unfolding story reveals that she links her loss of beauty, not with her age as the doctor will attempt to establish, but with her child. The woman tells the narrator:

> *C'est en soignant mon fils* que j'ai gagné cette épouvantable maladie, monsieur. Je l'ai sauvé, mais *je suis défigurée. Je lui ai donné ma beauté, à mon pauvre enfant.* Enfin, j'ai fait mon devoir, ma conscience est tranquille. Si je souffre, il n'y a que Dieu qui le sait. (II, 876; emphasis added)

The doctor gently strokes her cheeks with a paint brush, convincing her that he has removed all traces of the pock marks. This gesture is telling in its parallel to the power relationship in the story's narration; the doctor/narrator is indeed the "artist" who controls the viewer's/narratee's perspective on events. In addition, he is able to confine within a frame his "picture" of the female whose story *he* recounts. Just as the story's narrative frame serves to distance her from her story structurally, this distancing is also accomplished literally within the plot when the doctor closes the door, silencing Madame Hermet behind its frame. After closing the woman once again in her room, the doctor takes control of her story, saying, "Voici l'histoire atroce de cette malheureuse" (II, 876), and at this point the woman's self-diagnosis and the doctor's clinical one diverge.

When we leave the frame and enter into the framed narrative, the first-person narrator now assumes the role of the narratee to the doctor's story. As we have seen in the case of **"L'Enfant,"** the doctor/narrator has tremendous power as the voice of authority. He tells the narratee that his patient was the type of woman for whom beauty is the only measure of worth. Madame Hermet was left widowed with a son. Since the doctor was not an eye-witness to her years of suffering before the mirror as she watched her beauty fade, he recreates her life and her possible state of mind through a series of questions, beginning with: "Vit-elle venir la crise fatale, je n'en sais rien" (II, 877). This know-nothing posture is merely feigned, for the doctor's questions, which take up nearly two pages of text, become increasingly personal in detail. For example, he questions,

> S'est-elle enfermée dix fois, vingt fois en un jour, quittant sans raison le salon où causent des amis, pour remonter dans sa chambre et, sous la protection des verrous et des serrures, regarder encore le travail de destruction de la chair mûre qui se fane . . . ? (II, 877)

By the time the doctor asks his final question, the reader's eye glosses over the question mark and accepts as fact such a detailed account of what the woman must have suffered:

> Puis, comprenant qu'elle implore en vain l'inflexible Inconnu qui pousse les ans, l'un après l'autre, s'est-elle roulée, en se tordant les bras, sur les tapis de sa chambre, a-t-elle heurté son front aux meubles en retenant dans sa gorge des cris affreux de désespoir? (II, 878)

This is a remarkably vivid picture of her physical and psychological state considering the fact that the doctor was not even there to witness her behavior. The implied answer to this and all of the questions is, of course, yes indeed, for the reader gives credence to a psychological portrait based entirely on questions, and to accept the authority of the doctor as an actual eye-witness.

By his suggestion that the insane must be the only happy beings in the world—clearly not the case by now for Madame Hermet—the initial first-person narrator in the frame enticed the reader into expecting a story concerning bliss in madness. It will become evident that the doctor, too, misleads the reader by prefacing his tale with remarks concerning the effect old age has on this woman. However, when Madame Hermet was given the brief opportunity to reveal the source of her sorrow, she implicated, not the passing years, but the child. The thought that a mother could be driven mad by the loss of beauty due to a child is not palatable, and the doctor closes the door, dismisses her as insane, and proceeds to establish the more acceptable old age/insanity link, at least for the moment.

The doctor tells the narratee that Madame Hermet's son fell gravely ill at the age of fifteen. He is taken care of by an abbot, his preceptor Madame Hermet inquires about his health periodically, but refuses to stay with him herself. The description of Madame Hermet's neglect of her maternal duty is offset by an emphasis on her sexuality: "Elle entrait, en matin, *en peignoir de nuit, souriante, toute parfumée déjà,* et demandait dès la porte: 'Eh bien, Georget, allons-nous mieux?'" (II, 878; emphasis mine). Stating that she has urgent matters to attend to, she quickly slips out of the room, *"laissant derrière elle de fines odeurs de toi-*

GUY DE MAUPASSANT

———

Le Horla

———

QUINZIÈME ÉDITION

PARIS
PAUL OLLENDORFF, ÉDITEUR
28 *bis,* RUE DE RICHELIEU, 28 *bis*
1887
Tous droits réservés.

lette" (II, 878; emphasis mine). In the evening, *"elle apparaissait en robe décolletée,* plus pressée encore, car elle était toujours en retard. . . . " (II, 878; emphasis mine).

Upon learning that her son has smallpox, Madame Hermet terminates even her brief visits for fear of contracting the illness herself. She buys medicines designed to ward off the disease, and retreats to her room. Nearly two weeks later, the abbot tells her that her son is dying and is asking for his mother. She falls to her knees and cries as if in pain, "Ah mon Dieu! mon Dieu! Je n'oserai jamais! Mon Dieu! Mon Dieu, secourez-moi!" (II, 880). Two hours pass and Madame Hermet is still wailing on her knees when the abbot again comes to implore her to visit her son who is begging for his mother. Her son realizes what is happening and asks the doctor to tell his mother to go through the balcony to his window. She cannot bring herself to perform even this simple act which would reaffirm her maternity. Meanwhile, the child "attendait, les yeux tournés vers cette fenêtre, il attendait pour mourir qu'il eût vu une dernière fois *la figure douce et bien-aimée, le visage sacré de sa mère*" (II, 881; emphasis mine). The doctor ends the story by revealing that, after waiting all day in vain for this treasured glimpse of his mother, the child finally turns toward the wall and dies. The last lines of the story are: "Quand le jour parut, il était mort. Le lendemain elle était folle" (II, 881).

We have come a long way here from the initial suggestion by the frame's first-person narrator that this would be a story about the world of peace and tranquility inhabited by the insane. Implicitly, this is not a story of insanity, be it blissful or not, but of infanticide. **"Madame Hermet"** tells the story of women who refuse to relinquish their beauty in order to bear children and to sacrifice themselves for their children alone. The fact that Madame Hermet chose her sexual role over her maternal one is highlighted by the doctor's description of her state of (un)dress when she paid token visits to her dying son. The story of "folie," then, takes a new focus. Madame Hermet's insanity comes as a direct result of her selfishness, and is presumably meant to be viewed as a fitting punishment. Even though no explicit judgment is passed, the pitiful child is successfully made to bear witness against his mother. She is guilty of a crime against maternity. We have come a long way also from the doctor's suggestion that his story would involve the effect of old age in causing madness; the story's conclusion established the direct link between insanity and motherhood. The reader has been doubly deluded.

2.5 Mothers and Madness

In **"Madame Hermet,"** the first-person male narrator of the frame, who functions as the narratee in the framed tale, and the doctor/narrator of the framed tale attempt to answer the question: "Why is the woman mad"? In an article on women and madness, Shoshana Felman studies a remarkably similar tale of a woman's madness in a short story by Balzac entitled "Adieu" (1830). Felman's conclusions regarding the nature of Stéphanie's madness in Balzac's story are applicable to the tale of a woman's madness told by Maupassant nearly fifty years later. Of Balzac's story, Felman writes: "It is nonetheless striking that the dichotomy Reason/Madness, as well as Speech/Silence, exactly coincides in this text with the dichotomy Men/Women."[28]

Maupassant's treatment of female madness resembles Balzac's model. Like Stéphanie, Madame Hermet is cut short in her attempt to speak on her own behalf, for she is quickly hidden away behind closed doors by the doctor, the ultimate voice of authority in the tale. Felman adds:

> With respect to the woman's madness, man's reason reacts by trying to *appropriate* it: in the first place, by claiming to "understand" it, but with an external understanding which reduces the madwoman to a spectacle, to an object which can be *known* and *possessed*.[29]

The doctor plays the role of the voice of reason, the undisputed voice of authority, in **"Madame Hermet"** as well as in many of Maupassant's stories. Madame Hermet is reduced to a "spectacle" by the doctor who can pick and choose who her visitors will be, as well as how much of, and in what way, her story will be told. While this story offers one example of Maupassant's much-studied misogyny, it demonstrates not just a disdain for, but a fear of women. The mother who neglects her child is a frightening concept in the stories. In addition, the irrational quality which Maupassant sees as part of female nature is only shown briefly, and then quickly concealed behind closed doors literally, and figuratively within the safe distance afforded by the multiplication of layers of narration in the framed tale, so that the male will not lose his grasp on it.

Such well-known tales of horror as **"Le Horla"** have earned Maupassant the reputation as a writer obsessed with the theme of madness, but this theme has been the focus of scholarship mainly when it involves a male character. The madman dissects his own illness while suffering through its ravaging effects, and is given the chance to describe it himself as a result of the narrative structure which positions him as the voice of authority. It is interesting to note that in Maupassant's revised version of **"Le Horla"** published in 1887, several months after the original, the writer chose to give the male character, whose sanity is in question, even greater authority in telling his story, unlike the madwoman in **"Madame Hermet,"** and women in general who are denied the power of speech. The second version of **"Le Horla,"** which utilizes the diary form, is generally viewed as superior to the initial version, a simple first-person account of madness by the madman himself to four doctors designated in the frame as his narratees. Comparing the two versions Forestier affirms:

> Au compte rendu se substitue le journal, c'est-à-dire nullement l'observation au jour le jour, mais l'impression d'instant en instant: la lutte contre tout ce qui, vague à vague, vous étouffe et vous engloutit. Il faut une singulière lucidité pour écrire un naufrage que l'on ne vit pas encore. Car toute la différence entre les deux textes revient—qu'on me pardonne le truisme—à la forme qu'ils adoptent. Le récit est irrémédiablement clos. Le journal est ouvert, bien qu'il se sache voué à la finitude. Mieux, il est la forme même qui convient au moi déchiré puisque la conscience tente de s'y fixer dans sa mouvance et sa dispersion. (II, 1620)

All of Maupassant's major tales dealing with the mad*man* make use of a narrative structure which affords the insane male character the opportunity to explore his own illness and its effect on his perception of reality.[30] The altered state of consciousness experienced by the madman is, in fact, the source of almost mystical revelations, however frightening. The woman's experience with insanity does not offer her such insights, and is not the *raison d'être* of the tale at all. By contrast, as the madman documents the progression of his own illness, he addresses such universal concerns as human solitude and alienation, the possiblity of other worlds beyond the grasp of our sensory perceptions, the fragmentation of the self, and the resulting fear of the loss of one's identity. It is this last idea which Ross Chambers believes to be the most essential in the case of **"Le Horla."** The onset of insanity occurs when the protagonist looks in the mirror and fails to see his reflection. Although it is clear that madwomen in Maupassant's fiction already have no identity in their inability to control their text, Chambers offers the compelling argument that the madman in **"Le Horla"** fears this loss himself precisely, and paradoxically, as a result of the power he has in authoring his text:

> On voit immédiatement qu'écrire, c'est susciter l'"autre"—le Horla—sous la forme d'un lecteur; et c'est bientôt cet autre qui va se substituer dans la glace au reflet du narrateur. Ainsi, si le texte est, pour le narrateur lecteur, l'"autre" destructeur, le narrateur écrivain connaît à son tour un "autre" non moins dangereux en la personne du lecteur.[31]

In addition to granting a voice of authority to the madman, while silencing the madwoman, Maupassant's treatment of the theme of madness in a female-centered text is clearly only half of the equation. As noted in our study of **"La Mère sauvage,"** a failure to recognize the duality in thematic content, that is the combined treatment of war and maternity, robs the text of its potential richness. Likewise, **"Madame Hermet"** does not deal exclusively with madness: the juxtaposition of the themes of madness and maternity results in a story of implicit trial and judgment. Maupassant's portrayal here of a woman's insanity is used primarily to inculpate an unnatural mother. Her refusal to embrace her maternal role is a sign that she is indeed mentally "ill." Thus, insanity is both a metaphor for the "bad" mother, and fitting punishment for her transgression.

Maupassant's ambiguous feelings regarding female sexuality are evident in his fiction. Although a woman's sexuality is repeatedly defended against society's prudish norms—witness the doctor's argument with the baroness in **"Madame Hermet"**—it is nevertheless an empowering force much feared by the male. Maternity in its ideal form, on the other hand, is meant to be an ennobling and healing instinct, one which has the capacity even to cure a woman's insanity. In **"Berthe"** (1884), another mentally deficient woman comes under the scrutiny of a doctor and a curious male onlooker, and the structure is essentially the same as that of **"Madame Hermet."** Interestingly, it is **"Berthe"** which Forestier links to Balzac's "Adieu" (II, 1417). When Berthe reaches adolescence, the doctor is called upon to attempt to heal this woman who is nothing but a beautiful, but empty, shell. The doctor tells the narratee, "elle était superbe, et muette, muette par défaut d'intelligence" (II, 357). Berthe displays what in modern terms would be diagnosed as autistic behavior. Yet, her beauty captivates the doctor who, like the doctor in **"Madame Hermet,"** loses his scientific objectivity in her presence:

> Elle était devenue superbe; c'était vraiment un type de la race, une sorte de Vénus admirable et stupide. . . . J'ai dit une Vénus, oui, une Vénus, blonde, grasse, vigoureuse, avec de grands yeux clairs et vides, bleus comme la fleur du lin, et une large bouche aux lèvres rondes, une bouche de gourmande, de sensuelle, une bouche à baisers. (II, 360-1)

Berthe's father suggests that they marry her off so that she can bear a child, for maternity's healing power could offer a cure for mental illness:

> [. . .] mais réfléchissez, docteur . . . c'est que . . . peut-être . . . nous avons espéré . . . si elle avait des enfants . . . ce serait pour elle une grande secousse, un grand bonheur et . . . *qui sait si son esprit ne s'éveillerait pas dans la maternité?* (II, 360; emphasis mine)

The doctor agrees, saying:

> Il se pourrait que cette chose si nouvelle, que *cet admirable instinct des mères qui palpite au coeur des bêtes comme au coeur des femmes,* qui fait se jeter la poule en face de la gueule du chien, pour défendre ses petits, amenât une révolution, un bouleversement dans cette tête inerte, et mît en marche le mécanisme immobile de sa pensée. (II, 360; emphasis mine)

Unfortunately, the experiment goes awry, for instead of bearing a child through the arranged marriage, Berthe's sexual instincts are awakened. She exhausts her husband who beats her in frustration. When the doctor separates Berthe from him, Berthe's insatiable passion overcomes her, and, adding insult to injury, she goes mad: "Je la calmai avec des piqûres de morphine; et je défendis qu'elle revît cet homme, car je compris que le mariage la conduirait infailliblement à la mort. Alors elle devint folle! Oui, mon cher, cette idiote est devenue folle" (II, 363). This female Frankenstein-like monster spends her days locked away in an old hotel. The frame's narrator noticed this strange building in the beginning, providing the impetus for the tale's telling. The lower windows were covered "comme si on eût voulu empêcher les gens enfermés en ce vaste coffre de pierre de regarder dans la rue" (II, 356). Both Madame Hermet and Berthe are—to borrow the title from Sandra Gilbert and Susan Gubar's study of nineteenth century literary women—examples of "the madwomen in the attic" who are denied the power of the pen in writing their own stories.[32] Like Madame Hermet, Berthe is imprisoned both physically in her cell-like abode, and figuratively through a narrative structure which multiplies witnesses, and which distances her so completely from her story. Her *actual* inability to speak is mere icing on the cake.

It is important to recall that, although both Berthe and Madame Hermet are condemned to a life of silence, locked away and left alone with their madness, one is incriminated, and one is not. Maupassant never condemns the woman for her overt sexuality, as long as she remains childless. Along with the maternal instinct, it is a natural instinct. Her sexuality is, nonetheless, something to be feared by the male, and perhaps best locked away where it can be safely held in awe and fascination. Mothers who recognize sexuality as freedom in controlling their own stories, however, are condemned. They are no longer blessed with sexual power, for ideally, once they have given birth women are *supposed* to embrace their maternal role over their sexual one, or face condemnation as not only unnatural, but criminal. In this regard, Maupassant's mothers follow a long tradition of monstrous mothers going back to Medea of Greek mythology and Lilith of Hebrew legend.[33] Gilbert and Gubar analyze the story of Lilith as an example of the "monster woman" versus the "angel," binary opposites which have been used by men to define women through the ages, and from which Victorian women authors attempted to wrest themselves.[34]

2.6 Witnessing A Mother's Sexuality: The Male Child as Voyeur

Madame Hermet's desire to retain her sexual identity conflicts with her maternal status, and for this she is judged by her own child. A child's testimony against his or her own mother, however subtle, lies at the heart of stories involving a mother's violation of the sacred mother-child bond. Significantly, most of the children wronged by their mothers are male, a point we shall examine further. A notable exception is found in a short story entitled **"Yveline Samoris"** published in 1882, and rewritten in 1884 as **"Yvette,"** a long novella. An examination of these two stories dealing with the female child reveals the change in focus in stories centered on male children. In the second version published in mid-career, at a time when Maupassant appeared to be re-thinking his notion of the ideal mother, the female child who witnesses her mother's sexual nature learns from this behavior, rather than becoming its victim, as male children invariably are.

The first version, **"Yveline Samoris,"** contains the typical child-as-victim theme, without placing undue emphasis on the child's sex. The story is told by a male narrator to a male narratee in the first-person. The narratee asks the narrator if the woman in black whom they are staring at is indeed Madame la comtesse Samoris. The narrator responds: "Elle-même, elle porte le deuil de sa fille qu'elle a tuée" (I, 685). He adds that hers is a story, "toute simple, sans crime, et sans violences" (I, 685). Before telling the countess's story, the narrator reveals his source of information: the countess's former valet, Joseph, whom the narrator has hired. The distance separating the countess from her story is made manifest through the multiplication of voices which pass the story on, until it finally reaches the narratee: " . . . et voici tous les détails de cette mort que je tiens de Joseph, qui les tenait de son amie la femme de chambre de la comtesse" (I, 686).

While attending a ball, Yveline overhears a conversation between two men about her mother. They reveal that the young girl's father was a Russian count, and that the countess Samoris has since had many lovers whom she entertains for no more than a few weeks before moving on to the next man. Yveline is shocked at the news that her mother is nothing but a courtisan, and confronts the countess with her discovery. The countess denies all, but Yveline is unconvinced, and becomes a voyeur to her mother's sexuality: "Un soir elle n'eut plus de doute: elle surprit sa mère" (I, 687). She offers her mother an ultimatum which she has one month to carry out:

> Nous nous retirerons toutes les deux dans une petite ville ou bien à la campagne; nous y vivrons sans bruit, comme nous pourrons. Tes bijoux seuls sont une fortune. Si tu trouves à te marier avec quelque honnête homme, tant mieux; encore plus tant mieux si je trouve aussi. Si tu ne consens pas à cela, je me tuerai. (I, 687)

The countess cannot sacrifice her life of high-class prostitute for her child's sake, and Yveline commits suicide with chloroform. One has only to recall the opening words of the narrator to realize that implicitly, the mother committed infanticide, for Yveline is introduced as the daughter "qu'elle a tuée" (I, 685). Ironically, when the narratee asks what has become of the mother, the narrator responds: "Oh! elle a beaucoup pleuré. Elle recommence depuis huit jours seulement à recevoir ses intimes" (I, 687). Her remorse is obviously short-lived.

Rewritten as **"Yvette,"** the second version of the story is told in the third-person from the perspective of Servigny to his friend Saval. Servigny denies that he is in love with this courtisan's daughter, but admits to the troubling effect Yvette has on him. Servigny realizes that it is just a matter of time before Yvette succumbs to the lessons of her mother and the romance novels she devours, and follows in her mother's footsteps; he would like to be the first man to be there when she does. This story is quite different from **"Yveline Samoris"** in that the daughter is made to learn a lesson from her mother's pedagogy, instead of dying as its victim after first attempting to redeem the fallen mother. Yvette's mother warns her that Servigny's intentions do not involve marriage, but stops short of revealing the whole truth. As in **"Yveline Samoris,"** Yvette spies on her mother and Saval, and her voyeurism leads to a rude sexual awakening. She, like Yveline, offers her mother an ultimatum, but is somehow aware of the futility of her request. Yvette's suicide attempt merely provides a test for the male, which Servigny dutifully passes by climbing up the balcony to save her. We are to understand that Servigny has succeeded in his conquest, and that this female child has learned the lessons of her mother all too well. The mother is not judged, and the lesson is one regarding all females, beginning in childhood. Yvette is not the virtuous victim of a monstrous mother; therefore, she does not die in the end, but rather lives on to continue her mother's role as *femme fatale* in a world of men who are ensnared by her charms. Lorraine Gaudefroy-Demombynes makes the fatalism of this mother/daughter pedagogy clear:

> Elle a donc un rôle romanesque à jouer: sauver sa mère. Ici, son innocence et son honnêteté natives se teintent de cabotinage inconscient. . . . Son suicide est sans doute la conséquence logique de sa révolte intime et de son dégoût, et son désespoir est parfaitement sincère; mais il est un peu théâtral aussi. D'autant plus que c'est un suicide manqué, ce qui est bien fâcheux pour notre héroïne. Car sa mort aurait été en quelque sorte une victoire: la victoire de la vertu, et ce dénouement eût satisfait le lecteur moyen. . . . [35]

With the exception of **"Yveline Samoris,"** it is the male child who is the sacrificial victim of a mother's sexuality. In some of the earlier stories involving male children, the mother's guilt is lessened if she recognizes her sin, and attempts to atone for it. In **"L'Attente"** (1883), the frame of the story sets up an all-male jury: "On causait, entre hommes, après dîner, dans le fumoir" (I, 1059). Monsieur Le Brument, a lawyer, tells the story as the first-person narrator in the framed tale. He recounts the death-bed confession of a woman who promises him a handsome reward if he can find her son after her death. The woman's story is transcribed in the first-person by the narrator. She had married against her will, leaving behind her true love. The husband dies soon after the birth of their son. Although free now from marital responsibilities, the love of her maiden years was still married. The two consoled each other, eventually becoming lovers. She tells the narrator how happy her life was, and how her son loved this man who helped her raise him in her

widowhood. When the boy was seventeen, he surprised his mother and her lover in a passionate embrace, and fled his mother's house.

The son's silent condemnation of his mother fills her with "cette honte épouvantable qui tombe sur le coeur d'une mère en ces moments-là" (I, 1061). When he still does not return after much time has passed, she judges herself, for she experiences "une angoisse telle que je ne souhaiterais point au plus criminel des hommes dix minutes de ces moments-là" (I, 1062). The mother punishes herself by repressing her sexuality, refusing to see her lover until her son can be found. Twenty years pass, and her son still does not return. She asks the lawyer to tell her son to forgive his fallen mother: "Mon cher enfant, pardonne-lui et aime-la, maintenant qu'elle est morte, car elle a subi la plus affreuse des pénitences" (I, 1063). At the end of the tale, the layer returns in the frame to address his male narratees. Instead of judging the mother—for she has already been duly tried, convicted, and punished—he places blame on the son: "Je n'ai pas retrouvé le fils . . . ce fils . . . Pensez-en ce que vous voudrez; moi, je dis: ce fils . . . criminel" (I, 1064).

The horror experienced by the *male* child in Maupassant's fiction faced with the clandestine discovery of his mother's sexual nature certainly lends itself to psychoanalytic interpretations. The male protagonists in many nineteenth century texts are faced with such a conflict. Stendhal and Flaubert provide just two of the contemporary literary examples of the youthful male suitor who falls in love with a mature matronly woman. The incestuous possibilities inherent in Julien Sorel's pursuit of Madame de Rênal and Frédéric Moreau's idealization of Madame Arnoux are evident: the authority of the father figure in the story is undermined, and the violation of the image of the pure "asexual" mother threatens the very pursuit of the ideal. The mother herself is keenly aware of her guilt. For instance, Madame de Rênal believes that the illness of her child is punishment for her transgression of those bounds placed on her as a mother.

Maupassant repeatedly dramatized the male child's struggle for the attention of a mother who is also a sexual being. We have seen that she is invariably punished for privileging the sexual instinct over the maternal one. Symbols of the womb from which the male child is banished by the bad, or "sexual" mother abound in many of these stories. The son in **"L'Attente"** leaves the security of his mother's house after his discovery. In **"Le Mal d'André"** (1883) the male child's need for consolation at night in his mother's bed frustrates her lover. In a Pavlov-like experiment, the lover tricks the child into giving up this nightly source of comfort by repeatedly pinching him each time the mother takes him into the bed, as was her custom.

The most tragic tale of a male child's banishment from the symbolic womb appears in **"L'Armoire"** (1884). The frame sets up the fraternity of male listeners at a dinner conversation, and one of the men proceeds to tell a story. In the framed tale, the first-person narrator describes his feeling of solitude one winter night. He seeks comfort from a prostitute who leads him to her house, but who makes him wait outside. He hears the sound of two doors closing, and is finally allowed to enter. Once inside, the charm of the possible rendez-vous with a prostitute wears off, and instead, he asks her to tell him about her own life. The conversation is interrupted by a noise nearby: "Ça avait été d'abord un soupir, puis un bruit léger, mais distinct, comme si quelqu'un s'était retourné sur une chaise" (II, 403). The woman assures the narrator that it is just a neighbor heard through the thin walls, and she proceeds with her story. The narrator presses her for information about her first sexual encounter, but soon realizes that she is lying when she names an oarsman. He extracts a confession from her by pretending that he is a sorcerer who will cast a spell on her if she does not tell the truth. Frightened, she tells him that she was raped by a man hired as a temporary chef by her employers. She bore a son, Florentin, as a result of this encounter. Suddenly, a loud noise again interrupts the conversation. This time, the narrator locates the source:

> J'allais droit vers une porte cachée à la tête de notre lit et je l'ouvris brusquement . . . et j'aperçus, tremblant, ouvrant sur moi des yeux effarés et brillants, un pauvre petit garçon assis à côté d'une grande chaise de paille, d'où il venait de tomber. (II, 406)

The mother attempts to comfort the sobbing child, telling the narrator that she has no other way of entertaining her customers, and that the child has learned to remain still for an hour or two, but all-night clients make it difficult for him. However, she notes: "Il couche avec moi quand j'ai personne" (II, 407). This child is exiled from the warmth of his mother's bed, her womb, to the dark, detached womb which is the armoire. Such a discovery has a profound effect on the narrator:

> L'enfant pleurait toujours. Un pauvre enfant chétif et timide, oui, c'était bien l'enfant de l'armoire, de l'armoire froide et sombre, l'enfant qui revenait de temps en temps reprendre un peu de chaleur dans la couche un instant vide. (II, 407)

The desperation of the mother's situation does not exculpate her in the narrator's eyes for her treatment of the child, since the narrator is moved to tears with pity for him. This story shows further the disgust felt by the prostitute's male client faced with the functional aspect of her body. He can no longer separate the act from its biological function since this prostitute is also a mother.

2.7 From Monstrous Mothers to Monstrous Creator

When the stories dealing with maternal guilt are taken as a whole, there appears to be a chronological transformation in Maupassant's fictional representations of mothers. We have seen the concern up to 1884 with presenting the instinctive nature of motherhood (**"Histoire d'une fille de ferme"**), to the extent that mothers will commit murder in its name (**"Une Vendetta," "La Mère Sauvage"**). Later, the shift is away from incontestably guilty monstrous mothers found in the early and mid-career stories, to merely "unnatural" mothers whose rejection of their God-given nature is presented as an heroic act in the author's last works.

Apart from the few early stories (**"Une Vendetta," "La Mère sauvage"**) which actually portray the silent suffering Madonna-like woman, the existence of such a mother is merely hinted at later as an idealized conception, a point of comparison to her exact opposite, who *is* repeatedly depicted in the stories: the criminal mother. The condemnation of monstrous mothers relies on the reader's acceptance of an ideal model of maternal purity from which the fallen mother has deviated. But in repeatedly entertaining the thought that bad, even infanticidal, mothers do exist, Maupassant eventually began to call into question his own idealized conception of motherhood. With this comes a shift in blame from the mother to the Creator, for conception itself involves a physical act which is constantly portrayed as repugnant in Maupassant's fiction. In addition, Maupassant seemed to fear pregnancy and the pregnant body. Absolute purity in maternity, incarnated in the form of the Virgin Mother, becomes an illusion, an impossible model for human imitation.

This increasingly pessimistic view of mothers parallels Maupassant's darkening view of the world in general. Man has only inadequate physical means by which to reach a spiritual reality, as evidenced in **"Le Horla,"** but he struggles tragically nonetheless. Maupassant's deteriorating mental and physical health, causing him to suffer severe headaches and loss of vision, made him all too aware of the imperfections in nature, and this perhaps explains in part a somewhat greater compassion he expresses in the end toward women whom he views as essentially biological creatures. However, another explanation is to be found in the literary circle of which he was a part. On May 31, 1884, Maupassant wrote a letter to his friend, Huysmans, saying, "Je viens seulement de lire votre livre, mes yeux étant fort mauvais. Il m'a ravi, il m'a fait rire et rêver, m'a séduit par son style, par la vérité bizarre, par la philosophie cocasse et délicieuse."[36] The book in question was *A Rebours.* Here, Huysmans provides the ultimate expression of the decadent cult of artificiality over nature, and Maupassant was indeed greatly affected by it, as we shall see.

In the earliest stories, there appears to be little distinction between Nature, God, and Woman. As Mary Donaldson-Evans points out, woman is seen as Nature's accomplice in trying to thwart man's efforts to transcend the world of sense experience:

> The role of nature is not always innocent, however; its beauty awakens in human beings a feverish hunger for sexual union which throws them pell-mell into one another's arms in an act that is by definition the result of biological drive. Seen from this perspective, nature becomes an accomplice of love (understood in its sexual sense) and an ally of woman herself, the eternal temptress in Maupassant's work who lies in wait for men. . . . [37]

It is only very late in his career that Maupassant paints woman as a creature whose biological role as child-bearer makes her one who is even more a victim of nature's cruelty than man.

As noted, Maupassant followed his contemporaries in viewing the pregnant body and the newborn child with great revulsion. He dwells on this to an almost obsessive degree, however. When Benoist delivers his former lover's baby in **"La Martine,"** the passion he once felt for her dies suddenly: "Lui, il ne l'aimait plus, plus du tout. C'était fini. Pourquoi? Comment? Il n'eût pas su le dire. Ce qui venait de se passer l'avait guéri mieux que n'auraient fait dix ans d'absence" (I, 979). The pregnant woman in **"L'Enfant"** cannot bear the sight of her deformed body. The newborn child itself is not a beautiful creature, but rather is the incarnation of all that is ugly in nature. In **"L'Histoire d'une fille de ferme,"** Rose gives birth to "un petit squelette affreux, maigre à donner des frissons, et qui semblait souffrir sans cesse, tant il crispait douloureusement ses pauvres mains décharnées comme des pattes de crabe" (I, 231). The man who is unwittingly called upon to deliver a prostitute's baby in **"Nuit de Noël"** sees nothing but "un affreux petit morceau de chair ridée, plissée, geignante, miaulant comme un chat" (I, 698). The carnal act itself of procreation does not fare any better in the stories: it is compared to an illness in **"Enragée"** (1883) and to a crime in **"Les Caresses"** (1883).

All of these biological functions, from conception, to pregnancy, to childbirth, serve to imprison the woman in her body. She is a creature of the physical world, but one who slowly receives the author's pity, and who eventually triumphs over nature through artifice as the stories evolve. An examination of **"La Mére aux monstres"** (1883) and **"L'Inutile Beauté"** (1890), published at opposite chronological points in Maupassant's career, shows the evolution in his assessment of the monstrous mother's level of guilt. The different conclusions reached in the two works reflect the changes which took place in the author's world view over a relatively short period of time.

During a visit to a friend's country home, the male first-person narrator in the frame of **"La Mère aux monstres"** questions his friend about this woman. The narrator's male host replies that she is "une femme abominable, un vrai démon" who gives birth yearly to deformed children in order to sell them as side show freaks (I, 843). The narrator does not immediately believe his friend. Even after a brief visit to the woman's house, the narrator reserves judgment when pressed by his friend, but asks him to recount her story. At this point, the friend takes over as the first-person narrator of the story, and the original narrator assumes the role of narratee.

The listener learns that when the woman was employed as a servant, she tried to conceal an unwanted pregnancy, "avec un système qu'elle avait inventé, corset de force, fait de planchettes et de cordes" (I, 845). She gives birth to a monster-like creature, and becomes known as "la Diable." Neither pregnancy nor childbirth succeed in stirring up maternal feelings in this she-devil; in fact, this unnatural mother is on the brink of committing infanticide: "Elle éleva son monstre qu'elle haïssait d'ailleurs d'une haine sauvage et qu'elle eût étranglé peut-être, si le curé, prévoyant le crime, ne l'avait épouvantée par la menace de la justice" (I, 845-6). Once she is offered money for her child, la Diable makes a living by producing deformed children, and at the time of the story's unfolding, she has sold eleven such monsters.

At the end, the frame's narrator again takes over the narration. He finally has enough evidence now to condemn the woman in the tale he has just heard. Despite the horror he expresses at this crime against nature, the woman in the framed tale is not the only focus of judgment, for the tale continues in the ending frame. The memory of this awful woman fades away, until it is reawakened when the frame's narrator sees a society woman "sur une plage à la mode, une femme élégante, charmante, coquette, aimée, entourée d'hommes qui la respectent" (I, 847). His first reaction is one of pity for her and her three small children who are "difformes, bossus et crochus, hideux" (I, 847). However, he is disabused by his friend, a doctor, who tells him that this woman, like la Diable, is responsible for her offspring's deformities. They are the results of "des tailles restées fines jusqu'au dernier jour" through the use of corsets (I, 847). The doctor continues: "Elle sait bien qu'elle risque sa vie à ce jeu-là. Que lui importe, pourvu qu'elle soit belle, et aimée!" (I, 847). Maupassant shows here that women of all social ranks are capable of such a sin, and all are condemned equally, whether they commit the crime for the sake of money or to retain their sexual attractiveness to men. As Forestier states, "Il faudrait dire, plutôt, 'les mères' que 'la mère'; en effet, la femme du monde et la campagnarde sont associées dans la même réprobation" (I, 1536).

The mother in **"L'Inutile Beauté"** (1890), the countess Gabrielle de Mascaret, is a *femme du monde* whose desire to retain her beauty is judged with a very different eye. In the first section of this novella, Madame de Mascaret tells her husband that after eleven years of marriage and seven children, she will no longer be "la victime de l'odieux supplice de maternité" (II, 1207). She forces him to leave her alone once and for all by alleging that one of the children is not his. By the time we reach the third section of the story, six years have passed, and Madame de Mascaret is the topic of conversation of two male spectators who admire her beauty as she sits regally in her opera box. This section provides a definite rupture in the tale, for Madame de Mascaret merely provides a catalyst for a philosophical discussion between the two men. The evolution in Maupassant's view of a mother's vanity is made clear in the words of Roger de Salins, one of the spectators of both the artifice which is the opera, and the artificial beauty of Madame de Mascaret:

> Onze ans de grossesses pour une femme comme ça! quel enfer! C'est toute la jeunesse, toute la beauté, toute l'espérance de succès, tout l'idéal poétique de vie brillante, qu'on sacrifie à cette abominable loi de la reproduction qui fait de la femme normale une simple machine à pondre des êtres. (II, 1216)

Such a pronouncement would never have been made, especially by a male character, in the earlier stories. Although an emphasis on the physical degradation brought on by pregnancy is a constant of Maupassant's fiction, up to this point the author made it clear that a woman's natural duty was to accept this condition and to give up her sexual role. This is definitely not the case in this, one of his last stories. Roger de Salins becomes the vehicle through which the philosophy of Maupassant's last years is made manifest.

The artificial beauty of women at the opera, like Madame de Mascaret, overwhelms Salins who sees "les loges pleines de femmes décolletées, diamantées, emperlées, épanouies dans cette serre illuminée où la beauté des visages et l'éclat des épaules semblent fleurir pour les regards au milieu de la musique et des voix humaines" (II, 1214). Salins affirms that such man-made beauty is the only beauty that exists, for God's created world is one of ugliness:

> . . . je dis que la nature est notre ennemie qu'il faut toujours lutter contre la nature, car elle nous ramène sans cesse à l'animal. Ce qu'il y a de propre, de joli, d'élégant, d'idéal sur la terre, ce n'est pas Dieu qui l'y a mis, c'est l'homme, c'est le cerveau humain. (II, 1216)

He adds that the human mind is a tragic accident of creation, and that man is thus not suited for this, the animal world (II, 1218). Huysman's Des Esseintes takes

the idea of man's declaration of independence through artifice to the extreme, and Maupassant was, as noted, fascinated by this character. A. E. Carter points out that,

> after such a display of artificiality as *A Rebours,* in which every aspect of the theory [of decadence] was expressed and amplified, there was little more to be said; and indeed during the rest of the century little more was said: writers confined themselves to repetition.[38]

Maupassant rethought his ideas on motherhood in terms which follow Huysman's articulation of decadence.

The entire section of **"L'Inutile Beauté"** devoted to a heavy-handed philosophical discussion disrupts the tale, and makes plain how the ideal reader should judge the woman in the story. When we return to the husband-wife drama in the end, it is clear that Madame de Mascaret's defiance of nature is indeed heroic. It is important to realize, however, that this woman's maternal role has not been jeopardized. One could argue that since she already has fulfilled her role as a mother at the moment when she takes this symbolic vow of chastity, Maupassant has at last found his ideal Madonna, a Virgin Mother of sorts. As Mary Donaldson-Evans declares:

> Woman, free from phallocracy, rises to new heights of power in this story, and she does it without sacrificing either her femininity or her maternity. . . . [She] has become a self-determining being, an *inutile beauté* who refuses to remain an instrument of nature. An esthetic object (whence her likeness to a statue), she exists only to be admired, pure icon, cold, unfeeling.[39]

Rose, the farm girl in **"Histoire d'une fille de ferme"** was forced to deny her sexuality because of her maternal nature; Madame de Mascaret denies it in spite of her nature. It took Maupassant the span of his literary career to create such a defiant, heroic mother who is not found guilty for her revolt. Donaldson-Evans points out that although Maupassant died before completing the novel *L'Angelus,* one can conclude from the fragments that Maupassant was to have continued along this path by creating another such heroine for whom Madame de Mascaret was the *ébauche.*[40] . . .

Notes

[1] Until recently, much has been made of Maupassant's biography, including his mother/son relationship and its effect on his portrayal of such relationships in his fiction. Francis Steegmuller writes: "From the very beginning, Laure's maternity was marked by a jealousy that persisted to the end of her days." See Steegmuller, *A Lion in The Path* (New York: Random House, 1949), 6. Steegmuller goes so far as to blame Laure for Guy's

celebrated promiscuity: "It is a familiar spectacle—the absorption of a sensitive boy by a charming, cultivated, dignified mother not quite intelligent or selfless enough to know or to stop what she is doing. Of the two most usual, alternative consequences of such a relationship—physical indifference to women, or promiscuity—Guy from his teens did not display the former." (Steegmuller, 29). Paul Ignotus describes the feelings Maupassant had for his mother as bordering on the incestuous: "Guy adored his mother with a devotion that was touching, chivalrous and almost obscene. She was the only person to whom he was unreservedly attached all his life and from whom he never dissociated himself." See Paul Ignotus, *The Paradox of Maupassant* (London: University of London Press, 1966), p. 60.

[2] Steegmuller 6.

[3] Elisabeth Badinter, *L'Amour en plus* (Paris: Flammarion, 1980), 231.

[4] G. Hainsworth explains that, "frequently, the explicit theme is *prefigured* indirectly in the first paragraphs, or, in the text, a detail is preceded by a symbol which becomes comprehensible in light of the whole tale." See Hainsworth, "Pattern and Symbol in the Work of Maupassant," *French Studies* 5 (1951), 5.

[5] Hainsworth 8.

[6] In "Beginnings to Understand: The Narrative 'Come-On' in Maupassant's Stories" (*Neophilologus* 68 (1984), 37-47), Mary Donaldson-Evans studies the narrative techniques used by Maupassant in "Humble drame" to ensnare what she believes is the male portion of his reading public. Her study shows how this conscious reworking of the earlier "Rencontre" "bears witness not only to the progressive refinement of Maupassant's talent but to his growing awareness of form" (p. 47).

[7] Donaldson-Evans, *A Woman's Revenge: The Chronology of Dispossession in Maupassant's Fiction* (Lexington: French Foreign Publishers, 1986), 82.

[8] Donaldson-Evans 82.

[9] Emma has recourse to religion only insofar as it can satiate her sentimental yearnings. In fact, the potentially erotic interpretation of Catholic ritual is underscored in Flaubert's novel. This mixture of the sacred and profane characterizes a scene in which Emma's life at the convent school is described:

> Vivant donc sans jamais sortir de la tiède atmosphère des classes et parmi ces femmes au teint blanc, portant des chapelets à croix de cuivre, elle s'assoupit doucement à la langueur mystique qui s'exhale des parfums de l'autel, de la fraîcheur des bénitiers et du rayonnement des cierges. Au lieu de suivre la messe, elle regardait dans son livre les vignettes pieuses bordées d'azur, et elle aimait la brebis malade, le Sacré-Coeur percé de flèches aigues, ou le pauvre Jésus, qui tombe en marchant sous sa croix.—Flaubert, *Madame Bovary* (Paris: Livre de poche, 1972), 41-2.

One might also recall the tragicomic scene in which Madame Bovary grants her lover, Léon, a rendez-vous in the cathedral (*Madame Bovary,* 283-89).

[10] As in chapter 1, I am using Gerald Prince's terms which differentiate between the narrator (narrateur) who, in Maupassant's more complex tales, functions as the storyteller in the framed tale, and the narratee (narrataire) who positions himself in the surrounding frame as the internal listener of the narrator's story. See "Introductionà l'étude du narrataire," *Poétique* 14 (1973), 173-196. It is useful to recall here Angela Moger's summary of how this narrative technique functions in the short works: "Maupassant's invention of the narrator persona permits him, for example, to install a persona of his audience, a "listener" who is being told the internal narrator's story. The presence, in turn, of such a figure within the story enables him to influence our reading of his story—he can set things up in such a way that our reading must be a corrective of, or reaction to, the internal reader's response to what is told." See Angela S. Moger, "Narrative Structure in Maupassant: Frames of Desire," *PMLA* 100 (1985), 315.

[11] Mary Donaldson-Evans refers to this device of attracting the reader in the opening passage, only to proceed with a story with a decidedly different tone, as the narrative "come-on." She lists several examples of its appearance in such stories as "Cauchemar," "Le Horla," and "Madame Hermet." See "Beginnings to Understand," *Neophilologus,* 68 (1984), 39.

[12] J. H. Matthews, "Theme and Structure in Maupassant's Short Stories," *Modern Languages* 43 (1962), 138.

[13] Marie MacLean, "Baudelaire and the Paradox of Procreation," *Studi Francesi* 76 (1982), 88; author's emphasis.

[14] Baudelaire, "Sed Non Satiata," in *Les Fleurs du mal,* ed. Marcel Galliot (Paris: Didier, 1961), p. 31.

[15] Henri Peyre, "Baudelaire as a Love Poet," in *Baudelaire as a Love Poet and Other Essays,* ed. Lois B. Hyslop (University Park: Pennsylvania State University Press, 1969), 10.

[16] Charles Bernheimer, *Figures of Ill Repute: Representing Prostitution in Nineteenth-Century France* (Cambridge: Harvard University Press, 1989), 73.

[17] See Chapter I [of *Voices of Authority*] for a study of "Confessions d'une femme."

[18] As Forestier explains, "L'infanticide n'était pas rare et *Gil Blas* du 3 septembre 1883 signalait qu'une jeune femme, qui avait loué une chambre d'hôtel, n'avait pas reparu: vérifications faites, on trouva dans la cheminée de la chambre, un paquet contenant un enfant assassiné. Il y a lieu de tenir ce fait divers pour l'incitation directe à la rédaction du conte." (I, 1586.)

[19] Richard Lalou, "L'Infanticide devant les tribunaux français (1825-1910)," in *Dénatalité: l'antériorité française (1800-1914)*, Éditions des Hautes Études en Sciences Sociales (Paris: Seuil, 1986), 182.

[20] Philippe Ariès, *L'Enfant et la vie familiale sous l'Ancien Régime* (Paris: Seuil, 1973).

[21] Dominique Vallaud, "Le crime d'infanticide et l'indulgence des cours d'assises en France au XIXème siècle," *Histoire et Science Sociale/History and Social Science* 21 (1982), 475.

[22] The reference here to *women* on trial for infanticide is not accidental. This was viewed as a woman's crime throughout the nineteenth century: "Depuis l'article 302 du Code de 1810, qui subordonne la qualification du crime à la qualité de l'auteur, jusqu'à la loi du 18 novembre 1901, qui exclut l'usage du terme dans tous les cas où la mère est étrangère au crime, les législateurs se sont en effet toujours efforcés de définir l'infanticide comme un crime propre à la femme." (Lalou 184). Chapter 3 [of *Voices of Authority*] deals specifically with the child-directed crime most often associated with fathers in the text, namely, the procreation of bastard children.

[23] Vallaud mentions the following: the difficulty for the court of proving scientifically that the child died by its mother's hand; the harshness of the law of 1810 which only gave juries the choice of either issuing the death penalty or acquitting the woman, until, in 1832, the law allowed for extenuating circumstances, thus affording the jury alternative punishments to death; and the general view at the time that a woman in the throes of labor could not always be held accountable for her crime (Vallaud, 480-484).

[24] Vallaud 485.

[25] Vallaud 491.

[26] Vallaud 492.

[27] Further evidence of Mary Donaldson-Evans's notion of the narrative "come on" in Maupassant's stories. See note #11.

[28] Shoshana Felman, "Women and Madness: The Critical Phallacy," *Diacritics* 5.4 (1985), 7.

[29] Felman 7; author's emphasis.

[30] In "Lui?" (1883), the madman's painstaking self-analysis as he takes note of the progression of his insanity is transcribed in letter form to a *destinataire* known only as "mon cher ami" (I, 869). A doctor and the first-person narrator in the frame of "La Chevelure" (1884) become the madman's narratees as the two read the man's journal recounting his spiral into insanity. The journal itself forms the actual text of the story; thus, the madman is at once narrator and protagonist. The words of the madman in "Un fou?" (1884) are recounted by the narrator who was forced to listen to them. Once again, the madman analyzes his own illness and its devastating effects on his perception of reality. This is also the case in the first-person narrative structure of "Qui sait?" (1890).

[31] Ross Chambers, "La lecture comme hantise: *Spirite* et 'Le Horla,'" *Revue des Sciences Humaines* 177 (1980), 114. See my Chapter 3 for an analysis of "Le Horla."

[32] Sandra Gilbert and Susan Gubar, *The Madwoman in the Attic: The Woman Writer and the Nineteenth-Century Literary Imagination* (New Haven: Yale University Press, 1979).

[33] Gilbert and Gubar summarize the story of Lilith in the following: "Created not from Adam's rib but, like him, from the dust, Lilith was Adam's first wife, according to apocryphal Jewish lore. Because she considered herself his equal, she objected to lying beneath him, so that when he tried to force her submission, she became enraged and, speaking the Ineffable Name, flew away to the edge of the Red Sea to reside with demons. Threatened by God's. angelic emissaries, told that she must return or daily lose a hundred of her demon children to death, Lilith preferred punishment to patriarchal marriage, and she took her revenge against both God and Adam by injuring babies—especially male babies. . . . The figure of Lilith represents the price women have been told they must pay for attempting to define themselves." (*The Madwoman in the Attic*, 35).

[34] Gilbert and Gubar 35.

[35] Lorraine Gaudefroy-Demombynes, *La Femme dans l'oeuvre de Maupassant* (Paris: Mercure de France, 1953), 27-8.

[36] Maupassant, *Correspondance inédite,* eds. Artine Artinian and Édouard Maynial (Paris: Éditions Dominique Wapler, 1951), 285.

[37] Donaldson-Evans, *A Woman's Revenge,* 19.

[38] A. E. Carter, *The Idea of Decadence in French Literature* (Toronto: University of Toronto Press, 1958), 20.

[39] Donaldson-Evans, *A Woman's Revenge,* 100.

[40] Donaldson-Evans, *A Woman's Revenge,* 101.

P. W. M. Cogman (essay date 1997)

SOURCE: "Maupassant's Inhibited Narrators," in *Neophilologus,* Vol. 81, No. 1, January, 1997, pp. 35-47.

[*In the following essay, Cogman discusses how Maupassant, in his disgust for censorship of any kind, demonstrated his desire to expose the shocking and the explicit (especially with regard to sexual matters) in his work.*]

> "Ça se fait, tout le monde le sait, mais ça ne se dit pas, sauf nécessité."
>
> *Hautot père et fils*[1]

Early in his writing career, Maupassant had (like Flaubert before him) difficulties with the public censorship of the written word at the time. His poem *Une Fille* had been threatened with prosecution for "outrage à la morale publique et religieuse et aux bonnes moeurs" in 1880, and in 1883 Hachette had briefly banned *Une Vie* from sale on railway bookstalls. It is therefore not surprising to find him expressing vigorously opposition to censorship in his correspondence and his *chroniques*. He may be ready, as a writer seeking to live from his works and adjusting accordingly, to adapt his expression to the different constraints of newspapers and the greater freedom of publication in volume, and to angle different stories to different outlets,[2] though without compromising his vision.[3] Aware that the *nouvelle L'Héritage* might be a bit "vive" for the *Figaro*, Maupassant destined it otherwise for the *Gil Blas*[4] (though in the event, for reasons of timing, it appeared in *La Vie Militaire*). But he remains implacably opposed to any censorship by newspaper editors,[5] and in his *chroniques* frequently stresses the artist's duty to show the (brutal) truth, both as regards what is shown and how it is shown. He attacks the public's desire for a sentimental idealization and falsification of reality in a literature that is "invraisemblable, *sympathique* et *consolante*" (**"Autour d'un livre"**, *Chroniques,* I, 283), a literature that is ultimately hypocritical in that the reader knows that what it represents is not really the case.

> L'écrivain [. . .] cesse d'être consciencieux et artiste, s'il s'efforce systématiquement de glorifier l'humanité, de la farder, d'atténuer les passions qu'il juge déshonnêtes au profit des passions qu'il juge

honnêtes. [. . .] Il est indiscutable que les rapports sexuels entre hommes et femmes tiennent dans notre vie la plus grande place, qu'ils sont le motif déterminant de la plupart de nos actions.

> La société moderne attache une idée de honte au fait brutal de l'accouplement [. . .]. Et voilà que l'hypocrisie mondaine nous veut forcer à l'enguirlander de sentiment pour en parler dans un livre.
>
> (**"Les Audacieux"**, *Chroniques,* II, 280-81)

He attacks not just this falsification of "la chose", but also the equally hypocritical reluctance of society to talk about sex at all, the suppression of "le mot" (*Chroniques,* I, 356): "Le délit d'outrage aux bonnes moeurs ne vise guère que cet acte honorable et si naturel auquel tout le monde se livre régulièrement et sans lequel l'humanité n'existerait pas" (**"Chez le ministre"**, *Chroniques,* II, 146).

> Depuis quelques années les gens soi-disant honnêtes s'en prennent surtout à la littérature appelée pornographique. Nous n'avons plus le droit de parler franchement de l'accouplement des êtres, acte aussi utile à la race et aussi innocent en soi que celui de la nutrition, [. . .] sans exciter dans le public pudibond mais débauché un ouragan d'indignation.
>
> (**"Fille de fille"**, *Chroniques,* II, 329)

This refusal to acknowledge and name known realities, which leads either to silence and evasions, or to euphemisms, is satirized in a humorous *chronique* of 1882, **"Conflits pour rire"** (*Chroniques* II, 45-9), prompted by the new law of 2 August 1882 which represented a first restriction of the law of press freedom of 1881, and was intended to counter "un déferlement de publications obscènes à bon marchè".[6] A village priest, shocked by the primitive sculpture of a naked Adam and Eve on his church porch, attempts to conceal the "groupe trop naturel" by putting trousers on Adam (fixed with sealing wax), then, assisted by his *servante*, is caught "en train d'amoindrir Adam" by night. The priest is attempting to suppress sight of *la chose;* and in his narrative, Maupassant refers to the offending genitalia only by oblique expressions: "notre père à tous se dressait dans le costume originel"; the priest plans to "[diminuer] un peu notre père Adam, rien qu'un peu"; "le morceau que venait de perdre le générateur du genre humain" is kept as evidence. Maupassant is satirizing false modesty, but his euphemistic language ironically affects the very hiding that he mocks.

Maupassant may express his preference for sexual explicitness at times, for the "cru", "chaud", explicit older language (*Chroniques,* I, 288), and even call for explicit poetry on sexual variations, "l'amour défendu, raffiné, inventif":

Moi je voudrais, et ce serait de la bonne porno-
graphie, je voudrais qu'un poète, un vrai poète
les chantât audacieusement, un jour, en des vers
hardis et passionnés, ces choses qui font rougir
les imbéciles. Il ne faudrait là ni gros mots, ni
polissonneries, ni sous-entendus; mais une suite
de petits poèmes simples et francs, bien sincères.

("Celles qui osent!", *Chroniques*, II, 335)

But the satire of **"Conflits pour rire"**, shows paradoxically the advantages that lie in *not* naming the
contentious parts. The *jeu de cache-cache* that is the
subject of the article is operating on a linguistic level
too. Maupassant can exploit the restraints that inevitably exist both in the language of society, and in print,
in various ways, as he knew the writers of the past had
done. In a *chronique* of 1888, **"Le Style épistolaire"**,
discussing the correspondence of the maréchal de Tessé
published that year, he notes:

Les plaisanteries les plus osées sur les choses dont
il semble que l'on doive le moins parler, les
anecdotes les plus vives, dont M. de Rambuteau
[the editor] a dû même supprimer quelquesunes,
faisaient donc sourire, sans les fâcher, sans les
choquer, les princesses les plus augustes. [. . .]
Elles y sont contées, en effet, avec une adresse
spirituelle, qu'on appelait alors un tour galant, et
qui consistait à escamoter l'audace sous l'élégance
piquante de la phrase. Tessé, comme la plupart
des hommes et des femmes de ce siècle, avait
acquis une ingéniosité spéciale, pour faire passer
les plaisanteries les plus hardies, en attirant d'abord
l'attention par des cabrioles de rhétorique.

(*Chroniques*, III, 355-6)

The argument points two ways: the scabrous subjects
are both part of reality, but seemingly excessive and
unmentionable; the language, with its "sous-entendus"
(III, 356) both hides them and elaborates on them.
Maupassant develops the idea with a sustained comparison between a transparent *jupe de danseuse* and
the *nudité* it both hides and reveals: "la pensée s'égaye
de ce tour, s'amuse de cette farce, et accepte de voir
le dessous, à cause du dessus destiné, semblait-il, à le
dissimuler" (*Chroniques*, III, 356).

Shock is an essential ingredient of Maupassant's stories,
and not just simply on the level of the reader's reaction
to the *histoire* in Genette's sense,[7] of events and surprise
endings. Insofar as a recurrent preoccupation is, as Sullivan
has argued, the attempt "to lift the mask of appearance,
to expose hypocrisy, to provide an unobstructed view of
a piece of the world as it is, not as it is purported to be",[8]
it is perhaps natural that the characters whose blindness
(due to complacency, habit, or reluctance to see), or inhibitions, or more conscious hypocrisy, are being exposed,
should find this confrontation with reality shocking. Indeed, it has been argued that the only logical outcome for
such an experience is suicide or madness.[9]

Shock can of course take many forms: a character in
a heterodiegetic narrative discovers the shocking truth
(**Promenade**); a character tells of his or her discovery of the shocking truth to someone else (**Garçon,
un bock!**); a tale told by a character shocks the
narratee(s) (**La Chevelure, Miss Harriet**). What is
constant is Maupassant's construction of characters
both inside stories and in frame narratives to intensify the effect, as much by stressing their conventionality, constraints, or blindness, as by insistence
on the brutality of the truth they discover or the
deliberate provocativeness of the narrator. Such character construction can range from the conventional
Dufour family in **Une Partie de campagne,** whom
the two *canotiers* "épouvantèrent [. . .] par le récit
de leurs fatigues prodigieuses, de leurs bains pris en
sueur, de leurs courses dans le brouillard des nuits"
(I, 249), to the complacent bachelor in **L'Ermite** (II,
685), jolted out of his unawareness by his discovery
of his unwitting incest. Likewise the situation or
attitude of a frame narratee can be used to intensify
the potential to shock of the embedded tale. In **En
voyage** (I, 431), an anecdote of cruel and pointless
death, chance, and helplessness in the face of nature (a
boy has to watch his brother drown in a well in the
countryside, unable to help him or to get help) is told
to a female narratee distant and safe in a protected
urban room. In **La Veillée** (I, 445) the children who
read their dead mother's letters as they watch over her
body, letters that reveal an unsuspected passionate affair, represent the respectability of law and religion: a
magistrate "aux principes inflexibles" and a nun. Their
response is condemnation and rejection: the letters are
bundled back in a drawer. There is a similar response
in **La Confession** (II, 371) when the family discover,
this time with a posthumous reading of the *testament*
of the universally respected M. Badon-Leremincé, a
scandal of the past (the infanticide of his mistress's
child): they burn the will. The shocked response of
these narratees is in effect a desire not to hear, parallel
to the desire of the mass of humanity (as Maupassant
sees it) not to know, an "automatic hypocrisy":

Toute notre view, toute notre morale, tous nos
sentiments, tous nos principes sont hypocrites;
et nous le sommes inconsciemment, sans le savoir
[. . .]. Tout ce qui n'est plus hypocrite nous
blesse comme un outrage à notre honnêteté de
parade, à nos conventions mondaines, à nos usages
de fausses paroles, de fausses protestations, de
faux visages.

(*Chroniques*, I, 285)

Jean Rousset has noted how a fictional narratee
can react defensively to an embedded tale, showing
"réticences", or interrupting "pour se protéger de
la fascination du récit par une mise en distance
thérapeutique."[10] The response of Maupassant's narratees
frequently goes further in the desire not to know as

a sign of wilful social, sexual or moral blindness. The audience in *La Rempailleuse* (I, 546) is initially reluctant to hear the tale because of the social status of the heroine: a situation echoed in the story itself where the chemist and his wife are indignant at the devotion of the *rempailleuse*. At the end of *Une Ruse* (I, 560),[11] the female narratee is shocked by the doctor's tale of how he was faced with and solved the problem of getting the body of a woman's lover out of the house before the husband returns: "La jeune femme crispée demanda: / 'Pourquoi m'avezvous raconté cette épouvantable histoire?'" (II, 565). On a more frivolous level, narratees can manifest a superficial and hypocritical pretence of not wanting to know in ritual gestures and exclamations of shock to preserve appearances, as in *Joseph* (II, 506), where the successive stages of the baronne's revelation of her manipulation and seduction of the manservant are punctuated by the repeated shocked reactions of her (equally tipsy) narratee to her defiance of the conventions of marriage, class, and male initiative: "—Oh! ma chère! . . ." and "—Oh! Andrée".

Where the situation can produce more complex narrative interest is when limited and conventional moral or social attitudes produce, not just a narratee who does not want to hear, or know, but a narrator who does not want to tell (in both cases paradoxically reversing the expected norm of a narrative situation). This is arguably the case in some heterodiegetic narratives, where Maupassant echoes the characters' hypocritical reluctance to confront and express certain realities (both *la chose* and *le mot*) by a *récit* that teasingly refuses to say or show things. The narrator of *Boule de Suif* echoes the euphemisms ("Ces dames surtout trouvaient des délicatesses de tournures, des subtilités d'expression charmantes, pour dire les choses les plus scabreuses") and hypocrisy ("Elles s'épanouissaient dans cette aventure polissonne") (I, 111) of the characters by playing with focalization and ellipsis. The narrator keeps us largely with the group of travellers; all the exchanges between Boule de Suif and the Prussian take place "off stage". The dialogue between Cornudet and Boule de Suif in the corridor, when (we suppose) he too seeks her favours, is filtered through the eyes and ears of Loiseau, so that we have to guess Cornudet's request, and the return of Loiseau to his room and his wife is cut short at a testing point. During the celebratory dinner, Loiseau makes jokes "d'un goût déplorable" (I, 116) about the implied activities of Boule de Suif and the Prussian; Maupassant's humour is less coarse, but just as Loiseau appeals to the group's awareness of what is going on upstairs, so too the narrator appeals to the reader's awareness of what keeps the passengers awake:

> Et toute la nuit, dans l'obscurité du corridor coururent comme des frémissements, des bruits légers, à peine sensibles, pareils à des souffles, des effleurements de pieds nus, d'imperceptibles craquements. Et l'on ne dormit que très tard, assurément, car des filets de lumière glissèrent longtemps sous les portes. Le champagne a de ces effets-là; il trouble, dit-on, le sommeil. (I, 117)

In such a story (as in the more marked *grivoiserie* and double entendre of *L'Héritage* (II, 3), where the innuendos of a testing narrator match dishonest and salacious characters) narrators don't (quite) tell so that their euphemisms and evasions ironically highlight hypocrisy on the level of events. Other tales however accept the necessary inhibitions and constraints of language in society, without indignation, and derive a certain detached amusement from the incongruities that they throw up, and in particular with the complexities they offer for spinning tales and constructing a formally coherent short story. The frankness of the *histoire* (and critics from Lemaitre to Forestier have commented on his directness when talking about sex)[12] is filtered through and intensified by an awareness, by narrators as much as by the characters, of what cannot be said. These stories may seem slight in comparison to *Boule de Suif;* the use of allusion, double-entendre, euphemism, elision and restricted focalization can no doubt descend into a rather facile naughtiness appealing to the readership of *Gil Blas* but demanding little of them, and can represent just a way of subverting the required constraints imposed on published language by suggesting rather than stating, and relying on the imagination of the reader. Maupassant can however exploit the inhibitions of his characters to spin a tale out of minimal material, using the narratorial evasions and euphemisms to echo the hesitations and embarrassment of the characters.

In *La Serre* (I, 855),[13] the dormant love-life of the Lerebours is rejuvenated by their discovery (and watching) of their maid's rendez-vous in the greenhouse. Focalization and narrative ellipses are crucial in setting the tone. Having heard nocturnal noises in the house, interpreted as burglars, Mme Lerebour dispatches her husband to investigate: and we stay with her in the bedroom as her husband leaves (and is absent for 45 minutes), and she is gripped with fears, and have only his account, punctuated by the characteristic points of suspension of the inhibited narrator, when he returns: "C'était . . . c'était . . . Céleste qui avait un . . . un . . . rendezvous dans la serre . . . Si tu savais ce que . . . ce que . . . ce que j'ai vu . . . '"; and the following events are cut short by an ellipsis: "Mais lui, la tenant à pleins bras, l'entraînait document vers le lit . . .": followed by a *blanc* (I, 859) and a cut to the next morning. Likewise at the end as we see the couple, in an iterative present, revisiting the greenhouse:

Par les nuits claires quelquefois, les deux époux vont, à pas furtifs, le long des massifs et des plates-bandes jusqu'à la petite serre au bout du jardin. Et ils restent là blottis l'un près de l'autre contre le vitrage comme s'ils regardaient dedans une chose étrange et pleine d'intérêt. (I, 860)

Here it is not so much that the elided scenes or the spectacles cut off by the restricted focalization are imagined by a reader left free to his (or her) own devices; rather that they are provided by what Eco would argue is the reader's repertory of "intertextual scenarios",[14] of ready-made erotic memories or scenes.

It is however at the level of framed narration, or with clearly homodiegetic narrators, when an explicit fictional narrator (and generally a fictional narratee) are both present, that the potential of inhibited narrators for creating effects of tension or of comedy can be most fully exploited. Particularly, as one might expect, when the narratee is a woman. It is true that Maupassant can sometimes merely set up female narrators and narratees in such a way that their supposed inhibitions merely serve as a way of calling attention to *sous-entendus*, and that their euphemisms just highlight what is evaded, without any real thematic link with the story. In *Sauvée* (II, 651), for instance, the marquise de Rennedon gives a gleeful account to her friend the baronne de Grangerie of how she has hired a maid to set up her husband's capture *in flagrante delicto* in order to obtain a divorce. Maupassant here multiplies possible occasions of inhibition and embarrassment, and consequently of *sous-entendus*, evasions, and euphemisms, by exploiting situations of dialogue: either between narrator and narratee, as when Rennedon tells Grangerie of the shady intermediary approached to find a suitable maid: "'Comment dirais-je . . . [. . .] tu sais . . . de ces hommes qui font des affaires de toute . . . de toute nature . . .'" (II, 652); or with the discovery of the *flagrant délit*: "'J'ouvre la porte toute grande . . . Ah! ah! ah! ça y était en plein . . . en plein . . . ma chère . . .'" (II, 656); or between the narrator and a character in her story: as when she outlines tentatively to the intermediary the plan of finding a maid, or when Renndedon first meets the maid, or when the maid announces success "d'un air timide": "'Je fus un peu surprise, un rien émue même, non de la chose, mais plutôt de la manière dont elle me l'avait dite. Je balbutiai: "Et . . . et . . . ça s'est bien passé? . . . /—Oh! très bien, madame." '" (II, 655) But when Rennedon is reporting to Grangerie any such embarrassed encounter, she herself no longer shows any embarrassment before her narratee: the contrivance is clearly just to highlight the naughtiness; and one is above all aware, as Forestier notes of "la narration de ces secrets entre femmes", that they are for male consumers (II, 1491, about the similar *La Confidence*).

In other stories, however, there is a link between on the one hand the inhibitions of characters and the de-

lays of the narration, and on the other, the themes and the point of the *histoire*. In *La Bûche* (I, 352), the narrator is explaining to a woman friend why he has never married; he relates being left alone after dinner with his friend's wife, a prey to her advances; a falling log in the fire saves him from yielding and being caught by the husband's unexpected and premature return: blazing log saves from *flagrant délit*. He dwells on the "gêne singulière" of the evening, his vain attempts to fill the "silences embarrassants" of the conversation, to fend off her advances (I, 354). When the climax comes, the narrator finds the narration of events increasingly difficult: he can't explain to his female narratee what would have happened any more than his younger self was able to find a way of responding decisively to his friend's wife: should he betray his friend? or play the role of Joseph (with a clearly dangerous Potiphar's wife)?

. . . Enfin, une minute de plus . . . vous comprenez, n'est-ce pas? Une minute de plus et . . . j'étais . . . non, elle était . . . pardon, c'est lui qui l'était! . . . ou plutôt qui l'aurait été, quand voilà qu'un bruit terrible nous fit bondir. (I, 356)

And the narration resumes without further hesitation, with both problems solved: his young self is saved by the log and the husband's return, his narration can return to that of unembarrassing events. Similarly in *La Fenêtre* (I, 896), the narrator hesitates before revealing the full horror of his blunder at the climax of the tale (he mistakes from behind the respectable widow he is courting for her maid, whom he has seduced), and likewise intensifies the suspense of the moment and the awfulness of his act by reminding us at this point of the female narratee:[15]

Je la reconnus aussitôt, pleine, fraîche, grasse et douce, la face secrète de ma maîtresse, et j'y jetai, pardon, madame, j'y jetai un tendre baiser, un baiser d'amant qui peut tout oser. (I, 901)

More elaborately, in *Enragée?* (I, 939) the narratee has (conventionally) prompted the narrative ("Tu me demandes de te raconter mon voyage de noces") (I, 939). The subject as much as the narratee inhibits the narrator ("Comment veux-tu que j'ose?"; "Je prends du courage en écrivant et je me décide à tout dire" (I, 939). Her tale is one of comic misapprehensions: she cannot understand her husband's advances in bed, thinks that he is going mad and is going to kill her; she mistakes sexual pleasure for the onset of rabies. The mistakes spring from her ignorance. She has not been informed about sexual realities, first by her family, then by her husband, who assumes she is mischievously feigning ignorance (a lack of information that Maupassant treats elsewhere seriously, in *Une Vie*).[16] The reasons they have not told her are precisely the fears and inhibitions that constrain her as she gives the account of events to her friend: "Oh! ma chère, comment dire ça? Enfin voici" (I, 941). It is only obliquely and allusively that she can evoke her experiences, bringing out the rabies/orgasm parallel ("Les irritantes obsessions de mon mari déterminèrent un nouvel accès, qui fut plus long que le premier. J'avais envie de déchirer, de mordre, de hurler [. . .]") (I, 945). As Maupassant develops the story, it is permeated by a network of references to telling/not telling that draw out the protagonist's anxieties. Not only has her mother not dared to "effleurer ce sujet délicat" of sex (I, 939), her parents do not write to her about her pet dog, which had bitten her before she left, increasing her anxieties about rabies. She is of course reluctant to express her fears on this score to her husband: "Pour rien au monde je n'aurais voulu avouer la pensée qui me torturait" (I, 943); "Vingt fois je faillis lui dire mon abominable secret, mais je me tus" (I, 943). She hides her fears of rabies, they anxiously hide the realities of sex, and even her husband's tardy explanations are "sommaires" (I, 942) and do not prepare her to understand her physical sensations. Hence the confusions and misunderstandings, intensified by her vivid imagination.

The exploitation of inhibited narrators (teasing, suspense, emphasis, thematic complexity) is even more evident, when Maupassant underscores the problem of telling by a proliferation of retellings. The problem in *La Rouille* (I, 539), and the driving force behind events, is not so much male impotence, as the title might obliquely suggest,[17] but the reluctance of the male characters to face it openly and talk about it seriously. The baron Hector de Coutelier, now over 50, has a sole and "inapaisable passion": hunting, his only activity and subject of conversation: "dès qu'on parlait d'autre chose, il n'écoutait plus et s'essayait tout seul à fredonner des fanfares" (I, 540). His friend M. de Courville and his family plan to marry the baron to a widow. Having been won over by Mme Berthe de Vilers at her first erratic but successful shots, and apparently on the verge of committing himself, he puts off making his proposal without giving a reason to his friend: "Le baron se troubla soudain, et balbutiant: 'Non . . . non . . . il faut d'abord que je fasse un petit voyage . . . un petit voyage . . . à Paris'" (I, 542-3). It is his anxieties about his sexual competence (after sixteen years of inaction) that lead to this experimental trip to Paris, but its purpose remains undisclosed to M. de Courville, and to the reader. On his return, "changé, vieilli", he calls his friend in secret to a meeting, and "visiblement embarrassé", mysteriously declares to his friend: "'Je voulais vous dire . . . tout de suite . . . que cette . . . cette affaire . . . vous savez bien . . . est manquée'", refusing further explanation: "'Ce serait trop pénible à dire.'" The mystery prompts speculation in the friend's family: illegitimate children? an old affair? But three months later, drink helping, he reveals more of the situation, but still hesitantly:

"Depuis le temps que j'avais perdu l'habitude de . . . de . . . de l'amour, enfin, je ne savais plus si je serais encore capable de . . . de . . . , vous savez bien . . . Songez donc? voici maintenant seize ans exactement que . . . que . . . que . . . pour la dernière fois, vous comprenez. Dans ce pays ce n'est pas facile de . . . de . . . vous y êtes. Et puis j'avais autre chose à faire. J'aime mieux tirer un coup de fusil. Bref, au moment de m'engager devant le maire et le prêtre à . . . à . . . ce que vous savez, j'ai eu peur. Je me suis dit: Bigre, mais si . . . si . . . j'allais rater. [. . .] Enfin, pour en avoir le coeur net, je me suis promis d'aller passer huit jours à Paris." (I, 544)

His attempt to explain his predicament, with euphemisms (*l'amour*), periphrases ("ce que vous savez"), ellipses, appeals to his listener, conveys his inhibitions; he is only at ease and specific with a hunting vocabulary (which is not without generating appropriate double entendres, given the sexual sense of "tirer un coup"). His friend only superficially maintains an appearance of seriousness and sympathy: "M. de Courville se tordait pour ne pas rire"; and then retells the tale to his wife, "en suffoquant de gaieté" (I, 545). His wife does not laugh, but just proposes "avec un grand sérieux" to recall the planned bride. Maupassant has presented the baron's predicament in a series of different lights. Initially it is a puzzle (about the reasons for the trip to Paris, the cancelled proposal), created both by the baron (not telling his friend) and by the heterodiegetic narrator (who does not tell us); a puzzle that prompts the friend to seek a secret that would explain it. It then comes out successively as a source of private embarrassment to the baron, as male joke at the expense of another male's misfortune (as told by Courville to his wife), and is finally dismissed by her as a minor difficulty: "'Bah! Quand on aime sa femma, entendez-vous, cette chose-là . . . revient toujours'". This silences Courville, "un peu confus lui-même" (I, 545), and brings to a close a story generated not so much by an intimate problem, but by the problem and *avatars* of its disclosure to others.

Un Sage (I, 1087) in the same way exploits the combination of narration and inhibition to give interest to what would otherwise be little more than a mildly salacious story. Blérot, a childhood friend of the narrator, after the initial delights of marriage, finds his health being destroyed by the innocent but exhausting sexual demands of his wife; he follows his friend's blunt advice: "'Donne-lui des amants plutôt que de te laisser tuer ainsi'" (I, 1091), and is restored to health; he celebrates (on meeting his friend again) by a visit to the brothel. In terms of narrative content there is an obvious pattern: health → ill-health → health restored, reinforced by the appropriately named René Blérot saying at the end, of his refound friendship: "'Il me semble que je renais'" (I, 1092). But this surface pattern (Blérot's *histoire*) is echoed by a less obvious one (the narrator's *histoire*): intimacy with friend → lost intimacy → intimacy restored.

What provides the narrative interest is the multiple roles of the friend and initial homodiegetic narrator. He has been cut off from his previous open and intimate relationship with Blérot by his marriage. Before, "nous n'avions rien de secret"; now "c'est à peine si nous trouvions quelque chose à nous dire" (I, 1088). When he first meets the ill Blérot, he is puzzled by this mysterious transformation of his barely recognizable friend, and (in a pattern similar to *La Rouille*) forces the secret out of him in spite of his reluctance: "Il balbutia: 'Mais je n'ai rien à te dire'" (I, 1089). Embarrassed, Blérot reveals his secret through hints, allusions, evasions, a delaying suspense (which sustains the reader's and narratee's curiosity). The second time he meets Blérot, six months later, a transformation in his health as total as the one that had prompted his initial questions makes him again demand an explanation, and again leads to Blérot's embarrassment ("cramoisi"). The friend's comments on his healthy appearance are as unwelcome as were those on his ill-health: "Il balbutia très vite [. . .]" (I, 1091). Blérot's invitation to dinner and presentation of the lover, "un grand garçon [. . .] avec des joues velues et un aspect d'hercule mondain', explain all without Blérot having this time to say anything more (since the friend still pesters him with questions) than just: "'C'était trop bête de se laisser crever comme ça, à la fin'" (I, 1093). So the initial narrator/friend has become narratee to Blérot, but has not only become the means of forcing the confessions out of him, but also has a key role as active participant in saving his life (and his marriage?) with his blunt suggestion.[18] Their intimacy is now restored: "René ne cessait de me parler, familièrement, cordialement, franchement, comme autrefois" (I, 1092). Blérot's private sexual predicament, caused by "l'intimité du lit" (I, 1087), had cut Blérot off from intimacy with his friend. As Maupassant has developed the narrative, the story is perhaps less about restoring his health than about restoring that link between Blérot and his gynophobic friend (who formulates explicitly his anger, not just at Blérot's wife, but at "la femme, [. . .] cet être inconscient, charmant, terrible": I, 1091), and their ability to talk freely. The final proposed visit to the brothel provides a revenge on the female, and seals their refound intimacy, as well as providing a paradoxical twist for the end. Perhaps the story should be called not so much *Un Sage* as *Deux amis*.

Le Remplaçant (I, 700) is again, at the level of *histoire,* a simple tale: a respectable, *dévote* widow hires the regular sexual services of a soldier; when he cannot make the appointment one week, he sends a friend as a substitute; this prompts an initial quarrel over the sharing of the proceeds, then a resolution when both are taken on, providing the service twice a week. This could be summarized schematically: an arrangement is set up; → it is threatened (Silballe's absence); → substitute arrangement; → new threat (quarrel Silballe/ friend); → new arrangement. At the centre might seem to be the point that shocks the narratee in the frame narrative: the false respectability of Mme Bonderoi.

It is, however, not really just a story of "unmasking" of hypocrisy, with a playful element of gender role reversal (as the narrator suggests, we would not be surprised by the male version of what we see: the pursuit of youth of the other sex, sexual exploitation at work (Mme Bonderoi uses her husband's *clercs* while he is alive), or the prostitutes supporting their families on the proceeds, as the soldiers do their parents). Her "vices secrets" (I, 700) imply secrecy; but this secret is told; in fact, has to be told (to the appropriate persons) at various points if the supply of lovers is to be maintained. This creates a paradoxical pattern where characters are recurrently sworn to secrecy, then told something, and then themselves tell the forbidden story. Moreover the characters may want to tell, but circumstances and conventions place inhibitions on what they can say: neither Mme Bonderoi nor the soldiers can mention sex directly, which leads to a series of euphemisms and suggestions.

The initial frame sets up a conventional conversation in which the narratee's surprise prompts the second narrator to reveal "tous les détails" about some as yet unspecified surprising information about Mme Bonderoi. But rather than giving a direct account of "l'aventure invraisemblable arrivée jeudi dernier", the second narrator reveals that he has heard it from a friend, captain Jean d'Anglemare, who in turn had heard it from one of the soldiers in question: so that before we reach the embedded tale, the first-hand oral narration by Siballe (with its humorously contrasting style), we are aware of the story passing through a succession of narrators. Siballe relates his first encounter with Mme Bonderoi from the point of view of his innocent self at the time, initially unaware of what she is proposing (unlike the reader who has been told already: "Elle aimait les beaux garçons", and can guess). She swears him to secrecy: "'Alors ell' se fit comprendre ouvertement par des manifestations. Quand j'vis de quoi il s'agissait, je posai mon casque sur une chaise; et je lui montrai que dans les dragons on ne recule jamais, mon cap'taine'". He too, rather than saying explicitly, uses allusions and military metaphors.[19] The *remplaçant* is treated similarly: "'Elle le regarde, lui fait aussi jurer le secret.'" After the soldiers' quarrel and duel, Siballe now tells the captain, who tells his friend (the second narrator), "ria[nt] aux larmes"; and the friend repeats all this to his narratee: "Mais il [d'Anglemare] m'a fait aussi jurer le secret qu'il avait garanti aux deux soldats. 'Surtout, n'allez pas me trahir, gardez ça pour vous, vous me le promettez?'": and of course the friend both promises and tells his narratee of the promise to d'Anglemare . . . which he is now breaking: "'Oh! ne craignex rien'" (I, 703). So if on one level the story may seem to have at its centre the joke about the *remplaçant* (as Forestier notes, singularly appropriate for soldiers: I, 1502), or the revelation of "vices secrets" in bourgeois women, the *récit* is largely constructed around attempts to swear to secrecy (by Mme Bonderoi to both soldiers, by Siballe to the captain, by the captain to his friend) and their failure, without which there would be not only no story-telling, but no *histoire,* had not Siballe told his friend, desperate not to "lose" Mme Bonderoi.

The stories of *sous-entendus* and allusions that Maupassant wrote in this vein for *Gil Blas* tend to attract relatively little critical esteem and attention. For Marie-Claire Bancquart, the *clin d'oeil* of author to reader "agace facilement [. . .] le lecteur un peu exigeant".[20] Though some may deserve this, in many others what is interesting is Maupassant's ability to exploit the paradoxical narrative possibilities of inhibition. If a narrator's main aim is to get an idea across to a narratee whatever her (or his) resistance, it may be necessary to write "brutalement, sans ménagements galants", as does the narrator of *Les Caresses* (I, 952), when he attempts to overcome the woman's physiological revulsion at sex. But this produces in the event a tale lacking in tension and in narrative interest, and which concentrates simply and didactically on the ideas. Many other stories show that shockable narratees and inhibited narrators are more effective in generating thematic echoes, narrative complexity, and verbal play, out of a minimal anecdotal content—not to mention humour.

Notes

[1] Maupassant, *Contes et nouvelles,* ed. Louis Forestier, 2 vols, Bibliothèque de la Pléiade (Paris: Gallimard, 1988-89 (first edition 1974-79)), II, 1060. References in the text are to volume and page of this edition, and to *Chroniques,* Préface d'Hubert Juin, 3 volumes (Paris: Union Générale d'Editions, 1980).

[2] On the tone of different newspapers, see *La Parure et autres contes parisiens,* ed. M.-C. Bancquart (Paris: Garnier, 1984), pp. 22-24; Mary Donaldson-Evans, "*Nuit de Noël* and *Conte de Noël:* Ironic Diptych in Maupassant's Work", *French Review,* 54 (1980-81), 66-77; and on *Gil Blas, Contes et nouvelles,* I, 1379, and Claude Bellanger, Jacques Godechot, Pierre Guiral and Fernand Terrou (editors), *Histoire générale de la presse française,* 3 vols (Paris: PUF, 1969-1976), III (1972), 380-1.

[3] See David Bryant, *The Rhetoric of Pessimism and Strategies of Containment in the Short Stories of Guy de Maupassant* (Lewiston: Edwin Mellen, 1993), p. 34.

[4] *Correspondance inédite,* ed. A. Artinian and E. Maynial (Paris: Wapler, 1951), p. 177.

[5] "Tous les directeurs des journaux où j'ai écrit savent également que je n'ai jamais toléré qu'on supprimàt un seul mot. J'ai cessé ma collaboration régulière au *Gaulois* après une modification, ou plutôt une coupure faite *en mon absence,* à un article sur *Manon Lescaut,* cet article ayant paru *un peu vif*" (*Correspondance inédite,* p. 228; see also p. 231).

[6] *Histoire générale de la presse française,* III, 24. The effect was to make "outrages aux bonnes moeurs" in newspapers and posters punishable by a *tribunal correctionnel;* books still went before a jury.

[7] I use the distinction *histoire/récit,* and also homodiegetic/heterodiegetic, of Gérard Genette, "Discours du récit", in *Figures III* (Paris, Seuil, 1972).

[8] Edward D. Sullivan, *Maupassant: The Short Stories* (London: Edward Arnold, 1962), p. 57.

[9] Charlotte Schapira, "La Folie—thème et outil narratif dans les contes de Maupassant", *Neophilologus,* 74 (1990), 30-43.

[10] Jean Rousset, *Le Lecteur intime,* Paris, Corti, 1986, p. 63. On the role of the narratee generally, see notably Gerald Prince, "Introduction à l'étude du narrataire", *Poétique,* 4 (1973), 178-196; Ross Chambers, *Story and Situation: Narrative Seduction and the Power of Fiction* (Manchester: Manchester University Press, 1984). Recent studies on narrator and narratee in Maupassant include Andrea Calí, *Figures narratologigues dans 'La Maison Tellier'* (Lecce: Adriatica, 1981); Carmen Licari, "Le Lecteur des contes de Maupassant", *Francofonia,* 3 (1982), 91-103; Jaap Lintveldt, "Pour une analyse narratologique des *Contes et nouvelles* de Guy de Maupassant", in *Fiction, narratologie, texte, genre,* ed. Jean Bessière (New York: Lang, 1989); Tuula Lehman, *Transitions savantes et dissimulées: une étude structurelle des contes et nouvelles de Guy de Maupassant* (Helsinki: Societas Scientiarum Finnica, 1990). The emphasis tends to be on classification of technique rather than defining of effect.

[11] On the function of the frame and narrator/narratee relationships here, see Angela Moger, "That Obscure Object of Narration", *Yale French Studies,* 63 (1982), 129-138.

[12] Forestier in I, xlviii; Jules Lemaitre refers to "la franchise du récit, [. . .] la sensualité de l'artiste, laquelle au moins nous épargne la grivoiserie", in an article originally published in the *Revue Bleue,* which paradoxically obliged him to be euphemistic himself: "voulant les relire [les contes] en bonne compagnie [

. . .] je passerai vite où il faudra" ("Guy de Maupassant", *Les Contemporains,* lre série (Paris: Boivin, s.d.), pp. 285-310). The Pléiade notes (I, 1351-7) illustrate the extensive nature of the cuts necessary for *Histoire d'une fille de ferme* to be published in the *Revue Bleue:* nearly all the explicit sexual passages are deleted, even between cocks and hens.

[13] Compare *Le Crime au père Boniface* (II, 168) for another tale of inadvertent discovery that depends on picking up hints and double entendres, and where the reader has to guess what Boniface has failed to realize (he has heard, not a crime, but sounds of lovemaking), and where the narrator elides the explicit revelations (only alluding to the gestures of the *brigadier* and reducing what he finally says to a whisper that we are not allowed to hear).

[14] See Umberto Eco, *Lector in fabula. Le rôle du lecteur,* traduit de l'italien par Myriem Bouzaher (Paris: Livre de poche, 1990), pp. 101-105.

[15] In the original version of the story (*Gil Blas*), an introductory frame established the narratee as a woman who demands the story from a reluctant narrator. The final version cuts the frame; the two unexpected reminders of this narratee towards the close are thus odd (as Forestier notes: I, 1566), but all the more revealing of Maupassant's tactics.

[16] As Forestier notes (I, 1576).

[17] Given that *se dérouiller* could have the sense of 'to wanton: after a period of abstention' (John S. Farmer, *Vocabula Amatoria* [New York: University Books, 1966; first published anonymously, 1896].

[18] Compare the similar role of narrator/narratee who becomes agent in *Mademoiselle Perle,* albeit more destructively.

[19] With possible salacious overtones: 'Quand la corvée a été faite, mon cap'taine, je me suis mis en position de me retirer' (I, 702).

[20] *La Parure et autres contes parisiens,* p. 54.

FURTHER READING

Biography

Lerner, Michael G. *Maupassant.* New York: George Braziller, 1975, 301 p.

> Biography of Maupassant. Includes discussion of his period's social and literary evolution and how it affected his development as a writer.

Criticism

Abamine, E. P. "German-French Sexual Encounters of the Franco-Prussian War Period in the Fiction of Guy de Maupassant." *CLA Journal* 32, No. 3 (March 1989): 323-34.

> Considers the sexual aspect of the German military occupation of France following the Franco-Prussian War (1870-71) in three of Maupassant's stories—"Boule de suif," "Mademoiselle Fifi," and "Le Lit 29."

Bolster, Richard. "The Patriotic Prostitutes of Maupassant: Fact or Fantasy?" *French Studies Bulletin,* No. 51 (Summer 1994): 16-17.

> Briefly discusses the connection between Maupassant's characterization of the patriotic French prostitute in his works and a newspaper article published during the Franco-Prussian War.

Bowles, Thelma. "The Stacked Deck: A Study of Technique in Maupassant's Novels." *Romance Notes* 36, No. 1 (Fall 1985): 55-62.

> Using Maupassant's six novels, argues that although the characters seem to exist in a realistic framework, they are in fact unrealistic, being situated in a multilayered system of cultural codes.

Cogman, P. W. M. "Maupassant's Unacknowledgeable Puns." *French Studies Bulletin,* No. 53 (Winter 1994): 8-11.

> Briefly discusses the nature of Maupassant's use of "oblique" puns—words or expressions with obscene undertones likely grasped only by careful readers.

Donaldson-Evans, Mary. "Beginnings to Understand: The Narrative 'Come-On' in Maupassant's Stories." *Neophilologus* 68, No. 1 (January 1984): 37-47.

> Defends the value and importance of short stories in literary criticism through an examination of unusual beginnings in several of Maupassant's stories.

———. "The Matrical Marsh: A Symbol of Hope in Maupassant's Work." *French Forum* 2, No. 3 (September 1977): 255-62.

> Argues that understanding the metaphor of the marsh and how it stands apart from Maupassant's other aquatic images is essential to grasping the author's worldview.

Freimanis, Dzintars. "Maupassant as a Romantic." *The Romanic Review* 54, No. 3 (October 1963): 274-80.

> Argues that some of Maupassant's short stories mark him as somewhat of a romantic, rather than an entirely realist or objective author, as most critics contend.

Fusco, Richard. *Maupassant and the American Short Story: The Influence of Form at the Turn of the Century.* University Park: Pennsylvania State University Press, 1994, 230 p.

Traces the development of the short story form throughout Maupassant's oeuvre and argues for the significant influence of Maupassant's works on turn-of-the-century American short story writers.

Harris, T. A. Le V. "Repetition in Maupassant: Irony as Originality?" *Forum for Modern Language Studies* 25, No. 3 (July 1989): 265-75.

Provides a brief summary of two critical studies on Maupassant's reuse of textual material, then offers an interpretation of this narrative strategy, taking into account the author's ironic vision.

Issacharoff, Michael. "Telling Terror(?): Against Taxonomies." *Rivista di Letterature moderne e comparate* 49, No. 1 (January–March 1996): 1-11.

First examines the problematic nature of classifying works of literature as "fantastic" or "supernatural" (especially as pertaining to Maupassant's stories), then considers the possibility of Maupassant's stories as "terrorist."

Johnston, Marlo. Introduction to *A Parisian Bourgeois' Sundays and Other Stories,* by Guy de Maupassant, translated by Marlo Johnston, pp. 6-14. London: Peter Owen, 1997.

Introduces fifteen of Maupassant's early short stories, twelve of which had never before been published in English. Also includes a chronology.

MacNamara, Matthew. "A Critical Stage in the Evolution of Maupassant's Story-Telling." *Modern Language Review* 71, No. 2 (April 1976): 294-303.

Discusses the significance of the years 1880 to 1882 in Maupassant's development as a short-story writer.

McCrory, Donald. "Maupassant: Problems of Interpretation." *Modern Languages* 70, No. 1 (March 1989): 39-43.

Offers possible explanations for Maupassant's enduring popularity among literature teachers and students alike, noting Maupassant's literary skill, his clarity of style, and his brevity.

Moger, Angela. "Kissing and Telling: Narrative Crimes in Maupassant." In *Maupassant Conteur et Romancier,* edited by Christopher Lloyd and Robert Lethbridge, pp. 111-23. London: University of Durham, 1994.

Uses three of Maupassant's stories—"Le Modéle," "Découverte," and "Rose"—to discuss how the repetition or reenactment of plot elements reveals a metaphoric shift from nature to art.

Schapira, Charlotte. "Proper Names in Maupassant's Short Stories." *Names* 40, No. 4 (December 1992): 253-59.

Argues that Maupassant's creation and use of proper names for the characters in his works is an important yet unexamined area of study.

Stivale, Charles J. "Guy de Maupassant and Narrative Strategies of 'Othering'." *Australian Journal of French Studies* 30, No. 2 (May-August 1993): 241-51.

Examines several of Maupassant's stories, including "Mademoiselle Fifi" and "La Maison Tellier," to demonstrate the author's method of portraying women as "other" through their sexual, ethnic, and racial differences.

Sullivan, Edward D. *Maupassant: The Short Stories.* London: Edward Arnold (Publishers) Ltd., 1962, 64 p.

Examines various aspects of Maupassant's *contes,* such as narration, resonance, and atmosphere, then discusses several of his *nouvelles,* including "Boule de Suif" and "La Maison Tellier."

Traill, Nancy H. "Guy de Maupassant: The Scientific Cynic." In *Possible Worlds of the Fantastic: The Rise of the Paranormal in Fiction,* pp. 105-34. Toronto: University of Toronto Press, 1996.

Explores the fantastic in Maupassant's tales by analyzing three sets of narratives—traditional stories equating the unknown with the supernatural; tales revealing some consideration of the paranormal; and stories in which the paranormal is tangible.

Additional coverage of Maupassant's life and works can be found in the following sources published by the Gale Group: *Dictionary of Literary Biography,* Vol. 123; *Short Story Criticism,* Vol. 1; and *World Literature Criticism, 1500 to the Present.*

Alexander Pushkin

1799-1837

(Full name Alexander Sergeyevich Pushkin; also trans-literated as Alexsandr Puškin) Russian poet, novelist, short story writer, dramatist, essayist, and critic.

The following entry presents recent criticism on Pushkin. For additional information on Pushkin's career, see *NCLC*, Volume 3; for criticism devoted to his verse novel *Yevgeny Onegin* (1833; *Eugene Onegin*), see *NCLC*, Volume 27.

INTRODUCTION

An outstanding figure of nineteenth-century literature, Alexander Pushkin is recognized as the national poet of Russia. Emphasizing the simplicity and beauty of his native tongue, he transformed the literary language of his age, and helped Russian literature escape the domination of eighteenth-century neoclassicism. In his works, Pushkin absorbed many of the structural and stylistic characteristics of European writers—notably François Voltaire, Lord Byron, Shakespeare, and Sir Walter Scott—and recast them in a uniquely Russian mold. Known primarily for his long narrative poems, particularly *Eugene Onegin* and *Medny vsadnik* (1837; *The Bronze Horseman*), Pushkin additionally produced several collections of lyric poetry and completed a series of stage tragedies, and one full-length drama, *Boris Godunov* (1831). With his fiction, Pushkin established the foundation for the writings of the great Russian novelists—Leo Tolstoy, Fyodor Dostoevsky, and Ivan Turgenev.

Biographical Information

Born into the Russian aristocracy in 1799, Pushkin was brought up in an environment heavily influenced by European culture. From his early years in Moscow, Pushkin had easy access to French and British literature. After graduating from a government lycée at Tsarskoe Selo in 1817, he obtained an appointment to the Ministry of Foreign Affairs in St. Petersburg. While there he alternated between periods of reckless dissipation and intense writing, finishing his first full-length work *Ruslan i Lyudmila* (*Ruslan and Lyudmila*) in 1820. Just prior to its publication, however, Czar Alexander I exiled Pushkin to southern Russia for the allegedly revolutionary political sentiments expressed in his poetry. During the first four years of his six-year exile, he retained his civil service position and lived in various towns in the Caucasus and Crimea. Despite bouts of gambling and drinking, he was productive

during his years in southern Russia and wrote prolifically. Pushkin was eventually pardoned by Nicholas I in 1826, though the czar appointed himself the poet's personal censor, keeping him under strict observation and forbidding him to travel freely or leave Russia. In 1831 Pushkin married Natalia Nikolaevna Goncharova, and in the final ten years of his life he lived primarily in St. Petersburg where he produced *Eugene Onegin* and all of his shorter fiction. In 1837 he was severely wounded in a duel with George d'Anthès, an Alsatian nobleman who had openly made sexual advances toward Pushkin's wife. Pushkin died two days later.

Major Works

Critics generally divide Pushkin's poetic works into three periods. His early works, those written before his exile, include the narrative poem *Ruslan and Lyudmila*—a comic epic that celebrates freedom and love as it addresses the theme of youth coming to maturity—and numerous shorter poems, most of which were never published because of the bold attitudes he expressed concerning erotic love, politics, and religion. The second period in Pushkin's career roughly parallels his exile in southern Russia. Two of his narrative poems from this period, *Kavkazski plennik* (1822; *The Captive of the Caucasus*)—which contrasts civilized and primitive cultures as it addresses themes of the individual versus society—and *Bakhchisaraiski fontan* (1824; *The Bak-chesarian Fountain: A Tale of the Tauride*—which treats envy and jealousy—reveal the extensive influence of Lord Byron in terms of technique, character, and structure. Of Pushkin's poems on religious themes *Gavriiliada* (1821; *Gavriliada*) is the most infamous for its treatment of the Immaculate Conception as a love intrigue involving Mary, Satan, the angel Gabriel, and God. The principle poems from the last period of Pushkin's career are his most enduring works, *Eugene Onegin* and *The Bronze Horseman*. Described as a novel in verse and recognized for its technical precision and narrative complexity, *Eugene Onegin* is a story of twice-rejected love set against a detailed picture of Russian life in the early nineteenth century. *The Bronze Horseman* contrasts the omnipotence of Peter the Great with the helplessness of the protagonist, who is symbolic of the masses sacrificed for the construction of St. Petersburg and the glory of imperial Russia.

Among Pushkin's dramatic works, *Boris Godunov* is a historical play based on the work of Shakespeare. It opens with the accession of Godunov, a regent, to the Russian throne in 1598 and details the following seven years of intrigue, which culminate in his death and replacement by an ignoble pretender to the crown. Pushkin's "Little Tragedies," four one-act plays in blank verse, are numbered among his most abiding works of psychological realism. These dramas turn upon such themes as envy (*Motsart i Sal'eri*, 1831; *Mozart and Salieri*), avarice (*Skupoi rytsar*, 1836; *The Covetous Knight*), or lust (*Kammeny gost*, 1839; *The Stone Guest*). *Povesti Belkina* (1831; *The Tales of Ivan Belkin*) represents Pushkin's major contribution to the short story form. The volume consists of five tales framed by the commentary of a fictitious editor, Ivan Petrovich Belkin. The austere prose of this work, bereft of poetic embellishment, moves rapidly and with little psychological commentary. Demonstrative of these tales, "The Shot" is a story of revenge occasioned by the conflict of youthful brazenness with a more mature reflection. The novella *Pikovaya dama* (1834; *The Queen of Spades*) blends the tightly-plotted narrative technique and spare style of the *Tales* with a Gothic sensibility. Three successive games of cards, the curse of a dead countess, and the hero's eventual descent into madness, all figure prominently in this supernatural tale. *Kapitanskaya dochka* (1836; *The Captain's Daughter*), a largely realistic novella drawn from the historical events of the Pugachev peasant uprising, remains an important example of Pushkin's late prose work.

Critical Reception

Pushkin is considered by most critics to be the greatest and most influential Russian writer of the early nineteenth century. Still, much of Pushkin's work, particularly his lyric poetry, is rarely read outside of Russia—a reality most critics have attributed to the fact that his superlative style virtually defies translation. Although foreign readers may not be directly acquainted with Pushkin's writings, his influence is evident in the more widely-known books of Dostoevsky, Tolstoy, Turgenev, and Nikolai Gogol. In Russia and internationally, *Eugene Onegin* is generally regarded as Pushkin's masterpiece, and many commentators have noted that its realistic presentation of scene and character provided the model for the modern Russian novel. In his prose, scholars have observed, Pushkin rejected a stagnant literary tradition that counted fiction as an inferior genre; his ventures away from the sentimental fiction of the late eighteenth century thus signaled a new direction for Russian literature. Early critics in the West who read Pushkin outside of the context of his predecessors, however, often simply noted—as Gustave Flaubert did—the flatness of his prose. Modern critics of Pushkin's dramatic works have called for a reevaluation of their formal qualities, with many scholars emphasizing flaws in *Boris Godunov*, while acknowledging Pushkin's successes in the "Little Tragedies." Despite some negative appraisals, interest in Pushkin's fiction, narrative poetry, and drama in the twentieth century has remained strong, with contemporary scholars tending to rely on psychological analysis to reexamine these works, often highlighting the elements of irony and parody that they contain and evaluating Pushkin's experiments in narrative structure and technique.

PRINCIPAL WORKS

Ruslan i Lyudmila [*Ruslan and Lyudmila*] (poetry) 1820
Gavriiliada [*Gavriliada*] (poetry) 1821
Kavkazski plennik [*The Captive of the Caucasus*] (poetry) 1822
Bakhchisaraiski fontan [*The Bak-chesarian Fountain: A Tale of the Tauride*] (poetry) 1824
Stansy (poetry) 1826
Bratya razboiniki [*The Robber Brothers*] (poetry) 1827
Graf Nulin [*Count Nulin*] (poetry) 1827
Tsygany [*The Gypsies*] (poetry) 1827
Poltava [*Poltava*] (poetry) 1829
Boris Godunov [*Boris Godunoff*] [first publication] (drama) 1831
†*Motsart i Sal'eri* [*Mozart and Salieri*] [first publication] (drama) 1831

Povesti Belkina [*The Tales of Ivan Belkin*] (short stories) 1831

†*Pir vo vremya chumy* [*A Feast during the Plague*] [first publication] (drama) 1832

Domik v Kolomne [*The Little House in Kolomna*] (poetry) 1833

Yevgeny Onegin [*Eugene Onegin*] (verse novel) 1833

Pikovaya dama [*The Queen of Spades*] (novella) 1834

Shazki (fairy tales) 1834

Istoriya Pugacheva [*History of Pugachev*] (history) 1835

Kapitanskaya dochka [*The Captain's Daughter*] (novella) 1836

Puteshestvie v Arzrum [*A Journey to Arzrum*] (travel essay) 1836

†*Skupoi rytsar* [*The Covetous Knight*] [first publication] (drama) 1836

Arap Petra Velikogo [*The Negro of Peter the Great*] (unfinished novel) 1837

Istoriya sela Goryukhina [*History of the Village of Goryukhina*] (unfinished novel) 1837

Medny vsadnik [*The Bronze Horseman*] (poetry) 1837

†*Kammeny gost* [*The Stone Guest*] [first publication] (drama) 1839

Dubrovski [*Dubrovsky*] (unfinished novel) 1841

Rusalka [*The Water Nymph*] [first publication] (unfinished drama) 1841

Table Talk (essays) 1857

Polnoe sobranie sochienii. 16 vols. [*The Poems, Prose and Plays of Alexander Pushkin*] (poetry, drama, short stories, novellas, novels, essays, criticism, and letters) 1937-49

Pushkin's Poems (poetry) 1945

The Letters of Alexander Pushkin. 2 vols. (letters) 1963

The Critical Prose of Alexander Pushkin (criticism) 1969

Pushkin on Literature (letters, journals, and essays) 1971

---

*This work was widely circulated in manuscript form but never published by Pushkin.

---

†These works are collectively referred to as "The Little Tragedies."

CRITICISM

Nikolai Gogol (essay date 1832)

SOURCE: "A Few Words About Pushkin," in *Russian Literature Triquarterly*, Vol. 10, 1974, pp. 180-83.

[*In the following essay, originally published in 1832, Gogol lauds Pushkin as Russia's national poet.*]

The name of Pushkin immediately evokes the thought—Russian national poet. Indeed, none of our poets is higher than he and none deserves more to be called

"national"; this right decisively belongs to him. All the richness, power, and versatility of our language is contained in him, as if in a lexicon. More than anyone else he has further extended the limits of the language and has demonstrated its breadth. Pushkin is an extraordinary phenomenon and, perhaps, a singular phenomenon of the Russian spirit: a Russian of a development such as his won't appear for perhaps another two hundred years. In him, Russian nature, the Russian soul, Russian language and Russian character have been reflected in such purity, in such clean beauty, as might a landscape be reflected in the convex surface of an optical glass.

His life itself is completely Russian. That same revelry and open space toward which a Russian who has momentarily forgotten himself will sometimes strive and which is always pleasing to budding Russian youth were reflected in his raw years of entry into the world. Fate, as luck would have it, brought him to that spot where Russia's borders are distinguished by widely-spaced majestic features, where Russia's smooth immeasurability is abruptly broken by cloud-touching mountains and refreshed by the South. The gigantic, eternally snow-covered Caucasus, lying amidst burning valleys, struck him; he, one may say, summoned the strength of his soul and broke the final chains which were still weighing down free thoughts. He was captivated by the free poetic life of the daring mountaineers, their fights, their quick, irrepressible raids; and from then on his brush required that wide sweep, that quickness and boldness which so surprised and amazed a Russia that was only just beginning to read. Should he paint a fierce skirmish of a Chechenets with a Cossack—a syllable of his is lightning; and it shines so, like flashing sabres, and flies quicker than the very battle. Only he alone is the singer of the Caucasus: he is in love with it with all his soul and being; it imbues and saturates him with wonderful surroundings, the southern sky, the plains of splendid Georgia and the magnificent Crimean nights and gardens. Perhaps because of this he is so passionate and fiery in his works there, where his soul was touched by the South. In them he involuntarily directed all his energies, and because of this, his works, brimming with the Caucasus and the freeness of Circassian life and the nights of the Crimea, have possessed a wonderful, majestic power: they amazed even those who lacked the taste and development of spiritual faculty needed to understand him. Most bold of all it is accessible, more powerfully and spaciously extending the soul, especially that of youth, which still thirsts for only the unusual. No single poet in Russia has ever had so envious a lot as Pushkin. No one's glory has spread so quickly. In season and out of season it's been considered a duty to pronounce, and sometimes to mangle, some or other brightly glittering excerpts from his poems. His name has already taken on something electric, and has so spread itself out everywhere, that only someone of the idle low-life could use it to advantage in his work.[1]

He has been national from the very beginning because true nationalness consists not in the description of a sarafan, but in the very spirit of a people. A poet may even be national when he describes a completely foreign world, but looks on it with the eyes of his own national verse, with the eyes of the whole people, when he feels and speaks so that it seems to his compatriots as if they themselves are feeling and speaking. If one must say those virtues that constitute the properties of Pushkin and separate him from other poets, then they would be encompassed in an exceptional quickness of description and in the rare art whereby a few traits express a whole subject. His epithet is so distinct and bold, that sometimes one replaces an entire description; his brush flies. A shortish play of his is always worth an entire poem. It is hardly possible to say of any other poet's shortish play that it contains as much grandeur, simplicity, and power as any shortish play of Pushkin's.

But his latest poems, written in precisely that time when the Caucasus with all its terrible grandeur had stately lifted its summits behind clouds and had hidden itself from him, and after he had become absorbed in the heart of Russia, and her ordinary plains and devoted himself more deeply to an investigation of the life and customs of his compatriots, and wanted to be a national poet in the fullest sense—his poems had already begun to strike not all with that clarity and dazzling boldness so much a part of all his work away from Elbrus, the mountains, the Crimea, and Georgia.

It seems that this phenomenon is not so difficult to allow for: future admirers of the boldness of his brush and his paintings' enchantment will see that all his readers, educated and uneducated, tried in eager rivalry to make patriotic and historical events the subject of his poetry, forgetting that you can't represent the more calm and much less passion-filled everyday Russian life with the same colors used to paint the mountains of the Caucasus and their free and easy inhabitants. Representing the nation as one individual, the mass of the public is very strange in her desires; she cries: represent us as we are, in complete truthfulness, representing the work of our ancestors just the way it actually was. But should the poet, having heard her command, try to represent everything in complete truthfulness and just the way it actually was, she'll immediately pronounce: this is lifeless, weak, not good, and not very similar to the way it actually was. Here the mass of people is not a little similar to a woman who has ordered an artist to paint her portrait as a true likeness, but woe to him if he wasn't able to cover up all her defects. Only since coming under the direction of the emperors has Russian history acquired a vivid liveliness; before that, the character of the people was for the most part colorless; the various passions were little known to it. The poet can't be blamed; but among the people there is also the highly excusable desire to

exaggerate the works of its ancestors. There remain two possibilities for the poet: either to stretch one's style as high as possible, to give power to the powerless, to speak with animation about that which in itself retains no strong liveliness—then the throng of admirers, the throng of people is on his side, and together with it money; or to remain faithful to one truth, to be lofty where the subject is lofty, to be rough and bold where all is rough and bold, to be calm and quiet where there's no event in full swing. But in this case goodbye to popularity! He will not have it, even when the very subject being represented is already so lofty and rough that it cannot help but produce universal enthusiasm. This poet didn't choose the first possibility, because he wanted to remain a poet and because everyone who has felt in himself the spark of the sacred calling has a strict scrupulousness that doesn't permit him to express his talent in such a way. No one will deny that a wild, martially-dressed mountaineer, who is as free as can be and his own judge and master, is much more interesting a figure than some country judge and, though he has killed his enemy or burnt down a whole village, he appeals to our imagination and arouses our sympathies more powerfully than our own judges in their worn-out frock coats covered with tobacco stains, who have ruined hundreds of people, freeborn as well as serfs. But the one and the other belong to our world: both have the right to our attention though the things we see less frequently strike our imagination more powerfully, and to prefer the unusual to the usual is nothing more than the improvidence of the poet—improvidence before his numerous public and not before himself. He doesn't lose his dignity the least bit, and perhaps even acquires more, but only in the eyes of those few true connoisseurs. An event from my childhood occurs to me. I have always felt a small passion for painting. I worked for a long time on a landscape I had painted—in the foreground stood a dried-up tree. At the time I lived in the country; the local neighbors were my experts and judges. One of them looking at the picture, shook his head and said: "A good artist chooses a full-grown tree, a good one on which the leaves are fresh and growing well—not a dried-up one." In childhood it seemed annoying to hear such opinions, and later I drew wisdom from this: to know what pleases and what does not please the crowd. Pushkin's works that breathe with Russian nature are just as quiet and subtle as Russian nature herself. Only he whose soul cleanly conveys the Russian elements, to whom Russia is the Motherland, and whose soul is so delicately developed and sensitive that he is able to understand the not brilliant in appearance Russian songs and spirit, can completely understand them. The more ordinary the subject, the more lofty a poet must be in order to extract from it the unusual and in order that this unusual aspect be yet completely true. In all fairness, would his latest poems be highly valued? How would one find Boris Godunov, this lofty, deep work, encompassing within itself difficult poetry, and that rejected every coarse and motley decoration over which the crowd habitually fawns?—at the very least, there has been nothing published that truly reviews it, and it remains hitherto untouched.

In the minor works of his delightful anthology, Pushkin is unusually versatile and appears still more spacious and clear than in his poems. Several of these minor works are so sharply dazzling that anyone can understand them, even though most of them—particularly the very best of them—seem ordinary fare to the diverse crowd. One needs too fine a sense of smell to understand them. A higher sense is needed to understand the too sharp and the prominent characteristics together. For this, one must be in a sense a Sybarite who has long been satisfied with coarse and heavy viands, and who eats fowl only a bit at a time and delights in such food as would seem of an indistinct, strange, and totally unpleasant taste even to those accustomed to devouring the work of a prison cook. This collection of his minor poetry is a series of the most dazzling pictures. This is that clear world that breathes antiquity's traits and characters, and in which nature is as lively as in the stream of some or other silvery-river, in which there quickly and clearly gleam dazzling shoulders, or white arms, or an alabaster neck sprinkled by the night of dark curls, or transparent clusters of grapes, or myrtles and an arboreous canopy created for life. Here is everything: both enjoyment and simplicity, momentary loftiness of thought and the sacred cold of the reader's sudden profound inspiration. Here there is none of that assorted eloquent speech that fascinates through verbosity and in which every phrase through brute power deafens the masses by degradation when taken with others, but which, if taken separately, becomes weak and powerless. Here there is no eloquent speech, here there is only poetry; there's no affected luster: all is simple, all is proper, everything evinces an inner luster which doesn't reveal itself at once; all is the laconicism so characteristic of pure poetry. There are few words, but they are so precise that they convey everything. In every word there's an infinite space; every word is as boundless as the poet. Thus it is that you reread these minor works several times whereas a work where the main idea is too apparent doesn't merit it.

I always find it odd to hear the reputed experts and literateurs' judgment concerning them—I had generally trusted them before hearing their doctrine on the subject. One may term these minor works a touchstone on which one may experience the taste and esthetic sense of their nit-picking criticism. An incomprehensible matter! It would appear they think them intelligible to no one! They are so simply elevating, so vivid, so fiery, so voluptuous while childlike pure. How could one not understand them! Alas, it is an undeniable fact that the more a poet becomes a poet, the more he expresses feelings that are known only to poets, the more does the crowd round him dwindle and at last becomes so small that he can count his true admirers on the fingers of his hand.

Notes

[1] A variety of the most absurd verses have been scattered under Pushkin's name. This is the usual lot of talent that enjoys great fame. In the beginning this amuses, but later when you leave youth and see these unabating stupidities it is annoying. Such is the way they've lately begun to attribute to Pushkin: The medicine for cholera, on the first night is very similar.

Paul Debreczeny (essay date 1969)

SOURCE: "The Reception of Pushkin's Poetic Works in the 1820s: A Study of the Critic's Role," in *Slavic Review,* Vol. 28, No. 3, September, 1969, pp. 394-415.

[*In the following essay, Debreczeny explores early commentary on Pushkin's works in relation to the evolution of Russian literary criticism.*]

The relationship between Pushkin and his critics has been a subject of considerable interest and discussion since the poet's own time. Belinsky made it the focus of the introduction to his series of essays on Pushkin. The early biographers provided some further information, and scholarly attention dates from the 1889 monograph by S. S. Trubachev, *Pushkin v russkoi kritike, 1820-1880,* which appeared shortly after V. A. Zelinsky had published, between 1887 and 1889, his extremely, useful anthology of Pushkin criticism. The monograph is little more than a pedestrian rehearsal of reviews, digressing only to promulgate such myths as Pushkin's "aristocratic" attitude toward critics, but it remains valuable as a catalogue of criticism. Thereafter, both before the Revolution and during the Soviet period, the relevant published material becomes too extensive to list here. Recent comprehensive treatments of the subject may be found in N. I. Mordovchenko's *Russkaia kritika pervoi chetverti XIX veka* (1959) and in the Academy publication *Pushkin: Itogi i problemy izucheniia* (1966).

The published material offers a wealth of factual information, but, by contrast, a striking paucity of interpretations of the data—a situation not uncommon in Soviet scholarship. General critical studies of Pushkin's art, such as those by Tomashevsky and Gukovsky,[1] offer incidentally more in the way of interpretive treatment of the poet-critic relationship than do the works addressed directly to the subject. This article attempts an interpretation, with particular emphasis on Pushkin and his critics of the 1820s.

Social historians place great value on literary criticism. H. D. Duncan writes: "The critic is the key element in any consideration of literature as a social institution, because he is related in so many ways to both the author and the public."[2] Author, critic, and public, forming a kind of triangle, can assume a variety of positions relative to one another. It is quite possible for author and critic to interact while ignoring the public at large; in other situations the critic can represent society vis-à-vis the author or the author vis-à-vis society; or he can use the author's work as merely an excuse for publicizing his own ideas. The author himself can publicly engage with his critic or ignore him and speak to the reader over the critic's head. The relative position of the three parties can reveal something not only about patterns of literary taste in a particular age but also about the structure of a given society.

Early nineteenth-century Russian criticism displays several conceptions of the author-critic-public relationship. One is that of A. S. Shishkov and his followers, who, because of their classical and French-Russian neoclassical orientation, were called either classicists or neoclassicists, or sometimes pseudoclassicists, by their contemporaries.

Since Shishkov believed (with La Harpe, whom he translated) that the content of a literary work was determined by choice of genre, he took the role of the critic to consist simply in discussing whether or not the author had successfully followed the rules applicable to the genre and had chosen his words felicitously. Like Malherbe two centuries before, Shishkov could have been called *le tyran des mots et des syllabes.* Just as Malherbe had been aroused by the abundant coinages of the Pléiade, so was Shishkov enraged by the stylistic exuberance of Karamzin and Russian sentimentalism. His *Rassuzhdenie o starom i novom sloge rossiiskogo iazyka* (1803) was the fruit of his aversion to the sentimentalists' florid language; his critical attention remained entirely focused on linguistic problems.

Such a limitation of interest on the part of the neoclassical critics necessarily limited the audience addressed. Literature was the pastime of the few, and the critic spoke only to these few learned literati. When Shishkov organized his Society of Lovers of the Russian Word in 1811, the three hundred or so people who gathered in Derzhavin's home for the first meeting were virtually the whole audience the classicists could hope for; the contributions to the society, published periodically under the name *Talks,* sold in a hundred copies. Under these circumstances the critic was hardly in a position to assume the role of a middleman who could speak to the author in the name of the public or to the public in the name of the author and thus represent some kind of consensus of opinion or make an attempt to set up a public code of taste. He was merely a member of a small ingrown community in which any amateur might assume the role of either author or critic. Criticism

amounted to no more than a reinforcement of the standards accepted by the group, like rites performed by a congregation. And when Shishkov chose a target outside the group, chastising the sentimentalists for their practices, his predicament was like that of a minister scolding his congregation for lack of attendance at service: he could scold only those who attended.

Karamzin and his followers were not the right people to engage in debate. The aesthetics of sentimentalism left room only for the kind of deliberately uncritical criticism Madame de Staël practiced in her *De l'Allemagne,* that is, retelling the contents of works of art with feeling, interpreting them for the reader, popularizing them. Ever since Leibnitz remarked that he was more inclined to enjoy literature than to criticize it, representatives of the new sensibility had underplayed the function of the critic as a dissector and emphasized his usefulness as a gardener nurturing tender new shoots of poetry. Indeed the ideology of sentimentalism called for greater trust in sentiment than in reason. Many a thinker in the eighteenth century, from the Third Earl of Shaftesbury to Rousseau, advocated an education of the heart by indulging in noble sentiments. Man's heart was the natural depository of all the virtues—Rousseau found himself intoxicated by his innate virtue—and the poet's job was to open spontaneously the natural well of his feelings. Faced with a poetry that was the spontaneous revelation of man's inner worth, the critic found himself at a loss. How could he criticize when the ultimate measure of value—sentiment—was untouchable by external standards? Each work of art was a law unto itself; the supreme judge of values was the creative genius. The critic must humble himself before the poet's genius and try to convey to the reading public as much of the beauty of the poetry as he could, without dissecting it or presuming to judge it. Karamzin wrote in *Vestnik Evropy,* which he edited in 1802-3, that there was no need for a critical section in it, since Russian literature was not yet strong enough to be criticized; rather it needed encouragement and support.[3]

Although the sentimentalists were not sufficiently endowed with critical belligerence to meet the classicists in an out-and-out battle, they had a great advantage in commanding the attentions of a larger reading public. The rise of sentimentalism coincided with a tremendous growth in periodical literature: some eighty-four different journals, newspapers, and magazines sprang up in the two Russian capitals between 1801 and 1811. Most of them had a small circulation and soon disappeared, but others mushroomed in their place. Tales of sweet sensibility provided more enticing reading than the heavy-going *Rossiades* and solemn odes of the classical school. For the first time in history the Russian middle gentry and upper merchant class were attracted to reading. Literary criticism of the sentimental variety helped the situation by propagandizing rather than criticizing. As a result of the growth of literary journalism in the early 1800s, some fairly respectable periodicals were well established, with circulations up to a thousand, by the middle of the second decade. The best known among them were *Vestnik Evropy* (*Messenger of Europe*) and *Syn otechestva* (*Son of the Fatherland*).

Vestnik Evropy, although it had been edited for short periods by Karamzin and Zhukovsky, became, from a literary point of view, a conservative journal. *Syn otechestva,* on the other hand, assumed a more progressive role toward the end of the second decade of the century and eventually gave space to Pushkin and his associates. But the differences between these two periodicals no longer reflected the earlier division between classicism and sentimentalism. Sentimentalism had undergone several changes—a process ably described in Gukovsky's *Pushkin i russkie romantiki*—changes out of which two new trends emerged. On the one hand, Zhukovsky carried on the Karamzinite tradition of subjectivity, transforming it under fresh Western influences. Critics characterized Zhukovsky and his younger followers, such as P. A. Pletnev, as "mystics" until Pushkin emerged as the major representative of the group, from which time the term "romantic" came into use. On the other hand, patriotism and political liberalism combined to bring forth a "civic" (*grazhdanskii*) trend, represented by P. A. Katenin, A. S. Griboedov, V. K. Kiukhelbeker, K. F. Ryleev, and once more, Pushkin (whose dual role is one of Gukovsky's main points). The term "romantic" was applied to the civic trend, too. Indeed, romanticism became the fashionable catchword of the day, and Pushkin was right in complaining, as he did in several letters, that critics used the word without conceptual clarity. By and large, the term came to denote all literary effort that challenged the rules of classicism, aiming at freedom of expression rather than reasoned discipline.

The writers grouped around *Vestnik Evropy* were not classicists of the old stamp either. Russian periodical literature had gained the attention of the public during the sentimental period, and the classicists who subsequently moved in to take over some of the popular periodicals had to make adjustments. The result, in the twenties, was a peculiar blend of the two earlier tendencies. A new breed of critics emerged who held classical views but addressed a fairly wide middle-class audience; to distinguish them from the earlier classicists, I will call them conservatives. Critics of this generation were no longer writing for the privileged elite but rather for the village squire and his daughters, who were pictured as whiling away long winter evenings reading the latest volume of poetry or *Vestnik Evropy.* The favorite image of the critic was that of an old man who smilingly handed out words of wisdom to the young reader. Often he was not just an old man but, for greater effect, a wounded veteran of the Napoleonic War. Pushkin's comment on this stereotype was

that the loss of an eye and a hand is no excuse for blindness to beauty and inability to write.[4]

It was these *literaturnye starikashki* who continually assailed Pushkin's poetic works during the twenties. Their point of view manifested itself in their objections to the alleged disorderliness of the poet's works. The critic of *Vestnik Evropy* (no. 11, 1820), A. Glagolev, objected to **Ruslan and Liudmila** on the grounds that it was a romantic rehash of popular tales—tales that had no place in literature. He compared it to *Bova Korolevich, Eruslan Lazarevich,* and the tales of Kirsha Danilov, indicating that it belonged to a lowly genre outside the sphere of poetry as Boileau had understood it. What most disturbed critics like Glagolev was the impossibility of placing Pushkin's works in any of the accepted poetic categories. **The Prisoner of the Caucasus,** for instance, could not be classified as epic or lyric or satire; it was therefore incomprehensible. One of the most volatile representatives of the conservative movement, M. A. Dmitriev, summed up the objections against the poem (*Vestnik Evropy,* no. 3, 1825):

> A genuine author will never decide to publish a work from which you learn nothing except that *some*one was taken a prisoner and *some* young girl fell in love with him; that he could not return her affections because he had *lost his voluptuous love of life;* and finally that the girl helped him escape and threw herself in the river. Such poems, which are being called *music* with such fervor, will mean nothing to posterity; they mean nothing even to us contemporaries. Only truth, presented by a learned author in resplendent clarity, has been and will ever be beneficial to mankind.

Dmitriev and his associates frequently echoed Boileau in saying that the greatest literary virtues were Clarity, Good Sense, and Reason. The romantics most dismally failed in just these qualities. They mixed genres, did not care for a smooth development of plot, swiftly switched tone, and disregarded the gaps between the stylistic layers of language. The epitome of romanticism in the eyes of the conservatives was Pushkin. Dmitriev's indictment of the romantics' lack of clarity names no one poet, but the list of specific characteristics he deplores clearly indicates that he had Pushkin's works in mind (*Vestnik Evropy,* no. 5, 1824):

> The distinguishing traits of this school are not just a peculiar use of words and expressions and an imitation of the Germans, but also some kind of mixture of gloom with voluptuousness, of swift narration with immobility of plot, and of flaming passions with coldness of character. Bad imitators of the new school have still another trait, peculiar only to them; the fragments of their depictions are scattered, do not correspond to each other, and are incomplete; while the sentiments are undetermined and the language obscure.

The changes in Pushkin's style as the years went by escaped the eyes of the conservatives. *The Gypsies, Eugene Onegin,* and *Poltava* they regarded as no different from the earlier *Prisoner of the Caucasus* and *Fountain of Bakhchisarai;* all were simply "romantic." N. I. Nadezhdin's review of *Poltava* began with reflections on the lack of rules in romantic poetry and on the consequent lack of agreement about what is beautiful (*Vestnik Evropy,* no. 9, 1829). In *Poltava,* one did not know what to make of the character of Mazepa. Byron's Mazeppa at least was a powerful villain, a brave man who, calm and bold, made his pillow in an old oak's shade, disregarding dangers after a lost battle. Pushkin's Mazepa, on the other hand, fretted sleeplessly; his actions were motivated by petty hatred rather than the grand designs of a statesman—for instance he hated Peter I only because Peter had once pulled his beard—and he stupidly allied himself with Charles XII, whom he himself was soon to deride. If this characterization of Mazepa corresponded with historical truth, Nadezhdin said, then Mazepa was not worthy to be the hero of a narrative poem; but if the historical Mazepa was unlike the character, the mistake lay with Pushkin's inept characterization rather than his selection of a hero from history.

Nadezhdin pursued the comparison with Byron beyond the issue of appropriately great—even if villainously great—heroes. Byron himself was a Satanic genius, occupying a "bad eminence" to which Pushkin could make no claim:

> *Byron* really had genius, and what genius! . . . He is always true to himself, whether blasphemously trying to reveal the unsullied sacraments of *heaven and earth* or stooping to the scandalous barking of a vulgar pamphleteer. A gloomy universal hatred is seen everywhere; cheerless images of an orphan's existence which is shaken from its lethargic slumber only by wild outbursts of riotous life. *Byron's* poems are like deserted cemeteries in which carnivorous vultures furiously wrestle half-decayed skulls from hissing snakes. His world is hell; but how gigantic the greatness of Polyphemus must be if he has chosen the bottomless pit for his dwelling! . . . It is to our Poet's [Pushkin's] credit that such greatness is alien to him. He has not yet grown out of mankind's meager proportions, and his soul is on good terms—perhaps too good terms—with earthly life. Not one of his poems exudes that dampness of the grave which makes one's blood curdle reading *Byron.* His heroes—even in the somberest products of his imagination such as *The Robber Brothers* and *The Gypsies*—are imps rather than devils. And if he sometimes happens to protest against the world, he does it out of bad temper rather than hatred. How is it possible to compare him with *Byron?*

In his review of the seventh chapter of *Eugene Onegin* Nadezhdin claimed that Pushkin was not a genius but simply a poet of some talent who could write amusing and lively passages (*Vestnik Evropy,* no. 7, 1830). *Eugene Onegin* was not a novel in verse because there was nothing to hold it together, but here and there one could find some felicitous passages in it. The critic repeated what he had already said in his review of *Poltava:* Pushkin's talent lay in light humor and caricature and his works were acceptable as long as he maintained a Hogarthian style, but he inevitably slipped up when he tried his hand at anything serious. Thus Pushkin's poetry was relegated to some low genre that did not quite make literature as Nadezhdin understood it.

The argument against the romantics' incomprehensibility, disorderliness, and loose literary form was made in the name of reason and clarity, the crowning principles of classicism. But the critics of conservative leaning were now writing in what were for the standards of those years mass periodicals—*Vestnik Evropy* had a circulation of about twelve hundred copies. Their opinions were no longer the literary musings of connoisseurs but the voice of public opinion. The rationalism that for classicists of old had been an achievement attained by the select was now becoming middle-class common sense. What was present in the conservative school of the twenties was not the rarefied air and brilliant sparkle of the Enlightenment but the commonplace truisms of the country gentry. The literary critic was a middleman, but he spoke for the public to the author rather than to the public for the author. He was, in a sense, society's protest against changing taste and values.

Through the words of the critic a particular social group was asserting its opinions. The loose morality of *Ruslan* came under heavy fire; Dmitriev could not understand how a young man—the Prisoner of the Caucasus—could feel disillusioned and blase when a beautiful young woman was lavishing love on him; Nadezhdin exclaimed that it was a farce to make an old man like Mazepa fall passionately in love. A semi-educated public that thought it knew all the answers was asserting its commonplace morality. Its complacently self-satisfied and simple view of the world was being disturbed by complexities whose existence it was not willing to admit. It was thinking in prefabricated clichés and would not allow for anything else. For instance, it was agreed that spring is joyous; Nadezhdin was therefore unable to understand how Pushkin could write (*EO,* 7.3.1-4) . . . [otherwise]. And if spring required joy, the grave required solemnity; yet, as Nadezhdin indignantly pointed out, a shepherd sat on Lensky's tomb weaving a bast shoe.

It is, of course, hard to document just how far the critics represented the public. But the persistence of the periodicals and their relatively large circulation, together with the middle-class poses the critics assumed, all point to the existence of a literary public opinion in the middle strata of society. The conservatives by no means spoke for the whole reading public—we shall see other groups in connection with other literary trends—but they did succeed in creating, at least temporarily, a far larger following than the earlier classicists had attracted. An uneducated reading public and bad criticism were better than none at all, because both could be improved upon. When Pushkin wrote to Bestuzhev that there was no literary criticism in Russia (Pushkin, 9:158), he meant there was no criticism that could appreciate and explain good works of art. He was right, but even an exceptional poet like Pushkin could not have become popular if there had been no body of public opinion capable of gradual change toward higher levels of taste. The first appreciable body of Russian literary public opinion, created by a fusion of sentimentalism and classicism, showed a definite taste for the banal and mediocre. However distasteful to the poet such public sentiment might have been, its existence was important both as a foundation for the education of taste and as a force for modification of narrow, elitist criticism. In the first three decades of the century the exclusively linguistic interests of the early classicists were superseded by broader interests, still classically oriented, in subjects ranging from imagery to social standards.

Pushkin's conservative assailants were met head on by the romantic critics—a group whose militancy and self-assertiveness lasted only as long as the poet himself was willing to carry its banner. The romantic theory expounded in the course of polemics with the conservatives was largely negative—a denial of the assumptions and tenets of classicism. M. P. Pogodin's review of *The Prisoner of the Caucasus,* for instance, began with the assertion that long descriptions of nature and of native Caucasian mores, although they held up the movement of the plot, were in order in the poem simply because they were so beautiful (*Vestnik Evropy,* no. 1, 1823). This implied that the strict requirements of classical poetics could be violated if the poet were able spontaneously to provide disorderly yet irresistible beauty; that is, the creation of standards of beauty was really up to the poet. Similarly, Pletnev argued in his review of the poem that *The Prisoner of the Caucasus* belonged to the Byronic strain in poetry, which meant a stress on descriptive detail rather than action.[5] Pushkin's descriptive powers, the reviewer asserted, surpassed even Byron's. The most significant comments from this point of view were made by the leading critic of the romantic movement, Prince P. A. Viazemsky. His review of *The Prisoner of the Caucasus* is a veritable code of romanticism as it was understood in his day (*Syn otechestva,* no. 49, 1822). Neoclassicists, he argued, would not accept any kind of poetry that was not described in Aristotle, in the same way that some naturalists denied the existence of flowers not classified by Linnaeus. But the flowers grew and great poets went their own way regardless of

classification. It was particularly senseless for Russians to set up strict categories, Viazemsky said, since they had never had a respectable neoclassical literature from which to generalize. The French might be reluctant to part with their rich neoclassical tradition, but what had the Russians to lose? Their young literature could still follow any path it chose. The hero of Pushkin's poem, Viazemsky continued, was somewhat like Childe Harold, with this difference, that while Byron created autobiographical characters Pushkin drew on surrounding reality. His Prisoner is characteristic of a certain social sphere in which gifted people find no application for their talents. It is very much to Viazemsky's credit that he delineated at this early time what became later the well-known type of the "superfluous man" in Russian literature:

> A superabundance of power and of inner life whose ambitious demands cannot be satisfied by concessions to external life because the latter is bountiful enough only for the temperate desires of so-called good sense; the inevitable consequences of such dichotomy, that is, excitement without aim and consuming activity with no application to reality; hopes never fulfilled yet perpetually rising with renewed ardor—all this inevitably plants in the soul an ineradicable germ of boredom, mawkishness, and supersaturation, features characteristic of Childe Harold, the Prisoner of the Caucasus, and others of their kind.

Freedom to mirror reality as the poet saw fit rather than having to follow prescribed formulas lay at the very core of the romantic argument. Pushkin hailed the review in a letter to the critic: "All that you say about romantic poetry is charming; you did well in being the first to raise your voice for it."[6]

Viazemsky continued his defense of romanticism in his preface to *The Fountain of Bakhchisarai* (1824). He reasserted that romanticism meant freedom; it needed no rules because it was alive, and pedantry would only smother it. Maybe in a hundred years, he remarked, romanticism would also find its pedants who would set forth its rules; but for the time being it throve on spontaneous creation. If romantic works were not clear enough for the neoclassical mind it was just too bad; they were written for sharp-witted people and not for those who could not even be sure whether the Circassian girl had actually drowned in *The Prisoner of the Caucasus.*

Syn otechestva—the main haven of romantics—published an equally significant review of *The Fountain of Bakhchisarai,* written by M. N. Korniolin-Pinsky (no. 13, 1824). His most interesting statement concerned Pushkin's balladic, somewhat mysterious description of Maria's death: "If he had shown us the timid beauty under the dagger of the frenzied Georgian girl, he would have destroyed our enchantment and consequently his poem. Indignation would have exiled from our souls all other sensations called forth by the poem." This observation, showing great perceptiveness on the part of the critic, was related to Pogodin's idea that beauty excuses irregularity and to Pletnev's assertion of the importance of the descriptive detail rather than of action; all three critics insisted that the poet should be allowed to achieve a spontaneous effect, evoke a mood, create an atmosphere, even at the price of lesser clarity or lesser structural coherence of the component parts.

The growth of the romantic movement was reflected in the creation of a new periodical—*Moskovskii telegraf* (*Moscow Telegraph*), edited by N. A. Polevoi in collaboration with Viazemsky—which was to be completely devoted to the promotion of the new school. One of the first manifestations of its romantic policy was Polevoi's review of the first chapter of **Eugene Onegin** (no. 5, 1825), in which Pushkin was called, for the first time, "more than a talent," something like a genius, and the main principles of romanticism were reiterated: "The rules guiding the poet are innate in his creative imagination"; "the secret and the cause of so-called romantic poetry are to be found in an undetermined, inexplicable state of the human heart"; and "the poet is not free to choose the direction of his inspiration; what comes to him for a song, he sings."

Viazemsky's most important critical contribution to *Moskovskii telegraf* was his review of **The Gypsies** (no. 10, 1827). Here he described romanticism as a selective process. Details that had been indispensable in classical poetry, he argued, were passed over in an eagerness to reach the end, to draw conclusions, to show the essence. Romantic poetry was like a view from the top of a mountain: in its vision the unessential was blurred and only the most remarkable objects stood out.

Finally, an anonymous review of the first six chapters of **Onegin** in *Syn otechestva* (no. 7, 1828) should be mentioned as one of the last contributions to avowedly romantic criticism. The reviewer took up the novel's defense against those who had complained of its lack of plot. Maybe, he argued, a fast-moving plot was necessary for a short story, since it had room only for external details of life concentrating on a mere episode. The novel, however, depicted whole years in the lives of the characters and could afford to penetrate their inner world. Therefore, inner action and an undercurrent of spiritual events were more important for it than external plot. This opinion—so remarkably anticipating some of Chekhov's pronouncements on literature—once more conferred freedom on the poet in his choice of method, discarding the requirements of classical poetics.

Although the romantics' basic intent, that of discarding rules, was a negative one, there was a positive side to their mission. They took up the defense of the most important poet of the period and drove home to the public that judgment on the basis of rigid formalism was wrong. Their criticism moved in a direction exactly opposite to that of the conservatives. While the conservatives felt themselves delegated to voice the dissatisfaction of society with new trends in poetry and thought, the romantics did their best to justify and popularize these new trends. The conservatives spoke for the public to the author, the romantics for the author to the public. The romantics tried to wrest the public from the clutches of their literary opponents, and the success of such journals as *Moskovskii telegraf* (circulation 1,500 in 1825) testified to the success of their endeavors. What had seemed a fairly homogeneous reading public at the end of the second decade of the century became divided into two sections with differing opinions. The struggle had a beneficial effect on the conservative side too. Without the stimulus of opposition the conservative critics would never have grappled, as they were beginning to, with such complex subjects as imagery and thematic significance. But the real gain was what the romantics succeeded in conveying to the public. Such ideas as using a mystifying style to maintain a delicate atmosphere, indulging in beautiful but apparently gratuitous description, substituting inner action for external plot, letting reality pervade a poem without respect to preconceived forms, and so forth, represented entirely new departures not only in critical thinking but in the general view of life. These concepts had never been used before in Russian literature, and their inevitable effect was a broadening of the public mind. Thus, Russia of the 1820s provides an interesting example of a gradual but perceptible change in the pattern of public taste.

Despite their great services to Pushkin, however, the romantics did not fully understand him either. A. F. Voeikov, for instance, a poet and critic on the peripheries of the romantic movement, objected to Pushkin's humorous treatment of his heroine in **Ruslan and Liudmila:** "It is a pity that the author inopportunely ridicules her sensibility. His duty should be to instill in the reader a respect toward his heroine: she is not Farlaf, the clown of the poem. It is utterly indelicate to flaunt one's wit at the expense of a person felled by misfortune; and Liudmila is indeed unfortunate" (*Syn otechestva*, nos. 34-37, 1820). The playful ambivalence in the poet's attitude to his characters was too complex for Voeikov to comprehend, and the downright cynical passages in the poem evoked his indignation: "The educated public will be offended by these vulgar jokes." In the course of the discussion that followed his review in the pages of *Syn otechestva*, he was angered into an even sharper statement: "Would you really take it upon yourselves to read this poem to your virtuous mothers, sisters, or daughters, if you have such?" (no. 43, 1820). Similarly, N. I. Kutuzov, a member of the Union of Welfare, wrote in the same journal that Pushkin's pen was inspired "not by sensibility, but by sensuality" (no. 5, 1821).

The critics were puzzled by the nature of the central character of *The Prisoner of the Caucasus.* Both Pletnev and Pogodin, in the reviews I have quoted, insisted on logical questions about the causes of the young man's disillusionment. Did he reject the native girl's love because of the memory of a former unhappy love affair? If so, what is this talk about his not being worthy of her? Which was the main reason for his leaving: his love of freedom or his past affair that rendered him incapable of love? If he loved freedom, why did he not find his place among the freedom-loving Circassians? Pogodin even had a bright idea about improving the poem: the Prisoner's main motive should be homesickness. He wrote: "Pushkin could have indicated that the reason the Prisoner wished to escape was his love for his fatherland. Why did he not endow his hero with this wonderful Russian feeling: if to suffer, at least to suffer at home? Let sorrow, like lead, lay on his heart; but he wants to be on Russian soil, under a Russian sky, among Russian people, and he will feel better." Further, with reference to the Prisoner's words that love will pass, boredom will set in, and the maiden will fall in love anew, Pogodin commented: "To speak thus to a woman of fashion would be cruel; to do it to the innocent Circassian maiden is unpardonable." Even Viazemsky, the most ardent admirer of Pushkin's southern tales, charged that the Prisoner displayed inhuman cruelty in failing to attempt a rescue of the maiden from the waves. Thus he too seemed to think that Pushkin's poetry should conform to a generally accepted code of gallantry.

Although the romantic critics' main function was to disseminate a new taste and interpret its most prominent representative to the public, they became, like the conservative critics, the readers' spokesmen when they found fault. What they propagated was not so much Pushkin's poetry as a set of values partly distilled from it. Their theory, in short, failed to comprehend all the facets of Pushkin's poetic practice. If romantic criticism could not fully comprehend Pushkin during his most popular period, between 1820 and 1827, when his southern tales were published in succession, all hope of understanding was lost when he moved into the more rarefied region of his mature work, beginning with *Poltava* and *Boris Godunov.*

Although some purely personal hostilities had developed between Pushkin and some of his critics by the end of the twenties, that is insufficient explanation for the critics' failure to appreciate his new works. Clearly, Pushkin had soared to new heights of poetic achievement where his contemporaries could not follow. Furthermore, the likelihood of critical acceptance was diminished by two phenomena taking place at

that time—a new fusion of critical tastes and a further widening of the reading public, whose tastes tend inevitably to become more shallow as they widen. The leading periodicals of 1820 had emerged as a result of a fusion between classicism and sentimentalism; a similar process was now uniting the conservative and romantic trends of the late twenties. Romanticism had been an enormous success, and the periodicals that espoused it—*Severnaia pchela* (*The Northern Bee*) and *Moskovskii telegraf*—had become immensely popular. In 1830, the circulation of *Severnaia pchela* was four thousand, of *Moskovskii telegraf,* almost three thousand. (Of course, *Severnaia pchela*'s monopoly to print political news enhanced its popularity.) New strata of society were brought into the cultural life of the country. Whereas two decades before, the literary public had consisted of an elitist circle of literati, now a wide, far less well educated public had to be reckoned with. The taste of the avant-garde—the romantics of the early twenties—had filtered down to wide masses of readers. A taste that had become public property had lost all its revolutionary flavor and was easy to reconcile with conservative attitudes.

Despite the personal animosity of their respective editors, *Severnaia pchela, Moskovskii telegraf,* and *Vestnik Evropy* hardly differed in either their literary judgments or their growing vulgarity of tone. The crude jokes and clumsy "polemics" of Nadezhdin's reviews were more than matched by Bulgarin's lampoons and Polevoi's "New Painter" series. We have already seen Nadezhdin's views on *Poltava* and the seventh chapter of *Eugene Onegin;* Bulgarin's pronouncements on these works were in the same vein. Classicists, he argued in *Syn otechestva* (nos. 15-16, 1829), had bored the reader with their pedantry, and for this reason Byron's irregular balladic style had been welcome; but now this new mode of writing had become so widespread that it was just as monotonous as the work of the classicists. Pushkin—who had followed Byron but had not attained his master's excellence—resorted once more to fragmentary Byronic construction in his *Poltava* but could not bind his episodes and characters into a meaningful whole. His characters were not true to history: Kochubei appeared to be a revengeful blackguard, his wife, a fury; Mazepa turned against Peter just because Peter had once pulled his beard; all of which was a figment of Pushkin's imagination. Bulgarin's judgment of Maria, in particular, coincided with Nadezhdin's: "Maria, Kochubei's daughter, is an enigmatic creature. Why did she fall in love, head over heels, with a gray old man, why did she despise all youths and elope from her father's home in order to indulge in the decrepit, sick Hetman's caresses, as if he were Adonis?"

Bulgarin's notorious review of the seventh chapter of *Onegin* in *Severnaia pchela* (nos. 35, 39, 1830) claimed that the poet's talents had declined since he had begun the novel. The critic saw no action in this chapter, only the usual lyrical digressions which had by now become tiresome; he thought the stanzas describing the Larins' household effects prosaic; and he summed up the contents of the chapter in a banal little sestet about a marriageable maiden going to Moscow. Polevoi's review of the same chapter of the novel in *Moskovskii telegraf* (no. 6, 1830) claimed that the poet had grown tired, was repeating himself, and was clearly unable to create a comprehensive whole out of the scattered parts which made up **Onegin.** The critic of a less important periodical, *Galateia* (no. 14, 1830), also added his voice to the general condemnation of Pushkin, mentioning, among other objections, that it was improper for Tatiana to visit Onegin's house even though the young man was not there.

With the formerly romantic periodicals catering to a wider circle of middle-class readers, a need arose to satisfy more intellectual tastes, and new periodicals came into being, such as *Teleskop* and later Pushkin's *Sovremennik* (*The Contemporary*), but a discussion of these would lead us deep into the thirties. At the end of the twenties, deprived of the journals' support, Pushkin had to reach a cultivated audience without the critics.

One of the most promising subjects for a study of the "filtering" of taste down to wider masses is literary imitation. A consideration of Pushkin's epigones is beyond the scope of this essay, but this much should be mentioned: **Ruslan and Liudmila** was followed by a *Ratmir and Svetlana;* **The Prisoner of the Caucasus** was copied in *Cheka, a Tale of the Urals;* after **The Robber Brothers** came an imitative *Robber;* and soon after the publication of the first chapter of **Onegin,** novels in verse began appearing in print under such titles as *Eugene Velsky;* and so forth. It seems to me—and a detailed analysis might show—that these and other imitations lacked precisely those Pushkinian qualities that came under the critics' fire; in other words the imitators selected those elements of Pushkin's poetry that lent themselves most readily to stereotyping. Another example of such a selective—and simplifying—reproduction of his work is the fact that the description of Caucasian mores and the Circassian song from **The Prisoner of the Caucasus** (without the rest of the poem, i.e., without the controversial, difficult passages) were reprinted in six popular anthologies during the poet's lifetime alone. His fame with a wider public, outside the narrow circle of men of letters, rested on such fragments; and on such popularizations as the musical rendering of **The Black Shawl.** His wide fame did not necessarily mean that his poetic standards had become widespread, but rather that certain of their elements had penetrated the public mind and lost their pungency in the process. We have it on Apollon Grigoriev's testimony that some "provincial misses, or those of the Zamoskvarechye . . . continued

to expect that Lensky would reappear in the last chapter of **Onegin,** that he was not killed by Onegin but was only thought to be killed, and that he would be united with the widowed Ol'ga just as Onegin would be with Tat'yana."[7] Another indirect proof of the vulgarization of Pushkinian models is Grushnitsky in *A Hero of Our Time.* Pechorin, himself a Byronic hero on a higher level, was irritated by Grushnitsky precisely because the latter embodied a popular version of his own self-image. The type of the Prisoner of the Caucasus—Lermontov witnesses in his novel—had become commonplace among the golden youth by the thirties, although originally it had been one of the most difficult for the critics to comprehend. Literary criticism was both cause and victim of this process of popularization.

What was Pushkin's own reaction to the public opinion and literary criticism of his time? Dozens of epigrams, letters, lampoons, and articles testify that he could strike back—and strike back hard—when he wished to; and by the time he came to edit *Literaturnaia gazeta* with Delvig in 1830, he firmly believed that an author should not feel it below his dignity to engage in a "fist fight" with critics and journalists. As for learning from his critics, there is little evidence that he ever did that. When he asked his brother to send him reviews of the **Prisoner,** he said: "I hope that critics will not leave in peace the character of the Prisoner; he was created for them, my dear. I do not receive journals, so take the trouble to write me what they say—not for the sake of my correcting it, but for the sake of humbling my conceit" (**Letters,** 1:104). It might be argued that he did correct the mistakes critics found in the **Prisoner.** Vagueness in representation gave way to concreteness by the time he wrote, for instance, **The Gypsies.** But the change need not be interpreted as a response to the critics, since, after all, Pushkin himself, in the draft of a letter to Delvig, analyzed the flaws of the **Prisoner** better than anyone else (Pushkin, 9:383). More important, however, than his responses to individual instances of criticism are the larger questions of Pushkin's general attitude about public opinion and the kind of criticism that expressed it, and his conception of the poet's—his own—place in society.

To put the problem in perspective, it must be stated first of all that poets are quite capable of working in a hostile environment. Shelley wrote: "Even in modern times, no living poet ever arrived at the fulness of his fame; the jury which sits in judgment upon a poet, belonging as he does to all time, must be composed of his peers: it must be impanelled by Time from the selectest of the wise of many generations. A poet is a nightingale, who sits in darkness and sings to cheer its own solitude with sweet sounds. . . . "[8] The poet's primary concern is to define himself through the sound, image, and idea of his poetry, and while this obviously cannot be done in a social vacuum, it is quite possible that the poet's points of reference lie in ages or societies other than his own. Pushkin, it is certain, had Voltaire or André Chénier or any number of other poets of the past in his mind as an imaginary audience when he was writing poetry; he wrote more for them than for the critic of *Syn otechestva.* The shadow of Ovid provided for him the best poetic company in Bessarabia.

Yet contact with the living could not be dispensed with. Pushkin wrote to N. I. Gnedich from Kishinev: "Feel a little sorry for me: I live among Getae and Sarmatae; nobody understands me; I write as best I can, without hearing vivifying advice, praise, or blame" (**Letters,** 1:93). This "nobody understands me"—echoed later in Tatiana's letter to Onegin—was the greatest burden of the poet's southern exile. How highly he prized the approbation of his works by a few select friends is evident from a remark he made some years later about **Boris Godunov:** "Written in austere solitude, far from the chilling crowd, this tragedy has given me all the gratification a writer is allowed: brisk, inspired work, an inner conviction that I was sparing no effort, and finally endorsement by a small number of the select" (Pushkin, 6:300). A small number of the select could be more important than a whole chorus of critical voices in periodicals, for a privately gained security fortifies the writer to face a public storm. A case in point is the young Gogol, whose self-confidence as a writer was nurtured by Pushkin's circle in the early thirties. For Pushkin himself, the societies of Arzamas and the Green Lamp provided a good start in the second decade of the century, but exile tore him away from his friends and he suffered much as both man and artist. Despite his isolation, however, he corresponded with a few people who could be regarded as his "reference group." Letters concerning **The Prisoner of the Caucasus** illustrate the point.

The critics objected mainly to the character of the Prisoner: he was too blasé, incomprehensible in his *Weltschmerz,* and cruel in his relation to the Circassian maiden. Even Viazemsky, who belonged to Pushkin's inner circle, had some objections. However, other friends, P. Ia. Chaadaev and the Raevsky brothers foremost among them, approved of the Prisoner's type. As early as 1818, before he had ever read any of Byron's poetry, Pushkin wrote . . . a poem addressed to Chaadaev. . . .

A poetic attitude of disillusionment was connected in Pushkin's mind with Chaadaev, and if the poem he dedicated to this friend in 1821 is sufficient evidence, then it was Chaadaev whom he missed most during his exile. Chaadaev responded to the **Prisoner** just as the poet had desired. Pushkin reports his response in a letter to Viazemsky: "Do you see Chaadaev occasionally? He gave me a dressing down because of the **Prisoner;** he finds him insufficiently blasé. Chaadaev unfortunately is a connoisseur in that line; enliven his

beautiful soul, Poet!" (**Letters,** 1:109). This was not exactly praise for the poem, but it told Pushkin what he most wanted to hear: that the Prisoner's cynicism was legitimate; it could even have been sharper.

Contemporaries suspected that the person who inspired Pushkin's poem **"The Demon"** was Alexander Raevsky. Although Pushkin denied it (Pushkin, 4:262), there is no doubt that the Raevskys—who had introduced him to Byron—exercised an influence in a "demonic" direction. Nikolai Raevsky's reaction to the **Prisoner** was hardly unqualified praise: "One could not call your **Prisoner of the Caucasus** a good poem, but it has certainly opened up a path which mediocrity will. tumble over."[9] Nevertheless, Pushkin could find in the observation about mediocrity reassurance that he was moving in the right direction. If complacent mediocrity was to balk at his poem, it must be novel, shocking, fascinating—qualities he thought desirable in his romantic period. When he later recalls how he shared the Raevsky brothers' merriment over his lapses in the early works—Alexander roaring with laughter when he read in **The Fountain of Bakhchisarai** that in the midst of a heated battle sorrow petrified Girei—Pushkin's tone carries a ring of nostalgia for the security that an intimate and intelligently critical circle of friends can provide (Pushkin, 6:343-44). Such a circle, especially when it includes critics, as Pushkin's did—Viazemsky, Delvig, Katenin, N. Raevsky—is itself a social force insofar as their approval or disapproval determines the direction of the poet's work, which in turn may alter the patterns of public taste.

The social role of literature and the part criticism played were by no means lost on Pushkin. As early as 1820 he wrote concerning a conspicuous segment of the theater-going public in St. Petersburg: "These great people of our time carry on their faces the weary imprint of boredom, arrogance, worry, and stupidity, all of which are inseparable from their occupations. These perpetual spectators of the front rows frown over comedies, yawn over tragedies, slumber over operas, and pay attention, if at all, only to ballet performances. It it not inevitable that they should dampen the performance of the most fervent of our artists and induce indolence and apathy into their souls if nature blessed them with souls?" (Pushkin, 6:248-49). Although this statement concerns a medium in which physical confrontation makes interaction between audience and artist of primary importance, the idea of a chilling public apathy is relevant to literature in general, and Pushkin's concern could easily reflect his own fear of an unresponsive reading public. All through his life he remained sensitive to the public's demand: "I know very well the extent of the understanding, taste, and enlightenment of this public" (**Letters,** 1:113). "Do not praise me . . . but scold Russia and the Russian public" (**Letters,** 1:135). "I sincerely confess that I have been raised in fear of the estimable public and that I see no shame in playing up to it, harkening to the spirit of the time" (Pushkin, 6:281). "My tragedy will probably have no success. The journals resent me. I no longer possess what is most attractive to the public: youth and the novelty of literary name" (Pushkin, 6:350).

Sensitiveness to public opinion went hand in hand with concern about criticism. From among his many statements on the importance of criticism, two will serve for illustration. His remonstrance to Bestuzhev, to which I have already referred, reads as follows: "Just what are you calling criticism? *Vestnik Evropy* and *Blagonamerennyi?* Grech's and Bulgarin's bibliographical news? Your own articles? But admit it: this still cannot establish any kind of real opinion among our public; it cannot be considered a code of taste. Kachenovsky is dull-witted and boring; Grech and you are sharp-witted and amusing—that is all that can be said about the lot of you. But just where is the criticism? No. Let us turn your phrase around and say it: We have literature of a sort, but we have no criticism" (*Letters,* 1:222). His reference to "real opinion among our public" and "code of taste" implied that he did not need advice from his critic about techniques of writing or other such concerns of the workshop, but rather expected him to act as a mediator between the poet and the public. Thus criticism was a function needed by society at large rather than by the individual author. The idea was stated even more clearly in his article on literary criticism published in *Literaturnaia gazeta:* "Some will say that criticism should concern itself only with literary works which have evident merit; I do not think so. There are pieces of writing by themselves insignificant yet remarkable by their success and influence; in such cases observations about social mores are of greater import than literary comments. Last year several books were published (among them *Ivan Vyzhigin*) about which criticism could have said much that would have been enlightening and interesting. But were they analyzed or explained?" (Pushkin, 6:33). Why indeed had Bulgarin's banal novel become so popular—this was a question that really perplexed Pushkin—what was behind the whims of public taste, how could the situation be improved? The questions Pushkin asked himself were just those a student of the sociology of literature asks today.

Like most authors, however, Pushkin did not simply strive to win the favor of the public; his attitude was ambivalent. Russian literature at this time was undergoing the same radical changes as most other European literatures: from a Maecenas-supported institution, it was turning into a trade. What Adam Smith had said about products of the mind being sold for profit like shoes and stockings was understood by Pushkin. Several of his own remarks reflect the same idea: "I look at a finished poem of mine as a cobbler looks at a pair of his boots: I sell for profit" (*Letters,* 1:111). "Though I still write only under the capricious prompting of inspiration, I regard my verses, once written, as nothing but merchandise at so much per piece" (*Letters,* 1:158). And in an official document, submitted to Benkendorf, he characterized Russian literature after the ascension of Nicholas to the throne in these terms: "Literature was revitalized and it took its normal course, that is a *mercantile* course. Now it constitutes a branch of industry, protected by law" (Pushkin, 7:365). Toward the end of the twenties, as the pursuit of literature was becoming a profitable occupation, Pushkin's awareness of the market's fluctuations grew acute; for instance, he expressed anxiety that Bulgarin's unfavorable review of the seventh chapter of **Onegin** would affect sales (Pushkin, 9:330), and complained that *Severnaia pchela* alienated a great many of his potential readers (7:366). Dependence on the public's favor is naturally not to the writer's taste. We find, for instance, several English poets of the romantic period protesting the tyranny of public opinion. Wordsworth demanded: "Away . . . with the senseless iteration of the word *popular* applied to new works in poetry, as if there were no tests of excellence in this first of the fine arts but that all men should run after its productions, as if urged by an appetite, or constrained by a spell."[10] It is probably no coincidence that Pushkin wrote several poems in the spirit of "odi profanum vulgus"—such as **"The Poet," "Poet and Crowd," "To the Poet,"** and **"Unto Myself I Reared a Monument"**—in the late twenties and during the thirties when the commercialization of literature was striding forward. What Raymond Williams writes about the protests of the English poets of the time holds true for Pushkin: "At one level the defense is evidently compensatory: the height of the artists' claim is also the height of their despair."[11]

What I have so far described were social processes by no means unique to Russia of the first three decades of the nineteenth century. The respective positions of the neoclassical and sentimental critics were very similar elsewhere in Europe, the commercialization of literature was common to many countries, and the filtration of the elite's taste down to less educated strata of society is a phenomenon observable in almost any culture. Another common feature was that literature, and with it literary criticism, performed, among other functions, what sociologists call the function of pattern maintenance. This function meant the resolution of minor conflicts in a changing society. Minor conflicts arose, not from the great problems facing the nation, such as absolutism or serfdom, but from small shifts in private attitudes about life. Changing conditions brought forth new "type" situations which demanded new "strategies" for living (Kenneth Burke's expressions),[12] and literature provided just these strategies. It was not a political question how a St. Petersburg dandy went about his lady-killing or how provincial maidens chose husbands, yet these matters needed resolving if society was to function smoothly. When critics discussed the propriety of Tatiana's entering Onegin's house or the probability of Maria's falling in love with Mazepa, they were in effect trying to define the social code for such behavior. If the code changed, a minor adjustment had been made in society, or if it did not, society had succeeded in preserving its traditional values. In this process of adjustment, or attempted adjustment, the critic played an important role, tossing, as it were, the ball from writer to society and back and at the same time acting as arbitrator. This process was "pattern maintenance" in that it helped society effect minor adjustments without destroying its overall structure. It has been argued that a rigid society that does not allow even minor changes within its structure can easily reach a breaking point, whereas a flexible society can avoid violent upheavals by continually adjusting its structure.[13] Russian society, it appears, was similar to Western societies until the late 1820s in that it allowed literature and literary criticism to perform its function of pattern maintenance.

I do not mean to imply that Russian literature of the period performed no other function. Decembrist authors, and in many instances Pushkin himself, addressed themselves to the great political problems of society. Decembrists were indeed quite rigid in their demands for a civic trend in literature, which was the reason why they could not absorb the whole of Pushkin's many-sided literary output. Kiukhelbeker, for instance, attacked Zhukovsky's and Pushkin's elegies as serving no social purpose (*Mnemozina,* no. 2, 1824), and both Ryleev and Bestuzhev disapproved of Onegin, preferring an active antagonist of society such as Griboedov's Chatsky.[14] But the Decembrist trend did not so entirely dominate the literary scene as to prevent literature from performing its other functions.

In the late twenties, however, a change began which was to put Russian letters, and particularly Russian literary criticism, in a position that differed fundamentally from Western patterns. The first harbinger of change was a periodical I have not had occasion to mention so far, *Moskovskii vestnik.* The organ of some future Slavophiles and their fellow travelers—Pogodin, the Kireevsky brothers, A. S. Khomiakov, D. V. Venevitinov, S. P. Shevyrev—it reflected great interest in German idealist philosophy. Martin Malia has established that the sudden upsurge of interest in that philosophy from the second half of the twenties onward was due to a similarity of the Russian post-December predicament to that of Germany at the beginning of the nineteenth century.[15] In Russia the failure of the Decembrist uprising prompted the beginnings of a search for national identity. As in Germany, the effort grew out of disillusionment, shattered goals, and shame for the nation's backwardness.

As is well known, Pushkin had a brief courtship with *Moskovskii vestnik* and published a number of lyrics in it. But the heavy diet of philosophy was not for his palate. His works were reviewed by the *Liubomudry* in the spirit of their search for national identity. Shevyrev's review of Russian literature in 1827 and Ivan Kireevsky's similar survey of 1829 dealt with Pushkin in a more general way but with the same bias.[16] It has been noted in studies of the period that Ksenofont Polevoi's review of *Poltava* was written under the influence of *Moskovskii vestnik*'s general view (*Moskovskii telegraf,* no. 10, 1829). The most significant essay, however, was Ivan Kireevsky's "On the Character of Pushkin's Poetry" (*Moskovskii vestnik,* no. 6, 1828).

Kireevsky's essay would be significant for the sheer force of the author's reasoning and critical acumen alone, but its most striking feature is its nationalistic approach to its subject. His main contention is that Pushkin had gone through three stages of development: from the Italian and French influence of the *Ruslan* period he proceeded to a Byronic stage (the southern poems) and finally arrived at a Russian Pushkinian (*Russko-Pushkinskii*) period. As might be expected, this last period interested the critic most. He thought its main embodiments were Zemfira's father in *The Gypsies,* whom he regarded as typically Russian in his wisdom and humility; Tatiana and the descriptions of Russian life in *Onegin,* excluding, however, Onegin himself; and finally the monastery scene from *Boris Godunov,* which was the only part of the play published at the time he was writing the essay. From these fragments, he contended, one could glean the Russian national character: "In this third period of Pushkin's development one particularly notices an ability to be absorbed in the environment and in the passing moment. This same ability is the foundation of the Russian character: it lies at the very bottom of all the virtues and shortcomings of the Russian people. From this ability emanates courage, light heart, intractability of momentary impulses, generosity, intemperance, vehemence, sharpness, geniality, and so on and so forth." It is remarkable how this list of characteristics—and the whole essay—anticipates the views of Gogol and Dostoevsky. I submit, however, that they had little to do with Pushkin's poetry itself. Kireevsky approached Pushkin with a cherished preconception—once more anticipating a great successor, Belinsky—and his mission was to convey his own idea to the public, whether it were *à propos* of Pushkin or, if necessary, *malgré* Pushkin. Even though he made, I repeat, brilliant critical observations—pointing out, for instance, the relevance of the Finn's story to the general plot in *Ruslan* and the logical contradictions in the structure of *The Gypsies*—his basic concern was social, not literary.

The social emphasis of Kireevsky's essay points unmistakably toward the new functions literary criticism would assume in the following decades. Grave social and philosophical concerns pushed into the background (though never totally displaced) the more frivolous, "purely literary" matters of taste. Furthermore, under conditions of censorship that made overt social commentary impossible, literature was doomed to carry the enormous burden of social and political thought. Under the reign of a tsar who was capable of bursting into tears of gratitude over the prearranged "victory" of his troops in a military exercise, the possession of good taste alone became an act of political protest. The areas of cultural life in which a tolerant flexibility was allowed had shrunk considerably.

It is hazardous to speculate what the "healthy" functions are for certain structures in a society. The versatility of structures in assuming functions not normally carried by them is evident, if from nothing else, from the very fact that literary criticism in Russia *was* able to perform the task of political expression for over half a century. But it will perhaps not be too daring to claim that by depriving literary criticism—and to a lesser extent literature itself—of its pattern maintenance function, Russian society of the last century lost a powerful cohesive force.

Notes

¹ B. V. Tomashevsky, *Pushkin*, vol. 1, *1813-1824* (Moscow, 1956) and vol. 2, *1824-1837* (Moscow, 1961); G. A. Gukovsky, *Pushkin i russkie romantiki*, 2nd ed. (Moscow, 1965).

² *Language and Literature in Society* (Chicago, 1953), p. 73.

³ *Vestnik Evropy*, no. 6, 1802.

⁴ "Moi zamechaniia ob russkom teatre," *Sobranie sochinenii v desiati tomakh* (Moscow, 1959-62), 6:247. Unless otherwise stated, all subsequent references to Pushkin's works will be to this edition and will be given in parentheses within the text.

⁵ *Sorevnovatel' prosveshcheniia i blagotvoreniia*, no. 10, 1822.

⁶ *The Letters of Alexander Pushkin*, trans. J. Thomas Shaw, 3 vols. (Bloomington and Philadelphia, 1963), 1:108. All further references to Pushkin's letters will be to this edition.

⁷ *My Literary and Moral Wanderings*, trans. Ralph E. Matlaw (New York, 1962), p. 89.

⁸ *A Defense of Poetry*, ed. John E. Jordan (Indianapolis, 1965), p. 38.

⁹ Letter to Pushkin, May 10, 1825; quoted by Tomashevsky, 1:424.

¹⁰ *The Poetical Works of William Wordsworth*, ed. Thomas Hutchinson (Oxford, 1904), p. 952.

¹¹ *Culture and Society, 1780-1950* (London, 1958), p. 40.

¹² "Literature as Equipment for Living," *The Philosophy of Literary Form* (Baton Rouge, 1941).

¹³ For interesting examples, see Robert T. Holt, "A Proposed Structural-Functional Framework for Political Science," *Functionalism in the Social Sciences*, ed. Don Martindale (Philadelphia, 1965).

¹⁴ See Ryleev's letters to Pushkin, Feb. 12 and Mar. 10, 1825, in *Stikhotvoreniia, stat'i, pis'ma* (Moscow, 1956) and Bestuzhev's letter to Pushkin, Mar. 9, 1825, in *Sochineniia* (Moscow, 1958), vol. 2.

¹⁵ *Alexander Herzen and the Birth of Russian Socialism, 1812-1855* (Cambridge, Mass., 1961), chap. 5.

¹⁶ *Moskovskii vestnik*, no. 1, 1828, and *Dennitsa*, 1830, respectively.

Walter N. Vickery (essay date 1970)

SOURCE: "Lyric Poetry—1820-1836," in *Alexander Pushkin*, Twayne Publishers, 1970, 211 p.

[*In the following excerpt, Vickery studies Pushkin's mature lyric poetry.*]

The term *lyric* is sometimes used in Russian criticism to denote any poem belonging to the shorter genres—from the epigram to the elegy, from the personal theme to the patriotic or civic (anything, in effect, that can be listed under *stikhotvoreniya* or short poems, as opposed to the longer *poemy*). There is also the more limited and specific meaning of the word which envisages a *lyric* as a short poem in which the personal feelings of the author stand in the foreground: objective reality may well serve as a basis for such a poem, but it is the subjective feelings of the poet which receive the primary emphasis. It is in this latter narrower sense that Pushkin's lyrics are mainly treated in the present [essay]. Our concern will be with those poems which most directly reflect his intimate personal experiences, reactions, moods, and outlook. And of these only a relatively small percentage can here be mentioned.

In speaking of the subjective and personal as characteristic of the lyric, it should be borne in mind that the lyric element was by no means confined to Pushkin's shorter poems. It found expression, . . . in such diverse works as **The Prisoner of the Caucasus, Evgeny Onegin,** the "Little Tragedies," and **The Bronze Horseman.** So close was indeed at times the connection between his lyrics and his longer works—both narrative and dramatic—that, as early drafts show, short "lyric" passages were sometimes transposed into longer works, or excerpted therefrom to appear as lyrics.

At the same time, in Pushkin's case, the subjective and personal elements cannot be regarded as excluding wider issues of a political and social character. For not only was Pushkin's lyric poetry largely "autobiographical" in the broad sense that its many varied themes had as their focal, unifying point the author's own personality, but the author's moods and attitudes frequently reflected changes in the general Russian political climate, as well as the political hopes and disappointments not of Pushkin alone, but of many of his contemporaries. In many cases, Pushkin's lyrics yield insights not only into the poet's inner world, but into the larger world of Imperial Russia in which he lived.

One question which occupies Pushkin scholars is how best to divide Pushkin's lyric output into periods. This is inevitably a difficult problem. Themes treated in adolescence reappear in his mature work. New themes are added at certain points in time—without, however, the old themes necessarily disappearing. Among literary genres, that of the lyric is one of the most tradition-bound. Thus, the borderlines between periods are hopelessly blurred. Recognizing, nevertheless, that in the course of his creative life changes in Pushkin's lyric writing are observable, it is possible to offer as a very rough guide the following breakdown:

(1) *1813-1820.* This early period begins with Pushkin's juvenile experiments in the ready-to-hand Classical and Sentimentalist genres, particularly those practiced by the *Arzamas* group. In 1816-17 his elegies sound a hitherto unheard note of despondency produced by unhappiness in love. In 1817-20 there is some change in his love poetry which would seem to reflect the greater firsthand experience of his Petersburg years. But the most important innovation of these three years consists in the writing of liberal verses betokening his opposition to the regime.

(2) *1820-1826.* 1820 marks the beginning of the powerful influence of Byronism which accords perfectly with Pushkin's own attitudes: his sense of betrayal by friends, alienation from society, unhappiness in love, and hopelessness with regard to his future. The impersonal liberalism of his Petersburg years comes increasingly to be blended in with more personal themes, and around 1823 a newfound skepticism begins to be heard with regard to the liberal movement in the West and in Russia. By 1823-24 Pushkin has developed a more mature, objective, and critical view of the "Byronic" hero. The period of his exile is marked by an abundance of love poetry—less "literary" by now and more closely reflecting actual situations and specific emotions.

(3) *1827-1831.* The poetry of these years, which includes some of Pushkin's finest and most moving love poems, is marked by a growing awareness of the poet's isolated position in society, a profound disquiet with regard to life's aimlessness, a preoccupation with the past, with the passing of youth, and at times, with death. Pushkin's concern for the fate of the Decembrists also emerges in the poetry of these years, as do also his patriotic feelings prompted by the Polish uprising of 1831.

(4) *1831-1836.* In his last years there is a marked decrease in lyric output in general, particularly in lyrics devoted to intimate personal emotions; a tendency to "objectify" personal emotions is apparent; noteworthy is an increased interest in formal experimentation devoted to non-subjective themes and aiming at an extreme simplicity in style.

It cannot be overemphasized that this schema provides only the roughest of guides to thematic and stylistic development, not a series of watertight compartments.[1]

Pushkin's short poems written up to about 1820, as observed above, can, with a few exceptions, be treated as part of his apprenticeship. Elegance, technique, and feeling, although of a somewhat adolescent character, are clearly in evidence. But these early poems are, in the main, exercises in the literary tradition—both West European and Russian—in which Pushkin grew up. As Pushkin developed, he discarded many of the mannerisms of the *Arzamas* group, notably of Zhukovsky and Batyushkov. The formerly strong influence of Voltaire, Parny, and other eighteenth-century Classical poets diminished. The influence of André Chénier, Byron, and others was assimilated. Eventually, as we follow Pushkin's course, it no longer is meaningful to talk of influence. For though he continued all his life to experiment with non-Russian models, to borrow and to adapt, he reached a point where he was "using" models rather than "following" them, and his work became truly independent. But to this mature stage we shall come later.

The principal new important influence which Pushkin underwent in 1820 was that of Byron. This has been traced . . . [elsewhere] in connection with the "Southern poems." It made itself felt no less in Pushkin's lyric poetry. In fact, the first indication of Byronic influence occurs in a poem which in conception is undoubtedly indebted in some degree to Childe Harold's farewell to his native land (Canto I), and which Pushkin apparently wrote while sailing the Black Sea from Feodosia to Gurzuf:

> The frenzied love of former years I called to
>   mind,
> And all I've suffered, all that's dear unto my
>   heart,
> And all the weary pain of thwarted hopes,
>   desires. . . .
> Fly on, swift bark, and carry me to distant
>   lands
> At the dread bidding of the e'er treacherous
>   seas,
>   Yet not, not to the gloomy shores
>   That hem with mist my native land,

The land where first fierce passion's fire
Awoke, inflamed my youthful heart,
And where on me the tender muses secret
  smiled,
Where, battered by life's early storms,
My youth decayed, my youth was lost,
Where light-winged joy and happiness
  deceived, betrayed,
Marked, doomed to suffering my heart,
  benumbed and cold.
I go to seek new sights and sounds;
Far, from you I flee, my native land. . . .

And Pushkin goes on, in a vein with which we are familiar from the "Southern" poems, to deplore the follies and mistakes of his youth, and the young women who deceived him, all forgotten now; only not forgotten are the deep wounds of love inflicted on his heart, which nothing has been able to heal.

The corrosive "Byronic" skepticism, which leads to a negation of all positive values in life, is described in **"The Demon"** (1823):

In those past days when new to me
Were all the sights and sound of life—
The maiden's gaze, the tree leaves' rustle,
At night the nightingale's sweet song—
When feelings noble, lofty, proud,
When freedom, glory, yes, and love,
And when the arts' winged inspiration
So strongly made my blood to pulse—
Then was it that some evil spirit,
Casting upon my hopes and joys
A sudden shade of grief and pain,
Would come and sit alone with me.
Sad were the meetings 'twixt us two:
His smile and, yes, his beauteous gaze,
His venom-laden, biting words
Streamed a cold poison in my soul.
With calumny upon his lips
He tempted, challenged Providence;
Beauty he called an idle dream;
And inspiration he despised;
Did not believe in freedom, love;
He looked with mockery on life—
And for no thing in all the world
One word of blessing would he speak.[2]

The considerable number of poems written to different women during the first half of the 1820's show a wide range of feeling: grief at parting; jealousy; sorrow at the imminent death of a girl; the poet's reluctance to divulge the story of his mad passions and sufferings to the innocent and uncomplicated woman who has, for the moment, made him happy.

The theme of love is for Pushkin sometimes related to the theme of reborn inspiration: after a period of

spiritual flatness and boredom the poet is reawakened by his meeting with a woman, he experiences an almost Dionysiac *Lebensfreude,* his heart is unlocked, reopened to joy and sorrow, his whole being comes alive again, and he feels once more the urge to create. This is the theme of his famous lyric to Anna Petrovna Kern. Pushkin had been strongly impressed by her in a brief meeting in 1819 in Petersburg. In 1825, while Pushkin was in exile in Mikhaylovskoe, Anna Petrovna visited her relatives on the neighboring estate of Trigorskoye. The following poem was the fruit of the second meeting:

The wondrous moment I recall
When you appeared before my view;
You came, a dream ephemeral,
The spirit of pure beauty, you.

Through hopeless sorrows, somber, drear,
Through life's vain follies, whirls, alarms,
For long your gentle voice I'd hear,
And call to mind your tender charms.

Life's gusting storms—the years passed by—
Dispersed my dreams, and I forgot,
Forgot your gentle voice and I
Your face's heavenly charms forgot.

Remote, in gloomy isolation,
My days dragged by, the months, the years—
Without a god or inspiration,
With neither love nor life nor tears.

Thy soul, my soul to life recall!
Before me you appeared anew!
You came, a dream ephemeral,
The spirit of pure beauty, you.

And my heart beats in wild elation,
My spirit waked takes wing above;
Reborn are god and inspiration.
Reborn are life and tears and love.

But Pushkin's lyrics during the first half of the 1820's were not confined either to the theme of love or to the depiction of ennui and disillusionment. Pushkin is still the voice of Russian liberalism. In a verse epistle to his fellow poet Gnedich (1821), Pushkin compares his situation to that of Ovid in exile, but unlike the latter, "I to Octavius, in blind hope, / Pour forth no prayers of flattery." In his most famous political poem of this period, **"The Dagger"** (1821), Pushkin treats this weapon as a just means of retribution against tryanny and injustice. **"The Dagger"** is indeed a more outspoken, belligerent, and vengeful poem than the 1817 **"Ode to Freedom."** However, it is not, in this sense, entirely typical of the political verse written by Pushkin in the South and in Mikhaylovskoe. During the years 1820-25 two important changes are discernible in Pushkin's political verse. First, the narrowly political themes of 1817-20 are treated more broadly. The poet is, **"The Dagger"** excepted, no longer content to inveigh against tyranny, injustice, and serfdom, as though the setting right of these abuses would solve life's problems. These abuses are now viewed in the wider context of more general problems such as the processes of historical change, the meaning of life, and the destiny of man. At the same time these broader questions become interwoven with the personal emotions and reflections of the poet, and there occurs a fusion between the political theme and the truly lyric element in Pushkin's poetry. Secondly, from about 1823 a new note of skepticism is heard, skepticism both as to the successful outcome of any revolutionary attempt and as to the genuine determination of the people to achieve freedom.

This skepticism was undoubtedly induced in large measure by the failures in these years of the revolutionary movements in Portugal, Spain, and Naples. Pushkin's misgivings may also have arisen to some extent as a result of his contacts in the South with various members of the Russian revolutionary secret societies. His political skepticism is also to be seen as one facet of the tendency, noted above, to broaden the narrowly political theme, since it is applied not merely to political developments but to human nature in general. It is also tied in with the more specifically personal theme, since the poet complains that his call for freedom falls on deaf ears. This disillusioning dilemma, which seems to have provoked a spiritual crisis, is expressed in the following poem (1823), based on the parable of the sower:

> Sowing the seed of freedom I
> Early went forth, before the dawn,
> Into the wilds and with pure hand
> In furrows dark with slavery
> Freedom's life-giving seed I cast—
> I cast in vain; 'twas waste of time,
> Of labor and of noble thought . . .
> Graze on in peace, ye peoples, graze!
> You sleep and hear not honor's call.
> What use have herds for freedom's gifts?
> The butcher's or the shearer's knife
> Were better—and from age to age
> The yoke, the harness bells, the whip.[3]

"To the Sea" (1824) exemplifies perfectly Pushkin's growing tendency to combine the problem of freedom, presented now on a broad, almost philosophical base, with the problems of his personal life. Actually, this lyric started out as a meditation on the sea and the poet's destiny. The opening stanzas were written shortly before Pushkin's enforced departure from Odessa. The sea is seen as a symbol of freedom and power, and the poet recounts his own failure to carry out the plans he had nursed during the Odessa period—to escape from Russia by sea. The thought of Byron's death caused Pushkin, who had meanwhile arrived in Mikhaylovskoe, to enlarge his original theme to embrace both Byron, identified with the sea, as a symbol of freedom, and Napoleon.[4] Thus, in its final form, **"To the Sea"** is a lyric poem, which focuses on the poet's subjective emotions, but which defines these emotions by reference to the sea and to the world arena from which had recently passed two figures who had in different ways dominated the age:

> Farewell, thou freedom's element!
> For the last time before my gaze
> Thy blue waves rise and surge and sink
> And sparkle, beautiful and proud. . . .
>
> Alas, I wished but never left
> The dull and tedious earth-locked shore
> To hail thee with enraptured joy
> And through thy troughs, atop thy crests
> To speed full-sail a poet's flight!
>
> And thou didst call . . . but I was chained;
> In vain my soul was torn and rent:
> Held back by passion's powerful spell,
> Alas, I stayed upon the shore . . .
>
> Oh why regret? And whither now
> My carefree steps can I direct?
> One point in all your vasty wastes
> Would make an impress on my soul.
> One sea-swept rock, proud glory's tomb . . .
> There memories of majesty
> Waned and turned cold, were laid to sleep:
> 'Twas there Napoleon sank to rest.
>
> There with his grief Napoleon lies.
> And in his steps, like the storm's roar,
> A second ruler of men's minds
> Has sped away beyond our ken.
>
> Has gone—and Freedom mourns his death—
> Leaving the world his poet's wreath.
> Surge waves, storm seas, and thunder gales:
> He was thy bard, he sang of thee. . . .
>
> The world's grown empty . . . Whither now,
> Great ocean, could'st thou bear me? Where?
> Man's fate is everywhere the same:
> Where life seems blessed, there lies in wait
> Man's petty sway or tyrant's tread.
>
> Farewell, thou sea! I'll not forget
> The solemn beauty of thy waves;
> Long after this I still will hear
> Their crashing roar at eventide.
>
> Into the silent, lonely woods
> I'll carry in my memory

Thy cliffs, thy headlands and thy bays,
Thy sunlight, shades and sound of waves.

In this poem Pushkin bade farewell not only to the sea, not only to his life and loves in Odessa, but also in some measure to the early Byronic Romanticism which had taken such strong hold in 1820 at the start of his Southern exile. **"To the Sea"** expressed his regretful conviction that with the passing of such gigantic spirits as Napoleon—his ambition and despotism notwithstanding—and Byron, the poet of freedom, the world had somehow become a smaller and emptier place. It also expresses (in the last stanza but two) a certain skepticism, which was to reappear in Pushkin's work, as to the benefits which were allegedly to be obtained by replacing despotism by more liberal forms of government. At the root of this skepticism is the poet's suspicion that no form of government can make men free and happy, and that the essence of man's freedom and happiness lies outside the sphere of government—elsewhere, in some spiritual independence which Pushkin himself never achieved.[5]

One problem which was to preoccupy Pushkin throughout his creative life had to do with the role of the poet in society. Does the poet have a social mission to perform? Can the criteria of utilitarianism be applied to his work? Does poetic art have laws of its own, purely esthetic laws, independent of any message that may be propagated? What about art for art's sake? Is the poet answerable to himself alone for what he writes? And how does the poet fit into the outside world of society? A fair number of Pushkin's finest lyrics are attempts to deal with one or the other aspect of this broad problem. Over the years, as will be seen in the following pages, his answers were not entirely consistent, or, more precisely, there occurred shifts in his emphasis, dictated by his own circumstances and moods. In **"The Prophet"** (1826), perhaps the best known of all his short poems, the poet's role is seen as a highly dynamic one. Endowed through inspiration with an understanding of life's essence, the poet is charged to go forth like a biblical prophet and transform the heart of man:

With fainting soul athirst for Grace,
I wandered in a desert place,
And at the crossing of the ways
I saw the sixfold Seraph blaze;
He touched mine eyes with fingers light
As sleep that cometh in the night:
And like a frighted eagle's eyes,
They opened wide with prophecies.
He touched mine ears, and they were drowned
With tumult and a roaring sound:
I heard convulsion in the sky,
And flights of angel hosts on high,
And beasts that move beneath the sea,
And the sap creeping in the tree.

And bending to my mouth he wrung
From out of it my sinful tongue,
And all its lies and idle rust,
And 'twixt my lips a-perishing
A subtle serpent's forked sting
With right hand wet with blood he thrust.
And with his sword my breast he cleft,
My quaking heart thereout he reft,
And in the yawning of my breast
A coal of living fire he pressed.
Then in the desert I lay dead,
And God called unto me and said:
"Arise, and let My voice be heard,
Charged with My Will go forth and span
The land and sea, and let My Word
Lay waste with fire the heart of man."[6]

"The Prophet" was written in the late summer of 1826. At that time the sentencing of the Decembrists (five hanged and many exiled to Siberia) must have loomed large and fresh in the poet's mind. His very use of biblical style and imagery (see Isaiah 6) is in conformity with a Decembrist poetic tradition which depicted the Old Testament poet-prophet as scourging injustice and tyranny. This is not to impose on **"The Prophet,"** as some have sought to do, a narrowly political message. This poem lends itself rather to a broader, more general, almost philosophical interpretation. It has its roots in the distinction—already noted and a constantly recurring theme in Pushkin's work—between the poet in moments of inspiration and the poet reduced to mediocrity by the toils and snares of everyday petty preoccupations. The poet's superior wisdom and loftier view is granted him by virtue of his inspiration. This concept would appear to have something in common with the pantheism of Schelling which commanded support among Moscow intellectuals at that time. True, **"The Prophet"** reflects a basically Romantic view of the role of the poet. But Schelling's ideas on life and art were in essence alien to Pushkin's earthy outlook. Just as it is a mistake to see **"The Prophet"** in narrowly political terms, so also it would be wrong to read into this poem either Schellingian "otherworldliness" or any specifically religious appeal. The poet's inspiration is the foundation and keynote of the poem. With all this, "The Prophet" remains a challenging call to the poet to maintain the integrity of his vision and to speak out loud and clean on the side of truth and justice.[7]

The failure of the Decembrist uprising had important repercussions for Pushkin's political thinking. A nascent political skepticism was, as noted above, already apparent some time before December 14, 1825—in the short and bitter poem in which Pushkin likens himself to the sower in the New Testament parable, and in **"To the Sea."** After December 14 it was obvious to Pushkin and to others that the liberal cause had been defeated and that Nicholas I intended to rule with a firm hand. The poet's reaction was not, however, one of simple resignation. His interest in Russian history, exemplified in his work **Boris Godunov,** which was completed about a month before the Decembrist debacle, had been growing. He was beginning to ask himself the question, which was to preoccupy so many Russian minds in the nineteenth century, as to whether the Russian path of historical development had necessarily to follow along lines observed in other countries, particularly West European, or whether peculiarly Russian conditions might not demand peculiarly Russian solutions.

More specifically, Pushkin was conversant with the views of the Russian writer and historian, Karamzin, whose conservatism found its justification in the indisputable fact that progress and enlightenment had come to Russia not through the efforts of society or the people, but as a result of deliberate measures imposed by Russia's autocratic rulers, in particular Peter the Great. Add to this general line of speculation the gratitude Pushkin felt owing to his reprieve from exile, and it is not difficult to understand how Pushkin came to hope—and he was not alone in this hope—that, notwithstanding the brutal suppression of the Decembrist revolt, rational reforms would be forthcoming. But, these reforms would be introduced from above, as indeed the Tsar appears to have carefully stipulated in the September 8 interview in expressing to Pushkin his concern for the welfare of the Russian people. It is also understandable how Pushkin at times tended to draw a parallel between Nicholas I and Peter the Great. **"Stanzas,"** written in December 1826, at the outset of Nicholas' reign and shortly after the poet's reprieve, conveys Pushkin's initial optimism:

> In hope of happy days, renown,
> With confidence I gaze ahead:
> The start of Peter's glorious reign
> Was marred by risings crushed with blood.
>
> But he with truth won minds and hearts,
> With learning tamed the savage breast,
> Let Dolgoruky speak his mind,
> Saw not rebellion in his words.
>
> Boldly, with autocratic hand,
> He sowed the seeds of knowledge far
> And wide throughout his native land:
> Russia's proud destiny he knew.
>
> Now scholar and now man of war,
> Now carpenter, now mariner,
> His mind and hand encompassed all;
> A sovereign, he asked no rest.
>
> His the proud line from which you stem;
> Be proud, and follow in his steps:
> Like him, work tirelessly, be firm,
> Nor harbor rancor for what's past.

These noble sentiments bear testimony to Pushkin's delusions as to the amount of influence a poet's voice might be expected to have on his imperial master. The poem is also an appeal for clemency for the exiled Decembrists. Furthermore, as already noted, the poet's optimism was shared by others at the time. Yet this poem marks the beginning of a problem which was to plague Pushkin increasingly: it was widely regarded, even by some of the poet's friends, as a betrayal of his former convictions and an attempt to flatter the Tsar. It was, in fact, a compulsion to rebut charges of sycophancy which prompted Pushkin to write in 1828 a thirty-two line poem, **"To My Friends,"** which begins:

> No flatterer I when to the Tsar
> I freely write a poem of praise:
> I speak sincerely, unrestrained,
> I speak the language of the heart.

Pushkin goes on to say that he feels a genuine warm affection for his Tsar, who has returned him from exile and "liberated my thoughts." The real flatterers are those who would counsel the Tsar to repress a natural instinct for mercy, to despise the people, and to distrust enlightenment as the seed of depravity and rebellion. He concludes:

> Woe to the land where round the throne
> Only the slaves and flatterers stand,
> And where the poet, heaven's elect.
> Stays silent, with his eyes cast down.

"To My Friends" was submitted to Nicholas I, who caused to be conveyed to Pushkin his satisfaction, together with his wish that the poem not be published.

Pushkin's position with regard to the Decembrists, if not a particularly comfortable one, was natural enough. Pushkin was, of course, shocked and despondent. Many of the Decembrists had been his friends. But there was absolutely nothing he could do to help them now. He had been lucky not to be involved himself. He had himself asked the Tsar for pardon. He had made, roughly speaking, his peace with the regime. Sympathy with the exiles' sufferings, the exhortation to bear adversity with courage, and hope for the future was all that he or anyone else could offer. In January 1827 he handed to one of the Decembrist wives, who was leaving Moscow to join her husband in exile, his **"Message to Siberia":**

> In the depths of your Siberian mines
> Preserve your courage, patience, pride;
> Your toil, your burden's not in vain,
> Your noble vision shall not fail.
>
> True sister of misfortune, hope
> Shall in your gloomy dungeons keep
> Your spirits high and bring you cheer,
> Your long-awaited day will come:

The call of friendship and of love
Will penetrate your gloomy bars,
As my free voice now reaches you
Within your dark and somber lairs.

The heavy chains shall fall away,
Your prisons crumble—and in joy
Freedom shall greet you at the gate,
And brothers hand to you the sword.

Pushkin's return from exile brought obvious blessings. It ended his enforced isolation and reopened to him the pleasures of companionship and society. At the same time it complicated immeasurably his emotional life. Not only had the Decembrist affair left him with a feeling of unease, but it had removed from Moscow and Petersburg a goodly number of former friends, whose very names could now be mentioned only with caution. The reader is already familiar with other aspects of Pushkin's situation in the bachelor years following his reprieve. The freedom granted by the Tsar on September 8, 1826, was proving to be, at best, only partial. There were the constant pinpricks of Benkendorf's Third Section, and there was the grave threat of the *Gavriiliada* incident. In general, it soon became impossible to substantiate Pushkin's contention that the Tsar had "liberated my thought." But the most serious threat to Pushkin's peace of mind lay within him. By Pushkin's own admission, the dissipations of his early Petersburg years (1817-20) had brought him more distress than happiness. Now he was again exposed to similar temptations: his gambling was near-compulsive and costly. The companionship of men and the attractions of women were time-consuming, as was also his emotional need to cut a figure in society. If these types of distraction caused distress in 1817-20, when Pushkin's age might have seemed to justify the sowing of wild oats, it is not difficult to understand their more serious effects on a man who was now approaching thirty and felt that his youth, which he regarded as largely misguided and misspent, was slipping out from under him. He was afflicted by a sense of aimlessness: he seemed to have no niche and no purpose; either life in general was a futile exercise, or his own individual life had gone astray. Benkendorf's supervision and Pushkin's own weaknesses formed a ring of encirclement from which it was difficult to break free.

Such were, loosely speaking, the circumstances which provided the backdrop for some of Pushkin's finest mature lyrics. One particular aspect of a more general unease has to do with the problem, already mentioned, of the position of the poet in society. In **"The Poet"** (1827) Pushkin makes the distinction—referred to above—between the poet inspired and the poet immersed in the trivialities of everyday living:

Until Apollo summons him
Unto the sacred sacrifice,

Weakly the poet gives his heed
To life's vain cares and futile round;
And silent is his sacred lyre;
Cold and unfeeling sleeps his soul,
And 'mid the worthless of this world
More worthless still, perchance, is he.

But once Apollo's call divine
Reaches the poet's eager ear,
Like an eagle roused and taking wing,
The poet wakened soars in flight.
An alien to the world's vain joys,
And shunning man's society,
Before the idols of the crowd
He proudly keeps his head unbowed;
Austere and wild, the poet flees,
Yes, filled with strange alarms and sounds
Flees to the shore, the lonely waves,
Flees to the pathless, soughing woods.

In **"The Poet and the Throng"** (1828) Pushkin vehemently denies any obligation on the part of the poet to feed neatly packaged moral truths to the public. He concludes with the following quatrain:

Not for life's tumult and alarms,
Nor for life's struggle, nor for gain,
No, we were born for inspiration,
For prayer, and for harmonious sound.

The poor reception accorded to his *Poltava* and, in general, a feeling of being harassed by his critics caused Pushkin to emphasize increasingly the poet's independence. In **"To the Poet"** (1830) he insists that the poet pay no heed to the praise or foolish abuse of the public; he must go his own way without expecting any reward; he is his own "highest judge," answerable only to himself. Pushkin's poetry in the last five or six years of his life met with less and less understanding from the public, and the feeling of disaffection expressed in **"To the Poet"** was to become a more or less stable part of his attitude.

The disquiet which began to oppress Pushkin after his return from exile was both general and specific. Anxiety over the consequences which could have ensued from the *Gavriiliada* investigation is expressed in **"Foreboding"** (1828):

Once again above my head
The calm sky fills with clouds of bane
And envious fate with evil tread
Stalks my footsteps once again.
Can I still my fate deride?
Shall I still to fate oppose
The staunchness of my youthful pride
Unbowed before her sternest blows?

Bruised, battered by Life's cruel wind,
The storm, indifferent, I await;

Perhaps, saved even now, I'll find
Some port of refuge from my fate.
But parting's dread hour—I feel 'tis true—
Looms near, forbidding, merciless,
For the last time I haste to you,
And your hand, my angel, press.

Serene and gentle at the last.
Angel, bid a quiet farewell;
Let eyes uplifted or downcast
Tenderly your sorrow tell.
And your memory inside
For me the heart's lone flight will wage,
Replace the hope, the strength, the pride,
The daring of my youthful age.

The woman from whom Pushkin seeks courage in this poem is A. A Olenina, whom Pushkin was at the time courting with a view to marriage, but by whom he was rejected.

As we know, it was Natalia Nikolaevna Goncharova to whom Pushkin was eventually to become engaged and then married. His attitude to marriage and to his fiancée was extremely complicated psychologically. On the one hand, there was the hope of genuine happiness and spiritual rejuvenation; on a less ambitious level, there was the desire to organize his life on a firmer, more stable, more conventional footing. On the other hand, there were his grave misgivings and his doubts as to whether happiness could ever be his. At times he cast reluctant, at times nostalgic backward glances at his past and thought of the women he had once known and loved, still loved perhaps; and there was the sorrowful feeling that his youth now lay behind him. This stock-taking and the knowledge of the imminent change in his way of life gave rise to some of his most moving lyrics. **"Remembrance"** was written in 1828:

When the loud day for men who sow and reap
  Grows still, and on the silence of the town
The unsubstantial veils of night and sleep,
  The meed of the day's labour, settle down,
Then for me in the stillness of the night
  The wasting, watchful hours drag on their
  course,
And in the idle darkness comes the bite
  Of all the burning serpents of remorse;
Dreams seethe; and fretful infelicities
  Are swarming in my over-burdened soul,
And Memory before my wakeful eyes
  With noiseless hand unwinds her lengthy
  scroll.
Then, as with loathing I peruse the years,
  I tremble, and I curse my natal day,
Wail bitterly, and bitterly shed tears,
  But cannot wash the woeful script away.[8]

The pangs of remorse revealed in this poem were (as the unpublished continuation indicates) connected in the poet's mind with memories of past idleness and dissipation, of false friends, and of two women, now both dead, the remembrance of whom inspires in him— why, is not clear—feelings of guilt.

The realization that the time had come to adjust to a less exhilarating, more sober, and responsible way of life was not always expressed in the somber tones of **"Remembrance."** In a delightful verse epistle to Yazykov (1828), a fellow poet, Pushkin regrets that he is unable to join Yazykov and a mutual friend, N. D. Kiselev, in Derpt. His debts, incurred mainly by gambling, keep him in Petersburg:

For long I've wished to join you in
That German town whose praise you've sung,
To drink with you, as poets drink,
The wine whose praise you've also sung. . . .
Oh youth, brave, carefree days of youth!
I watch your passing with regret.
In youth, when to my ears in debt,
I'd give my creditors the slip,
Take to my heels, go any place;
But now I go to importune
My debtors who are far from prompt,
And staid and prudent how I curse
The heavy weight of debt and age!
Farewell, dear bard! Make merry, feast,
May Venus, Phoebus bring you cheer,
Heed not the pomp, conceit of rank,
Heed not your debtors' honied words,
Nor pay your debts: this is, you know,
A Russian noble's inborn right.

The lighthearted touch of the Yazykov epistle is, however, not characteristic of this period. The following short, famous poem (1828) reads like an act of painful renunciation:

I loved you once: love even now, maybe,
Love's embers still within my heart remain;
But trouble not; no, think no more of me;
I would not cause you sorrow, bring you pain.
I loved in silence, without hope, design;
Now shy, now jealous, torn by deep distress;
So tender and sincere a love was mine:
God grant some other love you no whit less.[9]

The sense of aimlessness and frustration which afflicted Pushkin at the time, produced moments in which the thought of death amounted almost to an obsession. There exists no more famous illustration of this mood than the following poem written in 1829, which was a far from happy year:

When'er I walk on noisy streets,
Or watch the crowd that throngs the church,
Or sit and feast with reckless youth,
Then to my mind come brooding thoughts.

I think: the years will swiftly pass
And, many though we now may be,
The grave's eternal vaults await,
And someone's hour is now at hand.

I see, perchance, a lonely oak,
I think: this forest patriarch will
Outlast my petty span as he
Outlasted those who went before.

A dear, sweet infant I caress,
At once I think: farewell! farewell!
To you my place on earth I yield:
For you shall bloom, while I decay.

To every day and hour I bid
Farewell and speed them on their way,
Wondering which day shall prove to be
The anniversary of my death.

And where will fate send death to me?
In battle, travel, on the sea?
Or will a neighboring vale receive
Me when I turn to earth's cold dust?

And though the unfeeling body knows
Not where it's laid, where it decays,
Still I would rather take my rest
Near places which I once held dear.

And at the entrance of the grave
May youthful life laugh, romp and play,
And may unheeding nature there
With everlasting beauty shine.

The productive autumn of 1830, when a cholera epidemic confined Pushkin to the Boldino estate, was shot through with nostalgic moods. Ekaterina Vorontsova, the wife of the governor-general of Odessa, has been one woman to leave a profound and lasting impression on the poet. It was with her in mind that on October 5 of that year he wrote **"Farewell"**:

For the last time I dare embrace
In thought your image dear to me,
To have my heart relive its dream
And with despondent, shy desire
To recollect once more your love.

The changing years pass swiftly by,
Bring change to all, bring change to us,
And for your poet you are now
Cloaked in sepulchral shade, while he—
For you—has vanished from the scene.

And yet accept, my distant friend,
A farewell greeting of my heart,
Just as some widowed wife might do,

Or friend embracing silent friend
Before the prison door is closed.[10]

His **"Elegy,"** written one month earlier on September 8, professes a desire to live and experience, but the mood is clouded and somber, the fragile pleasures and fleeting moments of inspiration he anticipates are outweighed by ominous forebodings, even the love he still hopes for will be flawed with the sadness of decline:

The extinguished merriment of madcap years
Weighs on me like a hangover's dull ache.
But—as with wine—the sadness of past days,
With age its strength increases in the soul.
My path is dark. The future's troubled sea
Holds little for me, mostly sorrow, toil.
But no, my friends, I do not wish to die;
I wish to live that I may think and suffer;
And I know too that pleasures will be mine.
Amid my troubles and my tribulation:
At times again the Muses will delight,
Creation's work will cause my tears to flow;
Perhaps once more my waning star will shine
Beneath the fleeting, farewell smile of Love.

One outgrowth of the increasingly tragic view of life expressed in Pushkin's lyrics at this time was a more devotional frame of mind. Pushkin was still capable of the irreverence of his *Gavriiliada* days. But more characteristic of the period around 1830 is a newfound respect for purity and sanctity. This is not, in the narrow sense, a religious feeling. It is, as always with Pushkin, partly esthetic, but it is also partly ethical in its aspiration for something pure and unchanging. A famous poem (1829) describes a poor knight who, after seeing an image of the Virgin Mary, will no longer look upon women or speak to them, but spends entire nights weeping before the image of the Virgin. Returning from Palestine, where he has fought bravely as a crusader, the knight secludes himself in his remote castle: "Still adoring, grieving ever, / And unshriven there he died." The Devil wishes to claim his soul, since the knight had neither prayed to God nor observed the fasts, and had adored unseemingly the Mother of Christ, but the Virgin intercedes and admits "her paladin" to heaven. Among other stimuli contributing to the makeup of this poem there is undoubtedly an underlying eroticism.

The same sublimated eroticism is clearly evident in Pushkin's **"Madonna"** (1830). In this poem, inspired by a painting of the Madonna and Child, as a letter written to his fiancée on July 30 of that year confirms, the Madonna of the poem is linked in the poet's emotions with the image of Natalia Nikolaevna.

The poet's marriage in February 1831 coincided with an abrupt change in his lyric output. Compared with the highly productive 1827-30 period, 1831 was a lean year:

of only five lyrics with serious pretensions, three are devoted to patriotic themes and reflect both Pushkin's support of Russia against Poland and his temporarily improved relationship with Nicholas I. Nor in the years that remained (1832-36) was Pushkin ever again to achieve that high level of productivity which characterizes his last bachelor period. Undoubtedly the social round interfered with his work and almost certainly, there were poems of a highly intimate nature which did not survive. Then, too, Pushkin was in his last years directing his efforts more and more to prose. But it is also reasonable to assume that Pushkin's pleasures and anxieties as a married man did not lend themselves as well by their very nature to lyric expression as had been the case in the 1827-30 period. An opposition as simple as that between happiness and unhappiness is not here involved—Pushkin was never very happy for very long. Nor should it be implied that unhappiness is the essential stuff of good poetry. It is, rather, that the problems which beset Pushkin in 1827-30, though very much his own, are also universal problems which inevitably beset grown thinking men. And it is this that makes this period, judged on quality and quantity, a highwater mark in his career as a lyric poet. After Pushkin's marriage, either these problems were less often in the foreground of his mind, or he felt inhibitions about writing about them—and certainly about publishing. Yet the less abundant poetry written in 1832-36, where it deals with the poet's intimate emotional life, reveals no falling-off of his powers. The relatively few personal poems of these years must rank among his finest.

One interesting illustration of the difficulties that can beset the married lyric poet is a small poem almost certainly inspired by Pushkin's wife, published posthumously, of uncertain date, but probably written early in his marriage:

Abandon's pleasures are not dear to me,
Frenzy, voluptuous rapture, ecstasy,
The young Bacchante who with groans and
  cries
Writhes in my grasp and with hot ardor tries
Her burning touch, her biting lips to lend
To haste the shudd'ring instant of the end.

How far more sweet the meekness of your
  kiss;
With you I know O what tormented bliss,
When yielding to long prayers, you tenderly
And without rapture give yourself to me.
Modestly cold, to my elation's cry
Heedless of all, you scarcely make reply
Then passion wakes, burns, blazes hotter, till—
You share at last my flame—against your will.[11]

Whenever Pushkin did permit himself to vent his personal feelings during the last years, the tragic impasse into which his married and social life had plunged him, is revealed with an appalling starkness. In one poem, written in 1833 or later, Pushkin—the epitome of intellectual sanity, balance, and restraint—is seen toying with the temptation of madness:

God grant that I not lose my mind.
Better the beggar's staff and pouch;
  Or better hunger, toil.
I do not mean that reason I
Now hold so dear; nor that with it
  I'd not be glad to part.

If only they would leave me free,
How swiftly, gaily would I flee
  Into the darkling woods!
I'd sing, delirious, possessed,
And lose myself enraptured in
  Chaotic, wondrous dreams.

And I would harken to the waves,
And I would gaze, in happiness,
  Up in the empty skies;
And I would be so strong and free
Like to a whirlwind cutting swathes
  Through fields and forest trees.

But here's the rub: if you go mad,
Then men will fear you like the plague,
  And, fearing, lock you up,
And they'll attach you with a chain,
And come and through the cage's bars
  Torment you like some beast.

And so by night I would not hear,
Not hear the nightingale's clear voice,
  The rustling of the trees—
I'd hear my comrades' shouts and cries,
The cursing of the nighttime guards,
  And shrieks and sounds of chains.

. . . An unpublished excerpt, written probably in June 1834, reflects the poet's extreme weariness with the life of the capital and his longing to retire to the country. This excerpt is clearly an appeal to his wife:

'Tis time, my friend, 'tis time! the heart has
  need of peace—
Days follow swiftly days, and each hour bears
  away
Some fraction of our being—while we all
  unawares,
Imagining we live, in life we are in death.

Happiness none knows—but calm, and
  freedom: these can be.
An enviable lot has long since been my dream,
Long since, a weary slave, I've contemplated
  flight
To some far-off abode of work and simple joys.

The manuscript contains Pushkin's plan for this unrevised and apparently unfinished excerpt: "Youth has no need of an *at home* [in English], mature age feels horror at *its own* isolation. Happy the man who finds a woman to share his life—he should make for *home*. Oh, shall I soon transfer my Penates to the country—fields, garden, peasants, books; poetic labors—family, love etc.—religion, death."[12]

But for Pushkin there was to be no escape. A visit to Mikhaylovskoe in September 1835, did not bring the hoped-for relief. In a somber poem Pushkin laments that his nurse, Arina Rodionovna, is now dead. He notes that young pines are beginning to grow up near the three tall pines he so often rode by. He himself will not live to see the young ones fully grown, but he hopes that his grandchild may see them and remember him.

As early as 1824, in his poem **"To the Sea,"** Pushkin had expressed some doubt as to the relationship between different forms of government and the true happiness of the individual. "Man's fate is everywhere the same," he had written. Now in 1836 he restates this thesis more explicitly in his poem **"From Pindemonte."** The poem, translated here only in part, gives also a clear picture of the sense of confinement and imprisonment which had taken hold of Pushkin, of the desperate need for the independence of mind and body which he craved in vain, and of those things which in his despair he treasured most and identified most closely with happiness:

> I set not too much store by those
>   high-sounding rights
> Proclaimed so loud by some, which dazzle
>   some men's minds. . . .
> For these, I understand, are *words, words,*
>   *words,* no more . . .
> Dependence on a tsar or on the people's will:
> It's one and the same thing. These are not
>   rights. To have
> To give account to none; to seek how best to
>   serve
> And please oneself alone; neither for power
>   nor pomp
> To bend the neck or compromise one's plans;
> As one's own fancy bids, to wander here and
>   there,
> Gaze on the sacred gifts, the beauty Nature
>   gives,
> And wonder at the fruits of art and inspiration
> With trembling joy, delight, enraptured
>   adoration,
> These things are happiness and freedom's
>   rights . . .

Beset by marital problems, at odds with society in which he was cutting an even sadder figure, and suffering from a neglect of his literary genius—which made him feel that as a writer he was regarded as having outlived his days of glory—the poet, through much of 1836, is plagued by a foreboding of imminent doom. A poem, written for the October 19, 1836 lycée anniversary, begins:

> There was a time: 'twas then our youthful
>   feast
> Shone, noisy, gay and garlanded with rose,
> The clink of glasses mingled with our
>   songs. . . .
> This is no longer so: our rakish feast,
> Like us, has with the years now run its
>   course,
> It has grown tamer, quieter and more staid,
> The toasts and clinking glasses ring less loud,
> Less playfully the conversation flows,
> Some seats are empty, sadder now we sit,
> More rarely 'mid the songs is laughter heard,
> More often now we sigh, and silence keep. . . .

What may be called Pushkin's final will and testament is a poem entitled **"Monument"** (1836). This poem is Pushkin's contribution to a longstanding literary tradition which, including in Russia Dershavin and Lomonosov, extends back to Horace's *Exegi monumentum*. The poem presents a sort of balance sheet of the poet's past achievements. It is born of that sadness caused, as noted above, by the lack of recognition accorded to his work during the 1830's—a lack of recognition which, added to his personal tribulations, and compounded by the journalistic polemics directed against him, embittered his last years. It is also the poet's last assertion of his freedom and independence.

> I've raised a monument no human hands could
>   build
> The path that leads to it can ne'er be
>   overgrown,
> Its head, unbowed, untamed, stands higher
>   from the ground
>   Than Alexander's column stands.
>
> Not all of me shall die: in verses shall my soul
> Outlive my mortal dust and shall escape
>   decay—
> And I shall be renowned so long as on this
>   earth
>   One single poet is alive.
>
> My hallowed fame shall spread through
>   Russia's mighty land,
> And each and every tribe shall venerate my
>   name:
> The proud Slav and the Finn, the still untamed
>   Tungus,
>   The Kalmuk, dweller of the steppe.

Long after this my name shall warm the
    people's heart,
Because my lyre has sung of feelings good
    and kind
And in my cruel age I sang blessed freedom's
    praise
    And for the fallen mercy begged.

Be thou obedient, Muse, to the command of
    God!
Not fearing hurt nor wrong, seeking no laurel
    crown,
Remain indifferent to calumny and praise,
    And do not quarrel with the fool.

Undoubtedly, Pushkin was right in predicting his own lasting fame. He was right, too, in the sense of timing which prompted him to write this poem—concealing beneath its traditional surface a mass of suffering—six months before his death.[13]

What, in conclusion, can be said of the best of Pushkin's lyric poetry? The sounds—in translation—elude us. Those to whom the privilege of reading Pushkin in the original is denied must take on faith that the sound patterns in his lyrics, though seldom obtrusive, are not only beautiful but also functional in that they harmonize with and contribute to the sense. The same must also be said, specifically, of the rhymes which play an important part in most of the lyrics—not merely as embellishments or line-markers but also as structural factors which shape the syntax and point up the thought, to which they are subordinated.

The themes and thoughts of Pushkin's lyrics speak largely for themselves. But some further understanding of his outstanding achievement as a lyric poet may be gained by comparing the best poems of his mature years with what he wrote in his youth. When, for example, in his 1816-17 elegies Pushkin speaks of unrequited love, of sorrow, and of death, though he is certainly sincere, one is aware that these are the moods of despair which sometimes beset the very young, moods which respond to the treatment of experience and adjustment, moods also, let it be said, which reflect a literary era. When in his mature work he speaks of such things, he speaks with his own voice, with a freshness, directness, and immediacy that give the impression that such emotions have not been treated in literature ever before. He speaks for himself in such a way that the natural and simple words he uses seem to emanate directly from the specific experiences and impressions of one man—experiences and impressions which could be precisely conveyed in those words alone. At the same time the balance, sense of proportion and self-restraint impart to his writings a universal quality. For Pushkin's writings are characterized—in form as well as content—by that self-restraint in dealing with deeply felt emotion which life demands of all men. Furthermore, this very self-restraint renders intelligible and doubly poignant to others the sufferings and tribulations which motivated Pushkin in writing of himself. And he wrote of things which are the common lot of grown man everywhere, of the limitations which life imposes on each and all, limitations which impart to life a tragic element which cannot be overlooked.

Notes

[1] See also B. P. Gorodetsky, *Lirika Pushkina* (Moscow-Leningrad, 1962), p. 29, and Gorodetsky, "Lirika," *Pushkin: itogi i problemy izucheniya* (Moscow-Leningrad, 1966), pp. 408-13.

[2] "The Demon" was widely interpreted as being a psychological portrait of Alexander Raevsky, a Russian "Byron" and a member of the family which had taken Pushkin to the Caucasus and Crimea in 1820, and introduced him to Byronism.

[3] This poem, unpublished during Pushkin's life, was prompted by the failure of the Spanish uprising which was suppressed by French troops.

[4] For details concerning the composition of this poem see N. Izmailov, "Strofy o Napoleone i Bayrone v stikhotvorenii 'K moryu,'" *Pushkin: Vremennik pushkinskoy komissii* (Moscow-Leningrad, 1941), VI, 21-29; also N. L. Stepanov, *Lirika Pushkina* (Moscow, 1959), pp. 310-26.

[5] "From Pindemonte" (1836), discussed later in this chapter, expresses more plainly the poet's misgivings as to the relationship between different forms of government and the true nature of human freedom and happiness.

[6] Translated by Maurice Baring, *Have You Anything To Declare?* (London, 1936: William Heinemann Ltd.), p. 246.

[7] The views here expressed on the ideas informing "The Prophet" are, in large measure, a condensation of N. L. Stepanov's evaluation. See N. L. Stepanov, *op. cit.,* pp. 347-63.

[8] Translated by Maurice Baring, *op. cit.,* p. 244.

[9] The woman to whom these eight lines were addressed remained unknown for many years, and her identity has still not been established with complete certainty. However, convincing evidence points to Karolina Soban'skaya whom Pushkin first met in Kiev or Odessa in 1821 (while on leave from Kishinev) and with whom he again became embroiled in Petersburg after his return from exile. See M. A. Tsyavlovsky, *Rukoyu Pushkina* (Moscow-Leniningrad, 1935), pp. 179-208. At the same time, it seems probable that

Pushkin copied this same poem into the album of A. A. Olenina who in 1828 rejected his marriage proposal; see T. G. Tsiavlovskaya, "Dnevnik Olenina," *Pushkin: Issledovaniya i materialy* (Moscow-Leningrad, 1958), II, 289-92.

[10] See B. P. Gorodetsky, *op. cit.,* pp. 289ff.

[11] The dating of this poem is uncertain. Gorodetsky (p. 359) gives it as January 19, 1830. On the assumption, which I am strongly inclined to accept, that it was addressed to Pushkin's wife, this date would be impossible. His wife's copy was dated 1831, and the poem may not have been written till 1832.

[12] *Ak. nauk,* III, 517.

[13] For an excellent study of this poem see M. P. Alekseyev, *Stikhotvorenie Pushkina "Ya pamyatnik sebe vozdvig . . ."* (Leningrad, 1967).

Barbara Heldt Monter (essay date 1972)

SOURCE: "Love and Death in Pushkin's 'Little Tragedies'," in *Modern Critical Views: Alexander Pushkin,* edited by Harold Bloom, Chelsea House Publishers, 1987, pp. 65-71.

[*In the following essay, originally published in 1972, Monter probes the thematic unity of Pushkin's "Little Tragedies" in their concern with "the recognition of love and the recognition of death."*]

A critical attempt to correlate separate works of the same author could hardly be more justified than in the case of Pushkin's four "Little Tragedies." All were completed in the fall of 1830: *The Miserly Knight (Skupoi rytsar'), Mozart and Salieri (Motsart i Sal'eri)* and *The Stone Guest (Kamennyi gost')* on October 23, October 26, and November 4 respectively. Pushkin may have been thinking about these three since 1826, but for such finished works their dates of completion are still remarkably close. The fourth play, *The Feast during the Plague (Pir vo vremia chumy),* was composed entirely during the 1830 autumn at Boldino where Pushkin was forced to stay later than he had expected because of a contemporary plague of cholera. Pushkin himself wished to unite the four plays under one heading, and he considered several less original generic titles before deciding finally upon "Malen'kie Tragedii" ("Little Tragedies"), a term which implies greater thematic as well as technical unity.

From the very beginning, critics said that these plays were for reading and not for acting. The "stage" history of *The Miserly Knight* is really the history of the baron's monologue, which the great actor Shchepkin loved to recite. Of the four plays only *Mozart and Salieri* was performed during Pushkin's lifetime and, unlike stagings of Pushkin's earlier poetic works (not meant as plays but containing some dialogue), it was not a success. Pushkin's popularity was waning by 1830, perhaps, as Akhmatova suggests, because it became more difficult for contemporaries to identify with his new, un-Byronic heroes. But with audiences of any age, these plays are too condensed, too highly "poetic" for the theater. Some critics defend their theatricality on the grounds of the sharp conflicts in each scene, but the "Little Tragedies" portray not conflict but the essence of conflict. As Bryusov wrote in 1915, "Pushkin gave in his dramas the elixir of poetry; the spectator must convert it into the living wine of poetry." Perhaps the most interesting of all the many failures to stage some of the "Little Tragedies" successfully is one which worked completely against this idea of the audience collaborating with the poet. The 1915 Stanislavsky production of all the plays except *The Miserly Knight* in one show underplayed the rhythm of the verses and stressed the famous actor's method of reexperiencing the role (*perezhivanie*). Alexander Benois's lavish costumes and decor for the Moscow Art Theater, accurate though they may have been, tended, as one critic noted, to use specific details that Pushkin himself could not have known. Thus, the feasters themselves were lost in a faithful reconstruction of the architecture of old London. Obviously, Pushkin relies less on specific detail than on the suggestiveness of his poetry. It is enough that his night in Madrid "smells of lemon and laurel" ("limonom i lavrom pakhnet").

Benois, unlike any of his predecessors, did look for a way to unite the plays. He made them into a "trilogy of death," beginning with *The Stone Guest* and *The Feast during the Plague* and ending with *Mozart and Salieri* as an "apotheosis," the "death of a genius, a demi-god." He saw the plays as allegory: "the human soul struggles with God and with other souls, conquers them and in the end becomes hopelessly damned, ruined." Benois could easily have included the miserly Baron in this synthesis.

Most of the excellent body of critical writing on the "Little Tragedies" stresses their similarities with the tradition of European literature rather than their internal unity. Indeed these plays, with their borrowed plots and characters, seem to exemplify the dictum that "the best writers expropriate best, they disdain petty debts in favor of grand, authoritative larcenies." Paradoxically, these works so clearly borrowed and so remote in time and place from Pushkin appear to be as close to the poet biographically and emotionally as anything he wrote. The two most personally motivated plays, *The Miserly Knight* and *The Stone Guest,* were published only in 1836 and 1939 (after Pushkin's death) respectively. In the fall of 1830 Pushkin was faced with a recurrent quarrel with his notoriously stingy father, adding material worries to psychological ones over his own impending marriage, over the prospect of becoming the husband rather than the Don Juan (Pushkin alters the legend to make the stone guest himself more of a presence, as the title reflects). As he sat out the cholera epidemic and waited to rejoin his fiancée, Pushkin thought about death and love, but not as separate categories. The intensity of his feelings distilled them into equally intense but abstract, impersonal art.

"Dread (*strakh*) is the uniting feeling in the four tragedies," claims one critic. Another speaks of the "pathological elements" in the "Little Tragedies." These elements lie just below the surface. Certainly it is naive to claim that "as in **Boris Godunov** Pushkin in the 'Little Tragedies' undertakes the complicated task of the construction of a tragedy without a love intrigue" in all of the plays except **The Stone Guest.** The love plot of the latter is something more than conventional, as we shall see, but in each of the other plays a distorted love does exist. An extraordinary passion for persons, things or abstractions gives each plays its dramatic momentum, until this passion finally consumes either its object or itself.

In each of Pushkin's probable sources for **The Miserly Knight** there is a double plot line: one involving the sexus avarus prototype and another conventional love plot with the younger generation triumphing. As Tomashevsky points out, Pushkin, aside from his famous remark that "Moliere's miser is miserly, and only that" ("U Mol'era Skupoi skup—i tol'ko"), must have noticed that "the character of Harpagon unites miserliness with amorousness." He states, however, that the love intrigue is generally external to the miser plot in most plays and Pushkin eliminates it. Not altogether. The most memorable scene of the play, the Baron's monologue, is in effect a perfect fusion of what had been two separate theatrical strains.

The Miserly Knight treats a conflict to the death between the miserly father and his son. If the father is the *skupoi,* the son is the covetous one; but, for both, poverty is shameful and money a means to power. There are other similarities between the two. Taking the love plot away from the son and giving it to the father in another form, Pushkin began an evening-out of audience sympathies, in spite of his own probable identification with the son. The duel, prevented by the Duke at the end, is actually fought between the Baron and Al'ber throughout the play. Each desires the death of the other and is obsessed by the fear that the other will outlive him. The son asks, "Will my father really outlive me?" ("Uzhel' otets menia perezhivet?"). The Baron says, "When I have scarcely died, he, he will go / . . . having stolen the keys from my corpse, / He will open the chests with a laugh" ("Edva umru, on, on soidet siuda / . . . ukrav kliuchi u trupa moego, / On sunduki

so smekhom otopret"). When tempted by the Jew in the first scene to poison his father, Al'ber attacks violently this incarnation of his own desire; but in the third scene he accepts the challenge of his father with such alacrity that he leaves his imprint on the glove he hurriedly picks up.

The father has greater insight into his own desires. He sees things clearly whenever he can focus the spotlight of his passion upon them. Pushkin's use of lover imagery in the knight's monologue makes it possible to regard the second scene as a magnificent perverted love story. The knight "like a young rake awaits a rendezvous" ("kak molodoi povesa zhdet svidan'ia"). He hastens to the "faithful chests" ("vernym sundukam"). Visions of nature are revealed to him from his dark cellar. The lines "I am above all desire, I am serene; / I know my power!" ("Ia vyshe vsekh zhelanii; ia spokoen; / Ia znaiu moshch moiu!") describe the consummation of love. It is important, however, to note that the real climax of the knight's passion is described in other terms, those of murder. The action of inserting the key in the lock is compared to that of plunging a knife into a victim. The feeling derived therefrom is "pleasant and terrifying at the same time" ("priiatno i strashno vmeste"). Death and love are united in one gesture. Finally, when the dying Baron calls for his keys, he is really calling for his life which has been concentrated in these objects. Pushkin's miserly knight, unlike the misers of Plautus and Molière, is not comic; his reactions are not mechanical in the Bergsonian sense. Rather they are symbolic of a love so great that it destroys itself in pursuing its object.

In **Mozart and Salieri** the theme of *nasledniki* is used more concretely as a pretext for murder itself, not just for the desire to murder, and in this play the poison is actually given. The "cherished gift of love" ("zavetnyi dar liubvi"), like the "first gift of (Al'ber's) father" ("pervyi dar ottsa") is the blow of death. Salieri's wife gives him poison instead of children. Symbolically, he carries this poison with him for eighteen years. Rationalizing that Mozart was useless because he left no artistic successors, Salieri kills the man he believes to be the greatest genius of the art both have loved from birth. But already in the first monologue Salieri speaks of killing music: "Having killed sounds, / I dissected music, like a corpse" ("Zvuki umertviv, / Muzyku ia raz"ial, kak trup"). Salieri dominates this play as does the Baron the previous one. Like the Baron, Salieri feels both pain and pleasure at the height of his passionate illusion: "It is both painful and pleasant / As if I had paid a heavy debt" ("i bol'no i priiatno / Kak budto tiazhkii sovershil ia dolg"). Killing what he loved has made Salieri free, but only as long as the final music lasts. His short-lived freedom from envy and doubt about his own talent is juxtaposed with the shortness of Mozart's life. But Mozart is aware of his coming death (he understands the man in black) and writes his *Requiem,* while Salieri sinks further into self-delusion at the end.

In the last three plays music is played or sung by men or women as an assertion of life in the face of death. Mozart plays his own music, hums a tune by Salieri, and listens to a beggar play a tune of his. In *The Stone Guest* Laura sings Don Juan's song and their affinity is thereby established. One of the entranced guests exclaims "But love itself is a melody" ("No i liubov' melodiia"). Later, Don Juan calls himself "an improvisor of love songs" ("Improvizatorom liubovnoi pesni"). Pushkin differs from his sources in stressing that the Don is a poet.

But love, which reaches the heights of music, is also tainted with death. Laura refuses to think of growing old: "why / Think of that?" ("zachem / Ob etom dumat'?"). Don Juan's words to Donna Anna: "What does death mean? for the sweet instant of a rendez-vous / I would give my life without a murmur" ("Chto znachit smert'? za sladkii mig svidan'ia / Bezropotno otdam ia zhizn' ") seem similar in tone, but there is, of course, much more to the Don than what he says to the woman he is seducing. In this play, more than in any of Pushkin's sources, Don Juan seems to be relentlessly courting his own death. He uses death to seduce Donna Anna, asking her to stab him, in what sounds like a parody of similar requests made in classical tragedy. He claims to have been reborn: "It seems to me that I am born anew" ("Mne kazhetsia, ia ves' pererodilsia"), a travesty on the romantic concept of redemption through love. Pushkin's irony stems from the fact that while the Don knows how to use life and death to serve the ends of love, he is not aware of how close his kind of love is bringing him to death.

He courts Donna Anna first in a cemetery, at the grave of her husband. Pushkin has made Don Alvaro the husband of Anna, not her father, and the Don invites him to his wife's bedroom, not to dinner at his house. Sexuality, traditionally associated with Don Juan's vigor and love of life, is here specifically connected with death. The statue is asked to "stand guard at the door" ("stat' na storozhe v dveriakh"). The image of death not just knocking at the door at the end, but actually keeping watch over Don Juan's activities is explicit with Pushkin. The Don's relationship with the statue is as intense, if not more intense, than his relationship to the women. At the beginning of scene 4, when he has Donna Anna alone in his room, he speaks again and again about her dead husband. Don Juan is different with different women, but one thing remains constant: with all his women he seeks the morbid. He remembers Inez for the "strange pleasure" ("strannuiu priiatnost' ") he found "In her sad gaze / And deadly pale lips" ("v ee pechal'nom vzore / I pomertvelykh gubakh") and in her weak voice. This "strange pleasure" is similar to that of the knight opening his treasure or of Salieri listening to Mozart's *Requiem.* He makes love to Laura in the presence of a corpse freshly killed by him. To have the corpse become a husband able to witness the seduction of a previously virtuous wife takes the pleasure three steps further. Anna, who says that "A widow should be faithful to the very grave" ("Vdova dolzhna i grobu byt' verna") is courted and first weakens "By that grave" ("Pri etom grobe"). The metonomy of the tomb standing for the dead one becomes a reality for her in exactly the way she fears.

For Don Juan much the same thing happens. Donna Anna asks him "What do you ask for?" ("Chego vy trebuete?"); he answers, "Death" ("Smerti"), meaning only the unreal romantic cliche of dying at her feet. Note how frequently he uses the conditional mood when talking to Donna Anna. In one speech toward the beginning of scene 3 the phrase "If I were a madman" ("Kogda b ia byl bezumets") is repeated three times. As in Pushkin's poem of 1833, "Ne dai mne Bog soiti s uma," the conditional mood is used to express the would-be freedom of the poet (here the lover) in madness. The poem ends with the possible consequences of madness: imprisonment by society, and divorce from the beloved sounds of nature; at the end of the play Don Juan is abruptly cut off from life: he calls to Donna Anna, but he has taken the hand of death.

In *The Feast during the Plague* love and death coexist, each intensifying the other. The play, like Wilson's *The City of the Plague,* concerns the attempt to deal not with the inevitable presence of death, but with the fear of death, which love of life only increases. As Thucydides wrote of the Athenian plague: "The most terrible thing of all was the despair into which people fell . . . for they would immediately adopt an attitude of utter hopelessness, and by giving in in this way, would lose their powers of resistance." Pushkin's way of treating the plague seems, however, to be unique. Unlike Boccaccio's heroes and heroines of the *Decameron,* Pushkin's characters do not attempt to remove themselves from the plague and create a pleasant life outside it. They hold their feast in the street where death's cart has the right of way. Wilson's drama has the same setting, but his Walsingham tries to dispel people's fears by saying that other kinds of death (death in battle or death at sea) are worse, and by wishing "Freedom and pleasure to the living." Pushkin's nameless "presider" ("predsedatel' ") celebrates death itself.

Close as he keeps to the parts of Wilson that he has chosen, Pushkin's play has a far greater intensity. Mary is no longer "sweet" but "pensive" ("zadumchivaia"), and the same word, which ends the play is also original with Pushkin. One effect of the brevity of the "Little Tragedies" is that, just as in a lyric poem, a repeated word becomes very important. One scholar has noted the repetition of the word *priiatno* in the other three plays, as well as its connection with murder and illness. In **The Feast during the Plague** the word is also used as part of an oxymoron: Mary's song is called "doleful and pleasant" ("unyloi i priiatnoi"). Since it is a song about death, one may and should connect it to the appearances of this word in the other three plays.

The two songs, Mary's and that of the presider, both honor love of life, but reflect different answers to the questions posed by the confrontation with death. Mary's song describes what the plague has done to life, with successive images of emptiness and quiet except in the cemetery where graves "like a frightened herd / Press together in a tight line" ("kak ispugannoe stado / Zhmutsia tesnoi cheredoi"). Thus, paradoxically, only death is given an attribute of life. The second part of the poem, in a strange mixture of the pathetic and the practical, urges Edmond not to court death by kissing the lips of his dying Jenny, but to wait until the plague is over to visit her grave. The song of the presider is completely original with Pushkin. This "hymn in honor of the plague" treats it not as something temporary, but as a recurring phenomenon like winter. The entire poem is an extended oxymoron epitomizing the paradox of the play itself. The "winter heat of feasts" ("Zimnii zhar pirov") is expanded to the deadly but beautiful breath of "rose-maidens" ("devy-rozy") and finally to the reason for the feast during the plague. The oxymoron illustrates the paradox of the "inexplicable pleasures" ("neiziasnimye naslazhden'ia") in a dark love, hinted at in the other three plays. Man is intoxicated by the very struggle with death: "There is an ecstasy in battle" ("Est' upoenie v boiu"), for in this struggle lies his greatest challenge, that of seeking a pledge of immortality ("Bessmert'ia, mozhet byt', zalog!"). The "deep pensiveness" ("glubokaia zadumchivost") of the presider at the end of the play is ambiguous. On the one hand, it should be connected with the same inspiration which enabled him to compose the hymn, the same genius which led Mozart to write his *Requiem*. But it is also close to that passion which gave the Baron his sensation of enacting a murder, spurred Salieri to kill Mozart, and brought Don Juan to invite death upon himself. The gap between immortal art and death is bridged only by an inspiration ever closer to madness. The four "Little Tragedies" explore this ground between the recognition of love and the recognition of death. Pushkin, when he asserts the former, also relentlessly implies the latter.

L. P. Grossman (essay date 1974)

SOURCE: "The Art of the Anecdote in Pushkin," in *Russian Literature Triquarterly,* Vol. 10, 1974, pp. 129-48.

[*In the following essay, Grossman views the centrality of the anecdote to Pushkin's prose and poetry.*]

Nowadays we look down upon these playthings of older children of an older time; but if there is the imprint of thought and art on the plaything, then it should be preserved in the Museum, just as those most minor trifles and artifacts, which have been excavated from beneath the ruins of Pompei, are preserved.

Prince P. A. Vyazemsky

Literary genres suffer their various fates. Some are doomed to disappear almost without a trace, depositing in our recollection only the abandoned technical term devoid of an ancient, often significant, rich and diverse meaning.

This is the fate of the anecdote. In our time this word has practically disappeared from the terminology of literary study. If in fact it is encountered in rare instances in critical treatises, then it is only as a specifically negative term. We speak about the anecdotal character of a *fabula,* of a presentation or a system of proofs in order to condemn them outrightly. The epithet "anecdotal" for us has become synonymous with the insignificant, the inconsequential, and is generally accepted as being of no value.

Yet there was a time when the anecdote represented a specifically artistic, and to a certain degree, even scientific genre, a source of abundant nourishment for historical studies, learned references, literary portraits, philosophical aphorisms, critical articles, satires and several types of novella. It was one of the widespread "genre-miniatures" which flourished in the eighteenth century side by side with the epigram, the fable, the aphorism, the madrigal, the literary epistle or signature to a portrait. Infusing various types of poetry and prose as a natural element, the anecdote enjoyed a completely independent existence as a special form of literary art that possessed its own laws, theory and traditions. There was a time when collections of anecdotes appeared as the most prolific of books and basic texts of a serious nature appeared with subtitles that are now but little understood, namely *anecdotes.*

The age of Diderot filled this word with an extensive and complicated content that practically eludes us today, but that was still disclosed and intelligible to the cultural minds at the beginning of the last century. It is difficult for us to comprehend why, for instance, Voltaire's historical treatise on Peter the Great, with its exacting selection of facts and various philosophical digressions where there is not a single anecdote in our sense of the word, is called *Anecdotes sur le czar Pierre le Grand.* Why one of the early stories of Karamzin, full of corpses, incense, sudden deaths and secluded prayers in monastery cells, is called simply "anecdote." Why the psychological novel of Benjamin Constant, *Adolphe,*—which by the way was highly esteemed by Pushkin and in the Russian translation is dedicated to him by Prince Vyazemsky—was published with the sub-title "Anecdote trouvée dans les papiers d'un inconnu." Why finally, Karl Marx placed his first political article in the Zurich philosophical collection "Anecdota." All this is incomprehensible to us without reference to the history of the genre and the evolution of the literary term.

In order to resolve several essential problems of modern literature it is essential to restore the forgotten meaning of this devalued word and as much as possible reestablish all its lost nuances more precisely. For an examination of the Russian *povest'* (tale) of the beginning of the past century, for the historical novel and various types of satire, it is necessary to take up anew this neglected and overgrown genre in the spirit of the age of its flowering.

Inquiring into the peculiarity of its former life full of glitter, gaiety, skeptical irony, wit and intellect, one experiences an involuntary need to rehabilitate this retired literary form which has been reborn in our day in the couplet, feuilleton, satirical humoresque or oral bagatelle. Perhaps our respect should be paid to it in one of the favorite forms of its time—in the form of the laudatory speech, the classical *Eloge,* the poetic panegyric. The sophisticated narrative qualities of this subtle and amusing form could inspire the investigator to a special praise of the anecdote. And it seems our praise would be more appropriate if in the annals of Russian literature this rejected genre be sanctified by the unassailable authority, the unmistaken taste and creative experience of Pushkin.

In the almanacs, books of rhetoric, lexicons or literary newspapers of the Pushkin era the anecdote was understood in a completely different fashion than in our time. In Russia this term experienced, from Karamzin to Chekhov, much the same evolution as in Germany did the word *Witz* which possessed in the eighteenth century an incomparably more extensive and deeper significance than in the twentieth century. When before the crystal goblet Faust intoned:

> *Ich werde jetzt dich keinem Nachbar reichen,*
>
> *Ich werde meinen Witz an deiner Kunst nicht zeigen—*

with the word *Witz* is here signified not a joke or witticism, but the ability to understand, as well as a profundity of discrimination. This is why Lessing could edit during the time of the *Vossische Zeitung* in Berlin in the middle of the eighteenth century the scientific-artistic monthly under the title *Das Neueste aus dem Reiche des Witzes.* This terminology has proven to be without currency in our time.

But what are the nuances that were invested in the concept of the anecdote in the Pushkin era?

By this term was understood above all a particular form of unestablished historical testimony. "By the designation of anecdotes," Golikov, who was well known to Pushkin, offered the definition, "are understood such narrations as are known only to a few persons." But to this classical definition there was soon added the requirement of a picturesque, witty and personal touch. The lyceum professor Koshansky in his *Rhetoric* defined the anecdote as something unestablished, deposited by history, forgotten in biographies, unknown among the people, but displaying a rare trait of character, intellect or the heart of a distinguished person. "The worthiness of the anecdote is to be found in its novelty, rarity, in its importance. Its purpose is to explain character, to show a feature of some virtue (sometimes a vice), to communicate a curious incident, occurrence, event."

Hence the proximity of the anecdote to historical composition and even frequently their coincidence in the eighteenth century. The recording of history at that time was not infrequently transformed into the collection of these unestablished features of character. "Anecdotes on Peter the Great" by Golikov, *Anecdotes on Shtelin, Russian State and Military Anecdotes,* by Sergei Glinka, the well known work by Rulhière, *Histoire ou anecdotes sur la revolution de Russie en 1762,* the less well known work of De la Marche, *Histoire et anecdotes de la vie de Pierre III*—all these books, contained in Pushkin's library, adequately display by their titles the significance of the historical tract ascribed to the collection of characteristic episodes of life. It is worthwhile perusing the older *Messenger of Europe* in order to be convinced of how common at that time had become the designation of historical articles and materials by this subtle and popular term. Tales of the bravery of hussars surrounded by French troops, of the self-sacrificing foot-soldiers and recruits, of the work feats of Peter the Great are all likewise enveloped in the general formula of the anecdote. According to the title of one of these ancient collections it is apparent that by "Russian anecdotes" is understood "the great memorable actions and edifying examples of glorious men." This is why we study Peter, Catharine, Suvorov, and, consequently, the foremost personalities of theater and literature principally in this form of the anecdotal anthology.

However, by the same word a completely different type of serious literature was denoted. Difficult instances of conscience, analyses of inner conflicts that grow into inner dramas, occasionally received the same designation. In this way the sub-title of Benjamin Constant's *Adolphe,* mentioned above, can be explained. At this point the refined psychological novel also is incorporated into the narrow term of the anecdote.

And, finally, the anecdote at the beginning of the nineteenth century was also understood in that broad sense in which it is used even nowadays in conversation, journalism and artistic prose. Then as now was understood as well the brief and witty story of an amusing occurrence or a pointed response. This form of the anecdote emerged from the European *fabliaux* and *facetiae,* from the Italo-French humorous novellas, and tales of jokes in the manner of the German stories of Till Eulenspiegel.

In Russia the anecdote appeared only in the second half of the eighteenth century in the form of an independent literary genre; however, it immediately enjoyed a wide popularity. The genre was defined quickly and distinctly.

The succinctness of the delivery, the mirthful and epigrammatic tone in the presentation of the unusual and unexpected incident, the waggishness or lampoonery of the final punch-line, the ability to build up and strengthen the effect of the ending, to concentrate the entire meaning of the small story on its point—such are the basic characteristics of this narrative miniature. The features of a caustic roguishness, as well as at times of a personal caricature, frequently transformed such a comic episode into outright satire.

In the 1830s Plyushar's lexicon seized upon and fixed all these features: "The instant should be entertaining, it must move, amaze . . . The major features of the well related anecdote are brevity, a lightness, the art of preserving the force or basic idea until the ending and then concluding it with something striking or unexpected." The subtlety and clarity of the formulation bears witness to the high development of the genre.[1]

In all three of its conceptions—as a picturesque element of history, as a serious psychological episode and, finally as a humorous story recalling the jesting medieval parable, modernized only by devices of wit, the anecdote was taken up by Pushkin and as we shall now see, penetrated deeply into the realm of his own artistic work.

In the poetics and artistic practice of Pushkin this literary form had an extensive and multiple significance. The poet used it as an amusing illustration in his articles and letters, readily illuminating with flashes of antique humor the fabric of his prose works. Not infrequently in his poems and even in his verses touching on historical *sujets,* that very same illustrative function of anecdotal testimonies from the past is most apparent. At times this uncomplicated material serves him as a seed which sends forth shoots and then provides a luxuriant growth, the *sujet* scheme of a brief *povest'* or an entire novel. Not infrequently, by means of it, the composition of an individual epigram or of an entire satiric lampoon is exploited almost in its entirety. Sometimes his use of the anecdote fulfills a supporting role in the compositional system, successfully tying together or untying its most important knots.

Of great interest to us are Pushkin's methods of using this versatile material. Often he simply introduces it into his story, relating without change the account which has come to him; he stores up and collects in great quantity these entertaining features of mores and intellectual culture. The entire character reference of the hero at times is dependent upon a skillful selection of anecdotes. In several cases, as, for example, in *The Captain's Daughter,* the notable episode from the past is subject to a thorough reworking. Here he uses the felicitous scheme of the episode, infusing it with a completely new and arbitrary scheme. Personages, concrete touches, the place of action—everything changes; there remains untouched only the familiar conjuncture of personages successfully woven by reality and legend and which provides in their confrontation the essential spark and combustion.

Frequently the poet adapts the striking device to a transposition of the anecdotal *fabula,* the transference of it from a distinct era to the present, developing and manipulating the forgotten curio in the setting of more contemporary mores and other psychological possibilities.

Curious is the particular device which could be called the "concealed anecdote": the interesting incident which remains unrelated even at the conclusion, opens for the author the possibility of indicating several erotic details of his *sujet,* and, thus, in no way offending literary decencies. One such example from these illustrative devices is in the biography of Ivan Petrovich Belkin which is distinguished by a "truly maidenlike modesty": "there follows an anecdote which we shall not relate, supposing it to be superfluous; incidentally, we assure the reader . . ." and so on.

Finally, in the process of artistic reworking, the anecdotal genre in Pushkin assumes dramatic features and unexpectedly provides purely tragic compositions in the form of a small *povest',* poem or philosophical drama. Thus from the archaic seed of the ancient anecdote there emerges in Pushkin a new form of the minor tragedy.

Let us attempt to orient ourselves in this extensive material that receives such an individualistic treatment.

Pushkin adopted this brief narrative form extensively in his poetics principally in its most widespread understanding as it is presented even to this day, namely, as a humorous, mirthful and witty story, briefly and succinctly relating a waggish or curious episode.

In general, Pushkin had a high estimation of the gift of witticism and himself demonstrated a consummate mastery. "Le jeune monsieur Arouet," as Katenin called Pushkin, justified his fame as the Russian Voltaire. "Young people recited his verses from memory, repeated his witticisms and related anecdotes about him"—reports Lev Sergeevich Pushkin. It was not by chance that when he met him in the palace gardens the grand prince would inquire of him "whether there are any new calembours." The innate talent of the poet, the lively and pointed humor, the cheerfulness of his conversation—all of this was combined with a special training and preparation for this greater play of the mind.

The culture of wit entered into the circle of requisite subjects for the upbringing of that time. The pedagogical system, which polished the Russian people of the eighteenth and the beginning of the nineteenth centuries, varied greatly from the later techniques of our intellectual education. The principal task of upbringing was not practicality, not the acquiring of information that was essential for coping with the world, but the addition of a greater polish and refinement to the future member of society, to the state official or courtier. This is why the concerns of an esthetic character were paramount in the pedagogical system of that time and in their fashion created the entire program of instruction: the ability to draw, declaim or fence was practically as obligatory for the cultivated person of that time as the knowledge is of foreign languages today. Even to this day Pushkin's and Lermontov's drawings continue to amaze us, bearing witness to the fact that in this area people at the beginning of the century were completely literate. We are astounded by Herzen's story of his lessons in declamatory art, the invitation extended to a French actor for instruction in scanning classical texts. And we are not at all cognizant of the fact that the wit and lively play in the conversations and letters of Pushkin's contemporaries appears as the result of a complex and consistent discipline defined by an intellectual tradition, whereas in its achievements in Vyazemsky, Griboedov, Tyutchev and Pushkin himself, this art of wittiness manifests the previous autumnal fruit of our literary creativity, abundantly assimilating into itself the rich juices of European intellectual culture. As was the case with drawing at the beginning of the nineteenth century, wit attended the familiar school, was worked out according to refined models, was regulated and nourished by books. The Russians of the Pauline and Alexandrian era were acquainted with a special cult of wit, loved and appreciated it. In this regard they appear as the direct recipients of the Parisian intellectual mores of the eighteenth century and no doubt with a great deal of success were able to reflect and creatively transform these mores in their conversations, letters, diaries and epigrams.

The intellectual traditions and artistic tastes of the eighteenth century, which surrounded him in his early years, transmitted to Pushkin effortlessly and naturally and this inclination to the art of the anecdote. According to the testimony of contemporaries, "his father was a rather pleasant conversationalist in the manner of the antique French school with anecdotes and word-plays." This art, together with poetic improvisations, charades and *bout-rimes,* the poet's uncle, Vasily Lvovich Pushkin, considered his sworn obligation in all the Moscow drawing rooms and poetic circles.

The representatives of the old literary generation, in the persons of Krylov, Prince Shakhovskoy or Dmitriev, paid their respects to this popular genre. In response to the demands of the enlightened minds, the eminent "Literary Handbook" of Kurganov placed side by side with the circumstantial presentations of philosophical and moral treatises—Epictetus, Seneca, Bacon and Wolf—"the brief schematic *povesti*" and "various jests." The reference encyclopedia as well could not pass by this most popular verbal form.

It is not surprising that this durable literary tradition had such a decisive impact on Pushkin and contemporaries. The "Russian Juvenal," Sobolevsky, was just as characteristic of his time as that friend of Pushkin whom the poet greeted in his epistle:

> *Barbed poet, intricate wit,*
> *Rich in brilliance, mind and jest,*
> *Most fortunate Vyazemsky, I envy you . . .*

In the succeeding generation this tradition of "brilliance" in mind and "jest" becomes noticeably impoverished. The antique and subtle art manifestly fades and degenerates. It flares up for the final time in a festive burst of pyrotechnics in the scintillating style of Herzen who was able to bring to life this dying genre in the new area of revolutionary journalism with an unparalleled brilliance. "For the sake of a felicitous witticism he was prepared to sacrifice all of world history,"—remarked Bodenstaedt after a conversation with him.

Herzen was our final wit in the spirit of the eighteenth century who was vividly connected with it in culture and tradition. By his time he found that his own contemporaries were jesting in a different fashion and laughed to a new tact. Minaev or Kurochkin were working out new forms of humor. The Pushkinian epigram was in its death throes, Tyutchev's aphorisms faded from print, discord arose over the term anecdote. Already in the criticism of the forties it was gaining the manifest reputation of being a cliché.

Incidentally it is essential to point out that even in the Pushkin era the old school of wit had begun to falter and degenerate. Even in **Onegin** there is a woeful remark concerning the crisis of the antique witticism:

> *Here there was in scented wig*
> *An old man, jesting in the ancient fashion*
> *With keen and perceptive excellence,*
> *Which nowadays seems somewhat amusing.*

A literary group was born which did not accept these delicate flowers of the thought and style of the times of Fontenelle. The attraction to the anecdote was alien to the romantic culture. Its religio-philosophical strivings did not react to the charms of this individualistic verbal form. Chateaubriand, Novalis or Venevitinov were likewise undisposed to it. Only the people organically connected with the age of Voltaire were able, in the atmosphere of new literary tastes, to comprehend, appreciate and adopt this bagatelle of an antique "oral literature." Only a few adopted the anecdote in their poetics, returned to it its former significance, deepened its antique literary meaning; such were Stendhal, Mérimée, Pushkin, and subsequently the Goncourts. They are all connected with the eighteenth century by powerful and complex bonds.

"Like a great number of the cultivated people of that period," Shevyrev says of Pushkin, "he was raised at first on French literature, and if it is at all fitting to speak of his philosophical education, then its source must be sought only in Voltaire, in the encyclopedists and generally in the French intellectual movement of the eighteenth century."

This is the invaluable testimony of a contemporary. In that intellectual movement about which Shevyrev is speaking the cult of the anecdote was especially of note. Voltaire himself was not only a first-class master of this art, but to a significant degree its legislator. His poetics include the anecdote among the number of important literary genres, placing it side by side with history, philosophy, the theater and the lyric. In his theoretic treatise on the study of style a separate heading is introduced for "anecdotes littéraires."

Another coryphaeus of the era—J. J. Rousseau—was likewise considered an inimitable virtuoso of anecdotal art. His "Confession" abounds with episodes of character and wit. Pushkin himself recognized the "epigrammatic tales" of Rousseau as a model of this genre.

Goethe was probably also indebted to this tendency, and not without the influence of the French literary modishness. At least his diaries bear witness to his express taste for the anecdote.

Our poet had a high regard as well for the eminent wit of that same period, Chamfort, the author of the aphorism which has survived even till today: "Peace to the huts, war to the palaces."

Pushkin apparently adopted from him the form of the collection of popular expressions and noteworthy incidents and perhaps according to the type of his **"Maximes"** and **"Anecdotes"** constructed the analogous entries of his diary, historical anecdotes, **"Table-Talk"** and so on. Finally the many almanacs, anthologies and collections of word-plays were no doubt familiar to Pushkin. All possible "boites à l'esprit," the collections of Chamfortiana, Voltairiana, Polissoniana, Arlequiniana and so on were sufficiently widespread in Russia, and their presence is distinctly felt in the intellectual culture of the Alexandrine period.

The circle of reading of the poet himself affirms his predilection for this literary genre.

Pushkin's library is full of collections of anecdotes or individual works of famous masters of this form. Here we find all its nuances and variations from Chamfort, Scarrone, Casti, Compistron to Fontenelle, Rivarol, Stendhal and Mérimée. In addition to the works indicated above there were present all possible *Anecdotes sur la Russie, Anecdotes sur le comte d'Espagne, The Russian Decameron of 1831, Chronique indiscrète du XIXe siècle* and even special encyclopedias, reference books and dictionaries in the manner of *Dictionnaire d'anecdotes, de traits singuliers et caracteristiques, historiettes, bon-mots, naivetés, saillies, réparties ingenieuses* . . . etc. etc.

Finally, there also was the classic model of the anecdotal genre, its most expressive type—*Les Historiettes de Tallemant des Reaux.* These memoirs of the seventeenth century, published not long before the death of Pushkin—in 1834-1835—were obviously adapted by the poet. Their publication was a major event in European literature: there unexpectedly appeared a significant writer who in the course of two centuries had remained completely unknown. In unlabored satirical sketches, where through jests and dialogues there passed almost all the eminent people of an era, from Cardinal Richelieu, Duc de Guise to Molière, LaFontaine and Bossuet, the author of the chronicle immediately leads us into the foyers and salons of the seventeenth century. Akin to Brantome in a great deal, Des Reaux with remarkable ease, freedom and mockery unfolds his scandalous chronicle of wanton morals and love intrigues, garnishing it abundantly with couplets, cynical episodes, waggish entanglements of persons and events. "Tallemant," says Saint Beuve, "was born an anecdotist, just as LaFontaine was a fablist; effortlessly he continues the race of tellers of tales and authors of the *fabliaux,* he exhibits the joyfulness of a Rabelais . . ."

Finally, in the hands of Pushkin there was no doubt also the eminent collection of witticisms, the "Bièvriana." Its author, one Bièvre, was considered the father of the word-play and its unexcelled master. His fame was based on entire works that were totally constructed on the play of words. In Russia his collection enjoyed a great popularity. Griboedov teased the avowed wits with him. Concerning Pushkin's acquaintance with him it is possible to judge according to one curious coincidence. The epigraph to the second chapter of *Onegin* which has not been explained even to our day and appears to introduce a new interpretation of the word "Rus' ": "O, rus! (Hor.)—O, rus'!" is doubtless taken out of the "Bièvriana." Here we find incidentally the following play on words as well: "When in the seventh year the arrival of the Russians was awaited in Paris, one of their supporters expressed his desire in a verse by Horace: "O rus (o Russes) quando ego te aspiciam!"

The Latin *rus* here is juxtaposed with the root "russkii." This anecdote by Bièvre apparently seems to be the source of the word-play in this Onegin epigraph.

Tallemant de Reaux or Bièvre both figured in that series of books which are so richly represented in Pushkin's library by the greatest classics of European wit and various encyclopedias of word-play. All this, judging by the selection and quantity of similar editions greatly preoccupied the poet and apparently, served him in some creative fashion, nourishing his inventions, infusing his compositions with wit and in every conceivable fashion ornamenting and enriching the basic fabric of his narratives.

This is evident above all in Pushkin's letters. The poet's correspondence with friends is full of such displays of brilliance which assume at times the characters of a simple play on words, but not infrequently presents the typical form of the humorous verbal miniature.

Of this type, for instance on the question of the choice of one of the capitals, we have the reference to the jester who in reply to the question "whether he prefers to be broken on the wheel or hanged," replies: "I prefer milk' soup." Similarly the pronouncement in a letter to Pletnev: "I, like Arthur Pototsky, to whom the offer was made to go fishing: *j'aime mieux m'ennuyer autrement.*" Or on the subject of the quarantine in Tsarskoe Selo during the cholera epidemic in Petersburg: "Thus was the custom in royal courts at times to cut down his page for the pranks of the son."

A special type of *anecdotes littéraires* adorn this correspondence in great quantity. Such is the story suggested by Pushkin for Vyazemsky's work on Fonvizin which he heard from Yusupov concerning the renowned dramatist who was "un autre Beaumarchais pour la conversation." In the letters to the same Vyazemsky, the well known wit whom Pushkin willingly entertained with felicitous aphorisms, there are, generally speaking, more than a few such analogous *dicta*. Here we find the final exclamation of André Chenier to the scaffold and the sarcastic protest of Chamfort on the subject of ruined epigrams. In the letter to Bestuzhev another eminent phrase of that same era is quoted: "Of our lyre one might say what Mirabeau spoke concerning Sièyes: *son silence est une calamité publique.*"

Here the play of words possesses no less of a significance. The mastery of the *calembour,* in the spirit of

the models of the classical anthology of Bièvre find for themselves an extensive adaptation here. Pushkin himself remarks on this in a letter to Küchelbecker: *"So zlosti dukhom prochel 'Dukhov' (calembour: reconnais-tu le sang?)"* In a letter to Pletnev: "The life of a thirty-year old groom is worse than 30 years of a gambler's life." And again in a letter to Vyazemsky: "Wherewith am I to treat you: here is my bon-mot for your amusement (for the sake of the point imagine that this was said to a sentimental girl of about 26 . . .): *Qu'est-ce que le sentiment? un supplement du temperament.*" Even in the letter to Natalya Nikolaevna Goncharova a reference to a bon-mot of Voltaire's is introduced.

Several of Pushkin's letters, such as those, for instance, to A. P. Kern, are almost entirely an outright play of words, humorous and light chit-chat riven throughout with jests, waggish hints and word-plays. "I was about to begin writing you some nonsense which would fairly make you laugh yourself to death," as Pushkin himself defines the character of his humorous letters.

In the face of the variety of these verbal twists, conversational *quid pro quo,* witty quotations and unexpected reversals, it is not difficult to seize upon a common feature in them: their proximity to the French eighteenth century which has cultivated this genre and elevated it to a degree of genuine literary mastery. The names of Beaumarchais, Mirabeau, Voltaire, Chamfort, the untranslatable French phrases scintillating throughout this friendly correspondence, all this points to the immediate connection of Pushkin with that intellectual culture in whose flowering the art of the anecdote possessed such an essential importance.

The short humorous story, refined and sharpened, plays a noticeable role even in the early experiments of Pushkin. Several lyceum verses are constructed on the basis of the anecdote.

Thus the composition of the first printed poem of Pushkin is defined, **"To My Friend, the Poet."** Written in the style of the classical epistle to Aristes it represents in itself the verbose friendly homily on the theme of whether it is worth it to be a poet. This typical deliberation in the antique didactic form with literary allusions (Rousseau, Kostrov, Camoens) with satirical sallies (against Rifmatov, Grafov, Bibrus), with reference to poetic models (Dmitriev, Derzhavin, Lomonosov), and finally, with laconic dicta-aphorisms of the type: "There are laurels on Pindar but there also are nettles" or: "Everyone praises poets but everyone reads only journals," and so on. This extensive material of queries, examples, maxims and proofs, which accumulate in the course of the verbose epistle could create the impression of excess. The fifteen-year-old poet apparently understood this danger only too well and with remarkable acumen circumvented it. In the interests of a successful resolution of this burden of argumentation he appends to the conclusion of the poem a parable concerning a drunken priest.

The episode of the peasants' encounter with the cheerful priest who has drained an inordinate number of glasses at a wedding concludes the long theoretical disputation with an animated humoresque. The ponderous style of the philosophical epistle is resolved in its conclusion. Thus, as early as his lyceum period the poet is using the anecdote as a successful device of poetic denouement.

But at the same time it serves him and the independent theme as a means of development. In this regard his lyceum poem **"Homeward bound on Easter Eve . . ."** is of interest. In essence this is a "seductive anecdote" (as Pushkin himself subsequently called this form of drollery), arranged in iambic pentameter with a cynically witty, concluding turnabout. Pushchin's testimony concerning the writing of this poem is worthy of note in many ways. As it turned out, the comrade-students at the lyceum, while sitting in the evening by the open window, were watching the people coming out of the church from all-night Easter vigil. Pushchin noticed in the crowd an old woman who was hotly disputing over something with a young girl and directed Pushkin's attention to them. The next day the poet met his friend with verses on the quarrel of Antipievna with Marfushka. Apparently the contrast of the frivolous and completely exposed *sujet* with the source of the verses—Easter vigil—moreover the reading of these verses on Easter Sunday, deeply embarrassed Pushchin.—"I became thoughtful for a while having listened to his verses in which the ending struck me," relates the author of "Zapiski" ("Notes"). As though sensing the tactlessness of his joke, the future author of the **"Gavriliada"** excused himself before his friend for his blasphemous experiment.

This episode is remarkable in many regards. It is important to point out the basic compositional device of Pushkin's in the construction of a poem on a given incident. Apparently more inclined to meditation, Pushchin would have treated in a completely different spirit the theme of the heated conversation of the two women on Holy Night. But even such a completely defined task presupposing and, as it were, prescribing a more profound lyrical style and a tone of elevated inspiration, is treated by Pushkin in the form of a bawdy yarn. The anecdotal form presents itself foremost to his consciousness and naturally informs the basis of his improvisation.

Subsequently, in 1825, Pushkin in a letter to Vyazemsky explains the laws and rules of such a poem defining it as an "epigrammatic tale," or even as a "bawdy epigram." If we recall the experiment probably written at the same time, "To a castrato there once came a violinist . . ." we shall see that at basis of this genre lies a droll, at times pornographic, yarn and that in essence all the works in this form appear as nothing else but droll anecdotes in verse form. Pushkin cultivated a definite proclivity for this genre.

It is not difficult to isolate that very anecdotal basis, at times plucked out of the dregs of contemporary life, in the series of satiric plays **"To the Tsar once was it said," "On Luculle's Recovery," "The Tsar, knitting his brows"** and in an entire series of Pushkinian epigrams which capture in a succinct line the typical anecdotal theme (for example, **"To Prince Shalikov," "The Parable," "The Curious Man," "To the Sultan's Accession," "To Count Razumsky"** and others).

The same paramount importance is shared by the anecdote in the construction of those works of Pushkin's which he prefers to call "humorous povesti" or "light, cheerful stories." This type embraces both poems and prose works. **"Count Nulin," "A Cottage in Kolomna," "Mistress into Maid"** are all likewise related to it. The models of the humorous *povest'* arise out of the treatment of some episodes concerning the unsuccessful love adventure of a contemporary Russian Parisian, the amorous cunning of a Kolomensky girl, and finally, a romantic episode which reconciles the hostile families.

Not only **"Mistress into Maid"** grew up out of this narrative seed. This is true of almost all of Pushkin's *povesti* which sprang from the fundamental principle of the anecdote even though it may have been subsequently masked by the dramatic effect of the reworked form. **"The Shot"** is a typical duelist's anecdote strewn with every possible curiosity from the arsenal of remarkable marksmen and cunningly weaves into the framework of the novella the engrossing episode concerning an unusual duel. **"The Snowstorm"** treats the fanciful anecdote concerning a hussar's prank which unfolds into a minor adventure novel with a seduction, a secret marriage and an entire chain of fatal coincidences leading to a happy denouement. **"The Gravedigger,"** constructed on the contrasts of the gloomy trade of the hero, his sullen character and the macabre dream with the surrounding lighthearted reality, appears, according to the definition of Pushkin himself, as a "tale" *(skazka)*, closely converging with the anecdote. Only the composition **"The Station-Master"** departs from this fundamental principle of the remainder of the *Tales of Belkin*.

It is remarkable that Pushkin himself viewed this suite of novellas in precisely this fashion. With his customary predilection for that literary genre which blossomed in the salon of Sergei Lvovich and was studied elaborately in the rhetorical lessons at the lyceum, Pushkin saw in these *povesti* brief experiments with an amusing and light narrative. The anecdote as the basis of *Tales of Belkin* is specifically recognized by their author. It turns out that the chronicler of the village of Goryukhino, having exhausted his powers in poetry, turns to prose and takes up the *povesti:* "But from habit not knowing how to arrange a fictitious occurrence," he informs the reader, "I have chosen remarkable anecdotes which I had heard at various times from various persons and I have attempted to adorn the truth with the vitality of the story, and sometimes with the flowers of my own imagination as well."

Emphasizing the anecdotal character of his series of *povesti* Pushkin wittily remarks in a note that the duelist's anecdote was related to him by a soldier, a coarse shopkeeper, while the two romantic ones were by some young maiden. In this way the typical feature of the anecdotal genre is exposed: its organically inherent character is that of a verbal curiosity.

In the same spirit, recollecting several years later his work on **Tales of Belkin,** the poet defines them with another characteristic term: during the cholera epidemic he locks himself in his study, "rereading Coleridge and composing short tales *(skazochki)* . . ." Pushkin often uses this term as a synonym for anecdote. Appreciative of the new form of the allegorical lampoon—the "Chinese anecdote," introduced into Russian journalism by Voeikov—Pushkin employs to this end the "children's tale," offering his readers in the figures of the "Little Fibber," the "Reformed Bully" and the "Windy-Headed Lad," caricatures of Svinin, Nadezhdin and Polevoi. All this represents different variations on the basic genre.

In anecdotal art there is a special category highly esteemed by Pushkin's contemporaries, and undoubtedly playing the most marked role in the verse and prose compositions of our poet. This is the historical anecdote as a particular form of narrative prose and one of the most operative catalysts in the novels of Walter Scott's time.

The highly artistic, and, in particular, the compositional value of this form is entirely understandable. The character episode of the past or the vivid pictorial outline sketching the person of the hero or the physiognomy of an entire society, can serve as the natural seed which presents in its development the complex composition of imagined dramas. The outstanding and colorful details of the past, dispersed throughout chronicles and memoirs, diaries and ambassadorial dispatches, biographies and letters, are capable of offering abundant food for the fantasy of the artist and to a significant degree facilitating the difficulty of romantic constructions.

This probably explains Pushkin's active interest in memoir literature, in the notes of Dashkova, Catherine, Napoleon or Talleyrand, and, moreover, the poet's declaration that for the memoirs of the eminent chief of Napoleon's police, Fouche, he is prepared to trade all of Shakespeare.

Among the writers of Pushkin's time we may observe the same tendency in Prosper Mérimée. Akin to Pushkin in a great deal, he attached overwhelming significance to the anecdote. Placing it at the basis of an entire series of his novellas he loved to weave out of these dispersed molecules of the past his extensive historical treatises. The popular *touches* of his age were more essential to him than multi-volumed sources or archival materials. He viewed history as a composition of well chosen anecdotes and he did not hesitate to adapt openly the methodology of his research to this device.

"I love in history only anecdotes," he confessed in the forward to one of his treatises, "and of these I prefer those in which I can reckon on finding a faithful depiction of the mores and characters of a specific era. This taste, perhaps, is not especially noble: but to my shame I confess that I would willingly have given Thucydides for the genuine memoirs of Aspasiya or of any slave of Pericles; for memoirs, these intimate conversations of the author with the reader, they alone communicate those human portraits which amuse and interest me. And of course, not according to the descriptions of Mezières, Monluc, Tavannes, La Noue and others is it possible to produce for oneself any conception of the French of the sixteenth century."

For people of the spiritual makeup of Mérimée, this acknowledgement is quite significant, and it is useful to take it into account in studying Pushkin. It is not by chance that his central hero, who has no desire to scrounge about "in the chronological dust of the history of the world," but entirely in the spirit of Mérimée, searches in his memory for: ". . . anecdotes of by-gone days, / From Romulus to our day." This was not at all as superficial and flippant as may appear at first glance. The fine cultural sense of Onegin and the extent of his reading justly promoted his interest in these keen-witted fragments of the past. He probably knew that the parliamentary orators of England made extensive use of them and in the hands of such masters of historical exposition as Tacitus or Gibbon, the cursory anecdote grew into the monumental style of the character reference and the literary portrait.

The enormous compositional and *sujet* role of the historical anecdote in the prose of Pushkin manifests itself to an undeniable degree in his prose sketches, unfinished studies and various literary fragments.

The preparatory fragments from **"Egyptian Nights," "Excerpts from the Biography of Nashchokin,"** and **"The Russian Pelham"** disclose a broad panorama of an entire series of such witty fragments of history. Displaying an artistic treatment, here are those character legends and facts which have remained beyond the pale of official annals. Pushkin makes extensive use of these living arabesques of the past for his *povesti.*

Ample testimony may further be found in his diary which is liberally sprinkled with historical anecdotes. Here also are the stories of Natalya Kirillovna Zagryazhskaya of which Pushkin made so much use: "From her he caught the echoes of generations and societies which had already disappeared from the face of the earth," says Vyazemsky, "and in his conversation with her he discovered an unusual historical and poetic charm . . ." Pushkin himself bears witness to the mastery of her stories: "Natalya Kirillovna told an anecdote (the confrontation of Ekaterina with Dashkova) with great vivacity."

With the same interest Pushkin listened to the oral stories of Speransky, with the same greed he captured the records of persons and mores of the past from the conversations of Poletika at dinner at Smirnova's or at the soirées of Karamzina. These table stories "about Paul I, our romantic emperor," occupied his imagination to the same degree as an archival document or a page from Plutarch.

Pushkin's diary is interspersed throughout with testimonies of the following type: "Wiegel related a curious anecdote to me" . . ."The grand prince told a multitude of *calembours*" . . ."Yesterday I was at Smirnova's. Tsitsianov anecdotes" . . . and so on. In the Pushkin collection **"Table-Talk,"** under many of the entries stand the remarks: ". . . heard from Prince VI. Nik. Golitsyn" . . . "from Count Belgorsky" . . . "from Prince Dolgorukov" . . . and so on. Vyazemsky testifies that Pushkin loved Engelgardt for the reason that he "played with words very successfully." The poet was frequently severe in his relations with Dmitriev but was always enthused with his witty speech.

It's not surprising that echoes from these conversations crop up in Pushkin's letters, in fragments from his notebook and in his historical remarks. From the volatile pages of his diary to his monumental treatise, records bear witness to this intellectual taste. Chiefly he gathers this material from conversations or forgotten chronicles completely on his own and quite independently, like Chamfort, under a simple rubric—"Historical anecdotes." The various features of character, pronouncements or pointed catchwords *(repliki)* of the historical figures of an entire century, a series of what are essentially "literary anecdotes" about Kheraskov and Kostrov, about Sumarokov and Barkov, about Gnedich and Milonov, about Lomonosov and Tredyakovsky—all these compose typical *chapelets d'anecdotes,* as Prosper Mérimée conceived of history.

These small fragments of Pushkin's literary heritage have remained in the dark to our day. All this time, however, the specific gift of the story is distinguished by an exclusive mastery: the compactness, the laconicism, the fluency of the transmission, the lucid pointedness of expression, the keen wit and the individuality of the passages of dialogue, the perfection and the conclusive

self-sufficiency of each miniature novella bordering at times on the portrait or character reference—all this elevates Pushkin's **"Historical Anecdotes"** to classical models of this genre. Here we have an analysis of a moving and unusually significant episode. Pushkin gives an account of the crucifix presented to the poet by the Franciscan prior, and of the significance which Byron attached to this holy object. This calls forth a series of thoughts on the "grief of the noble poet," on his faith, on his heroic death. All this is signified by the title **"An Anecdote on Byron."**

It is not surprising that for his obituary of Delvig, Pushkin demands "details, a presentation of his views, *anecdotes,* a choice of his verses" . . . And in fact, Pushkin introduces his article on the deceased Delvig with an anecdote.

Thus, the light literary genre assumes the features of profound dramatic effect. The anecdote in Pushkin makes the transition to drama. The core of the narrative, its original catalyst, the tiny seed of the many-faceted novella, it presented a complex flowering into several more profound, significant and consummate creations of Pushkin.

This is evident above all in **"The Queen of Spades."** This classic Russian *povest'* grows forth out of a model anecdote of Tomsky. Where did it come from, does it possess its own story, or was it composed by Pushkin? At the basis of the story of the Countess' secret is posited the ancient historical anecdote about Cagliostro. In the biography of the renowned adventurist there is a story about how he forecast without mistake three numbers for a lottery game. Apparently out of this kernel Pushkin's novella sent forth its own shoots. Instead of Cagliostro we find designated two other adventurists of that time—Count Saint-Germain and Casanova. The former becomes the principal hero of the fanciful tale concerning the mores of the eighteenth century.

The compositional problem here has led to the transferal of the anecdote concerning Cagliostro into the mores of contemporary gamblers. The connecting link between the milieu of horseguard rakes of the 1820s and the era of Richelieu is served by the figure of the old woman who intrudes into the contemporary scene with a vivid legend of a by-gone era. Into the episode itself, which is light, successful and not without certain playful nuances—this indispensable sharp spice of conversations of the eighteenth century—Pushkin introduces the beginning of the catastrophe, the *fatum,* the retribution, the somber maniacalness and fateful miscarriage momentarily transfiguring the frivolous anecdote of the Rococo era into the tragic Petersburg *povest'* which leads us directly to Dostoevsky.

This particular device of transposing the older anecdote into the setting of contemporary mores and entirely different conditions of life and thought was a strong enticement for Pushkin. He manipulated it as well during the creation of the later versions of **"Egyptian Nights."**

At their basis, according to Pushkin's own avowal, is posited an "entirely antique anecdote," the "Egyptian anecdote" which incidentally "George Sand would have refashioned for today's mores." Thus, the method is disclosed in its entirety whereby Pushkin operated during the refashioning of the legend about Cagliostro, dramatizing it within the setting of his own time. It is possible to suppose that the anecdote about Cleopatra was also to serve as the theme for a contemporary romantic drama recreating in the setting of the high society of Petersburg of the 1830s several features of the Alexandrian night.

In the preparatory fragments for **"Egyptian Nights"** the anecdote generally plays a marked role. It is represented here by both various concrete models as well as several theoretical considerations. Here the well known anecdote about Mme de Staël and Bonaparte is introduced and the critical *boutade* is made that in Russian social conversation now and then the "seductive anecdote" is heard without any relation to the truth, expounded, picked to pieces without any humor whatsoever. The forgotten testimony about Cleopatra, related in high society, assumes here the genuine character of the anecdote in the ancient sense of this word, i.e., of something "left behind by history," forgotten in the biography. Out of this historical fragment, dropped by ancient chroniclers, Pushkin creates his tragic poem about passion and death.

Finally, the third experiment with the same dramatic composition based on the unraveled anecdote provides a journalistic testimony of the sharp hissing which resounds at the premiere of **"Don Juan."** This intriguing curiosity from the musical past, buttressed by the legend of Salieri's pre-death confession of poisoning Mozart, assumes all the characteristics of a profoundly tragic design offering the poet the most felicitous material for a philosophical drama on the agonies of creativity. The legendary features emerging out of the biography of the Italian composer represent in themselves those specific facts, denied by official biographers, which are of double interest for the reader and poet. Out of this typical historico-anecdotal testimony sprouts forth the first and, perhaps even to our day, unexcelled Russian tragedy. The cold terror of the barren creator before the bursting power of the god-inspired genius knows no higher embodiment in world literature.

In all three instances Pushkin attains the heights of tragic art by proceeding from the anecdote. The cleverness of Cagliostro, the rapaciousness of Cleopatra, the envy of Salieri—these are the features of history, manners, characters out of which the *povest'*, poem and minor tragedy spring forth. **"The Queen of Spades," "Egyptian Nights"** and *Mozart and Salieri* display what profound, unexpected and rich possibilities were concealed for Pushkin in the art of the anecdote and to what heights his cultivation of this light genre soared.

Meanwhile the rich Pushkiniana of latter decades has completely circumvented this theme. And only the poet's contemporary critics were well aware of this character of Pushkin's narrative. It was not with the purpose of condemning the author, but in the interests of a correct formulation, that they frequently noted this peculiarity of many of his compositions. "*The Little House in Kolomna*"—wrote the critic Galatei— "is nothing more than an amusing anecdote which has been incorporated into Russian octaves in imitation of the Italian—and, it seems, written solely for their sake." " **'The Queen of Spades'** is not a *povest'* but a skillful story," wrote Belinsky, "in fact this is not a *povest'* but an anecdote . . . But the story, we repeat, is the height of mastery." " **'The History of the Village of Goryukhino'** is pointed farce in which, incidentally, there are also serious things," states that same Belinsky. In general *Tales of Belkin,* according to his definition, are "simply tales and yarns." **"The Gravedigger,"** in the opinion of *The Northern Bee,* is not a *povest'*, but merely an anecdote, and according to Polevoi's testimonial—an amusing farce. **"Mistress into Maid"** was compared with the farce or the French vaudville. Concerning *The History of the Pugachev Rebellion* a critic in *Library for Reading* noted that it was impossible to connect the great number of curious facts and anecdotes contained in the hundred and fifty pages. In raptures over *Count Nulin* as "a delightful plaything of poetry," *Son of the Fatherland* defined it as an "anecdotal *povest'*."

And it was all the easier for critics to establish this formula because Pushkin himself quite manifestly indicates it with his own reiterated pronouncements. Speaking of his works he did not cease to remark on this anecdotal basis of his *fabulae*. With *The History of the Pugachev Rebellion* he disclosed the basis of *The Captain's Daughter.* In the projected foreword to the novel he says: "The anecdote which serves as the basis of the *povest'* which we have published, is well known in Orenburg. It will be easy for the reader to discern the thread of the genuine incident running through the romantic fiction . . ."

In **"The Queen of Spades"** he says: "The anecdote of the three cards had a powerful effect on his imagination . . ." And further on in the words of Hermann: "And the anecdote itself? Could it be believed?"— "This was a jest, I swear to you, it was a jest," the Countess herself replies to him, more than once pointing out the anecdotal seed of the narrative. Precisely in the same manner at the beginning of Nashchokin's biography the device of the character reference for the father of the hero is openly conveyed: "Several anecdotes which have been preserved in legend offer some understanding of him." The original source of the *Tales of Belkin,* as we have seen, is in some "remarkable anecdotes," "heard at various times from various personages," and at the basis of **"Egyptian Nights,"** according to the definition of Pushkin, lies "an entirely ancient anecdote," a unique and rare offshoot of the genre, somewhat of a curiosity—the Egyptian anecdote.

We see that Pushkin himself in no way concealed the imposing role of this component in the development of his narrative art; he was not embarrassed at its genealogy, perhaps he saw in it an expedient and valuable principle and one would think that it would not at all be necessary for contemporary researchers to defend Pushkin from reproaches of "anecdotalism."

How did this secondary literary form entice him?

Above all it responded perfectly to Pushkin's basic problem as a writer: the creation of an engrossing *fabula.*

Criticism has repeatedly noted the non-verisimilitude of his *sujets,* but the author of **"The Snowstorm"** and *Dubrovsky* was himself least concerned with this aspect of his novellas. The verisimilitude of the *povest',* according to his literary esthetics, could be extremely relative and provisory. This is quite inconsequential.

The improbability of the *sujet,* its fantastic nature and the unnaturalness can freely extend to the boundary where this non-verisimilitude begins to spoil the interest of the story. This is what Pushkin is actually concerned with.

Let **"Mistress into Maid"** be a series of impossible *quid pro quos,* **"The Snowstorm"** a chain of improbable coincidences, **"The Queen of Spades"** a sequence of fateful chance happenings, and *Dubrovsky*—an outright melodrama: this is completely unimportant for their author. He requires above all a vivid, volatile, flowing and entertaining *fabula,* a fascinating dramatic intrigue which is capable of seizing immediately the reader and not releasing him for an instant during the course of the entire story. Hence, the particular devices which result in a stimulation of the reader's interest in what follows in the narrative: a sequence of intriguing epigraphs, the ability to cut off a chapter on an alluring question, and what is practically a complete absence of comments or digressions from the mainline of the *sujet.* All this creates an impetuous and quick tempo in the story, increasing fascination with the most improbable episodes, which, nonetheless, serve admirably the basic authorial purpose.

In this regard, Pushkin's response to Prince Vyazemsky, who in Zagoskin's *Roslavlev* did not find "truth either in a single thought, or in a single emotion, or in a single situation," is characteristic. Agreeing with Vyazemsky the poet all the same justifies the novel. To Vyazemsky's formula it is necessary to add only three lines: "that situations even though they are drawn out, are entertaining, that conversations, even though they be contrived, are vivid and that it is possible to read everything with pleasure." Entertainment, vividness, and the absorbing nature of the story, this is what condones the overstraining of situations and the contrived nature of characters and dialogues . . .

Pushkin's *povest'* is built on the entertaining fabula; this is its basic core and major impulse. In his treatment Russian prose doubtless assumes the veneer of the adventure story purged only from the excesses of this genre by high taste, a severe artistry and an admirable stylistic discipline which Pushkin has learned from the models of French prose of the eighteenth century.

This vast area of Pushkiniana—from the *Tales of Belkin* to the letters and notes of the poet—demands constant reference to the prose of Voltaire and Montesquieu. Outside of this tradition it defies explanation.

This is why the elements of sociological painting or psychological *etudes* are present in Pushkin's prose only incidentally, for obviously auxiliary purposes, retreating in all instances to the secondary scheme and nowhere masking the pointed and distinct core of the fabulistic character that rules all.

This is the basic, organic and profoundly conscious quality of the Pushkin story. For, of course, in his prose he is above all the raconteur, the storyteller, the collector and publisher of yarns, the master of anecdotes which are developed into *povesti,* and of *povesti* which recall brief tales. At the center of this art the *sujet* exercises its tyrannical reign.

This gift of story-telling, the ability to transmit, succinctly, and entertainingly a humorous or rare incident, to weave a novella, to introduce impetuously and pointedly an intrigue—this is what he was so deeply preoccupied with, particularly in the 1830s. What N. N. Raevsky called in one of his letters to Pushkin *narre rapide,* i.e., a swift unraveling of the *fabula,* the impetuous succession of events, the hastening tempo of narration, becomes the conscious task and organic requirement of his artistic nature.

The good *povest'* according to the views of Pushkin, should realize these principal requirements of a rapid tempo, succinct volume and an entertaining *sujet.* In a letter to Marlinsky he himself lets fall a significant definition: "quick-tempoed *povesti* with romantic transitions."

Is it at all surprising that Pushkin turned to the anecdote? Would it seem strange that this smallest but typical form of the novella which represents in the fabulistic sense a model of the accelerated, succinct and entertaining story, ought to occupy an outstanding place in the poetics and works of Pushkin?

The sophisticated and knowledgeable artist closely examined the artistic richness of this minor literary genre which goes back to the ancient novellette of the Trecento, with its requirements of a pointed novelty of *sujet* and a terse brevity in its treatment.

"In order to shine with wittiness," remarks one German scholar, "not only a power that can inspire flashes of brilliance is necessary, but the height as well from which they fall." This, so it would seem, is the best explanation of that high perfection which the forgotten art of the anecdote has attained in the work of Pushkin.

Notes

[1] We should mention yet another successful definition. Nikolai Grech associates with the category of "prosaic *povesti*" also the "shortest *povesti* or anecdotes of which the genuine ones belong to history. The character of their composition is brevity, clarity, simplicity. In anecdotes the pointed word or unexpected turnabout must occur at the end. They should be expressed as briefly as possible in order not to draw them out and render them flaccid. Nikolai Grech, *Textbook of Russian Literature (Uchebnaia kniga russkoi slovesnosti),* St. P., 1844, Part III, 386.

Valentin Nepomnyashchy (essay date 1974)

SOURCE: "On Pushkin's Evolution as a Poet in the 'Thirties (*The Tale of the Golden Cockerel*)," in *Soviet Literature*, No. 6 (315), 1974, pp. 141-67.

[*In the following essay, Nepomnyashchy examines Pushkin's verse fairy-tale,* The Tale of the Golden Cockerel, *acknowledging its significance to Pushkin's work of the 1830s.*]

The Tale of the Golden Cockerel is one of the strangest of Pushkin's compositions in the 'thirties.[1] Even alongside such works as **The Queen of Spades** or **The House at Kolomna** it is marked out by its mysterious, "hermetic" quality, by what you might describe as the difficulty of approaching it. Inseparably belonging to Pushkin's cycle of Russian fairy-tales, it stands on its own, markedly different from the

previous ones in the structure of its imagery, its stylistic features and its whole sombre-grotesque, puzzling and oddly unusual character.

For a long time the source of the plot was unknown. Almost a century after the fairy-tale first appeared, Anna Akhmatova discovered that Pushkin's source was the *Legend of the Arabian Astrologer,* a tale in Washington Irving's collection of short stories, *The Legends of the Alhambra*[2], now widely known to Russian readers. This discovery was the biggest and, in fact, the first serious step in studying **The Tale of the Golden Cockerel;** comparing it with its source, Akhmatova made several extremely important observations and conclusions (and I shall return to some of these) regarding the nature of the tale and its links with the dramatic circumstances of Pushkin's life in the 'thirties. In Akhmatova's view, what attracted Pushkin was a certain vitally real "outline," which rose in his imagination on reading Irving's story; then in 1834, one of the hardest years in his life, this "outline" was filled in with "autobiographical material"—and the tale was written; Akhmatova defined the theme as "the Tsar not keeping his promise," explaining the poet's interest in this theme by the sudden deterioration of the poet's relations with the tsar.

This is just a bare statement and it does not explain very much. We can hardly understand and explain anything in **The Tale of the Golden Cockerel** if we restrict the tale's content to its external biographical implications, which are in turn limited simply to the fact of "the tsar not keeping the promise" which Nicholas had given Pushkin in their conversation in 1826. The cause of a phenomenon and the phenomenon itself are not one and the same thing. And the "autobiographical material" to which Akhmatova refers is only the rightly disclosed "upper layer" through which, when it has been removed, we can go further and deeper, linking our analysis of this tale not only with the external facts of Pushkin's life, but also with his spiritual biography as a man and creative artist.

Among Pushkin's sketches in 1833 there is a wonderful fragmentary picture in rhyming couplets:

> *Near at hand the Tsar of fable*
> *Saw a chessboard on a table.*
>
> *On the board a troop of soldiers,*
> *Out of wax minutely moulded,*
> *He in even ranks arrayed.*
> *Proudly did the toys parade,*
> *Arms akimbo on their horses,*
> *Little fists in cotton gauntlets,*
> *Plumes in helmets made of wax,*
> *Sabres on their little backs.*
>
> *Then a basin at his order*
> *Straight away was filled with water;*

There he placed and left afloat
Many a splendid sailing boat,
Schooner, brigantine and frigate,
Each into a nutshell fitted. . . .

. . . . .

. . . . .

Sheer the sails were, small in size,
Like the wings of butterflies,
And the ropes. . . .

For many years the reason why this charming miniature remained unfinished was not clear, just as its very origin was unknown. As a result of Akhmatova's researches, it became evident that this episode is a preliminary to ***The Tale of the Golden Cockerel*** and bears an undisputed correspondence to Irving's *Legend of the Arabian Astrologer*. There a magician and astrologer has made a wonderful weathercock—a horseman who points his lance in the direction of danger—for a Moorish sultan named Aben Habuz, old and feeble but extremely warlike in the past; he also presents the sultan with a chessboard on which, without leaving the palace and even without sending his troops out, Aben Habuz can deal with his enemies by knocking the figures over with a magic wand.

Pushkin was fascinated by this episode, but soon gave up working on it—evidently because it was an unnecessary complication of the plot of the tale then taking shape in his imagination, based on Irving's theme.

But it was not only a question of plot. This fragment—with the wealth of its description, its love of detail and its good-natured humour ("Proudly did the toys parade . . ."), in its whole essence is rather near to ***The Tale of Tsar Saltan.*** In ***The Tale of the Golden Cockerel,*** instead of the picturesque and full-blooded world of the Island of Buyan over which a carefree sea breeze blows, another world has sprung up that is sketchily symbolic, almost unreal and yet nevertheless bears the imprint of a strange reality in which the impenetrability of mystery is combined with prosaic authenticity.

In this new reality there is no place for good-natured laughter and sly humour—here only lips are stretched in a smile, the eyes remain unsmiling. Vagueness, mystery, duality, uncertainty are imprinted with meticulous precision upon this new reality.

It is not just another fairy-tale. It is another dimension.

The living play of human faces and the riot of colour become a cold glitter, and phantoms come floating into the harmonious world of Russian fairy-tale.

Indeed, one does not know where Pushkin's all-knowing eunuch-astrologer comes from and disappears to, or what sort of a person he is; this "old man" is not characterised at all. He is featureless: his speech is colourless and does not contain a single characteristic, striking or personal expression; his monotone monologue which consists of long and complex sentences but is entirely devoid of *intonation*, contains nothing but bare technical instructions: and even in the later repetitive demands the old man makes: "Give me the maiden Queen of Shamakha in payment. . . . All I ask for is the maiden! . . ." one also hears an icily-dispassionate and inhuman note.

We do not know who this strange Queen of Shamakha is: she shines "like the morning star" and that is all—nothing more is known of her, she is featureless; one does not know why she appeared, what she needs Dadon for, why she was silent all the time, then suddenly chuckled when the astrologer was killed—and disappeared. . . .

We do not know, lastly, what the golden cockerel itself is: a sentinel or instrument of temptation, an executioner or judge? Why does it so insistently send Dadon against the Queen of Shamakha and why was the death of both Dadon's sons needed?

In this new reality phenomena, personages and events are not presented to us visually in the flesh, as in Pushkin's other fairy-tales, where even a little devil has his own features and a dog a character of its own—but are designated drily, in passing, in an undertone, as it were, and described as: "the neighbours," "rumour," "the people," "army," "city"—and as a result all this together, as it were, both exists and does not exist, it is assumed to exist and at the same time it is cast doubt upon with an ambiguous laugh.

And why did Pushkin suddenly need an Oriental legend in his cycle of Russian fairy-tales?

I am speaking here of the particular structure of the tale, of its artistic flesh.

It is plain, of course, that "flesh" is not the right word here—here there is least substance, least flesh of all compared with the other Pushkin's tales where the folklore "skeleton" is "covered" with the living material of human existence and three-dimensional characters.

Here there is no flesh, only a skeleton; no free fantasy but chill objectivity; no open frank emotion, not even an implication, but the riddle of bare fact.

The orientally-lavish and intricate design of Irving's Arab legend gives place here to an ascetic brevity, which creates a deceptive impression of un-pretentiousness and simplicity: the plot of the tale (which takes about 16-17 pages of a medium-sized book) is sharply reduced in length, connecting links are taken out, details removed, the exposition is compressed to twenty-five lines; the number of episodes is reduced to the minimum, particular moments of the action are not unfolded in detail but, on the contrary, tightened up, thereby intensifying the springing dynamics of the whole; the "bare simplicity" of expression, giving the semblance of an absence of premeditation or cunning, is brought to the extreme point of tension, the draperies of picturesque description and psychological nuance are torn away—and coming at the end of a series of full-blooded fairy-tale fantasies Pushkin's last tale seems to be a skeleton, with an ironic smile laying bare the formidable *root of the matter*. Without in any way explaining this root, the narrative rushes to its conclusion where we expect to find, at last, an unravelling of the mystery, some secret meaning revealed. . . .

But the conclusion comes as a fresh puzzle. And the thought crosses one's mind that the reader hunting for the truth has, like Dadon, been pursuing a phantom. A dizzy coda follows—the ringing flight of the Cockerel which suddenly dashes off its perch, Dadon's instant and frighteningly naturalistic death: he "cried once in agony—and died." And after this execution—as unexpected as thunder from a clear sky—for which the reader, busy solving the riddle of it all and put off his track by the general tone of irony, is unprepared—the headlong stream of happenings is cut short almost in mid-sentence. Everything collapses into emptiness— "like an illusion." The puzzling tale comes up against the no less puzzling "hint" which with a mocking smile ("Not a true tale") we are invited to decipher and understand and also draw from our understanding the necessary "lesson."

But to do this one must understand everything from the very beginning.

It may seem that the swift and purposeful advance to the root of the matter in which we are engaged, carries us in a circle not allowing us to approach the centre.

. . . . .

After the collapse of rationalism and the views of the Enlightenment on nature and history there began to take shape once again the facets of life upon which the 18th century with its ability to find an explanation for everything had turned its back. Carried away by Voltaire in his youth, in the 'thirties Pushkin already had quite a different attitude to the "pitiful sceptical intellectualising of the last century." *The Devils, The Wanderer* and *The Tales of Belkin* with their deceptive artlessness, *The Queen of Spades* and a number of other works show that the author of *The Song of Bacchus* and *The Tale of Tsar Saltan*

was increasingly interested in and drawn to what he himself defined as something "beyond the grasp of reason."

Lending an air of tragedy to this change, the situation which arose in the country after the watershed events of December 1825, gave real life an air of absurdity.

This absurdity affected Pushkin's behaviour in a particular way.

The absurdity lay in the fact that he still went on believing for some time in the possibility of enjoying "peace and freedom"; in the fact that while thirsting for peace he craved for activity.

But life without any hesitation quickly brought him to his senses. The surveillance, the constant interference in his life and activities, the conferring of a humiliating court post, lastly—and this was worse and more intolerable than anything else—the multiple censorship, the outcome of the tsar's gradual, deliberate and consistent violation of his own royal promise to remain Pushkin's sole censor. "In 1834 Pushkin knew what the Tsar's word was worth," Akhmatova correctly states, linking *The Tale of the Golden Cockerel* with this fact.

The year 1834 was the knot in which all the threads of this game drew together. By that time it had gradually become clear that not only was there "no happiness" for Pushkin "in this world," but also no "peace and freedom" either.

At no previous time does one find in Pushkin's letters so many recklessly-furious onslaughts on "the masters." Never until now had he been so soberly aware of the full depth of humiliation of a bard drawn close to the throne.

"Do not be angry, wife, and do not set a bad interpretation upon my complaints. I never thought to reproach you for my dependency. I had to marry you, because without you I would have been wretched all my life; but I should not have taken an official post and, what is even worse, entangled myself in financial obligations. . . . Like Lomonosov, I do not wish to be a jester for anyone, even for God himself. But it is not you who are to blame for all this— I am to blame as a result of my goodnaturedness, with which I am overflowing to the point of folly, despite the experience of life. Take care . . . no doubt your letters, too, are being opened: the state security requires this."

The letter is dated June 8, 1834, the year of soberness, of his new awareness of the nature of the world he is living in. And he administers the despairing reproof in his letter with an already complete realisation and even direct calculation that not only the eyes of Natalia Nikolayevna will read his letter with close attention.

. . . . .

. . . It is now, by the way, time we remembered the person who has long been considered the main character in the tale. In an unusual and colourless country, where no *individual people* exist, where the entourage of the Tsar himself is represented by a conventional "army commander," where even the Tsar's sons we see only when they are dead, along with other mysterious and almost fleshless figures of fantasy—in such a world the famous Tsar Dadon lives a full-blooded life, enjoys peace, gives orders, worries, goes into raptures, weeps, delights in honours paid to him, feasts, sleeps and even swears, quarrels, spits and even "thinks."

In the austere presentation of the story he is a bright patch of colour, his movements, gestures and reactions are characteristic, his language is expressive and juicy, rich in elements of common speech and foklore.

It seems as if certain features of the previous fairy-tales, some fragments of their style, are returned to us in Dadon for a special purpose. The living characteristics of a *Russian man* are set beside and grafted onto the "alien" manner of the tale with its literary stylisation and abstract drawing.

Yet Dadon is not simply a Russian fairy-tale character.

The contemporary words and phrases, which distinguish ***The Tale of the Golden Cockerel*** and have long been noticed in it, are not just "utilised" by the author, they are emphasised. Words of the present day, of contemporary conversation, letters and newspaper articles spring up here and there, like resounding blows, in the course of the fantastic plot, against a background of arid reticence and alongside folklorish, "fairy-tale" and "old-fashioned" words.

A jarring planned "dissonance" arises between the literary genre and the style. For the first time in the whole cycle the fairy-tale form is frankly presented as a mask on the face of contemporary man. The fairy-tale begins to border on comment upon news of the day.

Dadon's striking and colourful quality is the vividness of an expertly drawn and very neat caricature; his liveliness is the mobility of a puppet stitched together from motley rags.

And the main means used here prove to be elements of Russian folk poetry placed in an alien setting.

Nothing is easier than to note—as has been universally recognised—"the satirical use of folklore means."

But why are folk-poetry resources in Pushkin's last fairy-tale not used in various ways but linked exclusively with satire, why with emphatic vividness do they appear in their satirical function and set off the satire—and are reduced to nil where there is no need for satirical parody?

It is probably because in Pushkin's last fairy-tale the folklore style is itself the object of parody on a particular plane.

Akhmatova writes: "Pushkin squashed, as it were, the plot he borrowed from Irving." This is true, but there is more to it than that.

Everything was "squashed," shifted, moved about and given different fantastic configurations. The former characters, which were full of life, remained in a country of ancient invention; here reality was presented, on the one hand, in the shape of fleshless chimeras and, on the other, in the lively caricature of a despot, a father and a man. The "famous Tsar Saltan" has given place to "the famous Tsar Dadon"; the apotheosis of a strong family is replaced by the portrayal of fratricide; good-natured humour is twisted to irony and sarcasm, admiration of the beauty of the human body and soul—to a parody of the life of the spirit and of human feelings.

A *squashed* world has taken the place of a splendid, spacious world.

The vast, round universe with its blue sky and blue sea, at the heart of which are a mother and her child who grows "not by days but by the hour," had as its fixed centre the intimate world of the family and was transformed from chaos into cosmos *for the sake of man.*

But here we have the scale of a cubicle, a kitchenette, a hole whence comes the sound of something like the scurrying of mice.

In this world-hole everything is close to hand, with nowhere to turn in, with corners everywhere—and in every corner there is the same life reduced to "scurrying of mice" (Pushkin) and no room for man.

A "foul and pestilent congregation of vapours" (Hamlet), coming from without, has mingled with the pure air of fairy-tales, despite the resistance of the creator, who created the world as his dream. And the customary, old and simple words from which this world was built have begun to go to pieces, to ruffle, to lose their purity of meaning and finally cease to have their age-old message.

A tragic grotesque has emerged in the fairy-tale cycle which is a parody compared with the previous tales.

As Yuri Tynyanov pointed out in one of his early studies, "if comedy is a parody of tragedy, then tragedy can be a parody of comedy."

. . . . .

Only on one occasion, at the central moment when two realities are counterposed: the mysterious reality "beyond the grasp of reason," and the reality of ugly parody—on the boundary between them there comes a flash of lightning.

At the very mid-point of the tale it tears the plot into two, in its sharp light both the strange phantoms and the lively caricature disappear for an instant—and the voice of the narrator trembles; and instead of a headlong whirl, where everything is puzzle, ambiguity and mockery we read:

> *There a sight he saw appalling!*
> *Both his sons before him sprawling*
> *Motionless and deathly pale,*
> *On each other's sword impaled. . . .*

Pushkin has made his central episode the theme of "bloody fratricidal battle" which in the *Legend of the Arabian Astrologer* passes fleetingly in the background. The image of grass, red from blood, grows to a monstrous size in close-up, as it were, in the middle of a narrative shorn of colourful adjectives.

But at the sight of this silent and terrible scene the father-Tsar utters clownish howls. A minute later Dadon has "clean forgot" his two dead sons as lightheartedly as he "lamented," and "for a week" precisely he will now make merry with the "maiden."

The warning is forgotten, the "lesson" remains without consequence—and from this moment the Tsar is doomed.

The scene of fratricide which occupies the central place in the tale is not just a general broad symbol but also a tragic parody of the *theme of the family* as the centre of Pushkin's fairy-tale cycle. Dadon's parody of a reaction and his sacrilegious forgetfulness is a bitter mockery of the principal idea of the previous fairy-tale, *the idea of love and loyalty*—it is its perverted, "squashed" semblance. The last prop, the spiritual prop which held together the **Tale of the Dead Princess** is here destroyed.

And then man—the "beauty of the world," the "paragon of animals"—becomes a soulless puppet.

> *Proudly did the toys parade,*
> *Arms akimbo on their horses . . .*

And then it becomes quite clear why Pushkin rejected the fragment about the chessboard. The episode was needed only as an intermediary link between the legend and Pushkin's fairy-tale parody, it was needed as raw material, as a prototype of *the whole world* of this fairy-tale.

For the squashed world of Dadon is *in fact the chessboard.*

And all Dadon's actions and utterances from this point on bear the character of being quite obviously *sham.* Everything he says and does acquires either a paradoxical, contrary meaning or a secret, mockingly literal meaning which even he himself is unaware of.

He feasts like a victor, like the successful winner of a magnificent trophy—but his feast resembles a stupidly mechanical dance.

He returns with his armed men and with the young maiden, rumour races ahead of him, the people run along behind him—but who is this "maiden," what are all his "armed men" in face of her?

He meets his "old friend" the sage and condescendingly says to him: "Pray come closer! *What's your pleasure?*" and does not suspect that the phrase "what's your pleasure?" (in the Russian text—"what's your bidding?") has a literal meaning that spells his own fate.

Replying to the astrologer's demand he says in surprise: "A devil's in you . . ."—but the words refer to himself.

He says with irony: "You're going off your nut!"—not realising that he himself is the madman.

He admonishes the astrologer gravely: "I, of course, did promise, but there's a limit"—and is unaware that with the yardstick of his tiny chessboard he is trying to measure something that is *boundless;* and that he will soon reach his own "limit". . . .

Lastly—"And what good is she to you, sir?" he asks the old eunuch with murderous sarcasm. . . .

And what use is she indeed?

In Irving's story the wizard is a perfectly real old man with a character of his own and, moreover, a fastidious voluptuary, a chaser after Oriental luxury and feminine beauty. Pushkin's astrologer is a eunuch. And this is the only thing we really know about him. Nevertheless, rejecting the fabulous rewards which he is offered, he monotonously repeats: "Give me the maiden. . . . "

Because he is following *the rules of the game.*

And poor Dadon, shouting at the astrologer in his fury: "Nothing, that shall be your portion. Blame yourself for your misfortune . . ." (in the Russian text: "*You shall receive nothing.* You, *sinner,* bring trouble upon yourself . . ."), cannot understand this, he cannot grasp the rules of this game.

For it never enters his head that he himself is the "sinner" and that the astrologer *has no intention at all of "taking" anything from him.*

"That's enough now! *You know me!* Ask for anything you please—all my gold, a lofty title, or my finest horse and bridle . . ." he says grandly in front of the sage—and does not give a thought to the absurdity of what he says.

Dadon's triumph in his carriage is a celebration on top of a volcano, yet another "feast during the plague." And the strange chuckle of the Queen of Shamakha, who is apparently "unafraid of villainy" (in the Russian text: "Apparently does not fear sin") is the mockery of fate over the "sinner" who is celebrating his own doom.

Dadon is given only one opportunity to declare frankly and unambiguously the truth about himself—when, at the sight of the death and blood of his sons, who have fought over their trophy, he bursts out—in the midst of his mock-ritual laments—with a phrase to which even indifferent nature responds with a "groaning" but which remains only a ritual phrase for Dadon himself:

"Woe is me! I am undone! Now the time to die has come!"

And the time came but Dadon did not heed the warning, for he was blinded "like an owl" when the sunlight reaches.

The further he proceeds and the brighter it is around him, the more hopelessly blind he becomes. And when at the end of the road Dadon is offered salvation, he spits and brandishes his royal mace.

For the whole of his career, from his youth, from the very outset, has been that of an "unrighteous" man, of one for whom, according to the Koran, the supreme punishment waits:

"Allah *mocks them and confirms the error* in which they blindly wander!"

The confirmation of error is the most terrible punishment for one who has yielded to error from his youth. And here lies the "punitive" function of the irony with which the fairy-tale stresses the mysterious nature of what happens to the hero convinced that order exists all around him.

Only some of the *Imitations of the Koran,* which Pushkin wrote in exile, can compare with *The Tale of the Golden Cockerel* in their triumphant mercilessness. It had proved impossible to escape from the "devils" by making the sign of the cross or shunning them—one had to join open battle with them. *The Golden Cockerel,* the puppet-like, spiritless world of Dadon, records the world of *dead souls* which was being born.

In order not to become one of them, in order not "to turn stale and finally turn to stone," a man had to fight for his humanity, for his living soul and not become a puppet in the hands of puppets.

. . . . .

Gradually there emerges in clear outline one of the explanations why an Oriental legend appears in the cycle of fairy-tales.

A man of passion and ardour, Pushkin was not by poetic nature a "punitive" and "vengeful" person—his gift of artistic objectivity, his keen interest in studying life and men and not in passing sentence upon them, prevented this.

But the idea of retribution and of struggle presented itself to him on one occasion as a necessity: "They now look on me as a serf whom they can treat as they like . . ."; "But I can be a subject, even a slave, but not a serf or jester even for the Lord of Heaven."

At this point Pushkin, with his gift of re-incarnation, of changing into other bodies like Proteus, found support in the Oriental legend and in the militant spirit of the Koran with which he had long been familiar. . . .

Then indeed he found the "model" of his own fate in that of the astrologer-sage with his grey hair and swan whiteness—the colour of purity, light and wisdom, with the secret and precious gift that he entrusted to the Tsar "as to a friend" in return for a promise, and when the time came for the promise to be fulfilled, he received ("Pray come closer! What's your pleasure?") a blow from the royal mace on his forehead. . . .

Then another "model" began to "function," one in which a similar other-existence is acquired by the poet's prophetic gift, by his secret muse, "the mysterious maiden," and the formidable might of his priceless treasure—the "word" with which he is endowed, the power that grants gifts and punishments.

Starting as a ghostly whirl of half-statements and hints, the rush of events in the second half of the fairy-tale is accelerated. The triumphant flight of the Cockerel, the fall of the Tsar and his last groan are presented with solidly precise authenticity, with "poetic horror," as if this scene were swiftly brought before our eyes by a powerful hand and a firm voice were bidding "him who hath ears to hear."

When Dadon proudly tells the sage: "That's enough now! *You know me!*" (in the Russian text: "Do you know who I am?"), Dadon does not hear in his question the fateful *contrary meaning*. Does Dadon himself know who he is? And what lies ahead? And what sort of a game he takes part in?

. . . . .

The Golden Cockerel was not only a political satire.

Even in his most "non-personal" work Pushkin is writing about himself. His own life can be seen even in plots and situations that might seem to have no connection with him.

There is nothing surprising in this statement, it might seem. But the point is that I am now referring to *Dadon*.

Not only is the fairy-tale as a whole a parody-tragedy, but the fate of Dadon is a tragic self-parody and self-satire; judgement is carried out and the laughter of mockery is also aimed at the author himself.

Thus Pushkin, moving away from his Russian tales towards an Oriental legend retold by an American, moving away from his own self and his own humane objectivity to the supra-personal and fierce atmosphere of the Koran, again arrives back at himself.

This constitutes the tragic nature of *The Golden Cockerel.*

. . . . .

Let us now finish with the question of biographical applications and return to the fairy-tale as a literary fact of general significance.

Anna Akhmatova repeated the common error in pointing to "lack of clarity" in the story and to "discrepancies in the plot" of *The Golden Cockerel.* There is no such thing in the tale. The general error springs from regarding Tsar Dadon as the leading personage, proceeding only from the fact he is placed "in the foreground." People have thought the story is centred on Dadon and that the plot could be understood from studying Dadon's behaviour. They have tried to explain the meaning of what happens from the viewpoint of Dadon. But this is like explaining the meaning of Breughel's famous painting from the "viewpoint" of the blind persons portrayed in it.

Dadon is not the "main" character.

The plot of the tale cannot be understood from Dadon's actions, because there are *no such actions.* They are

illusions, throughout the whole story Dadon *performs no actions.* "Rule-and-doodle, Tsar, that's you!" (in the Russian text: "Rule, lying on your side!") is the formula of his whole life.

From the viewpoint of Dadon himself he is making progress, whereas in fact he is just going round in a circle to where he started from. He continually returns to himself, unwinds a single ball, reproducing in his "actions" one and the same *passive pattern:*

"In his old age" he "desired relaxation"—*without having any right to do so.*

To the mutual fratricide of his sons he responds only with wailing—and, instantly forgetting and betraying them, he plunges into pleasures which he is accustomed to take *"just like that," giving nothing in return.*

When, for the first and last time in his life, he is told he must *pay* and pay in full and that he has at last to perform an action, he takes it to be folly, an insult and nonsense.

And when with his royal mace he strikes the person to whom he should *make repayment,* it is the only blow in his life which does no harm to anybody—because the last circle has closed up and he has struck a blow at himself, at one stroke straight away paying for everything and surrendering everything. This is an instance of the suicide which Balzac described in *La peau de chagrin* and Oscar Wilde in *The Portrait of Dorian Grey,* where the hero himself pays "measure for measure" with his own life.

It is quite evident that it is not a question here of "covetousness," not a problem of "applied ethics" at all, indeed not a simply moral problem. " 'Poetry stands above morality," Pushkin wrote, "or is at any rate a totally different matter." Here there is a formula of life, the "metaphysics of fate." And from this angle the question of merciless punishment bearing down from outside—and the question of physical death—do not arise. For man unleashes that which he himself has wound up and we are confronted with a precise formula of the law, while physical death is only its particular instance. "Anatomy is not murder," wrote the author of the fairy-tale.

The general error in understanding *The Golden Cockerel* also sprang from regarding the astrologer, the "maiden" and the Cockerel as characters of secondary importance because, compared with Dadon, they are placed in the background—and from viewing them accordingly in distant perspective, so to say.

But it is not the "plane" that is decisive here. Pushkin's placing of his characters reveals the "method" of the ancient icon-painters which was much later given the name of "reverse perspective."

And for this reason, taking the "viewpoint" of Dadon, who knows nothing about himself, not to mention the astrologer, the Queen of Shamakha or his own Golden Cockerel, the reader will always see confusion and discrepancies and will never grasp what is evident from another "viewpoint," precisely that Pushkin's fairy-tale is *not a "tale" of Black chessmen* but that here *White* is "playing," and from such a viewpoint the story becomes remarkably well-knit.

The "coherence" consists above all in the fact that there are in the fairy-tale, apart from Dadon, *not three other* characters, as people think, but only *one* character; the wonderful Golden Cockerel, the Queen "shining like the morning star," the old man, grey as a swan and wearing a white hat—are not "connected" to each other but presented by Pushkin as a single whole. The consequent "clarity" lies above all in the fact that Dadon not only never was and never shall be "master" of the Queen of Shamakha, free to "give" or "not give" her away—from the very beginning nothing in the world belongs to Dadon. It is not he who can give or not give something to the astrologer, but *it is to him that presents are given* and his fate depends precisely on how he disposes of what he is given.

If Dadon had realised this, he would not have buried within himself the only force that belongs to himself—his own soul; that generous and salutary force, the lack of which makes him a parody of a father and of a man in the central episode of the "lamenting" of his sons and the feast beside their dead bodies.

If he had grasped this, he would not have been a heartless, passive plaything of fate, he would not have been truly alone in the face of destiny. And fate would not have appeared to him to be a riddle and nonsense.

But the fairy-tale proceeds differently and is about something different. Dadon understands none of this. Moreover, with Pushkin the misfortune of the Tsar is precisely that he understands everything in the reverse. And for this reason, regarding himself as master of the world, blinded by pride, he is not even master of himself, he is like a puppet. It is about this misfortune that the fairy-tale is written and not about Dadon himself. And its significance goes beyond the bounds not only of political satire, but much further still.

. . . . .

The image and symbol of a bird, often linked with notions of the creation of the world and of its end, occupy a great and often very important place in ancient philosophy, in mythology, in the metaphysics of ancient notions of the world, reflected in folk tales, too.

The cock is also the symbol of sun and light in the ancient beliefs of many peoples, from the Greeks and Slav tribes to the Chinese.

The same image is linked with the notion of the "Day of Judgement."

In the *Golubinaya Kniga*[3] one of the most important places is taken by the figure of the bird Straphil, which frequently has an eschatological connotation and is connected with the light-bearing theme of the cock.

The element of "accidental coincidence" in Pushkin's work was always close to the minimum. Pushkin had a fabulously great knowledge and we are still amazed to find ever new evidence of his learning in seemingly most unexpected fields. Some of these are easy to discover, others are hidden much deeper.

In those years Pushkin was closely in touch with Pyotr Kireyevsky, to whom he was drawn, as is well known, by a common interest in folklore. And there is no doubt he knew religious poetry well.

At any rate, *The Tale of the Fisherman and the Fish* (1833), which in spirit and content is the closest to *The Golden Cockerel* of all Pushkin's fairy-tales, is definite testimony to this acquaintance.

The author of *The Tale of the Golden Cockerel* knew, and knew well, the *Golubinaya Kniga*, which also specially interested Kireyevsky—it is a work which one researcher has described as "a pearl of Russian Biblical-mythological ballad."

It is worth noting the fact that in Pushkin's last fairy-tale the theme of the bird is *a theme running through the whole poem* and one which emerges at *turning-points in the plot.*

> *. . . and he shall*
> *Be your loyal sentinel,*
> *Shall my golden cockerel!*
>
> *. . . Like an owl the sunlight reaches,*
> *Hypnotised at once and speechless,*
> *In her presence Tsar Dadon . . .*

And the "venerable" astrologer-sage is described as being "all white *like a swan* . . ."

The last image, that of the white swan, which is unexpected and, it might seem, devoid of any explanation in this "dry land" fairy-tale, is now explicable. The explanation arises from a blending of the mythological theme of *the bird and the sea* in the poem of the "blue, swan" book—and the theme of the vast ocean expanses in *The Tale of Tsar Saltan,* of Pushkin's theme of "the free element," which in *The Tale of the Fisherman and the Fish* carries out its "absolute judgement." At the end of Pushkin's last fairytale, the tale of a squashed, blood-smeared world, defiled by fratricide and plunged in darkness, the theme of the swan, the colour of the white divine-sent cockerel, the radiance of purity, light and truth, erupts triumphantly.

. . . . .

Pushkin's last fairy-tale—this "mysterious" work, the sole work of his last autumn at Boldino and one of the most amazing examples of the laconism of Pushkin's major literary forms—occupies a particular place and is of unusually great significance in the poet's literary and emotional life. It is not the outline" (as Akhmatova describes it), which Pushkin took from Irving's Oriental legend, that was the receptacle he "filled" with autobiographical material—but on the contrary: the autobiographical "material," his personal living and spiritual experience served to give meaning to an "outline" of universal significance.

The process concluded with *The Tale of the Golden Cockerel* saw, on the one hand, a repetition—in an original, unique, reflected way—of the story of the destruction of the literary form of ancient fairy-tale, which had already long ago ceased its "active" existence in creative folk art, yielding to other forms of mankind's self-awareness and awareness of their proper place in the world. Accordingly, on the other hand, in Pushkin's work of the 'thirties the rebirth, evolution and destruction of this literary form—an inner destruction, for the outward form of it still remained—opened up new paths and made clear a "lesson" of immense significance. It is precisely in the interaction between Pushkin's developed "method" and one of the most ancient and "youthful" forms of folk art that a "model" was born that was, perhaps, the most expressive and internally compressed of all—and for that very reason capable of endless "development" in manifold significance and universality—a "model" which in certain respects plays, perhaps, a key role in the work of the later Pushkin.

Notes

[1] This article, published originally in the journal *Voprosy Literatury* ("Problems of Literature") No. 11, 1973, is reprinted in an abridged form for reasons of space.

[2] Anna Akhmatova, *Pushkin's Last Fairy-Tale; Zvezda* No. 1, 1933.

[3] *Golubinaya Kniga* is a Russian religious poem. *Kniga* means book. The adjective stems from *glubinnaya*—

profound, *glubokaya*—deep, and this suggests stillness and wisdom—*Ed.*

Robert Karpiak (essay date 1980)

SOURCE: "Pushkin's *Little Tragedies:* The Controversies in Criticism," in *Canadian Slavonic Papers,* Vol. XXII, No. 1, March, 1980, pp. 80-91.

[*In the following essay, Karpiak surveys twentieth-century thematic criticism of Pushkin's dramas* The Covetous Knight, Mozart and Salieri, *and* The Stone Guest.]

"There is nothing more difficult," wrote Vissarion Belinskii, "than to speak about a work of literature which is great in its totality and in its parts." "To such works," he continues, "belong *Skupoi rytsar', Motsart i Sal'eri,* and *Kamennyi gost'*."[1] The veracity of Belinskii's assessment of Alexander Pushkin's *Little Tragedies* (Malen'kie tragedii) as creations of high artistic merit and, at the same time, of high problematic complexity is well-substantiated. Important not only as masterpieces of Pushkin's *oeuvre,* but also as innovative developments in the evolution of Russian dramatic literature, this cycle of brief plays has long attracted the attention of scholars and has given rise to a voluminous body of critical commentary. Nevertheless, despite numerous efforts of critics, the task of providing a definitive and generally accepted understanding of the major conceptual problems presented in the *Little Tragedies* continues to evade solution.

Commenting on the state of the art in the early 1950s, B.P. Gorodetskii remarked that although the textological aspects had undergone quite thorough investigation, the problematic aspects (*problematika,* i.e., themes, ideas, characters, etc.) of these works still needed further study.[2] Much, however, has been written since then and, as the 150th anniversary of the famous "Boldino autumn" approaches, a new spate of critical commentary may well be expected. It is therefore timely, in anticipation of these commemorative events, to consider some of the fundamental problems posed by the *Little Tragedies* and to offer an overview of some of the critical responses to these problems. This paper is not intended as a comprehensive survey of studies on the *Little Tragedies.* Its purpose is simply to present a selected cross section of interpretative views chosen on the basis of general accessibility and representative quality. The dramas considered are *Skupoi rytsar'* (*The Covetous Knight*), *Motsart i Sal'eri* (*Mozart and Salieri*), and *Kamennyi gost'* (*The Stone Guest*). *Pir vo vremia chumy* (*The Feast During the Plague*), inasmuch as it is a translated excerpt from John Wilson's *The City of the Plague,* will not be included in this discussion.

N.S. Durylin's characterization of the *Little Tragedies* as "the epilogues of great and complicated lives filled with tremendous struggle and turmoil of the human soul," and as "the resolutions of great tragedies which have been played out before the raising of the curtain,"[3] conveys some idea of the complex foundation upon which these dramas have been built. This complexity is a result partially of the thematics of the plays, and partially of their extraordinary brevity and the celebrated laconicism of their style. Indeed, Pushkin entrusts a great deal of our appreciation of the *Little Tragedies* to the evocative quality of his poetry. This, in combination with the characterological complexity of the protagonists and their conflicting interests, has given rise to the controversies and polemics which are typical of the critical literature surrounding these intellectually challenging works.

The three major plays of the *Little Tragedies* cycle have been viewed by various critics, and indeed by Pushkin himself, as "dramatic investigations" of archetypal human obsessions: avarice, envy, and lust.[4] The problem of fundamental drives and passions, however, is formulated in terms of a juxtaposition, either in the form of collision or in the form of reconciliation, of two apparently incompatible concepts. Thus, in *Skupoi rytsar'* the moral problem of covetousness underlies an ethical question: is chivalry compatible with avarice? Similarly, the problem of envy emerges as a philosophical question in *Motsart i Sal'eri*: is genius compatible with criminality? Finally, in *Kamennyi gost'* the problem of lust manifests itself in the question: is don juanism, i.e., a behavioural pattern of compulsive infidelity, compatible with sincere love? This question is psychological in nature. It is thus not the obvious generalizations of the problems of avarice, envy, and lust that have generated the controversies of the *Little Tragedies,* but rather the formulation of these problems in the specific context and ambience of the dramas themselves.

In the very title of *Skupoi rytsar'* Pushkin underscores the juxtaposition of two seemingly mutually exclusive concepts: chivalry and avarice. Indeed, is the code of knighthood, founded on the lofty principles of valour, succour of the weak and defenceless, and service to a noble ideal, compatible with the image of the Baron as a cruel and egocentric moneygrubber? This ethical question emerges with deliberate and unmistakable intensity at the very climax of the drama where the Baron, challenging his own son to a duel, shouts in his frenzy "Am I a knight no longer?" just before collapsing to the floor and with his dying breath crying out: " . . . where, where are my keys? My keys, my keys!"[5] Where, we may ask, lies the tragedy of such a hero? The answer will depend both upon our understanding of the Baron as a knight and upon our interpretation of the nature of his avarice, of the real significance of gold in the drama.

Belinskii, one of the earliest commentators on *Skupoi rytsar'*, noted the dual role of gold as the object of the Baron's obsession. "You see," wrote Belinskii, "gold is this man's idol. He is filled with a pious reverence toward it; he speaks to it with words of veneration, serves it like a devoted, zealous priest. . . . He also looks at gold as a passionate young man looks at a woman whom he ardently loves and the possession of whom came at the price of some terrible crime, which renders her all the more precious."[6] Thus, gold in the drama fulfills not only the spiritual needs of the Baron, being an object of worship, a cult, but also responds to his sublimated physical needs as a symbol of womanhood. Carl Proffer, in a patently Freudian approach to the sexual symbolism in *Skupoi rytsar'*, asserts what Belinskii had simply suggested. "The trunks of gold are female symbols," declares Proffer. "The 'key' is a phallic symbol—the lock a vaginal symbol."[7] He even points out the homonymic relationship of the Russian words *grudy* (heaps, mounds) and *grudi* (breasts).

The peculiar sensuality of the Baron's obsession with gold has also been observed by D. Blagoi. Having already underscored the poignancy of the eros-thanatos motif in an early study of *Kamennyi gost'*, where he focusses on the perverse sensuality of Don Juan who always prefers love in the presence of death,[8] Blagoi returns to the love-death motif in a recent treatment of *Skupoi rytsar'*. "For the Baron," he writes, "gold is the source not only of a peculiar form of sensuality, but also of the greatest aesthetic pleasures. . . . In putting to rest, that is, in 'killing' his gold—the quintessence of the 'blood, sweat, and tears' that have been shed for it—the Baron 'kills' earthly life."[9] Thus, although he does not overtly state it, Blagoi leaves one with the impression that gold represents not only a woman, but a dead woman—a woman the Baron himself has immolated and derives from his visits to the crypt a sensual pleasure akin to necrophilia.

These two phenomena—the anthropomorphization of gold as a woman and the veneration of gold as a sacrament—are significant not only in terms of the chivalry-avarice juxtaposition, but also in terms of the paternal-filial relationship of Baron Philippe and his son Albert. The superficial conflict between a parsimonious father and his spendthrift progeny assumes the epic proportions of a champion preserving his Beautiful Lady from violation by a rival, of a high priest defending the sanctity of a shrine from desecration by an infidel. In Proffer's psychoanalytical interpretation of this conflict, "the libertine son will come, open his boxes, and 'he will smash the sacred vessels.' The son will be the father's rival for the favors of a (symbolic) woman. The son will murder the father and rob him of his masculinity."[10] In an analogous interpretation, Blagoi compares the Baron to Tsar Boris who is similarly threatened by a pretender.[11]

It is instructive to note that this particular view of the blood feud between the Baron and Albert is to be found even in certain Soviet interpretations of *Skupoi rytsar'*, despite a general avoidance of psychoanalytical and mythological approaches in favour of social ones. N.S. Durylin, for example, commenting on a performance of the Soviet actor Ostuzhev in the role of the Baron, reports that "Ostuzhev rendered an excellent portrayal of the agonizing love the miser bears his golden treasury. And his terror at the thought that his 'dissolute' son will descend into the vault is inspired not by the covetousness and greed of a time-worn skinflint, but by the jealousy of an aging lover toward his young rival."[12]

It would appear from the foregoing that with the ennoblement of the Baron's passion for gold comes the ennoblement of the Baron himself. The conclusion is that not only is knighthood compatible with avarice, but also that this compatibility is the substance of tragedy. The prerevolutionary critic N. Minskii wrote:

> The vulgar, superficial definition of avarice is refuted by Pushkin in the very title *Skupoi rytsar'*. It is possible to be avaricious and remain a knight. These two concepts, it would seem, are compatible. Avarice is one of the all-consuming obsessions, and, like all passions, is an expression of strength, and strength is the only source and the only pledge of honour.[13]

Minskii's interpretation of the problem of *Skupoi rytsar'*, which reflects that of Belinskii, is quite representative of pre-Soviet views on this *Little Tragedy*. As long as the Baron's idealization of gold is recognized, as long as it wields irresistible, mystical dominion over his soul, indeed, as long as gold is not a means to an end but the end itself, Pushkin's title presents no contradiction in terms and the play emerges as a tragedy. If, however, gold is simply a means to an end, if its intrinsic value is regarded only in materialistic terms, then the stature of the Baron declines and the image of the "knight-priest," as Blagoi calls him, degenerates to that of a bourgeois megalomaniac.

In diametric opposition to Minskii's hypothesis that gold is an end unto itself in Pushkin's drama, the Soviet comparativist I. Nusinov concludes that "gold is not an end, but a means. It is [the Baron's] means of defence against servility, against dependence, against disgrace. Gold is his way of satisfying every desire and whim, of realizing any dream. Insofar as gold was for the Baron not an end, but simply a means of realization of a noble human aspiration to independence, the Baron retains all human passions."[14] Here, even though pragmatic considerations have replaced the mystical, idealized significance of gold, the Baron, in Nusinov's interpretation, has preserved at least his humanity, if not his knighthood. But even the humanity of the Baron has been challenged by such recent Soviet critics as A.G. Gukasova who writes: "Avarice kills chivalry in the Baron. . . . To be a human being is to be a knight; but the Baron is a dehumanized man and he is a tragic figure because within him the knightly and the human principles die and he is in full cognition of this fact."[15] Finally, turning to the Baron's anguished question "Am I a knight no longer?", Gukasova reads herein the very verdict of the poet: "Yes, the Baron is no longer a knight, for he is no longer humane; everything chivalrous has degenerated in him. . . . In the finale of the play the miser definitively overcomes the knight, the man, the father."[16] It is clear that one has arrived here at the total rejection of any concordance of the concepts of knighthood and convetousness.

From Gukasova's conclusion, it can be inferred that the tragedy of *Skupoi rytsar'* is founded not as much on the conflict of two protagonists or two generations as it is on the crisis of a man in conflict with himself. Going somewhat further, it is not at all surprising to encounter in Marxist criticism the extrapolation of the crisis from the individual to society as a whole. The conflict of the knight and the usurer within the Baron represents the clash of two worlds: the chivalrous world of the Middle Ages and the mercantile world of the Renaissance. According to the Soviet writer S. Rassadin, "the world of the knight has turned into the world of the money-lender whose profession symbolizes the 'iron age' which later came to be known as the age of the bourgeoisie. This mentality is already incarnated in the knight, the bulwark and symbol of the retreating age of feudalism."[17]

The problem of genius and criminality in criticism of *Motsart i Sal'eri* is reflected not as much in the question whether or not Salieri is a genius as in the motivation for his murder of Mozart. Belinskii, whose perception of the fundamental problem of the drama as "the nature and mutual relationship of talent and genius" is popular even today, pointed out the love-hate dichotomy of Salieri's motivation: "Salieri is so intelligent; he loves and understands music to such a degree that he immediately comprehends that Mozart is a genius and that he, Salieri, is nothing."[18]

The primary motivation for Salieri's criminality, according to Belinskii, is envy, and this envy reaches its apogee with Mozart's ill-fated aphorism "genius is incompatible with villainy." Belinskii concludes that Salieri "knew himself to be capable of evil, and meanwhile a genius himself tells him that genius and crime are incompatible and that consequently he, Salieri, is no genius. So! I am no genius? Then take that—and the poison is slipped into the cup of genius."[19]

In time, however, pre-revolutionary criticism began to discern and indeed to emphasize new dimensions in the psychological make-up of Salieri and in the motivation of the crime. The fact that Salieri is no genius was rarely, if ever, disputed, but the tragic grandeur of a mediocre artist and self-proclaimed "Angel of Destruction" was found in other considerations, namely in Salieri's altruism and messianism. A. Gornfel'd writes of Salieri: "He imagines himself one chosen by historical providence; he must stop Mozart, otherwise not only he with his 'mute glory' but they all—the high priests of music—will perish."[20]

The continuation of this line of thinking is in evidence in early post-revolutionary Russian criticism of *Motsart i Sal'eri.* Referring to Salieri as the "knight-priest of art," Blagoi observed that "Salieri regards his intended murder of Mozart as a certain determinism, as a weighty duty that must be performed for the sake of the salvation of art."[21] I. Nusinov offered an interesting and noteworthy variation on this interpretation of Salieri's motive. "Please note," he writes, "that to kill Mozart is to fulfill that purpose for which he has been chosen by fate. However, for him this purpose is not out of concern for the fate of music itself, but rather for the fate of the servitors of Music."[22] This view clearly underscores the "humanity" of Salieri and his altruistic concern for his fellow man rather than for art as an abstraction. Genius is equated with abnormality, and abnormality which threatens the normalcy of the world must be destroyed.

The articles by Josephine Woll and Robert Louis Jackson are indicative of a divergence in the interpretation of Pushkin's drama between recent western and Soviet criticism. Woll, who focusses on the relationship of Salieri to Othello and Oedipus, underscores the tragic grandeur inherent in the heroes of this *Little Tragedy.* "In *Mozart and Salieri,*" to quote this critic, "the sphere of power is not earthly greatness but art. And in that sphere, Mozart and Salieri are the equivalent of kings or triumvirs. Their actions determine, or at least affect, the future and welfare of art; the artistic heights to which they belong (or aspire) magnify by that much more the consequences of their behaviour."[23] Similarly, Jackson perceives in Salieri the avatar of the mythical Satanic archetype. "Salieri and Satan," he writes, "share not only a superhuman malice, but a common descent from lofty heights. Both have experienced the sublime, both share a never-to-be-extinguished sensibility for the beauty and melody of an unattainable or lost paradise."[24]

The foregoing examples of western critical views of *Motsart i Sal'eri,* in which the theme and protagonists of the play are seen in terms of myth and archetype, contrast remarkably with recent Soviet criticism where is observed a phenomenon similar to that of *Skupoi rytsar',* that is, a decline in the stature of the hero and, consequently, in the stature of the tragedy as a whole. This is perhaps most strikingly represented in the writings of D. Blagoi, which reflect a rather drastic shift in the writer's understanding of the *Little Tragedies.* Blagoi, who in the 1920s wrote of Baron Philippe, of Salieri, and of Don Juan as heroic "knight-priests" in the service of an ideal, who spoke of their passions and deeds as veritable exploits,[25] apparently deferred to current trends in Soviet critical thought and, in the 1960s, retracted his previous judgement with this rather unconvincing attempt at sarcasm: "Salieri would have been very pleased to show this fool [Mozart] this man so insouciantly devoted to living, to what extent he, Salieri, is a fighter for justice in the world, to what extent he is a titan, a spiritual giant—more brilliant, more noble, more lofty, more chaste than he."[26] Further elaboration on this statement by a distinguished Pushkinist is perhaps superfluous, except to recall the judgement of Belinskii cited above: "Salieri is so intelligent . . . that he immediately comprehends that Mozart is a genius and that he, Salieri, is nothing." These contrasting views are suggestive of the limitations of contemporary Soviet critical approaches to the *Little Tragedies.* In neglecting the mythopoeic dimension, Soviet criticism has found it increasingly inconvenient to reconcile Pushkin's dramas with the classical concept of tragedy. As the stature of the protagonists is reduced to purely human proportions, as their drives and aspirations are reduced to mundane and pragmatic considerations, Pushkin's very purpose of dissociating the time, place, and action of the *Little Tragedies* from his contemporary Russian milieu seems to be disregarded or, worse yet, misunderstood.

By virtue of having been inspired by the fascinating figure of Don Juan, *Kamennyi gost'* is without a doubt the most famous play of the *Little Tragedies* cycle. Pushkin's treatment of this universal theme has consistently drawn the attention not only of Pushkinists, but also of specialists in comparative literature studies. Commentary on this work is as replete with controversies as it is with superlative epithets. Belinskii hailed *Kamennyi gost'* as the most beautiful of Pushkin's creations, while Gendarme de Bévotte, the notable authority on Don Juan, acknowledged its author to be the first great writer to have rehabilitated the hero after E.T.A. Hoffmann and Byron.[27]

Kamennyi gost' was written during the period of the most revolutionary and far-reaching changes in the entire history of the Don Juan theme. The first half of the nineteenth century saw the Classical image of the instinctive, hedonistic *burlador* radically transformed by the Romanticists' conception of the donjuanesque hero. Passing through such versions as Blaze de Bury's *Le Souper chez le Commandeur* (1834), Alexandre Dumas' *Don Juan de Marana* (1836), and José Zorrilla's *Don Juan Tenorio* (1844), the formerly unrepentant and condemned seducer effects a conversion and attains salvation through his love of a woman. Pushkin's Don Juan is clearly not saved at the end of the play; however, the possibility of his moral rebirth just before being dragged to hell has been suggested on the basis of the hero's confessions before Donna Anna:

> True, is it not, he's been described to you
> As an outrageous villain and a monster.
> O Dona Anna, rumor is perhaps
> Not wholly wrong; upon my weary conscience
> There weighs, perhaps, a heavy load of evil;
> I've long been an adept in lechery;
> But since I saw you first all that has changed:
> It seems to me, that I've been born anew!
> For, loving you, virtue herself I love—
> And humbly, for the first time in my life,
> Before her now I bend my trembling knees.

The major controversy of *Kamennyi gost'* can be formulated in the question: is don juanism compatible with sincerity in love? In other words, is Don Juan's courtship of Donna Anna in Pushkin's play merely his last seductive adventure before his punishment, or is it the burgeoning of true love and a genuine moral conversion to virtue? The "moral regeneration" theory, as one of the main interpretative approaches to *Kamennyi gost'*, springs not only from the words of Pushkin's hero (confessions of love by a Don Juan are traditionally suspect), but also from the following, apparently Hoffmann-inspired, suggestion by Belinskii:

> The most natural punishment for Don Juan could have been a true passion for a woman who either would not have reciprocated this passion, or who would have become its victim. This, it appears, is what Pushkin intended to do; at least this is what we are led to believe from the cry of Don Juan, which is torn from the very depth of his soul: "O, Donna Anna!"[28]

Since Belinskii, the moral regeneration hypothesis has found many supporters among Russian commentators of the pre-revolutionary period and appears to have been adopted as an official position in Soviet criticism. Among the former, N.P. Dashkevich and N. Kotliarevskii both conclude that Don Juan is truly ennobled and morally resurrected by Donna Anna.[29] B.P. Gorodetskii, of the latter camp, claims to see precisely in the moral rebirth of Don Juan the most significant innovation introduced by Pushkin into the Don Juan theme.[30] Anna Akhmatova arrives at an analogous conclusion and, once again suggesting a Hoffmannian interpretation, sees the tragedy of *Kamennyi gost'* as the sincere but unconsummated love between Don Juan and Donna Anna.[31]

The significance of the question of Don Juan's moral rebirth must be duly recognized as a fundamental issue not only in Pushkin's interpretation of the theme of compulsive infidelity (the *burlador* theme), but also in the full appreciation of the position *Kamennyi gost'* occupies in the historical evolution of the Don Juan myth in literature. Thus, if Don Juan's confession of love and devotion to virtue is but another stratagem of deceit designed to overcome the resistance of Donna Anna, Pushkin's protagonist reincarnates the archetypal *"dissoluto punito"* of the Classical tradition, If, on the other hand, he is indeed converted to true love, if his renunciation of don juanism is genuine, then he emerges as the prototype of the Don Juan of the Romantic period, on the road to redemption and salvation.

There is, to be sure, a very obvious trend to credit Pushkin with this innovation, particularly on the part of those commentators who view *Kamennyi gost'*, if not the whole of the *Little Tragedies* cycle, from an autobiographical perspective. The chronological proximity of the writing of this drama and of Pushkin's own marriage has led Kotliarevskii, among others, to the conclusion that "the words Don Juan speaks to Donna Anna [in his confession] were not addressed to her, but to Natalia Nikolaevna Goncharova."[32] And indeed, since the time that the nineteenth-century critic I. Shcheglov claimed to have discovered real-life prototypes for the *dramatis personae* of *Kamennyi gost'* among Pushkin's acquaintances and contemporaries,[33] the association of Pushkin and Don Juan and the concomitant hypothesis that Don Juan's confession represents Pushkin's own farewell to "don juanism" have found general acceptance among Soviet Pushkinists. A notable exception is Blagoi who categorically refutes the moral regeneration theory in stating that "if Pushkin's Don Juan indeed proved capable of loving one woman forever, he would *ipso facto* cease to be Don Juan. Thus, the problem of psychologically analyzing a character of this type would be eliminated, and yet, this problem is precisely the immediate objective of Pushkin's little tragedy."[34]

Some critics, who have not endorsed the autobiographical motivation for Don Juan's conversion in the debate over the compatibility of compulsive promiscuity and sincerity in love in *Kamennyi gost'*, have sought other factors to substantiate their argument. Of these factors, the most important is the character of Donna Anna, for she alone within the context of Pushkin's play might conceivably embody those rare qualities which would be necessary to effect the reform of the legendary seducer. And indeed, certain commentators claim to have found in Pushkin's heroine a counterpart of Hoffmann's Donna Anna who, in the story "Don Juan" (1813), had been destined to make Don Juan recognize the divine nature within him through love. Consequently, the hero of *Kamennyi gost'* must, as Janko Lavrin suggests, harbour an unconscious craving for the Ideal Woman.[35]

In concurrence with Blagoi, for whom Pushkin's Donna Anna bears not the slightest kinship with the Ideal

Woman Hoffmann envisaged in the heroine of Mozart's *Don Giovanni,* Frank Seeley dismisses the Donna Anna of *Kamennyi gost'* as quite an ordinary woman: "She proves much easier to 'conquer' than Ineza. . . . She is much less interesting than Laura, whose rich temperament, artistic talent, and proud courage and independence make her a feminine counterpart of the happier side of Juan himself. She is not more than conventional in her thinking and behaviour. . . . At the same time she is flutteringly curious, more than once ingenuously coy, and almost vulgar when she lets Juan take his first kiss."[36] As for Don Juan, asserts André Meynieux, not only does Pushkin's hero not nurture a love of a spiritual nature for Donna Anna, but is utterly incapable of such sentiment.[37]

The foregoing critical views on the highly contentious, yet fundamental issue of Pushkin's representation of the Don Juan type in *Kamennyi gost'* are obviously divided into two schools of thought. Commentators on this drama in the West have generally refuted the hypothesis of Don Juan's conversion to virtue and moral rebirth through love on the basis that Pushkin, inspired by the important Classical interpretations of the theme by Molière and Mozart, did not distort the traditional conception of the donjuanesque hero. On the other hand, Soviet criticism, with the outstanding exception of Blagoi, appears to have accepted the validity of the moral regeneration theory, partially on the basis of identifying Pushkin's own state of mind on the eve of his marriage to Natalia Goncharova with that of Don Juan when the latter renounces his dissolute past on his knees before Donna Anna, and partially with the intention of demonstrating Pushkin's penchant for innovation by effecting a revolutionary transformation in the character of a universal hero.

While the purpose of this paper has been to present an overview of some of the major problems in the interpretation of the *Little Tragedies,* it is not intended to attempt any solutions to these problems. In any case, such an attempt would amount to little more than the endorsement of one stated opinion and the refutation of another, or perhaps even the favouring of one critical approach while agreeing with the conclusions reached by another. It is, however, both gratifying and instructive to observe that a variety of critical approaches is represented in the expansive interpretative literature on the *Little Tragedies.* At the same time, it is regrettable that the tendency of Pushkin studies in the Soviet Union is to vote *en bloc,* as it were, on some of the most contentious issues, resulting in a monolithic and often predictable critical attitude toward these dramas.

It is hoped that this year's 150th anniversary of that fertile "Boldino autumn" will stimulate further investigation of Pushkin's productivity in this period among students of literature in the West. Such scholarly endeavour would have the highly important objective of enhancing our appreciation and understanding of some of Pushkin's aesthetically most rich and conceptually most challenging creations.

Notes

[1] V.G. Belinskii, *Sochineniia Aleksandra Pushkina* (Leningrad, 1937), p. 534.

[2] B.P. Gorodetskii, *Dramaturgiia Pushkina* (Moscow-Leningrad, 1953), p. 267.

[3] N.S. Durylin, *Pushkin na stsene* (Moscow, 1951), p. 94.

[4] This is reflected among some of the titles initially proposed for these plays: "Skupoi" (The Miser), "Zavist' " (Envy), and "Don-Zhuan."

[5] Excerpts from the *Little Tragedies* are quoted from the translation by A.F.B. Clark in Avrahm Yarmolinski (ed.), *The Poems, Prose and Plays of Alexander Pushkin* (New York, 1936).

[6] Belinskii, p. 537.

[7] Carl R. Proffer, "Pushkin and Parricide: *The Little Tragedies,*" *American Imago,* XXV, no. 4 (Winter 1968), 350.

[8] D. Blagoi, *Sotsiologiia tvorchestva Pushkina* (Moscow, 1929), pp. 225-26.

[9] D. Blagoi, *Tvorcheskii put' Pushkina 1826-1830* (Moscow, 1967), p. 594.

[10] Proffer, *American Imago,* XXV, no. 4 (Winter 1968), 351.

[11] Blagoi, *Tvorcheskii put',* p. 595.

[12] Durylin, p. 173.

[13] N. Minskii, "Skupoi rytsar'," in S.A. Vengerov (ed.), *Pushkin,* 6 vols. (St. Petersburg, 1909), III, 103.

[14] I. Nusinov, *Pushkin i mirovaia literatura* (Moscow, 1941), p. 66.

[15] A.G. Gukasova, *Boldinskii period v tvorchestve A.S. Pushkina* (Moscow, 1973), p. 83.

[16] *Ibid.,* pp. 85-86.

[17] St. Rassadin, *Dramaturg Pushkin* (Moscow, 1977), p. 61.

[18] Belinskii, p. 531.

[19] *Ibid.,* p. 533.

[20] A. Gornfel'd, "Motsart i Sal'eri," in Vengerov, *Pushkin,* III, 125.

[21] Blagoi, *Sotsiologiia,* p. 173.

[22] Nusinov, p. 109.

[23] Josephine Woll, " 'Mozart and Salieri' and the Concept of Tragedy," *Canadian-American Slavic Studies,* X, no. 2 (Summer 1976), 262.

[24] Robert Louis Jackson, "Miltonic Imagery and Design in Puškin's *Mozart and Salieri:* The Russian Satan," in Victor Terras (ed.), *American Contributions to the Seventh International Congress of Slavists,* 2 vols. (The Hague-Paris, 1973), II, 265.

[25] Blagoi, *Sotsiologiia,* p. 172.

[26] Blagoi, *Tvorcheskii put',* p. 629.

[27] Belinskii, p. 550; G. Gendarme de Bévotte, *La Légende de Don Juan,* 2 vols. (Paris, 1929), II, 13.

[28] Belinskii, p. 550.

[29] N.P. Dashkevich, "A.S. Pushkin v riadu velikikh poetov novogo vremeni," in V.S. Ikonnikov (ed.), *Pamiati Pushkina* (Kiev, 1899), pp. 133-34; N. Kotliarevskii, "Kamennyi gost'," in Vengerov, *Pushkin,* II, 146.

[30] Gorodetskii, p. 289.

[31] Anna Akhmatova, " 'Kamennyi gost'" Pushkina," in *O Pushkine* (Leningrad, 1977), pp. 89-109.

[32] Kotliarevskii, in Vengerov, *Pushkin,* II, 137.

[33] I. Shcheglov, *Novoe o Pushkine* (St. Petersburg, 1902), cited in *ibid.,* p. 138.

[34] Blagoi, *Tvorcheskii put',* p. 653.

[35] Janko Lavrin, *Pushkin and Russian Literature* (London, 1947), p. 176.

[36] Frank F. Seeley, "The Problem of *Kamennyy Gost'*," *The Slavonic and East European Review,* XLI, no. 97 (June 1963), 360.

[37] André Meynieux, "Pouchkine et Don Juan," *La Table Ronde,* no. 115 (November 1957), p. 101.

Paul Debreczeny (essay date 1980)

SOURCE: "The Execution of Captain Mironov: A Crossing of the Tragic and Comic Modes," in *Alexander Puskin: Symposium II,* Slavica Publishers, Inc., 1980, pp. 67-78.

[*In the following essay, Debreczeny considers the place of Captain Mironov's tragic execution in the otherwise comic* The Captain's Daughter.]

The Captain's Daughter (1836), even though its action is set in the midst of a bloody revolt, contains surprisingly little violence. Grinev's prophetic nightmare foreshadows a massacre, but only in a remote manner. Grinev is wounded quite seriously in his duel with Švabrin, but his wound turns out to be a blessing, for he awakes to find himself in the tender care of Maša. The first physical marks of cruelty appearing in the novel are the traces of torture on the body of the captive Bashkir; similar tokens of savage governmental repression are brought to our attention at the beginning of Chapter Ten as Grinev sees a group of mutilated convicts on his way to Orenburg and in Chapter Eleven when he is struck by Xlopuša's disfigured face. But all these faces had been deformed a long time ago, and they appear only as witnesses to a cruel past, far removed from the time of action, much the same way as Mironov's participation in the Turkish and Prussian campaigns seems to be a legend of bygone days.[1] In the present, as soon as the mutilated Bashkir opens his mouth showing a short stump in place of a tongue, his torture is stopped; moreover, Grinev the narrator hastens to soften the impact of the scene by reflecting on the progress that has been made since those ruthless days. Unmitigated violence, vividly represented before our eyes, appears only in Chapter Seven when the Cossack deserters hurl the Kalmyk Julaj's severed head over the log fence, that event serving as a prelude to the foremost violent scene in the novel: the execution of Captain Mironov; of his comrade in arms, Ivan Ignat'ič; and of his wife, Vasilisa Egorovna. Finally, the theme of beheading recurs at the very end of the novel, where we are told that Pugačev nodded to Grinev before his head was cut off; but that event, once more, is remote; it belongs to history, and it is narrated rather than represented vividly.

The execution of the Mironovs occurs exactly half-way through the novel, and indeed it occupies a central place in it. But as an unallayed scene of violence, it stands strangely isolated in the context of the narrative, which generally oscillates between the mildly comic and the mildly sentimental. The purpose of this paper is to examine how, if at all, the tragic note of the execution is brought into harmony with the novel's generally comic tone.

Commenting on several of the humorous devices Puškin used in *The Captain's Daughter,* critics have pointed out, above all, that most elements of the plot are so obviously conventional or melodramatic as to suggest parody. The salient examples are chance meetings (Grinev's with Pugačev and Zurin; Maša's with the empress);[2] a conflict between love and duty as in a neoclassical tragedy;[3] the sparing of a political enemy out of gratitude for a personal favor;[4] the introduction of a melodramatic villain;[5] the compulsion of the hero to withhold a secret as a device for slowing up the development of the plot;[6] and, last but not least, the ironic solution of the plot by a *dea ex machina.*[7] What makes the conventional elements comic is the artless naiveté of the narrator Grinev, whose character has been traced back not only to Puškin's earlier fictitious narrator, Ivan Petrovič Belkin, but also to satirical personages Puškin had created for parodying literary critics of his time.[8] The comedy is enhanced by references, either in the text or in the epigraphs, to eighteenth-century works such as Fonvizin's *The Young Hopeful* (1782) and Knjažnin's *The Eccentrics* (1790), which provide ironic contexts for the characters' actions.[9] Without enumerating further humorous devices which critics have seen in the novel, let us turn to one which has received relatively little attention: the device of frustrating expectations.

The title of Chapter One suggests that the young hero will become an officer of the Guards, an accomplishment which in his eyes would be "the height of human happiness." After his father's perverse decision to send him into the regular army instead, he feels that all his "brilliant hopes were shattered." But his new destination also raises certain expectations, though of a different kind, both in his and the reader's mind: we now think he will "learn to toil and drudge, to smell powder, and be a soldier, not an idler."[10] What in fact happens is that Zurin, claiming to be instructing him in the ways of the service, gets him drunk, robs him of a hundred rubles at billiards, and takes him to Arinuška's. Zurin's repeated insistence that all this is a lesson in the officer's mode of living reminds one of Ostap and Andrij Bul'ba's liquid initiation into the life of the Coassck *seč'*; and the whole scene, with the billiard marker on all fours under the table, has a Gogolesque flavor.

Having presented himself to Andrej Karlovič in Orenburg, the young Grinev realizes that he is being sent to "an out-of-the-way fort on the edge of the Kirghiz-Kaisak steppes." He is disappointed, but he imagines that his new surroundings will be impressive at least in their rugged severity: "I tried to picture Captain Mironov, my future commanding officer, and the image that came to my mind was that of a stern, short-tempered old man, oblivious to everything except the service, and ready to put me under arrest on bread and water for the merest trifle"; and "I expected to see fearsome bastions, towers, and a rampart." Instead, he arrives at "a small village bounded by a log fence" and commanded, not by a stern captain, but by a querulous Vasilisa Egorovna (strongly reminiscent of Vasilisa Kašporovna in Gogol's "Ivan Fedorovič Špon'ka and His Aunt" [1831]). She quarters Grinev

at the house of Semen Kuzov in order to punish the latter for having allowed his horse into her vegetable garden. The chief duty of Ivan Ignat'ič as an officer, it seems, is to hold a roll of thread on his outstretched hands for Vasilisa Egorovna to unwind. The main event of the day in the fort is that "Corporal Proxorov had a fight in the bathhouse with Ustin'ja Negulina over a bowl of boiling water,"[11] reminding us of such Gogolian women as Agaf'ja Fedoseevna, who bit off the assessor's ear or Gapka whom Ivan Ivanovič threatened to let loose on the mayor in the tale of the two Ivans. And, to continue the list of absurdities, the only cannon with which the fort is equipped has been in disuse for the last two years because its boom would frighten the Captain's daughter. The most farcical detail, however, twisting the style of the narrative beyond all pretense of realism into a gnarl of grotesque hyperbole, is the scene in which the Captain, clad in dressing gown and night cap, drills his veterans who, despite making a sign of the cross each time, cannot tell left from right, while Vasilisa Egorovna shouts that the drill should be over because dinner is ready and the cabbage soup is getting cold and because her husband doesn't know the first thing about drills anyway.[12] Grinev, who had hoped to become a dashing officer of the Guards in St. Petersburg, is justly "overcome by dejection," bemoaning that "I have been condemned to spend my youth in such a place."[13]

The one person who could bring a sense of adventure to this uninspiring village is the romantic villain Švabrin, and indeed it is his quarrel with Grinev which next raises the reader's expectations. He challenges Grinev with the ominous words, "You will not get away with this"; and Grinev, after responding to his adversary in kind, comments to the reader: "At that moment I could have torn him to pieces." But the only other officer in the fort, Ivan Ignat'ič, is stringing up mushrooms to be dried for the winter under Vasilisa Egorovna's orders when Grinev comes to ask him if he would serve as his second; the good old man refuses and suggests that if Grinev and Švabrin have any differences, they should just exchange a couple of blows: "If he hits you in the mug, you bash him on the ear."[14] In Belogorsk all romantic notions are soon translated into the prose of domestic reality. The young men's first attempt at dueling is thwarted by a handful of veterans commandeered to arrest them, not by the Captain, but by his wife, who berates the duelers as if they were naughty boys, tells the maid to lock their swords away in the pantry, and describes dueling simply as murder. Here is an early example of *ostranenie*— the device of looking at a familiar phenomenon with fresh eyes. Even the outcome of the eventual duel, though serious enough, is brought about by the comic Savel'ič, dashing to protect Grinev, whom he still regards as a little boy entrusted to his care.

Expectations are inflated to ludicrous proportions as Grinev prepares for the defense of the fort.[15] "It is our duty to defend the fort to the last breath," he declares. On the eve of the battle he is agitated by an "impatient expectation of danger and feelings of noble ambition." The next morning, when Maša smiles at him for the last time before the siege begins, his mental response is as follows: "I involuntarily grasped the hilt of my sword, remembering that I had received it from her hands the evening before, as if it had been given to me in order to defend my beloved. My heart burned. I imagined myself as her knight-protector. I longed to prove that I was worthy of her trust, and waited impatiently for the decisive moment."[16]

These chivalrous attitudes, however, are incongruous with the way the rest of the characters prepare to defend the fort. When Mironov receives information about Pugačev's approach, he has to trick his wife to get her out of the house in order to be able to hold a council with his officers without her; he has to lock up Palaška, the maid, in the pantry to prevent her from eavesdropping on the council; and when it is stated that he has "prepared for the onslaught,"[17] what is meant is that he is ready to take the barrage of his wife's questions. The ensuing description centers on how Vasilisa Egorovna wheedled the military secret out of the guileless Ivan Ignat'ič and on how Ivan Kuzmič failed to trick her for a second time. The tone of these descriptions befits, not preparations for a serious battle, but some farcical carryings-on like Ivan Ivanovič's scheme to saw the posts of Ivan Nikiforovič's goose pen.

Nevertheless, Grinev has promised to defend the fort to the last of his breath, and we await his heroic actions. He does dash out of the fort with Ivan Kuzmič and Ivan Ignat'ič, but the frightened garrison does not follow: "At that moment the rebels rushed upon us and burst into the fort. The drum fell silent; the garrison threw down their arms; I was hurled to the ground, but I got up again and entered the fort with the rebels. The commandant, wounded in the head, stood in the midst of a group of villains who demanded the keys from him. I was on the point of rushing to his aid when some hefty Cossacks seized me and bound me with their belts."[18] "I was on the point" is a phrase well chosen to describe Grinev's actions: he had been on the point of becoming a dashing officer of the Guards, of serving in a fort of austere magnificence, of teaching a villain a lesson in a duel, and of shedding his blood in defense of his beloved, but somehow, each time, something interfered.

Leaving aside the scene of Mironov's execution for the moment, let us follow the same pattern of frustrated expectations in further chapters of the novel. In Orenburg, Grinev awaits the meeting of the council "with impatience," just as he awaited battle earlier; and in front of the council he makes a strong case for offensive action, assuring his audience that Pugačev could not stand up to a professional army: what he gets in reply from the councilman who speaks after him is the sobering and prosaic suggestion that the town should act neither offensively, nor defensively, but "corruptively."[19] We are told that Grinev often participated in sorties against the besiegers of Orenburg, but the only time we actually see him in a raid he is "on the point of striking down"[20] a Cossack with his Turkish sword when the man takes his cap off, greets him cordially, and hands him a letter from Maša. The letter could be expected to encourage Grinev to fight her parents' murderers, but in fact it reproaches him for not taking enough care of himself during sorties; with its reproach it stands in the same relationship to Grinev's "heroism" as his mother's entreaties to take care of his health stood in relation to his father's command to guard his honor in Chapter One. Further, Grinev's earnest pleading of Maša's fate before the General elicits the unromantic suggestion that "it is better for her to be Švabrin's wife for the time being since he can protect her; later, after we execute him, god willing there will be suitors for her";[21] approaching Berdy, Grinev once more swings his sword at a sentry, but the latter is saved by his thick hat; Grinev tries to gallop away but has to come back because of his bungling servant; and he is threatened with execution once more, only to be spared once more.

Every unfulfilled expectation, it would seem, amounts to a lesson in realism. All fanciful notions are dashed against the prosaic facts of ordinary life. Scenes like Grinev's encounter with the Cossack Maksimyč even suggest that the simple affairs of individuals should take precedence over political allegiances and large issues of history. Indeed *The Captain's Daughter,* along with some of Walter Scott's novels, has been interpreted as a quest for simple humanitarian values amid conflicting fanaticisms.[22] This interpretation would be entirely convincing if history were presented in an unfalteringly comic vein throughout the novel; if chivalric sallies inevitably ended up in a joke while nobody got hurt—or at least if death and cruelty were only accessories to a stage setting, to be eluded by every character the reader knew intimately. But the reader cannot ignore the scene of the Mironovs' execution.

At first sight Grinev's behavior during the executions seems to fall into the same ironic pattern of unfulfilled expectations. He is captured with loud threats of retribution for not obeying the rebels' "Tsar"; he is led into Pugačev's presence to be tried along with Ivan Kuzmič and Ivan Ignat'ič. The other two are hanged for their defiance of the Pretender, and now it is Grinev's turn. "I looked at Pugačev boldly," we read, "ready to repeat the answer my courageous comrades had given"[23] (i.e., refusing to swear allegiance to Pugačev). He is not asked any questions, however, because Švabrin has denounced him and Pugačev does not even want to bother with him; he is being led to the gallows. He is "on the point" of becoming a martyr. But when Savel'ič throws himself at Pugačev's feet begging for his young master's life, Pugačev recognizes them both, and pardons Grinev. Once more, a personal gesture—gratitude for a hareskin coat—prevails over historical forces; human sympathy triumphs over fanaticism. What about Ivan Kuzmič and Ivan Ignat'ič, however?

They hang on the gallows, and continue hanging while the rebel leader, their murderer, tries to make friends with Grinev. Their corpses are brought into focus on several occasions: we see them in the daylight when some Bashkirs pull the boots off their feet and at dusk looming black and terrible as Grinev goes to see Pugačev; the moon lights them up when Grinev goes back to his lodging that evening; they hang over the next morning's gathering; and Grinev's last glance rests on them as he leaves for Orenburg. Even more horrifying is the body of Vasilisa Egorovna, who has been slashed by a saber for lamenting her husband's death and has been left lying stripped naked by the porch until the next day when someone throws a piece of matting over her.

Yet, despite these horrifying scenes, the narrator does not abandon his tone of light banter. The two older officers have already been hanged, and serious danger threatens Grinev's life when we read: "I was dragged to the gallows. 'Don't be scared,' repeated my executioners, wishing, in all truth perhaps, to give me courage." The young Cossack, sent to Grinev with Pugačev's invitation, describes the latter in the following terms: "Well, your Honor, everything shows that he is a person of distinction: at dinner he was pleased to eat two roast suckling-pigs, and he had his steam-bath so hot that even Taras Kuročkin could not bear it: he had to give the birch twigs to Fomka Bikbaev and he could just barely revive himself with cold water." The manner, once more, is Gogol's, down to the trick of casually mentioning two hitherto unheard-of characters with the assumption that the reader knows all about their habits. No less Gogolesque is the remark with which Andrej Karlovič receives the news of Vasilisa Egorovna's murder: "She was a good woman, and what an expert at pickling mushrooms!"[24] From among other similar details let us mention only the list of stolen goods Savel'ič presents to Pugačev in the shadow of the gallows: the act of presenting it is so improbable, and the list itself so funny, that the scene creates a farcical atmosphere.[25]

Some critics commenting on the scene of execution make the point that it is perceived relatively lightly because Grinev the narrator is an eighteenth-century man, used to cruelty, and because there is an element of justice in popular retribution against officers of governmental troops.[26] The chief question from the point of view of our investigation is not, however, to what extent the narrator should or should not condemn the cruelty under his eyes, but whether his description of it blends in with the stylistic context of the narrative.[27]

Marina Cvetaeva has suggested that we can accept the executions in their context as we accept violence in a fairy tale: Pugačev is not an ordinary human being in our perception but an incarnation of the evil of popular imagination, the wolf or robber of folklore.[28] It has indeed been demonstrated that the novel incorporates a number of fairy tale elements: Maša was described by one of Puškin's own contemporaries as a heroine out of a *bylina;* Pugačev has been likened to the fairy tale beast or robber that helps the hero; the motif of his generosity has been traced back to popular stories about him; Puškin himself hints in his epigraph to Chapter Twelve that Pugačev's rescue of the orphan Maša is rooted in folklore; Pugačev's hyperbolic, larger-than-life presentation is reminiscent of the presentation of folk heroes; even his physical appearance—in a red caftan, riding a white horse, with sword drawn—is evocative of popular *lubok* pictures; and finally Catherine II comes to the rescue of the hero and heroine as a fairy godmother.[29] One might add that the scene of execution itself is modeled on the trinary structure of the folk tale: Ivan Kuzmič and Ivan Ignat'ič perish in the clutches of the dragon, but the third "knight," Grinev, escapes.

Yet, despite the undoubted presence of these elements, a fairy tale atmosphere does not explain the problem under discussion. Cvetaeva would be right if Pugačev were an exclusively evil figure and if the violence were committed against some remote personages with whom the reader had no opportunity to identify; in that case "we" as readers would acknowledge the existence of evil in the abstract but would not ourselves be hurt by it; we would emerge victorious from a fight against it. But, in fact, the Mironovs were "us," endearing despite their laughable characteristics, and we cannot see their demise without pain. Moreover, Pugačev is far from being all evil: he is, in Cvetaeva's own description, the most enchanting character in the novel.

Pugačev's charm brings us to another related question, that of the romantic element in his presentation. It is perfectly plausible that he would, as did the real-life Pugačev,[30] spare a loyalist out of gratitude for a personal favor. It is still believable that he might invite the loyalist officer to an interview in the hope of gaining his allegiance. But it is beyond credibility that he would let the officer rejoin the opposite side; that he would send presents after him; that he would receive him with kindness a second time despite the suspicious circumstances of the officer's arrival in his camp; and that he would leave camp, army, siege, and all, in order to rescue the officer's bride, at once forgiving him for a fraud, offering himself as "father by proxy" for his wedding and making him privy to his innermost thoughts. It is precisely these unrealistic details that make Pugačev attractive, for he emerges as the eagle of the Kalmyk tale, as a lonely giant likely to be betrayed by his cohorts, a misunderstood hero seeking the friendship of a kindred spirit.[31] His greatness is that he is condemned from the beginning, and he knows it. His violent acts, it would seem, are redeemed by his acceptance of his own death in the concluding paragraph of the novel. But are they? Such a Pugačevian perspective is in jarring contrast to the lovingly mocking, intimately indulgent attitude which the narrator has shown towards them. Prior to the scene of the execution the only kind of romanticism we encountered was Grinev's "highfalutin" chivalry—put on display only in order to be debunked. The debunking was accomplished partly by frustrating expectations and partly by submerging fanciful notions in the quagmire of Russian provincial banality. But now, after the execution, notably with the evocative song Pugačev and his associates sing at the end of the evening, an entirely new, serious romantic strain enters the stylistic structure of the novel, and we are asked to accept the executions under the spell of its fairy tale atmosphere. The different stylistic strands which converge on the central scene of the executions are clearly incongruous.

Incongruity is the hallmark of the grotesque, and we have indeed seen some elements, especially in the description of the Mironovs, which brought the style close to the grotesque, but on the whole it is unlikely that Puškin was aiming here at the kind of grotesque effect which he had achieved, for example, in **"The Undertaker"** (1830).[32] Nor is *The Captain's Daughter* in the style of the *école frénétique,* and therefore it cannot treat the gory as gleefully as it is treated, for example, in *Notre-Dame de Paris* (1831) by Victor Hugo. It is more likely that Puškin simply failed to make the appropriate stylistic adjustments as he lifted raw material out of *A History of Pugačev* into the novel. If this is the case, then a certain stylistic incongruity is a flaw in the structure of *The Captain's Daughter.*[33] It is possible, however, that at least a partial solution to the problem can be found in the Grinev-Pugačev relationship.

It has been argued persuasively that in addition to the elder Grinev, both Mironov and Pugačev assume something of a fatherly role in relation to the young Petr and that the latter's progress through the novel is a process of gaining independence from paternal tutelage.[34] Andrej Grinev is a cross-grained father, bent on curbing his son's freedom, threatening to thrash him

for his duel as if he were a little boy, and thwarting his plans of marriage. When his son is convicted of treason, the elder Grinev accepts the verdict and will have nothing further to do with a "publicly dishonored traitor"[35]—a marked difference in attitude from that of the father in an early plan for the novel who would have gone to Petersburg to beg mercy for his son.[36] What is particularly remarkable about the old Grinev's belief in his son's guilt is that it persists even though he has heard from Maša and Savel'ič a full account of why Petr went over to the rebel side. One is reminded of Taras Bul'ba's condemning Andrij for his desertion of military duties in pursuit of love.

Young Petr, on his part, does everything contrary to his father's wishes. Behaving like "a boy let loose for the first time" in Simbirsk, he fails the first moral test upon leaving home; insisting on continuing the journey despite the threat of a blizzard, he fails the first test of wisdom to which he is exposed. He throws himself into the duel hotheadedly, clearly against his elders' wishes, as though it were some kind of rite of passage into manhood. He states explicitly that "I wanted to assert my independence" and show Savel'ič—a deputy of his father's—that "I was no longer a child," fearing that if "I did not gain the upper hand of the old man, it would be difficult to free myself from his tutelage later on." When Andrej Karlovič asks him what *"deržat' v ežovyx rukavicax"* means ("not to spare the rod"; literally "to hold in hedgehog-hide gloves"), he translates the phrase—reasserting his previous quest for independence—as "not to be too severe, to allow as much freedom as possible." Two reproachful statements by Savel'ič—"You're beginning your pranks early," pronounced after the Simbirsk episode, and "Why the haste? It would be understandable if you were hurrying to your wedding,"[37] when the travelers are caught in the blizzard—both express an effort to hold Grinev back from his headlong rush into independence, and both foreshadow his confrontation with his father over a plan of early marriage. Captain Mironov, too, plays a restraining role in relation to the young man both when he censures him for his duel and when he advises him to give up writing verse—that is, indulging in amorous sentiments.

One could go one step further and argue that Petr seeks liberation not only from paternal, but generally from parental tutelage. If he were more dutifully bound to his mother, he would not risk his life in a duel—an act which causes her to fall sick with fright and worry. Moreover, he fights the duel in defiance not so much of Captain Mironov as of Vasilisa Egorovna, who is the weightiest figure of authority in Belogorsk.

Pugačev is also something of a parental figure,[38] but his relation to Petr is nevertheless quite different from those of the elder Grinevs, Savel'ič, and the Mironovs. He appears in Grinev's life at a moment when the young man needs guidance both in escaping from the blizzard and in a new psychological orientation. Petr's search for new guidance was already apparent from his readiness to succumb to the older officer Zurin's seductive ploys, but the latter, of course, did not prove worthy of respect or sympathy; those feelings were to be reserved for the much more gallant Pugačev. A rapport between Petr and the rebels' future leader is established almost as soon as they meet for the first time; it is characteristic, for instance, that although Pugačev is strong and authoritative, he does in the blizzard just what the inexperienced and lost young man had recommended: to forge ahead despite dangers. Another reason why Grinev feels kinship for his guide is that the latter pawned his coat at an inn—having obviously behaved just as Grinev had in Simbrisk. Here is a different paternal figure to follow, and it is no accident that just as Pugačev is leading Grinev's sledge to safety, the latter has a dream in which his feared father ("My first thought was one of fear that my father would be angry with me") is replaced by Pugačev. This new father, though he heaps corpse upon corpse with his axe, gently invites Petr to receive his blessing. The same contrast between his violence to others and his kindness to the young Grinev is emphasized when Grinev visits him after the execution of the Mironovs, observing that "his features, regular and rather pleasant, had nothing ferocious about them." When eventually Pugačev makes Grinev laugh with him toward the end of that scene, we have the impression that the young man has in some way been seduced into betraying the dead Mironovs, who had been his substitute parents. The leader of the rebels has become Grinev's guide in rebelling against parental authority. Pugačev's liberating influence on the young hero and the latter's gratitude for it are emphasized several times: the rebellion is described as giving Grinev's soul "a powerful and salutary shock"; he says the happiness of his whole life depends upon Pugačev; and he becomes so attached to the rebel leader that he declares: "God is my witness that I would gladly repay you with my life for what you have done for me."[39]

Most important of all, Grinev could never have married his Maša if the rebellion had not occurred and Maša's parents had not been killed, because in that case his father would have had him moved to a different location and would have continued opposing his marital plans. What Grinev most abhors—the execution of his prospective in-laws—turns out to be the greatest benefaction to him. If we disregard the political meaning of the novel for the moment, we can describe it as the story of a young man's violent rebellion against parental restraints, with this peculiar feature, however, that he does not stain his hands with blood: it is Pugačev who commits the murder for him by proxy and suffers the punishment for it by proxy. Since Pugačev has murdered the Mironovs, Grinev does not have to raise his hand against his own parents.

It must be admitted that this interpretation does not solve the problem of the disunity of the various modes of presentation in the novel. Whichever way we interpret *The Captain's Daughter,* the execution scene retains a jarring quality. But if we take the novel's psychological dimensions into consideration, we can appreciate that the disunity we sense is a reflection in the artistic form of Puškin's probings into new, complex, even disconcerting contents.

Notes

[1] V. D. Skvoznikov writes convincingly that the participation of Ivan Kuzmič and Ivan Ignat'ič in these campaigns is a matter of "a distant past, beyond the framework of the narrative," unlikely to change our perception of these characters as peaceable ones. See: *"Stil' Puškina," Teorija literatury,* III (Moscow: Nauka, 1965), p. 78.

[2] *Ibid.,* p. 74.

[3] L. S. Sidjakov, *Xudožestvennaja proza A. S. Puškina* (Riga: Latvijskij gos. univ. im. P. Stučki, 1973), p. 192.

[4] M. Gofman, *"Kapitanskaja dočka"* in *Biblioteka velikix pisatelej: Puškin,* ed. S. A. Vengerov, IV (St. Petersburg: Brokgauz-Èfron, 1910), p. 368; and V. Šklovskij, *Zametki o proze Puškina* (Moscow: Sovetskij pisatel', 1937), p. 102.

[5] The description of Švabrin as "melodramatic" originates from V. G. Belinskij; see *Polnoe sobranie sočinenij,* 13 vols. (Moscow: AN SSSR, 1953-59), 7: 577.

[6] Šklovskij, *"V zaščitu sociologičeskogo metoda," Novyj Lef,* No. 3 (1927), p. 22.

[7] Among the varied comments on the denouement of the novel, I find Donald Davie's reference to a *dea ex machina* most illuminating. See *The Heyday of Sir Walter Scott* (New York: Barnes and Noble, 1961), p. 8.

[8] Once more, the literature on Grinev's connections with Belkin and with other possible antecedents in Puškin's *œuvre* is much diversified; I find the comments made by Šklovskij and Ju. G. Oksman most persuasive. See Šklovskij, *Zametki o proze Puškina,* pp. 100-101; and Oksman, *Ot "Kapitanskoj dočki" k "Zapiskam oxotnika"* (Saratov: Saratovskoe knižnoe izd., 1959), pp. 88-89.

[9] The most detailed consideration of Puškin's allusions to *Nedorosl'* can be found in D. D. Blagoj,

"*Puškin i russkaja literatura XVIII veka,*" in *Puškin rodonačal'nik novoj russkoj literatury,* ed. D. D. Blagoj and V. Ja. Kirpotin (Moscow, Leningrad: AN SSSR, 1941), pp. 159-60. About Puškin's use of *Čudaki* in the novel, see Šklovskij, *Zametki o proze russkix klassikov,* 2nd ed. (Moscow: Sovetskij pisatel', 1955), p. 80.

[10] P., 8/1, pp. 281-82.

[11] *Ibid.,* pp. 293-94 and 296, respectively.

[12] I. M. Tojbin has noted the grotesque nature of these descriptions; see "*Iz nabljudenij nad poètikoj Kapitanskoj dočki (Kapitanskaja dočka i Istorija Pugačeva),*" in *Voprosy literatury i metodiki prepo-davanija,* Učenye zapiski Kurskogo gos. ped. instituta, vol. 73 (Kursk, 1970), p. 84.

[13] P., 8/1, p. 296.

[14] *Ibid.,* pp. 301-02.

[15] John Bayley notes the technique of frustrating expectations in this instance; see *Pushkin: A Comparative Commentary* (Cambridge: Cambridge University Press, 1971), p. 338.

[16] P., 8/1, pp. 319 and 321-22, respectively.

[17] *Ibid.,* p. 315.

[18] *Ibid.,* p. 324.

[19] *Ibid.,* pp. 339-40.

[20] *Ibid.,* p. 341. Grinev's gesture of *almost* striking the Cossack Maksimyč reminds one of Girej of *Baxčisarajskij fontan* (1823), who halted his sword mid-air, distracted by the memory of his Marija. Puškin later recalled how his friend A. Raevskij roared with laughter over Girej's melodramatic gesture; see P., 11, p. 145.

[21] P., 8/1, p. 343.

[22] This is Ju. Lotman's interpretation of the novel; see "Idejnaja struktura *Kapitanskoj dočki,*" in *Puškinskij sbornik,* ed. M. Efimov et al. (Pskov: Pskovskij gos. ped. institut im. S. M. Kirova, 1962), pp. 3-20. For a similar interpretation of some of Scott's novels see Francis R. Hart, *Scott's Novels: The Plotting of Historic Survival* (Charlottesville: University Press of Virginia, 1966), chapters on *Waverly, The Heart of Midlothian,* and *Peveril,* especially pp. 19, 25, 29, 129, 144.

[23] P., 8/1, p. 325.

[24] *Ibid.,* pp. 325, 329, and 338, respectively.

[25] As is well known, Puškin used a real-life document as a source of Savel'ič's list, but the original had been written by a nobleman, not by a servant, and had been presented to the authorities, rather than to the rebel leader, in the hope of recovering some of the stolen goods. For details see Oksman, pp. 94-100.

[26] The argument that Grinev as an eighteenth-century man is less shaken by the sight of cruelty than a later reader would be is presented by V. G. Odinokov in his *Problemy poètiki i tipologii russkogo romana XIX v.* (Novosibirsk: Nauka, Sibirskoe otdelenie, 1971), pp. 56-7. G. P. Makogonenko draws attention to the circumstance that the simple village people who witness the executions in *Kapitanskaja dočka* behave differently from the populace horror-struck by the news of the murder of Boris Godunov's children in the tragedy by that name. Makogonenko attributes this difference to a perception of the Mironovs' execution as a just act. See *"Kapitanskaja dočka" A. S. Puškina* (Leningrad: Xudožestvennaja literatura, 1977), p. 53. M. Mal'cev, in his turn, argues that Grinev's relative equanimity in the face of the cruelties committed by the rebels testifies to his deep humanitarian concern for the cause of the simple people. See *Tema krest'janskogo vosstanija v tvorčestve A. S. Puškina* (Cheboksary: Šuvašskoe gos. izd., 1960), p. 185.

[27] V. Gusev, perceiving a polarity in modes of presentation, offers the suggestion, puzzling at least to me, that "the death of the Captain and of his wife 'reconciles' the two atmospheres—the serious and the laughable, tragedy and comedy." See *"Puškin i nekotorye problemy teorii stilja,"* in *V mire Puškina: Sbornik statej,* ed. S. Mašinskij (Moscow: Sovetskij pisatel', 1974), p. 569.

[28] *Moj Puškin* (Moscow: Sovetskij pisatel', 1967), p. 113. A similar view is expressed by Skvoznikov, pp. 79-81.

[29] See P. A. Vjazemskij, *Polnoe sobranie sočinenij,* ed. S. D. Šeremetev, II (St. Petersburg, M. M. Stasjulevič, 1879), p. 377; N. N. Petrunina and G. M. Fridlender, *Nad stranicami Puškina* (Leningrad: Nauka, 1974), pp. 112-14; Šklovskij, *Zametki o proze Puškina,* p. 118; Tojbin, *"Iz nabljudenij,"* p. 83; Tojbin, "*O Kapitanskoj dočke Puškina (K probleme nacional'-nogo svoeobrazija),*" in *Voprosy literatury,* ed. I. Z. Baskevič, Učenye zapiski Kurskogo gos. ped. instituta, vol. 94 (Kursk, 1972), pp. 124 and 136; and Davie, p. 8.

[30] It is well known that *Istorija Pugačeva* (pub. 1834) contains two episodes which served (in addition to popular stories) as sources for the scene of Pugačev's pardoning of Grinev. In the first one the rebel leader shows mercy to a Captain Bašarin at the urging of the latter's soldiers (see P., 9/1, p. 36); in the second

one he spares the life of a Protestant minister who gave him alms a year earlier, when he was a prisoner in Kazan (P., 9/1, p. 68).

[31] For a vivid characterization of Pugačev as a romantic hero see Cvetaeva, pp. 122-39.

[32] A. A. Zvoznikov writes that Puškin's treatment of Vasilisa Egorovna, shifting from mockery to compassion, is akin to Gogol's attitude to his characters in *"Starosvetskie pomeščiki"* (1835); see *"Osobennosti izobraženija russkogo nacional'nogo xaraktera v proze Puškina (Kapitanskaja dočka),"* *Russkaja literatura,* 1976, 19: 1, 125. Zvoznikov's comment is perceptive, but it still leaves open the question of whether Gogol's technique of combining incongruities is in accord with the overall atmosphere of Puškin's work.

[33] The only critic I am aware of who has stated this outright, claiming that "the horrors described in it [*Kapitanskaja dočka*] do not accord with Grinev's peaceable character and with the calm tone of his memoirs," is M. O. Lopatto. See *"Povesti Puškina: Opyt vvedenija v teoriju prozy,"* in *Puškinist: Istoriko-literaturnyj sbornik,* ed. S. A. Vengerov, III (Petrograd, A. F. Dressler, 1918), p. 14.

[34] Roger B. Anderson, "A Study of Petr Grinev as the Hero of Pushkin's *Kapitanskaia dochka,"* *Canadian Slavic Studies,* 5 (1971): 477-86.

[35] P., 8/1, p. 370.

[36] See the two outlines with Švanvič as central character, P., 8/2, p. 929.

[37] P., 8/1, pp. 283, 285, 292, 284, and 287, respectively.

[38] Anderson, p. 482. Gerald E. Mikkelson also considers Pugačev a paternal figure in relation to Grinev, but in his interpretation the leader of the uprising is more a historical father to "all the outcasts of the Russian empire" than a psychological one to Grinev the individual. See "The Mythopoetic Element in Pushkin's Historical Novel *The Captain's Daughter,"* *Canadian-American Slavic Studies,* 7 (1973): 309.

[39] P., 8/1, pp. 289, 330, 312, and 356, respectively.

Stephanie Sandler (essay date 1983)

SOURCE: "The Poetics of Authority in Pushkin's 'André Chénier'," in *Slavic Review,* Vol. 42, No. 2, Summer, 1983, pp. 187-203.

[*In the following essay, Sandler analyzes Pushkin's "André Chénier," and observes that the poem is indicative of a significant development in Pushkin's authorial voice.*]

During the spring and summer months of 1825, Aleksandr Pushkin intensified his efforts to end his exile in Mikhailovskoe. Though his friends urged him to produce work that might influence imperial opinion in his favor, Pushkin doubted that his poems could win him freedom.[1] His writings increasingly were concerned with what the function of poetry should be. Pushkin's "crisis" in 1825 turned not only on political issues (the Decembrist revolt at the end of the year upset him greatly) but also on literary decisions. Politics and poetry are intertwined in one of the most problematic poems of that year, **"André Chénier."** A poem now virtually forgotten, **"André Chénier"** shows Pushkin working out a formula for asserting his independence as a poet which was to organize his poetics for years to come.

The French poet André Chénier (1762-1794) was seen in the 1820s as an impassioned champion of political liberty who had been martyred for his ideals during the French Revolution. His poetry has strong formal and thematic ties to the classical tradition. Critics then as now have wavered between calling Chénier a neoclassical poet and the first romantic poet.[2] Pushkin and his contemporaries were struck by the fresh diction and large sweep of Chénier's poems. Because Chénier's poetry was suppressed after his death, the publication in 1819 of the first collection of his verse made him seem suddenly contemporary, all the more so since his ideas were consonant with those of free-thinking Russian aristocratic circles of the time.

Pushkin was fascinated by Chénier. He translated or adapted four of Chénier's poems into Russian.[3] The first mention of Chénier occurs in a letter Pushkin drafted to Prince Petr Viazemskii on July 6, 1824. Pushkin begins the letter with high praise for French historians, goes on to observe that romanticism has not really taken hold in France, and expresses admiration for two writers often cited as evidence of the growth of the romantic movement in France.[4] The mention of a poem about a dying poet by Lamartine begins an associative chain which leads to André Chénier, who symbolizes the heroic demise of a poet.

> Lamartine is quite good in his "Napoleon," and in "The Dying Poet" he is generally good in his use of a certain new harmony.

> No one cares more for the exquisite André Chénier than I do, but he is a classicist among classicists. He is just redolent of ancient Greek poetry.[5]

Pushkin first praises Chénier as the representative of a national literary tradition, and the sense of Chénier as a national poet emerges clearly in Pushkin's poem.

Pushkin polemicizes with those who would label Chénier a romantic either because his previously suppressed verse appeared only in 1819, when romanticism, especially in its Byronic varieties, was reaching new heights of popularity in Russia, or because his poetry was highly personal and often sad, always innovative. Pushkin noted in 1830:

> French poets have their concept of romanticism. They assign to it all works which bear the stamp of dreaminess or despair. Others even call neologisms and grammatical errors romanticism. In this manner André Chénier, a poet who has imbibed the spirit of antiquity, whose very insufficiencies derive from a desire to convey the forms of Greek prosody in the French language—they throw this poet in with the romantic poets.[6]

The sense of opposing an erroneous view of Chénier and of romanticism also emerges in Pushkin's poem about André Chénier's execution. To Pushkin, Chénier was a "classicist" because Chénier wrote in forms known to the ancient Greeks and Romans. The label is confirmed by the atmosphere and the events of Chénier's poetry, which recounts activities of gods and muses in elaborate periphrasis. In *L'Invention,* his long poem about the process of poetic creation, Chénier writes of the ancients, "Pour peindre notre idée empruntons leur couleurs."[7] The very title of the poem discloses Chénier's tendency to rely on the classical terms in aesthetic thought: it invokes the long-standing triad of invention, disposition, and elocution, recalling the stages of rhetorical composition and transmission which marked classical literature.

Pushkin wrote his poem about Chénier during the spring of 1825.[8] The poem is longer than his lyrics of the 1820s, most of which are less than a printed page long. Not only is the poem formally more complex than other lyrics from the 1820s, but several structural elements of the poem also strive toward a self-importance not found in other nonnarrative works. For example, **"André Chénier"** is dedicated to Nikolai Raevskii, the son of General Raevskii who befriended Pushkin during his southern exile. The French epigraph is taken from Chénier's late poem *La jeune captive:* "Ainsi, triste et captif, ma lyre, toutes fois / S'éveillait. . . ."[9] Chénier's poem is about a fellow prisoner, Aimée de Coigny.[10] The epigraph gives the first clue that Pushkin draws a parallel between his exile and Chénier's imprisonment: both poets are like the captive who sings despite her lack of freedom, and both have written poems about the sad captive who nevertheless sings on. **"André Chénier"** is also framed by an introduction and seven footnotes. Each of these components—dedication epigraph, introduction, footnotes—elevates the status of the poem, and each strengthens a reading of **"André Chénier"** as a statement about Pushkin's poetic development.

In the twelve lines which introduce **"André Chénier,"** Pushkin compares Chénier to a poet popular for his romantic temperament, Lord Byron. Pushkin admired Byron's most daring exercise in formal innovation, *Don Juan,* but it is the self-consciously exotic side of Byron which Pushkin imitated in *Kavkazski plennik* (*Prisoner of the Caucasus,* 1820) and *Bakhchissaraiskii fontan* (*The Fountain of Bakhchissarai,* 1823).[11] By 1825 Pushkin had largely outgrown the Byronic mood found in the southern poems. **"André Chénier"** appropriately begins by conjuring up Byron, who is now dead, not as Pushkin's point of departure but as one who continues to be the idol of others . . .

> Meanwhile, as the dumbfounded world
> Gazes at Byron's urn,
>
> . . . . .
>
> I am called by another shade,
> Long unsung, unlamented[12]
>
> . . . . .

Byron's tragic death aroused a sense of reverence which Pushkin mocked in a letter to Viazemskii.[13] Here he turns instead to a nearly forgotten poet. Because the poem begins with the word "meanwhile," it sets itself apart from other works from the beginning. The dedication to Nikolai Raevskii further accentuates the choice of Chénier over Byron: Raevskii introduced Pushkin to Byron's poetry, and his brother became a Russian paragon of Byronic behavior (Pushkin's poem **"Demon"** is about Aleksandr Raevskii).

The turn toward Chénier for poetic inspiration can be interpreted as an indication that Pushkin was moving away from romanticism; this is the approach taken by canonical Soviet criticism. But the final quatrain of the introduction portends other motivations . . .

> To the poet of love, leafy groves, and peace
> I carry graveside flowers.
> An unknown lyre resounds.
> I sing. I am heeded by him and by you.[14]

The one-word sentence in the final line creates a noticeable disjunction. Attention is drawn to the "reading" situation (literally a "listening" situation), which is triangular: the poet (Pushkin) sings, only Chénier and Raevskii listen. Implicitly a kind of eavesdropper status is conferred upon all others, specifically the readers of Pushkin's poem, a device that works well for the dramatic intensity of the scene which follows. Barriers are erected between poet and audience which reappear throughout the poem.

A narrative voice now sets the scene. Chénier awaits death in his prison cell. During the last night of his life, Chénier renews his commitment to the causes which led to his arrest. The narrator returns once more, as the dawn nears, to urge Chénier deeper into his past: Chénier "responds" by reliving happy times spent with friends and companions. The narrator then closes the poem with a lament as Chénier is led off for execution. The bulk of the poem, then, consists of two lengthy soliloquies presented as Chénier's own last words. (It is the first, politically more liberal of these soliloquies which was cut in half by the censors in 1826, and which circulated with the title "December 14" written across the top. Pushkin did not add the title.)

The first monologue consists of two apostrophes, the first of them addressed to the forces of freedom to which Chénier had dedicated himself as a revolutionary. It is a true apostrophe in the sense that an abstract idea (freedom) is personified in order that the poet may speak to it. Chénier then bids farewell to dear and distant friends. He begs them to read his poems and imagines himself as a silent listener in their midst. When Chénier projects himself among his friends while they recite his verse, another kind of personification takes place. So strongly does the poet identify with his verse that he suggests that he will himself live again whenever his poems are read.

The second monologue also hinges on two apostrophes. The first again strengthens the fusion of the poet with his poetry. After a long interlude during which the poet relives the golden days that preceded his fall into ignominy, he commences speaking directly to his poetry and, without any perceptible shift, to himself. As he encourages himself to be proud of his poetry, the monologue moves into the fourth and final apostrophe. Addressing the tyrants who have condemned him, Chénier enjoins them to follow him to the grave. Just as the first apostrophe to freedom culminated in the prophecy that the people would again find their way· to the spirit of freedom, so here a condemnation of the forces of evil leads Chénier to predict their violent demise.[15]

Several structural features are uncovered by this summary of the poem's narrative movement. First, the use of apostrophe controls and directs Chénier's monologue. The rhetorical device of turning the speaker's attention away from the scene at hand enjoys perfect psychological motivation: imprisoned, Chénier meditates upon his past actions and creates harmonious visions of the future. But by building the monologues around the trope of apostrophe, Pushkin also adds another level to the already complex "listening" situation. In the introduction, Pushkin claimed to be heard by Raevskii (his friend, the kind of comrade in ideas Chénier has in mind when he invokes *his* friends) and by Chénier. In the monologue, Chénier creates a situation that is nearly symmetrical. He does not identify

those who listen (literally, Chénier "speaks" to himself), but he directs his words toward forces which led to his present predicament. Those forces include dear friends (analogous to Pushkin's Raevskii), guiding concepts (Chénier serves as a source of poetic inspiration for Pushkin), and the false friends who betray Chénier in the end. The final role, that of the betrayer, seems to be played by Byron in the introduction, where he is rejected as the source of inspiration. The correspondence here is not political. Byron was himself a singer of freedom, and Pushkin had no reason to doubt the sincerity of Byron's commitment to liberal ideas. Byron does not resemble the Jacobins politically: they sang of freedom falsely, whereas Byron emerges as a false source of poetic inspiration. Pushkin creates an important parallel between false politics and false poetry. Thus the correspondence between the "listening" situations in the body of the poem and that in the introduction compares Chénier's victimization by false politicians with Pushkin's development beyond false theories of poetry. Chénier, the former revolutionary, repudiates Robespierre and his allies because they have failed to inaugurate a new era of freedom. Pushkin rejects Byron because he and like-minded romantics have failed to show the path toward a new, "true" (*istinnyi*) literature.

Pushkin accounts for the failure of romanticism by means of the imagery patterns in Chénier's monologues. In his first line, Chénier greets freedom as his guiding light (*svetilo*, l. 21). Attention is drawn to the line not only because it is the opening line but also because it is written in iambic pentameter. That meter appears in the narrator's two descriptions which begin the body of the poem (ll. 13-20), but Chénier's monologue uses only four- and six-footed iambic lines. The line "Privetstvuiu tebia moe svetilo!" ("I greet you my luminary!") begins Chénier's monologue, though its meter links it back to the narrator's lines; the line is markedly apostrophic, and it introduces the poem's central motif of light.

This light of freedom, which arose as a spark (l. 23), is predominantly *seen* by Chénier, in contrast to the chiefly aural imagery of the introduction. There, a chorus of European lyres and the call of another shade were heard. The last two lines, already noted for their asymmetrical cadence and compression, held completely aural appeal ("An unknown lyre resounds. / I sing. I am heeded by him and by you"). Although the introduction opens with the stunned world *looking* at Byron's urn, the onlookers seem to be dumbfounded (*izumlennyi*), looking only because they cannot speak.

In Chénier's monologue, verbs and images rely more on the quality of seeing. Though Chénier hears the holy thunder of freedom's storm (l. 25), this allusion to Zeus's thunder gives way instead to a "dark storm" (*buria mrachnaia*, l. 63) of those who have eclipsed freedom. The poet's relationship to his recollections is primarily one of seeing, as he remembers seeing the sons of freedom taking their oath, seeing the waves of rebirth which they proclaim (both times using the archaic verb *zret´*, ll. 29, 33). They swear and proclaim while he watches and listens: "Ia slyshal bratskii ikh obet" ("I heard their fraternal oath," l. 30) features heavy irony, since these "brothers" later betray Chénier. As the power of those who *say* that they are on the side of freedom increases, Chénier observes that the light of genuine freedom had already *shone* ("Uzhe siial tvoi mudryi genii," l. 37). Freedom is represented as purest light, disembodied and not of this world.

But it is the poet's participation in concrete verbal acts which implicitly leads to the demise of those working for freedom. When they proclaim equality, Chénier adds, "I my voskliknuli: *'Blazhenstvo!'* " ("And we exclaimed: *'Bliss!'* " l. 44).[16] The lament for lost freedom begins at this moment, triggered by Chénier's having joined the forces of those who proclaim rather than those who "see." These forces are characterized by blindness (l. 51) and darkness (l. 63).

Visual imagery emerges with new forcefulness in the second speech. Chénier comforts himself that his poetry has "shone forth" as it should . . .

> Your torch, flaming with menace,
> Lit with a cruel gleam
> The counsel of inglorious rulers
>
> . . . . .
>
> (ll. 146-48).

As the connection between poetry-writing and seeing tightens, Chénier moves to include the classical association of writing with singing (l. 153). The narrator also closes the poem "So *sang* the poet in exaltation" (l. 171, my emphasis).

When the executioners come in for Chénier, however, it is the lack of sound which is startling. The rattle of keys and locks precedes an important silence: "Ne slyshat´. Shestvie bezmolvno. Zhdet palach" ("Nothing is heard. The procession is soundless. The executioner waits," l. 182). This line breaks Pushkin's consistent use of the caesura in all of his hexametric lines with two stops and three two-word sentences.[17] The asymmetry is reminiscent of the final line of the introduction (l. 12) and equally significant, since the poem reaches it's emotional peak at this moment, as Chénier is led off to his death.

Indeed, the sound which does emerge from this silence as the representation of Chénier's poetry is exaggerated and unexpected. In the lines of prophecy which climax the final apostrophe, a sharp cry is heard, the kind of sound heretofore excluded from the poem . . .

> My cry, my furious laugh will torment you!
>
> . . . . .
>
> You will fall, tyrant! Indignation
> Will rise forth at last. The lament of the
> fatherland
> Will awaken weary fate.
>
> (ll. 163, 165-68).

Two conventional images are here invested with fresh meaning. Poetry as vision, a widespread notion during the romantic period, becomes poetry as prophetic judgment: Robespierre's government fell immediately after Chénier's execution. Pushkin may be using his advantage of hindsight to give Chénier the gift of prophecy, but the device is effective nonetheless. The other metaphor for poetry, singing, is transformed into utterly unharmonious shrieks and mad laughter. The classical poets and their followers are the ones to refer to poetry as singing, so that Pushkin rethinks both the classical and the romantic metaphors for writing in the space of a very few lines.

Other clusters of images also use conventional ideas or objects in new or newly appropriate ways. The tragedy of Chénier's death occasions all sorts of tears. For example, Chénier warns his friends not to let their tears for him be seen (l. 77). He adds, "V nash vek, vy znaete, i slezy prestuplen´e" ("In our age, you know, even tears are a crime," l. 78). Crying has become an act with consequences rather than an expression of grief. Tears of joy contribute to the poet's happier memories (ll. 83-84), especially as he recalls the misty but forgiving eyes of his chiding muse (ll. 124-26). When Chénier envisions himself among his friends as they reread his verse, he says that he will drink of their tears (ll. 99-100), but it is in the final line of **"André Chénier"** that the idea of weeping reaches its fullest expression. Here, the narrator offers his only apostrophe: he invokes the tears of the presiding muse of poetry ("Plach´, muza, plach´! . . ." ("Cry, muse, cry! . . ." l. 185). The line is rhythmically marked not by asymmetry but by the presence of only three iambs, the only such line in the entire poem. The emotional compression resulting from a line of such simple verse shows crying, a predictable activity in lyric poetry, as an act with deep meaning. The tears respond not only to the death of one man on the eve of a governmental change that would have freed him, but also to the very idea of sending poets to their death for political reasons.

One final image cluster, which follows a similar pattern, is the one built around the convivial banquet.

Feasts among friends occur often in André Chénier's Anacreontic poems. Pushkin oddly refers to the impending execution as a popular feast (l. 17). He then has the people imbibe nourishment (ll. 57-58), though it is freedom of which they figuratively partake. Feasts occur in Chénier's memories of happier days among friends, rounding out the generally positive association of nourishment with social and spiritual sustenance (ll. 107, 120). Once again, conventional metaphors are redefined in the poem's emotional conclusion. Just after the line in which Chénier describes his poetry as a shrill cry (l. 163), he jeers at the men who have sentenced him: "Pei nashu krov´, zhivi, gubia" ("Drink our blood, live by destroying," l. 164). Chénier indicts his accusers for their cruelty by contrasting their bloodthirstiness with the innocent feasts described in the first half of the poem.

By using these three image patterns—light suggesting poetic vision and political freedom, the tears of inspired lament, and the simple banquets of good people—Pushkin derives tremendous emotional impact from traditional metaphors in the closing lines of **"André Chénier."** Pushkin chooses these images in part because they recur in Chénier's verse and are thus appropriate to a poem about him.[18] Boris Tomashevskii has observed that these images also abound in Pushkin's early poetry and are therefore important elements in the growth of Pushkin's stock of poetic devices.[19] Tears, feasts, and morning luminaries are images associated with all elegiac poetry, and when Pushkin uses them in new ways he is, as always, consciously attempting to renew the genre.

It is the creation of an authentic elegy which motivates not only the imagery but also the structure of **"André Chénier."** The footnotes, for example, have a marked scholarly quality which becomes especially apparent in comparison to the note Konstantin Batiushkov appended to his *Umiraiushchii Tass* (*The Dying Tasso,* 1817).[20] Batiushkov simply weaves into a prose narrative details from Tasso's life that are not made clear in the poem. The Batiushkov elegy was Pushkin's chief Russian model for **"André Chénier."**[21] Pushkin studied *The Dying Tasso* carefully, and his marginal notes to the poem reveal that he paid attention to the modes of expression in the lament as well as to the music of Batiushkov's lines.[22]

Like Pushkin, Batiushkov was drawn to his subject for personal reasons (Batiushkov and Tasso both suffered bouts of insanity). A comparison of the footnotes to the two poems reveals how Pushkin goes beyond the personal connection between Chénier and himself. Pushkin's notes, seven in number, each brief, cite Henri de la Touche, whose introduction to the 1819 collection of Chénier's verse was a major source of information about the French poet. Pushkin also quotes Chénier's works to identify names which

figure in Chénier's monologues. The notes are written partly in French, partly in Russian. Pushkin uses French not only to quote de la Touche or Chénier; he writes "Voyez les odes qui lui sont addressées" (n. 2), and "Voyez ses iambes" (n. 4). The use of French here is doubly noticeable since previous notes are in Russian. Abel is identified as "odin iz druzei A. Sh." ("one of A. Sh.'s friends"), with Chénier's name spelled in the Russian way with *sh,* not *ch.*

The mixture of French and Russian in the footnotes has the same informality as some of Pushkin's Arzamas letters, where much banter is interspersed with serious discussions of poetry. The notes to **"André Chénier"** have the appearance of having been jotted down and never having been revised. Because **"André Chénier"** is written in Pushkin's most elevated style, the casual tone is all the more striking. But the footnotes do not threaten the serious character of the poem; rather, they elevate the portrait of Chénier by proving that the subject has been well researched, that Pushkin knows much about Chénier's life and work. These brief notes authenticate Pushkin's elegy in a way not attempted by the kind of marginal narrative which Batiushkov appended to his poem about Tasso. By telling his readers which sources he has consulted, Pushkin asserts that his poem about Chénier is "true," that its facts can be verified. Surely the notes address the wider reading audience, whom the introduction seemed to exclude. Here, then, is the final textual apostrophe, straight from the poet to his readers, directing them to the documentation for his poems It is in this sense that **"André Chénier"** is a historical elegy, as it is curiously labeled by most scholars: it uses information that can be checked in other documents.

While the footnotes suggest that **"André Chénier"** strives for a kind of historical authenticity, the discussion of poetry within the body of the poem speaks to the issue of poetic authenticity. After the monologue has listed various forces which led to Chénier's imprisonment, the poet turns to his own works as the ultimate repository of blame. Immediately after the narrator's interruption, Chénier begins a long series of couplets in hexameter. He asks, "Kuda, kuda zavlek menia vrazhdebnyi genii?" ("Where, where has my hostile genius lured me?" l. 110). The contrast between his days of naive freedom and the confined, frightening hours separating him from the guillotine is punctuated by such exclamations as "kak sladko zhizn´ moia lilas´ i utekala!" ("how sweetly my life has flowed and streamed past!" l. 127). Chénier begins to resent the poetry which led to his arrest, but when anger moves him to turn against his verse, an immediate reversal takes place. . . .

And what will I leave? Forgotten traces
Of insane jealousy and insignificant daring.

O perish, my voice, and you, false specter,
   You, the word, hollow sound . . .
         O no!
Silence, thou fainthearted complaint!
Poet, be proud and rejoice:

         . . . . .

                    (ll. 137-42)

In the very line which would assert the emptiness of
his poetry by calling it a "hollow sound" (l. 141), an
abrupt shift occurs from six- to four-footed iambs.

The shift is abrupt for several reasons. The preceding
thirty lines had moved smoothly in hexametric couplets without irregularities in caesura or in rhyme. At
line 141, a new grouping begins which mixes quatrain forms freely (AbAb, AbbA, and AAbb) through
the end of the poem. The "hollow sound" line fits into
neither series but subtly links them. "Pustoi" looks
back to the preceding couplet ending in "nichtozhnoi"
/ "lozhnyi" to form a kind of de facto rhyme. But the
rhyme is incomplete because of the end stress in
"pustoi" and because it would rhyme the ending
"oi" with a pair of feminine rhymes in "-ozhnoi" /
"-ozhnyi," and because the word falls technically in
the middle of the line. The actual last word, "net,"
could rhyme with the ensuing "poet" / "let" pair ("Ty
ne ponik glavnoi poslushnoi/ Pered pozorom nashikh
let"), but an odd fifth line would still result. "Ty,
slovo, zvuk pustoi . . . / O net!" ("You, the word,
hollow sound . . . / O no!") remains the marked line,
all the more so since it is broken off after the third
foot to correspond with the break in Chénier's thoughts.

That the line is marked in so many ways is curious in
itself. The poet who curses his work in a moment of
extreme despair would not seem noteworthy. It is the
radical dissociation of the poet from his poetry that is
new: Chénier addresses his verse as if it were an
entity separate from himself. Until this point, he has
identified his fate with that of his verse. Not only has
Chénier implied that he will live when his friends
recite his verse, he has told them to say as much:
"skazhite: eto on; / Vot rech´ ego" ("Say: it is he; /
These are his words" ll. 95-96). In this penultimate
apostrophe to his poems, Chénier separates himself
from them with sufficient distance to judge their success. As the apostrophe turns into an address to himself as the poet, Chénier moves toward a prophecy of
doom for his executioners . . .

   Singer, be proud, proud; and you, violent beast,
      Play now with my head;
   It is in your talons. But listen, know, godless one,
   My cry, my furious laugh will follow you!
                                    (ll. 160-63)

Chénier's moral superiority here is vast. His condemnation of those who would condemn him depends
on the assumption that his powers of prophecy as a
poet exceed the temporal might of any government.
Pushkin makes much of the contrast in *Boris Godunov*.[23]
The fact that he worked on that play and on **"André
Chénier"** at a time when his relationship with his
tsar was at a crisis point begins to explain the presence
of this conflict in both works. In **"André Chénier,"** it
is the dissociation of Chénier from his poetry which
enables him strongly to condemn his government. After
repudiating the idea that his poetry is a "hollow sound,"
Chénier affirms the power of the word to predict and to
encourage the unseating of tyrants. Thus, Chénier's
assertion of prophetic powers greater than those of
the rulers depends on the separation of his personal
fate from that of his poetry.

During the romantic period, a strong link between
the poet and his word was forged in an attempt to
justify the writing of short poems about the self. In
doubt about the validity of other kinds of experience, romantic poets could write with greatest certainty about their own lives. The trend begins as early
as Rousseau's *Confessions,* and it is Wordsworth
who sees how complex a task this actually was,
seeking to express himself " . . . by words / Which
speak of nothing more than what we are."

In Russia, poetry focusing on the self was closely associated with Lord Byron, especially his *Childe Harold,
Manfred,* and some of the more melancholy lyrics of
1816. Pushkin hence takes his very negative stance
against Byron in **"André Chénier"** in order to challenge excessive egoism in poetry. In a note about
Byron's dramas, Pushkin wrote: "Byron threw a one-
sided glance on the world and on the nature of man,
then turned away from them and became buried in himself. He presented us with the shade of his own self."[24]
Pushkin also describes Byron's poetry as self-indulgent
in a letter to Viazemskii. He refers to an article in
which Viazemskii lamented the fact that Thomas Moore
had carried out Byron's wish that his memoirs be
burned. Pushkin finds the loss good riddance: "Why
do you regret the loss of Byron's notes? the devil with
them! Thank God that they were lost. He was confess-
ing in his verse, unintentionally, carried away by the
ecstasy of the poetry."[25] Pushkin deprecates the public's
inordinate fondness for confessions and he mocks the
writers who pander to that taste: "There is no one one
loves, no one one knows like one's own self. An inex-
haustible subject."[26] The letter is not an attack on
Byron's writing in general—it opens with high praise
for *Don Juan.* Pushkin objects only to the works in
which Byron, and other writers, can write only, and
unselfconsciously, about themselves.

Pushkin condemns Byronic egoism with such force,
especially in the closing lines of the letter to Viazemskii

just cited, that one wonders whether he is not taking himself to task for some of his own youthful lyrics. Pushkin wrote a poem, for example, at the beginning of his southern exile (precisely when Raevskii introduced him to Byron's poetry), which qualifies easily as the kind of lyric repudiated in the letter to Viazemskii. "Pogaslo dnevnoe svetilo" ("Day's luminary has faded," 1820) invokes the fading morning sun, the lost confidantes of youth, and the tears of intense feeling.[27] Though the style differs noticeably from that of **"André Chénier,"** where rhetorical exclamations and Church Slavic diction elevate a highly complex message, the images in "Day's luminary has faded" are precisely those found in **"André Chénier."** In the first poem, there are countless ellipses, in contrast to the elaborations of **"André Chénier,"** as if the poet were so overpowered by the emotions of his poem that he could not write about his feelings in a more articulate manner. Here, too, apostrophe dominates, but it is to the supremely romantic image of the sea that Pushkin addresses "Day's luminary has faded." Pushkin's experience in the south was, of course, a journey to the sea, but the vast expanse of water is clearly associated with romantic poetry in this poem, and Byron's influence is readily apparent. In the poem traditionally cited as Pushkin's farewell to his Byronic period, **"K moriu"** (**"To the Sea,"** 1824), the sea is the object of the poet's address, the emblem of the south and all that it meant in Pushkin's early development as a poet.

Pushkin uses the same images that occur in "Day's luminary has faded" (except for the sea) when he writes **"André Chénier"** partly in parody of the earlier poem, whose emotions Pushkin might well have regarded as trivial in 1825. But in rejecting "Day's luminary has faded," Lord Byron, and all falsely self-oriented poetry, **"André Chénier"** also takes on the burden of replacing their subject matter. The poem sets out to explore and to exemplify the "true" elegy.

Although Pushkin himself appears to have had a clear idea of what the elegy represented as a metrical category in ancient times,[28] many writers in the 1820s regarded the elegy as synonymous with the "elegiac." Nikolai Grech's definition in his four-volume textbook on literature reflects the very general notions of the era: an elegy is defined as any "lyric poem depicting the mixed feeling of joy and sadness." Grech adds that the tone is to be *tomnyi* ("languid") and that a language of the heart designed to affect the reader should reign.[29]

Pushkin's textbook from his lycée days, Laharpe's *Cours de littérature ancienne et moderne,* gives an even broader definition of the elegy.

> Quoique le mot *élégie* vienne du grec [elegos] qui signifie *complainte* cependant elle n'était pas

toujours plaintive; elle fut originairement comme aujourd'hui, destinée à chanter différents objets, les dieux, le retour d'un ami ou le jour de sa naissance, ou, comme a dit Boileau, elle *gémissait sur un cercueil.* . . . L'élégie fut souvent le chant de l'amour heureux ou malheureux.[30]

Laharpe's definition seems designed to challenge the supposed narrowness of those who see elegies as inherently sad, but he conforms to the notion that a definition of the elegy can be achieved by looking at the emotions it seeks to evoke.

These definitions might apply best to Pushkin's early efforts in the genre poems which he called elegies and which mixed the languid tone of yearning for past loves and distant lands with the ever-present foreboding of death. A perfect example is his **"Elegiia"** of 1817 ("Opiat´ ia vash, o iunye druz´ia," "Again I am yours, o young friends"), though there are several others, including "Day's luminary has faded." When Pushkin uses the term "elegy" or even "elegiac" in his critical writings, it is usually in a broad sense, to label entire groups of poems, or to characterize the writings of poets like Del´vig or Baratynskii. There is no article of definition, as there is for such equally problematic terms as "romanticism," "nationalism," or for other modes of literature, like drama or fiction.

By the mid-1820s the elegy was clearly becoming problematic for Pushkin, partly because it became a vehicle for excesses of self-expression and thus was associated with the false definition of romanticism along thematic lines. Though Pushkin labeled several of his pre-1820 works as "elegies" (three in 1816, one each in 1817 and 1819), the only work called an elegy in 1825 was a disrespectful litany on the death of Anna L´vovna Pushkina. Pushkin disavowed this work in a letter to Viazemskii, claiming that it was more the doing of Del´vig.[31] Another poem of 1825, **"Solovei i kukushka"** (**"The nightingale and the cuckoo"**), also jokes about the ubiquity of elegiac sadness. Its last lines read, "Izbav´ nas bozhe, Ot elegicheskikh kuku!" ("Save us, o lord, / From the elegiac cuckoos!")[32] Other pejorative references to the elegy can be found in some of his letters,[33] and in *Evgenii Onegin,* when the narrator mocks Lenskii's devotion to his sad muse.[34]

Pushkin was impatient with the elegy, but he never rejected it completely. He went on to write at least one extremely successful poem which he called an elegy, **"Bezumnykh let ugasshee vesel´e"** (**"The faded joy of heedless years,"** 1830). Pushkin also wrote reviews about elegies and favorably mentioned such works by friends in letters to them.[35] In one letter, Pushkin concludes that the mere fact that imitators of elegies are intolerable does not mean that the genre itself should be banished from the "poetic oligarchy."[36]

"André Chénier" takes a stand against false elegies and, in a way typical of Pushkin's poetic principles, offers an alternative which may not be a pure elegy but which is somehow a more authentic elegiac poem. Certainly the poem is not an elegy in the classical sense: its meter approaches the elegiac distich only in the long section of couplets. "André Chénier" uses metrical transpositions freely to call attention to particular ideas or to achieve greater emotional intensity. The poem resembles the elegy defined by Grech, at least in terms of mood and subject matter. But the speaker moves farther into the realms of political indictment and impassioned prophecy than popular definitions of the elegy allow.

Tonally, "André Chénier" better fits Grech's definition of the ode: "A lyrical depiction of known feelings, in which the exalted Poet, forgetting all that is of the Earth, is transported into the eternal world of the mind."[37] The sense of soaring emerges in Chénier's exalted prophecy, and a feeling of imagined escape from the prison cell is present throughout his monologue. Moreover, the epigraph which Pushkin chooses is not from Chénier's elegies or even from his *Iambes,* but from *La jeune captive,* Chénier's last ode. In "André Chénier," the high diction, the stately progress of ideas, the burning prophecy at the last—all lift this poem out of the range of personal poetry associated with the elegy in the 1820s. Without the strophic divisions of the ode, and depending on narrative flow and dramatic intensity more than on the declamatory style of the ode, "André Chénier" still reaches far beyond the elegy as Pushkin knew it.[38]

There are several possible explanations for the mixing of ode and elegy in "André Chénier." First, the poem becomes a bridge between the eighteenth and nineteenth centuries by fusing the two genres which typified each age. In chapter 4 of *Evgenii Onegin,* Pushkin writes that he does not want to set two centuries quarreling by pitting the ode against the elegy.[39] Here Pushkin shows himself expressing the two genres as conflicting literary ideals, but it is the characteristic elegy which Pushkin wishes to temper with an admixture of elements from the ode. He seeks in "André Chénier" to avoid the false elegies which arise from false sentiments. Pushkin had judged Batiushkov's *The Dying Tasso* a failure for its lack of feeling.[40] In the movement away from Byron, Pushkin sought not purity of genre but purity of feeling. By evoking genuine significant emotions, Pushkin seeks a "true" elegy in "André Chénier" analogous to a "true" (*istinnyi*) romanticism. The presence of features from another genre does not diminish the intensity or purity of feeling in the poem; on the contrary, it elevates the meaning of these feelings.

While the false elegy is self-indulgent, "André Chénier" achieves another improvement in the genre by assuming a point of view other than that of Pushkin.[41] The poem's structure and complexities of apostrophe discussed above affirm that otherness by creating several barriers between Pushkin and the lines spoken by Chénier. The poem's reliance on apostrophe calls attention to its separate levels of speaker-listener relationships. Pushkin further validates the highly emotional content of the poem by adding footnotes which authenticate the information given about Chénier, and he intensifies the emotional impact of his poem by using traditional images with unexpected power.

A certain distance between Pushkin and his subject is encouraged, then, by several structural features of the poem. There is something typically Pushkinian about this act of distancing. Analyses of *Evgenii Onegin* normally comment on the narrator's claim that he is not to be confused with his hero. Dissociation is not limited to its playful varieties in the novel in verse: poetic distance is a key element of Pushkin's relationship to the dominant literary movement of his time, romanticism.

The presence of elements of the ode fortifies and magnifies Pushkin's argument for the powers of the poet in "André Chénier." The theme is not one which Pushkin annexed from Chénier's work; *La jeune captive* and the *Iambes* are nonpolemical works suffused with a kind of religious bliss. Pushkin's celebration of the power of the poet, the grand recognition toward which "André Chénier" as an ode builds, is marked in the poem by an opposition to the forces which rule France at the time of Chénier's death. By extension, Pushkin contrasts his own powers as a poet, demonstrated with great confidence in "André Chénier," with that of Russia's tsars.

Pushkin seems to have been meditating on some kind of connection between the tsar and himself in 1825. The theme is central to *Boris Godunov;* in this work no one commands the real authority to govern Russia, and characters like Pimen and the Holy Fool exemplify the potentially visionary power of art. In the notebook which contained the autographs of *Boris Godunov,* "André Chénier," and the fourth chapter of *Evgenii Onegin,* Pushkin also wrote out an imagined conversation with Alexander I, in which he imagines what he might say to himself if he were tsar.[42] Pushkin here suggests that fate connected him to Alexander I because they had the same first name: he even plays on the coincidence in a letter to his wife written in 1834 about their son, another Aleksandr.[43]

Pushkin depends on an opposition between the power of the poet and the authority of the government in some of his earlier political lyrics, for instance, "Vol´nost. Oda" ("Liberty. An Ode," 1817) and "Derevnia" ("The Countryside," 1819). In letters from the 1820s Pushkin uses metaphors that suggest deepened parallels between the political and poetic realms. He speculates about the "republic of letters," probably alluding to Chénier's *République des lettres*.[44] Pushkin calls the changes in prevailing artistic tastes a "change in the ministry on Parnassus."[45]

In another remark about his children's names, Pushkin's preference for literary over imperial names is telling. When Natal'ia Nikolaevna wanted to name their second son Nikolai, Pushkin objected. Rather than naming his son after the reigning tsar, Pushkin gave his wife a choice of two names full of personal significance: Gavrila and Grigorii.[46] Gavrila Pushkin was an ancestor who helped the False Dmitrii to the throne during the Time of Troubles; he is included in the cast of characters for *Boris Godunov.* Grigorii was the given name of the monk who became the False Dmitrii.

In **"André Chénier,"** Pushkin presents a poet with greater moral authority than that of the government which exerts overwhelming political force. While on the intertextual level **"André Chénier"** reveals an underlying conversation with Byron, in terms of political authority it suggests a conversation between Aleksandr Pushkin and Alexander I as one kind of ruler to another. The imagined conversation between Pushkin and his tsar, including both the possible conversation which he wrote out and the dialogue suggested by **"André Chénier,"** has as its subject the conditions for Pushkin's release from exile.

By displaying the powers of the poet in **"André Chénier,"** Pushkin offers new imperatives for his release. Rather than penning a work whose political ideology might please the tsar, as some of his friends urged, Pushkin may have sought to encourage his release by writing literature of such magnitude that no ruler would dare to keep him in Mikhailovskoe. Such personal reasons further account for the elevated style of **"André Chénier,"** as of *Boris Godunov,* works which Pushkin knew would have an imperial audience. **"André Chénier"** plays grandly with the trope of apostrophe, projecting its ultimate addressee as a ruler whose government is empowered to release the author from exile. Yet another triangle emerges, this one dependent on a reading, not a listening situation. Pushkin writes "about" Chénier for the benefit of his tsar. Distance from the subject remains crucial, since Pushkin cannot possibly win over Alexander I if he is too closely linked to the liberal ideas behind Chénier's monologues. We as readers again take on secondary status as witnesses to a complex exchange between poets and their governments, but once more the role only seems small. Without other readers and writers telling Alexander I that Pushkin is a great poet, his efforts may well be in vain. As later incidents provoked by Faddei Bulgarin sadly suggest, Russian tsars tended to trust others in judgments of literary talent and political intent.

As much as Pushkin played with the notion that his literary power might achieve his release, he was sufficiently realistic and politically aware to know that his talents were of no actual use to any ruler so long as he remained the independent poet he always was. Politics never overwhelm poetry in Pushkin's work, and it is his commitment to the priority of aesthetic considerations which separates Pushkin from the Decembrist poets. In **"André Chénier"** a sense of alienation from revolutionary poets emerges, especially when Chénier looks back at his poetry, amazed that it has been interpreted as a political act. **"André Chénier"** is a great poem precisely because it could not be "used" for any external aim, political or otherwise. Perhaps Pushkin sensed as much and included the parallel between poets and kings not only to show who was more important, but also to advance his own claims to a commanding position in the "republic of letters" which comprised Russian literature. Pushkin made impressive gains in the year 1825, and **"André Chénier"** shows Pushkin becoming a true "author"—a voice speaking with a sense of authority of its own definition.

Notes

[1] Pushkin responded with disbelief to letters from friends suggesting that *Boris Godunov* might bring about his release; see A. S. Pushkin, *Polnoe sobranie sochinenii* (Leningrad, 1939-1949), 13:172-73, 271. Among Pushkin's answers, the letter to P. A. Viazemskii, in which Pushkin compares himself to his Holy Fool, his ears sticking out of any conventional political cap, is the best known. See A. S. Pushkin, *Polnoe sobranie sochinenii* (hereafter *PSS*) (Leningrad, 1977-1979), 10:144-45. This, the most recent Academy edition of Pushkin, will be cited by volume and page number. References to the poem "André Chénier" are given in parentheses by line. All English translations are my own.

[2] Chénier's English biographer judges him to be strongly neoclassical; see Francis Scarfe, *André Chénier: His Life and Work* (Oxford, 1965). The introduction to his works in French takes a less firm stand but notes that he is usually seen as the first romantic. See André Chénier, *Oeuvres complètes* (Paris, 1950), xxxiii.

[3] V. B. Sandomirskaia outlines Pushkin's general interest in Chénier in "Perevody i perelozheniia Pushkina iz A. Shen'e," *Pushkin. Issledovaniia i materialy* (Leningrad, 1978) 8:90-106.

[4] An easily available source for Pushkin's ideas about romanticism is John Mersereau, Jr.'s study "Pushkin's Concept of Romanticism," *Studies in Romanticism*, 3, no. 1 (Autumn, 1963): 23-41. In Pushkin's essays, the central text is the drafted work on classical and romantic poetry (7:24-26) written, significantly, in 1825.

[5] *PSS,* 10:75-76.

[6] Ibid., 7:352-53.

[7] Chénier, *Oeuvres complètes,* p. 127.

[8] Some excellent research exists on the precise dating of "André Chénier." The issue is not without importance because 44 lines which were censored from Chénier's first speech were then circulated separately with the words "December 14" written across the top. As Pushkin pointed out in his own defense when the matter nearly came to public attention in 1828, the poem was completed months before the Decembrist uprising. See V. B. Sandomirskaia, "Andre Shen´e," *Stikhotvorenii A. Pushkina 1820-1830—kh godov* (Leningrad, 1974), pp. 14-18; and N. Eidel´man, *Pushkin dekabristy* (Moscow, 1979), pp. 314-27.

[9] *PSS,* 2:231.

[10] Francis Scarfe, *André Chénier,* pp. 326-35.

[11] Viktor Zhirmunskii's study *Bairon i Pushkin,* recently republished (Leningrad, 1978), still offers the clearest analysis of Pushkin's encounter with Byron as one facet of his struggle with romanticism.

[12] *PSS,* 2:231.

[13] Ibid., 10:107.

[14] Ibid., 2:231.

[15] Compare Michael Cooke's *Acts of Inclusion* (New Haven, Ct., 1979), pp. 12-18, where he theorizes that elegy and prophecy take up the same essential content during the romantic period.

[16] Compare the much-discussed closing of *Boris Godunov.* Pushkin ultimately removed the people's rousing cheers for the new Tsar Dmitrii and left only the comment "Narod bezmolvstvuet" ("The people are silent") as an implicit condemnation of the pretender's reign. An interesting article on this changed ending is M. P. Alekseev's "Remarka Pushkina 'Narod bezmolvstvuet,' " reprinted in his *Pushkin. Sravnitel´ no-istoricheskie issledovaniia* (Leningrad, 1972), pp. 208-39. All subsequent commentators follow Alekseev's conclusion that the people's silence demonstrates their awareness that their lot has not been improved by the change in rulers.

[17] On Pushkin's consistent use of the caesura in his hexametric line, see S. Bondi, "Pushkin russkii gekzametr," *O Pushkine* (Moscow, 1978), pp. 310-71.

[18] See L. P. Grossman, "Pushkin i Andre Shen´e," reprinted in his *Pushkin. Etiudy o Pushkine* (Moscow, 1928), pp. 194-96, for a discussion of images borrowed from Chénier.

[19] Boris Tomashevskii argues that the images are more from Pushkin's own early lyrics than from Chénier in his *Pushkin. Kniga vtoraia* (Moscow-Leningrad, 1961), p. 71. Both he and Grossman, as well as Sandomirskaia and Eidel´man in the essays cited above, have observed that Pushkin's metrical openness and stylistic informality were qualities learned from Chénier.

[20] K. N. Batiushkov, *Opyty v stikhakh i proze* (St. Petersburg, 1817) reprinted in the "Literaturnyi pamiatnik" series (Moscow, 1977), pp. 325-33.

[21] V. B. Sandomirskaia, "Andre Shen´e," p. 18, lists other "prison poems" written during the period, but she concludes that they also go back to Batiushkov for the basic model.

[22] *PSS,* 7:390-411.

[23] *Boris Godunov,* the fourth chapter of *Evgenii Onegin,* and "André Chénier" are as found in a single notebook, along with the poems "Ia byl svidetelem zlatoi tvoei vesny" ("I was witness to your golden spring"), "Segodnia bal u Satana" ("Today is a ball at Satan's"), and the imagined conversation with Alexander I. Comparisons of these works, for instance Eidel´man's *Pushkin i dekabristy,* emphasize the political connections among them.

[24] *PSS,* 7:37.

[25] Ibid., 10:148.

[26] Ibid.

[27] Ibid., 2:7-8.

[28] Ibid., 7:24, 37.

[29] Nikolai Grech, *Uchebnaia kniga russkoi slovesnosti* (St. Petersburg, 1830), 3:160.

[30] J. F. Laharpe, *Cours de la littérature ancienne et moderne* (Paris, 1816), 1:594.

[31] *PSS,* 10:144.

[32] Ibid., 2:250.

[33] Ibid., 10:90, 135, 210.

[34] See especially *Evgenii Onegin,* 4:31-33. Pushkin wrote chapter 4 in 1825, again in the same notebook mentioned above (n. 23).

[35] Examples are too numerous to cite in the text. Among them: 7:59-60, 81, 118, 153, 165, 184, 205, 244, 287; 10:36, 58, 314.

[36] *PSS,* 7:36.

[37] Nikolai Grech, *Uchebnaia kniga russkoi slovesnosti,* 3:34.

[38] Boris Tomashevskii has written about the "hybrid elegy" in Pushkin's time. See especially his "Strofika Pushkina," *Stikh i iazyk* (Moscow-Leningrad, 1959), p. 265. Compare the recent textbook by N. B. Fridman, *Romantizm v tvorchestve A. S. Pushkina* (Moscow, 1980), pp. 33-34, where "André Chénier" is viewed in the traditional way as a historical elegy, though Fridman cites many of the same facts which have caused me here to move away from that belief.

[39] *PSS,* 5:78-79.

[40] Ibid., 7:411.

[41] See Fridman, *Romantizm v tvorchestve A. S. Pushkina,* pp. 32-34. Fridman finds a poet's choice of historical subjects over contemporary themes typical of the romantic urge toward escape. Compare L. S. Fleishman, "Iz istorii elegii v pushkinskuiu epokhu," *Pushkinskii sbornik* (Rigd, 1968), pp. 31-35.

[42] *PSS,* 7:51-62.

[43] Ibid., 10:370.

[44] Ibid., 10:94; compare ibid., 10:98, 363.

[45] Ibid., 10:98.

[46] V. Veresaev, *Pushkin v zhizni* (Moscow, 1936), 2:232.

Paul Debreczeny (essay date 1983)

SOURCE: "Experiments with Narrative Modes," in *The Other Pushkin: A Study of Alexander Pushkin's Prose Fiction,* Stanford University Press, 1983, 386 p.

[*In the following essay, Debreczeny discusses innovative developments in the narrative technique of Pushkin's prose fiction.*]

I

Pushkin made his first serious attempt at writing fiction in the summer of 1827, when he completed six chapters of a proposed historical novel, now known to us as *The Blackamoor of Peter the Great.* The prototype for its central character, Ibrahim, was Pushkin's maternal great-grandfather, Abram Hannibal, an African who had been brought to Russia as a child during the reign of Peter I. Having been raised by Peter, Ibrahim (like the actual Hannibal) was sent to Paris to study military engineering. When we meet him in the opening chapter of the novel, he has already finished his training and distinguished himself in French military service, and would be ready to return to Russia if he were not involved in an adulterous affair with an elegant French lady, the Countess D. Their union even produces a baby—a black one, whom the Countess's attendants surreptitiously exchange for a white one in order to conceal the father's identity from her husband—but Ibrahim eventually returns to Russia, driven both by a sense of indebtedness to Peter and by a fear that the Countess will grow tired of him. He participates in Peter's efforts to build the new Russian empire and is treated kindly by his foster father: Peter even decides to find a bride for him. His choice falls on young Natalia Rzhevskaia, whose father is a high-ranking nobleman of the old school, opposed to Peter's reforms. Precisely because he has been in opposition, the old Rzhevskii dares not refuse his daughter's hand to the Tsar's favorite. When Natalia learns of her father's decision she falls ill, not so much because Ibrahim's unfamiliar appearance frightens her as because she is in love with a young man, Valerian, who had been brought up as an orphan at her father's house and lately joined the military. When we last see her, she has finally come around from a coma of two weeks' duration but is still unwell.

At this point in the narrative Pushkin's work on the novel came to a halt. He took up the project again in the spring of 1828, but this time succeeded in writing only one more page—showing Valerian's return to the Rzhevskii household—which is all that remains of Chapter Seven. Having given up hope of finishing the novel, he published two fragments from it, in 1829 and 1830.[1] The assembled text of all the extant parts (with a few minor omissions) was published posthumously by the editors of the journal *The Contemporary,* who also gave it its title.[2]

How much Pushkin identified with his great-grandfather can be seen from his verse epistle **"To Iurev"** (1820), in which he described himself as a descendant of Negroes. Fascinated by his ancestor, he had attempted to write about him several times before he set to work on the novel. As early as 1824 he wrote a fragment of a poem beginning with the line "As the Tsar's Blackamoor Thought of Marrying," and he also appended a footnote to the first edition of Chapter One of *Onegin* (6: 654-55) describing his ancestry in order to explain why he called the skies of Africa his own. This footnote, amounting to a brief biography of Hannibal (based on family tradition), might have been taken from Pushkin's autobiographical sketches.[3] Thus the material that was to lie at the foundation of Pushkin's historical novel had already been treated by him in a nonfictional way.

During 1825 and 1826 Pushkin had an opportunity to expand his knowledge—hitherto confined to family tradition—about Hannibal and his times. Not only did he acquire, from a great-uncle, a handwritten biography of Hannibal,[4] but he was also able to read I. I. Golikov's *The Deeds of Peter the Great* (1788-97), which his neighbors, the Osipovs, had in their library.[5] Furthermore, the text of **The Blackamoor** clearly shows that he had familiarized himself with A. O. Kornilovich's four sketches of Russian mores under Peter I, published in 1824.[6] In pursuing these sources, Pushkin probably had a historical essay, rather than fiction, in mind. Some of the material he had gathered for a historical study never became "fictionalized" as he worked on the novel: for example, the description of the Regency after the death of Louis XIV, given in Chapter One, is very close both stylistically and conceptually to Pushkin's purely essay-like **"Notes on Eighteenth-Century Russian History."**[7] It is not clear why Pushkin decided in the end to switch to fiction. Possibly he simply came across some unflattering details about Hannibal and thought he could handle them more easily in fiction than in a conscientious historical account.[8] In any case, having turned to fiction, he did not strictly adhere to facts: for instance, he made Peter propose to the Rzhevskiis on Ibrahim's behalf, though the real Hannibal did not marry until well after Peter's death; he made Ibrahim's bride a member of the ancient nobility in order to sharpen the social contrast with Peter's black officer; and he brought together such historical personalities as I. F. Kopievich and Feofan Prokopovich, who could not have been at Peter's Court at the same time.[9]

The most noticeable trace of Pushkin's original non-fictional approach to the story is the novel's detached mode of narration. In the text Pushkin left us, the author-narrator steps directly before the reader only twice: he begins Chapter Four with the words "I must now acquaint my gracious reader with Gavrila Afanasevich Rzhevskii" (8: 19); and toward the end of the same chapter he tells us that he is making an aside. Both of these first-person appearances of the author, however, are motivated purely by technical convenience, and no attempt is made to create a narrator with a personality of his own. Beyond this, there are a few occasions when the author's hand is revealed indirectly. Sometimes he introduces generalizations that are not attributable to any particular character in the novel and so must belong to him. He says, for instance, "Whatever you say, love without aspirations and demands touches the feminine heart more surely than all the wiles of seduction," and that "to follow the thoughts of a great man is a most engrossing mental exercise" (8: 5, 13).[10] At other times he attaches emotionally colored epithets to characters—"unfortunate" Ibrahim, "poor" Natasha (8: 9, 32)—or asks rhetorical questions—"What sensations filled Ibrahim's heart? Jealousy? Rage? Despair?" (8: 15)—both of which imply the presence of a sympathizing or interested author.

But his presence is nowhere obtrusive; nor does he ever enter into a dialogue with the reader.

Such a detached mode of narration, as we have seen, was a reaction on Pushkin's part to the conspicuous assumption of roles characteristic of his poetry. True, the author's own personality seemed to be hidden, as the contrasting lyrical personae—the Byronic poet and the patriotic bard—voiced their respective points of view in **The Prisoner of the Caucasus** and its Epilogue, but it was nevertheless obvious that the author was manipulating these lyrical personae. What was needed was not histrionics, but a detached narrator, rather like Father Pimen of **Boris Godunov,** who would simply record events as a "witness of many years" (7: 17). The narrator of **The Blackamoor** emerges as just such a chronicler.

The mode of narration Pushkin adopted for his novel was most unusual for the 1820's. Jane Austen had developed a similar authorial stance in the preceding decades, but Pushkin . . . was probably not familiar with her novels. Balzac and Stendhal had not yet published the novels that were to make their fame. In the fiction that Pushkin is known to have read before 1827, the convention was that the reader be initiated into the secrets of authorship, and that the author emerge as a distinct personality. As Washington Irving put it, "The public is apt to be curious about the sources from whence the author draws his stories, doubtless that it may know how far to put faith in them."[11]

Voltaire, whose prose Pushkin professed to admire the most (11: 18), attributed his *Candide* (1759) to a certain Doctor Ralph and claimed to have acquired additions to the manuscript from among the papers found in the doctor's pockets after his death. Horace Walpole, father of an altogether different tradition—that of the Gothic novel—whose writings were well known to Pushkin, claimed that he had found the manuscript of *The Castle of Otranto* (1764), written by a sixteenth-century monk, in the library of an ancient English family.[12] The manuscript of Benjamin Constant's *Adolphe* (1816)—much closer to Pushkin, both in time and in spirit—had been sent to the author by mistake.

Most interesting from the point of view of our investigation are the attitudes of the most popular novelist of the time, Sir Walter Scott, whom Pushkin praised for presenting history "in a domestic manner" (12: 195). Scott's *Tales of My Landlord,* a series that contained *The Black Dwarf* (1816), *Old Mortality* (1816), *The Heart of Midlothian* (1818), *A Legend of Montrose* (1819), and *The Bride of Lammermoor* (1819), was attributed to a whole set of fictitious narrators: the stories were supposed to have been told by the landlord of a public house in the town of Gandercleugh, written down by Peter Pattieson, the town's assistant schoolmaster, and published by Jedediah Cleishbotham, the schoolmaster, to whom the late Pattieson had bequeathed them. In addition, each tale was furnished with an introduction in which Cleishbotham gave particulars about the people from whom the landlord had heard the tale or who had at least contributed some details to it. Finally, two other fashionable writers of the day whose books Pushkin read—Washington Irving and E. T. A. Hoffmann—were notorious for their fictitious narrators, for their framed tales, and for the teasing relationship they created between the narrator and the reader.[13]

Russian writers contemporary to Pushkin or preceding him followed the dominant trend. N. M. Karamzin, whom Pushkin grudgingly acknowledged to have been the best Russian prose writer of the period (11: 19), had heard the story of "Poor Liza" (1792) from the heroine's repentant seducer, Erast. V. T. Narezhnyi's *Russian Gil Blas* (1814)—in keeping with the picaresque tradition—was characterized by a shifting narrative point of view and by the presence of inserted tales. And A. A. Bestuzhev-Marlinskii, whom Pushkin once admonished not to write in the manner of Scott (13: 80), claimed either to have derived his tales from historical sources (e.g. "Roman and Olga"; 1823) or to have gathered them by the campfire ("An Evening on Bivouac" and "A Second Evening on Bivouac"; 1823).

A frame for a tale or a fictitious narrator was, in itself, merely a technical device that authors sometimes dropped after a point; what made these devices important was that they were symptomatic of an overbearing authorial presence. Scott, for instance, could not leave it to the reader to simply follow the fate of his characters: as he said in his 1829 Preface to *Waverley* (1814), he liked to revert to first-person discourse with the reader even in a novel narrated in the third person:

> The author can only promise to be as little of an egotist as the situation will permit. It is perhaps an indifferent sign of a disposition to keep his word, that having introduced himself in the third person singular, he proceeds in the second paragraph to make use of the first. But it appears to him that the seeming modesty connected with the former mode of writing, is overbalanced by the inconvenience of stiffness and affectation which attends it during a narrative of some length, and which may be observed less or more in every work in which the third person is used, from the Commentaries of Caesar, to the Autobiography of Alexander the Corrector.[14]

In order to avoid the "stiffness" inherent in objective, third-person narration, Scott plays games with his reader. In Chapter Five of *Waverley,* for instance, he claims not to know whether it was "the merest accident in the world" that Cecilia Stubbs, daughter of the local squire, had taken up walking through Waverley-Chase—a place frequented by the dashing young Edward. The reader, of course, does know; he can see that the author is teasing him; and, as a result, a special author-reader relationship is formed. In Chapter Fifty-four of the same novel, when Edward is ready to fall in love with Rose Bradwardine, Scott reports how the young man suddenly discovers that Rose's manner is "most engaging," that "she has a more correct ear than Flora," and that "she has more feeling, too." Edward, so slow to realize the inclinations of his heart, appears to be somewhat on the silly side, but the reader, of course, is not so slow to perceive what is going on. A private joke has passed between author and reader, behind the character's back.

Given the conventions of the period—when the most popular novelist regarded a neutral, impersonal narrative as both stiff and affected—it was a bold undertaking on the part of Pushkin to begin his career as a prose writer with just such a narrative. In doing so, he anticipated a later trend in the development of nineteenth-century fiction, which was to be formulated in Flaubert's famous statement: "It is one of my principles that one must not be his own subject. The artist must be in his work like God in His creation: invisible and omnipotent; he should be everywhere felt, but nowhere seen."[15] Although this trend was not an exclusive one (authors have never abdicated their right to experiment with different narrative modes), its powerful influence on Russian literature is witnessed by such masterpieces—otherwise vastly different—as *Fathers and Sons* (1862), *Crime and Punishment* (1866), and *Anna Karenina* (1875-77).

What mattered most, as Pushkin sought a new manner of writing, was not just the question of whether the author was hidden from the reader or revealed to him, of whether he spoke in the first person or the third, but the question of whether he would be courageous enough to write as an intelligent chronicler, whose attitudes would be subtle and implicit, without clownish masks and false assumptions. In *The Blackamoor of Peter the Great* Pushkin projects the image of an author who does not have to pretend—for the sake of a joke with the reader or for any other reason—that he possesses only half of the truth about his characters. Unencumbered by a play-acting narrator's jocular or sentimental postures, he can reveal his characters' feelings in their full complexity. His narrator knows that human affairs are beset with both passion and compromise, and he does not feel obliged to apologize for this knowledge.

Stating that many a Parisian beauty looked at his black hero "with feelings more flattering than mere curiosity" (8: 5), he quite naturally assumes that members of different races can be attracted to each other.[16] But even as he depicts the Countess D.'s genuine love for Ibrahim, he does not attempt to conceal Ibrahim's own feelings of insecurity and fear of prejudice. Ibrahim's decision to return to Russia is motivated not only by his sense of duty and by his attachment to Peter I, but also by the anticipation of a break with the Countess, which would hurt him much more if he were not to initiate it himself.[17] After he leaves Paris, his burning passion fades into a cherished memory—a bold development indeed for an early-nineteenth-century novel. The news that his old friend Korsakov brings of the Countess—that she has taken a new lover—shocks him, but not enough to make him reject Peter's plan to find him a bride. He suspects that he will be unable to kindle the same feelings in Natalia Rzhevskaia as those he had kindled in the Countess, but he is willing to compromise in the hope of achieving, if not happiness, at least a respectable family life. Natalia, on her part, seems to be prepared to submit to her fate, which is also a compromise in the context of early-nineteenth-century literature: many an earlier heroine not only had hoped to pine away under the weight of sorrow, but had actually succeeded in doing so. How Pushkin would have treated the further events of his story, we do not know: all we have is a bare outline of a plan—calling for Ibrahim's unfaithful wife to deliver a white baby—which was recorded by Pushkin's friend A. N. Vulf in September 1827, just after Pushkin had completed the second chapter of the novel.[18]

Pushkin's attempt to present affairs of the heart in all their complexity was not entirely without precedent: he could borrow at least a few elements from a favorite novel of his younger days, Benjamin Constant's *Adolphe*. Pushkin's Countess D. (whose first name is Léonore) and Constant's Ellénore are both characterized as beautiful women though no longer in the first bloom of youth; they both fall in love with younger men, whose main attraction is their seemingly undemanding devotion; and they both have to face losing their young men.[19] Some of the very phrases Pushkin uses to describe Ibrahim's relations with the Countess are demonstrably taken from *Adolphe*. Constant's novel reveals the inner contradictions of his characters with a ruthlessness that, one feels, sometimes goes beyond his own intentions. Not only does Adolphe's love for Ellénore turn sour in the course of the narrative, but he and his mistress lacerate each other in a compulsive manner that anticipates Dostoevskii's heroes and heroines.

Although *Adolphe,* with its frank revelations, is a forerunner of the psychological novel, it seems that Constant was wary of the possible effect of such a narrative, and consequently clothed it in the most conventional style. Adolphe recounts his story with as much contrition as Karamzin's Erast; he moralizes; he bestrews the novel with high-flown rhetoric. Such a style—with its "Charme de l'amour, qui pourrait vous peindre?" and similar phrases—was obviously of no use to Pushkin, who strove for simplicity in prose. It is not surprising that Pushkin wrote "nonsense" in the margin of his copy of *Adolphe* where Constant has his hero throwing himself on the ground and wishing to be swallowed up by the earth (Chapter Three).[20] The ending of *Adolphe*—Ellénore's death on learning that her lover intends to desert her—must have also seemed nonsensical to Pushkin, for in **The Blackamoor** he depicted a passionate affair that terminated without fatal consequences and a maiden who tried to, but—at least according to the plan recorded by Vulf—could not die of grief.

Pushkin's attempt to develop an omniscient mode of narration was a pioneering venture, but it involved—because of its very novelty—enormous technical difficulties. These difficulties may well have contributed to his decision to abandon his novel, though there may have been other factors as well. Some scholars explain his failure to complete the work by the fact that Bulgarin published a lampoon claiming that Pushkin's ancestor Hannibal had been bought for a bottle of rum.[21] After the appearance of this lampoon, they suggest, it may well have been impossible for Pushkin to continue his novel without exposing himself to public ridicule. Yet against this is the fact that the lampoon did not appear until 1830, which is to say, two or three years after Pushkin had stopped working on the novel.[22] Other scholars argue that Pushkin had designed his novel as a lesson in good statesmanship to Nicholas I (Peter I being offered as a model) but grew more and more disillusioned with Nicholas, and seeing the futility of trying to influence him, simply lost interest in the novel.[23] Even if Pushkin's feelings toward Nicholas were changing, however, this explanation ascribes a much too narrowly utilitarian purpose to a work of art whose scope extends far beyond a didactic lesson to a tyrant. Although Peter I looms large in the novel, its protagonist is nevertheless his black officer, with whom Pushkin identified to a great extent. It has been shown that there is much in common between Ibrahim, wondering if he could win at least the respect and fidelity of Natalia, and Hannibal's great-grandson, who pondered the question of matrimony in very similar terms in his letter of December 1, 1826, to V. P. Zubkov.[24] This link between Pushkin's personal worries and Ibrahim's courtship problems by no means elucidates all aspects of the novel, but it is at least as important as the writer's attitude toward Nicholas.

Whatever the contribution of biographical factors to the interruption of the novel may have been, the difficulties that Pushkin encountered in the creative process itself must be taken into consideration.[25] Problems of the craft of prose writing were certainly on Pushkin's mind at the time. We have seen how he had complained to Liprandi about the difficulties of prose earlier in the decade. The same complaint—implying technical problems—is echoed in the confession he made to the writer and scholar V. I. Dal in 1833: "You wouldn't believe how much I long to write a novel, yet I cannot. I have begun three of them. I start off perfectly well, but then I run out of patience and cannot manage."[26] Among the problems of the creative process, the advantages and disadvantages of the narrative point of view Pushkin had chosen for *The Blackamoor* appear to be the crucial ones.

We may be able to get closer to the problem through a comparison of *The Blackamoor* with *Poltava*—the narrative poem in whose favor Pushkin abandoned his novel in the spring of 1828. The most obvious similarity between the two works is that they are both set in the epoch of Peter I, who himself plays an important role in each. Less obvious but equally important is the similarity between Ibrahim and Mazepa as incarnations of a certain side of Pushkin's personality. Both characters represent explorations of how disadvantaged men might fare in love—one disadvantaged by the color of his skin, the other by his age. The close link between the two characters was clearly revealed by Pushkin when he wrote—in answer to the critic N. I. Nadezhdin's objection to Maria's love for an old man[27]—that the ways of love are inscrutable: think of young Desdemona falling in love with the "old Negro," Othello (11: 164). Moreover, a sentence from *Othello*—"Transported . . . to the gross clasps of a lascivious Moor" (Act 1, Scene 1, line 137)—is paraphrased in *The Blackamoor* as "Don't throw Natashenka into the clutches of that black devil" (8: 25), which in turn reminds one of the image of Mazepa as an old kite preying on a young dove (5: 26). A further similarity, at least between *Poltava* and *Othello,* is that Maria's heart is touched by Mazepa's tales of vicissitudes just as Desdemona's is by Othello's tales. Othello, black and no longer young, was an inspiration to Pushkin in creating both Ibrahim and Mazepa.

Both heroes appear to enjoy success at first—Ibrahim with the Countess and Mazepa with Maria—only to encounter failure later, one in marriage, the other in his political career. In both cases, the germs of failure are hidden in the initial situations of seeming success. If Ibrahim leaves the Countess because he fears that prejudice against his color may awaken in her heart, it is also his fear of prejudice that drives him toward an unpropitious marriage, for it makes him blind to the possibility that some other woman might love him better than Natalia. If Mazepa wins Maria's heart with a passion belying his age, it is also a youthful overconfidence that leads him to his political error. Errors of judgment, springing from psychological causes, underlie the actions of both characters. A further parallel between the two works

is that both Natalia and Maria are excluded from their relatives' discussion of the respective marriage proposals; both faint on hearing the decision; and though Maria does not fall quite as ill as Natalia, she too refuses to eat and sleep, staggering around pale as a shadow for two days after her parents' decision. Thus, even though Pushkin switched from prose to poetry, he evidently retained some of his original ideas. And at least one of the reasons for this switch was that, innovative as his detached mode of narration might have been, Pushkin had failed to find the right compositional key for his novel.

For *Poltava* it was easier to find a compositional key, since poetry was familiar territory to Pushkin. One might say that he wrote the poem in a double key, much as he had *The Prisoner* and its Epilogue. On the one hand, Mazepa is attractive, able to fire the young Maria's imagination, has an air of somber dignity about him; he leads "sorrowful Little Russia" against "hated Moscow" (5: 24) at the urging of his fellow countrymen, and in this sense he appears to be, at least at first, the hero of a national liberation movement. What the objective narrator says about him is contradicted, however, by another narrative voice, that of a patriotic bard singing the praises of Peter I while heaping adjectives like "base," "cunning," and "deceitful" (5: 25) on Mazepa. This bard-author seems to enter into a contest with the author-narrator, who in turn strives to give out as much information, often favorable to Mazepa, as he can under the barrage of the bard's hostile epithets. We get two perspectives on reality, neither of which has absolute validity: Pushkin has risen to a height of detachment where he does not feel compelled to present one comprehensive, morally unified view of the world. But the image of Peter I, as presented by the bard, is entirely stylized. The contest between him and Mazepa, transcending the feud of two political leaders, becomes a contest between the forces of history and an individual, between idealized greatness and fallible humanity. With this double perspective, Pushkin anticipates his *Bronze Horseman* (1833).

Such a conspicuous use of contrasting authorial personalities—highly successful in *Poltava*—would have been incompatible with the mode of narration Pushkin had chosen for *The Blackamoor.* A detached chronicler writing in prose could not poeticize Peter the way a patriotic bard could. Pushkin's praise of Sir Walter Scott for showing history "in a domestic manner" and for presenting historical personalities "in the ordinary circumstances of life" (12: 195) suggests that he had hoped to make Peter a heroic figure without recourse to poetic stylization in his novel. The result of the experiment was that, in the six completed chapters of the novel, Peter emerged neither fully heroic nor entirely human. Pushkin must have felt that the "domestic" scenes he had chosen—

Peter having a nap after lunch, playing chess with an English sailor, finding a bride for his young officer—were not adding up to the image he had had in mind. They were endearing scenes, but they did not suggest the gigantic figure of the hero of Poltava. It must have been for this reason that he made some attempts to aggrandize Peter even at the price of sacrificing some of his principles of prose writing. For instance, the sentence "With every day he [Ibrahim] became more and more attached to the Emperor, more able to comprehend his lofty mind" (8: 13) had been written without the word "lofty" in the first draft (8: 525, note 5). It is not clear in the final version whether this word, carrying a value judgment, is a narrated thought of Ibrahim's or belongs to the author himself. We are left with the impression that the author is as much involved in the value judgment as his hero, which goes against the grain of a detached, neutral mode of narration.

Brought down to a domestic level as he is, Peter nevertheless fails to impress us as a real person. If Pushkin had truly wanted to portray him without idealization, he would have had to show the Tsar's savage cruelty along with his monumental achievements. As he appears in the novel, he is too good, too considerate, too moderate, to be convincing. Pushkin himself must have felt he was erring in this direction, for he proceeded to introduce some less flattering details about the Tsar. For example, the sentence " 'And now,' he continued, shaking his cudgel, 'walk with me to that scoundrel Danilych's house; I must talk to him about his latest pranks' " (8: 28) had been written without the words "shaking his cudgel" even in the second draft (8: 517). The word cudgel has such far-reaching implications for the image of Peter that its introduction into the text signals an entirely new departure.

A few years later Pushkin said to Dal with reference to Peter: "I am not yet able to comprehend, to grasp the whole of this giant at once: he is too large for us shortsighted people; we are still standing too close to him."[28] As is well known, Pushkin was soon to engage in a thorough historical study in order to come to a balanced understanding of the great Tsar, but at the time he was writing *The Blackamoor* he still stood too close to Peter to be able to portray him as a hero, yet too far to be able to depict him as an ordinary human being.

If Peter had emerged as a gigantic statue in the novel—as he was to do in *Poltava* and in *The Bronze Horseman*—the proportions of Ibrahim would have shrunk: his love affair in Paris, his ill-starred engagement to Natalia, and other personal concerns would have appeared dwarfed alongside the Tsar. This would have established a perspective on Ibrahim and could have served as the compositional key to the whole novel. As it turned out, Pushkin was not able to find the right angle from which to view his central character, any more than he was able to establish the right approach to Peter.

Having deliberately put the expressive means of poetry aside, Pushkin was unable to replace them with new ones appropriate to prose. He adopted a colorless narrator, as impersonal as the author of a historical treatise, but failed to develop the characters whose function it should have been to provide the color lacking in the narrator. Those independent attitudes that were expressed through contrasting lyrical personae in poetry should have been allowed to emerge as contrasting characters in prose. For this, however, Pushkin lacked the technique at this time.

What was needed was a new set of representational devices suited to prose fiction. As one such device, the heroes could have been endowed with speech characteristics that would have set them apart both from each other and from the author, creating a distance across which the reader could look with amusement, sympathy, or any other sentiment. One indication that Pushkin did not have the "feel" of his character is that he hardly ever made Ibrahim speak anywhere in the six chapters. The Regent speaks to him, Peter speaks to him, Korsakov pours out long tirades at him, but when the time comes for him to open his mouth, either he utters the tersest of sentences or Pushkin reports his statements for him. There are two exceptions to this rule: he gives full answers both to Peter, who offers to propose to Natalia for him, and to Korsakov, who counsels against his marriage. In the first case, he says he likes Natalia, and he mentions his appearance with anxiety—both of which details are revealing—but otherwise he speaks in the impersonal style of a courtier ("Your Majesty, I am blessed with Your Highest protection and favor"; 8: 27). In the second case, he responds to Korsakov with a Russian proverb ("It's not your duty to rock other people's babies"; 8: 30), a wholly unconvincing turn of phrase, coming as it does from the mouth of a foreign-born person who had spent only the years between his early childhood and his young manhood in Russia. One has the impression that Pushkin used this phrase, not in order to characterize Ibrahim, but in order to be able to include Korsakov's prophetic repartee to it: "Take care not to let it happen that you should illustrate this proverb in a literal sense." Two other passages that should reveal Ibrahim's character through his individual style are his letter to the Countess and his internal monologue about getting married, but both are abstract and impersonal. Thus Ibrahim does not emerge as a separate entity in a stylistic sense.

In addition to dialogues, letters, and internal monologues, the omniscient narrator of realistic fiction has at his disposal the opinions of the characters about each other. Pushkin made use of this device—for instance, Korsakov's comments on both Ibrahim and Peter provide amusing side views of these characters—but not with sufficient consistency. A case in point is the description of how Ibrahim's relations with the Countess develop. In the seventh paragraph of Chapter One (from line 10, p. 5, on), the point of view shifts from Ibrahim to the Countess, then to other people, then back to Ibrahim, in the eighth, from Ibrahim to the Countess, to the narrator, to the Countess's reputed former lover Merville, once more to the narrator, then back to Ibrahim, and finally to the Countess; in the ninth, from the narrator to other people, then to both Ibrahim and the Countess together, then to Ibrahim alone, then to the Countess alone, and so forth, with the result that no character's point of view is sufficiently established. There emerges a mosaic with no consistent perspective.

The best parts of the novel are those in which Pushkin succeeds in maintaining a consistent point of view. One of these is the description of the assembly at Peter's Court, which is seen mostly through Korsakov's eyes. "Korsakov was dumbfounded," says Pushkin at the opening of the scene, as if to emphasize the point of view, and the following two pages abound in phrases like "Korsakov could not regain his presence of mind," "Korsakov was struck by an unexpected sight," "Korsakov . . . stared wide-eyed," "Korsakov rejoiced," and "Korsakov grew more and more astonished" (8: 16, 17). The point of view is well chosen because Korsakov, a westernized fop, assumes he knows all about behavior in the best society, yet he discovers that his behavior is ridiculous by the standards of the recently westernized Russian Court. Another highly successful passage in the novel is the depiction of a dinner at Rzhevskii's house. Here the characters, voicing their opinions in detail, come fully alive.[29] It is not surprising that these were the two passages Pushkin decided to publish. Unfortunately, however, neither of them helped solve what seems to have been the main problem: the characterization of Ibrahim.

The lack of perspective is apparent also in the narrator's own descriptions of Ibrahim's feelings. This is, for instance, what Pushkin tells us about Ibrahim's thoughts concerning the Countess:

> It was more difficult to dismiss from his mind another, dear recollection: he often thought of the Countess D., imagined her just indignation, tears, and grief . . . At times a dreadful thought took his breath away: the distractions of high society, a new liaison, another lucky man—he shuddered. Jealousy began to seethe in his African blood, and burning tears were ready to course down his black face. (8: 13-14)

Are we to pity the man who worries about the possible infidelity of a former mistress he has abruptly deserted and may never see again? Some of the words chosen—such as "a dreadful thought took his breath away," "he shuddered," "jealousy began to seethe in his African blood," and "burning tears"—seem to indicate that the narrator expected as much. But barely two pages further on we are introduced to Korsakov's view that the Countess's infidelity was the most natural thing in the world, and Ibrahim's own tears seem to dry up fast as he hurries off to the assembly. Once more, the cause of the difficulty seems to lie in the difference between poetry and prose. A lyrical passage in a narrative poem or in a novel in verse can stand on its own, regardless of an ironic statement that may follow a few stanzas further on, for in poetry the presence of several lyrical personae facilitates quick transitions in mood; but a "novel in prose"—with a consistent, neutral, detached narrator—demands a steadier atmosphere. The quick transitions in mood inconsistent with the narrator's personality—added to the other problems—prevented Pushkin from getting a firm grip on Ibrahim's character. The outline of the character—strong passions yet weak compromises—was excellent, and the mode of narration augured the future development of the novel, but the technical difficulties of an entirely new way of writing were so enormous that Pushkin could not flesh out the well-conceived idea with appropriate details.

As he became conscious of his difficulties, he returned to his native element—poetry—and as a homecoming present to himself, he indulged in eight similes in a row in the second verse paragraph of *Poltava*—a practice he would never have allowed himself in "stern prose."

2

Far from being discouraged by his experience with *The Blackamoor of Peter the Great,* in the following years Pushkin endeavored to apply an omniscient mode of narration to a psychological study of "Contemporary man / With his immoral soul"—an even more formidable task. Two fragments, each in several drafts, and a number of plot outlines have remained of his efforts.

The first fragment is known by its opening words, as **"The Guests Were Arriving at the Dacha."** It consists of three chapters, written sometime between the fall of 1828 and the beginning of 1830.[30] Chapter One contains a conversation about Russian mores between a Spanish visitor and a young Russian called Minskii; introduces a restless young married woman by the name of Zinaida Volskaia; and hints at an incipient romance between her and Minskii. The other two chapters are fragmentary: Chapter Two shows

Minskii reading a note from Zinaida, which makes it clear that she is in love with him; and in Chapter Three the discussion between the Spaniard and Minskii is resumed.

The author-narrator of this fragment is as uncompromisingly intelligent as that of *The Blackamoor* was. He manages to reveal the complexity of his heroine in a mere few pages. Motherless since age five and left to the care of nurses and tutors by an indifferent father, she writes love letters to her dance teacher at age fourteen, which is enough to persuade her father to "bring her out" in society immediately. She soon marries the rich young Volskii, enjoys entertaining the whole town at her house, and develops a taste for shocking the best society with her pranks. Intent on taking a lover, she discusses prospective candidates with her confidant Minskii and ends up, predictably, in his arms. Unloved, she resorts to promiscuity as a means of drawing attention to herself, yet all the while "remained a fourteen-year-old at heart" (8: 39). This behavior is accompanied by a sense of guilt and inadequacy—the aspect of her character Pushkin emphasizes most. When she enters the drawing room at the dacha, she fails to take notice of anything; she refuses to engage in small talk; she sulks; her face is "changeable as a cloud" (8: 38); her general distractedness seems to indicate that she is engrossed in her inner problems. She awakens from her thoughts with a shudder (8: 38) and proceeds to the balcony to spend the rest of the evening alone with Minskii, which shocks the hostess and her other guests. One gets the feeling that she has sought her hostess's disapprobation as much as Minskii's company. Her anxious sense of inadequacy is revealed also in her note to Minskii, as she declares him vastly superior to herself, and complains and entreats (8: 41).

In the second draft (already corrected and copied out but not yet final) Pushkin had emphasized Zinaida's emotional problems even more openly. What was to become "her lively movements" had been "her restless movements" (8: 38, 536); the phrase "she got up" had been qualified by the adverb "impatiently" (8: 38, 536); and the gentleman conversing with Princess G. had said about her, "I look on her as if she were a sleepwalker, asleep yet walking on the roof: one would like to wake her but dares not" (8: 537; deleted from the final version). It is possible that Pushkin toned down the references to Zinaida's emotional problems because he feared that she might appear too far out of the range of normal to remain an attractive heroine. It is even more likely that he felt he could soften the tone of his description because he had found a subtler way to convey his meaning. In the drafts, Zinaida had entered the drawing room looking for Minskii, and her disquietude resulted from his absence. Deleting this detail from the final version proved to be a great gain, for the immediate cause of Zinaida's anxiety was now removed, and an impression of the general uneasiness of her mind was created. The change made it possible to put the rest of the characterization in a lower key.

Whether these were the considerations guiding Pushkin's hand or not, it is significant that he made such painstaking efforts to create a character of great psychological complexity. What we know of his further plans for the novel confirms that he wanted to continue it in the same vein: Zinaida's tragedy was to have been that, having lost Minskii to a young debutante, she would throw herself into a scandalous affair with a man she did not love (8: 554).

A second surviving fragment of a psychological novel begins with the words **"In the Corner of a Small Square."** It consists of one complete chapter and part of a second, both written sometime between November 1830 and March 1831. Chapter One consists of a dialogue between the heroine, once more called Zinaida, and her lover, Valerian Volodskii. It becomes clear from the dialogue that, having taken up with Volodskii, she has left her husband and set herself up in a remote quarter of the city, where Volodskii comes to visit her, though he is getting bored with her. The incomplete second chapter briefly summarizes how she left her husband and how Volodskii reacted to this unexpected development.

Most critics have regarded this fragment as a continuation of **"The Guests Were Arriving at the Dacha,"** since it is set against a similar social background and treats the same theme of adultery.[31] Moreover, the respective plot outlines associated with the two fragments both call for the heroine's lover to abandon her for the sake of an unmarried girl. However, as A. V. Chicherin, the critic who has studied these fragments most thoroughly, points out, the differences between the two fragments are greater than the similarities.[32] Indeed, the meek, submissive, pathetic Zinaida of the second fragment does not resemble her predecessor, even if we take into consideration a lapse of several years. She is older than her lover (an influence of *Adolphe*), which rules out the possibility that her Volodskii is a reincarnation of Minskii under a different name. Furthermore, although the first plot outline mentions Zinaida's confession to her husband, nowhere does it refer to her decision to leave him and to set up house on her own. One has to conclude that the second fragment represents, not a direct continuation of the first one, but a new attempt at handling the same theme.

In **"The Guests"** Pushkin concentrated most of his attention on his heroine, since it was she who had to make the decisions that were vital to the development of the plot. **"In the Corner"** presents the heroine at a stage in her life where her decisions have already been made: her fate now depends on what her lover decides to do. For this reason, Pushkin's attention here shifts to the hero; and the full range of Volodskii's feelings—from love through remorse to a desire for freedom and uncomplicated comfort—is at least sketched in, if not entirely developed.

The intricacy of characterization in these two fragments contradicts A. Z. Lezhnev's claim that Pushkin's prose in general concentrates "on actions rather than emotional experiences."[33] Nor does Lezhnev's monolithic view of Pushkin's style as always terse, austere, and simple hold true. Far from gravitating toward the barest subject-predicate-object structure, Pushkin's syntax is often complicated in these fragments, matching the nature of the material. Volskii's reasons for falling in love with Zinaida, for instance, are described in this sentence: "Volskii, a wealthy young man who usually let his feelings be governed by the opinions of others, fell head over heels in love with her because the Sovereign had once met her on the English Embankment and talked with her a full hour" (8: 39). Rather than whittling his phrase down to one precise, carefully chosen word, Pushkin tends in these fragments to pile synonym on synonym for cumulative effect, as in this sentence: "Volskaia reproached him for his coldness, his distrust, and the like; she complained and entreated, not knowing herself what about; showered on him a profusion of tender, affectionate assurances—and made an assignation to meet him in her box at the theater that evening" (8: 41). By no means anxious to avoid a profusion of qualifying epithets, Pushkin writes sentences like this one: "A pale lady, no longer in the first bloom of youth but still beautiful, dressed with great refinement, lay on a sofa strewn with cushions, in a room appointed with taste and luxury" (8: 143). Moreover, as Chicherin points out, in the unfinished works "the place of honor is occupied by the kind of epithet that denotes changeable, dynamic, relative qualities."[34] As an example, Chicherin cites the adjective "funny" (*smeshna;* 8: 39), applied to Zinaida, which has none of the fixed, absolute qualities that we find, for instance, in the word "haughty" (*nadmennyi;* 8: 162), applied to Troekurov in *Dubrovskii.* One might add that Pushkin, augmenting his epithets, compares Zinaida's face to a changeable cloud, aristocrats to Egyptian mummies, high society to a herd, and Volodskii to a restless schoolboy (8: 38, 41, 42, 144). All this testifies to a rich, varied style, by no means shorn of ornament.

Perceptive as Chicherin's comments on the early fragments are, he makes the error of referring to their stylistic features as "new" in comparison with those of the finished works, as if all the experimental pieces had been written after the publication of the main body of Pushkin's prose.[35] As Chicherin would have it, Pushkin first wrote a number of relatively uncomplicated works for publication and then began experimenting with more complex matters. This is a neat enough scheme—one would normally expect a writer to develop in this way—but it does not prove true in the case of Pushkin, who had already reached his full maturity in poetry when he turned to prose. Indeed it was **"In the Corner of a Small Square,"** conceived before *The Tales of Belkin,* that was to inspire Tolstoi in writing *Anna Karenina;*[36] and it was Zinaida of **"The Guests Were Arriving at the Dacha"** who foreshadowed many a heroine in the novels of Turgenev and Dostoevskii. In fiction, Pushkin began with the complex, and then—temporarily, never abandoning the hope of incarnating the complex—he descended to the simple.

The question arises once again: if the creation of significant new characters was within Pushkin's grasp, why did he stop working on his psychological novel? There are several possible answers: he may have lacked the settled circumstances and spiritual calm indispensable for a sustained effort in prose;[37] he may have anticipated difficulties with the censor;[38] he may even have been embarrassed by the closeness of Zinaida to her real-life model, A. F. Zakrevskaia;[39] but it must not be overlooked that in these fragments, as in *The Blackamoor of Peter the Great,* the highly original design involved formidable difficulties of craftsmanship.

In **"The Guests"** Pushkin makes an earnest effort to endow his heroes with speech characteristics. He is most successful with Zinaida's letter to Minskii, which reveals her desire to impress him with a style more "bookish" than her education would lead one to expect. Phrases like "[this] proves that you're invariably superior to me," as they are put in the Russian original (*eto dokazyvaet tvoe vsegdashnee prevoskhodstvo nado mnoiu;* 8: 41), do not sound like the words of a flighty society lady. How deliberately Pushkin was aiming at an awkward effect is witnessed by a change he made in the text. In the first draft of the letter, we read, "Your sophisms don't convince me" (*tvoi sofizmy ne ubezhdaiut menia;* 8: 539), which is a perfectly clear and natural phrase. In the final text, however, Pushkin changed this to "your sophisms don't convince my suspicions" (*tvoi sofizmy ne ubezhdaiut moikh podozrenii;* 8: 41), which makes little sense and in translation has to be rendered as something like "your sophisms don't allay my suspicions." One has the impression that Zinaida had conversed at parties with members of some of the intellectual groups of the day, such as the Archival Youths or the Lovers of Wisdom, and had learned some of their bookish phrases, without, however, understanding them.

Unfortunately, Pushkin cuts Zinaida's letter short and tells us about the rest of it in his own words, as if he had run out of breath trying to imitate her. As for dialogue, we hear her utter only two phrases: "I'd like to fall in love with R." and "How about the Baron W.?" (8: 40). The second of these is purely functional, with no marked speech characteristics. At first glance the other seems to reveal her character, but if we compare it with the style that is used by both Minskii and the author-narrator, we realize that it carries class, rather than individual, characteristics.

What strikes one most about Minskii's manner is his flippancy. The Spanish visitor's earnest praise of the northern night, for example, is not to his taste: he twists it into a comparison of northern and southern beauties, with a banal reference to "the old controversy between *la brune et la blonde*" (8: 37). Further, he cracks a joke about the purity of Petersburg morals, ascribed by a foreigner to the fact that "our winter nights are too cold and our summer nights too bright for amorous adventures" (8: 37). The Spaniard interposes with another earnest remark about Russian beauty, amicability, and purity, only to elicit the answer that amicability is "not in vogue" (8: 37). Later, in his conversation with Zinaida, Minskii counsels her not to get involved with R. because the man's "insufferable wife is in love with him" (8: 40). He recommends, instead, having an affair with L., *un homme à grands sentiments,* adding: "He'll be jealous and passionate; he'll torment you and amuse you: what more would you wish?" (8: 40). Finally, what makes him love Zinaida so sincerely, he says, is that she is "excruciatingly funny" (8: 39).

One might assume that Zinaida's phrase "I'd like to fall in love" is adapted to Minskii's flippant style, which would not be surprising since she clearly wants to impress him. What confounds the matter is that the narrator also resorts to the same style time and again. His statement, for instance, that Zinaida married Volskii because the man "was not repugnant to her" (8: 39), might just as well have been made by Minskii. In connection with rumors about Zinaida's love affairs, the narrator says: "According to the code of high society, plausibility equals verity, and to be the target of slander lowers us in our own estimation" (8: 39). This sentence reminds one of J.-F. Marmontel's phrase, "Les soupçons, dans le monde, valent des certitudes";[40] and it shows the dandy's penchant for borrowing aphorisms in order to shine at a social gathering. Further, explaining why Minskii was temporarily absent from society in his youth, the narrator says: "For a while passions muted the anguish of his wounded pride" (8: 40). The assumption is made that affairs of the heart are the transient aberrations of youth, but social vanities endure.

The attitudes of Minskii and Zinaida were obviously not Pushkin's own. A desire to expose the cynicism of a certain segment of Russian society is apparent in the fragment. Also, everything indicates that the emotional experiences of the characters were to be studied objectively, at a distance from the author. Yet instead of limiting the flippant tone of fashionable society to his characters, Pushkin allowed it to seep into the style of his narrator too. This failure to separate the narrator from the characters in a stylistic sense seems to have been the greatest problem Pushkin encountered in working on the novel.

This problem is most painfully obvious in Chapter Three of **"The Guests,"** where the Russian Minskii and the Spanish visitor discuss the characteristics of the Russian aristocracy. The opinions they voice can be found in Pushkin's 1830 lyric **"My Genealogy"** and in his **"Attempt to Rebut Some Non-Literary Charges"** (1830), as well as in other fictional fragments. They are plainly Pushkin's own; they were provoked by searing social experiences and have an air of petulance about them. Voicing them, Minskii and the Spaniard lose their identity, not only in a stylistic, but also in an ideological sense. Their conversation resembles Nadezhdin's critical essays written in the form of dialogues.

We must bear in mind that before Pushkin's time no Russian prose writer had attempted to use dialogue for characterization. To most writers, dialogue meant allowing the characters to say what the author himself would otherwise have said. It simply varied the form, enlivened the pace. In the eighteenth century Russian prose writers considered the use of numerous dialogues not only an unnecessary touch, but a positive flaw in craftsmanship.[41] Dialogue came into its own with the emergence of the detached, third-person narrative form. Pioneering this form, Pushkin also had to pioneer characterization through dialogue. In both, he encountered difficulties.

His great success in dialogue, in this early experimental period, was Chapter One of **"In the Corner of a Small Square."** Written about the same time as the last chapter of **"The Guests,"** this fragment also treats the theme of the Russian aristocracy, but infinitely more successfully. Here both speakers, descendants of ancient nobility, have personal reasons to resent those aristocrats of more recent vintage who set the tone in contemporary society. Zinaida has been ostracized for her adulterous affair. Volodskii, though not, as a man, formally excluded from society, has nevertheless been piqued by a Prince Goretskii who—obviously because of Volodskii's notorious affair—did not invite him to a party. Since both characters have perfect motivations for their irritability, we no longer feel that they are voicing Pushkin's own grievances. The argument about aristocracy is thus well motivated. But in addition, it has a well-designed place in the plot. While Zinaida bitterly reminds her lover that she has not frequented *his* aristocratic circles for quite some time, she is giving information to the reader about her situation. Her jealousy of his role in society reveals not only her hatred of that society, but also her premonition about his involvement with a younger society girl. Volodskii, in turn, not only vents his anger over the snub he received from Prince Goretskii, but seems to use this opportunity to discharge a great deal of accumulated hatred—hatred whose proper target should be Zinaida, since she is the one who has put him in an awkward social position. This perfectly constructed dialogue, then, characterizes the heroes, provides information about their past and present, hints at their incipient conflict, and at the same time conveys the author's social ideas in an unobtrusive way. It shows a situation, as one critic has aptly remarked, in which Tatiana might have found herself, had she yielded to Onegin's entreaties.[42] No wonder Tolstoi was so much impressed by it. Still, since this dialogue remained an isolated fragment of two and a half pages, one has to conclude that Pushkin was not yet able to sustain such a high level of writing throughout a novel. In the second chapter of **"In the Corner"** he turns to an extremely fast-moving narrative, with no dialogue.

This great speed of narration is another problem Pushkin encountered in his first attempts at prose. Chapter Two of **"In the Corner"** begins with the sentence "X. soon found out that his wife was unfaithful to him" (8: 145), which summarizes an experience that could have been expanded into several chapters. Tolstoi's Karenin, for instance, first notices that other people find Anna's behavior improper; he lectures her; his suspicions increase gradually; and he is not fully convinced of her infidelity until she tells him about it herself. The scene of confession itself, whose dramatic potentials are so skillfully exploited by Tolstoi, is summed up in one single sentence by Pushkin. Finally, Volodskii's reaction to Zinaida's precipitate action, described by Pushkin in one paragraph, could have occupied a whole volume, or more, as indeed the changes in Vronskii's attitudes were to do in *Anna Karenina*.

V. V. Vinogradov, in his monumental study of Pushkin's style, has likened Pushkin's prose to Russian chronicles, in which only essential events—like the pillars of a structure—were visible, nevertheless creating the impression of great latent wealth.[43] Another critic has drawn attention to the similarity between Pushkin's prose and the notes he jotted down while planning narrative poems.[44] In such notes—in those on Tatiana's letter, for instance—the barest essentials of the outline provide guideposts for the poetic development of the theme. These critical observations are valid at least in relation to those parts of the early fragments where the narration is rapid. With reference to these parts, one could say that Tolstoi's novel, realizing the potentials of Pushkin's sketch, filled out the space between the "pillars." What complicates

the issue, however, is that other parts of the fragments—Chapter One of **"In the Corner,"** for instance—present fully developed details rather than rapid outlines. This fact shows, once more, how difficult it is to characterize Pushkin's prose in general. He obviously tried to fill out his outlines with details—to transcend a merely essay-like presentation—but he did not always succeed, finding out in the process what a "devil of a difference" there was not only between the poetic development of a theme and its development in prose, but also between essay and fiction.

In order to examine the difference between poetry and prose once more, let us see how Pushkin introduces Tatiana in *Eugene Onegin*. She is first mentioned at the end of Stanza 23, Chapter Two, where the narrator asks the reader's permission to turn his attention to Olga's elder sister. In Stanza 24 Tatiana's name is given, and a digression about Russian girls' names follows. In the next stanza, six lines tell us what Tatiana was like (6: 42):

> Timid, sad, taciturn,
> Shy as a woodland fawn,
> She seemed to be a stranger
> In her own family.
>   . . .
> Often she sat alone all day
> Silently by the window.

The remaining eight lines of the stanza detail what she was *not* like: she did not have her sister's beauty and fresh complexion, she did not like to cuddle up to her parents, and even as a little girl, she would not run and play with other children. The following two stanzas contain a total of four and a half lines characterizing her directly—describing her pensive ways and her fondness for horror tales—with all the remaining lines again devoted to negative characterization, bringing to life everything she was not and did not do. Stanza 28 records that she loved to watch the sunrise from the balcony, which gives Pushkin an opportunity for a lyrical description of night and dawn. Finally, the first four lines of Stanza 29 contain the information that Tatiana loved novels, especially those of Richardson and Rousseau. With this, Pushkin considers her introduction and first characterization complete, and enters into the courtship and marriage of her parents. Put in prose, her description would amount to little more than an outline, but since a great wealth of poetry—witty digressions, lyrical descriptions, the charm of all the childish things Tatiana did not do (and which nevertheless remain associated with her in our minds)—fills out the gaps between the supporting pillars of design, we come away with the impression that she has been fully characterized.

What works in poetry, however, does not necessarily succeed in prose, at least not in the kind of prose

Pushkin cultivated. Almost as much information is provided about the Zinaida(s) of the two prose fragments as about Tatiana, yet the novel fails to get off the ground because Pushkin's concept of prose did not allow the kind of "padding" he used in poetry. All that the narrator of the fragments knows about his characters is revealed to the reader immediately; instead of saving some of his material for later, gradual release, he sets it all off in a single dazzling display of fireworks. This is connected with the fact that his narrator—even when he slips into the characters' style—is invariably an intelligent person who does not play games with the reader, but speaks directly to the point (as if writing an essay). Pushkin was soon to find that the manner of a somewhat dull-witted, semi-educated narrator—a "prosaic persona," so to speak—would be easier to handle.

3

The dull-witted narrator was shortly to be employed in *The Tales of Belkin.* But before Pushkin set himself to that task, he experimented with another narrative mode in the hope of overcoming the difficulties of detached, third-person narration. This was the epistolary form, which he put to use in the unfinished *A Novel in Letters,* written in the fall of 1829. As far as the letters take us, we become acquainted with Liza, an orphan brought up in a rich family, whose head was indebted to her late father. Although she has always been treated as an equal, she feels her inferiority, especially next to her foster mother's niece, the wealthy young Princess Olga. Tormented by a sense of her inferior social status, she has decided to retire to the country, where her grandmother, though reduced to modest circumstances, has received her with open arms. As her letters to her girl friend Sasha unfold, however, we realize that she had another reason for leaving St. Petersburg: she had fallen in love with a wealthy young man called Vladimir and feared that though he was obviously attracted to her, he would not marry her because of her poverty. Vladimir, missing her in the city, arrives at the house of a relative whose estate is adjacent to her grandmother's; the romance is renewed, but when the plot line breaks off we do not know what to expect because the relative at whose house Vladimir is staying has an attractive daughter, Masha.

Taking up the epistolary form marked a retreat: instead of pioneering an entirely new mode of writing, Pushkin was both drawing on his own experience as a correspondent and making use of existing literary models. Liza of *A Novel in Letters* says, of some eighteenth-century novels she has just been reading, that the action is entertaining but the characters speak in an unnatural language. "A clever man," she continues, "could adopt these ready-made plots and characters, amend the style, eliminate the absurdities,

supply the missing links—and the result would be a splendid original novel" (8: 50). This seems to be precisely what Pushkin set out to do in his epistolary novel; and he was to take his heroine's advice not only on this, but on other occasions.

In this particular case his chief models were *Julie, ou La Nouvelle Héloïse* (1761) by Jean Jacques Rousseau, which he had mentioned several times in *Onegin; Les Liaisons dangereuses* (1782), by Pierre Choderlos de Laclos,[45] to which he made an unflattering reference in **"The Guests"**; and *Clarissa* (1747-48) by Samuel Richardson. The last is discussed in *A Novel in Letters* itself: Liza reports to her friend that she has borrowed it from her neighbors and decided to plod her way through it despite the dullness of the first six parts, because the Preface to the translation promised that the last six would reward the industrious reader. "I bravely set about the task," she continues. "I read the first, the second, the third volumes . . . at last I reached the sixth one: dull beyond endurance. Well, thought I, now I shall be rewarded for my pains. And what happened? I read about the deaths of Clarissa and Lovelace, and that was the end of it. Each volume contained two parts, and I did not notice the transition from the six boring to the six entertaining ones" (8: 47).[46]

Despite this anecdote, Pushkin was making use of Richardson's technique. The choice was between it and that of Rousseau; each had its advantages and drawbacks. Unlike Julie and Saint-Preux, Pushkin's lovers do not correspond with each other, describing to each other how they kissed the day before. Their correspondents are friends, relatively uninvolved in their relationship and therefore needing information about it. This allows the reader to be initiated into the proceedings more naturally. On the other hand, describing events to friends—as Clarissa Harlowe does to Miss Howe, and Lovelace does to Belford—lacks the dramatic potential inherent in a correspondence between the lovers themselves. Pushkin might have objected to the behavior of Rousseau's lovers—arguing their sexual impulses as minutely and rigorously as if they were legal matters—but eliminating their direct exchange of letters meant depriving the novel of some lively moments. As used by Richardson and Pushkin, the letters quoted were not themselves the events: they were merely descriptions of events. The Richardsonian epistolary form came close to the first-person narrative of a journal or memoir, except for its more varied point of view.

It was perhaps the use of this form, lacking in dramatic opportunity, that hindered Pushkin in developing an otherwise promising plan. Liza of *A Novel in Letters* is potentially as interesting a person as Ibrahim or Zinaida. Her most characteristic trait is a morbid sensitivity, caused by her social position. When her friend the Princess refuses to wear expensive pearls, not wishing to outshine her, Liza resents this, just as Dostoevskii's Underground Man will resent Zverkov for refusing to be rude to him. When she desires her Vladimir to fall in love with Masha, she appears to be an early Nastasia Filippovna telling Myshkin to marry Aglaia (*The Idiot;* 1868-69). Her ambivalent feelings are matched by the ambiguous situation Pushkin places her in. It never becomes clear, at least not in the existing letters, whether she is right in her judgment of Vladimir as a flighty young man who is only leading her on. His behavior with Masha seems to indicate the correctness of this judgment, but Liza's friend Sasha implies that events might have taken a different turn if Liza had been bold enough to seize her opportunity earlier. Sasha's assessment of the situation may be simply a function of her vulgar mind—which is amply revealed in Letter 4—yet there is a prophetic ring to her words in Letter 7: "You're asking for misfortune: take care not to bring it on yourself" (8: 52). We cannot tell whether adversity coins Liza's character or her character generates adversity. The poet Valerii Briusov has aptly characterized her as another Tatiana, for whom "happiness is ever 'possible,' ever 'close at hand,' but never actually attainable."[47]

Her very style gives Sasha away as an empty-headed society girl, but Liza and Vladimir—perhaps because they lack the opportunity for dramatic confrontation—never develop a style of their own. It is noteworthy that Liza's description of Masha's family in Letter 3 was lifted, at least partially, from another fragment of Pushkin's, **"In the Beginning of 1812"** (1829), where the describer was a young officer. Liza's literary judgments are clearly Pushkin's own; her indignation over critical reviews in the *European Herald* anticipates Pushkin's **"Letter to the Editor of the *Literary Gazette*"** (1830); her claim that society ladies are not as prudish as some critics imagine them to be is a thought Pushkin expounds in **"An Attempt to Rebut Some Non-Literary Charges"**; and both her and Vladimir's discussions of the Russian nobility represent yet another attempt to convey Pushkin's own ideas on the topic.

In *A Novel in Letters,* Pushkin had given up the omniscient narrator of his other fragments, but he was still having difficulty with the narrative point of view. Having endowed his characters with his own lucid mind and critical judgments, he found it difficult to separate them from himself. This is why the letters of Liza and Vladimir appear to be Pushkin's own letters or essays, in spite of the individual and highly interesting psychological features that he intended to give to these characters. The stock of experience he had built up in writing his own letters was not, by itself, enough for fiction.

The same problem arose in connection with two more unfinished works: **"My Fate Is Sealed: I Am Getting Married"** and a short piece, known simply as **"A Fragment"** (both dated 1830), containing a discussion of the poet's place in society. Both are close to autobiography, written in the first person and illuminated by the insights of an intelligent mind. But neither gets off the ground as fiction. The second, in particular, comes quite close in style to an essay.

Pushkin's difficulty in the early fragments was that he insisted on treating complex material, though he had not found the right key, the right narrative point of view, the right technique for the new genres he was experimenting with. In order to find a solution, he had to lower his sights.

Notes

[1] *Severnye tsvety,* 1829, pp. 111-24; and *Literaturnaia gazeta,* 1830, No. 13: 99-100.

[2] *Sovremennik,* 6 (1837): 97-145. For full details about the dates and circumstances of Pushkin's work on the novel, see Lapkina [157].

[3] Feinberg [32], pp. 265-67.

[4] See *Rukoiu Pushkina* [10], pp. 34-49; and Pushkin [5], 12: 434-37. For further details about Abram Hannibal, see M. Vegner, *Predki Pushkina* (Moscow: Sovetskii pisatel', 1937), pp. 11-151; Veresaev [485], 1: 25-31; and V. Nabokov, "Pushkin and Gannibal: A Footnote," *Encounter,* 19, No. 1 (1962): 11-26.

[5] On the Osipovs' library, see M. Semevskii, "Progulka v Trigorskoe," *S-Peterburgskie vedomosti,* No. 139 (May 24, 1866).

[6] "O chastnoi zhizni Imperatora Petra I," "Ob uveseleniiakh russkogo dvora pri Petre I," "O pervykh balakh v Rossii," "O chastnoi zhizni russkikh pri Petre I," in A. O. Kornilovich, *Sochineniia i pis'ma* (Moscow: Akademiia Nauk SSSR, 1957), pp. 149-203 (originally published in *Russkaia starina* in 1824).

[7] Pointed out by Feinberg [32], pp. 306-7.

[8] Suggested by Arminjon [14], p. 70.

[9] For details on Pushkin's use of, and distortion of, historical materials, see Levkovich [54], pp. 181-88; and Iakubovich [114].

[10] It is interesting that both of these sentences betraying the author's presence can be traced to literary sources. The first one, as Akhmatova [150], p. 110, points out, was inspired by Adolphe's humble devotion to Ellénore in Chaps. 2 and 3 of Constant's novel. The second one, as Tomashevskii [84], p. 416, mentions, is a paraphrase of a sentence from Charles

Nodier's *Le Peintre de Saltzbourg* (1803): "C'est une chose admirable et pleine de charme que de suivre un grand génie dans son course" (entry for Oct. 9: [480], p. 78).

[11] From the Preface to *Tales of a Traveller* (1824); see Irving [478], 2: 12. In addition to Austen's novels, Johann Wolfgang Goethe's *Die Wahlver-wandtschaften* (1809) is an early example of a detached, third-person narrative, but there is no evidence that Pushkin had read this particular work.

[12] On Pushkin's familiarity with Walpole's works, see Vatsuro [91].

[13] On Irving's and Hoffmann's popularity in Russia, see Proffer [67]; Passage [65]; and Ingham [44].

[14] Scott [483], I: 3. Alexander the Corrector was a name assumed by Alexander Cruden (1701-70), best known for his *Complete Concordance to the Holy Scriptures* (1737). Among other works, he published *The Adventures of Alexander the Corrector* (in 3 parts, 1754-55).

[15] "C'est un de mes principes, qu'il ne faut pas s'ecrire. L'artiste doit être dans son oeuvre comme Dieu dans la creation, invisible et tout-puissant; qu'on le sente partout, mais qu'on ne le voie pas." See Flaubert's letter of March 18, 1857, to Mlle. Leroyer de Chantepie in Gustave Flaubert, *Oeuvres complètes* (Paris: L. Conrad, 1910-27), Correspondance, Série 4 (1854-61), p. 164. For a discussion of the author's disappearance into the background in the 19th-century novel, see Richard Stang, *The Theory of the Novel in England, 1850-1870* (New York: Columbia Univ. Press, 1959), pp. 91-110.

[16] This does not seem quite so natural to V. I. Lavretskaia, who writes ([52], p. 81): "The first time his [Ibrahim's] portrait is seen through the eyes of the frivolous, corrupt Countess. . . . The second time we perceive his features with the eyes of Natasha, a simple, unspoilt, pure Russian girl: it is understandable that she was frightened by the Negro's unusual appearance, which had appealed to the satiated Countess."

[17] Emphasized by Blagoi [22], p. 260.

[18] Dymshits [476], p. 325.

[19] Pointed out by Akhmatova [150], pp. 103, 110.

[20] Modzalevskii [479], p. 210. Pushkin was much more complimentary about Constant's language in his brief article announcing Viazemskii's forthcoming translation of *Adolphe* in 1830: "It will be interesting to see how Prince Viazemskii's experienced and lively pen has overcome the difficulties of metaphysical language—of a language that is always graceful, that is of high society, and that is often inspired"; [5], 11: 87. Although the epithets Pushkin chose are complimentary, they do not reflect his own aspirations as a prose stylist.

[21] F. V. Bulgarin, "Vtoroe pis'mo iz Karlova na Kamennyi ostrov," *Severnaia pchela*, 1830, No. 94: cols. 1-8.

[22] Bulgarin's lampoon is referred to by Oksman in his notes to *Arap Petra Velikogo* [4], 4: 713. Oksman also states that in the spring of 1828 Pushkin's attention was drawn away from prose by the idea of *Poltava*, and that he must have thought M. N. Zagoskin's work *Iurii Miloslavskii* (1829)—which had been published by the time Pushkin might have returned to his project in prose—solved the problem of creating a Russian historical novel. Pushkin's works of subsequent years, however, argue otherwise: it is clear that he was not about to cede the field to another historical novelist. Shklovskii [136], pp. 29-35, holds that Pushkin's "Plany povesti o strel'tse" represented a broader design for the theme of *Arap,* and that he abandoned the novel because this new design would have necessitated rewriting chapters already published. The "Plany" Shklovskii cites (dated 1833-34) seem to me to have only a tenuous connection with *Arap;* but even if they are connected with it, it is still not clear why Pushkin let his project lie for five or six years and then decided to redesign it.

[23] See Lapkina [157], p. 308; Lavretskaia [52], p. 86; and Blagoi [22], p. 273. See also Petrov [128], pp. 76-77.

[24] See Khodasevich [156], pp. 168 - 69.

[25] Pushkin's biographer N. L. Brodskii attributes Pushkin's difficulties to a problem in developing the plot: Pushkin, he conjectures, must have come to the conclusion that if he used the same situation twice—an unfaithful wife delivering a baby of an embarrassing color—he might not be able to maintain interest. See Brodskii, *A. S. Pushkin: Biografiia* (Moscow: GIKhL, 1937), p. 573. Brodskii's conjecture is hardly convincing: Pushkin's intention, quite clearly, was not simply to repeat the situation, but to reverse it ironically—a clever device indeed. Blagoi [22], p. 273, believes that the didactic purpose of giving Nicholas a lesson proved to be incompatible with the realistic principles of writing that Pushkin was beginning to espouse in the late 1820's. Further, Abramovich [149], p. 67, suggests that Pushkin could probably not reconcile his realistic presentation of history with his romantically colored portrait of Ibrahim. Skvoznikov [76], p. 71, connects Pushkin's difficulties with his inability, at this early stage, to contain the complexities of

the plot of a historical novel within the confines of his own stylistic principles of prose. And Petrunina [287], p. 102, argues that Ibrahim, of foreign origin and not psychologically bound up with Russian social groups, was not the right choice for Pushkin if his intention was to depict the social struggles of Peter's time. Closest to my own interpretation is that of Bocharov [24], pp. 115 - 24, which sees a tension between the narrative point of view and the historical theme in the novel.

[26] Dymshits [476], p. 455.

[27] See Nadezhdin's review of *Poltava* in *Vestnik Evropy,* 1829, Nos. 8 and 9: 287-302, 17-48.

[28] Dymshits [476], p. 455.

[29] For an analysis of the language of Rzhevskii and his circle, see Bogorodskii [154], pp. 211-19.

[30] Gladkova [112], p. 310, argues that Chap. 3 simply continues the conversation between Minskii and the Spanish tourist begun in Chap. I.

[31] See, for example, Vodovozov [230].

[32] Chicherin [102], p. 83.

[33] Lezhnev [119], p. 293.

[34] Chicherin [103], p. 132.

[35] Chicherin [102], pp. 84-85.

[36] See N. K. Gudzii, "Istoriia pisaniia i pechataniia *Anny Kareninoi,*" in L. N. Tolstoi, *Polnoe sobranie sochinenii* (Moscow: GIKhL, 1928-53), 20: 577-78. See also Gornaia [228]; and E. Maimin, "V spore s uchitelem," *Neva,* 2 (1962): 175-76.

[37] See Brodskii, *A. S. Pushkin* (cited in note 25, above), p. 588.

[38] See Gladkova [112], p. 313.

[39] See the comments of Oksman [4], 4: 762; and of Modzalevskii [2], 2: 304-7. The prototypes for several other characters in the unfinished novel have been identified by Vainshtein & Pavlova [229].

[40] From "Alcibiade," one of the *Contes Moraux* (1765). See *Oeuvres complètes de Marmontel,* nouvelle ed. (Paris: Verdière, 1818 - 19), 3: 19.

[41] See Odintsov [124], p. 411.

[42] Sidiakov [137], p. 38.

[43] Vinogradov [96], p. 523.

[44] Iu. N. Tynianov, *Arkhaisty i novatory* (Leningrad: Priboi, 1929), pp. 283-86.

[45] For details, see Vol'pert [445]. See also V. Shklovskii's brief discussion of Pushkin's models for the epistolary form in *Za i protiv: Zametki o Dostoevskom* (Moscow: Sovetskii pisatel', 1957), p. 28.

[46] Lotman [444] draws attention to the fact that Liza's description of *Clarissa* corresponds to the French translation of the novel, *Lettres angloises, ou Histoire de Miss Clarisse Harlowe* (Paris, 1777), with a Preface by the translator, the Abbé Prévost. The edition was in Pushkin's library.

[47] Briusov [100], p. 267. Ivanov-Razumnik [45], p. 83, claims that "the further development of the plot is clear: Vladimir will abandon both [girls] and will return to St. Petersburg in order to resume an Oneginian way of life."

John Mersereau, Jr. (essay date 1983)

SOURCE: "Pushkin's *Belkin Tales,*" in *Russian Romantic Fiction,* Ardis, 1983, 336 p.

[*In the following essay, Mersereau investigates the stories of Pushkin's* The Tales of Ivan Belkin.]

The best authors of the Romantic period began their careers as poets, and among them only Perovsky-Pogorelsky was exclusively a prose fictionist. Not surprisingly, Alexander Pushkin displayed an extraordinary gift for prose, although his talent in that area was hardly recognized during his lifetime—Marlinsky was more to the public taste. It was in the later twenties that Pushkin turned to prose with *The Negro of Peter the Great [Arap Petra Velikogo],* a fictionalized biography of the author's African great grandfather, Abraham Hannibal. The piece, which breaks off in the middle of the seventh chapter, displays from its first lines that laconicism so typical of all his prose:

> Among the young people sent to foreign countries by Peter the Great for the acquisition of the knowledge needed by the reformed State was his godson, the Negro Abraham. He was trained in a Parisian military academy, released as an artillery captain, distinguished himself in the Spanish war, and, severely wounded, returned to Paris. In the midst of his vast labors, the Emperor never ceased to keep himself informed of his favorite and always received flattering reports about his success and behavior. Peter was very satisfied with him and constantly called him back to Russia, but Abraham did not hurry.

Abraham's liaison with a French countess, the birth of their illegitimate child, his decision to return to Russia and subsequent journey are provided as reported background. The story really gets started after Abraham's arrival in Petersburg in Chapter II, when two dominant themes begin to develop, one stressing the role of Peter the Great as the creator of modern Russia and the other concerning Abraham's marriage to the daughter of the boyar Rzhevsky. The historical background includes descriptions of Peter's assemblies, where contemporary European social niceties were forced upon reluctant boyars and where those who broke the rules or incurred the Tsar's displeasure were obliged to down the contents of the huge Chalice of the Big Eagle.

In *The Negro of Peter the Great* Pushkin exercised his poetic license, changing circumstances to enhance the plot. Thus, Abraham's liaison with Countess D. was probably fictitious, and, though Peter himself serves as matchmaker for his Negro in the novel, history tells us that Abraham did not marry until a number of years following Peter's death, and, moreover, his wife was not a boyar's daughter. The novel ends at the point where Natalia, Rzhevsky's daughter, first glimpses her "official" fiancé, as she recovers from the shock of being told whom she must marry.

During Pushkin's life, only two parts of this work were published, but the entire piece, including the uncompleted seventh chapter, did appear in *The Contemporary* in 1837.[1] *The Negro of Peter the Great* had minimal effect on the course of Russian fiction, but it has been mentioned here primarily as the first extended example of Pushkin's imaginative prose.

A Novel in Letters [Roman v pismakh] was apparently intended to be a literary-political tract in the form of an epistolary society tale. The piece dates from 1829 and contains a number of Pushkin's ideas on literature and, especially, the author's personal views on the duties of the gentry with respect to their serfs, views which are reiterated in his personal correspondence, his criticism, and his notes on history written at about the same time. The literary opinions would hardly have excited the concern of the censors, but the remarks on the *parvenu* aristocracy and its indifference to the welfare of the serfs would have prevented publication of the work had Pushkin finished it. Probably this knowledge, and perhaps a realization that political tracts do not lend themselves to integration in a work of fiction, led the author to abandon his efforts.

The story's initial emphasis on the psychological state of the heroine, Liza, is of some interest, however. Raised and educated in Petersburg as the companion to a wealthy princess, she has recently joined her grandmother in the country, and it is there that she pens her first letter to her confidante, Sasha.

Of course, dear Sashenka, you are surprised at my unexpected withdrawal to the country. I hasten to explain everything frankly. The dependence of my position was always burdensome to me. Of course, Avdotya Andreevna raised me as her niece's equal. But in her house I was nonetheless a ward, and you cannot imagine how many petty miseries were unavoidable in that position.

She continues with some specific examples, and then adds: "Now, I live *at home,* I am the mistress—and you cannot believe what a real pleasure this is for me."

Pushkin's interest in the psychology of his character is visible also in a device which parallels one found in *Eugene Onegin:* Liza finds the books that her adorer, Vladimir, had read when he visited the country several years previously, and these books with his marginal notes reveal to her important facts about his personality. Sasha, Liza's correspondent, also provides comments upon the motivation of both Liza and Vladimir, which further deepens their characterization. This concern with inner motivation rather than external action is an important development in fiction and is a harbinger of Romanticism's evolution toward Realism.

The *Belkin Tales [Povesti Belkina]* are probably the best known of Pushkin's prose, with the exception of **"The Queen of Spades."** He composed the five stories and their introduction in several weeks during the fall of 1830 when he was confined to his father's estate at Boldino by a cholera quarantine. The introduction, which explains very circumstantially that the stories were transcribed by a provincial gentleman, Ivan Belkin, after he had heard them narrated by various persons, was apparently written as an afterthought to insulate Pushkin from any direct attacks by the critics. But the anonymity of the tales also led to their being ignored, and by the time Pushkin's name was connected with them the critics were distracted by more recent works.

The manuscript dates indicate that the *Belkin Tales* were composed in the following sequence: **"The Undertaker," "The Station Master," "Mistress Into Maid," "The Shot," "The Snowstorm"** [**"Grobovshchik," "Stantsionnyi smotritel", "Baryshnia-krest'-ianka," "Vystrel," "Metel"**]*;* the introduction was written last. The stories were arranged by the author with **"The Shot"** and **"The Snowstorm"** first and the rest following in the order of their composition. Some efforts have been made to justify Pushkin's plan in ordering the stories, but most explanations are unconvincing.

Pushkin was not only concerned with externally intriguing plots and characters but engaging in covert play with literary types, themes, and clichés. Unfortunately for his reputation as a prose writer, the critics of his time based their interpretations on the obvious externals, misunderstanding the stories and dismissing them as pleasant but unimportant trifles.

Professor Waclaw Lednicki has demonstrated[2] that the central figure in **"The Shot,"** the enigmatic Byronic Sylvio, is a psychological imposter, whose revenge against a truly natural leader of men, a certain Count D., becomes the entire purpose of his life. Thematically the story relates to Pushkin's *Mozart and Salieri*, one of the "little tragedies" written in Boldino that same fall, in which the composer Salieri, consumed by envy of Mozart's natural genius, poisons his rival. As for its structure, **"The Shot"** provides an interesting example of how a story can be organized to achieve the utmost in mystification, suspense, and characterization. Here we are given a multiple view of the central character, with the story presented by three narrators. Sylvio and the Count relate their tales of past events to a certain Lieutenant I.L.P. (remember, Belkin only wrote down stories told by others), who in turn incorporates their narratives into the framework of his story, which details his own meetings with both men. The character of the narrator himself is very important, for he must be naive enough to be attracted to Sylvio and yet sufficiently perceptive as a reporter to enable the reader to penetrate the real personality of the story's anti-hero.

"The Shot," all of which is presented retrospectively, opens in a provincial garrison town, where the narrator, at that time a junior officer, has become attached to Sylvio, a civilian retired from the army, who has acquired a reputation among the officers for his hospitality and skill with the pistol. However, the narrator is surprised and disappointed one evening when a newcomer to Sylvio's circle insults his host and does not even receive a challenge. One day Sylvio receives a letter and immediately announces his departure, at the same time inviting the officers to a farewell dinner. They all attend, and as they are leaving, Sylvio asks his young friend to remain. He then explains to the narrator that although he would surely have exterminated the rude newcomer in a duel under normal circumstances, he could not expose himself to the slightest risk because of a more pressing question of honor. Five years previously, he explains, he was serving in a cavalry regiment and had acquired quite a reputation for his abilities as duellist, drinker, and rake:

> "You know," continued Sylvio [to the narrator], "that I served in the *** Hussar regiment. My character is known to you: I am accustomed to be first in all respects, and this has been my passion since childhood. In our day brawling was fashionable, so I was the foremost brawler in the army. We prided ourselves on drunkenness, so I outdrank the famous Burtsov, whose praises were sung by Denis Davydov.

> In our regiment duels took place by the minute, and in all of them I was either a second or a participant. My comrades idolized me, and the regimental commanders, who were replaced by the minute, looked upon me as a necessary evil."

> "I was quietly (or unquietly) enjoying my fame, when a young man from a wealthy and well-known family (I don't want to name him) was assigned to us. From the day of my birth I had never met such a brilliant child of fortune! Imagine youth, intellect, good looks, the wildest kind of gaiety, the most reckless courage, a resounding name, and money, whose extent he did not know and which was never exhausted, and imagine what kind of effect he was bound to produce upon us. My prominence tottered. Seduced by my fame, he tried to gain my friendship. But I received him coldly, and without the slightest regret he withdrew from me. I came to hate him. His success in the regiment and in feminine society brought me to complete despair. I began to seek quarrels with him. He answered my epigrams with epigrams which always seemed to me more unexpected and sharper than mine. and which, of course, were incomparably more humorous. He was jesting while I was being spiteful."

Here in Sylvio's own words is the essence of his conflict with the Count, who, naturally and without trying, achieves what Sylvio has taken years of role-playing to accumulate. Finally, the exasperated Sylvio challenges the Count, who appears at the duelling site casually eating cherries and, having won the right to the first shot, just as casually puts a bullet through Sylvio's forage cap. Sylvio then aims at his adversary, but the Count faces him fearlessly, continuing to eat cherries and spitting the pits across the barrier.[3] This is too much for the would-be Byronic avenger, and he postpones his shot until such a time as the prospect of death will mean more to the Count. Now, five years later, Sylvio informs the narrator that he has heard of the Count's recent marriage and that he is leaving to take his revenge. The narrator remarks that Sylvio's tale caused "strange, conflicting feelings" to agitate him.

Another four or five years pass, during which the narrator retires to his estate in the country. His closest neighbor is a Countess B., who had been absent from her estate since shortly after her marriage several years before. However, one day she and her husband return to resume residence there, and the narrator visits them. In the course of their conversation, it turns out that the husband is Sylvio's old enemy, the Count, and he now tells the narrator what happened when the duel resumed. Sylvio had suddenly reappeared at the estate, demanded his shot, but hesitated as he aimed at the accommodating Count. Finally he determined they should begin anew. Once more they drew lots, the Count again winning first shot. Under some strange domination by Sylvio, the Count's shot pierced a picture on the wall. As Sylvio began to aim, the Countess rushed in and threw herself at his feet. The Count angrily told her to rise and demanded that Sylvio either shoot or stop his mockery. Sylvio responded that he would not shoot, since he was sufficiently satisfied with seeing the Count's agitation and apprehension. Hardly aiming, Sylvio put his bullet into the same hole made in the picture by the Count's shot and then departed. The narrator laconically reports that it was later said that Sylvio had died in battle during the Greek Insurrection.

The psychology of the envious, vindictive, obsessed Sylvio is naturally more intriguing than that of the Count, so it is on the former that Pushkin focused his story. And it is the manifold presentation of Sylvio, whose masks are peeled off to reveal his diseased soul, which makes this story so unusual, especially for the year 1830. Sylvio is seen from four different points of view: his own, which does not change and is lacking any self-awareness, the Count's and the narrator's which change as they learn more about Sylvio, and the reader's, which is abstracted from the others. Our view of Sylvio is continually evolving: at first we are intrigued by this mysterious figure who seems to be a natural leader, we are puzzled at his refusal to challenge the newcomer for his insult, and surprised at the extent of the malice revealed in his own story. Our feelings of dismay are further intensified when we learn that Sylvio spares the Count, but his act is not one of compassion. Rather, he does so because he expects that the Count will find his future life poisoned by the memory of Sylvio's domination. In declining his shot, Sylvio declares:

> "I am satisfied. I have seen your confusion, your alarm. I forced you to fire at me. That is enough. You will remember me, I leave you to your conscience."

But the irony is that Sylvio's long awaited "revenge" is ineffective, Sylvio attributes to the Count the kind of reaction which he, himself, would have had under the same circumstances, that is, a galling sense of frustration and humiliation. But the Count lives on happily, the episode with Sylvio reduced to the level of a bad dream. Although shaken, the Count has again proved his natural superiority to the psychological impostor.

Although **"The Shot"** incorporates Romantic themes and situations, and although its central character, Sylvio, is close kin to such excessive Romantic figures as Byron's Lara, Tieck's Eckbert, or even Scott's Black Monk, the tale's ultimate effect is quite unlike that of typical Romantic fiction. The mysterious and intriguing aura surrounding the central figure is the product of the naivete of the narrator, who is impressed by Sylvio's mask. But if the reader under-

stands the story, the fog gradually disappears and he gains a clear view of an obsessive personality, repulsive in its malignity and frightening in its violence.

The story concludes with Pushkin's private ironical twist:

> It is said that Sylvio led a detachment of hetaerists during the revolt of Alexander Ypsilanti and was killed in the battle of Skulyani.[4]

Skulyani was a disaster and a fitting apotheosis for Sylvio, whose personal qualities were insufficient to sustain his impersonation of the natural leader. The direct reference to Alexander Ypsilanti reinforces the irony, since Pushkin had a low opinion of him as a commander. In **"Kirdzhali,"** a historical sketch published in 1834, Pushkin had this to say about the Greek revolutionary:

> Alexander Ypsilanti was personally brave, but he did not have the qualities necessary for the role which he undertook so passionately and imprudently. He did not know how to get along with the people he had to lead. They had neither respect for nor confidence in him. After the unhappy battle in which the flower of Greek youth perished, Iordaki Olimbioti advised him to withdraw and himself took his place. Ypsilanti galloped to the borders of Austria and from there sent his curse to the people whom he called rebels, cowards, and scoundrels. These cowards and scoundrels for the most part perished within the walls of Seko monastery or on the banks of the Pruth, fighting desperately against an enemy ten times stronger.

Without suggesting any direct connection between Ypsilanti and Sylvio, it should be noted that neither name is Russian, and, like Sylvio himself, Ypsilanti served for a time as an officer in the Russian army.

"The Shot" is introduced with an epigraph from an anecdote included in Marlinsky's *An Evening on Bivouac* (1823): "I swore to shoot him in accordance with the duelling code (I still had a shot to follow his)." The earlier story is a sentimental tale involving an officer, Vladimir Lidin, who is gravely wounded in a duel with a captain who maligned the girl he loved. After a lengthy convalescence, Vladimir returns to his regiment to learn that his adversary and his girlfriend have been married. Since he still has one shot, he vows to continue the duel, but friends see to it that he is posted to some distant place. Later he learns that the wife was also the victim of the captain, who abandoned her to die penniless. Like **"The Shot,"** Marlinsky's tale has multiple narrators, but the potential for contrastive characterization is not exploited as it is in Pushkin's work. Further, Marlinsky seasons his work, as usual, with overt sentimentality and sententiousness, qualities antithetical to Pushkin's art. One may see **"The Shot,"** therefore, as Pushkin's restrained polemic with Marlinsky, the same plot nucleus built into a tightly crafted tale emphasizing the protagonist's obsessive personality and leaving it for the reader to decide the point.

"The Snowstorm" involves fate and mistaken identity, each theme emerging from the rather preposterous plot. Still, the atmosphere is more serious than frivolous, though not so serious as **"The Shot."** Mariya, the daughter of a wealthy provincial family, falls in love with their poor neighbor, Vladimir, but her parents prohibit their marriage. The two lovers scheme to elope, and one stormy night Vladimir sends his sleigh and coachman to convey Mariya and her maid to a nearby church, where arrangements had been made for their wedding. Meanwhile, Vladimir sets out alone and becomes hopelessly lost in the storm. A hussar officer on his way to Wilno also loses his way because of the blizzard and ends up at the church, where the fainting bride, the anxious priest, and witness mistake him for the tardy bridegroom. The officer nonchalantly permits himself to be married to the girl, who, only after they are wed, recovers sufficiently to discover that her husband is a total stranger. The hussar then drives away, and Mariya returns home. Her parents are blissfully ignorant of her adventure, and when she falls ill and raves deliriously about her love for Vladimir, they have a change of heart and reconsider their opposition to her marriage. They write this good news to the young man, but he responds madly that he will never see them again and wishes he were dead. Shortly afterwards they learn he has rejoined the army. Four years pass. Vladimir has perished in the War of 1812, and Mariya has moved to another village. There she meets a Colonel Burmin, a wounded veteran of the victory over Napoleon, and the two are quite attracted to each other. One day Burmin declares his love, but he explains that marriage is impossible because of a heedless act in the past, when during a snowstorm at some unknown village he had married an unknown woman. All is happily resolved when Mariya declares that she is his anonymous bride.

The caprice of fate is one of Pushkin's favorite themes. In Burmin's account there is a special note of his apparently *fated* role in the whole episode:

> "At the beginning of 1812," said Burmin, "I was hastening to Wilno, where our regiment was stationed. Having arrived at some post station once late in the evening, I was about to order that horses be harnessed as soon as possible when suddenly a terrible snowstorm arose, and the station master and the drivers advised me to wait. I followed their advice, but an inexplicable agitation took possession of me. *It seemed as if someone were pushing me.* [Italics mine]. Meanwhile, the storm did not abate. I became impatient, again ordered the horses to be harnessed, and set off into the tempest. The driver got the idea of traveling along the river, which would have shortened our way by three versts. The banks were drifted, and the driver passed the place where we should have turned onto the road, and in that way we ended up in some unknown region. The tempest did not abate. I saw a small light and ordered to be driven towards it. We drove into a village. There was a light in the wooden church. The church was open, behind the wall stood several sleighs, people were walking around the porch.

> 'This way, this way!' cried several voices. I ordered the coachman to drive up to them. 'For God's sake, where have you been?' someone said to me, 'the bride is in a faint, the priest doesn't know what to do. We were on the point of going back. Get out as fast as you can.' Without responding, I jumped from the sleigh and entered the church, which was weakly illuminated with two or three candles. The girl sat on a bench in a dark corner of the church. Another was rubbing her temples. 'Thank God,' she said, 'you've arrived at last. You almost tormented the young lady to death.' The old priest hurried. Three men and the maid supported the bride and were occupied exclusively with her. We were married. 'Kiss each other,' we were told. My wife turned her pale face toward me. I was on the point of kissing her. . . . She screamed, 'Ai, it isn't he, it isn't he!' and fell senseless. The witnesses fastened their frightened eyes upon me. I turned, left the church without any hindrance, jumped into my kibitka, and cried out, 'Drive on!' "

Is it fate again which reunites the husband and wife and leads them to discover their paradoxical relationship, or is it merely coincidence? Or is perhaps Pushkin playing with the whole Romantic concept of fated lovers, mistaken identity, and implausible coincidence? Notice the careful attention to details in the hussar's account, which seeks to justify Burmin's being mistaken for Vladimir: the darkness of the night, the dim candle light in the church, the fainting bride, who distracted everyone's attention from Burmin. If this story is a crypto-satire on outworn Romantic cliches, as its somewhat facetious tone might suggest, then all this justification is simply a red herring, a part of Pushkin's private joke.

Regardless of the author's intent, the story is cleverly constructed to keep the reader guessing until the very end. Burmin does not appear until the dénouement, and until his story is told we do not know what happened at the church on that fatal night, only that it brought about Mariya's spell of delirium and Vladimir's incoherent response to her parents' letter, incoherent not because he no longer loved the girl but because he knew he could never marry her: the morning after her marriage to Burmin he had learned that the wedding had taken place and that the groom had disappeared.

If we wished to see some special purpose in Pushkin's arrangement of the Belkin stories, we could claim that the third in the series, **"The Undertaker,"** is a work linking the sombre psychological study of **"The Shot"** and the less serious case of mistaken identity of **"The Snowstorm"** with the mock serious psychological study of **"The Station Master"** and the totally frivolous case of mistaken identity of **"Mistress Into Maid."** **"The Undertaker"** is a tale of the supernatural based on a variant of the cliché, "Speak of the devil and he shall appear."

Having moved to a new section of town, an undertaker, Adrian Prokhorov, is invited by a neighbor, the cobbler Schultz, to attend a party in honor of his silver wedding anniversary. At the celebration, which is thronged with German tradesmen of various callings, a great deal of beer is consumed, followed by toasts with sparkling wine. Finally a fat baker raises his glass "To the health of those for whom we work, *"unserer Kundleute!"* In jest, one of the guests calls out to the undertaker, "What's this? Drink up, little father, to the health of your corpses." Adrian is offended, and after the party is over he returns home angry and drunk. In a fit of pique, he declares that he won't invite his neighbors to his housewarming but rather "the people for whom I work, the Orthodox dead." Despite his servant's remonstrances, he persists and issues an invitation. The next evening the surprised undertaker finds his house crowded with his former customers. Although the spectres are somewhat macabre, there is no element of terror except for the host.

> The room was filled with corpses. Through the window the moon illuminated their yellow and blue faces, sunken mouths, dull, half-closed eyes, and projecting noses. With terror Adrian recognized in them the people buried through his services. . . . All of them, ladies and gentlemen, surrounded the undertaker with bows and greetings, with the exception of one poor fellow who had recently had a free funeral. Somewhat conscience stricken and embarrassed by his rags, he did not approach but stood quietly in a corner. . . .

> At this moment a small skeleton squeezed through the crowd and approached Adrian. Its skull smiled pleasantly at the undertaker. Bits of light green and red cloth and rotted linen hung here and there upon it as on a pole, and its bones rattled in its big jack boots like pestles in mortars. "You don't recognize me, Prokhorov," said the skeleton. "Do you remember the retired sergeant of the Guard, Peter Petrovich Kurilkin, the very one to whom in 1799 you sold your first coffin, moreover a pine one instead of oak?" With these words the corpse offered its bony embrace, but Adrian, collecting himself with difficulty, cried out and shoved it away. Peter Petrovich staggered, fell, and scattered about. A murmer of displeasure arose among the corpses. All

of them stood up for the honor of their comrade, they surrounded Adrian with abuse and threats, and the poor host, deafened by their cries and almost crushed, lost his presence of mind, and he himself fell onto the bones of the retired sergeant of the Guard and lost consciousness.

Descriptions of all this spectral haunting are quite facetious, even to the skeleton named Peter Petrovich who falls apart. The revelation that this was Adrian's dream, brought on by overindulgence at the cobbler's feast and irritation at the fancied insult to his profession, disarms the supernatural element.

Some efforts have been made to relate **"The Undertaker"** to works of E.T.A. Hoffmann, but the ties, if any, are tenuous. Pushkin's tale is more closely connected with his own *The Stone Guest,* one of the "little tragedies" written at Boldino in 1830, in which the brazen Don Juan invites the statue of the commander to stand guard over his rendezvous with the commander's widow:

> *(to the statue.)* I, commander, bid you come
> To the widow's house, where I'll tomorrow be,
> And stand and guard the doors. Well? Will you?
>   *(The statue nods its head)*
>   Oh, God!

Another source is indicated by an allusion in the story to the watchman Yurko, who "for twenty-five years served his calling with trust and truth, like Pogorelsky's postman." In *The Lafertov District Poppyseed Cake Vendor* (1825), Perovsky-Pogorelsky presented a story of the supernatural set against the background of the Moscow lower bourgeoisie, and, although the supernatural in that tale is "real," the tone is facetious, as it is in Pushkin's work. Pushkin's enthusiasm for Perovsky's work is indicated in a letter written to Leo Pushkin in March, 1825:

> My soul, grandmother's cat is really charming! I read the whole tale twice in one breath, and now I'm obsessed with Trifony Faleleyich Purrful. I move forward smoothly, squinting my eyes, rotating my head, and arching my back. Pogorelsky is certainly Perovsky, right?[5]

Generations of readers have been deceived by **"The Station Master,"** which only goes to prove that most readers see in a work what they wish to see. On the surface this story seems to be about a poor station master of the lowest rank, Samson Vyrin, whose beautiful daughter, Dunya, the light of her old dad's eyes, is abducted by an officer and taken to a life of sin in Petersburg. This touching tale is related by a traveler who visits the posting station on three occasions. The first time he is smitten, as are most voyagers, by the beauty and spontaneity of Dunya, whose charm animates the entire household. A second visit three years later reveals a haggard station master, a broken man, who when plied with punch tells of the perfidious officer, Minsky, who pretended to be ill in order to win Dunya. Tearfully he recounts how he urged his daughter to ride in Minsky's carriage to the village church and how she never returned. He followed her to Petersburg, learned where she was being kept, even saw her, but Minsky would not let him speak to her. The station master tells also of his anger when Minsky tried to buy him off with a handful of bills. The traveler-narrator leaves the station consumed with gloomy thoughts of Dunya's ultimate fate and the sorrowful image of her desolate father. A final visit discloses that the station master died from drink. The narrator's inquiries reveal that once a woman in an expensive carriage with children and servants had come to the village and visited his grave. The narrator also goes to the bleak cemetery and ruefully surveys the last resting place of Samson Vyrin, the victim of his daughter's sins and a rich man's callousness.

"The Station Master" presents an early example of the unreliable narrator. He does not deliberately try to deceive his audience but rather he is too naive, too conventional, to see the true import of the facts he relates. Happily, he is a comprehensive reporter who provides the reader with all essential information, but, unhappily, too many readers accept his judgment uncritically and, along with him, shed their tears pointlessly.

The meaning or point of any story must be developed from the entire story, and interpretations which are based on only a portion of the story are simply incorrect. A story is an organic whole, and its meaning derives from that whole. The Soviet scholar, M.O. Gershenzon, who is responsible for the dictum that the art of good criticism is the art of slow reading, was puzzled by one aspect of **"The Station Master"** which did not seem typical of Pushkin's prose. Gershenzon noted that one seldom finds digressions, inessential details, or superfluous qualifiers in Pushkin's fiction. Therefore, the critic was struck by the lengthy passage in which the narrator describes in detail the four pictures ornamenting the walls of the station. These depict the Parable of the Prodigal Son.

> At this point he [the station master] undertook to transcribe my travel orders, and I occupied myself by looking over the pictures which decorated his humble but tidy abode. They depicted the story of the prodigal son: in the first a venerable old man in a night-cap and robe is taking leave of a restless youth, who hastily accepts his blessing and a bag of money. In the second was depicted in clear features the dissolute behavior of the young person: he was sitting at a table surrounded by false friends and

shameless women. Further, the wastrel youth in rags and a three-cornered hat was herding swine and sharing their banquet. On his face was depicted deep sadness and repentence. Finally there was represented his return to his father. The kind old man in the same night-cap and robe was running out towards him: the prodigal son was kneeling, and in the background the cook was killing the fatted calf and the older brother was asking a servant the cause of all the joy. Under each picture I read appropriate German verses. Until now I have retained all this in my memory, along with the pots with balsam, and the bed with the motley screen, and the other things which surrounded me at that time. I see, as if now, the host himself, a man around fifty, fresh and vigorous, and his long green frock coat with three medals on faded ribbons.

In telling of his subsequent visit, the narrator again mentions these pictures, more or less in passing. But everything else has changed, for the station itself is gloomy and the master crushed. In Samson's story of Minsky's deception and the search for Dunya, he continually refers to his daughter as "my strayed lamb," "my poor Dunya," and the narrator in turn calls the master "the poor father," "the poor station master," "the unfortunate one." The old man concludes his tale with these pitiful observations:

> "It's already been three years," he concluded, "that I have been living without Dunya, and there's not been a word about her. Whether she's alive or not, God knows. Anything is possible. She's not the first or the last to be lured away by some traveling scoundrel, kept there a while, and abandoned. There are many of them in Petersburg, foolish young girls, today in thick silk and velvet, and tomorrow, take a look, they are sweeping the streets with tavern beggars. When I sometimes think that maybe this will happen to Dunya, then against my will I sin and wish her in the grave."

And so he takes to drink and dies. But why? Because he believed the pictures in his house, because he was certain that Dunya had to follow the descent of the prodigal and fall into poverty and misery. The irony is, however, that his dire prediction did not come true, quite the contrary. On the narrator's final visit, he asks to see Samson Vyrin's grave and is taken there by a small boy, who tells him:

> "Well, nowadays there are few travelers. . . . But in the summer a lady passed through, and she did ask about the old station master and went to his grave."

> "What lady?" I asked with curiosity.

> "A beautiful lady," answered the little boy. "She was traveling in a carriage with six horses, with three little young gentlemen and a wet nurse, and with a black pug dog. When they told her that the

old master had died, then she began to cry and said to the children, 'Sit quietly, and I'll visit the cemetery.' And I was about to lead her there. But the lady said, 'I know the way myself!' And she gave me a silver five kopek piece—such a kind lady!"

So Dunya is alive and well in Petersburg supported in style, with a coach and three children, a wet nurse, and a lapdog. And for that Samson Vyrin drank himself to death.

Nothing Pushkin ever wrote would suggest that his was a sentimental mentality. Rather, he always mocked that inclination, and often his characters were victims of their confidence in the verity of Sentimentalist cliches. He considered Richardson's Clarissa Harlowe an absolute fool (she willed herself to death after having been "dishonored" by Lovelace), and, regardless of the narrator's attitude toward Samson Vyrin, Pushkin must have seen the station master's self destruction as the epitome of folly.

All of the Belkin tales have their elements of irony, but in **"The Station Master"** irony becomes the essence of the piece. In addition to the irony of the pointless sacrifice, there are minor ironies, for example, the master's first name, Samson, which implies strength, and his surname, Vyrin, which possibly suggests *escavate* [vyryt']. In any case, Samson was done in by a woman and Vyrin does dig his own premature grave. Irony figures also in the origin of his tragedy, for it is he who insists that Dunya accompany Minsky to the church in his carriage: " 'What are you afraid of?' her father said, 'surely his honor is not a wolf and won't eat you up. Take a ride to church.' " And there is irony also in the scene of Samson's righteous indignation when Minsky tries to give him money to leave Dunya alone:

> For a long time he stood without moving. Finally he saw behind the fold of his cuff a roll of papers. He withdrew them and opened up several crumpled five and ten ruble bank notes. Again tears came to his eyes, tears of indignation! He wadded the notes into a ball, threw them to the ground, trampled them with his heels, and went on. . . . Having gone several steps, he stopped, thought a bit . . . and turned around . . . but the bank notes were not there. A well dressed young man, catching sight of him, ran up to a cabby, hurriedly took a seat, and cried out, "Drive on!"

Samson's second thoughts about the payoff money completely cancel out his earlier tears of indignation, and his heedless sacrifice of the banknotes, which is motivated by misplaced emotions, presages his later unnecessary death.

If one wishes further substantiation of Gershenzon's interpretation, note that **"The Station Master"** is a subtle parody of *Poor Liza,* with the victims raised one notch in social status. Instead of Liza's widowed mother, a peasant, we have Dunya's widowered father, a civil servant at the bottom of the scale.[6] Liza's mother and Vyrin are devoted to their offspring, who are not only uncommonly pretty but pretty free with their kisses. As malefactors we have Erast, a wishy-washy young gentleman who gambles to penury, and Minsky, who is obviously from the real *beau monde* and one who knows what he wants. Karamzin's refrain of "poor Liza" is matched by the station master's "poor Dunya," a phrase which Pushkin's narrator also reëchoes. The attempt to pay off the offended party is virtually the same in both stories. "[Erast] took her by the hand, led her to his study, locked the door. . . . ," while "Minsky took him by the hand, led him to the study, and locked the door behind him." Readers raised on Karamzin would certainly have expected that Dunya would come to no good end, but the wily Pushkin led them by the nose and reversed the anticipated ending.

"Mistress Into Maid," the last of the Belkin group, is yet another ironical treatment of *Poor Liza* and, at the same time, a variation on the themes of fate and mistaken identity found in **"The Snowstorm."** Its pervasive facetious tone implies its parodistic essence. Ivan Berestov, a widowed landowner of patriarchal principles, is at loggerheads with his neighbor, the Anglophile Grigory Muromsky, the father of seventeen-year-old Liza. When Alexey Berestov returns home from the university, he instantly captivates the local gentry misses with his Byronic poses:

> It is easy to imagine what kind of an impression Alexey was bound to create in the circle of our young ladies. He was the first among them to appear gloomy and disenchanted, he was the first to talk to them about lost happiness and about his faded youth. Moreover, he wore a black ring with the image of a death's head. All this was quite new in that province. Girls lost their heads over him.

Liza Muromskaya seeks an opportunity to meet this fascinating and handsome young neighbor, and, learning that he has an eye for peasant girls, she puts together a suitable costume, creates a cover story about being Akulina, the blacksmith's daughter, and goes into the forest to be encountered "accidentally" by Alexey. Their initial meeting leads to others, and Alexey is progressively more fascinated by his peasant beauty, whose moral rectitude and skill in learning to read and write (so they can correspond) are simply amazing. Meanwhile, their fathers have become reconciled, and Liza is forced to meet Alexey at her father's house. Heavy applications of powder and eyebrow pencil, in addition to an outlandish costume and artificial hair pieces, prevent Alexey from recognizing her. In fact, the impression she creates is so negative that Alexey flatly rejects his father's demand that he marry the girl. He then writes to his peasant Akulina proposing marriage. Hoping to enlist Liza to oppose the match which their parents are forcing on them, Alexey goes to Muromsky estate to talk to the young lady. Imagine his surprise to find his peasant maiden, now transformed into a pretty provincial miss, reading his letter in her father's drawing room.

There are several allusions to Karamzin in this story which suggest its parodic quality. Alexey teaches Liza Muromskaya "to read" using *Natalia, the Boyar's Daughter,* whose hero is also an Alexey and who eloped with Natalia to the Murom forests. The Liza of **"Mistress Into Maid"** is not destined to become yet another "poor Liza," and part of Pushkin's irony is in the fact that Liza-Akulina is not seduced and cast off. However, hidden in this story there is an actual victim of Alexey's attraction to lower class girls. Here there is a remark in passing about a letter written by Alexey:

> The young ladies looked at him and some feasted their eyes. But Alexey was little occupied with them, and they ascribed his insensitivity to a love affair. Indeed, there was passed from hand to hand a copy of the address of one of his letters:

> To Akulina Petrovna Kurochkina, Moscow, opposite the Alexeyev monastery, the house of the coppersmith Savelyev, and I most humbly request that you deliver this letter to A. N. R.

Who was this A.N.R., a gentry girl or something less elevated? Recall that when he arrived in the country Alexey immediately disdained the provincial misses and started chasing peasant girls. As Liza's maid reports:

> "They say the gentleman is handsome, he's such a kind person, so cheerful. One thing is bad: he likes to chase girls too much. Well, as for me, there's nothing wrong with that. In time he'll settle down."

One may surmise that this letter to A. N. R. contained expression of undying love, but that the next one would rationalize an end to their liaison. While Alexey and Liza are rejoicing in the provinces, somewhere in Moscow a young girl's dream has been shattered.

While writing the Belkin tales, Pushkin was also working on a satirical piece called *A History of the Village of Goriukhino [Istoriia sela Goriukhina].* He did not finish the work, but it did appear in *The Contemporary* soon after his death in 1837, and thus has a place in Romantic fiction.

The Petersburg literary mandarins, you will recall, were unhappy with Polevoy for his denigration of

Karamzin's *History of the Russian State,* expressed polemically in his own *History of the Russian People.* Pushkin's "history" is a parody of the pretensions of Polevoy's pedestrian work, and to some extent it is also a lampoon on that author-critic-publisher himself.

The village of Goriukhino was the ancestral holding of the Belkin family, and Ivan Belkin, transcriber of tales, retired there after an uneventful career in the army. The first part of *A History of the Village of Goriukhino* is an amusingly tedious account by Belkin of his efforts to serve literature, his original aspirations to be an epic poet yielding gradually to the realization that his talent, at best, was sufficient only to equip him as a village historian. He begins his history with a pseudo-scholarly explanation of his sources, which range from old calendars to village gossip:

> Here I put forth a list of sources which served me in compiling the History of Goriukhino Village: 1. A collection of antique calendars. *54 parts.* The first 20 parts are filled with antique script and titled. This chronicle was composed by my great grandfather, Andrey Stepanovich Belkin. It is distinguished by clarity and succinctness of style: for example: May 4. Snow. Trishka beaten for rudeness. 6. The chestnut cow croaked. Senka beaten for drunkenness. 8. Weather clear. 9. Rain and snow. Trishka beaten because of the weather. 11. Weather clear. Newly fallen snow. Hunted 3 hares. . . .

This register of incredible triviality continues in an exposition that is archaic, bookish, and naive, a marvelous exaggeration of Polevoy's style:

> The land which is named Goriukhino after its capital occupies more than 240 dessiatins on the earthly sphere. The number of its inhabitants extends to 63 souls. To the north it is bounded by the villages of Deriukhovo and Perkukhovo, whose inhabitants are poor, emaciated, and stunted, but the proud proprietors are devoted to the military exercise of coursing hares. To the south the river Sivka divides it from the holdings of the free Karachevsky grain framers—restless neighbors known for the turbulent cruelty of their customs. To the west it is surrounded by the flowering Zakharinsky fields which thrive under wise and enlightened landowners. To the east it comes in contact with wild, uninhabited places, an impassable swamp, where only bogberries grow and where legend proposes the habitation of a certain devil. N.B. This swamp is called *The Devil's Swamp.* It is related that a half-witted shepherdess used to stand watch over a herd of pigs not far from this remote spot. She became pregnant and was quite unable to explain satisfactorily this occurrence. Public opinion accused the swamp devil, but this fable is unworthy of a historian's attention, and after Niebuhr it would be unforgivable to believe it.

The benighted and earnest Belkin is also a perfect vehicle for Pushkin's gibes at serfdom. Later in his history, our chronicler tells how the villagers prospered when left largely to themselves but were impoverished virtually overnight when put under the control of a venal estate manager. Pushkin's social consciousness did not extend to the emancipation of the serfs, but he did demand elementary justice for them. In his unfinished *A Novel in Letters* (1829), he unequivocally expressed the conviction that the masters had a responsibility to ensure the welfare of those in their possession.

Notes

1 Chapter IV was printed in *Northern Flowers for 1829* but was unsigned.

2 *Russia, Poland and the West* (New York, 1954), 213 ff.

3 A Soviet acquaintance of mine once attributed this act of supreme *insouciance* to Lermontov at the time of his duel with Martynov, but that is simply a case of confusing fiction with fact.

4 At Skulyani 15,000 Turkish cavalry decimated a force of some 700 Greek liberationists.

5 Purrful's given name was actually Aristarchus.

6 Pushkin's parody of *Poor Liza* is also, paradoxically, a parody of Pyotr Mashkov's *Mariya, or the Tribulations of the Prodigal Daughter,* which was written three years *after* Pushkin's work.

Simon Karlinsky (essay date 1985)

SOURCE: "Pushkin and Neoclassical Drama," in *Russian Drama from Its Beginnings to the Age of Pushkin,* University of California Press, 1985, pp. 312-38.

[*In the following essay, Karlinsky characterizes Pushkin's works as "the culmination of Russian eighteenth-century neoclassicism."*]

> "Pushkin is our first classicist and romanticist, which makes him a realist." . . . (The latter definition depends upon the epoch, and also the temperament of the commentator.)
>
> Igor Stravinsky[1]

It has been the fate of many a great Russian writer to acquire in Western countries an image that is the very opposite of what he has actually stood for and believed. Ultraconservatives, such as Gogol and the mature Dostoevsky, are venerated as fearless indicters of tsarist tyranny. The humanitarian activist Anton

Chekhov, with his wide-ranging program of social betterment and environmental concern, is seen as a gloomy prophet of despair and doom. Vladìmir Mayakovsky, who detested anything bucolic and put his hopes for a better future in industrialization and urbanization, was depicted in an American educational film as a poet of farms, herds and open plains.

Most misunderstood of all in popular lore is Alexander Pushkin (1799-1837). A writer whose work represents the culmination of Russian eighteenth-century neoclassicism and is pervaded by it, Pushkin is usually seen as someone who finally and definitively put an end to the neoclassical tradition. More deeply steeped in French language and literature than any other Russian writer, Pushkin is often credited with emancipating Russian literature from French influence. Beneficiary of the advances in the development of literary Russian that were achieved earlier by Karamzin, Zhukovsky, Batiushkov, Krylov, and, eventually, by Shakhovskoy and Khmelnitsky, Pushkin is still often said to have created the modern literary language all by himself, with no outside help.

Pushkin was interested in drama and the theater from his childhood. He reputedly attempted composing comedies while he still lived at his parents' home, even before he was enrolled at the boarding school, the Lyceum of Tsarskoe Selo in the environs of St. Petersburg, at the age of twelve. His classmates at the Lyceum recalled that during his school years he began writing a verse comedy in the French neoclassical manner, a work that was later destroyed. The literary tastes of the teenaged Pushkin are outlined in detail in his poem **"Small Town"** (**"Gorodok"**), written when he was sixteen. The longest eulogy in the poem is reserved for Voltaire, "the rival of Euripides, the gentle friend of Erato [i.e., the muse of amorous poetry], and a descendant of Ariosto and Tasso." In a later passage devoted mainly but not totally to his favorite playwrights, Pushkin lists Ozerov, Racine, Molière ("the gigantic Molière"), Fonvizin, and Kniazhnin.

Kniazhnin (as the author of verse comedies) and Fonvizin were to remain Pushkin's lifelong favorites, as evidenced by the epigraphs from their plays and allusions to them in his prose works of the 1830s. Ozerov initially attracted Pushkin through Ekaterina Semyonova's performances in his tragedies and because of the myth that his untimely death was caused by harassment inflicted by his envious literary enemies. But in the essay **"My Remarks on the Russian Theater,"** which dates from January 1820 and usually opens the volume of Pushkin's critical essays in the academic editions of his collected works, we read of "the unfortunate Ozerov's imperfect creations," indicative of Pushkin's later disdain for Ozerov's tragedies, a disdain that led to disagreements with his friend and literary ally, Viazemsky, Ozerov's biographer and champion.

At the time of the opening of Shakhovskoy's *The Lipetsk Spa* Pushkin was the youngest member of the literary club "Arzamas," founded by Zhukovsky and Viazemsky to oppose the Archaists' attacks on sentimentalism and nascent Russian romanticism. With youthful fervor, Pushkin had earlier ridiculed Shakhovskoy in epigrams directed against the conservatism of the Archaists' literary position. Disgusted by Shakhovskoy's mockery of Zhukovsky, whom Pushkin regarded as his poetic teacher, and by the lampooning through the character of Countess Leleva's admirer, the retired hussar Ugarov, of two other people close to him—his uncle (the minor poet Vasily Pushkin) and Sergei Uvarov (later Pushkin's enemy, but at the time a fellow member of "Arzamas")—the teenaged Pushkin recorded in his diary for 1815 **"My Thoughts on Shakhovskoy,"** a murderous denunciation of the playwright, his personality, and his supposed technical deficiencies.[2]

In a few years, however, as Iury Tynianov has shown in his study "The Archaists and Pushkin," Pushkin's friendship and literary alliance with the junior Archaist Katenin put an end to his hostility to the Archaist camp. By 1819, Pushkin was introduced to Shakhovskoy by Katenin and became a regular visitor to Shakhovskoy's "garret," that is, the literary salon presided over by Shakhovskoy's mistress, Ekaterina Ezhova. In his letter to Katenin from his Mikhailovskoye exile, written on September 12, 1825, Pushkin recalled the reading by Katenin of his *Andromache* at the "garret" as one of the happiest evenings of his life. Pushkin's coining of the term "the Lipetsk flood" to describe the resurgent popularity of verse comedy after 1815 shows his awareness of the importance of Shakhovskoy's first verse comedy for this development. Subsequently, Pushkin not only authorized but even encouraged Shakhovskoy's dramatizations of his *Ruslan and Liudmila* in 1824, *The Fountain of Bakhchisarai* in 1825, and *The Queen of Spades* in 1836.

No initial unpleasantness marred Pushkin's personal and literary contacts with Nikolai Khmelnitsky. The record of their encounters is scant, especially in Pushkin's writings. In his letter to Nikolai Gnedich of May 13, 1823, Pushkin recalls being shown the manuscript of Khmelnitsky's comedy *The Irresolute Man* and offering Khmelnitsky his advice. Pushkin's letter of early May 1825 to his brother Lev mentions that the poet received a copy of the journal *The Russian Thalia* that contained some excerpts from a comedy by Khmelnitsky and adds: "And Khmelnitsky is my old love [Pushkin used the word *liubovnitsa* in the theatrical sense of "the woman with whom a character is in love"]. I have such a weakness for him that I'm prepared to place an entire couplet in his honor in the first chapter of *Onegin* (but what the deuce! They say he gets angry if one mentions him as a playwright)."

A possible cause for this purported anger may have been Khmelnitsky's rapid advancement in the civil service hierarchy, which was soon to lead to his appointment to the governorship of Smolensk. By failing to evoke Khmelnitsky's name in the first chapter of *Eugene Onegin,* Pushkin cheated him of the kind of immortality he had bestowed on Kniazhnin, Ozerov, Shakhovskoy, and Katenin by including theirs in stanza 18 of that chapter. But mentioned or not, Khmelnitsky is, as we shall see, very much present in the first chapter of *Eugene Onegin.* Pushkin's profession of love for Khmelnitsky's plays in the cited letter to his brother helps explain the impact Khmelnitsky had on the two major works that were being written or planned at the time, *Boris Godunov* and *Count Nulin.* The last mention of Khmelnitsky in Pushkin's correspondence occurs in the letter addressed to him on March 6, 1831, in his capacity as the governor of Smolensk, in response to a request that Pushkin donate copies of his books to the Smolensk municipal library. After a ceremonious first section of the letter addressed to His Excellency the Governor, Pushkin switches to an informal second section in which he protests that while he respects the governor, he loves Khmelnitsky the man as "my favorite poet."

Pushkin's supremacy in Russian literature was established with the publication in 1820 of *Ruslan and Liudmila,* a mock-heroic epic that incorporated what he had learned from the narrative poems of Ariosto and Voltaire, from Russian eighteenth-century humorous poems by Maikov and Bogdanovich, and, as Leonid Grossman has persuasively shown, from the ballets of his contemporary, the French choreographer Charles Didelot.[3] His narrative poem **"The Gabrieliad"** (1821) had its roots in the blasphemous and erotic eighteenth-century poems by Voltaire and Evariste Parny. With his hugely successful verse tales *The Prisoner of the Caucasus* (1820-21) and *The Fountain of Bakhchisarai* (1821-23), Pushkin turned to Byron for the model of his verse narratives and plunged into the typically romantic exoticism of the idealized Near East, made popular in France and England by Chateaubriand and Byron.

Pushkin's trajectory from this point on has been traditionally described by Russian scholars as a gradual overcoming of the romanticism of this period and finding his way to a realistic and socially critical depiction of the iniquities of Russian life of his time. Yet, a detailed examination of his dramatic projects that date from the same period as his "Southern" verse tales and an awareness of Pushkin's continuous fascination with the neoclassical verse comedy as practiced by Shakhovskoy, Khmelnitsky, and, eventually, Griboedov, indicate that Pushkin's neoclassical tastes remained alive and well throughout, despite the veneer of his later romantic and realistic orientation.

Pushkin's earliest surviving attempts to write for the stage date from his time of exile in the south of Russia, where Alexander I had banished him for some youthful revolutionary poems. Parallel with the composition of the ultraromantic *The Fountain of Bakhchisarai,* Pushkin made sketches for a comedy in couplets of iambic hexameter and for a neoclassical tragedy in five acts in the manner of Sumarokov and Kniazhnin. The latter project is all the more amazing because by that time Pushkin had made amply evident his disdain for the neoclassical tragedy not only of Sumarokov but even of Ozerov.

The subject he had selected was that of Vadim of Novgorod, the episode from the *Primary Chronicle* that had already been dramatized by the Empress Catherine and Kniazhnin. But where Catherine couched her version in the form of an imitation of Shakespeare and Kniazhnin draped the fragmentary legend of Vadim on a framework borrowed from Corneille and Metastasio, Pushkin was planning his own treatment of the situation, while retaining the usual anachronistic confusion between the pre-Christian Novgorod of the ninth century and the republican city-state that was destroyed by the rulers of Moscow five centuries later. Because Pushkin could not decide whether he wanted to write a tragedy or a narrative poem about Vadim and left sketches for both, we have a reasonably clear idea of his conception. Had the tragedy materialized, it would have been the familiar eighteenth-century love-versus-duty play, with a heroine named Rogneda (the Old Russian equivalent of the Scandinavian name Ragnhild, which was the name of the heroine of Kniazhnin's *Vladimir and Iaropolk*), who is torn between her duty to her father and her love for Vadim, the leader of the republican resistance to the autocratic rule of Riurik the Varangian. Interesting as an indication of the anti-monarchist sympathies of the young Pushkin, his play about Vadim had no future, as Pushkin himself must have realized. Had he completed it, it would, for all his genius, most likely have joined such other stillborn, belated exercises in neoclassical tragedy as Katenin's *Andromache* and Küchelbecker's *The Argives.*

Far more promising and giving greater cause for regret that it was not completed is the fragmentary comedy about gambling fever that Pushkin began sketching in his Kishinyov exile in 1821. Printed in academic editions of his writings under the title derived from its first words, **"Say, by What Chance"** (*Skazhi, kakoi sud'boi*), the fragment has been dubbed *The Gambler* by some scholars. There is only one completed scene, couched in the kind of

iambic hexameter in which Kniazhnin and Kapnist wrote their comedies. But in tone and diction it is far more reminiscent of Khmelnitsky. There also exists a disjointed but detailed outline of the other scenes, which has enabled Alexander Slonimsky, among others, to postulate the plot and the action of this unwritten comedy.[4] The milieu is of the kind that was more usually associated in the eighteenth century with melodrama than with high comedy: the world of addicted gamblers and of the cardsharps who prey on them. The characters bear the names of the actors of Shakhovskoy's St. Petersburg company, for whom Pushkin clearly intended this play.

The completed scene shows a young widow Valberkhova (i.e., the actress Maria Valberg, who had played young widows in *The Lipetsk Spa,* Khmelnitsky's *Castles in the Air* and, for that matter, in Molière's *The Misanthrope*), bickering with her gambler brother Sosnitsky (i.e., the part was intended for the actor Ivan Sosnitsky). In the unwritten portion, a young man in love with Valberkhova (he was to be played by the tragedian Iakov Briansky) plots to cure her brother of gambling in order to win Valberkhova's heart. His strategy is to induce a professional gambler (the character actor Alexander Ramazanov) to fleece Sosnitsky until he stakes on a card his old serf tutor (Mikhail Velichkin, who specialized in playing comical old men, such as Baron Volmar in *The Lipetsk Spa*). Horrified that he has gambled away the freedom of a trusted old servant who has looked after him since childhood, Sosnitsky renounces cards forever. Then the ruse is explained to him and everything ends happily. Similar in many ways to the worldly comedies of Shakhovskoy, Pushkin's projected *The Gambler* was also meant to sound a serious note about the abuses of serfowners' privileges, the theme of Pushkin's own impassioned poem, **"The Village"** (1819). In the 1920s, the Symbolist poet Valery Briusov did a reconstruction of this play, calling it *Urok igroku (A Lesson to a Gambler)*, which in the opinion of Slonimsky missed the point of the relationship between Valberkhova and her suitor.[5]

In his book *On Pushkin,* Sergei Bondi has proposed a four-step periodization for Pushkin's activity as playwright. Step one comprises his "Decembrist" projects, the unfinished tragedy and comedy of 1821-22; step two is the "realistic" *Boris Godunov;* step three is the plays of 1830, that is, the "little tragedies" and *Rusalka;* and step four is the unfinished drafts for "social dramas" set in medieval Western Europe that date from the mid-1830s.[6] Up to a certain point this periodization works, even though its transparent aim is to sustain the official Soviet conception of Pushkin moving toward ever greater realism, nationalism, and social awareness. Yet, it is unsatisfactory in the long run, not only because it distorts the progression of Pushkin's ideas, but because it ignores several other drafts that do not fit Bondi's scheme and fails to notice the mutual interpenetration of the dramatic and narrative genres that is so important in Pushkin's output in the 1820s.

While working on the drafts for his neoclassical tragedy about Vadim, Pushkin was at the same time introducing elements of romantic drama into his narrative poems. The center of *The Fountain of Bakhchisarai* is an impassioned melodramatic monologue by Zarema, one of the two heroines of the poem. This monologue later became the showpiece for Ekaterina Semyonova in Shakhovskoy's adaptation of this poem for the stage. Another narrative poem, *The Gypsies* (1824), is written for much of its length in the form of dramatic dialogues that read like a romantic play in verse. The diction of these dramatized poems owes nothing to any conceivable neoclassical model. But the case is very different with two other verse narratives dating from the first half of the 1820s, the opening chapters of *Eugene Onegin* and, especially, *Count Nulin* (1825).

The novel in verse *Eugene Onegin* is, of course, Pushkin's greatest achievement, an ever-fascinating poem that is also one of the central, most influential works of Russian literature. Volumes have been written about its style, so amazingly precise and so relaxed at the same time. Every possible source and influence have been analyzed by commentators. However, Pushkin himself acknowledged his debt to the two most important stylistic predecessors who helped shape the tone of *Eugene Onegin.* He encoded quotations from them in the first four lines of his novel . . .

> My uncle, a man of most honest principles,
> When he became so ill it was no joke,
> Forced me to respect him
> And could invent nothing better.

These somewhat opaque opening lines of *Eugene Onegin* can be recited by heart by most Russians. Numerous commentators have pointed out that the words *samykh chestnykh pravil* (of most honest principles) are a quotation from Ivan Krylov's fable "The Donkey and the Peasant," which Pushkin heard Krylov recite at a party in 1819, the year the fable was published.[7] The citation is usually interpreted as an act of homage to Krylov, whose fables Pushkin valued above La Fontaine's.

But the fourth line of this quatrain is also a paraphrased quotation, in this case from the third scene of Khmelnitsky's *Castles in the Air,* which Pushkin must have seen when it premiered in St. Petersburg in July of 1818. The maid Sasha, in praising her employer Aglaeva's late husband for having willed all his property to his widow, says: "Umnee nichego on vydumat' ne mog" ("He could invent nothing more intelligent").

In incorporating this Khmelnitsky phrase into the opening of his masterpiece, Pushkin both got around the obstacle of not being able to mention Khmelnitsky the playwright (about which he wrote to his brother) and paid Khmelnitsky as handsome an homage as he did to Krylov in the first line. Since Onegin's uncle and Aglaeva's husband are both characters whose main significance lies in their dying and leaving an inheritance to the protagonists, Pushkin connected the beginning of *Eugene Onegin* to Khmelnitsky's comedy on a deeper level than a mere citation of words.

It was after he had completed the opening chapters of *Eugene Onegin* in 1824-25 that Pushkin became interested in Shakespeare and began a serious study of his plays. As Mikhail Alexeyev has shown in his excellent study of the relationship of Pushkin to Shakespeare, it was a question of relinquishing the eighteenth-century prejudices against Shakespeare that Pushkin had inherited from La Harpe and Voltaire in favor of the more up-to-date French view of Shakespeare brought about by the critical writings of Mme de Staël and the commentary of François Guizot and Amedée Pichot in their revised 1821 edition of Pierre Letourneur's old translations, originally published in the 1770s.[8] "Mais quel homme que ce Schakespeare! [*sic*] Je n'en reviens pas. Comme Byron le tragique est mesquin devant lui!" Pushkin wrote to his friend Nikolai Raevsky in July of 1825. The full realization of Shakespeare's magnitude led Pushkin, as it did so many other writers of his generation, to lose his former high regard for both Molière and Byron.

Boris Godunov (1825, published 1830), Pushkin's only completed full-length play, was the result of his study of the man he came to call "our father Shakespeare." In honor of Shakespeare, Pushkin dispensed with the unities of time, place, and (though he denied it) action, something that only the Empress Catherine had had the audacity to do before in Russia. The violation of the unity of style, a unity previously taken for granted in Russian drama, is flaunted by mixing scenes in blank verse, rhymed verse, and prose. The central conception, however, is a profoundly eighteenth-century one, because *Boris Godunov* is an instance of "adaptation to our customs" of Shakespeare's historical plays just as Kniazhnin's *Vladimir and Iaropolk* was of Racine's *Andromaque.*

The overthrow of Tsar Boris in 1605 by the low-born pretender known as the False Dimitry became a subject for dramatic works within a few years after it occurred. From Lope de Vega's *El gran Duque di Moscovia,* published in 1617 but apparently written earlier, to Kotzebue's melodrama and Friedrich Schiller's unfinished last tragedy about the False Dimitry, both at the very end of the eighteenth century, there appeared in the West more than one hundred tragedies, novels, and even harlequinades about this series of events.⁹ In Russia, there were at least two plays called *Dimitry the Impostor,* one by Sumarokov (1771) and one by Narezhny (1800). Studying Shakespeare's *Richard II, Richard III,* and both parts of *Henry IV,* Pushkin must have noticed that all these plays deal with the toppling of an incumbent monarch whose claims to the throne are uncertain or tainted, by a self-appointed pretender whose claims are even less secure. Reading the story of Boris Godunov's fall in *The History of the Russian State* by Nikolai Karamzin (whose version of the events has been disproven by later historians), Pushkin realized its similarity to Shakespeare's histories and its suitability for a Shakespearean dramatization. He dedicated the play to Karamzin's memory.

Because it is a play about Russian history, written by Russia's national poet, there is general agreement among Russian commentators that **Boris Godunov** is one of the great masterpieces of Russian drama. Some critics, confusing Pushkin's play with the choral sections of Modest Musorgsky's opera, have described it as a folk tragedy, as a depiction of a people's revolution, or as a profound analysis of the dialectics of history.¹⁰ But patriotic homilies aside, **Boris Godunov** is on many levels an unsatisfactory play. Both Mirsky and Nabokov saw it as something of a failure. No director has ever been able to make it work on the stage. Although Pushkin copied many of Shakespeare's techniques, he somehow failed to notice that in each of the historic plays he imitated there is a dramatic arch that unites the activities of the antagonists and allows for the development of their characters and for a satisfactory final resolution of the play's action.

But in **Boris Godunov,** as John Bayley has aptly pointed out, "between Boris and the pretended Dimitry there is no dramatic relation at all. Not only do they never meet but each is absorbed in his own affairs, and their historical antagonism is not transposed into psychological terms but left in the realm of the accidental or the historically determined."¹¹ Individual scenes may contain wonderful poetry or function as effective self-contained dramatic units (e.g., the scene at the fountain between Dimitry and Marina or the scene at the inn on the Lithuanian frontier), but they do not add up to a viable continuum. The addition of Musorgsky's tense and haunting music does make Pushkin's tragedy work in a theater, but it is a music light years removed from the tone and the atmosphere of the original play. John Bayley was quite right when he wrote that Pushkin made a far better application of the dramatic principles of Shakespeare's stagecraft in his historical narrative poem **Poltava** (1828-29) than in his tragedy.¹²

In the midst of his work on **Boris Godunov,** Pushkin became acquainted with Griboedov's *The Misfortune of Being Clever.* Charmed by the new possibilities of rhymed iambic lines of varying lengths that Griboedov so effectively exploited for dramatic purposes in his comedy, Pushkin added to **Boris Godunov** the beautifully wrought scene in Marina Mniszech's dressing room. In the lilting dialogue between Marina and her maid Rózia (the Polish diminutive of Rose), Pushkin abandons Shakespeare's manner for Griboedov's and Shakespeare's and Karamzin's matter for that of the same third scene of Khmelnitsky's *Castles in the Air* already quoted in the first quatrain of **Eugene Onegin.** Marina's dreams of being a tsarina in Moscow, and Rózia's lively advice and comments closely follow Aglaeva's dreams of marrying a count and moving to St. Petersburg and her conversation with her maid. Despite having strayed into the beginning of the seventeenth century and having acquired a Polish name, Rózia is an unmistakable soubrette of early nineteenth-century Russian verse comedy in general and a near-twin of Sasha from *Castles in the Air* in particular. Pushkin must have understood that for all its charm, this scene did not belong in his Shakespearean tragedy. He removed it from the main text and relegated it to an appendix, where it now regularly appears.

The combination of Shakespeare and Khmelnitsky, ludicrous as such a conjunction may sound to most people, was also responsible for **Count Nulin,** a lively and witty narrative poem Pushkin wrote one month after completing **Boris Godunov.** As Pushkin put it in a later explanatory note on **Count Nulin,** the idea for this poem came to him as he was rereading "The Rape of Lucrece," which he qualified as "a rather feeble poem by Shakespeare." It set him wondering what would have happened if, instead of submitting to Tarquin, Lucrece had routed the man by slapping his face. Tarquin might have desisted and, Pushkin says, "the world and its history would have been different."

The beginning of **Count Nulin,** with its description of a lusty country squire's departure for the hunt with a pack of hounds and the boredom and loneliness of the wife he leaves behind, has no connection to either Shakespeare or Khmelnitsky. But then a carriage bell is heard, the carriage overturns, an unknown but attractive male traveler and his servant are invited into the house to recuperate, and we are suddenly in Pushkin's favorite Khmelnitsky comedy, *Castles in the Air.* The stratagem of having the male protagonist's carriage break down in front of the heroine's home in order to get them acquainted was in fact a trademark of Khmelnitsky's, to which he resorted, as Moisei Iankovsky has pointed out,¹³ in no less than three of his twelve plays. It was Khmelnitsky's own invention, because in Collin d'Harleville's *Les châteaux en Espagne,* on which two of these three plays were based, there are no carriage accidents. There, the young man blunders into the chateau by mistake, after having lost his way. That Pushkin borrowed the patented device of his "favorite poet" so openly to start the action of **Count Nulin** should leave no doubt that he wanted the connection of this poem to Khmelnitsky to be obvious. It may well be that **Count Nulin** is the equivalent of that couplet in honor of Khmelnitsky of which Pushkin had written to his brother a few months earlier.

Pushkin's treatment of *Castles in the Air* in **Count Nulin** is similar to the procedure Khmelnitsky applied to the full-length French comedies on which he based his brief Russian plays. Only the general situation and a few concrete details are retained. The characters placed in this situation are each writer's own. The bored wife in Pushkin is quite unlike Khmelnitsky's ambitious widow Aglaeva, and the serious, modest midshipman of *Castles in the Air* is nothing like the feather-brained fop Count Nulin. But the experiences that these two couples have during their encounter are, up to a point, remarkably alike. In both cases, the lady of the house hears a carriage bell, hopes it is a visitor, witnesses a carriage breakdown through the window, and invites the accident victim and his manservant into the house. In both cases, the man is pleasantly surprised to find himself hospitably received by an attractive and seeming available young woman, is encouraged by her to press his suit, and then, to his consternation, rejected and encouraged to leave.

The main difference is that Aglaeva dismisses the unlucky midshipman on the day of his arrival, after realizing that he is not the wealthy count for whom she took him. Count Nulin is invited to spend the night, and it is during his nocturnal visit to the bedroom of his hostess that the poem turns into a comical parody of the analogous scenes in "The Rape of Lucrece." The repulsed seduction is the dramatic high point of **Count Nulin** and because of it this poem is generally described as Pushkin's parody of Shakespeare.[14] But the allusions to Khmelnitsky's comedy (which also include the character of the heroine's soubrette confidante Parasha, not needed for the action of the poem except to serve as the counterpart of Sasha in *Castles in the Air;* and the discussion of the news and newspapers by the two protagonists), take up far more space and contribute more to the poem's narrative plot than do the elements drawn from Shakespeare.

Pushkin was to succumb to the temptation of the demon of neoclassical verse comedy on two more occasions, in a sketch for a play that dates from approximately 1827 and in a novella written in 1830. The sketch is an expository dialogue between a gentleman and the maid of the lady to whom he is engaged. It begins. . . .

> "It has taken you a long time to resolve
>   yourself to leave Moscow."

> "Have you been well, my dear?" "And you,
>   sir, are you well?"

The maid works for two sisters. The older, Olga Pavlovna, is a widow engaged to the traveler just arrived from Moscow. The younger, Sophia Pavlovna (the name and patronymic of the heroine of *The Misfortune of Being Clever*), has a suitor named Èlmirov. Finding an unsigned amorous note from Èlmirov to Sophia, the nameless protagonist tries to bribe the maid with a gift of jewelry so that she will pass the note to Olga. His apparent aim is to test Olga's fidelity.

Brief as it is, the fragment makes mincemeat of all the standard schemes of dividing Pushkin's work into classical, romantic, and realist stages, schemes that were mocked by the epigraph from Stravinsky's essay on Pushkin at the head of the present [essay]. If it really dates from 1827 (the dating is approximate), it is contemporary with the seventh chapter of **Eugene Onegin**. This is the chapter in which the impact of Griboedov's comedy on Pushkin is most evident, both in its epigraph from that comedy and in the satirical description of Tatiana's Moscow relatives, which echoes Chatsky's and Famusov's speeches about the elderly women and men who run Moscow society. (Tatiana's romantically surrealistic dream in the fifth chapter also owes something to the dream of Griboedov's Sophia.) The verse of the 1827 fragment is likewise derived from Griboedov.

The opening scene of *The Lipetsk Spa*, which shows Prince Kholmsky's conversation with Olenka's maid Sasha, was the probable model for the opening scene of this projected comedy. Bribing a maid with a gift of jewelry occurs in both Shakhovskoy's *Don't Listen . . .* and Griboedov's *The Misfortune of Being Clever*. A plot that involves an act of entrapment in order to test a woman's fidelity was already old in 1789 when Lorenzo da Ponte based his libretto for Mozart's *Cosí fan tutte* on it. In Russian neoclassical comedy of the nineteenth century it is central to Khmelnitsky's *Mutual Tests (Vzaimnye ispytaniia,* 1819) and Griboedov and Zhandr's *Pretended Infidelity*.

The itch to write a verse comedy in the Shakhovskoy-Khmelnitsky manner is also evident in the 1828 sketches for Pushkin's translation of *Le mari à bonnes fortunes* by Casimir Bonjour. This was to be an abridgment of a light French comedy that was a hit in Paris in 1824, rendered in couplets of rhymed iambic pentameter and with the action transposed to Moscow from Paris. But Pushkin must have realized that the day of this type of comedy was over in Russia. Shakhovskoy had not written in this form for almost a decade, Khmelnitsky was about to retire from playwriting, Alexander Pisarev (for whose vaudevilles and comedies Pushkin had a low regard) died in 1828. Though Pushkin had already written a masterful verse comedy with preservation of the classical unities in **Count Nulin,** his love affair with the genre did not find its final resolution until the 1830 prose novella **"Mistress into Maid"** (**"Baryshnia krest'ianka"**).

The cycle of five novellas Pushkin wrote in Boldino in the fall of 1830 is united by the framework of a fictitious narrator Ivan Belkin who has supposedly collected these stories. The cycle is therefore called **The Tales of Belkin.** As Vasily Gippius has shown in a masterful essay, these tales operate on two levels: as entertaining narratives and as witty parodies of literary and dramatic conventions.[15] Thus **"The Coffinmaker"** is a gentle debunking of Hoffmannesque tales of the supernatural. **"The Station Master,"** which Gippius says cannot be understood without knowing the sentimental dramas of Beaumarchais, Lessing, and Schiller, reverses the familiar plot of the seduction of a daughter of a lower-class family by a dissolute aristocrat, a plot that was also familiar in Russia from the dramatizations of Karamzin's "Poor Liza" by Ilyin and Fyodorov.

"The Snowstorm" plays with the improbable coincidences of sentimentalist drama, while **"The Shot,"** despite outward trappings that point to adventure tales by Bestuzhev-Marlinsky, is a parodistic retelling of Victor Hugo's *Hernani.*[16] **"Mistress into Maid"** is a neoclassical comedy turned into a prose narrative. Belinsky, who took a strong dislike to this story, discerned its origins when he described it as "improbable, vaudevillelike, showing the life of landowners from its idyllic side."[17] Pavel Katenin saw **"Mistress into Maid"** as a reworking of *Le jeu de l'amour et du hasard* by Marivaux into a short story in a manner analogous to Pushkin's later reworking of Shakespeare's *Measure for Measure* into his narrative poem "Angelo."[18] And yet, apart from the young noblewoman Silvia disguising herself as a servant—a widespread ploy in eighteenth-century opera and comedy, including *The Marriage of Figaro* and *She Stoops to Conquer*—there is little in common between Pushkin's novella and the comedy of Marivaux. The comedies that were on Pushkin's mind while he was writing **"Mistress into Maid"** were not by Marivaux but by Katenin's good friend Shakhovskoy.

The presence of Shakhovskoy is initially signaled by a quoted line from his First Satire (addressed to Molière) that appears on the first page of **"Mistress into Maid."** The passage from which this line comes ridicules Russian landowners who seek to improve the crop yields of their estates by introducing newfangled agricultural methods imported from England and go broke as a result. The thesis about the wastefulness and absurdity of imitating English-style farming, expressed in the 1807 satire, was developed by

Shakhovskoy in 1819 into a full-length comedy *The Prodigal Landowners,* which contrasted the silly Anglomaniac Prince Radugin with his uncle General Radimov, who prospers by staying with the traditional Russian farming methods.

This is precisely the theme of the opening pages of Pushkin's **"Mistress into Maid,"** which describe the feud between two neighboring landowners, the sensible traditionalist Berestov and the Anglomaniac Muromsky, who slowly ruins himself by forcing his serfs to farm *à l'anglaise.* The Shakhovskoy connection is further driven home by the information that Muromsky is a close relative of Count Pronsky, a distinguished and powerful statesman. This must be the one-time sentimentalist of *The New Sterne,* who has come to his senses and made an important career in the quarter century that separates Pushkin's novella from the play, rather than Colonel Pronsky of *The Lipetsk Spa,* who was not a count. The appearance of Berestov's son Alexei, a healthy and lusty young fellow who affects a Byronic pose of disappointment and dejection, is Pushkin's mocking of emotional stances that imitate literary fads, just as *The New Sterne* was Shakhovskoy's mockery of an earlier variant of the same phenomenon.

Muromsky's daughter Liza disguises herself as a peasant wench in order to meet the son of her father's enemy. The description of the two young people's romance moves away from Shakhovskoy and becomes a parody of all those Karamzinian plays where a young aristocrat woos a peasant maiden named Liza who later turns out to be a nobleman's daughter, a connection that is emphasized when Pushkin makes Alexei and Liza read Karamzin's "Natalia, the Boyar's Daughter." Pushkin's Liza is a mistress of numerous disguises, just as Shakhovskoy's Natasha was in *The Married Fiancée.* She has to impersonate not only a peasant but also an affected, bejeweled, and heavily made-up society lady. For each of these impersonations, Liza develops a new personality and a set of appropriate speech mannerisms. Despite her lack of any theatrical training, she is an accomplished comedienne, as inexplicably as Shakhovskoy's Natasha.

The resolution of **"Mistress into Maid,"** which involves the reconciliation of the feuding fathers, Alexei's plans to marry the young woman he thinks is a peasant, and the lucky chance that reveals her true identity to him, is worked out with the sure hand of a writer of eighteenth-century comedies of intrigue and disguise. Especially typical of that whole genre is the character of Liza's serf confidante and abettor in her disguises, the soubrette Nastya. Pushkin was capable of depicting believable, realistically observed Russian serfs and servants: Tatiana's nurse in **Eugene Onegin,** Masha's maid Palasha in **The Captain's Daughter,** and the hero's serf tutor in the same novel.

But whenever he writes something inspired by the tradition of the neoclassical verse comedy of the Shakhovskoy-Khmelnitsky-Griboedov type, we invariably get lively and witty soubrettes of the French and Russian comedic traditions who could not possibly have existed in actual Russian life. Nastya in **"Mistress into Maid"** is the last of this line, which also includes Rózia in the dressing-room scene of *Boris Godunov,* Parasha in *Count Nulin,* and the nameless maid in the 1827 draft for a comedy.

Writing **"Mistress into Maid"** must have exorcised Pushkin's fascination with the spirit of neoclassical comedy, for it is absent from his plays, verse tales, and prose narratives written from that point on. Within weeks after completing the last of *The Tales of Belkin,* Pushkin set to work on his cycle of "little tragedies" (this was during the miraculously productive Boldino autumn of 1830, when in a period of three months he produced, besides the cycle of stories and the cycle of plays, a large number of lyric poems and essays, in addition to writing **"The Little House in Kolomna"** and completing *Eugene Onegin*).

Inspired by a genre devised by Barry Cornwall (pen name of Bryan Waller Proctor, a rather pallid poet admired in his day by Byron and Keats) of brief dialogues in verse that combined features of drama and narrative poetry, Pushkin had been planning since 1826 to write a series of what he called "dramatic investigations" or "dramatic studies," each one concentrating on an analysis of one particular passion. In 1827, he listed the subjects he intended to use in these investigations: The Miser, Romulus and Remus (in which the she-wolf that raised them was to be a character), Mozart and Salieri, Don Juan, Jesus, Berald of Savoy, Tsar Paul I, A Devil in Love, Dimitry and Marina (whose relationship was left dangling in *Boris Godunov*), and Prince Kurbsky (the one-time adviser of Ivan the Terrible who later went over to the Poles and wrote the tsar famous vituperative letters; Kurbsky's son, invented by Pushkin, appeared in *Boris Godunov*).

Only three of these projects were realized in 1830. "The Miser" became *Skupoi rytsar',* the brief play Pushkin preferred for personal reasons to palm off as a translation of a nonexistent English play *The Covetous Knight* by William Shenstone.[19] The ruse was necessitated by the similarity between the disagreements on money matters between the old Baron and his rebellious son in the play and the actual situation between Pushkin and his father; "covetous" is not the right word to convey the Russian title, "avaricious" being much closer. *Mozart and Salieri,* converted in recent times into a London and New York hit play *Amadeus* by Peter Schaffer and stemming from newspaper reports about Antonio

Salieri's deathbed confession that he had poisoned Mozart,[20] is a study of envy.

The Stone Guest, the longest and most dramatic of the "little tragedies," derived, very remotely, from Molière's play about Don Juan and da Ponte's libretto for Mozart, investigates various kinds of amorous involvement between men and women. The three female characters are Inez (in an earlier draft she was a miller's daughter) whom Don Juan seduced and abandoned and who died because of it; the actress Laura, whose relationship with him is that of a friend and equal, despite their sexual involvement; and Donna Anna, who in this version is not the daughter, but the widow of the Comendador, a man Don Juan had killed in a duel. Donna Anna's particular attraction is her virtue and unavailability, which compel the famous seducer to love rather than merely desire her. In a provocative study of *The Stone Guest,* Anna Akhmatova has argued persuasively that this play, written just when Pushkin was to give up the sexual freedom of his earlier life in order to marry, contained elements of self-portraiture in both Don Juan and the Comendador.[21]

In addition to being studies of particular passions—avarice, envy, sexual drive—the three "little tragedies" are also united by the theme that was central to *Boris Godunov:* the incumbent defending his status from an aggressive usurper. Just as Boris had to defend his throne from the False Dimitry, the Baron in *The Covetous Knight* has to defend his hoard from his son Albert, Salieri has to defend his position in the musical world from Mozart, and the statue of the Comendador has to stop his murderer from possessing his wife. The outcome of this situation, common to all four plays, is variable. In *Boris Godunov* and *The Covetous Knight,* the usurpers triumph, while in *Mozart and Salieri* and *The Stone Guest* they are destroyed by the defending incumbents.

Usually grouped with the three "little tragedies," but only because it was written at the same time with them, is *Feast During the Plague,* Pushkin's compressed adaptation of several scenes from John Wilson's romantic drama *The City of the Plague.*[22] A dramatic poem rather than a play, it is a disturbing and beautiful meditation about our perpetual fascination with death. It treats in romantic terms what Ozerov had expressed in sentimentalist and neoclassical terms in *Polyxena.* It is also utterly unstageable (though its production has been tried). *Feast During the Plague* and the three "little tragedies" are philosophically complex works, they contain magnificent poetry, but none of them is very effective dramatically. Because they are by Pushkin, Russian theaters keep staging them. But like all of Pushkin's plays, the "little tragedies" function far better on the operatic stage than as spoken drama. The operatic setting of *The Stone Guest* is by Alexander Dargomyzhsky, of *Mozart and Salieri* by Rimsky-Korsakov (with the utilization of much of Mozart's own music), and of *The Covetous Knight* by Sergei Rakhmaninov.

Both Anna Akhmatova and Naum Berkovsky have connected the figure of the gentle Inez, the miller's daughter in the draft for the first scene of *The Stone Guest,* with the genesis of Pushkin's most effective play, dramatically and poetically: the regrettably unfinished folk drama *Rusalka.*[23] Like Shakespeare and Molière before him, Pushkin did not disdain borrowing themes from unimpressive sources. The magic operas about the water sprites of the Dnieper, based on *Das Donauweibchen* (see pp. 186ff.), took up residence on the stages of Russia when Pushkin was four years old and they remained there for at least a decade after he died. It was the plot of the first of the *Water Sprites* that Pushkin decided to convert into a drama couched in an idiom derived from his detailed studies of Russian folklore.[24]

In *Das Donauweibchen* and its four Russian avatars, the heroine is an elemental spirit who has had an affair with a mortal man, has a daughter by him, and objects to his plans to marry a mortal woman. In an early draft for *Rusalka* that dates from 1826, it can be seen that Pushkin intended to keep this situation. In the final version written in part in 1829 and in part in 1832, he chose to follow the widespread Slavic folk legend, which also served as the source for Adolphe Adam's ballet *Giselle,* about a peasant maiden who is seduced and abandoned by a nobleman and who then returns to haunt him as a supernatural creature.[25] Instead of having to choose between a woman and a mythological being, Pushkin's Prince is initially involved with a poor miller's daughter whom he abandons when dynastic reasons force him to take a bride of his own social standing.

The language of *Rusalka* is an expressive blend of high romantic poetry and of diction derived from traditional Russian songs and laments. Dramatically, it is enormously effective. *Rusalka* is the only play by Pushkin in which the principal characters really interact with one another. As in a folk legend, there are no proper names, yet the characters are individualized and their emotional predicaments are convincingly drawn. The miller's daughter, who drowns herself in the Dnieper after she is betrayed by her lover and is then reincarnated as a "*rusalka,* cold and powerful"; her scheming father, who is driven insane by the realization of what he had done to his daughter; her initially faithless and then penitent lover, the Prince; the Prince's neglected, anxious wife; the *rusalka's* young daughter, born into a supernatural world, but curious about her human origins—all these are splendid creations, believable on the psychological level, hauntingly poetic, and dramatically absorbing.

Rusalka was potentially the great and original folk drama that Pushkin's countrymen have credited him with having written in *Boris Godunov.* Its lack of an ending is so self-evidently deplorable that numerous hands have tried supplying it with one. Three amateurish attempts were made in the second half of the nineteenth century, and one of them was temporarily accepted by critics as the discovery of Pushkin's own manuscript for the conclusion of his play. In the twentieth century, final scenes for *Rusalka* were written by Valery Briusov and Vladimir Nabokov, but matching Pushkin's language proved beyond even their considerable talents. The ending Dargomyzhsky devised for his 1856 opera is at best a makeshift solution. Only Pushkin himself could have provided an appropriate finale, but in the last five years of his life he seems to have lost interest in writing drama in verse.

Pushkin's involvement with Shakespeare, which began in 1824, was crowned in 1833 by **"Angelo,"** his reworking of *Measure for Measure* into a narrative poem.[26] Pushkin himself considered it the finest of his narrative poems, but it remains to this day undeservedly neglected by both critics and general readers.[27] After abandoning *Rusalka,* Pushkin made sketches for three historical dramas in prose, set in Western Europe in medieval times. All three were to show persons of humble origins rising to great social prominence and then coming into conflict with the ruling elite of their time. In 1835 Pushkin wrote several scenes for the first of these projects, which had no title in his manuscript and was called by later editors *Scenes from the Time of Knighthood.* Like the majority of Pushkin's dramatic projects, it has literary sources, in this case *La Jacquerie* by Prosper Mérimée, the story "Tournament in Revel" by Alexander Bestuzhev-Marlinsky (1825), and one of the same author's critical essays.[28]

Set in Germany, the play was to include among its characters Berthold Schwartz, the semilegendary inventor of gunpowder, and to be centered on a revolt against the local feudal hierarchy led by a merchant's son who has become a minnesinger. The sketches are so pallid and undramatic that it is hard to believe they are the work of the mature Pushkin. The other two of this group of projects exist only as outlines. One is about the son of a hangman in France who ends up as a feudal lord. The other is based on the medieval legend of Pope Joan, an artisan's daughter whose love of learning led her to study theology in male attire and who was elected pope and then exposed as a woman when she gave birth to a child (by the Spanish ambassador to the Vatican) in a public place.[29] This was to be a Faustian drama, with devils and other supernatural beings participating in the action. Pushkin was not sure whether the subject was more suitable for a drama or a poem in the manner of Coleridge's "Christable."[30]

"The twentieth century began in the fall of 1914 together with the war, just as the nineteenth century began with the Congress of Vienna. Calendar dates mean nothing," wrote Anna Akhmatova in her "Fragments of Memoirs."[31] For the study of Russian literature, a far clearer picture emerges if we assume that the eighteenth century began in 1730 (Trediakovsky's proposal to use contemporary vernacular in imaginative literature) and ended in 1830, the date of publication of **Boris Godunov.** Poet-playwrights of Pushkin's generation may have been exposed to sentimentalist and romantic currents from the time of their adolescence, but they were all born in the eighteenth century and came to literary maturity when neoclassicism was still the norm. Some of them, such as Khmelnitsky and Alexander Pisarev, never quite emerged from it. Others were converted to romanticism, first Pushkin and after him, one by one, Katenin, Griboedov, and Küchelbecker. For these men, such a conversion was still a matter of choice.

But by 1830, the literary compass needle of Russian drama had permanently shifted from the pole of Molière to that of Shakespeare and Schiller (and, on a lower level, from Metastasio to Kotzebue and from there to Scribe). Playwrights born in the second and third decades of the nineteenth century turned their backs on neoclassical drama. The last to learn his craft from Russian neoclassical comedy was one of Russia's greatest playwrights, Nikolai Gogol. His *Inspector General* (1836) casts a long, lingering look of farewell at the theater of Fonvizin, Kapnist, and Shakhovskoy and then sets off, full sail, for the new shores of nineteenth- and twentieth-century drama, where Russian playwrights would become an integral part of the international theatrical world.

Notes

[1] Igor Stravinsky, "Pushkin: Poetry and Music," in Eric Walter White, *Stravinsky: The Composer and His Music* (Berkeley and Los Angeles, 1966), p. 542 (appendix). The quoted portion is Stravinsky's idea of a typical Russian muddle-headed view of Pushkin.

[2] See Gozenpud's introductory essay to his edition of A. A. Shakhovskoy, *Komedii, stikhotvoreniia* (Leningrad, 1961), pp. 35-37, for an analysis of allusions to Vasily Pushkin and Sergei Uvarov in *The Lipetsk Spa.*

[3] *Pushkin v teatral'nykh kreslakh* (Leningrad, 1926), pp. 122-31. Despite a few factual errors, Grossman's book is an excellent summary of Pushkin's early theatrical impressions that found wide reflections in his narrative poems of the 1820s.

[4] In his commentary to this fragment in A. S Pushkin, *Polnoe sobranie sochinenii* (Leningrad, 1935), vol. 7, pp. 673-77. The seventh volume of the edition of Pushkin's complete collected works, issued to commemorate the centenary of his death in 1937, was the first one of the series to be published. It contained both his completed and uncompleted dramatic works and included some 350 pages of detailed scholarly commentary by the finest Pushkin specialists of the period, among them Boris Tomashevsky, Mikhail Alexeyev, and Sergei Bondi. The scope and the scrupulously honest scholarship of this commentary make this volume the best single source of information on Pushkin the dramatist that has ever been published. But the objectivity of the commentators and the absence in their work of mandatory ideological and nationalistic biases angered the Soviet government. The commentary was dropped from subsequent printing of the volume (reportedly, on the personal order of Stalin), and the rest of the centenary edition was published without scholarly annotations.

The intellectual integrity of the editors of the 1935 volume contrasts heartbreakingly with the compulsory cliches that pervade some of their later publications on Pushkin (e.g., Sergei Bondi's book *O Pushkine* [Moscow, 1978]). In the notes that follow, this volume will be referred to as Pushkin, 1935.

[5] See Pushkin, 1935, p. 668.

[6] Bondi, *O Pushkine,* p. 179.

[7] In his annotated translation of *Eugene Onegin* (New York, 1964), Vladimir Nabokov devotes almost two pages to detailed explication of this three-word quotation from Krylov (vol. 2, pp. 29-31). For some reason, Nabokov chose to render "The Donkey and the Peasant" ("Osel i muzhik") as "The Ass and the Boor."

[8] M. P. Alexeyev, "Pushkin i Shekspir," in his book *Pushkin* (Leningrad, 1972), pp. 240-80. The same material is presented in *Shekspir i russkaia kul'tura,* ed. M. P. Alexeyev (Moscow and Leningrad, 1965), pp. 162 ff.

[9] For a survey of Western treatments, see M. P. Alexeyev, "Boris Gudunov i Dimitry Samozvanets v zapadno-evropeiskoi drame," in *"Boris Gudonov" A. S. Pushkina,* ed. K. N. Derzhavin (Leningrad, 1936), pp. 79-124.

[10] A rare instance of cogent argument for the originality of Pushkin's historical insights in *Boris Godunov* is Ilya Serman's fine essay "Paradoksy narodnogo soznaniia v tragedii A. S. Pushkina 'Boris Godunov' " ("Paradoxes of Popular Consciousness in Pushkin's *Boris Godunov*"), *Russian Language Journal* 35 (Winter 1981): 83-88.

[11] John Bayley, *Pushkin: A Comparative Commentary* (Cambridge, 1971), p. 166.

[12] Ibid.

[13] In *Russkaia stikhotvornaia komediia kontsa XVIII-nachala XIX v.* ed. Moisei Iankovsky (Moscow-Leningrad, 1964), pp. 24-25.

[14] George Gibian, "Pushkin's Parody On 'The Rape of Lucrece'," *The Shakespeare Quarterly* 1 (October 1950): 264-66.

[15] V. V. Gippius, "Povesti Belkina," in his book *Ot Pushkina do Bloka* (Moscow-Leningrad, 1966), pp. 7-45.

[16] See David M. Bethea and Sergei Davydov, "Pushkin's Saturnine Cupid: The Poetics of Parody in *The Tales of Belkin*," *PMLA* 96(1) (1981): 18-19 (note 11). This is an excellent study of the literary models and parodistic content of *The Tales of Belkin*. Its survey of earlier commentators shows that every possible source and resemblance has been explored, except for the Karamzinian drama and neoclassical comedy of Pushkin's time. "Mistress into Maid" ("The Lady Peasant" in this study) has been traced to sources as remote as *Romeo and Juliet* and Scott's *The Bride of Lammermoor* (note 24 on p. 20). Proximate sources, such as the plays about "Poor Liza" and Shakhovskoy's comedies remained outside the commentators' purview.

[17] V. G. Belinsky, *Sobranie sochinenii* (St. Petersburg, 1911), vol. 3, p. 489.

[18] Cited in Gippius, "Povesti Belkina," p. 26.

[19] On the possible connection between Pucshkin and Shenstone, see Richard A. Gregg, "Pushkin and Shenstone: The Case Reopened," *Comparative Literature* 17(2) (1965): 109-16.

[20] On the origins of the legend about Salieri's murder of Mozart and Pushkin's sources for the play, see Mikhail Alexeyev's detailed study in Pushkin, 1935, especially pp. 525 ff. It is curious that Pushkin's poetic genius unjustly convicted two people who had actually lived, Boris Godunov and Antonio Salieri, of murders they did not commit. On affinities between Pushkin and Mozart, see Vladimir Markov, "Mozart: Theme and Variations," in *The Bitter Air of Exile,* ed. Simon Karlinsky and Alfred Appel, Jr. (Berkeley and Los Angeles, 1977), pp. 455-57.

[21] Anna Akhmatova, " 'Kamennyi gost' Pushkina," in her book *O Pushkine* (Leningrad, 1977), pp. 89-109, and also note 7 on p. 168.

[22] See Henry Gifford, "Pushkin's *Feast in the Time of Plague* and Its Original," *American Slavic and East European Review* 8 (February 1949): 37-46.

[23] Akhmatova, *O Pushkine,* pp. 165 and 169. N. Berkovsky, " 'Rusalka,' liricheskaia tragediia Pushkina," in his book *Stat'i o literature* (Moscow-Leningrad, 1962), pp. 357-403.

[24] For a thorough analysis of *Rusalka's* connection to *The Water Sprite* comic operas, see Sergei Bondi's commentary in Pushkin, 1935, pp. 623-36.

[25] The manuscript of this play contained no title. The editors, recognizing the similarity of Pushkin's play to *The Water Sprite,* gave it the same title, *Rusalka.* The word *rusalka* refers in the Russian poetic and dramatic tradition to three different kinds of beings. In *The Water Sprite* operas, as in Zhukovsky's romance in verse *Undina,* it is an undine, a water sprite in female form. In Russian translations of Western fairy tales, such as Hans Christian Andersen's "The Little Mermaid," the word *rusalka* is used to denote a mermaid, a creature half-woman half-fish, who lives in the ocean. Neither an undine nor a mermaid was originally a human being.

But in Pushkin's play, just as in Gogol's story "May Night," *rusalka* is a young woman who is driven to drown herself because of her misfortunes and is only then reincarnated as a supernatural, water-dwelling being, whose aim is to punish those who have caused her suffering—a very different being from either an undine or a mermaid. Despite the similarity of the plot of Pushkin's play to *Water Sprite,* the heroine has a totally different nature and this is why I prefer to use the word *rusalka* for her, rather than water sprite or mermaid.

[26] See Alexeyev, *Pushkin,* pp. 276 ff.

[27] See George Gibian, "*Measure for Measure* and Pushkin's 'Angelo,' " *PMLA* 66 (June 1951): 426-31.

[28] See Bondi's commentary in Pushkin, 1935, pp. 652 ff. The excommunication of Alexander Bestuzhev (1797-1837; Marlinsky was his pen name) from Russian literature by Belinsky in 1840 prevents critics to this day from examining the impact on Pushkin of this important romantic critic and innovative prose writer, who was Pushkin's close friend and correspondent. The vast field of *Eugene Onegin* studies has still to discover the affinities between Bestuzhev's travelogue in verse and prose, *A Journey to Revel,* published in 1821, and Pushkin's celebrated novel in verse, begun in 1823.

[29] On the legend of Pope Joan and an account of Pushkin's interest in it, see Iulian Oksman's commentary in Pushkin, 1935, pp. 695-700.

[30] To demonstrate Pushkin's ties to the verse comedy of the Shakhovskoy-Khmelnitsky school, the present chapter has had to encompass discussions of the poet's nondramatic writings. The points could best be made through examining his literary practices and ignoring his theories about drama, which, though highly important, do not always reflect his

true stylistic orientation. The reader will find valuable discussions of the relationship between Pushkin's theories on drama (as stated in his essays and personal correspondence) and his plays in the chapter "The Drama" in John Bayley's *Pushkin* and in the other critical sources mentioned in the annotations to the present chapter. See also two of Pushkin's essays on drama theory in *Russian Dramatic Theory from Pushkin to the Symbolists, An Anthology,* ed. Laurence Senelick (Austin, 1981).

[31] Anna Akhmatova, *Sochineniia* (Paris, 1983) vol. 3, p. 146.

I. Z. Serman (essay date 1986)

SOURCE: "Paradoxes of the Popular Mind in Pushkin's *Boris Godunov,*" in *The Slavonic and East European Review,* Vol. 64, No. 1, January, 1986, pp. 25-39.

[*In the following essay, Serman focuses on the central importance of The Pretender, the false Tsarevich Dmitry, to* Boris Godunov—*a drama he sees as a folk-historical tragedy concerned with the changing consciousness of the Russian people.*]

One of the many constant problems for Soviet Pushkin scholars has been, who is the central character in Pushkin's ***Boris Godunov***? Indeed, is there a central hero at all? Most of those who have written on Pushkin's tragedy in the Soviet Union have found it more convenient to avoid confronting this question altogether and substitute for it another, more 'sociologized' approach. For example S. M. Bondi wrote in 1975: 'The fact that the central hero of Pushkin's tragedy is not Boris Godunov and his crime and not Grigory Otrep'yev and his remarkable fate but the people (*narod*) is apparent from the entire content and structure of the tragedy.'[1] To avoid repeating this banal opinion S. Rassadin suggested an original, but not very convincing solution to the problem. In his opinion, 'there is not one, but two pretenders in the tragedy'.[2] He elaborates this notion by suggesting that Dmitry the Pretender and Boris Godunov are 'usurpers not in relation to the severed dynasty of Ivan Kalita, nor to the future dynasty of the Romanovs . . . but *in relation to the people*'.[3] In other words, for all the unexpectedness of the critic's charge against Boris Godunov, his interpretation of the tragedy remains the standard one: the basic conflict is reduced to one between the people and authority.

N. Litvinenko, echoing Belinsky's words, wrote: '***Boris Godunov*** is an authentically folk-historical tragedy, which not only tells the story of the clash of Godunov, the Pretender, the Russian boyars and the Polish interventionists over the throne, but which also draws a picture of the people as the *basic agent of history*.'[4] N.

Balashov takes a similar view: 'Pushkin's tragedy is constructed as the radical conflict of the people and anti-people authority.'[5]

When did this interpretation of Pushkin's tragedy first arise? For our purposes this question is both interesting and relevant. This sociological and politicized view was directly connected with the events of the first Russian Revolution of 1905 and emerged as a result of reflecting, for the first time, on the experience of revolution (a defeated revolution, but a revolution nevertheless and not an uprising or rebellion as Russia had known before) with its impact on Russia and the Russian social consciousness. The historian Pavlov-Sil'vansky wrote in 1907 that '***Boris Godunov*** demonstrates for the first time, not only in Russian literature but in Russian historical scholarship as well, the decisive role of the people in the historical process, and the possibility of a victory over the autocracy'. In his tragedy Pushkin 'wants to show that such a disunity between people and authority' is a characteristic feature of all Russian history.[6] In the exhilarating pre-revolutionary atmosphere of 1916 B. N. Engel'gardt developed this idea further.[7]

Tantalizing in its own time because of its boldness and political relevance, this point of view later became a platitude in Soviet works on Pushkin's tragedy, although it was incorrect both with respect to the play itself and to a more general evaluation of the Russian folk consciousness in the seventeenth to nineteenth centuries. The conflict between autocracy and people is a very late phenomenon, born in the twentieth century. Before then all Russian social movements wanted another tsar, but not another form of rule; the slogan 'Down with the Autocracy' became popular only in 1905, after the Russo-Japanese War and the events of 9 January.

A solid piece of scholarship published by the Pushkinskiy dom in 1966 indicates how firmly entrenched the view of Pushkin's tragedy as the reflection of the historical conflict of the seventeenth century (as interpreted by Soviet historians) had become in Soviet Pushkin studies.[8] More recent works repeat this position, as for example, S. M. Bondi: 'The twenty-three scenes of ***Boris Godunov*** demonstrate vividly, and with historical accuracy, the evolution of the moods of the people of that era: at first political indifference, inertia, then a gradual growth of dissatisfaction, becoming stronger and stronger, and finally growing into a popular uprising, a rebellion that thrust the young tsar from the throne, after which the people, putting all their hopes on a new 'legitimate' tsar, again loses its sense of political activity and is transformed into a passive mob, awaiting the resolution of its fate by the tsar and the boyars.'[9]

It is characteristic of such an approach that the scholar himself apparently feels a certain awkwardness over the fact that his exposition has transformed the rebellious 'revolutionary' people into confirmed monarchists and legitimists. For this reason Bondi hastens to soften the impression of his words by an additional explanation: 'As is well known, all popular uprisings were of this nature until the appearance of the proletariat on the historical scene.'[10] This view of Pushkin's tragedy as a picture of the class struggle at the beginning of the seventeenth century supported the contention that the action in the play is not concentrated around a single person, whether Boris or the Pretender, but that each occupies only a part of the staged action and neither participates throughout the whole of the plot.[11]

The question of a major or central hero in Pushkin's tragedy is of primary importance. The interpretation of the play as a whole depends on it, for the basic conflict in the play is determined by the interaction of the characters and the degree to which each participates in the action—that is, in the development of the plot, in the struggle of the personalities and the forces standing behind them. Moreover, the transformation of the politicized, sociological approach into a commonplace of Pushkin scholarship demonstrates the power of stereotypes in thinking and the difficulty of breaking with traditional interpretations of Pushkin's text. The ideas set out below emerged from an attempt to read the play without the burden of either the prejudices held by the Romantic critics of Pushkin's time or the preconceptions of Soviet academic scholarship.

N. I. Nadezhdin, author of the first major article on *Boris Godunov,* considered the 'division of interest' between Godunov and the Pretender as a major shortcoming of the play: 'The main character is sacrificed utterly to another, who should have played a subordinate role.'[12] This conviction that the Pretender is 'insignificant' is even today generally accepted and deemed hardly worth discussing. This is despite the fact that Ivan Kireyevsky long ago made the subtle observation that Tsarevich Dmitry is present throughout the entire duration of the play: 'The shade of the murdered Dmitry reigns in the tragedy from beginning to end, governs the course of all events, serves as the link between all characters and scenes.'[13] The inspiration for this formulation came from Karamzin: 'The shade of Dmitry has risen from the grave.'[14]

No conclusions were drawn from Kireyevsky's observation, although, translated into the language of dramatic analysis, his idea might have provided the key both to the composition of the play as a whole, and to the problem of the central hero within it. Dmitry the Tsarevich really is the character who is present throughout the tragedy, but he is present in various capacities. In the beginning he is a person behind the scenes and acts off-stage; then he is transformed into a stage character, into an active participant. Before the scene in the Chudov Monastery, Dmitry the Tsarevich exists as a hypothesis: as a boy murdered on Boris Godunov's orders and buried in Uglich, and as a spectre that never for a moment abandons the consciousness of the criminal, Boris Godunov. Then he becomes the main topic of all conversations in the tragedy as the 'Impostor', until he finally appears himself in the scene 'Cracow. Vishnevetsky's House', as the living—or resurrected—and miraculously rescued Dmitry the Tsarevich, son of Ivan the Terrible. In terms of stage time and space, the Pretender is allotted no less than Boris Godunov, and for that reason alone critics should accord him no less attention. They have preferred, however, to dispose of him with a few scornful comments. In Rassadin's opinion he is only a 'usurper', although it is by no means clear what he usurped from the people—unless, perhaps, its affection for a legitimate tsar, whereas for Bondi 'Pushkin portrays Grigory Otrep'yev, unlike Boris Godunov, not as a serious statesman but as a political adventurer'.[15]

Bondi, of course, knew that Pushkin had modelled his Pretender, in type and period, on the French king Henri IV, and that G. O. Vinokur had written:

> The Pretender interested Pushkin primarily as rewarding material for romantic theatre. While the character of Boris was sustained in a single, predetermined, strict psychological profile, the character of the Pretender and his fate develops through the very course of the action. Pushkin did not give his Pretender any specific political physiognomy. This is an adventurer recalling Henry of Navarre . . . whose political role is revealed only in the way that others—the boyars, the people, Pater Chernikovsky—react to him. He himself, acting as a blind historical force, is the only one not carrying a definite political or social ideal.[16]

Bondi must also have recalled what Pushkin himself wrote about the Pretender in his preface to *Boris Godunov,* unpublished during his lifetime:

> Dmitry has a great deal in common with Henri IV. Like him he is brave, generous, and boastful, like him he is indifferent to religion—both of them abjure their faith for political reasons, both love their pleasures, and war, both are carried away by impossible plans, both become victims of conspiracies . . . [17]

In fairness it should be added that when Bondi feels less constrained in relation to the Pretender he softens his profile: 'He is clever, resourceful, talented, an ardent person, easily carried away, generous—and at the same time absolutely unprincipled in the political sense.'[18]

Bondi footnotes the word 'talented': 'He is also a poet'[19] without making reference to my article of 1969 where I drew attention to just this aspect.[20] In that early article I stressed the fact that there is not only the age boundary between Pimen and Grigory. The two represent different epochs of Russian life. Pimen is still entirely in the power of traditional concepts of tsarist authority; for him the personality of the tsar, even in such a tyrannical guise as Ivan the Terrible, was not to be judged by a human court. Pimen does not vindicate Ivan the Terrible, but his attitude towards him, not directly expressed, emerges clearly in his praise of Ivan's son Feodor . . . [21]

The image of Ioann, 'weary from his furious thoughts and executions' is set off by a contrast with the image of the 'ever praying' and 'meek' Feodor. Pride and submission, predatory and meek types, are embodied in Pimen's stories about these tsars, father and son. His attitude to Boris Gudunov, on the other hand, is quite free from any presumption about the unaccountability of tsars to human court. Boris was 'chosen' tsar, he was an elected tsar, and therefore Pimen considers himself justified in condemning him, while passing over in silence the crimes of Ivan the Terrible.

The idea of Pimen as a chronicler indifferent to good and evil is based on Grigory's words, and is eloquently refuted by the actual content of Pimen's speech. Pimen's political ideal—his idea of the Tsar-pilgrim—has not yet lost its vitality, although it is no longer in accord with the new political and moral spirit of the time. Pimen's story of the murder of the Tsarevich Dmitry—a story purporting to be that of an eyewitness—decisively convinces Grigory of Boris's guilt, and Pimen's comment that the 'murdered tsarevich' 'would have been your age and ruling' functions as an instant catalyst in Grigory's consciousness.

The Russian chronicles were compiled to fulfil certain political functions, as Ya. S. Lur'ye has pointed out:

> The chronicle was intended first of all not for posterity, but for contemporaries, and chronicle compilations were made use of in political struggles. But if tendentiousness was inherent in chronicle-writing throughout its history the character of this tendentiousness could change depending on the concrete purpose of the chronicle. Monastic chroniclers created special compilations which sometimes were independent of, and even in opposition to, the secular and ecclesiastical authorities; in other cases chroniclers supported one or another figure of authority, creating compilations of chronicles sympathetic to those in power (the ancient chronicles of Pechersky Monastery reveal just such an evolution—from the oppositional *Nachal'nyy svod* to the *Povest' vremennykh let*, friendly to royal power).

> Alongside the 'sympathizer chronicles' there existed in ancient Rus' chronicles enjoying complete official

approval and which came directly from a person of specific political authority or a corporation. This official nature of Grand Prince chronicling was most apparent at the end of the fifteenth and the beginning of the sixteenth centuries, and the practice led directly to the tsarist chronicling of Ivan the Terrible.[22]

Pimen's story, as Pushkin tells it, is an example of a free and imaginative reinterpretation of material painstakingly presented by Karamzin. The central point of the story—the repentance of the murderers at the corpse of the Tsarevich Dmitry—occurs completely naturally, under the influence of terror and pangs of conscience. Karamzin includes this quotation from the chronicle in his Notes:

> And immediately the murderers were all seized, and taken to the courtyard, and the people said: 'Sinful and evil men! How dared you commit such a deed?' And the sinful men stood and looked around and acknowledged their guilt, and said to the people: innocent blood has unmasked us; we obeyed the tempter Boris Godunov . . . and now we accept death for our deed. (XI, p. 41)

As we can see, in the chronicle to which Karamzin refers there is no miracle at all; the historian, a man of the eighteenth century, did not in any case place much trust in chroniclers' accounts of miracles: 'Leave superstition to our ancestors', Karamzin wrote, 'its imaginary terrors are nowhere near as varied as the real terrors in the history of nations'. (XI, p. 73)

The death of the Tsarevich Dmitry is described by Karamzin in this way: 'The nine-year-old holy martyr lay bloody in the embrace of her who had raised him and wanted to shield him with her own breast, he trembled like a dove, expiring, and died, without ever hearing the wailing of his desperate mother' (XI, p. 79). From this text Pushkin took the verb 'trembled' and, transferring it into Pimen's story, made a miracle the most important moment of the Uglich tragedy . . . [23]

Under the influence of Pimen's story—the story of an eyewitness, invented by Pushkin—Grigory's poetic imagination prompts him to a bold idea that would destroy all the popular beliefs and concepts: he would exploit these beliefs, he would take advantage of the people's faith in miracles to create his own miracle—the resurrection of the murdered tsarevich. Grigory's political imagination drives him to this risky act, forcing him to make a poem out of his own life, to compose his own 'song of destiny'.

Pushkin's Pretender, as a human type and as an individual, is a new phenomenon for seventeenth-century Russia. He is a person in whom personality triumphs over class structure, over the customary and the traditional. He represents an out-and-out violation of tradition: a monk who does not believe in God, a Russian who feels perfectly at home in Poland, amidst the most refined aristocracy, a Russian tsar (a claimant to the Russian throne) who behaves like a common adventurer, a statesman who is governed by poetic dreams. The Pretender lives by the principle of making the very most out of every minute of existence, with no glance back at the past and with calm faith in the future. But this rupture with every religious and ethical tradition of Russia, with all the forms of its everyday life, stands in opposition to the Pretender's desire to unite this new feeling of life with the name of the tsar, that is, with the overwheiming burden of tradition and custom accumulated over two centuries of the Muscovite autocracy. As Pushkin sees it, this clash in values laid the basis for the inevitable tragic failure of the Pretender, something not shown in the tragedy, but sensed. Pushkin's Pretender is not only a 'poet' in the strict sense of the word; he is a poet in the larger sense as well: he has a poetic nature, a poetic, artistic attitude towards life, towards all its manifestations, its joys, its beauty and vitality. The Pretender has an immediate sensuous perception of life. It is this, and not any abstract ideas of a political or ethical sort, that determines his behaviour, the choice of his way of life, the decisions he makes in critical situations.

The poetic nature of Grigory is won over by that very same element of the poetic in Pimen's story: that element of the miraculous without which, in the understanding of a person of the late sixteenth century, scarcely a single earthly event could be accomplished; it convinces Grigory decisively of Boris's guilt and prompts him to create a miracle himself, to 'resurrect' the murdered tsarevich, to place on the throne of the Russian tsars a 'legitimate' heir. The Pretender speaks frankly to Marina of his intention . . . [24]

The Pretender wants to realize a poetic dream by means of his whole life, he wants to exchange the prose of peaceful existence for the poetic fullness of life. That other Pretender of Pushkin's, Emel'yan Pugachov, develops the same thought to Grinyov, after telling him the familiar Kalmyk folk-tale about the eagle and crow. Pushkin saw the attractiveness of the Pretender precisely in those qualities which caused the critics to call his False Dmitry 'insignificant', to charge him with having no definite, concrete political idea. What Pushkin found attractive was the fact that power, for the Pretender, was not an aim but a means, not the crown of his achievement but only the first step, the starting point, after which the entire fullness of life must open up to him.

The Pretender himself is the result of that general spiritual crisis in Russian life at the beginning of the sevententh century which has long been noted by historians of religion:

The seventeenth century opens on the Time of Troubles in the Muscovite state. With the election of a new dynasty the Time of Troubles is not over. The entire century experiences extreme tension, uneasiness, dissent, arguments and quarrels. It was a century of popular uprisings and rebellions . . . But the Time of Troubles was not only a political crisis, not only a social catastrophe. It was even more a spiritual shock, or better, a moral turning point. In the *Smuta* the very psyche of the people is reborn. The people emerged from the *Smuta* changed, distraught, agitated, newly impressionable, very distrustful, even suspicious. It was the distrust of uncertainty. And this spiritual uncertainty or instability of the people was much more dangerous than all the social and economic difficulties which immediately engulfed the government of the first Romanovs.[25]

In his treatment of the personality of the Pretender, Pushkin freely reinterprets Karamzin. The historian calls Grigory's idea of pretendership *chudnaya,* that is strange, extraordinary: 'An extraordinary idea had taken root in the dreamer's soul' (XI, p. 75). Pushkin, as we have seen, turned the dreamer into a poet. He restored the original meaning of Karamzin's epithet *chudnaya,* replacing the 'extraordinary idea' by wonder, miracle (*chudo*). As the Pretender says of himself, 'I prepared the world a miracle'.

Pushkin carefully distinguishes between the concepts of *chudo* and *chudnyy/chudnaya.* The second concept is used most often in the sense of remarkable (*udivitel'nyy*). In addition to the above-mentioned example from the Pretender, there is another, from Basmanov (in the scene 'Moskva. Tsarskiye palaty'): 'No chto za chudnyy shum?' (What is that extraordinary noise?) The concept of *chudo* appears only in those scenes where there is talk of miracles in the strict sense of the word. That 'moral turning point' mentioned by Florovsky is especially evident in the fact that faith in miracles is disappearing, or rather, weakening. In Pushkin's tragedy not only the Pretender, but Prince Shuysky as well, do not believe in miracles. Shuysky is inclined to think that stories about miracles at the grave of the Tsarevich Dmitry are 'popular rumour' and that one must 'look into the matter diligently and dispassionately' before believing in their authenticity.

Once he has decided to realize his bold dream, on what does the Pretender rely? Soviet scholars avoid this interesting question, or give it a not entirely reasonable answer: they explain why the people rose up against Boris Gudunov, but not why they supported the Pretender. Litvinenko, for example, writes that in Pushkin's tragedy 'the people divined the anti-people essence of autocracy'[26] which, apparently, was rather easy for the people to do, insofar as that essence was 'anti-people'.

Karamzin, as a conscientious historian, could not avoid pondering the reasons for the Pretender's success. Karamzin knew that the folk consciousness lived by its faith in miracles. Karamzin's *History* provided the material for just such an explanation of the people's faith that Dmitry was really saved by a miracle. One piece of evidence that could convince the people of the Pretender's legitimate descent from Ivan IV was the sudden death of Boris, in which the popular consciousness—inclined to explain everything by a miracle—saw the manifest intervention of a Higher Will:

> Even those who had hitherto not believed the presumed Dmitry now began to believe in him, for they were struck by the sudden death of Godunov, and saw in that event new proof that it was not a Pretender but in fact the son of Ivan who demanded his legitimate inheritance; for the Almighty—so they thought—doubtless favoured him and was guiding him, through the grave of a usurper, to the throne. (XI, p. 113)

Karamzin apparently understood that this faith in the guilt of Boris and in the resurrection of the Tsarevich Dmitry cohabited, in some strange fashion, in the popular consciousness:

> No Russian before 1604 doubted in the death of Dmitry; he who grew up under the eyes of all Uglich, and whom all Uglich saw dead, and whose body was washed for five days with their tears: consequently the Russians could not reasonably believe in the resurrection of the Tsarevich; but *they did not love Boris* [my emphasis]! This unfortunate predisposition prepared them to be victims of a deception. (XI, p. 94)

But in this faith in miracles Karamzin sees only one of the reasons for the Pretender's success:

> Having no other examples of pretenders in their history and not understanding so bold a deception, loving the ancient line of tsars and greedily listening to the secret stories of the seeming virtues of the False Dmitry, Russians secretly began saying among themselves that God, by some miracle worthy of his wisdom, had actually been able to save Ioann's son for the murder of a hateful usurper and tyrant. (XI, p. 95)

Pushkin, in contrast to Karamzin, did not seek logic and consistency in the popular consciousness. He understood that a faith in miracles released the people from the tedious necessity of seeking a rational explanation for events. Pushkin's Grigory Otrep'yev understands that the Russian folk consciousness, convinced of Boris's crime, will believe with the same force of conviction in the resurrection of the Tsarevich Dmitry murdered by Boris—that it will believe in a miracle.

For in Pushkin's tragedy the people hold firmly and religiously to the conviction that Boris Godunov killed the Tsarevich Dmitry and that he was a criminal. But as soon as Grigory announced that he was the Tsarevich Dmitry who had been rescued from the hands of the assassins, the situation took a most unexpected and baffling turn—baffling, that is, for us. For if the people believe that the authentic living tsarevich has appeared, the very same person whom Boris Godunov had wanted to kill, it would seem to follow that Boris is not a murderer. But in the folk consciousness, as Pushkin shows it, there coexist, in utter defiance of logic, two mutually irreconcilable ideas. For if the Tsarevich Dmitry were alive and were truly the tsarevich and not a pretender, then Boris did not kill him, and was not a regicide, and in fact was not a criminal at all. If, on the other hand, Boris were a murderer and a criminal, then the person calling himself the tsarevich must be a pretender.

In the scene 'Ploshchad' pered soborom v Moskve' Pushkin very clearly portrays this strange and unexpected coexistence of two 'immobile' ideas in the popular consciousness. As the scene opens a conversation is going on between two people, most likely simple people of non-noble rank. They are in the square in front of the cathedral, not inside where the tsar and those permitted to enter are praying. The conversation between these two make clear precisely what is going on in the cathedral . . . [27]

Much is clarified in this conversation. We learn that the population of Moscow, or at any rate the greater part of it, is convinced that the tsarevich is alive and that he is not a pretender, not some Grishka Otrep'yev, but the real Tsarevich Dmitry. The remainder of the dialogue indicates just how strong that conviction is . . . [28]

Everything, it seems, is clear: the people think that the tsarevich is alive, that the one officially called a pretender is the Tsarevich Dmitry.

Pushkin does not end the scene with this, however; he introduces the *Yurodivy*. *Yurodstvo* (holy foolishness) was a very important phenomenon in Russian life in the fifteenth to seventeenth centuries, one of the most original forms of free expression for the people's hopes and opinions. After Panchenko's research into this question[29] a great deal has become clearer to us. Pushkin intuitively understood that holy fools expressed a great deal that could not have been expressed in any other way. And there in the scene in front of the cathedral, the *Yurodivy* casts the most serious accusation in the face of the tsar . . . [30]

Not 'as you ordered to slit', but 'as you slit'. In one and the same scene we hear two mutually irreconcilable assertions. Of course these two things are not said by one and the same person, and it is clear why: if it were not a holy fool who had said this, it would merely have demonstrated the inconsistency of the speaker. But from the lips of the *Yurodivy,* in Pushkin's treatment, it becomes a general characterization of the popular consciousness, which lives in a world with quite a different understanding of causal links than that governing a person of the Europeanized Russian culture of the 1820s.

Pushkin's originality can be seen in the way he portrays the thinking of the people: he shows how it is possible to unite in a single consciousness incompatible and contradictory elements; however, what seems to us to be a paradox is not regarded as such by the carriers of that consciousness. Pushkin gives the reason for this: according to him, the people's way of thinking is governed neither by cause and effect relations nor by correct views on Boris or on the False Dmitry (the Pretender), and it is precisely this coexistence of incompatible elements I propose to call the paradox of the folk mind.

One of the most interesting aspects of Pushkin's approach to portraying the popular consciousness in *Boris Godunov* is his attempt to find, in the structure of that consciousness, something unique to it, conditioned by national history. In a draft of an uncompleted critical article of 1825, that is during his work on *Boris Godunov,* Pushkin made more explicit the components of popular spiritual culture:

> Climate, type of government, and religion give each nation a particular physiognomy which to a greater or lesser extent is reflected in the mirror of poetry. There is a way of thinking and feeling, there is a multitude of customs, beliefs, and habits which belong exclusively to each individual nation.[31]

'A way of thinking'—that is what really interested Pushkin, and not the 'struggle of the people against the anti-people authorities'; a way of thinking, that is, the spiritual life of the nation, including the 'multitude of beliefs' whose often wondrous unity might indeed seem absurd to a person of the nineteenth century.

Pushkin recognized that ordinary Russian people of the seventeenth century believed in miracles and lived in expectation of a miracle. But it was only by the *hope* of a miracle that they were sustained. They never expected the actual course of history to turn out to be good for them, nor do they expect it now. Boris Godunov understands this well when he says: 'Zhivaya vlast' dlya cherni nenavistna' (Living authority is always hateful to the rabble). This waiting for a miracle was regarded by Pushkin as a general feature of the Russian folk mind—a feature which he had discovered in his studies of Russian life at the beginning of the seventeenth century. Evidently he had realized

even then that this faith in miracles was a universal and inseparable element of the popular consciousness. Of course Pushkin understood that the Russian people believed in miracles before the seventeenth century. His tragedy showed that this faith had always been characteristic of the people, that it was, moreover, a striking manifestation of the people's stagnation, inertia, inability to change; by its very nature the people were hostile to any dynamic force.

Nevertheless, despite the importance of Pushkin's discovery, it was impossible to construct a tragedy depicting only this unchanging state of mind. And so Pushkin set up in opposition to this world, this 'swarm-life' as Tolstoy called it, a new force embodying consciousness and personality, a force sceptical of miracles and in general rejecting the whole system of concepts in which miracle plays a major role. Pushkin's Pretender himself calls what he has accomplished a 'miracle', and indeed he has committed himself to an enterprise that is titanic in its daring: to resurrect the dead tsarevich, give life to the murdered child, and crown the posthumous miracles of Dmitry by emerging into the world as a living person.

Pushkin shows in his tragedy that at the beginning of the seventeenth century there appeared the first signs of a great gulf between the immobile weight of the mass mind, which sees in life only joyless sufferings from which one can occasionally be rescued by a miracle, and the dynamic currents of a new understanding and a new attitude towards life. Pushkin presented his Pretender as a new type of person in Russian life. The Pretender believes only in himself, and since in Pushkin's view he is not a mere adventurer but a poet, the Pretender has faith in his poetic dream of power. Under the influence of this dream he builds himself a life, by his own will, his own whim, subordinating political considerations to his poetic imagination. In Pushkin's portrait the Pretender is completely cut off from the sources of the people's religious beliefs, from traditional passivity, from the habit of waiting for a saviour and a miracle. The Pretender, in Pushkin's view, is the first Russian European.

It was a deliberate decision, as we have seen above, that Pushkin pictured his Pretender in similar terms to Henri IV. The Pretender's Europeanism resides in the force that tells him what methods to use to rally the masses behind him. But this strength becomes his weakness when he tries to draw the masses out of their customary ways of thinking and living. In his historical tragedy Pushkin shows he understood the significance of the conflict between the folk mind, with its traditional inertia, and the self-will of the solitary and self-sufficient individual. This conflict is foretold in the play, but not demonstrated in its action, and its significance extends far beyond the period of the Time of Troubles. In this opposition between the Europeanized Russian consciousness of the 'Russian European' and the traditions and customs of the people, Pushkin revealed the universal and perhaps chief conflict in the spiritual life of the Russian nation in general. This conflict was much more acute in Pushkin's time than at the beginning of the seventeenth century. In a more complex form this conflict continues in our time as well, and will continue as long as the people regard the course of life as a chain of misfortunes and calamities inflicted by evil forces, both foreign and native, from which one can be saved only by miracles.

Pushkin's tragedy can be correctly understood only in the light of Russia's historical experience, which tells us that the paradox of the folk mind as revealed by Pushkin is generated by the deep structure of the people's way of thinking. The people have been living in the traditional hope of a miracle; they are apparently incapable of taking a sober view of themselves and their own situation. Precisely this constitutes the prophetic significance of Pushkin's tragedy, and its sense of history.

Notes

[1] S. Bondi, 'Dramaticheskiye proizvedeniya Pushkina' in A. S. Pushkin, *Sobraniye sochineniy v desyati tomakh,* vol. 4, Moscow, 1975 (henceforth Bondi), p. 492.

[2] S. Rassadin, *Dramaturg Pushkin,* Moscow, 1977, p. 27.

[3] Ibid., p. 45, my emphasis.

[4] N. Litvinenko, *Pushkin i teatr. Formirovaniye teatral'nykh vozzreniy,* Moscow, 1974, pp. 210-11. Author's italics.

[5] N. Balashov, 'Struktura "Borisa Godunova" ' (*Izvestiya Akademii Nauk SSSR, seriya literatury i yazyka,* vol. 39, 1980, Moscow, p. 214).

[6] N. P. Pavlov-Sil'vansky, 'Narod i tsar' v tragedii Pushkina' in A. S. Pushkin, *Polnoye sobraniye sochineniy pod redaktsiyey S. A. Vengerova,* vol. 3, St Petersburg, 1910, p. 308.

[7] B. N. Engel'gardt, 'Istorizm Pushkina' in *Pushkinist: Istoriko-literaturnyy sbornik,* ed. S. A. Vengerov, vol. 2, Petrograd, 1916, pp. 58-75.

[8] *Pushkin. Itogi i problemy izucheniya,* AN SSSR, Moscow-Leningrad, 1966 (henceforth *Itogi*), pp. 446-49.

[9] Bondi, op. cit., pp. 491-92.

[10] Ibid., p. 492.

[11] *Itogi,* pp. 451-52.

[12] N. Nadoumko [Nadezhdin], 'Boris Godunov. Sochineniye A. S. Pushkina. Beseda starykh znakomtsev' (*Teleskop,* Moscow, 1831, part 1, no. 4, pp. 568-69).

[13] I. V. Kireyevsky, 'Obozreniye russkoy literatury za 1831 god' (*Yevropeyets,* Moscow, 1832, January, part 1, no. 1, p. 111). Quoted from I. V. Kireyevsky, *Polnoye sobraniye sochineniy v dvukh tomakh,* vol. 2, Moscow, 1911, p. 45.

[14] N. M. Karamzin, *Istoriya gosudarstva Rossiyskogo v 12 tomakh,* vol. 11, St Petersburg, 1892, p. 39. Henceforth pagination is given in the text.

[15] Bondi, op. cit., p. 494.

[16] G. S. Vinokur, 'Kommentariy k "Borisu Godunovu" A. S. Pushkina', in A. S. Pushkin, *Polnoye sobraniye sochineniy,* vol. VII: Dramaticheskiye proizvedeniya. AN SSSR, Moscow-Leningrad, 1935, p. 486.

[17] A. S. Pushkin, *Sobraniye sochineniy v desyati tomakh,* vol. 6, Moscow, 1975, p. 260.

[18] Bondi, op. cit., p. 495.

[19] Ibid.

[20] See I. Z. Serman, 'Pushkin i russkaya istoricheskaya drama 1830-kh godov', in *Pushkin. Issledovaniya i materialy,* vol. 6, AN SSSR, Leningrad, 1969, pp. 118-25.

[21] 'God loved the meekness of the Tsar/And Russia, under him, relaxed/in peaceful glory . . . ' ('Noch'. Kelya v Chudovom monastyre'): *Boris Godunov* in vol. 5, p. 235.

[22] Ya. S. Lur'ye, *Obshcherusskiye letopisi XIV-XV vv.,* Leningrad, 1976, pp. 15-16.

[23] 'The fleeing villains were seized/And brought before the warm corpse of the child/And lo, a miracle!—suddenly the corpse trembled—/"Confess!" the people cried:/And in terror of the axe the villains/confessed—and named Boris' (*BG,* p. 237).

[24] 'Weary of monastic servitude/I thought up beneath my cowl a bold design,/I prepared the world a miracle . . . ' (*BG,* p. 281).

[25] Prot. Georgy Florovsky, *Puti russkogo bogosloviya,* Paris, 1937, pp. 57-58.

[26] Litvinenko, op. cit., p. 212.

[27] '*First person:* What? They've already cursed *that one?* (emphasis Pushkin's).

Second person: I stood at the entry-way and heard what the Deacon was shouting: "Grishka Otrep'yev—anathema!"

First: Let them go ahead and curse—the Tsarevich has nothing to do with Otrep'yev!' (*BG,* p. 298).

[28] '*Second:* And now they are singing "Eternal Memory" to the Tsarevich.

First: "Eternal Memory" to a living man! That will end badly for them, godless ones!'

[29] A. M. Panchenko, 'Yurodstvo kak forma povedeniya', in D. S. Likhachev and A. M. Panchenko, *Smekhovoy mir Drevney Rusi,* Moscow-Leningrad, 1975, pp. 104-39.

[30] 'Order them to slit the boys' throats, just like you slit the throat of the little tsarevich' (*BG,* p. 300).

[31] Pushkin, 'O narodnosti v literature', *Sobraniye sochineniy v desyati tomakh,* vol. 6, p. 238.

A. D. P. Briggs (essay date 1986)

SOURCE: "Fallibility and Perfection in the Works of Alexander Pushkin," in *Problems of Russian Romanticism,* edited by Robert Reid, Gower Publishing Company, 1986, pp. 25-45.

[*In the following essay, Briggs presents a critical survey of Pushkin's works, concentrating on Pushkin's relation to romanticism.*]

I

There is every reason to associate the name of Alexander Pushkin with the artistic movement known as European romanticism. This movement, notoriously difficult to circumscribe either by general definition or by dates, arose from a dissatisfaction with the traditional constraints imposed by classical and neo-classical art, assisted as these were by the widespread devotion to rationalism which characterised eighteenth-century European sensibility. An impulse towards greater freedom, originality and imagination, by no means limited to the arts alone, gathered momentum and soon spread itself among the literate people of many countries, exciting men's and women's minds by its new possibilities. Each European literature, jealous of its individuality and ashamed of the bad name soon to be acquired by the movement because of excesses resulting from overindulgence in the newly acquired freedoms, is now reluctant to admit that it was ever host to romanticism in anything like a pure form. Russian literature denies this as volubly as any, though it remains true that approximately between 1820 and 1840 first the poetry and then the prose of that nation underwent a process of renewal which, although indigenous in its expression, nevertheless owed much to the general spirit of romanticism and to Byron and

Shakespeare in particular. These two decades, the heyday of romanticism in Russia, marked precisely the period of Pushkin's maturity, from the publication of **Ruslan and Lyudmila** when he was twenty, to his death by duelling—early in 1837. This is the first reason why he and the movement are linked together.

The second reason is that Pushkin was conscious of the new literary spirit and, as well as adapting it to suit his own purposes, he made a number of statements about the theory of romanticism. On the whole these comments do not yield many clues to an understanding of either the European literary scene or Pushkin's own achievement. Sometimes they encompass too much to be useful, as when he states that 'the Romantic school . . . is marked by the absence of all rules but not the absence of art'[1] or when he asks 'What forms of poetry are to be assigned to the Romantic school?' and gives his own answer: 'All those which were not known to the Ancients and those whose earlier forms have suffered change or been replaced by others'.[2] Elsewhere he is inclined to reject literary historicism altogether: 'in literature I am a sceptic . . . and . . . to me all its sects are equal, each exhibiting both good and bad sides'.[3] On another occasion he refers to the misuse of literary jargon as follows: 'Our journalists use the words "Classic" and "Romantic" as a term of general abuse like old women who refer to dissolute young men as "freemasons" or "Voltaireans" without knowing anything about Voltaire or freemasonry'.[4]

The first two of these comments were issued before Hugo's *Préface de Cromwell* (1827) and the last two before *Hernani* and the ensuing battle (1830). Heine's *Die Romantische Schule* appeared in 1836, only months before Pushkin's death. It is clear that Pushkin was still part of an unfolding process and we should not be surprised that his views on the overall movement do not provide us with penetrating insights into the relationship which existed between it and himself.[5] A useful summary of his attitude is provided by John Bayley:

> If the label 'romantic' meant anything for Pushkin, it could be applied in any age to a work which obeyed no rules but its own . . . the proper sense of romanticism was for him a literary technique, not a movement of the soul.[6]

If Pushkin's recorded opinions on romanticism are rather disappointing—the more so because of his acute perceptions on other literary topics—his manipulation of the possibilities opened up by the movement is quite the reverse. The third reason for considering Pushkin in relation to contemporary developments in European literature is the strongest. He is definable by his *de facto* treatment of the new liberties. Our understanding of this poet is sharpened by an awareness of what he did with romanticism and what he did not do, where he subscribed to its new traditions and where he departed from them, how he was betrayed by its false promises and how, more frequently, he resisted its blandishments. A study of Pushkin and romanticism will benefit the former more than the latter, by sharpening the definition of his exceptional literary quality. This quality is more variable than we are often led to believe, Pushkin having been guilty of more errors and lapses than are commonly acknowledged. These underadvertised shortcomings sometimes have their origin in his misuse or overuse of the energies newly released by romanticism. The purpose of this [essay] is to draw attention to a number of these imperfections and to take issue with those who seek to ignore or to disguise them. This may sound like the debasement of a great artist but the reverse is intended. Pushkin still has difficulty in gaining acceptance by world opinion as a literary master, despite the increase in attention paid to him over the last two decades. His genius lacks the commanding universality and consistency of Shakespeare; it cannot be neatly packaged and exported like that of Cervantes. It is not all that long since a distinguished reviewer expressed with some acuity the doubts and impatience which assail the foreign reader of Pushkin. His reference to 'Pushkin's notorious and unhappy pre-eminence as the least translatable of poets' was followed by the direct question, 'Is it all, perhaps, a confidence trick?'[7] Although much has been written on Pushkin since the time of that review the doubts linger on. They will not be dispelled by too great an insistence on the unchanging high quality of Pushkin's writing. Some indication of his shortcomings administered with due emphasis on the small proportion of his work for which they are accountable, should actually serve to enhance the poet's stature. Firstly, this might help to diminish the unduly reverential attitude so frequently adopted in his company, to which he never aspired and which he would have ridiculed out of existence. Secondly, it should project into greater prominence that small group of his works, including *Yevgeniy Onegin, The Bronze Horseman* (*Medniy vsadnik*), perhaps *The Queen of Spades* (*Pikovaya dama*) and certainly a couple of dozen lyric poems, which are properly described as unqualified masterpieces.

II

A commonplace in Pushkin criticism is the idea that his inborn, and carefully nurtured, classical instinct enabled him to avoid the worst temptations and pitfalls of romanticism. The idea is so obvious and has been so widely expressed that by now it amounts to a literary axiom. 'His style . . . , scarcely touched by Romanticism, is . . . classically perfect';[8] ' . . . a poet as naturally classical as Pushkin in an epoch fashionably and self-consciously romantic';[9] 'for all his flirtations

with Romanticism, he remained true to his literary education of Classicism';[10] 'the deep-lying . . . roots of Pushkin's style . . . are French and classical';[11] ' . . . Pushkin had finally broken with a false Romanticism which had never suited his classical spirit';[12] ' . . . pure, disinterested, classic art';[13] 'Russia's qualified successor of the antique world';[14] ' . . . poetry of classical precision and firmness';[15] 'this sense of balance and proportion . . . reminds the reader of Greek art when he reads Pushkin and gives us the impression that the poet is a classic, however much he may have employed the stock-in-trade of Romanticism'.[16] Such is the general view and there is little to be set against its underlying truth. All the same this collective judgement oversimplifies what is, in fact, rather a complicated question and, worse than that, it has led to an assessment of Pushkin which is too uniform and which sometimes refuses to see mistakes and deficiencies where they really do exist.

It is not quite true to say that Pushkin was 'scarcely touched' by romanticism or that his susceptibility to its temptations may be dismissed as mere 'flirtation'. Some of his deviations went deep, lasted long, and resulted in a number of works wholly or partly infected with what are commonly accepted as being among the more noxious romantic bacilli, exaggeration, oversimplification, excesses of passion and ambition, and so on. One of Pushkin's early poems, **"The Black Shawl"** (**"Chornaya shal"**, 1820), provides an arresting example of the mediocrity into which he was occasionally seduced by the new possibilities laid out so enticingly by European romanticism, and which he would one day transcend with triumph and consistency. Based on a Moldavian folk song, it recounts the murder of an unfaithful girl and her lover. The teller of the tale catches the two of them *in flagrante delicto*. The killing is described in the lurid terms which have come to be associated with the excesses of passion to which unrestrained romanticism was prone to lead and which scarcely typify the Pushkin whom we accept as the fountain-head of modern Russian literature:

> I entered the chamber in that remote place;
> The false maid was in an Armenian's
>   embrace.
>
> My head swam, and then . . . to my dagger's
>   refrain
> In mid-kiss the blackguard was taken and
>   slain.
>
> I stamped on the man's headless body and
>   stayed,
> Pale-faced and unspeaking, my eyes on the
>   maid . . .
>
>   (*Pol. sob.*, I, p. 278)

There is always a market for this sort of thing and the piece came rapidly to enjoy popular success. One of Pushkin's contemporaries, Vladimir Gorchakov, speaks of its early popularity with General Orlov in Kishinev.[17] Musical versions embellished fashionable drawing rooms.[18] There are several to choose from, solo songs and duets, a cantata, even a one-act pantomime-ballet.[19] In later years it fell from grace and this poem is now largely disowned. Mirsky described it as 'one of the crudest and least distinctly Pushkinian things he ever wrote'[20] and Nabokov as 'some indifferent couplets in amphibrachic tetrameter',[21] though more recently Bayley has implied that we should accept **"The Black Shawl"** as an efficient and equable exploitation of contemporary taste.[22] In fact although the poem does possess two easy virtues, an agreeable euphony and folkloric simplicity, these properties would not have been beyond the powers of any amateur poetaster of the period. Conversely, to the twentieth-century eye and ear it seems meretricious; its former glory has faded into an outworn fabric made up from sensational and sentimental material. It can be read nowadays only with indulgent amusement.

With **"The Black Shawl"** Pushkin seems to have fallen into a romantic pitfall. He did not do this often. It has been pointed out on many occasions that an array of safety devices normally protected him from such dangers. A perceptive essay by A. Slonimsky[23] gives some examples of how this is done. **"The Prisoner"** (**"Uznik,"** 1822) seems rather similar to **"The Black Shawl"** (especially in its use of the same rare metre) but fends off the attack from romanticism by 'features of realism' and 'compressed thinking' expressed in 'strictly logical forms'. Another poem, **"To the Sea"** (**"K moryu,"** 1824), on the other hand, culminates in a eulogy addressed to Napoleon and Byron, in which the praise is restrained and qualified; Slonimsky describes how further material on Napoleon was excised by the poet because of the danger to the balance of the poem and its main theme of valediction. Here we see Pushkin applying his much-advertised instinct for restraint and understatement. The sea in this poem is allowed a dual role; it becomes a symbol of freedom, but, before that, it is clearly a representation of the real sea, observed and experienced by Pushkin and recreated with every available poetic device. Bayley expresses the opinion that in this poem, 'The place becomes instant and intimate to us through sound',[24] and he extends the same idea to a poem written within a few days of **"The Black Shawl,"** 'The orb of day has died' ('Pogaslo dnevnoye svetilo', 1820), which by means of its 'acoustic opulence' recalls Horace's *Oceano Nox*.[25] Many other examples could be advanced from the earlier poems of Pushkin to show that he was usually capable either of drawing back from the worst temptations extended by ro-

manticism, or of turning necessity to advantage by applying romantic techniques such as opulent should effects to a relevant purpose.

Occasional lapses into unrestrained romanticism, with their attendant risibility, are, however, not restricted to the earliest of Pushkin's works. *The Fountain of Bakhchisaray (Bakhchisarayskiy fontan)* contains an example of romantic heroics embarrassing in its purity. Girey, left distraught following the death of the one he has loved and lost, is sometimes revisited by a recollection of her, even on the battlefield. When this occurs he freezes into immobility, even in mid-swipe:

> Often he lifts his sword, arm flailing,
> But then, poised, motionless he stays
> And glares round with demented gaze
> And terror-stricken air; then, paling,
> He whispers words that no one hears
> And yields to scalding, streaming tears.

(Pol. sob., II, pp. 333-4)

These lines alone, located towards the end of a poem by no means devoid of some of Pushkin's finer qualities, invalidate the whole piece. However successful the translation of them, it would never be possible to present them to a foreigner as part of the achievement of a literary master regarded in his own country as the equivalent of a Shakespeare, a Dante or a Cervantes.

These two brief examples come from Pushkin's early work. It is clear, however, that the romantic propensity towards overindulgence did not desert Pushkin along with his youth. Let us move forward to the period of his *Little Tragedies (Malen'kiye tragedii,* 1830). These are mature works and they are held in high esteem. Janko Lavrin describes them as being 'amongst the most condensed things Pushkin ever wrote'.[26] Bayley's claim is that they 'show most clearly a language realising the full potential of its simplest words'.[27] Richard Hare believed that they 'rise to the high level of his best work'.[28] There are four of them, all written during the celebrated Autumn period when Pushkin was incarcerated in Boldino by an outbreak of cholera: *The Miserly Knight (Skupoy ritsar'), Mozart and Salieri, The Stone Guest (Kamenniy gost'), The Feast during the Plague (Pir vo vremya chumy).* There is little doubt in the minds of the critics that *The Stone Guest* is not only the best of them, it is one of the finest works ever penned by the poet. E. J. Simmons describes it as 'in every respect . . . a masterpiece in miniature';[29] G. O. Vinokur as considered by many authorities 'the most accomplished of all his works';[30] Lavrin as 'an admirable masterpiece';[31] Oliver Elton as 'a miniature masterpiece'.[32] The French critical school does not dissent. Charles Corbet believes it to be ' . . . la plus intéressante, la plus vivante de ses "petites tragédies" ',[33] and André Meynieux sets it down as 'une oeuvre singulière et même insolite en Russie'.[34] If anything the acclaim directed at *The Stone Guest* has increased rather than declined. Mirsky states with full confidence that 'it shares with *The Bronze Horseman* the right to be regarded as Pushkin's masterpiece . . . it has no equal'.[35] Elsewhere he claims that '*The Stone Guest* is admirable and perfect *from whatever standpoint it be viewed*'.[36] One of the most recent comments on this work belongs to John Bayley, who says, 'the idea of the dramatic sketch . . . is elevated to the status of a master genre, culminating in *The Stone Guest,* a climax of perfection . . . '.[37]

Against these repeated claims, some of which amount to a suggestion that this is not merely an exquisite masterpiece but actually the finest work written by perhaps the finest literary artist ever to use the Russian language, it might be useful to consider by way of an example an extract taken from just before the middle of this dramatic sketch. Don Juan has entered Laura's room unexpectedly, interrupting a conversation between her and Don Carlos. Within seconds the two men have fought an impromptu duel with swords, Don Carlos has been killed, and Laura and Don Juan, reunited after a long separation, have discussed both the murder and the circumstances of Juan's return to Madrid. Now they embrace each other, and the following dialogue ensues:

> *Laura:*   My dear friend! . . .
>   Wait! Not before the dead! . . .
>   Where can we put him?
>
> *Don Juan:* Oh, leave him there. Ere dawn
>   tomorrow morning
>   I'll carry him away beneath my cloak
>   And lay him at the crossroads.
>
> *Laura:*   But take care
>   That no one sees you.
>
>   (*Pol. sob.*, III, p. 316)

Even this brief extract is enough to indicate something of the melodramatic content of *The Stone Guest.* It is not atypical. In the very first speech of the playlet Don Juan describes what he is about to do: fly down the familiar streets of Madrid with his moustaches hidden under his cape and his brows covered by the brim of his hat. The ending is the one familiar to students of the Don Juan legend; the Don is visited by the stone statue of the Commander whom he has killed and is taken down to Hell by him. Into this colourful material a number of ideas have been introduced by some critics apparently in justification of the extravagant praise so often extended to *The Stone Guest.* The suggestion is that these melodramatic characters should, after all, be taken seriously. Don

Juan is no odious betrayer of women and slayer of rivals; he proves capable of real love and is raised to the stature of a tragic hero overtaken by Nemesis at the very moment when he discovers true affection. In fact there is no evidence that his 'love' for Doña Anna, although expressed to her with great passion, differs from that which he has experienced so often before. It has even been imagined, erroneously, that the difference between Doña Anna and her predecessors is marked by her sinking down to Hell along with Juan;[38] in fact the final words 'they disappear' apply, in the traditional manner, only to the statue and his male victim.

The action and the characterisation of this playlet, from which Pushkin's well-known sense of everyday reality seems conspicuously absent, seem weak enough to disqualify *The Stone Guest* from any claim to absolute excellence. It is the poetry in the piece which must account for the way in which it has captivated so many minds. Don Juan comparing frigid northern women with sultry southern beauties and then recalling Doña Inez; the celebrated balcony scene between Laura and Don Carlos which includes her description of the beauty of the evening—there are one or two passages like these in which Pushkin's remarkable talents come into play. It is significant that in these brief moments the poet rediscovers some of those qualities which, under most circumstances, protect him against the dangers of romanticism. These are, briefly, a sense of style and structure (partly dependent on antithesis: contrasts between northern and southern women, the northern and southern climate); an instinct for brevity and understatement (the passages being short and unassertive); the insinuation of down-to-earth, everyday details, real and relevant ones rather than stock properties (smells of lemon and bay, the call of the night-watch); and the sophisticated manipulation of poetic sounds, providing both euphony and suggestiveness without overwhelming the listener.

The Stone Guest does possess poetic strength, but it seems to have been misapplied. Pushkin has made one of his rather rare literary miscalculations. He has taken hold of an old legend encrusted with fascinating preoccupations only too dear to the human heart. Sexuality, immortality, retribution for unethical conduct, humour and local colour, together with the magnificent idea of supernatural intervention by means of an animated statue, are all packed together into this small vessel. It is interesting to note that in all the hundreds of versions of this legend (even in Molière's *Dom Juan*), the mixture has proved too rich; there is not an unalloyed masterpiece among them—with the sole exception of *Don Giovanni*, in which it is clear that the triumph has everything to do with the wit and elegance of Da Ponte and the musical genius of Mozart, and nothing to do with the actual story. Pushkin has compounded the difficulties by choosing an even more condensed form than usual, the playlet, and it does not succeed. The result is not catastrophic failure but excessive saturation. The poetess Anna Akhmatova, intending to praise the work, refers to its *golovokruzhitel'nyy lakonizm,*[39] itself a nicely condensed phrase which means 'style so concise as to make the reader dizzy'; in fact she defines precisely the way in which the work goes wrong. So much is pressed upon the characters in so short a space that the actions they are required to perform, and the speeches they are required to pronounce, are telescoped together. Verisimilitude is the first casualty and misplaced humour the first undesirable intruder. Romantic theatricality is suggested by the familiar paraphernalia—moustaches, duels, corpses and graveyards. One of the faults easily diagnosed in many an outright failure of romantic literature is overambition, the attempt to include too much and solve too many problems at one stroke. In his own inimitable way Pushkin seems to be guilty of this in *The Stone Guest.* This alone is sufficiently disappointing; the misfortune is compounded every time someone attempts to present this work as one of his very finest.

An intriguing idea is that if Pushkin had chosen to spin out this material into a full-length play, or modernise and adapt it into a *poema,* it might have merited the suggested comparison with *The Bronze Horseman* which, as things stand, is inappropriate. This kind of speculation is normally fruitless but here the question of form is important. Liberation from the rules and regulations imposed upon earlier writers was one of the attractions offered by romanticism and Pushkin was not slow to avail himself of the new possibilities. One of his greatest triumphs, *Yevgeniy Onegin,* depends for its success partly on unusual properties of form; it is a novel yet it is written in verse and the stanza employed is an imaginative, malleable adaptation of the sonnet. This is one of the most glorious hybrids that literature has ever produced. However, there is no guarantee that the combination of traditional forms into new ones will always succeed. Pushkin's *Little Tragedies* are not suited to the stage, on which their unreality would obtrude even more strongly. Their more captivating qualities are poetic rather than theatrical; the soliloquies by Salieri (*Mozart and Salieri*) and the Baron (*The Miserly Knight*) include some of the poet's finest lines. There is a case for suggesting that Pushkin's playlets in verse are ill-conceived; the constituent forms do not mix and the result this time is a misshapen and ultimately sterile creation.

Pushkin's most important work for the theatre, *Boris Godunov,* was written half a decade earlier than *The Stone Guest.* In the case of this play the faults have been widely advertised, even to the extent of being overemphasised. They do have a strong connection with the romantic movement in the person of the one dramatist, William Shakespeare, whose universality and apparent disregard for the niceties of form held a great appeal to the artistic innovators of the period. Heinrich Heine summed up the appeal of Shakespeare by suggesting that 'with Protestant clearness [he] smiles over into our modern era'.[40] *Boris Godunov* was written under the smiling influence of Shakespeare whose history plays are recalled in many ways, by the theme of usurpation, the preoccupation with the author's national past and the serious attempt to portray reality rather than present stylised characters and situations. Pushkin's play has been widely discussed and the general conclusion is a negative one. It is held that, although a number of the scenes are beautifully wrought individual entities, they do not coalesce to form a unified work of art. If the centrifugal qualities of the play have been exaggerated this is perhaps for a good reason. It has been argued elsewhere[41] that there is greater unity to *Boris Godunov* than meets the eye and that this has been lost to view because of a deliberate step taken by Pushkin to disguise the shape of his play. It is in fact a five-act Shakespearean historical tragedy and was probably designed as such but Pushkin removed the divisions into acts and scenes, possibly in order to distance himself from Shakespeare whom he seemed to have been following too closely. For the same reason he took the otherwise strange decision to saddle his iambic pentameters with rigid observance of the second-foot caesura and constant end-stopping of his lines, two inhibiting features which result in a hobbled kind of poetry, far removed from the free-flowing blank verse of, for instance, the *Little Tragedies.* The miracle is that this play nevertheless includes several scenes of indisputably high literary and dramatic quality, it is anything but unstageable (though it is, in fact, rarely produced) and it includes, in Pimen's famous monologue, some of the (deservedly) best known verses in the treasure-house of Russian poetry. *Boris Godunov* is a complex phenomenon about which much remains to be said and written. For our present purposes it demonstrates again Pushkin's willingness to be drawn in directions favoured by other writers in the romantic period, his propensity for misjudgment and error and his tendency, when he is going wrong, to do so in his own manner rather than simply fall into a trap traditionally set for romantic writers.

III

Even in the period of his full maturity from 1830 until his death, Pushkin remained susceptible to lapses which, like some of those described above, not only have connections with romanticism but also remain underacknowledged. The tendency to overlook, disregard or misrepresent these shortcomings may be explicable in terms of what has been described as 'Pushkinolatry'. The phrase belongs to John Bayley, in this reference to *The Tales of Belkin* (*Povesti Belkina*): 'it was only when Pushkinolatry was well under way that they came to be treated with the same reverence as the rest of his work'.[42]

The Tales of Belkin is one such imperfect work, though it is true also that several critics have expressed misgivings as to its overall quality. Another, which has received substantial acclaim and less in the way of negative reservations, is *The Captain's Daughter* (*Kapitanskaya dochka*). It seems improbable that a serious literary commentator should express the opinion that Stendhal's *Scarlet and Black* is 'much overrated', dismiss Balzac in a passing remark as 'essentially mediocre' and then, in the same work, go on to describe *The Captain's Daughter* as a 'charming short novel' and 'an admirable novella', but this was achieved by Vladimir Nabokov.[43] More extreme pronouncements belong to the Soviet critic N. L. Stepanov who asserts that '*The Captain's Daughter* occupies a prime position in world literature',[44] and to Anna H. Semeonoff who suggests that 'in respect of its historical interest, as well as of its literary quality, [it] is one of the finest short novels of its kind'.[45] Judgements like these seem unduly biased in Pushkin's favour and likely to puzzle outsiders approaching his work for the first time, particularly since we are now speaking of the prose, which loses less in translation. On the other hand Pushkin's story *The Queen of Spades,* often described as one of the finest tales in the whole of Russian literature and itself hovering throughout near to the excesses of Gothic melodrama, may be said to justify the generous treatment accorded it. What are the differences between these three works? Which of them has a genuine claim to fame extendable beyond national confines into popularity on a world scale? To what extent is romanticism responsible for the shortcomings of Pushkin's best-known prose?

The Tales of Belkin (1830) and *The Queen of Spades* (1833) invite comparison in the present context because of the trappings of romanticism with which they are so strikingly decorated. Each of the five *Tales* contains a plot, characters, situations or attitudes which are outlandish; they are oversimplified or exaggerated to accord with the contemporary taste for the fantastic and the sentimental. For instance, the main character of **"The Shot"** (**"Vystrel"**), Silvio, is presented in these terms: 'His sombre pallor, the sparkle in his eyes and the thick smoke issuing from his mouth gave him a truly diabolical air' (*Pol. sob.,* IV, p. 50). Two other tales, **"The Snowstorm"** (**"Metel"**) and **"Mistress into Maid"** (**"Baryshnyakrest'yanka"**), are rather silly love stories based upon disguise, misunderstanding and coincidence. The one story which possesses some subtlety of character and situation, and the only one with an ending in which sadness predominates, is **"The Postmaster"** (**"Stantsionnyi smotritel'"**), and

even this tale contains a good deal of raw sentimentality, including an abduction, a pathetic parent left behind, his rejection and subsequent death followed by valedictory visits to the cemetery by his daughter and then the narrator. As for **"The Coffin-Maker"** (**"Grobovshchik"**), it contains a passage which begins,

> The room was full of corpses. Moonlight, shining in through the windows, lit up their faces all yellow and blue, their sunken mouths, their dim, half-closed eyes and protruding noses . . . Adrian was horrified to recognise them as people who had been buried by his own efforts . . . (*Pol. sob.,* IV, p. 71).

But what of *The Queen of Spades*? This story too deals with the supernatural; magic joins forces with murder and the outcome of it all is madness. Both works are well stocked with romantic preoccupations and methods; is there really any difference between them?

The difference, which is substantial, hides ironically within another shared similarity: the intention of both works to neutralise by parody the excesses of literature in the romantic period. This purpose is, in both cases, overtly expressed. **"The Snowstorm,"** for instance, includes a now celebrated assertion that 'Mariya Gavrilovna had been raised on French novels and was therefore in love' (*Pol. sob.,* IV, p. 57); later on she is referred to as 'a veritable heroine of a novel' (*Pol. sob.,* IV, p. 64). Similarly, a well-known exchange near the beginning of *The Queen of Spades* reminds us of the awfulness of recent popular literature. The Countess is speaking to her grandson:

> 'Paul . . . send me some sort of new novel, but, please, not one of those that are being written nowadays.'
>
> 'How do you mean, grand'maman?'
>
> 'I mean a novel that doesn't have the hero strangling his father or his mother and doesn't have any drowned bodies. Drowned bodies terrify me!'
>
> (*Pol. sob.,* IV, p. 197)

These amount to clear statements—though the point is obvious enough without them—that the writer is not wholly serious. Part of his purpose is to ridicule people who take literature too seriously, people with execrable literary taste and the writers who pander to them. This is a common practice for Pushkin who is at his best when toying with the literary illusion while simultaneously exploiting it to the full. A great deal of his work hovers tantalisingly between virtuosic fulfilment of chosen literary possibilities and a genial mockery of them. The best example of this is provided by the novel *Yevgeniy Onegin* which develops its story and examines the process, doing so at one and the same time in a light-hearted and off-hand manner worthy of its distinguished predecessor *Tristram Shandy*. Ever since the Russian formalist critic Viktor Shklovsky exposed this method more than half a century ago,[46] it has become increasingly clear that the attitude extends well beyond that novel. It is now possible for John Bayley to state without risk of exaggeration, 'The question and quality of parody is never far away in Pushkin . . . '.[47]

The question is, what lies beyond the parody? This is where *The Tales of Belkin* and *The Queen of Spades* part company. In the former the parody seems to have got out of hand. Again it is Bayley who expresses this cogently when he says that these stories 'escape into a dramatic limbo in which elements of parody appear and vanish without the apparent consent or intention of the compiler'.[48] As they do so they cannot avoid acquiring a resemblance to their despised targets which is too close for comfort. Furthermore, with the possible and partial exception of **"The Postmaster,"** they exclude extraneous material which might be held to possess greater value than mere parody, itself an excellent art-form but not one by means of which an artist can rise to the greatest heights. *The Tales of Belkin* are slender pieces. There is no denying their neatness. Perhaps for their style alone they even deserve to be called 'compact novels'[49] or 'the first stories of permanent artistic value in the Russian language'[50] though there is in such statements a sense of straining literary charity as far as it will go and of doing so in the knowledge that their author produced masterpieces on other occasions. The original readers and reviewers did not have that advantage since the *Tales* were not published under Pushkin's name. If one tries to imagine the now impossible task of reading and criticising these stories *ab ovo*, with no knowledge of the author's identity, it is hard to be too harsh on the contemporary critic who wrote of them:

> There is not the slightest point to any of these stories. You read them: they are nice, they run along harmoniously, but when you have finished nothing remains in your memory but a vague notion of the plot.[51]

Attempts to read more into *The Tales of Belkin* are fraught with danger, though they have been made. Mirsky dismissed them by accepting *The Tales* as masterpieces though 'not because of the deep hidden meanings which imaginative criticism has of late discovered in them'.[52] He would have been unimpressed by the most recent attempt which, setting aside literary considerations, sees this work as an elaborate code, furnished with reverberating clues and used by Pushkin to give voice to otherwise inexpressible political ideas.[53]

The Queen of Spades is different. The story does have a mischievous inclination towards parody. Pushkin used it to ridicule what one critic lists succinctly as 'the popular romantic themes of ghosts, the superman, madness and genius, unrequited love, demonic interference, the triumph of virtue, the midnight tryst, and so forth'.[54] Nevertheless all of this is played down. The accompanying explanations preserve verisimilitude until the very end. Complex ideas provide the story with sophisticated meanings beyond the scope of *The Tales of Belkin*—the illusory concept of human freedom, the contrary awareness of our rough-hewn ends being shaped by an outside destiny, the hidden power of human sexuality.[55] Meanwhile a feeling of the passage of time remains strong as the action alternates between two distinct ages, a sense of place is secured by the most judicious arrangement of detail, while the characterisation, although sketchy in the usual manner of Pushkin, is persuasively conducted in a series of differentiated portraits, each in its own way claiming attention or sympathy and justifying the assertion by Henry Gifford that '*The Queen of Spades* can be said to reveal much psychological finesse . . . '[56] All the time profound ironies, based particularly on a series of non-events or failures to achieve close objectives, are working on the reader's consciousness with a wry humour. Furthermore the qualities of this story are accessible to foreign readers. Its poetic language may be untranslatable, but its elegant structures, narrative interest and teasing questions of morality and psychology are all transmutable into other media. At the end of it all, and only on mature reflection, an awareness is gained of the delicacy of this operation. Pushkin has brushed against the grotesque, sailed near to melodrama, approached sensationalism, dallied with prurience and sentimentality, but at no time has he been guilty of an indiscretion. If *The Queen of Spades* has parodied the cheap tale of the supernatural it has done so in the most effective way, by demonstrating how a good one should be written.

We must not now be tempted to look for parody in every corner of the poet's work. Parody cannot rescue **"The Black Shawl,"** *The Fountain of Bakhchisaray*, *The Stone Guest* or *Boris Godunov* from whatever faults they possess. Nor has it any determining presence in Pushkin's historical story, *The Captain's Daughter*. This is another rather slender piece of writing, somewhat overvalued by general critical opinion, and important more for its historical role in Russian literature than its intrinsic artistic merit. *The Captain's Daughter* does not pretend to be a historical novel; it is properly described as a *povest'*, or novella, a title which should lead us to expect rather sketchier material than, for instance, Scott's *Waverley* (1814), Stendhal's *Scarlet and Black* (1830) or that outright masterpiece of historical fiction in the first third of the nineteenth century, Manzoni's *The Betrothed* (1827). For literary rather than historiographical reasons Pushkin's modest story ought to be excluded from comparison with these more substantial works, let alone with Tolstoy's. The deficiency which makes this so is precisely the opposite of the shortcoming identified as detracting from the merits of *The Stone Guest.* Whereas the latter is too densely packed with a surfeit of material, *The Captain's Daughter,* on the contrary, supports too rarefied an atmosphere. Pushkin has applied to it his famous formula, 'Precision and brevity—these are the two virtues of prose',[57] as if it were appropriate to all forms of prose at all times, which is not the case. It is no accident that all the best known and most successful literary-historical works (as well as most of the lesser known and less successful ones) are long. Length and leisure are fundamental requirements of this genre in order to build up convincing historical pictures as well as rounded literary characters. It was a mistake for Pushkin to believe that because precision and brevity had served him well on so many occasions before, in verse as in prose, these same qualities were needed to produce a good literary-historical romance. From this mistake arise both the minor irritations and the larger shortcomings of *The Captain's Daughter.* The minor irritations may not matter a great deal though one or two examples are worth citing. It would have been useful for us to have had more details of the processes by which young Grinyov fell in love with Masha; when this occurs and a proposal is made in Chapter 5, it seems premature and scarcely justified by the thinly described previous encounters. In the same way we thirst for details of the agony Grinyov must have experienced on the eve of his duel (Chapter 4), of the tactical thinking behind the apparently foolish sortie from the fortress which led to its easy capture (Chapter 5) and of the surprising decision (in Chapter 12) by Pugachov to spare the grovelling Shvabrin, caught out in his infamous treatment of Masha, which was expressed in the unconvincing sentence, 'I shall spare you this once, but don't you forget that the next time you commit any offence this one will also be remembered against you' (*Pol. sob.,* IV, p. 306). Most historical novels, if anything, lay on the detail too thickly, but in *The Captain's Daughter* we have a right to complain of short measure.

The same deficiency amounts to a major flaw when applied to Pushkin's depiction of character. It is true that, by some mysterious process worked by a fine artist, the major characters Grinyov, Savelich and Pugachov manage to appropriate sufficient detailed attention to establish themselves convincingly. The trouble occurs with the two characters who play parts of real significance but who do not appear often enough, or stay long enough in the forefront of our consciousness, to create the appearance of anything more than a simple personality presented to us in a single dimension and are thus divorced from our general impression of what human nature is like. Masha

and Shvabrin are characters from melodrama, the one a vulnerable and swooning heroine, the other a villain in everything he does. Not that everyone would agree with this statement. John Bayley, for instance, anticipates such criticism by stating the very opposite. According to this critic not only has Masha 'none of the artificial detachment of a Scott heroine' but 'Shvabrin's fictional villainy is convincingly established', and 'Certainly there is nothing of the stage villain in Pushkin's economical sketch of Shvabrin's nature'.[58] If the certainty implied in this last sentence (which forms part of a footnote) is well grounded one wonders why the contrary suspicion need be denied at all. In any case it is hard to see how such a charitable estimation of these two characters is to be justified. On almost every appearance Masha can be relied upon to blush, weep, swoon or hide away and we are not told of much else that she does. Similarly almost all Shvabrin's actions resound with caddishness; they tend to be qualified by expressions such as 'with sincere malice and feigned mockery' (*Pol. sob.,* IV, p. 287), 'in his bitterness' (p. 302), 'His face . . . expressive of sombre malice' (p. 309), 'vile' (p. 313), 'with a malign smile' (p. 317) and (in the omitted chapter) 'his face [expressing] malice and pain' (p. 327). In the character of Shvabrin Pushkin stands condemned by his own high standards. In an often-quoted comparison drawn between the characters of Shakespeare, who enjoy a rich complexity which is recognisably human, and those of Molière, who are so oversimplified that they carry over their monomaniacal characteristics into the simplest of everyday actions, Pushkin accuses the latter as follows: 'Molière's Miser is miserly—and that is all . . . Molière's Hypocrite trails after his patron's wife—hypocritically; takes on the care of an estate—hypocritically; asks for a glass of water—hypocritically'.[59] It may be that Shvabrin is not so bad as this. Perhaps he performs ordinary functions not like a villain but like an ordinary person; but if he does Pushkin has not seen fit to fill out this part of his personality. These two characters do have an air of oversimplification. As such they lend weight to the general feeling of discomfort which builds up throughout *The Captain's Daughter,* a feeling that we are being hustled too rapidly through complex events and are allowed only cursory glances at important issues and characters. Pushkin seems to have fallen into another literary pitfall; precision and brevity are not the two virtues of prose if you wish to create a masterpiece in the genre of historical fiction.

IV

The direction of this [essay] so far has been negative. Error and weakness have been paraded in an attempt to demonstrate that Pushkin was by no means immune from all the dangerous side effects which accompanied the new ideas ushered into European literature by romanticism. Much remains to be said on the positive side. In the first place there are unedifying aspects of romanticism in which Pushkin displayed no interest whatever. Although a lover of country life he never indulged in the worship of nature; the pathetic fallacy is absent from his work. Although superstitious and fascinated by the workings of destiny he shows no tendency towards transcendentalism, abstract philosophising, religious mysticism or any vague sense of idealism. There is some toying with the supernatural in his writings but this is dealt with satirically or in a lightly suggestive manner. He keeps a tight rein on emotion and sensation, and although some of his work is pessimistic he has no taste for lachrymose melancholy. In matters of form he was a sensible experimentalist, pushing existing possibilities towards their outer limits and combining them into new strands of potential, rather than trying to dazzle the onlooker with revolutionary pyrotechnics. Despite all that we have said he was protected by instinct and training against excess. Thus a large proportion of the ocean-tide of romanticism washed over him to little effect.

Secondly, even when emulating an admired romantic model, he relied on his innate classical spirit to reduce the risk of self-betrayal. This is seen at its clearest in his attitude to Byron. The 'Byronic' period lasts for four or five years (1820-4); it is unByronic to begin with, remote from Byron at its end and soon overtaken by a series of achievements of an entirely different order. There are two clear examples. If *Yevgeniy Onegin* began vaguely as an imitation of Byron's *Don Juan* it adopted even at the outset a more disciplined form and went on to develop over the years into a fully-fledged novel, elegant in design, filled with true-to-life characters and dialogue, raising serious moral issues and setting new standards in literature and language. Equally remarkable is Pushkin's development in the field of the narrative poem where his relationship with romanticism is most clearly demonstrated. Four southern narratives belong to the Byronic period: *The Caucasian Captive* (*Kavkazkiy plennik*, 1820-1), *The Robber Brothers* (*Brat'ya razboyniki*, 1821), *The Fountain of Bakhchisaray* (1822) and *The Gypsies* (*Tsygany*, 1824). The borrowings from European romanticism are obvious, particularly in the remote and exotic settings, among Circassian tribesmen, in a Crimean harem centuries ago, in a camp of outcasts beyond the Volga and among a band of gypsies wandering the plains of Bessarabia. Vagueness of motivation and characterisation, emphasis on local colour, stereotyped speech, cliché-ridden ideas of the corruption of civilisation as opposed to the purity of nature and those who live close to her—these, and other habitual romantic mannerisms, hover ominously in the air. However, they are kept largely at bay even at the outset and as Pushkin matures they are dissipated,

powerfully and forever. Even at this early stage Pushkin's descriptions of the extraordinary surroundings are restricted to an almost scientific deposition of relevant detail. His restraint is demonstrable in a number of ways. Sheer length is significant. Where Byron luxuriates in his use of language and allows most of his narrative poems to ramble on well beyond a thousand lines (in the case of *Childe Harold's Pilgrimage* well beyond four thousand) Pushkin starts with 777 lines in *The Caucasian Captive* and sees to it that every narrative poem afterwards gets shorter still. Interestingly enough, both poets produced at least one poem which is exceptional in this respect: Byron's *The Prisoner of Chillon* limits itself to 392 lines and much is gained in the process, whereas Pushkin loses a good deal when he allows *Poltava* (which is really two stories in one and they would have been better kept apart) to escape and run away to almost 1500 lines. To this we must add the fact that Byron normally uses a longer line than Pushkin, which is the case also when we compare *Don Juan*'s 16000 lines with *Yevgeniy Onegin*'s less than 6000. By such simple figures are garrulity and laconism brought face to face. Overindulgence and restraint are demonstrable by reference to a single quotation from the end of Byron's *The Giaour*,

> . . . the generous tear
> This glazing eye could never shed.
> Then lay me with the humblest dead,
> And, save the cross above my head,
> Be neither name nor emblem spread,
> By prying stranger to be read,
> Or stay the passing pilgrim's tread.

Pushkin at his lowest ebb could never have brought himself, for any reason, to rhyme six successive lines with the same sound. The very idea is offensive to him, a tawdry display of the easiest of the poet's skills. The whole span of Pushkin's dozen narrative poems consists of six or seven thousand lines of verse admirably rhymed in patterns which, without attracting obvious attention, vary the tone and support the meanings with efficiency and subtlety. Only on four or five occasions will this company extend temporary membership even to a *triple* rhyme, and on each occasion there is good reason for its entry. In *Count Nulin* (*Graf Nulin*) the device is used twice to humorous effect. Pushkin's forbearance in limiting the use of this firework (which is allowed only one appearance in the rollicking *Gavriiliada*) does him the greatest credit.

The Gypsies, already shortened to 569 lines, represents a great step away from Byron. Compared with *The Caucasian Captive* it is compressed, variform, imaginative and altogether more interesting, with real issues of human psychology and morality for us to ponder. Nevertheless the treatment of the main theme, freedom, is heavy-handed, the words *volya, vol'nyy* and *svoboda* cropping up with tedious regularity, and some of the language is stilted. There are too many unnecessary archaisms and poeticisms; this is the last narrative in which anyone will be allowed to say, 'Leave, children, your couch of bliss' (***Pol. sob.***, II, p. 345), instead of 'It is time to get up'. The poem stands out as a classic example of transitional work but there can be no doubting that it contains some excellent passages. Two of them are to be found where they count most, at the beginning and the end. Like a film director the poet zooms down and in from a long-distance aerial shot of the wandering gypsies and then approaches their camp from a curiously oblique angle by drawing attention to their glittering camp fires as seen from outside, through the waggon-wheels. Within moments we are whisked into the midst of one family and the story is under way. This is imaginative narration of a high order. It is matched by the zooming up and away at the conclusion of the poem as we leave Aleko's solitary waggon in the middle of the steppe, equating him, in one of Pushkin's sparingly used metaphors, with a wounded crane who cannot fly south with the rest of the flock.

An awareness of the limitations of these earlier poems enhances admiration for his mature ones. ***Count Nulin*** (1825) and ***The Bronze Horseman*** (1833) produce a double sense of wonderment, first that they sound so perfect, with every poetic means exactly attuned to the desired ends, and second that so much is included in so small a compass. Not a syllable seems to be wasted or wrongly deployed. It is significant that neither of them contains a wisp or a whiff of anything associated with Byronism or romanticism. Not that ***Nulin*** is in the same class as ***The Bronze Horseman***. It began as a direct parody of Shakespeare's *The Rape of Lucrece* and an amused look at the workings of chance events in human history. One appetising moment of parody remains; Nulin blunders through the darkness in his gaily coloured dressing-gown, knocking things over as he goes, and fails in his clumsy attempt at seduction; this is an amusing simulation of Tarquin's stallion-like progress through the castle and all-too-successful raping of Lucrece. Besides this the poem is full of sheer narrative interest and an infectious spirit of play. Pushkin casts an acute eye over the rural scene, epitomising in his finest manner as he goes. We are treated to the most elegant and delicate piece of satire, ranging wide, informative and devoid of acrimony. It is all told at a brisk pace and an unusually amusing twist is reserved for the last line. There is nothing amounting to a palpable flaw in this excellent poem, not even that of triviality; we are occasionally reminded, albeit through the tiniest hints, of social and family problems, awkward psychological truths and even ethical dilemmas. The main aim and achievement, however, centre around the unique pleasure of good story-telling which is what sets the poem below ***The Bronze Horseman***.

The multifarious claims made in substantiation of the importance of ***The Bronze Horseman*** have been drawn together into one bold assertion, that it is nothing less than 'the most remarkable of nineteenth-century poems'.[60] This is not a judgment made in haste. It would indeed be difficult to discover a poem written in that period which combines so many qualities, attempts so much without sounding a false note, and does so in such a short space. A detailed examination of the poem has been undertaken elsewhere, and will be again and again.[61] Even in summary form the qualities are impressive. Pushkin's manipulation of the resources of the Russian language, in at least three different styles, has been acknowledged as a remarkable example of instinctive musicality directed by a discriminating intelligence. The uncomplicated but moving story, and the ideas which accompany it, work themselves out in a complex system of hidden structures and cross-references which impart a sense of cohesion. The appearance of harmony and unity provides a flavour of paradox in view of the contrapuntal and antithetical methods by which the poem's arguments are presented. In modulating between these arguments, from theme to theme and between events concerning the protagonists, Peter, Yevgeniy, the city of St Petersburg and the river Neva, Pushkin shows that instinct for brevity, measurement and proportion with which his name is often equated and which is nowhere better exemplified. The seriousness of the poem, although uncharacteristic, is its greatest attribute; apart from some passing remarks on Yevgeniy as he is introduced and a little jibe at Count Khvostov, a contemporary poetaster, Pushkin dispels the accustomed atmosphere of flippancy or cynicism. No ponderous exertion of will appears to have been necessary for him to raise in the reader's mind a whole series of interesting ideas, some of them philosophical issues which, before this poem, had seemed to be beyond the poet's intellectual range. These concern issues of local, that is to say, Russian, significance, to do with the shaping and ordering of her society, past, present and future, a broader consideration of political questions such as the benefits and shortcomings of autocracy and democracy, a sad acknowledgement of the fragility of individuals, communities and even large institutions when they get in the way of the glacial movements of history and, overriding all of these ideas, a fearful reminder of the elemental powers belonging to the natural universe beside which humankind appears like a puny and short-lived irrelevancy. This latter notion, implicit throughout ***The Bronze Horseman*** and emphasised at the beginning and the end of the poem, shows how remote Pushkin has become, now at his most serious and significant, from the attitudes of the natural world adopted by European romanticism in general. All of these qualities are brought together in less than five hundred lines of memorable Russian verse.

V

The quality of Pushkin's achievement is to some extent measurable in negative terms. What he stopped doing, when he changed course, what he omitted—these non-existent attributes can contribute to an appreciation of his success. It is important to acknowledge that he did make wrong decisions, fall into error and produce some mediocre works. He sometimes allowed himself, in the broad sweep of his interests, to assimilate too much of the European romantic spirit. We have made an attempt to describe what went wrong in some of the flawed works which resulted, to trace Pushkin's movement away from misjudgment, and to isolate certain works of indisputable quality. Russians will argue that, even at his worst, Pushkin remains a great literary master. This is because his poetry *sounds* so perfect. Essentially minor works, like **The Caucasian Captive** and **The Fountain of Bakhchisaray,** are filled with a music so pleasing that it is easier to believe in their quality than to think of their immaturity. The beguiling euphony of all Pushkin's work, as well as being his hallmark and signal achievement, has been responsible for some misjudgment. To take an extreme example, his 'concord of sweet sounds' must surely be responsible for a pronouncement on Pushkin made by his most reliable critic in the English language which otherwise sounds idiosyncratic. 'The longer one lives,' Prince Mirsky confides, 'the more one is inclined to regard *King Saltan* as *the masterpiece of Russian poetry.'*[62] Happy memories of a Russian childhood, mingling with the recollection of the lovely music of this otherwise empty fairy tale, seem momentarily to have turned even Mirsky away from good sense. If we are to listen only to melody we shall repeat yesterday's mistakes by continuing to believe that some of Pushkin's works are better than they really are and that almost all the poet's *oeuvre* belongs to the category of surpassing excellence. This wrong supposition will continue to bemuse the non-Russian world and hinder rather than advance the spread of the poet's reputation.

In the last analysis, although Pushkin, as a contemporary of European romanticism, was deeply impressed by the new ideas liberated by the movement, he was neither dependent on it nor, in his best works, much affected by it. Some of Europe's finest artists who were active in the same period have also been subjected to close scrutiny in an attempt to determine how far they may be described as classical and how far romantic. Recent works have spoken as follows, for instance, about Goya (1746-1828) and Beethoven (1770-1827): the former 'is such an individual artist, and so much a genius that perhaps we should not think of him as part of a movement, still less the

exponent of a fashion',[63] and the latter 'simply did not speak the language of the romantics. He had started in the classic tradition and ended up a composer beyond time and space, using a language he himself had forged'.[64] For all his aberrations these remarks apply exactly to the achievement of Alexander Pushkin.

Notes

[1] 'Draft note on Tragedy' (1825), in Tatiana Wolff, *Pushkin on literature,* London, 1971, p. 130.

[2] 'Draft on Classical and Romantic poetry' (1825), ibid., p. 126.

[3] 'Draft article on Boris Godunov' (1828), ibid., p. 221.

[4] 'Literatura u nas sushchestvuyet, no kritiki yeshcho net' (prob. 1830), in A. S. Pushkin, *Polnoye sobraniye Sochineniy v shesti tomakh,* ed. M. A. Tsyavlovsky, Moscow-Leningrad, 1936, V, p. 303 (hereafter *Pol. sob.*).

[5] This subject is explored in detail in John Mersereau Jr's article, 'Pushkin's Concept of Romanticism' (*Studies in Romanticism,* III, 1, 1963, pp. 24-41), which ends however with the following sentence: 'We can hardly reproach Pushkin for failing to provide a viable interpretation of romanticism when, in fact, a century and a quarter after his death the phenomenon is still seeking its ultimate definition'.

[6] John Bayley, Introduction to A. Pushkin, *Eugene Onegin,* tr. Charles Johnston, Harmondsworth, 1979, p. 15.

[7] Donald Davie, 'Pushkin Plain', a review of *Pushkin: Selected Verse* (ed. John Fennell), *Guardian,* 20 March 1964.

[8] Marc Slonim, *The Epic of Russian Literature,* Oxford, 1964, p. 90.

[9] John Bayley, *Pushkin: a Comparative Commentary,* Cambridge, 1971, p. 91.

[10] Joe Andrew, *Writers and Society during the Rise of Russian Realism,* London, 1980, p. 13.

[11] Prince D. S. Mirsky, *Pushkin,* London, 1926, p. 22.

[12] John Fennell (ed.), *Pushkin,* Harmondsworth, 1964, p. xii.

[13] Oliver Elton, *Verse from Pushkin and Others,* London, 1935, p. 8.

[14] Col. G. V. Golokhvastoff, 'Poushkin, his place in letters', in *Pushkin: The Man and the Artist,* New York, 1937, p. 211.

[15] Edmund Wilson, 'In honour of Pushkin', in *The Triple Thinkers,* Harmondsworth, 1962, p. 44.

[16] Maurice Baring, *Landmarks in Russian Literature,* London, 1960, p. 193.

[17] David Magarshack, *Pushkin: a Biography,* London, 1967, p. 107.

[18] See, for instance, Henri Troyat, *Pushkin,* tr. N. Amphoux, London, 1974, p. 326.

[19] Details of the musical versions are given in N. Vinokur and R. A. Kagan, *Pushkin v muzyke: spravochnik,* Moscow, 1974, p. 160.

[20] D. S. Mirsky, op. cit., p. 75.

[21] A. Pushkin, *Eugene Onegin,* tr. with commentary by Vladimir Nabokov, New York, 1964, III, p. 155.

[22] Bayley, *Pushkin,* pp. 86-7.

[23] A. Slonimsky, *Masterstvo Pushkina,* Moscow, 1963, pp. 46-51.

[24] Bayley, *Pushkin,* p. 87.

[25] Ibid., p. 88.

[26] Janko Lavrin, *Pushkin and Russian Literature,* London, 1947, p. 161.

[27] Bayley, *Pushkin,* p. 206.

[28] Richard Hare, *Russian Literature from Pushkin to the Present Day,* London, 1947, p. 37.

[29] E. J. Simmons, *Pushkin,* New York, 1964, p. 328.

[30] G. O. Vinokur, 'Pushkin as a Playwright', in D. J. Richards and C. R. S. Cockrell, *Russian Views of Pushkin,* Oxford, 1976, p. 203.

[31] Lavrin, op. cit., p. 174.

[32] Oliver Elton, op. cit., Introduction, p. 11.

[33] Charles Corbet, 'L'originalité du *Convive de Pierre* de Pouchkine' (*Revue de la littérature comparée,* XXIX, 1955, p. 49).

[34] André Meynieux, 'Pouchkine et Don Juan' (*La Table Ronde,* November 1957, p. 99).

[35] D. S. Mirsky, *A History of Russian Literature,* New York, 1960, p. 97.

[36] Mirsky, *Pushkin,* p. 164 [my italics].

[37] Bayley, *Pushkin,* p. 208.

[38] Ibid., p. 199.

[39] Anna Akhmatova, *Sochineniya,* ed. G. P. Struve and B. A. Filippova, Washington, II, 1968, p. 259.

[40] Heinrich Heine, 'The Romantic School', in *Prose and Poetry,* ed. M. M. Bozman, London, 1934, p. 254.

[41] A. D. P. Briggs, 'The Hidden Forces of Unification in *Boris Godunov*' (*New Zealand Slavonic Journal,* 1, 1974, pp. 43-54).

[42] Bayley, *Pushkin,* p. 309.

[43] Nabokov, op. cit., II, pp. 90, 354, 290; III, p. 471.

[44] N. L. Stepanov, 'Pathos of the Novel', in Richards and Cockrell, op. cit., p. 226. (The editors cite this example in their Introduction, p. viii.)

[45] Anna H. Semeonoff, ed., *Kapitanskaya dochka,* London, 1962, pp. viii-ix.

[46] V. Shklovsky, '*Teoriya prozy* and *Pushkin i Stern*' (*Volya Rossii,* 6, Prague, 1922).

[47] Bayley, *Pushkin,* p. 245.

[48] Ibid., p. 309.

[49] Troyat, op. cit., p. 412.

[50] Nabokov, op. cit., III, p. 180.

[51] Quoted in Troyat, op. cit., p. 417.

[52] Mirsky, *Pushkin,* p. 179.

[53] Andrej Kodjak, *Pushkin's I. P. Belkin,* Ohio, 1979, p. 112.

[54] John Mersereau Jr, 'Yes, Virginia, there was a Russian Romantic Movement' (*Russian Literature Triquarterly,* 3, Spring 1972, p. 142).

[55] Some of these ideas have been explained more fully in another article. See A. D. P. Briggs, '*Pikovaya dama* and *Taman:* Questions of Kinship' (*Journal of Russian Studies,* 37, 1979, pp. 13-20).

[56] Henry Gifford, *The Novel in Russia,* London, 1964, p. 22.

[57] 'Draft article on Prose', in Tatiana Wolff, op. cit., p. 43.

[58] Bayley, *Pushkin,* p. 334.

59 From 'Table Talk' (*Sovremennik*, 8, 1837), quoted in T. Wolff, op. cit., pp. 464-5.

60 Bayley, *Pushkin*, p. 164.

61 The main points, as seen by the present author, are set out in greater detail in A. D. P. Briggs, 'The Hidden Qualities of Pushkin's *Mednyi vsadnik*' (*Canadian-American Slavic Studies*, Special Issue, *Pushkin I*, X, 2, Summer 1976, pp. 228-41).

62 D. S. Mirsky, *A History of Russian Literature*, New York, 1960, p. 93 [my italics].

63 Kenneth Clark, *The Romantic Rebellion*, London, 1974, p. 69.

64 Harold C. Schoenberg, *The Lives of the Great Composers*, London, 1971, p. 101.

Stephanie Sandler (essay date 1989)

SOURCE: "*Boris Godunov*: The Expectations of an Audience," in *Distant Pleasures: Alexander Pushkin and the Writing of Exile*, Stanford University Press, 1989, 263 p.

[*In the following essay, Sandler offers an interpretation of* Boris Godunov *that finds dramatic success and unity in its rhetoric of loneliness and separation.*]

> They were the players, and we who had
>   struggled at the game
> Were merely spectators, though subject to its
>   vicissitudes
> And moving with it out of the tearful stadium,
>   borne on shoulders, at last.
> Night after night this message returns.

>   —John Ashbery, "Soonest Mended"

What makes it profoundly difficult to write about *Boris Godunov* (1825) is the sense that one is reading the play alone, that no one who has written about this play has been able to read with the kind of sustained attention it demands.[1] There is no already existing "we" that a writer can suggest to her audience, no "we" to be implied as sharing in an experience of reading the play (as there is so fully created in, say, *Eugene Onegin*). Critics have never been quite sure what to do with *Boris Godunov*. At least since Vissarion Belinsky, most Pushkinists have spent their energy trying to explain why the play was not a popular success or writing commentaries aimed at translating archaic words and clarifying historical references.[2] There have also been some comparative studies, most notably on the Shakespearean elements of *Boris Godunov*.[3] Each approach has diverted attention away from the

text itself. Those who seek to explain its failure consider the audience, the construction of stages, the changing political climate. Those who write commentaries position themselves as prior to any act of interpretation by doing the work that should make reading easier. My goal is neither to annotate nor to defend the play, but instead to see how the play anticipates these approaches. The play's incomprehensibility, its need for scholarly apparatuses or comparative studies that seek analogies in other texts, these are effects of its strategies to keep readers at their distance. It is the play's guarantee that *Boris Godunov* will, as a text, have a worldly existence as solitary as that of its central characters.

Mine will not be the first attempt to "interpret" *Boris Godunov:* it is a favorite among Soviet scholars of Pushkin's supposed Realist texts. The dominant interpretation states that conflict in *Boris Godunov* comes not between major characters but between Tsar and people. Because of the kind of observations that this interpretation has stressed, a certain avoidance of the play again occurs: more attention is paid to one stage direction, the much-discussed conclusion, where the people (the *narod*) do not hail their new Tsar, than to what is said in all the preceding scenes.[4] How can a play recognized almost ritualistically as great have engendered diversionary tactics and an unsatisfying canonical interpretation?

One can learn valuable lessons from the play's reception by scholars. I turn to the play in order to ask what kind of audience it imagines for itself, to see how the idea of an audience (or its disappearance) motivates the rhetorical and dramatic strategies that make the play so difficult to write about. Pushkin dramatizes an audience's encounter with the play, but *Boris Godunov* can teach us how to be its pleased audience only with great difficulty because the play's currency is not pleasure but frustration.

As a genre drama arouses expectations of connections among characters on the stage and between spectacle and audience. In *Boris Godunov* Pushkin presents unsuccessful and isolated characters, and produces a dramatic structure where conflicts do not lead to confrontation and where the very anxiety about audience is itself an indicator of generic bewilderment. Caryl Emerson has written beautifully about later plays that "undo" Pushkin's *Boris Godunov*, yet the lesson of the play is that it undoes itself.[5] If, in the lyrics, I was able to study Pushkin's rhetoric of apostrophe as an organizing principle for his various modes of self-reference, then I should say at the outset that, in *Boris Godunov*, no single trope is so powerfully felt, nor could one be, given the play's immense centrifugal energy. I hope, though, to ease the transit from lyric apostrophe to dramatic address by my focus in this . . . [essay] on *Boris Godunov* on the play's audiences, that is, on how listeners are described, how they are presented onstage and imagined offstage.

My task is to discover how Pushkin's imagination of particular kinds of listeners transforms the idea of dramatic speech in ***Boris Godunov.*** To have begun by musing on my sense of separation from the play's other readers is of course to risk alluding to another way that ***Boris Godunov*** fails, that is, that it does not produce the bonding rituals typical of drama. (It is, after all, rather different for me to have pointed in the previous chapter to the discovery of solitude in Pushkin's lyrics, since lyric poetry typically makes us aware of a singer alone finding the language to express ideas and emotions and, for the most part, lyric poetry in the modern age is consumed in solitude.) Yet my goal, to repeat, is not to explain the play's failure, but to interpret anew its successful discontinuities. The play does not ignore conventions of connection and community in drama; it shows, repeatedly, their impossibility. Pushkin rejected verisimilitude as a principle in drama: "Quel diable de vraisemblance y a-t-il dans une salle coupée en deux dont l'une est occupée par 2000 personnes, sensées n'être pas vues par celles qui sont sur les planches?" (7: 113).[6] Pushkin here sees the theatrical presentation as an enclosed space that permits the self-conscious artifice of those performing and those observing. The theater is "cut in half," thus cutting the audience off from the stage. Dramatic success is achieved in ***Boris Godunov*** precisely in its rhetoric and designs of separation.

Boris Godunov takes place just at the outset of Russia's interregnum, known as the Time of Troubles (Smuta). The play begins with the accession to the throne of the Regent, Boris Godunov, in 1598; it also shows events leading to his sudden death in 1605. Concurrently, a monk, Grigory Otrepiev, decides to impersonate the young Tsarevich Dmitri, who had died in Uglich in 1591, before the action begins. Having proclaimed himself to be the Tsarevich, the False Dmitri is seen in Poland, where he seeks supporters and woos a Polish princess, then advances with his new army toward Moscow. Just as the False Dmitri is losing so badly as to seem defeated, Boris dies in Moscow's Kremlin, and Dmitri is hailed by the boyar princes as the new Tsar in the final scene. The Russian people, who witnessed Boris's hesitant rise to power in the opening scenes, are silent in the end.

Pushkin's play, twenty-three scenes in length, (Pushkin actually wrote 25 scenes; he excised two of them (a conversation between Grigory and an evil monk; another between Marina Mniszech and a servant) for the 1831 printed edition of ***Boris Godunov.***) without divisions into acts and with minimal staging instructions, conveys much of this information in full rejection of

the usual conventions of verisimilitude and dramatic unity. The play shows us characters as actors rather than the other way around, a fact that will interest me as I pursue the play's fascination with audiences. ***Boris Godunov*** shows characters taking up various pretenses in order to advance their political causes and in order to persuade their listeners (off and on the stage) that they are who they say they are. Such convictions are almost always hollow in the play; this omnipresence of failure is at the center of ***Boris Godunov.*** This open acceptance of, if you will, the theatricality of theater is oddly undermined within the play by a rhetoric of sincerity, by major characters whose speeches seem designed to convince their ever-elusive audiences and their own selves that they are who they say they are, not acting but "being themselves." Not an unexpected preoccupation, of course, in a play that has as one main character a pretender (a monk impersonating a Tsarevich), but there is an unease within ***Boris Godunov*** about the acceptability of pretense, just as there is mistrust in those who pretend to sincerity. Much of this [essay] will be devoted to two of Boris Godunov's soliloquies because it is in those moments when Boris speaks to himself, hence when he acts the parts of audience and actor at the same time, that the play most dramatically confronts its isolation from its imagined audiences. Boris is deaf to his own pretenses, something we feel again and again when he claims to be sincere; in his deafness the play shows the tragic consequences of an uncomprehending audience. The play's worst fear is that we will read it as naïvely as Boris reads himself.

. . . I will try finally to connect this sense of the play at odds with itself with the particular circumstances of Pushkin's life, with the role that he wished ***Boris Godunov*** to play in his life in 1825 and beyond. In the lyric poems it has been fairly clear how we could listen for Pushkin's voice, for the echoes of self-scrutiny that might resonate in poems about landscape, politics, and loss. But in drama one has to listen rather differently if one wants to hear the dramatist's voice. Just as I have indicated that it is more jarring to locate the sense of solitude in ***Boris Godunov*** because it is a drama, so it will be a test of the ways of reading Pushkin . . . for me to turn now to this dramatic text. There are thematic self-references to be found in this play, particularly in the plots of exile and impersonation, and in characters who are, in various ways, writers. More immediately at issue, though, is the rhetorical work of discontinuity in the play, the creation of a sense that we are as alone when we read ***Boris Godunov*** as Pushkin was when he wrote it.

Opening Lines

When ***Boris Godunov*** opens in the Kremlin, Prince Vorotynsky speaks to Prince Shuisky . . .

Together, we are appointed to oversee the city,
But there is no one, it seems, for us to watch
   over:
Moscow is empty; following after the
   patriarch,
All the people have also gone to the
   monastery.
What do you think: how will this crisis end?

(5: 187, SC. I)

As *Boris Godunov* begins, Vorotynsky calmly tells
Shuisky there is nothing to look at. It is remarkable
that *Boris Godunov* opens with the speeches of two
boyar princes saying that there is no dramatic spectacle, only their own speculation about an unseen event
of momentous political consequence. The boyars' first
concern is not the political drama, but those who
should be watching the drama: impatient to find out
whether Boris has become Tsar, the Russian people
have left for Novodevichy Monastery, where the announcement is anticipated. The popular audience is
as absent as the drama of Boris's ascent to the throne,
and their absence is noticed by two princes who are
themselves, for the moment, spectators.

I imagine a production of *Boris Godunov* opening on
a lit but totally empty stage; Shuisky and Vorotynsky
could speak their first lines from the audience or the
aisles, so fully are *they* spectators rather than actors
at this moment. Since what they wish to see is not
just the spectacle of power changing hands but another group of spectators, there might also be rows of
empty seats for the Russian people to sit among the
theatergoers, for the people are, even more than Shuisky
and Vorotynsky, initially present as beholders.

The stage has had to be emptied in order for the
performance to begin. What Shuisky and Vorotynsky
say about the city is that it is *empty* (*Moskva pusta*),
an epithet that recurs ominously in *Boris Godunov.*
Moscow's throne is empty; once he is Tsar, Boris
will be threatened by a pretender, whose appearance
as Dmitri implies that a grave is empty. The specter
of emptiness haunts *Boris Godunov* and will sometimes force it toward a false sense of plenitude: both
scenically, when the stage is filled with masses of the
Russian people (first seen only moments after this
opening dialogue), and rhetorically, in exchanges that
are over-determined because characters have emptied
their words of any finite meaning except that which
signifies façade.

Yet the play begins not so much by trying to hide from
the dangers of emptiness as by calling attention to
their importance in comprehending this drama. In beginning so utterly with nothing ("there is no one . . .
for us to watch over"), *Boris Godunov* disarms readers and potential viewers, leaving us as surprised to

find that there is nothing to see as Shuisky and
Vorotynsky are. Still, the two princes hold our attention briefly, for in the space that opens out before their eyes, they tell some of the story of how the
throne came to be vacant. As in the opening chorus
of a Greek tragedy, Vorotynsky now gives Shuisky,
and thus the play's listeners, those bits of background
facts necessary to understanding the drama, that is,
that Boris Godunov has been shut in a monastery for
a month, showing no sign of accepting the many
exhortations (which Vorotynsky lists) to rule Russia.
(It is ironic that Vorotynsky at first seems the infor-
mant of Shuisky, since Shuisky's pose is in every scene
determined by his knowing more than anyone else.
Among the boyar princes (who are not actors but spectators within *Boris Godunov*), Shuisky is a special
case. He keeps trying to be more active than passive,
more a performer than a watchful subordinate. Shuisky
effectively crosses the text's boundaries: readers know
that this apparently secondary figure himself ascends
the throne within a few years. Shuisky's political
instincts dominate his every sentence. Shuisky is the
first in Moscow to know of the appearance of the
pretender in Warsaw (sc. 9), and he is disappointed
to discover that he is not the first to bring these
admittedly infelicitous tidings to Tsar Boris.)

But we are not told much of the story, and as the play
proceeds, we come to doubt what we are told. A gesture that seems to acknowledge the audience's curiosity cannot satisfy. If Vorotynsky's opening lines
drew attention to the evacuation of stage and story
requisite to the beginning of *Boris Godunov,* then
the way in which Shuisky takes control of the scene
shifts attention to the play's rhetoric of evasion and
cunning. Vorotynsky and Shuisky demonstrate two
approaches to discerning what events mean, two ways
to uncover hidden intentions. The information about
Boris emerges in their questions and answers, but
Shuisky's answers are as cynical as Vorotynsky's
queries are innocent. Vorotynsky verbalizes naïvely
the changes transpiring around him: he believes that
Boris is reluctant to rule. When Shuisky predicts that
Boris will graciously agree to rule, Vorotynsky interrupts with evidence to the contrary. What if Boris
does not accept? Shuisky's answer reveals the cause
of his cynicism and ends Vorotynsky's recitations of
what he sees. If told that Boris irrevocably refuses
the throne, then Shuisky will say that . . .

... the blood
Of the infant Tsarevich was spilled in vain;
That if that is so, then Dmitri could have
   lived.

(5: 188, SC. I)

It is important to note what Shuisky does and does not
do here. Above all, he introduces the play's recurrent

interest in the death of the Tsarevich. Vorotynsky immediately wants to know whether Boris was really responsible for the death of the Tsarevich.

Rather than an answer, Shuisky provides the play's first and most tantalizing instance of rhetorical structures that obscure rather than clarify the truth . . .

> VOROTYNSKY:
>
> Come now, is it certain
> That it was Boris who killed the Tsarevich?
>
> SHUISKY:
>
> Who else?
> Who bribed Chepchugov in vain?
> Who sent both Bitiagovskys
> With Kachalov?

By creating a chain of rhetorical questions, Shuisky gains the usual advantage of this trope, intensified attention from his listener, who anticipates that the speaker will answer his own questions. Yet Shuisky's rhetorical questions turn away from the real issue. They fail to respond to Vorotynsky's question ("is it certain that it was Boris who killed the Tsarevich?"), and substitute three names for the only one concerned—Boris. A list of proper names swells to fill the gap left by Shuisky's evasion of Vorotynsky's question, yet it is not just a case of fullness covering over emptiness: Shuisky's rhetorical questions are a diversionary tactic and as such demonstrate how one character controls his listener by seeming to impart information.

Shuisky outdoes himself by undoing this entire conversation in scene 4. Boris Godunov has been crowned Tsar; Shuisky tries to take back the now-treasonous echoes in his scene 1 speech. He again diverts Vorotynsky from the topic of Dmitri's death, this time by claiming that he was only pretending to say slanderous things about the Tsar . . .

> . . . with made-up slander
> I was merely trying to test you,
> To know more surely your secret mode of
>   thought;

(5: 198, SC. 4)

When Shuisky claims to have been pretending in order to penetrate Vorotynsky's secrets, he epitomizes the disingenuous doubling so constitutive of *Boris Godunov,* a play about sincerity and pretense. Penetrating the pretenses of others becomes a necessary form of acquiring power, and penetration occurs through various forms of denial and passivity. The option of retracting troublesome or ineffective words will also be chosen by Dmitri when he courts Marina near the fountain (SC. 13).

The immediate consequences of Shuisky's revisions are for the play's increasingly confused audience. Shuisky's disclaimers cause us to look back to the opening exchanges and discover ourselves still less well-informed about the events to unfold. What seemed a choral-like imparting of (scanty) information becomes a feint, one character's "made-up slander" designed to "test" his companion. We either witness the onstage trickery or else become its target: how can we believe the attenuated allegations that Boris had Dmitri killed, especially once they are retracted, unless we disbelieve Shuisky's claim to have been "testing" Vorotynsky? The latter clearly seems a lie, but the former rings just as false yet goes strangely unrefuted. We have been drawn into the circle of curious uncertainty that encloses *Boris Godunov,* and we do not know any more than the actors what the play is trying to tell us about Dmitri's death in Uglich. This opening exchange, then, has managed to introduce its readers and viewers to the drama of *Boris Godunov* in ways that seem as valued for their ability to put us off as for their potential to draw us in. Shuisky and Vorotynsky are equally poor guides. Vorotynsky is busy trying to make sense of the events, while Shuisky seems to have secrets of his own.

If the boyar princes do not much key the audience about the way *Boris Godunov* is to be read or heard, then perhaps the *narod* will be more forthcoming. They are as unlike the boyars as possible. Compared with Shuisky's crafty denial of his allegations against Boris, the *narod,* when they are first seen in scenes 3 and 4, flee seriousness altogether. They escape from the difficulties of playing their role as audience by exaggerating the duplicity of the situation. In their appreciation of comedy the Russian people are more immediately present to us than the boyar princes (Shuisky and Vorotynsky saw nothing incongruous about their situation as the ones "appointed" to watch over people who had disappeared). Pushkin does not have to turn history into theater in *Boris Godunov;* once the *narod* are onstage, he can be content to show us how theatrical history can be. There must have been a pun in Pushkin's claim that the Time of Troubles was "one of the most dramatic epochs of modern history" (7: 114).

This is nowhere more evident than in the scenario of expectation that surrounds Boris's emergence as Tsar. Using material found in Nikolai Karamzin's *History of the Russian State,* Pushkin fashions a comedy of applause on command.[8] Here is part of the third scene . . .

> THE PEOPLE (*on their knees; howls and cries*):
> O, be merciful, our father! rule over us!
> Be our father, our Tsar!
>
> ONE OF THEM (*quietly*):
>
> What are they crying about there?

ANOTHER:
How should we know? that's for the boyars to
    know,
We're no match for such a task.

WOMAN (*with an infant*):
            Well? Now that it's time to cry,
You get quiet. I'll show you! Here's the
    bogeyman!
Cry, spoiled thing!
    (*Throws the child to the ground. The child
    squeals.*)
            There you go.

ANOTHER:
            Everyone's crying.
Let's start to cry too, brother.

ANOTHER:
            I'm trying, brother.
But I cannot.

FORMER:
            Me neither. Isn't there an onion?
We will rub our eyes with it.

LATTER:
            No, I will smear on some saliva.

(5:195-96, SC. 3)

The people try to cry and bow on command, acting
the part of audience, but Pushkin lets their pretense
show through: they grope for an onion to help along
their tears, or throw down a baby as if it were a stage
prop to make it cry with them. Later, when one of
them mutters, "Oh, who can figure them out?" just
before the cheers for Boris close the scene, the profound indifference of these spectators is brought, if
briefly, to the foreground, and we are reminded of
Shuisky and Vorotynsky's greater anxieties.

The class difference here is crucial: the people are
not privy to the details of this change in leadership,
which is one reason why they do not even try to figure out what is going on ("that's for the boyars to
know"). The *narod* only seem to be an audience because they react to an imagined spectacle. They do
not in fact watch much of anything but are aware of
always being watched. They are smart enough to
behave as if they cared, and perceptive enough to
know that their approval of the new Tsar has already
been written into the script. In contrast to Shuisky
and Vorotynsky, their lives will change little no matter
who wears the crown of the Monomakhs.

The Russian people have a special kind of power in
Boris Godunov, not a capacity to influence political
events, but an ability to convey their deepest reactions to political change at the same time that they
provide the expected responses. The kind of power
given to the people as an audience suggests one reason why we see them so vividly and so early in the
play and why they will close it as well. Audiences
and listeners have immense influence not on what
takes place in the arenas of public consequence, but
on how these events come to have meaning. The audience has a hermeneutic function, one could say,
which means that the listeners, depending on how
they listen and then on how they tell each other what
they have heard, control how an event takes on meaning. In dialogue that occurs in the ambiguous privacy of a theatrical stage, speakers can sometimes
be understood by how their words defend against a
listener's response (as Shuisky's do with Vorotynsky);
in soliloquy, speech may seem structured around an
imagined response, and in a way that Boris perfects, a
speaker can become the most aggressive audience
imaginable. Where political events are concerned, the
importance of a listener who has no political power
may be demonstrated in a double reaction, as in scene
3, or in the choice of silence, as in the final refusal
to hail Dmitri the Pretender. That silence, that refusal to perform, can only end *Boris Godunov,* and
it leaves the audience feeling that the play is broken
off, denied any cathartic sense of an ending as a
double murder occurs offstage. The silence of the
narod continues to work as interpretation; as readers
we are meant to share their horror.

In the Novodevichy Monastery scene, the *narod* comment on their own exclusion from the arenas of power
even as they pretend to cheer Boris's ascension to the
throne. Because the stage shows us listeners creating
their own commentary, while the rise of Boris to
power occurs offstage, what Pushkin does in the opening of *Boris Godunov* is to dramatize not Boris's
drama, but the process of trying to "figure out," as
the people call it, the drama. The play is, in a sense,
impudently there for us to watch. We sit literally and
figuratively in the dark, and the drama shows no inclination to help us "figure out" its many levels of
meaning. The onstage audiences, both boyar princes
and common people, are, for us, themselves the drama,
with paradoxical consequences. (Another group frequently called on to watch others act are the palace
guards. Just before Boris Godunov's famous soliloquy
"Dostig ia vysshei vlasti"/"I have attained the
highest power," the guards shoot questions back and
forth about where the Tsar is and what he is trying to
do. The question-and-answer structure even begins
the play. Vorotynsky asks questions that Shuisky
answers, often deviously.) We are, as I have said, put
off from the play by the explicit and implicit indications that we cannot know what is going on; yet we
are oddly drawn into the process of comprehending
what might be taking place in the monastery. We

watch mostly those who watch. We are like the readers in the text discovered by contemporary reader-response critics, but with one crucial difference: instead of allegorizing successful reading, this play shows us our own uncertainties.[9] When we do see and hear Boris, in scene 4, we discover that seeing things happen is little better as an indicator of secret events than was listening to the complaints of the excluded.

Boris in Soliloquy: Listening to the Self

When Boris takes the Russian crown in scene 4, he speaks his first lines with an openness meant to disarm . . .

> You, father patriarch, all of you, boyar princes,
> My soul is bared before you:
> You have seen how I accepted this great
>   power
> With fear and humility.

> (5: 197, SC. 4)

After Shuisky's speculations about Boris's guilty conscience and the people's feigned reverence outside Novodevichy Monastery, Pushkin embeds a necessary irony in Boris's statement that he is baring his soul. Boris tells his audiences in the church and off the stage (the words "all of you" add that embracing effect) how fearfully and humbly he has accepted the responsibility of rulership, but his claim has been undermined by the language of Shuisky's cynical predictions in scene I . . .

> Boris will wrinkle his brow a bit,
> Like a drunkard before a chalice of wine,
> And finally he will humbly agree
> To accept the crown; . . .

> (5: 187, SC. 1)

Shuisky views Boris as an actor (pretending indifference), but only a temporary one (he will "finally" reach for the wine); his similes define Boris by his weakness (for wine and for the crown). Shuisky also characterizes Boris's accession to the throne as a kind of transgression: *pereshagnet,* Shuisky affirms, confidently saying that Boris will step over or across anything to get onto the throne. Shuisky uses this particular verb in part because Vorotynsky has just asserted that the taint of Dmitri's death will prevent Boris from "stepping onto" the throne (5: 189). But Shuisky's answer, "he will step across," echoes the word for transgression (*prestuplenie*), as if Boris's stepping onto the throne will be another crime. Echoes of Shuisky's speech continue to discredit Boris even when Boris is alone on the stage. Both Boris and Prince Shuisky use the attribute of humility in describing the coronation, and again the effect is that

Shuisky's sarcasm forewarns the falseness of Boris's pose. Though we may not fully trust Shuisky, we cannot ignore his insinuations, as Pushkin ensures by having Boris echo Shuisky's diction in his first words.

Boris fills a role in a ritual mounted to demonstrate his power. He is lowered in stature by the very suggestion that he is acting because, in this religious ritual, he wants to seem as if he is baring his soul. Boris has all the conventions of royal investitures in hand: he confesses, he appeals to God for help, he recalls previous rulers and enjoins the boyars to serve him loyally, as they have served Ioann and Fyodor. The problem for Boris and for us as readers is that, in context, these conventions accentuate how illegitimate a ruler he is. We can barely believe that he now embarks on a time of rulership (though the historical Boris in fact did, but Pushkin will show us almost none of this period).

Boris's milieu is, from the beginning, sepulchral. The words that seem intended to bolster his claims to authenticity forewarn disaster and his future death. He goes to the coffins of past Tsars to pray, a living ruler seeking an authority endowed by the dead. He invites the assembled boyars to pay tribute to these sepulchres: "Now let us go bow to the tombs / Of Russia's rulers who have gone to rest" (5: 197). All Tsars in the previous dynasty would have paid homage to the tombs of their predecessors, but their deference would have signified dynastic continuity. Boris can only wish it were so easy. His desire to derive legitimacy from the dead will be grotesquely literalized in scene 5, where the monk Grigory first hears of the dead Tsarevich he will impersonate. Indeed, the ghost of the dead Dmitri already haunts the coronation scene, where Boris cannot pledge to work for his people without being drawn to a tomb.

For Boris these coffins are yet powerful signifiers, and he vainly invokes their fullness of meaning as if he could incorporate it. The drama shows, however, that power cannot be derived from the dead, even for Boris—or else that the dead, because abused (this will become true of the dead Tsarevich), have lost their capacity to signify authority.[10] Boris is already the man who will cry out "No matter who dies, I am everyone's secret murderer," and who will say of the masses that they only know how to love the dead (5: 208, sc. 7). If, in Romantic poetry, there is a temptation "for the self to borrow . . . the temporal stability that it lacks from nature"[11] (something one finds in **"To the Sea"**), then for Boris, it should be said, the temptation in this scene is to increase his potency by invocations of the dead. In Boris's imagination the coffins of dead rulers still transmit the reassurances of living symbols.

Boris's overwhelming anxiety about his capacity to rule and, in the soliloquies, to speak even in private about his sense of fearful inauthenticity leave him powerless in this scene ironically designed to celebrate his newfound power. Pushkin's Boris is doomed as Tsar not just because of his guilty conscience (as in Karamzin's version), but because his speeches can never convince him, his most critical audience, that he is the legitimate ruler he claims to be.[12] When Boris claims to be "bared," then, he speaks a paradoxical and unexpected truth. The scene shows him in all his uncertainties, despite his apparent conviction that his public self is fully intact. We are ready to hear the further revelations that should come in a soliloquy, even as we have learned to wonder what they and this theatrical self can possibly reveal.

Soliloquies are rare in *Boris Godunov.* In a play where the dramatis personae engage in elaborate acts of pretense, the actors demand an onstage audience for whom they consciously perform, and the readers or viewers of *Boris Godunov* benefit from that internal audience as it guides them in deciphering the actors' ambiguous behavior and speech. What is remarkable about Boris's soliloquy "I have attained the highest power" ("Dostig ia vysshei vlasti"), as well as his second, shorter one, is that he provides his own audience. He must perform both roles; the first soliloquy has become famous in part because, though he fails at so much else, Boris demonstrates impressive powers of multiplicity. An absence of authentic voice remains nevertheless. For Boris there can be only one source of sadness, and it is that wherever he turns he finds nothing he can encompass as his own.

Boris begins by a kind of clearing away of all distractions, which works much like the emptying of the stage at the start of the play. The speech opens with a recognition of emotional emptiness: achieved glory yields no pleasure . . .

> I have attained the highest
>   power;
> Six years have I reigned in peace.
> But there is no happiness in my soul.

(5: 207-8, SC. 7)

Boris's starting point for a speech of self-examination thus becomes the now-joyless pinnacle so desperately sought six years earlier. Rather clear expectations are thus created in the audience: we assume that he will come to understand his own unhappiness. But these expectations are quite frustrated. Although Boris repeats that he feels no pleasure, he practices on himself the distancing techniques that mark the opening of *Boris Godunov.* Boris is further from himself when the soliloquy ends than when he started out.

How the crossing from expectations of interior intimacy to sighs of failure occurs can be seen in the two-part movement of the soliloquy. There is, first, a long lament about Boris's failed attempts to win his subjects' love and loyalty. The soliloquy that begins with an admission that Boris feels no happiness repeats that fact ten lines later, and then continues in the following way . . .

>   I thought to calm my people
> With satisfaction and glory,
> To attract their love with generosity—
> But I have put aside that unfulfilled
>   willingness to care:
> Living power is hateful to the mob.
> They know how to love only the dead—
> We lose our minds when the people's clapping
> Or raging howl disturbs our heart!
> God sent famine to our land,
> The people started to wail, they were perishing
>   in torment;
> I opened the granaries to them, scattered
> Gold to them, found them work—
> Then they cursed me in their rage!
> Fires laid waste to their homes,
> So I built them new dwellings.
> Then they reproached me for the fires!
> That is the judgment of the mob: go try to
>   win its love.

(5: 208, SC. 7)

Boris sees himself as a nurturer, a protector, when he catalogues the protective gestures that he has made toward the Russian people, but they see in him a cause for all their trouble. The *narod,* as audience, demonstrate here their great interpretive powers, even when Boris has the stage seemingly to himself. Boris as much as confirms that the way his actions have been judged has made all the difference, especially since the morbidity for which he condemns the people ("they know how to love only the dead") infects his own language throughout the soliloquy—and, as his first speech at the coronation ceremony has just shown, throughout the play as well.

As the soliloquy continues, Boris finds his conscience eating away at him, poisoning his body with the death that seems to be everywhere around him. He twists that which is life-affirming into morbidity and failure, especially in the second half of the soliloquy, when he turns from popular adulation to the love of his family. With the sentence "that is the judgment of the mob," Boris seems to turn from public woes to domestic affairs. Our hopes for self-revelation are revived, since the family would seem a less vexed topic for Boris to explore. But the rhetorical signs are false: nothing is new as Boris turns to his family's failures. The metaphors do not change. Death comes like a "storm," thus recalling in a more aggressive way the clapping sound (as of waves against a shore, *plesk*) made by the people in the first half of the speech. The mob itself does not disappear: its rumors get repeated for more evidence that Boris is forever blamed . . .

> That is the judgment of the mob: go try to
>   win its love.
> I imagined finding joy in my family,
> I imagined making my daughter happy in
>   marriage—
> Like a storm, death carries away the groom . . .
> And here rumor slyly censures me
> Guilty of my daughter's widowhood—
> Me, me, the unlucky father!. .
> No matter who dies, I am everyone's secret
>   murderer:
> I hastened Feodor's demise,
> I poisoned my sister, the Tsaritsa,
> The humble nun . . . it is always I!
> Ah! I feel it: nothing can soothe us
> Amid worldly sorrows;
> Nothing, nothing . . . except perhaps
>   conscience alone.
> Thus, when healthy, it triumphs
> Over malice, over dark slander.
> But if there is a single spot on it,
> One, it appeared accidentally,
> Then—disaster! As if with the plague,
> The soul catches fire, poison pours into the
>   heart,
> Reproach pounds at the ears like a hammer,
> And everything sickens, and the head spins,
> And there are bloodied little boys before one's
>   eyes . . .
> And one would gladly flee, but there is
>   nowhere to go . . . horror!
> Yes, he who has an unclean conscience is
>   piteous.

(5: 208-9, SC. 7)

If the first half of the soliloquy culminates in the contrast between how Boris sees himself and how he is perceived, then the second half of the speech continues the contrast when Boris cries out that he is suspected as everyone's "secret murderer." But the real "spot" on Boris's conscience is represented as only that, a threat so grave that it cannot be named (as were the more preposterous crimes—that Boris "hastened Feodor's demise," poisoned his sister, and killed his future son-in-law). The dead Tsarevich is armed with a name too terrible to utter, as Boris will later say to his son: "He is dangerous, this unreal pretender, / He is armed with a terrible name" (5: 271, sc. 20). Boris even has trouble settling on a satisfactory metaphor to represent the murder of the Tsarevich figuratively. It is, serially, a "spot" on his conscience, the plague, a soul on fire, a poison-flooded heart, ears pounded by hammers. This rhetorical display dizzies Boris, until bloody male children, a

near-representation of the dead Dmitri but, as if to continue the lines' excesses, a multiplicity of children, loom before his eyes.[13]

The reliance on metaphors almost lets Boris escape reference to the child Dmitri, but the successful maneuvers to avoid naming him show how Boris is obsessed by this "spot" on his conscience. Boris disputes the guilt others thrust upon him, but he cannot defend himself. The spot on his conscience "appeared accidentally," a phrase that, by its parenthetic appearance, tries to lessen Boris's guilt. As elsewhere in the play the issue of responsibility is evaded, even when it hangs heaviest on Boris's head. The counterpoint to Boris's evasion of responsibility in soliloquy is his performance in conversation, the most poignant instance of which is his dying farewell to his son (sc. 20), where Boris is even less self-revealing than in his soliloquy. Overt talk about concealment frames that scene. Boris's opening lines mention his unclean conscience, and in a verbal echo of the first soliloquy, he continues: "But I have attained supreme power . . . / How? Don't ask" ("No ia dostig verkhovnoi vlasti . . . / Chem? Ne sprashivai"; 5: 271). In his final confession to the monks, he will ask forgiveness for his "voluntary and secret offenses" (*vol'nye i tainye obidy*; 5: 272), secret offenses that he will take to his grave. There is no final revelation of self brought on by the desperation of the moment.

In the dialogue with his son and in the first soliloquy, Boris seems to revel in the horror of his life, but the play reveals in him a sense of interiority that "discovers itself as too monstrous to be revealed."[14] The horror of what Boris sees within himself might be understood as the cause of a reluctance to articulate it as seen. Yet the complexity of the strategies by which he avoids a question like personal responsibility suggests that what we are really meant to see is the spectacle of someone pretending to self-confrontation, but longing for escape ("one would gladly flee, but there is nowhere to go").

The syntax in the second half of the soliloquy contains a revealing clue to the way Pushkin creates in Boris a character who wants to flee his own oppressive sense of self even as he discovers that he has no self to represent. Boris now refers to himself in the accusative case for the first time ("Me, me, the unlucky father!"), as if literalizing the etymological hint of accusation in the name for this grammatical category (the Russian term is *vinitel'nyi*). The accusations intensify a sense of guilt, but with them responsibility becomes easier to evade. Rather than sentences that place Boris as the agent of his actions, the play has him utter sentences where things are done to him. He is the victim of the dead child's dizzying appearance rather than the possible cause of the child's death.

As the judgment of the *narod* was disruptive in the first half of the speech, so self-judgment is Boris's fear in the end. Boris almost seems not to be talking about himself. After mentioning the word "conscience," Boris stops beginning his sentences with "I" and avoids self-reference altogether.[15] Impersonal sentences become keen indicators of Boris's struggle. In the gnomic last line, he talks about conscience as if it could be anyone else's, and he increases the distance between himself and his words when he feels pity for the one who has an unclean conscience. From sentences where he is the victim of others' actions and impersonal constructions, Boris brings himself around to a self-conceptualization that divorces its pathos from any admission of self-reference.

The grammatical shifts make us hear that last line ("Yes, he who has an unclean conscience is piteous") either as if Boris were talking about someone else or as if someone else were speaking about Boris. To have both meanings present suggests that his morbidity has turned back on him, that Boris is not present at all, as speaker or as subject. In that last line, he has so expanded the distance within as to implode out of the scene. The voice we hear intoning what should be the scene's most heartfelt line comes as if from outside the play. Distances grow increasingly overwhelming, and we as readers are also far, far away. Boris tells us that someone with an unclean conscience deserves our pity, but how can we sympathize with a character who cannot admit anything more than an "accidental" stain of guilt?

The underlying issue here is whether Boris is presented in Pushkin's play as bearing responsibility for the murder of the Tsarevich in Uglich, and there can be no easy answer to that question. There is much evidence to suggest that Pushkin believed Boris guilty: his source for historical information on Boris's age was Karamzin's *History of the Russian State,* and Karamzin quite unambiguously stresses the guilty conscience that ruined Boris's rule; moreover, Pushkin criticized other historians who deviated from Karamzin (7: 384-89). But a reading of the play makes these apparent beliefs problematic. I will delay until Chapter Three discussing the four occasions when the story of the murder of the Tsarevich is recounted in ***Boris Godunov;*** without these stories, one can say little about the historical conclusions Pushkin draws in the play. What can be said with some certainty, however, is that Boris expresses an anxiety about guilt; that his concern may be as much that he is not a legitimate ruler as it is that his accession to the throne is inevitably associated with the death of Dmitri; and finally, that his resentful speech about conscience stresses the imposition onto him of a popular belief in his guilt. The power of others to judge Boris guilty is so great that it can make him dizzy with fear.

Boris's refrain from the beginning has been that he is not happy . . .

> Neither power nor life has made me happy;
> I feel the coming heavenly thunder and woe.

> (5: 208, SC. 7)

What is most striking about these lines is their affirmation of feeling as prophecy in a speech where Boris largely denies his ability to feel anything. Perhaps this is the best way to sum up the source of our own emptiness as an audience as we listen to Boris's first soliloquy. Negations occur in each of his attempts to express emotion: Boris can only say what is lacking, never what is. Even the simile comparing his reign to a love affair (in the speech's opening) begins "isn't this the way" (*ne tak li*). Twice Boris says that "there is no happiness" in his soul; he repeats the word nothing three times in answer to his question of what can calm him ("nothing can soothe us / Amid worldly sorrows; / Nothing, nothing"). Whatever it is that Boris wants to say in this first soliloquy cannot, finally, be asserted.

In Boris's second soliloquy, the final line of which is well known ("Oh, you are heavy, crown of Monomakh!" / "Okh, tiazhela ty, shapka Monomakha!"), we are offered a chance to listen in on the thoughts of a man no longer questioning his right to rule, but still one whose rule is threatened and thus a man whose sense of authenticity remains incomplete. Boris has just heard that a young man claiming to be Dmitri has appeared in Poland and he is terrified. Because this speech is so much shorter, there is less chance for the elaborate evasions of the first soliloquy; more important, the final line would immediately seem much less a distancing summation than the impersonal conclusion "he who has an unclean conscience is piteous." I want to ask, then, whether Boris here attains an honesty of articulated emotion that eludes him in scene 7.

Here is Boris's second soliloquy in full . . .

> Oh, this is oppressive! . . let me catch my
>   breath . . .
> I felt it: all my blood rushed
> To my face and then heavily receded . . .
> So this is why for thirteen years in a row
> I keep dreaming about a murdered child!
> Yes, yes—this is it. Now I understand.
> But who is he, my terrible adversary?
> Who is against me? An empty name, a
>   shade—
> Will a shade really tear the porphyry from me,
> Or a sound deprive my children of their
>   inheritance?
> I am a madman! What am I afraid of?

Just blow on this ghost—and he will vanish.
So it is resolved: I will show no fear—
Though one should not disdain anything . . .
Oh, you are heavy, crown of Monomakh![16]

(5: 231, SC. 10)

With its stop-start rhythm the soliloquy shows Boris moving from declaration to reflection to resolution. This soliloquy seems an occasion of self-knowledge and successful self-scrutiny, more so than the longer first soliloquy. Boris says that he understands himself, he exclaims in recognition that "this is why" his dreams had tormented him. Narcissistic as ever, Boris gazes inward and momentarily finds a peculiar satisfaction in the sure knowing of what he beholds. He is, indeed, as badly off as he had previously feared. Earlier dreams of a murdered child are now interpreted as foreshadowing the "terrible adversary."

Paradoxically, Boris is relieved that his apprehensions were justified, even though the satisfaction of knowing that his nightmares were not causeless brings a heightened sense of anxiety about Dmitri. The speech moves forward motivated not by the pleasure of self-knowledge but by fear. As soon as Boris looks beyond himself, all certainty vanishes. Questions overpower the exclamations of the first six lines. Boris mixes rhetorical with genuine questions, so confused is he in stance. He cannot distinguish syntactically between what he wants to know ("who is he?," "what am I afraid of?") and what he wishes to persuade himself to believe (that Dmitri, as "shade" or "sound," cannot possibly deny Boris his right to rule). How can Boris believe that he understands anything at all? Boris's speech turns back upon itself in a way that once again denies him authentic power as a speaker. He claims to understand the significance of his recurring dream, but he denounces as void of significance the very event that has enabled his apparent comprehension. As in the first soliloquy's avoidance of the death in Uglich, the Tsar cannot name the pretender. Dmitri, the enemy, is an empty name, a shade, a sound, and a ghost. "Ghost" and "shade" recall the ubiquitous dead child. Dmitri is also a "terrible adversary," with the word terrible repeating the epithet for Ivan the Terrible, as if Dmitri were himself of royal lineage.

The "empty name" and the "sound" define the False Dmitri (as opposed to the dead child) as someone who has no identifiable origin or name, as a mystery devoid of knowable significance. Both terms ("empty name" and "sound") are empty shells, ghostlike in their own linguistic vagueness, suggestions of Boris's vain belief that Dmitri the Pretender has no personality that will win him followers, only the magnetism of a rumored identity. Dmitri becomes an unutterable name that Boris hopes will signify nothing, but the name's magic of popular appeal is effective because it can signify so much hope. What alternately terrifies and soothes Boris is the emotional resonance of the name (which is exactly what draws Grigory the monk toward impersonating the dead Tsarevich). There is little space in this play to consider seriously the possibility that the name Dmitri is empty: everyone, especially Boris, has burdened the name with emotional overtones. (Boris has a particular terror of empty language because he thinks it is inappropriate for a Tsar to speak unless his words are weighty. In his farewell speech to his son (sc. 20), Boris advises him to be "taciturn": "Be taciturn; the Tsar's voice / Should not get lost in the wind as if empty; / Like a sacred bell, it should only announce / Great sorrow or great rejoicing" (5: 272). Boris warns his son to speak only when his words will be significant, and it could be deduced that Boris's extreme fear of Dmitri comes in part from his attitude toward language as being always laden with significance. The name must signify the person; this is yet another reason why Boris cannot say Dmitri's name in these soliloquies, since to speak the name would be to admit that the person exists as named—if not to summon the person's spirit.) It is not the crown that is oppressive by the end of the speech, it is the unspeakable name. In retrospect, the absence of a specific referent in the opening line of the soliloquy, "Oh, this is oppressive!," seems ominous.

Boris reacts to these various forms of oppressiveness by reasserting his imaginary power over them. He stresses his ability to pretend, to hide his emotions, as part of his strategy. "I will show no fear," he resolves, saying not that he will feel no fear, but that he will not show it. With only the courage he hopes to feign, Boris seeks to sound firm ("it is resolved") because he cannot scorn Dmitri as insignificant. The appearance of the pretender is treated as an emotional, not a political, crisis, and it is emotional authenticity that Boris reaches for desperately in this scene.

Were there an achievement of emotional intensity here, it would need to be felt in the famous last line "Oh, you are heavy, crown of Monomakh!" The line ends the scene and thus comes at a climactic moment. Despite its lexicon of weightedness, the exclamation rhetorically seeks an elevated conclusion for the soliloquy. The line seems notable for its genuine expression of emotion, since Boris seldom permits such unmediated comments on how events make him feel. The tropes in this line seem less a turning from than a reach toward authenticity. Using the crown to represent the state is conventional and therefore does not slow the line's movement as a more complex figure might. The apostrophe to the crown as a symbol of Boris's sense of responsibility seems to enable rather than restrain his release of frustration. Yet Tsar Boris has just exclaimed, "I am a madman!," after which the apostrophe to his crown seems a diminished emotional gesture.

What makes the line so memorable, perhaps, is that it feels both natural (and therefore authentic) and fully staged. The line is an effective mechanism of repression by its very tropes. The crown lets Boris refer to his imperial power without really naming it in a way that reminds us of his many ploys for not naming Dmitri. The expression "crown of Monomakh" already hints at the unmentionable name, since any mention of Vladimir Monomakh is also a reference to the Rurik dynasty, of which Dmitri was the last descendant. The name also suggests that Boris has failed to live up to the greatness of Vladimir Monomakh. The crown, too, is important in Boris's facility with hidden references. He refers to Dmitri's threat as "tearing the porphyry" from him, a more striking usage of almost the same metonymy where costumes stand in for the power they signify. Boris can only invoke his power via articles of clothing, themselves bodily coverings that impersonally signify sovereign might. Clothes are a desired costume for this Tsar; being a Tsar, in some sense, is finally nothing more than looking the part.

When it is heard at last, the epithet heavy is also reduced in force by the very echoes that have given it resonance in the play. It recurs a fateful third time: Boris is oppressed by the news of Dmitri's appearance; he feels his blood sinking weightily within him; and he finally exclaims that the symbol of his rulership, his crown, weighs heavily on him.[17] Elsewhere in the play, the adjective finds several revealing contexts. The monk Pimen uses it in connection with the press of public duties that force Tsars to withdraw into monastic seclusion (5: 202). Pimen's words suggests that where responsibilities become oppressive, they soon end, a possibility that changes the exclamation "Oh, you are heavy, crown of Monomakh!" from a sign of exhaustion amid renewed determination into a proleptic vision that Boris's reign will shortly collapse. Perhaps more damning, though, is Boris's investiture speech, where he exclaims "How heavy is my obligation!" ("Skol' tiazhela obiazannost' moia!"; 5: 197). The sincerity of that speech was undercut by Shuisky's imputations, and despite Boris's professed honesty, he does not improve his image with the exclamation that his obligation is heavy. There, rulership is a much-desired and very new burden that could scarcely have begun to weigh on the just-crowned Tsar. One wonders, as a result, if the second complaint about feeling oppressed is similarly uttered for dramatic effect. Perhaps not, since the ruling Tsar now has cause for complaint. But the complaints are not heard here; they are figured as things as weightless as a shade or an empty name.

All of which means that when Boris tries to bring everything down to a sense of heaviness, we are inclined to disbelieve him, even though his assessment could be made plausible were the speech a different speech. As elsewhere in the play, the audience is at once drawn in by expectations of insight and put off by what sounds like an inevitable language of self-deception. In its very gesture of summation, distance is imposed in this final line, and what is seen is an exposed attempt at mastery rather than a release of emotion. Boris is frequently aphoristic. Earlier he told his son that "habit is the soul of sovereignty" ("Privychka—Dusha derzhav"; 5: 271), and Boris, enclosed in his own patterns, eagerly connects habit with might. Epigrammatic discourse presents itself as its own end, and covers a desire for control over a situation that inherently escapes summary.[18] Boris's introspection remains insular, emptied of any sense of discovery or even disclosure. That well-known final line begins with an exhalation of breath, a natural release of pent-up emotion. A physicality normally avoided in the play is nearly suggested in the speech's emphasis on breath, yet breath is an image that by its very insubstantiality does not add to Boris's might. Boris wishes to blow Dmitri away in one breath, and he begins the speech by hoping to catch his breath. The desires are in both instances paradoxically expressed; both seek to stifle the rhythm of life despite the suggested "breath" of air.

There is one other bodily detail that subverts Boris's claims to authority and, at the same time, could tell us what it is that makes him feel the crown so heavy on his head. To assure Boris that the child Dmitri died, Shuisky has just described his peaceful face. Boris then mentions his own face as reddened by the blood of emotion. When Boris speaks of the blood rushing to his own face, he appropriates the image of blood normally reserved for the dead child that his adversary now claims to incarnate. The dead child's face leads to Boris's face, then to the crown heavy on his head: the geography of description in this speech brings the Tsar ever closer to identifying with his apparent past victim and imminent adversary.

Such a reading of this soliloquy is dizzying, since nothing could be more threatening to Boris's sense of self-identity than for a listener to find in his words the suggestion that he is somehow like Dmitri. Others have suggested that Boris too is a pretender, thus undermining the most important sense of authority available to him in the play.[19] Named in the play's title, the character so obviously framed as its hero, Boris seems finally uncomfortable in the limelight. He is at his best when he talks to himself (or when he seems to, as in the farewell scene with his son), yet in the two soliloquies Boris uses his words as much to hide from as to probe the self he claims to seek. Split into actor and audience, Boris wants to run from the self who would listen, but as he himself says, there is nowhere to go. Listening carefully to his words, watching him consider the possibility of running away from himself, we as the play's readers gain insight not into Boris's character, but into why the play as a whole is so uncomfortable to read. The hero would gladly escape from the text, which contains him oppressively and cannot provide him with a means of self-discovery and self-expression. What we see in Boris, then, we come to recognize as characteristic of the play in its entirety. He is a character painfully compressed into roles that he knows he is only pretending to play; the play denies him the satisfactions of self-knowledge by continually facing him with a self that demands recognition for its personal authenticity.

The character is, then, an allegory for the play, which in its loneliness seems only to have itself as an audience. There is a further allegory to be read here, that of Pushkin's act of authorship. How his solitary labor is embedded into the play may be the most satisfying discovery that the play's readers can make, but it is a discovery that requires attention to writings about *Boris Godunov* by Pushkin and his friends.

Who Reads, Who Listens

When Pushkin began writing *Boris Godunov* near the end of 1824, he had been exiled for four years. Once finished, the play promised to stand as his major achievement during the years of exile (no small claim, considering the fame won by his narrative poems and the first chapters of *Eugene Onegin*). Letters from Pushkin's friends are encouraging, perhaps the most eloquent that of Pushkin's great contemporary, Evgeny Baratynsky. In a letter of December 1825, he wrote to Pushkin: "I'm dying for some idea of your *Godunov.* Our wonderful language is capable of everything; I feel this yet cannot carry it out. The language was created for Pushkin, and Pushkin for it. I am certain that your tragedy is filled with unusual beauty."[20] Zhukovsky even predicted that the play would bring about an end to Pushkin's long exile.[21] Pushkin responded with great pleasure, eager to believe Zhukovsky's predictions. "I will not die; it is impossible. God will not want *Godunov* to die with me. Give me some time: I accept your prophecy eagerly. Let the tragedy redeem me" (10: 145).[22] Pushkin speaks in terms of prophecy and redemption, but he is simply adopting Zhukovsky's usual religious language at the same time that he accepts Zhukovsky's predictions for the play's success. When Pushkin says that God would not want him to die before *Boris Godunov* is finished, he speaks his own lightly blasphemous language, and he does so in order to say how great his own hopes for the play really are.

Pushkin's letters show his pride in *Boris Godunov,* a work that sought to set new standards for Russian drama. He worried that the "timid taste" of his contemporaries would not appreciate the innovations he attempted in his "romantic tragedy" (7: 148), but it is not just that Pushkin wanted to rethink Russian drama. It is also the case that he wrote the play for a very small audience. He wrote to Viazemsky, the correspondent with whom Pushkin was regularly more honest than he was with Zhukovsky: "In the meantime, old soul, I have undertaken such a literary feat, one for which you will kiss me: a romantic tragedy! But careful, don't say a word. Only a very few people know about this" (10: 120). One can see in a more-often-mentioned letter to Viazemsky that Pushkin doubted Zhukovsky's prophecy of redemption. Part of the letter is familiar to Pushkin scholars for its reference to the Holy Fool, but I want to cite the entire paragraph where Pushkin talks about the play, for his description of himself and his relationship to the play is extremely revealing:

> I congratulate you, my dear, on a romantic tragedy, whose main character is Boris Godunov! My tragedy is finished; I reread it aloud to myself and clapped my hands and cried, good for you Pushkin, good for you, you son of a bitch! My Holy Fool is an exceedingly amusing fellow; my Marina will [give you an erection]—she's Polish and most excellent (a bit like Katerina Orlova—have I mentioned that to you?). The others are also very good; except for Captain Margeret, who swears obscenely all the time. The censor will never let him through. Zhukovsky says that the Tsar will pardon me for the tragedy, but hardly, my darling. Though it is written in good faith, I cannot hide all my ears under the Holy Fool's cap. They stick out! (10: 146)

Pushkin plays up the sexual possibilities for Viazemsky, but what we most notice in the letter is Pushkin's utter clarity about the unlikelihood of his work hastening his return to St. Petersburg. The play cannot bring Pushkin back into favor with the Tsar, he says: the censor will not even let the play be published both because of Captain Margeret's swearing and because Pushkin's free opinions "stick out."[23]

Yet the emotional position of the play in Pushkin's life is revealed by the way in which the play becomes his companion, the way that it stands in for the friends that exile keeps far away from him. Exile meant isolation, a painful truth that surfaces rarely in Pushkin's letters, but one that we see increasingly at this juncture. In 1830, when *Boris Godunov* had still not been published, Pushkin wrote in a discarded preface to the play: "It is with revulsion that I have decided to bring forth my tragedy for publication, and although I have always been rather indifferent to the success or failure of my writings, I must confess that the failure of *Boris Godunov* would be keenly felt by me. I am almost certain that it will fail. Like Montaigne, I can say about my work: C'est une oeuvre de bonne foi" (7: 114). By 1830, then, Pushkin wrote about *Boris Godunov* as a work he was unwilling to publish, and as he makes clear, one whose certain failure would be a source of great distress. The experience of writing the play seems intensely personal, almost fully enclosed by the writer's total isolation: "Written by me in strict isolation, far from chilling high society, the fruit of constant labor, this tragedy has given me everything that a writer is permitted to enjoy: a living and inspired sense of occupation, an inner conviction that I have applied all my efforts, and, finally, the approval of a small number of chosen people."

There is only one more paragraph in the preface, and it ends with the words "solitary labor." Images of solitude are not uncommon in these years. There is the telling refrain in the Lyceum anniversary poem of 1825, **"I drink alone"** ("The Nineteenth of October"/"19 oktiabria," 2: 244). Less eloquent, perhaps, if more straightforward, is the confession in a letter to N. N. Raevsky (the son), the French draft of which survives and is well known because it goes on to sketch out another preface to *Boris Godunov.* Here is Pushkin in July 1825: "Je suis très isolé: la seule voisine que j'allais voir est partie pour Riga et je n'ai à la lettre d'autre compagnie que ma vieille bonne et ma tragédie; celle-ci avance et j'en suis content" (10: 126).[24] Not surprisingly, Pushkin tried to retract the admission of sadness by saying that he was happy because his tragedy was progressing, but one remains struck by his having called the tragedy a "companion." The same thing occurs in a poem written when he finished *Eugene Onegin* in 1830— he called that novel in verse his "silent nighttime companion" (*molchalivyi sputnik nochi;* "Labor"/ "Trud," 3: 175). The text of *Boris Godunov* (and of *Eugene Onegin*) could do something no one else could do—provide him with the pleasure of company when there was no one else around. The solitude did not vanish. Indeed, I would argue that it was absorbed into a play that, though it had the power to vanquish Pushkin's solitude, leaves a reader feeling the overpowering sense of aloneness that I describe in the beginning of this [essay].

In the letter to Viazemsky Pushkin, alone, reads the play for his own pleasure, and claps his hands as if in applause, thus acting out the role of audience. In that single stroke several apparently separate strands of meaning in *Boris Godunov* come together. Pushkin is like the boyars or the *narod,* at once focused on the spectacle before him and aware that his own solitary performance is already part of the play. Whether we can take pleasure in reading or watching *Boris Godunov* depends on how much we are able to be like Pushkin: we must be content to read alone, the play itself our sole companion; we must be something other than a passive audience. When Pushkin as author becomes the clapping audience, we as listeners must work to imagine what it was like for Pushkin to write the play as he did. We need to find some

satisfaction (another word that Pushkin used in describing his feelings about the play; 10: 148) in perceiving the patterns of discontinuity and failure in the play's rhetoric as well as its themes. We must be willing to see ourselves in this play, willing to play the parts assigned to us, willing even to see how *Boris Godunov* has magnificently foreseen it all: our own doubts, our hesitations and frustrated revisions, our stunned silence in the end.

Notes

[1] I refer here, and throughout the [essay], to the experience of "reading" the play, a choice that is imperfect but to my mind unavoidable. I mean to suggest two things. First, since I am not writing a review of any particular performance of the play, nor can I assume that readers of my words will have anything more than a visualization of a performance in mind, I necessarily work from the published, printed script of the play. Yet Pushkin clearly wished for his play to exist as a performed piece of drama, and I will address myself throughout this chapter to the implications for performance of various features of the written text. Second, I "read" the play as a way to name my own cognitive activity of reacting to the play in writing. For a statement of method, see the Introduction and the beginning of Chap. 1, above. The term reading has taken on particular meanings in recent criticism, chiefly in opposition to the idea of "interpretation." "Reading" strives less for closure and seeks more actively to account for textual moments that make "interpretation" impossible. For a good description of the difference, as well as a fine example of such a "reading," see Burt, "Developments in Character."

[2] For an excellent summary and refutation of the arguments that *Boris Godunov* is unstageable, see Arkhangel'skii, "Problema stseny." One Western scholar who regards the play as "weak drama" is John Bayley; see his *Pushkin: A Comparative Commentary,* pp. 165-85. The best commentary is Gorodetskii, *Tragediia A. S. Pushkina.*

[3] See Alekseev, "Pushkin i Shekspir," pp. 240-80; and Verkhovskii, "Zapadnoevropeiskaia istoricheskaia drama." The most important recent comparative study of Pushkin's play is Emerson, *Boris Godunov,* pp. 88-141, and her comparisons in no way avoid what is most challenging about the play. Emerson places Pushkin's play alongside Karamzin's *History of the Russian State* (*Istoriia Gosudarstva Rossiiskogo;* 1818) and Mussorgsky's opera *Boris Godunov* (1869-72); she uses a Bakhtinian vocabulary to read brilliantly the play's generic innovations and its underlying views of history, character, and culture.

[4] The source of this approach, that the play's "hero" is the Russian people (the *narod*), is Filonov, *"Boris*

Godunov." Modern interpretations usually rely on the version of Filonov found in Gorodetskii, *Dramaturgiia Pushkina,* pp. 102-260. Whether that final stage direction should even be considered Pushkin's has been disputed. See Alekseev, *Pushkin,* pp. 221-52; and G. O. Vinokur's commentary to the play in Pushkin, *Polnoe sobranie sochinenii* (1935), 7: 430-31. Their positions are summarized in Emerson, *Boris Godunov,* p. 243 n. 120.

[5] Emerson, "Pretenders to History."

[6] "What the devil kind of verisimilitude is there in a room cut in half, the one part being occupied by 2,000 people who sense that they cannot be seen by those on the stage."

[7] I offer literal translations from the play here and in subsequent chapters, though I have used several formulations from Reeve's very careful, complete translation.

[8] Compare the indignant tones of Karamzin, *Istoriia Gosudarstva Rossiiskogo,* notes to vol. 10, p. 121: "In the manuscript document: 'women threw their suckling infants down to the ground, with crying sobs.' In one chronicle, it is said that some people, afraid not to cry but unable to feign tears, wiped saliva into their eyes!"

[9] For a good sample of reader-response theories, see Tompkins, *Reader in the Text;* and for the central text in this critical direction, Iser, *The Implied Reader.*

[10] My sense of the empty grave as a sign that gives everything else the possibility of meaning derives much from the work of Jacques Lacan. See, in particular, his essays "The Signification of the Phallus," in *Ecrits,* pp. 281-91, and "Desire and the Interpretation of Desire in *Hamlet.*"

[11] De Man, *Blindness and Insight,* p. 197.

[12] Excellent scholarship exists comparing Pushkin's historical account to that of his most important source, Karamzin's monumental history of Russia. See Luzianina, "Problemy istorii"; and Emerson, *Boris Godunov,* pp. 82-87. For an original, compelling argument that Pushkin's idea of Boris Godunov's "guilt" derives not from Karamzin, but from a profound understanding of popular legend, Christian sacrifice, and the collective unconscious, see Aranovskaia, "O vine Borisa Godunova."

[13] It is no accident that the soliloquy culminates in the high rhetoric (or *vitiistvo*) found in the end of "The Countryside" and discussed in the previous chapter. In "The Countryside" rhetorical display both proved and undermined the self-characterizations to-

ward which the poem was directed. In the soliloquy the rhetorical overload demonstrates, in a way that Boris cannot articulate, how self-characterization has become impossible.

[14] Kurrik, *Literature and Negation,* p. 40. Her reference is to Racinean tragedy, but it describes Boris's plight perfectly.

[15] The same observation about the "strange impersonality" of Boris's speech is made by Konick, "The Secrets of History," p. 58. For an extended analysis of the grammatical complexities of Boris's speech and their psychological consequences, see Aranovskaia, "O vine Borisa Godunova," pp. 138-49.

[16] The "crown" of this line is an accommodation, in English, to Russia's regal apparel. In Russian, *shapka* means cap or hat, and is still a common term for everyday clothing; the Tsar's "crown" is called a cap because it is not the jewel and metal structure of Western crowns, more like a jewel-adorned hat, made in this case of velvet.

[17] Aranovskaia, "O vine Borisa Godunova," p. 147, astutely suggests that the Tsar's heavy crown is parodied by the Holy Fool's helmet of heavy iron. In the passages that I go on to cite, Pushkin's word for heavy is either *tiazhkii* or *tiazhelyi,* terms that he used interchangeably. See Vinogradov et al., *Slovar' iazyka Pushkina,* 4: 611-15.

[18] These insights into the effects of epigrammatic discourse as a defense mechanism were clarified for me by Cameron, *Lyric Time,* especially pp. 32-35.

[19] See, for example, Rassadin, "Dva samozvantsa," in *Dramaturg Pushkin,* pp. 3-58; Nepomniashchii, *Poeziia i sud'ba,* pp. 226-31; and Emerson, *Boris Godunov,* pp. 99-105.

[20] *Perepiska A. S. Pushkina,* 1: 417.

[21] In a letter of April 12, 1826: "Write *Godunov* and things like it: they will open the doors of freedom." Ibid., p. 112.

[22] The letter begins by assuring Zhukovsky that Pushkin will not die because Pushkin had been exaggerating the seriousness of an aneurysm in order to obtain a visa for travel abroad. Zhukovsky never suspected that this was a maneuver to get him out of exile; see their correspondence in ibid., 2: 96 ff.

[23] Katenin predicts obstacles with the censor in a letter of March 14, 1826. Ibid., p. 215.

[24] "I'm very isolated: the only neighbor I've been going to see has gone to Riga, and I literally have no

companionship beyond my old servant and my trag-edy; that is progressing, and so I am content."

FURTHER READING

Anthologies

Pushkin, Alexander. *Complete Prose Fiction*, translated by Paul Debreczeny. Stanford, Calif.: Stanford University Press, 1983, 545 p.

> English translations of Pushkin's collected works of prose fiction. Includes a critical introduction to Pushkin's fiction by the translator.

———. *The Critical Prose of Alexander Pushkin*, edited and translated by Carl R. Proffer. Bloomington: Indiana University Press, 1969, 308 p.

> Contains selections from Pushkin's critical writings. Proffer introduces the essays with a survey of Pushkin's significance to Russian literary criticism.

———. *Pushkin Threefold: Narrative, Lyric, Polemic, and Ribald Verse*, translated by Walter Arndt. New York: E. P. Dutton & Co., Inc., 1972, 455 p.

> Collection of Pushkin's poetry in both Russian and English, preceded by a translator's introduction.

Biography

Vickery, Walter N. *Pushkin: Death of a Poet*. Bloomington: Indiana University Press, 1968, 146 p.

> Study of Pushkin's life, career, poetic decline, and death.

Criticism

Arndt, Walter. "*Ruslan i Ljudmila:* Notes from Ellis Island." In *Alexander Puskin: A Symposium on the 175th Anniversary of His Birth*, pp. 155-66. New York: New York University Press, 1976.

> Considers the sources and critical reception of Pushkin's first major work of poetry, *Ruslan and Lyudmila.*

Austin, Paul M. "The Exotic Prisoner in Russian Romant-icism." *Russian Literature* XVI (1984): 217-74.

> Examines the use of local color and the exotic in Pushkin's works and in those of his contemporaries.

Bayley, John. *Pushkin: A Comparative Commentary.* Cambridge: Cambridge University Press, 1971, 369 p.

> Comparative analysis of Pushkin's poetry, drama, and prose fiction.

Briggs, A. D. P. *Alexander Pushkin: A Critical Study.* Totowa, N. J.: Barnes & Noble Books, 1983, 257 p.

> Comprehensive critical re-evaluation of Pushkin's writings. Briggs finds that Pushkin's literary reputation has been largely distorted, especially as to the merit of his prose works.

Driver, Sam. *Pushkin: Literature and Social Ideas.* New York: Columbia University Press, 1989, 143 p.

> Examines Pushkin's works and thought in relation to the political and social climate of Russia in his day.

Kopelev, Lev. "Pushkin." *Russian Literature Triquarterly* 10 (1974): 185-92.

> Remarks on the power and music of Pushkin's poetry.

Shaw, J. Thomas. "Puskin's 'The Stationmaster' and the New Testament Parable." *Slavic and East European Journal* 21, No. 1 (Spring 1977): 3-29.

> Investigates Pushkin's extensive use of the New Testament Parable of the Prodigal Son in his "The Stationmaster."

Vickery, Walter N. "Pushkin: Russia and Europe." *Review of National Literatures (Russia: The Spirit of Nationalism)* III, No. 1 (Spring 1972): 15-38.

> Probes Pushkin's evolving attitude toward Russia.

Additional coverage of Pushkin's life and career is contained in the following sources published by the Gale Group: *Poetry Criticism*, Vol. 10; *Short Story Criticism*, Vol. 27; and *World Literature Criticism, 1500 to the Present.*

Nineteenth-Century Literature Criticism

Cumulative Indexes
Volumes 1-83

How to Use This Index

The main references

> Calvino, Italo
> 1923–1985 .... CLC 5, 8, 11, 22, 33, 39,
>   73; SSC 3

list all author entries in the following Gale Literary Criticism series:

BLC = *Black Literature Criticism*
CLC = *Contemporary Literary Criticism*
CLR = *Children's Literature Review*
CMLC = *Classical and Medieval Literature Criticism*
DA = *DISCovering Authors*
DAB = *DISCovering Authors: British*
DAC = *DISCovering Authors: Canadian*
DAM = *DISCovering Authors: Modules*
     DRAM: *Dramatists Module*; *MST*: *Most-Studied Authors Module*;
     MULT: *Multicultural Authors Module*; *NOV*: *Novelists Module*;
     POET: *Poets Module*; *POP*: *Popular Fiction and Genre Authors Module*
DC = *Drama Criticism*
HLC = *Hispanic Literature Criticism*
LC = *Literature Criticism from 1400 to 1800*
NCLC = *Nineteenth-Century Literature Criticism*
PC = *Poetry Criticism*
SSC = *Short Story Criticism*
TCLC = *Twentieth-Century Literary Criticism*
WLC = *World Literature Criticism, 1500 to the Present*

The cross-references

> See also CANR 23; CA 85-88;
>   obituary CA116

list all author entries in the following Gale biographical and literary sources:

AAYA = *Authors & Artists for Young Adults*
AITN = *Authors in the News*
BEST = *Bestsellers*
BW = *Black Writers*
CA = *Contemporary Authors*
CAAS = *Contemporary Authors Autobiography Series*
CABS = *Contemporary Authors Bibliographical Series*
CANR = *Contemporary Authors New Revision Series*
CAP = *Contemporary Authors Permanent Series*
CDALB = *Concise Dictionary of American Literary Biography*
CDBLB = *Concise Dictionary of British Literary Biography*
DLB = *Dictionary of Literary Biography*
DLBD = *Dictionary of Literary Biography Documentary Series*
DLBY = *Dictionary of Literary Biography Yearbook*
HW = *Hispanic Writers*
JRDA = *Junior DISCovering Authors*
MAICYA = *Major Authors and Illustrators for Children and Young Adults*
MTCW = *Major 20th-Century Writers*
NNAL = *Native North American Literature*
SAAS = *Something about the Author Autobiography Series*
SATA = *Something about the Author*
YABC = *Yesterday's Authors of Books for Children*

Literary Criticism Series
Cumulative Author Index

Androvar
See Prado (Calvo), Pedro

Angelique, Pierre
See Bataille, Georges

Angell, Roger 1920- .... **CLC 26**
See also CA 57-60; CANR 13, 44, 70; DLB 171, 185

Angelou, Maya 1928-**CLC 12, 35, 64, 77; BLC 1; DA; DAB; DAC; DAM MST, MULT, POET, POP; WLCS**
See also AAYA 7, 20; BW 2, 3; CA 65-68; CANR 19, 42, 65; CDALBS; CLR 53; DA3; DLB 38; MTCW 1, 2; SATA 49

Anna Comnena 1083-1153 ...._.......... **CMLC 25**

Annensky, Innokenty (Fyodorovich) 1856-1909 **TCLC 14**
See also CA 110; 155

Annunzio, Gabriele d'
See D'Annunzio, Gabriele

Anodos
See Coleridge, Mary E(lizabeth)

Anon, Charles Robert
See Pessoa, Fernando (Antonio Nogueira)

Anouilh, Jean (Marie Lucien Pierre) 1910-1987 **CLC 1, 3, 8, 13, 40, 50; DAM DRAM; DC 8**
See also CA 17-20R; 123; CANR 32; MTCW 1, 2

Anthony, Florence
See Ai

Anthony, John
See Ciardi, John (Anthony)

Anthony, Peter
See Shaffer, Anthony (Joshua); Shaffer, Peter (Levin)

Anthony, Piers 1934- .... **CLC 35; DAM POP**
See also AAYA 11; CA 21-24R; CANR 28, 56, 73; DLB 8; MTCW 1, 2; SAAS 22; SATA 84

Anthony, Susan B(rownell) 1916-1991 **TCLC 84**
See also CA 89-92; 134

Antoine, Marc
See Proust, (Valentin-Louis-George-Eugene-) Marcel

Antoninus, Brother
See Everson, William (Oliver)

Antonioni, Michelangelo 1912- .... **CLC 20**
See also CA 73-76; CANR 45, 77

Antschel, Paul 1920-1970
See Celan, Paul
See also CA 85-88; CANR 33, 61; MTCW 1

Anwar, Chairil 1922-1949 .... **TCLC 22**
See also CA 121

Anzaldua, Gloria 1942-
See also CA 175; DLB 122; HLCS 1

Apess, William 1798-1839(?) ... **NCLC 73; DAM MULT**
See also DLB 175; NNAL

Apollinaire, Guillaume 1880-1918**TCLC 3, 8, 51; DAM POET; PC 7**
See also Kostrowitzki, Wilhelm Apollinaris de
See also CA 152; MTCW 1

Appelfeld, Aharon 1932- .... **CLC 23, 47**
See also CA 112; 133; CANR 86

Apple, Max (Isaac) 1941- .... **CLC 9, 33**
See also CA 81-84; CANR 19, 54; DLB 130

Appleman, Philip (Dean) 1926- .... **CLC 51**
See also CA 13-16R; CAAS 18; CANR 6, 29, 56

Appleton, Lawrence
See Lovecraft, H(oward) P(hillips)

Apteryx
See Eliot, T(homas) S(tearns)

Apuleius, (Lucius Madaurensis) 125(?)-175(?) **CMLC 1**
See also DLB 211

Aquin, Hubert 1929-1977 .... **CLC 15**

See also CA 105; DLB 53

Aquinas, Thomas 1224(?)-1274 .... **CMLC 33**
See also DLB 115

Aragon, Louis 1897-1982**CLC 3, 22; DAM NOV, POET**
See also CA 69-72; 108; CANR 28, 71; DLB 72; MTCW 1, 2

Arany, Janos 1817-1882 .... **NCLC 34**

Aranyos, Kakay
See Mikszath, Kalman

Arbuthnot, John 1667-1735 .... **LC 1**
See also DLB 101

Archer, Herbert Winslow
See Mencken, H(enry) L(ouis)

Archer, Jeffrey (Howard) 1940- .. **CLC 28; DAM POP**
See also AAYA 16; BEST 89:3; CA 77-80; CANR 22, 52; DA3; INT CANR-22

Archer, Jules 1915- .... **CLC 12**
See also CA 9-12R; CANR 6, 69; SAAS 5; SATA 4, 85

Archer, Lee
See Ellison, Harlan (Jay)

Arden, John 1930- **CLC 6, 13, 15; DAM DRAM**
See also CA 13-16R; CAAS 4; CANR 31, 65, 67; DLB 13; MTCW 1

Arenas, Reinaldo 1943-1990**CLC 41; DAM MULT; HLC 1**
See also CA 124; 128; 133; CANR 73; DLB 145; HW 1; MTCW 1

Arendt, Hannah 1906-1975 .... **CLC 66, 98**
See also CA 17-20R; 61-64; CANR 26, 60; MTCW 1, 2

Aretino, Pietro 1492-1556 .... **LC 12**

Arghezi, Tudor 1880-1967 .... **CLC 80**
See also Theodorescu, Ion N.
See also CA 167

Arguedas, Jose Maria 1911-1969 .. **CLC 10, 18; HLCS 1**
See also CA 89-92; CANR 73; DLB 113; HW 1

Argueta, Manlio 1936- .... **CLC 31**
See also CA 131; CANR 73; DLB 145; HW 1

Arias, Ron(ald Francis) 1941-
See also CA 131; CANR 81; DAM MULT; DLB 82; HLC 1; HW 1, 2; MTCW 2

Ariosto, Ludovico 1474-1533 .... **LC 6**

Aristides
See Epstein, Joseph

Aristophanes 450B.C.-385B.C. .... **CMLC 4; DA; DAB; DAC; DAM DRAM, MST; DC 2; WLCS**
See also DA3; DLB 176

Aristotle 384B.C.-322B.C. **CMLC 31; DA; DAB; DAC; DAM MST; WLCS**
See also DA3; DLB 176

Arlt, Roberto (Godofredo Christophersen) 1900-1942 .... **TCLC 29; DAM MULT; HLC 1**
See also CA 123; 131; CANR 67; HW 1, 2

Armah, Ayi Kwei 1939-**CLC 5, 33; BLC 1; DAM MULT, POET**
See also BW 1; CA 61-64; CANR 21, 64; DLB 117; MTCW 1

Armatrading, Joan 1950- .... **CLC 17**
See also CA 114

Arnette, Robert
See Silverberg, Robert

Arnim, Achim von (Ludwig Joachim von Arnim) 1781-1831 .... **NCLC 5; SSC 29**
See also DLB 90

Arnim, Bettina von 1785-1859 .... **NCLC 38**
See also DLB 90

Arnold, Matthew 1822-1888 .... **NCLC 6, 29; DA; DAB; DAC; DAM MST, POET; PC 5; WLC**
See also CDBLB 1832-1890; DLB 32, 57

Arnold, Thomas 1795-1842 .... **NCLC 18**
See also DLB 55

Arnow, Harriette (Louisa) Simpson 1908-1986 **CLC 2, 7, 18**
See also CA 9-12R; 118; CANR 14; DLB 6; MTCW 1, 2; SATA 42; SATA-Obit 47

Arouet, Francois-Marie
See Voltaire

Arp, Hans
See Arp, Jean

Arp, Jean 1887-1966 .... **CLC 5**
See also CA 81-84; 25-28R; CANR 42, 77

Arrabal
See Arrabal, Fernando

Arrabal, Fernando 1932- .... **CLC 2, 9, 18, 58**
See also CA 9-12R; CANR 15

Arreola, Juan Jose 1918-
See also CA 113; 131; CANR 81; DAM MULT; DLB 113; HLC 1; HW 1, 2

Arrick, Fran .... **CLC 30**
See also Gaberman, Judie Angell

Artaud, Antonin (Marie Joseph) 1896-1948**TCLC 3, 36; DAM DRAM**
See also CA 104; 149; DA3; MTCW 1

Arthur, Ruth M(abel) 1905-1979 .... **CLC 12**
See also CA 9-12R; 85-88; CANR 4; SATA 7, 26

Artsybashev, Mikhail (Petrovich) 1878-1927 **TCLC 31**
See also CA 170

Arundel, Honor (Morfydd) 1919-1973 ... **CLC 17**
See also CA 21-22; 41-44R; CAP 2; CLR 35; SATA 4; SATA-Obit 24

Arzner, Dorothy 1897-1979 .... **CLC 98**

Asch, Sholem 1880-1957 .... **TCLC 3**
See also CA 105

Ash, Shalom
See Asch, Sholem

Ashbery, John (Lawrence) 1927-**CLC 2, 3, 4, 6, 9, 13, 15, 25, 41, 77, 125; DAM POET; PC 26**
See also CA 5-8R; CANR 9, 37, 66; DA3; DLB 5, 165; DLBY 81; INT CANR-9; MTCW 1, 2

Ashdown, Clifford
See Freeman, R(ichard) Austin

Ashe, Gordon
See Creasey, John

Ashton-Warner, Sylvia (Constance) 1908-1984 **CLC 19**
See also CA 69-72; 112; CANR 29; MTCW 1, 2

Asimov, Isaac 1920-1992 **CLC 1, 3, 9, 19, 26, 76, 92; DAM POP**
See also AAYA 13; BEST 90:2; CA 1-4R; 137; CANR 2, 19, 36, 60; CLR 12; DA3; DLB 8; DLBY 92; INT CANR-19; JRDA; MAICYA; MTCW 1, 2; SATA 1, 26, 74

Assis, Joaquim Maria Machado de
See Machado de Assis, Joaquim Maria

Astley, Thea (Beatrice May) 1925- .... **CLC 41**
See also CA 65-68; CANR 11, 43, 78

Aston, James
See White, T(erence) H(anbury)

Asturias, Miguel Angel 1899-1974**CLC 3, 8, 13; DAM MULT, NOV; HLC 1**
See also CA 25-28; 49-52; CANR 32; CAP 2; DA3; DLB 113; HW 1; MTCW 1, 2

Atares, Carlos Saura
See Saura (Atares), Carlos

Atheling, William
See Pound, Ezra (Weston Loomis)

Atheling, William, Jr.
See Blish, James (Benjamin)

Atherton, Gertrude (Franklin Horn) 1857-1948 **TCLC 2**
See also CA 104; 155; DLB 9, 78, 186

9

Baraka, Amiri 1934- **CLC 1, 2, 3, 5, 10, 14, 33, 115; BLC 1; DA; DAC; DAM MST, MULT, POET, POP; DC 6; PC 4; WLCS**
See also Jones, LeRoi
See also BW 2, 3; CA 21-24R; CABS 3; CANR 27, 38, 61; CDALB 1941-1968; DA3; DLB 5, 7, 16, 38; DLBD 8; MTCW 1, 2

Barbauld, Anna Laetitia 1743-1825 .... **NCLC 50**
See also DLB 107, 109, 142, 158

Barbellion, W. N. P. .... **TCLC 24**
See also Cummings, Bruce F(rederick)

Barbera, Jack (Vincent) 1945- .... **CLC 44**
See also CA 110; CANR 45

Barbey d'Aurevilly, Jules Amedee 1808-1889
NCLC 1; SSC 17
See also DLB 119

Barbour, John c. 1316-1395 .... **CMLC 33**
See also DLB 146

Barbusse, Henri 1873-1935 .... **TCLC 5**
See also CA 105; 154; DLB 65

Barclay, Bill
See Moorcock, Michael (John)

Barclay, William Ewert
See Moorcock, Michael (John)

Barea, Arturo 1897-1957 .... **TCLC 14**
See also CA 111

Barfoot, Joan 1946- .... **CLC 18**
See also CA 105

Barham, Richard Harris 1788-1845 ... **NCLC 77**
See also DLB 159

Baring, Maurice 1874-1945 .... **TCLC 8**
See also CA 105; 168; DLB 34

Baring-Gould, Sabine 1834-1924 .... **TCLC 88**
See also DLB 156, 190

Barker, Clive 1952- .... **CLC 52; DAM POP**
See also AAYA 10; BEST 90:3; CA 121; 129; CANR 71; DA3; INT 129; MTCW 1, 2

Barker, George Granville 1913-1991 **CLC 8, 48; DAM POET**
See also CA 9-12R; 135; CANR 7, 38; DLB 20; MTCW 1

Barker, Harley Granville
See Granville-Barker, Harley
See also DLB 10

Barker, Howard 1946- .... **CLC 37**
See also CA 102; DLB 13

Barker, Jane 1652-1732 .... **LC 42**

Barker, Pat(ricia) 1943- .... **CLC 32, 94**
See also CA 117; 122; CANR 50; INT 122

Barlach, Ernst (Heinrich) 1870-1938 . **TCLC 84**
See also CA 178; DLB 56, 118

Barlow, Joel 1754-1812 .... **NCLC 23**
See also DLB 37

Barnard, Mary (Ethel) 1909- .... **CLC 48**
See also CA 21-22; CAP 2

Barnes, Djuna 1892-1982 **CLC 3, 4, 8, 11, 29, 127; SSC 3**
See also CA 9-12R; 107; CANR 16, 55; DLB 4, 9, 45; MTCW 1, 2

Barnes, Julian (Patrick) 1946- .. **CLC 42; DAB**
See also CA 102; CANR 19, 54; DLB 194; DLBY 93; MTCW 1

Barnes, Peter 1931- .... **CLC 5, 56**
See also CA 65-68; CAAS 12; CANR 33, 34, 64; DLB 13; MTCW 1

Barnes, William 1801-1886 .... **NCLC 75**
See also DLB 32

Baroja (y Nessi), Pio 1872-1956 **TCLC 8; HLC 1**
See also CA 104

Baron, David
See Pinter, Harold

Baron Corvo
See Rolfe, Frederick (William Serafino Austin Lewis Mary)

Barondess, Sue K(aufman) 1926-1977 .... **CLC 8**
See also Kaufman, Sue
See also CA 1-4R; 69-72; CANR 1

Baron de Teive
See Pessoa, Fernando (Antonio Nogueira)

Baroness Von S.
See Zangwill, Israel

Barres, (Auguste-) Maurice 1862-1923 **TCLC 47**
See also CA 164; DLB 123

Barreto, Afonso Henrique de Lima
See Lima Barreto, Afonso Henrique de

Barrett, (Roger) Syd 1946- .... **CLC 35**

Barrett, William (Christopher) 1913-1992 **C L C 27**
See also CA 13-16R; 139; CANR 11, 67; INT CANR-11

Barrie, J(ames) M(atthew) 1860-1937 . **TCLC 2; DAB; DAM DRAM**
See also CA 104; 136; CANR 77; CDBLB 1890-1914; CLR 16; DA3; DLB 10, 141, 156; MAICYA; MTCW 1; SATA 100; YABC 1

Barrington, Michael
See Moorcock, Michael (John)

Barrol, Grady
See Bograd, Larry

Barry, Mike
See Malzberg, Barry N(athaniel)

Barry, Philip 1896-1949 .... **TCLC 11**
See also CA 109; DLB 7

Bart, Andre Schwarz
See Schwarz-Bart, Andre

Barth, John (Simmons) 1930- **CLC 1, 2, 3, 5, 7, 9, 10, 14, 27, 51, 89; DAM NOV; SSC 10**
See also AITN 1, 2; CA 1-4R; CABS 1; CANR 5, 23, 49, 64; DLB 2; MTCW 1

Barthelme, Donald 1931-1989 **CLC 1, 2, 3, 5, 6, 8, 13, 23, 46, 59, 115; DAM NOV; SSC 2**
See also CA 21-24R; 129; CANR 20, 58; DA3; DLB 2; DLBY 80, 89; MTCW 1, 2; SATA 7; SATA-Obit 62

Barthelme, Frederick 1943- .... **CLC 36, 117**
See also CA 114; 122; CANR 77; DLBY 85; INT 122

Barthes, Roland (Gerard) 1915-1980 **CLC 24, 83**
See also CA 130; 97-100; CANR 66; MTCW 1, 2

Barzun, Jacques (Martin) 1907- .... **CLC 51**
See also CA 61-64; CANR 22

Bashevis, Isaac
See Singer, Isaac Bashevis

Bashkirtseff, Marie 1859-1884 .... **NCLC 27**

Basho
See Matsuo Basho

Basil of Caesaria c. 330-379 .... **CMLC 35**

Bass, Kingsley B., Jr.
See Bullins, Ed

Bass, Rick 1958- .... **CLC 79**
See also CA 126; CANR 53; DLB 212

Bassani, Giorgio 1916- .... **CLC 9**
See also CA 65-68; CANR 33; DLB 128, 177; MTCW 1

Bastos, Augusto (Antonio) Roa
See Roa Bastos, Augusto (Antonio)

Bataille, Georges 1897-1962 .... **CLC 29**
See also CA 101; 89-92

Bates, H(erbert) E(rnest) 1905-1974 .... **CLC 46; DAB; DAM POP; SSC 10**
See also CA 93-96; 45-48; CANR 34; DA3; DLB 162, 191; MTCW 1, 2

Bauchart
See Camus, Albert

Baudelaire, Charles 1821-1867 **NCLC 6, 29, 55; DA; DAB; DAC; DAM MST, POET; PC 1; SSC 18; WLC**
See also DA3

Baudrillard, Jean 1929- .... **CLC 60**

Baum, L(yman) Frank 1856-1919 .... **TCLC 7**
See also CA 108; 133; CLR 15; DLB 22; JRDA; MAICYA; MTCW 1, 2; SATA 18, 100

Baum, Louis F.
See Baum, L(yman) Frank

Baumbach, Jonathan 1933- .... **CLC 6, 23**
See also CA 13-16R; CAAS 5; CANR 12, 66; DLBY 80; INT CANR-12; MTCW 1

Bausch, Richard (Carl) 1945- .... **CLC 51**
See also CA 101; CAAS 14; CANR 43, 61; DLB 130

Baxter, Charles (Morley) 1947- **CLC 45, 78; DAM POP**
See also CA 57-60; CANR 40, 64; DLB 130; MTCW 2

Baxter, George Owen
See Faust, Frederick (Schiller)

Baxter, James K(eir) 1926-1972 .... **CLC 14**
See also CA 77-80

Baxter, John
See Hunt, E(verette) Howard, (Jr.)

Bayer, Sylvia
See Glassco, John

Baynton, Barbara 1857-1929 .... **TCLC 57**

Beagle, Peter S(oyer) 1939- .... **CLC 7, 104**
See also CA 9-12R; CANR 4, 51, 73; DA3; DLBY 80; INT CANR-4; MTCW 1; SATA 60

Bean, Normal
See Burroughs, Edgar Rice

Beard, Charles A(ustin) 1874-1948 .... **TCLC 15**
See also CA 115; DLB 17; SATA 18

Beardsley, Aubrey 1872-1898 .... **NCLC 6**

Beattie, Ann 1947- **CLC 8, 13, 18, 40, 63; DAM NOV, POP; SSC 11**
See also BEST 90:2; CA 81-84; CANR 53, 73; DA3; DLBY 82; MTCW 1, 2

Beattie, James 1735-1803 .... **NCLC 25**
See also DLB 109

Beauchamp, Kathleen Mansfield 1888-1923
See Mansfield, Katherine
See also CA 104; 134; DA; DAC; DAM MST; DA3; MTCW 2

Beaumarchais, Pierre-Augustin Caron de 1732-1799 .... **DC 4**
See also DAM DRAM

Beaumont, Francis 1584(?)-1616 ...**LC 33; DC 6**
See also CDBLB Before 1660; DLB 58, 121

Beauvoir, Simone (Lucie Ernestine Marie Bertrand) de 1908-1986 **CLC 1, 2, 4, 8, 14, 31, 44, 50, 71, 124; DA; DAB; DAC; DAM MST, NOV; SSC 35; WLC**
See also CA 9-12R; 118; CANR 28, 61; DA3; DLB 72; DLBY 86; MTCW 1, 2

Becker, Carl (Lotus) 1873-1945 .... **TCLC 63**
See also CA 157; DLB 17

Becker, Jurek 1937-1997 .... **CLC 7, 19**
See also CA 85-88; 157; CANR 60; DLB 75

Becker, Walter 1950- .... **CLC 26**

Beckett, Samuel (Barclay) 1906-1989 **CLC 1, 2, 3, 4, 6, 9, 10, 11, 14, 18, 29, 57, 59, 83; DA; DAB; DAC; DAM DRAM, MST, NOV; SSC 16; WLC**
See also CA 5-8R; 130; CANR 33, 61; CDBLB 1945-1960; DA3; DLB 13, 15; DLBY 90; MTCW 1, 2

Beckford, William 1760-1844 .... **NCLC 16**
See also DLB 39

Beckman, Gunnel 1910- .... **CLC 26**
See also CA 33-36R; CANR 15; CLR 25;

TCLC 3
See also CA 104; 130; DLB 72
Bernard, April 1956- .... **CLC 59**
See also CA 131
Berne, Victoria
See Fisher, M(ary) F(rances) K(ennedy)
Bernhard, Thomas 1931-1989 ..... **CLC 3, 32, 61**
See also CA 85-88; 127; CANR 32, 57; DLB 85,
124; MTCW 1
Bernhardt, Sarah (Henriette Rosine) 1844-1923
TCLC 75
See also CA 157
Berriault, Gina 1926- ..... **CLC 54, 109; SSC 30**
See also CA 116; 129; CANR 66; DLB 130
Berrigan, Daniel 1921- .... **CLC 4**
See also CA 33-36R; CAAS 1; CANR 11, 43, 78;
DLB 5
Berrigan, Edmund Joseph Michael, Jr. 1934-1983
See Berrigan, Ted
See also CA 61-64; 110; CANR 14
Berrigan, Ted .... **CLC 37**
See also Berrigan, Edmund Joseph Michael, Jr.
See also DLB 5, 169
Berry, Charles Edward Anderson 1931-
See Berry, Chuck
See also CA 115
Berry, Chuck .... **CLC 17**
See also Berry, Charles Edward Anderson
Berry, Jonas
See Ashbery, John (Lawrence)
Berry, Wendell (Erdman) 1934- **CLC 4, 6, 8, 27,
46; DAM POET; PC 28**
See also AITN 1; CA 73-76; CANR 50, 73; DLB
5, 6; MTCW 1
Berryman, John 1914-1972 **CLC 1, 2, 3, 4, 6, 8, 10,
13, 25, 62; DAM POET**
See also CA 13-16; 33-36R; CABS 2; CANR 35;
CAP 1; CDALB 1941-1968; DLB 48; MTCW
1, 2
Bertolucci, Bernardo 1940- .... **CLC 16**
See also CA 106
Berton, Pierre (Francis Demarigny) 1920- **C L C
104**
See also CA 1-4R; CANR 2, 56; DLB 68; SATA
99
Bertrand, Aloysius 1807-1841 .... **NCLC 31**
Bertran de Born c. 1140-1215 .... **CMLC 5**
Besant, Annie (Wood) 1847-1933 .... **TCLC 9**
See also CA 105
Bessie, Alvah 1904-1985 .... **CLC 23**
See also CA 5-8R; 116; CANR 2, 80; DLB 26
Bethlen, T. D.
See Silverberg, Robert
Beti, Mongo .... **CLC 27; BLC 1; DAM MULT**
See also Biyidi, Alexandre
See also CANR 79
Betjeman, John 1906-1984 **CLC 2, 6, 10, 34, 43;
DAB; DAM MST, POET**
See also CA 9-12R; 112; CANR 33, 56; CDBLB
1945-1960; DA3; DLB 20; DLBY84; MTCW 1,
2
Bettelheim, Bruno 1903-1990 .... **CLC 79**
See also CA 81-84; 131; CANR 23, 61; DA3;
MTCW 1, 2
Betti, Ugo 1892-1953 .... **TCLC 5**
See also CA 104; 155
Betts, Doris (Waugh) 1932- .... **CLC 3, 6, 28**
See also CA 13-16R; CANR 9, 66, 77; DLBY 82;
INT CANR-9
Bevan, Alistair
See Roberts, Keith (John Kingston)
Bey, Pilaff
See Douglas, (George) Norman

Bialik, Chaim Nachman 1873-1934 .... **TCLC 25**
See also CA 170
Bickerstaff, Isaac
See Swift, Jonathan
Bidart, Frank 1939- .... **CLC 33**
See also CA 140
Bienek, Horst 1930- .... **CLC 7, 11**
See also CA 73-76; DLB 75
Bierce, Ambrose (Gwinett) 1842-1914(?)**TCLC 1,
7, 44; DA; DAC; DAM MST; SSC 9; WLC**
See also CA 104; 139; CANR 78; CDALB 1865-
1917; DA3; DLB 11, 12, 23, 71, 74, 186
Biggers, Earl Derr 1884-1933 .... **TCLC 65**
See also CA 108; 153
Billings, Josh
See Shaw, Henry Wheeler
Billington, (Lady) Rachel (Mary) 1942- **CLC 43**
See also AITN 2; CA 33-36R; CANR 44
Binyon, T(imothy) J(ohn) 1936- .... **CLC 34**
See also CA 111; CANR 28
Bioy Casares, Adolfo 1914-1999**CLC 4, 8, 13, 88;
DAM MULT; HLC 1; SSC 17**
See also CA 29-32R; 177; CANR 19, 43, 66; DLB
113; HW 1, 2; MTCW 1, 2
Bird, Cordwainer
See Ellison, Harlan (Jay)
Bird, Robert Montgomery 1806-1854 ... **NCLC 1**
See also DLB 202
Birkerts, Sven 1951- .... **CLC 116**
See also CA 128; 133; 176; CAAE 176; CAAS
29; INT 133
Birney, (Alfred) Earle 1904-1995**CLC 1, 4, 6, 11;
DAC; DAM MST, POET**
See also CA 1-4R; CANR 5, 20; DLB 88; MTCW
1
Biruni, al 973-1048(?) .... **CMLC 28**
Bishop, Elizabeth 1911-1979 **CLC 1, 4, 9, 13, 15,
32; DA; DAC; DAM MST, POET; PC 3**
See also CA 5-8R; 89-92; CABS 2; CANR 26, 61;
CDALB 1968-1988; DA3; DLB 5, 169; MTCW
1, 2; SATA-Obit 24
Bishop, John 1935- .... **CLC 10**
See also CA 105
Bissett, Bill 1939- .... **CLC 18; PC 14**
See also CA 69-72; CAAS 19; CANR 15; DLB
53; MTCW 1
Bissoondath, Neil (Devindra) 1955- .. **CLC 120;
DAC**
See also CA 136
Bitov, Andrei (Georgievich) 1937- .... **CLC 57**
See also CA 142
Biyidi, Alexandre 1932-
See Beti, Mongo
See also BW 1, 3; CA 114; 124; CANR 81; DA3;
MTCW 1, 2
Bjarme, Brynjolf
See Ibsen, Henrik (Johan)
Bjoernson, Bjoernstjerne (Martinius) 1832-1910
TCLC 7, 37
See also CA 104
Black, Robert
See Holdstock, Robert P.
Blackburn, Paul 1926-1971 .... **CLC 9, 43**
See also CA 81-84; 33-36R; CANR 34; DLB 16;
DLBY 81
Black Elk 1863-1950 ..... **TCLC 33; DAM MULT**
See also CA 144; MTCW 1; NNAL
Black Hobart
See Sanders, (James) Ed(ward)
Blacklin, Malcolm
See Chambers, Aidan
Blackmore, R(ichard) D(oddridge) 1825-1900
TCLC 27

See also CA 120; DLB 18
Blackmur, R(ichard) P(almer) 1904-1965**CLC 2,
24**
See also CA 11-12; 25-28R; CANR 71; CAP 1;
DLB 63
Black Tarantula
See Acker, Kathy
Blackwood, Algernon (Henry) 1869-1951**TCLC 5**
See also CA 105; 150; DLB 153, 156, 178
Blackwood, Caroline 1931-1996 .. **CLC 6, 9, 100**
See also CA 85-88; 151; CANR 32, 61, 65; DLB
14, 207; MTCW 1
Blade, Alexander
See Hamilton, Edmond; Silverberg, Robert
Blaga, Lucian 1895-1961 .... **CLC 75**
See also CA 157
Blair, Eric (Arthur) 1903-1950
See Orwell, George
See also CA 104; 132; DA; DAB; DAC; DAM
MST, NOV; DA3; MTCW 1, 2; SATA 29
Blair, Hugh 1718-1800 .... **NCLC 75**
Blais, Marie-Claire 1939- .. **CLC 2, 4, 6, 13, 22;
DAC; DAM MST**
See also CA 21-24R; CAAS 4; CANR 38, 75; DLB
53; MTCW 1, 2
Blaise, Clark 1940- .... **CLC 29**
See also AITN 2; CA 53-56; CAAS 3; CANR 5,
66; DLB 53
Blake, Fairley
See De Voto, Bernard (Augustine)
Blake, Nicholas
See Day Lewis, C(ecil)
See also DLB 77
Blake, William 1757-1827**NCLC 13, 37, 57; DA;
DAB; DAC; DAM MST, POET; PC 12; WLC**
See also CDBLB 1789-1832; CLR 52; DA3; DLB
93, 163; MAICYA; SATA 30
Blasco Ibanez, Vicente 1867-1928**TCLC 12; DAM
NOV**
See also CA 110; 131; CANR 81; DA3; HW 1, 2;
MTCW 1
Blatty, William Peter 1928- . **CLC 2; DAM POP**
See also CA 5-8R; CANR 9
Bleeck, Oliver
See Thomas, Ross (Elmore)
Blessing, Lee 1949- .... **CLC 54**
Blish, James (Benjamin) 1921-1975 ..... **CLC 14**
See also CA 1-4R; 57-60; CANR 3; DLB 8;
MTCW 1; SATA 66
Bliss, Reginald
See Wells, H(erbert) G(eorge)
Blixen, Karen (Christentze Dinesen) 1885-1962
See Dinesen, Isak
See also CA 25-28; CANR 22, 50; CAP 2; DA3;
MTCW 1, 2; SATA 44
Bloch, Robert (Albert) 1917-1994 .... **CLC 33**
See also AAYA 29; CA 5-8R, 179; 146; CAAE
179; CAAS 20; CANR 5, 78; DA3; DLB 44;
INT CANR-5; MTCW 1; SATA 12; SATA-
Obit 82
Blok, Alexander (Alexandrovich) 1880-1921
TCLC 5; PC 21
See also CA 104
Blom, Jan
See Breytenbach, Breyten
Bloom, Harold 1930- .... **CLC 24, 103**
See also CA 13-16R; CANR 39, 75; DLB 67;
MTCW 1
Bloomfield, Aurelius
See Bourne, Randolph S(illiman)
Blount, Roy (Alton), Jr. 1941- .... **CLC 38**
See also CA 53-56; CANR 10, 28, 61; INT CANR-
28; MTCW 1, 2

See also BW 1, 3; CA 85-88; 127; CANR 26; DA3;
DLB 48, 51, 63; MTCW 1, 2
Brown, Will
See Ainsworth, William Harrison
Brown, William Wells 1813-1884 **NCLC 2; BLC
1; DAM MULT; DC 1**
See also DLB 3, 50
Browne, (Clyde) Jackson 1948(?)- .... **CLC 21**
See also CA 120
Browning, Elizabeth Barrett 1806-1861 **NCLC 1,
16, 61, 66; DA; DAB; DAC; DAM MST,
POET; PC 6; WLC**
See also CDBLB 1832-1890; DA3; DLB 32, 199
Browning, Robert 1812-1889 **NCLC 19, 79; DA;
DAB; DAC; DAM MST, POET; PC 2; WLCS**
See also CDBLB 1832-1890; DA3; DLB 32, 163;
YABC 1
Browning, Tod 1882-1962 .... **CLC 16**
See also CA 141; 117
Brownson, Orestes Augustus 1803-1876 **NCLC
50**
See also DLB 1, 59, 73
Bruccoli, Matthew J(oseph) 1931- .... **CLC 34**
See also CA 9-12R; CANR 7; DLB 103
Bruce, Lenny .... **CLC 21**
See also Schneider, Leonard Alfred
Bruin, John
See Brutus, Dennis
Brulard, Henri
See Stendhal
Brulls, Christian
See Simenon, Georges (Jacques Christian)
Brunner, John (Kilian Houston) 1934-1995 **C L C
8, 10; DAM POP**
See also CA 1-4R; 149; CAAS 8; CANR 2, 37;
MTCW 1, 2
Bruno, Giordano 1548-1600 .... **LC 27**
Brutus, Dennis 1924-.... **CLC 43; BLC 1; DAM
MULT, POET; PC 24**
See also BW 2, 3; CA 49-52; CAAS 14; CANR 2,
27, 42, 81; DLB 117
Bryan, C(ourtlandt) D(ixon) B(arnes) 1936-**C L C
29**
See also CA 73-76; CANR 13, 68; DLB 185; INT
CANR-13
Bryan, Michael
See Moore, Brian
Bryan, William Jennings 1860-1925 .. **TCLC 99**
Bryant, William Cullen 1794-1878 **NCLC 6, 46;
DA; DAB; DAC; DAM MST, POET; PC 20**
See also CDALB 1640-1865; DLB 3, 43, 59, 189
Bryusov, Valery Yakovlevich 1873-1924 **TCLC 10**
See also CA 107; 155
Buchan, John 1875-1940 **TCLC 41; DAB; DAM
POP**
See also CA 108; 145; DLB 34, 70, 156; MTCW 1;
YABC 2
Buchanan, George 1506-1582 .... **LC 4**
See also DLB 152
Buchheim, Lothar-Guenther 1918- .... **CLC 6**
See also CA 85-88
Buchner, (Karl) Georg 1813-1837 ...... **NCLC 26**
Buchwald, Art(hur) 1925- .... **CLC 33**
See also AITN 1; CA 5-8R; CANR 21, 67; MTCW
1, 2; SATA 10
Buck, Pearl S(ydenstricker) 1892-1973 **CLC 7,
11, 18, 127; DA; DAB; DAC; DAM MST,
NOV**
See also AITN 1; CA 1-4R; 41-44R; CANR 1, 34;
CDALBS; DA3; DLB 9, 102; MTCW 1, 2;
SATA 1, 25
Buckler, Ernest 1908-1984 **CLC 13; DAC; DAM
MST**

See also CA 11-12; 114; CAP 1; DLB 68; SATA
47
Buckley, Vincent (Thomas) 1925-1988 . **CLC 57**
See also CA 101
Buckley, William F(rank), Jr. 1925- **CLC 7, 18,
37; DAM POP**
See also AITN 1; CA 1-4R; CANR 1, 24, 53; DA3;
DLB 137; DLBY 80; INT CANR-24; MTCW 1,
2
Buechner, (Carl) Frederick 1926-**CLC 2, 4, 6, 9;
DAM NOV**
See also CA 13-16R; CANR 11, 39, 64; DLBY 80;
INT CANR-11; MTCW 1, 2
Buell, John (Edward) 1927- .... **CLC 10**
See also CA 1-4R; CANR 71; DLB 53
Buero Vallejo, Antonio 1916- .... **CLC 15, 46**
See also CA 106; CANR 24, 49, 75; HW 1;
MTCW 1, 2
Bufalino, Gesualdo 1920(?)- .... **CLC 74**
See also DLB 196
Bugayev, Boris Nikolayevich 1880-1934**TCLC 7;
PC 11**
See Bely, Andrey
See also CA 104; 165; MTCW 1
Bukowski, Charles 1920-1994**CLC 2, 5, 9, 41, 82,
108; DAM NOV, POET; PC 18**
See also CA 17-20R; 144; CANR 40, 62; DA3;
DLB 5, 130, 169; MTCW 1, 2
Bulgakov, Mikhail (Afanas'evich) 1891-1940
TCLC 2, 16; DAM DRAM, NOV; SSC 18
See also CA 105; 152
Bulgya, Alexander Alexandrovich 1901-1956
TCLC 53
See Fadeyev, Alexander
See also CA 117; 181
Bullins, Ed 1935- ..... **CLC 1, 5, 7; BLC 1; DAM
DRAM, MULT; DC 6**
See also BW 2, 3; CA 49-52; CAAS 16; CANR
24, 46, 73; DLB 7, 38; MTCW 1, 2
Bulwer-Lytton, Edward (George Earle Lytton)
1803-1873 .... **NCLC 1, 45**
See also DLB 21
Bunin, Ivan Alexeyevich 1870-1953**TCLC 6; SSC
5**
See also CA 104
Bunting, Basil 1900-1985 **CLC 10, 39, 47; DAM
POET**
See also CA 53-56; 115; CANR 7; DLB 20
Bunuel, Luis 1900-1983**CLC 16, 80; DAM MULT;
HLC 1**
See also CA 101; 110; CANR 32, 77; HW 1
Bunyan, John 1628-1688 **LC 4; DA; DAB; DAC;
DAM MST; WLC**
See also CDBLB 1660-1789; DLB 39
Burckhardt, Jacob (Christoph) 1818-1897**NCLC
49**
Burford, Eleanor
See Hibbert, Eleanor Alice Burford
Burgess, Anthony**CLC 1, 2, 4, 5, 8, 10, 13, 15, 22,
40, 62, 81, 94; DAB**
See also Wilson, John (Anthony) Burgess
See also AAYA 25; AITN 1; CDBLB 1960 to
Present; DLB 14, 194; DLBY 98; MTCW 1
Burke, Edmund 1729(?)-1797**LC 7, 36; DA; DAB;
DAC; DAM MST; WLC**
See also DA3; DLB 104
Burke, Kenneth (Duva) 1897-1993 .... **CLC 2, 24**
See also CA 5-8R; 143; CANR 39, 74; DLB 45, 63;
MTCW 1, 2
Burke, Leda
See Garnett, David
Burke, Ralph
See Silverberg, Robert

Burke, Thomas 1886-1945 .... **TCLC 63**
See also CA 113; 155; DLB 197
Burney, Fanny 1752-1840 .... **NCLC 12, 54, 81**
See also DLB 39
Burns, Robert 1759-1796**LC 3, 29, 40; DA; DAB;
DAC; DAM MST, POET; PC 6; WLC**
See also CDBLB 1789-1832; DA3; DLB 109
Burns, Tex
See L'Amour, Louis (Dearborn)
Burnshaw, Stanley 1906- .... **CLC 3, 13, 44**
See also CA 9-12R; DLB 48; DLBY 97
Burr, Anne 1937- .... **CLC 6**
See also CA 25-28R
Burroughs, Edgar Rice 1875-1950 **TCLC 2, 32;
DAM NOV**
See also AAYA 11; CA 104; 132; DA3; DLB 8;
MTCW 1, 2; SATA 41
Burroughs, William S(eward) 1914-1997**CLC 1,
2, 5, 15, 22, 42, 75, 109; DA; DAB; DAC;
DAM MST, NOV, POP; WLC**
See also AITN 2; CA 9-12R; 160; CANR 20, 52;
DA3; DLB 2, 8, 16, 152; DLBY 81, 97; MTCW
1, 2
Burton, Sir Richard F(rancis) 1821-1890 **NCLC
42**
See also DLB 55, 166, 184
Busch, Frederick 1941- .... **CLC 7, 10, 18, 47**
See also CA 33-36R; CAAS 1; CANR 45, 73; DLB
6
Bush, Ronald 1946- .... **CLC 34**
See also CA 136
Bustos, F(rancisco)
See Borges, Jorge Luis
Bustos Domecq, H(onorio)
See Bioy Casares, Adolfo; Borges, Jorge Luis
Butler, Octavia E(stelle) 1947- ..... **CLC 38, 121;
BLCS; DAM MULT, POP**
See also AAYA 18; BW 2, 3; CA 73-76; CANR
12, 24, 38, 73; DA3; DLB 33; MTCW 1, 2;
SATA 84
Butler, Robert Olen (Jr.) 1945- ...**CLC 81; DAM
POP**
See also CA 112; CANR 66; DLB 173; INT 112;
MTCW 1
Butler, Samuel 1612-1680 .... **LC 16, 43**
See also DLB 101, 126
Butler, Samuel 1835-1902**TCLC 1, 33; DA; DAB;
DAC; DAM MST, NOV; WLC**
See also CA 143; CDBLB 1890-1914; DA3; DLB
18, 57, 174
Butler, Walter C.
See Faust, Frederick (Schiller)
Butor, Michel (Marie Francois) 1926- **CLC 1, 3,
8, 11, 15**
See also CA 9-12R; CANR 33, 66; DLB 83;
MTCW 1, 2
Butts, Mary 1892(?)-1937 .... **TCLC 77**
See also CA 148
Buzo, Alexander (John) 1944- .... **CLC 61**
See also CA 97-100; CANR 17, 39, 69
Buzzati, Dino 1906-1972 .... **CLC 36**
See also CA 160; 33-36R; DLB 177
Byars, Betsy (Cromer) 1928- .... **CLC 35**
See also AAYA 19; CA 33-36R; CANR 18, 36, 57;
CLR 1, 16; DLB 52; INT CANR-18; JRDA;
MAICYA; MTCW 1; SAAS 1; SATA 4, 46,
80; SATA-Essay 108
Byatt, A(ntonia) S(usan Drabble) 1936-**CLC 19,
65; DAM NOV, POP**
See also CA 13-16R; CANR 13, 33, 50, 75; DA3;
DLB 14, 194; MTCW 1, 2
Byrne, David 1952- .... **CLC 26**
See also CA 127

Chase, Mary (Coyle) 1907-1981 .... **DC 1**
See also CA 77-80; 105; SATA 17; SATA-Obit 29

Chase, Mary Ellen 1887-1973 .... **CLC 2**
See also CA 13-16; 41-44R; CAP 1; SATA 10

Chase, Nicholas
See Hyde, Anthony

Chateaubriand, Francois Rene de 1768-1848
NCLC 3
See also DLB 119

Chatterje, Sarat Chandra 1876-1936(?)
See Chatterji, Saratchandra
See also CA 109

Chatterji, Bankim Chandra 1838-1894**NCLC 19**

Chatterji, Saratchandra .... **TCLC 13**
See also Chatterje, Sarat Chandra

Chatterton, Thomas 1752-1770 . **LC 3, 54; DAM POET**
See also DLB 109

Chatwin, (Charles) Bruce 1940-1989**CLC 28, 57, 59; DAM POP**
See also AAYA 4; BEST 90:1; CA 85-88; 127;
DLB 194, 204

Chaucer, Daniel
See Ford, Ford Madox

Chaucer, Geoffrey 1340(?)-1400**LC 17; DA; DAB; DAC; DAM MST, POET; PC 19; WLCS**
See also CDBLB Before 1660; DA3; DLB 146

Chavez, Denise (Elia) 1948-
See also CA 131; CANR 56, 81; DAM MULT;
DLB 122; HLC 1; HW 1, 2; MTCW 2

Chaviaras, Strates 1935-
See Haviaras, Stratis
See also CA 105

Chayefsky, Paddy .... **CLC 23**
See also Chayefsky, Sidney
See also DLB 7, 44; DLBY 81

Chayefsky, Sidney 1923-1981
See Chayefsky, Paddy
See also CA 9-12R; 104; CANR 18; DAM DRAM

Chedid, Andree 1920- .... **CLC 47**
See also CA 145

Cheever, John 1912-1982**CLC 3, 7, 8, 11, 15, 25, 64; DA; DAB; DAC; DAM MST, NOV, POP; SSC 1; WLC**
See also CA 5-8R; 106; CABS 1; CANR 5, 27, 76;
CDALB 1941-1968; DA3; DLB 2, 102; DLBY
80, 82; INT CANR-5; MTCW 1, 2

Cheever, Susan 1943- .... **CLC 18, 48**
See also CA 103; CANR 27, 51; DLBY 82; INT
CANR-27

Chekhonte, Antosha
See Chekhov, Anton (Pavlovich)

Chekhov, Anton (Pavlovich) 1860-1904 **TCLC 3, 10, 31, 55, 96; DA; DAB; DAC; DAM DRAM, MST; DC 9; SSC 2, 28; WLC**
See also CA 104; 124; DA3; SATA 90

Chernyshevsky, Nikolay Gavrilovich 1828-1889
NCLC 1

Cherry, Carolyn Janice 1942-
See Cherryh, C. J.
See also CA 65-68; CANR 10

Cherryh, C. J. .... **CLC 35**
See also Cherry, Carolyn Janice
See also AAYA 24; DLBY 80; SATA 93

Chesnutt, Charles W(addell) 1858-1932**TCLC 5, 39; BLC 1; DAM MULT; SSC 7**
See also BW 1, 3; CA 106; 125; CANR 76; DLB
12, 50, 78; MTCW 1, 2

Chester, Alfred 1929(?)-1971 .... **CLC 49**
See also CA 33-36R; DLB 130

Chesterton, G(ilbert) K(eith) 1874-1936**TCLC 1, 6, 64; DAM NOV, POET; PC 28; SSC 1**
See also CA 104; 132; CANR 73; CDBLB 1914-

1945; DLB 10, 19, 34, 70, 98, 149, 178; MTCW
1, 2; SATA 27

Chiang, Pin-chin 1904-1986
See Ding Ling
See also CA 118

Ch'ien Chung-shu 1910- .... **CLC 22**
See also CA 130; CANR 73; MTCW 1, 2

Child, L. Maria
See Child, Lydia Maria

Child, Lydia Maria 1802-1880 .... **NCLC 6, 73**
See also DLB 1, 74; SATA 67

Child, Mrs.
See Child, Lydia Maria

Child, Philip 1898-1978 .... **CLC 19, 68**
See also CA 13-14; CAP 1; SATA 47

Childers, (Robert) Erskine 1870-1922 **TCLC 65**
See also CA 113; 153; DLB 70

Childress, Alice 1920-1994 **CLC 12, 15, 86, 96; BLC 1; DAM DRAM, MULT, NOV; DC 4**
See also AAYA 8; BW 2, 3; CA 45-48; 146; CANR
3, 27, 50, 74; CLR 14; DA3; DLB 7, 38; JRDA;
MAICYA; MTCW 1, 2; SATA 7, 48, 81

Chin, Frank (Chew, Jr.) 1940- .... **DC 7**
See also CA 33-36R; CANR 71; DAM MULT;
DLB 206

Chislett, (Margaret) Anne 1943- .... **CLC 34**
See also CA 151

Chitty, Thomas Willes 1926- .... **CLC 11**
See also Hinde, Thomas
See also CA 5-8R

Chivers, Thomas Holley 1809-1858 .... **NCLC 49**
See also DLB 3

Choi, Susan .... **CLC 119**

Chomette, Rene Lucien 1898-1981
See Clair, Rene
See also CA 103

Chopin, Kate**TCLC 5, 14; DA; DAB; SSC 8; WLCS**
See also Chopin, Katherine
See also CDALB 1865-1917; DLB 12, 78

Chopin, Katherine 1851-1904
See Chopin, Kate
See also CA 104; 122; DAC; DAM MST, NOV;
DA3

Chretien de Troyes c. 12th cent. - ..... **CMLC 10**
See also DLB 208

Christie
See Ichikawa, Kon

Christie, Agatha (Mary Clarissa) 1890-1976**CLC 1, 6, 8, 12, 39, 48, 110; DAB; DAC; DAM NOV**
See also AAYA 9; AITN 1, 2; CA 17-20R; 61-64;
CANR 10, 37; CDBLB 1914-1945; DA3; DLB
13, 77; MTCW 1, 2; SATA 36

Christie, (Ann) Philippa
See Pearce, Philippa
See also CA 5-8R; CANR 4

Christine de Pizan 1365(?)-1431(?) .... **LC 9**
See also DLB 208

Chubb, Elmer
See Masters, Edgar Lee

Chulkov, Mikhail Dmitrievich 1743-1792 . **LC 2**
See also DLB 150

Churchill, Caryl 1938- .... **CLC 31, 55; DC 5**
See also CA 102; CANR 22, 46; DLB 13; MTCW
1

Churchill, Charles 1731-1764 .... **LC 3**
See also DLB 109

Chute, Carolyn 1947- .... **CLC 39**
See also CA 123

Ciardi, John (Anthony) 1916-1986 . **CLC 10, 40, 44; DAM POET**
See also CA 5-8R; 118; CAAS 2; CANR 5, 33;
CLR 19; DLB 5; DLBY 86; INT CANR-5;

MAICYA; MTCW 1, 2; SAAS 26; SATA 1,
65; SATA-Obit 46

Cicero, Marcus Tullius 106B.C.-43B.C.**CMLC 3**
See also DLB 211

Cimino, Michael 1943- .... **CLC 16**
See also CA 105

Cioran, E(mil) M. 1911-1995 .... **CLC 64**
See also CA 25-28R; 149

Cisneros, Sandra 1954- ..... **CLC 69, 118; DAM MULT; HLC 1; SSC 32**
See also AAYA 9; CA 131; CANR 64; DA3; DLB
122, 152; HW 1, 2; MTCW 2

Cixous, Helene 1937- .... **CLC 92**
See also CA 126; CANR 55; DLB 83; MTCW 1, 2

Clair, Rene .... **CLC 20**
See also Chomette, Rene Lucien

Clampitt, Amy 1920-1994 .... **CLC 32; PC 19**
See also CA 110; 146; CANR 29, 79; DLB 105

Clancy, Thomas L., Jr. 1947-
See Clancy, Tom
See also CA 125; 131; CANR 62; DA3; INT 131;
MTCW 1, 2

Clancy, Tom .... **CLC 45, 112; DAM NOV, POP**
See also Clancy, Thomas L., Jr.
See also AAYA 9; BEST 89:1, 90:1; MTCW 2

Clare, John 1793-1864 ..... **NCLC 9; DAB; DAM POET; PC 23**
See also DLB 55, 96

Clarin
See Alas (y Urena), Leopoldo (Enrique Garcia)

Clark, Al C.
See Goines, Donald

Clark, (Robert) Brian 1932- .... **CLC 29**
See also CA 41-44R; CANR 67

Clark, Curt
See Westlake, Donald E(dwin)

Clark, Eleanor 1913-1996 .... **CLC 5, 19**
See also CA 9-12R; 151; CANR 41; DLB 6

Clark, J. P.
See Clark, John Pepper
See also DLB 117

Clark, John Pepper 1935-**CLC 38; BLC 1; DAM DRAM, MULT; DC 5**
See also Clark, J. P.
See also BW 1; CA 65-68; CANR 16, 72; MTCW
1

Clark, M. R.
See Clark, Mavis Thorpe

Clark, Mavis Thorpe 1909- .... **CLC 12**
See also CA 57-60; CANR 8, 37; CLR 30;
MAICYA; SAAS 5; SATA 8, 74

Clark, Walter Van Tilburg 1909-1971 .. **CLC 28**
See also CA 9-12R; 33-36R; CANR 63; DLB 9,
206; SATA 8

Clark Bekederemo, J(ohnson) P(epper)
See Clark, John Pepper

Clarke, Arthur C(harles) 1917-**CLC 1, 4, 13, 18, 35; DAM POP; SSC 3**
See also AAYA 4; CA 1-4R; CANR 2, 28, 55, 74;
DA3; JRDA; MAICYA; MTCW 1, 2; SATA
13, 70

Clarke, Austin 1896-1974**CLC 6, 9; DAM POET**
See also CA 29-32; 49-52; CAP 2; DLB 10, 20

Clarke, Austin C(hesterfield) 1934- **CLC 8, 53; BLC 1; DAC; DAM MULT**
See also BW 1; CA 25-28R; CAAS 16; CANR 14,
32, 68; DLB 53, 125

Clarke, Gillian 1937- .... **CLC 61**
See also CA 106; DLB 40

Clarke, Marcus (Andrew Hislop) 1846-1881
NCLC 19

Clarke, Shirley 1925- .... **CLC 16**

Clash, The

See also CA 85-88; CANR 28; MTCW 1

de Tolignac, Gaston
See Griffith, D(avid Lewelyn) W(ark)

Deutsch, Babette 1895-1982 .... **CLC 18**
See also CA 1-4R; 108; CANR 4, 79; DLB 45; SATA 1; SATA-Obit 33

Devenant, William 1606-1649 .... **LC 13**

Devkota, Laxmiprasad 1909-1959 .... **TCLC 23**
See also CA 123

De Voto, Bernard (Augustine) 1897-1955 **TCLC 29**
See also CA 113; 160; DLB 9

De Vries, Peter 1910-1993 CLC **1, 2, 3, 7, 10, 28, 46; DAM NOV**
See also CA 17-20R; 142; CANR 41; DLB 6; DLBY 82; MTCW 1, 2

Dewey, John 1859-1952 .... **TCLC 95**
See also CA 114; 170

Dexter, John
See Bradley, Marion Zimmer

Dexter, Martin
See Faust, Frederick (Schiller)

Dexter, Pete 1943- .... **CLC 34, 55; DAM POP**
See also BEST 89:2; CA 127; 131; INT 131; MTCW 1

Diamano, Silmang
See Senghor, Leopold Sedar

Diamond, Neil 1941- .... **CLC 30**
See also CA 108

Diaz del Castillo, Bernal 1496-1584 LC **31; HLCS 1**

di Bassetto, Corno
See Shaw, George Bernard

Dick, Philip K(indred) 1928-1982 CLC **10, 30, 72; DAM NOV, POP**
See also AAYA 24; CA 49-52; 106; CANR 2, 16; DA3; DLB 8; MTCW 1, 2

Dickens, Charles (John Huffam) 1812-1870 **NCLC 3, 8, 18, 26, 37, 50; DA; DAB; DAC; DAM MST, NOV; SSC 17; WLC**
See also AAYA 23; CDBLB 1832-1890; DA3; DLB 21, 55, 70, 159, 166; JRDA; MAICYA; SATA 15

Dickey, James (Lafayette) 1923-1997 CLC **1, 2, 4, 7, 10, 15, 47, 109; DAM NOV, POET, POP**
See also AITN 1, 2; CA 9-12R; 156; CABS 2; CANR 10, 48, 61; CDALB 1968-1988; DA3; DLB 5, 193; DLBD 7; DLBY 82, 93, 96, 97, 98; INT CANR-10; MTCW 1, 2

Dickey, William 1928-1994 .... **CLC 3, 28**
See also CA 9-12R; 145; CANR 24, 79; DLB 5

Dickinson, Charles 1951- .... **CLC 49**
See also CA 128

Dickinson, Emily (Elizabeth) 1830-1886 NCLC **21, 77; DA; DAB; DAC; DAM MST, POET; PC 1; WLC**
See also AAYA 22; CDALB 1865-1917; DA3; DLB 1; SATA 29

Dickinson, Peter (Malcolm) 1927- . **CLC 12, 35**
See also AAYA 9; CA 41-44R; CANR 31, 58; CLR 29; DLB 87, 161; JRDA; MAICYA; SATA 5, 62, 95

Dickson, Carr
See Carr, John Dickson

Dickson, Carter
See Carr, John Dickson

Diderot, Denis 1713-1784 .... **LC 26**

Didion, Joan 1934- CLC **1, 3, 8, 14, 32; DAM NOV**
See also AITN 1; CA 5-8R; CANR 14, 52, 76; CDALB 1968-1988; DA3; DLB 2, 173, 185; DLBY 81, 86; MTCW 1, 2

Dietrich, Robert
See Hunt, E(verette) Howard, (Jr.)

Difusa, Pati
See Almodovar, Pedro

Dillard, Annie 1945- CLC **9, 60, 115; DAM NOV**
See also AAYA 6; CA 49-52; CANR 3, 43, 62; DA3; DLBY 80; MTCW 1, 2; SATA 10

Dillard, R(ichard) H(enry) W(ilde) 1937- CLC **5**
See also CA 21-24R; CAAS 7; CANR 10; DLB 5

Dillon, Eilis 1920-1994 .... **CLC 17**
See also CA 9-12R; 182; 147; CAAE 182; CAAS 3; CANR 4, 38, 78; CLR 26; MAICYA; SATA 2, 74; SATA-Essay 105; SATA-Obit 83

Dimont, Penelope
See Mortimer, Penelope (Ruth)

Dinesen, Isak .... CLC **10, 29, 95; SSC 7**
See also Blixen, Karen (Christentze Dinesen)
See also MTCW 1

Ding Ling .... **CLC 68**
See also Chiang, Pin-chin

Diphusa, Patty
See Almodovar, Pedro

Disch, Thomas M(ichael) 1940- .... **CLC 7, 36**
See also AAYA 17; CA 21-24R; CAAS 4; CANR 17, 36, 54; CLR 18; DA3; DLB 8; MAICYA; MTCW 1, 2; SAAS 15; SATA 92

Disch, Tom
See Disch, Thomas M(ichael)

d'Isly, Georges
See Simenon, Georges (Jacques Christian)

Disraeli, Benjamin 1804-1881 . NCLC **2, 39, 79**
See also DLB 21, 55

Ditcum, Steve
See Crumb, R(obert)

Dixon, Paige
See Corcoran, Barbara

Dixon, Stephen 1936- .... CLC **52; SSC 16**
See also CA 89-92; CANR 17, 40, 54; DLB 130

Doak, Annie
See Dillard, Annie

Dobell, Sydney Thompson 1824-1874 .. **NCLC 43**
See also DLB 32

Doblin, Alfred .... **TCLC 13**
See also Doeblin, Alfred

Dobrolyubov, Nikolai Alexandrovich 1836-1861 **NCLC 5**

Dobson, Austin 1840-1921 .... **TCLC 79**
See also DLB 35; 144

Dobyns, Stephen 1941- .... **CLC 37**
See also CA 45-48; CANR 2, 18

Doctorow, E(dgar) L(aurence) 1931- . CLC **6, 11, 15, 18, 37, 44, 65, 113; DAM NOV, POP**
See also AAYA 22; AITN 2; BEST 89:3; CA 45-48; CANR 2, 33, 51, 76; CDALB 1968-1988; DA3; DLB 2, 28, 173; DLBY 80; MTCW 1, 2

Dodgson, Charles Lutwidge 1832-1898
See Carroll, Lewis
See also CLR 2; DA; DAB; DAC; DAM MST, NOV, POET; DA3; MAICYA; SATA ·100; YABC 2

Dodson, Owen (Vincent) 1914-1983 CLC **79; BLC 1; DAM MULT**
See also BW 1; CA 65-68; 110; CANR 24; DLB 76

Doeblin, Alfred 1878-1957 .... **TCLC 13**
See also Doblin, Alfred
See also CA 110; 141; DLB 66

Doerr, Harriet 1910- .... **CLC 34**
See also CA 117; 122; CANR 47; INT 122

Domecq, H(onorio Bustos)
See Bioy Casares, Adolfo

Domecq, H(onorio) Bustos
See Bioy Casares, Adolfo; Borges, Jorge Luis

Domini, Rey
See Lorde, Audre (Geraldine)

Dominique
See Proust, (Valentin-Louis-George-Eugene-) Marcel

Don, A
See Stephen, Sir Leslie

Donaldson, Stephen R. 1947- CLC **46; DAM POP**
See also CA 89-92; CANR 13, 55; INT CANR-13

Donleavy, J(ames) P(atrick) 1926- . CLC **1, 4, 6, 10, 45**
See also AITN 2; CA 9-12R; CANR 24, 49, 62, 80; DLB 6, 173; INT CANR-24; MTCW 1, 2

Donne, John 1572-1631 .... LC **10, 24; DA; DAB; DAC; DAM MST, POET; PC 1; WLC**
See also CDBLB Before 1660; DLB 121, 151

Donnell, David 1939(?)- .... **CLC 34**

Donoghue, P. S.
See Hunt, E(verette) Howard, (Jr.)

Donoso (Yanez), Jose 1924-1996 CLC **4, 8, 11, 32, 99; DAM MULT; HLC 1; SSC 34**
See also CA 81-84; 155; CANR 32, 73; DLB 113; HW 1, 2; MTCW 1, 2

Donovan, John 1928-1992 .... **CLC 35**
See also AAYA 20; CA 97-100; 137; CLR 3; MAICYA; SATA 72; SATA-Brief 29

Don Roberto
See Cunninghame Graham, R(obert) B(ontine)

Doolittle, Hilda 1886-1961 CLC **3, 8, 14, 31, 34, 73; DA; DAC; DAM MST, POET; PC 5; WLC**
See also H. D.
See also CA 97-100; CANR 35; DLB 4, 45; MTCW 1, 2

Dorfman, Ariel 1942- CLC **48, 77; DAM MULT; HLC 1**
See also CA 124; 130; CANR 67, 70; HW 1, 2; INT 130

Dorn, Edward (Merton) 1929- .... CLC **10, 18**
See also CA 93-96; CANR 42, 79; DLB 5; INT 93-96

Dorris, Michael (Anthony) 1945-1997 CLC **109; DAM MULT, NOV**
See also AAYA 20; BEST 90:1; CA 102; 157; CANR 19, 46, 75; CLR 58; DA3; DLB 175; MTCW 2; NNAL; SATA 75; SATA-Obit 94

Dorris, Michael A.
See Dorris, Michael (Anthony)

Dorsan, Luc
See Simenon, Georges (Jacques Christian)

Dorsange, Jean
See Simenon, Georges (Jacques Christian)

Dos Passos, John (Roderigo) 1896-1970 CLC **1, 4, 8, 11, 15, 25, 34, 82; DA; DAB; DAC; DAM MST, NOV; WLC**
See also CA 1-4R; 29-32R; CANR 3; CDALB 1929-1941; DA3; DLB 4, 9; DLBD 1, 15; DLBY 96; MTCW 1, 2

Dossage, Jean
See Simenon, Georges (Jacques Christian)

Dostoevsky, Fedor Mikhailovich 1821-1881 NCLC **2, 7, 21, 33, 43; DA; DAB; DAC; DAM MST, NOV; SSC 2, 33; WLC**
See also DA3

Doughty, Charles M(ontagu) 1843-1926 TCLC **27**
See also CA 115; 178; DLB 19, 57, 174

Douglas, Ellen .... **CLC 73**
See also Haxton, Josephine Ayres; Williamson, Ellen Douglas

Douglas, Gavin 1475(?)-1522 .... **LC 20**
See also DLB 132

Douglas, George
See Brown, George Douglas

Douglas, Keith (Castellain) 1920-1944 **TCLC 40**
See also CA 160; DLB 27

Douglas, Leonard

See Bradbury, Ray (Douglas)
Douglas, Michael
    See Crichton, (John) Michael
Douglas, (George) Norman 1868-1952 **TCLC 68**
    See also CA 119; 157; DLB 34, 195
Douglas, William
    See Brown, George Douglas
Douglass, Frederick 1817(?)-1895 . **NCLC 7, 55;**
    BLC 1; DA; DAC; DAM MST, MULT; WLC
    See also CDALB 1640-1865; DA3; DLB 1, 43, 50,
    79; SATA 29
Dourado, (Waldomiro Freitas) Autran 1926-**CLC**
    23, 60
    See also CA 25-28R; 179; CANR 34, 81; DLB 145;
    HW 2
Dourado, Waldomiro Autran 1926-
    See Dourado, (Waldomiro Freitas) Autran
    See also CA 179
Dove, Rita (Frances) 1952-.**CLC 50, 81; BLCS;**
    DAM MULT, POET; PC 6
    See also BW 2; CA 109; CAAS 19; CANR 27, 42,
    68, 76; CDALBS; DA3; DLB 120; MTCW 1
Doveglion
    See Villa, Jose Garcia
Dowell, Coleman 1925-1985 .... **CLC 60**
    See also CA 25-28R; 117; CANR 10; DLB 130
Dowson, Ernest (Christopher) 1867-1900**TCLC 4**
    See also CA 105; 150; DLB 19, 135
Doyle, A. Conan
    See Doyle, Arthur Conan
Doyle, Arthur Conan 1859-1930 .. **TCLC 7; DA;**
    DAB; DAC; DAM MST, NOV; SSC 12; WLC
    See also AAYA 14; CA 104; 122; CDBLB 1890-
    1914; DA3; DLB 18, 70, 156, 178; MTCW 1, 2;
    SATA 24
Doyle, Conan
    See Doyle, Arthur Conan
Doyle, John
    See Graves, Robert (von Ranke)
Doyle, Roddy 1958(?)- .... **CLC 81**
    See also AAYA 14; CA 143; CANR 73; DA3;
    DLB 194
Doyle, Sir A. Conan
    See Doyle, Arthur Conan
Doyle, Sir Arthur Conan
    See Doyle, Arthur Conan
Dr. A
    See Asimov, Isaac; Silverstein, Alvin
Drabble, Margaret 1939- **CLC 2, 3, 5, 8, 10, 22,**
    53; DAB; DAC; DAM MST, NOV, POP
    See also CA 13-16R; CANR 18, 35, 63; CDBLB
    1960 to Present; DA3; DLB 14, 155; MTCW 1,
    2; SATA 48
Drapier, M. B.
    See Swift, Jonathan
Drayham, James
    See Mencken, H(enry) L(ouis)
Drayton, Michael 1563-1631 **LC 8; DAM POET**
    See also DLB 121
Dreadstone, Carl
    See Campbell, (John) Ramsey
Dreiser, Theodore (Herman Albert) 1871-1945
    TCLC 10, 18, 35, 83; DA; DAC; DAM MST,
    NOV; SSC 30; WLC
    See also CA 106; 132; CDALB 1865-1917; DA3;
    DLB 9, 12, 102, 137; DLBD 1; MTCW 1, 2
Drexler, Rosalyn 1926- ....**CLC 2, 6**
    See also CA 81-84; CANR 68
Dreyer, Carl Theodor 1889-1968 .... **CLC 16**
    See also CA 116
Drieu la Rochelle, Pierre(-Eugene) 1893-1945
    TCLC 21
    See also CA 117; DLB 72

Drinkwater, John 1882-1937 .... **TCLC 57**
    See also CA 109; 149; DLB 10, 19, 149
Drop Shot
    See Cable, George Washington
Droste-Hulshoff, Annette Freiin von 1797-1848
    NCLC 3
    See also DLB 133
Drummond, Walter
    See Silverberg, Robert
Drummond, William Henry 1854-1907 **TCLC 25**
    See also CA 160; DLB 92
Drummond de Andrade, Carlos 1902-1987 . **C L C**
    18
    See also Andrade, Carlos Drummond de
    See also CA 132; 123
Drury, Allen (Stuart) 1918-1998 .... **CLC 37**
    See also CA 57-60; 170; CANR 18, 52; INT
    CANR-18
Dryden, John 1631-1700 .... **LC 3, 21; DA; DAB;**
    DAC; DAM DRAM, MST, POET; DC 3; PC
    25; WLC
    See also CDBLB 1660-1789; DLB 80, 101, 131
Duberman, Martin (Bauml) 1930- .... **CLC 8**
    See also CA 1-4R; CANR 2, 63
Dubie, Norman (Evans) 1945- .... **CLC 36**
    See also CA 69-72; CANR 12; DLB 120
Du Bois, W(illiam) E(dward) B(urghardt) 1868-
    1963**CLC 1, 2, 13, 64, 96; BLC 1; DA; DAC;**
    DAM MST, MULT, NOV; WLC
    See also BW 1, 3; CA 85-88; CANR 34, 82;
    CDALB 1865-1917; DA3; DLB 47, 50, 91;
    MTCW 1, 2; SATA 42
Dubus, Andre 1936-1999**CLC 13, 36, 97; SSC 15**
    See also CA 21-24R; 177; CANR 17; DLB 130;
    INT CANR-17
Duca Minimo
    See D'Annunzio, Gabriele
Ducharme, Rejean 1941- .... **CLC 74**
    See also CA 165; DLB 60
Duclos, Charles Pinot 1704-1772 .... **LC 1**
Dudek, Louis 1918- ....**CLC 11, 19**
    See also CA 45-48; CAAS 14; CANR 1; DLB 88
Duerrenmatt, Friedrich 1921-1990 . **CLC 1, 4, 8,**
    11, 15, 43, 102; DAM DRAM
    See also CA 17-20R; CANR 33; DLB 69, 124;
    MTCW 1, 2
Duffy, Bruce 1953(?)- .... **CLC 50**
    See also CA 172
Duffy, Maureen 1933- .... **CLC 37**
    See also CA 25-28R; CANR 33, 68; DLB 14;
    MTCW 1
Dugan, Alan 1923- ....**CLC 2, 6**
    See also CA 81-84; DLB 5
du Gard, Roger Martin
    See Martin du Gard, Roger
Duhamel, Georges 1884-1966 .... **CLC 8**
    See also CA 81-84; 25-28R; CANR 35; DLB 65;
    MTCW 1
Dujardin, Edouard (Emile Louis) 1861-1949
    TCLC 13
    See also CA 109; DLB 123
Dulles, John Foster 1888-1959 .... **TCLC 72**
    See also CA 115; 149
Dumas, Alexandre (pere)
    See Dumas, Alexandre (Davy de la Pailleterie)
Dumas, Alexandre (Davy de la Pailleterie) 1802-
    1870 **NCLC 11, 71; DA; DAB; DAC; DAM**
    MST, NOV; WLC
    See also DA3; DLB 119, 192; SATA 18
Dumas, Alexandre (fils) 1824-1895**NCLC 71; DC**
    1
    See also AAYA 22; DLB 192
Dumas, Claudine

See Malzberg, Barry N(athaniel)
Dumas, Henry L. 1934-1968 .... **CLC 6, 62**
    See also BW 1; CA 85-88; DLB 41
du Maurier, Daphne 1907-1989 .. **CLC 6, 11, 59;**
    DAB; DAC; DAM MST, POP; SSC 18
    See also CA 5-8R; 128; CANR 6, 55; DA3; DLB
    191; MTCW 1, 2; SATA 27; SATA-Obit 60
Dunbar, Paul Laurence 1872-1906 . **TCLC 2, 12;**
    BLC 1; DA; DAC; DAM MST, MULT, POET;
    PC 5; SSC 8; WLC
    See also BW 1, 3; CA 104; 124; CANR 79; CDALB
    1865-1917; DA3; DLB 50, 54, 78; SATA 34
Dunbar, William 1460(?)-1530(?) .... **LC 20**
    See also DLB 132, 146
Duncan, Dora Angela
    See Duncan, Isadora
Duncan, Isadora 1877(?)-1927 .... **TCLC 68**
    See also CA 118; 149
Duncan, Lois 1934- .... **CLC 26**
    See also AAYA 4; CA 1-4R; CANR 2, 23, 36;
    CLR 29; JRDA; MAICYA; SAAS 2; SATA 1,
    36, 75
Duncan, Robert (Edward) 1919-1988**CLC 1, 2, 4,**
    7, 15, 41, 55; DAM POET; PC 2
    See also CA 9-12R; 124; CANR 28, 62; DLB 5, 16,
    193; MTCW 1, 2
Duncan, Sara Jeannette 1861-1922 .... **TCLC 60**
    See also CA 157; DLB 92
Dunlap, William 1766-1839 .... **NCLC 2**
    See also DLB 30, 37, 59
Dunn, Douglas (Eaglesham) 1942- ... **CLC 6, 40**
    See also CA 45-48; CANR 2, 33; DLB 40; MTCW
    1
Dunn, Katherine (Karen) 1945- .... **CLC 71**
    See also CA 33-36R; CANR 72; MTCW 1
Dunn, Stephen 1939- .... **CLC 36**
    See also CA 33-36R; CANR 12, 48, 53; DLB 105
Dunne, Finley Peter 1867-1936 .... **TCLC 28**
    See also CA 108; 178; DLB 11, 23
Dunne, John Gregory 1932- .... **CLC 28**
    See also CA 25-28R; CANR 14, 50; DLBY 80
Dunsany, Edward John Moreton Drax Plunkett
    1878-1957
    See Dunsany, Lord
    See also CA 104; 148; DLB 10; MTCW 1
Dunsany, Lord .... **TCLC 2, 59**
    See also Dunsany, Edward John Moreton Drax
    Plunkett
    See also DLB 77, 153, 156
du Perry, Jean
    See Simenon, Georges (Jacques Christian)
Durang, Christopher (Ferdinand) 1949-**CLC 27,**
    38
    See also CA 105; CANR 50, 76; MTCW 1
Duras, Marguerite 1914-1996**CLC 3, 6, 11, 20, 34,**
    40, 68, 100
    See also CA 25-28R; 151; CANR 50; DLB 83;
    MTCW 1, 2
Durban, (Rosa) Pam 1947- .... **CLC 39**
    See also CA 123
Durcan, Paul 1944- ... **CLC 43, 70; DAM POET**
    See also CA 134
Durkheim, Emile 1858-1917 .... **TCLC 55**
Durrell, Lawrence (George) 1912-1990**CLC 1, 4,**
    6, 8, 13, 27, 41; DAM NOV
    See also CA 9-12R; 132; CANR 40, 77; CDBLB
    1945-1960; DLB 15, 27, 204; DLBY 90; MTCW
    1, 2
Durrenmatt, Friedrich
    See Duerrenmatt, Friedrich
Dutt, Toru 1856-1877 .... **NCLC 29**
Dwight, Timothy 1752-1817 .... **NCLC 13**
    See also DLB 37

See Betjeman, John

Fassbinder, Rainer Werner 1946-1982 . **CLC 20**
See also CA 93-96; 106; CANR 31

Fast, Howard (Melvin) 1914-**CLC 23; DAM NOV**
See also AAYA 16; CA 1-4R, 181; CAAE 181;
CAAS 18; CANR 1, 33, 54, 75; DLB 9; INT
CANR-33; MTCW 1; SATA 7; SATA-Essay
107

Faulcon, Robert
See Holdstock, Robert P.

Faulkner, William (Cuthbert) 1897-1962**CLC 1,
3, 6, 8, 9, 11, 14, 18, 28, 52, 68; DA; DAB;
DAC; DAM MST, NOV; SSC 1, 35; WLC**
See also AAYA 7; CA 81-84; CANR 33; CDALB
1929-1941; DA3; DLB 9, 11, 44, 102; DLBD 2;
DLBY 86, 97; MTCW 1, 2

Fauset, Jessie Redmon 1884(?)-1961**CLC 19, 54;
BLC 2; DAM MULT**
See also BW 1; CA 109; CANR 83; DLB 51

Faust, Frederick (Schiller) 1892-1944(?) **TCLC
49; DAM POP**
See also CA 108; 152

Faust, Irvin 1924- .... **CLC 8**
See also CA 33-36R; CANR 28, 67; DLB 2, 28;
DLBY 80

Fawkes, Guy
See Benchley, Robert (Charles)

Fearing, Kenneth (Flexner) 1902-1961 . **CLC 51**
See also CA 93-96; CANR 59; DLB 9

Fecamps, Elise
See Creasey, John

Federman, Raymond 1928- .... **CLC 6, 47**
See also CA 17-20R; CAAS 8; CANR 10, 43, 83;
DLBY 80

Federspiel, J(uerg) F. 1931- .... **CLC 42**
See also CA 146

Feiffer, Jules (Ralph) 1929- **CLC 2, 8, 64; DAM
DRAM**
See also AAYA 3; CA 17-20R; CANR 30, 59; DLB
7, 44; INT CANR-30; MTCW 1; SATA 8, 61,
111

Feige, Hermann Albert Otto Maximilian
See Traven, B.

Feinberg, David B. 1956-1994 .... **CLC 59**
See also CA 135; 147

Feinstein, Elaine 1930-........................... **CLC 36**
See also CA 69-72; CAAS 1; CANR 31, 68; DLB
14, 40; MTCW 1

Feldman, Irving (Mordecai) 1928- .... **CLC 7**
See also CA 1-4R; CANR 1; DLB 169

Felix-Tchicaya, Gerald
See Tchicaya, Gerald Felix

Fellini, Federico 1920-1993 .... **CLC 16, 85**
See also CA 65-68; 143; CANR 33

Felsen, Henry Gregor 1916-1995 .... **CLC 17**
See also CA 1-4R; 180; CANR 1; SAAS 2; SATA
1

Fenno, Jack
See Calisher, Hortense

Fenollosa, Ernest (Francisco) 1853-1908**TCLC 91**

Fenton, James Martin 1949- .... **CLC 32**
See also CA 102; DLB 40

Ferber, Edna 1887-1968 .... **CLC 18, 93**
See also AITN 1; CA 5-8R; 25-28R; CANR 68;
DLB 9, 28, 86; MTCW 1, 2; SATA 7

Ferguson, Helen
See Kavan, Anna

Ferguson, Samuel 1810-1886 .... **NCLC 33**
See also DLB 32

Fergusson, Robert 1750-1774 .... **LC 29**
See also DLB 109

Ferling, Lawrence
See Ferlinghetti, Lawrence (Monsanto)

Ferlinghetti, Lawrence (Monsanto) 1919(?)-**CLC
2, 6, 10, 27, 111; DAM POET; PC 1**
See also CA 5-8R; CANR 3, 41, 73; CDALB 1941-
1968; DA3; DLB 5, 16; MTCW 1, 2

Fernandez, Vicente Garcia Huidobro
See Huidobro Fernandez, Vicente Garcia

Ferre, Rosario 1942- .... **SSC 36; HLCS 1**
See also CA 131; CANR 55, 81; DLB 145; HW 1,
2; MTCW 1

Ferrer, Gabriel (Francisco Victor) Miro
See Miro (Ferrer), Gabriel (Francisco Victor)

Ferrier, Susan (Edmonstone) 1782-1854**NCLC 8**
See also DLB 116

Ferrigno, Robert 1948(?)- .... **CLC 65**
See also CA 140

Ferron, Jacques 1921-1985 .... **CLC 94; DAC**
See also CA 117; 129; DLB 60

Feuchtwanger, Lion 1884-1958 .... **TCLC 3**
See also CA 104; DLB 66

Feuillet, Octave 1821-1890 .... **NCLC 45**
See also DLB 192

Feydeau, Georges (Leon Jules Marie) 1862-1921
TCLC 22; DAM DRAM
See also CA 113; 152; CANR 84; DLB 192

Fichte, Johann Gottlieb 1762-1814 ...... **NCLC 62**
See also DLB 90

Ficino, Marsilio 1433-1499 .... **LC 12**

Fiedeler, Hans
See Doeblin, Alfred

Fiedler, Leslie A(aron) 1917- ...... **CLC 4, 13, 24**
See also CA 9-12R; CANR 7, 63; DLB 28, 67;
MTCW 1, 2

Field, Andrew 1938- .... **CLC 44**
See also CA 97-100; CANR 25

Field, Eugene 1850-1895 .... **NCLC 3**
See also DLB 23, 42, 140; DLBD 13; MAICYA;
SATA 16

Field, Gans T.
See Wellman, Manly Wade

Field, Michael 1915-1971 .... **TCLC 43**
See also CA 29-32R

Field, Peter
See Hobson, Laura Z(ametkin)

Fielding, Henry 1707-1754 **LC 1, 46; DA; DAB;
DAC; DAM DRAM, MST, NOV; WLC**
See also CDBLB 1660-1789; DA3; DLB 39, 84,
101

Fielding, Sarah 1710-1768 .... **LC 1, 44**
See also DLB 39

Fields, W. C. 1880-1946 .... **TCLC 80**
See also DLB 44

Fierstein, Harvey (Forbes) 1954- **CLC 33; DAM
DRAM, POP**
See also CA 123; 129; DA3

Figes, Eva 1932- .... **CLC 31**
See also CA 53-56; CANR 4, 44, 83; DLB 14

Finch, Anne 1661-1720 .... **LC 3; PC 21**
See also DLB 95

Finch, Robert (Duer Claydon) 1900- .... **CLC 18**
See also CA 57-60; CANR 9, 24, 49; DLB 88

Findley, Timothy 1930-**CLC 27, 102; DAC; DAM
MST**
See also CA 25-28R; CANR 12, 42, 69; DLB 53

Fink, William
See Mencken, H(enry) L(ouis)

Firbank, Louis 1942-
See Reed, Lou
See also CA 117

Firbank, (Arthur Annesley) Ronald 1886-1926
TCLC 1
See also CA 104; 177; DLB 36

Fisher, Dorothy (Frances) Canfield 1879-1958
TCLC 87

See also CA 114; 136; CANR 80; DLB 9, 102;
MAICYA; YABC 1

Fisher, M(ary) F(rances) K(ennedy) 1908-1992
CLC 76, 87
See also CA 77-80; 138; CANR 44; MTCW 1

Fisher, Roy 1930- .... **CLC 25**
See also CA 81-84; CAAS 10; CANR 16; DLB 40

Fisher, Rudolph 1897-1934**TCLC 11; BLC 2; DAM
MULT; SSC 25**
See also BW 1, 3; CA 107; 124; CANR 80; DLB
51, 102

Fisher, Vardis (Alvero) 1895-1968 .... **CLC 7**
See also CA 5-8R; 25-28R; CANR 68; DLB 9, 206

Fiske, Tarleton
See Bloch, Robert (Albert)

Fitch, Clarke
See Sinclair, Upton (Beall)

Fitch, John IV
See Cormier, Robert (Edmund)

Fitzgerald, Captain Hugh
See Baum, L(yman) Frank

FitzGerald, Edward 1809-1883 .... **NCLC 9**
See also DLB 32

Fitzgerald, F(rancis) Scott (Key) 1896-1940
**TCLC 1, 6, 14, 28, 55; DA; DAB; DAC; DAM
MST, NOV; SSC 6, 31; WLC**
See also AAYA 24; AITN 1; CA 110; 123; CDALB
1917-1929; DA3; DLB 4, 9, 86; DLBD 1, 15, 16;
DLBY 81, 96; MTCW 1, 2

Fitzgerald, Penelope 1916- .... **CLC 19, 51, 61**
See also CA 85-88; CAAS 10; CANR 56, 86; DLB
14, 194; MTCW 2

Fitzgerald, Robert (Stuart) 1910-1985 .. **CLC 39**
See also CA 1-4R; 114; CANR 1; DLBY 80

FitzGerald, Robert D(avid) 1902-1987 ... **CLC 19**
See also CA 17-20R

Fitzgerald, Zelda (Sayre) 1900-1948 ... **TCLC 52**
See also CA 117; 126; DLBY 84

Flanagan, Thomas (James Bonner) 1923- .. **C L C
25, 52**
See also CA 108; CANR 55; DLBY 80; INT 108;
MTCW 1

Flaubert, Gustave 1821-1880**NCLC 2, 10, 19, 62,
66; DA; DAB; DAC; DAM MST, NOV; SSC
11; WLC**
See also DA3; DLB 119

Flecker, Herman Elroy
See Flecker, (Herman) James Elroy

Flecker, (Herman) James Elroy 1884-1915**TCLC
43**
See also CA 109; 150; DLB 10, 19

Fleming, Ian (Lancaster) 1908-1964 **CLC 3, 30;
DAM POP**
See also AAYA 26; CA 5-8R; CANR 59; CDBLB
1945-1960; DA3; DLB 87, 201; MTCW 1, 2;
SATA 9

Fleming, Thomas (James) 1927- .... **CLC 37**
See also CA 5-8R; CANR 10; INT CANR-10;
SATA 8

Fletcher, John 1579-1625 .... **LC 33; DC 6**
See also CDBLB Before 1660; DLB 58

Fletcher, John Gould 1886-1950 .... **TCLC 35**
See also CA 107; 167; DLB 4, 45

Fleur, Paul
See Pohl, Frederik

Floogle buckle, Al
See Spiegelman, Art

Flying Officer X
See Bates, H(erbert) E(rnest)

Fo, Dario 1926-**CLC 32, 109; DAM DRAM; DC 10**
See also CA 116; 128; CANR 68; DA3; DLBY 97;
MTCW 1, 2

Fogarty, Jonathan Titulescu Esq.

DAMMULT
See also BW 2, 3; CA 109; CANR 25, 53, 75; DA3; DLB 67; MTCW 1

Gautier, Theophile 1811-1872NCLC **1, 59; DAM POET; PC 18; SSC 20**
See also DLB 119

Gawsworth, John
See Bates, H(erbert) E(rnest)

Gay, John 1685-1732 .... LC **49; DAM DRAM**
See also DLB 84, 95

Gay, Oliver
See Gogarty, Oliver St. John

Gaye, Marvin (Penze) 1939-1984 .... CLC **26**
See also CA 112

Gebler, Carlo (Ernest) 1954- .... CLC **39**
See also CA 119; 133

Gee, Maggie (Mary) 1948- .... CLC **57**
See also CA 130; DLB 207

Gee, Maurice (Gough) 1931- .... CLC **29**
See also CA 97-100; CANR 67; CLR 56; SATA 46, 101

Gelbart, Larry (Simon) 1923- .... CLC **21, 61**
See also CA 73-76; CANR 45

Gelber, Jack 1932- .... CLC **1, 6, 14, 79**
See also CA 1-4R; CANR 2; DLB 7

Gellhorn, Martha (Ellis) 1908-1998 CLC **14, 60**
See also CA 77-80; 164; CANR 44; DLBY 82, 98

Genet, Jean 1910-1986CLC **1, 2, 5, 10, 14, 44, 46; DAM DRAM**
See also CA 13-16R; CANR 18; DA3; DLB 72; DLBY 86; MTCW 1, 2

Gent, Peter 1942- .... CLC **29**
See also AITN 1; CA 89-92; DLBY 82

Gentile, Giovanni 1875-1944 .... TCLC **96**
See also CA 119

Gentlewoman in New England, A
See Bradstreet, Anne

Gentlewoman in Those Parts, A
See Bradstreet, Anne

George, Jean Craighead 1919- .... CLC **35**
See also AAYA 8; CA 5-8R; CANR 25; CLR 1; DLB 52; JRDA; MAICYA; SATA 2, 68

George, Stefan (Anton) 1868-1933 .. TCLC **2, 14**
See also CA 104

Georges, Georges Martin
See Simenon, Georges (Jacques Christian)

Gerhardi, William Alexander
See Gerhardie, William Alexander

Gerhardie, William Alexander 1895-1977CLC **5**
See also CA 25-28R; 73-76; CANR 18; DLB 36

Gerstler, Amy 1956- .... CLC **70**
See also CA 146

Gertler, T. .... CLC **34**
See also CA 116; 121; INT 121

Ghalib .... NCLC **39, 78**
See also Ghalib, Hsadullah Khan

Ghalib, Hsadullah Khan 1797-1869
See Ghalib
See also DAM POET

Ghelderode, Michel de 1898-1962CLC **6, 11; DAM DRAM**
See also CA 85-88; CANR 40, 77

Ghiselin, Brewster 1903- .... CLC **23**
See also CA 13-16R; CAAS 10; CANR 13

Ghose, Aurabinda 1872-1950 .... TCLC **63**
See also CA 163

Ghose, Zulfikar 1935- .... CLC **42**
See also CA 65-68; CANR 67

Ghosh, Amitav 1956- .... CLC **44**
See also CA 147; CANR 80

Giacosa, Giuseppe 1847-1906 .... TCLC **7**
See also CA 104

Gibb, Lee

See Waterhouse, Keith (Spencer)

Gibbon, Lewis Grassic .... TCLC **4**
See also Mitchell, James Leslie

Gibbons, Kaye 1960- ..... CLC **50, 88; DAM POP**
See also CA 151; CANR 75; DA3; MTCW 1

Gibran, Kahlil 1883-1931TCLC **1, 9; DAM POET, POP; PC 9**
See also CA 104; 150; DA3; MTCW 2

Gibran, Khalil
See Gibran, Kahlil

Gibson, William 1914-CLC **23; DA; DAB; DAC; DAM DRAM, MST**
See also CA 9-12R; CANR 9, 42, 75; DLB 7; MTCW 1; SATA 66

Gibson, William (Ford) 1948-CLC **39, 63; DAM POP**
See also AAYA 12; CA 126; 133; CANR 52; DA3; MTCW 1

Gide, Andre (Paul Guillaume) 1869-1951TCLC **5, 12, 36; DA; DAB; DAC; DAM MST, NOV; SSC 13; WLC**
See also CA 104; 124; DA3; DLB 65; MTCW 1, 2

Gifford, Barry (Colby) 1946- .... CLC **34**
See also CA 65-68; CANR 9, 30, 40

Gilbert, Frank
See De Voto, Bernard (Augustine)

Gilbert, W(illiam) S(chwenck) 1836-1911 TCLC **3; DAM DRAM, POET**
See also CA 104; 173; SATA 36

Gilbreth, Frank B., Jr. 1911- .... CLC **17**
See also CA 9-12R; SATA 2

Gilchrist, Ellen 1935- . CLC **34, 48; DAM POP; SSC 14**
See also CA 113; 116; CANR 41, 61; DLB 130; MTCW 1, 2

Giles, Molly 1942- .... CLC **39**
See also CA 126

Gill, Eric 1882-1940 .... TCLC **85**

Gill, Patrick
See Creasey, John

Gilliam, Terry (Vance) 1940- .... CLC **21**
See also Monty Python
See also AAYA 19; CA 108; 113; CANR 35; INT 113

Gillian, Jerry
See Gilliam, Terry (Vance)

Gilliatt, Penelope (Ann Douglass) 1932-1993CLC **2, 10, 13, 53**
See also AITN 2; CA 13-16R; 141; CANR 49; DLB 14

Gilman, Charlotte (Anna) Perkins (Stetson) 1860-1935 .... TCLC **9, 37; SSC 13**
See also CA 106; 150; MTCW 1

Gilmour, David 1949- .... CLC **35**
See also CA 138, 147

Gilpin, William 1724-1804 .... NCLC **30**

Gilray, J. D.
See Mencken, H(enry) L(ouis)

Gilroy, Frank D(aniel) 1925- .... CLC **2**
See also CA 81-84; CANR 32, 64, 86; DLB 7

Gilstrap, John 1957(?)- .... CLC **99**
See also CA 160

Ginsberg, Allen 1926-1997 CLC **1, 2, 3, 4, 6, 13, 36, 69, 109; DA; DAB; DAC; DAM MST, POET; PC 4; WLC**
See also AITN 1; CA 1-4R; 157; CANR 2, 41, 63; CDALB 1941-1968; DA3; DLB 5, 16, 169; MTCW 1, 2

Ginzburg, Natalia 1916-1991 . CLC **5, 11, 54, 70**
See also CA 85-88; 135; CANR 33; DLB 177; MTCW 1, 2

Giono, Jean 1895-1970 .... CLC **4, 11**
See also CA 45-48; 29-32R; CANR 2, 35; DLB 72;

MTCW 1

Giovanni, Nikki 1943-CLC **2, 4, 19, 64, 117; BLC 2; DA; DAB; DAC; DAM MST, MULT, POET; PC 19; WLCS**
See also AAYA 22; AITN 1; BW 2, 3; CA 29-32R; CAAS 6; CANR 18, 41, 60; CDALBS; CLR 6; DA3; DLB 5, 41; INT CANR-18; MAICYA; MTCW 1, 2; SATA 24, 107

Giovene, Andrea 1904- .... CLC **7**
See also CA 85-88

Gippius, Zinaida (Nikolayevna) 1869-1945
See Hippius, Zinaida
See also CA 106

Giraudoux, (Hippolyte) Jean 1882-1944TCLC **2, 7; DAM DRAM**
See also CA 104; DLB 65

Gironella, Jose Maria 1917- .... CLC **11**
See also CA 101

Gissing, George (Robert) 1857-1903TCLC **3, 24, 47; SSC 37**
See also CA 105; 167; DLB 18, 135, 184

Giurlani, Aldo
See Palazzeschi, Aldo

Gladkov, Fyodor (Vasilyevich) 1883-1958TCLC **27**
See also CA 170

Glanville, Brian (Lester) 1931- .... CLC **6**
See also CA 5-8R; CAAS 9; CANR 3, 70; DLB 15, 139; SATA 42

Glasgow, Ellen (Anderson Gholson) 1873-1945 TCLC **2, 7; SSC 34**
See also CA 104; 164; DLB 9, 12; MTCW 2

Glaspell, Susan 1882(?)-1948 . TCLC **55; DC 10**
See also CA 110; 154; DLB 7, 9, 78; YABC 2

Glassco, John 1909-1981 .... CLC **9**
See also CA 13-16R; 102; CANR 15; DLB 68

Glasscock, Amnesia
See Steinbeck, John (Ernst)

Glasser, Ronald J. 1940(?)- .... CLC **37**

Glassman, Joyce
See Johnson, Joyce

Glendinning, Victoria 1937- .... CLC **50**
See also CA 120; 127; CANR 59; DLB 155

Glissant, Edouard 1928-CLC **10, 68; DAM MULT**
See also CA 153

Gloag, Julian 1930- .... CLC **40**
See also AITN 1; CA 65-68; CANR 10, 70

Glowacki, Aleksander
See Prus, Boleslaw

Gluck, Louise (Elisabeth) 1943-CLC **7, 22, 44, 81; DAM POET; PC 16**
See also CA 33-36R; CANR 40, 69; DA3; DLB 5; MTCW 2

Glyn, Elinor 1864-1943 .... TCLC **72**
See also DLB 153

Gobineau, Joseph Arthur (Comte) de 1816-1882 NCLC **17**
See also DLB 123

Godard, Jean-Luc 1930- .... CLC **20**
See also CA 93-96

Godden, (Margaret) Rumer 1907-1998 . CLC **53**
See also AAYA 6; CA 5-8R; 172; CANR 4, 27, 36, 55, 80; CLR 20; DLB 161; MAICYA; SAAS 12; SATA 3, 36; SATA-Obit 109

Godoy Alcayaga, Lucila 1889-1957
See Mistral, Gabriela
See also BW 2; CA 104; 131; CANR 81; DAM MULT; HW 1, 2; MTCW 1, 2

Godwin, Gail (Kathleen) 1937- CLC **5, 8, 22, 31, 69, 125; DAM POP**
See also CA 29-32R; CANR 15, 43, 69; DA3; DLB 6; INT CANR-15; MTCW 1, 2

Godwin, William 1756-1836 .... NCLC **14**
See also CDBLB 1789-1832; DLB 39, 104, 142,

DAC; DAM MST; PC 2; WLC
See also CDBLB 1660-1789; DA3; DLB 109
Grayson, David
See Baker, Ray Stannard
Grayson, Richard (A.) 1951- .... **CLC 38**
See also CA 85-88; CANR 14, 31, 57
Greeley, Andrew M(oran) 1928- . **CLC 28; DAM POP**
See also CA 5-8R; CAAS 7; CANR 7, 43, 69;
DA3; MTCW 1, 2
Green, Anna Katharine 1846-1935 ..... **TCLC 63**
See also CA 112; 159; DLB 202
Green, Brian
See Card, Orson Scott
Green, Hannah
See Greenberg, Joanne (Goldenberg)
Green, Hannah 1927(?)-1996 .... **CLC 3**
See also CA 73-76; CANR 59
Green, Henry 1905-1973 .... **CLC 2, 13, 97**
See also Yorke, Henry Vincent
See also CA 175; DLB 15
Green, Julian (Hartridge) 1900-1998
See Green, Julien
See also CA 21-24R; 169; CANR 33; DLB 4, 72;
MTCW 1
Green, Julien .... **CLC 3, 11, 77**
See also Green, Julian (Hartridge)
See also MTCW 2
Green, Paul (Eliot) 1894-1981 ..... **CLC 25; DAM DRAM**
See also AITN 1; CA 5-8R; 103; CANR 3; DLB 7,
9; DLBY 81
Greenberg, Ivan 1908-1973
See Rahv, Philip
See also CA 85-88
Greenberg, Joanne (Goldenberg) 1932- . **CLC 7, 30**
See also AAYA 12; CA 5-8R; CANR 14, 32, 69;
SATA 25
Greenberg, Richard 1959(?)- .... **CLC 57**
See also CA 138
Greene, Bette 1934- .... **CLC 30**
See also AAYA 7; CA 53-56; CANR 4; CLR 2;
JRDA; MAICYA; SAAS 16; SATA 8, 102
Greene, Gael .... **CLC 8**
See also CA 13-16R; CANR 10
Greene, Graham (Henry) 1904-1991 CLC **1, 3, 6,
9, 14, 18, 27, 37, 70, 72, 125; DA; DAB; DAC;
DAM MST, NOV; SSC 29; WLC**
See also AITN 2; CA 13-16R; 133; CANR 35, 61;
CDBLB 1945-1960; DA3; DLB 13, 15, 77, 100,
162, 201, 204; DLBY 91; MTCW 1, 2; SATA 20
Greene, Robert 1558-1592 .... **LC 41**
See also DLB 62, 167
Greer, Richard
See Silverberg, Robert
Gregor, Arthur 1923- .... **CLC 9**
See also CA 25-28R; CAAS 10; CANR 11; SATA
36
Gregor, Lee
See Pohl, Frederik
Gregory, Isabella Augusta (Persse) 1852-1932
TCLC 1
See also CA 104; DLB 10
Gregory, J. Dennis
See Williams, John A(lfred)
Grendon, Stephen
See Derleth, August (William)
Grenville, Kate 1950- .... **CLC 61**
See also CA 118; CANR 53
Grenville, Pelham
See Wodehouse, P(elham) G(renville)
Greve, Felix Paul (Berthold Friedrich) 1879-1948

See Grove, Frederick Philip
See also CA 104; 141, 175; CANR 79; DAC; DAM
MST
Grey, Zane 1872-1939 .... **TCLC 6; DAM POP**
See also CA 104; 132; DA3; DLB 212; MTCW 1,
2
Grieg, (Johan) Nordahl (Brun) 1902-1943 **T C L C
10**
See also CA 107
Grieve, C(hristopher) M(urray) 1892-1978 **C L C
11, 19; DAM POET**
See also MacDiarmid, Hugh; Pteleon
See also CA 5-8R; 85-88; CANR 33; MTCW 1
Griffin, Gerald 1803-1840 .... **NCLC 7**
See also DLB 159
Griffin, John Howard 1920-1980 .... **CLC 68**
See also AITN 1; CA 1-4R; 101; CANR 2
Griffin, Peter 1942- .... **CLC 39**
See also CA 136
Griffith, D(avid Lewelyn) W(ark) 1875(?)-1948
TCLC 68
See also CA 119; 150; CANR 80
Griffith, Lawrence
See Griffith, D(avid Lewelyn) W(ark)
Griffiths, Trevor 1935- .... **CLC 13, 52**
See also CA 97-100; CANR 45; DLB 13
Griggs, Sutton Elbert 1872-1930(?) .... **TCLC 77**
See also CA 123; DLB 50
Grigson, Geoffrey (Edward Harvey) 1905-1985
CLC 7, 39
See also CA 25-28R; 118; CANR 20, 33; DLB 27;
MTCW 1, 2
Grillparzer, Franz 1791-1872 . **NCLC 1; SSC 37**
See also DLB 133
Grimble, Reverend Charles James
See Eliot, T(homas) S(tearns)
Grimke, Charlotte L(ottie) Forten 1837(?)-1914
See Forten, Charlotte L.
See also BW 1; CA 117; 124; DAM MULT, POET
Grimm, Jacob Ludwig Karl 1785-1863 **NCLC 3,
77; SSC 36**
See also DLB 90; MAICYA; SATA 22
Grimm, Wilhelm Karl 1786-1859 ..**NCLC 3, 77;
SSC 36**
See also DLB 90; MAICYA; SATA 22
Grimmelshausen, Johann Jakob Christoffel von
1621-1676 .... **LC 6**
See also DLB 168
Grindel, Eugene 1895-1952
See Eluard, Paul
See also CA 104
Grisham, John 1955- .... **CLC 84; DAM POP**
See also AAYA 14; CA 138; CANR 47, 69; DA3;
MTCW 2
Grossman, David 1954- .... **CLC 67**
See also CA 138
Grossman, Vasily (Semenovich) 1905-1964 **C L C
41**
See also CA 124; 130; MTCW 1
Grove, Frederick Philip .... **TCLC 4**
See also Greve, Felix Paul (Berthold Friedrich)
See also DLB 92
Grubb
See Crumb, R(obert)
Grumbach, Doris (Isaac) 1918- . **CLC 13, 22, 64**
See also CA 5-8R; CAAS 2; CANR 9, 42, 70; INT
CANR-9; MTCW 2
Grundtvig, Nicolai Frederik Severin 1783-1872
NCLC 1
Grunge
See Crumb, R(obert)
Grunwald, Lisa 1959- .... **CLC 44**
See also CA 120

Guare, John 1938-**CLC 8, 14, 29, 67; DAM DRAM**
See also CA 73-76; CANR 21, 69; DLB 7; MTCW
1, 2
Gudjonsson, Halldor Kiljan 1902-1998
See Laxness, Halldor
See also CA 103; 164
Guenter, Erich
See Eich, Guenter
Guest, Barbara 1920- .... **CLC 34**
See also CA 25-28R; CANR 11, 44, 84; DLB 5,
193
Guest, Edgar A(lbert) 1881-1959 .... **TCLC 95**
See also CA 112; 168
Guest, Judith (Ann) 1936-**CLC 8, 30; DAM NOV,
POP**
See also AAYA 7; CA 77-80; CANR 15, 75; DA3;
INT CANR-15; MTCW 1, 2
Guevara, Che .... **CLC 87; HLC 1**
See also Guevara (Serna), Ernesto
Guevara (Serna), Ernesto 1928-1967 ... **CLC 87;
DAM MULT; HLC 1**
See also Guevara, Che
See also CA 127; 111; CANR 56; HW 1
Guicciardini, Francesco 1483-1540 .... **LC 49**
Guild, Nicholas M. 1944- .... **CLC 33**
See also CA 93-96
Guillemin, Jacques
See Sartre, Jean-Paul
Guillen, Jorge 1893-1984 **CLC 11; DAM MULT,
POET; HLCS 1**
See also CA 89-92; 112; DLB 108; HW 1
Guillen, Nicolas (Cristobal) 1902-1989 **CLC 48,
79; BLC 2; DAM MST, MULT, POET; HLC
1; PC 23**
See also BW 2; CA 116; 125; 129; CANR 84; HW
1
Guillevic, (Eugene) 1907- .... **CLC 33**
See also CA 93-96
Guillois
See Desnos, Robert
Guillois, Valentin
See Desnos, Robert
Guimaraes Rosa, Joao 1908-1967
See also CA 175; HLCS 2
Guiney, Louise Imogen 1861-1920 ...... **TCLC 41**
See also CA 160; DLB 54
Guiraldes, Ricardo (Guillermo) 1886-1927**TCLC
39**
See also CA 131; HW 1; MTCW 1
Gumilev, Nikolai (Stepanovich) 1886-1921**TCLC
60**
See also CA 165
Gunesekera, Romesh 1954- .... **CLC 91**
See also CA 159
Gunn, Bill .... **CLC 5**
See also Gunn, William Harrison
See also DLB 38
Gunn, Thom(son William) 1929-**CLC 3, 6, 18, 32,
81; DAM POET; PC 26**
See also CA 17-20R; CANR 9, 33; CDBLB 1960
to Present; DLB 27; INT CANR-33; MTCW 1
Gunn, William Harrison 1934(?)-1989
See Gunn, Bill
See also AITN 1; BW 1, 3; CA 13-16R; 128;
CANR 12, 25, 76
Gunnars, Kristjana 1948- .... **CLC 69**
See also CA 113; DLB 60
Gurdjieff, G(eorgei) I(vanovich) 1877(?)-1949
TCLC 71
See also CA 157
Gurganus, Allan 1947- .... **CLC 70; DAM POP**
See also BEST 90:1; CA 135
Gurney, A(lbert) R(amsdell), Jr. 1930- **CLC 32,**

50, 54; DAM DRAM
See also CA 77-80; CANR 32, 64
Gurney, Ivor (Bertie) 1890-1937 .... **TCLC 33**
See also CA 167
Gurney, Peter
See Gurney, A(lbert) R(amsdell), Jr.
Guro, Elena 1877-1913 .... **TCLC 56**
Gustafson, James M(oody) 1925- .... **CLC 100**
See also CA 25-28R; CANR 37
Gustafson, Ralph (Barker) 1909- .... **CLC 36**
See also CA 21-24R; CANR 8, 45, 84; DLB 88
Gut, Gom
See Simenon, Georges (Jacques Christian)
Guterson, David 1956- .... **CLC 91**
See also CA 132; CANR 73; MTCW 2
Guthrie, A(lfred) B(ertram), Jr. 1901-1991 **C L C 23**
See also CA 57-60; 134; CANR 24; DLB 212;
SATA 62; SATA-Obit 67
Guthrie, Isobel
See Grieve, C(hristopher) M(urray)
Guthrie, Woodrow Wilson 1912-1967
See Guthrie, Woody
See also CA 113; 93-96
Guthrie, Woody .... **CLC 35**
See also Guthrie, Woodrow Wilson
Gutierrez Najera, Manuel 1859-1895
See also HLCS 2
Guy, Rosa (Cuthbert) 1928- .... **CLC 26**
See also AAYA 4; BW 2; CA 17-20R; CANR 14,
34, 83; CLR 13; DLB 33; JRDA; MAICYA;
SATA 14, 62
Gwendolyn
See Bennett, (Enoch) Arnold
H. D. .... **CLC 3, 8, 14, 31, 34, 73; PC 5**
See also Doolittle, Hilda
H. de V.
See Buchan, John
Haavikko, Paavo Juhani 1931- .... **CLC 18, 34**
See also CA 106
Habbema, Koos
See Heijermans, Herman
Habermas, Juergen 1929- .... **CLC 104**
See also CA 109; CANR 85
Habermas, Jurgen
See Habermas, Juergen
Hacker, Marilyn 1942-**CLC 5, 9, 23, 72, 91; DAM POET**
See also CA 77-80; CANR 68; DLB 120
Haeckel, Ernst Heinrich (Philipp August) 1834-
1919 .... **TCLC 83**
See also CA 157
Hafiz c. 1326-1389 .... **CMLC 34**
Hafiz c. 1326-1389(?) .... **CMLC 34**
Haggard, H(enry) Rider 1856-1925 ..... **TCLC 11**
See also CA 108; 148; DLB 70, 156, 174, 178;
MTCW 2; SATA 16
Hagiosy, L.
See Larbaud, Valery (Nicolas)
Hagiwara Sakutaro 1886-1942 **TCLC 60; PC 18**
Haig, Fenil
See Ford, Ford Madox
Haig-Brown, Roderick (Langmere) 1908-1976
CLC 21
See also CA 5-8R; 69-72; CANR 4, 38, 83; CLR
31; DLB 88; MAICYA; SATA 12
Hailey, Arthur 1920- .. **CLC 5; DAM NOV, POP**
See also AITN 2; BEST 90:3; CA 1-4R; CANR 2,
36, 75; DLB 88; DLBY 82; MTCW 1, 2
Hailey, Elizabeth Forsythe 1938- .... **CLC 40**
See also CA 93-96; CAAS 1; CANR 15, 48; INT
CANR-15
Haines, John (Meade) 1924- .... **CLC 58**

See also CA 17-20R; CANR 13, 34; DLB 212
Hakluyt, Richard 1552-1616 .... **LC 31**
Haldeman, Joe (William) 1943- .... **CLC 61**
See also Graham, Robert
See also CA 53-56, 179; CAAE 179; CAAS 25;
CANR 6, 70, 72; DLB 8; INT CANR-6
Hale, Sarah Josepha (Buell) 1788-1879**NCLC 75**
See also DLB 1, 42, 73
Haley, Alex(ander Murray Palmer) 1921-1992
CLC 8, 12, 76; BLC 2; DA; DAB; DAC; DAM MST, MULT, POP
See also AAYA 26; BW 2, 3; CA 77-80; 136;
CANR 61; CDALBS; DA3; DLB 38; MTCW 1, 2
Haliburton, Thomas Chandler 1796-1865 **N C L C 15**
See also DLB 11, 99
Hall, Donald (Andrew, Jr.) 1928- **CLC 1, 13, 37, 59; DAM POET**
See also CA 5-8R; CAAS 7; CANR 2, 44, 64;
DLB 5; MTCW 1; SATA 23, 97
Hall, Frederic Sauser
See Sauser-Hall, Frederic
Hall, James
See Kuttner, Henry
Hall, James Norman 1887-1951 .... **TCLC 23**
See also CA 123; 173; SATA 21
Hall, Radclyffe
See Hall, (Marguerite) Radclyffe
See also MTCW 2
Hall, (Marguerite) Radclyffe 1886-1943**TCLC 12**
See also CA 110; 150; CANR 83; DLB 191
Hall, Rodney 1935- .... **CLC 51**
See also CA 109; CANR 69
Halleck, Fitz-Greene 1790-1867 .... **NCLC 47**
See also DLB 3
Halliday, Michael
See Creasey, John
Halpern, Daniel 1945- .... **CLC 14**
See also CA 33-36R
Hamburger, Michael (Peter Leopold) 1924- **C L C 5, 14**
See also CA 5-8R; CAAS 4; CANR 2, 47; DLB 27
Hamill, Pete 1935- .... **CLC 10**
See also CA 25-28R; CANR 18, 71
Hamilton, Alexander 1755(?)-1804 ...... **NCLC 49**
See also DLB 37
Hamilton, Clive
See Lewis, C(live) S(taples)
Hamilton, Edmond 1904-1977 .... **CLC 1**
See also CA 1-4R; CANR 3, 84; DLB 8
Hamilton, Eugene (Jacob) Lee
See Lee-Hamilton, Eugene (Jacob)
Hamilton, Franklin
See Silverberg, Robert
Hamilton, Gail
See Corcoran, Barbara
Hamilton, Mollie
See Kaye, M(ary) M(argaret)
Hamilton, (Anthony Walter) Patrick 1904-1962
CLC 51
See also CA 176; 113; DLB 191
Hamilton, Virginia 1936- **CLC 26; DAM MULT**
See also AAYA 2, 21; BW 2, 3; CA 25-28R;
CANR 20, 37, 73; CLR 1, 11, 40; DLB 33, 52;
INT CANR-20; JRDA; MAICYA; MTCW 1,
2; SATA 4, 56, 79
Hammett, (Samuel) Dashiell 1894-1961**CLC 3, 5, 10, 19, 47; SSC 17**
See also AITN 1; CA 81-84; CANR 42; CDALB
1929-1941; DA3; DLBD 6; DLBY 96; MTCW 1, 2
Hammon, Jupiter 1711(?)-1800(?)**NCLC 5; BLC**

2; DAM MULT, POET; PC 16
See also DLB 31, 50
Hammond, Keith
See Kuttner, Henry
Hamner, Earl (Henry), Jr. 1923- .... **CLC 12**
See also AITN 2; CA 73-76; DLB 6
Hampton, Christopher (James) 1946- .... **CLC 4**
See also CA 25-28R; DLB 13; MTCW 1
Hamsun, Knut .... **TCLC 2, 14, 49**
See also Pedersen, Knut
Handke, Peter 1942- **CLC 5, 8, 10, 15, 38; DAM DRAM, NOV**
See also CA 77-80; CANR 33, 75; DLB 85, 124;
MTCW 1, 2
Handy, W(illiam) C(hristopher) 1873-1958**TCLC 97**
See also BW 3; CA 121; 167
Hanley, James 1901-1985 .... **CLC 3, 5, 8, 13**
See also CA 73-76; 117; CANR 36; DLB 191;
MTCW 1
Hannah, Barry 1942- .... **CLC 23, 38, 90**
See also CA 108; 110; CANR 43, 68; DLB 6; INT
110; MTCW 1
Hannon, Ezra
See Hunter, Evan
Hansberry, Lorraine (Vivian) 1930-1965**CLC 17, 62; BLC 2; DA; DAB; DAC; DAM DRAM, MST, MULT; DC 2**
See also AAYA 25; BW 1, 3; CA 109; 25-28R;
CABS 3; CANR 58; CDALB 1941-1968; DA3;
DLB 7, 38; MTCW 1, 2
Hansen, Joseph 1923- .... **CLC 38**
See also CA 29-32R; CAAS 17; CANR 16, 44, 66;
INT CANR-16
Hansen, Martin A(lfred) 1909-1955 .... **TCLC 32**
See also CA 167
Hanson, Kenneth O(stlin) 1922- .... **CLC 13**
See also CA 53-56; CANR 7
Hardwick, Elizabeth (Bruce) 1916-**CLC 13; DAM NOV**
See also CA 5-8R; CANR 3, 32, 70; DA3; DLB 6;
MTCW 1, 2
Hardy, Thomas 1840-1928**TCLC 4, 10, 18, 32, 48, 53, 72; DA; DAB; DAC; DAM MST, NOV, POET; PC 8; SSC 2; WLC**
See also CA 104; 123; CDBLB 1890-1914; DA3;
DLB 18, 19, 135; MTCW 1, 2
Hare, David 1947- .... **CLC 29, 58**
See also CA 97-100; CANR 39; DLB 13; MTCW 1
Harewood, John
See Van Druten, John (William)
Harford, Henry
See Hudson, W(illiam) H(enry)
Hargrave, Leonie
See Disch, Thomas M(ichael)
Harjo, Joy 1951- .. **CLC 83; DAM MULT; PC 27**
See also CA 114; CANR 35, 67; DLB 120, 175;
MTCW 2; NNAL
Harlan, Louis R(udolph) 1922- .... **CLC 34**
See also CA 21-24R; CANR 25, 55, 80
Harling, Robert 1951(?)- .... **CLC 53**
See also CA 147
Harmon, William (Ruth) 1938- .... **CLC 38**
See also CA 33-36R; CANR 14, 32, 35; SATA 65
Harper, F. E. W.
See Harper, Frances Ellen Watkins
Harper, Frances E. W.
See Harper, Frances Ellen Watkins
Harper, Frances E. Watkins
See Harper, Frances Ellen Watkins
Harper, Frances Ellen
See Harper, Frances Ellen Watkins

See also AAYA 24; AITN 1; CA 5-8R; CABS 1; CANR 8, 42, 66; DA3; DLB 2, 28; DLBY 80; INT CANR-8; MTCW 1, 2

Hellman, Lillian (Florence) 1906-1984**CLC 2, 4, 8, 14, 18, 34, 44, 52; DAM DRAM; DC 1**
See also AITN 1, 2; CA 13-16R; 112; CANR 33; DA3; DLB 7; DLBY 84; MTCW 1, 2

Helprin, Mark 1947- .. **CLC 7, 10, 22, 32; DAM NOV, POP**
See also CA 81-84; CANR 47, 64; CDALBS; DA3; DLBY 85; MTCW 1, 2

Helvetius, Claude-Adrien 1715-1771 .... **LC 26**

Helyar, Jane Penelope Josephine 1933-
See Poole, Josephine
See also CA 21-24R; CANR 10, 26; SATA 82

Hemans, Felicia 1793-1835 .... **NCLC 71**
See also DLB 96

Hemingway, Ernest (Miller) 1899-1961**CLC 1, 3, 6, 8, 10, 13, 19, 30, 34, 39, 41, 44, 50, 61, 80; DA; DAB; DAC; DAM MST, NOV; SSC 1, 25, 36; WLC**
See also AAYA 19; CA 77-80; CANR 34; CDALB 1917-1929; DA3; DLB 4, 9, 102, 210; DLBD 1, 15, 16; DLBY 81, 87, 96, 98; MTCW 1, 2

Hempel, Amy 1951- .... **CLC 39**
See also CA 118; 137; CANR 70; DA3; MTCW 2

Henderson, F. C.
See Mencken, H(enry) L(ouis)

Henderson, Sylvia
See Ashton-Warner, Sylvia (Constance)

Henderson, Zenna (Chlarson) 1917-1983**SSC 29**
See also CA 1-4R; 133; CANR 1, 84; DLB 8; SATA 5

Henkin, Joshua .... **CLC 119**
See also CA 161

Henley, Beth .... **CLC 23; DC 6**
See also Henley, Elizabeth Becker
See also CABS 3; DLBY 86

Henley, Elizabeth Becker 1952-
See Henley, Beth
See also CA 107; CANR 32, 73; DAM DRAM, MST; DA3; MTCW 1, 2

Henley, William Ernest 1849-1903 .... **TCLC 8**
See also CA 105; DLB 19

Hennissart, Martha
See Lathen, Emma
See also CA 85-88; CANR 64

Henry, O. .... **TCLC 1, 19; SSC 5; WLC**
See also Porter, William Sydney

Henry, Patrick 1736-1799 .... **LC 25**

Henryson, Robert 1430(?)-1506(?) .... **LC 20**
See also DLB 146

Henry VIII 1491-1547 .... **LC 10**
See also DLB 132

Henschke, Alfred
See Klabund

Hentoff, Nat(han Irving) 1925- .... **CLC 26**
See also AAYA 4; CA 1-4R; CAAS 6; CANR 5, 25, 77; CLR 1, 52; INT CANR-25; JRDA; MAICYA; SATA 42, 69; SATA-Brief 27

Heppenstall, (John) Rayner 1911-1981 . **CLC 10**
See also CA 1-4R; 103; CANR 29

Heraclitus c. 540B.C.-c. 450B.C. .... **CMLC 22**
See also DLB 176

Herbert, Frank (Patrick) 1920-1986**CLC 12, 23, 35, 44, 85; DAM POP**
See also AAYA 21; CA 53-56; 118; CANR 5, 43; CDALBS; DLB 8; INT CANR-5; MTCW 1, 2; SATA 9, 37; SATA-Obit 47

Herbert, George 1593-1633 . **LC 24; DAB; DAM POET; PC 4**
See also CDBLB Before 1660; DLB 126

Herbert, Zbigniew 1924-1998 . **CLC 9, 43; DAM POET**
See also CA 89-92; 169; CANR 36, 74; MTCW 1

Herbst, Josephine (Frey) 1897-1969 ..... **CLC 34**
See also CA 5-8R; 25-28R; DLB 9

Heredia, Jose Maria 1803-1839
See also HLCS 2

Hergesheimer, Joseph 1880-1954 .... **TCLC 11**
See also CA 109; DLB 102, 9

Herlihy, James Leo 1927-1993 .... **CLC 6**
See also CA 1-4R; 143; CANR 2

Hermogenes fl. c. 175- .... **CMLC 6**

Hernandez, Jose 1834-1886 ....**NCLC 17**

Herodotus c. 484B.C.-429B.C. .... **CMLC 17**
See also DLB 176

Herrick, Robert 1591-1674 ... **LC 13; DA; DAB; DAC; DAM MST, POP; PC 9**
See also DLB 126

Herring, Guilles
See Somerville, Edith

Herriot, James 1916-1995 .. **CLC 12; DAM POP**
See also Wight, James Alfred
See also AAYA 1; CA 148; CANR 40; MTCW 2; SATA 86

Herrmann, Dorothy 1941- .... **CLC 44**
See also CA 107

Herrmann, Taffy
See Herrmann, Dorothy

Hersey, John (Richard) 1914-1993**CLC 1, 2, 7, 9, 40, 81, 97; DAM POP**
See also AAYA 29; CA 17-20R; 140; CANR 33; CDALBS; DLB 6, 185; MTCW 1, 2; SATA 25; SATA-Obit 76

Herzen, Aleksandr Ivanovich 1812-1870 . **NCLC 10, 61**

Herzl, Theodor 1860-1904 .... **TCLC 36**
See also CA 168

Herzog, Werner 1942- .... **CLC 16**
See also CA 89-92

Hesiod c. 8th cent. B.C.- .... **CMLC 5**
See also DLB 176

Hesse, Hermann 1877-1962**CLC 1, 2, 3, 6, 11, 17, 25, 69; DA; DAB; DAC; DAM MST, NOV; SSC 9; WLC**
See also CA 17-18; CAP 2; DA3; DLB 66; MTCW 1, 2; SATA 50

Hewes, Cady
See De Voto, Bernard (Augustine)

Heyen, William 1940- .... **CLC 13, 18**
See also CA 33-36R; CAAS 9; DLB 5

Heyerdahl, Thor 1914- .... **CLC 26**
See also CA 5-8R; CANR 5, 22, 66, 73; MTCW 1, 2; SATA 2, 52

Heym, Georg (Theodor Franz Arthur) 1887-1912 **TCLC 9**
See also CA 106; 181

Heym, Stefan 1913- .... **CLC 41**
See also CA 9-12R; CANR 4; DLB 69

Heyse, Paul (Johann Ludwig von) 1830-1914 **TCLC 8**
See also CA 104; DLB 129

Heyward, (Edwin) DuBose 1885-1940 .. **TCLC 59**
See also CA 108; 157; DLB 7, 9, 45; SATA 21

Hibbert, Eleanor Alice Burford 1906-1993**CLC 7; DAM POP**
See also BEST 90:4; CA 17-20R; 140; CANR 9, 28, 59; MTCW 2; SATA 2; SATA-Obit 74

Hichens, Robert (Smythe) 1864-1950 . **TCLC 64**
See also CA 162; DLB 153

Higgins, George V(incent) 1939-**CLC 4, 7, 10, 18**
See also CA 77-80; CAAS 5; CANR 17, 51; DLB 2; DLBY 81, 98; INT CANR-17; MTCW 1

Higginson, Thomas Wentworth 1823-1911**TCLC 36**

See also CA 162; DLB 1, 64

Highet, Helen
See MacInnes, Helen (Clark)

Highsmith, (Mary) Patricia 1921-1995**CLC 2, 4, 14, 42, 102; DAM NOV, POP**
See also CA 1-4R; 147; CANR 1, 20, 48, 62; DA3; MTCW 1, 2

Highwater, Jamake (Mamake) 1942(?)- **CLC 12**
See also AAYA 7; CA 65-68; CAAS 7; CANR 10, 34, 84; CLR 17; DLB 52; DLBY 85; JRDA; MAICYA; SATA 32, 69; SATA-Brief 30

Highway, Tomson 1951- .... **CLC 92; DAC; DAM MULT**
See also CA 151; CANR 75; MTCW 2; NNAL

Higuchi, Ichiyo 1872-1896 .... **NCLC 49**

Hijuelos, Oscar 1951-**CLC 65; DAM MULT, POP; HLC 1**
See also AAYA 25; BEST 90:1; CA 123; CANR 50, 75; DA3; DLB 145; HW 1, 2; MTCW 2

Hikmet, Nazim 1902(?)-1963 .... **CLC 40**
See also CA 141; 93-96

Hildegard von Bingen 1098-1179 .... **CMLC 20**
See also DLB 148

Hildesheimer, Wolfgang 1916-1991 ...... **CLC 49**
See also CA 101; 135; DLB 69, 124

Hill, Geoffrey (William) 1932- **CLC 5, 8, 18, 45; DAM POET**
See also CA 81-84; CANR 21; CDBLB 1960 to Present; DLB 40; MTCW 1

Hill, George Roy 1921- .... **CLC 26**
See also CA 110; 122

Hill, John
See Koontz, Dean R(ay)

Hill, Susan (Elizabeth) 1942- **CLC 4, 113; DAB; DAM MST, NOV**
See also CA 33-36R; CANR 29, 69; DLB 14, 139; MTCW 1

Hillerman, Tony 1925- .... **CLC 62; DAM POP**
See also AAYA 6; BEST 89:1; CA 29-32R; CANR 21, 42, 65; DA3; DLB 206; SATA 6

Hillesum, Etty 1914-1943 .... **TCLC 49**
See also CA 137

Hilliard, Noel (Harvey) 1929- .... **CLC 15**
See also CA 9-12R; CANR 7, 69

Hillis, Rick 1956- .... **CLC 66**
See also CA 134

Hilton, James 1900-1954 .... **TCLC 21**
See also CA 108; 169; DLB 34, 77; SATA 34

Himes, Chester (Bomar) 1909-1984 **CLC 2, 4, 7, 18, 58, 108; BLC 2; DAM MULT**
See also BW 2; CA 25-28R; 114; CANR 22; DLB 2, 76, 143; MTCW 1, 2

Hinde, Thomas .... **CLC 6, 11**
See also Chitty, Thomas Willes

Hine, (William) Daryl 1936- .... **CLC 15**
See also CA 1-4R; CAAS 15; CANR 1, 20; DLB 60

Hinkson, Katharine Tynan
See Tynan, Katharine

Hinojosa(-Smith), Rolando (R.) 1929-
See Hinojosa-Smith, Rolando
See also CA 131; CAAS 16; CANR 62; DAM MULT; DLB 82; HLC 1; HW 1, 2; MTCW 2

Hinojosa-Smith, Rolando 1929-
See Hinojosa(-Smith), Rolando (R.)
See also CAAS 16; HLC 1; MTCW 2

Hinton, S(usan) E(loise) 1950-**CLC 30, 111; DA; DAB; DAC; DAM MST, NOV**
See also AAYA 2; CA 81-84; CANR 32, 62; CDALBS; CLR 3, 23; DA3; JRDA; MAICYA; MTCW 1, 2; SATA 19, 58

Hippius, Zinaida .... **TCLC 9**
See also Gippius, Zinaida (Nikolayevna)

Hiraoka, Kimitake 1925-1970
  See Mishima, Yukio
  See also CA 97-100; 29-32R; DAM DRAM; DA3;
  MTCW 1, 2

Hirsch, E(ric) D(onald), Jr. 1928- .... **CLC 79**
  See also CA 25-28R; CANR 27, 51; DLB 67; INT
  CANR-27; MTCW 1

Hirsch, Edward 1950- .... **CLC 31, 50**
  See also CA 104; CANR 20, 42; DLB 120

Hitchcock, Alfred (Joseph) 1899-1980 .. **CLC 16**
  See also AAYA 22; CA 159; 97-100; SATA 27;
  SATA-Obit 24

Hitler, Adolf 1889-1945 .... **TCLC 53**
  See also CA 117; 147

Hoagland, Edward 1932- .... **CLC 28**
  See also CA 1-4R; CANR 2, 31, 57; DLB 6; SATA
  51

Hoban, Russell (Conwell) 1925-**CLC 7, 25; DAM
  NOV**
  See also CA 5-8R; CANR 23, 37, 66; CLR 3; DLB
  52; MAICYA; MTCW 1, 2; SATA 1, 40, 78

Hobbes, Thomas 1588-1679 .... **LC 36**
  See also DLB 151

Hobbs, Perry
  See Blackmur, R(ichard) P(almer)

Hobson, Laura Z(ametkin) 1900-1986 **CLC 7, 25**
  See also CA 17-20R; 118; CANR 55; DLB 28;
  SATA 52

Hochhuth, Rolf 1931-**CLC 4, 11, 18; DAM DRAM**
  See also CA 5-8R; CANR 33, 75; DLB 124; MTCW
  1, 2

Hochman, Sandra 1936- .... **CLC 3, 8**
  See also CA 5-8R; DLB 5

Hochwaelder, Fritz 1911-1986 ..... **CLC 36; DAM
  DRAM**
  See also CA 29-32R; 120; CANR 42; MTCW 1

Hochwalder, Fritz
  See Hochwaelder, Fritz

Hocking, Mary (Eunice) 1921- .... **CLC 13**
  See also CA 101; CANR 18, 40

Hodgins, Jack 1938- .... **CLC 23**
  See also CA 93-96; DLB 60

Hodgson, William Hope 1877(?)-1918 **TCLC 13**
  See also CA 111; 164; DLB 70, 153, 156, 178;
  MTCW 2

Hoeg, Peter 1957- .... **CLC 95**
  See also CA 151; CANR 75; DA3; MTCW 2

Hoffman, Alice 1952- .... **CLC 51; DAM NOV**
  See also CA 77-80; CANR 34, 66; MTCW 1, 2

Hoffman, Daniel (Gerard) 1923- . **CLC 6, 13, 23**
  See also CA 1-4R; CANR 4; DLB 5

Hoffman, Stanley 1944- .... **CLC 5**
  See also CA 77-80

Hoffman, William M(oses) 1939- .... **CLC 40**
  See also CA 57-60; CANR 11, 71

Hoffmann, E(rnst) T(heodor) A(madeus) 1776-1822
  NCLC 2; SSC 13
  See also DLB 90; SATA 27

Hofmann, Gert 1931- .... **CLC 54**
  See also CA 128

Hofmannsthal, Hugo von 1874-1929 ... **TCLC 11;
  DAM DRAM; DC 4**
  See also CA 106; 153; DLB 81, 118

Hogan, Linda 1947- .... **CLC 73; DAM MULT**
  See also CA 120; CANR 45, 73; DLB 175; NNAL

Hogarth, Charles
  See Creasey, John

Hogarth, Emmett
  See Polonsky, Abraham (Lincoln)

Hogg, James 1770-1835 .... **NCLC 4**
  See also DLB 93, 116, 159

Holbach, Paul Henri Thiry Baron 1723-1789 **L C
  14**

Holberg, Ludvig 1684-1754 .... **LC 6**

Holden, Ursula 1921- .... **CLC 18**
  See also CA 101; CAAS 8; CANR 22

Holderlin, (Johann Christian) Friedrich 1770-1843
  NCLC 16; PC 4

Holdstock, Robert
  See Holdstock, Robert P.

Holdstock, Robert P. 1948- .... **CLC 39**
  See also CA 131; CANR 81

Holland, Isabelle 1920- .... **CLC 21**
  See also AAYA 11; CA 21-24R; 181; CAAE 181;
  CANR 10, 25, 47; CLR 57; JRDA; MAICYA;
  SATA 8, 70; SATA-Essay 103

Holland, Marcus
  See Caldwell, (Janet Miriam) Taylor (Holland)

Hollander, John 1929- .... **CLC 2, 5, 8, 14**
  See also CA 1-4R; CANR 1, 52; DLB 5; SATA 13

Hollander, Paul
  See Silverberg, Robert

Holleran, Andrew 1943(?)- .... **CLC 38**
  See also CA 144

Hollinghurst, Alan 1954- .... **CLC 55, 91**
  See also CA 114; DLB 207

Hollis, Jim
  See Summers, Hollis (Spurgeon, Jr.)

Holly, Buddy 1936-1959 .... **TCLC 65**

Holmes, Gordon
  See Shiel, M(atthew) P(hipps)

Holmes, John
  See Souster, (Holmes) Raymond

Holmes, John Clellon 1926-1988 .... **CLC 56**
  See also CA 9-12R; 125; CANR 4; DLB 16

Holmes, Oliver Wendell, Jr. 1841-1935**TCLC 77**
  See also CA 114

Holmes, Oliver Wendell 1809-1894**NCLC 14, 81**
  See also CDALB 1640-1865; DLB 1, 189; SATA
  34

Holmes, Raymond
  See Souster, (Holmes) Raymond

Holt, Victoria
  See Hibbert, Eleanor Alice Burford

Holub, Miroslav 1923-1998 .... **CLC 4**
  See also CA 21-24R; 169; CANR 10

Homer c. 8th cent. B.C.-**CMLC 1, 16; DA; DAB;
  DAC; DAM MST, POET; PC 23; WLCS**
  See also DA3; DLB 176

Hongo, Garrett Kaoru 1951- .... **PC 23**
  See also CA 133; CAAS 22; DLB 120

Honig, Edwin 1919- .... **CLC 33**
  See also CA 5-8R; CAAS 8; CANR 4, 45; DLB 5

Hood, Hugh (John Blagdon) 1928- .. **CLC 15, 28**
  See also CA 49-52; CAAS 17; CANR 1, 33; DLB
  53

Hood, Thomas 1799-1845 .... **NCLC 16**
  See also DLB 96

Hooker, (Peter) Jeremy 1941- .... **CLC 43**
  See also CA 77-80; CANR 22; DLB 40

hooks, bell .... **CLC 94; BLCS**
  See Watkins, Gloria
  See also MTCW 2

Hope, A(lec) D(erwent) 1907- .... **CLC 3, 51**
  See also CA 21-24R; CANR 33, 74; MTCW 1, 2

Hope, Anthony 1863-1933 .... **TCLC 83**
  See also CA 157; DLB 153, 156

Hope, Brian
  See Creasey, John

Hope, Christopher (David Tully) 1944- . **CLC 52**
  See also CA 106; CANR 47; SATA 62

Hopkins, Gerard Manley 1844-1889 . **NCLC 17;
  DA; DAB; DAC; DAM MST, POET; PC 15;
  WLC**
  See also CDBLB 1890-1914; DA3; DLB 35, 57

Hopkins, John (Richard) 1931-1998 .... **CLC 4**

See also CA 85-88; 169

Hopkins, Pauline Elizabeth 1859-1930**TCLC 28;
  BLC 2; DAM MULT**
  See also BW 2, 3; CA 141; CANR 82; DLB 50

Hopkinson, Francis 1737-1791 .... **LC 25**
  See also DLB 31

Hopley-Woolrich, Cornell George 1903-1968
  See Woolrich, Cornell
  See also CA 13-14; CANR 58; CAP 1; MTCW 2

Horatio
  See Proust, (Valentin-Louis-George-Eugene-)
  Marcel

Horgan, Paul (George Vincent O'Shaughnessy)
  1903-1995 .... **CLC 9, 53; DAM NOV**
  See also CA 13-16R; 147; CANR 9, 35; DLB 212;
  DLBY 85; INT CANR-9; MTCW 1, 2; SATA
  13; SATA-Obit 84

Horn, Peter
  See Kuttner, Henry

Hornem, Horace Esq.
  See Byron, George Gordon (Noel)

Horney, Karen (Clementine Theodore Danielsen)
  1885-1952 .... **TCLC 71**
  See also CA 114; 165

Hornung, E(rnest) W(illiam) 1866-1921**TCLC 59**
  See also CA 108; 160; DLB 70

Horovitz, Israel (Arthur) 1939- ..**CLC 56; DAM
  DRAM**
  See also CA 33-36R; CANR 46, 59; DLB 7

Horvath, Odon von
  See Horvath, Oedoen von
  See also DLB 85, 124

Horvath, Oedoen von 1901-1938 .... **TCLC 45**
  See also Horvath, Odon von
  See also CA 118

Horwitz, Julius 1920-1986 .... **CLC 14**
  See also CA 9-12R; 119; CANR 12

Hospital, Janette Turner 1942- .... **CLC 42**
  See also CA 108; CANR 48

Hostos, E. M. de
  See Hostos (y Bonilla), Eugenio Maria de

Hostos, Eugenio M. de
  See Hostos (y Bonilla), Eugenio Maria de

Hostos, Eugenio Maria
  See Hostos (y Bonilla), Eugenio Maria de

Hostos (y Bonilla), Eugenio Maria de 1839-1903
  TCLC 24
  See also CA 123; 131; HW 1

Houdini
  See Lovecraft, H(oward) P(hillips)

Hougan, Carolyn 1943- .... **CLC 34**
  See also CA 139

Household, Geoffrey (Edward West) 1900-1988
  CLC 11
  See also CA 77-80; 126; CANR 58; DLB 87;
  SATA 14; SATA-Obit 59

Housman, A(lfred) E(dward) 1859-1936 **TCLC 1,
  10; DA; DAB; DAC; DAM MST, POET; PC
  2; WLCS**
  See also CA 104; 125; DA3; DLB 19; MTCW 1, 2

Housman, Laurence 1865-1959 .... **TCLC 7**
  See also CA 106; 155; DLB 10; SATA 25

Howard, Elizabeth Jane 1923- .... **CLC 7, 29**
  See also CA 5-8R; CANR 8, 62

Howard, Maureen 1930- .... **CLC 5, 14, 46**
  See also CA 53-56; CANR 31, 75; DLBY 83; INT
  CANR-31; MTCW 1, 2

Howard, Richard 1929- .... **CLC 7, 10, 47**
  See also AITN 1; CA 85-88; CANR 25, 80; DLB
  5; INT CANR-25

Howard, Robert E(rvin) 1906-1936 .... **TCLC 8**
  See also CA 105; 157

Howard, Warren F.

See Pohl, Frederik

Howe, Fanny (Quincy) 1940- .... **CLC 47**
See also CA 117; CAAS 27; CANR 70; SATA-Brief 52

Howe, Irving 1920-1993 .... **CLC 85**
See also CA 9-12R; 141; CANR 21, 50; DLB 67; MTCW 1, 2

Howe, Julia Ward 1819-1910 .... **TCLC 21**
See also CA 117; DLB 1, 189

Howe, Susan 1937- .... **CLC 72**
See also CA 160; DLB 120

Howe, Tina 1937- .... **CLC 48**
See also CA 109

Howell, James 1594(?)-1666 .... **LC 13**
See also DLB 151

Howells, W. D.
See Howells, William Dean

Howells, William D.
See Howells, William Dean

Howells, William Dean 1837-1920 **TCLC 7, 17, 41; SSC 36**
See also CA 104; 134; CDALB 1865-1917; DLB 12, 64, 74, 79, 189; MTCW 2

Howes, Barbara 1914-1996 .... **CLC 15**
See also CA 9-12R; 151; CAAS 3; CANR 53; SATA 5

Hrabal, Bohumil 1914-1997 .... **CLC 13, 67**
See also CA 106; 156; CAAS 12; CANR 57

Hroswitha of Gandersheim c. 935-c. 1002 **CMLC 29**
See also DLB 148

Hsun, Lu
See Lu Hsun

Hubbard, L(afayette) Ron(ald) 1911-1986 **CLC 43; DAM POP**
See also CA 77-80; 118; CANR 52; DA3; MTCW 2

Huch, Ricarda (Octavia) 1864-1947 .... **TCLC 13**
See also CA 111; DLB 66

Huddle, David 1942- .... **CLC 49**
See also CA 57-60; CAAS 20; DLB 130

Hudson, Jeffrey
See Crichton, (John) Michael

Hudson, W(illiam) H(enry) 1841-1922 **TCLC 29**
See also CA 115; DLB 98, 153, 174; SATA 35

Hueffer, Ford Madox
See Ford, Ford Madox

Hughart, Barry 1934- .... **CLC 39**
See also CA 137

Hughes, Colin
See Creasey, John

Hughes, David (John) 1930- .... **CLC 48**
See also CA 116; 129; DLB 14

Hughes, Edward James
See Hughes, Ted
See also DAM MST, POET; DA3

Hughes, (James) Langston 1902-1967 **CLC 1, 5, 10, 15, 35, 44, 108; BLC 2; DA; DAB; DAC; DAM DRAM, MST, MULT, POET; DC 3; PC 1; SSC 6; WLC**
See also AAYA 12; BW 1, 3; CA 1-4R; 25-28R; CANR 1, 34, 82; CDALB 1929-1941; CLR 17; DA3; DLB 4, 7, 48, 51, 86; JRDA; MAICYA; MTCW 1, 2; SATA 4, 33

Hughes, Richard (Arthur Warren) 1900-1976 **CLC 1, 11; DAM NOV**
See also CA 5-8R; 65-68; CANR 4; DLB 15, 161; MTCW 1; SATA 8; SATA-Obit 25

Hughes, Ted 1930-1998 **CLC 2, 4, 9, 14, 37, 119; DAB; DAC; PC 7**
See also Hughes, Edward James
See also CA 1-4R; 171; CANR 1, 33, 66; CLR 3; DLB 40, 161; MAICYA; MTCW 1, 2; SATA

49; SATA-Brief 27; SATA-Obit 107

Hugo, Richard F(ranklin) 1923-1982 **CLC 6, 18, 32; DAM POET**
See also CA 49-52; 108; CANR 3; DLB 5, 206

Hugo, Victor (Marie) 1802-1885 **NCLC 3, 10, 21; DA; DAB; DAC; DAM DRAM, MST, NOV, POET; PC 17; WLC**
See also AAYA 28; DA3; DLB 119, 192; SATA 47

Huidobro, Vicente
See Huidobro Fernandez, Vicente Garcia

Huidobro Fernandez, Vicente Garcia 1893-1948 **TCLC 31**
See also CA 131; HW 1

Hulme, Keri 1947- .... **CLC 39**
See also CA 125; CANR 69; INT 125

Hulme, T(homas) E(rnest) 1883-1917 . **TCLC 21**
See also CA 117; DLB 19

Hume, David 1711-1776 .... **LC 7**
See also DLB 104

Humphrey, William 1924-1997 .... **CLC 45**
See also CA 77-80; 160; CANR 68; DLB 212

Humphreys, Emyr Owen 1919- .... **CLC 47**
See also CA 5-8R; CANR 3, 24; DLB 15

Humphreys, Josephine 1945- .... **CLC 34, 57**
See also CA 121; 127; INT 127

Huneker, James Gibbons 1857-1921 ... **TCLC 65**
See also DLB 71

Hungerford, Pixie
See Brinsmead, H(esba) F(ay)

Hunt, E(verette) Howard, (Jr.) 1918- .... **CLC 3**
See also AITN 1; CA 45-48; CANR 2, 47

Hunt, Francesca
See Holland, Isabelle

Hunt, Kyle
See Creasey, John

Hunt, (James Henry) Leigh 1784-1859 **NCLC 1, 70; DAM POET**
See also DLB 96, 110, 144

Hunt, Marsha 1946- .... **CLC 70**
See also BW 2, 3; CA 143; CANR 79

Hunt, Violet 1866(?)-1942 .... **TCLC 53**
See also DLB 162, 197

Hunter, E. Waldo
See Sturgeon, Theodore (Hamilton)

Hunter, Evan 1926- .... **CLC 11, 31; DAM POP**
See also CA 5-8R; CANR 5, 38, 62; DLBY 82; INT CANR-5; MTCW 1; SATA 25

Hunter, Kristin (Eggleston) 1931- .... **CLC 35**
See also AITN 1; BW 1; CA 13-16R; CANR 13; CLR 3; DLB 33; INT CANR-13; MAICYA; SAAS 10; SATA 12

Hunter, Mary
See Austin, Mary (Hunter)

Hunter, Mollie 1922- .... **CLC 21**
See also McIlwraith, Maureen Mollie Hunter
See also AAYA 13; CANR 37, 78; CLR 25; DLB 161; JRDA; MAICYA; SAAS 7; SATA 54, 106

Hunter, Robert (?)-1734 .... **LC 7**

Hurston, Zora Neale 1903-1960 . **CLC 7, 30, 61; BLC 2; DA; DAC; DAM MST, MULT, NOV; SSC 4; WLCS**
See also AAYA 15; BW 1, 3; CA 85-88; CANR 61; CDALBS; DA3; DLB 51, 86; MTCW 1, 2

Huston, John (Marcellus) 1906-1987 .... **CLC 20**
See also CA 73-76; 123; CANR 34; DLB 26

Hustvedt, Siri 1955- .... **CLC 76**
See also CA 137

Hutten, Ulrich von 1488-1523 .... **LC 16**
See also DLB 179

Huxley, Aldous (Leonard) 1894-1963 **CLC 1, 3, 4, 5, 8, 11, 18, 35, 79; DA; DAB; DAC; DAM MST, NOV; WLC**

See also AAYA 11; CA 85-88; CANR 44; CDBLB 1914-1945; DA3; DLB 36, 100, 162, 195; MTCW 1, 2; SATA 63

Huxley, T(homas) H(enry) 1825-1895 .. **NCLC 67**
See also DLB 57

Huysmans, Joris-Karl 1848-1907 ... **TCLC 7, 69**
See also CA 104; 165; DLB 123

Hwang, David Henry 1957- **CLC 55; DAM DRAM; DC 4**
See also CA 127; 132; CANR 76; DA3; DLB 212; INT 132; MTCW 2

Hyde, Anthony 1946- .... **CLC 42**
See also CA 136

Hyde, Margaret O(ldroyd) 1917- .... **CLC 21**
See also CA 1-4R; CANR 1, 36; CLR 23; JRDA; MAICYA; SAAS 8; SATA 1, 42, 76

Hynes, James 1956(?)- .... **CLC 65**
See also CA 164

Hypatia c. 370-415 .... **CMLC 35**

Ian, Janis 1951- .... **CLC 21**
See also CA 105

Ibanez, Vicente Blasco
See Blasco Ibanez, Vicente

Ibarbourou, Juana de 1895-1979
See also HLCS 2; HW 1

Ibarguengoitia, Jorge 1928-1983 .... **CLC 37**
See also CA 124; 113; HW 1

Ibsen, Henrik (Johan) 1828-1906 **TCLC 2, 8, 16, 37, 52; DA; DAB; DAC; DAM DRAM, MST; DC 2; WLC**
See also CA 104; 141; DA3

Ibuse, Masuji 1898-1993 .... **CLC 22**
See also CA 127; 141; DLB 180

Ichikawa, Kon 1915- .... **CLC 20**
See also CA 121

Idle, Eric 1943- .... **CLC 21**
See also Monty Python
See also CA 116; CANR 35

Ignatow, David 1914-1997 .... **CLC 4, 7, 14, 40**
See also CA 9-12R; 162; CAAS 3; CANR 31, 57; DLB 5

Ignotus
See Strachey, (Giles) Lytton

Ihimaera, Witi 1944- .... **CLC 46**
See also CA 77-80

Ilf, Ilya .... **TCLC 21**
See also Fainzilberg, Ilya Arnoldovich

Illyes, Gyula 1902-1983 .... **PC 16**
See also CA 114; 109

Immermann, Karl (Lebrecht) 1796-1840 **NCLC 4, 49**
See also DLB 133

Ince, Thomas H. 1882-1924 .... **TCLC 89**

Inchbald, Elizabeth 1753-1821 .... **NCLC 62**
See also DLB 39, 89

Inclan, Ramon (Maria) del Valle
See Valle-Inclan, Ramon (Maria) del

Infante, G(uillermo) Cabrera
See Cabrera Infante, G(uillermo)

Ingalls, Rachel (Holmes) 1940- .... **CLC 42**
See also CA 123; 127

Ingamells, Reginald Charles
See Ingamells, Rex

Ingamells, Rex 1913-1955 .... **TCLC 35**
See also CA 167

Inge, William (Motter) 1913-1973 **CLC 1, 8, 19; DAM DRAM**
See also CA 9-12R; CDALB 1941-1968; DA3; DLB 7; MTCW 1, 2

Ingelow, Jean 1820-1897 .... **NCLC 39**
See also DLB 35, 163; SATA 33

Ingram, Willis J.
See Harris, Mark

Innaurato, Albert (F.) 1948(?)- .... **CLC 21, 60**
See also CA 115; 122; CANR 78; INT 122
Innes, Michael
See Stewart, J(ohn) I(nnes) M(ackintosh)
Innis, Harold Adams 1894-1952 .... **TCLC 77**
See also CA 181; DLB 88
Ionesco, Eugene 1909-1994**CLC 1, 4, 6, 9, 11, 15, 41, 86; DA; DAB; DAC; DAM DRAM, MST; WLC**
See also CA 9-12R; 144; CANR 55; DA3; MTCW 1, 2; SATA 7; SATA-Obit 79
Iqbal, Muhammad 1873-1938 .... **TCLC 28**
Ireland, Patrick
See O'Doherty, Brian
Iron, Ralph
See Schreiner, Olive (Emilie Albertina)
Irving, John (Winslow) 1942- .. **CLC 13, 23, 38, 112; DAM NOV, POP**
See also AAYA 8; BEST 89:3; CA 25-28R; CANR 28, 73; DA3; DLB 6; DLBY 82; MTCW 1, 2
Irving, Washington 1783-1859 **NCLC 2, 19; DA; DAB; DAC; DAM MST; SSC 2, 37; WLC**
See also CDALB 1640-1865; DA3; DLB 3, 11, 30, 59, 73, 74, 186; YABC 2
Irwin, P. K.
See Page, P(atricia) K(athleen)
Isaacs, Jorge Ricardo 1837-1895 .... **NCLC 70**
Isaacs, Susan 1943- .... **CLC 32; DAM POP**
See also BEST 89:1; CA 89-92; CANR 20, 41, 65; DA3; INT CANR-20; MTCW 1, 2
Isherwood, Christopher (William Bradshaw) 1904-1986**CLC 1, 9, 11, 14, 44; DAM DRAM, NOV**
See also CA 13-16R; 117; CANR 35; DA3; DLB 15, 195; DLBY 86; MTCW 1, 2
Ishiguro, Kazuo 1954-**CLC 27, 56, 59, 110; DAM NOV**
See also BEST 90:2; CA 120; CANR 49; DA3; DLB 194; MTCW 1, 2
Ishikawa, Hakuhin
See Ishikawa, Takuboku
Ishikawa, Takuboku 1886(?)-1912**TCLC 15; DAM POET; PC 10**
See also CA 113; 153
Iskander, Fazil 1929-............................. **CLC 47**
See also CA 102
Isler, Alan (David) 1934- .... **CLC 91**
See also CA 156
Ivan IV 1530-1584 .... **LC 17**
Ivanov, Vyacheslav Ivanovich 1866-1949**TCLC 33**
See also CA 122
Ivask, Ivar Vidrik 1927-1992 .... **CLC 14**
See also CA 37-40R; 139; CANR 24
Ives, Morgan
See Bradley, Marion Zimmer
Izumi Shikibu c. 973-c. 1034 .... **CMLC 33**
J. R. S.
See Gogarty, Oliver St. John
Jabran, Kahlil
See Gibran, Kahlil
Jabran, Khalil
See Gibran, Kahlil
Jackson, Daniel
See Wingrove, David (John)
Jackson, Jesse 1908-1983 .... **CLC 12**
See also BW 1; CA 25-28R; 109; CANR 27; CLR 28; MAICYA; SATA 2, 29; SATA-Obit 48
Jackson, Laura (Riding) 1901-1991
See Riding, Laura
See also CA 65-68; 135; CANR 28; DLB 48
Jackson, Sam
See Trumbo, Dalton
Jackson, Sara
See Wingrove, David (John)

Jackson, Shirley 1919-1965**CLC 11, 60, 87; DA; DAC; DAM MST; SSC 9; WLC**
See also AAYA 9; CA 1-4R; 25-28R; CANR 4, 52; CDALB 1941-1968; DA3; DLB 6; MTCW 2; SATA 2
Jacob, (Cyprien-)Max 1876-1944 .... **TCLC 6**
See also CA 104
Jacobs, Harriet A(nn) 1813(?)-1897 ... **NCLC 67**
Jacobs, Jim 1942- .... **CLC 12**
See also CA 97-100; INT 97-100
Jacobs, W(illiam) W(ymark) 1863-1943**TCLC 22**
See also CA 121; 167; DLB 135
Jacobsen, Jens Peter 1847-1885 .... **NCLC 34**
Jacobsen, Josephine 1908- .... **CLC 48, 102**
See also CA 33-36R; CAAS 18; CANR 23, 48
Jacobson, Dan 1929- .... **CLC 4, 14**
See also CA 1-4R; CANR 2, 25, 66; DLB 14, 207; MTCW 1
Jacqueline
See Carpentier (y Valmont), Alejo
Jagger, Mick 1944- .... **CLC 17**
Jahiz, al- c. 780-c. 869 .... **CMLC 25**
Jakes, John (William) 1932-**CLC 29; DAM NOV, POP**
See also AAYA 32; BEST 89:4; CA 57-60; CANR 10, 43, 66; DA3; DLBY 83; INT CANR-10; MTCW 1, 2; SATA 62
James, Andrew
See Kirkup, James
James, C(yril) L(ionel) R(obert) 1901-1989 **C L C 33; BLCS**
See also BW 2; CA 117; 125; 128; CANR 62; DLB 125; MTCW 1
James, Daniel (Lewis) 1911-1988
See Santiago, Danny
See also CA 174; 125
James, Dynely
See Mayne, William (James Carter)
James, Henry Sr. 1811-1882 .... **NCLC 53**
James, Henry 1843-1916**TCLC 2, 11, 24, 40, 47, 64; DA; DAB; DAC; DAM MST, NOV; SSC 8, 32; WLC**
See also CA 104; 132; CDALB 1865-1917; DA3; DLB 12, 71, 74, 189; DLBD 13; MTCW 1, 2
James, M. R.
See James, Montague (Rhodes)
See also DLB 156
James, Montague (Rhodes) 1862-1936 . **TCLC 6; SSC 16**
See also CA 104; DLB 201
James, P. D. 1920- .... **CLC 18, 46, 122**
See also White, Phyllis Dorothy James
See also BEST 90:2; CDBLB 1960 to Present; DLB 87; DLBD 17
James, Philip
See Moorcock, Michael (John)
James, William 1842-1910 .... **TCLC 15, 32**
See also CA 109
James I 1394-1437 .... **LC 20**
Jameson, Anna 1794-1860 .... **NCLC 43**
See also DLB 99, 166
Jami, Nur al-Din 'Abd al-Rahman 1414-1492**LC 9**
Jammes, Francis 1868-1938 .... **TCLC 75**
Jandl, Ernst 1925- .... **CLC 34**
Janowitz, Tama 1957- .... **CLC 43; DAM POP**
See also CA 106; CANR 52
Japrisot, Sebastien 1931- .... **CLC 90**
Jarrell, Randall 1914-1965**CLC 1, 2, 6, 9, 13, 49; DAM POET**
See also CA 5-8R; 25-28R; CABS 2; CANR 6, 34; CDALB 1941-1968; CLR 6; DLB 48, 52; MAICYA; MTCW 1, 2; SATA 7
Jarry, Alfred 1873-1907 .... **TCLC 2, 14; DAM DRAM; SSC 20**
See also CA 104; 153; DA3; DLB 192
Jaynes, Roderick
See Coen, Ethan
Jeake, Samuel, Jr.
See Aiken, Conrad (Potter)
Jean Paul 1763-1825 .... **NCLC 7**
Jefferies, (John) Richard 1848-1887 .. **NCLC 47**
See also DLB 98, 141; SATA 16
Jeffers, (John) Robinson 1887-1962**CLC 2, 3, 11, 15, 54; DA; DAC; DAM MST, POET; PC 17; WLC**
See also CA 85-88; CANR 35; CDALB 1917-1929; DLB 45, 212; MTCW 1, 2
Jefferson, Janet
See Mencken, H(enry) L(ouis)
Jefferson, Thomas 1743-1826 .... **NCLC 11**
See also CDALB 1640-1865; DA3; DLB 31
Jeffrey, Francis 1773-1850 .... **NCLC 33**
See also DLB 107
Jelakowitch, Ivan
See Heijermans, Herman
Jellicoe, (Patricia) Ann 1927- .... **CLC 27**
See also CA 85-88; DLB 13
Jen, Gish .... **CLC 70**
See also Jen, Lillian
Jen, Lillian 1956(?)-
See Jen, Gish
See also CA 135
Jenkins, (John) Robin 1912- .... **CLC 52**
See also CA 1-4R; CANR 1; DLB 14
Jennings, Elizabeth (Joan) 1926- ..... **CLC 5, 14**
See also CA 61-64; CAAS 5; CANR 8, 39, 66; DLB 27; MTCW 1; SATA 66
Jennings, Waylon 1937- .... **CLC 21**
Jensen, Johannes V. 1873-1950 .... **TCLC 41**
See also CA 170
Jensen, Laura (Linnea) 1948- .... **CLC 37**
See also CA 103
Jerome, Jerome K(lapka) 1859-1927 .. **TCLC 23**
See also CA 119; 177; DLB 10, 34, 135
Jerrold, Douglas William 1803-1857 ... **NCLC 2**
See also DLB 158, 159
Jewett, (Theodora) Sarah Orne 1849-1909**TCLC 1, 22; SSC 6**
See also CA 108; 127; CANR 71; DLB 12, 74; SATA 15
Jewsbury, Geraldine (Endsor) 1812-1880 **NCLC 22**
See also DLB 21
Jhabvala, Ruth Prawer 1927- . **CLC 4, 8, 29, 94; DAB; DAM NOV**
See also CA 1-4R; CANR 2, 29, 51, 74; DLB 139, 194; INT CANR-29; MTCW 1, 2
Jibran, Kahlil
See Gibran, Kahlil
Jibran, Khalil
See Gibran, Kahlil
Jiles, Paulette 1943- .... **CLC 13, 58**
See also CA 101; CANR 70
Jimenez (Mantecon), Juan Ramon 1881-1958**TCLC 4; DAM MULT, POET; HLC 1; PC 7**
See also CA 104; 131; CANR 74; DLB 134; HW 1; MTCW 1, 2
Jimenez, Ramon
See Jimenez (Mantecon), Juan Ramon
Jimenez Mantecon, Juan
See Jimenez (Mantecon), Juan Ramon
Jin, Ha 1956- .... **CLC 109**
See also CA 152
Joel, Billy .... **CLC 26**
See also Joel, William Martin
Joel, William Martin 1949-

See also CA 134

Kant, Immanuel 1724-1804 .... **NCLC 27, 67**
See also DLB 94

Kantor, MacKinlay 1904-1977 .... **CLC 7**
See also CA 61-64; 73-76; CANR 60, 63; DLB 9, 102; MTCW 2

Kaplan, David Michael 1946- .... **CLC 50**

Kaplan, James 1951- .... **CLC 59**
See also CA 135

Karageorge, Michael
See Anderson, Poul (William)

Karamzin, Nikolai Mikhailovich 1766-1826
NCLC 3
See also DLB 150

Karapanou, Margarita 1946- .... **CLC 13**
See also CA 101

Karinthy, Frigyes 1887-1938 .... **TCLC 47**
See also CA 170

Karl, Frederick R(obert) 1927- .... **CLC 34**
See also CA 5-8R; CANR 3, 44

Kastel, Warren
See Silverberg, Robert

Kataev, Evgeny Petrovich 1903-1942
See Petrov, Evgeny
See also CA 120

Kataphusin
See Ruskin, John

Katz, Steve 1935- .... **CLC 47**
See also CA 25-28R; CAAS 14, 64; CANR 12; DLBY 83

Kauffman, Janet 1945- .... **CLC 42**
See also CA 117; CANR 43, 84; DLBY 86

Kaufman, Bob (Garnell) 1925-1986 .... **CLC 49**
See also BW 1; CA 41-44R; 118; CANR 22; DLB 16, 41

Kaufman, George S. 1889-1961 ...**CLC 38; DAM DRAM**
See also CA 108; 93-96; DLB 7; INT 108; MTCW 2

Kaufman, Sue .... **CLC 3, 8**
See also Barondess, Sue K(aufman)

Kavafis, Konstantinos Petrou 1863-1933
See Cavafy, C(onstantine) P(eter)
See also CA 104

Kavan, Anna 1901-1968 .... **CLC 5, 13, 82**
See also CA 5-8R; CANR 6, 57; MTCW 1

Kavanagh, Dan
See Barnes, Julian (Patrick)

Kavanagh, Julie 1952- ....**CLC 119**
See also CA 163

Kavanagh, Patrick (Joseph) 1904-1967 **CLC 22**
See also CA 123; 25-28R; DLB 15, 20; MTCW 1

Kawabata, Yasunari 1899-1972 . **CLC 2, 5, 9, 18, 107; DAM MULT; SSC 17**
See also CA 93-96; 33-36R; DLB 180; MTCW 2

Kaye, M(ary) M(argaret) 1909- .... **CLC 28**
See also CA 89-92; CANR 24, 60; MTCW 1, 2; SATA 62

Kaye, Mollie
See Kaye, M(ary) M(argaret)

Kaye-Smith, Sheila 1887-1956 .... **TCLC 20**
See also CA 118; DLB 36

Kaymor, Patrice Maguilene
See Senghor, Leopold Sedar

Kazan, Elia 1909- .... **CLC 6, 16, 63**
See also CA 21-24R; CANR 32, 78

Kazantzakis, Nikos 1883(?)-1957 **TCLC 2, 5, 33**
See also CA 105; 132; DA3; MTCW 1, 2

Kazin, Alfred 1915-1998 .... **CLC 34, 38, 119**
See also CA 1-4R; CAAS 7; CANR 1, 45, 79; DLB 67

Keane, Mary Nesta (Skrine) 1904-1996
See Keane, Molly

See also CA 108; 114; 151

Keane, Molly .... **CLC 31**
See also Keane, Mary Nesta (Skrine)
See also INT 114

Keates, Jonathan 1946(?)- .... **CLC 34**
See also CA 163

Keaton, Buster 1895-1966 .... **CLC 20**

Keats, John 1795-1821 .. **NCLC 8, 73; DA; DAB; DAC; DAM MST, POET; PC 1; WLC**
See also CDBLB 1789-1832; DA3; DLB 96, 110

Keene, Donald 1922- .... **CLC 34**
See also CA 1-4R; CANR 5

Keillor, Garrison ....**CLC 40, 115**
See also Keillor, Gary (Edward)
See also AAYA 2; BEST 89:3; DLBY 87; SATA 58

Keillor, Gary (Edward) 1942-
See Keillor, Garrison
See also CA 111; 117; CANR 36, 59; DAM POP; DA3; MTCW 1, 2

Keith, Michael
See Hubbard, L(afayette) Ron(ald)

Keller, Gottfried 1819-1890 .... **NCLC 2; SSC 26**
See also DLB 129

Keller, Nora Okja .... **CLC 109**

Kellerman, Jonathan 1949- **CLC 44; DAM POP**
See also BEST 90:1; CA 106; CANR 29, 51; DA3; INT CANR-29

Kelley, William Melvin 1937- .... **CLC 22**
See also BW 1; CA 77-80; CANR 27, 83; DLB 33

Kellogg, Marjorie 1922- .... **CLC 2**
See also CA 81-84

Kellow, Kathleen
See Hibbert, Eleanor Alice Burford

Kelly, M(ilton) T(errence) 1947- .... **CLC 55**
See also CA 97-100; CAAS 22; CANR 19, 43, 84

Kelman, James 1946- .... **CLC 58, 86**
See also CA 148; CANR 85; DLB 194

Kemal, Yashar 1923- .... **CLC 14, 29**
See also CA 89-92; CANR 44

Kemble, Fanny 1809-1893 .... **NCLC 18**
See also DLB 32

Kemelman, Harry 1908-1996 .... **CLC 2**
See also AITN 1; CA 9-12R; 155; CANR 6, 71; DLB 28

Kempe, Margery 1373(?)-1440(?) .... **LC 6**
See also DLB 146

Kempis, Thomas a 1380-1471 .... **LC 11**

Kendall, Henry 1839-1882 .... **NCLC 12**

Keneally, Thomas (Michael) 1935-**CLC 5, 8, 10, 14, 19, 27, 43, 117; DAM NOV**
See also CA 85-88; CANR 10, 50, 74; DA3; MTCW 1, 2

Kennedy, Adrienne (Lita) 1931-**CLC 66; BLC 2; DAM MULT; DC 5**
See also BW 2, 3; CA 103; CAAS 20; CABS 3; CANR 26, 53, 82; DLB 38

Kennedy, John Pendleton 1795-1870 ..... **NCLC 2**
See also DLB 3

Kennedy, Joseph Charles 1929-
See Kennedy, X. J.
See also CA 1-4R; CANR 4, 30, 40; SATA 14, 86

Kennedy, William 1928-**CLC 6, 28, 34, 53; DAM NOV**
See also AAYA 1; CA 85-88; CANR 14, 31, 76; DA3; DLB 143; DLBY 85; INT CANR-31; MTCW 1, 2; SATA 57

Kennedy, X. J. .... **CLC 8, 42**
See also Kennedy, Joseph Charles
See also CAAS 9; CLR 27; DLB 5; SAAS 22

Kenny, Maurice (Francis) 1929- . **CLC 87; DAM MULT**
See also CA 144; CAAS 22; DLB 175; NNAL

Kent, Kelvin
See Kuttner, Henry

Kenton, Maxwell
See Southern, Terry

Kenyon, Robert O.
See Kuttner, Henry

Kepler, Johannes 1571-1630 .... **LC 45**

Kerouac, Jack .... **CLC 1, 2, 3, 5, 14, 29, 61**
See also Kerouac, Jean-Louis Lebris de
See also AAYA 25; CDALB 1941-1968; DLB 2, 16; DLBD 3; DLBY 95; MTCW 2

Kerouac, Jean-Louis Lebris de 1922-1969
See Kerouac, Jack
See also AITN 1; CA 5-8R; 25-28R; CANR 26, 54; DA; DAB; DAC; DAM MST, NOV, POET, POP; DA3; MTCW 1, 2; WLC

Kerr, Jean 1923- .... **CLC 22**
See also CA 5-8R; CANR 7; INT CANR-7

Kerr, M. E. .... **CLC 12, 35**
See also Meaker, Marijane (Agnes)
See also AAYA 2, 23; CLR 29; SAAS 1

Kerr, Robert .... **CLC 55**

Kerrigan, (Thomas) Anthony 1918- .... **CLC 4, 6**
See also CA 49-52; CAAS 11; CANR 4

Kerry, Lois
See Duncan, Lois

Kesey, Ken (Elton) 1935-**CLC 1, 3, 6, 11, 46, 64; DA; DAB; DAC; DAM MST, NOV, POP; WLC**
See also AAYA 25; CA 1-4R; CANR 22, 38, 66; CDALB 1968-1988; DA3; DLB 2, 16, 206; MTCW 1, 2; SATA 66

Kesselring, Joseph (Otto) 1902-1967 .. **CLC 45; DAM DRAM, MST**
See also CA 150

Kessler, Jascha (Frederick) 1929- .... **CLC 4**
See also CA 17-20R; CANR 8, 48

Kettelkamp, Larry (Dale) 1933- .... **CLC 12**
See also CA 29-32R; CANR 16; SAAS 3; SATA 2

Key, Ellen 1849-1926 .... **TCLC 65**

Keyber, Conny
See Fielding, Henry

Keyes, Daniel 1927- ..**CLC 80; DA; DAC; DAM MST, NOV**
See also AAYA 23; CA 17-20R, 181; CAAE 181; CANR 10, 26, 54, 74; DA3; MTCW 2; SATA 37

Keynes, John Maynard 1883-1946 ...... **TCLC 64**
See also CA 114; 162, 163; DLBD 10; MTCW 2

Khanshendel, Chiron
See Rose, Wendy

Khayyam, Omar 1048-1131 ...... **CMLC 11; DAM POET; PC 8**
See also DA3

Kherdian, David 1931- .... **CLC 6, 9**
See also CA 21-24R; CAAS 2; CANR 39, 78; CLR 24; JRDA; MAICYA; SATA 16, 74

Khlebnikov, Velimir .... **TCLC 20**
See also Khlebnikov, Viktor Vladimirovich

Khlebnikov, Viktor Vladimirovich 1885-1922
See Khlebnikov, Velimir
See also CA 117

Khodasevich, Vladislav (Felitsianovich) 1886-1939
TCLC 15
See also CA 115

Kielland, Alexander Lange 1849-1906 .. **TCLC 5**
See also CA 104

Kiely, Benedict 1919- .... **CLC 23, 43**
See also CA 1-4R; CANR 2, 84; DLB 15

Kienzle, William X(avier) 1928- . **CLC 25; DAM POP**
See also CA 93-96; CAAS 1; CANR 9, 31, 59; DA3; INT CANR-31; MTCW 1, 2

Kierkegaard, Soren 1813-1855 ..... **NCLC 34, 78**

Kieslowski, Krzysztof 1941-1996 .... **CLC 120**
See also CA 147; 151

Killens, John Oliver 1916-1987 .... **CLC 10**
See also BW 2; CA 77-80; 123; CAAS 2; CANR 26; DLB 33

Killigrew, Anne 1660-1685 .... **LC 4**
See also DLB 131

Kim
See Simenon, Georges (Jacques Christian)

Kincaid, Jamaica 1949-**CLC 43, 68; BLC 2; DAM MULT, NOV**
See also AAYA 13; BW 2, 3; CA 125; CANR 47, 59; CDALBS; DA3; DLB 157; MTCW 2

King, Francis (Henry) 1923- .. **CLC 8, 53; DAM NOV**
See also CA 1-4R; CANR 1, 33, 86; DLB 15, 139; MTCW 1

King, Kennedy
See Brown, George Douglas

King, Martin Luther, Jr. 1929-1968**CLC 83; BLC 2; DA; DAB; DAC; DAM MST, MULT; WLCS**
See also BW 2, 3; CA 25-28; CANR 27, 44; CAP 2; DA3; MTCW 1, 2; SATA 14

King, Stephen (Edwin) 1947-**CLC 12, 26, 37, 61, 113; DAM NOV, POP; SSC 17**
See also AAYA 1, 17; BEST 90:1; CA 61-64; CANR 1, 30, 52, 76; DA3; DLB 143; DLBY 80; JRDA; MTCW 1, 2; SATA 9, 55

King, Steve
See King, Stephen (Edwin)

King, Thomas 1943-**CLC 89; DAC; DAM MULT**
See also CA 144; DLB 175; NNAL; SATA 96

Kingman, Lee .... **CLC 17**
See also Natti, (Mary) Lee
See also SAAS 3; SATA 1, 67

Kingsley, Charles 1819-1875 .... **NCLC 35**
See also DLB 21, 32, 163, 190; YABC 2

Kingsley, Sidney 1906-1995 .... **CLC 44**
See also CA 85-88; 147; DLB 7

Kingsolver, Barbara 1955-**CLC 55, 81; DAM POP**
See also AAYA 15; CA 129; 134; CANR 60; CDALBS; DA3; DLB 206; INT 134; MTCW 2

Kingston, Maxine (Ting Ting) Hong 1940- **C L C 12, 19, 58, 121; DAM MULT, NOV; WLCS**
See also AAYA 8; CA 69-72; CANR 13, 38, 74; CDALBS; DA3; DLB 173, 212; DLBY 80; INT CANR-13; MTCW 1, 2; SATA 53

Kinnell, Galway 1927-**CLC 1, 2, 3, 5, 13, 29; PC 26**
See also CA 9-12R; CANR 10, 34, 66; DLB 5; DLBY 87; INT CANR-34; MTCW 1

Kinsella, Thomas 1928- .... **CLC 4, 19**
See also CA 17-20R; CANR 15; DLB 27; MTCW 1, 2

Kinsella, W(illiam) P(atrick) 1935-**CLC 27, 43; DAC; DAM NOV, POP**
See also AAYA 7; CA 97-100; CAAS 7; CANR 21, 35, 66, 75; INT CANR-21; MTCW 1, 2

Kinsey, Alfred C(harles) 1894-1956 ... **TCLC 91**
See also CA 115; 170; MTCW 2

Kipling, (Joseph) Rudyard 1865-1936**TCLC 8, 17; DA; DAB; DAC; DAM MST, POET; PC 3; SSC 5; WLC**
See also AAYA 32; CA 105; 120; CANR 33; CDBLB 1890-1914; CLR 39; DA3; DLB 19, 34, 141, 156; MAICYA; MTCW 1, 2; SATA 100; YABC 2

Kirkup, James 1918-.............................. **CLC 1**
See also CA 1-4R; CAAS 4; CANR 2; DLB 27; SATA 12

Kirkwood, James 1930(?)-1989 .... **CLC 9**

See also AITN 2; CA 1-4R; 128; CANR 6, 40

Kirshner, Sidney
See Kingsley, Sidney

Kis, Danilo 1935-1989 .... **CLC 57**
See also CA 109; 118; 129; CANR 61; DLB 181; MTCW 1

Kivi, Aleksis 1834-1872 ....**NCLC 30**

Kizer, Carolyn (Ashley) 1925- . **CLC 15, 39, 80; DAM POET**
See also CA 65-68; CAAS 5; CANR 24, 70; DLB 5, 169; MTCW 2

Klabund 1890-1928 .... **TCLC 44**
See also CA 162; DLB 66

Klappert, Peter 1942- .... **CLC 57**
See also CA 33-36R; DLB 5

Klein, A(braham) M(oses) 1909-1972 .. **CLC 19; DAB; DAC; DAM MST**
See also CA 101; 37-40R; DLB 68

Klein, Norma 1938-1989 .... **CLC 30**
See also AAYA 2; CA 41-44R; 128; CANR 15, 37; CLR 2, 19; INT CANR-15; JRDA; MAICYA; SAAS 1; SATA 7, 57

Klein, T(heodore) E(ibon) D(onald) 1947-**CLC 34**
See also CA 119; CANR 44, 75

Kleist, Heinrich von 1777-1811**NCLC 2, 37; DAM DRAM; SSC 22**
See also DLB 90

Klima, Ivan 1931-............... **CLC 56; DAM NOV**
See also CA 25-28R; CANR 17, 50

Klimentov, Andrei Platonovich 1899-1951
See Platonov, Andrei
See also CA 108

Klinger, Friedrich Maximilian von 1752-1831
NCLC 1
See also DLB 94

Klingsor the Magician
See Hartmann, Sadakichi

Klopstock, Friedrich Gottlieb 1724-1803**NCLC 11**
See also DLB 97

Knapp, Caroline 1959- .... **CLC 99**
See also CA 154

Knebel, Fletcher 1911-1993 .... **CLC 14**
See also AITN 1; CA 1-4R; 140; CAAS 3; CANR 1, 36; SATA 36; SATA-Obit 75

Knickerbocker, Diedrich
See Irving, Washington

Knight, Etheridge 1931-1991 ... **CLC 40; BLC 2; DAM POET; PC 14**
See also BW 1, 3; CA 21-24R; 133; CANR 23, 82; DLB 41; MTCW 2

Knight, Sarah Kemble 1666-1727 .... **LC 7**
See also DLB 24, 200

Knister, Raymond 1899-1932 .... **TCLC 56**
See also DLB 68

Knowles, John 1926-**CLC 1, 4, 10, 26; DA; DAC; DAM MST, NOV**
See also AAYA 10; CA 17-20R; CANR 40, 74, 76; CDALB 1968-1988; DLB 6; MTCW 1, 2; SATA 8, 89

Knox, Calvin M.
See Silverberg, Robert

Knox, John c. 1505-1572 .... **LC 37**
See also DLB 132

Knye, Cassandra
See Disch, Thomas M(ichael)

Koch, C(hristopher) J(ohn) 1932- .... **CLC 42**
See also CA 127; CANR 84

Koch, Christopher
See Koch, C(hristopher) J(ohn)

Koch, Kenneth 1925- **CLC 5, 8, 44; DAM POET**
See also CA 1-4R; CANR 6, 36, 57; DLB 5; INT CANR-36; MTCW 2; SATA 65

Kochanowski, Jan 1530-1584 .... **LC 10**

Kock, Charles Paul de 1794-1871 .... **NCLC 16**

Koda Shigeyuki 1867-1947
See Rohan, Koda
See also CA 121

Koestler, Arthur 1905-1983**CLC 1, 3, 6, 8, 15, 33**
See also CA 1-4R; 109; CANR 1, 33; CDBLB 1945-1960; DLBY 83; MTCW 1, 2

Kogawa, Joy Nozomi 1935- **CLC 78; DAC; DAM MST, MULT**
See also CA 101; CANR 19, 62; MTCW 2; SATA 99

Kohout, Pavel 1928- .... **CLC 13**
See also CA 45-48; CANR 3

Koizumi, Yakumo
See Hearn, (Patricio) Lafcadio (Tessima Carlos)

Kolmar, Gertrud 1894-1943 .... **TCLC 40**
See also CA 167

Komunyakaa, Yusef 1947- ... **CLC 86, 94; BLCS**
See also CA 147; CANR 83; DLB 120

Konrad, George
See Konrad, Gyoergy

Konrad, Gyoergy 1933- .... **CLC 4, 10, 73**
See also CA 85-88

Konwicki, Tadeusz 1926- .... **CLC 8, 28, 54, 117**
See also CA 101; CAAS 9; CANR 39, 59; MTCW 1

Koontz, Dean R(ay) 1945- .. **CLC 78; DAM NOV, POP**
See also AAYA 9, 31; BEST 89:3, 90:2; CA 108; CANR 19, 36, 52; DA3; MTCW 1; SATA 92

Kopernik, Mikolaj
See Copernicus, Nicolaus

Kopit, Arthur (Lee) 1937- **CLC 1, 18, 33; DAM DRAM**
See also AITN 1; CA 81-84; CABS 3; DLB 7; MTCW 1

Kops, Bernard 1926- .... **CLC 4**
See also CA 5-8R; CANR 84; DLB 13

Kornbluth, C(yril) M. 1923-1958 .... **TCLC 8**
See also CA 105; 160; DLB 8

Korolenko, V. G.
See Korolenko, Vladimir Galaktionovich

Korolenko, Vladimir
See Korolenko, Vladimir Galaktionovich

Korolenko, Vladimir G.
See Korolenko, Vladimir Galaktionovich

Korolenko, Vladimir Galaktionovich 1853-1921
TCLC 22
See also CA 121

Korzybski, Alfred (Habdank Skarbek) 1879-1950
TCLC 61
See also CA 123; 160

Kosinski, Jerzy (Nikodem) 1933-1991 **CLC 1, 2, 3, 6, 10, 15, 53, 70; DAM NOV**
See also CA 17-20R; 134; CANR 9, 46; DA3; DLB 2; DLBY 82; MTCW 1, 2

Kostelanetz, Richard (Cory) 1940- .... **CLC 28**
See also CA 13-16R; CAAS 8; CANR 38, 77

Kostrowitzki, Wilhelm Apollinaris de 1880-1918
See Apollinaire, Guillaume
See also CA 104

Kotlowitz, Robert 1924- .... **CLC 4**
See also CA 33-36R; CANR 36

Kotzebue, August (Friedrich Ferdinand) von 1761-1819 .... **NCLC 25**
See also DLB 94

Kotzwinkle, William 1938- .... **CLC 5, 14, 35**
See also CA 45-48; CANR 3, 44, 84; CLR 6; DLB 173; MAICYA; SATA 24, 70

Kowna, Stancy
See Szymborska, Wislawa

Kozol, Jonathan 1936- .... **CLC 17**
See also CA 61-64; CANR 16, 45

See also CA 81-84; 147; CANR 72; DLB 13
Lunar, Dennis
  See Mungo, Raymond
Lurie, Alison 1926- .... **CLC 4, 5, 18, 39**
  See also CA 1-4R; CANR 2, 17, 50; DLB 2; MTCW 1; SATA 46
Lustig, Arnost 1926- .... **CLC 56**
  See also AAYA 3; CA 69-72; CANR 47; SATA 56
Luther, Martin 1483-1546 .... **LC 9, 37**
  See also DLB 179
Luxemburg, Rosa 1870(?)-1919 .... **TCLC 63**
  See also CA 118
Luzi, Mario 1914- .... **CLC 13**
  See also CA 61-64; CANR 9, 70; DLB 128
Lyly, John 1554(?)-1606 **LC 41; DAM DRAM; DC 7**
  See also DLB 62, 167
L'Ymagier
  See Gourmont, Remy (-Marie-Charles) de
Lynch, B. Suarez
  See Bioy Casares, Adolfo
Lynch, B. Suarez
  See Bioy Casares, Adolfo; Borges, Jorge Luis
Lynch, David (K.) 1946- .... **CLC 66**
  See also CA 124; 129
Lynch, James
  See Andreyev, Leonid (Nikolaevich)
Lynch Davis, B.
  See Bioy Casares, Adolfo; Borges, Jorge Luis
Lyndsay, Sir David 1490-1555 .... **LC 20**
Lynn, Kenneth S(chuyler) 1923- .... **CLC 50**
  See also CA 1-4R; CANR 3, 27, 65
Lynx
  See West, Rebecca
Lyons, Marcus
  See Blish, James (Benjamin)
Lyre, Pinchbeck
  See Sassoon, Siegfried (Lorraine)
Lytle, Andrew (Nelson) 1902-1995 .... **CLC 22**
  See also CA 9-12R; 150; CANR 70; DLB 6; DLBY 95
Lyttelton, George 1709-1773 .... **LC 10**
Maas, Peter 1929- .... **CLC 29**
  See also CA 93-96; INT 93-96; MTCW 2
Macaulay, Rose 1881-1958 .... **TCLC 7, 44**
  See also CA 104; DLB 36
Macaulay, Thomas Babington 1800-1859 **NCLC 42**
  See also CDBLB 1832-1890; DLB 32, 55
MacBeth, George (Mann) 1932-1992 **CLC 2, 5, 9**
  See also CA 25-28R; 136; CANR 61, 66; DLB 40; MTCW 1; SATA 4; SATA-Obit 70
MacCaig, Norman (Alexander) 1910- . **CLC 36; DAB; DAM POET**
  See also CA 9-12R; CANR 3, 34; DLB 27
MacCarthy, Sir (Charles Otto) Desmond 1877-1952 **TCLC 36**
  See also CA 167
MacDiarmid, Hugh .. **CLC 2, 4, 11, 19, 63; PC 9**
  See also Grieve, C(hristopher) M(urray)
  See also CDBLB 1945-1960; DLB 20
MacDonald, Anson
  See Heinlein, Robert A(nson)
Macdonald, Cynthia 1928- .... **CLC 13, 19**
  See also CA 49-52; CANR 4, 44; DLB 105
MacDonald, George 1824-1905 .... **TCLC 9**
  See also CA 106; 137; CANR 80; DLB 18, 163, 178; MAICYA; SATA 33, 100
Macdonald, John
  See Millar, Kenneth
MacDonald, John D(ann) 1916-1986 . **CLC 3, 27, 44; DAM NOV, POP**
  See also CA 1-4R; 121; CANR 1, 19, 60; DLB 8; DLBY 86; MTCW 1, 2

Macdonald, John Ross
  See Millar, Kenneth
Macdonald, Ross .... **CLC 1, 2, 3, 14, 34, 41**
  See also Millar, Kenneth
  See also DLBD 6
MacDougal, John
  See Blish, James (Benjamin)
MacEwen, Gwendolyn (Margaret) 1941-1987 **CLC 13, 55**
  See also CA 9-12R; 124; CANR 7, 22; DLB 53; SATA 50; SATA-Obit 55
Macha, Karel Hynek 1810-1846 .... **NCLC 46**
Machado (y Ruiz), Antonio 1875-1939 .. **TCLC 3**
  See also CA 104; 174; DLB 108; HW 2
Machado de Assis, Joaquim Maria 1839-1908 **TCLC 10; BLC 2; HLCS 2; SSC 24**
  See also CA 107; 153
Machen, Arthur .... **TCLC 4; SSC 20**
  See also Jones, Arthur Llewellyn
  See also CA 179; DLB 36, 156, 178
Machiavelli, Niccolo 1469-1527 .. **LC 8, 36; DA; DAB; DAC; DAM MST; WLCS**
MacInnes, Colin 1914-1976 .... **CLC 4, 23**
  See also CA 69-72; 65-68; CANR 21; DLB 14; MTCW 1, 2
MacInnes, Helen (Clark) 1907-1985 **CLC 27, 39; DAM POP**
  See also CA 1-4R; 117; CANR 1, 28, 58; DLB 87; MTCW 1, 2; SATA 22; SATA-Obit 44
Mackenzie, Compton (Edward Montague) 1883-1972 .... **CLC 18**
  See also CA 21-22; 37-40R; CAP 2; DLB 34, 100
Mackenzie, Henry 1745-1831 .... **NCLC 41**
  See also DLB 39
Mackintosh, Elizabeth 1896(?)-1952
  See Tey, Josephine
  See also CA 110
MacLaren, James
  See Grieve, C(hristopher) M(urray)
Mac Laverty, Bernard 1942- .... **CLC 31**
  See also CA 116; 118; CANR 43; INT 118
MacLean, Alistair (Stuart) 1922(?)-1987 **CLC 3, 13, 50, 63; DAM POP**
  See also CA 57-60; 121; CANR 28, 61; MTCW 1; SATA 23; SATA-Obit 50
Maclean, Norman (Fitzroy) 1902-1990 . **CLC 78; DAM POP; SSC 13**
  See also CA 102; 132; CANR 49; DLB 206
MacLeish, Archibald 1892-1982 **CLC 3, 8, 14, 68; DAM POET**
  See also CA 9-12R; 106; CANR 33, 63; CDALBS; DLB 4, 7, 45; DLBY 82; MTCW 1, 2
MacLennan, (John) Hugh 1907-1990 **CLC 2, 14, 92; DAC; DAM MST**
  See also CA 5-8R; 142; CANR 33; DLB 68; MTCW 1, 2
MacLeod, Alistair 1936- .. **CLC 56; DAC; DAM MST**
  See also CA 123; DLB 60; MTCW 2
Macleod, Fiona
  See Sharp, William
MacNeice, (Frederick) Louis 1907-1963 **CLC 1, 4, 10, 53; DAB; DAM POET**
  See also CA 85-88; CANR 61; DLB 10, 20; MTCW 1, 2
MacNeill, Dand
  See Fraser, George MacDonald
Macpherson, James 1736-1796 .... **LC 29**
  See also Ossian
  See also DLB 109
Macpherson, (Jean) Jay 1931- .... **CLC 14**
  See also CA 5-8R; DLB 53
MacShane, Frank 1927- .... **CLC 39**

See also CA 9-12R; CANR 3, 33; DLB 111
Macumber, Mari
  See Sandoz, Mari(e Susette)
Madach, Imre 1823-1864 .... **NCLC 19**
Madden, (Jerry) David 1933- .... **CLC 5, 15**
  See also CA 1-4R; CAAS 3; CANR 4, 45; DLB 6; MTCW 1
Maddern, Al(an)
  See Ellison, Harlan (Jay)
Madhubuti, Haki R. 1942- ... **CLC 6, 73; BLC 2; DAM MULT, POET; PC 5**
  See also Lee, Don L.
  See also BW 2, 3; CA 73-76; CANR 24, 51, 73; DLB 5, 41; DLBD 8; MTCW 2
Maepenn, Hugh
  See Kuttner, Henry
Maepenn, K. H.
  See Kuttner, Henry
Maeterlinck, Maurice 1862-1949 **TCLC 3; DAM DRAM**
  See also CA 104; 136; CANR 80; DLB 192; SATA 66
Maginn, William 1794-1842 .... **NCLC 8**
  See also DLB 110, 159
Mahapatra, Jayanta 1928- **CLC 33; DAM MULT**
  See also CA 73-76; CAAS 9; CANR 15, 33, 66
Mahfouz, Naguib (Abdel Aziz Al-Sabilgi) 1911(?)-
  See Mahfuz, Najib
  See also BEST 89:2; CA 128; CANR 55; DAM NOV; DA3; MTCW 1, 2
Mahfuz, Najib .... **CLC 52, 55**
  See also Mahfouz, Naguib (Abdel Aziz Al-Sabilgi)
  See also DLBY 88
Mahon, Derek 1941- .... **CLC 27**
  See also CA 113; 128; DLB 40
Mailer, Norman 1923- **CLC 1, 2, 3, 4, 5, 8, 11, 14, 28, 39, 74, 111; DA; DAB; DAC; DAM MST, NOV, POP**
  See also AAYA 31; AITN 2; CA 9-12R; CABS 1; CANR 28, 74, 77; CDALB 1968-1988; DA3; DLB 2, 16, 28, 185; DLBD 3; DLBY 80, 83; MTCW 1, 2
Maillet, Antonine 1929- ...... **CLC 54, 118; DAC**
  See also CA 115; 120; CANR 46, 74, 77; DLB 60; INT 120; MTCW 2
Mais, Roger 1905-1955 .... **TCLC 8**
  See also BW 1, 3; CA 105; 124; CANR 82; DLB 125; MTCW 1
Maistre, Joseph de 1753-1821 .... **NCLC 37**
Maitland, Frederic 1850-1906 .... **TCLC 65**
Maitland, Sara (Louise) 1950- .... **CLC 49**
  See also CA 69-72; CANR 13, 59
Major, Clarence 1936- .. **CLC 3, 19, 48; BLC 2; DAM MULT**
  See also BW 2, 3; CA 21-24R; CAAS 6; CANR 13, 25, 53, 82; DLB 33
Major, Kevin (Gerald) 1949- .... **CLC 26; DAC**
  See also AAYA 16; CA 97-100; CANR 21, 38; CLR 11; DLB 60; INT CANR-21; JRDA; MAICYA; SATA 32, 82
Maki, James
  See Ozu, Yasujiro
Malabaila, Damiano
  See Levi, Primo
Malamud, Bernard 1914-1986 **CLC 1, 2, 3, 5, 8, 9, 11, 18, 27, 44, 78, 85; DA; DAB; DAC; DAM MST, NOV, POP; SSC 15; WLC**
  See also AAYA 16; CA 5-8R; 118; CABS 1; CANR 28, 62; CDALB 1941-1968; DA3; DLB 2, 28, 152; DLBY 80, 86; MTCW 1, 2
Malan, Herman
  See Bosman, Herman Charles; Bosman, Herman

Author Index

DLB 14

Middleton, Thomas 1580-1627 .... **LC 33; DAM DRAM, MST; DC 5**
See also DLB 58

Migueis, Jose Rodrigues 1901- .... **CLC 10**

Mikszath, Kalman 1847-1910 .... **TCLC 31**
See also CA 170

Miles, Jack .... **CLC 100**

Miles, Josephine (Louise) 1911-1985 . **CLC 1, 2, 14, 34, 39; DAM POET**
See also CA 1-4R; 116; CANR 2, 55; DLB 48

Militant
See Sandburg, Carl (August)

Mill, John Stuart 1806-1873 .... **NCLC 11, 58**
See also CDBLB 1832-1890; DLB 55, 190

Millar, Kenneth 1915-1983 . **CLC 14; DAM POP**
See also Macdonald, Ross
See also CA 9-12R; 110; CANR 16, 63; DA3; DLB 2; DLBD 6; DLBY 83; MTCW 1, 2

Millay, E. Vincent
See Millay, Edna St. Vincent

Millay, Edna St. Vincent 1892-1950 **TCLC 4, 49; DA; DAB; DAC; DAM MST, POET; PC 6; WLCS**
See also CA 104; 130; CDALB 1917-1929; DA3; DLB 45; MTCW 1, 2

Miller, Arthur 1915- **CLC 1, 2, 6, 10, 15, 26, 47, 78; DA; DAB; DAC; DAM DRAM, MST; DC 1; WLC**
See also AAYA 15; AITN 1; CA 1-4R; CABS 3; CANR 2, 30, 54, 76; CDALB 1941-1968; DA3; DLB 7; MTCW 1, 2

Miller, Henry (Valentine) 1891-1980**CLC 1, 2, 4, 9, 14, 43, 84; DA; DAB; DAC; DAM MST, NOV; WLC**
See also CA 9-12R; 97-100; CANR 33, 64; CDALB 1929-1941; DA3; DLB 4, 9; DLBY 80; MTCW 1, 2

Miller, Jason 1939(?)- .... **CLC 2**
See also AITN 1; CA 73-76; DLB 7

Miller, Sue 1943- .... **CLC 44; DAM POP**
See also BEST 90:3; CA 139; CANR 59; DA3; DLB 143

Miller, Walter M(ichael, Jr.) 1923- .. **CLC 4, 30**
See also CA 85-88; DLB 8

Millett, Kate 1934- .... **CLC 67**
See also CA 1; CA 73-76; CANR 32, 53, 76; DA3; MTCW 1, 2

Millhauser, Steven (Lewis) 1943-**CLC 21, 54, 109**
See also CA 110; 111; CANR 63; DA3; DLB 2; INT 111; MTCW 2

Millin, Sarah Gertrude 1889-1968 .... **CLC 49**
See also CA 102; 93-96

Milne, A(lan) A(lexander) 1882-1956**TCLC 6, 88; DAB; DAC; DAM MST**
See also CA 104; 133; CLR 1, 26; DA3; DLB 10, 77, 100, 160; MAICYA; MTCW 1, 2; SATA 100; YABC 1

Milner, Ron(ald) 1938- .. **CLC 56; BLC 3; DAM MULT**
See also AITN 1; BW 1; CA 73-76; CANR 24, 81; DLB 38; MTCW 1

Milnes, Richard Monckton 1809-1885 **NCLC 61**
See also DLB 32, 184

Milosz, Czeslaw 1911-**CLC 5, 11, 22, 31, 56, 82; DAM MST, POET; PC 8; WLCS**
See also CA 81-84; CANR 23, 51; DA3; MTCW 1, 2

Milton, John 1608-1674**LC 9, 43; DA; DAB; DAC; DAM MST, POET; PC 19; WLC**
See also CDBLB 1660-1789; DA3; DLB 131, 151

Min, Anchee 1957- .... **CLC 86**
See also CA 146

Minehaha, Cornelius
See Wedekind, (Benjamin) Frank(lin)

Miner, Valerie 1947- .... **CLC 40**
See also CA 97-100; CANR 59

Minimo, Duca
See D'Annunzio, Gabriele

Minot, Susan 1956- .... **CLC 44**
See also CA 134

Minus, Ed 1938- .... **CLC 39**

Miranda, Javier
See Bioy Casares, Adolfo

Miranda, Javier
See Bioy Casares, Adolfo

Mirbeau, Octave 1848-1917 .... **TCLC 55**
See also DLB 123, 192

Miro (Ferrer), Gabriel (Francisco Victor) 1879-1930 .... **TCLC 5**
See also CA 104

Mishima, Yukio 1925-1970**CLC 2, 4, 6, 9, 27; DC 1; SSC 4**
See also Hiraoka, Kimitake
See also DLB 182; MTCW 2

Mistral, Frederic 1830-1914 .... **TCLC 51**
See also CA 122

Mistral, Gabriela .... **TCLC 2; HLC 2**
See also Godoy Alcayaga, Lucila
See also MTCW 2

Mistry, Rohinton 1952- .... **CLC 71; DAC**
See also CA 141; CANR 86

Mitchell, Clyde
See Ellison, Harlan (Jay); Silverberg, Robert

Mitchell, James Leslie 1901-1935
See Gibbon, Lewis Grassic
See also CA 104; DLB 15

Mitchell, Joni 1943- .... **CLC 12**
See also CA 112

Mitchell, Joseph (Quincy) 1908-1996 ... **CLC 98**
See also CA 77-80; 152; CANR 69; DLB 185; DLBY 96

Mitchell, Margaret (Munnerlyn) 1900-1949 **TCLC 11; DAM NOV, POP**
See also AAYA 23; CA 109; 125; CANR 55; CDALBS; DA3; DLB 9; MTCW 1, 2

Mitchell, Peggy
See Mitchell, Margaret (Munnerlyn)

Mitchell, S(ilas) Weir 1829-1914 .... **TCLC 36**
See also CA 165; DLB 202

Mitchell, W(illiam) O(rmond) 1914-1998**CLC 25; DAC; DAM MST**
See also CA 77-80; 165; CANR 15, 43; DLB 88

Mitchell, William 1879-1936 .... **TCLC 81**

Mitford, Mary Russell 1787-1855 .... **NCLC 4**
See also DLB 110, 116

Mitford, Nancy 1904-1973 .... **CLC 44**
See also CA 9-12R; DLB 191

Miyamoto, (Chujo) Yuriko 1899-1951 . **TCLC 37**
See also CA 170, 174; DLB 180

Miyazawa, Kenji 1896-1933 .... **TCLC 76**
See also CA 157

Mizoguchi, Kenji 1898-1956 .... **TCLC 72**
See also CA 167

Mo, Timothy (Peter) 1950(?)- .... **CLC 46**
See also CA 117; DLB 194; MTCW 1

Modarressi, Taghi (M.) 1931- .... **CLC 44**
See also CA 121; 134; INT 134

Modiano, Patrick (Jean) 1945- .... **CLC 18**
See also CA 85-88; CANR 17, 40; DLB 83

Moerck, Paal
See Roelvaag, O(le) E(dvart)

Mofolo, Thomas (Mokopu) 1875(?)-1948**TCLC 22; BLC 3; DAM MULT**
See also CA 121; 153; CANR 83; MTCW 2

Mohr, Nicholasa 1938-**CLC 12; DAM MULT; HLC**

2
See also AAYA 8; CA 49-52; CANR 1, 32, 64; CLR 22; DLB 145; HW 1, 2; JRDA; SAAS 8; SATA 8, 97

Mojtabai, A(nn) G(race) 1938- **CLC 5, 9, 15, 29**
See also CA 85-88

Moliere 1622-1673 **LC 10, 28; DA; DAB; DAC; DAM DRAM, MST; WLC**
See also DA3

Molin, Charles
See Mayne, William (James Carter)

Molnar, Ferenc 1878-1952**TCLC 20; DAM DRAM**
See also CA 109; 153; CANR 83

Momaday, N(avarre) Scott 1934- **CLC 2, 19, 85, 95; DA; DAB; DAC; DAM MST, MULT, NOV, POP; PC 25; WLCS**
See also AAYA 11; CA 25-28R; CANR 14, 34, 68; CDALBS; DA3; DLB 143, 175; INT CANR-14; MTCW 1, 2; NNAL; SATA 48; SATA-Brief 30

Monette, Paul 1945-1995 .... **CLC 82**
See also CA 139; 147

Monroe, Harriet 1860-1936 .... **TCLC 12**
See also CA 109; DLB 54, 91

Monroe, Lyle
See Heinlein, Robert A(nson)

Montagu, Elizabeth 1720-1800 .... **NCLC 7**

Montagu, Elizabeth 1917- .... **NCLC 7**
See also CA 9-12R

Montagu, Mary (Pierrepont) Wortley 1689-1762 **LC 9; PC 16**
See also DLB 95, 101

Montagu, W. H.
See Coleridge, Samuel Taylor

Montague, John (Patrick) 1929- ..... **CLC 13, 46**
See also CA 9-12R; CANR 9, 69; DLB 40; MTCW 1

Montaigne, Michel (Eyquem) de 1533-1592**LC 8; DA; DAB; DAC; DAM MST; WLC**

Montale, Eugenio 1896-1981**CLC 7, 9, 18; PC 13**
See also CA 17-20R; 104; CANR 30; DLB 114; MTCW 1

Montesquieu, Charles-Louis de Secondat 1689-1755 .... **LC 7**

Montgomery, (Robert) Bruce 1921(?)-1978
See Crispin, Edmund
See also CA 179; 104

Montgomery, L(ucy) M(aud) 1874-1942**TCLC 51; DAC; DAM MST**
See also AAYA 12; CA 108; 137; CLR 8; DA3; DLB 92; DLBD 14; JRDA; MAICYA; MTCW 2; SATA 100; YABC 1

Montgomery, Marion H., Jr. 1925- .... **CLC 7**
See also AITN 1; CA 1-4R; CANR 3, 48; DLB 6

Montgomery, Max
See Davenport, Guy (Mattison, Jr.)

Montherlant, Henry (Milon) de 1896-1972**CLC 8, 19; DAM DRAM**
See also CA 85-88; 37-40R; DLB 72; MTCW 1

Monty Python
See Chapman, Graham; Cleese, John (Marwood); Gilliam, Terry (Vance); Idle, Eric; Jones, Terence Graham Parry; Palin, Michael (Edward)
See also AAYA 7

Moodie, Susanna (Strickland) 1803-1885 **NCLC 14**
See also DLB 99

Mooney, Edward 1951-
See Mooney, Ted
See also CA 130

Mooney, Ted .... **CLC 25**
See also Mooney, Edward

Author Index

11, 29; DAM POET; PC 19
See also CA 13-16; 25-28R; CABS 2; CANR 35, 61; CAP 1; DLB 5, 16, 193; MTCW 1, 2

Olson, Toby 1937- .... CLC 28
See also CA 65-68; CANR 9, 31, 84

Olyesha, Yuri
See Olesha, Yuri (Karlovich)

Ondaatje, (Philip) Michael 1943-CLC 14, 29, 51, 76; DAB; DAC; DAM MST; PC 28
See also CA 77-80; CANR 42, 74; DA3; DLB 60; MTCW 2

Oneal, Elizabeth 1934-
See Oneal, Zibby
See also CA 106; CANR 28, 84; MAICYA; SATA 30, 82

Oneal, Zibby .... CLC 30
See Oneal, Elizabeth
See also AAYA 5; CLR 13; JRDA

O'Neill, Eugene (Gladstone) 1888-1953TCLC 1, 6, 27, 49; DA; DAB; DAC; DAM DRAM, MST; WLC
See also AITN 1; CA 110; 132; CDALB 1929-1941; DA3; DLB 7; MTCW 1, 2

Onetti, Juan Carlos 1909-1994 CLC 7, 10; DAM MULT, NOV; HLCS 2; SSC 23
See also CA 85-88; 145; CANR 32, 63; DLB 113; HW 1, 2; MTCW 1, 2

O Nuallain, Brian 1911-1966
See O'Brien, Flann
See also CA 21-22; 25-28R; CAP 2

Ophuls, Max 1902-1957 .... TCLC 79
See also CA 113

Opie, Amelia 1769-1853 .... NCLC 65
See also DLB 116, 159

Oppen, George 1908-1984 .... CLC 7, 13, 34
See also CA 13-16R; 113; CANR 8, 82; DLB 5, 165

Oppenheim, E(dward) Phillips 1866-1946 TCLC 45
See also CA 111; DLB 70

Opuls, Max
See Ophuls, Max

Origen c. 185-c. 254 .... CMLC 19

Orlovitz, Gil 1918-1973 .... CLC 22
See also CA 77-80; 45-48; DLB 2, 5

Orris
See Ingelow, Jean

Ortega y Gasset, Jose 1883-1955 TCLC 9; DAM MULT; HLC 2
See also CA 106; 130; HW 1, 2; MTCW 1, 2

Ortese, Anna Maria 1914- .... CLC 89
See also DLB 177

Ortiz, Simon J(oseph) 1941- .... CLC 45; DAM MULT, POET; PC 17
See also CA 134; CANR 69; DLB 120, 175; NNAL

Orton, Joe .... CLC 4, 13, 43; DC 3
See also Orton, John Kingsley
See also CDBLB 1960 to Present; DLB 13; MTCW 2

Orton, John Kingsley 1933-1967
See Orton, Joe
See also CA 85-88; CANR 35, 66; DAM DRAM; MTCW 1, 2

Orwell, GeorgeTCLC 2, 6, 15, 31, 51; DAB; WLC
See also Blair, Eric (Arthur)
See also CDBLB 1945-1960; DLB 15, 98, 195

Osborne, David
See Silverberg, Robert

Osborne, George
See Silverberg, Robert

Osborne, John (James) 1929-1994CLC 1, 2, 5, 11, 45; DA; DAB; DAC;DAM DRAM, MST; WLC

See also CA 13-16R; 147; CANR 21, 56; CDBLB 1945-1960; DLB 13; MTCW 1, 2

Osborne, Lawrence 1958- .... CLC 50

Osbourne, Lloyd 1868-1947 .... TCLC 93

Oshima, Nagisa 1932- .... CLC 20
See also CA 116; 121; CANR 78

Oskison, John Milton 1874-1947TCLC 35; DAM MULT
See also CA 144; CANR 84; DLB 175; NNAL

Ossian c. 3rd cent. - .... CMLC 28
See also Macpherson, James

Ostrovsky, Alexander 1823-1886 .. NCLC 30, 57

Otero, Blas de 1916-1979 .... CLC 11
See also CA 89-92; DLB 134

Otto, Rudolf 1869-1937 .... TCLC 85

Otto, Whitney 1955- .... CLC 70
See also CA 140

Ouida .... TCLC 43
See also De La Ramee, (Marie) Louise
See also DLB 18, 156

Ousmane, Sembene 1923- .... CLC 66; BLC 3
See also BW 1, 3; CA 117; 125; CANR 81; MTCW 1

Ovid 43B.C.-17 ...... CMLC 7; DAM POET; PC 2
See also DA3; DLB 211

Owen, Hugh
See Faust, Frederick (Schiller)

Owen, Wilfred (Edward Salter) 1893-1918T C L C 5, 27; DA; DAB; DAC; DAM MST, POET; PC 19; WLC
See also CA 104; 141; CDBLB 1914-1945; DLB 20; MTCW 2

Owens, Rochelle 1936- .... CLC 8
See also CA 17-20R; CAAS 2; CANR 39

Oz, Amos 1939- CLC 5, 8, 11, 27, 33, 54; DAM NOV
See also CA 53-56; CANR 27, 47, 65; MTCW 1, 2

Ozick, Cynthia 1928-CLC 3, 7, 28, 62; DAM NOV, POP; SSC 15
See also BEST 90:1; CA 17-20R; CANR 23, 58; DA3; DLB 28, 152; DLBY 82; INT CANR-23; MTCW 1, 2

Ozu, Yasujiro 1903-1963 .... CLC 16
See also CA 112

Pacheco, C.
See Pessoa, Fernando (Antonio Nogueira)

Pacheco, Jose Emilio 1939-
See also CA 111; 131; CANR 65; DAM MULT; HLC 2; HW 1, 2

Pa Chin .... CLC 18
See also Li Fei-kan

Pack, Robert 1929- .... CLC 13
See also CA 1-4R; CANR 3, 44, 82; DLB 5

Padgett, Lewis
See Kuttner, Henry

Padilla (Lorenzo), Heberto 1932- .... CLC 38
See also AITN 1; CA 123; 131; HW 1

Page, Jimmy 1944- .... CLC 12

Page, Louise 1955- .... CLC 40
See also CA 140; CANR 76

Page, P(atricia) K(athleen) 1916- .... CLC 7, 18; DAC; DAM MST; PC 12
See also CA 53-56; CANR 4, 22, 65; DLB 68; MTCW 1

Page, Thomas Nelson 1853-1922 .... SSC 23
See also CA 118; 177; DLB 12, 78; DLBD 13

Pagels, Elaine Hiesey 1943- .... CLC 104
See also CA 45-48; CANR 2, 24, 51

Paget, Violet 1856-1935
See Lee, Vernon
See also CA 104; 166

Paget-Lowe, Henry
See Lovecraft, H(oward) P(hillips)

Paglia, Camille (Anna) 1947- .... CLC 68
See also CA 140; CANR 72; MTCW 2

Paige, Richard
See Koontz, Dean R(ay)

Paine, Thomas 1737-1809 .... NCLC 62
See also CDALB 1640-1865; DLB 31, 43, 73, 158

Pakenham, Antonia
See Fraser, (Lady) Antonia (Pakenham)

Palamas, Kostes 1859-1943 .... TCLC 5
See also CA 105

Palazzeschi, Aldo 1885-1974 .... CLC 11
See also CA 89-92; 53-56; DLB 114

Pales Matos, Luis 1898-1959
See also HLCS 2; HW 1

Paley, Grace 1922-CLC 4, 6, 37; DAM POP; SSC 8
See also CA 25-28R; CANR 13, 46, 74; DA3; DLB 28; INT CANR-13; MTCW 1, 2

Palin, Michael (Edward) 1943- .... CLC 21
See also Monty Python
See also CA 107; CANR 35; SATA 67

Palliser, Charles 1947- .... CLC 65
See also CA 136; CANR 76

Palma, Ricardo 1833-1919 .... TCLC 29
See also CA 168

Pancake, Breece Dexter 1952-1979
See Pancake, Breece D'J
See also CA 123; 109

Pancake, Breece D'J .... CLC 29
See also Pancake, Breece Dexter
See also DLB 130

Panko, Rudy
See Gogol, Nikolai (Vasilyevich)

Papadiamantis, Alexandros 1851-1911 TCLC 29
See also CA 168

Papadiamantopoulos, Johannes 1856-1910
See Moreas, Jean
See also CA 117

Papini, Giovanni 1881-1956 .... TCLC 22
See also CA 121; 180

Paracelsus 1493-1541 .... LC 14
See also DLB 179

Parasol, Peter
See Stevens, Wallace

Pardo Bazan, Emilia 1851-1921 .... SSC 30

Pareto, Vilfredo 1848-1923 .... TCLC 69
See also CA 175

Parfenie, Maria
See Codrescu, Andrei

Parini, Jay (Lee) 1948- .... CLC 54
See also CA 97-100; CAAS 16; CANR 32

Park, Jordan
See Kornbluth, C(yril) M.; Pohl, Frederik

Park, Robert E(zra) 1864-1944 .... TCLC 73
See also CA 122; 165

Parker, Bert
See Ellison, Harlan (Jay)

Parker, Dorothy (Rothschild) 1893-1967CLC 15, 68; DAM POET; PC 28; SSC 2
See also CA 19-20; 25-28R; CAP 2; DA3; DLB 11, 45, 86; MTCW 1, 2

Parker, Robert B(rown) 1932- .... CLC 27; DAM NOV, POP
See also AAYA 28; BEST 89:4; CA 49-52; CANR 1, 26, 52; INT CANR-26; MTCW 1

Parkin, Frank 1940- .... CLC 43
See also CA 147

Parkman, Francis Jr., Jr. 1823-1893 .. NCLC 12
See also DLB 1, 30, 186

Parks, Gordon (Alexander Buchanan) 1912-CLC 1, 16; BLC 3; DAM MULT
See also AITN 2; BW 2, 3; CA 41-44R; CANR 26, 66; DA3; DLB 33; MTCW 2; SATA 8, 108

See also CANR 32; DAM MULT; DLB 209;
HLC 2; HW 1
Post, Melville Davisson 1869-1930 ...... **TCLC 39**
See also CA 110
Potok, Chaim 1929-**CLC 2, 7, 14, 26, 112; DAM
NOV**
See also AAYA 15; AITN 1, 2; CA 17-20R; CANR
19, 35, 64; DA3; DLB 28, 152; INT CANR-19;
MTCW 1, 2; SATA 33, 106
Potter, Dennis (Christopher George) 1935-1994
CLC 58, 86
See also CA 107; 145; CANR 33, 61; MTCW 1
Pound, Ezra (Weston Loomis) 1885-1972 **CLC 1,
2, 3, 4, 5, 7, 10, 13, 18, 34, 48, 50, 112; DA;
DAB; DAC; DAM MST, POET; PC 4; WLC**
See also CA 5-8R; 37-40R; CANR 40; CDALB
1917-1929; DA3; DLB 4, 45, 63; DLBD 15;
MTCW 1, 2
Povod, Reinaldo 1959-1994 .... **CLC 44**
See also CA 136; 146; CANR 83
Powell, Adam Clayton, Jr. 1908-1972 ... **CLC 89;
BLC 3; DAM MULT**
See also BW 1, 3; CA 102; 33-36R; CANR 86
Powell, Anthony (Dymoke) 1905- **CLC 1, 3, 7, 9,
10, 31**
See also CA 1-4R; CANR 1, 32, 62; CDBLB 1945-
1960; DLB 15; MTCW 1, 2
Powell, Dawn 1897-1965 .... **CLC 66**
See also CA 5-8R; DLBY 97
Powell, Padgett 1952- .... **CLC 34**
See also CA 126; CANR 63
Power, Susan 1961- .... **CLC 91**
Powers, J(ames) F(arl) 1917-1999**CLC 1, 4, 8, 57;
SSC 4**
See also CA 1-4R; 181; CANR 2, 61; DLB 130;
MTCW 1
Powers, John J(ames) 1945-
See Powers, John R.
See also CA 69-72
Powers, John R. .... **CLC 66**
See also Powers, John J(ames)
Powers, Richard (S.) 1957- .... **CLC 93**
See also CA 148; CANR 80
Pownall, David 1938- .... **CLC 10**
See also CA 89-92, 180; CAAS 18; CANR 49;
DLB 14
Powys, John Cowper 1872-1963**CLC 7, 9, 15, 46,
125**
See also CA 85-88; DLB 15; MTCW 1, 2
Powys, T(heodore) F(rancis) 1875-1953 **TCLC 9**
See also CA 106; DLB 36, 162
Prado (Calvo), Pedro 1886-1952 .... **TCLC 75**
See also CA 131; HW 1
Prager, Emily 1952- .... **CLC 56**
Pratt, E(dwin) J(ohn) 1883(?)-1964**CLC 19; DAC;
DAM POET**
See also CA 141; 93-96; CANR 77; DLB 92
Premchand .... **TCLC 21**
See also Srivastava, Dhanpat Rai
Preussler, Otfried 1923- .... **CLC 17**
See also CA 77-80; SATA 24
Prevert, Jacques (Henri Marie) 1900-1977 **C L C
15**
See also CA 77-80; 69-72; CANR 29, 61; MTCW
1; SATA-Obit 30
Prevost, Abbe (Antoine Francois) 1697-1763**LC 1**
Price, (Edward) Reynolds 1933-**CLC 3, 6, 13, 43,
50, 63; DAM NOV; SSC 22**
See also CA 1-4R; CANR 1, 37, 57; DLB 2; INT
CANR-37
Price, Richard 1949- .... **CLC 6, 12**
See also CA 49-52; CANR 3; DLBY 81
Prichard, Katharine Susannah 1883-1969 . **C L C**

46
See also CA 11-12; CANR 33; CAP 1; MTCW 1;
SATA 66
Priestley, J(ohn) B(oynton) 1894-1984 **CLC 2, 5,
9, 34; DAM DRAM, NOV**
See also CA 9-12R; 113; CANR 33; CDBLB 1914-
1945; DA3; DLB 10, 34, 77, 100, 139; DLBY 84;
MTCW 1, 2
Prince 1958(?)- .... **CLC 35**
Prince, F(rank) T(empleton) 1912- ...... **CLC 22**
See also CA 101; CANR 43, 79; DLB 20
Prince Kropotkin
See Kropotkin, Peter (Aleksieevich)
Prior, Matthew 1664-1721 .... **LC 4**
See also DLB 95
Prishvin, Mikhail 1873-1954 .... **TCLC 75**
Pritchard, William H(arrison) 1932- ... **CLC 34**
See also CA 65-68; CANR 23; DLB 111
Pritchett, V(ictor) S(awdon) 1900-1997**CLC 5, 13,
15, 41; DAM NOV; SSC 14**
See also CA 61-64; 157; CANR 31, 63; DA3; DLB
15, 139; MTCW 1, 2
Private 19022
See Manning, Frederic
Probst, Mark 1925- .... **CLC 59**
See also CA 130
Prokosch, Frederic 1908-1989 .... **CLC 4, 48**
See also CA 73-76; 128; CANR 82; DLB 48;
MTCW 2
Propertius, Sextus c. 50B.C.-c. 16B.C.**CMLC 32**
See also DLB 211
Prophet, The
See Dreiser, Theodore (Herman Albert)
Prose, Francine 1947- .... **CLC 45**
See also CA 109; 112; CANR 46; SATA 101
Proudhon
See Cunha, Euclides (Rodrigues Pimenta) da
Proulx, Annie
See Proulx, E(dna) Annie
Proulx, E(dna) Annie 1935- **CLC 81; DAM POP**
See also CA 145; CANR 65; DA3; MTCW 2
Proust, (Valentin-Louis-George-Eugene-) Marcel
1871-1922**TCLC 7, 13, 33; DA; DAB; DAC;
DAM MST, NOV; WLC**
See also CA 104; 120; DA3; DLB 65; MTCW 1, 2
Prowler, Harley
See Masters, Edgar Lee
Prus, Boleslaw 1845-1912 .... **TCLC 48**
Pryor, Richard (Franklin Lenox Thomas) 1940-
CLC 26
See also CA 122; 152
Przybyszewski, Stanislaw 1868-1927 . **TCLC 36**
See also CA 160; DLB 66
Pteleon
See Grieve, C(hristopher) M(urray)
See also DAM POET
Puckett, Lute
See Masters, Edgar Lee
Puig, Manuel 1932-1990 ... **CLC 3, 5, 10, 28, 65;
DAM MULT; HLC 2**
See also CA 45-48; CANR 2, 32, 63; DA3; DLB
113; HW 1, 2; MTCW 1, 2
Pulitzer, Joseph 1847-1911 .... **TCLC 76**
See also CA 114; DLB 23
Purdy, A(lfred) W(ellington) 1918-**CLC 3, 6, 14,
50; DAC; DAM MST, POET**
See also CA 81-84; CAAS 17; CANR 42, 66; DLB
88
Purdy, James (Amos) 1923- **CLC 2, 4, 10, 28, 52**
See also CA 33-36R; CAAS 1; CANR 19, 51; DLB
2; INT CANR-19; MTCW 1
Pure, Simon
See Swinnerton, Frank Arthur

Pushkin, Alexander (Sergeyevich) 1799-1837
**NCLC 3, 27, 83; DA; DAB; DAC; DAM
DRAM, MST, POET; PC 10; SSC 27; WLC**
See also DA3; DLB 205; SATA 61
P'u Sung-ling 1640-1715 .... **LC 49; SSC 31**
Putnam, Arthur Lee
See Alger, Horatio Jr., Jr.
Puzo, Mario 1920-1999**CLC 1, 2, 6, 36, 107; DAM
NOV, POP**
See also CA 65-68; CANR 4, 42, 65; DA3; DLB 6;
MTCW 1, 2
Pygge, Edward
See Barnes, Julian (Patrick)
Pyle, Ernest Taylor 1900-1945
See Pyle, Ernie
See also CA 115; 160
Pyle, Ernie 1900-1945 .... **TCLC 75**
See also Pyle, Ernest Taylor
See also DLB 29; MTCW 2
Pyle, Howard 1853-1911 .... **TCLC 81**
See also CA 109; 137; CLR 22; DLB 42, 188;
DLBD 13; MAICYA; SATA 16, 100
Pym, Barbara (Mary Crampton) 1913-1980 **C L C
13, 19, 37, 111**
See also CA 13-14; 97-100; CANR 13, 34; CAP 1;
DLB 14, 207; DLBY 87; MTCW 1, 2
Pynchon, Thomas (Ruggles, Jr.) 1937-**CLC 2, 3,
6, 9, 11, 18, 33, 62, 72; DA; DAB; DAC; DAM
MST, NOV, POP; SSC 14; WLC**
See also BEST 90:2; CA 17-20R; CANR 22, 46,
73; DA3; DLB 2, 173; MTCW 1, 2
Pythagoras c. 570B.C.-c. 500B.C. .... **CMLC 22**
See also DLB 176
Q
See Quiller-Couch, SirArthur (Thomas)
Qian Zhongshu
See Ch'ien Chung-shu
Qroll
See Dagerman, Stig (Halvard)
Quarrington, Paul (Lewis) 1953- .... **CLC 65**
See also CA 129; CANR 62
Quasimodo, Salvatore 1901-1968 .... **CLC 10**
See also CA 13-16; 25-28R; CAP 1; DLB 114;
MTCW 1
Quay, Stephen 1947- .... **CLC 95**
Quay, Timothy 1947- .... **CLC 95**
Queen, Ellery .... **CLC 3, 11**
See also Dannay, Frederic; Davidson, Avram
(James); Lee, Manfred B(ennington);
Marlowe, Stephen; Sturgeon, Theodore
(Hamilton); Vance, John Holbrook
Queen, Ellery, Jr.
See Dannay, Frederic; Lee, Manfred
B(ennington)
Queneau, Raymond 1903-1976 **CLC 2, 5, 10, 42**
See also CA 77-80; 69-72; CANR 32; DLB 72;
MTCW 1, 2
Quevedo, Francisco de 1580-1645 .... **LC 23**
Quiller-Couch, SirArthur (Thomas) 1863-1944
TCLC 53
See also CA 118; 166; DLB 135, 153, 190
Quin, Ann (Marie) 1936-1973 .... **CLC 6**
See also CA 9-12R; 45-48; DLB 14
Quinn, Martin
See Smith, Martin Cruz
Quinn, Peter 1947- .... **CLC 91**
Quinn, Simon
See Smith, Martin Cruz
Quintana, Leroy V. 1944-
See also CA 131; CANR 65; DAM MULT; DLB
82; HLC 2; HW 1, 2
Quiroga, Horacio (Sylvestre) 1878-1937 . **TCLC
20; DAM MULT; HLC 2**

See also CA 117; 131; HW 1; MTCW 1
Quoirez, Francoise 1935- .... **CLC 9**
See also Sagan, Francoise
See also CA 49-52; CANR 6, 39, 73; MTCW 1, 2
Raabe, Wilhelm (Karl) 1831-1910 ...... **TCLC 45**
See also CA 167; DLB 129
Rabe, David (William) 1940-**CLC 4, 8, 33; DAM DRAM**
See also CA 85-88; CABS 3; CANR 59; DLB 7
Rabelais, Francois 1483-1553 . **LC 5; DA; DAB; DAC; DAM MST; WLC**
Rabinovitch, Sholem 1859-1916
See Aleichem, Sholom
See also CA 104
Rabinyan, Dorit 1972- .... **CLC 119**
See also CA 170
Rachilde 1860-1953 .... **TCLC 67**
See also DLB 123, 192
Racine, Jean 1639-1699**LC 28; DAB; DAM MST**
See also DA3
Radcliffe, Ann (Ward) 1764-1823 .... **NCLC 6, 55**
See also DLB 39, 178
Radiguet, Raymond 1903-1923 .... **TCLC 29**
See also CA 162; DLB 65
Radnoti, Miklos 1909-1944 .... **TCLC 16**
See also CA 118
Rado, James 1939- .... **CLC 17**
See also CA 105
Radvanyi, Netty 1900-1983
See Seghers, Anna
See also CA 85-88; 110; CANR 82
Rae, Ben
See Griffiths, Trevor
Raeburn, John (Hay) 1941- .... **CLC 34**
See also CA 57-60
Ragni, Gerome 1942-1991 .... **CLC 17**
See also CA 105; 134
Rahv, Philip 1908-1973 .... **CLC 24**
See also Greenberg, Ivan
See also DLB 137
Raimund, Ferdinand Jakob 1790-1836 **NCLC 69**
See also DLB 90
Raine, Craig 1944- .... **CLC 32, 103**
See also CA 108; CANR 29, 51; DLB 40
Raine, Kathleen (Jessie) 1908- .... **CLC 7, 45**
See also CA 85-88; CANR 46; DLB 20; MTCW 1
Rainis, Janis 1865-1929 .... **TCLC 29**
See also CA 170
Rakosi, Carl 1903- .... **CLC 47**
See also Rawley, Callman
See also CAAS 5; DLB 193
Raleigh, Richard
See Lovecraft, H(oward) P(hillips)
Raleigh, Sir Walter 1554(?)-1618 ...... **LC 31, 39**
See also CDBLB Before 1660; DLB 172
Rallentando, H. P.
See Sayers, Dorothy L(eigh)
Ramal, Walter
See de la Mare, Walter (John)
Ramana Maharshi 1879-1950 .... **TCLC 84**
Ramoacn y Cajal, Santiago 1852-1934 **TCLC 93**
Ramon, Juan
See Jimenez (Mantecon), Juan Ramon
Ramos, Graciliano 1892-1953 .... **TCLC 32**
See also CA 167; HW 2
Rampersad, Arnold 1941- .... **CLC 44**
See also BW 2, 3; CA 127; 133; CANR 81; DLB 111; INT 133
Rampling, Anne
See Rice, Anne
Ramsay, Allan 1684(?)-1758 .... **LC 29**
See also DLB 95
Ramuz, Charles-Ferdinand 1878-1947 **TCLC 33**

See also CA 165
Rand, Ayn 1905-1982**CLC 3, 30, 44, 79; DA; DAC; DAM MST, NOV, POP; WLC**
See also AAYA 10; CA 13-16R; 105; CANR 27, 73; CDALBS; DA3; MTCW 1, 2
Randall, Dudley (Felker) 1914- **CLC 1; BLC 3; DAM MULT**
See also BW 1, 3; CA 25-28R; CANR 23, 82; DLB 41
Randall, Robert
See Silverberg, Robert
Ranger, Ken
See Creasey, John
Ransom, John Crowe 1888-1974 **CLC 2, 4, 5, 11, 24; DAM POET**
See also CA 5-8R; 49-52; CANR 6, 34; CDALBS; DA3; DLB 45, 63; MTCW 1, 2
Rao, Raja 1909- .... **CLC 25, 56; DAM NOV**
See also CA 73-76; CANR 51; MTCW 1, 2
Raphael, Frederic (Michael) 1931-... **CLC 2, 14**
See also CA 1-4R; CANR 1, 86; DLB 14
Ratcliffe, James P.
See Mencken, H(enry) L(ouis)
Rathbone, Julian 1935- .... **CLC 41**
See also CA 101; CANR 34, 73
Rattigan, Terence (Mervyn) 1911-1977 .. **CLC 7; DAM DRAM**
See also CA 85-88; 73-76; CDBLB 1945-1960; DLB 13; MTCW 1, 2
Ratushinskaya, Irina 1954- .... **CLC 54**
See also CA 129; CANR 68
Raven, Simon (Arthur Noel) 1927- .... **CLC 14**
See also CA 81-84; CANR 86
Ravenna, Michael
See Welty, Eudora
Rawley, Callman 1903-
See Rakosi, Carl
See also CA 21-24R; CANR 12, 32
Rawlings, Marjorie Kinnan 1896-1953 . **TCLC 4**
See also AAYA 20; CA 104; 137; CANR 74; DLB 9, 22, 102; DLBD 17; JRDA; MAICYA; MTCW 2; SATA 100; YABC 1
Ray, Satyajit 1921-1992**CLC 16, 76; DAM MULT**
See also CA 114; 137
Read, Herbert Edward 1893-1968 .... **CLC 4**
See also CA 85-88; 25-28R; DLB 20, 149
Read, Piers Paul 1941- .... **CLC 4, 10, 25**
See also CA 21-24R; CANR 38, 86; DLB 14; SATA 21
Reade, Charles 1814-1884 .... **NCLC 2, 74**
See also DLB 21
Reade, Hamish
See Gray, Simon (James Holliday)
Reading, Peter 1946- .... **CLC 47**
See also CA 103; CANR 46; DLB 40
Reaney, James 1926- **CLC 13; DAC; DAM MST**
See also CA 41-44R; CAAS 15; CANR 42; DLB 68; SATA 43
Rebreanu, Liviu 1885-1944 .... **TCLC 28**
See also CA 165
Rechy, John (Francisco) 1934-**CLC 1, 7, 14, 18, 107; DAM MULT; HLC 2**
See also CA 5-8R; CAAS 4; CANR 6, 32, 64; DLB 122; DLBY 82; HW 1, 2; INT CANR-6
Redcam, Tom 1870-1933 .... **TCLC 25**
Reddin, Keith .... **CLC 67**
Redgrove, Peter (William) 1932- ...... **CLC 6, 41**
See also CA 1-4R; CANR 3, 39, 77; DLB 40
Redmon, Anne .... **CLC 22**
See also Nightingale, Anne Redmon
See also DLBY 86
Reed, Eliot
See Ambler, Eric

Reed, Ishmael 1938- . **CLC 2, 3, 5, 6, 13, 32, 60; BLC 3; DAM MULT**
See also BW 2, 3; CA 21-24R; CANR 25, 48, 74; DA3; DLB 2, 5, 33, 169; DLBD 8; MTCW 1, 2
Reed, John (Silas) 1887-1920 .... **TCLC 9**
See also CA 106
Reed, Lou .... **CLC 21**
See also Firbank, Louis
Reeve, Clara 1729-1807 .... **NCLC 19**
See also DLB 39
Reich, Wilhelm 1897-1957 .... **TCLC 57**
Reid, Christopher (John) 1949- .... **CLC 33**
See also CA 140; DLB 40
Reid, Desmond
See Moorcock, Michael (John)
Reid Banks, Lynne 1929-
See Banks, Lynne Reid
See also CA 1-4R; CANR 6, 22, 38; CLR 24; JRDA; MAICYA; SATA 22, 75, 111
Reilly, William K.
See Creasey, John
Reiner, Max
See Caldwell, (Janet Miriam) Taylor (Holland)
Reis, Ricardo
See Pessoa, Fernando (Antonio Nogueira)
Remarque, Erich Maria 1898-1970 **CLC 21; DA; DAB; DAC; DAM MST, NOV**
See also AAYA 27; CA 77-80; 29-32R; DA3; DLB 56; MTCW 1, 2
Remington, Frederic 1861-1909 .... **TCLC 89**
See also CA 108; 169; DLB 12, 186, 188; SATA 41
Remizov, A.
See Remizov, Aleksei (Mikhailovich)
Remizov, A. M.
See Remizov, Aleksei (Mikhailovich)
Remizov, Aleksei (Mikhailovich) 1877-1957 **TCLC 27**
See also CA 125; 133
Renan, Joseph Ernest 1823-1892 .... **NCLC 26**
Renard, Jules 1864-1910 .... **TCLC 17**
See also CA 117
Renault, Mary .... **CLC 3, 11, 17**
See also Challans, Mary
See also DLBY 83; MTCW 2
Rendell, Ruth (Barbara) 1930-**CLC 28, 48; DAM POP**
See also Vine, Barbara
See also CA 109; CANR 32, 52, 74; DLB 87; INT CANR-32; MTCW 1, 2
Renoir, Jean 1894-1979 .... **CLC 20**
See also CA 129; 85-88
Resnais, Alain 1922- .... **CLC 16**
Reverdy, Pierre 1889-1960 .... **CLC 53**
See also CA 97-100; 89-92
Rexroth, Kenneth 1905-1982**CLC 1, 2, 6, 11, 22, 49, 112; DAM POET; PC 20**
See also CA 5-8R; 107; CANR 14, 34, 63; CDALB 1941-1968; DLB 16, 48, 165, 212; DLBY 82; INT CANR-14; MTCW 1, 2
Reyes, Alfonso 1889-1959 ... **TCLC 33; HLCS 2**
See also CA 131; HW 1
Reyes y Basoalto, Ricardo Eliecer Neftali
See Neruda, Pablo
Reymont, Wladyslaw (Stanislaw) 1868(?)-1925 **TCLC 5**
See also CA 104
Reynolds, Jonathan 1942- .... **CLC 6, 38**
See also CA 65-68; CANR 28
Reynolds, Joshua 1723-1792 .... **LC 15**
See also DLB 104
Reynolds, Michael Shane 1937- .... **CLC 44**
See also CA 65-68; CANR 9
Reznikoff, Charles 1894-1976 .... **CLC 9**

SMITH

Author Index

SATA 17

Tarkovsky, Andrei (Arsenyevich) 1932-1986**CLC 75**
See also CA 127

Tartt, Donna 1964(?)- .... **CLC 76**
See also CA 142

Tasso, Torquato 1544-1595 .... **LC 5**

Tate, (John Orley) Allen 1899-1979**CLC 2, 4, 6, 9, 11, 14, 24**
See also CA 5-8R; 85-88; CANR 32; DLB 4, 45, 63; DLBD 17; MTCW 1, 2

Tate, Ellalice
See Hibbert, Eleanor Alice Burford

Tate, James (Vincent) 1943- .... **CLC 2, 6, 25**
See also CA 21-24R; CANR 29, 57; DLB 5, 169

Tauler, Johannes c. 1300-1361 .... **CMLC 37**
See also DLB 179

Tavel, Ronald 1940- .... **CLC 6**
See also CA 21-24R; CANR 33

Taylor, C(ecil) P(hilip) 1929-1981 .... **CLC 27**
See also CA 25-28R; 105; CANR 47

Taylor, Edward 1642(?)-1729 . **LC 11; DA; DAB; DAC; DAM MST, POET**
See also DLB 24

Taylor, Eleanor Ross 1920- .... **CLC 5**
See also CA 81-84; CANR 70

Taylor, Elizabeth 1912-1975 .... **CLC 2, 4, 29**
See also CA 13-16R; CANR 9, 70; DLB 139; MTCW 1; SATA 13

Taylor, Frederick Winslow 1856-1915 **TCLC 76**

Taylor, Henry (Splawn) 1942- .... **CLC 44**
See also CA 33-36R; CAAS 7; CANR 31; DLB 5

Taylor, Kamala (Purnaiya) 1924-
See Markandaya, Kamala
See also CA 77-80

Taylor, Mildred D. .... **CLC 21**
See also AAYA 10; BW 1; CA 85-88; CANR 25; CLR 9, 59; DLB 52; JRDA; MAICYA; SAAS 5; SATA 15, 70

Taylor, Peter (Hillsman) 1917-1994**CLC 1, 4, 18, 37, 44, 50, 71; SSC 10**
See also CA 13-16R; 147; CANR 9, 50; DLBY 81, 94; INT CANR-9; MTCW 1, 2

Taylor, Robert Lewis 1912-1998 .... **CLC 14**
See also CA 1-4R; 170; CANR 3, 64; SATA 10

Tchekhov, Anton
See Chekhov, Anton (Pavlovich)

Tchicaya, Gerald Felix 1931-1988 .... **CLC 101**
See also CA 129; 125; CANR 81

Tchicaya U Tam'si
See Tchicaya, Gerald Felix

Teasdale, Sara 1884-1933 .... **TCLC 4**
See also CA 104; 163; DLB 45; SATA 32

Tegner, Esaias 1782-1846 .... **NCLC 2**

Teilhard de Chardin, (Marie Joseph) Pierre 1881-1955 .... **TCLC 9**
See also CA 105

Temple, Ann
See Mortimer, Penelope (Ruth)

Tennant, Emma (Christina) 1937- .. **CLC 13, 52**
See also CA 65-68; CAAS 9; CANR 10, 38, 59; DLB 14

Tenneshaw, S. M.
See Silverberg, Robert

Tennyson, Alfred 1809-1892 . **NCLC 30, 65; DA; DAB; DAC; DAM MST, POET; PC 6; WLC**
See also CDBLB 1832-1890; DA3; DLB 32

Teran, Lisa St. Aubin de .... **CLC 36**
See also St. Aubin de Teran, Lisa

Terence c. 184B.C.-c. 159B.C. . **CMLC 14; DC 7**
See also DLB 211

Teresa de Jesus, St. 1515-1582 .... **LC 18**

Terkel, Louis 1912-
See Terkel, Studs
See also CA 57-60; CANR 18, 45, 67; DA3; MTCW 1, 2

Terkel, Studs .... **CLC 38**
See also Terkel, Louis
See also AAYA 32; AITN 1; MTCW 2

Terry, C. V.
See Slaughter, Frank G(ill)

Terry, Megan 1932- .... **CLC 19**
See also CA 77-80; CABS 3; CANR 43; DLB 7

Tertullian c. 155-c. 245 .... **CMLC 29**

Tertz, Abram
See Sinyavsky, Andrei (Donatevich)

Tesich, Steve 1943(?)-1996 .... **CLC 40, 69**
See also CA 105; 152; DLBY 83

Tesla, Nikola 1856-1943 .... **TCLC 88**

Teternikov, Fyodor Kuzmich 1863-1927
See Sologub, Fyodor
See also CA 104

Tevis, Walter 1928-1984 .... **CLC 42**
See also CA 113

Tey, Josephine .... **TCLC 14**
See also Mackintosh, Elizabeth
See also DLB 77

Thackeray, William Makepeace 1811-1863**NCLC 5, 14, 22, 43; DA; DAB; DAC; DAM MST, NOV; WLC**
See also CDBLB 1832-1890; DA3; DLB 21, 55, 159, 163; SATA 23

Thakura, Ravindranatha
See Tagore, Rabindranath

Tharoor, Shashi 1956- .... **CLC 70**
See also CA 141

Thelwell, Michael Miles 1939- .... **CLC 22**
See also BW 2; CA 101

Theobald, Lewis, Jr.
See Lovecraft, H(oward) P(hillips)

Theodorescu, Ion N. 1880-1967
See Arghezi, Tudor
See also CA 116

Theriault, Yves 1915-1983 **CLC 79; DAC; DAM MST**
See also CA 102; DLB 88

Theroux, Alexander (Louis) 1939- .... **CLC 2, 25**
See also CA 85-88; CANR 20, 63

Theroux, Paul (Edward) 1941- **CLC 5, 8, 11, 15, 28, 46; DAM POP**
See also AAYA 28; BEST 89:4; CA 33-36R; CANR 20, 45, 74; CDALBS; DA3;DLB 2; MTCW 1, 2; SATA 44, 109

Thesen, Sharon 1946- .... **CLC 56**
See also CA 163

Thevenin, Denis
See Duhamel, Georges

Thibault, Jacques Anatole Francois 1844-1924
See France, Anatole
See also CA 106; 127; DAM NOV; DA3; MTCW 1, 2

Thiele, Colin (Milton) 1920- .... **CLC 17**
See also CA 29-32R; CANR 12, 28, 53; CLR 27; MAICYA; SAAS 2; SATA 14, 72

Thomas, Audrey (Callahan) 1935-**CLC 7, 13, 37, 107; SSC 20**
See also AITN 2; CA 21-24R; CAAS 19; CANR 36, 58; DLB 60; MTCW 1

Thomas, Augustus 1857-1934 .... **TCLC 97**

Thomas, D(onald) M(ichael) 1935-**CLC 13, 22, 31**
See also CA 61-64; CAAS 11; CANR 17, 45, 75; CDBLB 1960 to Present; DA3; DLB 40, 207; INT CANR-17; MTCW 1, 2

Thomas, Dylan (Marlais) 1914-1953 **TCLC 1, 8, 45; DA; DAB; DAC; DAM DRAM, MST, POET; PC 2; SSC 3; WLC**
See also CA 104; 120; CANR 65; CDBLB 1945-1960; DA3; DLB 13, 20, 139; MTCW 1, 2; SATA 60

Thomas, (Philip) Edward 1878-1917 ... **TCLC 10; DAM POET**
See also CA 106; 153; DLB 98

Thomas, Joyce Carol 1938- .... **CLC 35**
See also AAYA 12; BW 2, 3; CA 113; 116; CANR 48; CLR 19; DLB 33; INT 116; JRDA; MAICYA; MTCW 1, 2; SAAS 7; SATA 40, 78

Thomas, Lewis 1913-1993 .... **CLC 35**
See also CA 85-88; 143; CANR 38, 60; MTCW 1, 2

Thomas, M. Carey 1857-1935 .... **TCLC 89**

Thomas, Paul
See Mann, (Paul) Thomas

Thomas, Piri 1928- .... **CLC 17; HLCS 2**
See also CA 73-76; HW 1

Thomas, R(onald) S(tuart) 1913- **CLC 6, 13, 48; DAB; DAM POET**
See also CA 89-92; CAAS 4; CANR 30; CDBLB 1960 to Present; DLB 27; MTCW 1

Thomas, Ross (Elmore) 1926-1995 .... **CLC 39**
See also CA 33-36R; 150; CANR 22, 63

Thompson, Francis Clegg
See Mencken, H(enry) L(ouis)

Thompson, Francis Joseph 1859-1907 .. **TCLC 4**
See also CA 104; CDBLB 1890-1914; DLB 19

Thompson, Hunter S(tockton) 1939- **CLC 9, 17, 40, 104; DAM POP**
See also BEST 89:1; CA 17-20R; CANR 23, 46, 74, 77; DA3; DLB 185; MTCW 1, 2

Thompson, James Myers
See Thompson, Jim (Myers)

Thompson, Jim (Myers) 1906-1977(?) .. **CLC 69**
See also CA 140

Thompson, Judith .... **CLC 39**

Thomson, James 1700-1748**LC 16, 29, 40; DAM POET**
See also DLB 95

Thomson, James 1834-1882**NCLC 18; DAM POET**
See also DLB 35

Thoreau, Henry David 1817-1862**NCLC 7, 21, 61; DA; DAB; DAC; DAM MST; WLC**
See also CDALB 1640-1865; DA3; DLB 1

Thornton, Hall
See Silverberg, Robert

Thucydides c. 455B.C.-399B.C. .... **CMLC 17**
See also DLB 176

Thurber, James (Grover) 1894-1961 . **CLC 5, 11, 25, 125; DA; DAB; DAC; DAM DRAM, MST, NOV; SSC 1**
See also CA 73-76; CANR 17, 39; CDALB 1929-1941; DA3; DLB 4, 11, 22, 102; MAICYA; MTCW 1, 2; SATA 13

Thurman, Wallace (Henry) 1902-1934 . **TCLC 6; BLC 3; DAM MULT**
See also BW 1, 3; CA 104; 124; CANR 81; DLB 51

Tibullus, Albius c. 54B.C.-c. 19B.C. .. **CMLC 36**
See also DLB 211

Ticheburn, Cheviot
See Ainsworth, William Harrison

Tieck, (Johann) Ludwig 1773-1853 **NCLC 5, 46; SSC 31**
See also DLB 90

Tiger, Derry
See Ellison, Harlan (Jay)

Tilghman, Christopher 1948(?)- .... **CLC 65**
See also CA 159

Tillinghast, Richard (Williford) 1940- **CLC 29**
See also CA 29-32R; CAAS 23; CANR 26, 51

Timrod, Henry 1828-1867 .... **NCLC 25**

See also DLB 3

Tindall, Gillian (Elizabeth) 1938- .... **CLC 7**
See also CA 21-24R; CANR 11, 65

Tiptree, James, Jr. .... **CLC 48, 50**
See also Sheldon, Alice Hastings Bradley
See also DLB 8

Titmarsh, Michael Angelo
See Thackeray, William Makepeace

Tocqueville, Alexis (Charles Henri Maurice Clerel, Comte) de 1805-1859
.... **NCLC 7, 63**

Tolkien, J(ohn) R(onald) R(euel) 1892-1973 **C L C 1, 2, 3, 8, 12, 38; DA; DAB; DAC; DAM MST, NOV, POP; WLC**
See also AAYA 10; AITN 1; CA 17-18; 45-48; CANR 36; CAP 2; CDBLB 1914-1945; CLR 56; DA3; DLB 15, 160; JRDA; MAICYA; MTCW 1, 2; SATA 2, 32, 100; SATA-Obit 24

Toller, Ernst 1893-1939 .... **TCLC 10**
See also CA 107; DLB 124

Tolson, M. B.
See Tolson, Melvin B(eaunorus)

Tolson, Melvin B(eaunorus) 1898(?)-1966 .. **C L C 36, 105; BLC 3; DAM MULT, POET**
See also BW 1, 3; CA 124; 89-92; CANR 80; DLB 48, 76

Tolstoi, Aleksei Nikolaevich
See Tolstoy, Alexey Nikolaevich

Tolstoy, Alexey Nikolaevich 1882-1945 **TCLC 18**
See also CA 107; 158

Tolstoy, Count Leo
See Tolstoy, Leo (Nikolaevich)

Tolstoy, Leo (Nikolaevich) 1828-1910 **TCLC 4, 11, 17, 28, 44, 79; DA; DAB; DAC; DAM MST, NOV; SSC 9, 30; WLC**
See also CA 104; 123; DA3; SATA 26

Tomasi di Lampedusa, Giuseppe 1896-1957
See Lampedusa, Giuseppe (Tomasi) di
See also CA 111

Tomlin, Lily .... **CLC 17**
See also Tomlin, Mary Jean

Tomlin, Mary Jean 1939(?)-
See Tomlin, Lily
See also CA 117

Tomlinson, (Alfred) Charles 1927- **CLC 2, 4, 6, 13, 45; DAM POET; PC 17**
See also CA 5-8R; CANR 33; DLB 40

Tomlinson, H(enry) M(ajor) 1873-1958 **TCLC 71**
See also CA 118; 161; DLB 36, 100, 195

Tonson, Jacob
See Bennett, (Enoch) Arnold

Toole, John Kennedy 1937-1969 ...... **CLC 19, 64**
See also CA 104; DLBY 81; MTCW 2

Toomer, Jean 1894-1967 **CLC 1, 4, 13, 22; BLC 3; DAM MULT; PC 7; SSC 1; WLCS**
See also BW 1; CA 85-88; CDALB 1917-1929; DA3; DLB 45, 51; MTCW 1, 2

Torley, Luke
See Blish, James (Benjamin)

Tornimparte, Alessandra
See Ginzburg, Natalia

Torre, Raoul della
See Mencken, H(enry) L(ouis)

Torrence, Ridgely 1874-1950 .... **TCLC 97**
See also DLB 54

Torrey, E(dwin) Fuller 1937- .... **CLC 34**
See also CA 119; CANR 71

Torsvan, Ben Traven
See Traven, B.

Torsvan, Benno Traven
See Traven, B.

Torsvan, Berick Traven
See Traven, B.

Torsvan, Berwick Traven
See Traven, B.

Torsvan, Bruno Traven
See Traven, B.

Torsvan, Traven
See Traven, B.

Tournier, Michel (Edouard) 1924- **CLC 6, 23, 36, 95**
See also CA 49-52; CANR 3, 36, 74; DLB 83; MTCW 1, 2; SATA 23

Tournimparte, Alessandra
See Ginzburg, Natalia

Towers, Ivar
See Kornbluth, C(yril) M.

Towne, Robert (Burton) 1936(?)- .... **CLC 87**
See also CA 108; DLB 44

Townsend, Sue .... **CLC 61**
See also Townsend, Susan Elaine
See also AAYA 28; SATA 55, 93; SATA-Brief 48

Townsend, Susan Elaine 1946-
See Townsend, Sue
See also CA 119; 127; CANR 65; DAB; DAC; DAM MST

Townshend, Peter (Dennis Blandford) 1945- **CLC 17, 42**
See also CA 107

Tozzi, Federigo 1883-1920 .... **TCLC 31**
See also CA 160

Traill, Catharine Parr 1802-1899 .... **NCLC 31**
See also DLB 99

Trakl, Georg 1887-1914 .... **TCLC 5; PC 20**
See also CA 104; 165; MTCW 2

Transtroemer, Tomas (Goesta) 1931- **CLC 52, 65; DAM POET**
See also CA 117; 129; CAAS 17

Transtromer, Tomas Gosta
See Transtroemer, Tomas (Goesta)

Traven, B. (?)-1969 .... **CLC 8, 11**
See also CA 19-20; 25-28R; CAP 2; DLB 9, 56; MTCW 1

Treitel, Jonathan 1959- .... **CLC 70**

Tremain, Rose 1943- .... **CLC 42**
See also CA 97-100; CANR 44; DLB 14

Tremblay, Michel 1942- **CLC 29, 102; DAC; DAM MST**
See also CA 116; 128; DLB 60; MTCW 1, 2

Trevanian .... **CLC 29**
See also Whitaker, Rod(ney)

Trevor, Glen
See Hilton, James

Trevor, William 1928- **CLC 7, 9, 14, 25, 71, 116; SSC 21**
See also Cox, William Trevor
See also DLB 14, 139; MTCW 2

Trifonov, Yuri (Valentinovich) 1925-1981 **CLC 45**
See also CA 126; 103; MTCW 1

Trilling, Lionel 1905-1975 .... **CLC 9, 11, 24**
See also CA 9-12R; 61-64; CANR 10; DLB 28, 63; INT CANR-10; MTCW 1, 2

Trimball, W. H.
See Mencken, H(enry) L(ouis)

Tristan
See Gomez de la Serna, Ramon

Tristram
See Housman, A(lfred) E(dward)

Trogdon, William (Lewis) 1939-
See Heat-Moon, William Least
See also CA 115; 119; CANR 47; INT 119

Trollope, Anthony 1815-1882 .. **NCLC 6, 33; DA; DAB; DAC; DAM MST, NOV; SSC 28; WLC**
See also CDBLB 1832-1890; DA3; DLB 21, 57, 159; SATA 22

Trollope, Frances 1779-1863 .... **NCLC 30**

See also DLB 21, 166

Trotsky, Leon 1879-1940 .... **TCLC 22**
See also CA 118; 167

Trotter (Cockburn), Catharine 1679-1749 **LC 8**
See also DLB 84

Trotter, Wilfred 1872-1939 .... **TCLC 99**

Trout, Kilgore
See Farmer, Philip Jose

Trow, George W. S. 1943- .... **CLC 52**
See also CA 126

Troyat, Henri 1911- .... **CLC 23**
See also CA 45-48; CANR 2, 33, 67; MTCW 1

Trudeau, G(arretson) B(eekman) 1948-
See Trudeau, Garry B.
See also CA 81-84; CANR 31; SATA 35

Trudeau, Garry B. .... **CLC 12**
See also Trudeau, G(arretson) B(eekman)
See also AAYA 10; AITN 2

Truffaut, Francois 1932-1984 .... **CLC 20, 101**
See also CA 81-84; 113; CANR 34

Trumbo, Dalton 1905-1976 .... **CLC 19**
See also CA 21-24R; 69-72; CANR 10; DLB 26

Trumbull, John 1750-1831 .... **NCLC 30**
See also DLB 31

Trundlett, Helen B.
See Eliot, T(homas) S(tearns)

Tryon, Thomas 1926-1991 **CLC 3, 11; DAM POP**
See also AITN 1; CA 29-32R; 135; CANR 32, 77; DA3; MTCW 1

Tryon, Tom
See Tryon, Thomas

Ts'ao Hsueh-ch'in 1715(?)-1763 .... **LC 1**

Tsushima, Shuji 1909-1948
See Dazai Osamu
See also CA 107

Tsvetaeva (Efron), Marina (Ivanovna) 1892-1941 **TCLC 7, 35; PC 14**
See also CA 104; 128; CANR 73; MTCW 1, 2

Tuck, Lily 1938- .... **CLC 70**
See also CA 139

Tu Fu 712-770 .... **PC 9**
See also DAM MULT

Tunis, John R(oberts) 1889-1975 .... **CLC 12**
See also CA 61-64; CANR 62; DLB 22, 171; JRDA; MAICYA; SATA 37; SATA-Brief 30

Tuohy, Frank .... **CLC 37**
See also Tuohy, John Francis
See also DLB 14, 139

Tuohy, John Francis 1925-1999
See Tuohy, Frank
See also CA 5-8R; 178; CANR 3, 47

Turco, Lewis (Putnam) 1934- .... **CLC 11, 63**
See also CA 13-16R; CAAS 22; CANR 24, 51; DLBY 84

Turgenev, Ivan 1818-1883 **NCLC 21; DA; DAB; DAC; DAM MST, NOV; DC 7; SSC 7; WLC**

Turgot, Anne-Robert-Jacques 1727-1781 **LC 26**

Turner, Frederick 1943- .... **CLC 48**
See also CA 73-76; CAAS 10; CANR 12, 30, 56; DLB 40

Tutu, Desmond M(pilo) 1931- .. **CLC 80; BLC 3; DAM MULT**
See also BW 1, 3; CA 125; CANR 67, 81

Tutuola, Amos 1920-1997 **CLC 5, 14, 29; BLC 3; DAM MULT**
See also BW 2, 3; CA 9-12R; 159; CANR 27, 66; DA3; DLB 125; MTCW 1, 2

Twain, Mark **TCLC 6, 12, 19, 36, 48, 59; SSC 34; WLC**
See also Clemens, Samuel Langhorne
See also AAYA 20; CLR 58, 60; DLB 11, 12, 23, 64, 74

Tyler, Anne 1941- **CLC 7, 11, 18, 28, 44, 59, 103;**

See also AAYA 11; CLR 2; DLB 161; SAAS 3
Walter, Villiam Christian
    See Andersen, Hans Christian
Wambaugh, Joseph (Aloysius, Jr.) 1937- **CLC 3, 18; DAM NOV, POP**
    See also AITN 1; BEST 89:3; CA 33-36R; CANR 42, 65; DA3; DLB 6; DLBY 83; MTCW 1, 2
Wang Wei 699(?)-761(?) .... **PC 18**
Ward, Arthur Henry Sarsfield 1883-1959
    See Rohmer, Sax
    See also CA 108; 173
Ward, Douglas Turner 1930- .... **CLC 19**
    See also BW 1; CA 81-84; CANR 27; DLB 7, 38
Ward, E. D.
    See Lucas, E(dward) V(errall)
Ward, Mary Augusta
    See Ward, Mrs. Humphry
Ward, Mrs. Humphry 1851-1920 .... **TCLC 55**
    See also DLB 18
Ward, Peter
    See Faust, Frederick (Schiller)
Warhol, Andy 1928(?)-1987 .... **CLC 20**
    See also AAYA 12; BEST 89:4; CA 89-92; 121; CANR 34
Warner, Francis (Robert le Plastrier) 1937- **CLC 14**
    See also CA 53-56; CANR 11
Warner, Marina 1946- .... **CLC 59**
    See also CA 65-68; CANR 21, 55; DLB 194
Warner, Rex (Ernest) 1905-1986 .... **CLC 45**
    See also CA 89-92; 119; DLB 15
Warner, Susan (Bogert) 1819-1885 .... **NCLC 31**
    See also DLB 3, 42
Warner, Sylvia (Constance) Ashton
    See Ashton-Warner, Sylvia (Constance)
Warner, Sylvia Townsend 1893-1978 **CLC 7, 19; SSC 23**
    See also CA 61-64; 77-80; CANR 16, 60; DLB 34, 139; MTCW 1, 2
Warren, Mercy Otis 1728-1814 .... **NCLC 13**
    See also DLB 31, 200
Warren, Robert Penn 1905-1989 . **CLC 1, 4, 6, 8, 10, 13, 18, 39, 53, 59; DA; DAB; DAC; DAM MST, NOV, POET; SSC 4; WLC**
    See also AITN 1; CA 13-16R; 129; CANR 10, 47; CDALB 1968-1988; DA3; DLB 2, 48, 152; DLBY 80, 89; INT CANR-10; MTCW 1, 2; SATA 46; SATA-Obit 63
Warshofsky, Isaac
    See Singer, Isaac Bashevis
Warton, Thomas 1728-1790 **LC 15; DAM POET**
    See also DLB 104, 109
Waruk, Kona
    See Harris, (Theodore) Wilson
Warung, Price 1855-1911 .... **TCLC 45**
Warwick, Jarvis
    See Garner, Hugh
Washington, Alex
    See Harris, Mark
Washington, Booker T(aliaferro) 1856-1915 **TCLC 10; BLC 3; DAM MULT**
    See also BW 1; CA 114; 125; DA3; SATA 28
Washington, George 1732-1799 .... **LC 25**
    See also DLB 31
Wassermann, (Karl) Jakob 1873-1934 . **TCLC 6**
    See also CA 104; 163; DLB 66
Wasserstein, Wendy 1950- **CLC 32, 59, 90; DAM DRAM; DC 4**
    See also CA 121; 129; CABS 3; CANR 53, 75; DA3; INT 129; MTCW 2; SATA 94
Waterhouse, Keith (Spencer) 1929- ..... **CLC 47**
    See also CA 5-8R; CANR 38, 67; DLB 13, 15; MTCW 1, 2

Waters, Frank (Joseph) 1902-1995 .... **CLC 88**
    See also CA 5-8R; 149; CAAS 13; CANR 3, 18, 63; DLB 212; DLBY 86
Waters, Roger 1944- .... **CLC 35**
Watkins, Frances Ellen
    See Harper, Frances Ellen Watkins
Watkins, Gerrold
    See Malzberg, Barry N(athaniel)
Watkins, Gloria 1955(?)-
    See hooks, bell
    See also BW 2; CA 143; MTCW 2
Watkins, Paul 1964- .... **CLC 55**
    See also CA 132; CANR 62
Watkins, Vernon Phillips 1906-1967 .... **CLC 43**
    See also CA 9-10; 25-28R; CAP 1; DLB 20
Watson, Irving S.
    See Mencken, H(enry) L(ouis)
Watson, John H.
    See Farmer, Philip Jose
Watson, Richard F.
    See Silverberg, Robert
Waugh, Auberon (Alexander) 1939- .... **CLC 7**
    See also CA 45-48; CANR 6, 22; DLB 14, 194
Waugh, Evelyn (Arthur St. John) 1903-1966 **CLC 1, 3, 8, 13, 19, 27, 44, 107; DA; DAB; DAC; DAM MST, NOV, POP; WLC**
    See also CA 85-88; 25-28R; CANR 22; CDBLB 1914-1945; DA3; DLB 15, 162, 195; MTCW 1, 2
Waugh, Harriet 1944- .... **CLC 6**
    See also CA 85-88; CANR 22
Ways, C. R.
    See Blount, Roy (Alton), Jr.
Waystaff, Simon
    See Swift, Jonathan
Webb, Beatrice (Martha Potter) 1858-1943 **TCLC 22**
    See also CA 117; 162; DLB 190
Webb, Charles (Richard) 1939- .... **CLC 7**
    See also CA 25-28R
Webb, James H(enry), Jr. 1946- .... **CLC 22**
    See also CA 81-84
Webb, Mary Gladys (Meredith) 1881-1927 **TCLC 24**
    See also CA 182; 123; DLB 34
Webb, Mrs. Sidney
    See Webb, Beatrice (Martha Potter)
Webb, Phyllis 1927- .... **CLC 18**
    See also CA 104; CANR 23; DLB 53
Webb, Sidney (James) 1859-1947 .... **TCLC 22**
    See also CA 117; 163; DLB 190
Webber, Andrew Lloyd .... **CLC 21**
    See also Lloyd Webber, Andrew
Weber, Lenora Mattingly 1895-1971 ..... **CLC 12**
    See also CA 19-20; 29-32R; CAP 1; SATA 2; SATA-Obit 26
Weber, Max 1864-1920 .... **TCLC 69**
    See also CA 109
Webster, John 1579(?)-1634(?) **LC 33; DA; DAB; DAC; DAM DRAM, MST; DC 2; WLC**
    See also CDBLB Before 1660; DLB 58
Webster, Noah 1758-1843 .... **NCLC 30**
    See also DLB 1, 37, 42, 43, 73
Wedekind, (Benjamin) Frank(lin) 1864-1918 **TCLC 7; DAM DRAM**
    See also CA 104; 153; DLB 118
Weidman, Jerome 1913-1998 .... **CLC 7**
    See also AITN 2; CA 1-4R; 171; CANR 1; DLB 28
Weil, Simone (Adolphine) 1909-1943 .. **TCLC 23**
    See also CA 117; 159; MTCW 2
Weininger, Otto 1880-1903 .... **TCLC 84**
Weinstein, Nathan

See West, Nathanael
Weinstein, Nathan von Wallenstein
    See West, Nathanael
Weir, Peter (Lindsay) 1944- .... **CLC 20**
    See also CA 113; 123
Weiss, Peter (Ulrich) 1916-1982 **CLC 3, 15, 51; DAM DRAM**
    See also CA 45-48; 106; CANR 3; DLB 69, 124
Weiss, Theodore (Russell) 1916- ..**CLC 3, 8, 14**
    See also CA 9-12R; CAAS 2; CANR 46; DLB 5
Welch, (Maurice) Denton 1915-1948 .. **TCLC 22**
    See also CA 121; 148
Welch, James 1940- **CLC 6, 14, 52; DAM MULT, POP**
    See also CA 85-88; CANR 42, 66; DLB 175; NNAL
Weldon, Fay 1931- **CLC 6, 9, 11, 19, 36, 59, 122; DAM POP**
    See also CA 21-24R; CANR 16, 46, 63; CDBLB 1960 to Present; DLB 14, 194; INT CANR-16; MTCW 1, 2
Wellek, Rene 1903-1995 .... **CLC 28**
    See also CA 5-8R; 150; CAAS 7; CANR 8; DLB 63; INT CANR-8
Weller, Michael 1942- .... **CLC 10, 53**
    See also CA 85-88
Weller, Paul 1958- .... **CLC 26**
Wellershoff, Dieter 1925- .... **CLC 46**
    See also CA 89-92; CANR 16, 37
Welles, (George) Orson 1915-1985 **CLC 20, 80**
    See also CA 93-96; 117
Wellman, John McDowell 1945-
    See Wellman, Mac
    See also CA 166
Wellman, Mac 1945- .... **CLC 65**
    See also Wellman, John McDowell; Wellman, John McDowell
Wellman, Manly Wade 1903-1986 .... **CLC 49**
    See also CA 1-4R; 118; CANR 6, 16, 44; SATA 6; SATA-Obit 47
Wells, Carolyn 1869(?)-1942 .... **TCLC 35**
    See also CA 113; DLB 11
Wells, H(erbert) G(eorge) 1866-1946 **TCLC 6, 12, 19; DA; DAB; DAC; DAM MST, NOV; SSC 6; WLC**
    See also AAYA 18; CA 110; 121; CDBLB 1914-1945; DA3; DLB 34, 70, 156, 178; MTCW 1, 2; SATA 20
Wells, Rosemary 1943- .... **CLC 12**
    See also AAYA 13; CA 85-88; CANR 48; CLR 16; MAICYA; SAAS 1; SATA 18, 69
Welty, Eudora 1909- **CLC 1, 2, 5, 14, 22, 33, 105; DA; DAB; DAC; DAM MST, NOV; SSC 1, 27; WLC**
    See also CA 9-12R; CABS 1; CANR 32, 65; CDALB 1941-1968; DA3; DLB 2, 102, 143; DLBD 12; DLBY 87; MTCW 1, 2
Wen I-to 1899-1946 .... **TCLC 28**
Wentworth, Robert
    See Hamilton, Edmond
Werfel, Franz (Viktor) 1890-1945 .... **TCLC 8**
    See also CA 104; 161; DLB 81, 124
Wergeland, Henrik Arnold 1808-1845 . **NCLC 5**
Wersba, Barbara 1932- .... **CLC 30**
    See also AAYA 2, 30; CA 29-32R, 182; CAAE 182; CANR 16, 38; CLR 3; DLB 52; JRDA; MAICYA; SAAS 2; SATA 1, 58; SATA-Essay 103
Wertmueller, Lina 1928- .... **CLC 16**
    See also CA 97-100; CANR 39, 78
Wescott, Glenway 1901-1987 .. **CLC 13; SSC 35**
    See also CA 13-16R; 121; CANR 23, 70; DLB 4, 9, 102

DA3; DLBY 82; INT CANR-6; MTCW 1, 2
Wright, Charles (Penzel, Jr.) 1935- **CLC 6, 13, 28, 119**
See also CA 29-32R; CAAS 7; CANR 23, 36, 62; DLB 165; DLBY 82; MTCW 1, 2
Wright, Charles Stevenson 1932-**CLC 49; BLC 3; DAM MULT, POET**
See also BW 1; CA 9-12R; CANR 26; DLB 33
Wright, Frances 1795-1852 .... **NCLC 74**
See also DLB 73
Wright, Frank Lloyd 1867-1959 .... **TCLC 95**
See also CA 174
Wright, Jack R.
See Harris, Mark
Wright, James (Arlington) 1927-1980 **CLC 3, 5, 10, 28; DAM POET**
See also AITN 2; CA 49-52; 97-100; CANR 4, 34, 64; CDALBS; DLB 5, 169; MTCW 1, 2
Wright, Judith (Arandell) 1915-**CLC 11, 53; PC 14**
See also CA 13-16R; CANR 31, 76; MTCW 1, 2; SATA 14
Wright, L(aurali) R. 1939- .... **CLC 44**
See also CA 138
Wright, Richard (Nathaniel) 1908-1960**CLC 1, 3, 4, 9, 14, 21, 48, 74; BLC 3; DA; DAB; DAC; DAM MST, MULT, NOV; SSC 2; WLC**
See also AAYA 5; BW 1; CA 108; CANR 64; CDALB 1929-1941; DA3; DLB 76, 102; DLBD 2; MTCW 1, 2
Wright, Richard B(ruce) 1937- .... **CLC 6**
See also CA 85-88; DLB 53
Wright, Rick 1945- .... **CLC 35**
Wright, Rowland
See Wells, Carolyn
Wright, Stephen 1946- .... **CLC 33**
Wright, Willard Huntington 1888-1939
See Van Dine, S. S.
See also CA 115; DLBD 16
Wright, William 1930- .... **CLC 44**
See also CA 53-56; CANR 7, 23
Wroth, Lady Mary 1587-1653(?) .... **LC 30**
See also DLB 121
Wu Ch'eng-en 1500(?)-1582(?) .... **LC 7**
Wu Ching-tzu 1701-1754 .... **LC 2**
Wurlitzer, Rudolph 1938(?)- .... **CLC 2, 4, 15**
See also CA 85-88; DLB 173
Wyatt, Thomas c. 1503-1542 .... **PC 27**
See also DLB 132
Wycherley, William 1641-1715 . **LC 8, 21; DAM DRAM**
See also CDBLB 1660-1789; DLB 80
Wylie, Elinor (Morton Hoyt) 1885-1928**TCLC 8; PC 23**
See also CA 105; 162; DLB 9, 45
Wylie, Philip (Gordon) 1902-1971 .... **CLC 43**
See also CA 21-22; 33-36R; CAP 2; DLB 9
Wyndham, John .... **CLC 19**
See also Harris, John (Wyndham Parkes Lucas) Beynon
Wyss, Johann David Von 1743-1818 ... **NCLC 10**
See also JRDA; MAICYA; SATA 29; SATA-Brief 27
Xenophon c. 430B.C.-c. 354B.C. .... **CMLC 17**
See also DLB 176
Yakumo Koizumi
See Hearn, (Patricio) Lafcadio (Tessima Carlos)
Yamamoto, Hisaye 1921- . **SSC 34; DAM MULT**
Yanez, Jose Donoso
See Donoso (Yanez), Jose
Yanovsky, Basile S.
See Yanovsky, V(assily) S(emenovich)
Yanovsky, V(assily) S(emenovich) 1906-1989**CLC**

2, 18
See also CA 97-100; 129
Yates, Richard 1926-1992 .... **CLC 7, 8, 23**
See also CA 5-8R; 139; CANR 10, 43; DLB 2; DLBY 81, 92; INT CANR-10
Yeats, W. B.
See Yeats, William Butler
Yeats, William Butler 1865-1939**TCLC 1, 11, 18, 31, 93; DA; DAB; DAC; DAM DRAM, MST, POET; PC 20; WLC**
See also CA 104; 127; CANR 45; CDBLB 1890-1914; DA3; DLB 10, 19, 98, 156; MTCW 1, 2
Yehoshua, A(braham) B. 1936- .... **CLC 13, 31**
See also CA 33-36R; CANR 43
Yellow Bird
See Ridge, John Rollin
Yep, Laurence Michael 1948- .... **CLC 35**
See also AAYA 5, 31; CA 49-52; CANR 1, 46; CLR 3, 17, 54; DLB 52; JRDA; MAICYA; SATA 7, 69
Yerby, Frank G(arvin) 1916-1991 . **CLC 1, 7, 22; BLC 3; DAM MULT**
See also BW 1, 3; CA 9-12R; 136; CANR 16, 52; DLB 76; INT CANR-16; MTCW 1
Yesenin, Sergei Alexandrovich
See Esenin, Sergei (Alexandrovich)
Yevtushenko, Yevgeny (Alexandrovich) 1933-**CLC 1, 3, 13, 26, 51, 126; DAM POET**
See also CA 81-84; CANR 33, 54; MTCW 1
Yezierska, Anzia 1885(?)-1970 .... **CLC 46**
See also CA 126; 89-92; DLB 28; MTCW 1
Yglesias, Helen 1915- .... **CLC 7, 22**
See also CA 37-40R; CAAS 20; CANR 15, 65; INT CANR-15; MTCW 1
Yokomitsu Riichi 1898-1947 .... **TCLC 47**
See also CA 170
Yonge, Charlotte (Mary) 1823-1901 .... **TCLC 48**
See also CA 109; 163; DLB 18, 163; SATA 17
York, Jeremy
See Creasey, John
York, Simon
See Heinlein, Robert A(nson)
Yorke, Henry Vincent 1905-1974 .... **CLC 13**
See also Green, Henry
See also CA 85-88; 49-52
Yosano Akiko 1878-1942 .... **TCLC 59; PC 11**
See also CA 161
Yoshimoto, Banana .... **CLC 84**
See also Yoshimoto, Mahoko
Yoshimoto, Mahoko 1964-
See Yoshimoto, Banana
See also CA 144
Young, Al(bert James) 1939- .. **CLC 19; BLC 3; DAM MULT**
See also BW 2, 3; CA 29-32R; CANR 26, 65; DLB 33
Young, Andrew (John) 1885-1971 .... **CLC 5**
See also CA 5-8R; CANR 7, 29
Young, Collier
See Bloch, Robert (Albert)
Young, Edward 1683-1765 .... **LC 3, 40**
See also DLB 95
Young, Marguerite (Vivian) 1909-1995 . **CLC 82**
See also CA 13-16; 150; CAP 1
Young, Neil 1945- .... **CLC 17**
See also CA 110
Young Bear, Ray A. 1950- **CLC 94; DAM MULT**
See also CA 146; DLB 175; NNAL
Yourcenar, Marguerite 1903-1987**CLC 19, 38, 50, 87; DAM NOV**
See also CA 69-72; CANR 23, 60; DLB 72; DLBY 88; MTCW 1, 2
Yuan, Chu 340(?)B.C.-278(?)B.C. .... **CMLC 36**

Yurick, Sol 1925- .... **CLC 6**
See also CA 13-16R; CANR 25
Zabolotsky, Nikolai Alekseevich 1903-1958 **TCLC 52**
See also CA 116; 164
Zagajewski, Adam .... **PC 27**
Zamiatin, Yevgenii
See Zamyatin, Evgeny Ivanovich
Zamora, Bernice (B. Ortiz) 1938-**CLC 89; DAM MULT; HLC 2**
See also CA 151; CANR 80; DLB 82; HW 1, 2
Zamyatin, Evgeny Ivanovich 1884-1937**TCLC 8, 37**
See also CA 105; 166
Zangwill, Israel 1864-1926 .... **TCLC 16**
See also CA 109; 167; DLB 10, 135, 197
Zappa, Francis Vincent, Jr. 1940-1993
See Zappa, Frank
See also CA 108; 143; CANR 57
Zappa, Frank .... **CLC 17**
See also Zappa, Francis Vincent, Jr.
Zaturenska, Marya 1902-1982 .... **CLC 6, 11**
See also CA 13-16R; 105; CANR 22
Zeami 1363-1443 .... **DC 7**
Zelazny, Roger (Joseph) 1937-1995 ...... **CLC 21**
See also AAYA 7; CA 21-24R; 148; CANR 26, 60; DLB 8; MTCW 1, 2; SATA 57; SATA-Brief 39
Zhdanov, Andrei Alexandrovich 1896-1948**TCLC 18**
See also CA 117; 167
Zhukovsky, Vasily (Andreevich) 1783-1852**NCLC 35**
See also DLB 205
Ziegenhagen, Eric .... **CLC 55**
Zimmer, Jill Schary
See Robinson, Jill
Zimmerman, Robert
See Dylan, Bob
Zindel, Paul 1936- **CLC 6, 26; DA; DAB; DAC; DAM DRAM, MST, NOV; DC 5**
See also AAYA 2; CA 73-76; CANR 31, 65; CDALBS; CLR 3, 45; DA3; DLB 7, 52; JRDA; MAICYA; MTCW 1, 2; SATA 16, 58, 102
Zinov'Ev, A. A.
See Zinoviev, Alexander (Aleksandrovich)
Zinoviev, Alexander (Aleksandrovich) 1922-**CLC 19**
See also CA 116; 133; CAAS 10
Zoilus
See Lovecraft, H(oward) P(hillips)
Zola, Emile (Edouard Charles Antoine) 1840-1902 **TCLC 1, 6, 21, 41; DA; DAB; DAC; DAM MST, NOV; WLC**
See also CA 104; 138; DA3; DLB 123
Zoline, Pamela 1941- .... **CLC 62**
See also CA 161
Zorrilla y Moral, Jose 1817-1893 .... **NCLC 6**
Zoshchenko, Mikhail (Mikhailovich) 1895-1958 **TCLC 15; SSC 15**
See also CA 115; 160
Zuckmayer, Carl 1896-1977 .... **CLC 18**
See also CA 69-72; DLB 56, 124
Zuk, Georges
See Skelton, Robin
Zukofsky, Louis 1904-1978**CLC 1, 2, 4, 7, 11, 18; DAM POET; PC 11**
See also CA 9-12R; 77-80; CANR 39; DLB 5, 165; MTCW 1
Zweig, Paul 1935-1984 .... **CLC 34, 42**
See also CA 85-88; 113
Zweig, Stefan 1881-1942 .... **TCLC 17**
See also CA 112; 170; DLB 81, 118
Zwingli, Huldreich 1484-1531 .... **LC 37**
See also DLB 179

Literary Criticism Series
Cumulative Topic Index

This index lists all topic entries in Gale's *Classical and Medieval Literature Criticism, Contemporary Literary Criticism, Literature Criticism from 1400 to 1800, Nineteenth-Century Literature Criticism,* and *Twentieth-Century Literary Criticism.*

Topic Index

Topic Index

Topic Index

NCLC Cumulative Nationality Index

Goethe, Johann Wolfgang von **4, 22, 34**
Grabbe, Christian Dietrich **2**
Grimm, Jacob Ludwig Karl **3, 77**
Grimm, Wilhelm Karl **3, 77**
Hebbel, Friedrich **43**
Hegel, Georg Wilhelm Friedrich **46**
Heine, Heinrich **4, 54**
Hoffmann, E(rnst) T(heodor) A(madeus) **2**
Holderlin, (Johann Christian) Friedrich **16**
Immermann, Karl (Lebrecht) **4, 49**
Jean Paul **7**
Kant, Immanuel **27, 67**
Kleist, Heinrich von **2, 37**
Klinger, Friedrich Maximilian von **1**
Klopstock, Friedrich Gottlieb **11**
Kotzebue, August (Friedrich Ferdinand) von **25**
Ludwig, Otto **4**
Marx, Karl (Heinrich) **17**
Meyer, Conrad Ferdinand **81**
Morike, Eduard (Friedrich) **10**
Novalis **13**
Schelling, Friedrich Wilhelm Joseph von **30**
Schiller, Friedrich **39, 69**
Schlegel, August Wilhelm von **15**
Schlegel, Friedrich **45**
Schopenhauer, Arthur **51**
Storm, (Hans) Theodor (Woldsen) **1**
Tieck, (Johann) Ludwig **5, 46**
Wagner, Richard **9**
Wieland, Christoph Martin **17**

GREEK
Solomos, Dionysios **15**

HUNGARIAN
Arany, Janos **34**
Madach, Imre **19**
Petofi, Sandor **21**

INDIAN
Chatterji, Bankim Chandra **19**
Dutt, Toru **29**
Ghalib **39, 78**

IRISH
Allingham, William **25**
Banim, John **13**
Banim, Michael **13**
Boucicault, Dion **41**
Carleton, William **3**
Croker, John Wilson **10**
Darley, George **2**
Edgeworth, Maria **1, 51**
Ferguson, Samuel **33**
Griffin, Gerald **7**
Jameson, Anna **43**
Le Fanu, Joseph Sheridan **9, 58**

Lever, Charles (James) **23**
Maginn, William **8**
Mangan, James Clarence **27**
Maturin, Charles Robert **6**
Merriman, Brian **70**
Moore, Thomas **6**
Morgan, Lady **29**
O'Brien, Fitz-James **21**

ITALIAN
Collodi, Carlo **54**
Foscolo, Ugo **8**
Gozzi, (Conte) Carlo **23**
Leopardi, (Conte) Giacomo **22**
Manzoni, Alessandro **29**
Mazzini, Guiseppe **34**
Nievo, Ippolito **22**

JAPANESE
Higuchi, Ichiyo **49**
Motoori, Norinaga **45**

LITHUANIAN
Mapu, Abraham (ben Jekutiel) **18**

MEXICAN
Lizardi, Jose Joaquin Fernandez de **30**

NORWEGIAN
Collett, (Jacobine) Camilla (Wergeland) **22**
Wergeland, Henrik Arnold **5**

POLISH
Fredro, Aleksander **8**
Krasicki, Ignacy **8**
Krasinski, Zygmunt **4**
Mickiewicz, Adam **3**
Norwid, Cyprian Kamil **17**
Slowacki, Juliusz **15**

ROMANIAN
Eminescu, Mihail **33**

RUSSIAN
Aksakov, Sergei Timofeyvich **2**
Bakunin, Mikhail (Alexandrovich) **25, 58**
Bashkirtseff, Marie **27**
Belinski, Vissarion Grigoryevich **5**
Chernyshevsky, Nikolay Gavrilovich **1**
Dobrolyubov, Nikolai Alexandrovich **5**
Dostoevsky, Fedor Mikhailovich **2, 7, 21, 33, 43**
Gogol, Nikolai (Vasilyevich) **5, 15, 31**
Goncharov, Ivan Alexandrovich **1, 63**
Granovsky, Timofei Nikolaevich **75**
Herzen, Aleksandr Ivanovich **10, 61**
Karamzin, Nikolai Mikhailovich **3**
Krylov, Ivan Andreevich **1**

Lermontov, Mikhail Yuryevich **5**
Leskov, Nikolai (Semyonovich) **25**
Nekrasov, Nikolai Alekseevich **11**
Ostrovsky, Alexander **30, 57**
Pisarev, Dmitry Ivanovich **25**
Pushkin, Alexander (Sergeyevich) **3, 27, 83**
Saltykov, Mikhail Evgrafovich **16**
Smolenskin, Peretz **30**
Turgenev, Ivan **21**
Tyutchev, Fyodor **34**
Zhukovsky, Vasily (Andreevich) **35**

SCOTTISH
Baillie, Joanna **2**
Beattie, James **25**
Blair, Hugh **75**
Campbell, Thomas **19**
Carlyle, Thomas **22**
Ferrier, Susan (Edmonstone) **8**
Galt, John **1**
Hogg, James **4**
Jeffrey, Francis **33**
Lockhart, John Gibson **6**
Mackenzie, Henry **41**
Oliphant, Margaret (Oliphant Wilson) **11, 61**
Scott, Walter **15, 69**
Stevenson, Robert Louis (Balfour) **5, 14, 63**
Thomson, James **18**
Wilson, John **5**
Wright, Frances **74**

SPANISH
Alarcon, Pedro Antonio de **1**
Caballero, Fernan **10**
Castro, Rosalia de **3, 78**
Espronceda, Jose de **39**
Larra (y Sanchez de Castro), Mariano Jose de **17**
Tamayo y Baus, Manuel **1**
Zorrilla y Moral, Jose **6**

SWEDISH
Almqvist, Carl Jonas Love **42**
Bremer, Fredrika **11**
Stagnelius, Eric Johan **61**
Tegner, Esaias **2**

SWISS
Amiel, Henri Frederic **4**
Burckhardt, Jacob (Christoph) **49**
Charriere, Isabelle de **66**
Keller, Gottfried **2**
Meyer, Conrad Ferdinand **81**
Wyss, Johann David Von **10**

UKRAINIAN
Shevchenko, Taras **54**

Nationality Index

NCLC-83 Title Index